GUIDE TO THE DIPLOMATIC HISTORY OF THE UNITED STATES, 1775-1921

By

SAMUEL FLAGG BEMIS

FARNAM PROFESSOR OF DIPLOMATIC HISTORY
IN YALE UNIVERSITY

AND

GRACE GARDNER GRIFFIN

EDITOR OF "WRITINGS ON AMERICAN HISTORY"

UNITED STATES
GOVERNMENT PRINTING OFFICE
WASHINGTON : 1935

GLOUCESTER, MASS.
PETER SMITH
1959

L. C. Card 35—26001

To HERBERT PUTNAM, LL.D.

PREFACE

This book is what the title states. It is not a bibliography in the strict sense of the word. It is a guide. Its purpose is to put the reader quickly in directed and helpful touch with the already vast quantity of material, printed and unprinted, now available for the diplomatic history of the United States. It is surprising even to the authors of this guide that such a quantity should exist on what is only a comparatively small though not inconspicuous phase of modern history.

To accomplish our purpose we have thought it advisable to divide the guide into two parts: Part I, bibliographical chapters topically and chronologically arranged; Part II, Remarks on the Sources. Part I is intended to direct and assist the general student by revealing what has been written on the subjects outlined, with a modicum of comment when the title itself is not self-explanatory; to indicate the printed sources or how to get at them; and to give at least, and merely, suggestions for further sources in manuscript and archival collections, as well as for the study of pertinent maps (when those maps concern direct diplomatic relations of the United States in relation to its own territory or that of adjacent nations). These indications and suggestions immediately draw the investigator, by cross references, into contact with Part II, which contains an analysis of printed state papers and manuscript material, preceded by some textual remarks on the nature of the sources.

Two facts impelled us to bring the guide to a close with the year 1921 for the bibliographical chapters: that year, in which the United States concluded peace with Germany and Austria-Hungary, and in which assembled the Washington Conference, marks the end of a period in American as well as European diplomatic history; and in 1933 appeared Langer and Armstrong's *Foreign Affairs Bibliography*, covering the period 1919 to 1932.

We believe that our chapter headings and subdivisions within chapters of Part I substantially cover the history of American diplomacy to the peace treaties ending the World War. There may be some works that do not fall precisely into any of our chapters or subdivisions; and new topics, points of view, and emphases may appear in the future impossible to classify within the existing structure of our analysis. To claim otherwise would imply a certain omniscience. Nevertheless we think our method is the most practical and useful for a guide.

In citing titles in the bibliography we have assumed the responsibility of excluding things of ephemeral, insignificant, or useless nature, and we have presumed to draw a line that would exclude works not pertinent to the diplomatic history of the United States. Precisely where to draw such a line, perhaps no two persons would agree, but where there is doubt we include the title. *Where special bibliographies exist we do not repeat all their contents*—for only one example, on the Monroe Doctrine—but content ourselves with referring to the bibliographical aids and entering only the most important works. We do not cite textbooks except in very particular cases. We cannot hope that the bibliographical chapters are complete and final. We think them unusually comprehensive, however; and we are impressed with the fact that to serve our designs as a practical aid to scholarship and to justify the generous subventions which have made this guide possible, it should be brought within compass, printed, and put into use as soon as possible, rather than linger years for absolute perfection and then perhaps never be printed. For our own satisfaction, and against a possible reprinting, we would appreciate corrections and additions.

Use of the guide will reveal that only in exceptional instances do we cite American biographical works. This is because the generally available *Dictionary of American Biography* will be approaching completion by the time this is printed, and in view of the data included in the bibliographical notes appended to the sketches therein, it is deemed supererogatory to enter biographies of American statesmen and diplomatists. Exceptions are those biographies published since the relevant sketches in the *D.A.B.*, or occasionally a biography of really unusual value for depicting a particular phase of diplomatic history. We have tried to indicate the relevant British biographical material appearing since the publication of the *Dictionary of National Biography* and the principal biographical studies of other foreign statesmen and diplomatists, because these are not so readily located, and because of the comparative unavailability of the other foreign biographical dictionaries.

An historical source is the trace of an historical event; it is also the trace of an historical state of mind. Consequently the reader may find, among "printed sources" in the bibliographical sections of this guide, articles, pamphlets, and books which indicate states of mind about foreign policy, which otherwise might be classified as special works. Even though some such publications are academic in character, it is often difficult to classify them unequivocally as special monographs or as sources. We cannot quarrel with the specialist who might, in careful analysis, dispute items of our classification.

In pointing out the printed source material, and the manuscript and archival material, both in this country and abroad, we rely greatly on the various special bibliographical aids, guides, catalogues, indexes, checklists, and calendars which have been prepared for that purpose.

The organization of the guide makes it necessary in many instances to mention the same title more than once in different connections. Therefore to save space we have given each title when first entered in full a serial number printed in bold-faced type within brackets, thus: J. B. Moore, *History and digest of the international arbitrations to which the United States has been a party* (Wash.: Govt. Print. Off., 1898, 6 v.) [**5364**]. Later cross-references are by author or short title followed by repetition of the appropriate original serial number printed within parentheses in conventional type, thus: Moore, *Arbitrations* (no. 5364). The cross references may also be identified by consultation of the author index.

It has been necessary to limit the index to authors only; but we feel that the detailed scheme of classification, and the many cross-references will compensate for the lack of a comprehensive subject index.

The abbreviations for periodical references used in this *Guide* seem obvious in most cases, and in doubtful instances may be identified by the *Union list of serials* (no. 4993), below.

A work of this kind must depend on the advice and assistance of numerous scholars laboring in the field. Without desiring in any way to avoid full responsibility for any shortcomings of the following chapters we acknowledge with gratitude the valued help of:

Professor Jorge Basadre, of the University of San Marcos, Lima, Peru; Professor J. P. Baxter, 3d; Professor Robert C. Binkley, Dr. Philip C. Brooks; Miss Catherine A. Bryant; Dr. Eugenio Casanova, Superintendent of the Royal Italian Archives, Rome; Mr. James B. Childs, Chief of the Division of Documents, Library of Congress; President Tyler Dennett; Mr. John de Porry, of the Library of Congress; Dr. Arthur G. Doughty, Dominion Archivist, Ottawa, Canada; Dr. Worthington C. Ford; Dr. Jintaro Fujii, Editor, Bureau of Historical Research relating to the Imperial Restoration, Tokyo, Japan; Dr. Lothar Gross, Oberarchivrat, Haus-, Hof- und Staatsarchiv, Vienna; Professor Lawrence F. Hill; Dr. Arthur W. Hummel, Chief of the Division of Orientalia, Library of Congress; Dr. J. Franklin Jameson, Chief of the Division of Manuscripts, Library of Congress, and Benjamin Professor of American History; Mr. Cecil K. Jones, of the Library of Congress; Mr. James F. Kenney, Director of Historical Research, Public Archives of Canada; Miss Annita M. Ker, of the Library of Congress; Dr. Waldo G. Leland, Permanent Secretary of the American Council of Learned Societies; Mrs. Dorothy M. Louraine; Mr. Frank E. Louraine; Colonel Lawrence Martin, Chief of the Division of Maps, Library of Congress; Professor Percy Alvin Martin; Professor Frederick Merk; Dr. Hunter Miller, Historical Adviser, Department of State; Mrs. Roberta (Burnet) Newgarden; Professor Roy F. Nichols; Dr. Charles Oscar Paullin; Professor Julius F. Pratt; Dr. Erich Posner, Archivrat, of the Preussisches Geheimes Staats-Archiv, Berlin-Dahlem, Germany; Professor Herminio Portell Vilá, University of Havana, Havana, Cuba; Professor Herbert I. Priestley; Professor Lowell J. Ragatz; Mr. Seymour de Ricci, of Paris; Professor J. F. Rippy; Dr. James Alexander Robertson; Professor W. S. Robertson; Dr. Shio Sakanishi, of the Library of Congress; Professor France Scholes; Dr. Vernon G. Setser; Professor Charles Seymour; Mr. Charles L. Stewart, of Berkeley, California; Mrs. Grace Hammond Stowe; Professor Leonid Strakhovsky; Mrs. Natalia Summers, Archivist, Department of State; Professor Y. Takakai, of the Imperial University of Tokyo, Japan; Professor Charles C. Tansill; Miss Edna Field Vosper, Curator of Manuscripts, William L. Clements Library, Ann Arbor, Michigan; Professor Waldemar Westergaard; Dr. J. C. Westermann, Amsterdam, Holland; Professor A. Curtis Wilgus; Dr. Cyril Wynne, Chief of the Division of Research and Publications, Department of State.

Acknowledgments are made also to the following libraries and various persons on their staffs: The Library of Congress, Mr. Frederick W. Ashley, chief assistant librarian, Mr. Allen R. Boyd, executive assistant, Mr. Martin A. Roberts, superintendent of reading rooms, Mr. Robert A. Voorus; the Carnegie Endowment for International Peace and its librarian, Miss M. Alice Matthews; the Harvard College Library, Mr. Walter B. Briggs, assistant librarian, and Mr. Robert H. Haynes, superintendent of circulation; the Henry M. Huntington Library and its director, Dr. Max Farrand; the Hoover War Library and its director, Dr. Ralph H. Lutz; the William L. Clements Library and its director, Dr. Randolph G. Adams.

Unusually generous privileges were extended during several summers by the Harvard College Library.

Two institutions have made the work possible. The Social Science Research Council subsidized most of its expenses with a generous grant. The Library of Congress has published it; and without that national institution's unequaled facilities and cooperation the preparation of this volume would have been impossible.

Finally we make sincere acknowledgment to that organizer of opportunity, Dr. Herbert Putnam, Librarian of Congress.

S. F. B.
G. G. G.

CONTENTS

PART I. BIBLIOGRAPHY—Continued

PART I. BIBLIOGRAPHY—Continued

PART II. REMARKS ON THE SOURCES—Continued

PART I

BIBLIOGRAPHY OF THE DIPLOMATIC HISTORY OF THE UNITED STATES, 1775–1921

TOPICALLY AND CHRONOLOGICALLY
ARRANGED

CHAPTER I

THE REVOLUTION, 1775-1783 [1]

1. In General.
2. The Beginnings of American Foreign Contacts.
3. France and the American Revolution.
4. Spain and the American Revolution.
5. British Efforts at Reconciliation.
6. The Netherlands and the American Revolution.
7. The Armed Neutrality of 1780.
8. Scandinavia, Prussia, Northern and Central Europe.
9. Origin of the American Foreign Office.

1. In General

Bibliographical Aids

For general aids, see Evans (no. 4639); Sabin (no. 4655); Larned (no. 4657); Griffin (no. 4658); *Writings* (no. 4661); C. H. and T. (no. 4662); *Am. secs. state* (no. 4796), see " Bibliog. notes "; *Guide hist. lit.* (no. 4634); Myers (no. 5399), for collections of treaties. Miller, *Treaties* (no. 5371), v. I, 39–54, for " Bibliography of United States treaty collections."

Justin Winsor, *Reader's handbook of the American revolution, 1761–1783* (Boston, 1880; reprinted 1890, 1895, and 1899) [1]; "A list of treaties, conventions, and declarations concerning the American revolution and armed neutrality ", in the same author's *America* (no. 4782), v. VII, 82–88 [2]; also by the same author, " The manuscript sources of the history of the United States of America, with particular reference to the American revolution ", *ibid.*, v. VIII, 413–468 [3], which contains a note on foreign archives, now superseded by various later guides (see below, Pt. II, Ch. 3). Greene and Morris (no. 5531), 177–184. Cecil Headlam and C. T. Atkinson, " [Bibliography of] the American revolution ", in *The Cambridge history of the British Empire*, v. I (N.Y. and Cambridge, Eng., 1929), 876–888 [4].

General Works

Of general histories of the United States, see Bancroft (no. 4778); Hildreth (no. 4779); Von Holst (no. 4780); Winsor (no.

---

[1] See also Chapter II: " The Peace Settlement of 1782–1783."

4782); Channing (no. 4784). See also Wriston, *Executive agents* (no. 4799). We note here works on the American revolution as a whole:

Lord Mahon [Philip Henry Stanhope, Earl of Stanhope], *History of England, from the peace of Utrecht to the peace of Versailles, 1713–1783* (London, 1836–54, 7 v.), v. VII [5], a well-balanced and scholarly history which utilized such sources as were available at the time; prints useful documents in the appendix. John Fiske, *The American revolution* (N.Y., 1891, 2 v.) [6], a charming popular account now superseded by more recent works. W. E. H. Lecky, *The American revolution, 1763–1783; being the chapters and passages relating to America from the author's History of England in the eighteenth century*, ed. by J. A. Woodburn (N.Y. and Boston, 1898) [7], a scholarly, luminous work of philosophical insight, condensed as to foreign affairs. Sir George Otto Trevelyan, *The American revolution* (N.Y. and London, 1899–1907, 3 v. in 4; new ed., 1905–12) [8], which is continued and concluded in his *George the Third and Charles Fox, the concluding part of the American revolution* (London, 1912–14, 2 v.) [9], a masterly account by a sometimes oversympathetic Whiggish English historian. C. H. Van Tyne, *The American revolution, 1776–1783* (N.Y. and London, 1905) [10], now superseded in relevant parts by his *The founding of the American republic*, v. I: *The causes of the war of independence;* v. II: *The war of independence* (Boston and N.Y., 1922–29) [11], diplomatic portions of which volumes are based on much study of American and foreign archival sources; unfortunately this history stopped with the year 1778 because of the death of the author. S. G. Fisher, *The struggle for American independence* (Phila. and London, 1908, 2 v.) [12], one of the first dispassionate American accounts. Channing (no. 4784), v. III: *The American revolution*, the best review in any general American history. Wriston (no. 4799), of special value in this and all other periods of American diplomacy. Allan Nevins, *The American states during and after the Revolution, 1775–1789* (N.Y., 1924) [13], a valuable analysis of the political and constitutional evolution of the sovereign states and their confederation, of use to the intensive student of foreign relations.

Special Works

We note here works on the diplomacy of the revolutionary period as a whole.

Theodore Lyman, *The diplomacy of the United States; being an account of the foreign relations of the country from the first treaty with France, in 1778, to the treaty of Ghent, in 1814, with Great Britain* (Boston, 1826) **[14]**, now obsolete; it has the distinction of being the first historical study of American diplomacy. W. H. Trescot, *The diplomacy of the Revolution; an historical study* (N.Y., 1852) **[15]**, the first study based on unpublished MSS. in the Department of State. E. J. Lowell, "The United States of North America, 1775–1782; their political struggles and relations with Europe ", in Winsor, *America* (no. 4782), v. VII, 1–88 **[16]**, is accompanied by critical notes on material then available. E. C. Burnett, "Note on American negotiations for commercial treaties, 1776–1786 ", *Am. hist. rev.*, XVI (1911) 579–587 **[17]**, exceedingly valuable comments on American policy in regard to neutral rights, and exposition of the "Plan of 1776 " in relation to early American treaties; and by the same author, "Ciphers of the revolutionary period ", in *ibid.*, XXII (1917) 329–334 **[18]** contains hints only. Valentín Urtasún, *Historia diplomática de América*, pt. I: *La emancipación de las colonias británicas* (Pamplona, 1920–24, 2 v.) **[19]**, a pretentious study based on first-hand sources, particularly for French and English archives, but strangely not for Spanish archives. J. B. Scott, "Historical introduction ", in *Am. secs. state* (no. 4796), v. I, 3–111 **[20]**. C. H. Van Tyne, *England and America, rivals in the American revolution* (Cambridge, Eng., 1928) **[21]**, ch. 6: "The opposing diplomats of England and America ", a colorful lecture by an authority. A. E. Ingram, "Early American consular service notes ", *Am. foreign service jour.*, VI (1929) 114–117, 152–153, 186–187, 207–208 **[21a]**, biographical sketches of the sixteen consular officers appointed, 1780–1790, at the posts of Canton, Hispaniola, Liverpool, Madeira Island, Martinique, Nantes, Rouen, Bilboa, Hamburg, Marseilles, Cowes, Havre de Grace, London, and Fayal. S. F. Bemis, *The diplomacy of the American revolution* (N.Y., 1935) ("The foundation of American diplomacy [I] ") **[21b]**, a comprehensive and compact diplomatic history of the Revolution, based on existing printed material and very considerable archival sources at home and abroad.

For biographies of American statesmen and diplomatists who touched the diplomacy of the Revolution more or less (John Adams, Samuel Adams, Francis Dana, Silas Deane, John Dickinson, Benjamin Franklin, Alexander Hamilton, Benjamin Harrison, Ralph Izard, John Jay, Thomas Jefferson, Henry Laurens, Arthur Lee, William Lee, R. R. Livingston, John Lovell, James Madison, Gouverneur Morris, Robert Morris, Thomas Paine, Charles Thomson, and George Washington), see the relevant entries and bibliographical data in the *Dictionary of America biography* [2] (hereinafter cited as *D.A.B.* Other statesmen and diplomatists are listed under separate sections of this chapter, below.

Printed Sources

For American official documents and general source collections, see Sparks (no. 5337); Wharton, *Digest* (no. 5366), and *Corres.* (no. 5339); *Journals* (no. 5379); Moore's *Digest* (no. 5365); Burnett, *Letters* (no. 5380). Carlton Savage, *Policy of the United States toward maritime commerce in war.* v. I. *1776–1914* (Wash.: Govt. Print. Off., 1934) (Dept. of State) [22], a valuable official documentary survey by a specialist in the Department of State, publishing, after a factual commentary, the relevant documents in the following classification: enemy goods in neutral ships, neutral goods in enemy ships, definition of contraband of war, continuous voyage, validity of blockade, immunity of private property at sea.

For guides to British and foreign official publications, see below, Pt. II, ch. 2.

For bibliographies of American newspapers, see nos. 5007–5049, particularly Brigham (no. 5012). For English newspapers and periodicals, see Gabler (no. 5027).

For texts of treaties, see Miller, *Treaties* (no. 5371). Gilbert Chinard, ed., *The treaties of 1778, and allied documents* (Baltimore, 1928) [22a] is a convenient publication of the " plan of 1776 ", the treaties with France and the " act separate and secret ", and of the ratification.

Annual register (no. 5058), nos. 18–26, 1775–1783. *Affaires de l'Angleterre et de l'Amérique* (Antwerp, 1776–79, 15 v. in 17) [23], organ of American propaganda. *Parliamentary history* (no. 5410).

---

[2] For references to biographies of American statesmen and diplomatists we consider it supererogatory to do more than make reference throughout this guide (according to the above formula) to the *Dictionary of American biography* (no. 4927), publication of which is now well advanced, and completion of which is anticipated not long after our publication. After each entry in the *D.A.B.* is a note on existing biographies of the individual and his published writings.

Note also the third volume of Bernard Faÿ's *Benjamin Franklin,* comprising a *Bibliographie et étude sur les sources historiques à sa vie* (Paris, 1931) [21c], published after the issue of the *D.A.B.* containing the article on Benjamin Franklin.

For printed writings of the statesmen and diplomatists enumerated above (under " Special Works "), see our list on p. 756.

MSS.: Suggestions

The Papers of the Continental Congress, in the Library of Congress, containing the despatches and instructions of American agents abroad have been voluminously printed by Sparks (no. 5337) and Wharton (no. 5339), but a few are left in manuscript.

For collections of personal papers of men who dealt with American diplomacy throughout the Revolution, see our lists: (1) Papers of the Presidents (Washington, John Adams, Jefferson), p. 862, below. (2) Papers of the Secretaries of State (R. R. Livingston), p. 865, below. (3) Papers of American statesmen and diplomatists (Franklin), p. 868, below. Other personal papers are more appropriately indicated in the suggestions for MS. sources indicated in the following sections of this chapter.

The diplomacy of the American revolution may be traced also in the British (for guides, see p. 890), and French (for guides, see p. 915) archives, from which a wide collection of facsimiles was made in 1889 by B. F. Stevens, *Facsimiles of manuscripts in European archives relating to America, 1773–1783* (no. 5723), copies of which exist in the Library of Congress and some 30 other libraries throughout the world, but mostly in the United States. Mr. Stevens' facsimiles, and other transcript collections (mentioned below, p. 919) were based on a voluminous index, which was purchased by the United States Government, and is now in the Division of Manuscripts of the Library of Congress. Reordering and renumeration of some foreign archives since the preparation of this index makes it necessary to use a key to exploit many parts of it; it has become more of a paleographical curiosity than a useful catalogue. The French foreign office series (for guides see pp. 915–918) *Mémoires et documents, Amérique*, and *Mémoires et documents, États-Unis*, contain valuable material for the preliminaries of American diplomacy, which exists in facsimile in the Library of Congress. Jared Sparks had transcripts made of manuscript material much of it relating to foreign affairs, which is now in Harvard College Library, calendared by Justin Winsor, in the *Bibliographical contributions*, of the Library of Harvard University, no. 22 (Cambridge, Mass., 1889) [24]. The historian, George Bancroft, made a huge collection of transcripts from the archives of England, France, The

Netherlands, and Prussia, of material relating to the American revolution, particularly to foreign relations, which material is only meagerly used in his *History of the United States* (no. 4778). It is described in several places, most succinctly in *Manuscript collections in the New York Public Library* (no. 5555), 309. Decip{}hers of some of the despatches passing between foreign governments and their ministers in England, with cipher keys, 1740–1841, are in the British Museum.

Consult further, Pt. II, ch. 3 for other guides to foreign archive material.

Maps: Suggestions

John Jay, "Maps of North America, 1763–83 ", in Winsor, v. VII (no. 4782) [24a]. P. L. Phillips (no. 5137) shows the extent of European countries and of European colonies in America in 1775–83; his *List* (no. 5135) notes that "the manuscript maps of the revolutionary war, contained in the Faden, Force, and Rochambeau collections, many of them unknown to the historian, are in the Library and here noted." Hulbert, *Crown collection of American maps* (no. 5141). See also Paullin's *Atlas* (no. 213), p. 140, and plate 160.

For Spain and the American revolution, see the *Catálogo de mapas del Depósito de la Guerra* (no. 5139) which lists many maps and plans sent from Seville to Madrid in the early 19th century, including (v. II, 323–331) American maps. Torres Lanzas, *Archivo General de Indias* (no. 5140). Karpinski, *Maps in French, Spanish, and Portuguese archives* (no. 5149).

2. The Beginnings of American Foreign Contacts [3]

Bibliographical Aids

See Sec. 1, above.

Special Works

Gaillard Hunt, *The Department of State of the United States; its history and functions* (New Haven and London, 1914) [25] traces the earliest evolution of the "foreign office" of the United States. E. C. Burnett, "The name 'United States of America'",

---

[3] See also Sec. 3, below, for material regarding Beaumarchais, the Deane Affair, and French aid before the Alliance of 1778.

Am. hist. rev., XXXI (1925) 79-81 [26] gives historical origins of usage of the name. Margaret Miller, " The spy activities of Doctor Edward Bancroft ", *Jour. Am. hist.*, XXII (1928) 70-77, 157-170 [27], for Bancroft see also document printed at end of article by Bemis (no. 59). Ruth Y. Johnston, "American privateers in French ports, 1776-78 ", *Pa. mag. hist.*, LIII (1929) 352-374 [28]. Wriston (no. 4799), ch. 1. Dangerfield (no. 4835). Tyler, *Arthur Lee* (no. 74) shows that during the early months of 1776 Beaumarchais and Lee effected an agreement whereby military supplies were to be sent clandestinely to America by the French government. T. P. Abernethy, " Commercial activities of Silas Deane in France ", *Am. hist. rev.*, XXXIX (1934) 477-485 [29] deals with commercial speculations of Deane and other American representatives, as well as Frenchmen like Grand, Chaumont, *et alii*.

For biographies of John Adams, Samuel Adams, Francis Dana, Silas Deane, John Dickinson, Franklin, Benjamin Harrison, Jay, Jefferson, Arthur Lee, William Lee, R. R. Livingston, Wm. Lovell, and Thomas Paine, see the relevant entries and bibliographical data in the *D.A.B.*

Printed Sources

See Sec. 1, above, particularly Burnett's *Letters* (no. 5380), Wharton (no. 5339), and *Journals* (no. 5379). See also Sec. 3, below, " France and the American Revolution ", particularly Doniol (no. 40), and Secs. 5 and 7.

For the printed writings of American statesmen and diplomatists (enumerated above under " Special Works "), see our list on pp. 756-779.

MSS.: Suggestions

See Secs. 1 and 3, this chapter.

3. France and the American Revolution

Bibliographical Aids

For general bibliographical aids (American), see Sec. 1, above. See also French historical bibliographies (nos. 4732-4739).

A. P. C. Griffin, *List of works relating to the French alliance in the American revolution* (Wash., 1907) (Library of Congress) [30]. Bernard Faÿ, *Bibliographie critique des ouvrages français*

relatifs aux États-Unis, 1770–1800 (Paris, 1925) [31]. L. R. Gottschalk, "Lafayette", *Jour. modern hist.*, II (1930) 281–287 [32] is
a critical bibliographical essay on biographies, contemporary memoirs, and correspondence of Lafayette. S. W. Jackson, *La Fayette,
a bibliography* (N.Y., 1930) [33].

Special Works

We have eliminated from our text many of the titles listed in
Griffin (no. 30), to which the reader is referred for additional
material.

Louis de Loménie, *Beaumarchais et sons temps* (Paris, 1856, 2 v.;
also English ed.: London, 1856, 4v.) [34], the standard biography of
Beaumarchais, based on his papers. Cornélis de Witt, *Thomas Jefferson; étude historique sur la démocratie américaine* (Paris, 1862,
new ed.), also English translation (London, 1862), which has abstracts only of the useful documents printed in the French edition
[35], one of the first documentary studies. Adolphe de Circourt,
*Histoire de l'action commune de la France et de l'Amérique pour
l'indépendance des États-Unis*, par George Bancroft, traduit et an-
notée par le comte de Circourt (Paris, 1876, 3 v.) [36], published by
an *attaché* of the French foreign office who had assisted Bancroft in
his search for documents; contains matter not in Bancroft's original
English edition. Lewis Rosenthal, *America and France; the influence of the United States on France in the XVIIIth century*
(N.Y., 1882) [37], the first study of ideology. Friedrich Kapp,
Life of John Kalb, major-general in the revolutionary army (N.Y.,
1884) [38], an unbiased account of this interesting French observer
and soldier (of Prussian origin), based on his letters. Ludovic de
Colleville, *Les missions secrètes du général-major baron de Kalb et
son rôle de l'indépendance américaine* (Paris, 1885) [39] uses letters
and papers concerning de Kalb's missions to America, furnished by
his granddaughter. Henri Doniol, *Histoire de la participation de
la France à l'établissement des États-Unis d'Amérique* (Paris, 1886–
92, 5 v., and *Complément du tome V*, 1899) [40], a monumental work
voluminously documented with pieces and lengthy extracts from the
archives of the French ministry of foreign affairs, but it must be
used with caution because the author's admiration for Vergennes'
diplomatic successes as a worthy model for French statesmen during
the prostration of the Third Republic may have led him to make his

selections of documents accordingly; also by Doniol, " Le ministère des affaires étrangères de France sous le comte de Vergennes; souvenirs de Hennin sur ce ministre ", *Rev. hist. dipl.*, VII (1893) 528–560 [**41**], Hennin was one of Vergennes' principal functionaries in the newly reorganized foreign office. Albert Malet, " Un ministère des affaires étrangères aux XVIII° siècle; le comte de Vergennes," *Rev. pol. et lit.*, XLV (1890) 300–305 [**42**], a rapid and useful sketch. J. B. Perkins, *France in the American revolution* (Boston and N.Y., 1911) [**43**], a readable work now superseded by Corwin and Phillips. P. C. Phillips, *The West in the diplomacy of the American revolution* (Urbana, 1913) [**44**], a contributive study of French attitude toward expansive American claims to western boundaries. E. S. Corwin, " The French objective in the American revolution ", *Am. hist. rev.*, XXI (1915) 32–61 [**45**], which comprises the opening section of his *French policy and the American alliance of 1778* (Princeton, N.J., 1916) [**46**], a brilliant analysis, based mostly on the documents published by Doniol. C. H. Van Tyne, " Influences which determined the French government to make the treaty with America, 1778 ", *Am. hist. rev.*, XXI (1916) 528–541 [**47**] contends, contrary to Corwin, that France feared the effect of an Anglo-American reconciliation on the security of French and Spanish colonies. J. J. Jusserand, " Our first alliance ", *Nation. geog. mag.*, XXXI (1917) 518–548 [**48**]. Baron Hennet de Goutel, *Vergennes et l'indépendance américaine; Vergennes et Wilson* (Paris, 1918) [**49**]. Joachim Merlant, *La France et la guerre de l'indépendance américane (1776–1783)* (Paris, 1918) [**50**], this and the two previously listed titles are examples of historiography of the Franco-American alliance written during the period of fraternization of soldiers and diplomats, 1917–1918. Elizabeth S. Kite, *Beaumarchais and the war of American independence* (Boston, 1918, 2 v.) [**51**] popularizes Loménie (no. 34); also " Conrad Alexandre Gérard ", *Md. hist. mag.*, XV (1920) 342–344 [**52**] and other articles by the same author (based largely on Doniol) on the first French legation in the United States, published in the *Am. Cath. hist. soc. rec.*, XXXII (1921), 131–150, 274–294, XXXIII (1922) 54–91, XXXIX (1928) 155–174. Philippe Barrey, *Beaumarchais et ses armaments havrais* (Havre, 1919) [**53**]. Amy A. Bernardy, " La mission di Beniamino Franklin a Parigi nei dispacci degli ambasciatori Veneziani in Francia, 1776–1786 ", *Arch.*

storico ital., LXXVIII (1920) 237-262 [54]. Valentín Urtasún, *La alianza francesa* (Pamplona, 1920) [55], being vol. I of his work (see no. 19). C. E. Hill, *Leading American treaties* (N.Y., 1922) ch. 1 [56], a readable summary of the treaties of 1778. F. P. Renaut, *Le pacte de famille et l'Amérique; la politique coloniale franco-espagnole de 1760 à 1792* (Paris, 1922) [57] contains a chapter on the Family Compact and the war in America, by a writer who is exploring increasingly the French and Spanish archives. Alfred Dumaine, " Le comte de Vergennes et l'indépendance des États-Unis ", *Rev. hist. dipl.*, XXXVII (1923) 432-455 [58], an eulogistic essay on Vergennes' political character. S. F. Bemis, " The British secret service and the French-American alliance ",,*Am. hist. rev.*, XXIX (1924) 474-495 [59] uses records of the British secret service contained in Stevens' *Facsimiles* (no. 5723) ; also his *Hussey-Cumberland mission* (no. 113), which reveals from Spanish and other European archives a secret mission of considerable negative importance. Comte Wladimir d'Ormesson, *La première mission officielle de la France aux États-Unis; Conrad-Alexandre Gérard (1778-1779)* (Paris, 1924) [60], a dilletante production of a 20th century journalist habitué of the French foreign office. O. W. Stephenson, " The supply of gunpowder in 1776 ", *Am. hist. rev.*, XXX (1925) 271-297 [61] shows that through French assistance came the powder that enabled the United States to win the victory of Saratoga. C. H. Van Tyne, " French aid before the alliance of 1778 ", *Am. hist. rev.*, XXXI (1925) 20-40 [62] uses French archives, and Stephenson to emphasize the importance of this early secret French assistance. Bernard Faÿ, *L'esprit révolutionnaire en France et aux États-Unis à la fin du XVIII*[e] *siécle* (Paris, 1925; English ed.: N.Y., 1927) [63], a brilliant study which established the reputation of a French historian of our day; his " Les débuts de Franklin en France ", *Rev. de Paris*, XXXVIII (1931) 577-604 [64], and " Le triomphe de Franklin en France ", *ibid.*, 872-896 [65], useful chips from his larger labors. M. M. Lowes, " Les premières relations commerciales entre Bordeaux et les Etats-Unis d'Amérique, 1775-1789 ", *Rev. hist. Bordeaux*, XXI-XXII (1927-1928), passim. [66]. Réné Dalsème, *La vie de Beaumarchais* (Paris, 1928; Eng. edition: N.Y. and London, 1929) [67]. Roger Lafont, *Beaumarchais, le brilliant armateur* (Paris, 1928) [67a]. Beckles Willson, *America's ambassadors to France (1777-1927). A narrative of Franco-American diplo-*

matic relations (N.Y., 1928) [68]. W. B. Clark, *Lambert Wickes, sea raider and diplomat; the story of a naval captain of the revolution* (New Haven and London, 1932) [69] pieces together in a narrative voluminous excerpts, largely from Stevens' facsimiles, of documents relating to American abuses of French neutrality; and reports of British secret service operations. D. D. Irvine, " The Newfoundland fishery; a French objective in the war of American independence ", *Canad. hist. rev.*, XIII (1932) 268-284 [70] attaches much importance to the French desire for the fisheries as a motive for entering the war. Gaston Martin, " Commercial relations between Nantes and the American colonies during the war of independence ", *Jour. econ. and business hist.*, IV (1932) 812-829 [71] exploits departmental archives of Loire-Inférieure, to exhibit interest of commerce of port of Nantes in seeing overthrown the restrictions of the British Empire on American colonial commerce. Two studies by J. J. Meng: *The comte de Vergennes; European phases of his American diplomacy, 1774-1780* (Wash., 1932) [72], a study of the relation of European to American diplomacy, from the French archives; and " The place of Canada in French diplomacy of the American revolution ", *Bul. recherches hist.*, XXXIX (1933) 665-687 [73] uses sources, principally Doniol, to stress consistent French opposition to any conquest of Canada, despite Lafayette's ambitions for such. L. G. Tyler, "Arthur Lee, a neglected statesman ", *Tyler's quar. hist. and geneal. mag.*, XIV (1932-33) 65-76, 129-138, 197-216 [74] asserts that " the credit of initiating the important negotiations for getting supplies from France and Spain cannot be denied to Mr. Lee." Lewis Einstein, *Divided loyalties; Americans in England during the war of independence* (Boston, 1933) [75], this is a comprehensive and coherent study of American-born spies and informers utilized by George III in England and France. V. G. Setser, " Did Americans originate the conditional most-favored-nation clause?" *Jour. mod. hist.*, V (1933) 319-323 [76] concludes that France did. Bernard Faÿ, " La première légation des États-Unis en France ", *Rev. hist. dipl.*, XLVIII (1934) 470-476 [76a] identifies the various dwellings of the American agents in France during the years 1775-1778.

For biographies of American statesmen and diplomatists, see note in Sec. 1, above. Note also biographies of Lafayette and Thomas Paine.

For biographies of French statesmen, consult the *D.B.F.* (no. 4965) ; for Vergennes, see bibliography in Meng (no. 72 above).

Printed Sources

For American official documents and general source collections, see Sec. 1, above.

The best printed source for Franco-American diplomacy during the American revolution is Doniol's voluminous work (no. 40). For French instructions to ambassadors in Spain, too drastically abridged, but with useful editorial notes, see no. 5429, *Espagne*, III (1722–1793). See also, for note on printed French diplomatic documents, 1763–1783 : *The Cambridge history of the British Empire*, v. I (Cambridge, 1929), 834 [**77**]. Particular documents among printed sources are : *Exposé des motifs de la conduite du roi, relativement à l'Angleterre* (Paris, 1779) [**78**], an official manifesto justifying French intervention as a defensive measure. *Exposé des motifs de la conduite du roi de France, relativement à l'Angleterre; mémoire justificatif pour servir de réponse à l'exposé, &c. de la cour de France* (London, 1779) [**79**], written by the celebrated historian, Edward Gibbon, at the instigation of the British government as a reply to the French *Exposé* (no. 78). P. A. Caron de Beaumarchais, *Observations sur le Mémoire justificatif de la cour de Londres* (London and Phila., 1779) [**80**]. J. M. Gérard de Rayneval, *Observations sur le Mémoire justificatif de la cour de Londres* (Paris, 1780; and English edition : Phila., 1781) [**81**]. Arthur Lee, *Extracts from a letter written to the president of Congress, by the Honorable Arthur Lee, esquire, in answer to a libel published in the Pennsylvania gazette of the fifth of December, 1778, by Silas Deane, esquire* (Phila., 1780) [**82**] ; and by the same writer, *Observations on certain commercial transactions in France, laid before Congress* (Phila., 1780) [**83**]. Silas Deane, *Paris papers; or, Mr. Silas Deane's late intercepted letters to his brothers, and other intimate friends in America* (N.Y., 1782) [**84**], this being a reprint by James Rivington from his *Royal gazette*, for Oct. 24–Dec. 12, 1781 (the authenticity of these letters has been challenged) ; also by Deane, *An address to the United States of North America* (London, 1784) [**85**] ; these Deane documents all supplement Isham's printed collection (no. 5215). J. F. P. Maurepas, *Mémoires du comte de Maurepas*, 3d ed. (Paris, 1792, 3 v.) [**86**]. Comte C. G. de Vergennes, *Mémoire historique et politique sur la Louisiane, par M. de Vergennes, ministre de Louis XVI* (Paris, 1802) [**87**], regarding the authenticity of which see *Am. hist. rev.*, X (1905) 250, and Phillips (no. 44), 30. John Dickinson, *An address on the past, present, and eventual relations of the United States to France* (N.Y., 1803) [**88**]. Cornélis de Witt, *Thomas Jefferson* (no. 35) contains extracts from the correspondence of Vergennes and other French documents relating to American affairs, 1775-1776. *Papers in relation to the case of Silas Deane*, ed. by E. D. Ingraham (Phila., 1855) [**89**]. John Bigelow, *Beaumarchais the merchant; letters of Théveneau de Francey, 1777-1780* (N.Y., 1870) [**90**] includes extracts from the letters of Théveneau de Francey, confidential agent of Beaumarchais in America, addressed to Rodriguez, Hortalez and Co. (for replies see no. 99 below). De Circourt (no. 36), v. III: "Documents originaux inédits." John Durand, ed., *New materials for the history of the American revolution, translated from documents in the French archives* (N.Y., 1889) [**91**], the greater part of which relate to Beaumarchais' part in the revolution. Edward Bancroft, *A narrative of the objects and proceedings of Silas Deane, as commissioner of the United colonies to France; made to the British government in 1776*, ed. by P. L. Ford (Brooklyn, N.Y., 1891) [**92**]; for Dean and Bancroft, see also Bemis's article (no. 100). *Reply of William Lee to the charges of Silas Deane, 1779*, ed. by W. C. Ford (Brooklyn, N.Y., 1891) [**93**]. "Rapport du chevalier de la Luzerne, ministre de France à Philadelphie, sur la situation politique, militaire et commerciale des États-Unis à la fin de l'année 1781 ", *Rev. hist. dipl.*, V (1891) 421-436 [**94**], from the *Archives du Ministère des Affaires Étrangères, Correspondance politique, États-Unis*, XIX, 131 (see pp. 915-918, below). Jules Flammermont, *Les correspondances des agents diplomatiques étrangers en France avant la Révolution* (Paris, 1896) [**95**]. D. E. Huger Smith, "The mission of Col. John Laurens to Europe in 1781 ", *S.C. hist. mag.*, I (1900) 13-41, 136-151, 213-222, 311-322, and II (1901) 27-43, 108-125 [**96**], publishes 60 contemporary documents. Marquis de Lafayette, "Letters from Lafayette to Luzerne, 1780-1782 ", ed. by W. G. Leland and E. C. Burnett, *Am. hist. rev.*, XX (1915) 341-376, 576-612 [**97**]. *Warren-Adams letters; being chiefly a correspondence among John Adams, Samuel Adams, and James Warren* (Boston, 1917-25, 2 v.) (Mass. Hist. Soc. Coll., v. LXXII-LXXIII)

[98]. Jules Marsan, *Beaumarchais et les affaires d'Amérique; lettres inédits* (Paris, 1919) [99], consisting of 30 letters written by Beaumarchais to his agent in America, Théveneau de Francey. " Edward Bancroft's memorial to the Marquis of Carmarthen ", ed. by S. F. Bemis, *Am. hist. rev.*, XXIX (1924) 492–495 [100] publishes Bancroft's own summary of his espionage. C. M. Andrews, "A note on the Franklin-Deane mission to France ", *Yale univ. lib. gazette*, II (1928) 53–68 [101] includes a hitherto unprinted part of Deane's well known *Memorial* and 2 hitherto unprinted letters. " Beaumarchais et l'Amérique; une lettre inédite de Beaumarchais ", *France-Amérique*, n.s. XX (1929) 38–41 [102], a letter on the attitude of Beaumarchais toward the American colonies, addressed to Théveneau de Francey, which is not contained in the collection published in Marsan (no. 99). *The private papers of John, Earl of Sandwich, first lord of the admiralty, 1771–1782*, ed. by G. R. Barnes and J. H. Owen. v. II (London, 1933) (Navy Records Society) [103] throws light on the unpreparedness of the British navy for the crisis precipitated by the entry of the French into the American revolution. J. J. Meng, ed., *Conrad Alexandre Gérard: despatches and instructions (1778–1779)* (Wash., 1935) [103a] is a critically edited and translated printing of the correspondence of the first French minister to the United States with the Comte de Vergennes.

For the printed writings of American statesmen and diplomatists (enumerated in Sec. 1, above), also of Lafayette [4] and Thomas Paine, see our list on p. 756.

MSS.: Suggestions

See Sec. 1, above.

The official American diplomatic correspondence is in the Papers of the Continental Congress now in the Library of Congress (mostly printed by Sparks (no. 5337), Wharton (no. 5339), and in the printed writings of John Adams, Deane, Franklin, and Arthur Lee (see our list on p. 756)). For the diplomatic correspondence of the French foreign office with the United States, series *Correspondance politique*, and *idem, supplémentaire*, see below, p. 917. For a brief note on material in French archives, 1763–1783, see bibliography in *The Cambridge hist. Brit. Empire* (no. 77), v. I, 834. The correspond-

---

[4] A comprehensive collection of the correspondence of Lafayette, under the editorship of L. R. Gottschalk is being prepared.

ence of the French legation in the United States, from this series is contained in transcript in the Library of Congress: B. F. Stevens' Transcripts relating to the French Alliance, 1778–1784, which has been supplemented by interlading additional transcripts more recently secured (see below, no. 5724, and p. 7). See also the Stevens *Facsimiles* (no. 5723). *Correspondance politique, États-Unis* is partly calendared for the years 1778 to 1781, inclusive, in the *Report of the work of the Public archives [of Canada]*, for the years 1912 and 1913 (Ottawa, 1913–14, 2 v.) **[104]**. The significant series from the French foreign office, *Mémoires et documents, États-Unis*, and *Mémoires et documents, Amérique*, also exist in photocopy in the Library of Congress. The original minutes of the French legation in the United States, 1777–1796, are in the private library of Mr. William S. Mason, Evanston, Illinois. Photostats of the same exist in the Library of Congress. The Library of Congress possesses the original papers of Jean Holker, the first French consul in the United States. The William L. Clements Library, at Ann Arbor, Mich., has about 70 Holker papers supplementing the collection at the Library of Congress. The Library of Congress has also, in the series *United States finance*, two documents: *Account of bills drawn on the commissioners of the United States at Paris for interest of the monies lent to the public previous to the 1st of March 1778 and paid by Mr. Grand, banker, by order of Dr. Franklin*, and *Journal of cash for the commission at the court of France from Dec. 7, 1776, to Apr. 19, 1779*. The Stevens *Facsimiles* (no. 5723) contain much manuscript material relating to the formation of the French Alliance. The correspondence of the French foreign office with various European countries (notably Great Britain, The Netherlands and Spain) may also be consulted; for guides, (see below, p. 917). The original MSS. of the American diplomatic correspondence in the Papers of the Continental Congress, now in the Library of Congress, have been mostly printed by Sparks and Wharton (see Garrison, no. 5522). See also the Stevens *Index* (no. 5722), Bancroft transcripts of foreign archival material now in the New York Public Library (see Greene and Morris, no. 5531), and the Sparks transcripts of foreign archival material now in the Harvard College Library (no. 5543). Consult also the Franklin papers (p. 873), the Jay papers (p. 875), and the Deane papers (p. 872).

The Library of Congress has a fairly large collection (over 100 pieces) of original accounts and receipts relating to Deane's French mission. The New York Public Library has a journal or autobiography (in transcript) of Arthur Lee describing his diplomatic activities in 1777, interviews with foreign ministers, and his relations with Franklin and Deane. The papers of Robert Morris, also in the Library of Congress, include some of Beaumarchais' accounts during the Revolution. For calendars of the Arthur Lee MSS. in Harvard College Library, American Philosophical Society, and the Virginia Historical Society, see nos. 5542, 5537, and 5561. The papers of the Massachusetts clergyman, Samuel Cooper, in the Huntington Library at San Marino, California, also deal with the French Alliance (letters from Franklin, Luzerne, copies of correspondence of John Adams with Vergennes (printed)). The United States Treasury Department has in its unlisted and unindexed archives various important papers relating to the monies furnished to the United States by France.

4. Spain and the American Revolution

Bibliographical Aids

For general aids (American), see Sec. 1, above. See also (for Spain) Sánchez Alonso (no. 4759), and University of California Catalog (no. 4685).

Special Works

Manuel Dánvila y Collado, *Reinado de Carlos III* (Madrid, 1893–96, 6 v.), v. IV-V [105], based on archives of the Spanish foreign office; it is the most valuable for diplomatic history of the general histories of the reign of Charles III. François Rousseau, *La participation de l'Espagne à la guerre d'Amérique, 1779–1783* (Paris, 1902) also printed in *Rev. quest. hist.*, LXXII (1902) 444–489 [106], unreliable; and by the same author, *Règne de Charles III d'Espagne, 1759–1788* (Paris, 1907, 2 v.) [107]. F. E. Chadwick, *The relations of the United States and Spain, diplomacy* (N.Y., 1909) [108], an impartial and scholarly summary based largely on printed sources. Phillips (no. 44). Corwin (no. 45). Margaret B. Downing, "Oliver Pollock, patriot and financier", *Ill. Cath. hist. rev.*, II (1919) 196–207 [109], analysis of *A representation of the case of Oliver Pol-*

lock (Wash., 1803) [**110**], a brief written by an attorney, A. B. Woodward, presenting a claim to Congress, it exhibits many original papers bearing on Pollock's activities in New Orleans and Havana during the revolution securing military supplies. Manuel Conrotte, *La intervención de España en la independencia de los Estados Unidos de la América del Norte* (Madrid, 1920) [**111**], superseded by Yela Utrilla (no. 112). Renaut, *Pacte de famille* (no. 57). Urtazún (no. 19). J. F. Yela Utrilla, *España ante la independencia de los Estados Unidos* (Lérida, 1925, 2 v.) [**112**], of which v. II is documentary, a sort of Spanish supplement to Doniol (no. 40), it is the most important single book on Spanish-American relations during the Revolution. S. F. Bemis (no. 506), ch. 1; and his *The Hussey-Cumberland mission and American independence; an essay in the diplomacy of the American revolution* (Princeton, 1931) [**113**] which reveals for the first time, from Spanish and other European archives, the inner history of Spain's efforts to make a separate peace with England for Gibraltar, at the expense of France and of perfect American independence. Gustavo Otero Múñoz, "La independencia de la América y los proyectos de Aranda y Godoy", *Boletín de la historia y antigüedades*, XV (Bogota, 1926) [**114**]. S. G. Coe, *The mission of William Carmichael to Spain* (Baltimore, 1928) [**115-6**], the only study of the first accredited and accepted American diplomatic representative to Spain. J. A. James, *George Rogers Clark* (no. 232), which incorporates previous articles on Spain in the West during the revolution; and by the same writer, "Oliver Pollock, financier of the revolution in the West", *Miss. Valley hist. rev.*, XVI (1929) 67-80 [**117**], these works are illustrative of Spanish-American frontier relations. A. P. Nasatir, "The Anglo-Spanish frontier in the Illinois country during the American revolution, 1779-1783", *Ill. state hist. soc. jour.*, XXI (1928) 291-358 [**118**], the first of a series of studies by the author, utilizing Spanish sources. Richard Konetzke, *Die Politik des grafen Aranda; ein Beitrag zur Geschichte des spanisch-englischen Weltgegensatzes im 18. Jahrhundert* (Berlin, 1929) [**119**], a careful and balanced biography of the Spanish ambassador in France, based on his official correspondence. Kathryn T. Abbey, "Efforts of Spain to maintain sources of information in the British colonies before 1779", *Miss. Valley hist. rev.*, XV (1929) 56-68 [**120**]; and the same author's "Spanish projects for the reoccupation of the Floridas during the American revolution", *Hisp. Am. hist. rev.*, IX (1929) 265–285 [**121**] are both useful contributions. J. W. Caughey, "Bernardo de Gálvez and the English smugglers on the Mississippi, 1777", *Hisp. Am. hist. rev.*, XII (1932) 46–58 [**122**] uses Spanish colonial sources to show that captures of British ships were due to sporadic Spanish attempts to stop smuggling rather than to interference with navigation rights; and by the same writer, "Willing's expedition down the Mississippi, 1778", *La. hist. quar.*, XV (1932) 5–36 [**123**], based on the Pollock papers and other documents; and *Bernardo de Gálvez in Louisiana, 1776–1783* (Berkeley, Calif., 1934) [**123a**], as governor of the colony of Louisiana, he had an important role in the struggle between Spain and England. This work is based on MSS. in the *Archivo General de Indias*, Seville, and other repositories in Spain and the United States. P. H. Giddens, "Arthur Lee, first United States envoy to Spain", *Va. mag. hist.*, XL (1932) 3–13 [**124**]. Lawrence Kinnaird, "The Spanish expedition against Fort St. Joseph in 1781, a new interpretation", *Miss. Valley hist. rev.*, XIX (1932) 173–191 [**125**] analyses the capture of St. Joseph as a raid planned by the local commander at St. Louis. H. B. Bates, "Two Bourbon ministers and Arthur Lee", *Hisp. Am. hist. rev.*, XIII (1933) 489–492 [**126**], a very brief note, with archival references, of value only to one closely interested in Lee's activities.

For biographies of American diplomatists to Spain (Carmichael, John Jay, and Arthur Lee), see the relevant entries and bibliographical data in the *D.A.B.* Biographies of Spanish statesmen and diplomatists (Floridablanca and Aranda): A. Baquero, *Floridablanca, su biografía y bibliografía* (Murcia, 1909) [**127**]. C. Alcázar Molina, *El conde de Floridablanca; notas para su estudio* (Madrid, 1929) [**128**]. Segismundo Moret y Prendergast, "El conde de Aranda", *Revista de España*, LXI (1878) 394–414, 540–548 [**129**]. C. Carabias, *Bocetos históricos (casa de Borbón)* (Valladolid, 1886) [**130**] includes a sketch of Aranda. Konetzke, *Aranda* (no. 119).

Printed Sources

For American official documents and general source collections, see Sec. 1, above.

"Memorial presentado al rey Carlos III, y repetido a Carlos IV, por el Conde de Florida Blanca, renunciando el ministerio", in the *Obras originales del Conde de Floridablanca*, ed. by Antonio Ferrer del Río (Madrid, 1867), p. 307-350 [**131**], gives a résumé of the diplomatic negotiations preceding the signing of the peace between Spain and England. Flammermont (no. 95). *Recueil* (no. 273), *Espagne*, t. III, for notes (only) on French instructions to ambassadors in Spain. " Spanish correspondence concerning the American revolution ", ed. by J. A. Robertson, in *Hisp. Am. hist. rev.*, I (1918) 299-316 [**132**], a few documents only. Yela Utrilla (no. 112), v. II serves as a meager Spanish documentary supplement to Doniol (no. 40). For occasional documents note files of the *Hispanic American historical review, Mississippi Valley historical review*, and the *North Carolina historical review*.

For the printed writings of Franklin, Jay, Arthur Lee, and Washington, see list on p. 756.

MSS.: Suggestions

See Sec. 1, above.

The official correspondence of the American diplomatists having to deal with Spain during the Revolution (Arthur Lee, Franklin, John Jay, William Carmichael) is preserved in the Library of Congress, in the Papers of the Continental Congress, but is mostly printed in Sparks (no. 5337) and Wharton (no. 5339). For personal papers of Arthur Lee, Franklin, and Jay, see our list on pp. 868-883. The Library of Congress has a private journal of Arthur Lee (Dec. 16, 1776-Sept. 15, 1777) covering in part the period of his mission to Spain. As mentioned elsewhere (p. 865) Jay's letterbook, 1779 to 1782, now in the Huntington Library (photostat in the Library of Congress) is practically all printed in Wharton (no. 5339). The official correspondence of the Spanish Government in regard to the American revolution is now preserved in the *Archivo General de Simancas* and the *Archivo Histórico Nacional* at Madrid and in the *Archivo General de Indias*, at Seville. For further analysis, together with photocopies and transcripts, see below, p. 898. For Bancroft transcripts on Spanish affairs see Greene and Morris (no. 5331). For isolated Spanish pieces in the United States (mostly transcripts) see Robertson's *Guide* (no. 5560).

As to those portions of Jay's private correspondence which may still be unprinted, see our list, p. 865. In some of his last letters written just before his death early in 1795 in Madrid, Carmichael mentions that he had sent a trunk of his own correspondence to

Cadiz, whence he had expected to embark for the United States. We have no trace of the trunk or its contents since then. We note two lengthy Spanish memoirs, of Floridablanca, and one of Aranda: *Representación hecha al Augusto Monarca Rey de España por su ministro de estado Conde de Floridablanca*, 1789, preserved in the *Biblioteca Universitaria*, at Valencia, and *Representaciones de Floridablanca á Carlos III*, a summary of his ministerial labors, in 378 folio pages, preserved in the *Biblioteca del Monasterio Montserrat* (see Matteson's *Guide*, no. 5591); and (by Aranda) *Memoria secreta presentada al Rey de España sobre la independencia de las colonias después de haber firmado el tratado de Paris de 1783*, now preserved in the *Biblioteca Hispano-Ultramarina*, Madrid (see Sánchez-Alonso (no. 4759), item 8476). There are in the Library of Congress two volumes of MS. letters and accounts of Oliver Pollock, 1767–1781, relating in part to his financial dealings with Spanish colonial authorities. See also for Pollock's papers, no. 50 of the Continental Congress papers in that library. There are also unindexed and unlisted papers in the United States Treasury Department relating to monies furnished by Spain to the United States.

5. British Efforts at Reconciliation, 1774–1782

Bibliographical Aids

See Sec. 1, above.

Special Works

Timothy Pitkin, *A political and civil history of the United States of America, from the year 1763 to the close of the administration of President Washington in March 1797* (New Haven, 1828, 2 v.) [133] includes considerable discussion of the Carlisle peace mission. Jared Sparks, *The life of Gouverneur Morris* (Boston, 1832, 2 v.) [134]. Lord Mahon, *History of England* (no. 5), a general work with considerable material on the Carlisle mission. Mary A. M. Marks, *England and America, 1763 to 1783* (London, 1907, 2 v.) [135], a lively Whiggish history. Reginald Lucas, *Lord North, second earl of Guilford, K. G., 1732–1792* (London, 1913, 2 v.) [136], a record of North's career, drawn from familiar sources. Bemis (no. 59). W. T. Davis, *The Conference or Billopp house, Staten Island, New York* (Staten Island, 1926) [137], for an account of the conference of representatives of the American and British governments to discuss the war, at Staten Island, Sept. 11, 1776. G. H. Guttridge, *David Hartley, M. P., an advocate of conciliation, 1774–1783* (Berkeley, Calif., 1926) **[138]** uses Hartley's MS. papers and other, printed, sources to portray his attempts at conciliation, by means of letters to Franklin and unaccredited contacts with the British ministry. C. W. Rife, " Ethan Allen, an interpretation," *New Eng. quar.*, II (1929) 561–584 **[138a]**, a reliable picture of Ethan Allen as leader of the Vermont separatists during the Revolution, whose constituents would rather accept British rule than the jurisdiction of New York. Two recent biographies [5] of the Allen brothers are: J. B. Wilbur, *Ira Allen, founder of Vermont, 1751– 1814* (Boston and N.Y., 1928, 2 v.) **[138b]**, compilation rather than a biography, it publishes many documents relative to the separatist movement to exculpate the Allens from any treasonable implications; and John Pell, *Ethan Allen* (Boston and N.Y., 1929) **[138c]**, written without distortion or exculpation, deals with the opportunistic intrigues of Ethan and Ira Allen with the British. H. S. Wardner, " The Haldimand negotiations ", *Vt. hist. soc. proc.*, n.s. II, no. 1 (1931) 3–29 **[138d]**, the separatist movement in the Revolution based upon Capt. Justus Sherwood's official report of his initial diplomatic conference with Ethan Allen obtained by the writer from the Public Record Office, London.

Printed Sources

For American official documents and general source collections, see Sec. 1, above.

Joseph Reed, *Remarks on Governor Johnstone's Speech in Parliament; with a collection of all the letters and authentic papers, relative to his proposition to engage the interest of one of the delegates of the state of Pennsylvania, in the Congress of the United States of America, to promote the views of the British commissioners* (Phila., 1779) **[139]**. *The journal and correspondence of William, Lord Auckland* (London, 1861–62, 4 v.) **[140]**, as William Eden he was a member of the Carlisle peace commission of 1778. " Letters from Captain Sherwood on secret service, 1780–1781 ", in the *Report on Canadian archives*, by Douglas Brymner, 1882 (Ottawa, 1883) 8–10 **[140a]**, a brief calendar of documents, not the letters themselves, of Capt. Justus Sherwood's negotiations with the " state " of Vermont.

---

[5] Published too late for inclusion in the *D.A.B.*

"Some account of James Hutton's visit to Franklin, in France, in December of 1777 ", *Pa. mag. hist.*, XXXII (1908) 223–232 [**141**] consists of extracts from various letters written shortly after the visit, by Franklin, Hutton, and others, relating to Hutton's endeavors as confidential agent of the king to bring about a reconciliation of the colonies with the mother country.   S. E. Morison, *Sources and documents illustrating the American revolution, 1764–1788* (Oxford, 1923) [**142**] prints the "Royal instructions to the peace commission of 1778." *The correspondence of King George the Third, from 1760 to December 1783*, ed. by Sir John Fortescue (London, 1927–28, 6 v.) [**143**], printed from the original papers in the royal archives at Windsor, a highly important publication, indispensable, but unfortunately does not include the important enclosures referred to in the correspondence.

MSS.: Suggestions

See Sec. 1, above.

About one-third of the Stevens *Facsimiles* (no. 5723) relates to the Carlisle Peace Commission of 1778, consisting of reproductions from the British Colonial Office records, from the Carlisle MSS., the papers of William Eden (Lord Auckland), and other sources.   The papers of Lord North are in Rhodes House, Oxford, England.   The papers of the Earl of Carlisle, preserved at Castle Howard, are described and calendared in the *Fifteenth report of the Historical Manuscripts Commission*, Appendix, part VI (London, 1897) [**144**]. There is in the Library of Congress a MS. copy of the secret instructions to the Earl of Carlisle.   The Auckland papers (correspondence and papers of William Eden, first Baron Auckland) including many relating to the peace mission to America in 1778, are in the British Museum (Add. MSS. 34412–34471), for list of American material, see Andrews and Davenport (no. 5590), 145.   The papers of Sir Henry Clinton in the possession of Mr. William L. Clements include also the papers taken over by Clinton from Sir William Howe, his predecessor as commander-in-chief of the British army in America, both of whom were *ex officio* members of British peace commissions during the war.   The papers of Sir Guy Carleton, who succeeded Clinton, are now held by the Williamsburg Holding Corporation (for calendar, see no. 5598).   The Stopford-Sackville papers (Lord George Germain, secretary of state for colonial affairs, 1775–1782, are in the William L. Clements Library, and include material on the several peace offensives throughout the course of the war (for calendar, see no. 5596, below).

For guides to British Foreign Office and Colonial Office records, see below, nos. 5570–5583.

For French reactions, see " Manuscripts: Suggestions ", in Sec. 3, above.

6. The Netherlands and the American Revolution

Bibliographical Aids

For general aids (American), see Sec. 1, above. See also Fruin (no. 4750) ; Nijhoff (no. 4751).

Special Works

F. G. Slothouwer, " De erkenning van den Noord-Amerikaanschen staat door de Republiek der Vereenigde Nederlanden ", *Bijdragen voor Vaderlandsche geschiedenis en oudheidkunde*, 3d ser., v. VII (The Hague, 1893) 146–182 [145], now superseded by works of later investigators. Fauchille (no. 171). H. T. Colenbrander, *De Patriottentijd, hoofdzakelijk naar buitenlandsche bescheiden* (The Hague, 1897, 3 v.) [146], the standard authority and classical work on Dutch foreign relations, 1776–1787, based on exhaustive multiple archival research, indispensable for an understanding of the foreign policy of the Netherlands during the war of American independence. A. C. Buell, *Paul Jones, founder of the American navy* (N.Y., 1900, 2 v.) [147] contains a chapter on the " diplomatic duel in the Texel " between Sir Joseph Yorke, British ambassador to Holland, and Paul Jones, which involved the question of British neutrality and the possible recognition of the United States by Holland. J. F. Jameson, " St. Eustatius in the American revolution ", *Am. hist. rev.*, VIII (1903) 683–708 [148], a well-known and scholarly article on Dutch trade to America via St. Eustatius, giving valuable sidelights on Dutch-American relations during the Revolution. E. D. Baumann, " Het bezoek van Paul Jones aan ons land in 1779 ", *Tijdschrift voor geschiedenis, land- en volkenkunde*, XIX (1904) 249–272 [149], in which a Dutch scholar investigates the John Paul Jones episode. Friedrich Edler, *The Dutch Republic and the American revolution* (Baltimore, 1911) [150] depends, for Dutch sources, on Sparks, Bancroft, and Stevens transcripts. C. O. Paullin, *Diplomatic negotiations of American naval officers, 1778–1883* (Baltimore, 1912) **[151]** touches the diplomatic activities of John Paul Jones, 1778–1792. D. C. Seitz, *Paul Jones, his exploits in English seas during 1778–1780* (N.Y., 1917) **[152]** contains contemporary accounts collected from English newspapers, and a complete bibliography. F. W. van Wijk, *De republiek en Amerika, 1776–1782* (Leyden, 1921) **[153]** is a particular contribution for the William Lee–De Neufville project of a treaty, based principally on Dutch sources. Murk de Jong Hendrikszoon, *Joan Derk van der Capellen; staatkundig levensbeeld uit de wordingstijd van de moderne demokratie in Nederland* (Groningen and The Hague, 1922) **[154]** concerns American relations and political recognition. P. J. van Winter, "Onze eerste diplomatieke betrekkingen met de Vereenigde Staten", *Tijdschrift voor geschiedenis* XXXVIII (1923) 68–82 **[155]**; and his *Het aandeel van den Amsterdamschen handel aan den opbouw van het Amerikaansche gemeenebest* (The Hague, 1927–33, 2 v.) **[156]** uses Dutch and American unprinted sources to stress economic phases of diplomatic relations between Holland and the United States until 1803. F. P. Renaut, *La neutralité hollandaise devant la guerre d'Amérique, 1775–1780* (Paris, 1924) **[157]**; and by the same author, *Les Provinces-Unies et la guerre d'Amérique, 1775–1784* (Paris, 1924–32, 3 v.) **[158]**, each volume devoted to a specific subject as follows: *De la neutralité à la belligerance, 1775–1780; La propagande insurgente, C. W. F. Dumas, 1775–1780;* and *La marine hollandaise de 1776 à 1783.* Renaut's volumes, based on European multiple-archive research, are successively more thorough and scholarly.

For biographies of John Adams, Francis Dana, Benjamin Franklin, Henry Laurens, Arthur Lee, and William Lee, see the relevant entries and bibliographical data in the *D.A.B.*

Printed Sources

For American official documents and general source collections, see Sec. 1, above.

For guide to Dutch printed official documents, see no. 5431.

Peter Force, "Henry Laurens in England", *Hist. mag.,* XI (2d ser., I) (1867) 129–135 **[159]** prints a number of official documents and extracts from English newspapers, 1780–1782. *Missive van een Amsteladmsch burger aan zynen vriend t'Utrecht, rakende de memorie door den ridder Yorke, aan Haar Hoog Mogende over-*

gegeven op den 16de november 1780 (Utrecht and Amsterdam, 1780?) [**160**], a defence of the burgomaster P. J. van Berckel. "A narrative of the capture of Henry Laurens, of his confinement in the Tower of London, etc., 1780, 1781, 1782 ", *S.C. hist. soc. coll.*, I (1857) 18–68 [**161**] consists of Laurens' report to Benjamin Franklin, followed by documents, letters, etc., relating to his imprisonment in the Tower of London. *Brieven van en aan Joan Derck van der Capellen van de Poll* (Utrecht, 1879) (Historisch Genootschap, Utrecht, *Werken*, n.s., no. 27) [**162**], letters chiefly about the foreign relations of Holland, by a Dutch protagonist of American independence. *Dépêches van Thulemeyer, 1763–1788*, Robert Fruin and H. T. Colenbrander, eds. (Amsterdam, 1912) [**163**], the correspondence of Frederick the Great's diplomatic agent at The Hague. *Archives ou Correspondance inédite de de la maison d'Orange-Nassau*, 5th ser., v. 1–3, 1766–1789 (Leyden, 1910–15, 3 v.) [**164**], ed. by F. J. L. Krämer, the formidable collection of the correspondence of the Stathouder and his family. *Correspondance de la famille du Stathouder, 1777–1795*, edited by Johanna W. A. Naber (The Hague, 1932) [**165**] supplements the above with additional material, particularly correspondence of the *Stathouder's* wife and children. *Pol.-Corres. Friedrich's des Grossen* (no. 201). J. J. Meng, "A revolutionary fragment ", *Am. Cath. hist. soc. rec.*, XLII (1931) 191–196 [**166**], a detail showing the manner in which a certain despatch from an American secret agent in Holland was forwarded to Congress at Philadelphia, to be found in the official report no. 37, of the Abbé Desnoyers, French ambassador at The Hague, to Vergennes.

For the printed writings of American diplomatists (enumerated above under " Special Works "), see our list on p. 756.

MSS.: Suggestions

The official American sources for early contacts with The Netherlands are to be found in the Papers of the Continental Congress in the Library of Congress, mostly printed by Sparks (no. 5337) and Wharton (no. 5339). The Dutch sources are preserved in the Foreign Office papers in the *Rijksarchief*, at The Hague. For these and other Dutch archival sources, with guides and catalogues thereto, see below, p. 921. Among these a notable source consists of the papers of Charles William Frederick Dumas, acquired from descendants by the *Rijksarchief* (for calendar, see no. 5731). The Library of Congress has photocopies of both the official Dutch diplomatic correspondence and the Dumas papers. There are a few original Dumas pieces (outside the Papers of the Continental Congress) in the Library of Congress. The papers of Henry Laurens are in the library of the South Carolina Historical Society at Charleston. For the Adams papers, see our list of papers of the Presidents, p. 862. For John Paul Jones papers, see a *Calendar of John Paul Jones manuscripts in the Library of Congress* [mostly printed], comp. under the direction of C. H. Lincoln (Wash., 1903) (Library of Congress) [**167**]. Consult also the correspondence of the British, French, and Prussian foreign offices with The Netherlands (for guides, see p. 921 and summary given in Renaut (no. 158), 423–425). The Stevens *Facsimiles* (no. 5723) contain·selections from the first two. The Library of Congress has photostats of the last mentioned, which supplement the printed correspondence of Frederick the Great (no. 201). The Sparks (no. 5337) and Bancroft (see Greene and Morris, no. 5531) transcripts are selected from these British, French, and Prussian sources.

7. The Armed Neutrality of 1780

Bibliographical Aids

For general aids, see Sec. 1, above.

Winsor (no. 4782), ch. 2, sec. 1; the bibliographies given in Bergbohm (no. 170), Fauchille (no. 171), Scott (no. 182), and in C. F. Carusi and C. D. Kojouharoff, " The first armed neutrality ", *Nation. univ. law rev.*, IX (1929) 3–69 [**168**].

Special Works

Edvard Holm, " Om Danmarks deeltagelse i forhandlingerne om en væbnet neutralitet fra 1778–1780 ", *Hist. tidsskrift*, 3d ser., V (1866–1867) 1–164 [**169**], a very important monograph based on Danish archival MS. sources, from which several illuminating documents (in French originals) are reproduced, showing the Danish derivation of the principles of the Armed Neutrality. Carl Bergbohm, *Die bewaffnete Neutralität, 1780–1783; eine Entwickelungsphase des Völkerrechts im Seekriege* (Dorpat, 1883) [**170**] completely surveys and supersedes all previous literature on the subject, with thorough bibliographical notes. Paul Fauchille, *La diplomatie* *française et la ligue des neutres de 1780 (1776–1783)* (Paris, 1893) [**171**], a most important work with limitations because of the too close dependence on French archives. F. W. von Prittwitz und Gaffron, *Die bewaffnete Neutralität, ihre theoretische und praktische Bedeutung* (Borna-Leipzig, 1907) [**172**] is a juridical discussion. Emil Albrecht, " Die Stellung der Vereinigten Staaten von Amerika zur bewaffneten Neutralität von 1780 ", *Zeits. Völkerrecht*, VI (1912) 436–449 [**173**], a useful study of American attitude. Thorvald Boye, *De vaebnede neutralitetsforbund, et avsnit av folkerettens historie* (Christiania, 1912) [**174**], a very valuable study particularly to show the origin of the principles of the Armed Neutrality in the disquisitions of the Danish jurist, Professor Max Hübner, whose propositions were utilized by the Danish chancellor, Bernstorff. *Extracts from American and foreign works on international law concerning the armed neutrality of 1780 and 1800* (Wash., 1917) [**175**], pub. by the Carnegie Endowment for International Peace, gives views of accredited American and foreign publicists. W. S. Carpenter, " The United States and the League of Neutrals of 1780 ", *Am. jour. internat. law*, XV (1921) 511–522 [**176**] is much like Albrecht, *op. cit.* Dietrich Gerhard, *England und der Aufstieg Russlands: zur Frage des Zusammenhanges der europäischen Staaten und ihres Ausgreifens in die aussereuropäische Welt in Politik und Wirtschaft des 18. Jahrhundert* (Munich and Berlin, 1933) [**176a**], from the opening of the Black Sea in 1774 Russia strove to free herself from dependence on British capital and direction; the author regards the armed neutrality of 1780 as a step toward emancipation.

For biographies of John Adams and Francis Dana see the relevant entries and bibliographical data in the *D.A.B.* Also Cresson, *Francis Dana* (no. 197).

Printed Sources

For American official documents and general source collections, see Sec. 1, above.

August Hennings, *Sammlung von Staatsschriften, die, während des Seekrieges von 1776 bis 1783, sowol von den Kriegführenden, als auch von den neutralen Mächten, öffentlich bekannt gemacht worden sind; in so weit solche die Freiheit des Handels und der Schiffahrt betreffen* (Altona, 1784–85, 2 v.) [**177**] is a most useful compact collection of relevant treaties and proclamations. J. H. von Goertz (graf von), *The secret history of the armed neutrality; together with memoirs, official letters and state papers, illustrative of that celebrated confederacy, never before published, written originally in French by a German nobleman* (London, 1792; German ed.: Stuttgart and Tübingen, 1927–28, 2 v.) [178], Von Goertz was a Prussian diplomatist of the period. *Diaries and correspondence of James Harris, first Earl of Malmesbury; containing an account of his mission to the courts of Madrid, Frederick the Great, Catherine the Second, and The Hague*, ed. by his grandson, the third earl (London, 1844, 4 v.) [179], the celebrated papers of one of Britain's most able diplomatists. Doniol (no. 40), v. III, p. 701–742. *Recueil des documents russes concernants la neutralité armée de 1780 tirés des archives de Moscou* (Moscow, 1859), also published that year in the *Morskoi Sbornik* (Naval Review), nos. 9–12 (Sept.-Dec.) passim. [180]. *Bernstorffske Papirer, udvalgte Breve og Optegnelser vedrorende Familien Bernstorff i Tiden fra 1732 til 1835*, ed. by Aage Friis (Copenhagen, 1904–13, 3 v.) [181] includes the papers of the Danish chancellor, Andreas P. Bernstorff. J. B. Scott, *The armed neutralities of 1780 and 1800; a collection of official documents preceded by the views of representative publicists* (N.Y., 1918) [182]. Sir Francis Piggott and G. W. T. Omond, *Documentary history of the armed neutralities, 1780 and 1800; together with selected documents relating to the war of American independence, 1776–1783, and the Dutch war, 1780–1784* (London, 1919) [183], in which the selections reflect the bias of traditional British views.

For the printed writings of John Adams and Francis Dana, see our list on p. 756. See also Wharton (no. 5339) for letters of Francis Dana concerning his Russian mission.

MSS.: Suggestions

For any definitive study of the diplomacy of the Armed Neutrality the diplomatic archives of the several countries concerned (particularly Russia) must be searched. For indexes, and suggestions, see Pt. II, ch. 3, below.

The papers of Francis Dana are in the Massachusetts Historical Society, as are the Adams papers (closed to investigation). For papers of the Continental Congress, see Sec. 1, above.

8. Scandinavia, Prussia, Northern and Central Europe

Bibliographical Aids

See Sec. 1 above, and (for the Armed Neutrality), Sec. 7. See also the general historical bibliographies of the separate countries, Ch. XXIII, Sec. 1, c.

Special Works

Friedrich Kapp, *Johann Kalb* (no. 38) ; and by the same author, *Friedrich der Grosse und die Vereinigten Staaten von Amerika. Mit einen Anhang: Die Vereinigten Staaten und das Seekriegsrecht* (Leipzig, 1871) [**184**] has useful chapters on relations during the American revolution. Hanns Schlitter, *Die Beziehungen Oesterreichs zu den Vereinigten Staaten von Amerika*, I. (*1778–1787*) [no more published] (Innsbrück, 1885) [**185**] describes, from documents in Austrian archives, the visit of William Lee and Austrian efforts for mediation. Oscar Browning, " Une mystère diplomatique; Hugh Elliot à Berlin ", *Rev. hist. dipl.*, II (1888) 255–273 [**186**] exploits Elliot's official correspondence, using copious extracts to reveal the circumstances of his theft of Arthur Lee's despatches. H. P. Gallinger, *Die Haltung der deutschen Publizistik zu dem amerikanischen Unabhängigkeitskriege, 1775–1783* (Leipzig, 1900) [**187**], a most useful analysis of the attitude of contemporary German publications. P. L. Haworth, " Frederick the Great and the American revolution ", *Am. hist. rev.*, IX (1904) 460–478 [**188**], based on Bancroft's transcripts of selected documents in the Prussian archives and on the printed (still incomplete) correspondence of Frederick the Great, it is still the best treatise. J. C. Hildt, *Early diplomatic negotiations of the United States with Russia* (Baltimore, 1906) [**189**] discusses Dana's mission to Russia, without Russian sources. J. G. Rosengarten, *Frederick the Great and the United States* (Lancaster, Pa., 1906) [**190**]. W. E. Lingelbach, " Saxon-American relations, 1778–1828 ", *Am. hist. rev.*, XVII (1912) 517–539 [**191**], from documents in the *Königliches Sächsisches Hauptstaatsarchiv* in Dresden shows the persistent interest of the Saxon ministry in the possibilities of trade with an independent United States. F. A. Golder, " Catherine II and the American revolution ", *Am. hist. rev.*, XXI (1915) 92–96 [**192**], summary impressions by a scholar who had done much work in Russian archives. Beatrice M. Victory, *Benjamin Franklin and Germany* (Phila., 1915) [193], a stringing together of copious quotations from interesting relevant documents and prints found in Germany and America. K. E. Carlson, *Relations of the United States with Sweden* (Allentown, Pa., 1921) [194]. S. J. M. P. Fogdall, *Danish-American diplomacy, 1776–1920* (Iowa City, 1922) [195], this and the preceding study are not definitive because they do not go much beyond printed sources. F. P. Renaut, *La politique de propagande des Américains durant la guerre d'indépendance, 1776–1783*, t. I: *Francis Dana à Saint Petersbourg* (Paris, 1922) [195a] uses illuminating material from French but not Russian archives. A. B. Benson, *Sweden and the American revolution* (New Haven, 1926) [196] has little on diplomatic relations. W. P. Cresson, *Francis Dana, a Puritan diplomat at the court of Catherine the Great* (N.Y., 1930) [197] uses papers of Dana, and of John Adams, hitherto published. E. F. S. Hanfstaengl, *Amerika und Europa von Marlborough bis Mirabeau* (Munich, 1930) [198], one of the earliest political intimates of the present Chancellor Hitler of Germany notes the relation of the War of the Bavarian Succession to the diplomacy of the American revolution, and goes out of his way to make disparaging remarks on the United States. Stolberg-Wernigerode, *Deutschland und Verein. Staaten* (no. 4314).

For biographies of John Adams, J. Q. Adams, William Carmichael, Francis Dana, Benjamin Franklin, Arthur Lee, and William Lee, see the relevant entries and bibliographical data in the *D.A.B.*

Printed Sources

For American official documents and general source collections, see Sec. 1, above.

For guides to printed official documents of the European countries, see below, p. 836.

Malmesbury's *Diaries and correspondence* (no. 179). *Joseph II., Leopold II. und Kaunitz; ihr Briefwechsel*, ed. by Adolf Beer (Vienna, 1873) [199], a source for Austrian mediation policy. Circourt (no. 36), v. III, contains selections of the letters between Frederick the Great and his ministers at the courts of Russia and France.

Correspondance secrète du comte de Mercy-Argentau avec d'Empereur Joseph II. et le Prince de Kaunitz, ed. by Alfred d'Arneth and Jules Flammermont (Paris, 1889–91, 2 v.) [**200**], source for Austrian mediation policy. *Bernstorffske Papirer* (no. 181), an edition of the personal papers of the Danish chancellor. *Politische Correspondenz Friedrich's des Grossen*, XXXVII–XLIII Bd., 1775–1779 (Berlin, 1918–1933, 7 v. (in progress)) [**201**], ed. by G. B. Volz, and published by the "Preussische Akademie des Wissenschaften" (this monument of editing now (1934) reaches December, 1779, with its 43d volume. *British diplomatic instructions* (no. 5422), v. V : *Sweden, 1727–1789* [**202**]. " Revolutionary correspondence of Charles Carroll of Carrollton with William Carmichael ", ed. by Elizabeth S. Kite, *Am. Cath. hist. soc. rec.*, XLII (1931) 1–11 [**203**], prints instructions of Silas Deane to Carmichael, on a secret mission to Amsterdam and Berlin, 1776.

For the printed writings of American diplomatists (enumerated above under " Special Works "), see our list on p. 756.

MSS.: Suggestions

The official manuscript records of American contacts, or attempted diplomatic contacts, with Scandinavia, Prussia, Austria, and Russia repose in the papers of the Continental Congress, and the despatches and instructions are mostly printed by Sparks (no. 5337), Wharton (no. 5339), and in the *Journals of the Continental Congress* (no. 5379). For papers of John Adams, Dana, Arthur Lee, Wm. Lee, see below, pp. 862 ff. See Greene and Morris (no. 5531) for Bancroft transcripts from Prussian and other European archives; and calendar of Sparks transcripts (no. 5543). Stevens' *Facsimiles* reproduce the correspondence of the British agent, Liston, at Berlin, about his sifting of Arthur Lee's despatches. The Library of Congress has photostats of all the MS. material in Prussian archives in regard to the American revolution as listed in M. D. Learned's *Guide* (no. 5746); similarly from Austrian archives as listed in A. B. Faust's *Guide* (no. 5764); and some pieces from Russian archives, as listed in F. A. Golder's *Guide* (no. 5779). See below, Pt. II, ch. 3, for guides to Prussian, Austrian, Russian, and Scandinavian archives.

9. Origin of the American Foreign Office

Bibliographical Aids

See Sec. 1, above.

Special Works

E. R. Johnson, "The early history of the United States consular service, 1776–1792", *Pol. sci. quar.*, XIII (1898) 19–40 [**204**], a convenient and useful statement drawn from obvious published sources like Wharton and the *Journals*.   G. C. Wood, *Congressional control of foreign relations during the American revolution, 1774–1789* (Allentown, Pa., 1919) [**204a**] analyses the committee system.   Gaillard Hunt, *The Department of State of the United States; its history and functions* (New Haven, 1914) [**205**] is the standard history; also by the same writer, "The genesis of the office of Secretary of State", *Am. hist. assoc. ann. rep.* for 1922, v. I (1926) 335–343 [**206**].   M. L. Bonham, jr., "Robert R. Livingston", in *Am. secs. state* (no. 4796), v. I, 115–189 [**207**] describes the office of foreign affairs in its embryonic days.   J. B. Sanders, "The development of the executive departments in the Continental Congress, 1774–89", in *Abstracts of theses, humanistic series, . . . University of Chicago*, v. VII (Chicago, 1930) 283–288 [**208**] traces the evolution of administrative organs in the Continental Congress.

For biographies of John Adams, John Dickinson, Benjamin Franklin, Benjamin Harrison, John Jay, Thomas Jefferson, R. R. Livingston, James Lovell, Robert Morris, and Washington, see the relevant entries and bibliographical data in the *D.A.B.*

Printed Sources

For American official documents and general source collections, see Sec. 1, above.

For the printed writings of American statesmen and diplomatists (enumerated above, under "Special Works"), see our list on p. 756.

MSS.: Suggestions

The papers of the Continental Congress, in the Library of Congress are the prime source, many of which have been published in the above-mentioned printed sources.   The papers of Robert Morris, one of the Committee on Foreign Affairs, are in the Pennsylvania

Historical Society, and the Library of Congress. For papers of John Adams, Franklin, John Jay, R. R. Livingston, and Gouverneur Morris, see below, p. 862. One might consult the correspondence of the French ministers in the United States (see p. 16, above), and of the Spanish observers (see Hill's *Catalogue*, no. 5650), and Gómez del Campillo's MS. list (no. 5627). See also Sparks, Bancroft, and Stevens transcripts (above p. 7).

CHAPTER II

THE PEACE SETTLEMENT OF 1782–1783

1. In General.
2. Anglo-American Negotiations.
3. Anglo-French Negotiations.

4. Anglo-Spanish Negotiations.
5. Anglo-Dutch Negotiations.

1. In General

Bibliographical Aids

For general aids, see Evans (no. 4639); Sabin (no. 4655); Larned (no. 4657); Griffin (no. 4658); *Writings* (no. 4661); C., H. and T. (no. 4662); *Am. secs. state* (no. 4796), v. I, see "Bibliographical notes"; *Guide hist. lit.* (no. 4634); Winsor, *Handbook Am. revolution* (no. 1), 264–273; and his *America* (no. 4782), v. VII, 170–184.

W. C. Abbott, *An introduction to the documents relating to the international status of Gibraltar 1704–1934* (N. Y., 1934) [**208a**].

General Works

See the entries in Ch. I, sec. 1.

The Cambridge history of British foreign policy, 1783–1919, ed. by Sir A. W. Ward and G. P. Gooch (Cambridge, Eng., 1922–23, 3 v.), v. I: 1783–1815 [**209**], a co-operative work recognized by scholars, authoritative, but American problems are necessarily condensed as only one feature of multifarious British diplomacy. Hill, *Treaties* (no. 4794). *Am. secs. state* (no. 4796), v. I. *The Cambridge history of the British Empire*, v. VI: *Canada and Newfoundland* (Cambridge, Eng., 1930) [**210**], ch. 7: "British North America and the American revolution", by D. A. McArthur, an authoritative Canadian scholar. E. M. Douglas, *Boundaries, . . . of the United States*, 2nd ed. (Wash.: Govt. Print. Off., 1930) [**211**], a factual outline of expanding American boundaries.

Printed Sources

See the entries in Ch. I, sec. 1. See also Doniol (no. 40 above); and for text of treaties, Miller, *Treaties* (no. 5371).

MSS.: Suggestions

See separate sections below.

36

Maps: Suggestions

For a statement, prepared by Col. Lawrence Martin, Chief of the Division of Maps of the Library of Congress, concerning the various editions and impressions of Mitchell's map of North America, and the impressions of it used in the negotiations of 1782–1783, see the notes attached to the Anglo-American treaties of September 29, 1827, and August 9, 1842, in Hunter Miller's *Treaties* (no. 5371), v. III[1] and IV. For note regarding Library of Congress copies of Mitchell's map, and Aranda's transcription of Franklin's red-line map of Dec. 5 or 6, 1782, see the *Report of the Librarian of Congress*, 1933 (Wash., 1933), p. 69 [212].

The various boundary proposals have been worked out, on Mitchell's map as a base, in *Atlas of the historical geography of the United States*, by C. O. Paullin, ed. by J. K. Wright, published jointly by the Carnegie Institution of Washington and the American Geographical Society of New York (Wash. and N.Y., 1932) [213], plates 89–90; see also p. 52–55, for textual matter on boundaries at the " Negotiations for peace, 1779–1783."

From the British Public Record Office the Library of Congress has secured reproductions of several MSS. dealing with various copies of Mitchell's map and their use in American boundary disputes. They include the correspondence between the British consul general in New York and the Foreign Office, by which the Steuben copy of Mitchell's map is definitely identified.

See also, for information regarding maps relative to the proposed Spanish-American boundary lines, Yela Utrilla (no. 112), v. I, 461–482, discussing the boundary between Spanish possessions and the United States, and maps used at the negotiations, and v. II, 355–364, for the " Diario de Aranda sobre los límites con las colonias agosto 1782 (original remitido con carta no. 2266)" [213a], the original of this letter is in *A. H. N., Estado* 3885. Bemis, *Pinckney's treaty* (no. 506), 38–39, and map 1, for Aranda's proposal given to Jay, 1782; but, for correction, see the same writer's communication relative to the proposed Spanish-American boundary lines, 1782, in the *Hisp. Am. hist. rev.*, VII (1927) 386–389 [214], giving a map

---

[1] Col. Martin has collected a barrel of information of all kinds about Mitchell's map of North America which it is hoped will some day appear in print.

showing boundary lines suggested by Jay, Aranda, Vergennes, and Rayneval, 1782.   See also Torres Lanzas (no. 1257) ; and Karpinski (nos. 5149 and 5150).

2. Anglo-American Negotiations

Bibliographical Aids

For general aids, see Sec. 1, above.

General Works

See Sec. 1, above.   Miller, *Treaties* (no. 5371), v. II, for historical notes of great value.

Special Works

Mahon (no. 5), v. VII.   Lord John Russell, *The life and times of Charles James Fox* (London, 1859–66, 3 v.) **[215]**.   Earl Stanhope, *Life of the Right Honourable William Pitt* (London, 1861–62, 4 v.) **[216]**.   Sir George Cornewall Lewis, *Essays on the administrations of Great Britain from 1783 to 1830*, ed. by Sir Edmund Head (London, 1864) **[217]**, ch. 1 is a critical review of Russell's *Fox* (no. 215), and Buckingham's *Memoirs* (no. 357).   Lord Edmond Fitzmaurice, *Life of William, earl of Shelburne, afterwards first marquess at Lansdowne; with extracts from his papers and correspondence* (London, 1875–76, 3 v.; 2nd and rev. ed., London, 1912, 2 v.) **[218]** contains a scholarly study of Shelburne's diplomacy, with excerpts from his papers.   John Jay, *The peace negotiations of 1782 and 1783* (N.Y., 1884) **[219]**, appendix (p. 121–239) consists of documentary and source material; also by the same author, with same title, but a separate study, " The peace negotiations of 1782–1783 ", in Winsor (no. 4782), v. VII, 89–184 **[220]**, the " Jay papers " cited do not seem to be other than transcripts collected from various official archival sources by the author.   Mellen Chamberlain, " New England's interest in the fisheries in 1781 ", *Mass. hist. soc. proc.*, 2d ser., IV, 1887–1889 (1889) 48–54 **[221]**, comments on the printed text of a circular sent by Boston to other towns in Massachusetts to inspire identical instructions by towns to delegates in the General Court to work for the fisheries as a treaty *right*.   Thomas Hodgins, *British and American diplomacy affecting Canada* (Toronto, 1900) **[222]**, with maps; an important study based on wide research.   It has a tendency to see Anglo-American settlements too frequently made at the expense of Canadian interests. Mary A. M. Marks (no. 135). C. M. Burton, " The boundary lines of the United States under the treaty of 1782 ", in *Historical papers delivered before the Society of Colonial Wars of the State of Michigan* (Detroit, 1908), 21–32, also published in *Mich. hist. soc. coll.*, XXXVIII (1912) 130–139 [**223**], a dilettante but stimulating paper based on vacation researches in English archives. W. L. Grant, " Pitt's theory of empire ", *Queen's quar.*, XVI (1908) 32–43 [**224**] discusses Pitt's economic views on the preliminaries of peace. R. L. Schuyler, *The transition in Illinois from British to American government* (N.Y., 1909) [**225**] contains discussion of " The peace negotiations and the West." Lucas, *Lord North* (no. 136). P. C. Phillips (no. 44), ch. 11 : " Vergennes and the negotiations for peace." James White, " Boundary disputes and treaties ", in *Canada and its provinces*, Adam Shortt, A. G. Doughty, general editors (Toronto, 1914), v. VIII, 749–958 [**226**] discusses negotiations and differences regarding the international boundary that commenced in the peace of 1782. E. R. Johnson and others, *History of domestic and foreign commerce of the United States* (Wash., 1915, 2 v.) [**227**], v. II, pt. 2 : " The fisheries ", by T. W. Van Metre, discusses the fisheries as an international question, beginning with the treaty of 1783. Corwin (no. 45) gives an acute analysis of French policy. Hill, *Treaties* (no. 4794), ch. 2, a good summary based on printed sources. C. W. Alvord, *Lord Shelburne and the founding of British American goodwill* (London, 1926) [**228**], a stimulating but not sententious lecture by a man who had worked over a great body of English and American as well as French sources. Temple Bodley, *George Rogers Clark, his life and public services* [2] (Boston and N.Y., 1926) [**229**] cannot settle the question how much Clark had to do with the diplomatic victory of 1782. G. H. Guttridge, *David Hartley* (no. 138). E. C. Burnett, " Edward Langworthy in the Continental Congress ", *Ga. hist. quar.*, XII (1928) 211–235 [**230**], as a supporter of the Deane faction he played an important part in the controversy over the terms of peace. G. W. Brown, " The St. Lawrence in the boundary settlement of 1783 ", *Canad. hist. rev.*, IX (1929) 223–238 [**231**], a most useful and scholarly contribution. J. A. James, *The life of George Rogers Clark* (Chicago, 1928) [**232**] incorporates his previ-

---

[2] This, and Pease (no. 234) were written too late for inclusion in the bibliographical note on G. R. Clark at the end of the article in *D.A.B.*, *q.v.*

ous articles on Spain in the West during the revolutionary period; and by the same author, "An appraisal of the contributions of George Rogers Clark to the history of the West ", *Miss. Valley hist. rev.*, XVII (1930) 98–115 [**233**], the author is persuaded Clark's military activities contributed to the diplomatic victory of 1782. W. E. Stevens, *The Northwest fur trade, 1763–1800* (Urbana, Ill., 1928) [**233a**], a careful dissertation which stresses "Big business and the treaty of 1783 ", and after study of Canadian archival sources and transcripts of the Shelburne papers, among other sources, shows there is no evidence that Shelburne took any account of the fur-trade in the preliminary negotiations. T. C. Pease and Marguerite J. Pease, *George Rogers Clark and the revolution in Illinois, 1763–1787* (Springfield, Ill., 1929) [**234**] ascribes the diplomatic victory of 1782 not to Clark's operations but to the general turn of the war. Eunice Wead, " British public opinion of the peace with America, 1782 ", *Am. hist. rev.*, XXXIV (1929) 513–531 [**235**]. Dora M. Clark, *British opinion and the American revolution* (New Haven, 1930) [**236**], both these last works are based on study of British newspapers and periodicals. Bernard Faÿ, " Une paix sans victoire: la paix de 1783 ", *Rev. hist. dipl.*, XLIV (1930) 213–220 [**237**], a pithy summary by a well-known French scholar. J. J. Meng, *Vergennes* (nos. 72, 73, 238) ; and " Franco-American diplomacy and the treaty of Paris, 1783 ", *Am. Cath. hist. soc. rec.*, XLIV (1933) 193–219 [**238**], this latter stressing Vergennes' ingenuousness. S. .F. Bemis, " Canada and the peace settlement of 1782–3 ", *Canad. hist. rev.*, XIV (1933) 265–284 [**239**] arrays printed and unprinted sources and analyses the progress of the Anglo-American negotiations to show why more of Canada was not included in American territory. A. L. Burt, *The old province of Quebec* (Toronto and Minneapolis, 1933) [**239a**], a scholarly narrative by a Canadian professor in an American university. Its interest to the student of diplomatic history consists of the author's fresh appraisal óf the reason for failure of Canada's claim to more expansive boundaries in 1782–1783, and his attributing of the Indian menace as one of the reasons for refusal promptly to evacuate American soil as required by the treaty. Gilbert Chinard, *Honest John Adams* (Boston, 1933) [**240**] is the latest review of John Adams' diplomacy, but is obliged to rely mostly on familiar printed material (the Adams papers not being open to historical scholars). Einstein, *Divided loyalties* (no. 76).

For biographies of American statesmen and diplomatists and other figures (John Adams, G. R. Clark, Franklin, Alexander Hamilton, John Jay, Thomas Jefferson, Henry Laurens, R. R. Livingston, James Madison, James Monroe, George Washington, Witherspoon) see the relevant entries and bibliographical data in the *D.A.B.*

For biographies of British statesmen and diplomatists (Lord Carmarthen (Leeds), Alleyn Fitzherbert, Charles James Fox, Thomas Grenville, Lord North, Richard Oswald, the Duke of Portland, Lord Rockingham, Lord Shelburne, Henry Strachey, Thomas Townshend, and Benjamin Vaughan), consult the *D.N.B.* (no. 4927). Note also John Drinkwater's *Charles James Fox* (N.Y., 1928) [**241**]. For British prime ministers (Rockingham and Shelburne) see Clive Bigham, *The prime ministers of Britain, 1712-1921* (London, 1922) [**242**] which has a useful bibliography.

Printed Sources

For American official documents and general source collections, see Sec. 1, above.

British official documents: *Parliamentary history* (no. 5410); *Corres. Geo. III* (no. 143), v. V-VI.

Annual register (no. 5058), nos. 25-26. *A full and faithful report of the debates in both houses of Parliament, on Monday the 17th of February, and Friday the 21st of February, 1783, on the articles of peace,* 2d ed. (London, 1783) [**243**]. *The speeches of the Right Honourable Charles James Fox, in the House of Commons,* ed. by John Wright (London, 1815, 6 v.), v. II [**244**]. *Memoirs of the Marquis of Rockingham and his contemporaries, with original letters and documents now first published,* by George Thomas, Earl of Albemarle (London, 1852, 2 v.) [**245**]. *Memoirs of the court and cabinets of George the Third, from original family documents,* by the Duke of Buckingham and Chandos (London, 1853-55, 4 v.), v. I [**246**]. *Memorials and correspondence of Charles James Fox,* ed. by Lord John Russell (London, 1853-57, 4 v.) [**247**]. " Monsieur Rayneval's letter to Mr. Monroe, vindicating the conduct of France in the negotiations for peace in 1782 ", in W. C. Rives, *History of the life and times of James Madison* (Boston, 1859-68, 3 v.), v. I,

655–660 [248], a letter dated Paris, Nov. 14, 1795. Horace Walpole, *Journal of the reign of King George the Third from the year 1771 to 1783*, ed. by Dr. Doran (London, 1859, 2 v.; later edition, ed. by A. F. Steuart: London and N.Y., 1910, 2 v.) [249]. *Corres. Auckland* (no. 140). Lewis, *Essays* (no. 217) gives portions of Oswald's diary in May and June, 1782, and memoranda given by Shelburne to Oswald, 1782. "Letter of Count de Marbois, 1782", *Mass. hist. soc. proc.*, VII (1864) 262–266 [250] is a copy, in English translation, of the intercepted letter of Marbois to Vergennes on the fisheries (also pub. in Jay's *Life*, no. 5244 below, v. I, 490–494, and Timothy Pitkin, *A political and civil history of the United States* (New Haven, 1828), v. II, 528–531). The original letter is in the British Public Record Office, and a copy in the Library of Congress. Fitzmaurice, *Shelburne* (no. 218). Circourt (no. 36). William Jay, "The treaty of peace, 1783; correspondence between William Jay and John Quincy Adams", *Mag. Am. hist.*, III (1879) 39–44 [251], five letters written in the year 1832 during the preparation by the former of his *Life* of his father, John Jay. *The political memoranda of Francis, fifth Duke of Leeds*, ed. by Oscar Browning (London, 1884) (Camden Society Publications, XXXV) [252]. *The historical and the posthumous memoirs of Sir Nathaniel William Wraxall, 1772–1784*, ed. by H. B. Wheatley (London, 1884, 5 v.), v. II [253] contains a discussion of Lord Shelburne's policy and further references to the peace negotiations. John Jay, *On the peace negotiations of 1782–1783, as illustrated by the secret correspondence of France and England* (N.Y., 1888), reprinted from the *Papers* of the American Historical Association, v. III, no. 1, 1888 [254] is a summary of sources of information on the subject. Stevens' *Facsimiles* (no. 5723, see also p. 7, above). Doniol (no. 40), v. V. *The life, public services, addresses and letters of Elias Boudinot, LL.D., president of the Continental Congress* (Boston and N.Y., 1896, 2 v.) [255] gives commentaries on the peace negotiations. *Autobiography and political correspondence of Augustus Henry, third duke of Grafton, K.G.*, ed. by Sir W. R. Anson (London, 1898) [256]. *The Whitefoord papers; being the correspondence and other manuscripts of Colonel Charles Whitefoord and Caleb Whitefoord, from 1739 to 1810*, ed. by W. A. S. Hewins (Oxford: Clarendon press, 1898) [257], Caleb Whitefoord was secretary to the British peace commission at Paris, 1782–83. "Letters of

Benjamin Vaughan to the Earl of Shelburne ", ed. by C. C. Smith, *Mass. hist. soc. proc.*, 2d ser., XVII (1903) 406–438 [**258**], copies of private letters from Vaughan, unofficial agent of Lord Shelburne, written during the negotiations for peace, 1782–83. *Warren-Adams letters* (no. 98), v. II. L. J. Carey, ed., " Franklin is informed of Clark's activities in the Old Northwest ", *Miss. Valley hist. rev.*, XXI (1934) 375–378 [**258a**] prints a letter (translated) of Peter Sargé addressed to Franklin, from La Rochelle, France, July 6, 1779, apprising him of Clark's capture of the Illinois and the post of Vincennes, and its recapture. *The diary of John Jay during the peace negotiations of 1782*, with introduction by Frank Monaghan (New Haven, 1934) [**259**], a short diary much of which was hitherto unpublished.

For faithful text of the treaty (with notes), see Miller, *Treaties* (no. 5371).

For the printed writings of American statesmen and diplomatists (enumerated above, under " Special Works "), see our list on p. 756.

The printed writings of British statesmen and diplomatists are entered above. Consult also the *D.N.B.* (no. 4969).

MSS.: Suggestions

The official American sources are preserved in the papers of the Continental Congress (mostly printed by Sparks (no. 5337), Wharton (no. 5339), and in the *Journals* (no. 5379)). A special collection of Franklin's papers was acquired by the State Department and is now, with other Franklin MSS. in the possession of the Library of Congress. They include a transcript of " Oswald's journal." See also for Franklin papers, p. 873 below. For John Adams, Jay, and Laurens MSS., see pp. 862, 865, and 877, respectively.

The English official sources have been preserved in the Public Record Office (Foreign Office papers) (for guides, see below, p. 890). The Library of Congress has photocopies of the British Foreign Office correspondence with Oswald, 1782–83 (F. O. 97, vol. 157), and some volumes of British documents, F. O. 27 (France) important for understanding the peace negotiations at Paris, 1782–83. The Canadian Archives has copies of F. O. Miscellaneous, vol. 511 (letters of Oswald, Strachey, Shelburne, Townshend, and miscellaneous diplomatic correspondence and papers) relating to the treaty negotiations. It is not known whether the papers of Charles James

Fox in Holland House pertain to the peace negotiations, and the same may be said of the Lord North papers in Rhodes House, Oxford. There are still other North papers in the possession of Sir Leicester Harmsworth. The William L. Clements Library, Ann Arbor, Mich., has the original political papers of Lord Shelburne (for calendars, see Royal Commission on Historical Manuscripts, *Third report* (London, 1872) 125–147; *Fifth report* (London, 1876) 215–260; and *Sixth report* [3] (London, 1877) 235–243 [260]; and *Report of the Canadian archives for the year 1921* (Ottawa, 1922) 229–281 [261], and some valuable pieces from the papers of Thomas Townshend. The Clements Library is planning the publication of a comprehensive documentary history of the peace negotiations of 1782–1783, and to that end is collecting material from many sources. The Huntington Library has two volumes of correspondence of Townshend with George III, relative to American independence, including minutes of the Cabinet in connection with the negotiations with the commissioners of the United States. The Library of Congress has some original odd pieces from the Townshend papers, which supplement those at Ann Arbor. David Hartley's papers formerly in Washington, D.C., in the possession of the estate of the late Joseph Leiter are now in the William L. Clements Library (for calendar, by H. A. Morrison, see *The Leiter library; a catalogue of the books, manuscripts and maps . . . , collected by the late Levi Ziegler Leiter* (Wash., 1907) [262–3]). The papers of Caleb Whitefoord, secretary to the British peace commissioners, are in the British Museum. The Hardwicke (Yorke) papers are in the British Museum, for letters regarding the peace negotiations, see Paullin and Paxson's *Guide* (no. 5577), 552. For calendar of the papers of Sir Henry Strachey, under secretary of state in the Colonial Office, 1782–83, and special envoy to the peace conference, see no. 5595 below. For transcripts of British state papers, see Sparks transcripts (for calendar, see no. 24), Bancroft transcripts (see Greene and Morris, no. 4665). A comprehensive collection of transcripts from British, French, and Dutch archives, is the Stevens *Transcripts relating to the peace of 1782–1783* (no. 5724), in the Library of Congress.

---

[3] The personal correspondence listed in the *Sixth report* is still at Bowood, in the possession of the Marquis of Lansdowne.

The correspondence between the French foreign minister and the French diplomatic representatives in the United States, Holland, Spain, Austria, and Russia contains important material on the Anglo-American settlement. See series *Correspondance Politique*, and *idem, supplémentaire, États-Unis, Espagne, Hollande, Prusse, Russie, Austrie*, and the relevant parts of series *Mémoires et Documents* (for lists, etc., see below, p. 915). The series *Etats-Unis* is in the Stevens *Transcripts relating to the French alliance* (no. 5724) see also below, p. 920. One should also consult the " Minutes of the French legation in the United States, 1777–1795 ", now in the William S. Mason Library at Evanston, Ill., photocopies in the Library of Congress.

3. Anglo-French Negotiations

Bibliographical Aids

See Sec. 1, above. For French historical bibliographies, see nos. 4732–4739.

Special Works

Comte de Garden, *Histoire générale des traités de paix* (Paris, 1848–87, 15 v.), v. IV, 284–345 [**264**] for an old treatise on the Anglo-French treaty of 1783. Fitzmaurice's *Shelburne* (no. 218). Doniol (no. 40), also by the same writer, " La première négociation de la paix de 1783 entre la France et la Grande-Bretagne ", *Rev. hist. dipl.*, VI (1892) 56–61 [**265**]; and " Tentatives de l'Angleterre en 1781 et 1782 pour amener la France à traiter de la paix ", *ibid.*, XIV (1900) 161–198 [**266**]. Urtasún (no. 19). Renault (no. 57). Yela Utrilla (no. 112). Cresson (no. 197). Faÿ (nos. 63 and 237). Meng (no. 238).

For Austrian and Russian mediation, see references in Ch. I, sec. 8.

For biographies of French statesmen and diplomatists (Luzerne, Marbois, Montmorin, Vergennes) see the *D.B.F.;* also for Vergennes, see Meng (no. 72).

Printed Sources

Correspondence of Charles James Fox (no. 247). Fitzmaurice, *Shelburne* (no. 218). " Conférences de M. de Rayneval avec les ministres anglais [1782] ", *Rev. hist. dipl.*, VI (1892) 62–89 [**267–8**], drawn from documents in the *Archives des Affaires Étrangères*.

Doniol (no. 40).   Flammermont, *Corresp. agents dipl. en France* (no. 95).   *Corres. George III* (no. 143).

For text of the Anglo-French treaty of 1783 (in English), see *A collection of all the treaties of peace, alliance, and commerce between Great Britain and other powers, 1648–1783*, v. I (London, 1785, 3 v.) [269], and George Chalmers, *A collection of treaties between Great Britain and other powers*, v. II (London, 1790, 2 v.) [270]; (in French), see *Recueil des traités de la France*, publié sous les auspices du Ministre des Affaires Étrangères, ed. by A. J. H. de Clercq, v. I (Paris, 1864) [271]; Karl von Martens, *Recueil manuel et pratique de traités* (Leipzig, 1846–57, 7 v.), v. I, 301–308 [272].

MSS.: Suggestions

The Stevens *Transcripts relating to the peace negotiations of 1782* (no. 5724, see also below, p. 892) contain copious selections from British, French, and Dutch official archives and from the Lansdowne (Shelburne) papers then preserved at Bowood, England; of these the political papers, now known as the Shelburne papers are today in the possession of the William L. Clements Library at Ann Arbor, Mich. (see above, "MSS: Suggestions", sec. 2, this chapter). These are replete with material on Anglo–French affairs. The official archives of the British and French foreign offices (for guides and indexes (see Pt. II, ch. 3), contain the main order of sources, to be supplemented by the Spanish, Dutch, Prussian, and Austrian archives (for partial guides and indexes, see Pt. II, ch. 3).

4. Anglo-Spanish Negotiations

Bibliographical Aids

For general aids, see Sec. 1, above.   See also Spanish historical bibliographies, nos. 4758–4760.

Special Works

Doniol (no. 40).   Dánvila y Collado (no. 105).   Flammermont (no. 95) contains an account of the mission of Aranda in Paris. Rousseau (nos. 106 and 107).   Phillips (no. 44).   Corwin (no. 45). Conrotte (no. 111).   Renaut (no. 57).   Yela Utrilla (no. 112). Bemis (nos. 113 and 506).   Urtasún (no. 19).   Konetzke (no. 119).

For biographies of British statesmen and diplomatists, see Sec. 2, above; for Spanish (Floridablanca and Aranda), Ch. I, sec. 4; for American, Sec. 1, above; for French, Sec. 3, above.

Printed Sources

For American official documents and general source collections, see Sec. 1, above.

Fox (no. 247). Fitzmaurice (no. 218). Doniol (no. 40). Flammermont (no. 95) lists the Aranda correspondence in the archives at Simancas (*Secretaría de Estado*). *Correspondence . . . Duke of Grafton* (no. 256) discusses the Spanish efforts to take Gibraltar. *Recueil des instructions* (no. 5429), XII bis: *Espagne*, v. III (1722–1793) [**273**] for French instructions (too much abridged) to her ambassador to Spain, Count de Montmorin. " Dictámen del Conde de Aranda ", *Inst. estud. am. bol.*, I (1913) 53–57 [**274**] is a memorandum of Aranda to the King regarding the independence of the English colonies in America, found in the *Archivo General de Indias*. Yela Utrilla (no. 112), v. II. *Corres. George III* (no. 143), v. V.

For text of the treaty of Aranjuez (in English), *Am. secs. state* (no. 4796), I; (in Spanish), Alejandro del Cantillo, *Tratados, convenios, y declaraciones de paz y de comercio* (Madrid, 1843) 574–590 [**275**]; and (in French), *Recueil des traités de la France* (no. 271), and Martens, *Recueil manuel* (no. 272), v. I.

MSS.: Suggestions

The records of the foreign offices of Great Britain (for indexes, see below, p. 890), France (for indexes, see below, p. 915) ; and Spain (for indexes, see below, p. 898) must be consulted. Mr. Gómez del Campillo's list of Floridablanca-Aranda correspondence in the *Archivo Histórico Nacional* (no. 5627) enumerates the pieces in this, the most important single collection of sources relating to the Anglo-Spanish peace settlement. The Library of Congress has photocopies of only a few of these pieces. Jay's letterbook (see p. 865) is printed in Wharton (no. 5339). See also " MSS: Suggestions " in Secs. 2 and 3 above.

5. Anglo-Dutch Negotiations

General Works

Colenbrander, *Patriottentijd*, v. I (no. 146) is the most satisfactory and scholarly, multiple-archive treatise. Urtasún, *Historia diplomática*, v. II (no. 19).

Special Works

Fauchille (no. 171). Edler (no. 150). Renaut (no. 158).

Printed Sources

For American official documents and general source collections, see Sec. 1, above.

For guides to British and Dutch printed official documents, see below, pp. 838 and 843, respectively.

Malmesbury's *Diaries and corres.*, v. I (no. 179). Fox, *Memorials* (no. 247). Beaufort, *Brieven van der Capellen* (no. 162). Fitzmaurice, *Shelburne* (no. 218). *Dépêches van Thulemeyer* (no. 163). *Corres. George III* (no. 143).

For text of the definitive treaty of May 20, 1784, see Karl von Martens, *Recueil manuel* (no. 272), v. 1. For the preliminary articles of peace signed at Paris, Sept. 2, 1783, see Georg F. von Martens, *Recueil des traités d'alliance, de paix* . . ., 2d ed., rev. and enl. (Gottingen, 1817–35, 8 v.) [**276**], v. III.

MSS.: Suggestions

Consult the Stevens *Transcripts relating to the French alliance* (no. 5724, and see also above, p. 7) and Bancroft transcripts (see Greene and Morris, no. 5531). For the Dutch peace settlement, the records of the British (for indexes, see below, p. 890), Dutch (for indexes, see below, p. 921), and French (for indexes, see below, p. 915) foreign offices should be consulted.

CHAPTER III

THE CONFEDERATION, 1783-1789

1. In General

Bibliographical Aids

For general aids, see Evans (no. 4639); Sabin (no. 4655); Larned (no. 4657); Griffin (no. 4658); *Writings* (no. 4661); C. H. and T. (no. 4662); *Am. secs. state* (no. 4796), see " Bibliographical notes "; *Guide hist. lit.* (no. 4634); Myers (no. 5399), for collections of treaties. Miller's *Treaties* (no. 5391), v. I, 39-54, for " Bibliography of United States treaty collections." See also Winsor, *America* (no. 4782), v. VII, 233-235.

For guides to American newspapers, see nos. 5004-5047, particularly Nelson (no. 5009); Brigham (no. 5012); and Library of Congress (no. 5031).

General and Special Works

Of general histories of the United States, see Bancroft (no. 4778); Von Holst (no. 4780); McMaster (no. 4781); Winsor (no. 4782); Channing (no. 4784). See also *Am. secs. state*, v. I (no. 4796); and Wriston (no. 4799).

Lyman (no. 14). John Fiske, *The critical period of American history, 1783-1789* (Boston and N.Y., 1888) [**277**], a classical study of the political ineptitude of the Confederation in domestic and foreign affairs. A. C. McLaughlin, *The Confederation and the constitution, 1783-1789* (N.Y. and London, 1905) [**278**], a well-balanced study having the advantage of scholarship after Fiske. Nevins, *American states* (no. 13). W. K. Woolery, *The relation of Thomas*

Jefferson to American foreign policy, 1783–1793 (Baltimore, 1927) [279], a useful analysis of Jefferson's diplomacy based on his private papers and official records in the Department of State. Ingram, *Am. consular service* (no. 21a).

For biographies of John Adams, Thos. Barclay, Carmichael, Franklin, David Humphreys, Hamilton, Jay, Jefferson, R. R. Livingston, Madison, Monroe, Robert Morris, Short, Charles Thomson, and Washington, see the relevant entries and bibliographical data in the *D.A.B.;* and *Am. secs. state* (no. 4796).

Printed Sources

For American official documents and general source collections, see *Dipl. corres. U.S., 1783–1789* (no. 5340); Wharton, *Digest* (no. 5366); *Journals* (no. 5379); Moore's *Digest* (no. 5365); Burnett, *Letters* (no. 5380).

For texts of treaties, see Miller, *Treaties* (no. 5371).

For guides to American newspapers, see nos. 5004–5047; particularly Nelson (no. 5009); Brigham (no. 5012); and Library of Congress (no. 5031).

For the printed writings of the American statesmen and diplomatists abroad enumerated above, under " Special Works ", see our list on p. 756.

MSS.: Suggestions

The American MS. sources for the diplomacy of the Confederation are extensively preserved. The bulk of the official diplomatic correspondence is found in the Papers of the Continental Congress in the Library of Congress (mostly printed); and the papers of the several diplomatists are in careful custody. For personal papers of President Washington, see p. 862. For papers of John Adams, Franklin, Hamilton, Jay, and Jefferson, the American diplomatists of the period, see our lists on pp. 862–883. The foreign collections are discussed below under separate sections.

For guides, catalogues, and indexes, note Van Tyne and Leland (no. 5495); Library of Congress, *Handbook* (no. 5520); Garrison (no. 5522); and Greene and Morris (no. 5531); and see below, Pt. II, ch. 3.

2. Evolution of the American Foreign Office

Bibliographical Aids

See Sec. 1, above

Special Works

J. C. Guggenheimer, " The development of the executive depart-
ments, 1775–1789 ", in *Essays in the constitutional history of the
United States in the formative period, 1775–1789*, by graduates and
former members of Johns Hopkins University, ed. by J. F. Jameson
(Boston and N.Y., 1889) 116–185 [**280**] discusses the Committee of
Foreign Affairs, and the organization of the Department of Foreign
Affairs. Johnson, *U.S. consular service* (no. 204). H. B. Learned,
*The President's cabinet; studies in the origin, formation, and struc-
ture of an American institution* (New Haven, 1912) [**281**], the
standard work. Gaillard Hunt (nos. 205 and 206). Wood, *Cong.
control* (no. 204a). J. M. Mathews, *The conduct of American foreign relations* (N.Y., 1922) [**282**] has a chapter on the Department
of State. *Am. secs. state* (no. 4796), v. I, 193–208. Sanders, *Exec.
depts.* (no. 208). Dangerfield, *Defense of the Senate* (no. 4836).

Printed Sources

See Sec. 1, above. Note particularly the *Corres. and public papers
of John Jay* (no. 5244).

MSS.: Suggestions

See Sec. 1, above.

3. The New Treaties (Sweden, Prussia, Morocco) and other Commercial Negotiations (Austria, Denmark, The Netherlands)

Bibliographical Aids

See Sec. 1, above.

Special Works

Friedrich Kapp (no. 184), for an account of the German side of
the negotiations of the treaty with Prussia, of 1785. Schlitter (no.
185), for negotiations with the government of Emperor Joseph II,
of Austria, in regard to a treaty of commerce. G. F. Zook (no. 409),
for material regarding the proposed treaty with France. A. A.
Giesecke, *American commercial legislation before 1789* (N.Y., 1910)

[283–4] has a useful summary of unsuccessful attempts of Congress to work out among the States a uniform shipping and trade control, 1783–1789. Burnett, *Note* (no. 17), a very valuable exposition of the " Plan of 1776 " in relation to early American treaties. Lingelbach, *Saxon-Am. relations* (no. 191), based on the reports of Philip Thieriot, special commissioner from Saxony to the United States, 1784–1785. S. E. Baldwin, " Franklin and the rule of free ships, free goods ", *Am. antiq. soc. proc.*, n.s. XXV, pt. 2 (1915) 345–357 [285] is concerned with Franklin's part in the negotiations of the treaty with Prussia, 1785. E. R. Johnson, *History of domestic and foreign commerce of the United States* (Wash., 1915, 2 v.) [286], v. I, pt. 1: "American commerce to 1789." J. S. Reeves, " The Prussian-American treaties ", *Am. jour. internat. law*, XI (1917) 475–510 [287], a history of their application rather than their negotiation. A. B. Benson, " Our first unsolicited treaty ", *Am. Scandinavian rev.*, VII (1919) 43–49 [288] deals with the treaty with Sweden, 1783. Carlson (no. 194). Fogdall (no. 195) discusses negotiations for a treaty with Denmark, 1783–1784, and negotiations for claims based on the Bergen prizes, through John Paul Jones, 1783–1788. A. L. Kohlmeier, " The commerce between the United States and The Netherlands, 1783–1789 ", *Ind. univ. stud.*, v. XII, June-Dec. 1925 (Bloomington, Ind., 1926) 1–47 [289]. Woolery (no. 279).

For biographies of the American commissioners to negotiate treaties (John Adams, Benjamin Franklin, and Thomas Jefferson), David Humphreys, secretary to the commission, and Thomas Barclay (Morocco), see the relevant entries and bibliographical data in the *D.A.B.*

For biographies of the foreign diplomatists and statesmen concerned with these negotiations see the biographical dictionaries of the several countries involved (listed below, nos. 4920–4987), and follow up (if necessary) in the several national historical bibliographies, *ibid.*, p. 688.

Printed Sources

See Sec. 1, above.

For indexes and guides to printed European official documents (meager for this period) see below, p. 836.

De Circourt (no. 36), v. III. *Die Berichte des ersten Agenten Österreichs in den Vereinigten Staaten von Amerika, Baron de*

Beelen-Bertholff und die Regierung der Österreichischen Niederlande in Brüssel, 1784–1789, ed. by Hanns Schlitter (Vienna, 1891) ("Fontes Rerum Austriacarum", Abth. 2., Bd. XL^V) [**290**] contains his reports, in the original French, giving information upon the negotiations between Austria and the United States in regard to a treaty of commerce. "American commercial conditions, and Negotiations with Austria, 1783–1786", ed. by Hubert van Houtte, *Am. hist. rev.*, XVI (1911) 567–578 [**291**] prints documents from the national archives at Brussels relating to a proposed treaty between Austria and the United States, including the proposition of the Austrian chancellor, Kaunitz-Rittberg, concerning the treaty, and the instructions of Joseph II, Feb. 27, 1786. J. B. Scott, *The treaties of 1785, 1799, and 1828 between the United States and Prussia, as interpreted in opinions of attorneys general, decisions of courts, and diplomatic correspondence* (N.Y., 1918) [**292**], published by the Carnegie Endowment for International Peace. S. G. Hermelin, "Report about the mines in the United States, 1783", *Swed., Am. hist. bul.*, IV (Feb. 1931) 7–54, (June 1931) 13–33 [**292a**], Hermelin was sent by the Swedish government as commercial investigator.

For the printed writings of John Adams, Benjamin Franklin, David Humphreys, and Thomas Jefferson, see our list on pp. 756–779.

For the printed writings of European diplomatists and statesmen concerned in the negotiations see the biographical dictionaries of the several countries involved (nos. 4920–4987), unless specifically entered above.

For texts of treaties, see Miller, *Treaties* (no. 5371).

MSS.: Suggestions

See Sec. 1, above. For negotiations with Sweden and with Denmark,[1] we have no guide to the sources in their foreign offices (for meager index, see pp. 931–932); but one should consult the correspondence of the Swedish ambassador in Paris (Comte de Creutz), who negotiated the treaty with Franklin. The papers of J. H. E. Bernstorff and A. P. Bernstorff, successive foreign ministers of Denmark, are in family archives (printed, see no. 181). For Austrian

---

[1] At the *Rigsarkivet,* Copenhagen, see *Akter vedrörende Forhandlingerne om en Handelstraktat mellem Danmark og Nord Amerika, 1783–1786,* Dept. F. A., Nordamerika, I, a. (see Fogdall (no. 195), 23).

and Prussian sources, photostats of unprinted portions of which are
in the Library of Congress, see Faust's *Guide* (no. 5764), Learned's
Guide (no. 5746) and below, pp. 924–931. For material relating to
Austrian-American commerce in the Belgian archives see editorial
notes accompanying publication by Van Houtte in the *Am. hist. rev.*
(no. 291). The Saxon sources are described in bibliographical notes
in Lingelbach (no. 191). There are no known manuscript records
left of the Moroccan foreign office for this period; negotiations must
be traced in the American sources, and reflections may be found in
the correspondence of the representatives in Morocco, of France,
Great Britain, and Spain.

4. Franco-American Affairs, 1783–1789

Bibliographical Aids

For general aids (American) see Sec. 1, above. See also French
national historical bibliographies (nos. 4732–4739); and Faÿ,
Bibliographie critique (no. 31).

Special Works

Renaud de Moustier, "Les Etats-Unis au lendemain de la guerre
de l'indépendance d'après la correspondance diplomatique inédite du
comte de Moustier", *Rev. hist. dipl.*, VI (1892) 518–540 [**293**], a most
valuable article for topic suggested by the title, which should be read
in connection with Duniway (no. 294) and Bourne's edition (no.
302). Cornélis de Witt (no. 35). C. A. Duniway, "French influence on the adoption of the federal Constitution", *Am. hist. rev.*,
IX (1904) 304–309 [**294**] uses records of the French foreign office
to show that France, though preferring the continuance of an
impotent American confederation, did not interfere with the fram-
ing of the Constitution of 1787. Zook, *Comm. treaty* (no. 409).
Three studies by F. L. Nussbaum deal with relation of Franco-
American commerce and diplomacy during the Confederation:
"American tobacco and French politics, 1783–1789", *Pol. sci. quar.*,
XL (1925) 497–516 [**295**]; "The French colonial arrêt of 1784",
So. Atlan. quar., XVII (1928) 62–78 [**296**], a study of the re-
adjustment of French policy in regard to commerce with her West
Indian colonies and the United States; and "The revolutionary
Vergennes and Lafayette versus the farmers general", *Jour. mod.
hist.*, III (1931) 592–613 [**297**]. Renaut (no. 57), 366–390. Woolery

(no. 279). Beckles Willson (no. 68). L. R. Gottschalk, "Lafayette as commercial expert", *Am. hist. rev.*, XXXVI (1931) 561-570 [**298**] includes a memoir by him. R. L. Jones, "America's first consular convention", *Southw. soc. sci. quar.*, XIII (1932) 250-263 [**299**] uses printed American but no French sources. J. A. Baisnée, *France and the establishment of the American Catholic hierarchy; the myth of French interference (1783-1784)* (Baltimore, 1934) [**299a**], there is an extended summary of this by Maurice Casenave in *Rev. hist. dipl.*, XLVIII (1934) 477-498.

For biographies of Ralph Izard, Thomas Jefferson, Rufus King, R. H. Lee, and Washington, see the relevant entries and bibliographical data in the *D.A.B.*

For biographies of French diplomatists and statesmen (Montmorin, Moustier, Otto, and Vergennes[2] see the *D.B.F.* (no. 4965).

Printed Sources

For American official documents and general source collections, see Sec. 1, above.

For guides to French official documents (meager for this period), see p. 842.

For guides to American newspapers, see Sec. 1, above; for English, see *Tercentenary handlist* (no. 5013); Crane and Kaye (no. 5015); Gabler (no. 5017); Library of Congress (nos. 5031-2).

George Bancroft, *History of the formation of the Constitution of the United States of America* (N.Y., 1882, 2 v.) [**300**], v. II, 369-501, contains selected portions of the correspondence of the French ministers to the United States, 1786-1787. De Moustier (no. 293) prints copious selections from Moustier's official correspondence, to be read with those printed by Bancroft and H. E. Bourne (no. 302). "Letters of Stephen Higginson, 1783-1804", ed. by J. F. Jameson, *Am. hist. assoc. ann. rep.* for 1896, v. I (1897) 704-841 [**301**] reveal "long before 1793, the propension toward England and the distrust of France." "Correspondence of the Comte de Moustier with the Comte de Montmorin, 1787-1789", ed. by H. E. Bourne, *Am. hist. rev.*, VIII (July 1903) 709-733, and IX (Oct. 1903) 86-96 [**302**] serves to supplement the correspondence given in Bancroft (no. 300), and Moustier (no. 293), printing letters "selected with a view of bringing out the attitude of France toward the attempt

---

[2] See Meng (no. 238), 119-121, for a comprehensive bibliography of Vergennes.

to consolidate the new republic, and of showing the embarrass-
ments of diplomacy prior to the organization of an effective
central government." " Letters of Rufus King to Jonathan
Jackson ", *Mass. hist. soc. proc.*, XLIX (1916) 83–89 [**303**] discuss particularly relations with France, 1786. Lieut. Col. Gom-
bault, " Les États-Unis au lendemain de la guerre d'indépendance
d'après la correspondance d'Otto ", *Carnet de la Sabretache*, XXIII
(Paris, 1920) 9–12 [**304**], notes from the correspondence of Louis
Guillaume Otto, Comte de Mosloy, 1779–1792. Morison (no. 142)
includes " Reports of Otto, 1786 ", from the *Archives des Affaires
Etrangères*, Paris. Albert Mathiez, " Lafayette et le commerce
franco-américain à la veille de la révolution ", *Ann. hist. révol. franç.*,
n.s. III (1926) 474–484 [**305**] consists of documents of 1786–1787,
from the papers of the " Compagnie Nouvelle des Indes ", in the
national archives. Henri Sée, " Commerce between France and the
United States, 1783–1784 ", *Am. hist. rev.*, XXXI (1926) 732–752
[**306**] prints 9 enlightening documents from the chamber of commerce of Nantes. Gottschalk (no. 298), for memoir of **Lafayette**,
probably 1783, in advocacy of improved commercial relations with the
United States.

For the printed writings of Ralph Izard, Thomas Jefferson, Rufus
King, R. H. Lee, and Washington, see our list on p. 756.

For printed writings of the French diplomatists and statesmen
(Montmorin, Moustier, Otto, and Vergennes), supplementary to
those listed above, see the *D.B.F.* (no. 4965).

MSS.: Suggestions

See Sec. 1, above.

The principal series in the archives of the *Ministère des Affaires
Etrangères*, at the Quai d'Orsay, Paris, are *Correspondance Politique,
Etats-Unis*, and *idem, Amérique;* but one should consult also the
corresponding English (*Angleterre*), and Spanish (*Espagne*) series
for valuable supplementary sources. For guide see below, p. 915.
For manuscript sources in the *Bibliothèque Nationale* and other Paris
libraries, see Leland, *Guide* (no. 5704). The letterbooks of the
French Legation, 1778–1796, in the private library of Mr. William S.
Mason, of Evanston, Illinois (copies in the Library of Congress)
contain a few interesting memoranda and statistics.

The Library of Congress has photostats or transcripts of all the American material indicated in the above paragraph, with the exception of such pieces as might be drawn from the English and Spanish corridors of the Quai d'Orsay archives.

There are 3 letters of De Moustier, French minister, written during his mission to the United States, 1788–89, in the Bibliothèque Municipale, Angers, France.

5. Spanish-American Affairs, 1783–1789

Bibliographical Aids

For general aids (American), see Sec. 1, above. See also (for Spain) Sánchez Alonso (no. 4759), and Univ. of Calif. catalogue (no. 4685). Special aids are: Bemis (no. 506), 359–368; Whitaker (no. 502), 223–245; and F. J. Turner and Frederick Merk, *List of references on the history of the West*, 5th impression of rev. ed. (Cambridge, 1928) **[307]**.

Special Works

Charles Gayarré, *History of Louisiana* (N.Y., 1854–66, 4 v.; issued in several eds., 4th ed., 1903) **[308]**, composed of transcripts of original documents in French and Spanish archives woven together with a slender thread of narrative; though much of it is now superseded by more intensive research by later scholars, it is still a valuable record. J. M. Brown, *Political beginnings of Kentucky* (Louisville, 1889) **[309]**, written primarily to clear the memory of John Brown of the charge of complicity in the plan to separate Kentucky from the Union and unite it with Spanish Louisiana. Theodore Roosevelt, *The winning of the West* (N.Y. and London, 1889–96, 4 v.), v. III, ch. 3 **[310]** unfolded some previously neglected relations of the American frontiersmen with Spain and England; "The special student" (said F. J. Turner), "must regret that Mr. Roosevelt does not find it possible to make history a more jealous mistress." Justin Winsor, *The westward movement* (Boston and N.Y., 1897), chs. 15–17 **[311]**, a standard summary of a limited period by a careful scholar, with useful facsimile maps. F. A. Ogg, *The opening of the Mississippi; a struggle for supremacy in the American interior* (N.Y., 1904) **[312]**, a popular and readable account. W. R. Shepherd, "Wilkinson and the beginnings of the Spanish conspiracy",

Am. hist. rev., IX (1904) 490–506 [**313**], the first account from damning Spanish sources. Chadwick (no. 108). Manuel Serrano y Sanz, *El brigadier Jaime Wilkinson y sus tratos con España para la independencia del Kentucky (años 1787 á 1797)* (Madrid, 1915) [**314**], by no means a complete study of Wilkinson; and by the same writer, *España y los indios Cherokis y Chactas en la segunda mitad del siglo XVIII* (Seville, 1916) [**315**] prints representative documents. Jane Berry, " Indian policy of Spain in the southwest, 1783–1795 ", *Miss. Valley hist. rev.*, III (1917) 462–477 [**316**] shows the importance of the Indians in the diplomacy of the period. James Wilkinson (the grandson), " General James Wilkinson ", *La. hist. quar.*, I (1917) 79–166 [**317**], a collection of quotations mostly from secondary authorities, uncritically joined together in an effort to whitewash the grandfather—the incriminating documents are omitted. Renaut, *Conflit hispano américain* (no. 500), and *Pacte de famille* (no. 57), 366–390. Conrotte (no. 111), ch. 7, discussing the navigation of the Mississippi, Gardoqui mission, and Pinckney's mission to Spain. Coulter, *Navigation of the Mississippi* (no. 511). A. P. Whitaker has thrown a flood of new light, particularly from documents in Spanish archives, on Spanish political interests in the Southwest, and on Spanish-American relations, in the following articles: " Spanish intrigue in the old southwest: an episode, 1788–89 ", *Miss. Valley hist. rev.*, XII (1925) 155–176 [**318**]; " The Muscle Shoals speculation, 1783–1789 ", *ibid.*, XIII (1926) 365–386 [**319**] gives light on relation to the Spanish conspiracy of James White, and John Sevier; " Spain and the Cherokee Indians, 1783–98 ", *N.C. hist. rev.*, IV (1927) 252–269 [**320**]; *Span.-Am. frontier* (no. 502), ch. 5: " Gardoqui's mission "; "Alexander McGillivray, 1783–1793 ", *N.C. hist. rev.*, V (1928) 181–203, 289–309 [**321**]; " James Wilkinson's first descent to New Orleans in 1787 ", *Hisp. Am. hist. rev.*, VIII (1928) 82–97 [**322**]; and *Documents* (no. 333), for its " Historical introduction." Bodley, *Clark* (no. 229), for Wilkinson's plot and the Louisiana expedition. Bemis, *Pinckney's treaty* (no. 506), for the Mississippi question and the southern boundary. Coe, *William Carmichael* (no. 115), for the mission of Carmichael as chargé d'affaires to Spain, 1783–1795. R. E. McClendon, " Origin of the two-thirds rule in Senate action upon treaties ", *Am. hist. rev.*, XXXVI (1931) 768–772 [**323**] shows the influence of the Mississippi question. Charles Warren, " The Mississippi river and the treaty clause of the

Constitution ", *George Washington law rev.*, II (1934) 271–302 [323a] stresses the recently established connection of the Mississippi question with that clause of the Constitution which requires ratification of treaties by a two-thirds majority of the senators present.

For biographies of John Adams, William Carmichael, G. R. Clark, Alexander Hamilton, Thomas Jefferson, Rufus King, R. H. Lee, James Madison, Washington, Wilkinson, and others, see the relevant entries and bibliographical data in the *D.A.B.*

For biographies of Floridablanca (nos. 127, 128) and Aranda (nos. 119, 129, 130).

Printed Sources

For American official documents and general source collections, see Sec. 1, above. For Spanish printed official documents, see *Gaceta de Madrid* (no. 5127c).

For guides to American newspapers, see Sec. 1, above.

James Wilkinson, *Memoirs of General Wilkinson* (Wash., 1810) (Half-title: *Burr's conspiracy exposed; and General Wilkinson vindicated*) [324], the memoirs of the scoundrel are thoroughly unreliable. Florida Blanca, *Memorial* (no. 326). " Letter of Rufus King to Elbridge Gerry, 1786 ", *Mass. hist. soc. proc.*, IX (1867) 9–12 [325] discusses the question of the navigation of the Mississippi, and the treaty with Spain. *Obras originales del Conde de Floridablanca* (Madrid, 1899) (" Bibliotecas de Autores Españoles, v. L ") [326] contains the confidential instructions given by the king to the council of state, July 8, 1787, in regard to commerce with America, and the Mississippi river navigation controversy. " Papers bearing on Wilkinson's relations with Spain, 1787–1789 ", ed. by W. R. Shepherd, *Am. hist. rev.*, IX (1904) 748–766 [327], from Spanish archives. " Charles Pinckney's reply to Jay, August 16, 1786, regarding a treaty with Spain ", ed. by W. C. Ford, *Am. hist. rev.*, X (1905) 817–827 [328] is a copy of a speech delivered in Congress, not elsewhere recorded, and is found printed as a broadside in the Madison papers in the Library of Congress. Louis Houck, *The Spanish régime in Missouri; a collection of papers and documents relating to upper Louisiana* (Chicago, 1909, 2 v.) [329] consists of 128 documents (1767–1800) from the Spanish archives and other sources. " Papers relating to Bourbon county, Georgia, 1785–1786 ", ed. by E. C. Burnett, *Am. hist. rev.*, XV (1909–10) 66–111, 297–353

[330–1], bearing on Georgia and the Spanish frontier. Robertson, *Louisiana, 1785–1807* (no. 705). Juan Ventura Morales, " Informe relativo á los actos de agresión, hostilidad, etc., cometidos por el gobierno de los Estados Unidos de Norte América contra los dominios de España en las Floridas y sus dependencias ", *Arch. nac. bol.*, XIII (Havana, 1914) 9–21 [**332**], copy of an official communication from Juan Ventura Morales, Havana, Nov. 3, 1817, describing American aggressions during the period 1783 to 1817. *Letters of Rufus King* (no. 5248) discuss the proposed treaty with Spain. *Documents relating to the commercial policy of Spain in the Floridas, with incidental reference to Louisiana,* ed. by A. P. Whitaker (Deland, Fla., 1931) [**333**] is a valuable collection of Spanish documents *circa* 1776 to 1808. John Caughey, "Alexander McGillivray and the Creek crisis, 1783–1784 " in *New Spain and the Anglo-American west;* historical contributions presented to Herbert Eugene Bolton, v. I (Los Angeles, Calif., 1932), 263–288 [**334**] includes 16 documents from the *Papeles de Cuba* (Archivo General de Indias) showing McGillivray's intimacy with Spanish officials.

For the printed writings of John Adams, Alexander Hamilton, Thomas Jefferson, Rufus King, R. H. Lee, James Madison, and Washington, see our list, p. 756.

MSS.: Suggestions

See Sec. 1, above.

The personal papers of the first American *chargé d'affaires*, William Carmichael, 1784–1795, were, as above mentioned, in a trunk which has been traced only as far as Cadiz, whither it had been sent in 1795 when death interrupted his departure from Madrid for his homeland. Papers presented to the House of Representatives with the claim of Carmichael are included among the *House of Representatives collection* in the Library of Congress.

The records of the Spanish foreign office at the *Archivo Histórico Nacional*, Madrid, are indicated very generally in Shepherd's *Guide* (no. 5635), and specifically by subheads and *legajo* numbers in Campillo's typescript guide (see p. 904). The papers of the Spanish legation in the United States (containing signed instructions and copies of despatches) (including those of Diego de Gardoqui) are preserved (but damaged by mildew) in the archives of the *Departa-*

mento de Estado, in the Plaza de Santa Cruz, Madrid. The incoming despatches and drafts of the outgoing papers are in the *Archivo Histórico Nacional*, Madrid. For the legation papers at the *Departamento de Estado* there is nothing but a MS. list of *legajo* numbers in the possession of the archivist. Shepherd's *Guide* (no. 5635) is very general and lacks *legajo* numbers. In the *Archivo Histórico Nacional* is considerable supplementary American material in the form of ministerial *dossiers* (*expedientes*) grouped in bundles (*legajos*). The American material for this archive before the year 1800 has been catalogued, *legajo* by *legajo* by the present chief, Mr. Miguel Gómez del Campillo, in typed MS. cards, a copy of which is in the Division of Manuscripts in the Library of Congress. The correspondence of the Spanish colonial authorities in Louisiana and Florida, relayed via Cuba, is largely contained in the *Papeles de Cuba*, now in the *Archivo General de Indias*, at Seville, and is carefully catalogued, with analysis of separate *legajos* particularly relating to the United States, in R. R. Hill's *Catalogue* (no. 5650). The Library of Congress has photostats of the American documents in the *Archivo Histórico Nacional* and the *Papeles de Cuba*. For guides and indexes to Spanish archives, see below, p. 898. The Library of Congress also has a photographic collection of the despatches of the Spanish governors of Louisiana, 1766–1791, but without enclosures. For bibliographical notes see Bemis (no. 506) and Whitaker (no. 502). For transcripts and original MS. pieces existing in the United States in 1910, see Robertson's *Guide* (no. 5532). For note regarding Floridablanca MSS., see Ch. I, sec. 4, p. 22.

The original MSS. of the local East Florida archives, delivered by Spain to the United States with the province, are now in the Library of Congress, described by Mabel M. Manning (no. 1007). A single piece in original MS. in the Library of Congress is *Rapport au Comte de Luzerne, ministre de la marine, au sujet du passage du Mississippi, projété par le Général Wilkinson*, March 27, 1788. Another, in the Bibliotheca Nacional, Madrid (among the Gayangos MSS.) is *Dictamen dado en 1788, por D. Juan Bautista Múñoz, sobre la pretensión de los Anglo-Americanos respecto á la navegación del Misisipi.* Definitive research must cover the various MS. collections in and relating to the Mississippi Valley region. For indexes to MS. collections in local libraries, etc., see below, p. 886.

Maps: Suggestions

See Ch. IV, Sec. 5.

6. Anglo-American Affairs, 1783-1789

Bibliographical Aids

See Sec. 1, above; also Canadian historical bibliographies (nos. 4671-4677). *Political history of England*, ed. by William Hunt and R. L. Poole, v. X, 1760-1801 (N.Y. and London, 1905) [335], for notes on authorities. Bemis, *Jay's treaty* (no. 551), 347-367. Three bibliographies by L. J. Ragatz: *H. C. sess. papers Brit. W. Indies* (no. 5407); *H. Lords sess. pap. Brit. W. Indies* (no. 5409); and *Guide* (no. 4721). Turner and Merk (no. 307). R. G. Trotter, *Canadian history; a syllabus and guide to reading* (N.Y., 1926; new and enl. ed., Toronto, 1934) [336]. T. C. Pease, *English and French materials for a history of the northwest, 1783-1815* (in preparation) [337-8].

For lists of American newspapers, see Sec. 1, above. For lists of English newspapers, see *Tercentenary handlist* (no. 5013); Crane and Kaye (no. 5015); and Gabler (no. 5027).

Special Works

A. C. McLaughlin, "The western posts and the British debts", *Am. hist. assoc. ann. rep.*, for 1894 (1895) 413-444 [339], the pioneer study in this field, but the writer did not have available all the Canadian and British MS. sources. De Witt (no. 35). Edward Smith, *England and America after independence; a short examination of their international intercourse, 1783-1872* (Westminster, Eng., 1900) [340], by an avowed advocate of the propriety of English dealings with America. I. J. Cox, "The Indian as a diplomatic factor in the history of the Old Northwest", *Ohio archaeol. and hist. quar.*, XVIII (1909) 542-565 [341], an early study of ground considerably reworked since. F. H. Severance, "The Niagara peace mission of Ephraim Douglass in 1783", *Buffalo hist. soc. pub.*, XVIII (1914) 115-142 [342], Douglass was commissioned by Congress in 1783 to visit the western Indian tribes and make known to them the peaceful disposition of the United States. In this mission he came in contact with the British officials in the occupied posts. Orpha E. Leavitt, "British policy on the Canadian frontier, 1782-92; mediation and an Indian barrier state", *Wis.*

hist. soc. proc., 1915 (1916) 151-185 [**343**], the writer believes instructions given by the ministry manifest a constant desire for peace with the United States. H. C. Bell, " British commercial policy in the West Indies, 1783-93 ", *Eng. hist. rev.*, XXXI (1916) 429-441 [**344**]. *Camb. hist. Br. for. pol.* (no. 209), v. I, 143-215, for " Pitt's first decade, 1783-1792 ", by J. H. Clapham [**345**] which discusses briefly Anglo-American relations. Bemis, *Jay's treaty* (no. 551) for an account of British-American relations during the " critical period ", based on English archives; and the same writer in *Am. secs. state* (no. 4796), v. I, 209-231. J. H. Rose, *Life of William Pitt* (N.Y., 1924) [**346**] discusses relations between John Adams and Pitt. Anna L. Lingelbach, " The inception of the British Board of Trade ", *Am. hist. rev.*, XXX (1925) 701-727 [**347**], for the early history of the Committee for Trade and Plantations, organized in 1784, which controlled the regulation of commercial relations with America. R. B. Mowat, *The diplomatic relations of Great Britain and the United States* (London, 1925) [**347a**], a summary account of varying quality, intended for the general reader, by a scholar not sufficiently grounded in American history to escape occasional misstatements. Stevens, *N.W. fur trade* (no. 233). Rife, *Ethan Allen* (no. 138a). Wilbur, *Ira Allen* (no. 138b). Pell, *Ethan Allen* (no. 138c). Beckles Willson, *America's ambassadors to England (1785-1928)*; *a narrative of Anglo-American diplomatic relations* (London, 1929) [**348**], ch. 1: " John Adams, 1785-1788." *Camb. hist. Br. Emp.*, (no. 210), v. VI, chs. 7, 8, and 9, by Duncan McArthur contain brief summaries of Anglo-American frontier disputes by a fair-minded historian who utilizes original sources generously for such a general work. S. J. Buck, *The story of the grand portage* (Minneapolis, 1931?) [**349**], an interesting sketch of a locality which assumed much significance in the diplomacy of the Anglo-American frontier. A. L. Burt, "A new approach to the problem of the western posts ", *Canad. hist. assoc. ann. rep.* (1931) 2-17 [**350**] regards danger of backbite by former Indian allies as one of the principal reasons for refusal of Great Britain to relinquish the posts; also his *Quebec* (no. 239a). G. H. Payne, *England; her treatment of America* (N.Y., 1931) [**351-2**], polemic reviewing Anglo-American relations in a bitter spirit to show the impossibility of any Anglo-American alliance today, an antidote to Smith (no. 340).

For biographies of John Adams, Alexander Hamilton, Ralph Izard, Benjamin Franklin, John Jay, Thomas Jefferson, R. H. Lee, Washington, *et alii*, see the relevant entries and bibliographical data in the *D.A.B.*

For biographies of British diplomatists and statesmen (Sir John Temple, consul-general to the United States; Lord Carmarthen (Leeds), Lord Dorchester, Charles James Fox, Sir Frederick Haldimand, and William Pitt, the younger) see the *D.N.B.*[3] Note also these more recent works in the "Makers of Canada" series: Jean N. McIlwraith, *Sir Frederick Haldimand* (London and Toronto, 1904; 2nd ed., 1926) [**353**]; and A. G. Bradley, *Lord Dorchester* (London and Toronto, 1907) [**354**].

For British prime ministers, see Bigham (no. 242).

Printed Sources

For American official documents and general source collections, see Sec. 1, above. Note particularly Moore's *Internat. arbitrations* (no. 5364), v. I, and *Internat. adjudications* (no. 5367), v. I–II, for the northwest boundary question. For British official documents, see House of Commons *Journals* and House of Lords *Journals* (no. 5418); *Parl. hist.* (no. 5410); *London Gazette* (no. 5127a); Ragatz (nos. 5407, 5409) for lists of British parliamentary papers relating to the West Indies. The *Reports on Canadian archives* (for contents, see *Index to Reports on Canadian archives from 1872 to 1908* (Ottawa, 1909) [**355**] contain many relevant documents; note particularly: *Report on Canadian archives, 1890*, by Douglas Brymner (Ottawa, 1891), 97–175 [**356**], for "Relations with the United States after the peace of 1783", consisting of abstracts of 38 documents from the British archives, 1787–1791, which relate mainly to Indian affairs, the retention of the western posts, and commercial relations.

For bibliographical note regarding contemporary writings useful in tracing commercial relations with Great Britain before 1789, see Channing (no. 4784), v. III, 428–429.

Lord Sheffield, *Observations on the commerce of the American states* (London, 1784) [**356a**], an essay full of statistics written for the purpose of defending the British commercial monopoly against American privileges. Sheffield is said (by Benns (no. 1343)) to have been assisted with data by the American Silas Deane. *Corres.*

---

[3] We endeavor to note significant ones which have appeared since the *D.N.B.*

C. J. Fox (no. 247), v. II. " Letters of the Marquis of Buckingham ", *Mass. hist. soc. proc.*, IX (1867) 69-80 [**357**], to Sir John
Temple, British consul-general to the United States, 1785-1787.
Bancroft (no. 300) contains selection of the correspondence of
Temple and Carmarthen, 1786-1789, of Sydney to Dorchester, 1787,
and of Grenville to Dorchester, 1789. For a calendar of " Correspondence relating to the exchange of prisoners and to Vermont, 1780-1784 ", see the *Report on Canadian archives*, by
Douglas Brymner, 1888 (Ottawa, 1889), 775-794 [**357a**]. *Michigan pioneer and historical collections*, v. XX, XXIV, XXV (Lansing, Mich., 1892-96, 3 v.) [**358**] contain voluminous printings from
Canadian transcripts of material in British colonial office records in
regard to relations with the American Indians about the occupied
American posts. " Letters of Phineas Bond, British consul at Philadelphia, to the foreign office of Great Britain, 1787, 1788, 1789 ", ed.
by J. F. Jameson, *Am. hist. assoc. ann. rep.*, for 1896, v. I (1897)
513-659, and *ibid.*, for 1897 (1898) 454-568 [**359**]; and the same
editor's S. Higginson's *Letter* (no. 301). " The Bowdoin and Temple papers ", Pt. II, *Mass. hist. soc. coll.*, 7th ser., v. VI (Boston,
1907) [**360**], letters to and from Governor Bowdoin and his son-in-
law, Sir John Temple, British consul-general to the United States,
1785-1798. " Marbois on the fur trade, 1784 ", *Am. hist. rev.*, XXIX
(1924) 725-740 [**361**], a letter and report in the archives of the
ministry of foreign affairs at Paris. *An Englishman in America,
1785; being the diary of Joseph Hadfield*, ed. by D. S. Robertson
(Toronto, 1933) [**362**], he travelled via the Hudson River route to
Canada, and up the St. Lawrence to Lake Ontario and Niagara when,
during the hold-over period, the forts on the south shores of the
Great Lakes were yet occupied by the British.

For the printed writings of American statesmen and diplomatists
(enumerated above, under " Special Works "), see our list on pages
756-779.

For the printed writings of British diplomatists and statesmen,
other than those entered above, see the bibliographical notes appended to relevant articles in the *D.N.B.*

MSS.: Suggestions

See Sec. 1, above.

The Fortescue edition of the *Corres. George III* (no. 143) stops
with 1783, but the William L. Clements Library, Ann Arbor, Mich.,

has typescripts which continue the edition to 1820. There was no British legation in the United States during this period, but the reports of the consuls (Sir John Temple, Phineas Bond, and George Miller) and of unaccredited observers, secret and open (Edward Bancroft, P. Allaire, and George Beckwith) are preserved among the Foreign Office papers in the British Public Record Office; see no. 5578. Of great importance is the correspondence of the British Colonial Office with its officials in British North America and the West Indies; see no. 5586. The correspondence with the governors-general of Canada (Haldimand and Dorchester) in the Colonial Office, and in transcript in the Canadian Archives, is calendared in the *Reports* of the Canadian Archives for 1884–1889 (published 1885–1890 (see *Index to Reports of Canadian Archives from 1872 to 1908* (Ottawa, 1909)). The original papers of Governor Haldimand, 1758–1785, are in the British Museum (transcripts in Canadian Archives); for volumes containing materials for American history after 1782, see Paullin and Paxson (no. 5577), 536–544. For correspondence of Canadian officials with frontier agents, Indian service, and British agents in the United States, see *ibid*. The Chatham papers, and the papers of the Board of Trade, both in the Record Office, throw light on commerce with the United States. The British Museum has the Liverpool papers (Robert Banks Jenkinson, Lord Hawkesbury, 2d Earl of Liverpool), also miscellaneous letters and papers relating to American affairs (western forts and the Indians), 1718–1796. The Library of Congress has photostats of miscellaneous papers relating to the history of Vermont and Ira Allen, 1774 to about 1800.

For guides, catalogues, indexes, and calendars of MS. material in British archives and libraries, see below, p. 890. See also Parker (no. 5610) for guide to materials in Canadian archives. There is a bibliographical note in Bemis, *Jay's treaty* (no. 551).

Maps: Suggestions

For the Northeast Boundary, see p. 287, below. For Canadian maps, see Holmden (no. 5144); for maps in British archives, see Andrews, *Guide* (no. 5576), Andrews and Davenport, *Guide* (no. 5590), Paullin and Paxson, *Guide* (no. 5577), and Phillips (no. 5135). See also Karpinski (no. 5150) for maps of the northwest during this period.

7. The Netherlands, 1782–1789

Bibliographical Aids

For general aids (American) see Sec. 1, above.

For Dutch historical bibliography see Fruin (no. 4750).

Special Works

Kohlmeier, *U.S. and Netherlands* (no. 289). Van Winter, *Amsterdamschen Handel* (no. 156).

For biographies of John Adams, John Jay, Thomas Jefferson, and Washington, see the relevant entries and bibliographical data in the *D.A.B.*

Printed Sources

For American official documents and general source collections, see Sec. 1, above.

For guide to Dutch official documents, see p. 843.

For the printed writings of John Adams, C. W. F. Dumas, John Jay, Thomas Jefferson, and Washington, see our list on p. 756.

MSS.: Suggestions

See Sec. 1 above.

For index to correspondence of the Dutch foreign office with its American legation, and exchange with the American *chargé* at The Hague, see no. 5728. For C. W. F. Dumas papers, see no. 5731. The Library of Congress has photocopies of these documents. For indexes, etc., to Dutch archives, see below, p. 921.

CHAPTER IV

THE FEDERALIST PERIOD, 1789–1801

1. In General

Bibliographical Aids

For general aids, see Evans (no. 4639); Sabin (no. 4655); Larned (no. 4657); Griffin (no. 4658); *Writings* (no. 4661); C., H. and T. (no. 4662); *Am. secs. state* (no. 4796), see " Bibliographical notes "; *Guide hist. lit.* (no. 4634); Myers (no. 5399), for collections of treaties. Miller, *Treaties* (no. 5371), v. I, 39–54, for " Bibliography of United States treaty collections." See also Winsor (no. 4782), v. VII, 513–525, for notes on the sources of information regarding the diplomacy of the period. A. W. Greely, *Public documents of the early Congresses* (Wash., 1897) [363] for list of government publications, including messages and state papers of presidents omitted from Richardson's compilation. Bassett, *Federalist system* (no. 366), ch. 20: " Critical essay on authorities." Greene and Morris (no. 5531).

For guides to newspapers, see Brigham (no. 5012), and Library of Congress *Checklist* (no. 5031); and (for English newspapers), *Tercentenary handlist* (no. 5013); Crane and Kaye (no. 5015); and Gabler (no. 5027).

General and Special Works

Of general histories of the United States, see Hildreth (no. 4779); Von Holst (no. 4780); McMaster (no. 4781); Winsor (no. 4782); Channing (no. 4784). See also *Am. secs. state*, v. I–II (no. 4796); and Wriston (no. 4799).

Lyman (no. 14). W. H. Trescot, *The diplomatic history of the administrations of Washington and Adams, 1789–1801* (Boston, 1857) [**364**], Trescot was probably the first historian to use the archives of the Department of State, to which he was officially attached. Sorel, *L'Europe et la révolution française* (no. 396). J. B. Angell, " The diplomacy of the United States, 1789–1850 ", in Winsor, *America* (no. 4782), v. VII, 461–525 [**365**]. J. S. Bassett, *The federalist system, 1789–1801* (N.Y., 1906) [**366**]. H. E. Bourne, *The revolutionary period in Europe, 1763–1815* (N.Y., 1914) [**367**], a useful and scholarly summary with abundant references and suggestions for further reading and investigation. Johnson, *Hist. commerce U.S.* (no. 641), ch. 22: " Survey of American commerce at the beginning of the national period." J. H. Latané, " Jefferson's influence on American foreign policy ", *Univ. of Va. alumni bul.*, 3d ser., XVII (1924) 245–269 [**368**] contains provocative suggestions and generalizations. Woolery (no. 279). Ingram, *Am. consular service* (no. 21a). Savage, *U.S. maritime policy* (no. 22).

For biographies of American presidents, secretaries of state, and diplomatists abroad (for names and tenure see latest *Register* of the Dept. of State (no. 5122)), see relevant entries and bibliographical data in *D.A.B.;* and *Am. secs. state* (no. 4796). Note also biographies of Alexander Hamilton, Oliver Wolcott, and James McHenry.

Printed Sources

For American official documents and general source collections, see *Jour. exec. proc. Sen.*, v. I (no. 5387) ; *A.S.P., F.R.*, v. I–II (no. 5341) ; *Ann. Cong.* (no. 5382) ; Wharton, *Digest* (no. 5366) ; *Abridg. debates* (no. 5386) ; Richardson (no. 5335) ; Moore's *Arbitrations* (no. 5364) ; *Repts. Sen. Com. for. rel.* (no. 5388), meager and poorly arranged record previous to 1816. Moore's *Digest* (no. 5365). Myers (no. 5399), for collections of treaties.

For text of treaties, with notes, see Miller, *Treaties* (no. 5371).

For guides to newspapers, see nos. 5004–5044.

For printed writings of American presidents, secretaries of state, and diplomatists abroad (for names and tenure, see latest *Register* of the Dept. of State (no. 5122)), see our list on p. 756.

The embargo laws (Boston, 1809) [**369**], a handy print in English, of the British orders in council, French decrees, and American laws restricting commerce, 1793–1808. Timothy Pickering, *A review of*

*the correspondence between the Hon. John Adams, late president of
the United States, and the late Wm. Cunningham*, 1803–12 (Salem,
1824) [370] for Pickering's own account of his removal, with ani-
madversions on the mission to France in 1799. William Sullivan,
*Familiar letters on public characters, and public events, from the
peace of 1783 to the peace of 1815* (Boston, 1834) [371] contains
biased sketches of contemporaries written by an irreconcilable
Federalist. George Gibbs, *Memoirs of the administrations of
Washington and John Adams* (N.Y., 1846, 2 v.) [372] gives
voluminous selections from the papers of Oliver Wolcott, 2nd
secretary of the treasury, illustrative of Federalist attitude on
foreign policy. *The journal of William Maclay, United States senator from Pennsylvania, 1789–1791*, ed. by E. S. Maclay (N.Y.,
1890; new ed.: N.Y., 1927) [373]. Farrand, *Federal convention*
(no. 5381). *The Windham papers; the life and correspondence of the
Rt. Hon. William Windham, 1750–1810* (London, 1913, 2 v.) [374],
v. I, 121–136, contains a letter from " an unknown correspondent "
(recently identified as the Vicomte de Noailles, cf. *Am. hist. rev.*,
XXXVIII, 633) written from Philadelphia to William Windham,
June 1, 1793, giving a close-up on American statesmen and their outlook on domestic and foreign affairs.

MSS.: Suggestions

There are abundant general collections, official and private, covering various phases of American diplomacy, 1789–1801. The official
archives of the Department of State are intact, and are described
below, pp. 788 ff. and 858 ff., and are analyzed in Van Tyne and
Leland (no. 5495). For personal papers of presidents (Washington,
John Adams), secretaries of state (Jefferson, Randolph, Pickering,
Marshall), and diplomatists abroad (for names and tenure see latest
Register of the Department of State (no. 5122)), see our lists on
pp. 862–883. The papers of Secretary of War Henry Knox are in
the New England Historic Genealogical Society; those of his successor James McHenry, were acquired in 1931 by the Library of
Congress. The main collection of Alexander Hamilton's papers is
in the Library of Congress, that of his successor Oliver Wolcott is in
the Connecticut Historical Society at Hartford. For further leads
to general MS. material in the United States, see the various guides,
catalogues, and indexes listed below in Pt. II, ch. 3, pp. 886–890.

Deciphers of some of the despatches passing between foreign governments and their ministers in England, with cipher keys, 1740–1841, are in the British Museum.

In " Manuscript Suggestions " to the separate topical sections following in this chapter we give more particular suggestions.

2. The New Department of State and the Constitutional Conduct of Foreign Affairs [1]

Bibliographical Aids

See Sec. 1, above.

Special Works

Foster, *Am. diplomacy* (no. 4788), 103–135, for " The organization of the Department of State." Mary L. Hinsdale, *A history of the President's cabinet* (Ann Arbor, Mich., 1911) [375]. H. B. Learned (no. 281). Hunt (no. 205). Ralston Hayden, *The Senate and treaties, 1789–1817* (N.Y. and London, 1920) [376]. Fleming, *Treaty veto* (no. 4834). R. E. McClendon on *The two-thirds rule in Senate action upon treaties* (no. 4835). Dangerfield, *Defense of the Senate* (no. 4836), for Washington's intercourse with the Senate concerning foreign relations and treaty making. Holt, *Defeated treaties* (no. 4837).

Printed Sources

For general collections, see Sec. 1, above. Alexander Hamilton, James Madison, John Jay, *The Federalist* (N.Y., 1788, 2 v. and many subsequent editions) [376a] contains interpretations of the powers of the federal government by the classic expositors of the Constitution of 1787. *Journal of Wm. Maclay* (no. 373) for debate in the Senate on the bill for organizing the Department of Foreign Affairs. Farrand, *Federal convention* (no. 5381).

For printed writings of Hamilton, Jefferson, Madison, and Washington, see our list on p. 756.

MSS.: Suggestions

For the organization of the State Department see the papers of Washington and Jefferson. The entire archives of the Department for this period are intact, and are described in Van Tyne and Leland

---

[1] See also Ch. III, Sec. 2, above.

(no. 5495). The significance of the new office, and of the constitution, is reflected in the correspondence of the French, Spanish, and Dutch diplomatic representatives in the United States, 1787–90 (see Secs. 4, 5, and 7 below). Note also the papers of Washington, Jefferson, Madison, and Hamilton, in the Library of Congress, and MS. day-book of President Washington's official acts as executive (*Journal of the proceedings of the President, 1793–1797*) in the same library.

3. Problem of Neutrality, 1793–1794

Bibliographical Aids

For general aids, see Sec. 1, above.

See also Faÿ, *Bibliographie* (no. 31); and there is a useful and comprehensive bibliography in Thomas, *Am. neutrality* (no. 385).

Special Works

See Secs. 1, above and 4, below ("Franco-American Relations"), particularly Sorel (no. 396); Hazen (no. 399); Schalch de la Faverie (no. 642); and Woolery (no. 279).

George Bemis, *Precedents of American neutrality* (Boston, 1864) [377] discusses the expulsion and seizure of Genet's privateers in 1793, and American treatment of French and British Alabamas in Washington's administration. C. G. Fenwick, *The neutrality laws of the United States* (Wash., 1913) [378], a convenient analysis. A. H. Washburn, "The American view of neutrality", *Va. law rev.*, II (1914) 165–177 [379] traces the evolution of American policy in regard to neutrality. H. C. Lodge, "Washington's policies of neutrality and national defence", in his *War addresses* (Boston and N.Y., 1917) 117–136 [380]. L. M. Sears, "Jefferson and the law of nations", *Am. pol. sci. rev.*, XIII (1919) 379–399 [381]. S. F. Bemis, "The United States and the abortive armed neutrality of 1794", *Am. hist. rev.*, XXIV (1918) 26–47 [382] deals with the reasons why the United States did not accept the Swedish invitation to join the Dano-Swedish treaty of 1794; his "The United States and Lafayette", *D. A. R. mag.*, LVIII (1924) passim. [383] emphasizes Washington's refusal to entangle the United States in European politics in order to get Lafayette out of Prussian and Austrian prisons, 1792–1794; his *Jay's treaty* (no. 551); and his account in *Am. secs. state* (no. 4796) v. II, ch. 4. C. M. Thomas, *American neutral-*

ity in 1793; a study in cabinet government (N.Y., 1931) [**384**], a good treatment of problems of neutral rights and duties in the year 1793 only. C. S. Hyneman, *The first American neutrality; a study of the American understanding of neutral obligations during the years 1792 to 1815* (Urbana, Ill., 1934) [**385**], a detailed analysis.

Printed Sources

For American official documents and general source collections see Sec. 1, above. See also Sec. 4 (" Franco-American Relations "), noting particularly Turner (nos. 472, 476); Sec. 5 (" Spanish-American Relations "), and Sec. 6 ("Anglo-American Relations ").

Embargo laws (no. 369). *Dropmore MSS.* (no. 5602), v. I contains some private letters to and from the British foreign secretary, Lord Grenville. C. R. Fish, *The foundations of American neutrality* (Madison, 1922) [**386**] reprints, not impeccably, most significant papers on neutrality 1778-1794.

For the printed writings of John Adams, Hamilton, Jay, Jefferson, Madison, and Monroe, see our list on p. 756.

MSS.: Suggestions

See in detail the MS. suggestions in this chapter, Secs. 4 and 6, particularly the papers of Washington, John Adams, Hamilton, Jay, and Jefferson, and E. Randolph, and the Genet papers in the Library of Congress. Note also President Washington's official *Journal of the proceedings of the President, 1793-1797,* above (sec. 2) referred to. The fundamental source consists of the notes exchanged between the Secretary of State and the diplomatic representatives of the belligerent powers. They are preserved in the Department of State archives, and are not all printed in *A.S.P., F.R.,* I (no. 5341). The diplomatic correspondence of the belligerent powers with their American agents is of course indicated (see Secs. 4, 5, 6, and 7).

4. Franco-American Relations

Bibliographical Aids

For general aids, see Secs. 1 and 3, above.

For French historical bibliographies, see nos. 4732-4739.

Jameson, *Bibliography of Monroe and the Monroe doctrine,* (no. 1139). A bibliography of " French spoliations ", in *Boston pub. lib. bul.,* VI (1885) 393-402 [**387**]. Maurice Tourneur, " Les sources bibliographiques de l'histoire de la révolution française ", *Bibliographie moderne*, I (1897) 249–289, 329–368 [**388**]. Pease (no. 337). Kircheisen, *Bibliog. Napoléons* (no. 629); also his *Bibliog. napoléon. Zeitalters* (no. 630). F. J. Turner, in his introduction to " *Corres. Fr. ministers* " (no. 476) gives a useful bibliography of French-American diplomacy. Pierre Caron, *Manuel pratique pour l'étude de la révolution française* (Paris, 1912) [**389**], most valuable, containing a description of the archives of foreign affairs, and of manuscripts dealing with foreign affairs of the period, as well as printed works. Faÿ, *Bibliographie critique* (no. 31). André Monglond, *La France révolutionnaire et impériale; annales de bibliographie méthodique et description des livres illustrés* (Grenoble, 1930–) [**390**] is a bibliography (in course of publication) of works appearing in the years 1789–; to date (1934), three volumes have been published (v. III, 1933), extending through the year 1796. Dutcher, *Napoleonic studies* (no. 631) and *Napoleonic period* (no. 632).

Special Works

For the principal general histories of France during the French Revolution and the early Bonapartist years, see Caron, *Manuel* (no. 389); Kircheisen, *Bibliographie* (no. 629); and (best of all) *Guide hist. lit.* (no. 4634).

Among these general histories Sorel (no. 396) is of supreme value, to be corrected in certain details of the diplomatic history of the French Revolution, especially Panton's diplomacy, by the later studies of A. Mathiez, *La révolution française* (Paris, 1922–1927, 3 v.; Eng. translation, N.Y., 1928) [**391**], and for the Directory, by Guyot (no. 412).

C. W. Goldsborough, *The United States' naval chronicle*, v. I (Wash., 1824) [**392**], for an early account of the hostilities with France. Gibbs (no. 372) for reflections of Federalist foreign policy. G. F. Emmons, *The navy of the United States, 1775 to 1853* (Wash., 1853) (known as *Statistical history of the United States navy*) [**393**]. Gayarré (no. 308). Trescot (no. 364). De Witt, *Jefferson* (no. 35). James Parton, " The exploits of Edmond Genet in the United States ", *Atlantic*, XXXI (1873) 385–405 [**394**], an interesting narrative by an eminent writer who lacked French sources since printed. Frédéric Masson, *Le département des affaires étrangères pendant la révolution, 1787–1804* (Paris, 1877) [**395**], for notes regarding men dealing with American affairs. Albert Sorel, *L'Europe et la révolution française* (Paris, 1885–1904, 8 v.) [**396**], a great masterpiece which incorporates in this general history of French diplomacy, 1793–1815, his previous article on " La diplomatie française et l'Espagne de 1792 à 1796 ", in *Rev. historique*, XI–XIII (1879–1880). H. von Wilke, " Gouverneur Morris, amerikanischer Gesandter in Paris, während der Schreckenszeit", *Hist. Zeitschrift*, LXVII (n.s., XXXI) (1891) 192–211 [**397**], an article excited by the appearance of A. C. Morris' *Diary and letters of Gouverneur Morris*, in 1888, supplementing the earlier and more imperfect edition by Sparks of Morris' correspondence. A. T. Mahan, *The influence of sea power ʊʌon the French revolution and empire, 1798–1812* (Boston, 1892, 2 v.) [**398**], a great classic. Roosevelt, *West*, v. IV (no. 310). C.D. Hazen, *Contemporary American opinion of the French revolution* (Baltimore, 1897) [**399**] gives opinions of Americans abroad (Jefferson, G. Morris, and Monroe), and Americans at home, and contains a useful bibliography. Winsor, *Westward movement* (no. 311). G. F. Hoar, "A famous fête ", *Am. antiq. soc. proc.*, n.s. XII (1898) 240–259 [**400**], fête given by Joseph Bonaparte, Oct. 3, 1800 on the conclusion of the treaty with the United States. J. H. Rose, *Revol. and Napoleonic era* (no. 635) ; *Napoleon and sea power* (no. 636) ; and *Brit. W. India commerce* (no. 813). Ludovic Sciout, " La révolution à Saint-Domingue; les commissaires Sonthonax et Polverel ", *Rev. quest. hist.*, LXIV (1898) 399–470 [**401**] describes the terrible insurrection in San Domingo from the records of the French commissioners sent to deal with it, and is valuable for an understanding of French island colonies in Franco-American relations. F. J. Turner published several articles in which he combined his rare knowledge of the history of the Mississippi Valley—and of the United States—with the documents from French archives edited by him in *Corres. Fr. ministers* (no. 476) : " The origin of Genet's projected attack on Louisiana and the Floridas ", *Am. hist. rev.*, III (1898) 650–671, also published in his *The significance of sections in American history* (N.Y., 1932) 52–85 [**402**] ; " The diplomatic contest for the Mississippi valley ", *Atlantic*, XCIII (1904) 676–691, 807–817 [**403**], for criticism, see P. C. Phillips (no. 44), p. 30^n and Mildred S. Fletcher (no. 438) ; and " The policy of France toward the Mississippi valley in the period of Washington and Adams ", *Am. hist. rev.*, X (1905) 249–279, also published in his *The significance* *of sections in American history* (N.Y., 1932) 138–182 [**404**]. G. C. Genet, *Washington, Jefferson and "citizen" Genet, 1793* (N.Y., 1899) [**405**]. A. Cans, " Les idées de Talleyrand sur la politique coloniale de la France au lendemain de la révolution ", *Rev. hist. mod.*, II (1900) 58–63 [**406**]. Marc de Villiers du Terrage, *Les dernières années de la Louisiane française* (Paris, 1904) [**407**]. Alphonse Bertrand, " Les Etats-Unis et la révolution française ", *Rev. deux mondes*, 5th ser., XXXIII (1906) 392–430 [**407a**], an informing narrative elicited by the appearance of Turner's edition of the correspondence of the French ministers, 1791–1792 (no. 476). B. W. Bond, jr., *The Monroe mission to France 1794–1796* (Baltimore, 1907) [**408**], of limited value because indispensable French sources were not available to author. W. S. Robertson, *Miranda* (no. 556). G. F. Zook, " Proposals for new commercial treaty between France and the United States, 1778–1793 ", *So. Atlan. quar.*, VIII (1909) 267–283 [**409**], though this is a very valuable monograph, it would be more valuable if the writer had had the French sources. Paul Mantoux, " Le comité de salut public et la mission de Genet aux Etats-Unis ", *Rev. hist. mod.*, XIII (1909–10) 5–35 [**410**], by an eminent French scholar, later the official interpreter at the Versailles Peace Conference of 1919, who utilized both the French and American sources. Driault, *Napoléon* (no. 639). Brooks Adams, " The convention of 1800 with France ", *Mass. hist. soc. proc.*, XLIV (1911) 377–428 [**411**], an Adams discusses as a lawyer's brief legal implications in the history of the dispute between France and the United States, 1794–1800. Raymond Guyot, *Le directoire et la paix de l'Europe . . ., 1795–1799* (Paris, 1911; also 1912 edition) [**412**], a most scholarly history of French foreign policy based on French archival sources, touches American affairs. Kircheisen, *Napoleon I.* (no. 640). C. I. Crawford, *A review of the history of the French spoliation claims and some of the principles of international law applying to them*, prepared for the use of the committee on claims, U.S. Senate (Wash.: Gov't. Print. Off., 1912) [**412a**], apparently a legal brief supporting the justice of the claims, with historical statement. L. Didier, " Le citoyen Genet " *Rev. quest. hist.*, XCII–XCIII (1912– 1913) passim. [**413**], scholarly account based on archives of the French foreign office and the documents published by Turner (see below, next section). S. E. Morison, *The life and letters of Harrison Gray Otis, federalist, 1765–1848* (Boston and N.Y., 1913, 2 v.)

[**414**], for expressions of Federalist opinion in regard to France; and "A Yankee skipper in San Domingo, 1797 ", *Mass. hist. soc. proc.*, XLIX (1916) 268–273 [**415**] prints a letter written by Capt. Samuel Morris, at Cape François in 1797, which describes the difficulties of neutral commerce; and " Elbridge Gerry, gentleman, democrat ", *New Eng. quar.*, II (1929) 3–33 [**416**]. J. A. James, " French diplomacy and American politics, 1794–1795 ", *Am. hist. assoc. ann. rep.*, for 1911, v. I (1913) 151–163 [**417**] deals with Fauchet's mission; his " Louisiana as a factor in American diplomacy, 1795–1800 ", *Miss. Valley hist. rev.*, I (1914) 44–56 [**418**] points out that the desire to control Louisiana was conspicuous among the causes in bringing about the treaty of 1800; and his " French opinion as a factor in preventing war between France and the United States, 1795–1800 ", *Am. hist. rev.*, XXX (1924) 44–55 [**419**]. G. Vauthier, " Notes sur les relations commerciales de la France et les Etats-Unis de 1789 à 1815 ", in *Mémoires et documents pour servir à l'histoire du commerce . . . en France*, ed. by Julien Hayem, 3d ser. (Paris, 1913) 91–106, and in *Rev. internat. commerce*, XV (1913) 83–98 [**420**] contains a few statistics, apparently of American origin, undocumented, and is of little contributive value. F. T. Hill, "Adventures in American diplomacy—I. The affair of X, Y, and Z ", *Atlantic*, CXIII (1914) 533–545 [**421**], a popular account based on the printed despatches of the American commissioners. G. A. King, *The French spoliation claims* (Wash., 1916) [**422**], a history of the disposal of the assumed claims by the United States government, evidently by a lawyer who had much concerned himself with this class of business. Channing, *Hist. U.S.*, IV (no. 4784) gives in several chapters what is still the best account of Franco-American relations, 1795–1800. Oscar Hallam, " Citizen Genet, his contribution to international law ", *Am. law rev.*, LI (1917) 321–344 [**423**], a very useful analysis of the crystallization of American interpretation of neutral obligations in 1793–1794. Schalck de la Faverie, *Napoléon et l'Amérique* (no. 642). Charles Warren, *History of laws prohibiting correspondence with a foreign government and acceptance of a commission* (Wash., 1917) [**424**], for the immediate causes of the Logan act of 1799. Renaut, *Question de Louisiane* (no. 675a) publishes the instructions given by the *Directoire* to Gen Pérignon, and other diplomatic documents. Hayden (no. 376) for the Senate and the Convention of 1800 with France. Archibald Henderson,

"Isaac Shelby and the Genet mission ", *Miss. Valley hist. rev.*, VI
(1920) 451–469 [425] explains lukewarmness of Governor Shelby
of Kentucky in cooperating with the federal government against
Genet's operations in the West as designed to alarm the administration into action in solving the diplomatic problem of the
Mississippi, but see S. M. Wilson, *A review . . . of "Isaac
Shelby and the Genet mission"*, by Dr. Archibald Henderson
(Lexington, Ky., 1920) [426] who, diffusely, disagrees with
Henderson's conclusions and considers Shelby ingenuous in his
explanations of lack of constitutional power and deprecation of the
gravity of French designs on American neutrality.   Ernest Lavisse,
ed., *Histoire de France contemporaine depuis la révolution jusqu'à
la paix de 1919* (Paris, 1920–22, 10 v.) [427], a recent review by a
leading French scholar in a remarkably successful cooperative series,
v. II (1920) : *La révolution (1792–1799)*, par G. Pariset, a well digested narrative abreast with recent research (except for Mathiez's
most recent contributions on the period 1789–1794).   E. M. Coulter,
"Elijah Clarke's foreign intrigues " and the " Trans-Oconee republic ", *Miss. Valley hist. rev.*, extra no. (Nov. 1921) 260–279, also
issued (Athens, Ga., 1922) (University of Georgia Bulletin, v.
XXIII, no. 4) [428] discusses Clarke's associations with Genet in the
scheme for an invasion of the Floridas by a force raised in Georgia,
1793–1794.   Hill, *Treaties* (no. 4794), good summary of the convention
of 1800.   F. L. Nussbaum, *Commercial policy in the French revolution; a study of the career of G. J. A. Ducher* (Wash.: Am. Hist. Assoc.,
1923) [429] traces the evolution of the new French navigation system.   A. S. Lanier, " The French spoliation claims ", *Va. law reg.*,
n.s. X (1924) 12–23 [430], an argument against payment by the
United States of claims for indemnification of insurance companies,
still unpaid, arising out of French spoliations before 1801.   Bodley,
G. R. Clark (no. 229).   Woolery (no. 279).   Giuseppe Caraci, " Il
generale francese Giorgio Enrico Vittorio Collot ed il suo viaggio
nell' America Settentrionale, 1796 ", in *Atti d. XXII Cong. Internazionale degli Americanisti, Roma, settembre 1926*, v. II (1928)
619–648 [431] is more concerned with Collot's contributions to geographical knowledge than with the political significance of his activities, which would have been more apparent if the author had
had available French sources other than Collot's own *Voyage*.
Regina K. Crandall, " Genet's projected attack on Louisiana and the

Floridas, 1793–94 ", *Abstracts of theses, humanistic series*, pub. by the University of Chicago, v. V (1928) 263–270 [**432**]. F. R. Hall, "Genet's western intrigue, 1793–1794 ", *Ill. state hist. soc. jour.*, XXI (1928) 359–381 [**433**] is especially concerned with the George Rogers Clark aspect of the enterprise. Meade Minnigerode, *Jefferson, friend of France, 1793; the career of Edmond Charles Genet, . . . as revealed by his private papers, 1763–1834* (N.Y. and London, 1928) [**434**], a vivid but none too critical narration of the " new " biographical type which depicts Genet putting " all his eggs so trustfully in Jefferson's false-bottom basket." A. P. Whitaker, " The commerce of Louisiana and the Floridas at the end of the eighteenth century ", *Hisp. Am. hist. rev.*, VIII (1928) 190–203 [**435**] stresses economic factors revealed by extensive studies in Spanish archives; his " France and the American deposit at New Orleans ", *ibid.*, XI (1931) 485–502 [**436**] states that the basis of French policy in regard to Louisiana, 1795–1803, was economic interest; see also his *Mississippi question* (no. 505). Beckles Willson (no. 68). John Rydjord, " The French revolution and Mexico ", *Hisp. Am. hist. rev.*, IX (1929) 60–98 [**437**] is concerned with Genet and the Louisiana border. Mildred S. Fletcher, " Louisiana as a factor in French diplomacy from 1763 to 1800 ", *Miss. Valley hist. rev.*, XVII (1930) 367–376 [**438**] opposes older conceptions of Turner *et alii* that Vergennes urged the recovery of Louisiana. Hyneman, *Neutrality* (no. 384). J. J. Jusserand, " La jeunesse du citoyen Genet d'après des documents inédits ", *Rev. hist. dipl.*, XLIV (1930) 237–268 [**439**]. Georges Lefebvre, Raymond Guyot, and Philippe Sagnac, *La révolution française* (Paris, 1930) [**440**] includes a recent analysis of French relations with the United States. Two scholarly studies by C. L. Lokke: " French dreams of colonial empire under Directory and Consulate ", *Jour. mod. hist.*, II (1930) 237–250 [**441**]; and " The Trumbull episode; a prelude to the 'XYZ' affair ", *New Eng. quar.*, VII (1934) 100–114 [**442**], Col. John Trumbull (the celebrated artist) had been *persona non grata* in France because of his connection with Jay's treaty in 1794–95; and when he visited there in 1797, Talleyrand considered him full of guile and suspected his presence to be connected with hidden intrigues of Marshall, Pinckney, and Gerry. J. C. Parish, " The intrigues of Doctor James O'Fallon ", *Miss. Valley hist. rev.*, XVII (1930) 230–263 [**443**] deals with an associate of Clark in Genet's threatened attack upon Louisiana. Maude H. Woodfin, " Citizen Genet and his mission ", in *Abstracts of theses, humanistic series*, pub. by the University of Chicago, v. VII (1930) 305–311 [**444**]. Clauder, *Am. commerce and Napoleon* (no. 814). Lord Craigmyle (Thomas S., baron), *John Marshall in diplomacy and in law* (N.Y. and London, 1933) [**444a**], lectures by a distinguished English jurist to American university audiences. The lecture on Marshall as a diplomatist is based mostly on Beveridge's biography and contributes nothing. Bernard Faÿ, *The Two Franklin's: fathers of American democracy* (Boston, 1933) [**445**], brilliant style (after the influence of Gertrude Stein) but, this time, looser history; it gives a colorful picture of Genet's reception in Philadelphia (but says little about his intrigues, nothing about the West). Few American scholars are likely to accept the thesis of the parentage of American democracy. Bemis, *Washington's farewell address* (no. 619).

For biographies of American diplomatists to France (Wm. Short, G. Morris, J. Monroe, C. C. Pinckney, J. Marshall, Elbridge Gerry, Oliver Ellsworth, Wm. Vans Murray, W. R. Davie), see the relevant entries and bibliographical data in the *D.A.B.* Note particularly A. J. Beveridge, *The Life of John Marshall* (Boston and N.Y., 1916–1919, 4 v.) [**445a**]. V. C. Miller, *Joel Barlow; revolutionist, London, 1791–92* (Hamburg, 1932) [**445b**].[2] There is an English translation (by Elinore Denniston) of Daniel Walther's *Gouverneur Morris* (Lausanne, 1932) (N.Y. and London, 1934) [**445c**].[2]

For biographies of French diplomatists and consuls to the United States (Adet, Fauchet, Genet, Létombe, Otto, and Ternant) and of French statesmen, see the *D.B.F.* (no. 4965). See also Masson (no. 395). A summary of recent biographies of persons prominent in the Napoleonic period is given in Dutcher, *Napoleon and Napoleonic period* (no. 632). See also Kircheisen, *Bibliog. Napoléons* (no. 629) for memoirs and biographies of this period. Note particularly G. Lacour-Gayet, *Talleyrand, 1754–1838* (Paris, 1928–34, 4 v.) [**446**].

Printed Sources

For American official documents and general source collections, see Sec. 1, above; and *Court of claims reports*, v. XXII–L (Wash., 1886–1915) [**447**] for French spoliation claims.

---

[2] Published too late for inclusion in the *D.A.B.*

For guide to French official publications see below, pp. 836 and 842; note particularly *Despatches from Paris, 1784–1790* (no. 5422). There are the following notable publications of French laws, decrees, and parliamentary proceedings for the revolutionary period: J. B. Duvergier and others, *Collection complète des lois, décrets, ordonnances, règlemens . . . 1788 . . . et des notes sur chaque loi* (Paris, 1834–) **[448]**; *Lois et actes du gouvernement, 1789–1794* (Paris, 1834–35, 8 v.), continued by the *Bulletin des lois de la république française*, 1793 to date **[449]**; *Archives parlementaires de 1787 à 1860; recueil complet des débats législatifs et politiques des chambres françaises* (Paris, 1862–1914, 209 v., still incomplete, to date (1934) runs through July 17, 1839) **[450]**; *Recueil des actes du Comité de Salut Public, avec la correspondance officielle des réprésentants en mission et le registre du Conseil Exécutif Provisoire*, ed. by F. A. Aulard (Paris, 1889–1911, 26 v.) **[451]**; and *Recueil des actes du Directoire Exécutif (procès-verbaux, arrêtés, instructions, lettres et actes divers)* ed. by A. Debidour (Paris, 1910–11, 2 v.) **[452]**.

For documents illustrating intrigues of French agents in Canada, see the *Reports on the Canadian archives* (no. 5611), particularly for 1890, 1891, and 1894.

For text of the treaty of Mortefontaine, see Hill, *Treaties* (no. 4794); and Miller, *Treaties* (no. 5371).

The correspondence between Citizen Genet, . . . and the officers of the federal government; to which are prefixed the instructions from the constituted authorities of France to the said minister (Phila., 1793) and French and English editions (Phila., 1794) **[453]** contains additional correspondence and includes some letters not printed in *A.S.P., F.R.*[3] Joseph Fauchet, *A translation of Citizen Fauchet's intercepted letter no. 10, to which are added*

---

[3] A considerable amount of French diplomatic correspondence was published in the United States at the time for the purpose of influencing public opinion. Most of this is included in *A.S.P., F.R.*, and is also to be found in the catalogues of the larger lbraries in this country. We have not attempted to list it here.

Nor have we included all the contemporary pamphlet literature; for this material consult Jameson, *Bibliog. Monroe* (no. 1139), and Faÿ, *Bibliog. critique* (no. 31). Contemporary French pamphlets, and articles in the *Moniteur* (*Gazette nationale, ou Moniteur universel. 1789—an VIII* (Paris, 1789, 24 v.), and a convenient reprint, *Réimpression de l'ancien Moniteur, seule histoire authentique et inaltérée de la révolution française depuis la réunion des Etats-généraux jusqu'au Consulat (mai 1789–November 1799)* (Paris, 1858–63, 32 v.) **[453a]**, the official journal of the Consulat, containing French decrees, correspondence, etc.) are given in the bibliography in Nussbaum (no. 429), and in Faÿ (no. 31). We list here a few items.

extracts of no. 3 and 6 (Phila., 1795) [**454**]; also his *A sketch of the present state of our political relations with the United States of North America* (Phila., 1797) [**455**] which is a translation of Paris edition (1797) entitled *Coup d'œil sur l'état* [etc.] giving an analysis of Franco-American relations reinforced by selected French diplomatic documents and the writer's own prepossessions. Edmund Randolph, *A vindication of Mr. Randolph's resignation* (Phila., 1795), published anonymously; with new ed., under author (Richmond, 1855) [**456**], regarding his resignation from the office of secretary of state, caused by suspicions of improper relations with the French minister. Richard Beresford (supposed author), *Sketches of French and English politicks in America, in May, 1797* (Charleston, 1797) [**457**]. James Monroe, *View of the conduct of the executive in the foreign affairs of the United States connected with the mission to the French republic, 1794–6* (Phila., 1797) [**458**] gives Monroe's account of his mission to France. Joel Barlow, *Letters from Paris, to the citizens of the United States, on the system of policy hitherto pursued by their government relative to their commercial intercourse with England and France, &c.* (London, 1800), also published separately (Phila., 1800 and 1801) with title, *Joel Barlow to his fellow citizens . . .* [**459**]. *Rapport fait par P. A. Adet, sur la convention conclue entre la République Française et les Etats-Unis d'Amérique* (Paris, 1801) [**460**]. *Mémoire ou coup-d'œil rapide sur mes différens voyages et mon séjour dans la nation Crëck,* par le général Milfort (Paris, 1802) [**461**], written by an adventurer who went to Paris in 1795 and secured attention to his plans for French alliance with the Creek Indians. *Actes et mémoires concernant les négociations qui ont eu lieu entre la France et les Etats-Unis de l'Amérique, 1793–1800,* comp. by A. G. Gebhardt (London, 1807, 3 v.); an English edition entitled, *State papers relating to the diplomatick transactions between the American and French governments, 1793–1800* (London, 1816, 3 v.) [**462**] consists of a reprint for French readers of documents, in original English and French, previously published in the United States. Talleyrand, *Memoir* (no. 568) and *Letter* (no. 569). J. M. Antepara, *South American emancipation; documents, historical and explanatory, shewing the designs . . . and the exertions made by General Miranda for the attainment of that object* (London, 1810) [**463**], edited from Miranda's papers. G. H. V. Collot, *Voyage dans l'Amérique Septentrionale, ou Description des pays arrosés par le Mississippi, l'Ohio, le Missouri et autres rivières affluentes* (Paris, 1826), and an English translation (Florence, Italy, 1924) [**464**] is the journal of General Collot, Adet's agent, who made a secret French military survey of the Mississippi valley. *Extract from the " Code diplomatique ", par [Louis] Portiez . . . relative to the convention of September 30, 1800, between the United States and France* (translation) (Wash., 184?) [**465**]. *Corres. Napoléon Ier* (no. 646). Albert du Casse, *Histoire des négociations diplomatiques relatives aux traités de Mortfontaine, de Lunéville et d'Amiens* (Paris, 1855, 3 v.) [**466**] strings together (in Vol. I), with a thread of narrative, documents from French archives relating to the negotiation of the Franco-American treaty of 1800. H. C. Lodge, *Life and letters of George Cabot* (Boston, 1877) [**467**] give the views of a Federalist leader of moderate type on foreign affairs, particularly French relations. De Witt, *Jefferson* (no. 35), for correspondence of Genet with the Directory. " Portions of the journal of André Michaux, botanist, written during his travels in the United States and Canada, 1785 to 1796 ", ed. by C. S. Sargent, *Am. phil. soc. proc.*, XXVI (1889) 1-145 [**468**] gives brief references to his part in the Genet project and meetings with Clark, Shelby, Jefferson, and others. *Correspondance diplomatique de Talleyrand: La mission de Talleyrand à Londres, en 1792; correspondance inédite de Talleyrand avec le Département des Affaires Étrangères, le général Biron, etc.; ses lettres d'Amérique à Lord Lansdowne*, ed. by George Pallain (Paris, 1889) [**469**]. " Lettres de M. de Talleyrand à Mme. de Staël ", *Rev. hist. dipl.*, IV (1890) 209-211 [**470**], letters written from the United States, 1794-96, mostly personal, but showing quick appreciation of the nature of Anglo-American issues: " With some reparations and indemnities for prizes made in such an unjust manner, they will wind up the matter." Higginson, *Letters* (no. 301). " Letters of John Marshall when envoy to France, 1797, 1798 ", *Am. hist. rev.*, II (1897) 294-306 [**471**] prints three letters to George Washington. The late Professor F. J. Turner edited the following publications: " Carondelet on the defense of Louisiana, 1794 ", *Am. hist. rev.*, II (1897) 474-505 [**472**], a letter from Baron Carondelet, governor of Louisiana and West Florida, which shows the governor's preparation for resisting the proposed French expedition (Genet-Clark) against New Orleans in 1793–94; "Selections from the Draper collection in the possession of the State Historical Society of Wisconsin, to elucidate the proposed French expedition under George Rogers Clark against Louisiana, in the years 1793–94 ", *Am. hist. assoc. ann. rep.*, for 1896, v. I (1897) 930–1107 [**473**]; " The Mangourit correspondence in respect to Genet's projected attack upon the Floridas, 1793–94 ", *ibid.*, for 1897 (1898) 569–679 [**474**], Mangourit was French consul at Charleston, South Carolina, during the period of the correspondence; " Documents on the relations of France to Louisiana, 1792–1795 ", *Am. hist. rev.*, III (1898) 490–516 [**475**], 12 documents from the *Archives des Affaires Étrangères*, Paris, which elucidate the attempts of Genet upon Louisiana; *Correspondence of the French ministers to the United States, 1791–1797* (Wash., 1904) (Am. Hist. Assoc. Ann. Rep., for 1903, v. II) [**476**], printed from transcripts which, while very copious, are not complete; omits instructions (except the first set for each agent) and enclosures to despatches; but is highly important for the main series of despatches. *The X.Y.Z. letters*, ed. by H. V. Ames and J. B. McMaster (Phila., 1899) [**477**], a reprint of letters in *A.S.P., F.R.*, v. I. " Letters of James Monroe, 1798–1808 ", *N.Y. pub. lib. bul.*, IV (1900) 41–61 [**477a**], three or four letters on minor details of Monroe's mission to France printed from the Cadwalader collection. " Letters of Toussaint Louverture and of Edward Stevens, 1798–1800 ", *Am. hist. rev.*, XVI (1910) 64–101 [**478**], letters from the consular despatches preserved in the Department of State showing diplomatic relations between Santo Domingo and the United States, and the encouragement lent to Louverture by the United States. *Letters of Harrison Gray Otis* (no. 414), for Federalist sentiment against France. *Mémoires et documents pour servir à l'histoire du commerce et de l'industrie en France*, 3d ser., ed. by Julien Hayem (Paris, 1913) [**479**] publishes documents on the commercial relations of France and the United States, 1789–1815. *Windham papers* (no. 374). " Letters of William Vans Murray to John Quincy Adams, 1797–1803 ", ed. by W. C. Ford, *Am. hist. assoc. ann. rep.*, for 1912 (1914) 343–715 [**480**], letters from Murray taken from the Adams papers, to which have been added the more important private letters which passed between Timothy Pickering, then secretary of state, and Murray, from the Pickering papers in the Massachusetts Historical Society. " Du Pont, Talleyrand, and the French spoliations ", ed. by S. E. Morison, *Mass. hist. soc. proc.*, XLIX (1916) 63–79 [**481**] prints a report (*mémoire*) from Victor Du Pont to Talleyrand, July 21, 1798, which " exposes the American policy of France, the value of American neutrality to the Republic, and her designs on Louisiana." *The controversy over neutral rights between the United States and France, 1797–1800; a collection of American state papers and judicial decisions*, ed. by J. B. Scott (N.Y., 1917) [**482**], pub. by the Carnegie Endowment for International Peace; as is also *Opinions of the attorneys generals and judgments of the Supreme Court and Court of Claims of the United States relating to the controversy over neutral rights between the United States and France, 1797–1800* (Wash., 1917) [**483**]. " Les Etats-Unis et la France au début de 1793 ", *Annales révol.*, IX (1917) 411–412 [**484**] is a brief communication from the minister of marine and colonies to the president of the Convention, Mar. 8, 1793, informing him of evidence of friendship and sympathy of the American people in the war with Austria and Prussia. Heloise H. Cruzat, " General Collot's reconnoitering trip down the Mississippi and his arrest in New Orleans in 1796, by order of the Baron de Carondelet, governor of Louisiana ", *La. hist. quar.*, I (1918) 302–320 [**484a**] prints translation of some documents bearing on the arrest of General Collot. Albert Mousset, *Un témoin ignoré de la révolution; le comte de Fernan Nuñez, ambassadeur d'Espagne à Paris, 1787–1791* (Paris, 1923) [**485**], significant for scarcity of mention of Louisiana. *Prize cases decided in the United States Supreme Court, 1789–1918*, prepared . . . under the supervision of James Brown Scott (Oxford, 1923) [**486**], pub. by the Carnegie Endowment for International Peace, is a convenient reprint from cases scattered among 250 volumes of Supreme Court reports; contains decisions on French prizes. " Letter of Thomas Paine, 1793 ", ed. by Louise P. Kellogg, *Am. hist. rev.*, XXIX (1924) 501–505 [**487**] deals with George Rogers Clark and the Louisiana expedition. " Talleyrand and Jaudenes, 1795 ", *Am. hist. rev.*, XXX (1925) 778–787 [**488**], two despatches from Josef de Jaudenes, Spanish envoy to the United States, and other memoranda, from the

Archivo Histórico Nacional, Madrid, relating to Talleyrand's stay in the United States. " Une lettre du Duc de Liancourt à Talleyrand, 1797 ", ed. by Jean Marchand, *Rev. hist. dipl.*, XLIII (1929) 466–472 [**489**] describes the attitude in the United States towards England and France at the time; also under same editorship, " Trois lettres inédites du Duc de Liancourt, Philadelphie, 1796–1797 " *ibid.*, XLIV (1930) 383–398 [**490**]; and " Le journal du Duc de Liancourt à Philadelphie, 1794–1795 ", *ibid.*, XLV (1931) 342–360, 430–448 [**491**], consisting of extracts from the journal. Chinard, *Letters of Lafayette and Jefferson* (no. 5246). C. M. Thomas, " Date inaccuracies in Thomas Jefferson's Writings ", *Miss. Valley hist. rev.*, XIX (1932) 87–90 [**492**] notes two instances in Ford's edition of the *Writings of Thomas Jefferson*, for the year 1793, where erroneous dates of cabinet meetings lead to wrong conclusions in regard to the Genêt intrigues and our status as a neutral nation. C. L. Lokke, ed., " Three letters of Charles Cotesworth Pinckney during the X Y Z mission ", *S. C. hist. and geneal. mag.*, XXXV (1934) 43–48 [**492a**], from the Elbridge Gerry French commission MSS. in the Pierpont Morgan Library, New York; the first two manifest Pinckney's desire to be helpful in every way, the third communication (Paris, Feb. 2, 1798) has a different tone, outwardly friendly but showing resentment against Gerry.

For the printed writings of American presidents, secretaries of state, and diplomatists to France (for names and tenure, see latest *Register* of the Dept. of State (no. 5122)), see our list on p. 756. See also *Works of Fisher Ames* (no. 5184); and *Corres. Rufus King* (no. 5248).

For the printed writings of the French diplomatists and statesmen listed above, under " Special Works ", see the bibliographical notes appended to relevant articles in the *D.N.B.* One may further consult the French historical bibliographies (nos. 4732–4739). For memoirs, writings, correspondence, etc., of personalities of the period, see Kircheisen's *Bibliographie du temps de Napoléon* (no. 630). A list of memoirs of French statesmen is given in Rose, *Revolutionary era* (no. 635); and a list of writings of contemporary French travellers in this country who discussed its relations to France is given in Turner, *Corres. Fr. ministers* (no. 476).

MSS.: Suggestions

See Sec. 1, above.

The official diplomatic records of France are preserved in the *Archives du Ministère des Affaires Etrangères*, in the series *Correspondance Politique, Etats-Unis*. The series *Correspondance Politique, Etats-Unis, Supplémentaire* contains ancillary material of the legation and the foreign office, as does also the series *Mémoires et Documents, Etats-Unis*, and *Mémoires et Documents, Amérique*. The similar series, *Espagne*, cannot be ignored, nor French negotiations with England during this period, *Angleterre*. (For useful bibliographical remarks see R. Guyot (no. 412) above). For description of these archives see below, p. 915. The Library of Congress has photocopies of all these French series, except for such part of the *Correspondance Politique, Etats-Unis* (i.e. the main despatches) as is printed by Turner (no. 476). It has also photocopies of *Archives Nationales, Colonies* F, vol. 285 (" Code historique, colonies, 1792–1795 ") containing documents respecting French refugees from Santo Domingo in Charleston; letters from Mangourit, consul at Charleston, to: Gen. Moultrie, governor of South Carolina, La Forest, Genet, and others; and letters to Mangourit from: La Forest, Monge, Genet, and others. The minutes of the French legation in the United States, 1777 to 1796, are in the private library of Wm. S. Mason, of Evanston, Ill. The Library of Congress has photostats of them. The George Rogers Clark papers are in the Draper collection of the State Historical Society of Wisconsin. For MS. material in the *Bibliothèque Nationale* and other Paris libraries, see Leland's *Guide* (no. 5704). For Ford transcripts of French material (printed by Turner (no. 476)) and other material in New York, see Greene and Morris (no. 5531).

For papers of American ministers in France (William Short, Gouverneur Morris, James Monroe, C. C. Pinckney, John Marshall, Elbridge Gerry, Oliver Ellsworth, Wm. Vans Murray, Wm. R. Davie), see our list on pp. 868–883. Note Sec. 6 for papers of American diplomatists in England during the same period, notably Rufus King.

The Huntington Library has a letter book (contemporary copy from the Department of State) containing correspondence dealing with relations with France, 1794–96, also a letter book (contemporary copies) of the "X.Y.Z." commissioners, 1797–98.

The Library of Congress has several important collections of Genet papers, and there are others in the New York Historical Society. The papers of André Michaux are in the American Philosophical Society. For French intrigues in Canada see the *Report on Canadian archives* (no. 5611), for 1890, 1891, and 1894. French intrigues in Louisiana and the American Southwest are abundantly reflected in the papers of the Spanish colonial administration of Louisiana and Florida (see "MSS.: Suggestions", sec. 5, below).

There are several Genet pieces in the Bibliothèque Municipale, Aix, France; some papers of Genet *père* and some of the son, Edmond Genet, which deal with Franco-American anti-British propaganda among other things in the Bibliothèque Méjane at Aix–en–Provence; and "Minute d'une lettre de Mangourit au citoyen Pelletier à la Nouvelle Orléans, auquel il soumet un plan pour opérer la révolution à la Louisiane (Charleston, 1er août 1793)" in the Bibliothèque Municipale, Rheims, France.

Maps: Suggestions

See Ch. II, sec. 1.

5. Spanish-American Relations

Bibliographical Aids

See Sec. 1, above; also Spanish historical bibliographies (nos. 4758–4760). Bemis, *Pinckney's treaty* (no. 506), and Whitaker, *Sp.-Am. frontier* (no. 502) and *Documents* (no. 333), for useful bibliographical notes. Brooks, *Bibliog. Georgia hist.* (no. 710). T. M. Owen, *Bibliog. Alabama* (no. 650); and his *Bibliog. Mississippi* (no. 651). *Check-list Floridiana* (no. 711).

Special Works

T. M. Green, *The Spanish conspiracy; a review of early Spanish movements in the southwest* (Cincinnati, 1891) **[493]**, still a most valuable narrative for Spanish intrigues in Kentucky, though the author did not have available all the Spanish documents which would have supported his conclusions. B. A. Hinsdale, "The establishment of the first southern boundary of the United States", *Am. hist. assoc. ann. rep.*, for 1893 (1894) 329–366 **[494]**, the first study, based on American printed state papers without advantage of essential Spanish material. Roosevelt, *West* (no. 310). Winsor, *Westward movement* (no. 311). Chambers, *West Florida* (no. 714). F. L. Riley, " Spanish policy in Mississippi after the treaty of San Lorenzo ", *Am. hist. assoc. ann. rep.*, for 1897 (1898) 175-192 [**495**], lacked necessary records in Spanish archives; and his " Transition from Spanish to American rule in Mississippi ", *Miss. hist. soc. pub.*, III (1900) 261-311 [**496**], though Spanish sources were not available to the author, it is a useful narrative of the evacuation by Spain of the territory north of 31°, utilizing Ellicott's *Journal*. G. L. Rives, " Spain and the United States in 1795 ", *Am. hist. rev.*, IV (1898) 62-79 [**497**] also lacked necessary Spanish sources. Ogg, *The Mississippi* (no. 312). Fuller, *Purchase Florida* (no. 977). B. W. Bond, jr., " Monroe's efforts to secure free navigation of the Mississippi river during his mission to France, 1794-96 ", *Miss. hist. soc. pub.*, IX (1907) 255-262 [**498**], based on Monroe's correspondence without the Spanish side of the story. Chadwick, *U.S. and Spain* (no. 108), the earlier introductory chapters on the period to 1800 are now superseded by Whitaker (no. 502), Bemis (no. 506), and others. James, *Louisiana* (no. 418). I. J. Cox, " Wilkinson's first break with the Spaniards ", in the *Eighth annual report* of the Ohio Valley Historical Association, 1914 (Charleston, W.Va., 1915), 49-56 (This report is published in the *Biennial report* of the Dept. of Archives and History of the State of West Virginia, 1911-12, 1913-14 (Charleston, W.Va.) [**499**] refers to the " break " in 1798; and his *West Florida controversy* (no. 719). Serrano y Sanz, *Wilkinson* (no. 314), and *España y Cherokis* (no. 315), limited to Spanish sources. Three studies by F. P. Renaut, who sees Louisiana as a European problem as well as an American one, and has traces of work in French and Spanish original sources: *Louisiane* (no. 675a) ; " Le premier conflit hispano-américain; la navigation du Mississippi, 1783-1795 ", *Rev. études hist.*, LXXXV (1919) 44-68 [**500**], and *Pacte de famille* (no. 57), 366-390. E. M. Coulter, " The efforts of the democratic societies of the west to open the navigation of the Mississippi ", *Miss. Valley hist. rev.*, XI (1924) 376-389 [**501**] deals with the agitation in 1793-94 to force Congress and the President to secure from Spain the right of navigation of the Mississippi. Several studies by A. P. Whitaker, based on careful and detailed research in Spanish archives: *Spanish intrigues* (no. 318) ; *Chero-*

kee Indians (no. 320); *Spanish-American frontier, 1783–1795; the westward movement and the Spanish retreat in the Mississippi Valley* (Boston and N.Y., 1927) [**502**], in contrast to Bemis (no. 506) attributes Spain's diplomatic surrender to pressure of American frontiersmen; *Alexander McGillivray* (no. 321); *Harry Innes* (no. 531); " New light on the treaty of San Lorenzo: an essay in historical criticism", *Miss. Valley hist. rev.*, XV (1929) 435–454 [**503**] argues from archival documents that Godoy " in all human probability " knew the text of Jay's treaty when he signed with Pinckney; " Godoy's knowledge of the terms of Jay's treaty ", *Am. hist. rev.*, XXXV (1930) 804–810 [**504**] presents conflicting documents recently found to confirm his belief that Godoy knew the text of Jay's treaty when he signed with Pinckney; and *The Mississippi question, 1795–1803; a study in trade, politics, and diplomacy* (N. Y. and London, 1934) [**505**], a brilliant description of the broad background of Spanish-American relations, and of French intrusion, in the Mississippi Valley during the Federalist period, with a new and valuable analysis of the Louisiana purchase, based on diligent and clever research in Spanish, French, British, and American archives as well as exhaustion of printed material. S. F. Bemis, *Pinckney's treaty; a study of America's advantage from Europe's distress, 1783–1800* (Baltimore, 1926) [**506**] explains the diplomatic victory of the United States in the treaty of 1795 as due to Spain's involvement in European difficulties centering about the Franco-Spanish treaty of Basle (1795), (note correction of map by another map [see no. 214]); *Am. secs. state* (no. 4796), v. II. S. G. Coe, *Carmichael* (no. 115). A. P. Nasatir has published several very useful articles from a study of original documents, Spanish and English, on Anglo-Spanish rivalry in the upper Mississippi Valley: *Anglo-Span. frontier during Am. revolution* (no. 118); "Anglo-Spanish rivalry on the upper Missouri ", *Miss. Valley hist. rev.*, XVI (1929–1930) 359–382, 507–528 [**507–8**]; " Ducharme's invasion of Missouri; an incident in the Anglo-Spanish rivalry for the Indian trade of upper Louisiana ", *Mo. hist. rev.*, XXIV (1929–1930), 3–25, 238–260, 420–439 [**509**]; "Anglo-Spanish rivalry in the Iowa country, 1797–1798 ", *Ia. jour. hist.*, XXVIII (1930) 337–389 [**510**]. Posey, *Blount conspiracy* (no. 555). Hamer, *British and Indians* (no. 586). Thompson, *Blount conspiracy* (no. 560). Aiton, *La. cession* (no. 685), for explanation of the cession of 1763. J. A. James, " Oliver Pollock and the free navigation of the Mississippi river ", *Miss. Valley hist. rev.*, XIX (1932) 331–347 **[511]**. Lawrence Kinnaird, "American penetration into Spanish Louisiana ", in *New Spain . . .* historical contributions presented to H. E. Bolton (Los Angeles, Calif., 1932), v. I, 211–237 **[512]**, utilizing American sources and Spanish transcripts, and calling attention to further work to be done in the archives; prints here 8 documents, 1778–1797.

For material regarding Miranda's project for concerted action against Spain at the time of the Nootka Sound affair, see entries in Sec. 4 ("Anglo-American Relations "), nos. 533, 535, 538, 556; and Renaut, *Pacte de famille* (no. 57).

For biographies of American diplomatists to Spain (Wm. Carmichael, Wm. Short, Th. Pinckney, and David Humphreys), see the relevant entries and bibliographical data in the *D.A.B.*

For the Spanish diplomatists in the United States (José de Viar, José de Jaudenes, and Carlos M. de Irujo), we have found no biographical accounts. There is no satisfactory biography of Godoy for our purpose; for a brief biographical sketch see *Enciclopedia universal* (no. 4974), and recent studies by E. B. d'Auvergne, *Godoy, the Queen's favorite* (Boston, 1913) **[513]**, uncritical, undocumented; H. R. Madol, *Godoy, das Ende des alten Spanien* (Berlin, 1932) **[514]**, the best study to date. It is also issued in Spanish translation (Madrid, 1933), and in English (London, 1934).

Printed Sources

For American official documents and general source collections, see Sec. 1, above. See *A.S.P., Misc.*, I, for " Correspondence concerning intrigues between Spanish officers in Louisiana and others, for a dismemberment of the Union, 1808 "; Report of the House of Representatives on "Inquiry into the conduct of Harry Innis, district judge of the United States for the district of Kentucky, in being a party to intrigues of the Spanish officers in Louisiana against the United States, 1808 "; and report " On the subject of an illicit connexion between Gen. James Wilkinson and the Spanish government, 1808 " **[515]**. Moore, *Adjudications* (no. 5367), v. V, for Spanish spoliations, commission under article 21 of the treaty between the United States and Spain, 1795.

For Spanish official publications, see *Gaceta de Madrid* (no. 5127c). *Correspondance qui dévoile la trahison du senateur américain W. Blount; les intrigues du ministre anglais Liston; et l'étrange neutralité observée par le secrétaire d'état des Etats-Unis, Timothy Pickering* (Phila., 1797) [516], the English original is printed in *A.S.P., F.R.*, II, 66–77. *A letter to Timothy Pickering, esq., secretary of state, from the Chevalier de Yrujo . . . July 11, 1797* (Phila., 1797) [517], also in *A.S.P., F.R.*, II. *Letters of Verus* [pseud.] *addressed to the Native American* (Phila., 1797) [518], the authorship has been attributed to (1) Irujo, the Spanish minister to the United States, and (2) to Philip Fatio, secretary of the minister. *The journal of Andrew Ellicott, late commissioner on behalf of the United States . . . 1796, . . . 1800: for determining the boundary between the United States and the possessions of His Catholic Majesty in America* (Phila., 1803) [519], in 1796 he was commissioner to survey the boundary between the United States and Florida. *Mr. Rowan's motion, for an inquiry into the conduct of Harry Innis, district judge of the United States for the district of Kentucky* (Wash., 1808) [520] includes a resolution introduced in Congress for an inquiry into the relations of Judge Innes with the Spanish government, and other relevant documents. (See also *A.S.P., Misc.*, I, for report of the House of Representatives on this inquiry). Daniel Clark, *Proofs of the corruption of General James Wilkinson* (Phila., 1809) [521]. Wilkinson's *Memoirs* (no. 324). *Mémoires du Prince de la Paix, Don Manuel Godoy*, traduits en français d'après le manuscrit espagnol par J. B. d'Esménard (Paris, 1836, 4 v.; Eng. translation, London, 1836) and a Spanish edition (Madrid, 1908), annotated by Ivan Peters [522], written in his very old age by a man who was inveterately reckless with the truth, they must be used with great caution. W. C. Ford, *The United States and Spain in 1790. An episode in diplomacy described from hitherto unpublished sources* (Brooklyn, 1890) [523] gives opinions of members of Washington's cabinet and the chief justice in regard to the attitude to be taken by the United States in the event of war between Spain and Great Britain (Nootka Sound affair). "The correspondence of Gen. James Robertson", *Am. hist. mag.*, I–V (1896–1900) passim. [524] consists of letters of 1784 to 1814, a large number being from William Blount. *Carondelet on the defence of Louisiana, 1794* (no. 472). "Concerning Philip Nolan", *Texas state hist. assoc. quar.*,

VII (1904) 308–317 [525], documents from the Department of State, 1798–1801, dealing with Philip Nolan, leader of the first Anglo-American invasion of Texas. *Letter of Gen. James Wilkinson* (no. 778), written to José de Iturrigaray, from Natchez, Nov. 17, 1806. "An interview of Governor Folch with General Wilkinson ". *Am. hist. rev.*, X (1905) 832–840 [526] is a letter from Gov. Folch of Florida to the governor general of Cuba, Marquis de Someruelos, June 25, 1807, which throws new light on the relations between Wilkinson and the Spanish. Turner, ed., *Blount conspiracy* (no. 580). *Boundary line between Florida and Georgia; certain documents and reports relating to the locating and marking of the line between the territory and state of Florida and the state of Georgia* (Wash., 1908) (60th Cong., 1st sess. Sen. Doc. no. 467) [527] reprints documents of the years 1827–1830, in regard to the boundary line under article 2 of the treaty with Spain, in 1795. " Military journal of Captain Isaac Guion, 1797–1799 ", in the *Seventh annual report of the Dept. of archives and history of Mississippi and state of Florida* (Nashville, Tenn., 1909) 27–113 [528], by the agent of the United States in the final negotiations for the evacuation of the Spanish military posts east of the Mississippi and the fixing of the boundary. Houck, *Spanish régime* (no. 329). Robertson, *Louisiana* (no. 705), select documents with valuable notes. Manuel Serrano y Sanz, *Documentos históricos de la Florida y la Luisiana* (Madrid, 1912) [529]. Renaut, *Louisiane* (no. 675a), 196–240, for documents, 1796–1806. " The democratic societies of 1793 and 1794 in Kentucky, Pennsylvania, and Virginia ", *Wm. and Mary coll. quar.*, 2d ser., II (1922) 239–256 [530], from the MSS. in the Library of Congress. " Harry Innes and the Spanish intrigue, 1794–1795 ", ed. by A. P. Whitaker, *Miss. Valley hist. rev.*, XV (1928) 236–248 [531], two letters showing the connection of U.S. Judge Harry Innes with the Spanish intrigue, and by the same (as editor), *Docs. Sp. comm. policy, Fla. and La.* (no. 333). Hamer (no. 586).

Of the American diplomatists in Spain (Wm. Carmichael, Wm. Short, T. Pinckney, D. Humphreys) there exists published writings of only Humphreys: *Life and times of David Humphreys* (no. 5241a) which prints most of his despatches from Madrid.

The text of the treaty of 1795 (in English and in Spanish) is given in Bemis, *Pinckney's treaty* (no. 506), and most recent authentic original texts are printed in Miller, *Treaties* (no. 5371).

MSS.: Suggestions

The official diplomatic correspondence is rather completely preserved in both the United States and Spain. Bemis (no. 506) has bibliographical notes on these sources. See Pt. II, ch. 3, for various catalogues and indexes to official American, Spanish, French, and British,
archives, and for Library of Congress transcripts and photocopies of
the diplomatic correspondence for this period. J. A. Robertson's
Documents (no. 705) lists transcripts and originals of Spanish MSS.,
existing in the United States up to date of publication (1911). For
more recent transcripts in possession of the North Carolina Historical Commission, see no. 5558. The Missouri Historical Society,
at St. Louis, possesses 500 pages of transcripts of Spanish documents
relating to upper Louisiana contained in the *Archivo General de
Indias.* The East Florida papers of the Spanish regime, acquired
by the United States at the time of the cession, are now in the Library of Congress, see note by Mabel M. Manning (no. 1007).

Collections of private papers are less methodically preserved in
Spain, and not at all traceable in guides and catalogues for scholars.
We do not know of the whereabouts (if existing) of the private
papers of Godoy, Gardoqui, Viar, and Jaudenes. The personal
papers of Carlos de Irujo, minister of Spain in the United States,
1796–1806, are preserved, in the possession of the Duke of Sotomayor, in Spain. For notes regarding a few Floridablanca MSS.,
see Ch. I, Sec. 4, "MSS.: Suggestions." For papers of American
presidents, secretaries of state, and diplomatists in Spain (Wm.
Carmichael, Wm. Short, T. Pinckney, D. Humphreys, and Wm. L.
Smith, who was an American representative in Portugal and Spain),
see our list on pp. 862–883. In the Library of Congress are the
Harry Innes papers and Andrew Ellicott's correspondence during
his survey of the southern boundary, 1797–1800 (400 letters). The
papers of Rufus King (p. 876) contain matter on the navigation of
the Mississippi River. The papers of the Rutledge family (John
Rutledge, American chargé in Spain) are in the Pennsylvania
Historical Society. Search among the collections in the Mississippi
Valley (for indexes, see pp. 886–890) will reward the investigator.

Maps: Suggestions

The Library of Congress (Division of Maps) has acquired
photographs of several Spanish MS. maps relating to the Missis-

sippi Valley and the southern boundary, from the *Archivo Histórico Nacional*, Madrid, and other Spanish archives. [4]   For description of several of these, see *Noteworthy maps, no. 2*, compiled by Lawrence Martin and Clara Egli (Wash., 1929) (Library of Congress) [532], nos. 6, 8, 9, and 13, and 90.   One of these is reproduced in facsimile in Bemis, *Pinckney's treaty* (no. 506), map 1.   Other maps illustrating Spanish diplomacy in the Mississippi Valley are in the same volume, but map 1 should be corrected by referring to note in *Hisp. Am. hist. rev.*, VII (1927) 386–389 (no. 214).   See also Chambers, *West Florida* (no. 714); Phillips, *Maps in Library of Congress* (no. 5135); *Lowery collection* (no. 5145); Torres Lanzas (no. 5140); Hill's *Catalogue* (no. 5650) (for maps in the Spanish archives); and Karpinski (no. 5149).

See also Ch. II, sec. 1.

6. Anglo-American Relations, 1789–1801

Bibliographical Aids

For general aids, see Sec. 1, above.
For special aids, see Ch. III, sec. 6.

Special Works

For general works, see Sec. 1, above.

H. H. Bancroft, *History of the northwest coast* (San Francisco, 1884, 2 v.) [533], for the Nootka Sound affair.   *Treaties and conventions concluded between the United States of America and other powers* (Wash., 1889) (48th Cong., 2d sess. Senate. Exec. doc. no. 47) [534], the appendix contains valuable notes, especially for the commissions under Jay's treaty.   McLaughlin, *Western posts* (no. 339).   Roosevelt, *West* (no. 310).   Smith, *England and America* (no. 340).   Winsor, *Westward movement* (no. 311).   Hubert Hall, " Pitt and General Miranda ", *Athenaeum*, I (1902) 498–499 [535], for the Nootka Sound affair.   F. A. Ogg, " Jay's treaty and the slavery interests of the United States ", *Am. hist. assoc. ann. rep.*, for 1901 (1902) 273–298 [536], the best study, but lacks British sources.   E. D. Adams, *The influence of Grenville on Pitt's foreign policy, 1787–1798* (Wash.: Carnegie Institution of Washington) [537].   W. R. Manning, " The Nootka Sound controversy ", *Am.*

---

[4] *Report of the Librarian of Congress,* for 1927 (Wash., 1927).

hist. assoc. ann. rep., for 1904 (1905) 279–478 [**538**], a definitive monograph based on American, British, and Spanish archives. R. R. Rankin, " The treaty of amity, commerce, and navigation between Great Britain and the United States, 1794 ", *Univ. of Cal. chron.*, IX, no. 2, suppl. (1907) [**539**] lacks British sources. Cox, *Indian as dipl. factor* (no. 341). C. E. Slocum, *The Ohio country between the years 1783 and 1815* (N.Y. and London, 1910) [**540**] gives running account of English and American rival activities in the Ohio country. Three studies by W. R. Riddell: " Settlement of international disputes by and between English-speaking nations " *Yale law jour.*, XXII (1913) 545–553, 583–589 [**541**]; " When international arbitration failed ", *Canad. law times*, XL (1920) 351–360 [**542**] discusses the failure of the international commission under Jay's treaty, in 1797, to settle claims owing in the United States to British subjects; and " Interesting notes on Great Britain and Canada with respect to the negro ", *Jour. negro hist.*, XIII (1928) 185–198 [**543**], for Jay's treaty and the negro slaves. C. A. Beard, *Economic origins of Jeffersonian democracy* (N.Y., 1915) [**544–5**] has a good chapter on Jay's treaty. H. C. Bell, *Brit. comm. policy* (no. 344) uses English records carefully to show how during the war the governors of the British West Indian colonies were allowed, even forced, to violate the navigation acts which excluded American ships. Leavitt, *Brit. pol. on Canad. frontier* (no. 343). G. C. Davidson, *The Northwest company* (Berkeley, Calif., 1918) [**546**] is useful for the history of the early Canadian fur trade. Margaret Woodbury, *Public opinion in Philadelphia, 1789–1801* (Durham, N.C., 1919) [**547**] discusses briefly public opinion in regard to Jay's treaty. Hayden, *Senate and treaties, 1789–1817* (no. 376), a competent study, useful for Jay's treaty in the Senate. A. G. Lindsay, " Diplomatic relations between the United States and Great Britain bearing on the return of the negro slaves, 1783–1828 ", *Jour. negro hist.*, V (1920) 391–419 [**548**], written apparently in ignorance of Ogg (no. 536), it takes up the question of embarked negroes after the Revolution, and also after the war of 1812, as revealed in abundant printed sources. Five studies by S. F. Bemis: *Abortive armed neutrality* (no. 382); "Alexander Hamilton and the limitation of armaments ", *Pacific rev.*, II (1922) 587–602 [**549**] attributes the American idea of limitation of armaments to Hamilton in 1794; " Jay's treaty and the northwest boundary gap ", *Am. hist. rev.*, XXVII (1922) 465–484 [**550**] concerns the gap of about 150 miles in the northwest boundary, 1783–1818; *Jay's treaty; a study in commerce and diplomacy* (N.Y., 1923) **[551]** interprets the negotiation of Jay's treaty as controlled by the necessity in 1794 to Great Britain and to the United States of a continuation of prosperous Anglo-American relations; and "The London mission of Thomas Pinckney, 1792–1796 ", *Am. hist. rev.*, XXVIII (1923) 228–247 **[552]** deals with diplomatic issues over neutral rights and impressment, 1793–1795. *Camb. hist. Br. for. pol.* (no. 209). Hill, *Treaties* (no. 4794). Renaut, *Pacte de famille* (no. 57), for the Nootka Sound crisis, 1789–90. Mowat, *Gt. Brit. and U.S.* (no. 347a). Anna Lingelbach, *Board of trade* (no. 347). W. C. Morey, *Diplomatic episodes; a review of certain historical incidents bearing upon international relations and diplomacy* (N.Y., 1926) **[552a]** has a chapter on the diplomatic controversy leading up to the Jay treaty. *Am. secs. state*, v. II (no. 4796). W. A. Mackintosh, "Canada and Vermont; a study in historical geography ", *Canad. hist. rev.*, VIII (1927) 9–30 **[553]**, the Vermont separatists and the connection of the Allen brothers; review of the Vermont border from 1779 (Haldimand negotiations to the end of the war of 1812), drawn from Canadian archives. H. L. Osgood, "The British evacuation of the United States ", *Rochester hist. soc. pub.*, VI (1927) 55–63 **[554]**, a paper read in 1900 by an eminent American historian, useful as a record of the evacuation of the western posts. Stevens, *N.W. fur trade* (no. 233). W. B. Posey, "The Blount conspiracy ", *Birmingham-Southern coll. bul.*, XXI (1928) 11–12 **[555]**, little new; utilizes Blount documents printed by Turner. Willson, *Ambassadors* (no. 348) ; and *Friendly relations; a narrative of Britain's ministers and ambassadors to America (1791–1930)* (Boston, 1934) **[556]** consists of short sketches of the personalities of the forty men who represented Great Britain in the United States, with selections from their diplomatic correspondence and private letters, emphasizing, for the most part, the friendly relations they had with the United States. Little analysis of the diplomatic problems involved. Rife, *Ethan Allen* (no. 138a). Wilbur, *Ira Allen* (no. 138b). Pell, *Ethan Allen* (no. 138c). W. S. Robertson, *The life of Miranda* (Chapel Hill, N.C., 1929) **[557]** traces Miranda's relation to Pitt and Nootka Sound in 1790 and to British and American concepts of revolution in Spanish America in 1797–98 (The author has published earlier article on phases of Miranda's career in *Am.*

hist. assoc. ann. rep., for 1907, v. I). N. A. Mackenzie, "The Jay treaty of 1794", *Canad. bar rev.*, VII (1929) 431–437 [**558**] contains historical commentary on decision of the U.S. Supreme Court, in recent immigration case of A. J. Karnuth *et alii* vs. U.S., April 8, 1929, in reference to article III of Jay's treaty, arguing that this article was never abrogated. G. S. Graham, *British policy and Canada, 1774–1791; a study in 18th century trade policy* (London and N.Y., 1930) [**559**], chiefly concerned with the development of trade policy in the new British empire after 1783. Hyneman, *Neutrality* (no. 384). Isabel Thompson, "The Blount conspiracy", *East Tenn. hist. soc. pub.*, no. 2 (1930) 3–21 [**560**], a short account based principally on *A.S.P.* Payne (no. 351). Moore's *Arbitrations* (no. 5364) contains a fine narrative summary of the history of the work of the mixed commissions set up by Jay's treaty; but that is now to be supplemented by the much more elaborate and definitive account, containing also the documents, in his *Adjudications* (no. 5367), v. I–IV, *viz:* v. I–II: *Saint Croix river arbitration* (no. 1697); v. III: *Arbitration of claims for compensation for losses and damages resulting from lawful impediments to the recovery of prewar debts; mixed commission under article VI of the treaty between Great Britain and the United States of November 19, 1794;* v. IV: *Compensation for losses and damages caused by the violation of neutral rights, and by the failure to perform neutral duties; mixed commission under article VII of the treaty between Great Britain and the United States of November 19, 1794.* This series contains history of the cases, combined with documents. Newcomb, *Jay's treaty* (no. 587a).

For material dealing with the St. Croix commission, 1796, see "Northeast Boundary Controversy", Ch. XI, Sec. 3, below.

For note regarding biographies of American statesmen, see Sec. 1, above. For biographies of American diplomatists to Great Britain (Gouverneur Morris, Thomas Pinckney, Jay, Rufus King, and Christopher Gore), and of John Trumbull, member of commission under article VII of Jay's treaty, see the relevant entries and bibliographical data in *D.A.B.*

For biographies of British diplomatists in the United States (George Hammond, Robert Liston, Sir George Beckwith (agent); also Lord Dorchester, governor general of Canada, and J. G. Simcoe, lieutenant governor of the Province of Upper Canada, and British statesmen (Pitt, Lord Carmarthen, Lord Grenville), consult the *D.N.B.* For British prime ministers of the period, see Bigham, *Prime ministers* (no. 242). Note also A. G. Bradley, *Lord Dorchester* (Toronto, 1907) [**561**]; D. C. Scott, *John Graves Simcoe* (Toronto, 1907) [**562**]; and W. R. Riddell, *The life of John Graves Simcoe, first lieutenant governor of the province of Upper Canada, 1792–96* (Toronto, 1926) [**563**]. Note also Rose, *William Pitt* (no. 346); E. K. Chatterton, *England's greatest statesman, a life of William Pitt, 1759–1806* (Indianapolis, 1930) [**564**]; and P. W. Wilson, *William Pitt, the younger* (Garden City, N. Y., 1930) [**565**]. A biographical sketch of Thomas Barclay, British consul general in the United States, is in the *D.A.B.*

Printed Sources

For American official documents and general source collections, see Sec. 1, above. For documentary history of the mixed commissions under articles of Jay's treaty, see Moore, *Adjudications* (no. 5367), v. III (pre-war debts, article 6), v. IV (neutral rights and neutral duties, article 7).

For British official documents, see *Annual register* (no. 5058); House of Commons, *Journal*, and House of Lords, *Journal* (no. 5418); *Parl. hist.* (no. 5410); and *Official gazette* (no. 5127a). British Parliamentary (sessional) papers regarding claims of British subjects provided for in Jay's treaty are: *Report[s] from select committee* . . . (1812 (134) II; 1812–13 (66) III, 319; and 1813 (335) III) [**566**].

There is a voluminous contemporary pamphlet literature of opponents and advocates of Jay's treaty which we cannot list here. It is to be found in the catalogue of the Library of Congress, and in other large libraries. Such as was printed in the United States is listed in Evans (no. 4639). Such as relate to the West Indies in any way are noted in Ragatz (no. 4721). For selected English pamphlets see Bemis (no. 551), 362.

T. Coxe, *Brief examination of Lord Sheffield's observations* (Phila., 1791) [**567**] is an American refutation of Lord Sheffield's famous *Observations on the commerce of the United States* (no. 356a) in which Sheffield defends the British colonial navigation system. C. M. de Talleyrand-Périgord, *Memoir concerning the commercial relations of the United States with England* (Boston, 1809) [**568**], a famous memoir reflecting little good in America; and " Les Etats-Unis et l'Angleterre en 1795; lettre de M. de Talleyrand ", *Rev. hist. dipl.*, III (1889) 64–77 [**569**], a letter written to Lord Lansdowne, 1795, in which he expresses his conviction that the Americans are attached to England, and that France must have Louisiana. Gibbs (no. 372) for expressions of Federalist policy. Benjamin Lincoln, " Journal of a treaty held in 1793, with the Indian tribes northwest of the Ohio, by commissioners of the United States ", *Mass. hist. soc. coll.*, 3d ser., V (1836) 109–176 [**570**]. " Correspondence relating to affairs in Canada, 1783–1795 ", in *Statutes, documents and papers bearing on the discussion respecting the northern and western boundaries of the Province of Ontario* (Toronto, 1878) 306–320 [**571**] consists of extracts from the Upper Canada MSS. and the Simcoe papers in the Canadian archives (see also no. 584 for Simcoe papers). *The St. Clair papers; the life and public services of Arthur St. Clair*, ed. by W. H. Smith (Cincinnati, 1882, 2 v.) [**572**], for American military operations and the western fur trade. J. G. Wilson, " Judge Bayard of New Jersey, and his London diary of 1795–1796 ", *N.J. hist. soc. proc.*, 2d ser., VIII (1884) 204–216 [**573**] includes extracts from the diary of the American agent to prosecute claims before British admiralty courts. Ford, *U.S. and Spain* (no. 523), documents showing relation of the United States to the Nootka controversy; and by the same editor, " Edmund Randolph on the British treaty, 1795 ", *Am. hist. rev.*, XII (1907) 587–599 [**574**], documents showing attitude of Randolph toward ratification of Jay's treaty, but compare with Hammond's MS. despatches, and printed French despatches in Turner (no. 476). " Vermont negotiations ", in *Report on Canadian archives*, by Douglas Brymner, 1889 (Ottawa, 1890) 53–58 [**575**] prints 4 documents of 1791–1794, from British archives, dealing with the negotiations of the Allens (Ethan, Levi, Ira) of Vermont; *Report on Canadian archives*, 1890 (Ottawa, 1891) [**576**] contains 38 documents from the British archives bearing on relations with the United States, 1787–1791 (relating mainly to Indian affairs, retention of the western posts, and commercial relations) and includes important documents concerning Beckwith's secret mission to the United States; see also *Report*, for 1891 (Ottawa, 1892) for a few documents bearing on the English plan to seize Louisiana and Florida in 1797; and *Report*, for

1930–31, by A. G. Doughty (Ottawa, 1931–32, 2v.) [576a] containing a "calendar of state papers, addressed by the secretaries of state for the colonies to the governors general or officers administering the Province of Lower Canada, from 1797 until 1841", with copious extracts of correspondence; and a similar calendar for the Province of Upper Canada (Ontario), 1796 to 1820, in the *Report*, for 1933 (Ottawa, 1934) [576b]. *Mich. pioneer and hist. coll.* (no. 358), documents from the British colonial office, 1760–1794. The Dropmore MSS. (*Manuscripts of J. B. Fortescue, esq., preserved at Dropmore*), published by the Historical Manuscripts Commission of Great Britain, v. II–III (London: H. M. Stationery Off., 1894–99) [577] contain important documents from the personal papers of Lord Grenville relating to Jay's treaty. *Selections from the correspondence of Thomas Barclay, formerly British consul-general at New York*, ed. by G. L. Rives (N.Y., 1894) [578]. *Letters of Phineas Bond* (no. 359). *Letters of Stephen Higginson* (no. 301). F. J. Turner, "English policy toward America in 1790–1791", *Am. hist. rev.*, VII (1902) 706–735, VIII (Oct. 1902) 78–86 [579] gives documents from the Public Record Office, which illustrate England's American policy, particularly at the period of the Nootka Sound episode, also a report on the petition of Vermont for a commercial treaty; his *Corres. French ministers* (no. 476), for the Blount conspiracy and the Miranda affair; and by the same editor, "Documents on the Blount conspiracy, 1795–1797", *Am. hist. rev.*, X (1905) 574–606 [580], American, British, and French documents illustrating the proposed attack upon Spanish possessions by frontiersmen expecting aid from Great Britain. *The memoirs of Rufus Putnam and certain official papers and correspondence*, ed. by Rowena Buell (Boston and N.Y., 1903) [581], for Indian affairs in the Northwest. *Bowdoin and Temple papers* (no. 360). S. F. Bemis, "Relations between the Vermont separatists and Great Britain, 1789–1791", *Am. hist. rev.*, XXI (1916) 547–560 [582], 6 documents from the Public Record Office and Canada Archives, relative to negotiations of the Allen brothers of Vermont in regard to an alliance with Great Britain. *David Thompson's narrative of his explorations in western America, 1784–1812*, ed. by J. B. Tyrrell (Toronto, 1916) [583], for early British penetration of the upper Mississippi country and its relation to the northwest boundary. *The correspondence of Lieu-*

tenant Governor John Graves Simcoe, with allied documents, relating to his administration of the government of Upper Canada, 1789–1796, ed. by E. A. Cruikshank (Toronto: Ontario Historical Society, 1923–31, 5 v.) [584], the first four volumes print letters mostly from originals or trustworthy copies in the Canada Archives, the fifth volume prints 82 additional letters preserved by Simcoe's descendants and now in the possession of Mr. W. P. Cole of Southampton,, England (highly valuable) ; and by the same editor, *Records of Niagara; a collection of contemporary letters and documents, 1790–92* (Niagara, Ont.: Niagara Historical Society, 1930) [585], for American-British Indian relations; and *The correspondence of the Honourable Peter Russell; with allied documents relating to his administration of the government of Upper Canada during the official term of Lieut. Governor J. G. Simcoe while on leave of absence,* Vol. 1, *1796–1797,* edited for the Ontario Historical Society by E. A. Cruikshank and A. F. Hunter (Toronto, 1932) [585a], the index reveals a few items regarding the United States. P. M. Hamer, "The British in Canada and the southern Indians, 1790–1794", *East Tenn. hist. soc. pub.,* II (1930) 107–134 [586], transcripts of correspondence of Col. Alexander McKee, British Indian agent at Detroit, from the Canadian Archives. R. C. Werner, "War scare and politics in 1794", *N.Y. state hist. assoc. quar. jour.,* XI (1930) 324–335 [587] prints a letter reflecting the tense situation on the Canadian frontier, 1794. J. T. Newcomb, "New light on Jay's treaty", *Am. jour. internat. law,* XXVIII (1934) 685–692 [587a] reveals for the first time the hitherto unpublished text of the British order-in-council of April 25, 1795, ordering capture of neutral cargoes of provisions "on enemy account." Whitaker, *Mississippi question* (no. 505).

For authentic text of Jay's treaty, see Miller, *Treaties* (no. 5371), v. II.

For the printed writings of American diplomatists to Great Britain and to France (for names and tenure, see latest *Register* of the Dept. of State (no. 5122)), see out list on p. 756. Note also the *Writings of John Quincy Adams* (no. 5180), containing a few letters regarding the ratification of Jay's treaty; *Writings of A. J. Dallas* (no. 5211); *Letters of R. H. Lee* (no. 5255); and *Letters of Harrison Gray Otis* (no. 414).

MSS.: Suggestions

See Sec. 1, above.

For analysis of MS. sources in official and private collections available in 1920 relating to the negotiations of Jay's treaty, see Bemis (no. 551).

The official records are manifold. For American, British, and Canadian archival sources, and guides and indexes thereto, see pp. 855–898. The various MS. records of the proceedings of the mixed commissions set up under the terms of Jay's treaty have been traced and printed in Moore's *Adjudications*, v. I–IV (no. 5367). The Library of Congress has, in addition to the facsimiles and transcripts from foreign archives described on pp. 892–893, a folio volume of transcripts from British, French, and Spanish archives relating to the Nootka Sound controversy, made by Dr. W. R. Manning. For papers of the Presidents (Washington, Adams), and secretaries of state (Jefferson, Randolph, Pickering, Marshall, Madison, Monroe), and American diplomatists abroad (for complete list of persons and tenure, see most recent edition of *Register* of the Department of State (no. 5122), see our list on pp. 862–883. The Library of Congress also has the papers of Secretary of War James McHenry, and, most important (but mostly printed) the papers of Alexander Hamilton; and a letter book of John Trumbull, 1796–1802, containing letters mainly on the subject of Jay's treaty. For other MS. sources, in New York, see Greene and Morris (no. 5531). For papers of Wm. Blount, governor of the territory south of the Ohio, 1790–1796, in the State Historical Society of Wisconsin, see its *Descriptive list* (no. 5565), 83–84; there are also copies of other MS. papers of Blount in the MS. collections of Mr. T. M. Owen, Montgomery, Ala., (originals in the possession of Mr. W. D. Stephens, of Los Angeles, Cal.).[5]

The Fortescue edition of the *Correspondence of George III* (no. 143) stops with 1783, but the William L. Clements Library has typescripts which continue the edition to 1820. The personal papers of William Pitt (the younger) are included in the Chatham papers now in the British Record Office. The multitudinous private papers of Lord Grenville during his long tenure of office are described (and extensively printed, though not many of the letters relating to America) by the British Historical Manuscripts Commission in *Dropmore*

[5] Cf. *Miss. Hist. Soc. Pub.*, V (1902) 233, 276.

MSS. (no. 5602). The British Museum contains the Liverpool papers, being the correspondence of Robert Banks Jenkinson, 2nd Earl of Liverpool, some letters of Gouverneur Morris to the Duke of Leeds and J. B. Burges, 1790, treating of sentiments of Great Britain regarding a treaty of commerce, impressment, etc.; letters of Wm. Tatham, U.S. agent in Spain, to Gen. Charles Rainsford, London, 1796; also miscellaneous letters and papers relating to American affairs (western forts and the Indians), 1718–1796. The Library of Congress has an autobiography of Edward Thornton, a secretary (later minister) of the British legation in the United States. The Lawrence collection in the Canadian Archives has a letter book of the collector and the comptroller of customs, Prince Edward Island, 1789–1809, which has some items on trade relations with the United States. There is a MS. letterbook of J. G. Simcoe, 1792–1793, in the Huntington Library at San Marino, California. The Library of Congress has a memorial to the commissioners for carrying into effect the 6th article of the treaty of Nov. 1794, by Lt. Gen. James Grant of the British army. The same library has transcripts of the negotiations with Great Britain respecting the eastern boundary, including the journal of the commissioners, Aug. 30, 1796–Oct. 25, 1798, with an appendix containing all the papers and documents laid before them.

Maps: Suggestions

Paullin's *Atlas* (no. 213). For a map first depicting the northwest boundary gap, see *A.S.P., F.R.* (no. 5341), v. I, 492. This map is missing from some copies. For MS. maps in the Canadian Archives relating to the frontier, see Holmden (no. 5144). For maps relating to the Northeast Boundary Dispute, see Ch. XI, below. There are some interesting MS. maps of the Canadian frontier in the British Colonial Office Library. For enumeration and description of contemporary maps, see *Statutes respecting boundaries of Ontario* (no. 571), 135–140.

7. The Other European States

Bibliographical Aids

See Sec. 1, above, for general historical bibliographies. For special bibliographical aids, see (The Netherlands), no. 4750, 4751; and Ch. III, Sec. 7; (Danish, Norwegian, and Swedish) nos. 4730, 4731;

4752; 4761; also bibliographies in Carlson (no. 194) and Hovde (no. 4365); (Germany and Austria) nos. 4740-4734 and 4726; and (Portugal) no. 4754.

Special Works

THE NETHERLANDS: G. W. Vreede, *Inleidung tot eene geschiedenis der nederlandsche diplomatie* (Utrecht, 1856-65, 6 v.) [588], v. IV-VI deal with the European diplomatic relations of the Batavian Republic and the reign of Louis Bonaparte, 1795-1810. Van Winter, *Amsterdamschen handel* (no. 156), v. II.

SCANDINAVIAN COUNTRIES: Bemis, *The U.S. and abortive armed neutrality of 1794* (no. 382). Carlson, *U.S. and Sweden* (no. 194) touches the Armed Neutrality of 1794 as revealed by printed sources, but overlooking Bemis. Fogdall, *Dan.-Am. relations* (no. 195).

PRUSSIA AND SAXONY: Hayden, *Senate and treaties* (no. 376), for the treaty of 1799 with Prussia in the U.S. Senate. Lingelbach, *Saxon-American relations* (no. 191).

For biographies of American diplomatists to The Netherlands (William Short, J. Q. Adams, and Wm. Vans Murray), Norway and Sweden (J. Q. Adams), Prussia (J. Q. Adams), and Portugal (David Humphreys, J. Q. Adams, and Wm. L. Smith), see the relevant entries and bibliographical data in the *D.A.B.*

Printed Sources

For American official documents and general source collections, see Sec. 1, above.

For guides to foreign official documents, see below, p. 836. See also (for The Netherlands) Ch. III, sec. 7; (for Sweden) Carlson (no. 194) which lists official and semi-official documents, diaries, and memoirs.

THE NETHERLANDS: *Letters of William Vans Murray* (no. 5272). *Writings of J. Q. Adams* (no. 5180). *Letters of T. B. Adams* (no. 5182). *Archives ou Corres. inédite maison d'Orange-Nassau* (no. 164). *Corres. famille du Stathouder* (no. 165).

DENMARK: *Bernstorffske Papirer* (no. 181).

PRUSSIA: *The treaties of 1785, 1799, and 1828*, ed. by J. B. Scott (no. 292).

PORTUGAL: " Correspondence of William Smith, American minister to Portugal ", ed. by B. C. Steiner, *Sewanee rev.*, XIV (1906)

76–104 [**589**], letters to James McHenry, secretary of war, 1797–99. *Life and times of David Humphreys* (no. 5241a) includes most of his despatches from Lisbon. "Letters of William Smith, minister to Portugal", *S.C. hist. mag.*, XXV–XXVI (1924–1925) passim. [**590**], letters to Timothy Pickering, secretary of state, 1798–1800, in which he gives the news of Europe in a manner more intimate than in his official despatches.

For the printed writings of American statesmen (see Sec. 1, above) and diplomatists (Wm. Short, J. Q. Adams, Wm. Vans Murray) for The Netherlands; (J. Q. Adams) for Norway, Sweden, and Prussia, see our list on p. 756.

MSS.: Suggestions

See Sec. 1, above.

For guides, indexes, etc., to Dutch, German, Austrian, and Scandinavian archives, and transcripts and photocopies from same in the Library of Congress, see Pt. II, ch. 3.

For the personal papers of the successive American ministers at The Hague (Wm. Short, 1792–1794, J. Q. Adams, 1794–1797, Wm. Vans Murray, 1797–1801) ; Prussia and Sweden (J. Q. Adams, 1797–1798) ; Portugal (D. Humphreys, 1791–1797, Wm. L. Smith, 1797–1801), see our list on p. 868. The diary of T. B. Adams, who served as secretary to his brother, J. Q. Adams, in Prussia (1798) now in the New York Public Library, is printed, as well as a few of his letters (no. 5182). The business, diplomatic, and political correspondence of Sylvanus Bourne, consul at Amsterdam, *circa* 1790–1800, is in the Library of Congress. Some of the letters give news of the depredations on American commerce and information on the policy of Great Britain and Napoleon toward America and American trade; include letters of Wm. Vans Murray, minister to Holland. There are in the New York Historical Society (Rufus King papers) a few letters written from Hamburg by the American consul, Joseph Pitcairn, to King, discussing Prussian-American relations.

8. Liquidation of International Debts [6]

Bibliographical Aids

For general aids, see Sec. 1, above.

---

[6] For the background of the debt liquidation, see Ch. I, Secs. 3 and 4.

Special Works

C. J. Stillé, *Beaumarchais and " the lost million "* (Phila., 1890), also pub. in the *Pa. mag. hist.*, XI (1887) 1-36 [**591**] explains in a definitive way the discrepancies between Franklin's receipts for two million and later French documents indicating that three million had been given to him before 1778 for the United States (for other material on Beaumarchais, see Ch. I, sec. 3). A. S. Bolles, *The financial history of the United States, from 1789 to 1860* (N.Y., 1883; 4th ed., 1894) [**592**] devotes some pages to the funding and the payment of the revolutionary debt. D. E. Huger Smith, " Commodore Alexander Gillon and the frigate South Carolina ", *S. C. hist. mag.*, IX (1908) 189-219 [**593**], for the source of the Luxembourg claims; and by the same writer, " The Luxembourg claims ", *ibid.*, X (1909) 92-115 [**594**] for an analysis of the claims. Alice G. Waldo, " Continental agents in America in 1776-1777 ", *Americana*, VI (1911) 1137-1151, VII (1912) 41-51, 141-149 [**595**] shows the service rendered by the agents in furnishing supplies. D. R. Dewey, *Financial history of the United States* (N.Y., 1915) [**596**] furnishes a general setting for the study of any question of public finances of the United States. Eloise Ellery, *Brissot de Warville; a study in the history of the French revolution* (Boston and N.Y., 1915) [**597**], for correspondence in regard to his speculation in the debt of the United States. Two studies by Marcel Marion: " De la participation financière de la France à la guerre de l'indépendance américain ", *Rev. dix-huitième siècle*, III (1918) 1-7 [**598**] estimates, on basis of a statement found in the MSS. of the *Bibliothèque Nationale*, the cost of the war to France, 1776-1782 (1,200 to 1,500 million *livres*) ; " La France créancière des Etats-Unis, 1781-1795 ", *Rev. deux mondes*, 7th pér., XLIV (1928) 830-847 [**599**], a popular essay which adds nothing to the more scholarly researches of Fliniaux and Aulard. André Fliniaux, *Quelques précisions sur les dettes des Etats-Unis envers la France ou des Français pendant la guerre de l'indépendance et sur leur remboursement* (Toulouse, 1922) [**600**], a short summary based on printed state papers. Nussbaum, *Commercial policy* (no. 429) shows the efforts of Ducher to get the debt commuted. A. Aulard, " La dette américaine envers la France sous Louis XVI et sous la révolution ", *Rev. Paris*, XXXII, no. 3 (1925) 319-338, 534-550, and a supplementary article in the *Révolution franç.*, n.s., no. 26 (1925) 111-124 [**601**], a most authoritative history, from the French

archives, of the payment in full by the United States of the monies
which were borrowed from France during the Revolution. W. E.
Borah and W. C. Bruce, "The French debt", in the *Congressional
record*, LXVI (Jan. 22, 1925) 2279–2284 [**602**] is a very, very curious
dialogue between Senators Borah and Bruce on the French loans.
J. H. Latané, *How Senator Borah handles the facts; our revolutionary debt to France* (Phila., 1925) [**603**] shows the mistakes made
by Senator Borah in the above-mentioned dialogue. S. F. Bemis,
"Payment of the French loans to the United States, 1777–1795",
Current hist., XXIII (1926) 824–831 [**604**], a short summary, which
has some faulty arithmetic in one detail, based largely on Aulard;
also same author in *Am. secs. state* (no. 4796), v. II, 59–93, and his
Pinckney's treaty (no. 506), 369–381, for "The financial debt of the
United States to Spain and its payment; loans and subsidies." H.
L. Bourdin, "How French envoys sought payment of America",
Current hist. mag., XXIII (1926) 832–836 [**605**], from French
sources. Van Winter, *Amsterdamschen Handel* (no. 156), for the
debt of the United States to the Dutch bankers, 1782–1788. Gilbert
Chinard, "Gallo-American commerce and the debt question" in his
Thomas Jefferson (Boston, 1929), 176–193 [**606**]. R. R. La Follette,
"The American revolutionary foreign debt and its liquidation", in
George Washington university bulletin, summary of theses, 1929–31
(Washington, 1931), 78–82 [**607**]. B. U. Ratchford, "An inter-
national debt settlement: the North Carolina debt to France", *Am.
hist. rev.*, XL (1934) 63–69 [**607a**], the debt to the Marquis de
Bretigney, agent for North Carolina in the French West Indies,
for war supplies from Martinique during the American revolution.
The debt was paid in 1802.

For biographical references see Sec. 1, above.

Printed Works

For American official documents and general source collections,
see Sec. 1, above. See also *A.S.P.*, *Finance*.

For guides to French official documents, see pp. 836 and 842. See
also Doniol (no. 40).

For contemporary French pamphlets, articles in the *Moniteur*,
and detailed references to *Corres. pol.*, *Etats-Unis* (p. 917), see
the bibliography in Nussbaum (no. 429); also, for contemporary
pamphlets, Jameson, *Bibliog. Monroe* (no. 1139), and Faÿ, *Bibliog.
critique* (no. 31).

J. G. A. Ducher, *De la dette publique en France, en Angleterre et dans les Etats-Unis de l'Amérique* (Paris, 1791) [608], in which he advocates the immediate liquidation of the whole of the debt. J. P. Brissot, *Nouveau voyage dans les Etats-Unis* (Paris, 1791, 3 v.; Eng. tr.: Boston, London, 1794, and 1797) [609] has two chapters on the American debt; see also *J. P. Brissot, correspondance et papiers*, by Claude Perroud (Paris, 1912) [610] for material on the relation of Brissot to speculations on the foreign debt of the United States in 1788. *The national loans of the United States, from July 4, 1776, to June 30, 1880*, by Rafael A. Bayley, as prepared for the tenth census of the United States (Wash.: Govt. Print. Off., 1881, 2d ed., 1882) [611] has a helpful tabulation of the loans. *Corres. de Moustier* (no. 302). *Corres. Fr. ministers* (no. 476).

For references to printed writings of American statesmen and diplomatists, see Sec. 1 above. Note also *Letters of George Cabot* (no. 5198).

MSS.: Suggestions

See Sec. 1, above. The official American sources for the study of the liquidation of the revolutionary debt are to be found in: (1) The Department of State, for guides and indexes, see p. 858. (2) Treasury Department, account of Ferdinand Grand, the banker through whose agency the United States carried on financial operations abroad, particularly in France, 1777–1785; estimates and statements, 1790–1802; statement of the accounts of the United States during the administration of the Superintendent of Finance, 1781–1784; and statement of accounts of the United States Board of Treasury from 1781 to the commencement of the present government. (3) General Accounting Office of the United States, for vouchers of accounts of John Holker, French consul general and supply agent in America during the American revolution. For the Jefferson, Robert Morris,[7] and Short papers see our lists, pp. 862–883. See also the Continental Congress papers in the Library of Congress.

The French official sources are to be found in the series, *Correspondance politique, Etats-Unis*, and *Correspondance politique, Etats-Unis, Supplémentaire*, also the series *Mémoires et Documents, Etats-*

---

[7] For description of the papers of Robert Morris, see H. A. Homes, *Description and analysis of the remarkable collection of the unpublished manuscripts of Robert Morris, the first financial minister of the United States from 1781 to 1784, including his official and private diary and correspondence* (Albany, 1876) [612].

Unis of the *Archives du Ministère des Affaires Etrangères*. For guides and indexes to French archives, see p. 915. The Library of Congress has photocopies of this series covering the period of the debt liquidation.

The minutes of the French legation in the United States, 1777 to 1796, are in the private library of William S. Mason, of Evanston, Ill.; photostats in the Library of Congress.

9. Washington's Farewell Address

Bibliographical aids.

For general aids, see Sec. 1, above.

Special Works [8]

Horace Binney, *An inquiry into the formation of Washington's farewell address* (Phila., 1859) [613], one of the first critical essays in American historiography reconstructs the documentary evolution of the text of the Address. R. G. Usher, " Washington and entangling alliances ", *No. Am. rev.*, CCIV (1916) 29–38 [614] analyses precise meaning of Washington's famous dictum about " entangling alliances." E. J. Benton, " The spirit of Washington's foreign policy ", *Review*, I (1910) 469–471 [615] emphasizes the "American character " of Washington's foreign policy. W. E. Borah, " Washington's foreign policy ", in *D.A.R. mag.*, LIII (1919) 187–191 [616], valuable only for facsimile of a portion of the original MS. in Washington's hand, of the text which went to the printer. Morison, *Origin of the Monroe doctrine, 1775–1823* (no. 1170), a lecture, delivered at the London School of Economics, to show the relationship of the principles of the Farewell Address to the later Monroe Doctrine. J. F. Rippy and Angie Debo, " The historical background of the American policy of isolation ", *Smith coll. stud. in hist.*, IX (1924) 71–165 [617], assemble the expressions (both private and official) of isolation sentiment and fear of entangling alliances, from 1775 to 1793. Three studies by S. F. Bemis: *U.S. and Lafayette* (no. 383), Washington's cautions dealing with Lafayette's imprisonment in Prussia and Austria, 1792–1797, illustrate his anti-entanglement ideas; " The background of Washington's foreign policy ", *Yale rev.*, n.s. XVI (1927 316–336 [618]; and " Washington's farewell address; a foreign pol-

---

[8] We are indebted to Mr. Frank Louraine, of the Library of Congress, for some of the suggestions in this section.

icy of independence ", *Am. hist. rev.*, XXXIX (1934) 250–268 [**619**], employs hitherto unused material from French archives to show that Washington issued his farewell address to frustrate French control of American domestic politics; and to suggest that the motive of the address was to establish independence of the United States from French tutelage as well as abstention from European entanglements. H. M. Wriston, " Washington and the foundations of American foreign policy ", *Minn. hist.*, VIII (1927) 3–26 [**620**], a popular lecture. Leonardo Vitetti, " Le origini della politica di isolamento degli Stati Uniti ", *Politica*, anno XII (1930) 89–143, anno XIII (1931) 322–379, anno XIV (1932) 164–221 [**621**], a rather expansive review of American policy in this respect, from printed state papers and secondary authorities. A. H. Wheeler, " The origin of the isolation policy of the United States ", in Clark University, *Thesis abstracts, 1929* (Worcester, 1930) 120–122 [**622**], J. G. Randall, " George Washington and 'entangling alliances ' ", *So. Atlan. quar.*, XXX (1931) 221–229 [**623**] professes to establish Jefferson in 1801, rather than Washington in 1796, as author of the phrase " entangling alliances." Savelle, *Am. dipl. principles* (no. 4823a), for precedents for American foreign policy. St. G. L. Sioussat, " The Farewell Address in the twentieth century ", *General mag. and hist. chron.* (Univ. of Penn.), XXXIV (1932) 319–330 [**623a**], one of the best analyses of Washington's mentality and the Address. Whitaker, *Mississippi question* (no. 505).

For biographical references see Secs. 1 and 3, above. See *D.A.B.* for bibliographical references to Thomas Paine.

Printed Works

For American official documents and general source collections, see Sec. 1, above.

Thomas Paine, *Common sense* (Phila., 1776), issued in many editions [**624**]. " Papers relative to the valedictory address of President Washington ", *Memoirs of the Historical society of Pennsylvania*, I, pt. 2 (1826) 231–257 [**625**], letters written by various persons concerning the drafting of the Address. *Washington's farewell address, with Hamilton's revised draft*, ed. by W. C. Ford (N.Y., 1892) [**626**], from v. XII of the *Writings of Washington. Claypoole's American daily advertiser* (Phila.), Sept. 19, 1796 [**627**] contains the Farewell Address as published at the time. Facsimile of the first and last pages of Washington's farewell address is given in E. M. Avery, *History of the United States*, v. VII, appendix (Cleveland, 1910) [628]. V. H. Paltsits, *Washington's farewell address, in facsimile, with transliterations of all the drafts of Washington, Madison, & Hamilton, together with their correspondence and other supporting documents*, edited, with a history of its origin, reception by the nation, rise of the controversy respecting its authorship, and a bibliography (N.Y.: The New York Public Library, 1935) [628a].

For the printed writings of Hamilton, Jay, Jefferson, Madison, and Washington, see our list on p. 756.

MSS.: Suggestions

See Sec. 1, above.

The evolution of the Farewell Address may be traced in manuscript letters and drafts in the Washington, Hamilton, and Madison papers in the Library of Congress. Certain other pieces are in the manuscript collections of the New York Public Library. See Paltsits (no. 628a).

CHAPTER V

THE JEFFERSONIAN PERIOD AND THE WAR OF 1812

1. In General.
2. Diplomacy of the Louisiana Purchase.
3. Spain: West and East Florida.
4. Aftermath of the Louisiana Purchase: Boundaries; Border Intrigues.

5. Impressment and Neutral Rights.
6. Anglo-American Frontier; War of 1812 and Peace of Ghent.

1. In General

Bibliographical Aids

For general aids, see Evans (no. 4639); Sabin (no. 4655); Larned (no. 4657); Griffin (no. 4658); *Writings* (no. 4661); C., H. and T. (no. 4662); *Am. secs. state* (no. 4796), see "Bibliographical notes"; *Guide hist. lit.* (no. 4634); Myers (no. 5399), for collections of treaties. Miller, *Treaties* (no. 5371), v. I, 39–54, for "Bibliography of United States treaty collections."

Winsor, *America* (no. 4782), v. VIII, 513–525. Channing, *Jeffersonian system* (no. 638), ch. 21: "Critical essay on authorities"; and his *History*, v. IV (no. 4784) for useful bibliographical notes. Turner and Merk (no. 307).

For Napoleonic material, see F. M. Kircheisen, *Bibliographie Napoléons* (Berlin, 1902; Eng. ed.: London, 1902) [629], also his *Bibliographie des napoleonischen Zeitalters einschliesslich der Vereinigten Staaten von Amerika* (Berlin, 1908–12, 2 v.; French ed.: Paris, 1908–12, 2 v.), and supplement in the *Revue des études napoléoniennes*, II (1912) (continued for current bibliographical notes in Napoleonic studies, in the same *Revue*, 1912–) [630]. G. M. Dutcher, "Tendencies and opportunities in Napoleonic studies", *Am. hist. assoc. ann. rep.*, for 1914, v. I (1916) 181–220 [631]; also his "Napoleon and the Napoleonic period", *Jour. mod. hist.*, IV (1932) 446–462 [632] which gives a survey of primary and secondary sources for the study of the subject. Monglond, *France révol. et impér.* (no. 390).

For periodical references, see *Poole's index* (no. 4995).

For lists of newspapers, see nos. 5004–5044; particularly Brigham (no. 5012); and Library of Congress check list (no. 5030).

General and Special Works

Of general histories of the United States, see Hildreth (no. 4779); Von Holst (no. 4780); McMaster (no. 4781); Winsor (no. 4782); Channing (no. 4784). See also *Am. secs. state*, v. III (no. 4796); and Wriston (no. 4799).

Lyman (no. 14). Adolphe Thiers, *Histoire du consulat et de l'empire* (Paris, 1845–74, 21 v.; Eng. translation: London, 1845–62, 20 v.) [633], a work now superseded by Sorel, but once of great political influence because of its apotheosis of Napoleon's career. Sorel (no. 396). Henry Adams, *History of the United States during the administrations of Jefferson and Madison* (N.Y., 1889–91, 9 v.) [634], the chapters on diplomacy, which constitute perhaps one-half of the work, are based principally on foreign office records, printed and unprinted. More intensive archival research by later writers is correcting details but is not likely to alter very much the broad outlines of one of the greatest classics in American historiography by one of the greatest minds America has yet produced. A. T. Mahan, *Sea power and the French revolution* (no. 398), and his *Sea power in its relations to the war of 1812* (Boston, 1905, 2 v.) [635] are also among the greatest pieces of American scholarly writing, stressing with able subordination of detail the fundamental significance of sea power to the diplomacy and to the general history of the Napoleonic period, itself considered in its proper place in history. J. H. Rose published three studies based on extensive research in English archives: *The revolutionary and Napoleonic era, 1789–1815* (Cambridge, Eng., 1898) [636], also his " Napoleon and sea power ", *Cambridge hist. jour.*, I (1924) 138–157 [636a], and his " British West India commerce as a factor in the Napoleonic war ", *ibid.*, III, no. 1 (1929) 34–46 [637], clear-cut studies of diplomatic facts of Napoleonic history by an eminent British scholar who spent many happy years reading manuscripts in the British Record Office. Channing, *History*, v. IV (no. 4784) gives on the whole the clearest and most succinct summary of the position of the United States between the opposing European belligerent maritime systems (superseding his earlier *The Jeffersonian system, 1801–1811* (N.Y. and London, 1906) [**638**]).   Edouard Driault, *Napoléon et l'Europe* (Paris, 1910–27, 5 v.) [**639**], a rapidly moving narrative of the international relations of those stirring times by the leading Napoleonic scholar of France.   F. M. Kircheisen, *Napoleon I., sein Leben und seine Zeit* (Munich, 1911–32, 8 v.) [**640**], this most recent elaborate study now extends through 1811, and gives extensive treatment, among other things, of Anglo-French relations and problems of sea power.   Bourne, *Revolutionary period* (no. 367) is a well-designed and authoritative one-volume summary, 1789–1815, most useful for beginning students of this mighty period of history.   Johnson, *Domes. and for. commerce* (no. 286), ch. 23: "The first quarter century, 1790 to 1815," by G. G. Huebner [**641**], a trustworthy and careful summary in a cooperative history.   Alfred Schalck de la Faverie, *Napoléon et l'Amérique; histoire des relations franco-américaines spécialement envisagée au point de vue de l'influence napoléonienne (1688–1815)* (Paris, 1917) [**642**], after 1800 this work appears to be more or less a French abridgment of Henry Adams.   Ernest Lavisse, *Histoire de France,* v. III: *Le consulat et l'empire (1799–1815)* (Paris, 1921) [**643**], a well-digested narrative abreast with recent research.   A. F. Fremantle, *England in the nineteenth century, 1801–1810* (N.Y., 1929–30, 2 v.) [**644**], the latest and somewhat erratic political history of the period.   Louis Madelin, *Le consulat et le l'empire* (Paris, 1932–33, 2 v.) [**645**], a very recent work of solid merit, equalled by very few accounts of the Napoleonic period.

For biographies of American presidents (Jefferson and Madison), secretaries of state (Madison and Monroe), and diplomatists abroad (for names and tenure, see latest *Register* of the Dept. of State (no. 5122)), see the relevant entries and bibliographical data in the *D.A.B.*, and *Am. secs. state* (no. 4796).

For bibliographical note regarding British statesmen of the period, see Sec. 5, below.   For biographies, memoirs, etc., of French (and other European) statesmen, see Kircheisen, *Bibliographie Napoléons* (no. 629); Dutcher (no. 631), which gives a summary of recent biographies of persons prominent in that period; the general bibliographies of the Napoleonic period, and French general historical bibliographies (nos. 4732–4739).

Printed Sources

For American official documents and general source collections, see *Jour. exec. proc. Sen.* (no. 5387); *A.S.P., F.R.*, (no. 5341); *Ann. Cong.* (no. 5382); *Abridg. debates* (no. 5386); Richardson (no. 5335); Moore's *Arbitrations* (no. 5364); Moore's *Digest* (no. 5365). Myers (no. 5399), for collections of treaties.

For texts and notes, see Miller, *Treaties* (no. 5371).

For lists of American newspapers, see nos. 5004-5044; particularly Brigham (no. 5012); and Library of Congress check list (no. 5030).

For the printed writings of American presidents, secretaries of state, and diplomatists abroad (for their names and tenure, see latest *Register* of the Dept. of State (no. 5122)), see our list on p. 756.

For several important collections of French official documents, see Ch. IV, Sec. 4 (nos. 448-452). *Correspondance de Napoléon Iᵉʳ; publiée par ordre de l'empereur Napoléon III* (Paris, 1858-70, 32 v.) [646], the official edition, published by order of Napoleon III (for other editions of correspondence, memoirs, writings, etc., of Napoleon, see Kircheisen's *Bibliographie Napoléons* (no. 629). This veteran scholar is said to be now preparing a definitive edition of the writings of Napoleon).

Some of the more important contemporary pamphlets dealing with international relations are noted in Channing, *Jeffersonian system* (no. 638). For complete list of contemporary American pamphlets, consult Evans, *Am. bibliog.* (no. 4639).

Many of the diplomatic notes reprinted in *A.S.P., F.R.* (no. 5341) were originally printed at the time of delivery, either in the press or particular pamphlets, for the sake of influencing public opinion, and collected in printed editions from time to time in the successive editions of T. B. Wait's *State Papers* (Boston, 1814, 1815, 1819) [647]. Though they are significant, because of the date of their publication, we cannot cite these numerous prints here. They may be found by consulting Evans, *Am. bibliog.* (no. 4639), and in the catalogues of the Library of Congress and other large libraries.

William Sullivan, *Letters on public characters* (no. 371). *William Plumer's memorandum of proceedings in the United States senate, 1803-1807*, ed. by E. S. Brown (N.Y., 1923) [648] is of value because of the lack of detailed official records of the debates in the Senate during this period. Savage, *U.S. maritime policy* (no. 22).

For memoirs, etc., of French statesmen, see note on p. 86. Comte G. de Caraman, "Les États-Unis il y a quarante ans", *Rev. contemporaine*, III (1852) 208–234 [**649**] consists of reminiscences (1810–12) of the secretary of the French legation in Washington under the Sieur Sérurier.

MSS.: Suggestions

The groups of MS. sources which apply to this period in general are: the archives of the Department of State, analyzed in Van Tyne and Leland (no. 5495) and described below, p. 858; the papers of the three presidents, Thomas Jefferson, James Madison, and James Monroe, who were also secretaries of state (Jefferson, 1789–1793) (see p. 862), and of Robert Smith, the only other secretary of state of the period (see p. 866).

Other departmental archives than those of the Department of State are noted in Van Tyne and Leland. Deciphers of some despatches passing between foreign governments and their ministers in England, with cipher keys, 1740–1841, are in the British Museum.

More particular indications of MS. sources are noted below in the appropriate sections following in this chapter.

2. Diplomacy of the Louisiana Purchase

Bibliographical Aids

See Ch. IV, sec. 4; also Sec. 1, above. See also French historical bibliographies (nos. 4732–4739); Spanish historical bibliographies (nos. 4758–4760). Jameson, *Bibliog. Monroe* (no. 1139) contains material on the Louisiana purchase and Spanish mission. T. M. Owen, "A bibliography of Alabama", *Am. hist. assoc. ann. rep.*, for 1897 (1898) 777–1248 [**650**]; also his "Bibliography of Mississippi", *ibid.*, for 1899, v. I (1900) 633–828 [**651**]. T. P. Thompson, *Catalogue of Americana, consisting principally of books relating to Louisiana and the Mississippi Valley (Louisiana Purchase)* (New Orleans, 1903) [**652**]. J. A. Robertson,[1] *Louisiana* (no. 705). Marshall (no. 768), and Brown (no. 676), for their bibliographies. J. L. Mecham, "The northern expansion of New Spain, 1522–1822; a

---

[1] Dr. Robertson, for many years Secretary of the Florida State Historical Society, and editor of the Hispanic American Historical Review, is preparing a *Bibliography of Florida to 1821*, a comprehensive bibliography of books, with some MSS., and lists of libraries having rare volumes.

selected bibliographical list", *Hisp. Am. hist. rev.*, VII (1927) 233–276 [**653**].

Special Works

Jared Sparks, "The history of the Louisiana treaty", *No. Am. rev.*, XXVIII (1829) 389–418, XXX (1830) 551–556 [**654**], which is a review of Barbé-Marbois's history (no. 694). J. W. Monette, *History of the discovery and settlement of the valley of the Mississippi, . . . and the subsequent occupation, settlement, and extension of civil government by the United States, until the year 1846* (N. Y., 1846, 2 v.) [**655**], an early work, once standard, now superseded by later studies having richer access to archival records. Gayarré (no. 308). Masson, *Département des affaires étrangères* (no. 395). Sorel (no. 396). Henry Adams, "Napoléon Ier et Saint-Domingue", *Rev. hist.*, XXIV (1884) 92–130 [**656**], with numerous extracts from French archives and Napoleon's *Correspondance*. C. F. Robertson, *The Louisiana purchase in its influence upon the American system* (N.Y., 1885) (Am. Hist. Assoc. Pap., v. I, no. 4) [**657**]. C. A. Geoffroy de Grandmaison, *L'ambassade française en Espagne pendant la révolution, 1789–1804* (Paris, 1892) [**658**] rests on the unprinted correspondence of the French foreign office with its representatives in Spain, but dismisses the retrocession negotiations in a very summary way. Mahan, *French revolution* (no. 398). Roosevelt, *West* (no. 310). Winsor, *Westward movement* (no. 311). M. J. Wright, "Some account of the transfer of the Territory of Louisiana from France to the United States", *So. hist. assoc. pub.*, II (1898) 17–28 [**659**] indicates that Jefferson's government was preparing to mobilize militia for the forcible occupation of Louisiana in case Spain should not lend herself to the execution of the cession. N. P. Langford, "The Louisiana purchase and preceding Spanish intrigues for dismemberment of the union", *Minn. hist. soc. coll.*, IX (1901) 453–508 [**660**], nothing new. Max Farrand, "The commercial privileges of the treaty of 1803", *Am. hist. rev.*, VII (1902) 494–499 [**661**] analyses the diplomatic aftermath of article VII (giving certain commercial privileges to French and Spanish ships in Louisiana ports). J. K. Hosmer, *The history of the Louisiana purchase* (N.Y., 1902) [**662**], a popular account, prepared in advance of the St. Louis exposition (1903), undocumented, based on general historical narratives and a few unmentioned monographs. F. J.

Turner, " The significance of the Louisiana purchase ", *Rev. of rev.*, XXVII (1903) 578–584 [**663–4**] contains thoughtful observations, as does another popular magazine article of his, *Diplomatic contest* (no. 403). Marc Villiers du Terrage, *Dernières années de la Louisiane française* (407), a voluminous general history written pretty exclusively from French sources, but with only a summary account of the diplomacy of 1800–1803; and by the same writer, *La Louisiane, histoire de son nom, etc.* (no. 770). P. Coquelle, *Napoléon et l'Angleterre, 1803–1813* (Paris, 1904; Eng. tr., London, 1904) [**665**], an authoritative work based on British and French archival sources. Alcée Fortier, *A history of Louisiana* (N.Y. and Paris, 1904) [**666**], a "de-luxe " edition of a general history of Louisiana, elegantly illustrated. The chapter dealing with the Louisiana cession relies on the printed despatches of Livingston and Monroe, and on Barbé Marbois' history, from which extensive excerpts are published. Ogg, *Opening of the Mississippi* (no. 312). E. O. Randall, " The Louisiana purchase ", *Ohio archaeol. and hist. quar.*, XIII (1904) 248–262 [**667**], a straightforward summary with nothing new. W. R. Shepherd, " The cession of Louisiana to Spain ", *Pol. sci. quar.*, XIX (1904) 439–458 [**668**] deals with Franco-Spanish diplomacy anent the transfer of 1763, but see Aiton (no. 685) for new light. W. M. Sloane, " The world aspects of the Louisiana purchase ", *Am. hist. assoc. ann. rep.*, for 1903, v. I (1904) 85–104, rewritten in *Am. hist. rev.*, IX (1904) 507–521 [**669**], this summary is valuable for its stimulating reflections rather than for any original contribution. Two studies by I. J. Cox: *The early exploration of Louisiana* (Cincinnati, 1906) [**670**], ch. 14, for note on " The diplomatic correspondence of Louisiana exploration "; and *The Louisiana-Texas frontier* (Austin, Tex., 1906–13, 2 v.), reprinted from the *Quarterly* of the Texas State Historical Association (later the Southwestern Historical Association) [**671**] which discusses diplomatic intrigues for the possession of Louisiana, and the diplomacy of the cession; (see also nos. 670, 671, 703, 718, 719, 720, 763, 765 below, for studies by the same writer on boundary disputes of the Louisiana purchase). Fuller (no. 977). Chadwick (no. 108). Guyot (no. 412). Kircheisen, *Napoléon I.* (no. 640). Louis Pelzer, " Economic factors in the acquisition of Louisiana ", *Miss. Valley hist. assoc. proc.*, VI (1913) 109–128 [**672**] stresses American commerce on the Mississippi, now superseded by Whitaker, *Mississippi ques-*

tion (no. 505). J. A. James, *Louisiana* (no. 418). T. L. Stoddard.
French revolution in San Domingo (Boston, 1914) [**673**], a standard
account, resting on laborious research in French archives, by a student who saw in the subject a prototype of the world-wide " conflict
of color " which seemed to him a fundamental problem of the twentieth century; it is useful for the proper understanding of the relation of conditions in San Domingo, but weak on American diplomacy thereto relating; (see also nos. 656, 675a, 683, 694 for other
studies on Napoleon and San Domingo). G. Labouchère, " L'annexion de la Louisiane aux États-Unis et les maisons Hope et Baring ", *Rev. hist. dipl.*, XXX (1916) 423–455 [**674**], for diplomatic
and financial phases of the transaction; also by the same writer,
" Bonaparte et la Louisiane ", *Nouvelle revue*, 4th ser., XXV (1918)
passim. [**675**], leans heavily on Schalck de la Faverie (who in turn
depended on Henry Adams) and apparently on Labouchère. F. P.
Renaut, *La question de la Louisiane, 1796–1806* (Paris, 1918) [**675a**],
reprinted from the *Revue de l'histoire des colonies française*, 1918; a
valuable, but not definitive, study of the part played by Louisiana in
French and Spanish policy during those years. E. S. Brown, *The
constitutional history of the Louisiana purchase, 1803–1812* (Berkeley, Calif., 1920) [**676**], for a special phase; also his " Jefferson's
plan for a military colony in Orleans Territory ", *Miss. Valley hist.
rev.*, VIII (1922) 373–376 [**677**]. Hayden, *Senate and treaties* (no.
376), for the Senate and the Louisiana treaty. Cardinal Goodwin,
*The trans-Mississippi West (1803–1853); a history of its acquisition
and settlement* (N.Y. and London, 1922) [**678**] contains a not un-
useful summary based on secondary accounts. Hill, *Treaties* (no.
4794). Bécker, *Historia* (no. 723). André Lafargue, " 'A reign of
twenty days'; Pierre Clement de Laussat ", *La. hist. quar.*, VIII
(1925) 398–410 [**679**] deals with the administration of De Laussat
as colonial prefect of Louisiana during the twenty days that intervened between the retrocession of Louisiana by Spain to France and
the transfer from France to the United States. C. L. Lokke,
" Jefferson and the Leclerc expedition ", *Am. hist. rev.*, XXXIII
(1928) 322–328 [**680**] is concerned with the attitude of Jefferson in
regard to the French expedition to San Domingo in 1801. J. E.
Winston and R. W. Colomb, " How the Louisiana purchase was
financed ", *La. hist. quar.*, XII (1929) 189–237 [**681–2**], a de-

tailed history of the payment of the purchase price of $11,500,000 to the French government, based upon *Papers appertaining to the purchase of the Louisiana province, collected and edited by the United States Treasury Department in 1875 for use in the Centennial Exposition at Philadelphia.* Mildred S. Fletcher, *Louisiana in French diplomacy* (no. 438) reviews the literature and printed documents critically, and concludes that French policy for the reacquisition of Louisiana does not antedate 1793, possibly 1795. André Fugier, *Napoléon et l'Espagne, 1799–1808* (Paris, 1930, 2v.) [683], based on impressive multiple archival study. Dunbar Rowland, " Mississippi in the transfer of the Louisiana purchase ", *La. hist. quar.*, XIII (1930) 235–245 [684] ascribes to the southwestern colonization movement the real cause for the purchase. A. S. Aiton, " The diplomacy of the Louisiana cession ", *Am. hist. rev.*, XXXVI (1931) 701–720 [685] deals with the transfer of 1763, to question that Louisiana was then a colonial " white elephant." A. P. Whitaker, " France and the American deposit at New Orleans ", *Hisp. Am. hist. rev.*, XI (1931) 485–502 [686], and Lyon (no. 708) state, after examination of Spanish and French archives, that there is no evidence of Franco-Spanish collusion preceding the cloture of the Mississippi. Also by A. P. Whitaker, " The retrocession of Louisiana in Spanish policy ", *Am. hist. rev.*, XXXIX (1934) 454–476 [687], the thesis is that, far from being bullied into retroceding Louisiana in 1800, Spain was trying to trade Louisiana to France for as good a bargain as possible—supported by abundant work in French and Spanish archives. Whitaker, *Mississippi question* (no. 505) contains an important chapter on the retrocession of Louisiana, attributing it to Spanish desires astutely marked. R. B. Guiness, " The purpose of the Lewis and Clark expedition ", *Miss Valley hist. rev.*, XX (1933) 90–100 [688] shows that Jefferson did not contemplate the purchase of Louisiana when he proposed to Congress, Jan. 18, 1803, the Lewis and Clark expedition; scientific motives were but incidental to the main objective which was to expand the American fur trade on the upper reaches of the Missouri, in rivalry to British trading activities there. E. W. Lyon, *Louisiana in French diplomacy, 1759–1804* (Norman, Okla., 1934) [689], a very valuable work. The author incorporates the results of fresh study of relevant French, British, Spanish, and American archives to depict the European background of the Louisiana cessions of 1800 and 1803. Van Winter, *Amsterdamschen handel* (no. 156), v. II, for mobilization of Dutch capital to support the Louisiana purchase.

For biographies of American statesmen (Jefferson, Rufus King, R. R. Livingston, James Madison, James Monroe, and Gouverneur Morris), see the relevant entries and bibliographical data in the *D.A.B.*

For note regarding biographies of French statesmen of the Napoleonic period, see Sec. 1, above, p. 115.

Printed Sources

For American official documents and general source collections, see Sec. 1, above. Documents regarding the transfer of Louisiana to France and again to the United States are in *A.S.P.*, *Public Lands*, V and VII. See *A.S.P.*, *Misc.*, I, 344–356, 362–384, for " Description of Louisiana ", which was also printed separately (Wash., 1803) under title, "An account of Louisiana, being an abstract of documents, in the offices of the Departments of State, and of the Treasury ", a compilation made by direction of President Jefferson. This was also published as *Old South leaflets*, gen. ser., v. 5, no. 105 (Boston, 1902) [**690**].

For guides to French official documents, see below, pp. 836 and 842. Consult also *Journal officiel* (no. 5127b).

For contemporary pamphlets and speeches, see Jameson, *Bibliog. Monroe* (no. 1139), the bibliography in Robertson, *Louisiana* (no. 705), and Evans, *Am. bibliog.* (no. 4639).

Vergennes, *Mémoire* (no. 87). [C. B. Brown], *Monroe's embassy, or, The conduct of the government, in relation to our claims to the navigation of the Mississippi,* . . . (Wash., 1803) [**691**], published anonymously, signed " Poplicola." Wm. Duane, *Mississippi question; report of a delegate in the Senate of the United States, on the 23d, 24th, and 25th February, 1803, on certain resolutions concerning the violation of the right of deposit in the island of New Orleans* (Phila., 1803) [**692**]. *Reflections on the cession of Louisiana to the United States*, by " Sylvestris " [pseud. for James Madison] (Wash., 1803), also pub. in the *Magazine of history, with notes and queries,* extra number, no. 171 (1931) [**693**]. Marquis de Barbé-Marbois, *Histoire de la Louisiane et de la cession de cette colonie par la France aux Etats-Unis de l'Amérique Septentrionale* (Paris, 1829;

Eng. translation, Phila., 1830) [**694**], written 25 years after by a participant in the cession who was a vivid and dramatic writer, but who takes occasion to justify a political necessity that compelled France to make the cession.   Pierre Clément Laussat, *Mémoires sur ma vie* (Pau, 1831) [**695**], for reminiscences of the colonial prefect of Louisiana for France on the retrocession by Spain of that province. *Corres. Napoléon* (no. 646).   Henry Adams, *Documents relating to New England federalism, 1800–1815* (Boston, 1877; reprinted, 1905) [**696**]; also his *Napoléon Ier* (no. 656).   Théodore Iung, *Lucien Bonaparte et ses mémoires* (Paris, 1882–1883, 3 v.) [**697**] in which Napoleon's brother gives opinion on reasons for selling Louisiana. Charles Whitworth (Earl Whitworth), *England and Napoleon in 1803, being the despatches of Lord Whitworth and others*, ed. by Oscar Browning (London, 1887) [**698**].   Léonce de Brotonne, *Lettres inédites de Napoléon Ier* (Paris, 1898) [**699**] contains a few letters concerning Louisiana which do not appear in Napoleon's collected correspondence.   Rufus Blanchard, *Documentary history of the cession of Louisiana to the United States till it became an American province* (Chicago, 1903) [**700**]. *State papers and correspondence bearing upon the purchase of the territory of Louisiana* (Wash., 1903) (57th Cong., 2d sess.   House.   Doc. no. 431) [**701**], documents (1801–1804), particularly diplomatic correspondence of the United States, reprinted on the occasion of the centenary exposition at St. Louis.   William Salter, "The Louisiana purchase in the correspondence of the time", *Ann. Iowa*, 3d ser., VI (1904) 401–415 [**702**] consists of extracts from *State papers* (no. 701), with additions from the " Works " of public men of the day.   " The transfer of Louisiana and the Burr conspiracy, as illustrated by the Findlay letters ", ed. by I. J. Cox, *Ohio hist. and phil. soc. quar. pub.*, IV, no. 3 (1909) 91–138 [**703**], correspondence of G. P. Torrence, members of the Findlay family, and others.   Alexandre Tausserat-Radel, *Papiers de Barthélemy*, v. VI (Paris, 1910) [**704**] prints reports of the French negotiator at the treaty of Basel containing allusions to French efforts to obtain Louisiana in 1795.   Houck, *Spanish régime* (no. 329).   J. A. Robertson, *Louisiana under the rule of Spain, France, and the United States, 1785–1807, as portrayed in hitherto unpublished contemporary accounts* (Cleveland, O., 1911, 2 v.) [**705**] for a few selected documents dealing with the retrocession of Louisiana and transfer to the United States, from the correspondence of the French and Spanish officials (especially Talleyrand, Laussat, Casa Irujo, and Ceballos) as well as that of the English ministers to the United States. Hayem (no. 479). Renaut (no. 675a) publishes 8 documents, including " Rapport de Talleyrand à l'empereur, au sujet du ' Mémoire sur les Florides ', remis par Monroe ", from the *Archives du Ministère des Affaires Étrangères, États-Unis.* Gilbert Chinard, *Volney et l'Amérique, d'après des documents inédits et sa correspondance avec Jefferson* (Baltimore, 1923) [**705a**] has a chapter on " Volney et Bonaparte; La cession de la Louisiane; traduction des ' Ruines ' par Jefferson." " Despatches from the United States consulate in New Orleans, 1801–1803 ", ed. by J. F. Jameson, *Am. hist. rev.*, XXXII (1927) 801–824, XXXIII (1928) 331–359 [**706**], official despatches of the American consuls at New Orleans (Evan Jones, William S. Hulings, and Daniel Clark) in regard to commercial affairs and relations with the Spanish authorities in Louisiana just before cession; supplemented by "Another dispatch from the United States consulate in New Orleans ", ed. by A. P. Whitaker, *ibid.*, XXXVIII (1933) 291–295 [**707**], which gives valuable information regarding the activities of the writer, Daniel Clark, and an account of the transfer of Louisiana from Spain to France. *Corres. Jefferson and Du Pont de Nemours* (no. 5246), hitherto unpublished letters throw new light on Jefferson's New Orleans diplomacy, particularly on the origin of the idea of a purchase. " The closing of the port of New Orleans ", ed. by E. W. Lyon, *Am. hist. rev.*, XXXVII (1932) 280–286 [**708**], document from the *Archivo Histórico Nacional,* Madrid, comprising the complete text of a report to the king on the closing of the port of New Orleans to Americans, drawn up in the *Ministerio de Estado,* which, the editor believes, shows that the initiative did not come from Napoleon and Talleyrand, but was a Spanish affair alone (note also Whitaker, no. 686).

For printed writings of American statesmen (enumerated above, under " Special Works "), see our list on p. 756.

For printed writings of foreign statesmen (Napoleon, Marbois, Talleyrand, Laussat, and Godoy): nos. 470, 488, 522, 569, 646, 694, 695. See also bibliographical note in Sec. 1, above.

MSS.: Suggestions

See Sec. 1, above. Note also papers of Rufus King (U.S. minister to Great Britain) in our list on p. 876.

For indication as to original MSS., and transcripts and facsimiles thereof, of diplomatic papers pertaining to the subject in the United States, Spanish, French, and British archives, see notes given above, Chs. III and IV, which apply also to the period of the Louisiana Purchase. There is an extended analysis of a diplomatic nature in A. Fugier (no. 683), v. I, xiii-xliv.

The Henry Adams transcripts, in long hand, in the Library of Congress, are of documents selected by that writer for his celebrated *History* (no. 634) from the diplomatic archives of France, Spain, and Great Britain. The Bemis typed transcripts, in the same library, supplement these with material (despatches and enclosures) copied from the Spanish foreign office papers in the *Archivo Histórico Nacional*, and (instructions) from the legation papers now in the *Departamento de Estado*. The Missouri Historical Society at St. Louis, has 500 pages of transcripts from Spanish archives relating to upper Louisiana, some of which concern the French sale of that territory to the United States. For other Spanish MSS. and transcripts in the United States, see Robertson's *List* (no. 5560). Some particular accounts of pertinent collections are: Miguel Gómez del Campillo, " Chronological statement of papers and documents relative to Louisiana in the national historical archives of Madrid ", *La. hist. soc. pub.*, IV (1908) 124–144 [**709**]; and Mabel M. Manning, *East-Florida papers* (no. 1007). The Chicago Historical Society (Gunther collection) has some original documents of the cession of Louisiana from Spain to France and from France to the United States.

3. Spain:² West and East Florida, 1801–1815

Bibliographical Aids

See Sec. 1, above. See also Spanish historical bibliographies (nos. 4758–4760).

R. P. Brooks, *A preliminary bibliography of Georgia history* (Athens, Ga., 1910) [**710**]. Owens, *Bibliog. Alabama* (no. 650); also his *Bibliog. Mississippi* (no. 651). " Preliminary check list of Floridiana, 1500–1865, in the libraries of Florida ", *Florida lib.* [*assoc.*] *bull.* (Jacksonville), v. II, no. 2 (1930) 4–16 [**711**], includ-

---

² For Diplomacy of the Louisiana Purchase, see Sec. 2 above; for border intrigues, Sec. 4 below. See also Ch. IV, Sec. 5, for Spanish-American Relations, 1789–1801.

ing books, manuscripts, newspapers and periodicals, and maps. *Catalogue of the Wymberley Jones de Renne Georgia library at Wormsloe, Isle of Hope, near Savannah, Georgia* (Wormsloe, Ga., 1931, 3 v.) [712], a catalogue of books relating to the history of Georgia, which includes also newspapers and maps.

Special Works

See Sec. 1, above.

Hinsdale, *Southern boundary* (no. 494). H. L. Favrot, " The West Florida revolution ", *La. hist. soc. pub.*, I, pts. 2–3 (1895–96) *passim.* [713], remarks on the causes of the Baton Rouge revolution of 1810, based on the written proceedings of the insurrectionists. H. E. Chambers, *West Florida and its relations to the historical cartography of the United States* (Baltimore,1898) [714] endeavors to show the unsoundness of Livingston's and Madison's claim that West Florida was included in the Louisiana purchase. Farrand (no. 661). Fuller (no. 977). Chadwick (no. 108). F. L. Riley, "Mississippi river as a political factor in American history ", *Miss. hist. soc. pub.*, XI (1910) 31–60 [715], a review which does not improve on Turner (no. 403). W. R. de Villa Urrutia, *Relaciones entre España y Inglaterra durante la guerra de la independencia; apuntes para la historia diplomática de España de 1808 á 1814* (Madrid, 1911–14, 3 v.) [716] has little on the subject of Florida. Four studies by I. J. Cox, " The American intervention in West Florida ", *Am. hist. rev.*, XVII (1912) 290–311 [717]; " General Wilkinson and his later intrigues with the Spaniards ", *ibid.*, XIX (1914) 794–812 [718]; *The West Florida controversy, 1798– 1813; a study in American diplomacy* (Baltimore, 1918) [719], too voluminous; and " The border missions of General George Mathews ", *Miss. Valley hist. rev.*, XII (1925) 309–333 [720] contribute a great deal from American printed and unprinted sources and from transcripts from Spanish archives, together with the researches by the author in the Archives of the Indies at Seville. Schalck de la Faverie (no. 642), for Napoleon's relations to Florida. F. A. Ogg and Dunbar Rowland, " The American intervention in West Florida ", *Miss. Valley hist. assoc. proc.*, IV (1912) 47–58 [721] justifies American intervention in 1810 on ground of complete breakdown of Spanish sovereignty. F. P. Renaut, " La politique des Etats-Unis dans l'Amérique du Nord espagnole sous le règne de Joseph Bonaparate, 1808–1814 ", *Rev. sci. pol.*, XXXIX (1918) 76–93 [**722**], an undocumented narrative describing how " the plans of annexation [of West Florida] sketched out between Vicente Folch and Madison in 1810 " were realized, thanks to the war of 1812. Jerónimo Bécker, *Historia de las relaciones exteriores de España durante el siglo XIX* (Madrid, 1924–26, 3 v.) [**723**], by the late archivist of the Spanish foreign office, contains a wealth of material drawn from the archives, but the author was not abreast of historical works done in other countries on his subject. Caroline M. Brevard, *A history of Florida from the treaty of 1763 to our own times,* . . . ed. by J. A. Robertson, v. I (Deland, Fla.: Florida State Hist. Soc.,1924) [**723a**], dealing generally with the period from the treaty of 1763 to the admission to statehood. C. A. Geoffroy de Grandmaison, *L'Espagne et Napoléon* (Paris, 1925–31, 3 v.) [**724**], a most scholarly analysis of Franco-Spanish relations, based on extensive archival work, but pays little attention to Florida and the United States. J. W. Pratt, *Expansionists of 1812* (N.Y., 1925) [**725**] discusses the rise in the Southwest of the plan to declare war on England in order to annex the Floridas and possibly Mexico from England's ally, Spain, as a balance to annexation of Canada also; valuable for crystallizing an important and now generally accepted new emphasis on the causes of the war of 1812. A. H. Phinney, " First Spanish-American war ", *Fla. hist. soc. quar.*, IV (1926) 114–129 [**726**] deals with the attempted seizure of St. Augustine by Americans in 1812. R. K. Wyllys, " The East Florida revolution of 1812–1814 ", *Hisp. Am. hist. rev.*, IX (1929) 415–445 [**727**], a study of the abortive East Florida filibustering attempt based principally on material contained in printed Congressional documents. Rippy, *Rivalry* (no. 1077), for British opposition to U.S. acquisition of the Floridas and Louisiana. T. F. Davis, " Elotchaway, East Florida, 1814 ", *Fla. hist. soc. quar.*, VIII (1930) 143–155 [**728**] deals with General Mathews and the " patriot invasion ", one of the abortive efforts to take East Florida from Spain, with documents of the putative state-makers. F. P. Burns, " West Florida and the Louisiana purchase ", *La. hist. quar.*, XV (1932) 391–416 [**729**], another examination of the question of whether it was included in the territory ceded by the treaty of 1803. Whitaker, *Mississippi question* (no. 505), the latest examination of the same problem, gives evidence to show France did not get West Florida with Louisiana.

For biographies of American statesmen of the period (J. Q. Adams, J. C. Calhoun, Langdon Cheves, H. Clay, W. C. C. Claiborne, governor of Mississippi Territory, Andrew Jackson, Jefferson, Madison, Monroe, Robert Smith, *et alii*) and diplomatists (to Spain: Chas. Pinckney, James Bowdoin, Geo. W. Erving; to France: R. R. Livingston, John Armstrong, Joel Barlow, Wm. H. Crawford; to England: Rufus King, Wm. Pinkney, Jonathan Russell) see the relevant entries and bibliographical data in the *D.A.B.*

For Spanish representatives in the United States (Irujo and Valentín de Foronda) we know of no biographical sketches. Useful lists of governors of Spanish East Florida, 1784–1821, and West Florida, 1781–1821, are given in *Fla. hist. soc. quar.*, VI (1927) 117–119 [730].

Printed Sources

For American official documents and general source collections, see Sec. 1, above. Consult the *Gaceta de Madrid* (no. 5127c) for Spanish official notices.

Ellicott, *Journal* (no. 519) is the record of his official survey of the boundary between the United States and Florida under the commission of 1796. *West Florida* (n.p., 1810?) [731], and *Observations on the conduct of our executive towards Spain* (n.p., 1812?) [732] are two contemporary pamphlets issued under the signature "Verus" (identified as Luis de Onís, Spanish minister to the United States) in support of the Spanish claim to title in West Florida as opposed to the American official position—a third pamphlet is published in Onís's *Memoria* (below). A. L. Latour, *Historical memoir of the war in West Florida and Louisiana in 1814–15*, tr. by H. P. Nugent (Phila., 1816, 2 v.) [733]. H. M. Brackenridge, *Views of Louisiana: containing geographical, statistical, and historical notices of that vast and important portion of America* (Pittsburgh, 1814; 2d ed., Baltimore, 1817) [734]. Benjamin Vaughan, *Remarks on a dangerous mistake as to the eastern boundary of Louisiana* (Boston, 1814) [735] argues against the claim of the United States to West Florida. "Lettre sur Cuba (juin 1807) ", *Rev. révolution*, VIII (1886) docs., 65–70 [736], a letter of Turreau, French minister in the United States, to Talleyrand. "West Florida and its attempt on Mobile,

1810–1811 ", *Am. hist. rev.*, II (1897) 699–705 [**737**], 5 letters which have to do with the short-lived State of West Florida. For the official activities of Governor Claiborne, *The Mississippi territorial archives, 1798–1803*, ed. by Dunbar Rowland, v. I (Nashville, Tenn.: Pub. by the Mississippi Dept. of Archives, 1905) [**738**], containing the " Executive journals of Governor Winthrop Sargent and Governor William Charles Coles Claiborne "; also *Official letter books of W. C. C. Claiborne, 1801–1816*, ed. by Dunbar Rowland (Jackson, Miss., 1917, 6 v.) [**739**] including documents and papers concerning West Florida. *Bowdoin and Temple papers* (no. 360), Part II, 1783–1812, some of which relate to the abortive efforts between 1806 and 1808 for the acquisition from Spain of East and West Florida and the settlement of the western boundary of Louisiana. *Secret statutes of the United States; a memorandum,* by David Hunter Miller, special assistant in the Dept. of State (Wash.: G.P.O., 1918) [**740**], for secret discussions and resolutions of the 11th and 12th Congresses in regard to Florida, 1811–13. " James Monroe, secretary of state, to George Matthews ", *Fla. hist. soc. quar.*, VI (1928) 235–237 [**741**], a letter of Apr. 4, 1812, to Gen. George Matthews, removing him from his position as commissioner in Florida, on account of the Amelia Island affair. Whitaker, *Documents* (no. 333).

For the printed writings of American statesmen and diplomatists (enumerated above, under " Special Works "), see our list on p. 756.

MSS.: Suggestions

See particularly Secs. 1 and 2, above, and bibliographical notes in Pratt, *Expansionists of 1812* (no. 725). The Library of Congress has photocopies of most of the material in the *Papeles de Cuba* listed by Hill's *Catalogue* (no. 5650), which deals with East and West Florida. For guide to British, French, and Spanish archives, see below, Part II, ch. 3. *Alabama hist. comm.* (no. 5525), for MSS. in Mobile and Spain. Robertson, *Spanish manuscripts* (no. 5540). Dunbar Rowland, *Miss. archives* (no. 5525). Mabel M. Manning (no. 1007).

Maps: Suggestions

John Melish, *Military and topographical atlas of the United States* (Phila., 1813) [**742**] includes a " Description of East and West

Florida and the Bahama Islands." *Catálogo Depósito de la Guerra* (no. 5139) lists many maps and plans sent from Seville to Madrid in the early 19th century, including Louisiana and Florida. Torres Lanzas, *Relación descriptiva* (no. 5140). *The Lowery collection* (no. 5145). Karpinski, *Maps in Spanish archives* (no. 5149), and his " Mapping Florida ", *Print connoisseur*, IX (1929) 291–310 [**743**], a brief historical sketch of maps of Florida, 1502–1823. *Floridiana* (no. 711) includes maps. Casteñeda and Martin, *MS. maps of Texas* (no. 790). A. F. Harley, " Bernard Romans's map of Florida engraved by Paul Revere, and other early maps in the library of the Florida Historical Society ", *Fla. hist. soc. quar.*, IX (1930) 47–57 [**744**] (see also P. L. Phillips, *Notes on the life and works of Bernard Romans* (Deland, Fla., 1924) [**745**], which contains a reproduction of the Bernard Romans map of Florida, 1774, from the only known copy, in the Library of Congress). Library of Congress, *Noteworthy maps*, no. 3 (Wash., 1930) [**746**], for photostats of MS. maps relating to Louisiana and West Florida.

4. Aftermath of the Louisiana Purchase: Boundaries; Border Intrigues

Bibliographical Aids

See Secs. 1 (" In General ") and 2 (" Diplomacy of the Louisiana Purchase "), above.

H. B. Tompkins, *Burr bibliography; a list of books relating to Aaron Burr* (Brooklyn, 1892) [**747**]. T. M. Marshall (no. 768) has a bibliography on the western boundary. C. W. Raines, *A bibliography of Texas; being a descriptive list of books, pamphlets, and documents relating to Texas in print and manuscript since 1536, . . with an introductory essay on the materials of early Texan history* (Austin, 1896) [**748**].

Special Works

J. J. Anderson, *Did the Louisiana purchase extend to the Pacific ocean?* (N.Y., 1881) [**749**] begins a controversy by contending that the Oregon country was not a part of the Louisiana purchase. W. A. Mowry, " Did the Louisiana purchase include Oregon? " *Am. hist. assoc. pap.*, II (1888) 40–43 [**749a**] is an abstract of a paper published in the *Mag. Am. hist.*, XVI (1886) 333–341, contending that the Rocky Mountains was the western boundary of the Louisiana purchase. E. L. Berthoud, *The boundaries of Louisiana in 1803*

(Golden, Colo., 1897) **[750]** argues that Louisiana could be considered, from historical documents cited, as extending to the Pacific. J. O. Broadhead, *The Louisiana purchase; extent of territory acquired by said purchase* (St. Louis, 1897) (Mo. Hist. Soc. Coll., v. I, no. 13) **[751]** argues against extension of Louisiana to the Pacific and criticizes the map published by the Department of the Interior in 1896. Binger Hermann, *The Louisiana purchase and our title west of the Rocky Mountains, with a review of annexation by the United States* (Wash.: G.P.O., 1898) **[752]**, the commissioner of the General Land Office reviews the principal facts in the history of Louisiana and its acquisition by the United States to support his contention that the next map published by the Department of the Interior be corrected so as not to include the Pacific slope in the Louisiana purchase (which was so ordered). J. R. Ficklen, " The northwestern boundary of Louisiana, with special reference to the French cession of 1803 ", *La. hist. soc. pub.*, II, pt. 2, 1898 (1899) 26–39 **[753]**, another argument against basing the claim to Oregon on the Louisiana purchase; and his " Was Texas included in the Louisiana purchase? " *So. hist. assoc. pub.*, V (1901) 351–387 **[754]** argues from documents and maps against the inclusion of Texas. S. M. Davis, " The dual origin of Minnesota ", *Minn. hist. soc. coll.*, IX (1901) 519–548 **[755]**, nothing new; the dual origin referred to is the treaty with Great Britain of 1783 and the Louisiana cession of 1803. Louis Houck, *The boundaries of the Louisiana purchase; a historical study* (St. Louis, Mo., 1901) **[756]** reviews the historical controversy to conclude that all of Montana, Oregon, and Washington should be placed in the galaxy of states included within the Louisiana purchase; also his *History of Missouri* (Chicago, 1908, 3 v.) **[757]**, which is a painstaking comprehensive history of the provincial and territorial periods, illustrated by a wealth of documentary material, particularly from Spanish archives; ch. 20 summarizes the diplomacy of the Louisiana territory and Mississippi valley, and boundary questions. H. H. Chittenden, *The American fur trade of the far West* (N.Y., 1902, 3 v.) **[758]**, a pioneer and informing work indispensable to the student of trans-Mississippi expansion. Two studies by W. F. McCaleb: *The Aaron Burr conspiracy; a history largely from original and hitherto unused sources* (N.Y., 1903) **[759]**, the hitherto unused sources are Mexican archives and Spanish diplomatic correspondence. The author maintains that Burr had in mind no treasonable design against the United States but rather a filibustering expedition into Spanish territory; and "The Aaron Burr conspiracy and New Orleans", *Am. hist. assoc. ann. rep.*, for 1903, v. I (1904) 131-144 [**760**], which discounts the theory of a plotted uprising in New Orleans; (see also Beveridge's *Marshall* (no. 445a) for the Burr conspiracy). Victoriano Salado Álvarez, *La conjura de Aaron Burr y las primeras tentativas de conquista de México por americanos del oeste* (Mexico, 1908) [**761**] elaborates McCaleb's thesis by use of documents in the Mexican archives, and represents Burr as the precursor of Houston in 1836. Six studies by I. J. Cox develop various details of border diplomacy and intrigue from patient study of multifarious sources: "The significance of the Louisiana-Texas frontier", *Miss. Valley hist. assoc. proc.*, III (1911) 198-213 [**762**]; "The Louisiana-Texas frontier", *Southw. hist. quar.*, XVII (1913) 1-42, 140-187 [**763**] (See also nos. 670 and 671); "The Pan-American policy of Jefferson and Wilkinson", *Miss. Valley hist. rev.*, I (1914) 212-239 [**764**]; "The Louisiana-Texas frontier during the Burr conspiracy", *Miss. Valley hist. rev.*, X (1923) 274-284 [**765**]; and "Hispanic-American phases of the 'Burr conspiracy'", *Hisp. Am. hist. rev.*, XII (1932) 145-175 [**766**] portrays Burr's persistent plottings, through the uncertain intermediary, Ch. Williamson, for English (and later for French) assistance for filibustering enterprises against Spanish colonial dominions. J. P. Brady, *The trial of Aaron Burr* (N.Y., 1913) [**767**], written from original records in United States court at Richmond. T. M. Marshall, *A history of the western boundary of the Louisiana purchase, 1819-1841* (Berkeley, Cal., 1914) [**768**], rests primarily on printed material. Bemis, *N.W. boundary gap* (no. 550). Goodwin, *Trans-Mississippi West* (no. 678), ch. 3. Shackelford Miller, "The Wilkinson-Burr conspiracy", in the *Proceedings of the twenty-first annual meeting of the Kentucky State Bar Association*, 1922 (Louisville, 1922), 182-223 [**769**], a very rambling review of the relations of Wilkinson and Burr, with a plethora of quotations from secondary authorities and from the record of Burr's trial. Bécker (no. 723). Marc de Villiers, *La Louisiane, histoire de son nom et de ses frontières successives (1681-1819)* (Paris, 1929), reprinted from the *Journal de la Société des Américanistes de Paris*, n.s. XXI (1929) 1-70 [**770**], the latest review, with "simplified sketches" of historical maps, and author's own map, illustrating historical boundaries of Louisiana. Douglas, *Boundaries* (no. 211). Richard Stenberg, " The western boundary of Louisiana, 1762–1803 ", *Southw. hist. quar.*, XXXV (1931) 95–108 [**771**] suspects a secret treaty of about 1762 between France and Spain in which the western boundary of Louisiana was definitely specified. The writer believes that " French statesmen possessed much more knowledge of the basis of France's claim to Texas than they vouchsafed to the American purchasers." Also by the same writer, " The boundaries of the Louisiana purchase ", *Hisp. Am. hist. rev.*, XIV (1934) 32–64 [**772**], new material to strengthen the hypothesis that Spain and France bounded Louisiana by the Mississippi and the lower Rio Grande in 1762; and a new interpretation of the diplomacy of the cession articles of the treaties of 1800 and 1803, suggesting that Florida was within the purchase. J. C. Parish, *The emergence of the idea of manifest destiny* (University of California at Los Angeles, 1932) [**773**], the author sees an unchristened manifest destiny in Thomas Jefferson's utterances. Morrison Shafroth, " The Aaron Burr conspiracy ", *Am. bar assoc. jour.*, XVIII (1932) 669–673 [**774**] believes the original sources show that Burr conspired with both English and Spanish emissaries, but does not reveal any sources not hitherto printed by Henry Adams and reports of the Burr treason trial.

For biographies of American diplomatists and statesmen, see Secs. 2 and 3. For biographies of other officials and persons (Blennerhassett, Burr, Claiborne, William Clark, Andrew Ellicott, Meriwether Lewis, Zebulon Pike, James Wilkinson, *et alii*) see the relevant entries and bibliographical data in the *D.A.B.*

Printed Sources

For American official documents and general source collections, see Sec. 1, above. *A.S.P.*, *Misc.*, I, for " Proceedings relative to the connexion of General James Wilkinson with Aaron Burr and his illicit intercourse with the Spanish government, 1808 " [**775**], and others regarding the Burr conspiracy; *ibid.*, II, 79–127, " Report of a Committee of the House of Representatives on an inquiry into the conduct of Brigadier General James Wilkinson, 1810 " [**775a**].

See also Sec. 2, above, and Ch. VII, Sec. 2.

Reports of the trials of Colonel Aaron Burr . . . for treason . . . in the circuit court of the United States, held at the city of Richmond, 1807, taken in shorthand, by David Robertson (Phila., 1808,

2 v.), also pub. as v. IV–V of the series *Causes célèbres* (N.Y., 1875, 2 v.) [**776**]. Wilkinson, *Memoirs* (no. 324). W. H. Safford, *The Blennerhassett papers, embodying the private journal of Harman Blennerhassett, and the hitherto unpublished correspondence of Burr, Alston, Comfort Tyler, Devereaux, Dayton, Adair, Miro, Emmett, Theodosia Burr Alston, Mrs. Blennerhassett, and others, . . . developing the purposes and aims of those engaged in the attempted Wilkinson and Burr revolution* (Cincinnati, 1861; and later editions) [**777**], Blennerhassett was a fellow conspirator with Burr. "A letter of Gen. James Wilkinson, 1806 ", *Am. hist. rev.*, IX (1904) 533–537 [**778**], written to José de Iturrigaray, viceroy of Mexico, from Natchez, Nov. 17, 1806. *Original journals of the Lewis and Clark expedition, 1804–1806*, printed from the original manuscripts in the library of the American Philosophical Society, . . . together with manuscript material of Lewis and Clark from other sources . . . ed. by R. G. Thwaites (N.Y., 1904–05, 8 v.) [**779**], now the standard edition superseding others; see also F. J. Teggart, " Notes supplementary to any edition of Lewis and Clark ", *Am. hist. assoc. ann. rep.*, for 1908, v. I (1909) 185–195 [**780**], a most valuable commentary. *Bowdoin and Temple papers* (no. 360), containing material on the settlement of the western boundary of Louisiana. "Papers of Zebulon M. Pike, 1800–1807 ", ed. by H. E. Bolton, *Am. hist. rev.*, XIII (1908) 798–827 [**781–2**], from originals in the archives of the ministry of foreign relations in Mexico,[3] being the papers taken in 1807 from Pike by the Spanish authorities at Chihuahua. *Torrence papers . . . Burr conspiracy* (no. 703). *Spanish régime in Missouri*, ed. by Louis Houck (no. 329), translations from the Spanish documents in the Archives of the Indies at Seville. Robertson, *Louisiana* (no. 705). *Letter books of W. C. C. Claiborne* (no. 739). *The Southwestern expedition of Zebulon M. Pike*, ed. by M. M. Quaife (Chicago, 1925) [**783**], a reprint of Pike's journal of 1805, 1806, 1807 (printed first in Philadelphia in 1810) without the original maps and charts. "Documents bearing upon the northern frontier of New Mexico, 1818–1819 ", ed. by A. B. Thomas, *New Mexico hist. rev.*, IV (1929) 146–164 [**784**] reveal the interest officials of New Spain took in the activities of Americans who were disturbing New Mexico. A. B. Thomas, " The Yellow-

---

[3] See Prof. Bolton's comments on these archives in *ibid.*, 523.

stone river, James Long and Spanish reaction to American intrusion into Spanish dominions, 1818–1819 ", *ibid.*, 164–177 [**785**] prints a document consisting of a digest of various official reports from Philadelphia to Acapulco, Mexico, which give details of the threatened American invasion, and the Spanish point of view in regard to it. *Pichardo's treatise on the limits of Louisiana and Texas*, ed. by C. W. Hackett (Austin, Tex., 1931–34, 2 v.) [**786**], an argumentative historical treatise with reference to the verification of the true limits of the provinces of Louisiana and Texas, written by Father José Antonio Pichardo, to disprove the claim that Texas was included in the Louisiana purchase of 1803. For comment on its diplomatic use, see P. C. Brooks, "Pichardo's treatise and the Adams-Onís treaty ", *Hisp. Am. hist. rev.*, XV (1935) 94–99 [**786a**]. *Zebulon Pike's Arkansaw journal: in search of the southern Louisiana purchase boundary line (interpreted by his newly discovered maps)*, ed. with bibliographical resumé, 1800–1810, by S. H. Hart and A. B. Hulbert (Colorado Springs and Denver, 1932) [**787**] includes an account of Pike's life and papers, by S. H. Hart, and of the purpose of Pike's expedition, by A. B. Hulbert.

For the printed writings of American diplomatists and statesmen, see Secs. 2 ("Louisiana Purchase Diplomacy ") and 3 ("Spain: East and West Florida "). For journal and memoirs of Aaron Burr, see no. 5197.

MSS.: Suggestions

See Secs. 1, 2, and 3, above, particularly material in United States, British, Canadian, and Spanish archives, to be examined through the guides, catalogues, and indexes therein referred to. Note collections of the Mississippi Archives (see below, no. 5525); the Spanish Archives of New Mexico (no. 5525); *Historical collections in New Orleans* (no. 5553); Texas Archives and MSS. (nos. 5525, 5560); Claiborne papers in the Library of Congress; Durrett papers and Melville papers in the University of Chicago (Newberry Library), and Wilkinson papers in the Chicago Historical Society. The Library of Congress has a scrap book volume of papers of Isaac Briggs, surveyor general of the Southwestern Dept. during Jefferson's administration, which contains depositions and papers regarding Gen. James Wilkinson's part in the Burr conspiracy. The State Historical Society of Wisconsin has authorized the preparation of a calendar of George Rogers Clark papers in the Draper collection. Note bibliographical data in the articles on Burr, Claiborne, William Clark, Ellicott, Lewis, Pike, etc., in the *D.A.B.*

Maps: Suggestions

See Ch. II, sec. 1, Ch. III, sec. 1, and Ch. VI, sec. 3, above.

Bibliographies of maps relating to Louisiana and Florida and boundaries are: *MS. maps, Brit. Museum* (no. 5129); *Printed maps, Brit. Museum* (no. 5131); Winsor, *America* (no. 4782), v. V, 79–86, also his *Westward movement* (no. 311), with full cartographical illustrations from contemporary sources; *Depósito de la guerra* (no. 5139); Torres Lanzas, *Relación descriptiva* (no. 5140); Phillips (no. 5135); Holmden (no. 5144); *Lowery collection* (no. 5145); (Canada) Geographic Board (no. 5146).

For notes regarding Louisiana boundary maps in particular: "Curious correspondence of De L'Isle, the geographer, as to the limits of Louisiana ", *Historical magazine*, III (1859) 231–233 [788], comprising letters (1715–1716) of Rev. Mr. Bobé, to De L'Isle, the geographer to the King of France, which reveal the care of the French government not to allow any boundaries to be assigned to Louisana, New Mexico, or California. Justin Winsor, " Cartography of Louisiana and the Mississippi basin under the French domination ", in his *America* (no. 4782), v. V, 79–86 [789]. J. H. Ficklen (no. 753) notes specific maps brought forward by Monroe and Pinckney, and Señor Cevallos, to support their respective contentions in 1805 (see *A.S.P., F.R.*, II, 662–665), and certain other maps cited by J. Q. Adams and the Spanish minister, Onís, in the negotiations of 1818–19. Robertson, *Louisiana* (no. 705). Marshall, *Western boundary* (no. 768). Karpinski, *French and Spanish maps* (no. 5149). C. E. Castañeda and Early Martin, jr., *Three manuscript maps of Texas by Stephen F. Austin; with biographical and bibliographical notes* (Austin, Tex., 1930) [790] describes also maps prior to those of Austin, which were drawn by José M. Puelles and other Spaniards, to indicate the boundaries of West Florida, Louisiana, Texas, etc., and prints a " list of manuscript maps of Texas, 1822–1835." *Pichardo's treatise* (no. 786), for maps to accompany his report, found in the archives of the *Departamento de Relaciones Exteriores* in the City of Mexico. Stenberg, *Western boundary* (no. 771) cites two maps of 1762 which may be noted as bearing possibly an official aspect. *Pike's Arkansaw journal* (no. 787), for his newly discovered maps of the southwestern boundary of the Louisiana purchase.

5. Impressment and Neutral Rights, 1803–1812

Bibliographical Aids

For general aids, see Sec. 1, above. See also French historical bibliographies, nos. 4732–4739.

Camb. mod. hist., v. VIII (no. 795), 791–796, for bibliography of the "Struggle for commercial independence." C. T. Harbeck, *A contribution to the bibliography of the history of the United States navy* (Cambridge, Mass., 1906) [**791**], "Right of search and impressment, 1799–1859" (U.S. documents) (p. 36–39). H. H. B. Meyer, *List of references on embargoes* (Wash., 1917) (Library of Congress) [**792–3**]. Melvin, *Napoleon's navigation system* (no. 802) contains an extensive bibliography for this period, both of printed and MS. material. See also the bibliographies in Heckscher, *Continental system* (no. 806), and Sears, *Jefferson and the embargo* (no. 811).

Special Works

See Sec. 1, above, for general works, particularly: Channing (no. 4787), McMaster (no. 4781), Mahan (no. 398), Henry Adams (no. 634), Sorel (no. 396), Kircheisen (no. 640), Driault (no. 639), *Am. secs. state*, v. III (no. 4796).

De Witt, *Jefferson* (no. 35). Smith, *England and America* (no. 340). W. M. Sloane, "The continental system", *Pol. sci. quar.*, XIII (1898) 213–231 [**794**], an enlightening essay, but with little in regard to the relation of the United States to the system. J. B. McMaster, "The struggle for commercial independence, 1763–1812", in *Cambridge modern history*, v. VII: *The United States* (Cambridge, Eng., 1903), 305–334 [**795**] discusses briefly the French decrees, British orders in council, etc. C. B. Elliott, "The doctrine of continuous voyages", *Am. jour. internat. law*, I (1907) 60–104 [**796**], a lengthy essay and commentary, showing that the doctrine "was developed by the English courts to defeat the devices of American merchantmen" to violate the Rule of 1856, and continuing to American application of the doctrine in the civil war. L. H. Woolsey, "Early cases on the doctrine of continuous voyages", *ibid.*, IV (1910) 823–847 [**797**], considers relation of the doctrine to blockade in cases "half a century prior to the civil war ", in 1805 and 1808. Updyke, *Dipl. war of 1812* (no. 887). G. W. Daniels, " The American cotton trade with Liverpool under the embargo and nonintercourse acts ", *Am. hist. rev.*, XXI (1916) 276-287 [**798**]. G. W. T. Omond, *The law of the sea; a short history of some questions relating to neutral merchant shipping, 1756-1916* (London, 1916) [**799**], written during the bitter Anglo-German maritime war of 1914-1918 by a champion of British sea power. A. H. Stockder, " The legality of the blockades instituted by Napoleon's decrees, and the British orders in council, 1806-1813 ", *Am. jour. internat. law*, X (1916) 492-508 [**800**] analyzes the more salient features of blockade during this period as set forth and laid down by statesmen of the United States, Great Britain, and France. W. E. Lingelbach, " England and neutral trade ", *Mil. hist. and econ.*, II (1917) 153-178 [**801**] indicates the important distinction between British policy of using belligerency to exploit neutral commerce in 1803-1815, and that of 1914-1917 of constricting neutral commerce solely to harass the enemy. Schalck de la Faverie (no. 642). F. E. Melvin, *Napoleon's navigation system; a study of trade control during the continental blockade* (N.Y., 1919) [**802**], a notable contribution, albeit inartistically presented, tracing, after wide and deep study in American, French, and English archives, the detailed development of Napoleon's continental system and showing its relation to American diplomacy (a main feature of the writer's thesis is that the determining factor in the economic strife of Napoleon with England was the position of the United States as the chief neutral). Carlson, *U.S. and Sweden* (no. 194), for the Stralsund claims and commercial negotiations of the period. W. W. Jennings, *The American embargo, 1807-1809; with particular reference to its effect on industry* (Iowa City, 1921) [**803**], no contribution because it ignores a great body of American and foreign MS. sources as well as some important secondary material. Morison, *Maritime history* (no. 1720). Fogdall, *Dan.-Am. dipl.* (no. 195), ch. 2: " Problems of the Napoleonic era, 1800-1815," *Camb. hist. Br. for. pol.* (no. 209), v. I, ch. 3. W. F. Galpin, " The American grain trade to the Spanish Peninsula, 1810-1814 ", *Am. hist. rev.*, XXVIII (1922) 24-44 [**804**]; and his study *The grain supply of England during the Napoleonic period* (N.Y. and London, 1925) [**805**], ch. 8: " The Anglo-American grain trade, 1800 to 1813 ", discuss, after scholarly archival research, the international and legal aspects of this trade (grain for the British troops). E. F. Heckscher, *The Continental system; an economic interpretation*, ed. by Harald Westergaard (Oxford, 1922) **[806]**, an important, readable, and lucid presentation, which shows the significance to belligerents of swollen war-time commerce of neutrals, particularly in the case of the United States. The author has not been sufficiently familiar with some of the important American studies of the period, like Henry Adams. Mowat (no. 347a), meager. J. F. Zimmerman. *Impressment of American seamen* (N.Y., 1925) **[807]** has utilized American archives, but was not able to consult the necessary British manuscript records. H. W. Briggs, *The doctrine of continuous voyage* (Baltimore, 1926) **[808]**, an analysis of cases and commentary. Virginia D. Harrington, " New York and the embargo of 1807 ", *N. Y. state hist. assoc. jour.*, VIII (1927) 143–151 **[809]** shows how the embargo stimulated manufactures, injured agriculture, and prostrated commerce. Robert McElroy, *Pathway of peace; an interpretation of some American and British crises* (N.Y., 1927) **[810]**, a series of popular lectures given by an American professor on the Oxford faculty to English audiences, ch. 5: " Economic pressure as a substitute for war " concludes that the war of 1812 was not caused, nor was it prevented, by Jefferson's substitute for war. L. M. Sears, *Jefferson and the embargo* (Durham, N.C., 1927) **[811]**, a helpful study. Elizabeth B. White, *American opinion of France, from Lafayette to Poincaré* (N.Y., 1927) **[812]**, for analysis and digest of public opinion in regard to our relations with France, as seen in contemporary diaries, letters, newspapers, etc. J. H. Rose, " British West India commerce as a factor in the Napoleonic war ", *Cambridge hist. soc. jour.*, III, no. 1 (1929) 34–46 **[813]** utilizes records of the British Colonial Office to analyze the importance of British West Indian conquests and commerce as a relief against Napoleon's Continental System. Hyneman, *Neutrality, 1792–1815* (no. 384). Anna C. Clauder, *American commerce as affected by the wars of the French revolution and Napoleon, 1793–1812* (Phila., 1932) **[814]**, a Univ. of Penn. doctoral thesis supplementing Heckscher (no. 806) with more particular emphasis of the effect of belligerent decrees on the United States. Savage, *U.S. maritime policy* (no. 22).

For biographies of American presidents (Jefferson and Monroe), and secretaries of state (Madison, Monroe, Robert Smith), ministers to France (John Armstrong, Joel Barlow, W. H. Crawford), to Great Britain (Monroe, Wm. Pinkney, Jonathan Russell, *chargé*), see the relevant entries and bibliographical data in the *D.A.B.* For brief biographical sketches, see Beckles Willson, *America's ambassadors to England* (no. 348), and by the same writer, *America's ambassadors to France* (no. 68). Other biographies are: W. E. Dodd, *The life of Nathaniel Macon* (Raleigh, N.C., 1903) [815]; Edmund Quincy, *Life of Josiah Quincy of Massachusetts* (Boston, 1867, 6th ed., 1874) [816]; Octavius Pickering, *The life of Timothy Pickering* (Boston, 1867–73, 4 v.) [817]; *Life and letters of Joseph Story*, ed. by his son, W. W. Story (Boston, 1851, 2 v.) [818]; Hugh Garland, *The life of John Randolph* (N.Y. and Phila., 1850, 2 v.) [819].

For biographies of British statesmen (secretaries of state for foreign affairs: Lord Hawkesbury, Lord Harrowby, Lord Mulgrave, C. J. Fox, Lord Grey, George Canning, Lords Bathurst, Wellesley, and Castlereagh), and diplomatists (ministers to the United States: Anthony Merry, D. M. Erskine, F. J. Jackson, and A. J. Foster), see the *D.N.B.*, and the bibliographical notes therein. See also Bigham, *Prime ministers of Britain* (no. 242); P. M. Thornton, *Foreign secretaries of the XIX. century to 1834*, 2d ed. (London, 1881–83, 3 v.) [820]; and, for a sketch of Castlereagh, Algernon Cecil, *British foreign secretaries, 1807–1916* (London, 1927) [821]. A more recent biography of Canning is H. W. V. Temperley, *Life of Canning* (London, 1905) [822].[4]

Printed Sources

For American official documents and general source collections, see Sec. 1, above (note also *A.S.P.*, *Commerce* (no. 5341)).

For British orders in council, French decrees, and American laws and proclamations restricting commerce, beginning with 1793, see *The embargo laws* (no. 369); convenient summaries are given in Channing, *History*, v. IV (no. 4784); British orders in council, 1807 (14 in number) are printed in Heckscher (no. 806), reprinted from Hansard, v. X, 126–148. For U.S. embargo acts, see *Statutes at Large* (no. 5377).

A useful list of contemporary magazines and newspapers (American and European) is given in Galpin, *Grain supply* (no. 805), 272–

---

[4] The special studies by Temperley (no. 1152) and Webster (no. 893), of the foreign policy of Canning and Castlereagh refer to a later period, 1815–1827.

276.   Note in particular: *Annual register* (no. 5058); and *Niles'*
weekly register, 1811–1849 (Baltimore [etc.], 1811–49, 75 v.) **[822a]**.
For catalogues of newspapers, see nos. 5004–5047, notably Brigham
(no. 5012).   Some extracts from contemporary papers reflecting
public opinion in regard to our relations with France are given in
Elizabeth B. White, *Am. opinion of France* (no. 812).

BRITISH OFFICIAL DOCUMENTS: *Journals* of the House of Lords, and
House of Commons (no. 5418); *Parliamentary debates* (no. 5410);
London gazette (no. 5127a); *Brit. and for. state pap.* (no. 5416).

BRITISH DIPLOMATIC CORRESPONDENCE AND PARLIAMENTARY PAPERS
(HOUSE OF COMMONS SESSIONAL PAPERS): *Order of council respecting*
commerce with America (1807, IV, 1) **[823]**. *Papers respecting*
discussions with America (1808, XIV, 1, 13, 21, 33. 1809, IX, 391,
431. 1810, XV, 363, 395) **[824]**. *Correspondence respecting certain*
orders in council (1809, IX, 375) **[825]**. *Minutes of evidence* . . .
respecting the orders in council (1808, X, 81; reprinted 1812,
III, 689) **[826]**. *Papers respecting Austria, . . . and the United*
States, presented to Parliament in 1808 (Foreign Office) (London,
1808) **[827]**. *Papers presented to the House of Commons, re-*
lating to the encounter between His Majesty's ship Leopard,
and the American frigate Chesapeake (F.O.) (London, 1809)
[828]. *Papers presented to the House of Commons, by Mr.*
Secretary Canning, relating to America [*1809*] (F.O.) (London,
1809) **[829]** contain instructions by Canning, to D. M. Erskine,
British minister to the United States, with correspondence between
Mr. Erskine and Robert Smith, secretary of state of the United
States. *Further papers, presented to the House of Commons, by Mr.*
Secretary Canning, relating to America (F.O.) (London, 1809)
[830], 4 letters, Canning to Pinkney, and Pinkney to Canning, 1808.
Papers presented to Parliament in 1809 (by the War Office) (Lon-
don, 1809) **[831]** contain Canning's correspondence with the
United States on the subject of the orders in council, 1808.
Papers presented to the House of Commons, relating to the encounter
between His Majesty's ship Leopard, and the American frigate
Chesapeake, by the Foreign Office (London, 1809) **[832]**. *Corre-*
spondence between Mr. Secretary Canning and the Hon. D. Erskine
(London, 1810) **[833]**. *Papers relating to America,* presented to the
House of Commons, 1809 (F.O.) (London, 1810) **[834]** deal with
the Chesapeake-Leopard encounter and the embargo. *Correspondence*

relating to America, presented to Parliament in 1810 (London, 1811) [835]. *Correspondence on the French decrees and British orders in council* (1812–13, XIV, 5, 41, 105, 135, 209) [836]. *Minutes of evidence ... relating to orders in council* (1812, III, 1) [837]. *Papers presented to Parliament in 1813* (F.O.) (London, 1813?) [838], containing the correspondence of the Marquess Wellesley, the Earl of Liverpool, and Viscount Castlereagh, with the American ministers in London, 1810–1812, and other correspondence regarding American relations.

FRENCH OFFICIAL PUBLICATIONS: *Bulletin des lois* (no. 449). *Moniteur* (no. 453a), the official journal of the Consulate and Empire, containing French decrees, correspondence, etc. The primary French source for the period is: *Corres. Napoléon* (no. 646).

James Stephen, *War in disguise; or, The frauds of neutral flags* (London, 1805; reprinted, 1917) [839], one of the most important political pamphlets of the time, revealing the desires of the British navigation and trade interests to take advantage of the war not only to control but to exploit neutral commerce. *An examination of the British doctrine which subjects to capture a neutral trade not open in time of peace* (Phila., 1806) [840], published anonymously, was written by Madison. *An essay on the rights and duties of nations, relative to fugitives from justice; considered with reference to the affairs of the Chesapeake,* by an American [David Everett] (Boston, 1807) [841]. *Collection of interesting and important reports and papers on the navigation and trade of Great Britain,* published by the Society of Ship-owners of Great Britain (London, 1807) [842] contains two reports framed by the Earl of Liverpool, president of the Committee of the Lords of the Privy Council, on the trade of Great Britain with the United States. *A true picture of the United States of America, being a brief statement of the conduct of the government and people of that country towards Great Britain,* by a British subject (London, 1807) [843]. Alexander Baring (Lord Ashburton), *An inquiry into the causes and consequences of the orders in council; and an examination of the conduct of Great Britain towards the neutral commerce of America* (London, 1808; 1st Am. ed., N.Y., 1808) [844]. [C. B. Brown] *The British treaty, with an appendix of state papers which are now first published* (London, 1808) [844a], supposed to have been printed in Philadelphia in 1807, reprinted in London in 1808, with an appendix of state papers. Deals with the Monroe-Pinkney treaty. *Thoughts upon the conduct of our administration, in relation both to Great Britain and France, more especially in reference to the late negotiation, concerning the attack on the Chesapeake*, by a friend of peace [John Lowell] (Boston, 1808) [845] charges Jefferson with being pro-French and anti-English; also by John Lowell, *Interesting political discussion; the diplomatic policy of Mr. Madison unveiled, in a series of essays containing strictures upon the late correspondence between Mr. Smith and Mr. Jackson,* by a Bostonian, (n.p., 1810) [846]. *Observations on the American treaty, in eleven letters, . . . under the signature of Decius* [T. P. Courtenay] (London, 1808) [847], an attack from the British point of view on Monroe's rejected treaty. Lewis Goldsmith, *An exposition of the conduct of France towards America* (London, 1810: 2d ed., N.Y., 1810) [848], a comparative analysis of French and English decrees and their effect on the United States, with digests of 26 American spoliation cases in French courts. [A. C. Hanson], *Reflections upon the late correspondence between Mr. Secretary Smith, and Francis James Jackson, esq., minister plenipotentiary of his Britannic Majesty* (Baltimore, 1810) [849]. *Translation of a letter from General Turreau to the Secretary of State, dated 14th November, 1810* (n.p., 1810?) [850]. *Aperçu sur la situation politique des Etats-Unis d'Amérique*, par le général Turreau (Paris, 1815) [851]. *Ten hints addressed to wise men; concerning the dispute which ended, on Nov. 8, 1809, in the dismission of Mr. Jackson, the British minister to the United States*, by Benjamin Vaughan (Boston, 1810) [852]. William Coleman, *An appeal to the people; being a review of the late correspondence and documents, relating to the rejection of the British minister* [F. J. Jackson] (N.Y., 1810) [853]. *Robert Smith's address to the people of the United States* (Baltimore, 1811) [854], survey of his career as secretary of state. "Orders in council, and the American embargo", *Quar. rev.* (London), VII (1812) 1–34 [855–6], a contemporary discussion of the orders. Robert Mayo, *Synopsis commercial system of the U.S.* (no. 1377), 60–68, for a synopsis of neutrality regulations and regulations of commercial intercourse with England and France, 1793–1839. *Docs. rel. to New Eng. federalism, 1800* (no. 696), exhibiting the ominous opposition of New England Federalists to the diplomacy of the administration. "Plan pour la conquête de Saint Domingue (1806)", *Revue de la révolution,* VIII (1886) docs. sec., 89-96, 97-113 [857], from the MSS. of Turreau, the originator of the plan. "Anticipation of the war of 1812", in the *Report on Canadian archives,* by Douglas Brymner, archivist, 1896 (Ottawa, 1897) 24-75 [858], transcripts of documents from the Public Record Office, giving information on the differences with the United States, 1804-1813. *Reports of prize cases determined in the High Court of Admiralty, before the Lords Commissioners of Appeals in prize causes . . . 1745 to 1859,* ed. by E. S. Roscoe (London, 1905, 2 v.) [859]. *The autobiography of Captain Zachary G. Lamson* (Boston, 1908) [860] gives a short account of commercial troubles of the period before the war of 1812. R. G. Albion, "Admiralty prize case briefs", *Am. hist. rev.,* XXXIII (1928) 593-595 [861] describes briefs prepared for 84 cases of American ships condemned in the High Court of Admiralty, 1803-08, which published briefs have recently been acquired by the New York Public Library, and are of great value for the study of international law and diplomatic relations. "Jefferson to William Short on Mr. and Mrs. Merry, 1804", *Am. hist. rev.,* XXXII (1928) 832-835 [862] gives an explanation of a famous episode in Jefferson's presidency, that of the dinner of Dec. 2, 1803, and the resulting conflict respecting official etiquette. Savage, *U.S. maritime policy* (no. 22).

For the printed writings of American statesmen (John Q. Adams, Fisher Ames, Joel Barlow, Geo. Cabot, Henry Clay, A. J. Dallas, Albert Gallatin, Jefferson, Rufus King, Madison, Monroe, Gouverneur Morris, H. G. Otis, Wm. Pinkney, and Josiah Quincy) see our list on p. 756. The correspondence of John Adams concerning the British doctrine of impressment, originally published in the *Boston Patriot* is printed in his *Works* (no. 5180).

Printed writings of British statesmen: *Memoirs and correspondence of the most noble Richard, Marquess Wellesley,* by R. R. Pearce (London, 1846, 3 v.) [863] contains correspondence of 1810-11 between Wellesley in his capacity as British secretary of state for foreign affairs, and the American minister in London (Wm. Pinkney). *Memoirs and correspondence of Viscount Castlereagh, second marquess of Londonderry,* ed. by Charles Vane, Marquess of Londonderry (London, 1850-53, 12 v.) [864], last four volumes (*Correspondence and despatches*) include his diplomatic activities. *Memoirs of the Whig party during my time,* by Henry Richard

Lord Holland, ed. by his son, Henry Edward Lord Holland (London, 1852–54, 2 v.) [865] includes an account (brief) of the negotiation of the treaty with Monroe and Pinkney, 1806. *The life and administration of Robert Banks, second Earl of Liverpool*, comp. from original documents by C. D. Yonge (London, 1868, 3 v.) [866] includes copious extracts from his correspondence. *The Bath archives; a further selection from the diaries and letters of Sir George Jackson, K. C. H., from 1809 to 1816*, ed. by Lady Jackson (London, 1873, 2 v.) [867] contains letters from his brother, Francis James Jackson, British minister to the United States, 1809–1810. *The life of the Rt. Hon. Spencer Perceval, including his correspondence*, by his grandson, Spencer Walpole (London, 1874, 2 v.) [867a], correspondence of the British prime minister, 1809–12, has a chapter on the orders in council, 1812. *Dropmore MSS.* (no. 5602), v. VII–X. *Corres. Thomas Barclay* (no. 578). *The Wellesley papers; the life and correspondence of Richard Colley Wellesley, marquess Wellesley . . . secretary of state for foreign affairs, 1809–1812*, by the editor of " The Windham papers " (London, 1914, 2 v.) [868], while covering the years at the foreign office has nothing of importance regarding American affairs.

MSS.: Suggestions

See Sec. 1, above.

The MS. material on this subject is most voluminous. For a description of American (only) sources relating to impressment, see footnotes in Zimmerman (no. 807). For archives of Departments of State and Navy of the United States, see Van Tyne and Leland's *Guide* (no. 5495). A collection of miscellaneous papers of the House of Representatives now in the Library of Congress, includes petitions and memorials regarding questions of commerce, the political situation in Europe, the embargo and non-intercourse acts, in the years preceding the War of 1812. For British sources, consult Paullin and Paxson's *Guide* (no. 5577), and the serial lists and indexes of the British Public Record Office (nos. 5578, 5584–5588), including XVIII (Admiralty) and LII (Foreign Office). In addition to the official diplomatic papers, the latter list notes the private collection of papers of Francis James Jackson in the Record Office. For further analysis of guides to English and French archives, see below, pp. 890 and 915. The Library of Congress has transcripts of the main series of British despatches and instructions to 1806 (inclusive), and photostats of the same, 1806 through 1870.

The controversy over neutral rights involved all Europe. A detailed analysis of possible MS. material relating to the subject even limited to matters affecting the United States would require an extended treatise. The archives of the French foreign office, particularly the American correspondence (for indexes, see below, p. 915), reveal American relations with the Continental System. The Library of Congress now has facsimiles of the main series of diplomatic correspondence with the French legation in America to and including 1814. One should also examine American sources in Russia and the Baltic countries, and the French satellite states (Batavian Republic, Hanseatic Cities, etc.). For analysis of indexes, see below, Pt. II, ch. 3. W. E. Lingelbach, " Historical investigation and the commercial history of the Napoleonic era ", in *Am. hist. rev.*, XIX (1914) 257-281 [869] is a notable discussion of the value of consular and diplomatic correspondence, customs records, etc., in the investigation of our commercial relations with European nations at the time. There are useful bibliographies in Melvin (no. 802), and Galpin (no. 805).

Several collections of MSS. in the British Museum touch the subject: Papers of William Huskisson; of the Marquess of Wellesley (secretary of state for foreign affairs, 1809-12); of the second Earl of Liverpool (Robert Banks Jenkinson, Baron Hawkesbury). The British Historical Manuscripts Commission's *Report on the manuscripts of Earl Bathurst, preserved at Cirencester Park* (London, 1923) [870] describes a collection containing important material on British-American diplomacy, particularly in regard to the policy embodied in the orders in council. There is a collection of papers (letters and diaries, and " Notes on the United States of America collected in the years 1804-1807, 1811, 1812 ") by Sir Augustus John Foster, British minister to the United States, 1811-12, in the Library of Congress, and of Thomas Barclay (British consul general for the northeastern states before the War of 1812) in the New York Historical Society. There are other Barclay papers in the Huntington Library at San Marino, California.

The British Museum has also intercepted letters in cipher from Maret, duc de Bassano, French minister of foreign affairs, to Serurier, French minister to the United States, with letters from M. Serurier and M. Lescalier, French consul general in the United States, to the duke, regarding relations between the United States and France, Jan. 15, 1812–April 29, 1813.

See our list, p. 868, for papers of American diplomatists in Great Britain: Rufus King (minister plenipotentiary, 1796–1802), James Monroe and William Pinkney (joint ministers plenipotentiary, 1803–1811); in France: John Armstrong (minister plenipotentiary, 1804–1810), Jonathan Russell (chargé, 1810–1811), Joel Barlow (minister plenipotentiary, 1811–1812). The Library of Congress has the papers of Sylvanus Bourne (U.S. consul at Amsterdam) and of D. B. Warden (first consul general at Paris)—another smaller collection is in the Maryland Historical Society.

6. Anglo-American Frontier; War of 1812, and Peace of Ghent

Bibliographical Aids

For general aids, see Sec. 1, above. Note also Canadian historical bibliographies (nos. 4671–4677).

"Bibliography of the war of 1812", *Bostonian soc. proc.*, 1899 (Boston, 1899) 57–64 [871]. For material on the international boundary and border relations, the following indexes: *Index to volumes I–XX of the Wisconsin historical collections* (Madison, 1915) (State Historical Society of Wisconsin, *Collections*, v. XXXI) [872]; *Index to the reports and collections of the Michigan Pioneer and Historical Society*, v. I–XXX, 1874–1906 (Lansing, 1904–07, 2 v.) [873]; *Index to reports of Canadian archives, from 1872 to 1908* (Ottawa, 1909) [874–5]. Hill, *Treaties* (no. 4794), for selected bibliography of treaty of Ghent. Pratt (no. 725) has a good bibliography on border relations preceding the war of 1812. Trotter, *Canadian history; syllabus and guide* (no. 336).

Special Works

P. Murav'ev, "Anglo-Amerīkanskaia voĭna 1812–1815 [The Anglo-American war of 1812–1815]", *Biblioteka dlīa chteniīa [A reading library]*, XXXI (1838) 27–57 [876], a description of the military activities, also the political and diplomatic background, favourable to the United States. A. J. Hill, "How the Mississippi river and the Lake of the Woods became instrumental in the establishment of the northwestern boundary of the United States", *Minn. hist. soc.*

coll., VII (1893) 305-317 [877], a valuable summary, with maps, from printed sources of the history of the northwest boundary gap from 1782 until the final closing of the gap in 1823 and the final designation of the "northwesternmost point" of the Lake of the Woods in 1842. V. Tīmīrīâzev, "The emperor Alexander I as an arbiter in international disputes", *Īstorīcheskīĭ Vîestnīk* (1897) [877a] discusses the Russian arbitration under the treaty of Ghent. U. S. Grant, "The international boundary between Lake Superior and the Lake of the Woods", *Minn. hist. soc. coll.*, VIII (1898) 1-10 [878], a description of the physiography of the boundary region by an experienced geologist who had done field work in that territory. A. N. Winchell, "Minnesota's northern boundary", *ibid.*, 185-212 [879], negotiations concerning the northwest boundary, 1783 to 1842, based chiefly on *Am. state papers*, Congressional journals and documents, and Sparks' *Dipl. correspondence*. Moore, *Arbitrations* (no. 5364), v. I, for the Russian arbitration; and *Adjudications* (no. 5367), v. VI, for the "Arbitration of the title to islands in Passamaquoddy Bay and the Bay of Fundy, under article 4 of the treaty of Ghent. Hodgins, *Brit. and Am. dipl. affecting Canada* (no. 222). Smith, *England and America* (no. 340). Mahan, *Sea power and war of 1812* (no. 398), ch. 18 (v. II, 409-437) : "The peace negotiations" incorporates his article on "The negotiations at Ghent in 1814", published in *Am. hist. rev.*, XI (1905) 68-87 [880]. K. C. Babcock, *The rise of American nationality, 1811-1819* (N.Y. and London, 1906) [881], ch. 10: "Peace negotiations (1813-1815)", a summary account. Hildt, *U.S. and Russia* (no. 189), for Russian offer of mediation (1813) and Russian arbitration under the treaty of Ghent (indicates that the Russian offer of mediation was made to prevent an alliance between the United States and France). C. P. Lucas, *The Canadian war of 1812* (Oxford, Eng., 1906) [882] has a judicious and inspiring chapter on the treaty of Ghent and valuable reflections on the significance of the war in Anglo-American relations. White, *Boundary disputes* (no. 226). M. F. Ware, "A sidelight on the war of 1812", *Hist. teach. mag.*, V (1914) 319-323 [883] suggests plausibly that England was largely influenced in continuing the war after 1813, by expectations of territorial aggrandizement. F. T. Hill, "The treaty of Ghent", *Atlantic*, CXIV (1914) 231-241 [884], a delightful description of the personalities of the negotiators and the local color of the negotiation. Jules Basdevant, "Deux conventions peu connues sur le droit de la guerre (Etats-Unis d'Amérique et Grande-Bretagne, 12 mai 1813–Colombie et Espagne, 26 novembre 1820)", *Rev. gén. droit internat.*, XXI (1914) 5–29 [**885**] considers the significance in international law of the Anglo-American cartel for the exchange of prisoners. Dunning, *Brit. Emp. and U.S.* (no. 1335). W. C. Ford, "The treaty of Ghent, and after", *Wis. hist. soc. proc.*, LXII (1915) 78–106 [**886**], a thought-provoking lecture by an always luminous writer who supplemented the obvious printed American material with some of the then unprinted correspondence of J. Q. Adams. F. A. Updike, *The diplomacy of the war of 1812* (Baltimore, 1915) [**887**], a temperate and judicious study, infelicitously presented and too lengthy, presenting a rather thorough survey from the principal American and British sources, printed and unprinted. C. S. Blue, "John Henry the spy", *Canad. mag.*, XLVII (1916) 3–10 [**888**], he was sent to the United States by the governor general of Canada a few years before the war of 1812. F. A. Golder, "The Russian offer of mediation in the war of 1812", *Pol. sci. quar.*, XXXI (1916) 380–391 [**889**] is based on archives of the Russian ministry of foreign affairs, and mainly concerned with the part played by Russian diplomatists, in particular the chancellor Romanzoff. C. B. Coleman, "The Ohio Valley in the preliminaries of the war of 1812", *Miss. Valley hist. rev.*, VII (1920) 39–50 [**890**] advances the theory that it was the Ohio Valley section that virtually brought on the war and that the aim was the conquest of Canada. Lindsay, *Return of negro slaves* (no. 548) adds little to what may be found in Moore's *Arbitrations* (no. 5364). Dudley Mills, "The Duke of Wellington and the peace negotiations at Ghent in 1814", *Canad. hist. rev.*, II (1921) 19–32 [**891**] considers that a compromise peace with the United States was dictated not only by the advice of Wellington that the military and diplomatic situation of 1814 after the battle of Plattsburgh did not warrant severer British demands, but also by a very proper abandonment of a spirit for "revenge." Bemis, *N. W. boundary gap* (no. 550). Hill, *Treaties* (no. 4794) a convenient summary. C. K. Webster, "The American war and the treaty of Ghent, 1812–1814", ch. 5 (p. 522–542) in *Camb. hist. Brit. for. pol.*, v. I (no. 209) [**892**], by a profound student of this period of British diplomacy; and his *The foreign policy of Castlereagh, 1812–1815; Britain and the reconstruction of Europe* (London, 1931) [**893**], a magnificent piece of research but has little if anything regarding the United States. Also by C. K. Webster, and H. W. V. Temperley, " British policy in the publication of diplomatic documents under Castlereagh and Canning ", *Camb. hist. jour.*, I (1924) 158–169 **[893a]** which has a few comments of value regarding Castlereagh's desire for conciliation with the United States. J. F. Cady, " Western opinion and the war of 1812 ", *Ohio archaeol. and hist. quar.*, XXXIII (1924) 427–476 **[894]** anticipates the thesis independently reached by Pratt (below), except for the southern expansionist urge for Florida. L. M. Hacker, " Western land hunger and the war of 1812; a conjecture ", *Miss. Valley hist. rev.*, X (1924) 365–395 **[895]**. Mowat (no. 347a), thin. Pratt, *Expansionists of 1812* (no. 725), a very noteworthy contribution which shows that the war of 1812 was voted by the very section which suffered least from it, the West, which hoped to annex Canada and Florida, and opposed by the seaboard sections who suffered most from the maritime insults of Great Britain. C. W. Brown, *Opening of the St. Lawrence* (no. 1649). E. A. Cruikshank, " The ' Chesapeake ' crisis as it affected Upper Canada ", *Ont. hist. soc. pap.*, XXIV (1927) 281–322 **[895a]** discusses military preparations made in 1807–9 for the defense of Canada in case of war with the United States and relations with the Indians as regards a possible conflict. White, *Am. opinion of France* (no. 812). H. L. Keenleyside, *Canada and the United States* (N.Y., 1929) **[896]**, a methodical and careful historical summary based on thorough use of printed sources. Douglas, *Boundaries* (no. 211).

For biographies of American diplomatists: Peace commission (J. Q. Adams, J. A. Bayard, Albert Gallatin, Henry Clay, Jonathan Russell), ministers to Great Britain (Wm. Pinkney, Rufus King), to France (Wm. Crawford, Joel Barlow, John Armstrong), and other statesmen (Madison, Monroe, George Cabot, A. J. Dallas, H. G. Otis, Timothy Pickering), see the relevant entries and bibliographical data in the *D.A.B.* See also Beckles Willson, *Ambassadors to England* (no. 349), and his *Ambassadors to France* (no. 68).

For biographies of British diplomatists: Peace commission (Admiral Lord Gambier, Henry Goulbourn, William Adams), British minister to the United States, 1811–1812: A. J. Foster; to Russia, Lord Cathcart, see the *D.N.B.* with relevant bibliographical notes.

See also Bigham, *Prime ministers* (no. 242) ; Thornton, *Foreign sec-retaries* (no. 820) ; and Cecil, *British foreign secretaries* (no. 821).

Printed Sources

For American official documents and general source collections, see Sec. 1, above. *A.S.P., Misc.*, II, 938–956, for message of the president, with Jonathan Russell's account, and John Quincy Adams' reply, relating to certain proceedings of a majority of the American commissioners who negotiated the treaty, 1822 [**897**]. British official publications: *Brit. and for. state pap.* (no. 5416) ; H. of L., *Journals* and H. of C., *Journals* (no. 5418) ; *Parl. hist.* (no. 5410) ; *London gazette* (no. 5127a).

[John Henry], *Message from the President of the U. States, trans-mitting copies of certain documents obtained from a secret agent of the British government, employed in fomenting disaffection to the constituted authorities* (Wash., 1812) [**898**], John Henry, a British agent, was sent to New England in 1809 to report upon the political feeling in that section. In February 1812, disappointed at lack of a proper recompense, he sold the letters and documents connected with his mission to President Madison, who transmitted them to Congress. *Papers presented to Parliament in 1813* (London, 1813?) [**899**] con-sists of British foreign office correspondence relating to the war with the United States (correspondence of the Marquess Wellesley, the Earl of Liverpool, and Viscount Castlereagh, with the American ministers in London, Jan. 1810 to July 1812, etc.). [Nathaniel Atcheson], *A compressed view of the points to be discussed, in treat-ing with the United States of America, A.D. 1814* (London, 1814) [**900**], apparently compiled for the benefit of the Canadian fur trade. *State papers, on the negotiation and peace with America, 1814* (London, 1815) [**901**] consists of a statement of Madison's instruc-tions to the American plenipotentiaries for the negotiation of peace, and the correspondence between the British and American plenipo-tentiaries, Aug. 19 to Oct. 13, 1814, at Ghent. *Papers relating to the war with America* (Gt. Brit. Parl. H. of C. sess. pap., 1814–15, IX: 481, 501, 513) [**902**]. J. Q. Adams, *The duplicate letters, the fisheries and the Mississippi; documents relating to transactions at the negotiation of Ghent* (Wash., 1822; 2d ed., Louisville, 1823) [**903**], regarding the proposition at Ghent to grant to the British the right to navigate the Mississippi in return for the Newfoundland fisheries. Amos Kendall, *Letters to John Quincy Adams, relative to the fisheries and the Mississippi* (Lexington, Ky., 1823) [**904**]. *The treaty of Ghent, and the fisheries; or, The diplomatic talents of John Quincy Adams, candidly examined*, anon. (Boston, 1824) [**905**]. *Honorable Jonathan Russell's letter to John P. Van Ness, Esq.*, with an appendix (dated Milton, Sept. 10, 1828) [**906**], pamphlet in the Harvard College Library and the John Hay Library of Brown University; Russell defends himself against the charge of plotting with Clay either for the latter's political advancement or for Adams' political injury, in the discussions concerning the fisheries and the Mississippi. Henry Adams, ed., *Docs. relating to New Eng. federalism* (no. 696). "Le Canada sous le premier empire ", *Revue de révolution*, VII (1886) 97–103 [**907**] is a report written by the French minister to the United States, Turreau, probably in 1810, proposing French conquest of Canada. *Copies of papers on file in the Dominion archives at Ottawa, Canada, pertaining to the relations of the British government with the United States during [and subsequent to] the period of the war of 1812* (Lansing, Mich., 1889–90, 2 v.) (Mich. Pioneer and Hist. Soc. Coll., v. XV–XVI [**908**]. Henry Adams, "Count Edward de Crillon ", *Am. hist. rev.*, I (1895) 51–69 [**909**] prints a number of documents from the French archives regarding this Frenchman, " patron " of John Henry, the British secret agent in the United States. "Anticipation of the war of 1812 ", in the *Report on Canadian archives*, 1896 (Ottawa, 1897), 24–75 [**910**], transcripts of documents from the British archives of the years 1804–1813, including the reports of John Henry, giving information on political disagreements with the United States; and also documents concerning British relations with the American Indians (see Preface). "Records of the vice-admiralty court at Halifax, Nova Scotia; the condemnation of prizes and recaptures of the revolution and war of 1812 ", *Essex inst. hist. coll.*, XLV–XLVII (1909–1911) passim. [**911**], judgments on maritime captures. "Letters of John Quincy Adams, from Ghent, 1814 ", *Am. hist. rev.*, XV (1910) 572–574 [**912**], of interest for its spirited statement of the author's position at one of the darkest periods of the peace negotiations. "Letters of Jonathan Russell, 1815 ", *Mass. hist. soc. proc.*, XLIV (1911) 304–322 [**913**], written to Henry Clay and J. Q. Adams, in regard to American politics and relations with Great Britain. "Secret reports of John Howe, 1808", ed. by D. W. Parker, *Am. hist. rev.*, XVII (Oct. 1911, Jan. 1912) 70-102, 332-354 [914], Howe was a secret observer reporting on American political conditions to Sir Geo. Prevost, lt. governor at Halifax, somewhat similarly to the reports of John Henry to Sir James Craig, governor at Montreal. James Gallatin, *A great peacemaker* (no. 5227) includes in "Appendix", correspondence between Albert Gallatin and Alexander Baring, showing the state of feeling in England towards America and the possibilities of the success of the mission. "Letters relating to the negotiations at Ghent, 1812-1814", *Am. hist. rev.*, XX (1914) 108-129 [915], two from the Russian archives, others from the Crawford, Adams, and Bayard papers; nearly all are private letters. "Letters to Jonathan Russell, 1801-1822", *Mass. hist. soc. proc.*, XLVII (1914) 293-310 [916]. *Papers of J. A. Bayard*, ed. by Elizabeth Donnan (no. 5188) include instructions to Bayard from the secretary of state, 1813, and contain two MSS. not given in instructions first published in *A.S.P.*, *F.R.* "British Ghent commission; intended instructions", ed. by W. C. Ford, *Mass. hist. soc. proc.*, XLVIII (1915) 138-162 [917] consists of unpublished instructions and despatches of the British Ghent commission, from the British Public Record Office. *John Quincy Adams and others on the peace of Ghent, 1814*, ed. by S. E. Morison (Boston, 1917?) (Old South Leaflets, no. 211) [918], extracts from the writings of Adams, despatches of the Duke of Wellington, and other documents. *The treaty of Ghent and negotiations that followed, 1814-1818*, ed. by S. E. Morison (Boston, 1917?) (Old South Leaflets, no. 212) [919] is another selection of documents. "Otis Ammidon to Jonathan Russell", *Mass. hist. soc. proc.*, LIV (1922) 78-79 [920], a letter of Feb. 20, 1815, discussing the termination of the war and the conclusion of peace. "Jonathan Russell to John N. Forbes", *ibid.*, 76-77 [921], a letter of Jan. 21, 1815, mainly devoted to a discussion of the treaty. "Robert M. Patterson to Jonathan Russell", *ibid.*, 79-80 [922], letter of Feb. 20, 1815, dealing with the treaty of peace.[5]

---

[5] A paper by J. P. Pritchett, on "The Red River valley and the war of 1812", was read at the 46th Annual Meeting of the American Historical Association, 1931. It gave the history of an abortive scheme to restrict the limits of Louisiana Territory and to claim the Red River valley for the English.

For authentic text of the treaty, see Miller, *Treaties* [6] (no. 5371).
For the printed writings of American diplomatists and statesmen
(enumerated above, under " Special Works ", biographies), see our
list on p. 756.

" Writings " (memoirs, correspondence, etc.) of British statesmen: *Memoirs and corres. of Castlereagh* (no. 864), v. IX–XII. include many letters from Charles Bagot, Lord Bathurst, and others,
to Castlereagh, regarding affairs in America (Ghent treaty, etc.).
Dropmore MSS. (no. 5602), v. VII–X, for letters of this period
relating to American affairs. *Supplementary despatches and memoranda of Field Marshal Arthur, Duke of Wellington*, ed. by his son,
the Duke of Wellington (London, 1858–72, 15 v.) **[924]**, v. IX includes a series of letters from Goulbourn to Bathurst written during
the negotiations at Ghent (not published in the *Bathurst papers* (no.
870, above) ; (see also Dudley Mills (no. 891), based on the *Supplementary despatches*). *Corres. Thomas Barclay* (no. 578).

MSS.: Suggestions

See Secs. 1, 2, and 5, above.

The official papers of the British (including Canadian) and American governments are therein indicated. The papers of the British
commission at Ghent are listed in no. 5578, p. 6. The papers of the
American commissioners at Ghent have been preserved in great part,
and extensively printed (see " Printed Sources " immediately above).
For personal papers of commissioners (J. Q. Adams, James A.
Bayard, Henry Clay, Wm. H. Crawford, and Albert Gallatin), and
of William Shaler, attached to the Ghent commission, see our list
on p. 868 below. There are in the Library of Congress some letters
of John Randolph of Roanoke to James Monroe, regarding the treaty
of Ghent; and copies, transferred from the Department of State,
of the papers of the British emissary, John Henry, relating to the
New England intrigue, 1809–1812. For Federalist sentiment, see
papers of Timothy Pickering (p. 865) and others in the Massachusetts Historical Society. The Papers of Jonathan Russell are in the
Wheaton collection in Brown University Library.

The Public Archives of Canada has a volume of private letters to
Lord Bathurst (not calendared in its *Reports*), including among

---

[6] The text of the treaty has also been published recently in *Treaties and agreements
affecting Canada in force between His Majesty and the United States of America, with
subsidiary documents*, 1814–1925 (Ottawa, 1927) **[923]**.

them 21 letters from Henry Goulbourn, dated from Ghent, 1814, some of them printed in *Supplementary despatches of Wellington* (no. 924). The same Archives has also the papers of the Court of Vice-Admiralty at Halifax from about 1787 to about 1820 (181 volumes and portfolios); these include the records of prize cases during the war of 1812. For description of photocopies in the Library of Congress from the Canadian archives (Diplomatic correspondence of ministers or *chargés* at Washington with governors and other officials in Canada), see p. 898.

For the notable private collections of British statesmen: Grenville. Bathurst, Portland, see the 13th, 14th, 15th, and 18th *Reports* of the Historical Manuscripts Commission (nos. 5593 and 5603). The Liverpool papers (above, p. 146), and the papers of the Marquess of Wellesley are in the British Museum.

CHAPTER VI
THE BARBARY STATES, 1775–1815

Bibliographical Aids

For general aids, see Evans (no. 4639); Sabin (no. 4655); Larned (no. 4657); Griffin (no. 4658); *Writings* (no. 4661); C., H. and T. (no. 4662); *Am. secs. state* (no. 4796), see "Bibliographical notes". *Guide hist. lit.* (no. 4634).

Winsor, *America*, v. VII (no. 4782), 418–419, for Tripolitan war. H. S. Ashbee, *A bibliography of Tunisia* (London, 1889) [925]. Sir R. Lambert Playfair, "The bibliography of the Barbary States, pt. I: Tripoli and the Cyrenaica", in Royal Geographical Society, *Supplementary papers*, v. II (London, 1889), 557–614 [926]; supplemented by the author's *Bibliography of Algeria, . . . to 1887* (London, 1889), from the *Supplementary papers* of the Royal Geographical Society, v. II, pt. 2, p. 129–430; and *Supplement . . . to 1895* (London, 1898) [927]. Sir R. L. Playfair and Robert Brown, "A bibliography of Morocco, from the earliest times to the end of 1891", in the Royal Geographical Society, *Supplementary papers*, v. III, pt. 3 (London, 1892), 201–476 [928]. Federico Minutilli, *Bibliografia della Libia; catalogo alfabetico e metodico di tutte le pubblicazioni . . . sulla Tripolitania, la Cirenaica, il Fezzan e le confinanti regioni del deserto* (Turin, 1903) [929]. Harbeck, *Bibliog. U.S. navy* (no. 791), "Tripoli expedition" (p. 12–14), and "War with Algiers" (p. 26). Ugo Ceccherini, *Bibliografia della Libia* (Rome, 1915) [930]. E. Rouard de Card, *Livres françaises des XVII*e *& XVIII*e *siècles concernant les états Barbaresques* (Paris, 1911; suppl., 1917) [931]. Irwin (no. 943) has a useful bibliography which analyses the MS. sources in the Department of State.

Special Works

For general historical works, see Sec. 1 of Chapts. III, IV, and V, each.

Robert Greenhow, *The history and present condition of Tripoli, with some accounts of the other Barbary states* (Richmond, Va.,

1835) [**932**] includes the history of their relations with the United States to 1830; the author was a versatile and able scholar, who as an employee in the Department of State had available original records, which, while not cited methodically, seem to have been used. Greenhow had pretentions to a stately style in a period greatly influenced by Walter Scott. " The United States and the Barbary states ", anon., *Atlantic mo.*, VI (1860) 641-657 [**933**]. Stanley Lane-Poole, *The story of the Barbary corsairs* (N.Y., 1890) [**934**], a most absorbing general history of the piratical depredations of the Barbary corsairs, based on secondary accounts. Paul Deslandres, *L'ordre des Trinitaires pour le rachat des captifs* (Paris, 1903) [**935**] traces the history of captivity of Christians by the Barbary corsairs as revealed in the archives of this benevolent ecclesiastical order. G. W. Allen, *Our navy and the Barbary corsairs* (Boston and N.Y., 1905) [**936**], the standard account of the naval operations attendant upon diplomacy. R. S. Rodgers, " Closing events of the war with Tripoli, 1804-1805; McMaster's account compared with official records and with other reliable authorities ", *U.S.N. inst. proc.*, XXXIV (1908) 889-916 [**937**] reprints numerous and lengthy extracts from relevant state papers to show that the eminent historian was mistaken in stating that Eaton withdrew from Derne because of Commodore Rodgers. Émile Dupuy, *Etudes d'histoire d'Amérique Américains & Barbaresques (1776-1824)* (Paris, 1910) [**938**], the clearest and best proportioned account to date, resting on printed sources. C. O. Paullin, *Diplomatic negotiations of American naval officers, 1778-1883* (Baltimore, 1912), 43-121 [**939**] covers the diplomacy of the United States with the Barbary States, illuminated by his skilful use of the archives of the Navy Department—an unusually creditable account. Lord Teignmouth (Henry Noel Shore), " British protection of American shipping in the Mediterranean, 1784-1810 ", *Unit. ser. mag.*, n.s. LXX (1919) 169-178 [**940**], written at the time of the Versailles peace discussions in the U.S. Senate, and using American activities against the Corsairs to preach a sermon on the text that no " great " people can command respect who " shirk their part with impunity when civilization is at stake." Hayden, *Senate and treaties* (no. 376), for the treaties with Algiers, Tunis, and Tripoli. P. J. Foik, " In the clutches of the Barbary corsairs ", *Ill. Cath. hist. rev.*, IX (1926) 162-176 [**941**] reprints from contemporary newspapers, documents (mostly diplomatic and consular reports, many of which may be found in *Dipl. corres.*, *1783–1789* (no. 5340)), and letters of captured American sea captains. *Am. secs. state*, v. I–III (no. 4796). Woolery, *Jefferson and foreign policy* (no. 279) has a chapter on the negotiations with the Barbary States, 1789–1793, drawn largely from Jefferson's letters printed and unprinted. Enrico de Agostini, " Una spedizione americana in Cirenaica nel 1805 ", *Riv. colonie ital.*, II (1928) 721–732, III (1929) 41–56 [942], only value is a photograph of ruins of the American fort at Derne. Wriston, *Executive agents* (no. 4799), for material relating to the special agents to the Barbary States (John Paul Jones, Thos. Barclay, David Humphreys, Joel Barlow, etc.). R. W. Irwin, *The diplomatic relations of the United States with the Barbary powers, 1776–1816* (Chapel Hill, N.C., 1931) [943], so far the only attempt to write a history from unpublished sources in the Department of State. Miller, *Treaties* (no. 5371), v. II has historical notes of great value.

For biographies of Wm. Bainbridge, Thos. Barclay, Joel Barlow, James Barron, J. L. Cathcart, Richard Dale, Stephen Decatur, Wm. Eaton, Isaac Hull, David Humphreys, Ralph Izard, John Jay, Jefferson, Rufus King, John Lamb, Tobias Lear, Madison, Marshall, Mordecai M. Noah, Richard O'Brien, David Porter, Edward Preble, John Rodgers, and Wm. Shaler, see the relevant entries and bibliographical data in the *D.A.B.* Note also, H. A. S. Dearborn, *The life of William Bainbridge, esq., of the United States navy*, ed. by James Barnes (Princeton, 1931) [944], a biography prepared while the subject was alive (completed in 1816) by an author who appears to have had some access to papers and information supplied by the commodore, now printed for the first time from the (recently found) original manuscript. F. R. Rodd, *General William Eaton; the failure of an idea* (N.Y., 1932) [945] contains little original work, and many long quotations from previously printed letters of Eaton and official publications.

Printed Sources

See Chs. III, IV, and V, Sec. 1 in each.

For American official documents and general source collections, see *A.S.P., F.R.*, v. I–IV (no. 5341) ; *A.S.P., Nav. aff.*, v. I (no. 5341b) ; *Dipl. corres. U.S.* (no. 5340) ; *Ann. Cong.* (no. 5382) ; *Abridg. debates* (no. 5386) ; Wharton, *Revol. dipl. corres.* (no. 5339) ; Richardson (no. 5335); *Repts. Sen. com. for. rel.* (no. 5388), meager and poorly arranged record previous to 1816; *Jour. Cont. Cong.* (no. 5379); Burnett, *Letters* (no. 5380).

For texts of the Barbary treaties of the United States, 1786–1816, see Miller, *Treaties* (no. 5371), which has important corrections in translations, with some original Arabic texts, accompanied by most enlightening notes.

For guides to American newspapers, see Brigham (no. 5012); and Library of Congress (nos. 5030, 5031).

[Mathew Carey], *A short account of Algiers, . . . with a concise view of the origin of the rupture between Algiers and the United States* (Phila., 1794) **[946]**, appendix contains letters of 1793–94. John Fess, *Journal of the captivity and sufferings of John Fess, several years a prisoner in Algiers* (Newburyport, 1797) **[947]**. Jonathan Cowdery, *American captives in Tripoli; or, Dr. Cowdery's journal in miniature, kept during his late captivity in Tripoli*, 2d ed. (Boston, 1806) **[948]**. William Ray, *The American tars in Tripolitan slavery; containing an account of the loss and capture of the United States frigate Philadelphia; treatment and sufferings of the prisoners; . . . public transactions of the United States with that regency . . .* (Troy, 1808; reprinted, N.Y., 1911) **[949]**, by one of the captured and enslaved seamen. Charles Prentiss, *The life of the late Gen. William Eaton; several years an officer in the United States' army, consul at the regency of Tunis* (Brookfield, 1813) **[950]** consists mainly of his letters. M. M. Noah, *Correspondence and documents relative to the attempt to negotiate for the release of the American captives at Algiers,* 1813–1814 (Wash., 1816) **[951]**; and by the same writer, who had been consul in Tunis, *Travels in England, France, Spain, and the Barbary States, in the years 1813–14 and 15* (N.Y., 1819) **[952]**. C. W. Goldsborough, *The United States' naval chronicle,* v. I (Wash., 1824) **[953]** contains documents of the years 1790–1796 relating to the depredations of the Barbary corsairs and diplomatic negotiations with the Barbary States. William Shaler, *Sketches of Algiers, political, historical, and civil* (Boston, 1826) **[954]** prints extracts from his journal kept while consul-general at Algiers, 1823–24. C. C. Felton, *The life of William Eaton* (Boston, 1838) **[955]** prints selections from Eaton's letters and official correspondence. "Nathaniel Cutting's journal of an embassy to Algiers in 1793, under Col. David Humphreys", *Historical magazine, IV*

(1860) 262–264, 296–298, 359–363 [**956**], in 1793 he was appointed by President Washington to proceed to Lisbon, with secret despatches to Col. Humphreys and to act as secretary of that commission to Algiers. "Commodore Preble and Tripoli", *Am. hist. record*, I (1872) 53–60 [**957**] contains the diary of Commodore Preble, 1803–1805. J. R. Soley, "Operations of the American squadron under Commodore Edward Preble in 1803–04", *U.S. naval inst. proc.*, V (1879) 51–98 [**958**] prints several of Preble's letters and journal of operations before Tripoli in 1804 (this journal is also pub. in the *Magazine of American history*, III (1879). C. B. Todd, *Life and letters of Joel Barlow* (N.Y., 1886) [**959**] reproduces a considerable number of Barlow's letters, written in Algiers. *Corres. of Rufus King* (no. 5248), for letters dealing with his activities in regard to the Barbary States during his mission to England. J. L. Cathcart, *The captives*, comp. by his daughter, J. B. C. Newkirk (La Porte, Ind., 1899) [**960**] is an account of Cathcart's experiences while a prisoner in Algiers, from 1785 to 1796; also by the same writer, *Tripoli . . . letter book by James Leander Cathcart, first consul to Tripoli, and last letters from Tunis*, comp. by his daughter, J. B. C. Newkirk (La Porte, Ind., 1901) [**961**], consisting of letters of 1799–1802. *The Hull-Eaton correspondence during the expedition against Tripoli, 1804–1805;* ed. from a letter book in the library of the American Antiquarian Society, by C. H. Lincoln (Worcester, Mass., 1911) [**962**]. F. L. Humphreys, *David Humphreys* (no. 5241a) prints numerous letters.

For the printed writings of persons connected with Barbary diplomacy (enumerated above under "Special Works") consult our list on p. 756 and the *D.A.B.* We have, however, listed above the outstanding prints of journals, correspondence, etc., dealing specifically with this subject.

MSS.: Suggestions

See Chs. III, IV, and V, above. Paullin (no. 151) and Irwin (no. 943) have analyses of relevant material respectively in the archives of the Departments of the Navy and State (see below, Pt. II, ch. 3) for further guides and indexes thereto. The diplomatic and consular correspondence of the European nations, particularly France, Great Britain, and Spain (see below, Pt. II, ch. 3 for guides and indexes) with the Barbary States, should prove revealing of the relations of the United States with the Corsair states; so far as we are aware it has never been worked.

The papers of Washington, John Adams, John Quincy Adams, Franklin, Jefferson, Rufus King, Gouverneur Morris, James Monroe, Thomas Pinckney, William Short, and other prominent American statesmen and diplomatists of the period touch this subject (for discussion, see our lists of papers of the presidents (p. 862), secretaries of state (p. 865), and American diplomatists (p. 868). Some particular collections of private papers are: in the Library of Congress, the letter book of Chas. D. Coxe, 1806–1809, consul at Tunis; 26 vols. of correspondence of Gen. Wm. Eaton, 1801–1806; a few pieces from Tobias Lear, 1797–1813; the papers of Commodore David Porter; in the Harvard College Library, the papers of Joel Barlow; in the Huntington Library, correspondence and letter books (1794–1805) of William Eaton, while agent to the Barbary States (9 volumes, not yet catalogued); in the New York Public Library, the papers of Consul James L. Cathcart. For the papers of William Shaler (commissioner to conclude peace, 1815, and consul general at Algiers, 1815–1829), see p. 881.

CHAPTER VII

FLORIDA, HISPANIC AMERICA, AND THE MONROE DOCTRINE
1815–1826

1. In General

Bibliographical Aids

For general aids, see Evans (no. 4639) ; Sabin (no. 4655) ; Larned (no. 4657) ; Griffin (no. 4658) ; *Writings* (no. 4661) ; C. H. and T. (no. 4662) ; *Am. secs. state* (no. 4796), for " Bibliographical Notes "; *Guide hist. lit.* (no. 4634) ; Myers (no. 5399), for collections of treaties. Miller, *Treaties* (no. 5371), v. I, 39–54, for " Bibliography of United States treaty collections."

For contemporary periodical references (notably *Niles' register*), consult *Poole's index* (no. 4995).

For lists of newspapers, see Brigham (no. 5012), Library of Congress *Check list* (no. 5030), and nos. 5004–5047.

See also Spanish historical bibliographies (nos. 4758–4760) ; and Spanish-American historical bibliographies (nos. 4678–4725).

General Works

Of general histories of the United States, see Hildreth (no. 4779) ; Von Holst (no. 4780) ; McMaster (no. 4781) ; Winsor (no. 4782) ; Channing (no. 4784). See also *Am. secs. state*, v. IV (no. 4796) ; and Wriston (no. 4799). Miller, *Treaties* (no. 5371), v. III, for historical notes of great value.

F. E. Chadwick, *U.S. and Spain* (no. 108). J. H. Latané, *The United States and Latin America* (Garden City, N.Y., 1920) [963] cites few Spanish sources or references, and for later period and contemporary discussion is now superseded by Lockey, and by Stuart. J. B. Lockey, *Pan-Americanism; its beginnings* (N.Y., 1920; in

Spanish translation, with added notes (Caracas, 1927)) **[964]**, a painstaking study, based almost wholly on printed sources; its scope extends beyond the title to include a general history of the United States and the movement for independence in Hispanic America. *Camb. hist. Brit. for. pol.* (no. 209), v. II, chs. 1 and 2. G. H. Stuart, *Latin America and the United States*, 2d ed., thoroughly rev. (N.Y. and London, 1928) **[965]**, so far the best summary account by a scholar who has a command of the relevant literature from both continents, but stresses the more recent at expense of earlier periods. Bécker, *Relaciones exteriores* (no. 723).

For an enumeration, without assessment, of general histories of Hispanic America, see A. C. Wilgus, *The histories of Hispanic America; a bibliographical essay*, issued by the Columbus Memorial Library of the Pan American Union (Wash., 1932) **[966]**.

For biographies of J. Q. Adams, J. C. Calhoun, Henry Clay, Andrew Jackson, Jefferson, Madison, and Monroe, see the relevant entries and bibliographical data in the *D.A.B.*, and (except Jackson) in *Am. secs. state* (no. 4796). Note also, B. C. Clark, *John Quincy Adams, " Old man eloquent "*[1] (Boston, 1932) **[967]**, an edifying and well-written " human-interest " biography, based on standard secondary works and obvious printed sources.

For British statesmen, see Thornton, *Foreign secretaries* (no. 820); Bigham, *Prime ministers* (no. 242); Cecil, *British foreign secretaries* (no. 821); the *D.N.B.;* Temperley, *Canning* (no. 1152); Webster, *Castlereagh* (no. 893).

Printed Sources

For American official documents and general source collections, see *Jour. exec. proc. Sen.* (no. 5387); *A.S.P., F.R.* (no. 5341); *Ann. Cong.* (no. 5382); Wharton, *Digest* (no. 5366); *Abridg. debates* (no. 5386); Richardson (no. 5335); *Repts. Sen. com. for. rel.* (no. 5388), meager and poorly arranged record previous to 1816; Moore's *Digest* (no. 5365). Myers (no. 5399), for collections of treaties.

For texts of treaties, see Miller, *Treaties* (no. 5371).

For lists of American newspapers, see nos. 5004–5047; particularly Brigham (no. 5012); and Library of Congress *Check list* (no. 5030).

For contemporary pamphlets, etc., consult Evans, *American catalogue* (no. 5639).

---

[1] Published since the volume of the *D.A.B.* which contains the article on Adams.

T. H. Benton, *Thirty years' view; or, A history of the working of the American government for thirty years, from 1820 to 1850, chiefly taken from the Congress debates, the private papers of General Jackson, and the speeches of ex-Senator Benton* (N.Y., 1854–56, 2 v.) [968] for contemporary views.

For printed writings of J. Q. Adams, J. C. Calhoun, Henry Clay, Andrew Jackson, Jefferson, Madison, and Monroe, see our lists on pp. 862–883.

For printed writings of British statesmen, see *Castlereagh* (no. 864); *Liverpool* (no. 866); and *Some official correspondence of Lord Canning*, ed. by E. J. Stapleton (London, 1887, 2 v.) [969], containing correspondence of 1821–1825.

MSS.: Suggestions

For the archives of the Department of State, see Pt. II, chs. 1 and 3. The diplomatic, and other archives of Great Britain, France, and Spain (including Cuba) are indispensable for the proper investigation of any of the topics included in this chapter.[2] For the appropriate guides, catalogues, and indexes, and American facsimiles, see below: Great Britain, p. 890; France, p. 915; and Spain, p. 898.

The important papers of John Quincy Adams are inaccessible insofar as they are not printed (see our list, p. 863). For the papers of Jefferson, Madison, Monroe, Henry Clay, J. C. Calhoun, and Andrew Jackson, see our lists of the papers of presidents, and secretaries of state, below, pp. 862–867.

2. The Florida Question and the Transcontinental Boundary [3]

Bibliographical Aids

For general aids, see Sec. 1, above.

For special bibliographies on Florida, see Ch. V, Sec. 3.

Special Works

C. B. Vignoles, *The history of the Floridas, 1497–1821* (Brooklyn, 1824), originally published as *Observations upon the Floridas* (N.Y.,

---

[2] Perkins (no. 1172) has shown how the sources extend even into other state archives.

[3] See also Ch. V, sec. 2 (Diplomacy of Louisiana), sec. 3 (Spain; West and East Florida), and sec. 6 (War of 1812 and Peace of Ghent) above.

We are indebted for suggestions in this section to Dr. Philip C. Brooks, who is preparing a publication on *The Adams-Onís treaty of 1819* (no. 984).

1823) **[970]**, an early history of the Floridas, based on such information as was then available, apparently written to satisfy the demand in the United States for general information about the newly acquired territory, contains official papers, etc., 1783-1823. J. L. Williams, *A view of West Florida, embracing its geography, topography . . . with an appendix treating of its antiquities, land titles, and canals . . . with maps* (Phila., 1827) **[971]**. Gayarré (no. 308). Daniel Webster, "Acquisition of the Floridas", *Mass. hist. soc. proc.*, XI (1871) 329-330 **[972]**, "probably written as a college exercise." J. L. M. Curry, "The acquisition of Florida", *Mag. Am. hist.*, XIX (1888) 286-301 **[973]**, an undocumented narrative apparently based on the documents printed in *A.S.P., F.R.*; and by the same writer (minister to Spain, 1885-8), *Diplomatic services of George William Erving* (Cambridge, 1890) (communicated to the Massachusetts Historical Society) **[974]**, though the documents are not specifically cited this article is stated, in Mr. R. C. Winthrop's preface to it, to be based on material in the archives of the U.S. legation in Madrid. Hinsdale, *Southern boundary* (no. 494). James Schouler, "Monroe and the Rhea letter", in his *Historical briefs* (N.Y., 1896), 97-120, also pub. in the *Mag. Am. hist.*, XII (1884) 308-322 **[975]**, John Rhea asserted in 1831 that President Monroe, in 1818, had sent by Rhea to Andrew Jackson private instructions allowing Jackson to invade Spanish Florida even into Spanish garrisons in response to a suggestion of Jackson that this could be done without implicating the government. Monroe on his deathbed denied this under oath. Schouler discusses the evidence and concludes the "Rhea letter" was probably never written. Moore, *Arbitrations* (no. 5364), v. V, 4487-4531, for payment of claims assumed by the United States under the Florida treaty. Callahan, *Cuba* (no. 1804-1805), for Cuba's relation to the Florida question. R. C. H. Catterall, "A French diplomat and the treaty with Spain, 1819", *Am. hist. rev.*, XI (1906) 495-496 **[976]** is an abstract of a paper dealing with the part played by Hyde de Neuville, French minister at Washington, in securing a peaceful settlement of the disputed issues between the United States and Spain. H. B. Fuller, *The purchase of Florida; its history and diplomacy* (Cleveland, 1906) **[977]**, a full account, but is blind to the Spanish archives. Jerónimo Bécker, "La cesión de las Floridas", *España moderna*, CCXL (1908) 41-70 **[978]** is mostly reproduced in his *Historia* (no. 723). Chadwick, *U.S.*

and Spain (no. 108), ch. 7, for the Florida treaty and Jackson's invasion of Florida. F. W. Hackett, *The Meade claim* (Wash., 1910) **[979]** is a brief survey of facts attending the ratification by Spain of the treaty. Marshall, *Western boundary* (no. 768). Hill, *Treaties* (no. 4794), a readable summary. Brevard, *Florida* (no. 723a). Hoskins, *Hisp. Am. policy of Clay* (no. 1071). T. F. Davis, *MacGregor's invasion of Florida, 1817; together with an account of his successors, Irwin, Hubbard, and Aury on Amelia Island, East Florida* (Jacksonville, Fla., 1928), reprinted from the *Quarterly* of the Florida Historical Society, v. VII **[980]**, a rather detailed account, resting on *A.S.P., F.R.*, and contemporary Savannah and Charleston newspapers, with a useful map of operations on Amelia Island. R. K. Wyllys, " The filibusters of Amelia Island ", *Ga. hist. quar.*, XII (1928) 297-325 **[981]** is concerned with their share in bringing about the occupation of East and West Florida in 1817-18. Rippy, *Rivalry* (no. 1077) for the English attempt at mediation between Spain and the United States. Douglas, *Boundaries* (no. 211). Lindley, *Foreign policy of Henry Clay* (no. 1083). W. R. de Villa-Urrutia, *Fernán-Núñez, el embajador* (Madrid, 1931) **[982]**, the 7th Count of Fernán Núñez was ambassador to Great Britain, 1812-17. P. C. Brooks, " The Pacific Coast's first international boundary delineation, 1816-1819 ", *Pacific hist. rev.*, III (1934) 62-79 **[983]** utilizes hitherto unexploited Spanish archives to show the significance of the Adams-Onís negotiations in establishing a transcontinental boundary, and the various alternate lines, suggested during those negotiations, in the Pacific Northwest. This is part of his study nearing completion of *The Adams-Onís treaty of 1819* **[984]**, the only adequate study of the subject because it has thoroughly digested the Spanish archives as well as those of the United States. It correctly pictures the treaty of 1819 with Spain not as " the Florida treaty " but as a treaty which delimited a transcontinental frontier. J. B. Lockey, " The Florida intrigues of José Álvarez de Toledo ", *Fla. hist. soc. quar.*, XII (1934) 145-178 **[984a]**, wide research in many scattered sources shows Toledo was probably acting in the interests of Spain while professing to be a Mexican revolutionist in the United States.

For biographies of American statesmen (J. Q. Adams, Henry Clay, Albert Gallatin, Andrew Jackson, James Monroe) and diplomatists (ministers to Spain: G. W. Erving, 1814-1819, and John

Forsyth, 1819–1823; to Great Britain: J. Q. Adams, 1815–1817, and Richard Rush, 1817–1825; to France: A. Gallatin, 1815–1823), see the relevant entries and bibliographical data in the *D.A.B.*

Brief biographical notes regarding Francisco D. Vives, Spanish minister to the United States, 1820–1821, and E. Pérez de Castro, Spanish minister of state, are found in Espasa (no. 4974). For sketch of diplomatic activities of José García de Léon y Pizarro, Spanish minister of state, see Villa Urrutia, *Fernán Núñez* (no. 982). A brief biographical sketch of Luis de Onís, Spanish minister to the United States, 1809–1819, is given in *Appleton's* (no. 4925), v. IV, 582.

For brief sketches of Hyde de Neuville, French minister to the United States, 1816–1822, see M. A. Boullée, *Biographies contemporaines* (Paris, 1868, 2 v.), v. I, 256–274 [985], and Edmond Biré, *Mémoires et souvenirs (1789–1830)*, 1st ser. (Paris, 1894), no. 3599 [985a].

Printed Sources

For American official publications and general source collections, see Sec. 1, above.

Benjamin Vaughan, *Eastern boundary of Louisiana* (no. 735). *Mr. Adams' defence of General Jackson's conduct in the Seminole war* n.p., 1818?) [986], also pub. in *A.S.P.*, *F.R.*, v. IV, 539–554, John Quincy Adams's letter, as secretary of state, to G. W. Erving, American minister to Spain, on the subject of Jackson's invasion of Florida and the execution of Arbuthnot and Ambrister. *Official correspondence between Don Luis de Onís . . . and John Quincy Adams . . . in relation to the Floridas and the boundaries of Louisiana, with other matters in dispute between the two governments* (London, 1818) [987], also printed in *A.S.P.*, *F.R.*, IV, 450–479. Vicente Pazos, *Exposition, remonstrance and protest* (no. 1100). *Narrative of a voyage to the Spanish Main [1819] in the ship " Two Friends "; the occupation of Amelia Island by McGregor, etc., sketches of the Province of East Florida and anecdotes illustrative of the habits and manners of the Seminole Indians, with an appendix containing a detail of the Seminole war and the execution of Arbuthnot and Ambrister* (London, 1819) [988]. J. F. Rattenberry, " Remarks on the cession of the Floridas to the United States of America, and on the necessity of acquiring the island of Cuba by Great

Britain ", in the *Pamphleteer* (London), XV (1819) 261–280 [989]. *Memorial of Major General Andrew Jackson, March 6, 1820*, printed by order of the Senate (Wash., 1820) (16th Cong., 1st sess., Sen. Doc. 73) [990], in justification of his course in the first Seminole war. Luis de Onís, *Memoria sobre las negociaciones entre España y los Estados-Unidos de América, que dieron motivo al tratado de 1819* (Madrid, 1820, 2 v.) [991] was the author's defense of his negotiation of the treaty of 1819 against attacks of his countrymen. It has an appendix containing many documents (including the 3 publications signed " Verus "), not printed in the English translation, *Memoir upon the negotiations between Spain and the United States . . .*, in 1 vol. (Wash., 1821). José Callava, *Manifiesto sobre las tropelías y bejaciones que cometió el gobernador americano de Panzacola . . . contra . . . nombrado para la entrega de Florida occidental a los Estados Unidos* (Havana, 1821) [992]. *Message from the President . . . transmitting a report of the secretary of state, with the documents relative to a misunderstanding between Andrew Jackson and Elijius Fromentin, judge of a court therein; also the correspondence between the secretary of state and the minister of Spain, on certain proceedings in that territory & c.c.* (Wash., 1822) (17th Cong., 1st sess. House. Doc. 42) [993], in regard to proceedings for carrying into effect the treaty of 1819. M. L. de Vidaurre, *Cartas americanas, políticas y morales, que contienen muchas reflecciones sobre la guerra civil de las Américas* (Phila., 1823, 2 v.) [994] contains one or two letters from Madrid with highly subjective reflections on the cession of the Floridas. *Concise narrative of Gen. Jackson's first invasion of Florida*, by "Aristides " (N.Y., 1827) [995] (Library of Congress ascribes it to W. P. Van Ness), an election pamphlet calculated to show the blamelessness of Jackson's military conduct in Florida. *Correspondence between Gen. Andrew Jackson and John C. Calhoun . . . on the subject of the course of the latter, in the deliberations of the cabinet of Mr. Monroe, on the occurrences in the Seminole war* (Wash., 1831) [996], ventilating a famous political quarrel which broke out in 1830 when Calhoun's enemies informed President Jackson that Calhoun, as secretary of war in Monroe's cabinet in 1818, favored punishing Jackson for his invasion of Florida. The documents are valuable for question of American aggression in 1818. Benton, *Thirty years* (no. 968), v. I, for Jackson's exposition of the Florida conquest, and other contemporary material. [C. B. Collier], *Spain and the United States. The treaty of 1819. To the Senate and House of Representatives: Spain calls upon the United States for the fulfillment of the ninth article of the said treaty* (Wash., 1880) [997–8]. *Statement showing the payments and awards of the commissioners appointed under the conventions between the United States and France, April 30, 1803, and July 4, 1831, and between the United States and Spain, Feb. 22, 1819* (Wash.: Govt. Print. Off., 1886) [999].[4] *Monroe's messages on Florida* (Boston, 1902) (Old South Leaflets, no. 129) [1000]. "Informe relativo a los actos de agresión, hostilidad, etc., cometidos por el gobierno de los Estados Unidos de Norte América contra los dominios de España en las Floridas y sus dependencias", *Boletín del Archivo Nacional* (Havana), XIII (1914) 9–21 [1001], Juan Ventura Morales to Alexandro Ramírez, signed Havana, Nov. 3, 1817. "Letter of William Wirt, 1819 ", *Am. hist. rev.*, XXV (1920) 692–695 [1002] gives the writer's opinion in regard to the measures proposed to meet the refusal of the king of Spain to ratify the treaty, namely, the occupation of the Floridas. Brevard, *Florida* (no. 723a), for correspondence of American and Spanish officials, 1818, and correspondence concerning the transfer of government. Gregor MacGregor and John Skinner, " Letters relating to MacGregor's attempted conquest of East Florida, 1817", *Fla. hist. soc. quar.*, V (1926) 54–57 [1003], communicated to John Quincy Adams apprising him of MacGregor's design for a filibustering expedition to bring Florida ultimately into the United States as an independent state. *Pichardo's treatise* (no. 786).

For authentic text of the treaty and useful notes, see Miller, *Treaties* (no. 5371), v. II.

For the printed writings of American statesmen and diplomatists (enumerated above, under " Special Works "), see our list on p. 756.

Memoirs, etc., of foreign diplomatists: *Castlereagh* (no. 864); and *The diary and correspondence of Henry Wellesley, first lord Cowley, 1790–1846*, ed. by F. A. Wellesley (London, 1930) [1004], giving brief reference to the reception of the treaty by the King and Council of State, in the diary of the British minister to Spain at this time. J. G. Hyde de Neuville, *Mémoires et souvenirs* (Paris, 1890–92, 3 v.), and English translation and abridgment, *Memoirs of Baron Hyde de Neuville; outlaw, exile, ambassador* (London, 1913,

---

[4] For history of these claims, see Moore's *Arbitrations* (no. 5364), V, 4481–4531.

2 v.) [1005], the memoirs of the French minister to the United
States, 1816–22; deal meagerly with his good offices between Adams
and Onís in the negotiations of 1817–19. *Memorias de la vida del
Exmo. Señor D. José García de León y Pizarro escritas por el
mismo* (Madrid, 1894–97, 3 v.) [1006], the autobiographical memoirs
of the Spanish minister of state at the time of the negotiations,
which includes also (v. III) important letters and documents relative to the treaty.

MSS.: Suggestions

See Sec. 1, this chapter, for references to American and foreign
archives, and papers of American presidents and secretaries of
state, 1815–1826, and of Andrew Jackson, and J. C. Calhoun.

Particularly important is Hill's *Catalogue* (no. 5650) and Mabel
M. Manning, "The East Florida papers in the Library of Congress",
Hisp. Am. hist. rev., X (1930) 392–397 [1007], which describes the
collection of original MSS. comprising the official correspondence
of the government of East Florida from the time of the Spanish
recovery of that region in 1784 to its acquisition by the United States
in 1821.

See particularly Ch. V, sec. 3.

The Library of Congress now has photocopies of the main
series of signed despatches, with enclosures, and drafts of instructions (from the *Archivo Histórico Nacional*) of the correspondence
of the Spanish foreign office with Onís, its minister in Washington,
and typescripts of the signed instructions (from the *Departamento
de Estado*); as well as of much of the relevant material on Florida
listed by Hill's *Catalogue* (no. 5650). It also has photocopies of the
documents in *legajo* 8294, "*Embajada de Inglaterra*", *Sección de
Estado*, in the *Archivo General de Simancas*, consisting of papers
relating to the proposed mediation of Great Britain between Spain
and the United States in 1817–1819. Dr. James A. Robertson, Secretary of the Florida Historical Society, has called our attention to a
most informing MS. now in the possession of the Huntington Library,
San Marino, Calif., and of which Dr. Robertson possesses a photostat copy: *Informe sobre la cesión de las Floridas, estipulada en el
tratado de Washington de 22 de febrero de 1819*", dated Sept. 30
and Oct. 5, 1820. It is the secret report of a committee of the
Spanish Cortes to that body, reviewing the whole Florida question,
and presenting reasons why the Cortes should ratify the treaty.

D. W. Parker's *Guide* (no. 5511) gives a general description of the papers in Washington relating to the territories of the United States, of which much more detailed indications are to be expected in the notes to the forthcoming edition of selections from those papers now being prepared for publication by the Department of State.[5]

The Library of Congress has the expense account of John Forsyth, while minister to Spain, 1819–1823. Leland's *Guide* (no. 5704) notes in the *Bibliothèque Nationale*, a letter of Hyde de Neuville, May 8, 1841, communicating details of a biographical character respecting his conduct toward Napoleon.

The personal papers of Carlos M. de Irujo, minister of Spain in the United States, 1796–1806, are preserved, in the possession of the Duke of Sotomayor, in Spain. The personal papers of Luis de Onís, Spanish minister in the United States, 1809–1819 (recognized December 1815), whose family has included other famous Spanish diplomatists, are at the ancestral home in Cantalapiedra, Spain. Some biographical information about Luis de Onís is in the possession of his great grandson, Professor Federico de Onís, of Columbia University.

Maps: Suggestions

See Ch. V, Sec. 4, above.

The treaty of 1819 stipulated that the boundary line west of the Mississippi was to be drawn in accordance with "Melish's map of the United States, published at Philadelphia, improved to the first of January, 1818." See [*Map of*] *The United States of America, compiled from the latest and best authorities*, by John Melish (Phila., 1818) [**1007a**], which is listed in Phillips, *Maps* (no. 5135), 880. See also John Melish, *A geographical description of the United States, with the contiguous British and Spanish possessions, intended as an accompaniment to Melish's map of these countries* (Phila., 1816; new ed., rev. and enl., Phila., 1826) [**1008**]. Notes regarding maps of the Floridas in relation to the treaty with Spain of 1819 and a map of the Floridas in relation to the treaty with Spain of 1819, including land grants, are given in Miller, *Treaties* (no. 5371), v. III, 41.

---

[5] The progress of this work, being edited by Professor C. E. Carter, is described in the reports for 1931 and 1932, of the committee (of the American Historical Association) on the Documentary Historical Publications of the United States Government, see *Annual reports* of the American Historical Association, 1931, 1932. See also no. 5511a.

3. United States and Hispanic America to 1826

Bibliographical Aids

For general American historical bibliographies, see Sec. 1, above. For Spanish-American historical bibliographies, see nos. 4678–4725; particularly Sánchez Alonso (no. 4759) for Spanish-American historical material.

A. P. C. Griffin, *List of references on recognition in international law and practice* (Wash., 1904) (Library of Congress) [1009], for material on recognition of the Spanish-American colonies. Lockey, *Pan-Americanism* (no. 964) has a comprehensive bibliography of printed material. Trelles, *Bibliografía cubana* (no. 1141), p. 174–206: "Historia de las relaciones diplomáticas y políticas de los Estados Unidos con España y Cuba." W. S. Robertson, *Hisp.-Am. relations* (no. 1206), "Bibliography": p. 431–455. Childs, *Hisp. Am. govt. docs.* (no. 5425); also his *Memorias* (no. 5424). L. W. Bealer, "Contribution to a bibliography on Artigas and the beginnings of Uruguay, 1810–1820", *Hisp. Am. hist. rev.*, XI (1931) 108–134 [1010]. *Theses on Pan American topics* (no. 5106). Wilgus, *Histories* (no. 966).

For Spanish-American newspapers, see bibliography in Robertson, *Hisp.-Am. relations* (no. 1206); *Newspapers in Pan American Union* (no. 5037); and other guides to newspapers (nos. 5004–5047).

Special Works

See Secs. 1, above, and 4, below.

See particularly Ch. VIII for general histories of the several Hispanic-American states.

Benjamín Vicuña Mackenna, *Ostracismo de los Carreras* (Santiago de Chile, 1857) [1011], one of the earliest narratives of Gen. José Miguel Carrera, interesting Chilean revolutionist, and agent to the United States. Bartolomé Mitre, *Historia de Belgrano y de la independencia argentina* (Buenos Aires, 1858–59, 2 v.; see latest edition, 1927–28, 4 v.) [1012], a history of the war for independence in the Argentine region to 1820, by a celebrated Argentine historian who made extensive use of public and private archives in that country. It is of value particularly for the beginning of Argentine contacts with Europe, but also mentions more briefly the United States. The same author's *Historia de*

San Martín y de la emancipación sudamericana (Buenos Aires, 1887–88; 2nd rev. ed., Buenos Aires, 1890, 4 v.) **[1013]**, also in an English abridgment by William Pilling (London, 1893) surveys similarly the independence movement as framed about the figure of San Martin. C. J. Stillé, *The life and services of Joel R. Poinsett* (Phila., 1888), reprinted from the *Pa. mag. of hist.*, XII (1888) 129–164, 257–303 **[1014]**, a sketch based on the great mass of Poinsett papers in the Historical Society of Pennsylvania. Matías Romero, " The United States and the liberation of the Spanish-American colonies ", *No. Am. rev.*, CLXV (1897) 70–86 **[1015]**, the author, the Mexican minister to the United States, asserts that the " United States government did not render either material or moral assistance to the cause of the independence of the South American colonies." See also a reply to the article, by H. D. Money, " The United States and the Spanish-American colonies ", *ibid.*, 356–363 **[1016]**; and a rejoinder by Mr. Romero in *ibid.*, 553–571 **[1017]**. Callahan, *Cuba* (no. 1805). W. F. McCaleb, " The first period of the Gutierrez-Magee expedition ", *Tex. hist. assoc. quar.*, IV (1901) 218–229 **[1018]**, filibustering expedition against Mexico, 1811–12. Manuel de Oliveira Lima, *Historia diplomatica do Brazil; reconhecimento do imperio*, 2d ed. (Rio de Janeiro and Paris, 1902) **[1019]**, this none-too-critical work, based on printed sources, gives a fairly good treatment of recognition of Brazil by the United States; thereafter only the high points in Brazilian-American relations receive attention; also his *O movimento da independencia, 1821–1822* (São Paulo, 1922) **[1020]**, there is a bare mention of the influence of the American Revolution on the movement for Brazilian independence, but a fuller analysis of the Graham-Rodney mission and its influence. F. L. Paxson, *The independence of the South-American republics; a study in recognition and foreign policy* (Phila., 1903) **[1021]**, a pioneer study in which the author exploited the archives of the United States Department of State, and the British Foreign Office, but not European or Hispanic-American archives. Diego Mendoza, " Estudios de historia diplomática; el tratado de 1824 entre Colombia y los Estados Unidos ", *Boletín de historia y antigüedades*, II (Bogotá, 1904) 389–402, 458–476 **[1022]**. Alberto Palomeque, *Oríjenes de la diplomacia arjentina; misión Aguirre á Norte América* (Buenos Aires, 1905, 2 v.) **[1023]**, this is a very valuable study of early contacts of the Argentine and the United States preliminary to the recognition of

the independence of the former by the latter, based on the archives
of the Argentine foreign office, the personal papers of the agent
Aguirre, and printed American and English state papers. A valu-
able supplement to American studies resting on the archives of the
Department of State. J. S. Reeves, *The Napoleonic exiles in
America; a study in American diplomatic history, 1815–1819* (Baltimore, 1905) [1024–5], for transactions with the French minister at
Washington in regard to schemes of the French exiles, in Texas,
directed against the Mexican possessions of Spain. Temperley,
Later Am. policy of Canning (no. 1150) shows that Canning's later
American policy was intended to defeat certain claims of the Monroe Doctrine and that his motives in recognizing the Spanish-American republics, and in sending an envoy to the Congress of Panama
were all influenced by that idea. Rio Branco, *Brazil, U.S. and Monroe Doctrine* (no. 1155) includes material on the mission of José
Silvestre Rebello, chargé d'affaires of Brazil to the United States,
1824–29. Seven studies by W. S. Robertson: *Life of Miranda* (no.
556), for the projects of European governments in regard to Spanish
America and the attitude of statesmen in the United States on various occasions; " The beginnings of Spanish-American diplomacy ",
in *Essays in American history dedicated to Frederick Jackson
Turner* (N.Y., 1910), 231–267 [1026–7] is concerned with the efforts
of the Spanish-American insurgents to initiate diplomatic relations
with foreign nations from 1810 to 1816, with special attention to
Venezuela; " The first legations of the United States in Latin America ", *Miss. Valley hist. rev.*, II (1915) 183–212 [1028] sees in the
recognition by the United States, and the establishment of seven legations in Latin America in a critical period of Hispanic history (without asking for favors) a significant event, not sufficiently appreciated,
which laid the foundations for Pan Americanism; *S.Am. and Monroe
Doctrine* (no. 1162) describes the reception of Monroe's message to
Congress of Dec. 2, 1823, by the republic of Colombia, the empire of
Brazil, and the provinces of the Rio de la Plata; " The United States
and Spain in 1822 ", *Am. hist. rev.*, XX (1915) 781–800 [1029] considers Spanish-American relations with regard to the recognition of
the independence of the new Hispanic-American nations, from study
of American and Spanish sources; " The recognition of the Hispanic
American nations by the United States ", *Hisp. Am. hist. rev.*, I (1918)
239–269 [1030], a careful study of the motives, policy, and process of

the United States in recognizing the independence of the Hispanic-American Republics; *Hisp.-Am. relations with U.S.* (no. 1206) deals more generally with the period after recognition. Chadwick, *U.S. and Spain* (no 108). Diego Barros Arana, " El primer cónsul estranjero en Chile, Mr. Joel Roberts Poinsett ", in his *Obras completas*, v. XI (Santiago de Chile, 1911), 41-58 [**1031**], a most readable sketch of Poinsett's unusual career by a distinguished Chilean historian who had no access to Poinsett's official or private papers (now available in the United States) but who used the diary of José Miguel Carrera, and the correspondence of the revolutionary *junta* of Buenos Aires to throw light on Poinsett's singular adventures in Chile. Miguel Varas Velásquez, *Don José Miguel Carrera en los Estados Unidos* (Santiago de Chile, 1912) [**1032**], for Carrera's mission to the United States, 1816-1818, for munitions, etc. C. K. Webster, " Castlereagh and the Spanish colonies, I: 1815-1818 ", *Eng. hist. rev.*, XXVII (1912) 78-95 [**1033**], and his " Castlereagh and the Spanish colonies, II: 1818-1822 ", *ibid.*, XXX (1915) 631-645 [**1034**], the substance of these two articles later incorporated in his *Castlereagh* (no. 1171). I. J. Cox, " Monroe and the early Mexican revolutionary agents ", *Am. hist. assoc. ann. rep.*, for 1911, v. I (1913) 197-215 [**1035**] is concerned with the activities of three agents of the Mexican revolutionists (José Bernardo Gutiérrez de Lara, José Álvarez de Toledo, and John Hamilton Robinson), 1811-1814; and by the same writer, *Pan-American policy, Jefferson and Wilkinson* (no. 764), for Wilkinson's intrigues against Spanish America, 1807-09. Fenwick, *Neutrality laws* (no. 378). Daniel Antokoletz, *Histoire de la diplomatie argentine*, t. I, *La diplomatie pendant la révolution* (Paris and Buenos Aires, 1914) [**1036**], originally delivered as lectures at the University of Buenos Aires. It includes an undocumented account of the missions of Diego Saavedra and Juan Pedro Aguirre to the United States. Curtis, *Hostile military expeditions* (no. 1797). C. A. Villanueva, *Fernando VII y los nuevos estados* (Paris, 1914) [**1037**], for Cuban affairs. Julius Goebel, *The recognition policy of the United States* (N.Y., 1915) [**1038**], p. 116-143: " The recognition of the Spanish American states." J. B. Moore, " Henry Clay and Pan-Americanism ", *Columbia univ. quar.*, XVII (1915) 346-362 [**1039**], a lecture by the celebrated jurist on Henry Clay's advocacy of the cause of Hispanic-American independence as the pedestal of the later Pan-American movement. Raimundo Rivas, *Relaciones internacionales entre Colombia y los Estados Unidos, 1810–1850* (Bogotá, 1915) [**1040**], based on the Bogotá archives, is one of the most important books on the subject because of its utilization of the archives of Colombia, though the author betrays no familiarity with sources outside of Bogotá. Alejandro Álvarez, *Diplomacia de Chile durante la emancipación* (Santiago, 1916) [**1041**], which was published under title, *Rasgos generales de la historia diplomática de Chile, 1810–1910*, t. I (Santiago, 1911), the portions which deal with Chilean-American relations are based on secondary support (Barros Arana, *Historia* (no. 1314)) and American state papers—no archival investigation. R. D. Skinner, " The first Americanist ", *Nation*, CII (1916) 98 [**1042**] treats briefly of the diplomatic activities of Manuel Torres, first minister from Colombia to the United States. Five studies by C. L. Chandler : *Inter-American acquaintances*, 2d ed. (Sewanee, Tenn., 1917) [**1043**] discusses the beginning of Pan American relations and the Pan Americanism of Henry Clay; " United States merchant ships in the Rio de la Plata (1801–1809) as shown by early newspapers ", *Hisp. Am. hist. rev.*, II (1919) 26–54 [**1044**]; " The United States shipping in the La Plata region, 1809–1810 ", *ibid.*, II (1920) 159–176 [**1045**]; " Commercial relations between the United States and Brazil, 1798–1812 ", *Revista de Instituto histórico e geographico brasileiro*, tomo especial, *Congresso internacional de historia da America* (1922), v. I (Rio de Janeiro, 1925), 397–414 [**1046**]; and " United States commerce with Latin America at the promulgation of the Monroe Doctrine ", *Quar. jour. econ.*, XXXVIII (1923) 466–487 [**1047**] deals with the years prior to 1823, statistics compiled largely from American newspapers. W. R. Shepherd, " Bolívar and the United States ", *Hisp. Am. hist. rev.*, I (1918) 270–298 [**1048**], an apotheosis after wide reading of Bolivariana, with copious quotations from the Liberator's utterances. Enrique Loudet, " César Auguste Rodney, algo sobre la trascendencia de son misión ", *Revista histórica* (Montevideo), IX (1919) 514–520 [**1049**], a eulogy of Rodney's services in Buenos Aires on the occasion of the centenary of his death. Lockey, *Pan Americanism* (no. 964). " La question cubane en 1825 ", *Nouv. rev.*, 4th ser., L (1920) 115–133 [**1050**] is a discussion of the Cuban question from the viewpoint of international law and the application of the Monroe Doctrine thereto, and prints two documents from the Russian archives. W. W. Pierson, "Alberdi's views on the Monroe Doctrine", *Hisp. Am. hist. rev.*, III (1920) 362–374 [**1051**] is a brief summary of the opinions of the Argentine publicist in regard to the influence of the Monroe Doctrine (*i.e.*, the United States) on Hispanic America in the revolutionary and early nationalistic periods. Gabriel Porros Troconis, "Relaciones diplomáticas de Colombia y los Estados Unidos en la guerra de independencia", *Cuba contemporánea*, XXII (1920) 153–169 [**1052**] relies principally on Monroe's messages and published proceedings of the U. S. Congress to outline the history of the early Colombian missions to the United States and the reception of their first diplomatic representative. C. Parra Pérez, "La diplomacia de Bolívar", *Revista del Instituto histórico y geográfico del Uruguay* (Montevideo), II, no. 2 (1922) 863–895, also pub. in *Rev. Amérique latine*, VI (1923) 103–109 [**1053**], later incorporated in his study of *Bolívar*, tr. by N. A. N. Cleven (Paris, 1928; Span. ed., *ibid.*) [**1054**], mainly concerned with Bolivar and the Panama Congress. Zacarias de Góes Carvalho, "Silvestre Rebello em Washington", in *Archivo diplomatico da independencia* (no. 1123), v. V (1922), vii-xlvii [**1055**], a sketch of the career of the first acknowledged Brazilian envoy to the United States, with his official correspondence. Henriques, *Correia da Serra* (no. 1420) prints an official letter of the Portuguese minister to the United States (1816–1820) relating to American filibustering ships. Norberto Piñero, *La política internacional argentina* (Buenos Aires, 1924) [**1056**], disparate essays on Argentine foreign policy from the period of the revolution to the present; there are chapters on the early relations between the United States and Argentine. Pedro A. Zubieta, *Apuntaciones sobre las primeras misiones diplomáticas de Colombia* (*primero y segundo períodos—1809–1810–1830*) (Bogotá, 1924) [**1057**], an account of the first diplomatic missions of Colombia to Europe, the United States, and the new republics of Hispanic-America, 1811–1826, based on their correspondence as preserved in Colombian archives. Joseph Agan, *Corrêa da Serra* (no. 1421), account of the activities of José Francisco Corrêa da Serra, minister from Portugal at Washington, 1816–20, and his efforts to check privateering enterprises during the South American struggle for independence; and *The diplomatic relations of the United States and*

Brazil, v. I. *The Portuguese court at Rio de Janeiro* (Paris, 1926) [**1058**] which is based on the then unpublished diplomatic correspondence of the United States government, and the conventional printed sources and secondary authorities. This is the only work in English on this subject. The early death of the author prevented the publication of sequent volumes. Nicolás García Samudio, *Capítulos de historia diplomática* (Bogotá, 1925) [**1059**], for the mission of Don Manuel Torres to the United States and early relations. This work pursues further the Colombian and American archival sources used by Rivas (nos. 1040 and 1261), Urrutia (no. 4051), and Zubieta (no. 1057), and exploits the printed *Diary* of John Quincy Adams (no. 5180) and the *Archivo Santander* (no. 1116), some selected diplomatic documents are printed in the appendix. Temperley, *For. pol. Canning* (no. 1152), for Cuban affairs, 1822–26. Three studies by A. C. Wilgus: " Spanish American patriot activity along the Gulf coast of the United States, 1811–1822 ", *La. hist. quar.*, VIII (1925) 193–215 [**1060**] discusses violations of American neutrality, utilizing *A.S.P.*, *F.R.*, contemporary periodicals, and secondary material; " Some notes on Spanish American patriot activity along the Atlantic seaboard, 1816–1822 ", *N. C. hist. rev.*, IV (1927) 172–181 [**1061**], a sequel to the last-mentioned article; " Some activities of United States citizens in the South American wars of independence, 1808–1824 ", *La. hist. quar.*, XIV (1931) 182–203 [**1062**], from Manning (no. 1124) and other printed sources including narratives of adventures in South America, the author details many instances of American individuals participating in the revolutionary movement. W. C. Collier and Guillermo Feliú Cruz, *La primera misión de los Estados Unidos de América en Chile* (Santiago de Chile, 1926) [**1063**], for the mission of J. R. Poinsett to Chile, 1811–14; and by Feliú Cruz, " Poinsett en Méjico y en Chile ", *Rev. chilena* (Santiago de Chile), XII (1928) 37–46 [**1064**]; to these authors were available some very valuable MS. sources previously not used: the papers and diary of José Miguel Carrera, the Chilean patriot and revolutionist, during his contacts with Joel R. Poinsett in Chile and during his mission to the United States in 1816–1818, papers of Commodore Porter in the possession of one of the authors, Mr. Collier (American ambassador to Chile at the time), and other documents in the *Biblioteca Nacional* of Chile, etc. The book is a very valuable contribution. The article is apparently a reply to Puga y Acal (no. 1062a). Carlos Correa Luna, *Alvear y la diplomacia de 1824–1825 en Inglaterra, Estados Unidos y Alto Perú, con Canning, Monroe, Quincy Adams, Bolívar y Sucre* (Buenos Aires, 1926) [**1065**], for the first Argentine mission to the United States. This is a reprint of popular articles which appeared in 1924–1925 in *La Prensa* (Buenos Aires) the material for which came in large part from the diplomatic archives of the Argentine in the process of investigations for a more pretentious work. Isidro Fabela, *Los precursores de la diplomacia mexicana* (Mexico: Publicaciones de la Secretaría de Relaciones Exteriores, 1926) [**1066**], foreign relations of Mexico, 1785–1824. W. R. Sherman, *The diplomatic and commercial relations of the United States and Chile, 1820–1914* (Boston, 1926) [**1067**], based on American sources only and weak in use of Spanish secondary material compared with Evans. C. M. Trelles y Govín, " Un precursor de la independencia de Cuba: Don José Álvarez de Toledo ", in *Discursos leídos en la recepción pública del Sr. Carlos M. Trelles y Govín*, 1926 (Havana, 1926), 8–180 [**1068**], revolutionist who played an important role in Mexican-American relations, 1811–14. Prints 35 documents, mainly from the *Archivo General de Indias, Papeles de Cuba*, the *Memorias* of García de León y Pizarro, also an exhaustive bibliography of Toledo. H. C. Evans, jr., *Chile and its relations with the United States.* (Durham, N.C., 1927) [**1069**], a concise narrative insofar as one can be drawn from the great array of printed matter in English and Spanish and the MS. archives of the Department of State of the United States, but not of Chile. G. G. Johnson, " The Monroe doctrine and the Panama congress ", *James Sprunt hist. stud.*, XIX, no. 2 (1927) 53–73 [**1070**], an analysis of the interpretations given the Monroe message by the executive and legislative departments of the United States government and by the Hispanic American countries concerned with the Panama Congress. H. L. Hoskins, " The Hispanic American policy of Henry Clay, 1816–1828 ", *Hisp. Am. hist. rev.*, VII (1927) 460–478 [**1071**], a useful review based on the printed sources available in the United States. João Pandíá Calogeras, *A política exterior do imperio* (Rio de Janeiro, 1927–28, 2 v.) [**1072**], a general history of Brazilian diplomacy to about 1828. Volume II has instructive chapters on early missions of Brazil to the United States and to Europe, with lengthy excerpts from the diplomatic correspondence. Manuel Puga y Acal, " Poinsett en

Méjico y en Chile ", *Rev. chilena* (Santiago de Chile, 1927) 43–58 [**1073**], an argumentative article based on secondary accounts. N. A. N. Cleven, " The first Panama mission and the Congress of the United States ", *Jour. negro hist.*, XIII (1928) 225–254 [**1074**], lengthy analysis of the debates in Congress on the question of sending a mission to the Panama Congress, stressing the solid opposition against any effort to consider there the emancipation of negro slaves. C. W. Hackett, " The development of John Quincy Adams's policy with respect to an American confederation and the Panama congress, 1822–1825 ", *Hisp. Am. hist. rev.*, VIII (1928) 496–526 [**1075**], as revealed in the recent documentary publication of Manning (no. 1124) and *A.S.P.*, *F.R.* J. F. Rippy, *Latin America in world politics* (N.Y., 1928; rev. ed., 1931) [**1076**] is an outline survey which, while using many primary sources, relies much on secondary works. It is valuable for the period 1823–1860, as for the later period. More definitive archival researches of the author are set forth in his *Rivalry of the United States and Great Britain over Latin America, 1808–1830* (Baltimore, 1929) [**1077**], which, in the light of the unpublished records of the British Public Record Office and the Department of State of the United States, throws into relief the animosities between Great Britain and the United States during this period in regard to certain phases of their relations with the new republics of Hispanic America. Maurice Casenave, " Les émigrés bonapartistes de 1815 aux Etats-Unis ", *Rev. hist. dipl.*, XLIII (1929) 20–32, 131–154 [**1078**], an undocumented essay by a French diplomatist, discusses the rôle which Bonapartist *émigrés* in the United States played in filibustering in Hispanic America and the question of neutrality (cf. Reeves, no. 1024). T. S. Currier, *Los corsarios del Río de la Plata* (Buenos Aires, 1929) [**1079**], important preliminary study by a North American writer of American privateering after the war of 1812 as affecting the relations between the United States and the provinces of the Rio de la Plata, based upon newspapers and other contemporary sources. A valuable appendix lists the privateers. Watt Stewart exploits the newly published documents in Manning (no. 1124) in: " The South American commission, 1817–1818 ", *Hisp. Am. hist. rev.*, IX (1929) 31–59 [**1080**]; and "Argentina and the Monroe doctrine, 1824–1828 ", *ibid.*, X (1930) 26–32 [**1081**]; " The United States-Argentine commercial negotiations of 1825 ", *ibid.*, XIII (1933) 367–379 [**1082**], the unsuccessful efforts of J. M. Forbes, American consul at Buenos Aires, to offset the British-Argentine commercial treaty of 1825 by a reciprocity arrangement to be effected by legislation; based on consular correspondence, mostly printed by Manning (no. 1124) ; and "The diplomatic services of John M. Forbes at Buenos Aires", *ibid.*, XIV (1934) 202–218 [**1082a**], a *précis* of his despatches describing his mission as commercial agent and consul, 1820–1831; principal issues were over privateering and impressment. L. C. Lindley, "Some aspects of the foreign policy of Henry Clay", in Clark University, *Thesis abstracts*, 1929 (Worcester, 1930), 117–120 [**1083**], believes Clay's policy exercised no signal influence on a foreign policy determined by factors other than his "oratory" and "persistence." E. J. Pratt, "Anglo-American commercial and political rivalry on the Plata, 1820–1830 ", *Hisp. Am. hist. rev.*, XI (1931) 302–335 [**1084**] enlarges on Rippy (no. 1077) with use of Manning (no. 1124) and other records in the Department of State and British Record Office. Hill, *U. S. and Brazil* (no. 1277). John Rydjord,[6] "Napoleon and the independence of New Spain ", in *New Spain . . .*, contributions presented to Herbert E. Bolton (Los Angeles, Calif., 1932), v. I, 289–312 [**1085**] prints 3 documents (Onís's report of the arrival of Napoleon's agents in Baltimore, 1809; Precautions taken by the audiencia of Guatemala against Napoleon's agents, 1810; and Napoleon's instruction to d'Amblimont, 1810), with textual introduction. Lillian E. Fisher, "American influence upon the movement for Mexican independence ", *Miss. Valley hist. rev.*, XIII (1932) 463–478 [**1086**] shows that the American example, and American writings inflamed a revolutionary spirit, but most of the article is devoted to detailing the various filibustering expeditions and trespasses upon Spanish territory adjacent to the United States. R. F. Nichols, "Trade relations and the establishment of the United States consulates in Spanish America, 1779–1809 ", *Hisp. Am. hist. rev.*, XIII (1933) 289–313 [**1087**] uses archives of the Department of State and facsimiles from Spanish *Archivo Histórico Nacional* to show how blocking of sea-ways by enemies during periodic wars, 1779–1808, caused the Spanish government to tolerate emergency trade with the United States, and the acceptance of "agents " (consuls) particularly in Cuba. Dorothy M. Parton, *The diplo-*

---

[6] John Rydjord, *International interest in the revolutionizing of New Spain* is announced for publication.

matic career of Joel Roberts Poinsett (Wash., 1934) [**1087a**], thesis (Ph. D.) of the Catholic University of America, based on original material in United States and British archives, and the Poinsett papers.

For the Panama Congress [7] of 1826: J. M. Torres Caicedo, *Unión latino-americana; pensamiento de Bolívar para formar una liga americana; su origen y sus desarrollos* (Paris, 1865) [**1088**], written by a Venezuelan publicist. L. A. Otero, *El Congreso internacional de Panamá en 1826* (Bogotá, 1906) [**1089**]. P. A. Zubieta, *Congresos de Panamá y Tucubaya* (Bogotá, 1912) [**1090**], mostly a Spanish reprint of the protocols, treaties, and other well-known acts of the Congress, to which is added the instructions to the Colombian delegate and other documents drawn from the archives at Bogota. D. F. O'Leary, *El congreso internacional de Panamá en 1826; desgobierno y anarquía de la Gran Colombia* (Madrid, 1920) [**1091**]. G. H. Stuart, " Simón Bolívar's project for a league of nations ", *Southw. pol. sci. quar.*, VII (1926) 238-252 [**1092**], the most recent sketch by a scholarly admirer of Bolívar's audacity in attempting to give to the American republics a system of international law " almost simultaneously with the establishment of their internal governmental organizations." Porras Barrenechea, *Congreso de Panamá* (no. 1136) has a long historical introduction to his publication of the relevant Peruvian diplomatic correspondence. Ferrara, *El Panamericanismo* (no. 4069) opens with a discussion of the origins of the early conferences. Barcía Trelles, *Doctrina de Monroë* (no. 1174) is the most penetrating analysis of the relation of the foreign policy of the new Hispanic-American states, particularly the Pan-American Congress, to the early Monroe Doctrine. Carlos Ibarguren, "La misión de Aguirre á los Estados Unidos," in his *En la penumbra de la historia argentina* (Buenos Aires, 1932), 87-96 [**1092a**].

For biographies of American statesmen (J. Q. Adams, J. C. Calhoun, Henry Clay, Jefferson, Madison, Monroe) and diplomatists (including agents to Spanish America prior to recognition: T. L. Halsey, R. K. Lowry, J. B. Prevost, Alexander Scott, Wm. Shaler, W. G. D. Worthington; commissioners to South America: C. A.

---

[7] R. F. Arragón. *The Congress of Panama* [1087b] is an unprinted doctoral dissertation in the Harvard College Library, which treats in particular of the relations of the United States to the congress.

Rodney, Theodorick Bland, H. M. Brackenridge, John Graham; and first envoys: (Argentina) C. A. Rodney and J. M. Forbes; (Brazil) Condy Raguet; (Central America) Wm. Miller and John Williams; (Colombia) R. C. Anderson and B. T. Watts; (Chile) Heman Allen; (Mexico) J. R. Poinsett; (Peru) James Cooley), see, in addition to entries given above in this section, the relevant entries and bibliographical data in the *D.A.B.*

Spanish American biographical material is meager. Of the early agents (M. H. Aguirre, Telésfero de Orea, Manuel Palacio, José R. Revenga, for identification, see Robertson, *Beginnings of Span.-Am. diplomacy* (no. 1027)), and first envoys: (Argentina) Carlos M. de Alvear; (Brazil) José Silvestre Rebello; (Central America) Manuel I. Arce, J. M. Rodríguez, Antonio J. Cañaz; (Colombia) Manuel Torres and José M. Salazar; (Mexico) José M. B. Zozoya), we note in addition to monographs entered above: Sketches of "Manuel Palacio", in Ramón Aspurúa, *Biografías de hombres notables de Hispano-América* (no. 4932), v. II, 186-195 [1093]; of José R. Revenga, in *ibid.*, v. IV, 317-330 [1094]; "Silvestre Rebello em Washington", by Heita Lyra, in *Archivo diplomatico da independencia* (no. 1123), v. V, i-lxxiii [1095]; Francis Drake, *Dictionary of American biography* (Boston, 1874) [1096], for sketch of C. A. Rodney.

Printed Sources

For American official documents and general source collections, see Sec. 1, above.

For guides to Hispanic-American official documents, see nos. 5424-5427.

[H. M. Brackenridge], *South America; a letter on the present state of that country, to James Monroe, President of the United States* (Wash., 1817) [1097], written (pub. anonymously) by the secretary of the South American mission consisting of C. A. Rodney, J. Graham, and T. Bland, 1817-18; also by the same writer, *Voyage to South America, performed by order of the American government, in the years 1817 and 1818* (Baltimore, 1819, 2 v.) [1098] is concerned with the same mission, and includes the "letter" noted above. *Message from the President . . . November 17, 1818* (Wash., 1818) (15th Cong., 2d sess., House doc. 2) [1099] includes reports of C. A. Rodney and John Graham, two of the three commissioners sent to investigate affairs in the Spanish provinces of South America. Vicente Pazos, *The exposition, remonstrance and protest of Don Vicente Pazos, commissioner on behalf of the republican agents established at Amelia Island, in Florida, under the authority and in behalf of the independent states of South America,* tr. from the Spanish (Phila., 1818) [1100]. *Message from the President . . .,* February 2, 1819 (Wash., 1819) (15th Cong., 2d sess., House doc. 48) [1100a], reports on the viceroyalty of Buenos Aires and Chile by T. Bland, member of the commission sent to South America to investigate affairs. *Message from the President . . . transmitting . . . Report of Theodorick Bland, esquire, on South America* (Wash., 1819), reprinted with the title, *The present state of Chili; from the report laid before Congress by Judge Bland, the commissioner sent to that country by the government of the United States in 1818* (London, 1820), also Spanish edition, tr. by Domingo Amunátegui Solar. in *Anales de la Universidad de Chile,* 2d ser., IV (1926) 927–980, and V (1927) 1–53 [1101]. *Strictures on a voyage to South America as indited by the " Secretary to the (late) mission " to the La Plata . . . In a series of letters* (Baltimore, 1820) [1102], a bitter attack on Brackenridge and his book (no. 1098), Brackenridge believed it to be the joint production of Theodorick Bland, member of the South American commission, J. S. Skinner, Dr. Moreno (one of the South American exiles), and Baptis Irvine.[8] [Dominique de Fourt] de Pradt, *Europe and America, in 1821; with an examination of the plan laid before the Cortes of Spain for the recognition of the independence of South America,* tr. from the French of the abbé de Pradt by J. D. Williams (London, 1822, 2 v.) [1103]. Bernardo Monteagudo, *Ensayo sobre la necesidad de una federación jeneral entre los estados hispano-americanos, y plan de su organización* (Lima, 1825) [1104]. Benjamin Chew, *A sketch of the politics, relations, and statistics, of the western world, and of those characteristics of European policy which most immediately affects its interests: intended to demonstrate the necessity of a grand American confederation and alliance* (Phila., 1827) [1105]. P. I. Cadena, *Anales diplomáticos de Colombia* (Bogotá, 1878) [1106], selections from the diplomatic correspondence, 1820–21, of Manuel Torres, first minister of New Granada to the United States. *Sesiones de los cuerpos legislativos de Chile* (no. 1188). " Diary and letters of Henry Ingersoll,

---

8 See J. Q. Adams, *Memoirs* (no. 5180), v. V, 56–57.

prisoner at Carthagena, 1806–1809 ", ed. by E. E. Sparks, *Am. hist. rev.*, III (1898) 674–702 [**1107**], Ingersoll was taken captive in 1806, on Miranda's filibustering expedition against Spanish America. "Miranda and the British Admiralty, 1804–1806 ", *ibid.*, VI (1901) 508–530 [**1108–1109**], documents from the Public Record Office, London (despatches to the Secretary of the Admiralty by British commanders). *Papers of Sir Charles R. Vaughan* (no. 1380) throw light on the problems growing out of the South American conditions. " Calendar of the Manuel de Salcedo correspondence, 1810–1812 ", in the *Thirty-first annual report* of the [Texas] Commissioner of Agriculture, . . . and History, for the year ending August 31, 1906 (Houston, Tex., 1906) Pt. II, 31–56 [**1110**], the documents, of which abstracts are here given, deal with relations with the Americans on the border, filibustering expeditions, etc. "Los Estados Unidos y la independencia argentina; como nació la doctrina de Monroe; comprobaciones históricas, publicadas en ' La Nación ' en los días 12, 13 y 14 de julio de 1906 ", in J. J. Biedma, *Los Estados Unidos de América y la independencia argentina* (Buenos Aires, 1906), 29–67 [**1111**], mainly a reprint in Spanish of well-known United States official correspondence, 1817–23, following a popular essay. L. M. Pérez, ed., " Relations with Cuba ", *So. hist. assoc. pub.*, X (1906) 203–214, 378–380 [**1112**], letter of Gov. Claiborne, 1809, and report of J. R. Poinsett to the President, 1823 (both from Dept. of State archives), and an anonymous letter of 1820 regarding a supposed expedition fitting out in Great Britain for an invasion of Cuba (from national archives of Cuba). *Canning and Cuba, 1812* (no. 1196) ; and " Canning to Vaughan ", *Mass. hist. soc. proc.*, XLVI (1913) 233–235 [**1113**], letter from George Canning, Feb. 8, 1826 (*F. O., America,* 209, no. 10) in regard to Cuba. *Brazil, U.S. and Monroe Doctrine* (no. 1155) includes a translation of the instructions of José Silvestre Rebello, Brazilian chargé d'affaires in Washington, 1824. *Papers of Zebulon M. Pike* (no. 781). *La diplomacia mexicana*, ed. by Enrique Santibáñez, pub. by the " Secretaría de Relaciones Exteriores " (Mexico, 1910–13, 3 v.) [**1114**] is a collection of documents from the Mexican foreign office, extending only through the early part of 1825— some deal with Poinsett's mission, others with S. S. Wilcocks, D. G. Ingraham, and William Taylor, early American consuls in Mexico. Joaquín de Anduaga, "A Spanish protest against the United States' recognition of Latin-American independence ", *Jour. Am. hist.*, VIII

(1912) 411–415 [1115] is a communication from the Spanish minister, Don Joaquín de Anduaga, to the American secretary of state (J. Q. Adams), Mar. 9, 1822, and the reply of the secretary. *Archivo Santander*, published by the "Academia Nacional de Historia" of Colombia (Bogotá, 1913–1925, 22 v.) [1116] contains the correspondence of the guiding personality of Colombian politics and diplomacy during this period. W. S. Robertson, "Documents concerning the consular service of the United States in Latin America, with introductory note", *Miss. Valley hist. rev.*, II (1916) 561–568 [1117] prints a letter of Robert Smith, secretary of state, to William Shaler, June 16, 1810, and a letter from James Monroe, secretary of state, to Luis Goddefroy, consul for Buenos Aires, Apr. 30, 1811. "Protocols of conferences of representatives of the allied powers respecting Spanish America, 1824–1825", *Am. hist. rev.*, XXII (1917) 595–616 [1118], documents from the archives of the French foreign office, dealing with conferences of the European powers for the purpose of adjusting Spanish-American affairs, and revealing an apparently unauthorized proposal of James Brown, American minister to France, that the United States join with the maritime powers in guaranteeing Spanish possession of Cuba on condition that Spain accept the mediation of those powers between herself and her South American revolted colonies. F. J. Urrutia, *Páginas de historia diplomática; los Estados Unidos de América y las Repúblicas hispanoamericanas de 1810 á 1830* (Bogotá, 1917; another ed., Madrid, 1918) [1119] is a documentary collection of importance, though much of the material is included in Manning (no. 1124 below). *Correspondencia generales de la Provincia de Buenos Aires relativas á relaciones exteriores (1820–1824)*, ed. by Emilio Ravignani (Buenos Aires, 1921) (*Documentos para la historia Argentina*, t. XIV, of the Facultad de Filosofía y Letras, Universidad Nacional, Buenos Aires) [1120]. Nicolás García Samudio, "Relaciones entre Colombia y los Estados Unidos; la primera nota de 1810", *Pan Am. Unión bol.*, LV (1922) 388–391 [1121] prints a note of José Miguel Pey, vicepresidente of the "Junta Suprema de Santa Fé," to the President of the United States, 1810, with comment. Also García Samudio, *Capítulos* (no. 1059), 159–222: "Documentos relativos á la misión de don Manuel Torres en Washington y al reconocimiento de la Repúblicas hispanoamericanas por los Estados Unidos, 1819–1822." Fabián Velarde and F. J. Escobar, *El congreso de Panamá en 1826* (Panama,

1922) [**1122**], after a short introduction reprints various relevant
diplomatic documents, particularly of Colombia. *Archivo diplomatico da independencia*, pub. by the "Ministerio das Relações Exteriores" of Brazil, v. V (Rio de Janeiro, 1923) ed. by Góes Carvalho
[**1123**] includes the diplomatic correspondence of the Brazilian government with its first recognized mission in the United States, under
Silvestre Rebello, minister, 1822–1827, from the Brazilian archives.
W. R. Manning, *Diplomatic correspondence of the United States
concerning the independence of the Latin-American nations* (N.Y.,
1925, 3 v.) (Publications of the Carnegie Endowment for International Peace) [**1124**], a definitive printing of all relevant material. "Diary of José Gutiérrez de Lara, 1811–1812", ed. by Elizabeth H. West, *Am. hist. rev.*, XXXIV (1928) 55–77 [**1125**], a translation from the Spanish of the diary of a Mexican republican leader,
covering his activities in Washington in the patriot cause. *Archivo
del General Miranda* (Caracas, 1929– (to date (1934), 14 v.) [**1126**]
the papers of General Francisco de Miranda recently purchased by
the Venezuelan Government from Lord Bathurst, and now being
published by that government, under the editorship of a committee
headed by Vicente Dávila. *Cartas del Libertador,*⁹ ed. by Vicente Lecuna (Caracas, 1929–30, 10 v.) [**1127**] is the official edition
of the letters of Bolivar, 1799–1830, among which are some reflecting his policy in regard to foreign affairs and inter-American
relations. "Correspondence between General William Winder and
President Monroe with reference to proposals made by the
United Provinces of South America", ed. by Mary M. Kenway,
Hisp. Am. hist. rev., XII (1932) 457–461 [**1129**] consists of 2 letters (1818) from the papers of Gen. Winder in the possession of
Johns Hopkins University, which throw some light on the early re-
lations of the United States with these provinces, and especially on
the attitude of President Monroe, as expressed to a personal friend.
J. B. Lockey, ed., "An early Pan-American scheme", *Pacific hist. rev.*,
II (1933) 439–447 [**1130**], scheme proposed by William Shaler, sub-
mitted to Sec. Monroe in 1812, now in the Department of State.
      For the Panama Congress of 1826: [Dominique de Fourt] de
Pradt, *Congrès de Panama* (Paris, 1825) [**1131**], for contemporary

---

⁹ For an account of the official edition here noted and earlier editions of the letters of
Bolivar, see Julio Planchart, "The letters of the liberator," *Pan Am. union bul.*, LXIV
(1930) 1313–1331 [**1128**].

comments on the forthcoming Panama Congress by one who seemed to be in intimate touch with Bolivar himself. *The executive proceedings of the Senate of the United States, on the subject of the mission to the Congress of Panama, together with the messages and documents relating thereto* (Wash., 1826) (19th Cong., 1st sess. Senate. Doc. 68) [**1132**]. *The congress of 1826, at Panama, and subsequent movements toward a conference of American nations*, pub. by the 1st International American Conference, Washington, D.C. (Wash.: Govt. print. off., 1890) (*Its* Reports of Committees and Discussions thereon, v. IV. Historical Appendix) (51st Cong., 1st sess., Senate. Exec. doc. 232, pt. 4) [**1133**] reprints American state papers, diplomatic correspondence, reports, etc., thereon, together with the protocols and treaty of the congress. Francisco Centeno, " El Congreso de Panamá y la diplomacia armada de Bolívar ", *Rev. derecho, hist., y letras*, XLIII (1912) 507–515, XLIV (1913) 42–68, 189–223, 358–368, 523–554 [**1134**] prints important Peruvian, Chilean, and Argentine documents anent the congress, together with the minutes of the congress. Zubieta (no. 1090) for Colombian instructions, etc. *El Congreso de Panamá y algunos otros proyectos de unión hispano-americana*, ed. by Antonio de la Peña y Reyes (Mexico, 1926) (Archivo Histórico Diplomático Mexicano, núm. 19) [**1135**] consists of Mexican documents dealing with the Panama Congress. *El Congreso de Panamá (1826)*, ed. by Raúl Porras Barrenechea (Lima, 1930) (Archivo Diplomático Peruano, t. I) [**1136**], pub. by the " Ministerio de Relaciones Exteriores " of Peru, consists of official documents of the Peruvian ministry of foreign affairs, 1825–26.

For the printed writings of American statesmen and diplomatists (enumerated above, under " Special Works "), see our list on p. 756.

MSS.: Suggestions

See Secs. 1 and 2, this chapter, particularly for European archives, also Sec. 4 for papers of British ministers in the United States during discussion of the question of recognition of the independence of the Spanish-American states. For guides and indexes to the archives and other collections in England, France, Mexico, and Cuba, see below, Pt. II, ch. 3; note particularly Bolton (no. 5674), for Mexican archives, and Pérez (no. 5682) for Cuban archives. There is no guide to material relating to American history in the other Hispanic-American archives; but the investigator is referred to the few published guides and indexes to the archives of those states (see below, p. 909). See also Herbert Friedenwald, "A synoptical catalogue of manuscripts in the Library of Congress relating to Cuba ", in Griffin, *List of books relating to Cuba* (no. 4722), 58–61 **[1137]**. For a calendar of documents in the. Spanish archives regarding the independence of the Spanish-American states, see Torres Lanzas, *Independencia de América* (no. 5640). The papers of Miranda, acquired from Lord Bathurst by the Republic of Venezuela, are now at Caracas and are described by W. S. Robertson, " The lost archives of Miranda ", *Hisp. Am. hist. rev.*, VII (1927) 229–232 **[1138]**, and Edouard Clavery, " Les archives de Miranda à Caracas ", *Rev. Amérique latine*, XVII (1929) 113–119 **[1138a]**. They are now being published (no. 1126), as are the papers of Bolívar (no. 1127).

For papers of American presidents and secretaries of state, see Sec. 1, above, and our lists, on pp. 862–867. For papers of American diplomatists to Hispanic-American states (J. M. Forbes, commissioner to Argentine, and later *chargé d'affaires*, 1817–1825; Caesar A. Rodney, commissioner to the Argentine, 1823–1824; Joel R. Poinsett, agent for seamen and commerce, to Buenos Aires and Chile, 1810–1811, and consul general for Buenos Aires, Chile, and Peru, 1811–18??; Jeremy Robinson, agent for commerce and seamen at Lima, Callao, and other places in South America, in 1817, and William Shaler, agent for commerce and seamen at Havana and Vera Cruz in 1810–13), see our list on p. 868.

Many papers of José Miguel Carrera, Chilean agent sent to the United States in 1816–1818, are said to be in the possession of a descendant, Mr. Alejandro Fierro Carrera, of Chile.

The papers of Sir R. Wilson, relating to the Spanish colonies in South America, Mexico, and Texas, and their recognition as independent states, 1811–1841, are in the British Museum.

4. The Origin of the Monroe Doctrine, 1823–1826

Bibliographical Aids

For general aids, see Sec. 1, above.

J. F. Jameson, " Bibliography of Monroe, and the Monroe Doctrine ", in D. C. Gilman, *James Monroe* (rev. ed.) (Boston and N.Y.,

1898), 260–294 [**1139**]. H. H. B. Meyer, *List of references on the Monroe Doctrine* (Wash., 1919) (Library of Congress) [**1140**]. C. M. Trelles y Govín, *Estudio de la bibliografía cubana sobre la Doctrina de Monroe* (Havana, 1922) [**1141**] includes more than 1,300 titles with commentary on works in Spanish (but less commentary on those in English) of books, periodical articles, and official documents bearing on the Monroe Doctrine, on the Hispanic-American relations of Cuba, and on Cuba's relations with the United States.[10] Pan American Union, Columbus Memorial Library, *Bibliography on the Monroe Doctrine* (Wash., 1924) [**1142**], a mimeographed list; deals mainly with its expressions and interpretation. Lockey, *Pan-Americanism* (no. 964). Perkins, *Monroe Doctrine* (no. 1172), 263–269. Phillips Bradley, *A bibliography of the Monroe Doctrine, 1919–1929* (London: London School of Economics, 1929) [**1143**] supplements the bibliography published by the Library of Congress (no. 1140).

Special Works

The literature on the Monroe Doctrine is so vast that it is practical here to refer mainly to the bibliographical aids above listed. None of these aids restricts itself to the origin of the doctrine, except the notes given by Perkins in his *Monroe Doctrine* (no. 1211) and "J. Q. Adams" in *Am. secs. state*, IV (no. 4796). Professor Perkins's monograph on the origin of the doctrine is already a classic, and except for the most detailed requirements sufficiently covers the ground. From this and the above aids we select the following references, including also some of the works very recently published. We omit here many titles which we do not regard important.

Ernest Caylus, *Doctrine Monroë* (Paris, 1865) [**1144**], these letters from New York, elicited by Buchanan's message of 1859 constitute one of the first special treatments of the Monroe Doctrine. Comte de Boislecompte, " M. Canning et l'intervention des Bourbons en Espagne ", *Rev. hist. dipl.*, VII (1893) 414–427 [**1145**], an undocumented study printed from a history of French diplomacy left incomplete by the author. It suggests that Canning was outwitted by French diplomacy during the Spanish intervention of 1823 and

---

[10] We have included in our bibliography only a selection of the more important works contained in this very detailed bibliographical study, to which the reader is referred for further material.

therefore turned to the United States, and to South America, for compensation. W. F. Reddaway, *The Monroe Doctrine* (Cambridge, Eng., 1898; 2d ed., N.Y., 1905) **[1146]**, before Perkins (nos. 1172 and 1211) this was the best general treatment of the Monroe Doctrine, though the scholar might wish to find more notes as to the sources used. Its thesis is: " that the evolution of the Monroe Doctrine was gradual: that the peculiar form of the message of 1823 was due to John Quincy Adams; that he, and he alone, applied it to politics; and that it produced its desired effect as an act of policy, but in no way modified the Law of Nations." In comments on the relation of Cuba and Hawaii, in 1898, to the Monroe Doctrine the author is less objective. W. C. Ford, " John Quincy Adams and the Monroe Doctrine ", *Am. hist. rev.*, VII (1902) 676–696, VIII (Oct. 1902) 28–52 **[1147]** emphasizes, after careful study of the American sources, official and unofficial, the intimate relationship of John Quincy Adams to the pronouncement of the doctrine. (See also no. 1193, below.) E. M. Lloyd, " Canning and Spanish America ", *Royal hist. soc. trans.*, n.s. XVIII (1904) 77–105 **[1148]** rests on Stapleton and other secondary material, and may now be said to be superseded by Temperley (no. 1152). T. B. Edgington, *The Monroe Doctrine* (Boston, 1904) **[1149]**, chiefly valuable as a reprint of easily available documents and of lengthy excerpts from publicists. Four studies by H. W. V. Temperley, resting on thorough examination of British sources, and foreign archival sources: " The later American policy of George Canning ", *Am. hist. rev.*, XI (1906) 779–797 **[1150]**, shows that the later American policy of Canning was intended to defeat certain claims of the Monroe Doctrine (the non-colonization principle and the principle which tended to make America a separate world from Europe), see also his *Canning and Cuba* (no. 1196) ; " Canning and the conferences of the four allied governments in Paris, 1823–1826 ", *Am. hist. rev.*, XXX (1924) 16–43 **[1151]** traces from multiarchival records the breakdown of this last device for prolonging the European concert (see also no. 1153) ; *The foreign policy of Canning, 1822–1827 ; England, the neo-Holy alliance, and the New World* (London, 1925) **[1152]** ; " French designs on Spanish America in 1820–5 ", *Eng. hist. rev.*, XL (1925) 34–53 **[1153]**, the earlier articles are to a great extent incorporated in the later book, which may be considered definitive and is especially valuable for British diplomacy and the Monroe Doctrine. F. J. Turner, *Rise of the new West, 1819–1829* (N.Y. and London, 1906) [1154] has a chapter on "The Monroe Doctrine (1821–1823)." [Baron Rio Branco], *Brazil, the United States and the Monroe Doctrine* (Wash.? 1908) [1155], article reprinted from the *Jornal do Commercio*, of Rio de Janeiro, Jan. 20th, 1908, and generally attributed to Baron Rio Branco, the foreign minister of Brazil; it is evidently reprinted from an article printed in *For. relations* (no. 5345), 1906, pt. 1, 116–124; it presents historical evidence to show that 59 days after the reading of President Monroe's message, the Brazilian government issued instructions to its representative in Washington to propose to the United States an alliance. Georg Heinz, *Die Beziehungen zwischen Russland, England und Nord-amerika im Jahre 1823; Beiträge zur Genesis der Monroedoktrin* (Berlin, 1911) [1156], based on secondary works and such sources as J. Q. Adams's *Memoirs* and Rush's *Residence. Canning and his friends* (no. 1179). C. A. Villanueva, *La Santa Alianza* (Paris, 1912) [1157]; and his *La monarquía en América* (Paris, 1912–13, 4 v.) [1158], based on careful research in French archives and containing much important documentary material. Herbert Kraus, *Monroe-Doktrin, in ihren Beziehungen zur amerikanischen Diplomatie und zum Völkerrecht* (Berlin, 1913) [1159], this is a typical German dissertation, written in the United States under the guidance of John Bassett Moore. It rests on printed state papers and its historical review of the doctrine in American foreign policy, to 1905 is suggestive of the array of documents on that subject published in Mr. Justice Moore's *Digest* (no. 5365). Overstresses the expansive evolution of the doctrine. W. R. Manning, "Statements, interpretations, and applications of the Monroe Doctrine, etc., 1823–1845", in the *Proceedings of the American Society of International Law at its eighth annual meeting*, 1914 (Wash., 1914) 34–59 [1160], a scholarly article, the result of much research in archives of Mexico and the United States as well as in printed sources. Four works of W. S. Robertson deal in a scholarly way with various aspects of the origin of the doctrine: "The Monroe doctrine abroad in 1823–24", *Am. pol. sci. rev.*, VI (1912) 546–563 [1161] considers briefly the reception accorded Monroe's message in England, France, Spain, and Austria; "South America and the Monroe Doctrine, 1824–1828",

Pol. sci. quar., XXX (1915) 82–105 [**1162**] describes briefly the reception of the message of Dec. 2, 1823, by Colombia, Brazil, and the provinces of the Rio de la Plata; *United States and Spain in 1822*, (no. 1029) deals with the immediate antecedents of the Monroe Doctrine message. *Miranda* (no. 556). A. B. Hart, *The Monroe Doctrine; an interpretation* (Boston, 1916) [**1163**], this work is replete with excerpts from official utterances on the Monroe Doctrine, to 1915, many of which may be found in Moore's *Digest* (no. 5365) for the period before 1906, and in the published writings of American statesmen. The author interprets these statements in multifarious ways under numerous rubrics. It is encyclopedic rather than a contribution of original scholarship. Lockey, *Pan-Americanism* (no. 964). W. A. Phillips, *The Confederation of Europe; a study of the European alliance, 1813–1823* (London and N.Y., 1920) [**1164**], a polished and scholarly study of the European peace settlement of 1815, the accompanying and sequent alliances including the genesis of the Monroe Doctrine. Constantin Rados, " Webster, Monroë et le philhellénisme aux États-Unis pendant la guerre de l'indépendance grecque ", *Acropole*, I (Athens, 1920) 39–48 [**1165**] attaches much significance to the paragraph in Monroe's message, to Webster's speeches, and the activities of the philhellenic " Samuel Owe " of Boston as encouragements to the Greek cause; light. W. P. Cresson, *The Holy alliance; the European background of the Monroe Doctrine* (N.Y., 1922) [**1166**] no improvement on Phillips, and superseded by Perkins; and his " Chateaubriand and the Monroe Doctrine ", *No. Am. rev.*, CCXVII (1923) 475–487 [**1167**], nothing new. L. A. Lawson, *The relation of British policy to the declaration of the Monroe Doctrine* (N.Y., 1922) [**1168**], " an instructive recapitulation of a familiar story rather than an original contribution to historical knowledge." W. A. MacCorkle, *The personal genesis of the Monroe Doctrine* (N.Y. and London, 1923) [**1169**] is written to " submit the proof that James Monroe held no trumpet through which any other man should blow his defiance to the world." S. E. Morison, " The origin of the Monroe Doctrine, 1775–1823 ", *Economica*, IV (1924) 27–51 [**1170**], a useful summary with a recapitulation of " anti-entanglement " philosophy of American statesmen from 1776, translated into French, in " Les origines de la doctrine de Monroe ", *Rev. sci. pol.*,

XLVII (1924) 52–84. C. K. Webster, *The foreign policy of Castlereagh, 1815–1822,*[11] *Britain and the European alliance* (London, 1925) [**1171**], another definitive multiarchival study, companion to Temperley's *Foreign policy of Canning,* indispensable for the European background of the Monroe Doctrine. Dexter Perkins, *The Monroe Doctrine, 1823–1826* (Cambridge, 1927) [**1172**], one of the most solid pieces of research in the diplomatic history of the United States, based on thorough archival research in all relevant countries. It incorporates earlier articles published in the *American historical review.* An abridgment, in effect, may be found in same author's *John Quincy Adams,* in *Am. secs. state,* v. IV (no. 4796). No one will question the definitiveness of the study. Some have attributed more influence to J. Q. Adams in the pronouncement of the doctrine. W. F. Craven, jr., " The risk of the Monroe Doctrine, 1823–1824 ", *Hisp. Am. hist. rev.,* VII (1927) 320–333 [**1173**] points out what Perkins also showed: that " there was very little prospect of European intervention and, therefore, little risk assumed by the United States." Earle, *Am. interest in Greek cause* (no. 1428). Johnson, *Monroe Doctrine and Panama congress* (no. 1070). Cline, *Am. attitude toward Greek war* (no. 1436). Camilo Barcía Trelles, *Doctrina de Monroë y cooperación internacional* (Madrid, 1931) [**1174**], also published in French in the *Recueil des cours,* of the Académie de Droit International, 1930, t. II (Paris, 1931) 391–605, a voluminous disquisition which links the Monroe Doctrine with the idea of the intangibility of America originating as far back as the writings of Francisco Vitoria in the 16th century; suggests that the United States made a great error, 1823–1826, in failing to accept the proffered cooperation of the new Hispanic-American republics in the Monroe Doctrine: followed by a penetrating analysis of the significance of the Monroe Doctrine in the 20th century. Watt Stewart, *Argentina and Monroe Doctrine* (no. 1081). Rippy, *Latin America in world politics* (no. 1070). C. H. Salit, " La política de no intervención de Canning en la América española ", *Inst. investigaciones hist. bol.* (Buenos Aires. Universidad Nacional, Instituto de Investigaciones Históricas), año XI, t. XV (no. 54) (1932) 432–457 [**1175**], based on the published American and English sources and standard secondary authorities (Stapleton, Webster, Temperley) to

---

[11] His later, 1931, notable study of Castlereagh's foreign policy from 1812–1815 (no. 893) does not touch the United States.

suggest that Canning was a glorious statesman who in extending British diplomacy and commerce asked nothing for Great Britain which he would not have gladly conceded to others. Savelle, *Am. dipl. principles* (no. 4823a), for precedents for some principles of American foreign policy. T. R. Schellenberg, "Jeffersonian origins of the Monroe Doctrine", *Hisp. Am. hist. rev.*, XIV (1934) 1–32 [**1176**], an important article, which traces the influence of the writings of du Pradt on Jefferson's conception of the political system of the old world as distinct from the new, particularly du Pradt's discernment (1819) of an American system as distinct from the European system, and Jefferson's conversations and writings with and to Monroe on this subject, 1820–23.

For biographies of American statesmen and diplomatists (Adams, Calhoun, Clay, Jefferson, Madison, Monroe, Richard Rush), see the relevant entries and bibliographical data in the *D.A.B.*, and *Am. secs. state* (no. 4796).

For biographies of George Canning, see the *D.N.B.*. Biographies of Canning since the *D.N.B.* are: J. A. R. Marriott, *George Canning and his times; a political study* (London, 1903) [**1177**]; H. W. V. Temperley, *Life of Canning* (London, 1905) [**1178**] (not to be confused with his more mature *Foreign policy of Canning*, no. 1152). *George Canning and his friends, containing hitherto unpublished letters, jeux d'esprit, etc.*, ed. by Captain Josceline Bagot (London, 1909, 2 v.) [**1179**]; and Sir Charles Petrie, *George Canning* (London, 1930) [**1180**]. Webster, *Foreign policy of Castlereagh* (no. 1171). See also, for European statesmen, W. P. Cresson, *Diplomatic portraits; Europe and the Monroe Doctrine one hundred years ago* (Boston and N.Y., 1923) [**1181**].

Printed Sources

For American official documents and general source collections, see Sec. 1, above. Note particularly Moore's *Digest* (no. 5365), v. VI, 368–604, for a survey of the Monroe Doctrine, with copious extracts from state papers relating to its promulgation, principles, and special applications.

For British official documents, see p. 838.

Appeal of Messenian Senate of Calamata to citizens of the United States, May 1821, printed in English translation in *No. Am. rev.*, XVII (1823) 415–416 [**1182**], asking assistance to purge Greece from the Barbarians. Vicomte de Chateaubriand, *Congrès de Vérone*, 2 éd. (Paris, 1838, 2 v.), and English edition, *The Congress of Verona* (London, 1838, 2 v.) [1183], mainly memoirs, and correspondence; also "Some unedited letters of Chateaubriand printed as the 'Supplément au Congrès de Vérone'" in the *Revue politique et littéraire*, L (1912) 513–518, 545–551 [1184] contains correspondence with the Prince de Polignac, 1823–1824; and his *Œuvres complètes* (Paris, 1865–73, 12 v.) [1185]. Richard Rush, *Residence at the court of London* (no. 5288), for the conversations between Canning and Rush, the latter's despatches, etc. *Corres. Castlereagh* (no. 864), v. XII (1818–1822) contains letters of Bagot regarding the Monroe Doctrine. Wellington, *Supplementary despatches* (no. 924). Yonge, *Liverpool* (no. 866), v. III, 297–304: "Memorandum by Lord Liverpool" reviewing the state of the relations of Great Britain with the provinces of Spanish America, 1824 [1186]. D. F. O'Leary, *Memorias . . .*, ed. by his son, S. B. O'Leary (Caracas, 1879–1914, 32 v.) [1187] is a voluminous collection of correspondence of Bolívar and his associates, useful for the South American aspects of the Monroe Doctrine, but difficult to use, as it is without index of any kind, despite its many volumes. *Sesiones de los cuerpos legislativos de la República de Chile, 1811 á 1845*, ed. by Valentín Letelier (Santiago, 1887–1908, 37 v.) [1188] includes debates on foreign affairs, and drafts of instructions to Chilean diplomatic envoys. *Official corres. Canning* (no. 969). Comte Jean de Villèle, *Mémoires et correspondance* (Paris, 1888–90, 5 v.) [1189]. *Mémoires Hyde de Neuville* (no. 1005). A. B. Hart and Edward Channing, eds., *Extracts from official declarations of the United States embodying the Monroe Doctrine, 1789–1891* (N.Y., 1892) [1190]. [S. M. Hamilton, ed.], *The Hamilton facsimiles in the national archives relating to American history.* Part I. *The Monroe Doctrine; its origin and intent* (N.Y., 1896) [1191], facsimiles of the correspondence between Monroe and ex-presidents Jefferson and Madison relating to Canning's proposals to Rush in 1823. Gabriel Festing, *John Hookam Frere and his friends* (London, 1899) [1192] prints several letters of George Canning to Frere, including one of Jan. 8, 1825, discussing American affairs. W. C. Ford, *J. Q. Adams and Monroe Doctrine* (no. 1147) includes documents; also his "Some original documents on the genesis of the Monroe Doctrine", *Mass. hist. soc. proc.*, 2d ser., XV

(1902) 373-436 [**1193**], which was also published separately under title, *John Quincy Adams; his connection with the Monroe Doctrine* (Cambridge, Mass., 1902), consisting of hitherto unpublished documents found among the J. Q. Adams papers, and from the Department of State. A. A. Polovtsov, *Correspondance diplomatique des ambassadeurs et ministères de Russie en France et de France en Russie* (Paris, 1902-07, 3 v., also issued (in Russian), St. Petersburg, 1904) [**1194**]. *Papers of Sir Charles R. Vaughan* (no. 1380). *Proceedings Alaska boundary tribunal* (no. 2610) v. II, 31-93 : " Diplomatic correspondence relating to the treaty of 1824 between the United States and Russia " [**1195**]. Edgington (no. 1149) reprints extracts of the correspondence of Rush with the Department of State. " Canning and Cuba, 1812 ", *So. hist. assoc. pub.*, XI (1907) 1-5 [**1196-7**] prints two unpublished despatches from George Canning to Stratford Canning, British minister at Washington, which relate to Canning's American policy in regard to Cuba, and should be read in connection with Temperley's article (no. 1150). *George Canning and his friends* (no. 1179) contains letters by and to Canning, and other correspondence. *Corres. Russian ministers in Washington, 1818-1823* (no. 1448). *Corres. Provincia de Buenos Aires* (no. 1120), for South American aspects of the Monroe Doctrine. Brazil, *Arch. dipl. independencia* (no. 1123). *Camb. hist. Brit. for. pol.* (no. 209), v. II, Appendix B contains " The suppressed parts of Polignac memorandum, October 9th, 1823 " [**1198**]. Harold Temperley, " Documents illustrating the reception and interpretation of the Monroe Doctrine in Europe, 1823-4 ", *Eng. hist. rev.*, XXXIX (1924) 590-593 [**1199**] deal with Austrian policy, French policy, and United States policy. *Protocols of conferences . . . of the allied powers respecting So. Am.* (no. 1118). Manning, *Dipl. corres.* (no. 1124). *Archivo Mirando* (no. 1126). *Cartas libertador* (Bolívar) (no. 1127). *Corres. Henry Wellesley* (the British ambassador to Austria, 1822-31) (no. 1565) includes some items relating to the consideration of Spanish-American affairs at Vienna, 1822-25.

For the printed writings of American statesmen and diplomatists (J. Q. Adams, Calhoun, Clay, Gallatin, Jefferson, Madison, Monroe, and Rush)[12] see our list on p. 756.

---

[12] Rush's despatches of 1823, " some of which are known, but all of which are not printed in the *State papers*", are printed in the *Writings* of Monroe (Hamilton edition), v. VI, 356-419.

The printed writings (memoirs, correspondence, etc.) of foreign statesmen are entered above.

For extracts from leading European newspapers reflecting the reception of the message abroad in 1823–24, see Robertson (no. 1161).

MSS.: Suggestions

See Sec. 1, above, particularly for references to American and foreign archival guides and indexes and references to papers of presidents and secretaries of state. We have, preserved, the personal papers of the successive British ministers to the United States at this time: Charles Bagot, 1816–1819, private papers now in the possession of Col. Bagot of Levens Hall (temporarily deposited in the Public Record Office for copying), official papers in the Public Record Office; copies of both in the Canadian Archives, for list see *Report of the work of the [Canadian] archives branch for the year 1910* (Ottawa, 1911), 28–50 [**1200**]. Stratford Canning, 1820–1823, in the British Public Record Office; and Sir Charles Vaughan, 1825–1831, described and copiously printed by J. A. Doyle (see no. 1380). Perkins (no. 1172) has given in his bibliographical note a brief statement of the MS. sources in Washington and in European archives, but any investigator must supplement this by a use of the guides and indexes to British, French, Russian, Prussian, Austrian, and Spanish archives (see below, Pt. II, ch. 3) and also for transcripts and facsimiles of same in the United States. Note particularly Torres Lanzas (no. 5640, below).

CHAPTER VIII

THE UNITED STATES AND HISPANIC AMERICA[1]
1826–1861

1. In General

Bibliographical Aids

For general bibliographical aids (American), see Sabin (no. 4655); Larned (no. 4657); Griffin (no. 4658); *Writings* (no. 4661); C. H. and T. (no. 4662); *Am. secs. state* (no. 4796), for " Bibliographical notes "; *Guide hist. lit.* (no. 4634); Myers (no. 5399), for collections of treaties. Miller, *Treaties* (no. 5371), v. I, 39–54, for " Bibliography of United States treaty collections."

For contemporary periodical references (notably *Niles's register*), consult *Poole's index to periodical literature* (no. 4995).

See also Spanish historical bibliographies (nos. 4758–4760), particularly Sánchez Alonso (no. 4759); and Spanish American historical bibliographies (nos. 4678–4725a).

General Works

Of general histories of the United States, see Von Holst (no. 4780); McMaster (no. 4781); Channing (no. 4784). See also *Am. secs. state*, v. IV–VI (no. 4796); and Wriston, *Exec. agents* (no. 4799). Miller, *Treaties* (no. 5371), v. III, for historical notes of great value.

For critical appraisals and comments on leading Hispanic-American histories, carefully chosen and analyzed, see *Guide hist. lit.* (no.

---

[1] Except Mexico. For Mexico and Texas, see below, Chapt. X.

4634). For a convenient list of general histories of Hispanic America, consult Wilgus, *Histories of Hispanic America* (no. 966), noting in particular: Juan Ortega y Rubio, *Historia de América* (Madrid, 1917, 3 v.) [1201]; Carlos Pereyra, *Historia de América española* (Madrid, 1920–26, 8 v.) [1202] C. E. Akers, *A history of South America*, new ed., with additional chapters bringing the work down to 1930 (N.Y., 1930; 1st ed., London, 1904) [1203]; and J. F. Rippy, *Historical evolution of Hispanic America* (N.Y., 1932) [1204], the latest of a number of textbooks on the subject, which devotes a large part to a survey of the international relations of the states of Hispanic America.

G. W. Crichfield, *American supremacy; the rise and progress of the Latin American republics and their relations to the United States under the Monroe Doctrine* (N.Y., 1909, 2 v.) [1205], a hodge-podge of quotations, statistics, and dates. Latané, *U.S. and Lat. Am.* (no. 963). Lockey, *Pan Americanism* (no. 964). W. S. Robertson, *Hispanic-American relations with the United States* (N.Y. and London, 1923) [1206] has an historical survey by a competent scholar familiar with foreign writers. Rippy, *Latin America in world politics* (no. 1070). Stuart, *Latin America and U.S.* (no. 965).

Special Works

J. M. Callahan, " Statements, interpretations, and applications of the Monroe Doctrine and of more or less allied doctrines from 1845 to 1870 ", in the *Proceedings of the American Society of International Law*, at its eighth annual meeting (Wash., 1914) 59–105 [1207]. C. H. Wesley, " The struggle for the recognition of Haiti and Liberia as independent republics ", *Jour. negro hist.*, II (1917) 369–383 [1208], brief summary from U.S. published documents. Rippy, *Rivalry of U.S. and Gt. Brit. over Latin America* (no. 1077). J. T. Lanning, " Great Britain and Spanish recognition of the Hispanic-American states ", *Hisp. Am. hist. rev.*, X (1930) 429–456 [1209] shows the uneasiness caused in Washington in 1836 by the influence of Great Britain in persuading Spain to recognize the American republics. A. C. Wilgus, " Official expression of manifest destiny sentiment concerning Hispanic America, 1848–1871 ", *La. hist. quar.*, XV (1932) 486–506 [1210], as revealed in debates of Congress, messages of the presidents, etc. Dexter Perkins, *The Monroe Doctrine,*

1826–1867 (Baltimore, 1933) [**1211**], a sequel to the author's other notable volume on the origins of the doctrine, 1823–1826 (no. 1172).

For biographies of American presidents, secretaries of state, and diplomatists to the Hispanic American states (for names and tenure, see latest *Register* of the Dept. of State (no. 5122)), see the relevant entries and bibliographical data in the *D.A.B.* and *Am. secs. state* (no. 4796). Note also Clark, *John Quincy Adams* (no. 967).

For list of Hispanic American diplomatists to the United States, see the *Register* of the Dept. of State, 1874 (no. 5122). The comparatively few biographical studies of Hispanic American diplomatists to the United States are cited by us in the appropriate sections of this bibliography.

Printed Sources

For American official documents and general source collections, see *Jour. exec. proc. Sen.* (no. 5387); *Reg. debates Cong.* (no. 5383); *Cong. Globe* (no. 5384); Wharton, *Digest* (no. 5366); *Abridg. debates* (no. 5386); Richardson (no. 5335); *Repts. Sen. com. for. rel.* (no. 5388); Moore's *Arbitrations* (no. 5364), and *Digest* (no. 5365); note particularly Hasse (no. 5344) for index to the United States documents relating to foreign affairs.

For list of treaty collections, see Myers (no. 5399); for texts of treaties, see Miller, *Treaties* (no. 5371).

For guides to newspapers, see nos. 5004–5044; particularly Library of Congress *Check-list* (no. 5030); and Pan American Union *Catalogue* (no. 5037); and for list of early Hispanic American newspapers, see Robertson (no. 1206), 452–453. An analysis of the principal American newspapers and periodicals, 1848 to 1871, is given in J. G. Gazley (no. 1424).

For guides to Hispanic American official documents, see Childs (nos. 5424 and 5425), and Gregory (no. 5400) for a check-list, only, of the serial publications of the Hispanic American nations, noting particularly the publications of the ministries of foreign affairs.

Robertson, *Docs. consular service U.S. in Latin America* (no. 1117). Manning, *Dipl. corres. indep. Latin America* (no. 5342) contains documents to 1830; and his *Dipl. corres. U.S.; inter-American affairs* (no. 5343), v. I–IV, (Argentina, Bolivia, and Brazil, Central America having appeared to date (1934); they cover the period 1831 to 1860, and include (with a few exceptions) all the documents in the archives of the Department of State bearing upon the international relations of the Hispanic American states. Urrutia, *Páginas hist. diplomática* (no. 1119). *Cartas del Libertador* (Bolívar) (no. 1127).

For the printed writings of American presidents, secretaries of state, and diplomatists to Hispanic America (for names and tenure, see latest *Register* of the Dept. of State (no. 5122)), see our list on p. 756.

MSS.: Suggestions

Suggestions of unprinted material must be meager for this relatively undeveloped phase of the diplomatic history of the United States, because of the lack of spade work done in the inventorying and indexing of the archives of the various states of South and Central America. On the other hand the MS. material in the United States is readily indicated; much of the official material is now being printed.[2] For guide to MS. material in the Department of State, see Pt. II, chs. 1 and 3. For the few indexes to Hispanic American archival collections, see p. 909. The diplomatic relations of the several Hispanic American states with Europe often touch or overlap the relations of the United States; consequently the investigator may find it necessary to consult European archives and collections; for guides, indexes, etc., to these see our notes below, Pt. II, ch. 3.

For papers of presidents of the United States (in this period; J. Q. Adams, Andrew Jackson, Martin Van Buren, W. H. Harrison, John Tyler, J. K. Polk, Zachary Taylor, Millard Fillmore, Franklin Pierce, and James Buchanan), and secretaries of state (Henry Clay, Van Buren, Edward Livingston, Louis McLane, John Forsyth, Daniel Webster, A. P. Upshur, J. C. Calhoun, James Buchanan, J. M. Clayton, Edward Everett, W. L. Marcy, Lewis Cass, and Jeremiah S. Black), see our notes below, p. 862 (presidents), and p. 865 (secretaries of state). There is in the Library of Congress a small portfolio of papers of Wm. H. Trescot, assistant secretary of state, June to

---

[2] W. R. Manning's first series (no. 5342) printed the diplomatic correspondence of the United States in regard to the several Hispanic-American states, 1809 to 1830. The second series (no. 5343) will cover the period 1831 to 1861, grouped by states. Of this the volumes on the Argentine, Bolivia and Brazil, Central America, Chile and Colombia, have already (1935) appeared. The American Historical Association in 1932 passed a resolution importuning the Carnegie Endowment for International Peace and the Pan American Union to stimulate the several republics to publish in an organized fashion the Hispanic-American counterparts to Manning. This is a consummation devoutly to be wished.

December 1860, on diplomatic and political affairs. The correspondence of President Buchanan and Cave Johnson, nominated by Buchanan as commissioner to Paraguay to settle disputed claims of citizens against the United States and the Paraguayan Navigation Company, in 1860, is in the Historical Society of Pennsylvania.

Diplomatic representatives of the United States to Hispanic American states in this period, who have left collections of papers are: Wm. H. Harrison (later President), *chargé* to New Granada in 1828 (see p. 863 for his papers); M. B. Lamar (former President of Texas), minister to Nicaragua and Costa Rica, 1858–59; E. G. Squier, *chargé* to Central America, 1849; and E. L. Plumb, secretary of legation at Mexico, 1866–67, and *chargé d'affaires*, 1867–68; for papers see our list on p. 868.

2. Cuban Question

For the Cuban Question, 1826–1861, see Ch. XII: " Slavery and Expansion ", sec. 2 (" The Cuban Question, 1826–1860 "). For the Cuban Question before 1826, see Ch. VII, sec. 3 (" The United States and Hispanic America, to 1826 ") and sec. 4 (" The Origin of the Monroe Doctrine ").

3. Central America:[3] Isthmian Diplomacy

Bibliographical Aids

For general aids, see Sec. 1, above.

War Dept. Library, *Mexico* (no. 4712), pt. 2: " Interoceanic canals and railroads." H. A. Morrison, *List of books and articles in periodicals relating to interoceanic canal and railway routes (Nicaragua; Panama, Darien, and the valley of the Atrato; Tehuantepec and Honduras; Suez Canal* (Wash., 1900) (Library of Congress) [**1212**], appendix: *Bibliography of United States public documents*, prepared in the office of the Superintendent of Documents, which lists documents of 1827–1899. Travis, *Clayton-Bulwer treaty* (no. 1229), " Bibliography ": p. 309–312. Phillips, *Central America* (no. 4703). J. C. Frank, *American interoceanic canals; a list of references in the New York Public Library* (N.Y., 1916), reprinted from its *Bulletin*, January 1916 [**1213**]. Williams, *Isthmian diplomacy* (no. 1235), " Bibliography ": p. 331–345. Two lists by H. H. B.

---

[3] For material regarding William Walker and Nicaragua, see Ch. XII, sec. 4.

65215—35——15

Meyer: *Monroe Doctrine* (no. 1140), and *List of references on the Panama Canal and the Panama Canal Zone* (Wash., 1919) Library of Congress) [1214].

General Works

See Sec. 1, above, for general histories of the United States and general works on American diplomacy.

During his diplomatic career in Central America, 1849–1853, E. G. Squier [4] profited from his experiences and observations by writing then and later a number of books which taken together afford a compendium of information then available on social, economic, and political conditions of the Central American republics: *Nicaragua, its people, scenery, monuments, and the proposed interoceanic canal* (N.Y., 1852, 2 v.) [1215]; *Travels in Central America* (N.Y., 1853, 2 v.) [1216]; *Notes on Central America; particularly the states of Honduras and San Salvador* (N.Y., 1855) [1217]; *The States of Central America* (N.Y., 1858) [1218]; *Honduras; descriptive, historical, and statistical* (London, 1870) [1219], enlarged from his *Notes on Central America.* Lorenzo Montúfar y Rivera Maestre, *Reseña histórica de Centro-América* (Guatemala, 1878–87 ['88], 7 v.) [1219a], this work covers the period from 1812 to 1860, and is valuable as a Central American view of the rivalry of the United States and Great Britain in the area, as well as of Walker and the filibusters. H. H. Bancroft, *History of Central America* (San Francisco, 1882–87, 3 v.) [1220], under the direction of the nominal author, more material than previously amassed was available for this narrative, but the haste which forced the work prevented it from reaching the higher standards of scholarship now demanded. It is valuable for its variety of data. A. R. Gibbs, *British Honduras; an historical and descriptive account of the colony from its settlement, 1670* (London, 1883) [1221], an undocumented narrative said to be " readable and apparently trustworthy." W. F. Johnson, *Four centuries of the Panama Canal* (N.Y., 1906) [1222], by a facile and informative writer of voluminous books for popular consumption. Alcée Fortier and J. R. Ficklen, *Central America and Mexico* (Phila., 1907) [1223], for a brief account of Central American history. Koebel, *Central America* (no. 3774).

---

[4] For a bibliography compiled by Rafael Heliodoro Valle, of the various books and pamphlets published by Squier, see *Hisp. Am. hist. rev.*, V (1922), 776–789.

Special Works

A number of the special studies of the diplomacy of the United States with Panama, entered more fully later, have introductory chapters on earlier Isthmian diplomacy: Viallate (no. 2651); Huberich (no. 2653); Tavernier (no. 3679); Müller-Heymer (no. 2655); Arias (no. 3681); Bunau-Varilla (no. 3739); Kennedy (no. 2664); Tower (no. 2671).

Two articles published in the *Democratic review*, XXXI (n.s. I) (1852): "The islands of the Gulf of Honduras; their seizure and organization as a British colony" (p. 544–552), and "Our foreign relations. Central America—The Crampton and Webster project" (p. 337–352) [**1224**]. L. M. Keasbey, *The early diplomatic history of the Nicaragua canal* (Newark, N.J., 1890) [**1225**], a scholarly thesis, served as apprentice work for his later *The Nicaragua canal and the Monroe Doctrine; a political history of Isthmus transit, with special reference to the Nicaragua canal project and the attitude of the United States government thereto* (N.Y. and London, 1896) [**1226**], a book written to inspire American control over the future canal route, as against Great Britain and the estoppel of the Clayton-Bulwer treaty. The investigations were restricted to printed sources and works, principally American. Also by the same writer, "The national canal policy", *Am. hist. assoc. ann. rep.*, for 1902, v. I (1903) 275–288 [**1227**], a cogent plea for control of the canal by the United States, and for the Nicaraguan route rather than Panama. I. D. Travis, *British rule in Central America; or, A sketch of Mosquito history* (Ann Arbor, Mich., 1895) [**1228**], a short thesis which serves as an approach to the author's formidable, *The history of the Clayton-Bulwer treaty* (Ann Arbor, Mich., 1900) [**1229**], the first objective study, based on American and British printed state papers, now superseded by Williams (no. 1235). M. W. Hazeltine, "The Clayton-Bulwer treaty", *No. Am. rev.*, CLXV (1897) 452–459 [**1230**]. J. G. Whiteley, "The diplomacy of the United States in regard to Central American canals", *ibid.*, 364–378 [**1231**], substantially a plea for our adherence to the Clayton-Bulwer treaty. Smith, *England and America* (no. 340), "Clayton-Bulwer treaty": p. 296–313. Eduardo Posada and P. M. Ibáñez, *Vida de Herrán* (Bogotá, 1903) [**1232**], Pedro A. Herrán, minister of New Granada at Washington, 1855–63. Latané, *U.S. and Co-*

lombia (no. 963) analyses later American official discussions and interpretations of the treaty of 1846. Raúl Pérez, " The treacherous treaty; a Colombian plea ", *No. Am. rev.*, CLXXVII (1903) 934–946 [**1233**], a Colombian's analysis of the later history of the treaty of 1846 with New Granada, particularly in relation to the Hay-Herrán unratified treaty of 1903. C. M. Colby, " Diplomacy of the quarter deck ", *Am. jour. internat. law*, VIII (1914) 443–476 [**1234**] deals with the diplomatic activities of naval officers at Panama in regard to the treaty with New Granada in 1846. Rivas, *Colombia y los Estados Unidos* (no. 1040). Mary W. Williams, *Anglo-American Isthmian diplomacy, 1815–1915* (Wash., 1916; another ed.: Baltimore, 1916) [**1235**] is the standard authority, one of the outstanding studies in the diplomatic history of the United States, which embodies scholarly researches in English and American printed and unprinted sources. John Bigelow, *Breaches of Anglo-American treaties* (N.Y., 1917) [**1236**] is mainly devoted to the Clayton-Bulwer treaty. J. A. Hoyos, *Les Etats-Unis et la Colombie* (Paris, 1918) [**1236a**] shows the policy of New Granada to have been friendly to the United States at this early period. Munro, *Central America* (no. 3775), a good summary of the early political history of the Isthmus in the first chapters. *Camb. hist. Brit. for. pol.* (no. 209), v. II, p. 265–283 : " The Clayton-Bulwer treaty, 1849–1856." Hill, *Treaties* (no. 4794), p. 347–387 : " The Panama canal treaties." W. W. Pierson, " The political influences of an interoceanic canal, 1826–1926 ", *Hisp. Am. hist. rev.*, VI (1926) 205–231 [**1237**]. Hellmuth von Cramon, " Der diplomatische Kampf Englands und der Vereinigten Staaten um Nicaragua ", *Europaische Gespräche*, V (1927) 342–355 [**1237a**], undocumented essay on the events of 1848–50. Stuart, *Lat. America and U.S.* (no. 965), ch. 3. J. B. Lockey, " Diplomatic futility ", *Hisp. Am. hist. rev.*, X (1930) 265–294 [**1238**] discusses the diplomatic careers of the eleven appointees to Central America before 1849, of whom only one prolonged his stay more than a few months, the others having suffered various misfortunes. R. R. MacGregor, " The treaty of 1846 (seventeen years of American-Colombian relations, 1830–1846)", in Clark University, *Thesis abstracts, 1929* (Worcester, 1930) 35–39 [**1239**], written primarily from the archives of the Department of State, but not overlooking Rivas' Colombian monograph (no. 1040). Rippy, *Latin America in world* *politics* (no. 1070).   G. F. Hickson, "Palmerston and the Clayton-Bulwer treaty", *Cambridge hist. jour.*, III (1931) 295–303 [**1240**] a reexamination of foreign office papers in the British Public Record Office yields a little new light, for one thing: the British government preferred to negotiate at Washington because Secretary of State Clayton had informed Crampton, British minister, that he did not hold to the principles of President Monroe in regard to non-colonization.   J. D. Ward, "Sir Henry Bulwer and the United States archives", *ibid.*, 304–313 [**1241**] discusses alleged insertion of a fraudulent document.   Perkins, *Monroe Doctrine* (no. 1211), ch. 4: "The Central American question and the doctrine, 1849–1863."

For biographies of American presidents: (Jackson, Van Buren, Harrison, Tyler, Polk, Taylor, Fillmore, Pierce, Buchanan) secretaries of state (Forsyth, Webster, Upshur, Calhoun, Buchanan, Clayton, Everett, Marcy, Cass), and diplomatists (to Great Britain: Edward Everett, Geo. Bancroft, Abbott Lawrence, James Buchanan, and G. M. Dallas; to Central America: B. A. Bidlack, Solon Borland, Alex. Dimitry, Elijah Hise, E. G. Squier), see the relevant entries and bibliographical notes in the *D.A.B.*

For biographies of British statesmen (Palmerston, Lord John Russell) and diplomatists (Sir Henry Bulwer, J. P. Crampton, Earl of Clarendon), see the *D.N.B.* and appended bibliographical notes.

Printed Sources

For American official documents and general source collections, see Sec. 1, above.

For a list of U.S. public documents relating to interoceanic communication, 1827–1900, see Morrison's bibliography (no. 1212).   For an index to U.S. documents relating to canal diplomacy, to 1801, see Hasse's *Index* (no. 5344).

For vote on ratification of the Clayton-Bulwer treaty in the United States Senate, see the *Congressional Globe*, Appendix, 32d Cong., 2d sess., Senate special session, 27, 1852–53, p. 267 [**1241a**].

For guides to British official documents, see below, p. 838.   British Parliamentary (House of Commons Sessional) Papers: *Correspondence respecting the Mosquito Territory* (1847–1848, LXV) [**1242**]; *Correspondence with the United States respecting Central America* and *Further correspondence* . . . (1849–56) (1856, LX) [**1243**],

p. 155–158, for the Webster-Crampton project; and *idem* (1856–60) (1860, LXVIII); and *Bay Islands* (1856, XLIV) [**1244**].

For guides to Central American documents, see Childs, *Memorias* (no. 5424); and Gregory (no. 5400).

Adolphe Dénain, *Ensayo sobre los intereses políticos y comerciales del istmo de Panamá considerandoles bajo el punto de vista de la Nueva Granada* (Panamá, 1844), photostat reproduction . . . of an original in the library of the Ministère des Affaires Etrangères, Paris (Wash., 1931) [**1245**]; and French edition, *Considérations sur les intérêts politiques et commerciaux qui se rattachent à l'isthme de Panama* (Paris, 1845) [**1246**]. Three works by Felipe Molina (Costa Rican minister to the United States, 1851–53): *Der Freistaat Costa Rica in Mittel-Amerika und seine Wichtigkeit für den Welthandel, den Ackerbau und die Kolonisation nach Französischen des F.M.*, ed. by Freiherr A. v. Bülow (Berlin, 1850) [**1247**]; *Memoir on the boundary question pending between the republic of Costa Rica and the state of Nicaragua* (Wash., 1851) [**1248**]; and *Costa Rica and New Granada; an inquiry into the question of boundaries, which is pending between the two republics* (Wash., 1853) [**1249**] includes " documentary evidence in support of the ancient title of Costa Rica." " Letters of Bancroft and Buchanan on the Clayton-Bulwer treaty, 1849, 1850," ed. by G. E. Belknap, *Am. hist. rev.*, V (1899) 95–102 [**1250–1**]. *Duke of Argyll . . . memoirs* (no. 1976) discusses briefly (v. II, 47–48) the Nicaraguan question, 1856. Lord Stanmore [Arthur Hamilton Gordon], *Sidney Herbert, Lord Herbert of Lea; a memoir* (London, 1906, 2 v.) [**1252**] contains a letter from Gladstone, June 16, 1856, discussing the Dallas negotiation of Central American affairs. Richard Olney (secretary of state, 1895–97), *The Clayton-Bulwer treaty; memorandum* (Wash., 1900) [**1253**], the treaty at this time was still in full binding force and vigor. *Vaughan papers* (no. 1380) throw light on the question of the interoceanic canal. A. B. Hart, *Extracts from official papers relating to the Isthmian canal, 1515–1909* (N.Y., 1910) (American History Leaflets, no. 34) [**1254**]. *Compilation of executive documents and diplomatic correspondence relative to a trans-isthmian canal in Central America; with specific reference to the treaty of 1846 between the United States and New Granada (U.S. of Colombia) and the " Clayton-Bulwer " treaty of 1850* (N.Y., 1905, 3 v.) [**1255**], published (significantly) by Sullivan and Cromwell, general counsel for the

New Panama Canal Company. " Letters of E. George Squier to John M. Clayton, 1849–1850," ed. by M. W. Williams, *Hisp. Am. hist. rev.*, I (1918) 426–434 [**1256**], letters written to the secretary of state by the American *chargé* in Central America, relating mainly to difficulties with Great Britain, found among the Clayton papers in the Library of Congress.

For texts of the treaties with New Granada (1846), and Great Britain (1850), see Miller, *Treaties* (no. 5371).

For printed writings of American statesmen and diplomatists (enumerated above, under " Special Works "), see our list on p. 756.

MSS.: Suggestions

See Sec. 1, above; also Ch. IX, sec. 1, for papers of British statesmen. Note also the photocopies of the political and commercial reports from Prussian representatives in Central America during the eighteen fifties, in the Library of Congress.

Maps: Suggestions

Pedro Torres Lanzas, *Relación descriptiva de los mapas, planos, etc., de la audiencia y capitanía general de Guatemala (Guatemala, San Salvador, Honduras, Nicaragua, y Costa Rica) existentes en el Archivo General de Indias* [1590–1892] (Madrid, 1903) [**1257**], reprinted from the *Revista de archivos*, for 1903. Phillips, *Maps relating to Central America* (no. 4703). *Cartografía de la América Central*, published by the Guatemalan " Comisión de Límites " (Guatemala, 1929) [**1258**] contains maps submitted in the Guatemala-Honduras boundary mediation of 1918, and includes 20 maps published 1840–1860, among them 3 maps of Central America, by E. G. Squier, 1849, 1853, and 1858. American Geographical Society, *Maps Hispanic America* (no. 5153).

4. New Granada and Colombia [5]

Bibliographical Aids

See Sec. 1, above.

General Works

For general histories, see Sec. 1, above. For a general history of Colombia: Jules Humbert, *Histoire de la Colombie et du Véné-*

---

[5] See also Sec. 3, above (" Central America : Isthmian Diplomacy ").

zuéla des origines jusqu'à nos jours (Paris, 1921) [**1259**], a "well ordered sketch presenting alternately the development of each republic." J. M. Henao and Gerardo Arrubia, *Historia de Colombia para la enseñanza secundaria,* 5th ed., revised and enlarged (Bogotá, 1929, 2 v. in 1) [**1260**], probably the best survey of the history of Colombia, but foreign relations are sketched rather briefly.

Special Works

Raimundo Rivas, *Colombia y los Estados Unidos* (no. 1040), important for Colombian sources used. A. C. Rivas, *Ensayos de historia política y diplomática* (Madrid, 1916) [**1261**] includes a section on " La diplomacia de los Estados Unidos y la monarquía en Colombia " (p. 161–242), which is concerned with the missions of Gen. W. H. Harrison and T. P. Moore, 1828–1831, and their anxiety about a possible monarchial coup d'état in Colombia. The author uses, and prints, Spanish translations of selected despatches of these ministers to the secretaries of state; the *Memorias* of O'Leary, and the above-mentioned work of Raimundo Rivas. Zubieta, *Primeras misiones dipl. Colombia* (no. 1057). Rippy, *Rivalry* (no. 1077), ch. 5: " Rivalry in northern South America "; and *Capitalists* (no. 3696), for early interests and activities of capitalists in Colombia.

For biographies of American statesmen and diplomatists, see note in Sec. 1, above.

Biographies of Colombian envoys to the United States: Soledad Acosta de Samper, *Biografía del general Joaquín Acosta, prócer de la independencia, historiador, geógrafo, hombre científico y filántropo* (Bogotá, 1901) [**1262**], Acosta was minister to the United States in 1842. Eduardo Posada and Pedro M. Ibáñez, *Vida de Herrán* (Bogotá, 1903) [**1263**], Herrán was minister to the United States in 1847. The other Colombian envoys, as yet unhonored and unsung by biographers, are listed in the *Register* of the Department of State, for 1874 (no. 5122).

Printed Sources

For general collections, see Sec. 1, above, including Hasse's *Index* (no. 5344).

W. H. Harrison, *Remarks of General Harrison, late envoy extraordinary and minister plenipotentiary of the United States to the Republic of Colombia, on certain charges made against him by that government* (Wash., 1830) **[1264]**. Colombia (Republic of New Granada), *Nueva Granada i los Estados-Unidos de América; final controversia diplomática con relación a los sucesos de Panamá, del día 15 de abril de 1856* (Bogotá, 1857) **[1265]**, in English, French, and Spanish (and reprint, in English: Liverpool, 1857), state papers issued by the government of New Granada, in regard to the combat between American citizens and Granadians on Apr. 15, 1856. *Protesta del general Pedro Alcántara Herrán, enviado extraordinario y ministro plenipotenciario de la Confederación granadina cerca del gobierno de los Estados Unidos de América, contra la dictadura del titulado "Presidente de los Estados Unidos de Colombia", Tomás C. de Mosquera* (Bogotá, 1865) **[1266]**. Urrutia, *Estados Unidos y las repúblicas hisp.-am.* (no. 1119), for the missions to Colombia of C. S. Todd, R. C. Anderson, B. J. Watts, W. H. Harrison, and T. P. Moore, to 1833. Manning, *Dipl. corres.; inter-American affairs* (no. 5343), v. V (1935) for volume of documents, 1831–1860, in regard to Colombia.

5. Venezuela

Bibliographical Aids

For general aids, see Sec. 1, above.
M. S. Sánchez, *Bibliografía venezolanista* (no. 4719).

General Works

For general histories, see Sec. 1, above. For a general history of Colombia and Venezuela: Humbert (no. 1259). José Gil Fortoul, *Historia constitucional de Venezuela*, 2nd ed., rev. (Caracas, 1930–33, 3 v.) **[1267]**, although the constitutional phases are stressed, considerable attention is given to Venezuela's social and economic history and to its foreign relations. Recognized generally as the best.

Special Works

We know of no special works dealing with relations between Venezuela and the United States during this period.

Printed Sources

For general collections, see Sec. 1, above, including Hasse's *Index* (no. 5344).
Mariano Briceño, *Memoria justificativa de la conducta del gobierno de Venezuela en la questión Isla de Aves, presentada al excmo.*

señor secretario de estado de los Estados Unidos, por el enviado estraordinario y ministro plenipotenciario de Venezuela, dr. Mariano Briceño (Caracas, 1854), also published in English (Wash. 1858) [**1268**]. Manning, *Dipl. corres.; inter-American affairs* (no. 5343), for volume of documents, 1831–1860, in regard to Venezuela, now in preparation.

6. Brazil

Bibliographical Aids

For general aids, see Sec. 1, above.

Catalogo da Bibliotheca Municipal [Rio de Janeiro] (no. 4698). *Catalogo da exposição de historia do Brazil* (no. 4699). *Catalogo . . . bibliotheca do Senado Federal da . . . Brazil* (no. 4700). Garraux, *Bibliog. brésilienne* (no. 4700 a). *Catalogo da bibliotheca do Archivo Publico Nacional* (no. 4701). Phillips, *Brazil* (no. 4702). Hill, *U.S. and Brazil* (no. 1277), "Bibliography": p. 306–316, listing sources, secondary material, newspapers and magazines.

General Works

For general histories, see Sec. 1, above. For general histories of Brazil in particular: J. F. da Rocha Pombo, *Historia do Brazil* (Rio de Janeiro, 1905, 10 v.) [**1269**]; R. M. Galanti, *Historia do Brasil* (São Paulo, 1910–13, 5 v.) [**1270**].

Special Works

Schuyler, *Am. dipl. and commerce* (no. 4786), ch. 6, 329–344, for relations with Peru and Brazil in regard to the navigation of the Amazon, in the 1850's and 1860's. Manuel de Oliveira Lima, *Nos Estados Unidos* (Leipzig, 1899) [**1271**], a recapitulation of newspaper articles which has one chapter, "Relações do Brasil com os Estados Unidos", very general in nature. Helio Lobo, *Cousas diplomaticas* (Rio de Janeiro, 1918) [**1272**], pt. I: " Uma velha amizade internacional (Brasil, Estados-Unidos da America, 1822–1916)" is brief and sketchy. W. R. Manning, "An early diplomatic controversy between the United States and Brazil", *Am. jour. internat. law*, XII (1918) 291–311, and *Hisp. Am. hist. rev.*, I (1918) 123–145 [**1273**], for the activities of the American *chargé* at Rio de Janeiro, Condy Raguet, in regard to interference with American commerce wrought by the Brazilian blockade of Argentine ports during the war of 1825–1828, drawn from *A.S.P.*, *F.R.* and other printed U.S.

government documents. P. A. Martin, "The influence of the United States on the opening of the Amazon to commerce ", *Hisp. Am. hist. rev.*, I (1918) 146–162 [1274], as revealed to the author in the printed documents of the United States and of Brazil. Jane E. Adams, "Abolition of the Brazilian slave trade ", *Jour. negro hist.*, X (1925) 607–637 [1275]. *Am. secs. state* (no. 4796), v. V, for discussion of the mission of Henry A. Wise to Brazil in 1844 with special reference to the slave trade. L. F. Hill, "The abolition of the slave trade to Brazil ", *Hisp. Am. hist. rev.*, XI (1931) 169–197 [1276]; also his *Diplomatic relations between the United States and Brazil* (Durham, N.C., 1932) [1277], an authoritative study in the preparation of which the author exhausted the printed sources, and the archives of the Department of State of the United States. It is the only real scholarly study of the diplomatic relations between the two countries. The author thinks Brazilian archives may later possibly reveal supplementary information, but he has carefully worked through a vast mass of printed Brazilian documents. It seems certain that any further study will be only supplementary in small detail. A. K. Manchester, *British preëminence in Brazil, its rise and decline* (Chapel Hill, N.C., 1933) [1278] is a scholarly study of Anglo-Brazilian relations which is based upon British archives (but not Brazilian) and parallels Hill (no. 1277).

For biographies of American statesmen and diplomatists, see note in Sec. 1, above.

For list of Brazilian ministers to the United States (to 1874), see *Register* of the Dept. of State for 1874 (no. 5122), and (to 1912), Raul de A. de Campos, *Relações diplomaticas do Brasil, contendo os nomes dos representantes diplomaticos do Brasil no estrangeiro e os dos representantes diplomaticos dos diversos paizes no Rio de Janeiro de 1808 a 1912* (Rio de Janeiro, 1913) [1279]. For list of Brazilian ministers of foreign affairs, see " Indice dos presidentes de conselho e dos ministros de estado da repartição dos negocios estrangeiros, ora das relações exteriores ", in Cardoso de Oliveiro, *Actos diplomaticos* (no. 1281), v. II, 505–511 [1279a].

Printed Sources

For general collections, see Sec. 1, above, including Hasse's *Index* (no. 5344).

Colección de los documentos relativos a la navegación fluvial del Río de la Plata, el Amazonas, y sus afluentes, publicados en las di-

versas memorias del ministerio de relaciones exteriores del imperio del Brazil, traducidos y ofrecidos a la consideración de las repúblicas de la América del Sur, que en ella tienen interés, por un Sur Americano (Caracas, 1857) [1280]. J. M. Cardoso de Oliveira, *Actos diplomaticos do Brasil; tratados do periodo coloniale e varioses documentos desde 1493* (Rio de Janeiro, 1912, 2 v.) [1281], a calendar of papers (1493–1912), not copies of texts. Antonio Pereira Pinto, *Apontamentos para o direito internacional, ou, Collecção completa dos tratados celebrados pelo Brasil com differentes nações estrangeiros; acompanhada de uma noticio historica e documentada sobre as convenções mas importantes* (Rio de Janeiro, 1864–66, 4 v.) [1282]. W. R. Manning, *Dipl. corres. U.S.: inter-American affairs* (no. 5343), v. II. *Bolivia and Brazil* (Wash., 1932) [1283], a comprehensive, valuable, and notable collection.

7. Argentine Republic

Bibliographical Aids

For general aids, see Sec. 1, above.

Pedro de Angelis, *Colección de obras impresas y manuscritas que tratan principalmente del Río de la Plata* (Buenos Aires, 1853) [1284], an extensive and valuable bibliography which covers practically all printed and manuscript works then in existence on the La Plata region. Antonio Zinny, *Efemeridografía argiro metropolitana hasta la caída del gobierno de Rosas* (Buenos Aires, 1869) [1285], a valuable detailed survey of the periodical literature of Buenos Aires from 1801 to 1852. Andrés Lamas, *Biblioteca del Río de la Plata; colección de obras, documentos, y noticias . . . para servir a la historia, física, política, y literaria del Río de la Plata* (Buenos Aires, 1873) [1286]. *Catálogo métodico,* of the "Biblioteca Nacional" of Argentine (no. 4693). Cady, *Rio de la Plata* (no. 1297), "Bibliography": p. 272–289.

General Works

For general works, see Sec. 1, above, particularly Robertson (no. 1206); Stuart (no. 965).

General histories of the Argentine Republic:[6] V. F. López, *Historia de la República Argentina; su origen, su revolución y su*

---

[6] There are some critical appraisals of the lives and works of Argentine historians in Ricardo Rojas, *Obras,* XIV. *La literatura argentina. Los modernos,* 2d ed. (Buenos Aires, 1925) 153–223 [1287].

desarrollo político (Buenos Aires, 1883–93, 10 v.) [**1288**], strongly nationalistic, somewhat disdainful of archives and method, goes only to 1829. C. A. Villanueva, *Historia de la República Argentina* (Paris, 1924, 2 v.) [**1289**], a useful account, by a Venezuelan scholar, that quotes rare material from the French archives. Enrique Vera y Gonzáles, *Historia de la República Argentina* (Buenos Aires, 1926, 2 v.) [**1290**]. Ricardo Levene, *Lecciones de historia argentina*, 12. ed. (Buenos Aires, 1929, 2 v.) [**1291**], " a good epitome of the history of Argentina . . . emphasizes diplomatic, political, and military history." F. A. Kirkpatrick, *A history of the Argentine Republic* (Cambridge, Eng., 1931) [**1292**], an excellently written compendium of four centuries of Argentine history designed to interpret that country to English readers, and based principally on the works of Argentine historians.

V. G. Quesada, *Historia diplomática latino-americana* (Buenos Aires, 1918–20, 3 v.) [**1293**], this is confined to the relations of the Argentine with limitrophal countries; the author was minister to the United States, 1885–92. Piñero, *Política internac. argentina* (no. 1056) is a general history of Argentine diplomacy, deals only briefly with relations with the United States.

Special Works

Caleb Cushing, " English and French intervention in the Río de la Plata ", *U.S. mag. and Democratic rev.*, XVIII (1846) 163–184 [**1294**], American diplomatist (commissioner to China, 1843–45) expresses opposition to the policy of the European powers. Schuyler, *Am. diplomacy and commerce* (no. 4786), for relations with the Argentine in regard to the free navigation of the river Plate in 1852. Carlos Pereyra, *Rosas y Thiers; la diplomacia europea en el Río de la Plata, 1838–1850* (Madrid, 1919) [**1295**] shows prejudice against the United States in the matter of the foreign intervention in the Rio de la Plata. Julius Goebel, *The struggle for the Falkland Islands; a study in legal and diplomatic history* (New Haven, 1927) [**1296**], an elaborate and prodigious piece of research which includes an account of the trouble with Argentina over the seal fisheries in the Falkland Islands, caused by the seizure of an American sealer in 1831. J. F. Cady, *Foreign intervention in the Rio de la Plata, 1838–50; a study of French, British, and American policy in relation to the Dictator Juan Manuel Rosas* (Phila. and London. 1929) [**1297**], this is the best work so far done on relations between the Argentine and the United States, although treating of a limited period. The author made use of archival sources in the United States and Europe, but his work on Argentine sources is restricted to the printed material. P. D. Dickens, " The Falkland Islands dispute between the United States and Argentina ", *Hisp. Am. hist. sev.*, IX (1929) 471–487 [**1298**] adds little to Goebel's more thorough study. Stewart, *Argentina and the Monroe Doctrine* (no. 1081). Pratt, *Anglo-Am. rivalry on the Plata* (no. 1084). S. A. Radaelli, " La cuestión de las islas Malvinas ", in his *Capítulos de historia argentina* (Buenos Aires, 1931) 235–242 [**1299**].

For biographies of American statesmen and diplomatists, see note in Sec. 1, above.

For list of Argentine diplomatists to the United States, see the *Register* of the Department of State, for 1874 (no. 5122).

For a list of presidents and ministers of foreign relations of the Argentine from 1852 to 1910, see the *Catálogo de la biblioteca, mapoteca y archivo* (no. 4694), 920–942.

Printed Sources

For general collections, see Sec. 1, above, including Hasse's *Index* (no. 5344). For a bibliography of Argentine consular and diplomatic correspondence, arranged chronologically by countries, see the *Catálogo de la biblioteca, mapoteca y archivo* (no. 4694), 689–745.

For contemporary newspapers and periodicals, see the bibliography in Cady (no. 1297).

Papers relative to the origin and present state of the questions pending with the United States of America, on the subject of the Malvinas (Falkland Islands), laid before the legislature of Buenos Ayres by the government of the province charged with the direction of the foreign relations of the Argentine Republic (Buenos Ayres, 1832; also issued in Spanish: Buenos Ayres, 1832) [**1300**], published by the " Ministerio de Relaciones Exteriores " of the Argentine Republic. *Correspondencia sostenida entre el excmo. gobierno de Buenos Aires encargado de las relaciones exteriores de la confederación argentina y el sr. Juan B. Nicolson, capitán comandante de las fuerzas navales de los Estados Unidos sobre la costa del Brazil y Río de la Plata, sobre la cuestión promovida por los ss. agentes de la*

Francia (Buenos Aires, 1839) [**1301**], for American mediation in a dispute between Argentina and France in 1839. *Archivo americano y espiritu de la prensa del mundo*, ed. by Pedro de Angelis (Buenos Aires, 1843–51) [**1302**], the official organ of the Provincial Government of Buenos Aires; contains copies of much diplomatic correspondence, with Spanish, French, and English translations. *Memorandum du gouvernement de Buenos Aires sur les traités conclus par les ministres de France, d'Angleterre, et des Etats-Unis avec le général Justo José de Urquiza touchant la libre navigation des rivières le Parana et l'Uruguay* (Buenos Aires, 1853) [**1303**]. *Documentos relativos a la navegación fluvial* (no. 1280). Hopkins, *Historico-political memorial upon la Plata* (no. 1213) for discussion of relations with Argentina in respect to the free navigation of rivers under the treaty of 1853. Confederación Arjentina, *Documentos oficiales, mediación del encargado de negocios de los Estados Unidos de América, d. Benjamin Yancey, en la cuestión de la integridad nacional y proclama del presidente de la confederación arjentina* (Montevideo, 1859) [**1304**], for the attempted mediation of the United States in a dispute over Argentine affairs during the internecine war between Pres. Urquiza of Argentina and the province of Buenos Aires in 1859. *Correspondencia diplomática del doctor don Manuel Herrera y Obes con los principales hombres públicos americanos y europeos de 1847 a 1852*, ed. by Alberto Palomeque (Montevideo, 1901, 3 v.) [**1305**], for the defense of Montevideo. Juan Manuel Rosas, *Papeles de Rosas*, ed. by Adolfo Saldías (La Plata, 1904–07, 2 v.) [**1306**], for the intervention in the Rio de la Plata. W. R. Manning, *Dipl. corres. Latin America* (no. 5342); and his *Dipl. corres.; inter-American affairs* (no. 5343), v. I: *Argentina*, print authoritatively and comprehensively the relevant documents from the archives of the Department of State.

For printed writings of American statesmen and diplomatists, see note in Sec. 1, above.

8. Uruguay

Bibliographical Aids

For general aids, see Sec. 1, above.

B. Fernández y Medina, *La imprenta y la prensa en el Uruguay, 1807–1900* (Montevideo, 1900) [**1307-8**].

General Works

For general histories, see Sec. 1, above. For general history of Uruguay: Eduardo Acevedo, *Historia del Uruguay* (Montevideo, 1916–23, 5 v.) **[1309]**, a "voluminous narrative based on extensive documentary sources, to which, however, there are few definite references." Stresses economic and administrative subjects.

Special Works

There are no special works on the relations between the United States and Uruguay during this period.

For biographies of American statesmen and diplomatists, see note in Sec. 1, above.

For list of Uruguayan diplomatists in the United States, see *Register* of the Dept. of State, for 1874 (no. 5122).

Printed Sources

For general collections, see Sec. 1, above, including Hasse's *Index* (no. 5344).

Documentos relativos a la navegación fluvial (no. 1280), for documents in regard to the opening to free navigation of the rivers in this region. W. R. Manning, *Dipl. corres. inter-American affairs* (no. 5343), for volume of documents, 1831–1860, in regard to Uruguay, now in preparation.

9. Paraguay

Bibliographical Aids

For general aids, see Sec. 1, above.

J. S. Decoud, *Books . . . relating to Paraguay* (no. 4715).

General Works

For general histories, see Sec. 1, above. For general history of Paraguayan diplomacy: Cecilio Báez, *Historia diplomática del Paraguay* (Asunción, 1931–32, 2 v.) **[1310]** includes some discussion of relations with the United States.

Special Works

Schuyler, *Am. diplomacy* (no. 4786), for relations with Paraguay resulting in two treaties, for the settlement of claims, in 1853, and of commerce and navigation, in 1859. Crichfield, *American supremacy* (no. 1205), p. 275–278: "Convention between the United States and Paraguay, February 4, 1859."

For biographies of American statesmen and diplomatists, see note in Sec. 1, above.

For list of Paraguayan diplomatists to the United States, see *Register* of the Dept. of State, for 1874 (no. 5122).

Printed Sources

For general collections, see Sec. 1, above, including Hasse's *Index* (no. 5344).

Documentos a la navegación fluvial del río de la Plata, el Amazonas y sus afluentes (no. 1280), for the treaty with Paraguay conceding the free navigation of the Paraguay and Paraná rivers throughout her jurisdiction, in 1859. *Historia documentada de las cuestiones entre el gobierno del Paraguay y el de los Estados Unidos* (Asunción, 1858) [**1311**]. E. A. Hopkins, *Historico-political memorial upon the regions of the Río de la Plata and conterminous countries, to James Buchanan, president of the United States* (N.Y., 1858) [**1312–3**], the writer was special agent (1844–45), and later (1853) consul to Paraguay; the memorial includes an account of the Paraguayan difficulties with the American consul in 1856, Colonel Fitzpatrick's mission to Paraguay, and other matters. W. R. Manning, *Dipl. corres.; inter-American affairs* (no. 5343), for volume of documents, 1831–1860, in regard to Paraguay, now in preparation.

10. Bolivia

Bibliographical Aids

For general aids, see Sec. 1, above.

Gabriel René-Moreno, *Biblioteca boliviano* (no. 4696). *Books . . . relating to Bolivia in the Columbus Memorial Library* (no. 4697).

General Works

For general works, see Sec. 1, above. Note particularly W. S. Robertson (no. 1206).

Special Works

We know of no special works dealing with relations between Bolivia and the United States during this period.

For biographies of American statesmen and diplomatists, see note in Sec. 1, above.

For list of Bolivian diplomatists to the United States, see the *Register* of the Dept. of State, for 1874 (no. 5122).

Printed Sources

For general collections, see Sec. 1, above, including Hasse's *Index* (no. 5344).

W. R. Manning, *Dipl. corres.; inter-American affairs* (no. 5343), v. II : *Bolivia and Brazil.*

11. Chile

Bibliographical Aids

For general aids, see Sec. 1, above.

N. Anrique Reyes, *Bibliografía de Chile* (no. 4704). Phillips, *Books . . . relating to Chile* (no. 4705). *Catálogo de la Biblioteca del Congreso Nacional* (no. 4706). Sherman, *U.S. and Chile* (no. 1067), 219–224. Evans, *Chile and the U.S.* (no. 1069), 221–234.

General Works

For general histories, see Sec. 1, above. For a general history of Chile: Diego Barros Arana, *Historia jeneral de Chile* (Santiago de Chile, 1884–1902, 16 v.; 2nd ed., " corregida por el ejemplar que dejó revisado el autor e impresa en homenaje a su centenario " (Santiago de Chile, 1930–33, 7 v. (in progress)) [**1314**], by the most distinguished and scholarly of Chilean historians, this is one of the greatest monuments of Hispanic American historiography, but goes only to 1833, after which one may follow in the same author's *Un decenio de la historia de Chile, 1841–1851* (Santiago de Chile, 1905–06, 2 v.) [**1315**]. A less detailed but well balanced and broader narrative is Luis Galdámes, *Estudio de la historia de Chile* (Santiago de Chile, 1906, 2 v.; and successive editions) [**1316**]. Domingo Amunátegui y Solar, *Nacimiento de la república de Chile (1808–1833)* (Santiago, 1930) [**1316a**].

Special Works

Alberto Cruchaga Ossa, " Don Joaquín Campino, first Chilean minister to the United States, 1827 ", *Pan-American magazine*, XXXIX (1926) 37–42 [**1317**] ; and *ibid.*, 157–161, for " Impressions of the first Chilean minister to Washington, 1827–1830 ", drawn from his official communications. Sherman, *U.S. and Chile* (no. 1067). Evans, *Chile and U.S.* (no. 1069). Charles Pergler, " Early diplomatic relations of the United States and Chile ", *Nation. univ. law* *rev.*, X (1930) 65–79 [**1318**], as drawn off from the United States documents published by Manning (no. 1124).

For biographies of American statesmen and diplomatists, see note in Sec. 1, above.

For list of Chilean diplomatists to the United States, see (to 1874), *Register* of the Dept. of State, for 1874 (no. 5122); also (to 1911), Sherman (no. 1067), 217–218.

Printed Sources

For general collections, see Sec. 1, above, including Hasse's *Index* (no. 5344).

Cuerpos legislativos de Chile, 1811 a 1845 (no. 1188). Alberto Cruchaga Ossa, " Impressions of the first Chilean minister to Washington, 1827–1830 ", *Pan-American magazine*, **XXXIX** (1926) 157–161 [**1319**] consists of extracts from the official communications of Don Joaquín Campino to the Chilean government. Manning (no. 5343), v. V: *Chile and Colombia*.

12. Peru

Bibliographical Aids

For general aids, see Sec. 1, above.

René-Moreno, *Biblioteca peruana* (no. 4716). *Catálogo de la biblioteca*, of the " Camara de Senadores " of Peru (no. 4717).

General Works

For general works, see Sec. 1, above. Note particularly W. S. Robertson (no. 1206).

General histories of Peru: M. Nemesio Vargas, *Historia del Perú independiente* (Lima, 1903–17, 8 v.) [**1319a**], one of the best general histories of Peru. Carlos Wiesse, *Historia del Perú* (Lima, 1925–28, 4 v.) [**1320**], a very general work designed for university students, based on secondary writings. Vol. III deals with the emancipation period and immediately thereafter, with most meager mention of the United States. Jorge Basadre, *La iniciación de la república* (Lima, 1928–29, 2 v.) [**1321**] is a manual which traces the internal politics of the formation of the republic of Peru.

Arturo García Salazar, *Resumen de historia diplomática del Perú, 1820–1884* (Lima, 1928) [**1322**] is a general history of Peruvian diplomacy, devoted mainly to inter-Hispanic-American relations, and does not touch relations with the United States at this period.

Special Works

Schuyler, *Am. diplomacy* (no. 4786), for relations with Peru in regard to the free navigation of the Amazon in the late 1850's.

For biographies of American statesmen and diplomatists, see Sec. 1, above.

For list of Peruvian diplomatists to the United States, see the *Register* of the Dept. of State, for 1874 (no. 5122). For chronological list of the presidents, ministers of foreign affairs, and diplomatic representatives of Peru, to 1917, see Arturo García Salazar, *Guía práctica para los diplomáticos peruanos* (no. 5127a).

Printed Sources

For general collections, see Sec. 1, above, including Hasse's *Index* (no. 5344).

No special collections, but note W. R. Manning, *Dipl. corres.; inter-American affairs* (no. 5343), for volume of documents, 1831–1860, in regard to Peru, now in preparation.

13. Ecuador

Bibliographical Aids

For general aids, see Sec. 1, above.

Catálogo de la Bibliografía nacional del Dr. Carlos A. Rolondo (no. 4710).

General Works

For general histories, see Sec. 1, above. General history of Ecuador: Federico González Suárez, *Historia general de la república del Ecuador* (Quito, 1890–1903, 9 v.) [**1323**], a "compendious account based on archival sources, with special emphasis on the colonial period and the wars of independence; marked ecclesiastical bias."

Special Works

No special works dealing with relations between Ecuador and the United States during this period.

For biographies of American statesmen and diplomatists, see note in Sec. 1, above.

For list of Ecuador's diplomatists to the United States, see *Register* of the Dept. of State, for 1874 (no. 5122).

Printed Sources

For general collections, see Sec. 1, above, including Hasse's *Index* (no. 5344).

Documentos relativos a la navegación fluvial (no. 1280), for material regarding the opening to foreign commerce and navigation of the Amazon and its tributaries within her jurisdiction by Ecuador. Note also W. R. Manning, *Dipl. corres.; inter-American affairs* (no. 5343), for volume containing relations with Ecuador to 1860, now in preparation.

CHAPTER IX

COMMERCE; CLAIMS; EXPANSION IN EUROPE OF AMERICAN FOREIGN RELATIONS [1]
1815-1861

1. In General

Bibliographical Aids

For general aids (American), see Evans (to 1820) (no. 4639); Sabin (no. 4655); Larned (no. 4657); Griffin (no. 4658); *Writings* (no. 4661); C. H. and T. (no. 4662); *Am. secs. state* (no. 4796), for "Bibliographical notes"; *Guide hist. lit.* (no. 4634); Myers (no. 5399), for collections of treaties. Miller, *Treaties* (no. 5371), v. I, 39–54, for "Bibliography of United States treaty collections." See also the general historical bibliographies of foreign countries, nos. 4726 to 4765.

For contemporary periodical references (notably *Niles's register*), consult *Poole's index* (no. 4995).

For lists of newspapers, see nos. 4004–5047; particularly Brigham (no. 5012), to 1820; and Library of Congress checklists (nos. 5030–5032).

There is no formal bibliography of the history of the commerce of the United States, but see Johnson, *Hist. commerce U. S.* (no. 227), 363–386, for a useful classified list of books on American and foreign commerce.

General Works

Of general histories of the United States see Hildreth (no. 4779) to 1821; Von Holst (no. 4780); McMaster (no. 4781); Channing (no.

---

[1] For Hispanic American States, see Ch. VIII. For Texas and Mexico, see Ch. X. For the Far East, see Ch. XVII.

4784). See also *Am. secs. state* (no. 4796); and Wriston, *Executive agents* (no. 4799). Miller, *Treaties* (no. 5371), v. III, for historical notes of great value.

Schuyler, *Am. diplomacy* (no. 4786). Alfred Stern, *Geschichte Europas seit den Verträgen von 1815 bis zum Frankfurter Frieden von 1871* (Berlin, 1894–1904, 10 v.) **[1324]**, standard and authoritative general history of Europe during this period. W. P. Stearns, " Foreign trade of the United States from 1820 to 1850 ", *Jour. pol. econ.*, VIII (1899) 34–57 **[1325]**, an essay on the relation of improved inland transportation, agricultural development, and tariff policy, in short the " American system " to foreign trade. W. W. Bates, *American navigation; the political history of its rise and ruin* (Boston and N.Y., 1902) **[1326]**, a chauvinistic survey, replete with copious quotations from American state papers; includes chapters on navigation and nonintercourse bills, and reciprocity acts and conventions. J. Laurence Laughlin and H. Parker Willis, *Reciprocity* (N.Y., 1903) **[1327]**, a general treatise by two competent American authorities. Johnson, *Hist. Commerce U. S.* (no. 227), v. II, pt. 1: " The foreign trade of the United States since 1789 ", by G. G. Huebner. A general account and still the standard one. Morison, *Maritime history* (no. 1720), a splendid and scholarly study of the part of Massachusetts shipping in the history of the American merchant marine. L. W. Maxwell, *Discriminating duties and the American merchant marine* (N.Y., 1926) **[1328]**, for discussion of the history of discriminating duties in America, and of American policy shown by commercial treaties. J. H. Frederick, *The development of American commerce* (N.Y. and London, 1932) **[1329]** has chapters, based largely on trade statistics, on foreign commerce, 1815–1860, and commercial policy.

For biographies of presidents, secretaries of state, and diplomatists abroad (for list, see latest *Register* of the Dept. of State (no. 5122)), see relevant entries and bibliographical data in the *D.A.B.* and *Am. secs. state* (no. 4796). For American ambassadors to England and France, see Beckles Willson (nos. 348 and 68 respectively).

For list of foreign diplomatic envoys to the United States, see the *Register* of the Dept. of State, 1874 (no. 5122). For British statesmen, see Bigham, *Prime ministers* (no. 242); Thornton, *Foreign secretaries* (no. 820); Cecil, *Foreign secretaries* (no. 821), and *D.N.B.*

A recent biography of Stratford Canning, British minister to the United States, 1820–23, is *The life of Stratford Canning* (*Lord Stratford de Redcliffe*), by Elizabeth F. Malcolm-Smith (London, 1933) [**1330**].

Printed Sources

For American official documents and general source collections, see *Jour. exec. proc. Sen.* (no. 5387); *A.S.P., F.R., A.S.P., Commerce and Navigation* (nos. 5341, 5341a); *Annals Cong.* (no. 5382); *Reg. debates Cong.* (no. 5383); *Cong. Globe* (no. 5384); *Abridg. debates* (no. 5386); Wharton, *Digest* (no. 5366); Richardson (no. 5335); Moore's *Arbitrations* (no. 5364); Moore's *Digest* (no. 5365); *Rep. Sen. com. for. rel.* (no. 5388); Hasse's *Index* (no. 5344), for documents relating to foreign affairs; Myers (no. 5399), for collections of treaties. United States Tariff Commission (by H. G. A. Braver), *Handbook of commercial treaties, digests of commercial treaties, conventions, and other agreements of commercial interest between all nations* (Wash., 1922) [**1331**].

For guides to foreign official publications, see pp. 836–849.

For guides to and bibliographies of newspapers, see nos. 5004–5047. For an analysis of the principal American newspapers and periodicals of the period from 1848 to 1871 expressive of American opinion, see "The sources of American opinion in the mid-nineteenth century", in J. G. Gazley, *Am. opinion* (no. 1424), 524–566.

For indexes to periodicals, see nos. 4995–5003.

For texts of treaties, see Miller, *Treaties* (no. 5371).

T. H. Benton, *Thirty years'* (no. 968) for contemporary account of foreign affairs of the period.

For printed writings of American presidents, secretaries of state, and diplomatists abroad (for list, see the latest edition of the *Register* of the Department of State (no. 5122)), see our list on p. 756.

For list of foreign diplomatic envoys to the United States, see the *Register* (no. 5122), for 1874.

MSS.: Suggestions

Notes here concerning MS. sources in this broad field may be supplemented by references to suggestions for MSS. noted in Chapters X–XII. For official diplomatic correspondence as preserved in the Department of State and other foreign offices, see below: United

States, p. 857; Canada, p. 896 (see also no. 1200, and the important Baring papers now in the Canadian Archives), which include discussions on Canadian relations with the United States, such as the Maine boundary dispute, McLeod affair, reciprocity treaty, civil war relations, Alabama claims, Fenian activities, for description see G. E. Shortt, "The House of Barings and Canada", *Queen's quar.*, XXXVII (1930) 732–743 [**1331a**]; the official and private papers of Joseph Howe (secretary of state for the Provinces, 1869–73) in the same archives contain material regarding the fisheries under the reciprocity treaty of 1854; Great Britain, p. 890; Spain, p. 898; Portugal, p. 908; France, p. 915; The Netherlands and Belgium, p. 921; Germany, p. 924; Austria-Hungary, p. 928; Scandinavian Countries, p. 931; Russia, p. 933; Italy and the Papal States, p. 937. Deciphers of some despatches passing between foreign governments and their ministers in England, 1740–1841, with cipher-keys, are in the British Museum. A voluminous group of miscellaneous papers from the House of Representatives acquired by the Library of Congress in 1910 contains numerous items on claims.[2]

The Princeton University Library has the minutes of the French *Commission de liquidation*, 1816–1819, for American claims arising out of the Napoleonic wars; and in the Library of Congress are photostatic copies of some correspondence (from Prussian archives) between the United States and Prussia concerning the law of the sea. For voluminous photostatic copies in the Library of Congress of official diplomatic correspondence of the European governments with the United States, see Pt. II, ch. 3 (under separate countries).

For personal papers of American presidents and secretaries of state, see p. 862 ff. The following particular collections of American diplomatists may be noted (for notes regarding location and contents of papers, see below, p. 868): (Austria) Nathaniel Niles, 1837–38; J. Randolph Clay, 1840–42; (Belgium) H. S. Legaré, 1832–37; Virgil Maxcy, 1837–42; H. W. Hilliard, 1842–44; T. G. Clemson, 1844–51; R. H. Bayard, 1850–53; (Denmark) Henry Wheaton, 1827–35; (France) Albert Gallatin, 1815–23; Nathaniel Niles, 1832–35; Edward Livingston, 1833–35; Lewis Cass, 1836–42; W. R. King, 1844–46; Richard Rush, 1847–49; J. Y. Mason, 1853–59; C. J. Faulk-

---

[2] A. S. Tilton, *House miscellaneous papers in the Library of Congress* (Madison, 1913) [**1332**], reprinted from the *Proceedings of the State Historical Society of Wisconsin*, for 1912, 227–245.

ner, 1860–61; (German States: Bavaria, Hesse Cassel, Saxony, Württemberg) Henry Wheaton, 1843; (Great Britain) Richard Rush, 1817–25; Rufus King, 1825–26; Albert Gallatin, 1826–27; James Barbour, 1827–28 and 1845–46; Martin Van Buren, 1831–32; Andrew Stevenson, 1836–41; Abbott Lawrence, 1849–52; J. C. Bancroft Davis, 1849–52; George Bancroft, 1846–49; Benjamin Moran, 1856–76; (Muscat) Edmund Roberts, 1832; (Netherlands) William Eustis, 1814–18; Harmanus Bleecker, 1839–42; Christopher Hughes, 1842–45; (Papal States) Lewis Cass, Jr., 1849–58; (Portugal) Edward Kavanagh, 1835–41; Benjamin Moran, 1855–56; (Prussia) A. J. Donelson, 1846–49; D. D. Barnard, 1850–53; P. D. Vroom, 1853–57; (Russia) 1813–18; Wm. Pinkney, 1816–18; G. W. Campbell, 1818–20; T. B. Watts, 1828–29; John Randolph, 1830–31; C. S. Todd, 1841–46; John Randolph Clay (secretary) 1830–31; (Sardinia) Nathaniel Niles, 1838–50; W. B. Kinney, 1850–53; (Spain) Hugh Nelson, 1823–25; A. H. Everett, 1825–29; Washington Irving, 1842–46; J. H. Eaton, 1836–40; A. C. Dodge, 1855–59; (Sweden and Norway) J. M. Forbes (consul), 1818–19; Christopher Hughes, 1819–26, and 1830–42; H. W. Ellsworth, 1845–49; (Tunis) W. P. Chandler, 1854–56; (Turkey) D. S. Carr, 1843–49; G. P. Marsh, 1849–53; (Two Sicilies) Wm. Pinkney, 1816–31.

In the Library of Congress are the papers (1806–1843) of D. B. Warden, first consul general at Paris (some also in the Maryland Historical Society) ; a photostat of a draft of a report from John Randolph Clay, U.S. envoy to Russia, 1834. The reports as American consul at Malaga, Spain, 1840–66, of T. M. Newsom, are in the Minnesota Historical Society. For papers of early merchants trading to Europe and the Far East which should throw sidelights on international affairs, one should look to the collections of the Essex Institute at Salem, Mass., and in the Baker Library of the Harvard School of Business Administration, Cambridge.

We may note some collections of personal papers of foreign statesmen and diplomatists who had to do with American affairs. The Sir Charles Bagot papers in the Canadian Archives during the periods when he was British minister at Washington, 1816–19, and governor-general of Canada, 1838–42, are (1) from the official correspondence in the British Public Record Office (F.O.), and (2) from the private papers in the possession of Col. Bagot of Levens Hall, temporarily deposited in the Record Office for copying. For calendar, see no.

1200. In the British Museum are to be found the papers of the great free trader, Richard Cobden, a few papers of George Canning (secretary of state for foreign affairs, 1807-09, 1822-27) (letters to J. H. Frere), the Earl of Liverpool (secretary of state for foreign affairs, 1801-04), Sir Robert Peel (prime minister, 1834-35, 1841-46), the Earl of Aberdeen (secretary of state for foreign affairs, 1841-46); official and personal papers of Wiliam Huskisson, president of the Board of Trade, 1823-1827, which include material on the northeast boundary question, the regulation of the trade of the United States with the British West Indies, etc. The main collection of Aberdeen papers is in the possession of his grandson, the Marquess of Aberdeen and Temair, of Tarlan, Aberdeenshire, and of Lord Stanmore, of Loughton, Essex.[3] A copy of a privately printed, but never published, collection of Aberdeen papers [1332a] is in the British Museum; a nearly complete set of the same is in Harvard College Library; and portions of the set are also in the Library of Congress, (Rare Book Room), and the W. L. Clements Library of the University of Michigan. The papers of Lord Clarendon, president of the Board of Trade, 1846-47, secretary of state for foreign affairs, 1853-58, 1865-66, and 1868-70, are in the possession of the present Lord Clarendon—index in the Public Record Office. Palmerston's (secretary of state for foreign affairs, 1830-41, 1846-51; prime minister, 1855-58, 1859-65) papers are in the custody of Sir Wilfrid Ashley, at Broadlands, Romsey, Hampshire, England. The principal body of George Canning's personal papers are understood to be in the possession of Lord Lascelles at Chesterfield House, London, but contain little on American affairs and nothing not duplicated in the Record Office. In the Public Record Office are the personal papers of Stratford Canning (minister to the United States, (1820-23), and Earl Russell (prime minister, 1846-52, 1865-66, and secretary of state for foreign affairs, 1852-53, 1859-65). Some of the letters of G. T. L. Poussin (minister of France, 1848-49) are in the Library of Congress. A curious collection is that of E. M. A. Martini, secretary of the Dutch legation in Washington and chargé d'affaires, 1833-42, in the Library of Congress, consisting of scrapbooks preserving the visiting cards of diplomatic and political notables with whom he was associated.

---

[3] See preface to Lady Frances Balfour's *Aberdeen* (no. 1383).

2. Commerce and Diplomacy

A. Great Britain [4]

Bibliographical Aids

For general aids, see Sec. 1, above; and Canadian historical bibliographies (nos. 4671–4677).

A. P. C. Griffin and H. H. B. Meyer, *List of references on reciprocity* (Wash., 1910) (Library of Congress) [**1333**], this 2d edition incorporates the *Select list . . . on reciprocity with Canada*, by A. P. C. Griffin, pub. in 1907, and includes a list of public documents, by which the legislative history of the reciprocity treaties or projects from the year 1815 may be traced; also *Additional references to reciprocity* (no. 2941). Benns, *West India carrying-trade* (no. 1343), "Bibliography": p. 189–200. Ragatz, *H.C.sess.pap. slave trade* (no. 5407); his *H.L.sess.pap. slave trade* (no. 5409); and *Guide Brit. Caribbean hist.* (no. 4721).

General Works

See Sec. 1, above.

Smith, *England and America* (no. 340), presents the "case" of Great Britain in Anglo-American relations. Laughlin and Willis, *Reciprocity* (no. 1327). Babcock, *Am. nationality* (no. 881), ch. 16: "Negotiations with England, 1815–1818." D. R. Moore, *Canada and the United States, 1815–1830* (Chicago, 1910) [**1334**], informative but not definitive; a useful dissertation, unique in its field and scope, which made much use of MSS. in Canada and Ontario archives, and of printed government documents and other published sources. W. A. Dunning, *The British Empire and the United States; a review of their relations during the century of peace following the treaty of Ghent* (N.Y., 1914) [**1335**], general, lucid. Hill, *Treaties* (no. 4794), ch. 7: "The convention of 1818 with Great Britain." *Camb. hist. Br. for. pol.*, v. II (no. 209). Maxwell, *Discriminating duties* (no. 1328), analysis of present day conditions with historical background discussing the workings of the commercial agreement of 1830 with England, and American policy shown by commercial treaties. Mowat, *G.Brit. and U.S.* (no. 347a). Keenleyside, *Canada and U.S.* (no. 896).

---

[4] For the "Fisheries Dispute", see Ch. XVI, sec. 7, below, particularly Schuyler (no. 4786), Elliott (no. 2815), Henderson (no. 2821), Balch (no. 2823), Wormwith (no. 2832), Johnson (no. 227). For the "Slave Trade", see Ch. XII, sec. 3, below. For the Isthmian question, see Ch. VIII, sec. 3.

Special Works

H. A. Hill, " The navigation laws of Great Britain and the United States ", *Jour. soc. science*, IX (1878) 101–116 **[1336]**, for a general account of the navigation laws of the early 19th century. F. E. Haynes, *The reciprocity treaty with Canada of 1854* (Baltimore, 1892) **[1337]**, the first study of the subject, limited to printed documents of the United States government. Sidney Webster, " Franklin Pierce and the Canadian reciprocity treaty of 1854 ", *Grafton and Coös county bar assoc. proc.*, 1892 (Concord, N.H., 1893) 358–385 **[1338]**, a well-informed and thoughtful essay by one of the chief defenders of the foreign policy of the Pierce administration. Chalfont Robinson, *A history of two reciprocity treaties* (New Haven, 1904) **[1339]**, dealing with the treaty with Canada in 1854, and the treaty with Hawaii in 1876, based on a wider use of government printed documents, monographs, and British parliamentary sessional papers of 1844–1852, and debates. Porritt, *Protection in Canada, 1846–1907* (no. 2943). Moore, *Canada and U.S., 1815–1830* (no. 1334). C. D. Allin and G. M. Jones, *Annexation, preferential trade and reciprocity; an outline of the Canadian annexation movement of 1849–50, with special reference to the questions of preferential trade and reciprocity* (Toronto, 1912) **[1340]**, for the economic and political (annexation) rather than the diplomatic phase, with much attention to public opinion as reflected in Canadian newspapers. *Reciprocity and commercial treaties*, pub. by the U.S. Tariff Commission (Wash., 1919) **[1341]**, for a study of the reciprocity and tariff agreements of the United States, covering the reciprocity treaty with Canada of 1854. C. C. Tansill, *The Canadian reciprocity treaty of 1854* (Baltimore, 1922) **[1342]**, the first study of the subject to make use of Canadian and American archives, and of the voluminous papers of Secretary Marcy, in fact, it was originally designed as part of a biography of Marcy. F. L. Benns, *The American struggle for the British West India carrying-trade, 1815–1830* (Bloomington, Ind., 1923) **[1343]** traces, principally from American printed sources, the diplomatic and legislative struggle of the United States government to regain for American merchants the right to trade with the British colonies in the West Indies. T. P. Martin, " The influence of trade (in cotton and wheat) on Anglo-American relations, 1829–1846 ", one of a series of articles printed in

18 consecutive Sunday issues of the Louisville (Ky.) *Courier-Journal*, beginning Feb. 12, 1923, under the title of "19th century history" [**1344**] has some suggestive conclusions concerning relationship of trade and diplomacy. Trotter, *Canad. federation* (no. 2933). Culbertson, *Internat. econ. policies* (no. 4811a). Maxwell, *Discriminating duties* (no. 1328). L. J. Ragatz, *The fall of the planter class in the British Caribbean, 1763–1833; a study in social and economic history* (N.Y., 1928) [**1345**] contains chapters depicting the devastating effect on the prosperity of the British island plantations in the West Indies of the British navigation laws which excluded American shipping. Phelps, *Anglo-Am. peace* (no. 4228). Laura White, *U.S. in 1850's as seen by Brit. consuls* (no. 1653), from their official correspondence. W. D. Overman, "I. D. Andrews and reciprocity in 1854; an episode in dollar diplomacy", *Canad. hist. rev.*, XV (1934) [**1345a**] shows that during the years preceding the reciprocity treaty of 1854, Andrews was engaged in the dual role of special agent of the United States in Canada and the lower provinces to report upon trade conditions, and propagandist.

For biographies of American and British statesmen and diplomatists, see note in Sec. 1, above.

Biographies of Canadian statesmen: Sir J. G. Bourinot, *Lord Elgin* (Toronto, 1903) [**1346**]; G. M. Wrong, *The Earl of Elgin* (London, 1905) [**1347**]; J. L. Morison, *The eighth Earl of Elgin; a chapter in nineteenth-century imperial history* (London, 1928) [**1348**], ch. 4: "Canada: economic developments to the reciprocity treaty of 1854." Skelton, *Sir Alexander T. Galt* (no. 1928), Canadian minister of finance, 1858–62, 1864–66, 1867. Biographies of Sir John A. Macdonald (nos. 2494–2496).

Printed Sources

For general collections, see Sec. 1, above.

For a convenient list of United States public documents, diplomatic correspondence, etc., regarding the reciprocity treaty with Canada, see Griffin and Meyer (no. 1333). Also U.S. Treasury Dept., *British North American colonies. Communication in compliance with resolution of Senate of Mar. 8, 1851; report of Israel D. Andrews, on trade and commerce of British North American colonies* (Wash., 1854) [**1349**], and *Extracts from Congressional debates on the reciprocity treaty of 1854 with Canada, together with* *message of the President transmitting the treaty to Congress* (Wash., 1911) (61st Cong., 3d sess., House Doc. 1350) **[1350]** which includes the legislation to terminate the treaty and proceedings in Senate and House. For fuller references to government documents, see Hasse, *Index* (no. 5344).

For texts of treaties, see Miller, *Treaties* (no. 5371).

Great Britain, House of Commons Sessional Papers: *Four accounts of ships and tonnage cleared outwards and entered inwards in the British colonies in the West Indies and North America, for the last 11 years, 1816 to 1826* (1826–27, XVIII, 309) **[1351]**. *Correspondence between Great Britain and the United States relative to commercial intercourse between America and the British West India colonies, Aug. 1826 to 1827* (1826–27, XXV, 21) **[1352]**. *Papers relating to the tariffs published in the United States in the years 1824 and 1828* (1928, XIX, 1) **[1353]**. *Correspondence relative to commercial intercourse between the United States of America and the British West India colonies, June to October 1827* (1828, XIX, 596) **[1354]**. *Number of imperial gallons of rum and molasses annually exported from the British West India colonies to the United States and British North America, 1812 to 1829* (1830, XXII, 277) **[1355]**. *Papers relating to the shipping, imports and exports, value of cargoes, &c.; also statements relative to the population &c. of the United States* (1837–38, XLVII, 381), **[1356]**. *Papers relative to tariffs published in the United States and presented . . . 1828* (1846, XLVIII, 1) **[1357]**. *Commercial tariffs and regulations, resources, and trade, of the several states of Europe and America* (1846, XLIX, Pts. 1 and 2, 729, 1–2) **[1358]**. *Exports to and imports from the United States, for 1845* (1846, LXIV, 329) **[1359]**. *Statements showing the entries inwards and clearances outwards in the ports of the United States of America, . . . also total amount of American and foreign tonnage employed in the commerce of the United States* (1847–48, XX, Pt. 2, 371) **[1360]**. *Number and tonnage of shipping . . . from and to the United States of America, 1815 to 1847* (1847–48, XX, Pt. 2, 1) **[1361]**. *Return of the alterations made in the tariffs of foreign states since 1st January 1844* [includes the United States] (1847–48, LVIII, 281) **[1362]**. *Account of British produce and manufactures exported to the West India colonies in the year 1847, . . . similar*

returns for the United States of America (1847–48, LVIII, 451)
[**1363**]. *Accounts of the total quantity of cotton wool imported into
the United Kingdom in each year, 1815 to 1847, . . . with similar
account, showing the exports of cotton goods and yarn to the United
States of America* (1847–48, LVIII, 325) [**1364**]. *Return of the
principal articles imported into the United Kingdom from the United
States, 1843 to 1847* (1847–48, LVIII, 447) [**1365**]. *Correspondence with the minister from the United States respecting the
navigation laws* (1847–48, LIX, 31) [**1366**]. *Despatch from Mr.
Pakenham, Her Majesty's minister, at Washington, to Viscount Palmerston, dated 29 March 1847, on the customs revenue of the United
States under the new tariff* (1847, LIX, 369) [**1367**]. *Correspondence with foreign states relative to the proposed relaxation of the
British navigation laws (. . . and the United States)* (1849, LI,
179) [**1368**]. *Reply of the United States government respecting the
proposed relaxation of the British navigation laws* (1849, LI, 235)
[**1369**]. *Correspondence respecting the light dues levied on the
shipping of the United States in the United Kingdom* (1851, LVII,
409) [**1370**]. *Copies of acts recently passed by the legislatures of
Canada, Nova Scotia, New Brunswick, and Prince Edward Island,
for giving effect on the part of those provinces to the recent reciprocity treaty with the United States* (1855, XXXVI) [**1371**].

Canadian Parliamentary Papers dealing with the Reciprocity
Treaty: For a list of Ontario Parliamentary " Bills relative to the
United States of America " (mainly in regard to commercial intercourse), see the *General index to the Journals of the House of Assembly of the late Province of Upper Canada . . . 1825–1839/40*
(Montreal, 1848), 574–575 [**1372**]. *Report on trade and commerce*
by Committee to inquire into Commercial Intercourse between Canada and . . . the United States, of the Legislative Assembly of the
Parliament of Canada (Quebec, 1855) [**1373**]; and *Return to an
address of the Legislative Assembly, dated 28th March, 1860; for
copy of correspondence which may have taken place in reference to
the working of, or the repealing of, the reciprocity treaty*, April 3,
1860 (Canada. Sess. pap., v. IV, Sess. 1860) [**1374**].

For Canadian and British documents dealing with the termination of the treaty, in 1865, see Griffin and Meyer, *List of references
on reciprocity* (no. 1333), 60–61.

" British colonial and navigation system " (anon.), *Am. quar. rev.*, II (1827) 267–306 **[1375]** is a contemporary historical résumé and analytical exposition of the question between the United States and Great Britain concerning colonial trade, as introduction to a contemplated review of the then recently published (1826) official correspondence of the Dept. of State relative to colonial trade. It has been established that the president, John Quincy Adams, was the author of this article. L. W. Tazewell, *A review of the negociations between the United States of America and Great Britain, respecting the commerce of the two countries, and more especially concerning the trade of the former with the West Indies* (London, 1829) **[1375a]** reflects the anti-Adams viewpoint. Timothy Pitkin, *A statistical view of the commerce of the United States of America* (New Haven, 1835) **[1376]**, a valuable compendium of information on trade; it incidentally reflects the attitude of the New England commercial interests. Dallas, *Letters from London 1856–60* (no. 5212). Robert Mayo, *A synopsis of the commercial and revenue system of the United States, as developed by instructions and decisions of the Treasury Department for the administration of the revenue laws* (Wash., 1847, 2 v.) **[1377]**, for Treasury Dept. instructions regarding commercial intercourse. *The reciprocity treaty between the United States and Great Britain of June 5, 1854*, report of a special committee of the Boston Board of Trade, submitted and adopted Jan. 2, 1865 (Boston, 1865) **[1377]**. Haliburton, *International trade* (no. 1664), a plea for the development of general international trade by Canada as a substitute for, and improvement upon, the expired reciprocity with the United States. *Letters and journals of James, eighth Earl of Elgin,* ed. by Theodore Walrond (London, 1872) **[1379]**, for the Canadian reciprocity treaty. " The papers of Sir Charles R. Vaughan, 1825–1835 ", ed. by J. A. Doyle, *Am. hist. rev.*, VII (1902) 500–503 **[1380]**, for the disputes with Great Britain over commercial affairs, particularly the West India trade. " Israel D. Andrews' claims under the reciprocity treaty of 1854 ", *N.Y. pub. lib. bul.*, IX (1905) 445–447 **[1381–2]**, three letters dealing with the claims of I. D. Andrews, United States consul in Canada, who was selected by Webster to help in negotiating the treaty of 1854 with Great Britain, but payment of the claims was disputed in Congress four years later. Anderson, *Canadian questions* (no. 2641). *Corres. Sir John Mac-*

donald (no. 2509). Frances Balfour, *The life of George, fourth Earl of Aberdeen* (London, 1922, 2 v.) **[1383]** is really a publication of diary and letters. For printed writings of American statesmen and diplomatists, see note in Sec. 1, above.

B. Other European States

Bibliographical Aids

For general aids, see Sec. 1, above.

Special Works

Charles Edwards, " Duties on Portuguese wines," *Merchant's magazine* (Hunt's) XI (1844) 395–411 **[1384]**, a discussion of the issue arising over the attempt of the United States Treasury Dept. to collect higher duties on Portuguese wines than justified by the most-favored-nation clauses of the treaty with Portugal; with documents. Moritz Linderman, " Zur Geschichte der älteren Handelsbeziehungen Bremens mit den Ver. Stadten von Nordamerika ", *Bremisches Jahrbuch*, X (1878) 124–146 **[1385]**, details regarding negotiation of treaties of friendship, commerce, and navigation with Hanseatic Republics, 1827 and 1828, based on archives of Bremen, and others in Berlin. Ernst Baasch, *Beiträge zur Geschichte der Handelsbeziehungen zwischen Hamburg und Amerika* (Hamburg, 1892) bound with *Hamburgische Festschrift zur Errinnerung an die Entdeckung Amerika's*, hrsg. vom Wissenschaftlichen Ausschuss des Komités für die Amerika-Feier. Bd. I (Hamburg, 1892) **[1386]**, the librarian of the Hamburg Kommerzbibliothek exploits the archives of the city to construct a scholarly history of the beginnings of German commercial overseas contacts, particularly with North and South America. G. M. Fisk, *Deutschland u. Vereinigten Staaten* (no. 4292) ; and " German-American diplomatic and commercial relations historically considered ", *Review of reviews*, XX (1902) 323–328 **[1387]**, a summary equivalent to a college classroom lecture, by a one-time secretary of the American embassy in Berlin, which would be useful to a diplomatist unexpectedly transferred to Germany. Hoekstra, *Holland-Am. relations* (no. 1412). Reeves, *Prussian-Am. treaties* (no. 287), for the treaty of 1828 and its applications. Hovde, *U.S. and Sweden and Norway* (no. 4365). Carlson, *Relations with Sweden* (no. 194), for the treaty of 1816. Fogdall,

Dan.-Am. diplomacy (no. 195), for negotiation of treaties, settlements of claims, and the abolition of the Sound dues. Karl Brinkmann, *Die preussische Handelspolitik vor dem Zollverein und der Wiederaufbau vor hundert Jahren* (Berlin and Leipzig, 1922) **[1387a]**, a study, based upon Prussian archival material (principally from the foreign office) of the re-orientation of Prussian commercial policy and trade relations between 1810 and 1818, and of the transition from an " isolated " policy to the " Zollverein " policy, 1818–24. Includes analysis of trade arrangements made or contemplated with the United States. G. J. Kloos, *De handelspolitieke betrekkingen tusschen Nederland en de Vereenigde Staten van Amerika, 1814–1914* (Amsterdam, 1922) **[1388]**, the author sees his subject from the commercial viewpoint and undeniably from the Dutch side. A good survey for general information, based on printed works on both sides, but only Dutch MSS. Wallace McClure, " German-American commercial relations ", *Am. jour. internat. law*, XIX (1925) 689–701 **[1389]**, analysis of treaty relationships, particularly most-favored-nation clauses, and the treaty of 1828. Maxwell, *Discriminating duties* (no. 1328). Tilberg, *U.S. and Sweden* (no. 4366) devotes some pages to the " Diplomacy of Swedish-American commerce, 1783–1925." W. H. Walker, *Franco-American commercial relations, 1820–1850* (Hays, Kans., 1931) **[1390]**, replete with statistical information and details of trade, reaches the not startling conclusion that the United States was the center of French interest in American commerce. Stolberg-Wernigerode, *Deutschland und Vereinigten Staaten* (no. 4314). Gordon, *Relations with Turkey* (no. 4377). J. A. Greenlee, " The Webster land claims in New Zealand ", *Pacific hist. rev.*, III (1934) 416–432 **[1390a]**, claims of William Webster, a citizen of the United States. R. H. Luthin, " St. Bartholomew . . .", *Hisp. Am. hist. rev.*, XIV (1935) 307–324 **[1390b]**, includes Swedish-American relations involving questions of trade and neutrality in the period following the Napoleonic wars.

Printed Sources

For general collections, see Sec. 1, above; particularly Hasse's *Index* (no. 5344) for published U.S. documents.

" Letters of John Quincy Adams to Alexander Hill Everett, 1811–1837 ", *Am. hist. rev.*, XI (1905–1906) 88–116, 332–354 **[1391]**, consisting of 26 letters written from Russia, The Netherlands, and Spain, of which nos. 4, 6, 8–14 incl., are published in the Ford ed. of *Writings of John Quincy Adams*. N. W. Posthumus, " Gegevens over de handelsrelaties van Nederland met de Vereenigde Staten van Noord-Amerika in de eerste jaren na het herstel ", in *Economisch-historisch Jaarboek*, published by the " Nederlandsch Economisch-Historisch Archief ", v. I (The Hague, 1916) 199–240 [1392], consisting mainly of new source material (1815–1817) from the Dutch archives; and by the same editor, *Documenten betreffende de buitenlandsche handelspolitiek van Nederland in de negentiende eeuw* (The Hague, 1919–31, 6 v.) [1393], consisting of documents of the years 1813 to 1870 concerning the commercial policy of the Netherlands with foreign powers, including some dealing with American relations. Scott, *Treaties with Prussia* (no. 292).

For printed writings of American statesmen and diplomatists, see note in Sec. 1, above.

For lists of European diplomatic envoys to the United States, see the *Register* of the Dept. of State, 1874 (no. 5122).

3. Claims [5]

Bibliographical Aids

See Sec. 1, above. Boston Public Library list on *French spoliations* (no. 387).

Special Works [6]

Moore, *Arbitrations* (no. 5364), the history of all adjudicated claims for this period, including also historical and legal notes on the domestic commissions of the United States for the adjustment of international claims, is found in this authoritative work. Also his *Adjudications* (no. 5367), v. V. *Spanish spoliations, 1795. French indemnity, 1831.* Fredrik Bajer, " L'arbitrage dit ' Butterfield ' ", *Rev. hist. dipl.*, XV (1901) 88–108 [1394], historical sketch of the claim against Denmark for detention, in 1854, of 2 vessels at Saint Thomas, dismissed by decision of the arbitrator, Sir Edmund Mon-

---

[5] Denmark, France, Great Britain, Naples, The Netherlands, Portugal, Spain, Sweden. For claims controversies with the Hispanic American States, see Ch. VIII; with Mexico, see Ch. X.
[6] There is a paucity of monograph material, but the reader is referred (in addition to some of the general works included here) to the general histories cited in Sec. 1, particularly *Am. secs. state* (no. 4796) and *Camb. hist. Brit. for. pol.* (no. 209).

son, in 1900.   J. W. Williams, " The French question ", in his *Articles on social and political science* (West Chester, Pa., 1916) 63–139, originally published in the *Am. quar. rev.*, XVII (1835) [**1395**], an excellent contemporary (1835) discussion of our relations with France in regard to French spoliations, based on published state papers then available.   Hoekstra, *Holland-American relations* (no. 1412), ch. 6: " The spoliations claims against Holland."   Carlson, *Relations with Sweden* (no. 194), ch. 3: " The Stralsund claims." Fogdall, *Danish-American diplomacy* (no. 195), for Danish claims. Hill, *Treaties* (no. 4794), for claims under the convention of 1818 with Great Britain.   Marcel Marion, " Un épisode des relations pécuniaires franco-américaines ", *Rev. deux mondes*, 7th ser., XXXVII (1926) 46–64 [**1396**] discusses the negotiations of 1834–1835.   P. C. Perrotta, *The claims of the United States against the Kingdom of Naples* (Wash., 1926) [**1396a**], United States but not Neapolitan sources were available to the writer.   C. K. Webster, " British mediation between France and the United States, 1834–1836 ", *Eng. hist. rev.*, XLII (1927) 58–78 [**1397**] deals with the French spoliations dispute, and is based on American, Austrian, British, and French archives.   R. E. Spiller, " Fenimore Cooper and Lafayette; the financial controversy of 1831–1832 ", *Am. literature*, III (1931) 28–44 [**1398a**]. R. A. McLemore, *The French spoliation claims, 1816–1836; a study in Jacksonian diplomacy* ([Nashville, Tenn.] 1933), reprinted from the *Tennessee historical magazine*, ser. 2, v. II, no. 4 [**1398b**], thesis (Ph.D.), Vanderbilt University; a useful study of the purely American correspondence and other papers dealing with the subject, with brief reflections by the author.   Miller, *Treaties* (no. 5371) in successive volumes have valuable notes on claims and claims agreements.   R. C. McGrane, *Foreign bondholders and American state debts* (N.Y., 1935) [**1398c**].   For biographies of American statesmen, see note in Sec. 1, above.

Printed Sources

For general collections, see Sec. 1, above.   Note particularly Moore's *Arbitrations* (no. 5364) and *Adjudications* (no. 5367), v. V, for the French indemnity, 1831.   Miller, *Treaties* (no. 5371) for claims agreements.

Letter . . . relating to the claims of American citizens upon Great Britain, under the treaty of Ghent and convention of St. Peters-

burgh, for slaves and property captured during the war, 1825 (Gt. Brit. H. of C. Sess. pap., 1825, XXIV) [**1399**]. *Documens, communiques à l'appui du projet de loi relatif au traité du 4 juillet, 1831,* par M. le Ministre Secrétaire d'Etat au Département des Affaires Étrangères, séance du 21 janvier, 1835 (Paris, 1835) [**1400**], published with G. M. Gibbes, *Traité du 4 juillet, 1831, entre la France et les Etats-Unis, mémoire aux Chambres* (Paris, 1835) [**1401**]. " Les Réclamations des Etats-Unis envers la France ", *Rev. deux mondes,* 4th ser., I (1835) 311–330 [**1402–3**], a contemporary letter (anon.) discussing the French spoliations dispute. *Extract from " Code diplomatique ", par Portiez . . . Convention of September 30, 1800, between the U.S. and France* (no. 465), (Translation) tr. for the Committee on Foreign Affairs of the House of Representatives. *French spoliations prior to 1800; synopsis of the claims . . ., including the correspondence between the United States and France on that subject* (Wash., 1858?) [**1404**].

For printed writings of American statesmen and diplomatists, see note in Sec. 1, above.

MSS.: Suggestions

See Sec. 1, above.

The Bibliothèque Thiers (Paris) has a dossier of MSS. entitled " affaires d'Amérique, 1834–5 ", of Adolphe Thiers when he was minister of the interior which give an interesting sidelight on the sentiment of the French government regarding the negotiations with America in 1834–35. Thiers confided everything to his mother-in-law, Madame Dosue, and she recorded (Boswell-like) his impressions.

4. Expansion in Europe of American Foreign Relations [7]

Bibliographical Aids

See Sec. 1, above.

Special Works

F. Feddersen, *Danmark og Nordamerika om Oeresund* (Copenhagen, 1856) [**1405**], Danish view, opposed to the American demand for cancellation of the Sound dues. J. B. Moore, " Kossuth; a sketch of a revolutionist ", *Pol. sci. quar.,* X (1895) 95–131, 257–291

---

[7] See also Sec. 2b, this chapter.

[1406] includes an account of the efforts of the United States Government in behalf of the leader of the Hungarian revolution of 1848 and diplomatic complications. M. J. Wright, "Some bold diplomacy in the United States in 1861", *Am. hist. assoc. ann. rep.*, for 1895 (1896) 405–410 [1407] is concerned with the intervention with the Egyptian government by the American consul in Egypt (W. S. Thayer) in behalf of one Faris-al-Hakim, a Syrian, acting as agent of American missionaries. S. M. Stroock, "Switzerland and American Jews", *Am. Jew. hist. soc. pub.*, XI (1903) 7–52 [1408], an account of an episode affecting the rights of American Jewish citizens in Switzerland, anent a clause in the treaty of 1855 restricting the privileges and rights of American Jews in that country. Hildt, *Diplomatic relations with Russia* (no. 189), for the question of consular immunity (Kosloff affair, 1815–16), and other matters of Russian-American diplomacy. H. Nelson Gay, *Le relazioni fra l'Italia e gli Stati Uniti* (Rome, 1907), reprinted from *Nuova antologia*, CCXI (1907) 657–671 [1409] deals with the period 1847 to 1871, from the printed diplomatic correspondence of the United States and the letters of George P. Marsh, United States minister in Italy, 1861–1882; also by the same writer, *Uno screzio diplomatico fra il governo pontificio e il governo americano e la condotta degli svizzeri a Perugia il 20 giugno 1859* (Perugia, 1907), reprinted from the *Archivo storico del risorgimento umbro*, anno III (1907) 113–201 [1410] utilizes printed American and Italian state papers, and other sources, supplemented by the papers of Antonelli, Cardinal Secretary of State, in the *Fondo risorgimento* of the *Biblioteca Vittorio Emanuele*, at Rome. R. E. Prime, *American territory in Turkey; or, Admiral Farragut's visit to Constantinople, and the extraterritorialty* [sic.] *of Robert College* (N.Y., 1908) [1411], recollections concerning the foundation of Robert College and the parcel of land "practically American, within the Turkish dominion" in which it was established. Callahan, *Alaska purchase* (no. 2231), for Russian-American relations during the Crimean war. Heinz, *Russland, England und Nordamerika* (no. 1156). Paullin, *Diplomacy of naval officers* (no. 151), ch. 9: "Early relations with Africa and the Pacific, 1821–1872." Peter Hoekstra, *Thirty-seven years of Holland-American relations, 1803 to 1840* (Grand Rapids, Mich., and Paterson, N.J., 1916) [1412], a thorough study, after extensive researches in Dutch and

American archives traces the evaporation of American claims against Holland arising out of the Napoleonic intervention. Elihu Root, " The treaty of 1832 with Russia ", in his *Addresses* (no. 5287), 313–326 [**1413**], address in the Senate, Dec. 19, 1911. Reeves, *Pruss.-Am. treaties* (no. 287). Wesley, *Recognition of Liberia* (no. 1208). Hovde, *U.S. and Sweden and Norway* (no. 4365). R. C. McGrane, " The American position on the revolution of 1848 in Germany ", *Hist. outlook*, XI (1920) 333–339 [**1414**] stresses wisdom in 1848 of traditional policy of abstention from European politics; utilizes MSS. of A. J. Donelson, U.S. minister to Germany. E. N. Curtis, " La révolution de 1830 et l'opinion publique en Amérique ", *Révolution de 1848*, XVII (1921) 64–73, 81–118 [**1415**]; and "American opinion of the nineteenth century revolution ", *Am. hist. rev.*, XXIX (1924) 249–270 [**1416**] analyses public sentiment in the United States in 1830, 1848, and 1870 regarding the French revolutions of those years. Fogdall, *Dan.-Am. dipl.* (no. 195), for the Sound dues and other problems, 1841–1860. Three studies by L. F. Stock, based on archives of the Department of State (the Papal archives are not yet fully available) : " The United States at the court of Pius IX ", *Cath. hist. rev.*, n.s. III (1923) 103–122 [**1417**], dealing with diplomatic relations with the Vatican, 1848 to 1867; "American consuls to the Papal States, 1797–1870 ", *ibid.*, n.s. IX (1929) 233–251 [**1418**]; " The United States and the Vatican—past diplomatic relations ", in the Carnegie Institution of Washington, *News Service bulletin*, 1929 series, nos. 10, 11, 12; serial numbers 41, 42, 43 (1929) 57–61 [**1419**]. J. A. Henriques, *Corrêa da Serra* [8] (Coimbra, 1923), reprinted from the *Boletim da Sociedade Broteriana*, 2d ser., II (1923) 83–125 [**1420**], a biographical sketch of the celebrated Portuguese naturalist who was minister-plenipotentiary to the United States, 1816–1820, with a bibliography of his writings and some of his private, and two official letters from the United States, the former relating to botany, the latter to American filibustering ships. Joseph Agan, " Corrêa da Serra ", *Pa. mag. hist.*, XLIX (1925) 1–43 [**1421**] gives an account of the activities of José F. Corrêa da Serra, minister from Portugal at Washington, 1816–1820, based principally on American sources, notably the papers of Thomas

---

[8] See also, for a good sketch of the life of Corrêa da Serra, the *Biographic universelle*, IX, 258–259 ; and *Nouvelle biographie générale*, XI, 923–926.

Jefferson. McClure, *Ger. Am. com. rel.* (no. 1389). Two studies by M. E. Curti: *Austria and the United States, 1848–1852; a study in diplomatic relations* (Northampton, Mass., 1926) (Smith College Studies in History, v. XI, no. 3) **[1422]** is based on diplomatic archives at Vienna and in Berlin, and treats of Austria and manifest destiny, the Mann mission, and the Kossuth affair; and " George N. Sanders—American patriot of the fifties ", *So. Atlan. quar.*, XXVI (1928) 79–87 **[1423]** describes his activities in the interests of the Hungarian revolutionary movement, while he was American consul to London, in the early 1850's. J. G. Gazley, *American opinion of German unification, 1848–1871* (N.Y., 1926) **[1424]** includes also chapters on American opinion of Hungary (Kossuth affair, etc.), and of France. Fidelino Figueiredo, " Alguma coisa sobre as relações Luso-Norte-americanas ", *Revista de historia* (Lisbon), XV (1926) 167–181 **[1425]**, this is, it seems, the only attempt ever made in Portugal to study the diplomatic relations between that country and the United States; it is very general in character, contains a short reference to Humphreys' mission. F. A. Golder, " Russian-American relations during the Crimean war ", *Am. hist. rev.*, XXXI (1926) 462–476 **[1426]**, based on material found in the Russian foreign office in 1917. C. E. Hill, *The Danish Sound dues and the command of the Baltic; a study of international relations* (Durham, N.C., 1926) **[1427]** is a learned historical study, based on a mass of Danish source material. The last chapter deals with " The United States and the Sound dues ", based on printed sources and unprinted material in the archives of the Department of State. E. M. Earle, "American interest in the Greek cause, 1821–1827 ", *Am. hist. rev.*, XXXIII (1927) 44–63 **[1428]**, as revealed in printed writings of contemporaries and in newspapers and periodicals. For activities and policy of the United States government, see the same writer's " Early American policy concerning Ottoman minorities ", *Pol. sci. quar.*, XLII (1927) 337–367 **[1429]**. H. de C. Ferreira Lima, " Garrett diplomata ", *Jornal do comercio e das colonias* (Lisbon) August 1927 **[1430]**, A. Garrett negotiated and signed the treaty with Portugal in 1840. Perkins, *Monroe Doctrine* (no. 1172), for the controversy with Russia in the course of which the noncolonization principle was laid down. J. A. Hawgood, *Politische und wirtschaftliche Beziehungen zwischen den Vereinigten Staaten von Amerika und der deutschen provisorischen*

Central–regierung zu Frankfort am Main, 1848–49 (Forest Gate [Eng.] 1928) [**1430a**], a Heidelberg thesis printed in English by an English student, who has examined German archival records. It stresses the unique recognition by the United States of the Provisional Central Government at Frankfort in 1848–49, and the influence of the American example. Two studies by L. M. Sears: "The Neapolitan mission of Enos Thompson Throop, 1838–1842", *N.Y. state hist. assoc. jour.*, IX (1928) 365–379 [**1431**], from the MS. official instructions and despatches of Throop in the Department of State; and "Robert Dale Owen's mission to Naples", in the *Proceedings of the tenth annual Indiana history conference, . . . 1928* (Indianapolis, 1929) 43–51 [**1432**], describing his mission as *chargé d'affaires* to the Two Sicilies, 1853–54, based on similar material in the archives of the Department of State. *100 years of the American consulate at Frankfort-on-the-Main, 1829–1929*, published by the Dept. of Economics in commission from the magistracy of the city of Frankfort-on-the-Main (Frankfort, 1929; in Eng. and Ger. eds.) [**1433**], popular essays, some of them utilizing consular letters. Rudolph Said-Ruete, *Said bin Sultan (1791–1856), ruler of Oman and Zanzibar: his place in the history of Arabia and East Africa* (London, 1929) [**1434**], for the treaty with Muscat (Oman), 1833. Wriston, *Exec. agents* (no. 4799). A. B. Benson, "Henry Wheaton's writings on Scandinavia", *Jour. Eng. and Germ. philol.*, XXIX (1930) 546–561 [**1435**], Wheaton was our first regular diplomatic agent to Denmark, as *chargé*, 1827–35, and became an earnest student of Scandinavian history and literature. Myrtle A. Cline, *American attitude toward the Greek war of independence, 1821–1828* (Atlanta, Ga., 1930) [**1436**], based principally on newspaper and periodical sources, and printed state papers, but the author also consulted the archives of the Department of State and various personal papers. L. Lucile Morse, "The relations between the United States and Turkey", in Clark University, *Thesis abstracts*, 1929 (Worcester, 1930) 174–178 [**1437**], abstract of a thesis covering the whole period, without indicating sources. B. P. Thomas, *Russo-American relations, 1815–1867* (Baltimore, 1930) [**1438**], a typical doctoral thesis. The author was able to avail himself of Golder and other special studies, and to use a limited collection of photostats of Russian documents in the Library of Congress, and in the archives of the Dept. of State. J. F. Thorning, "American notes in Vatican diplomacy" in United States Catholic Historical Society, *Records and Studies*, XX (1931) 7-27 **[1439]**, based on L. F. Stock's studies (nos. 1417-1419), and printing several letters of 1867 from the legation of the United States at Rome, showing how the American mission to the Vatican came to an end; and by the same writer, " The Pope's first consul general in the United States ", *Thought*, VII (1933) 637-645 **[1440]** clears up doubt formerly existing in regard to identity of the first consular representative of the Pope in the United States, and shows him to have been Don Ferdinand Lucchesi, appointed in 1826, not J. B. Sartori; based on material in the Vatican archives. Gordon, *Am. rel. with Turkey* (no. 4377), primarily a study of economic relations, is weak on the history of diplomatic relations. H. R. Marraro, *American opinion on the unification of Italy, 1846-1861* (N.Y., 1932) **[1442]**, as digested principally from American newspapers. Sister Loretta C. Feiertag, *American public opinion on the diplomatic relations between the United States and the Papal States (1847-1867)* (Wash., 1933) **[1443]**, the writer had available Stock's edition of *Instructions and despatches* (no. 1451), and worked carefully through American newspapers and periodicals, and the *Cong. Globe;* but the records of the Vatican seem to have been unavailable to her. Nasim Sousa, *The capitulatory régime of Turkey; its history, origin and nature* (Baltimore, 1933) **[1443a]**, particular attention is paid to relations between the United States and Turkey on this subject. Stolberg-Wernigerode, *Deutschland und Vereinigten Staaten* (no. 4314). J. C. Westermann, " Een Amerikaansch oordeel over ons land omstreeks, 1820 ", *Tijdschrift voor Geschiedenis*, XLIX (1934) 42-55, 161-178 **[1444]**, A. H. Everett's mission to the Netherlands. The author, who has done much research both in the Netherlands and this country, has recently published his valuable and comprehensive work, *The Netherlands and the United States; their relations in the beginning of the nineteenth century* (Berlin, 1935).

For biographies of American statesmen and diplomatists, see the note in Sec. 1, above. A recent biography is, Linda Rhea, *Hugh Swinton Legaré, a Charleston intellectual* (Chapel Hill, N.C., 1934) **[1444a]**[9], Legaré was *chargé d'affaires* in Belgium, 1832-35, and secretary of state ad interim in 1843, after Webster's resignation.

---

[9] Published too late for inclusion in the D.A.B.

This work is based on his personal papers as well as archives of the Department of State.

For lists of foreign diplomatic envoys to the United States, see (to 1874) the *Register* of the Dept. of State, 1874 (no. 5122). A list of Danish representatives at Washington, to 1921, is given in Fogdall (no. 195), 157–158.

Printed Sources

For general collections, see Sec. 1, above. Hasse's *Index* (no. 5344), for guide to published United States documents.

For a convenient list of United States documents regarding Danish-American relations, see the bibliography in Fogdall (no. 195); for the same dealing with American relations with Italy, 1818–1861, see Marraro (no. 1442), 331–332.

P. Svīnīn. " Vzglīad na respublīku Soedīnennykh Amerīkanskīkh oblasteī [An outlook on the republic of the United States of America] ", in *Syn Otechestva* [*Son of the Fatherland*], XVII–XVIII (1814) passim. [1445] is a travel description of the United States with comments on Russo-American relations of that date. *Writings of Legaré* (no. 5257) includes extracts from his private and diplomatic correspondence (he was *chargé d'affaires* in Belgium, 1832–35). Harro Harring, *Russland und die Vereinigten Staaten Nord-Amerika's* (N.Y., 1854) [1446] is anti-Czarist propaganda. [H. F. McDermott], *Letters on the Sound-dues-question* (N.Y., 1855) [1447] consists of 7 letters, issued anonymously, written for the New York Daily Times, in 1855, by a non-official citizen. " Correspondence of the Russian ministers in Washington, 1818–1823 ", *Am. hist. rev.*, XVIII (1913) 309–345, 537–562 [1448] consists of documents from the central archives at St. Petersburg and the archives of the embassy at Washington, containing letters of the ministers Pierre de Polética and Baron de Tuyll van Serooskerken. F. S. Rodkey, " The opinions of three American diplomats on the character of Tsar Nicholas I.", *Slavonic rev.*, VI (1927) 434–437 [1449], James Buchanan's report of his farewell audience with the Emperor, 1833, and despatches of Buchanan and Dallas, 1833 and 1837, respectively. "A diplomatic incident; when Washington closed our Vatican ministry ", *Atlantic mo.*, CXLIV (1929) 500–510 [1450] prints significant diplomatic correspondence concerning the last American relations with the Papal court, 1867. L. F. Stock, *United*

States ministers to the Papal States; instructions and despatches (Wash., 1933) (American Catholic Historical Association Documents, v. I) [**1451**], a complete publication of despatches, instructions, and enclosures, from the Dept. of State, with illuminating preface.

For printed writings of American statesmen and diplomatists, see note in Sec. 1, above.

MSS.: Suggestions

See Sec. 1, above.

CHAPTER X

TEXAS AND MEXICO, 1828–1861

1. In General

Bibliographical Aids

For general aids, see Sabin (no. 4655); Larned (no. 4657); Griffin (no. 4658); *Writings* (no. 4661); C. H. and T. (no. 4662); bibliographies in *Am. secs. state* (no. 4796); *Guide hist. lit.* (no. 4634). Myers (no. 5399) for collections of treaties. Miller, *Treaties* (no. 5371), v. I, 39–54, for " Bibliography of United States treaty collections."

For lists of newspapers, see nos. 5004–5047; particularly Library of Congress checklists (no. 5030–5032). For index to periodical material (including *Niles's Register*) see *Poole's index* (no. 4995). Winsor (no. 4782), v. VII, 527–672. War Dept. Library, *Mexico* (no. 4712), pt. III: " Mexican war, 1846–48, and Texan-Mexican war." Griffin, *References on recognition* (no. 4801). N.Y. Public Library, *Mexico* (no. 4713). Also the bibliographies in the following monographs: Rives, *U.S. and Mexico* (no. 1460); Marshall, *Western boundary* (no. 768); Manning, *U.S. and Mexico* (no. 1476); Priestley, *Mexican nation* (no. 1462); Rippy, *U.S. and Mexico* (no. 3548). Tinker, *Bibliog. Fr. newspapers of La.* (no. 5020).

General Works

Of general histories of the United States, see Von Holst (no. 4780); McMaster (no. 4781); Rhodes (no. 4783); Channing (no. 4784). See also *Am. secs. state* (no. 4796); and Wriston (no. 4799).

For general histories of Hispanic America, see Ch. VIII, sec. 1.

248

Three works by H. H. Bancroft: *History of Mexico* (San Francisco, 1883–88, 6 v.) [1452]; *History of California* (San Francisco, 1884–90, 7 v.) [1453], one of the more notable of the works written by Bancroft's employed writers; and *History of the North Mexican states and Texas* (San Francisco, 1884–89, 2 v.) [1454], similar in method to his *Central America* (no. 1220).

Luis Pérez Verdía, *Compendio de la historia de México* (Mexico, 1884; 5th ed.: Mexico, 1911) [1455], perhaps the best, though now old. This is a condensation of Vicente Riva Palacio, ed., *México a través de los siglos* (Mexico and Barcelona, 1887–89, 5 v.) [1456], the most recent of the larger sets on Mexican history and still in great part valid for its period. Nicolás León, *Compendio de la historia general de México* (Mexico, 1902; and several later editions) [1457] is not free from error especially in treating of relations with foreign countries wherein the *amour propre* of the Mexican has been touched. G. P. Garrison, *Westward extension* (N.Y., 1906) [1458], now largely superseded by later more intensive studies. J. S. Reeves, *American diplomacy under Tyler and Polk* (Baltimore, 1907) [1459], the first scholarly study of the subject, from materials available in the United States, it must be supplemented by later special works. G. L. Rives, *The United States and Mexico, 1821–1848; a history of the relations between the two countries from the independence of Mexico to the close of the war with the United States* (N.Y., 1913, 2 v.) [1460], comprehensive in scope, judicious and cheerful in tone (if not in style), the author used the archives of the Department of State to advantage, but those of Mexico and Great Britain only very meagerly. Does not always place Mexico in the right and put the United States in the wrong. Now largely superseded by Manning (no. 1476) and Smith (nos. 1519 and 1592). A. M. Carreño, *México y los Estados Unidos de América; apuntaciones para la historia del acrecentamiento territorial de los Estados Unidos a costa de México desde la epoca colonial hasta nuestros días* (Mexico, 1922) [1461], this work, written in 1913 (before the appearance of Justin Smith's scholarly studies) reviews Mexican-American relations from Mexican printed and archival sources, with lengthy extracts from the latter. Goodwin, *The Trans-Mississippi West* (no. 678) has a useful short account of the Texas question and the Mexican war. *Camb. hist. Brit. for. pol.*, v. II (no.

209). H. I. Priestley, *The Mexican nation* (Mexico City, 1923) [**1462**], the best recent general history of Mexico in English. Carlos Pereyra, *Historia de la América española*, III. *Méjico* (Madrid, 1924) [**1463**] deals with Mexico in bold strokes, the history is synthetic, the attitude is modern, the relations with the United States recognized as fixed by economic motives rather than prejudice. Rippy, *Latin America* (no. 1076) and *U.S. and Mexico* (no. 3548). E. C. Barker, " On the historiography of American territorial expansion " in the *Trans-Mississippi West*, papers read at a Conference on the history of the trans-Mississippi West held at the University of Colorado, 1929 (Boulder, Colo., 1930), 219–247 [**1464**] has a critical and very wholesome analysis of the tendency of some American historians of western expansion at the expense of former Spanish and Mexican territory toward hyper-derogation of motives and morals of the United States. Douglas, *Boundaries* (no. 211). J. M. Callahan, *American foreign policy in Mexican relations* (N.Y., 1932) [**1465**], the author bases his text upon laborious research and detailed study of the printed and unprinted archives of the Department of State, but ignores the Mexican archives, and a vast amount of important monographic material in Spanish and English, including Justin Smith: Reading this book it is not always possible clearly to understand precisely what the foreign policy was. F. S. Dunn, *The diplomatic protection of Americans in Mexico* (N.Y., 1933) [**1466**], an iconoclastic juridical approach to a subject much investigated—the author still finds fresh materials in the archives of the Department of State. Perkins, *Monroe Doctrine, 1826–67* (no. 1211).

For biographies of American statesmen and diplomatists to Mexico and Texas (for names and tenure, see latest *Register* of the Dept. of State (no. 5122)), see relevant entries and bibliographical data in the *D.A.B.*

For list of Mexican diplomatic envoys to the United States, see the *Register* of the Dept. of State, 1874 (no. 5122). A list of Mexican secretaries of foreign affairs, 1821–1924, is given in *Personas que han tenido a su cargo la secretaría de relaciones exteriores desde 1821 hasta 1924* (Mexico: Secretaría de Relaciones Exteriores, 1924) (Archivo Histórico Diplomático Mexicano, no. 6) [**1467**]. For lists of biographical dictionaries, see nos. 4953–4956.

Printed Sources

For American official publications and general source collections, see *Jour. exec. proc. Sen.* (no. 5387); *A.S.P., F.R.* (only to 1828) (no. 5341); *Ann. Cong.* (no. 5382); *Reg. debates Cong.* (no. 5383); *Cong. Globe* (no. 5380); Wharton, *Digest* (no. 5366); *Abridg. debates Cong.* (no. 5386); Richardson (no. 5335); Moore, *Arbitrations* (no. 5364); *Repts. Sen. com. for. rel.* (no. 5383); Moore's *Digest* (no. 5365); for index to United States official documents, see Hasse's *Index* (no. 5344).

For texts of treaties, see Miller, *Treaties* (no. 5371).

For guides to Mexican official publications, see below, p. 841; Myers, *Treaties* (no. 5399), and Gregory (no. 5400), noting particularly the *Memorias* of the Foreign Office, which contain the reports of the department, diplomatic correspondence, and miscellaneous material of value.

For guides to newspapers, see nos. 5004–5047; particularly Library of Congress checklists (nos. 5030, 5032).

For printed writings of American presidents, secretaries of state, and diplomatists to Mexico and Texas (for names and tenure, see latest *Register* of the Dept. of State (no. 5122)), see our list on p. 756. Note particularly *Corres. Andrew Jackson* (no. 5243), and Rowland, *Jefferson Davis . . . papers and speeches* (no. 5214).

MSS.: Suggestions

The archives of the Dept. of State (which have been exhaustively used by Rives (no. 1460), Manning (no. 1476), Smith (no. 1592), Rippy (no. 3548), and Callahan (no. 1465) are described in Van Tyne and Leland (no. 5495).

H. E. Bolton, " Material for southwestern history in the central archives of Mexico ", *Am. hist. rev.*, XIII (1908) 510–527 **[1468]** describes very briefly the contents of the archives devoted to the period of the Texan question. For detailed list see his *Guide* (no. 5674). For guides to British and French official archives and photostats from those archives, see below: British, p. 890, and French, p. 915.

For private MSS. of the presidents (J. Q. Adams, Jackson, Van Buren, W. H. Harrison, Tyler, Polk, Taylor, Fillmore, Pierce, Buchanan), see p. 862; and secretaries of state (Clay, Van Buren,

E. Livingston, McLane, Forsyth, Webster, Upshur, Calhoun, Buchanan, Clayton, Everett, Marcy, Cass, Black), see p. 865. Secs. 2–4 of this chapter contain further suggestions for MS. material. For elaborate list of MSS. dealing with relations between the United States and Mexico, see Smith (no. 1592), v. II, 517–524. The same author discusses the sources particularly in no. 1572. Twenty volumes of transcripts of the material used by Justin H. Smith in writing his *War with Mexico* (no. 1592) are contained in the García collection in the University of Texas library at Austin. The same library has 18 folders of MSS. of Valentín Gómez Farías, 1821–57, containing commentaries on Anglo-American activities in Texas and during the Mexican war.

Maps: Suggestions

See Ch. VII, sec. 2, above. Consult also the bibliographies of maps listed in Ch. XXIII, sec. 12; particularly War Dept. Library (no. 4712).

Manuel Orozco y Berra, *Materiales para una cartografía mexicana* (Mexico: Imprenta del Gobierno, 1871) **[1469]**. For secondary maps illustrating the southwestern boundary discussions and issues, see Paullin (no. 213), plates 93g–95d, with accompanying text; Marshall, *Western boundary* (no. 768); and Garber (no. 1628).

Noteworthy original maps: S. F. Austin, *Mapa original de Texas por el ciudadano Estevan F. Austin, presentado al Exmo. Sor. Presidente, por su autor, 1829*, the original in the archives of the "Secretaría de Fomento", Dept. of cartography, photocopy in the Bolton Collection, University of California **[1470]**; Castañeda and Martin, *Maps of Texas by Stephen F. Austin* (no. 790).

Two maps were attached to the treaty of Guadalupe Hidalgo: (1) *Mapa de los Estados Unidos de México según lo organizado y definido por las varias actas del congreso de dicha república y construido por las mejores autoridades.* Lo publican, J. Disturnell, . . . Nueva York, 1847. Revised edition **[1471]**. There are at least five 1847 editions of Disturnell, but the one attached to the treaty can be identified by the two inserts (not four) in the Gulf of Mexico. A facsimile will be published in v. V of Miller's *Treaties* (no. 5371). See Douglas, *Boundaries* (no. 211) for copy of " Part of the map of Mexico prepared by J. Disturnell and published in New York in 1847." (2) *Plano del Puerto de S. Domingo en la costa setentl. de*

Californˢ. Leventado por el 2°. Piloto de la Armada D. Juan Pantoja. Año *1782,* in the *Atlas* to the voyage of the schooners " Sutil " and " Mexicana " (José Espinosa y Tello, *Relación del viage hecho por las goletas Sutil y Mexicana en el año de 1792* (Madrid, 1802)) **[1472]**.

2. Mexico, to 1836

Bibliographical Aids

See Sec. 1, above.

Special Works

Paxson (no. 1021), for recognition of Mexican independence. Temperley, *Later Am. policy of Canning* (no. 750), for British influence in Mexico and Poinsett's struggle against it. Joceline Bagot, *Canning and friends* (no. 1179). Alleine Howren, " Causes and origin of the decree of April 6, 1830 ", *Southw. hist. quar.,* XVI (1913) 378–422 **[1473]**, the decree of Apr. 6, 1830 was an attempt of Mexico to save Texas to the Mexican nation by strengthening the ties of that state with Mexico. Marshall, *Western boundary* (no. 768). J. H. Smith, " The drama of our diplomacy in Mexico ", *World's work,* XXVII (1914) 308–312 **[1474]** is concerned with the mission of J. R. Poinsett and later periods; see also his " Poinsett's career in Mexico ", *Am. antiq. soc. proc.,* n.s. XXIV, pt. 1 (1914) 77–92 **[1475]**. W. S. Robertson, *First legations in Latin America,* (no. 1028). W. R. Manning, *Early diplomatic relations between the United States and Mexico* (Baltimore, 1916) **[1476]**, author used Mexican and United States Dept. of State archives carefully to cover the period from 1821 to 1830, and incorporates earlier articles on the same subject. Two studies by J. F. Rippy : " Some precedents of the Pershing expedition into Mexico ", *Southw. hist. quar.,* XXIV (1921) 292–316 **[1477]** discusses the occupation of Nacogdoches, Texas, in 1836; and " Britain's role in the early relations of the United States and Mexico ", *Hisp. Am. hist. rev.,* VII (1927) 2–24 **[1478-9]**. Bécker, *Relaciones exteriores España* (no. 723). Fabela, *Precursores dipl. mex.* (no. 1066) deals with Mexican foreign relations prior to 1824. Manuel Puga y Acal, " Poinsett en Méjico y en Chile ", *Rev. chilena,* XI (Santiago de Chile, 1927) 43–58 **[1480]**, an argumentative article based on secondary accounts. E. C. Barker, *Mexico and Texas, 1821–1835* (Dallas, Tex., 1928)

[1481], primarily a searching study of the political and constitutional phases of the Texan revolution, it shows how efforts of Adams
and Jackson to purchase Texas alarmed Mexico into repressive
measures there. Guillermo Feliú Cruz, " Comprobaciones histó-
cas; Poinsett en Méjico y en Chile ", *Rev. chilena*, XII (1928)
37–46 [1482], apparently a reply to the article above (no. 1480).
Bernard Mayo, "Apostle of manifest destiny," *Am. mercury*, XVIII
(1929) 420–426 [1483], caustic survey of Butler's Mexican diplomacy. H. T. Thompson, *Waddy Thompson, jr., member of Congress,
1835–1841, minister to Mexico, 1842–44*, rev. ed. (Columbia, S.C.,
1929) [1484], brief sketch by a descendant. R. R. Stenberg, " Jackson, Anthony Butler, and Texas ", *Southw. soc. sci. quar.*, XIII
(1932) 264–286 [1485], author reviews the sources on Butler's mission and concludes that Butler has been made a scapegoat for Jackson's intrigues; and a later article by the same writer: " The Texas
schemes of Jackson and Houston, 1829–1836 ", *ibid.*, XV (1934)
229–250 [1485a] presents Jackson as a master of subtle intrigue and
duplicity in collusion with Houston, but the evidence is circumstantial and fragmentary.

For biographies, see note in Sec. 1, above.

Printed Sources

For general collections, see Sec. 1, above.

*Memoria que el secretario de estado y del despacho de relaciones
esteriores é interiores presenta al soberano Congreso constituyente
sobre los negocios de su cargo leída en la sesión de 8 de noviembre de
1823*, by Lucas Alamán (Mexico, 1823) [1486], translated (in part,
and dated Nov. 1 instead of Nov. 8) in *British and foreign state
papers*, X, 1822–23 (London, 1828) 1070–1076. It discusses the state
of the relations of Mexico with other countries. J. R. Poinsett, *Notes
on Mexico, made in the autumn of 1822, . . . by a citizen of the
United States* (Phila., 1824) [1487] gives his observations during
unofficial travels in Mexico prior to his official mission; also his
*Exposición de la conducta política de los Estados Unidos, para con
las nuevas repúblicas de América* (Mexico, 1827) [1488], issued
(July 4, 1827) in answer to the attacks made upon him in the Vera
Cruz manifesto. *The speeches of the Right Honourable William
Huskisson, with a biographical memoir* (London, 1831, 3 v.) [1489]
contains an exposition of the political and commercial relations of

Great Britain with Mexico, 1830; which is also included in *Select speeches of the Right Honourable William Windham, and the Right Honourable William Huskisson,* ed. by Robert Walsh (Phila., 1837) **[1490]**. Lucas Alamán, *Defensa del ex-ministro de relaciones D. Lucas Alamán, en la causa formada contra él y contra los ex-ministros de guerra y justicia del vice-presidente D. Anastasio Bustamente* (Mexico, 1834) **[1491]**. Mexico, Comisión de Límites, *Diario de viage de la Comisión de límites que puso el gobierno de la República, bajo la dirección del Exmo. Sr. general de división D. Manuel de Mier y Terán,* written by order of the commission by Louis Berlandier and Rafael Chovel (Mexico, 1850) **[1492]**, Mexican commission to survey the Texas-Louisiana boundary, following the treaty of 1819 between the United States and Spain. J. M. Tornel y Mendivil, *Breve reseña histórica de los acontecimientos más notables de la nación mexicana desde el año 1821 hasta nuestros días* (Mexico, 1852) **[1493]**, antagonistic to Poinsett. *Some official correspondence of Canning* (no. 969). J. M. de Bocanegra, *Memorias para la historia de México independiente, 1822-1846* (Mexico, 1892-97, 2 v.) **[1494]** includes a contemporary account of Poinsett's reception. *Papers of Sir Charles R. Vaughan* (no. 1380) includes correspondence with the British representative in Mexico, Sir H. G. Ward, and reveals the attitude of Mexico towards Great Britain and the United States. F. L. Paxson, " England and Mexico, 1824-1825 ", *Texas hist. assoc. quar.,* IX (1905) 138-141, and *Univ. of Colo. stud.,* III (1906) 115-118 **[1495]**, extracts from British foreign office correspondence showing the British activities in Mexico. *La diplomacía mexicana,* ed. by Enrique Santibáñez (Mexico, 1910-13, 3 v.) **[1496]** presents documents from archives of the foreign office of Mexico concerning the first mission of the United States to Mexico and first mission of Mexico to the United States. " Message of President Monroe [1818] and documents relative to the imprisonment of certain American citizens at Santa Fe by the Spanish authorities in 1811-1817 ", *Old Santa Fe,* I (1914) 369-385 **[1497]** deals with the imprisonment of A. P. Chouteau, for having entered Spanish territory without the necessary passport. *Lucas Alamán; el reconocimiento de nuestra independencia por España y la Unión de los países hispano-americanas,* ed. by Antonio de la Peña y Reyes (Mexico: Publicaciones de la Secretaría de Relaciones Exteriores, 1924) (Archivo Histórico Diplomático Mexicano, no. 7) **[1498]**, selections from the official correspondence of Alamán while minister of foreign relations, with a few other letters. Joaquín Moreno, *Diario de un escribiente de legación,* ed. by Genaro Estrada (Mexico: Secretaría de Relaciones Exteriores, 1925) (Archivo Histórico Diplomático Mexicano, no. 16) [1499] is the diary of an attaché of the Mexican legation in Paris and Rome, 1833-1836, and throws light on American affairs at the time. Manning, *Dipl. corres.* (no. 5342). Luis Chávez Orozco, *Un esfuerzo de México por la independencia de Cuba* (Mexico: Secretaría de Relaciones Exteriores, 1930) (Archivo Histórico Diplomático Mexicano, no. 32) [1500] contains correspondence of. the Mexican legation in the United States of J. R. Poinsett, U. S. minister to Mexico, of Francisco Pizarro Martínez, Mexican secret agent in New Orleans, and other documents.

For printed writings of American presidents, secretaries of state, statesmen, and diplomatists to Mexico and Texas, see Sec. 1, above.

MSS.: Suggestions

See Secs. 1 and 3, this chapter.

The *Second biennial report 1911-1912* of the Texas Library and Historical Commission (Austin, 1914) [1500a] contains a list of transcripts from the Mexican archives dealing with diplomatic relations between the United States and Mexico, 1820 to 1830. Lota M. Spell, " Mier archives ", *Hisp. Am. hist. rev.,* XII (1932) 359-375 [1501] includes a calendar, 1820-1822, and description of the collection in the University of Texas of the papers of José Servado Teresa de Mier Noriega y Guerra, who played an important part in the struggle for Mexican independence, and lived in Philadelphia for several months after he was banished from Mexico.

Of the personal papers of diplomatic agents [1] of the United States to Mexico the following may be noted: William Shaler (consul, 1810-13); Joel Poinsett (1825-29); Anthony Butler (1829-36); and Powhatan Ellis (1839-42).

3. Texas Question, 1836-1845

Bibliographical Aids

See Sec. 1, above.

Raines, *Bibliog. of Texas* (no. 748).

---

[1] For list of extant collections of papers of such agents (giving location and analysis of contents), see p. 868.

General Works

See Sec. 1, above; note particularly, Carreño (no. 1461), Goodwin (no. 678), Reeves (no. 1459), Rippy (no. 3548), Callahan (no. 1465).

Henderson Yoakum, *History of Texas from its first settlement in 1685 to its annexation to the United States in 1846* (N.Y., 1856, 2 v.) [**1502**], the writer used critical contemporary material which has since disappeared. Bancroft, *Texas* (no. 1454). *The Earl of Aberdeen*, by Sir Arthur Gordon [1st Baron Stanmore] (N.Y., 1893) [**1503**]. Z. T. Fulmore, " History of Texas geography ", *Tex. state hist. assoc. quar.*, I (1897) 9-25 [**1504**], for boundaries of Texas (includes a map showing boundaries as claimed by Texas, 1836 to 1850). D. G. Wooten, *A comprehensive history of Texas, 1685 to 1897* (Dallas, 1898, 2 v.) [**1505**]. R. M. McElroy, *The winning of the far West; a history of the regaining of Texas; of the Mexican war, and the Oregon question* (N.Y. and London, 1914) [**1506**], heroic. Balfour (no. 1383), really a publication of diary and letters. Holt, *Defeated treaties* (no. 4837).

Special Works

Vicente Filisola, *Memorias para la historia de la guerra de Tejas* (Mexico, 1848-49, 2 v.) [**1507**], a contemporary narrative by a Mexican general, and later president of the supreme court, of military and naval affairs, who prints many documents. Z. T. Fulmore, " The annexation of Texas and the Mexican war ", *Tex. state hist. assoc. quar.*, V (1901) 28-48 [**1508**], a glorification of the Texan pioneer and his revolution, superseded by the more careful works of Rives, Manning, and Justin Smith, *post*. I. J. Cox, " The southwest boundary of Texas ", *Tex. state hist. assoc. quar.*, VI (1902) 81-102 [**1509**], largely from the Spanish and Mexican point of view. Whitelaw Reid, *The Monroe doctrine, the Polk doctrine, and the doctrine of anarchism* (N.Y., 1903) [**1510**], analysis of Polk's policy regarding Texas. B. H. Carroll, *Die Annexion von Texas; ein Beitrag zur Geschichte der Monroe-Doktrin* (Berlin, 1904) [**1511**] exploits the then unpublished diplomatic correspondence of Texas to show that annexation was controlled by an expansionist policy rather than the slavery question. G. P. Garrison, " The first stage of the movement for the annexation of Texas ", *Am. hist. rev.*, X (1904) 72-96 [**1512**], a careful narrative of the first Texan proposal for annexation and its rejection by the United States in 1837, very largely resting on the diplomatic correspondence of Texas, then being edited by the author for publication (no. 1555). J. L. Worley, " The diplomatic relations of England and the Republic of Texas ", *Tex. state hist. assoc. quar.*, IX (1905) 1–40 [**1513**], based on MS. collection of diplomatic, consular, and domestic correspondence in the State Library at Austin. Two studies by E. C. Barker : " President Jackson and the Texas revolution ", *Am. hist. rev.*, XII (1907) 788–809 [**1514**] defends Jackson against charges of unneutral conduct ; and his " The United States and Mexico, 1835–1837 ", *Miss. Valley hist. rev.*, I (1914) 3–30 [**1515**], dealing with relations which grew out of the Texas revolution. E. D. Adams, *British interests and activities in Texas, 1838–1846* (Baltimore, 1910) [**1516**], based on documents in the Public Record Office, London. Ethel Z. Rather, " Recognition of the Republic of Texas by the United States ", *Tex. state hist. assoc. quar.*, XIII (1910) 155–255 [**1517**], the writer did not have access to records in the Dept. of State or archives in the city of Mexico. Two studies by T. M. Marshall : " Diplomatic relations of Texas and the United States, 1839–1843 ", *Tex. state hist. assoc. quar.*, XV (1912) 267–293 [**1518**], based on the *Diplomatic correspondence of the Republic of Texas* and *Secret journals of the Senate, Republic of Texas;* and *Western boundary La.* (no. 768), challenges the purity of Andrew Jackson's motives. Justin H. Smith, *The annexation of Texas* (N.Y., 1911) [**1519**], an outstanding and important study, based on archives of France, Great Britain, Mexico, Texas, and the United States, a work of prodigious scholarship and array of archival sources, his conclusions are sometimes debatable. E. D. Adams, *The power of ideals in American history* (New Haven, 1913) [**1519a**], for thought provoking analysis of the dogma of " manifest destiny." Two studies by G. L. Rives : " Mexican diplomacy on the eve of the war with the United States ", *Am. hist. rev.*, XVIII (1913) 275–294 [**1520**], based on documents in the Mexican archives ; dealing with relations with Great Britain and France in regard to prevention of annexation of Texas by the United States; and *U.S. and Mexico* (no. 1460). Goebel, *Recognition policy* (no. 1038) examines the recognition of Texas. J. E. Winston, " The attitude of the newspapers of the United States towards Texan independence ", *Miss. Valley hist. assoc. proc.*, VIII (1916) 160–175 [**1521**]. Carlos Pereyra, *Tejas; la primera desmembración de Méjico* (Madrid, 1917 ?) [**1522**], polemic and journalistic, it shows how the author hates the United States because of Texas; and how he distrusts United States historians. Two studies by C. S. Boucher: " The annexation of Texas and the Bluffton movement in South Carolina ", *Miss. Valley hist. rev.*, VI (1919) 3–33 [**1523**], for the controversy over the annexation of Texas particularly as it appeared in the presidential campaign of 1844; and " In re that aggressive slavocracy ", *Miss. Valley hist. rev.*, VIII (1921) 13–79 [**1524**] leans on a " vast mass " of personal correspondence of southern statesmen (cited only in a general group) to show that the South had no aggressive hankering after Texas before 1843. A.K. Christian, " Mirabeau Buonaparte Lamar ", *Southw. hist. quar.*, XXIV (1920–1921) *passim.* [**1525**] uses local Texas sources for a study of the administration of President Lamar, particularly foreign affairs, in the early years of the Republic of Texas. Annie Middleton, " Donelson's mission to Texas in behalf of annexation ", *ibid.*, 247–291 [**1526**], study of the final stage of annexation, based on Texas diplomatic correspondence, correspondence of Calhoun, and other documents. Rippy, *Precedents of Pershing expedition* (no. 1477), for the occupation of Nacogdoches, Texas, in 1836. N. W. Stephenson, *Texas and the Mexican war; a chronicle of the winning of the Southwest* (New Haven, 1921) [**1527**], a popular sketch, with an implication in the title. R. S. Hicks, " Diplomatic relations with Mexico during the administration of James K. Polk ", *So. Cal. hist. soc. pub.*, XII, pt. 2 (1922) 5–17 [**1528**] relies on Polk's diary and the Larkin papers to show Polk's determination to go the limit to get California. Martin, *Trade and Anglo-American relations* (no. 1344). W. C. Binkley, *The expansionist movement in Texas, 1836–1850* (Berkeley, Cal., 1925) [**1529**], a valuable study of the adjustment of the western (Mexican) boundary of Texas to include California. Harriet Smither, " English abolitionism and the annexation of Texas ", *Southw. hist. quar.*, XXXII (1929) 193–205 [**1530**], English interference in Texas affairs in 1843, based on *Diplomatic correspondence of the Republic of Texas*, and *Correspondence of J. C. Calhoun.* Alma H. Brown, " The consular service of the Republic of Texas ", *ibid.*, XXXIII (1930) 184–230, 299–314 [**1531**], based on Texan consular correspondence now in the Texas State Library, the *Diplomatic correspondence of the Republic of Texas* and the *Secret journals of the senate of Texas.* Two studies by J. E. Winston: " Notes on commercial relations between New Or-

leans and Texan ports, 1838-1839 ", *ibid.*, **XXXIV** (1930) 91-105
[**1532**]; and "New Orleans newspapers and the Texas question,
1835-1837 ", *ibid.*, **XXXVI** (1932) 109-129 [**1533**]. Mary K.
Chase, *Négociations de la République du Texas en Europe 1837-1845* (Paris,
1932) [**1534**], based on protracted research in the archives in Paris,
Brussels, and The Hague, contains hitherto unpublished letters of
Texan envoys in Europe and of European diplomatists interested
in Texas. It reproduces documents which supplement Garrison
(no. 1555) and Adams (no. 1516). H. D. Jordan, "A politician of
expansion: Robert J. Walker ", *Miss. Valley hist. rev.*, **XIX** (1932)
362-381 [**1535**] shows that Walker was one of the president's foremost allies in the efforts of 1843-45 to secure Texas. C. T. Neu,
" The annexation of Texas ", in *New Spain and the Anglo-American
West;* historical contributions presented to Herbert Eugene Bolton
(Los Angeles, Calif., 1932), v. II, 71-102 [**1536**] deals with the last
phase of the annexation movement, with documents heretofore unpublished. R. R. Stenberg, " President Polk and the annexation
of Texas ", *Southw. soc. sci. quar.*, **XIV** (1934) 332-356 [**1537**] to
show that Polk went back on pre-inauguration promise to senators
to carry through annexation by optional mode of negotiation; and
" The failure of Polk's war intrigue of 1845 ", *Pacific hist. rev.*, **IV**
(1935) 39-68) [**1537a**] shows how Polk covertly urged Texas to
come into the United States still at war with Mexico for the Rio
Grande. J. W. Pratt, " John L. O'Sullivan and manifest destiny ",
N.Y. hist., **XIV** (1933) 213-232 [**1538**], interesting biographical and
political information about the author of the phrase.

For biographies of American statesmen and diplomatists, see
note in Sec. 1, above.

For biographies of presidents of the Republic of Texas (Gen. Sam
Houston, M. B. Lamar, and Anson Jones), and diplomatic envoys
to the United States (for names and tenure, see *Register* of the Dept.
of State, 1874 (no. 5122)), see relevant entries and bibliographical
data in the *D.A.B.*

Note J. M. Roa Bárcana, *Datos y apuntamientos para la biografía
de D. Manuel Eduardo de Gorostiza* (Mexico, 1876) [**1539**], minister
plenipotentiary and envoy extraordinary of Mexico to the United
States, 1836.

Printed Sources

For general collections, see Sec. 1, above.

U.S. official documents relating to the Texan question are conveniently listed in Binkley (no. 1529), 224–226; see also Hasse (no. 5344), for index to same.

For guide to British official documents, see p. 838. For treaties with Great Britain, see Hertslet's *Commercial treaties* (no. 5417).

Two works by José María Tornel [y Mendivil], Mexican minister to the United States, 1830–31: *Manifestación del C. José María Tornel* (Mexico, 1833) [**1540**], an exposition of the facts and motives of the author's public career; and *Tejas y los Estados Unidos de América, en sus relaciones con la República Mexicana* (Mexico, 1837) (translation published in *The Mexican side of the Texan revolution*, ed. by C. E. Castañeda (Dallas, Tex. 1928) [**1541**], political pronouncements. *Correspondencia que ha mediado entre la legación extraordinaria de México y el Departamento de Estado de los Estados-Unidos, sobre el paso del Sabina por las tropas que mandaba el general Gaines* (Mexico, 1837) [**1542**], the correspondence of M. E. de Gorostiza, Mexican minister, with the American Department of State, it includes also " Documentos relativos al pedido que hizo de su pasaporte el honorable Sr. Powhatan Ellis, encargado de negocios de los Estados Unidos de América." *Examination and review of a pamphlet printed and secretly circulated by M. E. Gorostiza, late envoy extraordinary from Mexico; previous to his departure from the United States, and by him entitled " Correspondence between the legation extraordinary of Mexico and the Department of State of the United States, respecting the passage of the Sabine, by the troops under the command of General Gaines "* (Wash., 1837) [**1543**] includes a translation of Gorostiza's pamphlet. *Journals of the consultation held at San Felipe de Austin, October 16 [-November 14] 1835*, pub. by order of Congress [of the Provisional Government of Texas] (Houston, 1838) [**1544**]. *Journal of the proceedings of the General Council of the Republic of Texas, held at San Felipe de Austin, November 14th, 1835 [-March 11th, 1836]* (Houston, 1839) [**1545**]. William Kennedy, *Texas; the rise, progress and prospects of the Republic of Texas* (London, 1841, 2 v.) [**1546**], written by one of the English diplomatic agents in Texas, represents contemporary opinion on Texas. M. E. de Gorostiza,

Dictamen leído el 3 de junio de 1840 en el Consejo de Gobierno sobre le cuestión de Tejas (Mexico, 1844) [**1547**]. Waddy Thompson, *Recollections of Mexico* (N.Y. and London, 1846) [**1548**], by the American minister to Mexico, 1842–44. *Correspondence between the governments of Great Britain and the United States relative to the general abolition of slavery in Texas, 1843–1844* (Gt. Brit. House of Commons. Sess. pap., 1847–48, LXIV) [**1549**] prints Calhoun-Pakenham correspondence. Benton, *Thirty years' view* (no. 968). Anson Jones, *Memoranda and official correspondence relating to the Republic of Texas, its history and annexation, including a brief autobiography of the author* (N.Y., 1859) [**1550**]. A. Fourier de Bacourt, *Souvenirs d'un diplomate; lettres intimes sur l'Amérique* (Paris, 1822; Eng. tr.: N.Y., 1885) [**1551**], being the letters from America of the French minister to the United States, 1840–42. Sam Houston, " The annexation of Texas ", *Tex. state hist. assoc. quar.*, I (1897) 79–86 [**1552**], letter from Gen. Houston, to Major A. J. Donelson, U.S. *chargé d'affaires* in Texas, Apr. 9, 1845. Alex. Dienst, " The New Orleans newspaper files of the Texas revolutionary period ", *ibid.*, IV (1900) 140–151 [**1553**], items from the New Orleans press relating to Texas. Antonio López de Santa Anna, *Mi historia militar y política, 1810–1874; memorias inéditas* (Mexico, 1905) [**1554**]. *Diplomatic correspondence of the Republic of Texas*, ed. by G. P. Garrison (Wash., 1908–11, 3 v.) (Am. Hist. Assoc. Ann. Rep. for 1907–1908) [**1555**]. *Secret journals of the Senate, Republic of Texas, 1836–1845*, ed. from the original records in the State Library and the Department of State, by E. W. Winkler (Austin, Tex., 1911) [**1556**]. J. M. Puelles, " Report given to his excellency, the president of the Mexican republic with regard to the boundaries of the province of Texas with that of Louisiana (Zacatecas, 1828) ", *La. hist. quar.*, I (1917) 21–43 [**1557**], report of a survey of the boundary between Texas and Louisiana, published in 1828. *British diplomatic correspondence concerning the Republic of Texas, 1838–1846*, ed. by E. D. Adams (Austin, Tex., 1918) reprinted from the *Journal* of the Texas State Historical Association, v. XV, 1912, and the *Southwestern historical quarterly*, v. XVI–XXII, 1912–1917 [**1558**], consisting of letters and reports of the two British officials in Texas (Charles Elliot, and William Kennedy). *Corres. Nicholas Biddle* (no. 1699). *The papers of Mirabeau Buonaparte Lamar*, ed. from the original papers in the Texas State Library by C. A. Gulick, jr., with the assistance of Katherine Elliott (Austin, Tex., 1921–27, 6 v.) [**1559**]. *Don Manuel Eduardo de Gorostiza y la cuestión de Texas; documentos históricos*, ed. by Antonio de la Peña y Reyes (Mexico: Secretaría de Relaciones Exteriores, 1924) (Archivo Histórico Diplomático Mexicano, no. 8) [**1560**], selections from the official correspondence between Gorostiza as minister from Mexico to the United States and the U.S. Dept. of State, with a few other letters. "Some Texas correspondence [1832–1835], ed. by J. M. Winterbotham, *Miss. Valley hist. rev.*, VI (1924) 99–127 [**1561**] illustrates Anthony Butler's intrigues in Mexico. *Lord Aberdeen, Texas y California; colección de documentos*, ed. by Antonio de la Peña y Reyes (Mexico: Secretaría de Relaciones Exteriores, 1925) (Archivo Histórico Diplomático Mexicano, no. 15) [**1562**], the correspondence here printed had already been exploited by Rives (no. 1460) and Smith (no. 1592). *The Austin papers*, ed. by E. C. Barker (Wash., 1924–28, 3 v.) (Am. Hist. Assoc. Ann. Rep., for 1919, v. II: for 1922, v. II) [**1563**]. *The Mexican side of the Texan revolution (1836) by the chief Mexican participants, General Antonio López de Santa Anna, D. Ramón Martínez Caro, General Vicente Filisola, General José Urrea, General José María Tornel*, tr. with notes by C. E. Castañeda (Dallas, Tex., 1928) [**1564**] mostly military documents, but contains the "Relations between Texas, the United States of America, and Mexico", by J. M. Tornel y Mendivil (for original Spanish edition, see no. 1541 above). *The diary and correspondence of Henry Wellesley, first Lord Cowley, 1790–1846*, ed. by his grandson, F. A. Wellesley (London, 1930) [**1565**] contains items regarding conversations with Guizot ["the real chief of the government"] re the question of the annexation of Texas (the writer was British ambassador at Paris). *Journals of the fourth Congress of the Republic of Texas, 1839–1840*, ed. by Harriet Smither (Austin, Tex., 1931 ?, 3 v.) [**1566–7**]. Chase, *Négociations Texas en Europe* (no. 1534) contains letters, hitherto unpublished, of Texan envoys to Europe and European diplomatists interested in the problems of the Republic of Texas, and supplements admirably the two chief collections: Garrison, *Dipl. corres.* (no. 1555), and Adams, *British dipl. corresp.* (no. 1516).

For printed writings of American presidents, secretaries of state, statesmen, and diplomatists, see Sec. 1, above. Note particularly

Corres. of Calhoun (no. 5199), and the *Diary of James K. Polk* (no. 5282) for intimate revelations of Polk's diplomacy and policy of expansion.

MSS.: Suggestions

See Secs. 1 and 2, above.

For the official records of Texas under the Spanish and Mexican régimes, see E. C. Barker, " Report on the Bexar archives ", *Am. hist. assoc. ann. rep.*, for 1902, v. I (1903) 357–363 [**1568**].

The diplomatic correspondence of the Republic of Texas has been printed (see no. 1555) ; the consular correspondence is in the Texas State Library. The *Second biennial report, 1911–1912*, of the Texas Library and Historical Commission (Austin, Tex., 1914) [**1569**] contains a list of transcripts from the British Public Record Office of letters written by Charles Elliot, British *chargé-d'affaires* in Texas, William Kennedy, British consul, and others, 1840 to 1845.

Of the personal papers of diplomatic agents of the United States, we have located the following: A. J. Donelson, *chargé d'affaires*, 1844–45, in the Library of Congress. Papers of presidents of the Republic of Texas: Sam Houston (1836–38, 1841–44), widely scattered, the chief collections are in Austin, Texas (an unpublished calendar by A. J. Stephenson (thesis) in the University of Texas) ; M. B. Lamar, 1838–41 (see list of extant collections of papers of American diplomatic agents, p. 868 below) ; Anson Jones, 1844–45, papers were published in 1859, under title, *Memoranda and official correspondence relating to the Republic of Texas* (no. 1550), the MSS. are in the possession of members of the family in San Antonio. See also the papers of A. J. Burnley, commissioner of the Republic of Texas, in the Texas State Library; of Memucan Hunt, member of commission to mark the boundary between Texas and the United States, in the same library; and the Duff Green papers in the Library of Congress.

The García collection in the University of Texas Library includes 9 folders of correspondence of Mariano Paredes y Arrillaga, 1825–1846, containing important material on the revolution led by Paredes in 1844 and its relations with the American government. The same collection includes 1 folder of MSS., 1837, of J. M. Tornel, for his *Tejas y los Estados Unidos* (no. 1547).

4. Diplomacy of the War with Mexico, 1845-1848

Bibliographical Aids

For general aids, see Sec. 1, above.

R. E. Cowan and R. G. Cowan, *A bibliography of the history of California and the Pacific west, 1510-1906* (San Francisco, 1914) [**1570**]. H. E. Haferkorn, *The war with Mexico, 1846-1848; a select bibliography on the causes, conduct, and the political aspect of the war* (Wash., 1914) [**1571**]. J. H. Smith, " Sources for the history of the Mexican war, 1846-1848 ", *Mil. hist. and econ.*, I (1916) 18-32 [**1572**], a most valuable survey; and his *War with Mexico* (no. 1592) containing a voluminous list of manuscripts, periodicals, books and pamphlets relating to the United States and Mexico, to 1848. C. L. Camp, "Western history; a checklist of recent items relating to California and the West ", *Calif. hist. soc. quar.*, IX- (1930-) passim. [**1573**], a current bibliographical list (in progress).

General Works

See Sec. 1, above.

Josiah Royce, *California from the conquest in 1846 to the second vigilance committee in San Francisco (1856), a study of American character* (Boston, 1886) [**1574**], a most perspicuous account, remarkable for the penetrating criticism of Frémont's claims as to his part in the acquisition of California. Moore's *Arbitrations* (no. 5367), v. II, ch. 28: " United States and Mexican claims commission; convention of April 11, 1839." Reeves, *Tyler and Polk* (no. 1549). I. B. Richman, *California under Spain and Mexico, 1535-1847* (Boston and N. Y., 1911) [**1575**], based on Spanish and Mexican archives, has a chapter on the acquisition of California. Rives, *U.S. and Mexico* (no. 1460). Carreño, *México y los Estados Unidos* (no. 1461). R. G. Cleland, *The history of California, American period* (N. Y., 1922) [**1576**], a good short account of the conquest. Hill, *Treaties* (no. 4794), ch. 10: " The treaty of Guadalupe Hidalgo." Antonio de la Peña y Reyes, *La diplomacia mexicana; pequeña revista histórica* (Mexico, 1923) [**1577**], a short sketch introducing the series of archival documentary publications since in progress, quoting some documents anent Slidell's mission of 1845-46.

Special Works

R. S. Coxe, *Review of the relations between the United States and Mexico, and of the claims of citizens of the United States against Mexico* (N.Y., 1846) **[1578]**, *ex parte* indictment of incompetence of Mexican nation and government. Albert Gallatin, *Peace with Mexico* (N.Y., 1847) also published in his *Writings* (no. 5226), v. III **[1579]**, contemporary wisdom of an elder statesman. William Jay, *A review of the causes and consequences of the Mexican war* (Boston, 1849) **[1580]**, anti-slavery view. John Currey, *Treaty of Guadalupe Hidalgo and private land claims and titles existing in California at the date of the treaty* (San Francisco? 1891) **[1581]**, a lawyer's brief. Two studies by E. G. Bourne: " The proposed absorption of Mexico in 1847–48 ", *Am. hist. assoc. ann. rep.*, for 1899 (1900) 155–169 (reprinted in his *Essays in historical criticism* (N.Y., 1901) **[1582]**; and his " The United States and Mexico, 1847–1848 ", *Am. hist. rev.*, V (1900) 491–502 **[1583]**, these somewhat similar articles explain how the United States escaped from annexation of all of Mexico in 1847–48. Julius Klein, " The making of the treaty of Guadalupe Hidalgo, on February 2, 1848 ", *Univ. of Calif. chron.*, VII (1905) 247–318 **[1584]**, a suggestive essay, from printed sources, which interprets the treaty as the cause of the failure of the " all-of-Mexico " movement. C. H. Owen, *The justice of the Mexican war* (N.Y., 1908) **[1585]**, verdict for the United States by one who did not have available sources since uncovered. E. D. Adams, " English interest in the annexation of California ", *Am. hist. rev.*, XIV (1909) 744–763 **[1586]** declares English archives reveal no British appetite for California (also printed in his *British interests in Texas* (no. 1516)). R. W. Kelsey, *The United States consulate in California* (Berkeley, 1910) **[1587]** uses Larkin's papers to expose Polk's intrigue to instigate rebellion in California and acquire it *à la* Texas. Two studies by L. M. Sears: " Slidell's mission to Mexico ", *So. Atlan. quar.*, XII (1913) 12–26 **[1588]** contends that American diplomacy was a serious manful endeavor to achieve great ends by liberal means; and " Nicholas P. Trist, a diplomat with ideals ", *Miss. Valley hist. rev.*, XI (1924) 85–98 **[1589]**, a rehabilitation, based upon the Trist papers. C. C. Kohl, *Claims as a cause of the Mexican war* (N.Y., 1914) **[1590]** gives a full treatment of this issue, but it is largely based on Moore's *Arbitrations* (no. 5367). Justin H.

Smith was the leading American scholar on this subject. Note his "Great Britain and our war of 1846–1848", *Mass. hist. soc. proc.*, XLVII (1914) 451–462 [**1591**], and his *The war with Mexico* (N.Y., 1919, 2 v.) [**1592**], a classic based on prodigious erudition and multiple archival sources, the general thesis being Mexico, rather than the United States, was responsible for the war, in opposition to earlier writers, led by Von Holst (no. 4780), who condemn Polk's policy. His conclusions are sometimes less objective than his research. Also his "La república de Río Grande", *Am. hist. rev.*, XXV (1920) 660–675 [**1593**] describes the movement for independence in the northeastern provinces of Mexico in 1840. Stephenson, *Texas and Mexican war* (no. 1527). R. D. Hunt, "A prize and a national policy; the contest for California", *So. Cal. hist. soc. pub.*, XII, pt. 3 (1923) 128–139 [**1594**], based largely on E. D. Adams (no. 1909). Binkley, *Expansionist movement* (no.1529). M. E. Curti, "Pacifist propaganda and the treaty of Guadalupe Hidalgo", *Am. hist. rev.*, XXXIII (1928) 593–598 [**1595**], the treaty of Guadalupe Hidalgo considered as introducing the idea of the permanent arbitration of future disputes. A. P. Nasatir, "French activities in California before statehood", *Proceedings of the Pacific Coast branch of the American Historical Association*, 1928, 76–88 [**1596**] lists French voyages and other evidence of interest, but makes apparently no use of French archives; but see also his *French consulate* (no. 1618). M. W. Williams, "Secessionist diplomacy of Yucatan", *Hisp. Am. hist. rev.*, IX (1929) 132–143 [**1597**], the diplomatic mission of José Rovira to Washington to ask official recognition of Yucatec neutrality in 1846. R. K. Wyllys, "French imperialists in California", *Calif. hist. soc. quar.*, VIII (1929) 116–129 [**1598**], question of French designs in California, 1830–50; thinks France was feeling out things there, but doubts positive intentions—the article is not definitive for lack of recourse to French archives. L. B. Lesley, "The international boundary survey from San Diego to the Gila river, 1849–1850", *ibid.*, IX (1930) 3–15 [**1599**], the joint survey to carry out the provisions of article V of the treaty of Guadalupe Hidalgo. E. A. Wiltsee, "The British vice consul in California and the events of 1846", *ibid.*, X (1931) 99–128 [**1600**] uses papers of J. A. Forbes (British vice-consul) to narrate request of Gov. Pío Pico for British intervention. J. D. P. Fuller, "The slavery question and the movement to acquire Mexico, 1846–48 ", *Miss. Valley hist. rev.*, XXI (1934) 41–48 [**1600a**] shows that southern Whigs and a group of southern Democratic leaders, including Calhoun, opposed absorption of all of Mexico because they feared.it would be geographically and socially hostile to their institutions; at the same time some northern antislavery opinion can be found which advocated taking all of Mexico for the same reasons.

For biographies of American statesmen and diplomatists, see note in Sec. 1 above. Two recent biographies of Fremont throw some light on his reconnaissance in California in 1845–46: Cardinal Goodwin, *John Charles Frémont; an explanation of his career* (Stanford University, 1930) [**1601**] which reappraises Frémont's activities in California: and Allan Nevins, *Frémont, the West's greatest adventurer* (N.Y., 1928, 2 v.) [**1602**]. See also E. A. Sherman, *The life of the late Rear-Admiral John Drake Sloat, of the United States navy, who took possession of California and raised the American flag at Monterey on July 7th, 1846* (Oakland, Cal., 1902) [**1603**]; . and S. J. Bayard, *A sketch of the life of Com. Robert F. Stockton; with an appendix, comprising his correspondence with the Navy Department respecting his conquest of California* (N.Y., 1856) [**1604**].

Printed Sources

For general collections, see Sec. 1, above.

UNITED STATES OFFICIAL DOCUMENTS: 30th Cong., 1st sess., *House exec. docs.*, nos. 38, 40, 56, and 60; 2d sess., *House exec. doc.* no. 50 30th Cong., 1st sess., *Senate exec. doc.* no. 52. Indexed in Hasse (no. 5344). Buchanan's official instructions to the various diplomatic representatives of the United States are printed in his *Works* (no. 5196).

MEXICAN OFFICIAL DOCUMENTS: *Exposiciónes dirigidas al supremo gobierno por D. Tadeo Ortiz, relativas á la seguridad de los límites de esta república mandadas imprimir por acuerdo de la Cámara de Diputados* (Mexico, 1841) [**1605**]. Two *Memorias* of the " Ministerio de Relaciones Exteriores ": *Memoria del secretaría de estado y del despacho de relaciones exteriores y de gobernación de la república mexicana, correspondiente á la administración provisional en los años de 1841, 42 y 43*, leída en las cámaras del Congreso Constitucional desde el día 12 al 17 de enero de 1844, signed: T. M. de Bocanegra (Mexico, 1844) [**1606**], with documents. *Memoria de la primera secretaría de estado y del despacho de relaciones interiores y exteriores de los Estados Unidos Mexicanas, 1846* (Mexico, 1846) [**1607**]. A document of the Mexican " Supremo Corte de Justicia ": *Breve impugnación a las observaciones acerca del parecer fiscal y acuerdo de la Suprema Corte sobre el ocurso que le dirigieron once señores diputados reclamando la inconstitucionalidad de los tratados de paz celebrados con gobierno anglo-americano*, signed: Mariano Aguilar y López (Mexico, 1848) [**1608**]. A publication of the " Ministerio de Relaciones Exteriores ": *Comunicación circular que el exmo. Sr. D. Manuel de la Peña y Peña, estendió en el año de 1845 como ministro de relaciones, para dirigirla á los gobiernos y asambleas departamentales, sobre la cuestión de paz ó guerra, según el estado que guardaban en aquella epoca* (Queretaro, 1848) [**1608a**]. M. C. Rejón, *Observaciones del diputado saliente Manuel Crecencio Rejón, contra los tratados de paz, firmados en la ciudad de Guadalupe el 2 del proximo pasado febrero, precididas de la parte histórica relativa á la cuestión originaria* (Queretaro, 1848) [**1609**]. G. M. Dallas, *Mr. Dallas's letter on the Mexican treaty;* reprinted from the Public Ledger of June 15, 1849 (Phila., 1849) [**1610**]. Benton's *Thirty years* (no. 968). Luis de la Rosa, *Impresiones de un viage de México á Washington en octubre y noviembre de 1848* (N.Y., 1849) [**1611**]. " *Letters of General Antonio López de Santa Anna relating to the war between the United States and Mexico, 1846–1848*, ed. by J. H. Smith ", *Am. hist. assoc. ann. rep.*, for 1917 (1920) 355–431 [**1612**], principally military. Two volumes under the editorship of Antonio de la Peña y Reyes: *Aberdeen, Texas y California* (no. 1562), full documentation of the Anglo-Mexican correspondence from Mexican archives; and *Algunos documentos sobre el tratado de Guadalupe y la situación de México durante la invasión americana* (Mexico: Secretaría de Relaciones Exteriores, 1930) [**1613–4**], 55 documents, 1845–48, from Mexican archives (some previously printed). *La gestión diplomática del Doctor Mora*, comp. by Luis Chávez Orozco (Mexico, 1931) [**1615**], documents from the minister from Mexico at London, 1845–48. Cardinal Goodwin, " Thomas Oliver Larkin: description of California " in *New Spain*, historical contributions presented to H. E. Bolton (Los Angeles, Calif., 1932), v. II, 103–120 [**1616**], " Larkin's description of California, June 15, 1846 ", contains significant analysis of the

political state of California in 1845–46, and expectations of " some
of the Californias " for " possession by the United States." Aaron
Leggett, "An important letter: Aaron Leggett to William Marcy,
October 16, 1845 ", *Calif. hist. soc. quar.*, XI (1932) 33–34 [**1617**]
deals with the possibility of British intervention in California.
A. P. Nasatir, ed., " The French consulate in California, 1843–1856 ",
ibid., XI–XIII (1932–1934) passim. (in progress) [**1618**], documents
(with historical introduction and notes) from the French foreign
office (*correspondance consulaire*), which show that French activities
were sufficiently great to cause grave excitement not only to Mexico,
but also in greater extent to Great Britain and the United States.
George Tays, ed., " Pío Pico's correspondence with the Mexican
government, 1846–1848 ", *Calif. hist. soc. quar.*, XIII (1934) 99–149
[**1618a**], correspondence of the last governor of Mexican California,
found in the Mexican foreign office archives. " Lately it seems the
whole folder has been stolen from the archives and the documents
are being offered for sale by a Mexico city dealer."

For printed writings of American statesmen, see Sec. 1, above.
Note particularly *Corres. Calhoun* (no. 5199) ; and *Diary of J. K.
Polk* (no. 5282).

MSS.: Suggestions

See Secs. 1–3, above.

For thorough summary of the MS. sources, note J. H. Smith
(no. 1572), who comments on the MS. material in official archives
of the United States, Mexico, Great Britain, France, and Spain.
The Library of Congress has some photostats of Prussian reports
and documents on the arbitration between the United States and
Mexico, 1838–41 (Preussisches Geheimes Staats-Archiv (Berlin-
Dahlem), Auswärtiges Amt III, Rep. 3, Gemischte Differenzen, vols.
1 and 2).

There is a diary of Pres. Franklin Pierce during the Mexican
war, 1847, in the Huntington Library (photostat in the Library
of Congress) ; and a Texas MS., 1844, of Daniel Webster in the
Worcester Historical Society (formerly the Worcester Society of
Antiquity), Worcester, Mass. Among private collections of American diplomatists (not indicated in Secs. 1–3 above) are papers of
Nicholas Trist (U.S. peace commissioner) in the Library of Congress; papers of T. O. Larkin (U.S. consul at Monterey) in the

Bancroft collection, University of California), and of Waddy Thompson (U.S. minister to Mexico, 1842–44) in the library of the University of Texas, at Austin. The personal and official papers of W. A. Leidesdorff (after 1845, U.S. vice-consul in San Francisco) relating to the early history of American California, are in the Huntington Library, San Marino, Calif., and in the same library, 207 documents and letters, for the most part addressed to or written by Gen. M. G. Vallejo, dealing (in part) with political affairs during the 1840's. The papers of J. R. Bartlett in connection with his service as U.S. commissioner on the Mexican boundary commission, 1849–53, are in the John Carter Brown Library, at Brown University. The correspondence and official papers of Commodore David Conner, U.S.N., during and immediately after the Mexican war, including secret diplomatic papers, are in the New York Public Library. The Library of Congress has the MSS. of Commander J. L. Saunders, U.S.N., covering his services on the Mexican coast, 1844–47, including his correspondence with the Navy Dept. and naval commanders, British, French, and American consuls, all pertaining to marine movements in Mexican waters, blockade of the Mexican ports, and the transportation of American agents and despatches.

The papers of Maj. Guillaume T. Poussin, French envoy to the United States, 1848–49, containing nearly 50 letters from Americans of prominence are in the Library of Congress.

5. Gadsden Treaty, and Relations with Mexico, 1848–1861

Bibliographical Aids

For general aids, see Sec. 1, above.

Morrison, *List relating to interoceanic canals and railway routes* (no. 1212). Frank, *Interoceanic canals* (no. 1213), "Tehuantepec "route": p. 79–81. Garber (no. 1628) has a very extensive bibliography.

General Works

See Sec. 1, above; particularly Rippy (no. 3548), and Callahan (no. 1465).

Special Works

Two articles by Alejandro Villaseñor y Villaseñor, in his *Obras* (Mexico, 1897–1906, 2 v.) [1619], "Tratado MacLane-Ocampo"

(v. I, 71–334) reviews this unratified treaty between the United States and Mexico, 1859, from a Mexican patriotic point of view ("Shall the future of Mexico be to live free, Latin and Catholic: or shall it languish and die under the subjection of heretical Anglo-Saxon influence?"); and "El tratado Wyke-Zamacona" (v. II, 61–167), British-Mexican treaty for the adjustment of debts, 1861, which the author thinks bad but necessary at the time. H. L. Wilson, "President Buchanan's proposed intervention in Mexico", *Am. hist. rev.*, V (1900) 687–701 [**1620**] (based on documentary sources) considers its American phases and its reception in Europe. J. M. Callahan, "The Mexican policy of southern leaders under Buchanan's administration", *Am. hist. assoc. ann. rep.*, for 1910 (1912) 125–161 [**1621**], mission of Forsyth, 1857–59, and of Robert McLane, 1859–60 (unratified treaty negotiated by McLane in 1860). Six scholarly studies by J. F. Rippy, now embodied in his *U.S. and Mexico* (no. 3548): "The Indians of the southwest in the diplomacy of the United States and Mexico, 1848–1853", *Hisp. Am. hist. rev.*, II (1919) 363–396 [**1622**], efforts of the United States to meet its obligations regarding the Indians, under the treaty of Guadalupe Hidalgo; "Diplomacy of the United States and Mexico regarding the Isthmus of Tehuantepec, 1848–1860", *Miss. Valley hist. rev.*, VI (1920) 505–532 [**1623**]; "The boundary of New Mexico and the Gadsden treaty", *Hisp. Am. hist. rev.*, IV (1921) 715–742 [**1624**]; "A ray of light on the Gadsden treaty", *Southw. hist. quar.*, XXIV (1921) 235–242 [**1625**], two documents written by Santa Anna; "Anglo-American filibusters and the Gadsden treaty", *Hisp. Am. hist. rev.*, V (1922) 155–180 [**1626**]; and "The negotiation of the Gadsden treaty", *Southw. hist. quar.*, XXVII (1923) 1–26 [**1627**]. P. N. Garber, *The Gadsden treaty* (Phila., 1923) [**1628**], the most complete study so far, makes full use of British and American printed and MS. sources, but the writer was unable to consult Mexican archives.

For biographies of American statesmen and diplomatists, see note in Sec. 1, above.

Printed Sources

For general collections, see Sec. 1, above.

For a complete list of the relevant U.S. Congressional documents, see Garber (no. 1628), 189–195; for index, see Hasse (no. 5344).

For newspapers, see Garber (no. 1628), 198–199.

For text of treaty, see Miller, *Treaties* (no. 5371).

Dictamen de la comisión especial de Tehuantepec del Senado, encargada de examinar las varias resoluciones dictadas con motivo del privilegio exclusivo concedido á D. José Garay, issued by the Mexican Senate [Mexico, Congreso, Senado] (Mexico, 1851) [**1629**]. *Cuestión de Tehuantepec,* signed: Manuel Payno, Ramón Olarte, José Joaquín Pesado (Mexico, 1852) [**1630**]. *Documentos relativos á la apertura de una vía de comunicación ínter-oceánica por el istmo Tehuantepec,* printed by order of the "Cámara de Diputados" of the "Congreso de México" (Mexico, 1852) [**1631**]. Manuel Larrainzar, *La cuestión de Tehuantepec, contiene dos notas del enviado extraordinario y ministro plenipotenciario de la República Mexicana en Washington, y algunos artículos que sobre esta materia se han publicado* (N.Y., 1852) [**1632**]; and his *Análisis del dictamen de la comisión de negocios estrangeros del Senado de los Estados Unidos sobre el negocio de Tehuantepec* (N.Y., 1852), also issued in English, *A review of the report of the committee of foreign affairs of the Senate of the United States, relative to the Tehuantepec matters* (N.Y., 1852) [**1633**]. *A memorial setting forth the rights and just reasons on the part of the government of the United States of Mexico for not recognizing the validity of the privilege granted to D. José Garay, for opening a way of communication between the Atlantic and Pacific oceans by the Isthmus of Tehuantepec, nor the legality of the transfer of said privilege which the latter made to citizens of the United States of North America,* published by the Minister of [Foreign] Relations ("Ministerio de Relaciones") (Mexico, 1852) [**1634**], includes also Spanish text; and by the same ministry, *Decreto del supremo gobierno para la apertura del istmo de Tehuantepec, contrato celebrado con la compañía mixta y comunicaciones diplomáticas relativas al asunto* (Mexico, 1853) [**1635**]. J. F. Ramírez, *Memorias, negociaciones y documentos, para servir á la historia de las diferencias que han suscitado entre Mexico y los Estados Unidos, los tenedores del antiguo privilegio, concedido para la comunicación de los mares Atlántico y Pacífico, por el istmo de Tehuantepec* (Mexico, 1853) [**1636**] prints many selected documents calculated to ventilate the secret diplomacy associated with the Garay claim and Tehuantepec isthmian negotiations. *The life of J. J. Crittenden, with selections from his correspondence and speeches,* ed. by his daughter, Mrs.

Chapman Coleman (Phila., 1871, 2 v.) [1637], U.S. senator (from Kentucky) who took a prominent part in the discussions on the Texan and Mexican question. F. G. Palacio, *Claims of Mexican citizens against the United States for Indian depredations, being the opinion of the Mexican commissioner in the joint claims commission under the convention of July 4, 1868, between Mexico and the United States* (Wash., 1871) [1638]. República Mexicana, *Informes y manifestos de los poderes ejecutivo y legislativo de 1821 a 1904*, v. I: *Mensajes y sus respuestas desde 28 setiembre de 1821 hasta 31 de mayo de 1863* (Mexico, 1905) [1639]. López de Santa Anna, *Memorias inéditos* (no. 1554). *The official correspondence of James S. Calhoun while Indian agent at Santa Fé and superintendent of Indian affairs in New Mexico* [1849–1852] ed. by Annie H. Abel (Wash., 1915) [1640].

MSS.: Suggestions

Aside from the MS. sources indicated in Sec. 1, above, note our list on p. 868 for papers of Nathan Clifford (U.S. minister to Mexico, 1848–49) and James Gadsden (U.S. minister to Mexico, 1853–56). See also papers of Senators John Bell and J. J. Crittenden (for calendar, see no. 1834), and of Jefferson Davis, in the Library of Congress.

CHAPTER XI

THE CANADIAN BOUNDARY, 1815–1861

1. In General.
2. The Northern Frontier (Rush-Bagot Agreement of 1817; Boundary Treaty of 1818; Relations with Canada to 1861).
3. Northeastern Boundary, and Webster-Ashburton Treaty.
4. Oregon Question.

1. In General

Bibliographical Aids

For general aids, see Sabin (no. 4655); Larned (no. 4657); Griffin (no. 4658); *Writings* (no. 4661); C. H. and T. (no. 4662); bibliographies in *Am. secs. state* (no. 4796); *Guide hist. lit.* (no. 4634); and Canadian historical bibliographies (nos. 4671–4677), particularly *Canadiana* (no. 4675), and Lewin (no. 4676). Myers (no. 5399), for collections of treaties. Miller, *Treaties* (no. 5371), v. I, 39–54, for "Bibliography of the United States treaty collections."

For lists of newspapers, see nos. 5004–5047.

General and Special Works

Of general histories of the United States, see Von Holst (no. 4780); McMaster (no. 4781); Rhodes (no. 4783); Channing (no. 4784). See also *Am. secs. state*, v. IV-V (no. 4796); and Wriston, *Executive agents* (no. 4799).

Hodgins, *Brit. and Am. diplomacy affecting Canada* (no. 222). Smith, *England and America* (no. 340). Reeves, *Tyler and Polk* (no. 1459). Moore, *Canada and U.S., 1815–1830* (no. 1334). Dunning, *Brit. Emp. and U.S.* (no. 1335). James White, "Boundary disputes and treaties", in *Canada and its provinces*, Adam Shortt, A. G. Doughty, eds., v. VIII (Toronto, 1914) [1641], a scholarly account by the leading Canadian authority, based on Moore's *Arbitrations* (no. 5364), *A.S.P., F.R.*, (no. 5341) and other printed sources. Hill, *Treaties* (no. 4794). *Camb. hist. Brit. for. pol.*, v. II,

1815–1866 (no. 209). Mowat, *Gt. Brit. and U.S.* (no. 347a). Keenleyside, *Canada and U.S.* (no. 896). Douglas, *Boundaries* (no. 211). Miller, *Treaties* (no. 5371) for erudite notes.

For biographies of American presidents, secretaries of state, and diplomatists abroad (for names and tenure, see the latest *Register* of the Dept. of State (no. 5122)), see relevant entries and bibliographical data in the *D.A.B.*

For biographies of British statesmen and diplomatists to the United States (for names and tenure, see the *Register* of the Dept. of State, 1874 (no. 5122), or the latest *Foreign office list* (no. 5578)), consult the *D.N.B.* See also Thornton, *Foreign secretaries* (no. 820); Bigham, *Prime ministers* (no. 242); Cecil, *Foreign secretaries* (no. 821); Beckles Willson, *Ambassadors to England* (no. 348).

Printed Sources

For American official publications and general source collections, see *Jour. exec. proc. Sen.* (no. 5387); *A.S.P., F.R.* (no. 5341); *Annals Cong.* (no. 5382); *Reg. debates Cong.* (no. 5383); *Cong. Globe* (no. 5384); Wharton, *Digest* (no. 5366); *Abridg. debates* (no. 5386); *Richardson* (no. 5335); Moore's *Arbitrations* (no. 5364); *Repts. Sen. com. for. rel.* (no. 5388); Moore's *Digest* (no. 5365); Hasse, *Index* (no. 5344).

For texts of treaties, see Miller, *Treaties* (no. 5371).

For guides to newspapers, see nos. 5004–5047; to periodicals, see nos. 4982–5003. For analysis of the principal American newspapers and periodicals, 1848 to 1871, see Gazley, *Sources of American opinion* (no. 1424).

For printed writings of American presidents, secretaries of state, and diplomatists abroad (for names and tenure, see latest *Register* of the Dept. of State (no. 5122), see our list on p. 756.

For guides to British official publications, see Myers (no. 5399), *Am. lib. Paris* (no. 5399a), Gregory (no. 5400); and in particular, see p. 838, below.

For guides to Canadian official publications, see p. 838 below.

MSS.: Suggestions

For official archival records of the United States, Great Britain, and Canada, see below: United States, p. 857; Great Britain, p. 890; Canada, p. 896.

For personal papers of presidents and secretaries of state, see below: presidents, p. 862, secretaries of state, p. 865. For personal papers of American diplomatists in Great Britain (for names, see latest *Register* of the Dept. of State (no. 5122)) see our list, p. 868; and British diplomatists in the United States, p. 228.

See also " MSS.: Suggestions " under separate sections of this chapter.

2. The Northern Frontier: (Rush-Bagot Agreement of 1817; Boundary Treaty of 1818; Relations with Canada to 1861)

Bibliographical Aids

See Sec. 1, above, and Secs. 3–4, below.

Special Works

A. J. Hill, *Mississippi river and northwestern boundary* (no. 877). J. M. Callahan, *The neutrality of the American lakes and Anglo-American relations* (Baltimore, 1898) **[1642]** uses American sources, and such Canadian and British sources as were available in print; and his "Americo-Canadian relations concerning annexation, 1846–1871 ", in *Studies in history inscribed to James Albert Woodburn* (Bloomington, Ind., 1926) (Ind. Univ. Stud., v. XII, 1925) p. 185–214 **[1643]**, an informing survey which utilized American sources, including the archives of the Department of State, but little first-hand Canadian material. Reeves, *Tyler and Polk* (no. 1459). Moore, *Canada and the U.S.* (no. 1334). Schafer, *Brit. attitude on Oregon* (no. 1735) is exceptionally good for the treaty of 1818. C. H. Levermore, *The Anglo-American agreement of 1817 for disarmament on the Great Lakes* (Boston: World Peace Foundation, 1914) **[1644]**, a useful summary by a distinguished proponent of disarmament who finds a valuable lesson in this chapter of diplomatic history. The author consulted all principal sources except the unprinted correspondence of the British foreign office. W. E. Culkin, " Northern Minnesota boundary surveys in 1822 to 1826, under the treaty of Ghent ", *Minn. hist. soc. coll.*, XV (1915) 379–392 **[1645]**, mostly derived from Moore, *Arbitrations* (no. 5364). Robert Wild, " The Rush-Bagot convention ", in *Report of the proceedings of the meeting of the State Bar Association of Wisconsin for the year 1915* (Milwaukee, 1916) 100–111 **[1646]**, a thoughtful wartime address on the significance of the convention. Bemis, *N.W.*

boundary gap (no. 550). C. O. Paullin, "The early choice of the forty-ninth parallel as a boundary line", *Canad. hist. rev.*, IV (1923) 127–131 [**1647**], a note on early cartography and the Anglo-French commission following the treaty of Utrecht of 1713, which first hit upon the line of 49° as a possible boundary. Webster, *Castlereagh* (no. 893), for brief but competent discussion of Rush-Bagot convention. Trotter, *Canad. federation* (no. 2933). Morey, *Dipl. episodes* (no. 552a), ch. 2: "Federalism and international liability: the case of the 'Caroline'." W. P. Shortridge, "The Canadian-American frontier during the rebellion of 1837–1838", *Canad. hist. rev.*, VII (1926) 13–26 [**1648**], a careful paper which considers the disturbances in Canada in relation to the prose-lyting character of the American population adjacent to the Cana-dian boundary. G. W. Brown, "The St. Lawrence waterway as a factor in international trade and politics, 1783–1854", in Uni-versity of Chicago, *Abstracts of theses, Humanistic series*, v. III (Chicago, 1927) 179–184 [**1649**], an unusually good thesis, based on printed sources and MS. material in the Canadian archives; a small part of it is printed in "The opening of the St. Lawrence to American shipping", *Canad. hist. rev.*, VII (1926) 1–4 [**1650**]. J. B. Brebner, "Joseph Howe and the Crimean war enlistment controversy between Great Britain and the United States", *Canad. hist. rev.*, XI (1930) 300–327 [**1651**] used the Joseph Howe papers in the Public Archives of Canada. Emily S. Whiteley, "The small-talk of a great affair", *Va. quar. rev.*, VI (1930) 21–36 [**1652**] anent the successful negotiation of the Rush-Bagot treaty agreement. Laura A. White, "The United States in the 1850's as seen by British consuls", *Miss. Valley hist. rev.*, XIX (1933) 509–536 [**1653**], the consuls in general, though prejudiced against the United States, were intelligent observers, and their despatches con-tain valuable descriptions of economic conditions, immigration, movement of population, and the phenomenon of the West. Miller, *Treaties*, v. IV (no. 5371).

For biographies of American and British statesmen and diplo-matists, see note in Sec. 1, above. See also J. W. Longley, *Joseph Howe* (Toronto, 1904) [**1654**]. for biography of a Canadian official who figured in the recruitment controversy.

Printed Sources

For general collections, see Sec. 1, above.

British Parliamentary (House of Commons Sessional) Papers dealing with the recruitment controversy: *Papers relative to recruiting in the United States* (1856, v. LX) [**1655**]. *Further papers relative to recruiting in the United States* (1856, v. LX). *Papers respecting recruiting in the United States, not already published in the papers laid before Parliament, May 2, 1856* (1856, v. LX) [**1656**] which were reprinted from a collection of papers entitled *Messages of the President ordered to be printed by the Senate of the United States.*

Corres. Castlereagh (no. 864).   J. W. Foster, *Limitation of armament on the Great Lakes* (Wash., 1914) (Carnegie Endowment . . . Pamphlet no. 2) [**1657**], report of the secretary of state, J. W. Foster, 1892, relative to the agreement of 1817.   "A secret military document, 1825", ed. by J. J. Talman, *Am. hist. rev.*, XXXVIII (1933) 295–300 [**1658**], report submitted to the Duke of Wellington on the state of the defenses of Canada, in which the possibility of war between the United States and the British provinces is considered to be very real.   Miller, *Treaties*, v. IV (no. 5371).

For printed writings of American statesmen and diplomatists, see note in Sec. 1, above.   See also the *Works of Rufus Choate* (no. 5203), v. II, 4–23, for speech on the McLeod case.

MSS.: Suggestions

Copies of the personal papers of Charles Bagot are in the Canadian Archives (see no. 1200).   The *Report of the Public Archives [of Canada]* for 1930–31 (Ottawa, 1931–32, 2 v.) [**1659**] contains a "Calendar of state papers, addressed by the secretaries of state for the colonies to the governors general or officers administering the province of lower Canada, from 1787 until 1841", and there is a parallel calendar for the Province of Upper Canada (Ontario), 1796 to 1820, in the *Report,* for 1933 (Ottawa, 1934).   The *Report* for 1923 contains a calendar, with comprehensive analyses of contents, of the collection of the papers of Lord Durham, during his stay in Canada in 1838, including the report made to Durham by Col. Charles Grey of his mission to Washington.   The papers of Joseph Howe, Canadian official who had charge of recruitment, are in the Public Archives of Canada. For photostat copies at the Library of Congress of correspondence between the Canadian governor general and the British minister in Washington to 1875, see below, p. 898.

Maps: Suggestions

For Northeast Boundary, and Oregon Boundary, see below, Secs. 3 and 4. For general bibliographical data, see Winsor, v. VII (no. 4782); Phillips, *List* (no. 5135); *Maps in Brit. Col. Off.* (no. 5143); Holmden (no. 5144); Karpinski (nos. 5149, 5150). Moore's *Arbitrations* (no. 5364) has comprehensive reference (with volume VI, of 61 facsimile maps) to maps used in working out boundaries under articles VI and VII of the Treaty of Ghent. Paullin's *Atlas* (no. 213), plate 91 B, text 57, plate 93 B, text 60 gives authentic representations of lines claimed by British and by American commissioners in working out the boundary from Lake Superior to the Lake of the Woods and thence to 49° north latitude.

3. Northeastern Boundary,¹ and Webster-Ashburton Treaty ²

Bibliographical Aids

For general aids, see Sec. 1, above.

Joseph Williamson, *A bibliography of the state of Maine, from the earliest period to 1891* (Portland, 1896, 2 v.)³ [1660], v. II, p. 16–25, for material on the northeastern boundary. A. R. Hasse, " The northeastern boundary ", *N.Y. pub. lib. bul.*, IV (1900) 391–411 [1661] consists of references to (selected) maps, documents, reports, and other papers in the New York Public Library relating to the northeastern boundary controversy.

Special Works

W. B. Lawrence, *The history of the negotiations in reference to the eastern and northern boundaries of the United States* (N.Y.,

---

¹ This section deals with the Northeastern boundary dispute from the treaty of 1783 to 1842, and includes the several commissions for the settlement of specific points in dispute under Jay's treaty (St. Croix River Commission, 1796–1798, to decide upon the true St. Croix river designated in the treaty of 1783), and the commissions under the Treaty of Ghent.

² For provision of the treaty in regard to the Slave Trade, see Ch. XII, sec. 3.

³ A supplementary volume continuing the bibliography through 1933, compiled by Elizabeth Ring, under the auspices of the University of Maine, is announced for publication in 1935.

1841) [**1662**], an article published in the *New York review* for Jan. 1841, embodying a cursory history inspired by the writer's earlier review of Albert Gallatin's argument (no. 1690). "Guillaume I, roi de Pays-Bas, arbitre du différend territorial anglo-américain (1829–1831)", *Conservateur; revue de droit internat.*, I (Utrecht, 1868) 111–120 [**1663**] consists of a few remarks and observations, accompanying the publication of some official diplomatic correspondence, already published in the United States. R. G. Haliburton, *International trade, our only safeguard against disunion* (Ottawa, 1868) [**1664**], a plea for the development of general international trade by Canada as a substitute for, and improvement upon, the expired reciprocity with the United States. Israel Washburn, *The north-eastern boundary* (Portland, 1881) [**1665**], a belated but strong argument against the convention of 1842; especially concerned with the position of Maine in the controversy. Gordon, *Earl of Aberdeen* (no. 1503). Three studies by H. S. Burrage: "The St. Croix commission, 1796–98 ", *Maine hist. soc. coll.*, 2d ser., VI (1895) 225–251 [**1666**]; "The attitude of Maine in the northeastern boundary controversy ", *Maine hist. soc. coll.*, 3d ser., I (1904) 353–368 [**1667**], defense of the attitude of Maine against a " Shylockian " policy charged by Professor Ganong (see no. 1670); and *Maine in the northeastern boundary controversy* (Portland, 1919) [**1668**], a book of the " local history " variety, with some contributions in fact and corrections in error concerning the northeast boundary controversy. The author utilized the archives of Maine but ignores several British and American monographs. T. C. Mendenhall, " Twenty unsettled miles in the northeast boundary ", *Am. antiq. soc. proc.*, n.s. XI, pt. 2 (1897) 188–210 [**1669**] discusses omission in the treaty of 1842 of accurate definition of the boundary from the mouth of the St. Croix through Passamaquoddy Bay to the Atlantic Ocean (settled by convention in 1892). Moore, *Arbitrations* (no. 5364), v. I, 1–161. W. F. Ganong, "A monograph of the evolution of the boundaries of the province of New Brunswick ", *Royal soc. Canada proc.*, 2d ser., VII (1901) sec. 2, 139–449 [**1670**] based on original sources; a standard Canadian monograph which has done much to correct mistaken Canadian impressions. O. E. Tiffany, " The relations of the United States to the Canadian rebellion of 1837–1838 ", *Buffalo* *hist. soc. pub.*, VIII (1905) 1–147 [**1671**], policy of the Van Buren administration in regard to violation of neutrality on the border, the Caroline affair, and McLeod case. Anderson, *Canadian questions* (no. 2641) " includes a condensed history of the chief points in the controversy known as northeastern boundary questions, of the negotiations, and of the settlement by article 1 of this treaty [Webster-Ashburton]. The report was written for Secretary of State Root in connection with the negotiations that resulted in the treaty with Great Britain of April 11, 1908." Reeves, *Tyler and Polk* (no. 1459). H. T. Gordon, *The treaty of Washington, concluded August 9, 1842, by Daniel Webster and Lord Ashburton* (Berkeley, Calif., 1908) [**1671a**], printed prize essay, a commendable summary of the subject drawn from printed sources, and stressing the value of the extradition articles among others. Dudley Mills, " British diplomacy and Canada—the Ashburton treaty ", *United Empire*, n.s. II (1911) 683–712 [**1672**], an unusually good study of maps; contains a useful bibliography. E. D. Adams, " Lord Ashburton and the treaty of Washington ", *Am. hist. rev.*, XVII (1912) 764–782 [**1673**], based on printed official sources and MS. material in the Public Record Office. White, *Boundary disputes* (no. 1641), a Canadian historian shows that the northeast boundary issue arose only after the need for a strategic military road was discovered. For an account of the Indian Stream Republic, in territory at the head of the Connecticut river, which territory was later in dispute between Great Britain and the United States, see the *Collections of the New Hampshire Historical Society*, v. XI, ed. by O. G. Hammond (Concord, N. H., 1915) [**1673a**]; and an unsigned article, " Some forgotten constitutions : Indian Stream Republic ", in the *Constitutional review* (H. C. Black, editor), XI (Wash., 1927) 53–58 [**1673b**]. J. F. Sprague, " The northeastern boundary controversy, 1783–1842 ", in L. C. Hatch, ed., *Maine, a history* (N.Y., 1919, 3 v.), v. I, 247–281 [**1674**]. Balfour, *Aberdeen* (no. 1383) touches briefly upon the matter. Edward Gray, " Ward Chipman, loyalist ", *Mass. hist. soc. proc.*, LIV (1922) 331–353 [**1675–6**], a sketch of a Boston loyalist settled in New Brunswick, who acted as counsel for the Crown in the northeastern boundary dispute and settlement in 1797 and commission under the treaty of Ghent regarding the Passamaquoddy Bay islands. Martin, *Anglo-Am. relations* (no. 1344). E. L. Harvey, " Sir

Howard Douglas and the Maine boundary ", in the *Proceedings of the Pacific coast branch of the American Historical Association, 1929* (1930) 41–47 [**1677**] shows how the governor of New Brunswick succeeded in getting the matter submitted to arbitration by the King of the Netherlands. Alastair Watt, " The case of Alexander McLeod ", *Canad. hist. rev.*, XII (1931) 145–167 [**1678**] would correct certain errors in fact and expressions of unwarranted opinion previously published, notably to show that McLeod was not a vainglorious boaster. Miller's *Treaties*, v. IV (no. 5371) gives most valuable notes.

For biographies of American and British statesmen and diplomatists, see note in Sec. 1, above.

Brief biographical notes regarding the persons (33 in number) actively engaged in the negotiations for the settlement of the boundary covering the entire period of the controversy are given in Dudley Mills (no. 1672).

Note also S. J. Reid, *Life and letters of the first Earl of Durham, 1792–1840* (London and N.Y., 1906, 2 v.) [**1679**]; and C. W. New, *Lord Durham; a biography of John George Lambton, first Earl of Durham* (Oxford, 1929) [**1680**].

Printed Sources

For general collections, see Sec. 1, above. Note particularly Miller, *Treaties*, v. IV (no. 5371).

The American official sources on the negotiation of the treaty are found in *27th Cong., 3d sess., Senate doc.*, no. 1 (serial 413), and the same papers, but with different pagination are in *27th Cong., 3d sess., House exec. doc.*, no. 2 (serial 418) [**1681**]. For itemized list of source material (1755–1842) as found in American official publications and writings of statesmen and diplomatists, see Hasse's *Bibliography* (no. 1661). For a list of United States official documents regarding the " Caroline " affair, see Moore's *Digest* (no. 5365), v. II, 409–411, and Miller's *Treaties* (no. 5371), v. IV, 443–457, for authoritative account of the case as it came " within the negotiations of Webster and Ashburton, though not mentioned in the treaty."

British Parliamentary Papers (House of Commons Sessional Papers) dealing with the northeastern boundary and Webster-Ashburton treaty: *Correspondence relating to the boundary between the British possessions in North America and the United States of*

America, under the treaty of 1783, subsequently to the reference to arbitration of the disputed points of boundary, under the convention of the 29th September, 1827, and the fifth article of the treaty of Ghent, and *Proceedings and correspondence relating to the pretensions of the states of Maine, Massachusetts, and New Hampshire; and to the question of jurisdiction within the disputed territory from 1831–1837* (1837–38, v. XXXIX) [**1682**]. *Correspondence relating to the boundary between the British possessions in North America and the United States of America under the treaty of 1783* (1840, v. XXXII) [**1683**]. *Supplementary reports relating to the boundary between the British possessions in North America and the United States of America under the treaty of 1783* (1842, v. XXVIII) [**1684**]. *Correspondence between Great Britain and the United States relative to the treaty lately concluded at Washington, including instructions from the Earl of Aberdeen to Lord Ashburton, 1842–43;* and *Papers relative to the special mission of Lord Ashburton to the United States of America in 1842;* and *Correspondence relating to the boundary between the British possessions in North America and the United States of America, under the treaty of 1783 (in continuation of Paper presented to Parliament in 1840)* (1843, v. LXI) [**1685**]. *Correspondence respecting the operations of the commission for running and tracing the boundary line between Her Majesty's possessions in North America and the United States, under the VI. article of the treaty, signed at Washington, August 9, 1842,* and *Despatch from Lord Sydenham to Lord John Russell, dated August 9, 1841, respecting the provisional occupation of the disputed territory, and the consequent correspondence thereon* (1845, v. LII) [**1686**].

[Ward Chipman], *Remarks upon the disputed points of boundary under the fifth article of the treaty of Ghent, principally compiled from the statements laid before the King of the Netherlands, as arbiter* (Saint John, N.B., 1838) [**1687**], published anonymously; an exposition of the British claim. General Court of Massachusetts, *Report and resolves in relation to the northeastern boundary* (Boston, 1838) (Mass. General Court. Senate doc., no. 67) [**1688**]. Albert Gallatin, *The right of the United States of America to the northeastern boundary claimed by them, principally extracted from the statements laid before the King of the Netherlands, and revised* (N.Y., 1840) [**1689**] includes eight maps; and *A memoir on the*

*northeastern boundary in connection with Mr. Jay's map; . . . to-
gether with a speech on the same subject by the Hon. Daniel Webster, delivered . . . April 15, 1843* (N.Y., 1843) [**1690**] are valuable
as the work of the ablest American diplomatist of the time who had
immersed himself in the subject as American agent in the arbitration of 1829. *Report of the Committee on the northeastern boundary* (of the Legislature of Maine) (Augusta, 1841) (Twenty-first
legislature. No. 19. Senate) [**1691**], signed C. S. Daveis. G. W.
Featherstonhaugh, *Observations upon the treaty of Washington,
signed August 9, 1842* (London, 1843) [**1692**] [Jared Sparks],
" The treaty of Washington ", *No. Am. rev.*, LVI (1843) 452–496
[**1693**]. "Aspinwall papers, part II ", *Mass. hist. soc. coll.*, 4th ser.,
v. X (1871) 830–851 [**1694**], several letters to and from, and
memorandum of, George Chalmers, 1816–1817, regarding the Passamaquoddy Bay Islands survey. *Life of J. J. Crittenden* (no. 1637),
Crittenden was attorney general of the United States at the time
of the McLeod affair. Ashley, *Palmerston* (no. 1969) denounces the
Ashburton treaty. *The correspondence and diaries of the late Right
Honourable John Wilson Croker, LL.D., F.R.S., secretary to the
admiralty from 1809 to 1830*, ed. by L. J. Jennings (London, 1884,
3 v.) [**1695**], v. II, 393–403, for several letters of 1843 from Aberdeen
and Ashburton in regard to the boundary dispute and treaty, and the
question of the maps. *Sir Robert Peel, . . . from his private correspondence*, ed. by C. S. Parker (London, 1891–99, 3 v.) [**1696**] contains a few letters regarding the boundary question. *Corres. of
Thomas Barclay* (no. 578) is of value in studying the negotiations of
the St. Croix commission of 1790–98. Moore's [4] *Arbitrations* (no.
5364), and *Adjudications* (no. 5367), v. I–II: *Saint Croix river arbitration; mixed commission under article V of the treaty between
Great Britain and the United States of November 19, 1794* [**1697**]
give between them a definitive account of the Canadian boundary controversies which were submitted to arbitration, with official maps and
documents. For voluminous printed documents of the United States
Government relating to the northeast boundary, see no. 2644. *Papers
of Sir Charles Vaughan* (no. 1380) reveal the course of the dispute
after the rejection of the arbitration by the King of the Netherlands,
in 1829. " Letters of James Lloyd, 1815–1824 ", *Mass. hist. soc.*

---

[4] See also his *A treatise on extradition and interstate rendition; with appendices containing the treaties and statutes relating to extradition* (Boston, 1891, 2 v.) [**1696a**]

proc., XLV (1912) 375–408 [**1698**] include brief discussion of the northeastern boundary dispute. *The correspondence of Nicholas Biddle dealing with national affairs, 1807–1844*, ed. by R. C. Mc-Grane (Boston and N.Y., 1919) [**1699**]. *Letters of David Thompson* (no. 1770). *The Greville diary, including passages hitherto withheld from publication*, ed. by Philip W. Wilson (Garden City, N.Y., 1927, 2 v.) [**1700**], the diary of Charles Greville, contains an interesting mention of the map in the British Public Record Office that figured in the negotiations of the Webster-Ashburton treaty. *Letters from Lord Sydenham, governor general of Canada, 1839–41, to Lord John Russell*, ed. by Paul Knaplund (London, 1931) [**1701**] presents an unabridged edition of nearly all the letters from Lord Sydenham to Lord John Russell, 1839–41, found among the Russell papers at the Public Record Office, including a number discussing relations between British North America and the United States.

For printed writings of American statesmen and diplomatists, see note in Sec. 1, above.

MSS.: Suggestions

See Secs. 1 and 2, above, and 4, below.

The records (memoranda kept by Griffith Evans) of the mixed commission under article VI of Jay's treaty are in the Huntington Library. The papers of the mixed commission under article VII of Jay's treaty are in the Public Record Office, London, duplicates of some of them with other important documents are in the Department of State. This material is now printed by Moore, in *Adjudications* (no. 5367).

Note the Baring papers in the Canadian Archives (no. 1331a). The Canadian Archives also has acquired from Mr. J. W. Lawrence of St. John, N.B., 7 portfolios of papers relating to the northeastern boundary, 1796–1843. This material centers about the commissions appointed under the treaties of 1794 and 1814, and includes many of the papers of Ward Chipman, who was British agent to the boundary commission under the treaty of Ghent. The Maine State Library at Augusta has volumes of MS. correspondence and documents relating to the boundary controversy. The Maine Historical Society at Portland has among its papers relating to the northeastern boundary: Papers of Ward Chipman (boundary commissioner),

1796–1800; Thomas Barclay (boundary commissioner), 1816–1842; Pagan letters, and letters of John Gilmore Deane (" Cato ", "Ishmael"); and the journal of the Passamaquoddy Bay boundary commission. Another collection of MSS. used by agents in boundary commissions, formerly belonging to Edward Winslow and Ward Chipman was (in 1901) understood to be in the possession of the Rev. W. O. Raymond, St. John, N.B. The Gallatin papers and Webster papers (see p. 874 and 866 respectively) have many papers relating particularly to the northeastern boundary. The Buffalo Historical Society has a collection of reports of surveys, correspondence, and miscellaneous notes concerning the boundary, 1817–1829, including the report of the British commissioners under the 7th article of the treaty of Ghent, and minutes of the Proceedings of the commissioners in deciding that boundary, kept by Donald Fraser, secretary, 1824–27. The Library of Congress has the personal papers (44 pieces) of Albert Smith, M.C., of Maine, who was appointed to run the northeast boundary between the United States and New Brunswick and Canada, and photostats (from the *Rijksarchief* at The Hague) relating to the arbitration by the King of the Netherlands in 1829.

For papers of British statesmen, see Ch. IX, sec. 1. The British Museum has a memorandum on the Canadian-American frontier, 1826, by Henry U. Addington (secretary of legation at Washington); also the papers of William Huskisson, president of the Board of Trade, 1823–37, and secretary of state for war and the colonies, 1827–38, including some on questions of the northeastern boundary.

Maps: Suggestions

The diplomacy of the northeastern boundary rests heavily on maps as sources. See above, Chapts. III, sec. 6, IV, sec. 6; and V, sec. 6; particularly Phillips' *List* (no. 5135). Hasse (no. 1661), 391–392, for list of maps of the northeastern boundary. Holmden (no. 5144); Brit. Col. Off., *Catalogue of maps* (no. 5143); and notes by Lawrence Martin in Miller's *Treaties*, v. III and IV (no. 5371). *The Register of debates in Congress*, v. VIII (Wash., 1833), 1406–1410 [**1702**] gives a list of British maps bearing on the question of the northeast boundary.

For an account, by Jared Sparks, to be used with great caution, of maps regarding the northeastern boundary, including Franklin's red-line map, see no. 1693.   Justin Winsor, *The cartographical history of the northeastern boundary controversy between the United States and Great Britain* (Cambridge, 1887) [**1703**] consists of remarks in regard to a manuscript belonging to the Massachusetts Historical Society (therein printed), which contains a statement of the controversy, in 1796, by Egbert Benson, one of the commissioners under article V of the treaty of 1794.

Moore's *Arbitrations* (no. 5364), v. I, 1–195, has a most comprehensive discussion of maps relating to the various phases of the northeastern boundary question, with facsimiles, supplemented by his *Adjudications* (no. 5367). Williamson's *Bibliography of the state of Maine* (no. 1660), v. II, 26–28, indicates maps and charts. One of the most valuable treatises is D. A. Mills (no. 1672). *The Greville diary* (no. 1700) contains contemporary comment on the maps (" King George's ") in the British Public Record Office which favored the American contention on the northeastern boundary. Maps relating to the boundary are noted in *Noteworthy maps . . .* accessions of the Library of Congress for 1926, comp. by Lawrence Martin (Wash., 1926) 2–3; for 1927 (Wash., 1927) 17–19 [**1704**]; and *Report of the Librarian of Congress*, 1926 (Wash., 1926) 106–107; 1928 (Wash., 1928) 105 [**1705**]. Hunter Miller, "An annotated Dashiell's map ", *Am. hist. rev.*, XXVIII (1932) 70–73 [**1706**] describes an interesting map directly connected with the Webster-Ashburton treaty, which came to light in 1932 in the archives of the Department of State. The only adequate atlas with textual explanations of sources, and facsimiles of Mitchell's map is Paullin's *Atlas* (no. 213), see particularly plates 90, 91A, 91B, 92A, 93A, with corresponding text. See also maps in House of Commons, *Sessional Papers*, 1837–38, v. XXXIX; and 1843, v. LXI.

The Library of Congress has photostats of two MS. maps describing the northeast boundary (F.O. 5, vol. 360)—" map of the northern part of the state of Maine and of the adjacent British provinces, 1830 ", showing the portion of that state claimed by Great Britain, and "map of the disputed territory reduced from the original of Messrs. Featherstonhaugh and Mudge, British commissioners, 1839."

4. Oregon Question [5]

Bibliographical Aids

For general aids, see Sec. 1, above.

Winsor, *America* (no. 4782), v. VII, 527-672.   Katherine B. Judson, *Subject index to the history of the Pacific Northwest and of Alaska as found in the United States government documents, congressional series, in the American state papers, and in other documents, 1789-1881*, pub. by the Washington State Library (Olympia, Wash., 1913) [**1707**].   Cowan, *Pacific west* (no. 1570).   C. W. Smith, *Pacific northwest Americana; a check list of the books and pamphlets relating to the history of the Pacific northwest*, 2d ed., rev. and enl. (N.Y., 1921) [**1708**].   Turner and Merk, *References on the history of the West* (no. 307).   R. L. Reid, " British Columbia; a bibliographical sketch ", *Bibliog. soc. Am. pap.*, XXII, pt. 1, 1928 (Chicago, 1929) 20-44 [**1709**].   R. J. Kerner, " Russian expansion to America; its bibliographical foundations ", *ibid.*, XXV (1931) 111-129 [**1710**].   " Bibliography relating to the Russians in California ", *Calif. hist. soc. quar.*, XII (1933) 210-216 [**1711**]. Miller, *Treaties* (no. 5371), v. V (in press) has many bibliographical references, particularly to American and British printed documents.

General Works

See Sec. 1, above.

Robert Greenhow, *Memoir, historical and political, on the northwest coast of North America* (Wash., 1840) [**1712**], and *The history of Oregon and California* (Boston, 1844; several editions, 4th ed., rev., cor. and enl.: Boston, 1847) [**1713**] are still valuable treatises by a former clerk in the Department of State who had unusual access at least to American source materials, together with a historical mind.   T. J. Farnham, *History of the Oregon Territory* (N.Y., 1844) [**1714**] upholds American claims.   C. G. Nicolay, *The Oregon Territory* (London, 1846) [**1715**], exponent of British claims.   Washington Irving, *Astoria*, author's rev. ed.

---

[5] See Florida Treaty of 1819, Ch. VII, sec. 2, for treaty basis of American claim to territory to the Pacific coast, formerly included in the Spanish domain.   For early Russian expansion to America, see Ch. XIV, sec. 2 (The Alaska Purchase).   For the San Juan Boundary Dispute, see Ch. XVI, sec. 3, a, below.

(N.Y., 1849) [**1716**], for a long time a classic on Astoria. The writer had access to documents since destroyed, but this work now should be supplemented by Porter's recent biography of Astor (no. 1758a). Bancroft, *Northwest coast* (no. 533); and *History of Oregon* (San Francisco, 1886–88, 2 v.) [**1717**], these two works, by Bancroft himself, are among the best of the products of his historical establishment and constitute a very useful general history— until C. H. Carey (no. 1721) they were the best general history of the northwest coast. Gordon, *Aberdeen* (no. 1503). Joseph Schafer, *History of the Pacific Northwest* (N.Y., 1905), see later edition, revised and rewritten (N.Y., 1918) [**1718**], a good summary of the early history of the Oregon country, by a scholar who had worked much in the archives of Great Britian and the United States, and who stressed emigration and diplomacy. Much investigation has been done since then. Garrison, *Westward extension* (no. 1458). Temperley, *Later Am. policy Canning* (no. 1150). E. O. S. Scholefield and F. W. Howay, *British Columbia, from the earliest times to the present* (Vancouver, 1914, 4 v.) [**1718a**], v. I (by Scholefield) has chapters on " The Nootka Sound controversy " and " The Oregon question." J. C. Bell, *Opening a highway to the Pacific, 1838–1846* (N.Y., 1921) [**1719**], a study of the social and economic forces behind the frontiersmen's trek to Oregon, of some value to suggest that they did not consciously go out there to " save " Oregon for the United States. Balfour, *Aberdeen* (no. 1383). S. E. Morison, *The maritime history of Massachusetts, 1783–1860* (Boston and N.Y., 1921) [**1720**], already a classic; it connects Massachusetts maritime history with the development of American interests on the northwest coast. C. H. Carey, *History of Oregon* (Chicago and Portland, 1922) [**1721**], best general account at date, but must now be supplemented, for diplomacy, with Merk's recent articles, *post*. Goodwin, *Trans-Mississippi West* (no. 678). Webster, *Castlereagh* (no. 1171). G. W. Fuller, *A history of the Pacific Northwest* (N.Y., 1931) [**1722**], a good history, but has a minimum on diplomatic affairs. F. W. Howay, "An outline sketch of the maritime fur trade ", *Canad. hist. assoc. ann. rep.*, 1932 (1932) 5–14 [**1723**], by the leading authority on the subject, an indefatigable investigator and discriminating user of sources. Two works by H. R. Wagner: *Spanish voyages to the northwest coast* *of America* (San Francisco: California Historical Society, 1929) **[1724]**, authoritative account based on records of Spanish explorers; and *Spanish explorations in the Strait of Juan de Fuca* (Santa Ana, Calif., 1933) **[1724a]**, a learned and authoritative treatment of the Spanish explorations of 1790–93, with translations of original accounts and facsimiles of thirteen maps and plans. Miller, *Treaties* (no. 5371), v. V (in press) has a voluminous treatise on the negotiation of the Oregon treaty, replete with relevant documents.

Special Works [6]

Adam Thom, *The claims to the Oregon Territory* (London, 1844) **[1725]**. Thomas Falconer, *The Oregon question* (London, 1845) **[1726]**. William Sturgis, *The Oregon question* (Boston, 1845) **[1727]**. Travers Twiss, *The Oregon question examined, in respect to the facts and the law of nations* (London, 1846) **[1728]**. E. J. Wallace, *The Oregon question determined by the rules of international law* (London, 1846) **[1729]**. Thom, Falconer, Twiss, and Wallace are arguments to support the English claim; Sturgis for the American side. William Barrows, *Oregon, the struggle for possession* (Boston, 1884) **[1730]**, utterly unreliable as a history of the Oregon question, because based on the fictitious accounts of the efforts of Marcus Whitman to save Oregon first published by H. H. Spalding, and later exposed by E. G. Bourne, *post*. Mowry, *Louisiana purchase and Oregon* (no. 749). Ficklen, *Northw. boundary Louisiana* (no. 753), an argument to demolish the claims that the Louisiana Purchase included Oregon. Two studies by E. G. Bourne: "The legend of Marcus Whitman", *Am. hist. rev.*, VI (1901) 276–300, and in his *Essays in historical criticism* (N.Y., 1901) **[1731]**, by painstaking research with original sources breaks down the legend of Whitman's ride across the continent to save Oregon to the Union; and "Aspects of Oregon history before 1840", *Oreg. hist. quar.*, VI (1906) 255–275 **[1732]** stresses, among other phases of the Oregon movement, Senator Benton's resolute opposition to any boundary compromises such as considered by Webster and Tyler. Reeves, *Tyler and Polk* (no. 1459). Gertrude Ather-

---

[6] For treatises on the relation of the Louisiana Purchase to Oregon, see Ch. V, sec. 4.

There are numerous articles on the Oregon question, of varying value, which we have not included here, and on the early explorations on which rival American and British claims were based, which we do not include here, in the *Quarterly* of the Oregon Historical Society, passim, and the *Washington historical quarterly*, passim.

ton, "Nicolai Petrovich Rezanov", *No. Am. rev.*, CLXXXIX
(1909) 651-661 [**1733**], official of the Russian-American Fur
Company who visited San Francisco in 1806, and planned to secure control of the country for Russia. Heinz, *Russland, England, and Nordamerika* (no. 1156). W. I. Marshall, *Acquisition
of Oregon and the long suppressed evidence about Marcus
Whitman* (Seattle, 1911, 2 v.) [**1734**], a devastating, if somewhat vituperative, attack on the Marcus Whitman legend. Joseph
Schafer, "The British attitude toward the Oregon question,
1815-1846", *Am. hist. rev.*, XVI (1911) 273-299 [**1735**], written after a careful reading of the correspondence of the British
foreign office, it must now be supplemented by the later studies
of Merk, who used additional material. R. L. Schuyler, "Polk
and the Oregon compromise of 1846", *Pol. sci. quar.*, XXVI (1911)
443-461 [**1736**], the Oregon question in the light of information
contained in Polk's diary. D. W. Howe, "The Mississippi Valley in
the movement for fifty-four forty or fight", *Miss. Valley hist. assoc.
proc.*, V (1912) 99-116 [**1737**], particularly as revealed in the
debates of Congress. White, *Boundary disputes* (no. 1641). R. G.
Cleland, "Asiatic trade and the American occupation of the Pacific
coast", *Am. hist. assoc. ann. rep.*, for 1914, v. I (1916) 283-289
[**1738**], Asiatic trade as a motive for annexation in Oregon, based
on original sources. T. C. Elliott, "An event of one hundred years
ago", *Oreg. hist. soc. quar.*, XIX (1918) 181-187 [**1739**], a link in
the chain of title by which Oregon finally became a part of the
United States, U.S. exploring expedition under Capt. James Biddle; and by the same writer, "The surrender at Astoria in 1818",
ibid., XIX (1918) 271-282 [**1740**], surrendered by the British according to terms of treaty of Ghent. L. B. Shippee, "Oregon and
the diplomacy of 1821-1827", *ibid.*, 189-214 [**1741**], Russian
interests on the northwest coast and the controversy with Great
Britain. Katharine B. Judson, "The British side of the restoration
of Fort Astoria", *ibid.*, XX (1919) 243-260, 305-330 [**1742**], based
on British archival sources, controverts the point of view hitherto
taken by writers that the restoration was gained by American
cleverness as against British intrigue. V. J. Farrar, "The reopen-
ing of the Russian-American convention of 1824", *Wash. hist. quar.*,
XI (1920) 83-88 [**1743**], phases of relations of the United States
and Russia in regard to trade on the northwest coast then under

Russian control, based on official correspondence. Bemis, *N.W. boundary gap* (no. 550). Two studies by G. Verne Blue: "The Oregon question—1818-1828; a study of Dr. John Floyd's efforts in Congress to secure the Oregon country", *Oreg. hist. soc. quar.*, XXIII (1922) 193-219 [**1744**], as observed in the *Annals of Congress* and *Niles' Register;* and "France and the Oregon question", *ibid.*, XXXIV (1933) 39-50, 144-163 [**1745**], based on despatches of Pageot, French *chargé* in the United States, describing the Oregon controversy between Great Britain and the United States; contains also an important instruction by Guizot resisting Polk's interpretation of the Monroe Doctrine. T. P. Martin, *Anglo-Am. relations* (no. 1344); and his "Free trade and the Oregon question, 1842-1846", in *Facts and factors of economic history* (E. F. Gay memorial volume) (Cambridge, Mass., 1932) 470-491 [**1746**] considers free-trade policies in England and America as assisting settlement of the Oregon question. Six studies by Frederick Merk:[7] "The Oregon pioneers and the boundary", *Am. hist. rev.*, XXIX (1924) 681-699 [**1747**], from English MS. sources, including archives of the Hudson Bay Company, shows decisive effect on British diplomacy of the removal of their post from Ft. Vancouver on the Columbia river to Ft. Victoria on Vancouver Island; *Fur trade and empire; Sir George Simpson's journal; remarks connected with the fur trade in the course of a voyage from York Factory to Fort George and back to York Factory, 1824-1825* (Cambridge, Mass., 1931) [**1748**], together with accompanying documents; "British party politics and the Oregon treaty", *Am. hist. rev.*, XXXVII (1932) 653-677 [**1749**], the treaty of 1846 from a British point of view was not a compromise but a surrender, which required delicately balanced understandings between opposing party leaders; "The British corn crisis of 1845-46 and the Oregon treaty", *Agric. hist.*, VIII (1934) 95-123 [**1749a**], a most important article effectively demolishing a widely accepted recent thesis that British necessities for importations of American foodstuffs, particularly maize, forced that government to make concessions for the settlement of the Oregon question in order to preserve peace and uninterrupted importations of indispensable food; "British government propaganda and the Oregon treaty", *Am. hist. rev.*,

---

[7] Professor Merk is understood to be now preparing what is expected to be a definitive study of the Oregon controversy.

XL (1934) 38–62 [**1749b**] details the way in which the British government, having decided to make the concession of the line of 49°, set about preparing the public for that with carefully arranged press propaganda; and "Snake Country expedition, 1824–25; an episode of fur trade and empire", *Miss. Valley hist. rev.*, XXI (1934) 49–62 [**1749c**] describes methodical plans of the Hudson's Bay Company to trap out the beaver country south and east of the Columbia, and the upper Missouri streams, in order to protect British fur preserves in the Oregon country by a sterile buffer against advance of American trappers into the northwest. R. C. Clark, "British and American tariff policies and their influence on the Oregon boundary treaty", *Pacific Coast branch Am. Hist. Assoc. proc.*, 1926 [**1750**]. Henry Commager, "England and the Oregon treaty of 1846", *Oreg. hist. soc. quar.*, XXVIII (1927) 18–38 [**1751**] considers the English political situation the decisive factor in the settlement of the controversy. J. W. Pratt, "The origin of 'manifest destiny'", *Am. hist. rev.*, XXXII (1927) 795–798 [**1752**] shows that the phrase first appeared in an editorial in the *Democratic review*, for July 1845, in reference to the Oregon question; and his *Sullivan and manifest destiny* (no. 1538). C. A. Duniway, "Daniel Webster and the West", *Minn. hist.*, IX (1928) 3–15 [**1753**], Webster as a deprecator of "manifest destiny." L. M. Scott, "Influence of American settlement upon the Oregon boundary treaty of 1846", *Oreg. hist. quar.*, XXIX (1928) 1–19 [**1754**] gives statistics of American immigration to Oregon: 1842, 137; 1843, 875; 1844, 1475; 1845, 3000. P. Gronsky, "L'établissement des Russes en California", *Rev. hist. moderne*, IV (1929) 401–415, V (1930) 101–123 [**1755**], drawn largely from Tikhemenev (no. 2228) and Resanov (no. 2228a). F. H. Soward, "President Polk and the Canadian frontier", in Canadian Historical Association, *Report of the annual meeting . . . May 23, 1930* (Ottawa, 1930) 71–80 [**1756**] uses Polk's *Diary* and secondary writings to acquit the president of the charge of sacrificing a national interest to a sectional slavery policy in the settlement of the Oregon question. The *Quarterly of the California Historical Society*, v. XII, no. 3 (San Francisco, 1933) [**1757**] is devoted to a series of articles on the Russian settlements in California, by E. O. Essig, Adele Ogden, and C. J. Du Four. Miller's *Treaties* (no. 5371), v. V, has most valuable notes.

For biographies of American and British statesmen and diplomatists, see Sec. 1, above. Note also F. V. Holman, *Dr. John McLoughlin, the father of Oregon* (Cleveland, O., 1907) [**1758**]; and K. W. Porter, *John Jacob Astor, business man* (Cambridge, Mass., 1931, 2 v.) [**1758a**].

Printed Sources

For general collections, see Sec. 1, above. Note particularly Miller, *Treaties* (no. 5371), v. V (in press), the most important expository of official sources (many here printed for the first time) on the negotiation of the Oregon treaty.

Moore's *Arbitrations* (no. 5364), v. I, 237-270, for " Claims of the Hudson's Bay and Puget's Sound agricultural companies: commission under the treaty of July 1, 1863." For indexes to U.S. official documents and printed diplomatic correspondence, see Judson's *Index* (no. 1707), and Hasse's *Index* (no. 5344). Buchanan's official instructions to the various diplomatic agents of the United States are printed in his *Works* (no. 5196).

British state papers dealing with the Oregon dispute are contained in: *Correspondence relative to the negotiation of the question of disputed right to the Oregon Territory, on the northwest coast of America, subsequent to the treaty of Washingon, 9 August 1842* (Gt. Brit. House of Commons. Sess. pap., 1846, v. LII) [**1759**]. See also *Brit. and for. state papers* (no. 5416), v. XXXIV, for documents regarding the Oregon question.

The speeches of the Right Honourable George Canning, with a memoir of his life, by R. Therry (London, 1828, 6 v.) [**1760**]. Charles Wilkes, *Narrative of the United States exploring expedition, during the years 1838, 1839, 1840, 1841, 1842*, by Charles Wilkes, U.S.N., commander of the expedition (Phila., 1844, 5 v. and *Atlas* of 5 maps; various editions) [**1761**]. Also " Report on the territory of Oregon, by Charles Wilkes, commander of the United States exploring expedition, 1838-1842 ", *Oreg. hist. soc. quar.*, XII (1911) 269-299 [**1761a**], report made to the secretary of the navy, June 1842. Albert Gallatin, *The Oregon question* (N.Y., 1846) also pub. (Wash., 1846) under title, *Letters of the Hon. Albert Gallatin, upon the Oregon question* [**1762**], by a veteran contemporary diplomatist who participated in the earlier phases. British and American Joint Commission for the Final Settlement of the Claims of the Hudson's

Bay and Puget's Sound Agricultural Companies, *Papers* . . . (Wash.: Govt. Print. Off., 1865–69, 14 v. in 13) [1763] contains a wealth of historical material embodied as evidence in the arguments. J. J. Crittenden, *Correspondence* (no. 1637), U.S. senator who took a prominent part in the discussions on the Oregon dispute. Stapleton, *Official corres. Canning* (no. 969). " Documents on the abrogation of the treaty of joint occupation of Oregon ", *Oreg. hist. soc. quar.*, IX (1908) 388–411 [1764], reports of " Oregon " public meetings, 1842–43, etc. " Letters of Sir George Simpson, 1841–1843 ", *Am. hist. rev.*, XIV (1908) 70–94 [1765], reports of conditions in the Hudson's Bay Company's territory at the time of the final steps of the Oregon boundary controversy. Joseph Shafer, ed., " Documents relative to Warre and Vavasour's military reconnoissance in Oregon, 1845–6 ", *Oreg. hist. soc. quar.*, X (1909) 1–99 [1765a]. Katharine B. Judson, " Polk and Oregon; with a Pakenham letter ", *Oreg. hist. soc. quar.*, XX (1919) 301–302 [1766], letter written during the debates in Congress on the Oregon question by Richard Pakenham, British minister at Washington, Mar. 29, 1846. " Secret mission of Warre and Vavasour ", *Wash. hist. quar.*, III (1912) 131–153 [1767], letters of Sir George Simpson and others, from the Public Record Office, dealing with the expedition of the British officers, Warre and Vavasour, into the Oregon country in 1846. T. C. Elliott, " The northern boundary of Oregon ", *Oreg. hist. soc. quar.*, XX (1919) 25–34 [1768] consists mainly of a letter from the governor of the Hudson's Bay Company to Lord Canning, Dec. 9, 1825; and by the same writer, " The northwest boundaries (some Hudson's Bay company's correspondence)", *ibid.*, XX (1919) 331–344 [1769], documents of the years 1825–26, of special interest as showing the intimate connection of the Hudson's Bay Company with the British cabinet. Balfour, *Aberdeen* (no. 1383). " Some letters of David Thompson ",[8] ed. by L. J. Burpee, *Canad. hist. rev.*, IV (1923) 105–126 [1770], 5 letters addressed to Sir Robert Peel, Lord Stanley, and Gladstone, in 1840, which reflect the national irritation of the time. They represent an old explorer's unreliable recollections; Thompson was British surveyor of the boundary line under the 6th and 7th articles of the treaty of Ghent from 1816 to 1826. " Hudson's Bay company claims in the Northwest ", *Wash.*

---

[8] For other " Thompson " material, see T. C. Elliott, in *Oreg. hist. soc. quar.*, passim.

hist. quar., XIX (1928) 214–217 [**1771**], letters of 1857 and 1859 relating to lands and improvements for which the Hudson's Bay company and its subsidiary, the Puget Sound Agricultural Company, were awaiting compensation from the United States Government. L. M. Scott, "Report of Lieutenant Peel on Oregon in 1845–46", *Oreg. hist. quar.*, XXIX (1928) 51–76 [**1772**] includes the report of this British naval officer, some of his letters, and letters of Capt. John Gordon, and John McLoughlin in regard to the Oregon question. G. V. Blue, "Unpublished portions of the mémoires of Duflot de Mofras", in the *Proceedings* of the Pacific Coast branch of the American Historical Association, 1928 (1929) 89–102 [**1773**], drawn from documents in the Archives des Affaires Etrangères, Paris; reveals the attention of the minister of foreign affairs on that part of the world in 1839. F. W. Howay, ed., *The Dixon-Meares controversy* (N.Y., 1929) [**1774**], rare pamphlets and MS. journals dealing with the disputes and claims of these two fur trading voyagers to the northwest coast in the 1780's. Rita Dielmann, "Data on 'Opposition to claiming and occupying Oregon country, as shown in the congressional debates on the negotiations with Great Britain and on the treaty of July 17, 1846'", in the *Congressional record*, v. LXXII, no. 137 (1930) 3824–3825 [**1775**]. R. C. Clark, ed., "Aberdeen and Peel on Oregon, 1844", *Oreg. hist. quar.*, XXXIV (1933) 236–240 [**1776**], correspondence between Sir Robert Peel, prime minister, and Lord Aberdeen, foreign minister, showing that the British had given up hope of obtaining the Columbia as the boundary, but were determined to retain access to the ports in Puget Sound and free navigation of the Columbia. For selections from the correspondence of Aberdeen (printed but never published), see no. 1332a, above. Wagner, *Span. explorations* (no. 1724).

For printed writings of American statesmen and diplomatists, see Sec. 1, above. Note particularly, Richard Rush, *Memoranda* (no. 5288); *Writings of Gallatin* (no. 5226); *Corres. Calhoun* (no. 5199); *Diary of Polk* (no. 5288).

MSS.: Suggestions

See Secs. 1, 2, 3, above, for official archival collections, private papers, etc. See also D. W. Parker's *Calendar* (no. 5511), for papers in the Washington archives relating to Oregon during the territorial period.

The papers of Senator J. J. Crittenden, who took a prominent part in the discussions on the Oregon boundary dispute, are in the Library of Congress (for calendar, see no. 1834).

The University of Oregon Library at Eugene, Oreg., has a collection of typescript copies made by Dr. Joseph Schafer of documents in the British Record Office relating to the Oregon boundary question, 1813-1846.

In addition to the British MSS. noted in sections 1 and 3, there is a voluminous collection of MSS. of great importance in the papers of the Hudson's Bay Company, London. A minor small collection of Hudson's Bay Company papers, relating to the Puget Sound Agricultural Company is in the Huntington Library at San Marino, California.[9] The Library of Congress has photostats of correspondence of Lieutenants Warre and Vavasour during their expedition to the Oregon country, 1845-46, with survey maps (F.O. 5, vol. 457).

The Washington State Library, at Olympia, has the MS. of the court exhibit in the case of the Puget Sound Agricultural Company, under the British-American Joint Commission, including 11 maps and 7 drawings, prepared by Edward Lander, counsel for the Hudson's Bay Company (never printed).

The archives of the American Board of Commissioners for Foreign Missions at Boston should be noted.

The British Museum has a Survey of the Oregon Territory between latitude 45° and 54°, by David Thompson, astronomer and surveyor (Add. MSS. 27363) and accompanying maps.

Maps: Suggestions

For lists of maps, see nos. 5128-5154; Judson, *Subject index to . . . Alaska* (no. 1707), 199-201; J. F. Guillén, *Repertorio de los MSS. cartas, planos y dibujos relativos a las Californias existentes en este museo* (Madrid, 1932) (Publicaciones del Museo Naval, I) [1777], this covers the collection formerly in the Depósito Hidrográfico.

There was never any particular cartographical difficulty concerning the Oregon boundary settlement of 1846, except for the location of the line out through Juan de Fuca Straits (see below, p. 413). The boundaries mentioned in various offers and counter-offers during the Oregon negotiations, 1818-1846, are worked out with great

---

[9] Also a collection of several hundred books and pamphlets not yet catalogued.

precision in C. O. Paullin's authoritative *Atlas* (no. 213), plate 93c, text p. 61. The traces of various explorations made by nationals of the rival nations on the Pacific coast involve a multitude of maps which are more pertinent to the history of exploration and of which a bibliography would be a useful service. The British Museum has 4 maps accompanying a survey of the Oregon Territory between 45° and 54° latitude, by David Thompson, of which there are photostats in the Library of Congress. Among the more noteworthy of those enumerated below are those of Dixon, Meares, Vancouver, and those reproduced in the *Journals of the Lewis and Clark expedition*. George Dixon, *Voyage autour de monde*, tr. from the Eng. by M. Lebas (Paris, 1789) [**1778**] has "Carte des voyages du King George et de la Reine Charlotte, aux côtes nord oueste de l'Amérique en 1786–1787", made by George Dixon. John Meares, *Voyage made in the years 1788 and 1789, from China to the northwest coast of America* (London, 1791, 2 v.) [**1779**]. José Espinosa y Tello, *Relación del viage hecho por las goletas Sutil y Mexicana en el año de 1792 para reconocer el estrecho de Fuca* (Madrid, 1802) [**1780**], perfect copies should have map; reproductions are in Cecil Jane, *Span. voyage* (no. 1790). Robert Greenhow, *Memoir* (no. 1712), and *Geography of Oregon and California and the other territories of the northwest coast of North America*, illustrated by a new and beautiful map of those countries (N.Y., 1845) [**1781**]. Samuel Parker, *Journal of an exploring tour beyond the Rocky Mountains* (Ithaca, N.Y., 1842) [**1782**] has a map of the Oregon Territory by Parker, 1838. M. Duflot de Mofras, *Exploration du territoire de l'Orégon des Californies et de la Mer Vermeille, executée pendant les années 1840, 1841 et 1842* (Paris, 1844) [**1783**] has an atlas. John Dunn, *History of the Oregon Territory and British North-American fur trade* (London, 1844) [**1784**] has a map of the Oregon country. Wilkes, *U.S. exploring expedition* (no. 1761) has in its *Atlas* a map of the Oregon territory dated 1841. Thomas Farnham, *Oregon Territory* (no. 1714), accompanied by a map. Mons. Fédix, *L'Orégon et les côtes de l'Océan Pacifique du Nord, aperçu géographique, statistique et politique* (Paris, 1846) [**1785**]. Alexander Ross, *Adventures of the first settlers on the Oregon or Columbia river, being a narrative of the expedition fitted out by John Jacob Astor* (London, 1849) [**1786–7**]. Thwaites, *Journals of Lewis and Clark expedition* (no. 779), v. III: "Atlas accompanying the original journals

of the Lewis and Clark expedition, 1804–1806, being facsimile reproductions of maps, chiefly by William Clark . . . now for the first
time published." E. S. Meany, *Vancouver's discovery of Puget
Sound* (N.Y., 1907) [**1788**] has several early maps. F. A. Mourelle,
*Voyage of the Sonora in the second Bucareli expedition to explore
the northwest coast, survey the port of San Francisco and found
Franciscan missions and a presidio and pueblo at that port* (San
Francisco, 1920) [**1789**]. Howay, *Dixon-Meares controversy* (no.
1774) has section of Meare's map, Cooke's map, and Duncan's sketch
of the entrance of the Strait of Juan de Fuca, and others. Douglas,
Boundaries (no. 211). Cecil Jane, *A Spanish voyage to Vancouver
and the northwest coast of America, being the narrative of the
voyage made in the year 1792 by the schooners Sutil and Mexicana
to explore the strait of Fuca* (London, 1930) [**1790**], translated from
the original Spanish edition of 1802. Wagner, *Span. explorations*
(no. 1724). Miller, *Treaties* (no. 5371), v. V (in press).

CHAPTER XII

SLAVERY AND EXPANSION [1]

1. In General

Bibliographical Aids

For general aids, see Sabin (no. 4655); Larned (no. 4657); Griffin (no. 4658); *Writings* (no. 4661); C. H. and T. (no. 4662); bibliographies in *Am. secs. state* (no. 4796); *Guide hist. lit.* (no. 4634). Myers (no. 5399) for collections of treaties. Miller, *Treaties* (no. 5371), v. I, 39–54, for "Bibliography of United States treaty collections".

For lists of newspapers, see nos. 5004–5047.

For index to periodical material (particularly *Niles's Register*) see *Poole's index* (no. 4995).

General Works

Of general histories of the United States, see Von Holst (no. 4780); McMaster (no. 4781); Channing (no. 4784). See also Henry Wilson, *History of the rise and fall of the slave power in America* (Boston, 1872–77, 3 v.) [1791], a polemic abolitionist narrative; *Am. secs. state*, v. VI (no. 4796); Wriston, *Exec. agents* (no. 4799); Perkins, *Monroe Doctrine, 1826–1867* (no. 1211).

For biographies of American presidents, secretaries of state, and diplomatists abroad (for names and tenure, see latest *Register* of the Dept. of State (no. 5122)), see relevant entries and bibliographical data in the *D.A.B.*, and *Am. secs. state* (no. 4796). Note particularly R. F. Nichols, *Franklin Pierce* (Phila., 1931) [1792].

Printed Sources

For American official publications and general source collections, see *Jour. exec. proc. Sen.* (no. 5387); *A.S.P., F.R.* (no. 5341); *Ann.*

---

[1] See also Ch. X: "Mexico and Texas, 1823–1861."

Cong. (no. 5382) ; *Reg. debates Cong.* (no. 5383) ; *Cong. Globe* (no. 5384) ; Wharton's *Digest* (no. 5366) ; *Abridg. debates* (no. 5386) ; *Richardson* (no. 5335) ; Moore's *Arbitrations* (no. 5364) ; *Repts. Sen. com. for. rel.* (no. 5388) ; Moore's *Digest* (no. 5365) ; Hasse (no. 5344).

For text of treaties, with valuable notes, see Miller, *Treaties* (no. 5371).

For guides to newspapers, see nos. 5004–5047. Note particularly, Kenny, *Am. newspaper directory* (no. 5004a). An analysis of the principal American newspapers and periodicals, 1848 to 1871, is given in J. G. Gazley (no. 1424).

Helen T. Catterall (Mrs. R. C. H. Catterall), *Judicial cases concerning American slavery and the negro* (Wash.: Carnegie Institution, 1926–32, 3 v. (in progress) [**1793**], though primarily illustrating social and economic phases of slavery, includes also cases involving British search and seizures of American vessels. Elizabeth Donnan, *Documents illustrative of the history of the slave trade to America* (Wash.: Carnegie Institution, 1930–35, 4 v.) [**1794**], containing documents from 1441 to 1807.

For printed writings of American presidents, secretaries of state, and diplomatists abroad (for names and tenure, see latest *Register* of the Dept. of State (no. 5122)), see our list on p. 756.

For guides to British, French, and Spanish state papers, see below: British, p. 838; French, p. 842; and for Spanish, consult Gregory, *Serial publications of foreign governments* (no. 5400).

2. Cuban Question, 1826–1860

Bibliographical Aids

For general aids, see Sec. 1, above. See also Griffin, *Cuba* (no. 4722) ; Trelles y Govín, *Bibliog. cubana* (no. 4723) ; and Sánchez Alonso (no. 4759).

Special bibliographies are given in Caldwell (no. 1808), 123–138; G. H. Stuart, *Cuba* (no. 3335), 22–23; "Bibliografía revolucionaria cubana, relativa a la independencia, 1809–1830 ", in *Discursos leídos en la recepción pública del Sr. Carlos M. Trelles y Govín, 1926* (Havana, 1926), 139–150 [**1795**]; Guerra y Sánchez, *Independencia de Cuba* (no. 3366) ; and Ettinger (no. 1814), 502–526, giving an admirable bibliography of histories, monographs, and printed and MS. sources of the diplomacy of slavery and expansion.

General Works

See Sec. 1, above.

Mariano Torrente, *Política ultramarina, que abraza todos los puntos referentes á las relaciones de Españas con los Estados Unidos, con la Inglaterra, y las Antillas* (Madrid, 1854) [**1796**], contemporary tract emphasizing necessity of defenses of Cuba. Chadwick, *U.S. and Spain* (no. 108). R. E. Curtis, "The law of hostile military expeditions as applied by the United States", *Am. jour. internat. law*, VIII (1914) 224–255 [**1797**]. W. F. Johnson, *History of Cuba* (N.Y., 1920, 5 v.) [**1798**], perhaps not acceptable to the critical scholar, this is still the best general history of Cuba. Latané, *U.S. and Latin America* (no. 963). Bécker, *Relaciones exteriores* (no. 723). Rippy, *Rivalry* (no. 1077). Thomas, *Russo-American relations* (no. 1438), ch. 4: "Cuba and Russo-American relations."

Special Works [2]

"La question de Cuba, jugée au point de vue américaine", *Rev. brittanique*, 7th ser., XXII (1854) 257–290 [**1799**] summarizes a number of contemporary expositions of the question. J. M. Philippo, *The United States and Cuba* (London, 1857) [**1800**]. Sidney Webster, "Mr. Marcy, the Cuban question and the Ostend manifesto", *Pol. sci. quar.*, VIII (1893) 1–32 [**1801–2**], a defense of Marcy's diplomacy and of the foreign policy of the Pierce administration by Pierce's private secretary. Benoist, *Cuba et les Etats-Unis* (no. 3420), written on the eve of the Spanish-American war, to show that from 1815 or 1820 to 1897, the United States in dealing with Spain on the subject of Cuba has pushed two policies: an official, proper one; and a popular, impulsive and unbridled one. J. H. Latané, "The diplomacy of the United States in regard to Cuba", *Am. hist. assoc. ann. rep.*, for 1897 (1898) 217–278 [**1803**], early applications of the Monroe Doctrine to Cuba, and schemes of annexation, based entirely on printed English and American sources. J. M. Callahan, "Cuba and Anglo-American relations", *ibid.*, 195–215 [**1804**] deals with the period 1819–1829, without having available the principal English sources; now partially superseded by Rippy (no. 1077); and his *Cuba and international relations* (Baltimore, 1899) [**1805**], Cuba in American history and international relations; it

---

[2] We have not attempted to list all the contemporary periodical literature regarding the Cuban question. For this, consult *Poole's index*, v. I, 1802–1881 (no. 4995).

is evidently restricted mainly to American printed sources. Rodríguez, *Anexión de Cuba* (no. 3427), written by a rabid partisan
of annexation, gives interesting data, especially of the proposed
López constitution of Cuba. A. C. Quisenberry, *Lopez's expeditions
to Cuba, 1850 and 1851* (Louisville, Ky., 1906) [**1806**], not reliable,
but does not aim to be critical, and has used no Cuban sources. Of
value to show the representatives of prominent southern families
recruited in Lopez's filibusters. H. L. Janes, " The Black Warrior
affair ", *Am. hist. rev.*, XII (1907) 280–289 [**1807**], authoritative account using newly discovered material (papers in the letter-
files of the captain-general of Cuba preserved in the *Archivo Nacional* at Havana, and correspondence, official and private, of Americans residing in Havana). R. G. Caldwell, *The Lopez expeditions
to Cuba, 1848–1851* (Princeton, 1915) [**1808**], emphasizing military
events, it utilized Cuban archives, but should now be supplemented
by Portell Vilá, *post.* J. B. Moore, "A great secretary of state; William L. Marcy ", *Pol. sci. quar.*, XXX (1915) 377–396 [**1809**], but for
much new light on Marcy see also H. B. Learned in *Am. secs. state*,
v. VI (no. 4796). Three works by Herminio Portell Vilá : *Historia de
Cárdenas* (Havana, 1928) [**1810**], p. 97–126, for an account of the
López expedition to Cárdenas in 1850; *Narciso López y su época*
(Havana, 1930) [**1811**] (1 vol., 2 more volumes already partially
completed are yet to be published), uses Cuban archives and places
López in the category of Cuban heroes and patriots, rather than a
filibuster and annexationist; and " Cubí y Soler y el Presidente
Monroe ", *Rev. bimestre cubana*, XXIX, no. 3 (1932) 327–331 [**1812**]
tells of the first translation of the Monroe Doctrine into Spanish and
the man who translated it (letter of Mariano Cubí y Soler to Monroe,
Dec. 17, 1823, found in the Monroe papers). Guerra y Sánchez,
Camino de la independencia (no. 3366). Roque E. Garrigo, *Historia
documentada de la conspiración de los soles y rayos de Bolívar*
(Havana, 1929, 2 v.) [**1813**], notwithstanding imperfections this
work gives ample information on the international aspects of the
first revolutionary schemes in Cuba. A. A. Ettinger, *The mission to
Spain of Pierre Soulé, 1853–1855; a study in the Cuban diplomacy
of the United States* (New Haven, 1932) [**1814**], based on prodigal
research in European (except Spanish !) and American archives and
libraries, presented in voluminous and not unreadable array; adds
surprisingly little new to the many outlines already presented by

Learned's " Marcy " in *Am. secs. state*, v. VI (no. 4796), but does reveal interesting oral commitments of Fillmore and Webster to British and French ministers, 1852, conveniently forgotten after Webster's death. J. A. Reinecke, jr., " The diplomatic career of Pierre Soulé ", *La. hist. quar.*, XV (1932) 283–329 [**1815**], based on American printed sources, it is superseded by Ettinger.

For biographies of American presidents, secretaries of state and diplomatists abroad, see note in Sec. 1, above. See also biographies of Jefferson Davis, as given in the *D.A.B.*

For accounts of J. A. Miralla, envoy from the Cuban revolutionists to treat with President Monroe in 1823, see Antonio Iraizoz, " Un precursor olvidado: el argentino José Antonio Miralla ", *Cuba contemporánea*, XXXI (1923) 331–344 [**1816**]; and Eduardo Labougle, *José Antonio Miralla* (Buenos Aires, 1924) [**1817**].

Printed Sources

For general collections, see Sec. 1, above. U.S. official documents relating to the Cuban question are conveniently listed in Ettinger (no. 1814); and (for Lopez's expedition to Cuba) in Caldwell (no. 1808). The official text of the Ostend manifesto, with the correspondence is to be found in 33d Cong., 2d sess., *House exec. doc. 93*, v. X [**1818**]; this same document also contains the correspondence dealing with the *Black Warrior* case.

For guides to British, French, and Spanish official publications, see below, Pt. II, ch. 2, pp. 836 ff.

British Parliamentary Papers dealing with the Cuban question: *Correspondence between the United States, Spain, and France concerning alleged projects of conquest, and annexation of the Island of Cuba* (Gt. Brit. House of Commons. Sess. pap. 1852-53, v. CII) [**1819**]. Spanish official publication dealing with the Cuban question: *Negociaciones diplomáticas encaminadas á guarantizar á España la posesión de la isla de Cuba, de 1825 á 1853* (Madrid, 1853?) [**1820**], at head of title: " Ministerio de Estado. Sección Política. Reservado."

For an analysis of contemporary newspapers (American and foreign), see Ettinger (no. 1814). An indispensable source for the study of the period is the Cuban newspaper, *La Verdad*, printed in both English and Spanish, in New York from 1848 to 1853; it was published by the annexationist Junta as its official organ.

F. J. Grund, *The Americans, in their moral, social, and political relations* (London, 1837, 2 v.; another ed.: Boston, 1837, 2 v. in 1) [**1820a**] advocates the acquisition of Cuba, a larger navy, construction of an Isthmian canal and control of the Pacific; by a Bohemian immigrant publicist. W. H. Trescot, *A few thoughts on the foreign policy of the United States* (Charleston, S.C., 1849) [**1821**] advocates, Washington's advice notwithstanding, a partnership, even alliance, of the United States and Great Britain on policy in the Far East, and also to guarantee the independence of Cuba. The author was really the father of the writing of diplomatic history in the United States (see his nos. 364 and 15) and was later in the diplomatic service of the United States and of the Confederacy. Two articles in the *Democratic review* (Wash.): "The Cuban debate", (n.s. II, 1852, p. 433–456) [**1822**], debate in the U.S. Senate, Dec. 23, 1852; and "The late Cuba state trials" (n.s. I, 1852, p. 307–319) [**1823**], review of the filibuster trials in New Orleans and New York, of the Cárdenas expedition of Gen. López, 1850. José de la Concha, *Memorias sobre el estado político, gobierno y administración de la isla de Cuba* (Madrid, 1853), 133–298 [**1824**], for the Spanish point of view; written by the governor and captain general of Cuba of the period. Edward Everett, *Correspondence on the proposed tripartite convention relative to Cuba* (Boston, 1853) [**1825**]. *Life of J. J. Crittenden* (no. 1637) includes letters while acting secretary of state,[3] October 22, 1851, to M. Sartiges, French minister in Washington, in regard to filibusters captured and executed by France (filibusters from New Orleans to Cuba), on Cuba and the European powers, and a few others regarding Cuba and the filibusters. M. B. Field, *Memories of many men* (N.Y., 1874) [**1826**], Field was secretary of the American legation at Paris, 1854–55, and this volume of his reminiscences is "exceedingly valuable for its first-hand impressions of Soulé in Madrid at the time of the rejection of the Ostend manifesto and his ultimate resignation" (Ettinger). Stapleton, *Corres. of Canning* (no. 969). *The Ostend manifesto, 1854* (N.Y., 1892) (American History Leaflets, no. 2) [**1827**], text of the manifesto. Rodríguez, *Anexión de Cuba* (no. 3427), a reprint of documents illustrating American policy toward Cuba, 1776–1898. [D. H. Burtnett] "Lopez's expeditions to Cuba, 1850–51. Betrayal of the

---

[3] Attorney general in Fillmore's cabinet, acting secretary of state, and uncle of Wm. L. Crittenden who perished with Lopez's filibusters.

Cleopatra, 1851 ", ed. by L. M. Pérez, *So. hist. assoc. pub.*, X (1906) 345–362 [**1828–9**], document, dated New York, July 26, 1851, signed by Duncan Smith (name assumed by Dr. D. H. Burtnett), printed from a copy in the National Archives of Cuba; the contemporary Spanish translation was printed in the *Boletín del Archivo Nacional* (Havana), v. V, 1906.   Manning, *Monroe Doctrine* (no. 1160), early application of the Monroe Doctrine to Cuba.   " Papeles inéditos relativos a las expediciones del general Narciso López [1845–1852] ", *Boletín del Archivo Nacional* (Havana), XVI (1917) 256–283, 373–437, XVII (1917) 67–91 [**1830**], a series of important documents from the "Archivo Nacional " of Cuba.   " Correspondencia reservada de los cónsules de España en los Estados Unidos de América con el gobernador y capitán general de la Isla de Cuba ", *ibid.*, XXVII (1928) 129–273 [**1831**], documents of the years 1819–34. J. A. Saco, *Contra la anexión* (Havana, 1928) [**1832**], collection of papers of a Cuban patriot active in the period 1835–1860 and later. " Letter from Alexander M. Clayton to J. F. H. Claiborne relative to Cuban affairs ", *Hisp. Am. hist. rev.*, IX (1929) 364–368 [**1833**], document written by the American consul in Cuba discussing the relations of the United States and Cuba in 1853–54.   Garrigo, *Conspiración* (no. 1813), v. II consists of documents, some dealing with international aspects of early revolutionary schemes in Cuba.

For printed writings of American statesmen and diplomatists, see Sec. 1, above.   See also the *Letters, papers, and speeches* of Jefferson Davis (no. 5214).

MSS.: Suggestions

For official archives of the United States, Cuba, Spain, France, and Great Britain, and photocopies therefrom, see below: United States, p. 857; Cuba, p. 912; Spain, p. 898; France, p. 915; and Great Britain, p. 890.   There is an excellent analysis of American, British, and French MS. sources for the Cuban question and Ostend manifesto in Ettinger (no. 1814).   A facsimile of the original report of the meeting at Ostend, in Buchanan's handwriting, is in Nichols, *Franklin Pierce* (no. 1792).

For personal papers of American presidents (Polk, Taylor, Fillmore, Pierce, and Buchanan), secretaries of state (Calhoun, Buchanan, Clayton, Everett, Marcy, Cass), and diplomatists (for names and tenure, see latest *Register* of the Dept. of State (no. 5122)) see below: presidents, p. 862; secretaries of state, p. 865; and diplomatists, p. 868.

For some extant personal papers of English and French statesmen and diplomatists, see Ch. X, Sec. 1.

J. J. Crittenden papers in the Library of Congress (see *Calendar of the papers of John Jordan Crittenden* (Wash.: Govt. Print. Off., 1913) [1834]). The principal collections of personal and official papers of Jefferson Davis (Secretary of War, and, of course, later President of the Confederate States) are in the Confederate Memorial Hall, New Orleans, and in the Dept. of Archives and History of the State of Mississippi, at Jackson (now printed, see no. 5214).

Note Herbert Friedenwald, "A synoptical catalogue of manuscripts in the Library of Congress relating to Cuba ", in Griffin, *Cuba* (no. 4722), 58–61. See also Paz, *Catálogo* (no. 5656).

3. Slavery and the Slave Trade [4]

Bibliographical Aids

For general aids, see Sec. 1, above. Trelles, *Biblioteca hist. cubana* (no. 4723), v. I, 94–104, for a list of references regarding slavery. Soulsby (no. 1850).

For the British West Indian phase of the movement for the abolition of the slave trade there are three valuable bibliographical contributions by L. J. Ragatz: *H. L. sess. papers rel. Brit. West Indies* (no. 336); *H. L. sess. papers rel. Brit. West Indies* (no. 337); and the comprehensive and authoritative *Guide Brit. Carib. hist.* (no. 4721).

There is a useful bibliographical note regarding the diplomatic phases of the slave trade in the *Am. secs. state* (no. 4796), v. V, 362–363.

Special Works

W. B. Lawrence, *Visitation and search; or, An historical sketch of the British claim to exercise a maritime police over the vessels of all nations, in peace as well as in war, with an inquiry into the expediency of terminating the eighth article of the Ashburton treaty* (Boston, 1858) [1835], the first publication of a careful examination of this

---

[4] We are aware of no published comprehensive study of the diplomatic history of the abolition of the slave trade.

" historic problem " of American diplomacy, by a capable American legal scholar strong in his defense against arbitrary visit and search. **J. A.** Saco, *Historia de la esclavitud de la raza africana en el Nuevo Mundo y en especial en los países américo-hispanos* (Barcelona, 1879) also published (Havana, 1932, 2 v.) as *Colección de libros cubanos*, v. XXVIII–XXIX [**1836**], a fundamental work on the history of slavery in the New World. Schuyler, *Am. diplomacy* (no. 4786). **W. E. B.** DuBois, *The suppression of the African slave trade to the United States of North America, 1638–1870* (N.Y., 1896) [**1837**], ch. 9: " The international status of the slave trade, 1783–1862 ", a useful summary account, based on printed sources (*A.S.P.*, and *Brit. and For. State Pap.*), but the author is concerned more with the illegal trade than with the diplomatic efforts to suppress it. Queneuil, *Traite des noirs* (no. 2400). Reeves, *Tyler and Polk* (no. 1459). Dunning, *Brit. Emp. and U.S.* (no. 1335). Three papers by T. P. Martin: *Anglo-American relations* (no. 1344), shows cooperation between British and American antislavery societies; " Some international aspects of the antislavery movement, 1818–1823 ", *Jour. econ. and business hist.*, I (1928) 137–148 [**1838**] treats of American cotton supremacy in British markets; " The upper Mississippi Valley in Anglo-American antislavery and free-trade relations, 1837–1842 ", *Miss. Valley hist. rev.*, XV (1928) 204–220 [**1839**] deals with the economic basis of the American protest against the British corn laws and relations between British and American antislavery leaders. A. P. Newton, " The slave-trade and frontier difficulties, 1815–1841 ", in the *Camb. hist. Brit. for. pol.* (no. 209), v. II, 220–247 [**1840**]. Mowat, *Gt. Brit. and U.S.* (no. 347a). Temperley, *Canning* (no. 1152). Webster, *Castlereagh* (no. 1171). F. J. Klingberg, *The antislavery movement in England* (New Haven, Conn., 1926) [**1841**], diplomatic negotiations are only touched upon. Three works by W. L. Mathieson: *British slavery and its abolition, 1823–1838* (London and N.Y., 1926) [**1842**], confined to the West Indian group of colonies; *Great Britain and the slave trade, 1839–1865* (London, N.Y., and Toronto, 1929) [**1843**], depends on the Parliamentary papers; *British slave emancipation, 1838–1849* (London, N.Y., etc., 1932) [**1844**], a continuation of his no. 1842. R. W. Van Alstyne, " The British right of search and the African slave trade ", *Jour. mod. hist.*, II (1930) 37–47 [**1845**], a brief summary, from a study of printed

British and American documents, and the opinions of publicists, emphasizing that the British " right " of search was a treaty right not a right by international law *per se.* St. George L. Sioussat, " Duff Green's ' England and the United States ';[5] with an introductory study of American opposition to the quintuple treaty of 1841 ", *Am. antiq. soc. proc.*, n.s. XL, pt. 2 (1931) 175–276 [**1846**], contribution to hitherto obscure aspects of Anglo-French-American relations, 1841–1842, and frustration of the quintuple treaty. Hill, *U.S. and Brazil* (no. 1277), with a scholarly treatment (without access to Brazilian archives) of " The abolition of the African slave trade to Brazil ", the most important chapter of American-Brazilian relations. W. R. Riddell, "An international complication between Illinois and Canada arising out of slavery ", *Ill. state hist. soc. jour.*, XXV (1932) 123–126 [**1847**], a curious instance of slavery in the Old Northwest in 1829. A. T. Milne, " The slave trade and Anglo-American relations, 1807–1862 ", *Inst. hist. research bul.*, IX, no. 26 (1931) 126–129 [**1848**], abstract of thesis which utilized original records in the Public Record Office; regards slavery as explaining uneasy relations during the half century preceding the civil war. The appendix gives chronology of British suppression of the slave trade, 1807–1863, with principal laws and treaties made by Great Britain on the subject (see also his *Lyons-Seward treaty* (no. 1988)). R. E. McClendon, " The *Amistad* claims: inconsistencies of policy ", *Pol. sci. quar.*, XLVIII (1933) 386–412 [**1849**], the diplomatic history of the still unsettled *Amistad* case and claims, as revealed by printed and unprinted correspondence of the Dept. of State. H. G. Soulsby, *The right of search and the slave trade in Anglo-American relations, 1814–1862* (Baltimore, 1933) [**1850**], based on the pertinent correspondence, much of it unpublished and hitherto unused, of the Dept. of State and the British Foreign Office. A tolerably complete and unusually clear treatment not likely to be superseded. Miller, *Treaties* (no. 5371), v. IV, 438–441, for a discussion and documentary extracts regarding article 8 of the Webster-Ashburton treaty, dealing with the question of visit and search in connection with the suppression of the slave trade.

For biographies of American statesmen and diplomatists (to France and Great Britain), see note in Sec. 1, above. See also biographies of Jefferson Davis, as given in the *D.A.B.*

---

[5] See no. 1854.

Printed Sources

For general collections, see Sec. 1, above. Note particularly Moore's *Digest* (no. 5365), for cases involving the slave trade, and Hasse's *Index* (no. 5344), for index to United States public documents.

See Ragatz (nos. 336–337) for British sessional papers. Particular volumes of British sessional papers (House of Commons) are: *Correspondence with British ministers and agents in foreign countries, and with foreign ministers in England, relating to the slave trade, from April 1, 1850 to March 31, 1851* (1851, v. LVI, pt. II, no. 1) [**1851**]; and *Correspondence with the United States government on the question of right of visit* (1857–58, v. XXXIX) [**1852**].

[Lewis Cass], *An examination of the question, now in discussion, between the American and British governments, concerning the right of search*, by an American (Paris, 1842) [**1853**], written anonymously by Lewis Cass, then American minister to France, protesting against the British policy in regard to right of search in the suppression of the slave trade. [Duff Green], *The United States and England*, by an American (London, 1842) [**1854**], a series of letters discussing the issues pending between the two nations, particularly the slave trade. For commentary on this work, see Sioussat (no. 1846). [Sir W. G. Ouseley], *Reply to an "American's examination" of the "right of search"; with observations on some of the questions at issue between Great Britain and the United States, and on certain positions assumed by the North American government*, by an Englishman (London, 1842) [**1855**], pub. anonymously in answer to Cass (no. 1853) and exhibits the extreme British point of view. Henry Wheaton, *Enquiry into the validity of the British claim to a right of visitation and search of American vessels suspected to be engaged in the African slave trade* (Phila., 1842) [**1855a**], an able refutation by the American publicist, then minister to Berlin. Benton's *Thirty years'* (no. 968). *Corres. of J. J. Crittenden* (no. 1637). *Documents relatifs à la traite des esclaves* (no. 2439). *Papers of Sir Ch. Vaughan* (no. 1380) include despatches on the question of the slave trade. Catterall, *Judicial cases on slavery* (no. 1793). Annie H. Abel and F. J. Klingberg, eds., *A sidelight on Anglo-American relations, 1839–1858* (Lancaster, Pa., 1927) [**1856**], published by the Association for the Study of Negro Life and History, prints a considerable correspondence of Lewis Tappan, secretary of the American and Foreign Anti-Slavery Society, with the British and Foreign Anti-Slavery Society, illustrating the cooperation of British and American antislavery forces particularly, rather than the diplomatic aspects. Donnan, *Documents on slave trade* (no. 1794). Milne, *Lyons-Seward treaty* (no. 1988). Miller, *Treaties* (no. 5371), v. IV, 438–441, for documentary extracts regarding article 8 of the Webster-Ashburton treaty dealing with the question of visit and search in connection with the suppression of the slave trade.

For printed writings of American statesmen and diplomatists abroad (for names and tenure, see latest *Register* of the Dept. of State (no. 5122)) see our list on p. 756. Note particularly writings of J. Q. Adams, Buchanan, J. C. Calhoun, Lewis Cass, Richard Rush, and Daniel Webster; also Jefferson Davis and other southern leaders.

MSS.: Suggestions

See Sec. 2, above, for reference to American and foreign official archives and other collections.

The almost unexplored series, *F.O., Slave Trade* (F.O. 84) in the Public Record Office throws much light on Anglo-American relations in this regard.

The variety of MSS. relating to slavery is vast; but source collections of great value to show the effect on Anglo-American relations of antislavery organizations in England and America, are the minutes of the British and Foreign Anti-Slavery and Aborigines Protection Societies, 1823–1911, at Denison House, London (photostats in the Library of Congress), and of the Committee for the Abolition of the Slave Trade, 1787–1819, in the British Museum (photostats in the Library of Congress).

Note particularly the Liverpool and Wm. Huskisson papers in the British Museum and the papers of Duff Green in the Library of Congress.

4. Filibusters, 1848–1861 [6]

Bibliographical Aids

For general aids, see Sec. 1, above. For López expedition, see Caldwell (no. 1808).

---

[6] For Filibusters to Cuba, see Sec. 2, above. For Filibusters in Mexico, see also Ch. X, Sec. 2. See also Ch. VIII, Sec. 3.

Special Works

August Nicaise, *Les flibustiers américains; Walker et l'Amérique Centrale* (Paris, 1861) [**1857**], an European indictment of Walker and the slavocracy which animated him. Lorenzo Montúfar, *Walker en Centro-América* (Guatemala, 1887) [**1858**], the most important of the accounts by Central American historians, by a Costa Rican who attempts an impartial history. He prints selected documents from some Central American archives, but he had access only to part of the necessary material, and does not specifically document his narrative which suffers from deficiencies in style and construction. D. B. Lucas, *Nicaragua; war of the filibusters* (Richmond, 1896) [**1859**], an undocumented study which sees in the defeat of Walker a turning point from chaos to order in Central America. Travis, *Clayton-Bulwer treaty* (no. 1229). Curtis, *Hostile military expeditions* (no. 1797). Caldwell, *Lopez expeditions* (no. 1808), and Portell Vilá, *López* (no. 1811). W. O. Scroggs, *Filibusters and financiers; the story of William Walker and his associates* (N.Y., 1916) [**1860**], the standard work. After exhaustive study of printed and MS. sources in the United States, concludes that Walker was not a big enough man to take advantage of a great opportunity to make Central America into a stable state commanding the best canal route. J. F. Rippy, " Border troubles along the Rio Grande, 1848–1860 ", *Southw. hist. quar.*, XXIII (1919) 91–111 [**1861**], a carefully worked out paper from a multitude of printed sources. Isidro Fabela, " El filibusterismo americano en Centro América ", *Rev. mex. derecho internac.*, III (1921) 1–57 [**1862**]. Carreño, *Mexico y los EE. UU.* (no. 1461). Garber, *Gadsden purchase* (no. 1628). Callahan, *Mexican relations* (no. 1465). Wilgus, *Manifest destiny* (no. 1210). Two studies by R. K. Wyllys, *The French in Sonora (1850–1854)* ; *the story of French adventurers from California into Mexico* (Berkeley, Calif., (1932) [**1863**] describes filibustering attempts of the California French in Sonora, particularly that of Raousset-Boulbon and their not inharmonious relationship with American filibusters; based on Mexican archival sources, printed documents, and works; and " The republic of Lower California, 1853–1854 ", *Pacific hist. rev.*, I (1932) 194–213 [**1864**], revealing the connection of this movement with Walker's filibustering schemes. Pratt, *Manifest destiny* (no. 1752). J. M. Clarke, "Antonio Meléndrez, nemesis of William Walker in Baja California ", *Calif. hist. soc. quar.*, XII (1933) 318–322

[1864a], account of Walker's filibustering expedition to Lower California in 1853 and 1854; based mainly on newspapers (Los Angeles *Southern California*, San Diego *Herald*, San Francisco *Daily Herald*). Deals with the military rather than the diplomatic phase. Hallie M. McPherson, " The plan of William McKendree Gwin for a colony in north Mexico, 1863–1865 ", *Pacific hist. rev.*, II (1933) 357–386 [1865], Senator Gwin was one of the most notorious of slavery-expansionists whose grand designs were interrupted by the civil war. The author has used such Gwin papers as remain in the Bancroft Library and other sources, to show how Gwin hoped to enlist Napoleon III in his schemes during the civil war.

Printed Sources

For general collections, see Sec. 1, above.

For U.S. public documents, see Hasse's *Index* (no. 5344). Garber (no. 1628) has in his bibliography a list of U.S. government documents relating to Mexico, 1853–1861.

See Childs, *Memorias* (no. 5424), for Central American official publications. W. V. Wells, *Walker's expedition to Nicaragua; a history of the Central American war; and the Sonora and Kinney expeditions, including all the recent diplomatic correspondence* (N.Y., 1856) [1866], a book put together in 20 days to extol filibuster Walker and his government. William Walker, *The war in Nicaragua* (Mobile and N.Y., 1860) [1867], as told by the filibuster himself. Hostile critics of his enterprise acknowledge the general accuracy of such facts as he chooses to present in this narrative. Vidal Morales y Morales, *Iniciadores y primeros mártires de la revolución cubana* (Havana, 1901; also issued (in 3 v.), Havana, 1931) [1867a], a large collection of documents ill arranged, many now inaccessible, with comments by the author, who was director of the archives at Havana. "A short sketch of my life for the last four years in Nicaragua ", being the reminiscences of Elleanore (Callaghan) Ratterman, a female filibuster in Nicaragua who concluded that " with such a country, our U.S. would have a ' Garden of Eden ' ", published in *Tenn. hist. mag.*, I (1915) 315–330 [1868]. W. O. Scroggs, ed., " Walker-Heiss papers; some diplomatic correspondence of the Walker régime in Nicaragua ", *ibid.*, 331–345 [1869], mainly official papers of Major John Heiss, who was intimately connected with the Walker regime in Nicaragua, 1856–60; Heiss went to Nicaragua in 1856 as bearer of despatches from the Dept. of State, and returned as a " naturalized " citizen of Nicaragua. R. K. Wyllys, "An expansionist in Baja California, 1855 ", *Pacific hist. rev.*, I (1932) 477–482 [**1870**], a letter from an American commercial agent (Thomas Sprague) at La Paz and other points in Baja California, describing a project for the acquisition of Baja California by the United States, under the doctrine of " manifest destiny."

MSS.: Suggestions

See particularly Secs. 2 and 3, above.

Garber, *Gadsden treaty* (no. 1628) cites important collections for American slavery expansionist tendencies toward northern Mexico. For Mexican archives, see below, p. 910. In the Bancroft Library of the University of California are thousands of transcripts from archives in Mexico dealing with western filibusters. We know of no guides or indexes to Central American archives. The same library has the original memoirs of Senator W. M. Gwin, of California, slavery-expansionist.

A collection of papers left by Major John Heiss, intimately associated with the Walker regime in Nicaragua, was (according to the *Tenn. hist. mag.*, I (1915), 331) in the possession of Robert Lusk, Esq., of Nashville, Tenn. For printing of some of the documents, see no. 1869 above.

CHAPTER XIII

THE CIVIL WAR, 1861–1867

1. In General

Bibliographical Aids

For general aids, see Sabin (no. 4655); Larned (no. 4657); Griffin (no. 4658); *Writings* (no. 4661); C. H. and T. (no. 4662); *Guide hist. lit.* (no. 4634); and bibliographies in *Am. secs. state* (no. 4796).

For indexes to periodical literature, see nos. 4995–5003.

For lists of newspapers, see nos. 5004–5047; particularly Kenny, *Am. newspaper directory* (no. 5004a), and Library of Congress check lists nos. 5030, 5032.

J. R. Bartlett, *The literature of the rebellion. A catalogue of books and pamphlets relating to the civil war in the United States, and on subjects growing out of that event . . . and essays from reviews and magazines on the same subjects* (Boston, 1866) [1871]. James Kelly, *The American catalogue of books, . . . published in the United States from Jan., 1861, to Jan., 1871* (N.Y., 1866–71, 2 v.) [1872], *Supplement* to Vol. I contains pamphlets, sermons, and addresses on the civil war. Griffin, *List on recognition* (no. 4801), for material on the recognition of the Confederate states by European governments. Morrison, *Off. pub. Confed. states* (no. 5352). Griffin and Meyer, *List on reciprocity* (no. 1333). *Camb. hist. Brit. for. pol.* (no. 209), v. II, 656. Jordan and Pratt (no. 2092), 271–290, particularly for newspapers, periodicals, and pamphlets. Owsley (no. 2117), 579–591.

General Works

Of general histories of the United States, see Rhodes (no. 4783), v. III–IV, a standard account, but much has been uncovered since;

316

Channing (no. 4784), v. VI, a more recent and masterly survey; and Oberholtzer (no. 4785). See also *Am. secs. state* (no. 4796), v. VI; and Wriston (no. 4799).

Wilson, *Slave power* (no. 1791). Stern, *Geschichte Europas* (no. 1324). Emile Ollivier, *L'empire libéral* (Paris, 1895–1915, 17 v.) [**1873**], an elaborate but defensive history by the head of the " tiers parti " and head of Napoleon III's responsible ministry in 1870. Pierre de la Gorce, *Histoire du second empire* (Paris, 1899–1905, 7 v.) [**1874**], the best account of the second empire, strong on foreign policy. John Nicolay and John Hay, *Abraham Lincoln, a history* (N.Y., 1902, 10 v.) [**1875**], the authors, Lincoln's private secretaries, were devoted admirers. The biography is really a general history of the civil war, and has much to do with diplomatic history in which the President played a major part. Nicolay also wrote the chapters on the civil war in Vol. VII of the *Cambridge modern history*. Sidney Low and L. C. Sanders, *The history of England during the reign of Queen Victoria (1837–1901)* (London, 1907) (The Political History of England, ed. by William Hunt and R. L. Poole, III) [**1876**], a comprehensive political history coöperatively written by British scholars. *The Cambridge modern history*, v. XII. *The latest age* (Cambridge, 1910) [**1877**], ch. 2: " Foreign relations of the United States during the civil war ", by J. Westlake, stresses, particularly, questions of maritime law. Now supplanted in details by more refined researches. Dunning, *Brit. Emp. and the U.S.* (no. 1335). J. F. Rhodes, *History of the civil war, 1861–1865* (N.Y., 1917) [**1878**] is a one volume abridgment of his larger history (no. 4783). *Camb. hist. Brit. for. pol.* (no. 209), v. II, 488–521: "Anglo-American relations during the civil war, 1860–1865 ", by A. P. Newton [**1879**]. Bécker, *Relaciones exteriores* (no. 723). Mowat, *Gt. Brit. and U.S.* (no. 347a). J. B. McMaster, *A history of the people of the United States during Lincoln's administration* (N.Y. and London, 1927) [**1880**], a continuation of his standard *History* (no. 4781). Payne, *Eng. treatment of Am.* (no. 351). C. R. Fish, Sir Norman Angell, and C. L. Hussey, *The United States and Great Britain* (Chicago, 1932) [**1881**], a symposium with stimulating generalities.

For biographies of American presidents, secretaries of state, and diplomatists abroad (for names and tenure, see latest *Register* of the Dept. of State (no. 5122)), see relevant entries and bibliographical data in the *D.A.B.* W. M. Brigance, *Jeremiah Sullivan Black; a defender of the Constitution and of the Ten Commandments* (Phila., 1934) [1881a] is a recent biography of the secretary of state, Dec. 1860 to March 4, 1861. Note also: W. L. Whittlesey, "William Lewis Dayton, 1825", *Princeton alumni weekly*, XXX (1930) 797-802 [1882], for brief account of the minister to France, 1861-1865. Consult the *D.A.B.* also for biographies of Senator Charles Sumner, chairman of the committee on foreign relations of the U.S. Senate, 1861-1871.

Printed Sources

For American official documents and general source collections, see p. 810; particularly *Jour. exec. proc. Sen.* (no. 5387); *Cong. Globe* (no. 5384); *For. relations* (no. 5345), this does not contain all the material which was published, generally after being submitted to Congress; for this one must consult the various indexes and catalogues of U.S. government documents (for analysis of these, see pp. 817-820), and some of these are listed in H. C. and T. (no 4662). Wharton's *Digest* (no. 5366); Richardson (no. 5335); Moore's *Arbitrations* (no. 5364); *Repts. Sen. com. for. rel.* (no. 5388); Moore's *Digest* (no. 5365).

For guide to foreign official publications, see below, p. 836. We have segregated below British and French official publications of diplomatic correspondence and other state papers dealing with the civil war and the United States. Lists of British sessional papers are given in Bartlett's *Literature* (no. 1871).

For lists and indexes of newspapers, domestic and foreign, see nos. 5004-5047, particularly Library of Congress check lists (5030, 5032); for English newspapers, *Tercentenary handlist* (no. 5013).

There is a voluminous array of pamphlet material, much of which may be found listed in Bartlett's *Literature* (no. 1871), and Kelly (no. 1872). Lutz (no. 2084) lists pamphlet material in German; and West (no. 2090) in French. In the Library of Congress is a collection of bound "political pamphlets" of which nos. 91 and 92 contain several more published in England, particularly on maritime questions; and nos. 93 and 94, those published in France. The Harvard College Library has a large collection of contemporary pamphlet literature on the civil war.

For contemporary periodical material, see *Poole's index* (no. 4995). Jordan and Pratt (no. 2092) lists the more noteworthy English and French periodicals and classifies them as favoring the North or the South.

The *Official records of the Union and Confederate navies in the war of the rebellion* . . . Ser I, v. 1–27; ser. II, v. 1–3 (Wash.:) Govt. Print. Off., 1894–1927, 30 v., and Index) [**1883**], published by the Navy Department, is a voluminous alcove for printed sources for the naval history of the civil war, but contains also much material relating to diplomacy, particularly in connection with naval affairs (see index to series, under France, Great Britain, etc.). Note particularly, for Confederate diplomatic correspondence, etc., no 2110 below. *The Rebellion record; a diary of American events, with documents, narratives, illustrative incidents, poetry, etc.*, ed. by Frank Moore (N.Y., 1861–68, 11 v.) and *Supplement* (N.Y., 1864) [**1884**] begun in 1862 a week-by-week annal, full of all kinds of source material, but chiefly concerned with military events.

For the printed diaries, correspondence, and other writings of American presidents (Buchanan, Lincoln, Johnson), secretaries of state (J. S. Black and W. H. Seward), and of American diplomatists during the civil war (C. F. Adams, minister plenipotentiary, Great Britain, 1861–68; Benjamin Moran, secretary of U.S. legation, London, 1855–73; W. L. Dayton, minister plenipotentiary to France, 1861–65; John Bigelow, consul general in Paris, and minister plenipotentiary, 1865–66; for complete list of other officials at other posts, see latest *Register* of the Dept. of State (no. 5122)), see our list on p. 756; and bibliographical list in Owsley (no. 2117). See also the *Reminiscences* of F. W. Seward (no. 5291); and the *Autobiography* of Thurlow Weed (no. 5309). Note also the printed diaries of two Cabinet members in Lincoln's government: *Diary of Gideon Welles, secretary of the navy under Lincoln and Johnson*, ed. by J. T. Morse, jr. (Boston and N.Y., 1911, 3 v.) [**1885**], discursive diary by the secretary of the navy, gives occasional " inside " information on foreign affairs (for criticism of textual rendition, see Beale (no. 5332)). *The diary of Edward Bates, 1859–1866*, ed. by H. K. Beale (Wash.: Govt. Print. Off., 1933) (Annual Report of the American Historical Association for 1930, v. **IV**) [**1886**], the diary of Lincoln's attorney general, reveals cabinet discussions of the Trent affair, blockade, Mexican relations (Maximilian affair). For the letters of Charles Sumner, chairman of the Senate committee on foreign relations, see no. 5297. *The diary of Orville Hickman Browning*, ed. by T. C. Pease and J. G. Randall (Springfield, Ill., 1925–33, 2 v.) [1887], Browning was senator from Illinois, 1861–63, and his diary refers briefly to such matters as the Alabama claims, and the Maximilian affair.

Adam Gurowski, *Diary* (Boston, N.Y., and Wash., 1862–66, 3 v.) [1888], day-by-day (1861 to 1865) comments by a Washington observer familiar with political personalities, it has current appraisals of foreign policy, particularly Anglo-American affairs; Gurowski was a radical Polish refugee, who was a translator in the Dept. of State, 1861–63. *My diary North and South*, by William Howard Russell (N.Y., 1863) [1889], by the American correspondent for the London *Times*, contains many comments on the diplomatists and diplomacy. For further letters of W. H. Russell, see L. M. Sears, " The London Times' American correspondent in 1861; unpublished letters of W. H. Russell ", *Hist. outlook*, XVI (1925) 251–257 [1889a].

We have listed below (Sec. 5) the printed writings of Confederate officials and diplomatists.

MSS.: Suggestions

For guides and indexes to the files of official diplomatic correspondence of the Department of State, and of the foreign offices of the European powers, which constitute the base of sources for the diplomatic history of the United States during this period, see below, Pt. II, ch. 3.

For papers of President Lincoln, and Secretary of State Seward, see our lists below, pp. 862 and 865, and also our list of personal papers known to be extant, of American diplomatists (for names and tenure, see latest *Register* of the Dept. of State (no. 5122)), p. 868. The papers of Charles Sumner, who served as chairman of the Senate committee on foreign relations from 1861 to 1871, are in the Harvard College Library. The Francis Lieber papers in the Huntington Library are of value for their discussions of many problems of international relations and international law of the civil war and reconstruction period (much on the " Trent " affair), by a professor of international law at Columbia, who was in frequent communica-

tion with Sumner. For description and evaluation of these papers, see C. B. Robson, " Papers of Francis Lieber ", *Huntington lib. bul.*, no. 3 (1933) 135–152 [**1890**].
Further more detailed suggestions for MSS. are given in following sections of this chapter.

2. Anglo-American (including Canadian) Relations

Bibliographical Aids

See Sec. 1, above. Jordan and Pratt (no. 2092), 273–288, for list of British pamphlets and books bearing on the civil war.

Special Works

George Bemis, *Hasty recognition of rebel belligerency; and our right to complain of it* (Boston, 1865) [**1891**]. Two addresses by Goldwin Smith, one of the greatest friends of the United States ever born in England: *England and America*, a lecture read before the Boston Fraternity and published in the *Atlantic Monthly* for December, 1864 (Boston, 1865) [**1892**]; and *The civil war in America*, an address read at the last meeting of the Manchester Union and Emancipation Society (London, 1866) [**1893**], a staunch defense of the American political system against attacks by the friends of absolutism and autocracy; and by the same writer, " England and the war of secession ", *Atlantic*, LXXXIX (1902) 303–311 [**1894**], an entirely sympathetic review. Mountague Bernard, *A historical account of the neutrality of Great Britain during the American civil war* (London, 1870) [**1895**], the author was professor of international law at Oxford, and agent of Great Britain in the Alabama claims arbitration. W. C. Teichmann, *Englands und Frankreichs Stellung zum Bürgerkriege in den Vereinigten Staaten von Amerika, 1861–65* (Munich, 1885) [**1896**], very inadequate. J. M. Callahan, " The northern lake frontier during the civil war ", *Am. hist. assoc. ann. rep.*, for 1896, v. I (1897) 335–359 [**1897**], incorporated in his *Neutrality of the American lakes* (no. 1642), neutrality of the Great Lakes as revealed in the archives of the Dept. of State and printed sources, but does not use Canadian archives. Smith, *England and America* (no. 1892). Charles Francis Adams, Jr., son of the minister to Great Britain, and brother to Brooks Adams and the historian Henry Adams, and one-time president of the Massachusetts Historical Society, made an extensive study of Anglo-American diplomacy during the civil war, based on official printed and MS. records of both governments and his father's diary and papers, and other private records in England and the United States. His researches are really the point of departure for the later special study (no. 1909) of Professor E. D. Adams (no relation) who was at one time associated with C. F. Adams, Jr., in his investigations. C. F. Adams, Jr., died before his work could be embodied in a projected biography of his father, but much of his work is left in the form of special essays published in the *Proceedings* of the Massachusetts Historical Society, and republished in other forms (see also Sec. 3) : " Queen Victoria and the civil war ", *Mass. hist. soc. proc.*, 2d ser., XVII (1903) 439-448; XVIII (1905) 123-154; XX (1907) 454-474, reprinted (" revised, largely recast and materially added to, as well as compressed "), in his *Studies, military and diplomatic* (N.Y., 1911) 375-413 [1898], this was written before the publication of the *Letters of Queen Victoria* (no. 1985). Also by the same author, "A crisis in Downing Street ", *Mass. hist. soc. proc.*, XLVII (1914) 372-424 [1899], a study of the decision of the British Cabinet (October 1862), and of C. F. Adams and the projected Anglo-French program of intervention in the American civil war. This article was also published separately (Boston, 1914) under title, *The crisis of foreign intervention in the war of secession, September-November 1862.* Also by C. F. Adams, " The British proclamation of May 1861 ", *Mass. hist. soc. proc.*, XLVIII (1915) 190-241 [1900], the proclamation concerning Confederate belligerancy, from material in the Public Record Office, the papers of Lord Lyons, and the Russell papers. Henry Clews, " England and Russia in our civil war ", *No. Am. rev.*, CLXXVIII (1904) 812-819 [1901], by citing a letter written to the author in 1889 by W. E. Gladstone, endeavors to show that England did not consider recognizing the Confederacy in 1862 (at which time we now know Gladstone was favorable to such a move). John Bigelow, *Lest we forget; Gladstone, Morley, and the Confederate loan of 1863* (N.Y., 1905) [1902] ventilates the " mysterious reserve " held by Gladstone's " distinguished biographer " as to that statesman's subscription to the Confederate loan. George Haven Putnam, " The London ' Times ' and the American civil war ", *Putnam's*, V (1908) 183-191 [1903], a helpful essay analyzing the " Times " columns for those years. Brooks Adams, " The seizure of the Laird rams ", *Mass.*

hist. soc. proc., XLV (1912) 243-333 [**1904**] uses official correspondence, C. F. Adams' *Diary*, and Morley's *Gladstone* as background for his relation of C. F. Adams' efforts to stop the rams from sailing and war from following. Lord Newton, *Lord Lyons; a record of British diplomacy* (London, 1913, 2 v.) [**1905**], a publication of the relevant private and official papers of the British minister in Washington, 1859-64, cleverly strung together by informing narrative. S. E. Baldwin, " The ' continuous voyage ' doctrine during the civil war, and now ", *Am. jour. internat. law*, IX (1915) 793-801 [**1906**]. Goebel, *Recognition policy* (no. 1038) studies the legal aspect of the question of the possible foreign recognition of the Confederacy. L. B. Schmidt, " The influence of wheat and cotton on Anglo-American relations during the civil war ", *Iowa jour. hist.*, XVI (1918) 400-439 [**1907**], the writer thinks English requirements for northern wheat, rather than for southern cotton, moulded English diplomacy toward the civil war; but see Owsley (no. 2117). Brougham Villiers (*pseud.* for F. J. Shaw) and W. H. Chesson, *Anglo-American relations, 1861-1865* (London, 1919) [**1908**], hands-across-the-sea type of historical essay. *Camb. hist. Br. for. pol.* (no 1879). E. D. Adams, *Great Britain and the American civil war* (London and N.Y., 1925, 2 v.) [**1909**], this is so far the most important work on the subject, though it must be supplemented and corrected by Owsley (no. 2177), and Baxter (no. 2006). Though the author presents the evidence he refuses to come to the unpleasant conclusion that what stopped Anglo-French diplomatic intervention in 1862 was the battle of Antietam. Based on British official and private archives. W. H. Dawson, *Richard Cobden and foreign policy* (London, 1926) [**1910**]. Helen G. Macdonald, *Canadian public opinion on the American civil war* (N.Y., 1926) [**1911**], digested from the essential parts of despatches, books, periodicals, and newspapers. Fred Landon, " The American civil war and Canadian confederation ", *Royal soc. Canad. trans.*, 3d ser., XXI, sec. 2 (1927) 55-62 [**1912**], how the spectacle of the civil war in the United States stimulated the movement for Canadian confederation. T. L. Harris, *America and England in 1861* (Baldwin City, Kans., 1928) [**1913**], a mimeographed thesis, based on printed sources, which certainly adds nothing to E. D. Adams. J. H. Kiger, " Federal government propaganda in Great Britain during the American civil war ", *Hist. outlook*, XIX (1928) 204-209 [**1914**].

a very useful summary of the activities of Thurlow Weed, W. M. Evarts, A. D. White, R. J. Walker, and other agents of Unionist propaganda in England; and of the efforts in that direction, in England and France of regularly accredited diplomatic officials. Keenleyside, *Canada and U.S.* (no. 896), for the American civil war and the Fenian raids. F. H. Underhill, " Canada's relations with the empire as seen by the Toronto Globe, 1857–1867 ", *Canad. hist. rev.*, X (1929) 106–128 [1915], the *Globe* was the outstanding newspaper in Upper Canada at the time. Owsley, *King Cotton diplomacy* (no. 2177). E. H. Pieper, *The Fenian movement* (Urbana, Ill., 1931) [1916], abstract of thesis (Ph.D.), University of Illinois; the author used files of the Department of State, newspaper organs of the Fenian brotherhood, proceedings of conventions, and printed controversial sources. A. E. Taylor, " Walker's financial mission to London on behalf of the North, 1863–1864 ", *Jour. econ. and business hist.*, III (1931) 296–320 [1917], R. J. Walker, an antislavery southerner, and financier of ability, was sent to Europe by Secretary of the Treasury Chase to maintain the credit of the United States abroad, and to strike whenever possible at the Confederate position in European financial circles. D. C. Masters, " Reciprocity and the genesis of Canadian commercial policy ", *Canad. hist. rev.*, XIII (1932) 418–428 [1918], intensive study of Canadian archives which shows how Canada constructed the framework of a commercial policy in 1864. J. P. Smith, *The republican expansionists of the early reconstruction era* (Chicago, 1933) [1918a], a modest and valuable analysis of Canadian-American relations, 1864–1867, based on a considerable amount of hitherto unexploited material. W. O. Henderson, *The Lancashire cotton famine, 1861–1865* (Manchester, Eng., 1934) [1918b], a scholarly analysis of the causes and consequences of the cotton famine, showing that it was not due solely to the civil war, but complicated by the overproduction of 1859–60.

For biographies of President Lincoln, Secretary of State Seward, and C. F. Adams, minister to Great Britain, see relevant entries and bibliographical data in the *D.A.B.* Note also, J. T. Adams, *The Adams family* (Boston, 1930) [1919].

For biographies of British statesmen (Lord Palmerston, Earl Russell, Lord Lyons, John Bright, W. E. Gladstone, Lord Granville, Duke of Argyll, Disraeli, W. H. Russell, correspondent of the London *Times* in the United States, and of Queen Victoria) and others, see the relevant entries and bibliographical data in the *D.N.B.* More recent biographical writings are: *Life and correspondence of John Duke Lord Coleridge, Lord Chief Justice of England*, written and ed. by Ernest Hartley Coleridge (London, 1904, 2 v.) **[1920]**. John Morley, *Life of Richard Cobden* (London, 1908) **[1921]**. G. M. Trevelyan, *The life of John Bright* (Boston and N.Y., 1913) **[1922]**. J. A. Hobson, *Richard Cobden, the international man* (N.Y. and London, 1919) **[1923]**. Newton, *Lord Lyons* (no. 1905). Lytton Strachey, *Queen Victoria* (London and N.Y., 1921) **[1924]**. Sir Arthur Hardinge, *The life of Henry Howard Molyneux Herbert, fourth Earl of Carnarvon, 1831–1890*, ed. by Elisabeth Countess of Carnarvon (London, 1925, 3 v.) **[1925]**. Dawson, *Cobden* (no. 1910). Philip Guedalla, *Palmerston* [1] (London, 1926) **[1926]**. A. Wyatt Tilby, *Lord John Russell* (London, 1930) **[1927]**, with a chapter on " The Alabama."

O. D. Skelton, *The life and times of Sir Alexander Tilloch Galt* (Toronto, 1920) **[1928]** is the biography of a Canadian statesman (minister of finance in the 1850's and 1860's) who took an active part in reciprocity negotiations and other Canadian-American matters. Pope's *Macdonald* (no. 2494), Macdonald was first prime minister of the Dominion of Canada, 1867–1873, and 1878–1891.

Printed Sources

See Sec. 1, above, for general collections and for political pamphlets. See also Sec. 3, below.

For guide to British official documents (state papers, *Parliamentary debates, Brit. and for. state papers*, etc.), see below, p. 838. British Parliamentary (sessional) papers: *Correspondence respecting the case of the fugitive slave Anderson* (Commons, 1861, LXIV) **[1929]**. *Correspondence relating to the civil war in the United States of North America* (Commons, 1862, LXII, and Lords, 1862, XXV) **[1930]**. *Correspondence relating to the civil war in the United States of North America* (Commons, 1863, LXXII, and Lords, 1863, XXIX) **[1931]**. *Account of guns and other munitions of war shipped from Liverpool to America during 1861 and 1862* . . . (Commons, 1864, LVIII) **[1932]**. *Correspondence respecting the capture of the " Saxon " by U.S. ship " Vanderbilt "* (Commons,

---

[1] Professor H. C. Bell, of Wesleyan University, Middletown, Conn., has nearly ready for publication a biography of Palmerston, based on much new material.

1864, LXII) [1933]. *Correspondence respecting enlistment of British seamen* . . . (Commons, 1864, LXII) [1934]. *Correspondence respecting recruitment in Ireland for military service of United States* (Commons, 1864, LXII) [1935]. *Return of claims of British subjects against the U.S. gov't., from commencement of civil war to 31st March, 1864* (Commons, 1864, LXII) [1936]. *Correspondence respecting enlistment of British subjects in U.S. army* (Commons, 1864, LXII) [1937]. *Correspondence respecting attack on St. Albans, Vermont, and naval force on North American Lakes* (Commons, 1865, LVII) [1938]. *Correspondence on cessation of civil war in North America* (Commons, 1865, LVII) [1939]. *Correspondence respecting proclamation issued by U.S. President, 22nd May, 1865* (Commons, 1865, LVII) [1940]. *Despatch from Mr. Seward to Mr. Adams, arising out of the late civil war in the United States* (Commons, 1867, LXXIII) [1941]. *Correspondence respecting British and American claims arising out of the late civil war in the United States* (Commons, 1867, LXXIV; 1867–68, LXXIII) [1942]. These are reprinted, with important material, in the 7 vol. Appendix to the British *Case* (no. 2531).

British Parliamentary (sessional) papers regarding the termination of the Canadian reciprocity treaty: *Despatch from Lord Lyons respecting reciprocity treaty* (Commons, 1862, LXII) [1943]; and *Papers respecting the termination of the reciprocity treaty of June 5, 1854, between Great Britain and the United States* (Commons, 1865, LVII) [1944]. Canadian Parliamentary papers: *Return of an address of the Legislative Assembly, dated 28th March, 1860, for copy of correspondence which may have taken place in reference to the working of, or the repealing of, the reciprocity treaty, Apr. 3, 1860* (Canada. Parliament. Sess, pap., v. IV. 3rd sess. of the 6th Parl., Sess. 1860) [1945] and *Report of the Minister of Finance on the reciprocity treaty with the United States,* . . . Mar. 28, 1862 (*ibid.,* 1st sess. of the 7th Parl., Sess. 1862), prepared by Sir Alexander Galt [1946]. *Correspondence between the government of Canada and the United States or the British ambassador at Washington, and* . . . *despatches from the Home government, and orders in council, on the subject of the reciprocity treaty,* Feb. 17, 1865 (Canada. Parliament. Sess. pap., 1865, no. 26) [1947]. *Correspondence relating to the Fenian invasion, and the rebellion of the southern states* (Ottawa, 1869) [**1948**], a document published by the Dept. of the Secretary of State, of Canada.

T. C. Grattan, *England and the disrupted states of America* (London, 1861) [**1949**], author was formerly British consul in Massachusetts. C. G. Loring and E. W. Field, *Correspondence on the present relations between Great Britain and the United States of America* (Boston, 1862) [**1950**], correspondence between an English lawyer (E. W. Field) and an American lawyer (C. G. Loring). Also by C. G. Loring, *Neutral relations of England and the United States* (Boston, 1863) [**1951**], written to justify American complaints of breaches of neutrality because of English aid to Confederate ships-of-war; and *England's liability for indemnity* (Boston, 1864) [**1952**], a rebuttal to " Historicus ", exculpations printed in the London *Times*. " Historicus " was the pseudonym used by Sir William Vernon-Harcourt. J. S. Mill, *The contest in America* (Boston, 1862) [**1953**]. James Spence, *On the recognition of the southern confederation*, 2d ed. (London, 1862) [**1954**] argues for recognition of the Confederate States. W. H. Russell, *Diary* (no. 1889), see also his despatches to the London *Times*. Boston, Board of Trade, Special Committee, *The reciprocity treaty between the United States and Great Britain of June 5, 1854;* report of a special committee of the Boston Board of Trade submitted and adopted Jan. 2, 1865, and ordered to form a part of the eleventh annual report (Boston, 1865) [**1955**], committee: Lorenzo Sabine and others. Arthur Harvey, *The reciprocity treaty; its advantages to the United States and Canada* (Quebec, 1865) [**1956**], a prize essay. Joseph Howe, *The reciprocity treaty, its history, general features, and commercial results;* a speech by the Hon. Joseph Howe of Nova Scotia, July 14, 1865, at the Great International Commercial Convention, at Detroit (Hamilton, Ont., 1865) [**1957**], a plea for continuance of reciprocity. Two publications issued by the Treasury Department: *A preliminary report on the treaty of reciprocity with Great Britain, to regulate the trade between the United States and the provinces of British North America* (Wash., 1866) [**1958**], report on the treaty about to expire, prepared by E. H. Derby, special agent; and *Canadian non-intercourse*, reply by Secretary of the Treasury to inquiry by foreign affairs committee of the House of Representatives (Wash., 1867) [**1959**]. Great Britain, Neutrality Laws Commission, *Report of the Neu-*

trality laws commissioners (London, 1868) [1960] includes " regulations and instructions published by Her Majesty's Government
during the civil war in America." John Bright, *Speeches on questions of public policy*, ed. by J. E. T. Rogers (London, 1868, 2 v.)
[1961] has 7 speeches on relations with America, 1861–67. *John
Bright and the American civil war*, ed. by L. V. Roth (Boston, 1900)
(Old South Leaflets, no. 218) [1962], extracts from letters and
speeches of John Bright. "Letters of John Bright, 1861–1862 ",
Mass. hist. soc. proc., XLV (1912) 148–159 [1963]; and " Bright-
Sumner letters, 1861–1872 ", *ibid.*, XLVI (1913) 93–166 [1964], let-
ters to Charles Sumner, from the Sumner papers in Harvard College
Library. Trevelyan, *John Bright* (no. 1922) includes numerous
extracts from his letters describing the British attitude towards the
United States. *The diaries of John Bright*, ed. by Philip Bright
(London, 1930) [1965] has extracts from his diary describing his
campaign for the cause of the North. Lord John Russell, *Recollections and suggestions, 1813–1873* (Boston, 1875) [1966]. Sir
Spencer Walpole, *The life of Lord John Russell* (London and N.Y.,
1891, 2 v.) [1967] includes numerous extracts from Russell's writings
in regard to the war. *The later correspondence of Lord John
Russell, 1840–1878*, ed. by G. P. Gooch (London and N.Y., 1925)
[1968] has practically nothing on American affairs. We understand this otherwise admirable edition has overlooked several important letters in the Russell papers. Evelyn Ashley,
*The life and correspondence of Henry John Temple, Viscount
Palmerston* (London, 1879, 2 v.) [1969]. A. T. Rice, "A famous
diplomatic dispatch ", *No. Am. rev.*, CXLII (1886) 402–410 [1970–1]
reproduces the original despatch of Seward, as corrected by Lincoln,
conveying to C. F. Adams, minister in London, his first full instructions after the outbreak of the war. T. H. Dudley, *Diplomatic
relations with England* (no. 2078), colorful recollections of men and
measures. *Memorials . . .* by Roundell Palmer, Earl of Selborne (London and N.Y., 1896–98, 2 v. in 4) [1972]. " Letters of Richard Cobden to Charles Sumner, 1862–1865 ", *Am. hist. rev.*, II (1897) 306–319
[1973] discuss the attitude in England toward the war and interviews
with Lord Russell. Coleridge, *Life and corres. Lord Coleridge* (no.
1920) has 16 letters to and from Coleridge regarding the American
civil war, 1861–1866. *Forty years of friendship as recorded in the
correspondence of John Duke. Lord Coleridge, and Ellis Yarnall*

during the years 1856 to 1895, ed. by Charlton Yarnall (London, 1911) [**1974**], Yarnall was the American correspondent of the *Guardian*, the leading church paper in England during the civil war. Sir Spencer Walpole, *The history of twenty-five years* (London, 1904–08, 4 v.) [**1975**]. *George Douglass, eighth Duke of Argyll, K.G., K.T. (1823–1900); autobiography and memoirs*, ed. by Dowager Duchess of Argyll (London, 1906, 2 v.) [**1976**] has letters to and from John Morley, Gladstone, and others regarding the war. "Letters of the Duke and Duchess of Argyll to Charles Sumner", ed. by H. G. Pearson, *Mass. hist. soc. proc.*, XLVII (1914) 66–106 [**1977**], letters of 1861–66, discuss in particular the escape of the "Alabama" and the attitude of the foreign secretary, Lord Russell. Sir H. E. Maxwell, *The life and letters of George William Frederick, fourth Earl of Clarendon* (London, 1913) [**1978**] contains occasional desultory reflections on American affairs by the Chancellor for the Duchy of Lancaster. Lord Newton, *Lord Lyons* (no. 1905) contains hitherto unpublished correspondence of the British minister in Washington during the civil war. J. W. Foster, *Limitation of armament on the Great Lakes* (Wash.: Carnegie Endowment for International Peace, 1914) [**1979**], correspondence of 1864–65, regarding projected termination of the agreement of 1818. "Extracts from the diary of Benjamin Moran, 1860–1868", *Mass. hist. soc. proc.*, XLVIII (1915) 431–492 [**1980**], Moran was secretary of the American legation in London. "Letters of Goldwin Smith to Charles Eliot Norton [1863–1872]", *ibid.*, XLIX (1916) 107–160 [**1981**], some discuss the attitude of the English toward America during the war. "Earl Granville to C. A. Spring Rice", *ibid.*, XLIX (1916) 62 [**1982**], letter written Apr. 10, 1887, regarding the attitude of the British cabinet in respect to the recognition of the Confederacy. *The education of Henry Adams; an autobiography* (Boston, 1918?) [**1983**] contains a few philosophical comments of political significance relating to his sojourn in England as his father's (C. F. Adams) secretary during the war. Ford, *Adams letters* (no. 5178). *Correspondence of Sir J. A. Macdonald* (no. 2509). Edith J. Archibald, *Life and letters of Sir Edward Mortimer Archibald . . .; a memoir of fifty years of service* (Toronto, 1924) [**1984**], British consul at New York, 1857–1883, describes his watching and reporting of the Fenian conspiracy. *The letters of Queen Victoria. Second series. A selection from Her*

Majesty's correspondence and journal between the years 1862 and 1878, published by authority of His Majesty the King, ed. by G. E. Buckle (London, 1926–28, 3 v.) **[1985]**. *The Palmerston papers; Gladstone and Palmerston; being the correspondence of Lord Palmerston and Mr. Gladstone, 1851–1865,* ed. by Philip Guedalla (London, 1928) **[1986]** contains correspondence dealing with the war in the United States. *The Paris embassy during the Second Empire; selections from the papers of Henry Richard Charles Wellesley, 1st Earl of Cowley, ambassador at Paris, 1852–1867,* ed. by his son, Colonel the Hon. F. A. Wellesley (London, 1928; Am. edition, N.Y., 1929) (under title, *Secrets of the Second Empire*) **[1987]**, for problems of Anglo-French policy toward the American civil war. " The Lyons-Seward treaty of 1862 ", ed. by A. T. Milne, *Am. hist. rev.,* XXXVIII (1933) 511–525 **[1988–9]** publishes correspondence from British archives showing that the Anglo-American treaty of 1862 concerning the African slave trade was the result of American initiative, rather than of British, as commonly supposed.

For the printed writings of President Lincoln, Secretary of State Seward, C. F. Adams, minister to England, and of other personalities (see note regarding biographies on p. 324), see our list on p. 756.

MSS.: Suggestions

For guides and indexes to official American and British diplomatic correspondence and archives (also French and other European archives), see Pt. II, ch. 3. For Canadian archives, see p. 896. The Library of Congress now has a complete photostatic reproduction of the main despatches and instructions of the British ministers in the United States, 1806–1870, inclusive, and of the correspondence between the British minister in Washington and the Governor-General of Canada, 1791–1875.

In addition to the papers of Presidents Lincoln and Johnson, and Secretary of State Seward, important collections of the private papers of American, British, and Canadian statesmen and diplomatists are preserved. The papers of Charles Francis Adams (minister to England, 1861–67) are among the (interdicted) Adams papers now deposited in the Massachusetts Historical Society. The papers (about 5,000 pieces) of Thomas Haines Dudley, U.S. consul at Liverpool, 1861–72, and some of the vice-consul, Henry Wilding, are in the Huntington Library at San Marino, California, and include much material in regard to the construction of Confederate cruisers, and claims on that account. The Library of Congress has the very important diary of Benjamin Moran, successively clerk, assistant-secretary, and chargé of the United States legation in London (printed extracts in no. 1980), 1851–74, with day-to-day record of the legation's business, and valuable sidelights on Anglo-American diplomacy.

Of English statesmen who had a hand in American affairs we may note: the papers of Queen Victoria, preserved, as royal archives, in the Round Tower of Windsor Castle (partly printed in no. 1985); Palmerston, see above, p. 229; Gladstone, at Hawarden Castle, Hawarden, Flintshire; Lord Lyons (British minister at Washington, 1859–64), at Old Norfolk House, St. James' Square, London; Earl Russell (British minister of foreign affairs), at the Public Record Office; Sir A. H. Layard (under-secretary of state for foreign affairs, 1861–66), with Lords Russell and Palmerston, 1861; with Sir William Stuart, secretary of legation in Washington, 1863–65; and other letters and papers relating to the American civil war, in the British Museum (Add. MSS. 38987–38996).

Noteworthy pertinent collections of MSS. at the Canadian archives are: Papers of Sir John A. Macdonald, first prime minister of the Dominion of Canada; and the Baring papers; both for commercial affairs. Note also the *Inventory of the military documents in the Canadian archives* (no. 5617). The private papers of Sir Alexander T. Galt, Canadian minister of finance during this period, who was active in the reciprocity negotiations, are in the possession of his son, Elliott T. Galt, of Montreal.

3. Neutral Rights and Maritime Law [2]

Bibliographical Aids

See Sec. 1, above.

Harbeck, *Bibliog. U.S. Navy* (no. 791). Boston Public Library, *Freedom of the seas* (no. 4392).

---

[2] See also Secs. 2, 4, and 5. For arbitration of the "Alabama" claims, see Ch. XVI, sec. 2. It is announced in the *Am. hist. rev.,* XXXVII (July 1932), 829, that Prof. F. L. Owsley is preparing (assisted by a subvention from the Social Science Research Council) a publication on the United States and the Freedom of the Seas, 1861–1865.

Special Works

Gideon Welles, " The capture and release of Mason and Slidell ", *Galaxy*, XV (1873) 640–651 [1990]. J. R. Soley, *The blockade and the cruisers* (N.Y., 1883) [1991], the first and one of the best descriptions of the blockade; must now be supplemented by E. D. Adams (no. 1909), Baxter (no. 2006), and Owsley (no. 2117). T. L. Harris, *The Trent affair, including a review of English and American relations at the beginning of the civil war* (Indianapolis, 1896) [1992], according to C. F. Adams, Jr., who had studied the matter very considerably, this is a very complete review of the essential facts of the case; but it should now be supplemented by Baxter (no. 2006). F. R. Stark, *The abolition of privateering and the Declaration of Paris* (N.Y., 1897) [1993], a Columbia University dissertation, written without benefit of the pertinent unprinted archives, but a useful summary. A. Constable, " Comment on the Trent affair ", *Westminster rev.*, CLVIII (1902) 640–642 [1994], takes issue with Harris' book (no. 1913). See also a " Rejoinder ", by A. P. Gilmour, *ibid.*, CLIX (1903) 338–340 [1995]. Four studies by C. F. Adams, who had access to the papers of his father, the minister, and other extensive sources: " A historical residuum ", in his *Studies, military and diplomatic* (N.Y., 1911) 344–374 [1996], this paper is printed under the title " The Laird rams " in the *Proceedings* of the Massachusetts Historical Society, 2d ser., XIII (1900) 177–197, and in its present form has been recast, abbreviated in parts, and elsewhere developed by the use of new material since brought to light; " The seizure of the Laird rams ", *Mass. hist. soc. proc.*, XLV (1912) 243–333 [1997]; *Seward and the Declaration of Paris; a forgotten diplomatic episode, April-August, 1861* (Boston, 1912), reprinted from the *Proceedings* of the Massachusetts Historical Society, XLVI (1913) 23–84 [1998], after lengthy analysis of the negotiation, based on printed sources and Adams papers, considers Seward's diplomacy in the premises as ill-considered, not creditable, and, in short, emotional; and " The Trent affair ", *Mass. hist. soc. proc.*, XLV (1912) 35–148 [1999] adds little to the essential facts or conclusions presented by Harris (no. 1913), but has some interesting observations on the psychological reaction of the North to Capt. Wilkes' seizure of Mason and Slidell. R. H. Dana, *The Trent affair; an aftermath* (Cambridge, 1912) [2000], from the

Proceedings of the Massachusetts Historical Society, XLV (1912) 508–522, is an answer to a paper by C. F. Adams (no. 1999) emphasizing that his father, R. H. Dana, Jr., must have meant legal according to British precedent, when he exclaimed to C. F. Adams, Jr., in 1862, that the seizure was legal. This is followed by a note in reply by Mr. Adams, confirming his recollection by his diary. Helio Lobo, *Cousas diplomaticas* (no. 1272), 81–212, for account of the Confederate cruisers in Brazilian waters. Sir F. T. Piggott, *The Declaration of Paris, 1856; a study, documented* (London, 1919) [2001], by an inveterate proponent of classical British traditions of maritime practice. J. W. Pratt, " The British blockade and American precedents ", *U.S. naval inst. proc.*, XLVI (1920) 1789–1802 [2002], a cogent elucidation and commentary on the significance of the principal civil war cases (*Bermuda, Springbok, Peterhoff*) for Anglo-American diplomacy in regard to the British blockade during the world war. Albert Gleaves, " The affair of the Blanche (October 7, 1862), an incident of the civil war ", *ibid.*, XLVIII (1922) 1661–1676 [2003], destruction of the Confederate blockade runner *Blanche* by the U.S. cruiser *Montgomery*, with brief account of the diplomatic controversy with Spain subsequent upon violation of her neutral jurisdiction. Hyde, *International law* (no. 4810). J. E. G. de Montmorency, " Sea-policy and the Alabama claims, 1861–1907 ", in the *Camb. hist. Brit. for. pol.*, v. III (1923) 54–71 [2004]. E. D. Adams, *Gt. Brit. and Am. civil war* (no. 1909). Cleven, *James Watson Webb* (no. 3965) touches lightly the subject of the Confederate cruisers in Brazilian waters. Briggs, *Continuous voyage* (no. 808). Three works by J. P. Baxter, 3rd: " The British government and neutral rights, 1861–1865 ", *Am. hist. rev.*, XXXIV (1928) 9–29 [2006] examined instruction of Admiral Milne—shows he was instructed to acquiesce in the blockade, to provide a useful precedent for future British wars; and by the same author, " Some British opinions as to neutral rights, 1861 to 1865 ", *Am. jour. internat. law*, XXIII (1929) 517–537 [2007] uses new material including opinions of the law officers of the Crown, and the correspondence between the Admiralty and the Foreign Office, and between the Admiralty and the commander in chief in American waters; and *The introduction of the ironclad warship* (Cambridge, 1933) [2008], a masterly technical study; the parts

of the volume that treat of the effect of the new naval inventions
upon foreign relations in the late fifties and early sixties are especially valuable to the student of Anglo-American diplomacy during
the civil war. Van Alstyne, *Right of search and slave trade* (no.
1845). Owsley (no. 2117) concludes that "Old Abe" sold his
country's "birthright for a mess of pottage", by proclaiming and
persisting in a blockade which, the author argues, was ineffective;
ignores Baxter's important contribution (no. 2006) on British
policy and the American blockade. Hill, *U.S. and Brazil* (no. 1277),
more thorough account of Confederate cruisers in Brazilian waters.
T. A. Bailey, *Trent affair* (no. 4463). Savage, *U.S. maritime policy*
(no. 22).

Printed Sources

For general collections, see Sec. 1, above. Particularly, for published United States diplomatic correspondence (in part) relating
to neutral rights, see *For. relations* (no. 5345) for years 1860-1865.
For special collections dealing with the "Trent", see below (nos.
2031-2037). Other noteworthy special publications of documents
are: *Correspondence between the State Department and the representative of Her Britannic Majesty's government in relation to
the capture of British vessels sailing from one British port to
another, having on board articles contraband of war for the use
of the so-called Confederate States* (37th Cong., 3d sess. Sen.
Ex. doc. no. 27) [**2009**]. *Dockyards and ironworks of Great Britain
and France. Letter from the Secretary of the Navy, in answer to
a resolution of the House of 20th instant, transmitting report of
Chief Engineer King, as also May, in relation to iron-clad vessels
and dockyards of Europe* (38th Cong., 2d sess. House. Ex. doc.
no. 14) [**2010**].

British Parliamentary (House of Commons sessional) papers relating to various phases of neutral rights and maritime law: *Letter
from Foreign Office to Admiralty, Colonial, War, and India offices,
interdicting armed cruisers and privateers whether of the U.S.A.
or so-styled Confederate States, from carrying prizes into British
ports, 1 June 1861* (1861, XXXVIII) [**2011**]. *Correspondence with
the United States respecting blockade* (1861, LXV) [**2012**]. *Correspondence relative to the overtures addressed to contending parties
in the United States with a view to adhesion to principles of mari-*

time law, as laid down by Congress of Paris in 1856 (1862, LXII) **[2013]**. *Despatch from Lord Lyons respecting obstruction of southern harbours* (1862, LXII) **[2014]**. *Papers relating to blockade of the ports of Confederate States* (1862, LXII) **[2015]**. *Papers respecting " Emily St. Pierre ", of Liverpool* (1862, LXII) **[2016]**. *Correspondence respecting instructions given to U.S. naval officers in regard to neutral vessels and mails* (1863, LXXII) **[2017]**. *Correspondence with Mr. Adams respecting neutral rights and duties* (1863, LXXII) **[2018]**. *Correspondence respecting despatch of letters by private ships to Matamoras* (1863, LXXII) **[2019]**. *Letters or other communications between collector of customs at Liverpool and any department of the government in reference to detention of vessel " Gibraltar "* (1863, LXXII) **[2020]**. *Correspondence respecting trade with Matamoras* (1863, LXXII) **[2021]**. *Additional instructions to colonial governors on the subject of belligerent cruisers* (1864, XL) **[2022]**. *Correspondence respecting the "Alabama " (in continuation of correspondence presented to Parliament in March 1863)* (1864, LXII) **[2023]**. *Communications between collector of customs at Liverpool and Messrs. Klingenden and co., respecting shipment of guns on board the " Gibraltar "* (1864, LXII) **[2024]**. *Correspondence respecting iron-clad vessels building at Birkenhead* (1864, LXII) **[2025]**. *Correspondence respecting the " Tuscaloosa "* (1864, LXII) **[2026]**. *Papers on seizure of the U.S.'s steamer " Chesapeake "* (1864, LXII) **[2027]**. *Correspondence respecting the " Shenandoah "* (1866, LXXV) **[2028]**. *Correspondence between Her Majesty's government and Messrs. Laird brothers* (London, 1864) **[2029]**. *Correspondence respecting the seizure of the British vessels " Springbok " and " Peterhoff " by United States cruisers in 1863* (1900, CV (Cd. 34)) **[2030]**, correspondence of 1863–66.

The following sources relate specifically to the Trent affair: (U.S. official documents)—*Correspondence between the Secretary of State and the authorities of Great Britain and France in relation to the recent removal of certain citizens of the United States from the British mail-steamer Trent* (Wash., 1862) (37th Cong., 2d sess. Sen. Ex. doc. 8) **[2031]**. *Correspondence between the governments of the United States and Great Britain in relation to the British mail-steamer Trent* (37th Cong., 2d sess. House. Ex. doc. 46) **[2032]**, not identical with no. 2031 above. *Correspondence between the min-*

*ister from Austria and the Secretary of State of the United States, in
relation to the taking of certain citizens of the United States from
on board the British steamer Trent* (1862) (37th Cong., 2d sess. Sen.
Ex. doc. 14) [**2033**]. *Correspondence between the minister of Prussia and the Secretary of State, in relation to the . . . Trent* (1862)
(37th Cong., 2d sess. Sen. Ex. doc. 18) [**2034**]. *Translation of an
instruction to the minister of His Majesty the King of Italy accredited to this government, and a copy of a note to that minister
from the Secretary of State, relating to the . . . Trent* (1862) (37th
Cong., 2d sess. Sen. Ex. doc. 30) [**2035**]. " Notes of Austria,
France, and Prussia to the United States regarding the Trent affair, 1861 ", *Am. jour. internat. law*, X, supplement (1916) 67–72
[**2036**], (1) M. Thouvenel to Mr. Mercier, Paris, Dec. 3, 1861; (2)
Count Bernstorff to Baron Gerolt, Berlin, Dec. 25, 1861; (3) Count
Rechberg to M. de Hulsemann, Vienna, Dec. 18, 1861. British Parliamentary papers: *Correspondence respecting seizure of Messrs.
Mason, Slidell, M'Farland, and Eustis from on board the Royal mail
packet Trent by commander of U.S.'s ship " San Jacinto "* (London,
1862) (Commons, 1862, LXII) [**2037**].

For commentary on the Trent affair, see J. G. Phillimore,
Case of the seizure of the southern envoys, reprinted, with
additions, from the " Saturday Review " (London, 1861) [**2038**].
The case of the Trent examined (London, 1862) [**2039**]. Edwin De
Leon, *Three letters from a South Carolinian relating to secession,
slavery, and the Trent case* (London, 1862) [**2040**]. Comte A. de
Gasparin, *A word of peace on the American question* (London,
1862) [**2041**], a translation of the writer's *Une parole de paix sur
le différend entre l'Angleterre et les Etats-Unis* (Paris, 1861).
Giovanni de Gionnis, *Sull' arresto dei commissari americani del
Sud, Mason e Slidell a bordo del legno inglese* (Cagliari, 1862)
[**2042**]. H. W. Lord, *The highway of the seas in time of war*
(Cambridge, Eng., 1862) [**2043**]. *Maritime capture*, by a lawyer
(London, 1862) [**2044**]. Heinrich von Marquardsen, *Der Trent-
Fall* (Erlangen, 1862) [**2045**]. Joel Parker, *International law, case
of the Trent* (Cambridge, Mass., 1862) [**2046**]. P. A. Smith, *The
seizure of the southern commissioners considered with reference to
international law* (London, 1862) [**2047**]. David Urquhart, *Analysis of M. Thouvenel's despatch* (London, 1862) [**2048**]. Sir William Vernon-Harcourt, *Letters by Historicus on some questions of*

international law, reprinted from "The Times" with considerable addition (London, 1863) [**2049**], written under the pseudonym of "Historicus." C. G. Loring, *Neutral relations* (no. 1951), and *Remarks on the letter of "Historicus"* (no. 1952), a rebuttal to the exculpations in the *Letters by Historicus* (no. 2049). A. M. Costi, *Memoir of the Trent affair* (Wash., 1865) [**2050**].

For civil war prize cases before the Supreme Court of the United States, see J. W. Wallace's *Cases argued and adjudged in the Supreme Court of the United States, 1863–1874* (Wash., 1870–76, 23 v.) [**2051**] (notably the *Bermuda,* III, 514; the *Springbok,* V, 1; the *Peterhoff,* V, 28). District Court of the United States for the Southern District of New York, *The United States vs. The bark Springbok and her cargo. In prize. Opinion of the court, by Judge Betts* (N.Y., 1863) [**2052**]. *The seizure of the "Peterhoff"; being a statement of the facts, the reason, the law, and the consequences, with the correspondence* (London, 1863) [**2053**]. *Papers relating to the condemnation of the British barque "Springbok" and her cargo, by the District court of New York, U.S., with the opinions of the press thereon* (London: Printed for the owners, 1864) [**2054**]. *Papers relating to the illegal seizure of the British barque "Springbok", by an American cruiser, and the wrongful condemnation of her cargo by the Supreme Court of the United States* (London: Printed for the owners, 1868) [**2055**]. *Judgments des cours de prises des États-Unis d'Amérique dans l'affaire de la barque anglaise "Springbok" et de son chargement, commentés par D.C.L.* (Paris, 187–?) [**2056**]. *Correspondence respecting the seizure of the British vessels "Springbok" and "Peterhoff" by United States' cruisers in 1863* (London, 1900) (Parliament. Papers by Command. Cd. 34) [**2057**]. Thomas Baty, ed., *Prize law and continuous voyage; containing . . . Brief in the Springbok case, by the Hon. W. M. Evarts, sometime state secretary. Analysis of the Springbok judgment, by D.C.L.* (London, 1915) [**2058**].

Professor Mountague Bernard, who held the newly established chair of international law at Oxford, later was one of the commissioners who signed the treaty of Washington, 1871, and who helped to present the British case at Geneva, wrote during the war the following brochures which reflect contemporary British judicial opinion: *On the principle of nonintervention;* a lecture delivered in the hall of All Souls' College (Oxford and London, 1860) [**2059**].

Two lectures on the present American war (Oxford and London, 1861) [**2060**]. *Notes on some questions suggested by the case of the "Trent"* (Oxford, 1862) [**2061**]. *A lecture on alleged violations of neutrality by England in the present war* (London, 1863) [**2062**]. *Four lectures on subjects connected with diplomacy* (London, 1868) [**2063**]. *Neutrality of Great Britain* (no. 1895). L. B. Hautefeuille, *Quelques questions de droit international maritime à propos de la guerre d'Amérique* (Leipzig and Paris, 1861) [**2064**]. Joel Parker, *The domestic and foreign relations of the United States* (Cambridge, 1862) [**2065**], also published in the *North American review*, XCIV (1862) 196–258, on maritime law and civil war incidents, by a Harvard Law School professor. David Urquhart, *Answer to Mr. Cobden on the assimilation of war and peace. Also analysis of the correspondence with the United States, showing the Declaration of Paris to have been violated by England and France* (London, 1862) [**2066**]. " Vopros o blokadîe morskikh beregov, voznikshiĭ po povodu voĭny v Severo-Amerikanskikh Shtatakh " [The question of the blockade of sea coasts with relation to the war in the United States], *Morskoĭ Sbornik* [The Naval review], no. 8 (1862) 33–43 (supplement) [**2067**], a criticism of the United States government for action contrary to the principles of international law that a blockade should be effective. F. M. Edge, *The destruction of the American carrying trade;* a letter to Earl Russell, K.G., Her Majesty's principal secretary of state for the foreign department (London, 1863; 2d ed., London, 1864) [**2068**], an analysis by an Englishman of the formidable damage done by the Confederate cruisers built in England, which gives strong support for later American argument for " indirect damages." F. W. Gibbs, *The foreign enlistment act* (London, 1863, 2d ed.) [**2069**] opines that the act prevents the ports of England from being made either directly or indirectly stations of hostility. J. E. Cairnes, *England's neutrality in the American contest* (London, 1864) [**2070**], a professor of jurisprudence and political economy in Queen's College, Galway, discourses not on what the law is (*i.e.* uncertain), but what it ought to be, by a revised statute. Sir Hugh Cairns, *Claim asserted by the government to detain ships upon suspicion;* a speech delivered in the House of Commons, February 23, 1864 (London, 1864) [**2071**]. [William Vernon-Harcourt] " Historicus ", *American neutrality* (N.Y., 1865), reprinted from *The*

Times [London], December 22, 1864 [**2072**], an argument for the correctness of British neutrality, based on American examples in 1818, 1819. *The foreign enlistment acts of England and America; the "Alexandra" and the rams*, by " Vigilans " (London, 1864) [**2073**], an anonymous " layman's " plea for no interruption. James Lorimer, *The rights and duties of belligerents and neutrals* (Edinburgh, 1865) [**2074**]. " O neĭtralītetiê Anglī v posliêdneĭ voĭne Soedīnennykh Shtatov " [Concerning the neutrality of England in the late United States' war], *Morskoĭ Sbornīk* [The Naval review], no. 7 (July 1865) 1–18 (supplement) [**2075**], comments on the Alabama case, stating that if England had broken her pledge of neutrality by arming ships, the United States government had relieved England of its pledge by making recruitments in Ireland. " Narushīla-lī Angliïâ svorĭ neĭtralītet v diêliê Shenandoah? [Did England break her pledge of neutrality in the affair of the Shenandoah?], *ibid.* (1866), no. 2, 1–7 [**2076**], comments on an article in the *British nautical magazine*, with the conclusion that England did not break her pledge of neutrality in the affair of the *Shenandoah*. *Rept. Neutrality laws commissioners* (no. 1960). *Casual papers upon the "Alabama" and kindred questions and, incidentally, upon national amenities*, 2d ed. (Hongkong, 1869) [**2077**], first published in the Hongkong *Daily Press*, 1862–65. Gideon Welles, *Lincoln and Seward* (N.Y., 1874) [**2077a**], an analysis, by the secretary of the navy, of Seward's policy which would have desired, if the exigencies of war permitted, to be circumspect toward neutrals in order to preserve the future position of the United States as a neutral. Thouvenel, *Secret de l'Empereur* (no. 2207), correspondence of the French minister of foreign affairs. T. H. Dudley, " Three critical periods in our diplomatic relations with England during the late war; personal recollections of Thomas H. Dudley, late United States consul at Liverpool ", *Pa. mag. hist.*, XVII (1893) 34–54 [**2078**], recollections of minor value about the *Trent* case, Franco-British projected mediation, Confederate rams, with a note (p. 47) that consul Dudley reported 130 steamers which left England to run the blockade with war material. C. F. Adams, *Trent affair* (no. 1999), includes (p. 76–148) contemporary documents from the Adams and Winthrop MSS. W. H. Trescot, " The Confederacy and the Declaration of Paris ", *Am. hist. rev.*, XXIII (1918) 826–835 [**2079**] prints important documents from the papers of W. H. Trescot, principally a memorandum of his contact with the English and French consuls in the South, in regard to the Confederacy and the Declaration of Paris. *Union and Confederate navies* (no. 1883) contains the operations of Union cruisers, blockading squadrons, and other matters, and (Ser. 2, v. II) correspondence of the Confederate Navy Dept. J. P. Baxter, 3rd, ed., " Papers relating to belligerent and neutral rights, 1861–1865 ", *Am. hist. rev.*, XXXIV (1928) 77–91 [2080], documents from the Admiralty papers in the British Public Record Office, London, the Archives de la Marine, Paris, and the Department of State, Washington; and *Some Brit. opinions* (no. 2007).

MSS.: Suggestions

See Sections 1, 2, and 5. There is no adequate index to the records of the U. S. Navy Department. For most helpful notes on marine archives of the United States, Great Britain, and France, see J. P. Baxter, 3rd, *The ironclad warship* (no. 2008).

Note also *List of Admiralty records* (no. 5584), and Didier Neuville, *Inventaire des archives de la marine* (no. 5708).

4. The United States and Europe, 1861–1865 [3]

Bibliographical Aids

See Sec. 1, above, for general aids. Note also the historical bibliographies of European countries (nos. 4726–4765). Jordan and Pratt (no. 2092) has a comprehensive bibliography.

Special Works

John Bigelow, *France and the Confederate navy, 1862–1868; an international episode* (N.Y., 1888) [2081], by the U.S. consul general in France during the civil war, who uses letters and papers of Slidell and others that he purchased in France at the time, supplemented by the Slidell-Benjamin correspondence found in the Confederate archives. Deals with the scheme of the Confederate agents for having ships built in French navy yards for the Confederate navy, with the connivance of the French authorities. R. C. Hawkins, " Coming of the Russian ships in 1863 ", *No. Am. rev.*, CLXXVIII (1904) 539–544 [2082], the writer professes to know of documents showing cool reception to the Russian Grand Duke by President Lincoln, on the

---

[3] See also Sec. 6, below.

occasion of the visit of the Russian fleet. J. M. Callahan, *Russo-American relations during the American civil war* (Morgantown, W.Va., 1908) [2083] is based on American sources. R. H. Lutz, *Die Beziehungen zwischen Deutschland und den Vereinigten Staaten während des Sezessionskrieges* (Heidelberg, 1911) [2084], in addition to printed German and American sources the author made use of the reports of Schleiden, 1861–64, Hanseatic minister to the United States, from the archives at Bremen. Also by the same author, " Rudolf Schleiden and the visit to Richmond, April 25, 1861 ", *Am. hist. assoc. ann. rep.*, for 1915 (1917) 207–216 [2085], as revealed in his despatches. F. A. Golder, " The Russian fleet and the civil war ", *Am. hist. rev.*, XX (1915) 801–812 [2086], by official unpublished archives of the Russian foreign office, shows that the purpose of the visit of the fleet was to find shelter on the Atlantic and Pacific in anticipation of a war with Great Britain over the Polish question; and " The American civil war through the eyes of a Russian diplomat ", *ibid.*, XXVI (1921) 454–463 [2086a], as revealed in the correspondence of the Russian minister at Washington, Edouard de Stoeckl, with the Russian foreign office. Three studies by L. M. Sears, " French opinion of our civil war ", *Mid-West quar.*, II (1915) 357–366 [2087], useful, but the study by West (no. 2090) is much more complete; "A neglected critic of our civil war ", *Miss. Valley hist. rev.*, I (1915) 532–545 [2088], the critic was the editor of the *Revue des deux mondes;* and "A Confederate diplomat at the court of Napoleon III ", *Am. hist. rev.*, XXVI (1921) 255–281 [2089], " it is with Slidell's share in this correspondence [Mason papers in the Library of Congress] that the present paper is primarily concerned. Its object is . . . to show what contribution toward the making of that history [Confederate diplomacy in Europe] may be derived from this one source, recently made available to the student." Fogdall, *Danish-Am. diplomacy* (no. 195), for complications resulting from the civil war. Gleaves, *Affair of the Blanche* (no. 2003), for brief account of a diplomatic controversy with Spain. W. R. West, *Contemporary French opinion on the American civil war* (Baltimore, 1924) [2090], an adequate study, based principally on a voluminous collection of French newspapers, periodicals, debates in the legislature, supplemented by original correspondence of the Confederate State Department and the Pickett papers in the Library of Congress. White, *Am. opinion of France*

(no. 812).   E. A. Adamov, " Russia and the United States at the
time of the civil war ", *Jour. mod. hist.*, II (1930) 586–602 [**2091**], by
an archivist in the Central Archives at Moscow, duplicates Golder,
Russian fleet (no. 2086).   Thomas, *Russo-Am. relations* (no. 1438).
Donaldson Jordan and E. J. Pratt, *Europe and the American civil
war* (Boston and N.Y., 1931) [**2092**], largely a study of public
opinion in reaction to the various problems of the civil war, from
European sources; stresses cultural and economic relations, as well
as constant danger of European intervention.   Poultney Bigelow,
"John Bigelow and Napoleon III ", *N.Y. history*, XIII (1932)
154–165 [**2093**] contrasts the success of his father, consul-general at
Paris during the civil war, with the failure of C. F. Adams to gain
public support in England.   Stolberg, *Deutschland und die V.S.*
(no. 4314).

For biographies of President Lincoln, Secretary of State Seward,
and American diplomatists abroad (for names and tenure, see latest
Register of the Dept. of State (no. 5122)), see the relevant entries
and bibliographical data in the *D.A.B.*

Printed Sources

For general collections, see Sec. 1, above.   For guides and indexes
to European official publications, see nos. 5398–5438.

French diplomatic correspondence is found in: *Documents diplomatiques*, 1861, 1862, 1863, published by the " Ministère des Affaires
Étrangères " (Paris, 1862–63, 3 v.) [**2094**].   *Austria and the Trent*
(no. 2033).   *Italy and the Trent* (no. 2035).   *Prussia and the Trent*
(no. 2034).   Félix Aucaigne, *L'alliance russo-américaine* (Paris, 1863)
[**2095**], sarcastic and indignant observations on a supposititious
alliance.   Michel Chevalier (supposed author), *La France, le Mexique et les États Confédérés* (Paris, 1863), also English translation,
France, Mexico, and the Confederate States (N.Y., 1863) [**2096**]
sets forth the general theory of American affairs at the court of
Napoleon III.   E. J. Kiehl, *Ons verdrag met Amerika; tractaat van
vriendschap en commercie tusschen haar hoog mogende, de Staten-
Generaal der Vereenigde Nederlanden, en de Vereenigde Staten van
Americka d. 8 October 1782* (The Hague, 1863) [**2097**], a treatise
of political and international law, on the question whether in 1863,
the Dutch-American treaty of 1782 should be enforced or not, and on
the nature of its stipulations; written from printed sources, with an

occasional historical sidelight. Emile Nouette-Delorme, *Les Etats-Unis et l'Europe; rupture de l'union, reconnaissance du Sud, abolition de l'esclavage* (Paris, 1863) [**2098**], an argument for intervention. C. B. Boynton, *English and French neutrality and the Anglo-French alliance, in their relations to the United States and Russia, including an account of the leading policy of France and of England for the last hundred years—the origin and aims of the alliance, the meaning of the Crimean war, and the reason of the hostile attitude of these two powers toward the United States, and of the movement on Mexico,* . . . (Cincinnati, 1864) [**2099**], a fervent and unscholarly emphasis on the community of pious interests of Russia and the United States; a revised edition (Cincinnati, 1866), under title, *The four great powers.* Rudolf Schleiden, *Reise-erinnerungen aus den Vereinigten Staaten von Amerika* (N.Y., 1873) [**2100**], and *Jugend-erinnerungen eines Schleswig-Holsteiners* (Wiesbaden, 1886–94, 4 v.) [**2101**], Schleiden was representative of the Hanseatic Cities in the United States during the civil war and these reminiscences relate thereto. J. P. Grund, " Bismarck and Motley—with correspondence till now unpublished ", *No. Am. rev.*, CLXVII (1898) 360–376, 481–496, 569–572 [**2102**], the author, an American journalist, visited Bismarck at Friedrichsruh during his retirement, and Bismarck, while burning his own papers, gave Grund nine letters (mostly personal) from his old schoolmate, Motley, including some while minister to Austria in 1862. *Memoirs of " Malakoff " [pseud.] being extracts from the correspondence and papers of the late William Edward Johnston,* ed. by his son, R. M. Johnston (London, 1907, 2 v.) [**2103**], Johnston, who wrote under the name " Malakoff ", was correspondent for the New York *Times* during the reign of Napoleon III. Several chapters are devoted to his correspondence from Paris during the American civil war. *Notes of Austria, France, and Prussia regarding Trent* (nos. 2033–2035). Cowley, *Paris embassy* (no. 1987). E. A. Adamov, ed., " Documents relating to Russian policy during the American civil war ", *Jour. mod. hist.*, II (1930) 603–611 [**2104**].

For the printed writings of President Lincoln, Secretary of State Seward, and American diplomatists abroad (for names and tenure, see the latest *Register* of the Dept. of State (no. 5122)), see our list on p. 756.

MSS.: Suggestions

See Sections 1, 2, 5, and 6.

For guides and indexes to the official archives of the United States and European countries (France, The Netherlands, Belgium, Spain, Denmark, Sweden, Germany, Austria, Russia, and Italy) and photocopies thereof in the Library of Congress, see Pt. II, ch. 3, below.

There are known to be extant the following collections of diplomatists at European courts during this period: John Bigelow (France); G. P. Marsh (Italy); J. L. Motley (Austria); J. S. Pike (The Netherlands); H. S. Sanford (Belgium). For description and location of collections, see our list of MSS. of American diplomatists (p. 868).

5. Diplomatic Efforts of the Southern Confederacy [4]

Bibliographical Aids

See Sec. 1, above, for general aids.

D. S. Freeman, *A calendar of Confederate papers, with a bibliography of some Confederate publications; preliminary report of the Southern Historical Manuscripts Commission*, prepared under the direction of the Confederate Memorial Literary Society (Richmond, Va., 1908) [**2105**]. H. A. Morrison, *Off. pub. Confed. States* (no. 5352). Bonham, *Brit. consuls* (no. 2114), 262–267. *Off. pub. Confed. States in Va. state lib.* (no. 5351). C. N. Baxter and J. M. Dearborn, *Confederate literature; a list of books and newspapers, maps, music, and miscellaneous matter printed in the South during the Confederacy, now in the Boston Athenaeum* (Boston: The Boston Athenaeum, 1917) [**2106**]. West, *Fr. opinion* (no. 2090), 153–156. W. O. Waters, " Confederate imprints in the Henry E. Huntington Library unrecorded in previously published bibliographies of such material ", *Bibliog. soc. Am. pap.*, XXIII, pt. 1, 1929 (1930) 18–109 [**2107**]. Jordan and Pratt (no. 2092), 269–290. Owsley (no. 2117), 579–591.

Special Works

J. D. Bulloch, *The secret service of the Confederate States in Europe, or, How the Confederate cruisers were equipped* (N.Y.,

---

⁴ See also Sections 1, 2, 3, 4, and 6.

1884, 2 v.) [**2108**], the writer was the agent of the Confederate government to direct naval operations in Europe, and chief representative of the navy department of the Confederacy abroad. Bigelow, *Fr. and Confed. navy* (no. 2081). J. M. Callahan, " Diplomatic relations of the Confederate States with England (1861–1865)", *Am. hist. assoc. ann. rep.*, for 1898 (1899) 265–283 [**2109**], abridgment of material embodied in the author's subsequent book, following, *The diplomatic history of the Southern Confederacy* (Baltimore, 1901) [**2110**], based on the diplomatic correspondence of the Confederacy, supplemented by that of the United States, and various printed sources; nothing from important foreign archives, and therefore in part superseded by E. D. Adams (no. 1909) and Owsley (no. 2117). J. C. Schwab, *The Confederate States of America, 1861–1865; a financial and industrial history of the South during the civil war* (N.Y., 1901) [**2111**], for the Confederate foreign loan; this incorporates his earlier " The Confederate foreign loan ", *Yale rev.*, I (1892) 175–186. L. Q. Washington, " Confederate State Department ", *Indep.*, LIII (1901) 2218–2224 [**2112**], a brief description. J. H. Latané, " The diplomatic relations of the Confederacy ", in *The South in the building of the Nation*, v. IV (Richmond, 1909) 525–544 [**2113**], brief summary arranged to fit into a publisher's enterprise. M. L. Bonham, *The British consuls in the Confederacy* (N.Y., 1911) [**2114**], the author used diplomatic correspondence of the Confederacy, and of the United States, but not the correspondence of the consuls themselves. C. F. Adams, " The Confederate cotton campaign, Lancashire, 1861–1862 ", in his *Trans-Atlantic solidarity* (Oxford, 1913) 57–84, followed by an article on England and Confederate relations, " Dis aliter visum ", *ibid.*, 87–129 [**2115**]. Sears, *Confed. diplomat* (no. 2089). L. F. Stock, " Catholic participation in the diplomacy of the southern Confederacy ", *Cath. hist. rev.*, XVI (1930) 1–18 [**2116**], missions of Bishop Lynch to the Pope, of Father John Bannon to Ireland, and of other agents to Ireland in 1863 (Robert Dowling, Edwin De Leon, and J. L. Capston) to endeavor to check the flow of emigration to the North. F. L. Owsley, *King Cotton diplomacy; foreign relations of the Confederate States of America* (Chicago, 1931) [**2117**], history of the Confederacy's efforts to coerce Europe with giving aid to the rebellion by threat of a cotton famine. King Cotton could not coerce English diplomacy because of a surplus on hand that lasted well into 1862. English failure to intervene with France in 1862 was due to the Confederate defeat at Antietam. After 1862 English contentment with war profits produced complacency about the blockade. The author has made extensive use of foreign MS. records, including the archives of the French foreign office, then just opened to historical research. Uneven in style and expression. Beckles Willson, *John Slidell and the Confederates in Paris (1862–65)* (N.Y., 1932) [**2118**].

For biographies of Confederate statesmen (Jefferson Davis, President; A. H. Stephens, Vice-President; Robert Toombs, R. M. T. Hunter, and J. P. Benjamin, secretaries of state; S. R. Mallory, secretary of the navy), and diplomatists abroad (John Slidell, France; J. M. Mason, Great Britain; Bishop Lynch, Rome; L. J. C. Lamar, Russia; P. A. Rost, Spain; Father John Bannon, agent to Ireland; D. P. Kenner, A. D. Mann, and W. L. Yancey; Henry Hotze, consul-general in London) ; and J. D. Bulloch, agent of the Navy Dept. abroad, and M. F. Maury, agent for purchasing and arming vessels, see the relevant entries and bibliographical data in the *D.A.B.* See also, for bibliographical references to biographical material regarding Jefferson Davis, A. H. Stephens, J. P. Benjamin, John Slidell, Robert Toombs, and M. F. Maury: F. M. Green, *Studies in Confederate leadership; . . . an outline for individual group study* (Chapel Hill, N.C., 1931) [**2119**]. A recent biography of J. P. Benjamin is Rollin Osterweis, *Judah P. Benjamin; statesman of the lost cause* (N.Y. and London, 1933) [**2120**]. For a convenient list see M. J. Wright, *General officers of the Confederate army; officers of the executive departments of the Confederate States, members of the Confederate Congress by states* (N.Y., 1911) [**2121**].

For a list of " Consuls and agents from foreign countries to the Confederate States, 1861–1865 ", see *Official records war of the rebellion* (no. 1883), ser. 2, v. III (1922), 12. A list of " British consular officials in the South, 1860–65 ", is given in Bonham (no. 2114), 259–261.

Printed Sources

For general collections, see Sec. 1, above. See also Secs. 4 and 6.

For a list of Confederate " newspapers and periodicals ", see the Boston Athenaeum list (no. 2106), 155–179.

OFFICIAL PUBLICATIONS OF THE CONFEDERATE STATES OF AMERICA: *Correspondence of the Department of State in relation to the British consuls resident in the Confederate States* (Richmond, 1863) [**2122**], published by the Confederate Department of State. *Jour. Cong. Confed. States* (no. 5387a). Richardson, *Pap. Confed., incl. dipl. corres.* (no. 5350). U.S. Official publications: *Official records of the Union and Confederate navies* (no. 1883), the most important collection of the diplomatic correspondence of the Confederacy.

BRITISH PARLIAMENT (HOUSE OF COMMONS SESSIONAL) PAPERS: *Correspondence with Mr. Mason respecting blockade and recognition of Confederate States* (1863, LXXII; same, Lords, 1863, XXIX) [**2123**]. *Correspondence with Mr. Adams respecting Confederate agents in England* (1863, LXXII) [**2124**]. *Despatch from Lord Lyons referring to alleged report of Secretary of Navy of so-styled Confederate States* (1864, LXII) [**2125**]. *Correspondence respecting removal of British consuls from so-styled Confederate States of America* (1864, LXII) [**2126**]. *Correspondence with Mr. Mason, commissioner of so-styled Confederate States of America (in continuation of Papers presented to Parliament in March 1863)* (1864, LXII) [**2127**].

For contemporary periodical and pamphlet material, particularly Confederate propaganda in England and France, see bibliographical notes in Jordan and Pratt (no. 2092), and Owsley (no. 2117).

F. W. Gibbs, *Recognition* (London, 1863) [**2128**], an historical examination of previous cases of recognition to show that the Confederate government had not achieved the independence to warrant recognition. Bulloch, *Secret service Confederacy* (no. 2108). *Memoirs of " Malakoff "* (no. 2103). W. W. Henry, " Kenner's mission to Europe ", *Wm. and Mary quar.*, XXV (1916) 9–12 [**2129**], a copy of a MS. in the Library of Congress, of W. W. Henry, reporting a conversation with D. F. Kenner, in which he gave an account of his mission to England and France in 1864–5, as special envoy from President Jefferson Davis. J. T. Pickett, " Letter from Colonel John T. Pickett, of the Southern Confederacy, to Señor Don Manuel de Zamacona, minister of foreign affairs, Mexico ", *Hisp. Am. hist. rev.*, II (1919) 611–617 [**2130**], with introduction by Mary W. Williams; Pickett was sent to Mexico as diplomatic agent of the Confederate States early in 1861 (the letter was written Sept. 16, 1861). J. F. Jameson, ed., "The London expenditures of the Confederate secret service ", *Am.*

hist. rev., XXXV (1930) 811–824 [**2131**], a letter written by Henry Hotze, Confederate commercial agent in London, to J. P. Benjamin, secretary of state, Dec. 31, 1864, enclosing a series of accounts of his expenditures for the secret service of the Confederacy.

Printed writings of Confederate statesmen and diplomatists: *Jefferson Davis . . . letters, papers, and speeches* (no. 5214). *Correspondence of R. M. T. Hunter, 1826–1876*, ed. by C. H. Ambler (Wash., 1918) (Am. Hist. Assoc. Ann. Rep., for 1916, v. II) [**2132**] contains no material on his activities as secretary of state.

MSS.: Suggestions

The rather complete official records of the diplomacy of the Confederacy, the so-called Pickett papers, are in the Library of Congress, fully printed (no. 1883). These must be used with the diplomatic archives of the United States government and of the various European governments and Mexico (see MSS. suggestions in Secs. 1, 2, 3, 4, and 6).

The scattered papers of President Jefferson Davis have been brought together (principal collection in Confederate Memorial Hall, New Orleans) by the Mississippi Department of Archives and History, and edited by Rowland (no. 5214). Some papers of Vice-President A. H. Stephens are in the Historical Society of Pennsylvania. His correspondence as printed in the *Annual Report* of the American Historical Association for 1911, v. II (1913) has nothing of significance for foreign affairs. Very little is known to be extant of the personal papers of the three successive Confederate secretaries of state: Robert Toombs (*Correspondence*, published in *Annual Report* of American Historical Association, for 1911, v. II (1913) contains nothing for foreign affairs) ; R. M. T. Hunter (a small collection in the State Library of Virginia, at Richmond, has little on diplomacy) ; J. P. Benjamin, although Benjamin's *Diary of events, 1862–1864*, is to be found in the Pickett papers.

The Library of Congress has a rich collection of personal papers relating to Confederate diplomatic efforts: J. M. Mason (envoy to England) ; Henry Hotze (" consul-general " in London) ; John Slidell (envoy to France) ; copy of a MS. narrative of " The diplomacy of the Confederate cabinet of Richmond and its agents abroad ", by Paul Pecquet du Bellet, written about 1868, by an ambitious Louisianian who professed to be a volunteer supporter of Confederate diplomacy in Paris and who believed he was exposing the deficiencies and mistakes of the Confederate agents, after the war; J. T. Pickett (envoy to Mexico); A. D. Mann (envoy to Spain and the Papal States); M. F. Maury (agent for naval activities in Europe); W. W. Henry's memorandum on his conversation with Duncan Kenner on the subject of the latter's instructions as the last Confederate envoy to Europe (see no. 2129).

Other collections: D. F. Kenner (secret mission to England and France, 1864-65), at The Cabildo, New Orleans; W. L. Yancey (envoy to Spain, with P. A. Rost and A. D. Mann), in the Department of Archives and History, Montgomery, Alabama; P. A. Rost, in the *Academia de la Historia*, Madrid.[5] Some of the papers of Bishop Lynch (envoy to Rome) are in the Cathedral at Charleston, South Carolina.

6. Mexico and Maximilian; The Monroe Doctrine [6]

Bibliographical Aids

Jameson, *Bibliog. Monroe Doctrine* (no. 1139). A. P. C. Griffin, "List of works on the relations of the United States and France during the French occupation of Mexico, 1861-1867", in his *International arbitration* (no. 4188), 101-105 [**2134**]. Caron, *Bibliographie . . . 1866 à 1897* (no. 4737), 398-401: "Expédition du Mexique (1862-1867)." Treudley (no. 2161a), for bibliography of the United States and Santo Domingo, to 1866. Meyer, *List on Monroe Doctrine* (no. 1140). Corti (no. 2165), v. II, 949-963, a voluminous bibliography on "Maximilian of Mexico." Perkins (no. 1211), 549-560, for a choice bibliography of the Monroe Doctrine, 1826-1867.

Special Works

R. Lepelletier de Saint-Rémy, *Saint-Domingue; étude et solution nouvelle de la question haïtienne* (Paris, 1846, 2 v.) [**2135**]. Gustave d'Alaux, *L'empereur Soulouque et son empire* (Paris, 1856), originally published in a series of articles in the *Revue des deux*

---

[5] Rost left a portfolio of his official correspondence in Madrid, at the close of the war, which was later given to the *Academia*. See Ignacio Bauer, "Lista cronológica de documentos encontrados en la cartera C. S. A., iniciales que significan ' Confederate States of America ', y abandonados por el delegado del presidente Jefferson Davis en España, Mr. P. A. Rost ", *Real acad. hist. bol.*, LXXVI (1920) 161-162 [**2133**].

[6] See also Sec. 4, above.

mondes, 1850–1851 **[2136]** gives French views on the Dominican question; it was also published in English, *Soulouque and his empire*, from the French of Gustave d'Alaux, tr. and ed. by J. H. Parkhill (Richmond, 1861). " The Monroe Doctrine ", *No. Am. rev.*, LXXXII (1856) 478–512 **[2137–8]**, published anonymously; said to be the first article in which the title " Monroe Doctrine " was used, it declares that " the principles now advocated in its name [Monroe Doctrine] are wholly unhistorical, and without foundation in any legitimate interpretation of his guarded language." Two articles by Charles de Mazade, " La question du Mexique dans le parlement espagnol ", *Rev. deux mondes*, 2e pér., XLII (1863) 505–512 **[2139]**; and L'expédition du Mexique et la politique française ", *ibid.*, 2e pér., XLVIII (1863) 675–706 **[2140–1]**. J. M. Hidalgo, *Apuntes para escribir la historia de los proyectos de monarquía en México desde el reinado de Carlos III hasta la instalación del Emperador Maximiliano* (Paris, 1868) **[2142]**, Hidalgo was one of the leading Mexican monarchists who first approached the French court. Friedrich von Hellwald, *Maximilian I., Kaiser von Mexico; sein Leben, Wirken und sein Tod, nebst einem Abriss der Geschichte des Kaiserreichs* (Vienna, 1869, 2 v.) **[2143]**, a mournful history of a lost cause dated in Vienna on the first anniversary of Maximilian's execution. Francisco de Paula de Arrangóiz, *Apuntes para la historia del segundo imperio mexicano* (Madrid, 1869) **[2144]**, by a Mexican reactionary and monarchist who enjoyed confidences with many political personalities of the day. Henri de Suckau, *Deux interventions en Amérique; Mexique et Honduras* (Paris, 1869) **[2145]**. Vice-Admiral D. D. Porter, " Secret missions to San Domingo ", *No. Am. rev.*, CXXVIII (1879) 616–630 **[2146]** contains important data relative to the secret missions of Porter to the Dominican Republic in 1846 and 1847. José de la Gándara [y Navarro], *Anexión y guerra de Santo Domingo*, por el general Gándara (Madrid, 1884, 2 v.) **[2147]**, by a Spanish general who participated in the attempted conquest but who was opposed to a policy of outright annexation; prints a good many relevant documents. Paul Gaulot, *La verité sur l'expédition du Mexique* (Paris, 1889–90, 3 v., new ed., Paris, 1906, 2 v.) **[2148]**, based on original documents collected by Ernest Louet, by an officer of the French expeditionary corps. The author has used uncompromising selections from the correspondence of Napoleon III. with Bazaine.

Frederic Bancroft, "The French in Mexico and the Monroe Doctrine", *Pol. sci. quar.*, XI (1896) 30–43 [2149] states that the Monroe Doctrine, though constantly appealed to at the time of the Maximilian affair by the sensational newspapers and the politicians, seems not once to have been mentioned in any of the official despatches of the United States. J. G. García, *Compendio de la historia de Santo Domingo*, 3d ed., enl. and rev. (Santo Domingo, 1896, 3 v.) [2150], a general text, undocumented, by a Dominican historian. A. de St. Mérant, *Samana et ses projets de cession, 1844–91* (Paris, 1896) [2151], a hostile French review of American projects for annexation. Two essays by Alejandro Villaseñor y Villaseñor, published in his *Obras* (Mexico, 1897–1906) [2152]: "Anton Lizardo" (v. I, 1–70) on the incident at Anton Lizardo, 1860, in which United States naval forces stopped two vessels, the *General Miramón* and *Marqués de la Habana*, to show that it was done at the instigation of the Juárez regime (to which this author is historically hostile); and "Juárez y la Baja California" (v. II, 395–463), thinks Juárez was too ready to open up Lower California to American adventurers. Hilarión Frías y Soto, *México y los Estados Unidos durante la intervención francesa* (Mexico, 1901) [2153], the author was abused by the Mexican press for having made a speech in Chicago recognizing the aid of American diplomacy in ridding Mexico of French troops; this book justifies his contention. H. Léonardon, "Espagne et la question du Mexique", *Ann. sci. pol.*, XVI (1901) 59–95 [2154], how secret Spanish desire to place a Bourbon on the Mexican throne was thwarted by Napoleon III's pronouncement for Maximilian. C. A. Duniway, "Reasons for the withdrawal of the French from Mexico", *Am. hist. assoc. ann. rep.*, for 1902, v. I (1903) 313–328 [2155] shows that the attitude of the United States was only one contributing cause; there were other far-reaching influences, notably the rise of Prussia, and the strain on the French treasury. Ernst Schmit, ritter von Tavera, *Geschichte der Regierung des Kaisers Maximilian I. und die Französische Intervention in Mexiko* (Vienna and Leipzig, 1903, 2 v.) [2156], the book was written about 1874 to fulfill a pledge to the unfortunate Maximilian made by the author, then an attaché of the Austrian legation in Mexico, but not published till 30 years later. It is rather a history of Maximilian's government than of diplomacy connected with that venture; but the earlier chapters deal with the London convention of 1861. Fernando Iglesias Calderón, *El egoísmo norte-americano durante la intervención francesa* (Mexico, 1905) [2157], a reply to Frías y Soto (no. 2153). Fernando Iglesias Calderón, *Las supuestas traiciones de Juárez; cesión de territorio. Generalísmo americano. Antón Lizardo. El tratado Mac-Lane* (Mexico, 1907) [2158], written, after Francisco Bulnes' " El verdadero Juárez ", to defend Juárez against the attacks by Bulnes, *cf.* also Villaseñor (no. 2152). J. M. Callahan, *Evolution of Seward's Mexican policy* (Morgantown, W.Va., 1909) [2159], worked out from documents in the Department of State, now incorporated in his *U.S. and Mexico* (no. 1465). J. W. Foster, "Maximilian and his Mexican empire", *Columbia hist. soc. rec.*, XIV (1911) 184–202 [2160], undocumented and now wholly superseded by later more critical and scholarly works (Martin, Corti, Callahan). P. F. Martin, *Maximilian in Mexico; the story of the French intervention (1861–1867)* (N.Y., 1914) [2161], until Corti (no. 2165), the most complete account, based on printed sources only. Only the last two chapters deal with American diplomatic attitude. Hart, *Monroe Doctrine* (no. 1064). Mary Treudley, *The United States and Santo Domingo, 1789–1866* (Worcester, Mass., 1916) [2161a], based on the printed sources; has an excellent bibliography of such material. Latané, *U.S. and Latin America* (no. 963). H. L. Hoskins, " French view of the Monroe Doctrine and the Mexican expedition ", *Hisp. Am. hist. rev.*, IV (1921) 677–689 [2162], the armed invasion of Mexico by the French as a striking case to show the attitude of European states toward the Monroe Doctrine. Carreño (no. 1461). Louis Sonolot, " L'agonie de l'empire du Mexique, d'après des lettres et des notes inédites du général Castelnau ", *Rev. Paris*, XXXIXe ann. (1927) 590–625, 862–898 [2163], an account of the last days of the Maximilian empire in Mexico drawn from the letters written to Napoleon III by the French general Castelnau in 1866. L. F. Stock, " The Empress of Mexico visits Rome; a diplomatic episode ", *America*, XXXVII (1927) 226–227 [2164], visit of the Emperor Maximilian and the Empress Charlotte to receive the parting benediction of Pius IX. Count Egon Caesar Corti, *Maximilian and Charlotte of Mexico*, tr. from the German by Catherine A. Phillips (N.Y. and London, 1928, 2 v.; German ed., Zurich, 1924, 2 v.) [2165], the principal account of Maximilian's venture, and European diplomacy relating thereto, based chiefly on Maximilian's own archives, those of his Mexican government, and those of Austria-Hungary; has comparatively little on the United States, certainly nothing from important American sources. An abridgment, more or less, of this work is his *Die Tragödie eines Kaisers* (Leipzig, 1933) [**2165a**]. Antonio de la Peña y Reyes, *La labor diplomática de D. Manuel María de Zamacona como secretario de relaciones exteriores* (Mexico, 1928) [**2166**], Mexico's secretary for foreign relations, July 13 to Nov. 26, 1861; one brief section bears upon Seward's proposed treaty designed to forestall intervention by a loan well secured by a mortgage upon Mexico's public lands. Sumner Welles, *Naboth's Vineyard; the Dominican Republic, 1844–1924* (N.Y., 1928) [**2167**], so far the most comprehensive and authoritative work, by an able American diplomatist who digested the printed sources and utilized the MS. records of the Department of State, but whose quotations therefrom are occasionally imperfectly collated. Wriston (no. 4799), for special agents to Santo Domingo. Ruth L. Benjamin, " Marcus Otterbourg, United States minister to Mexico in 1867 [*i.e.* consul, 1861–1867] ", *Am. Jew. hist. soc. pub.*, no. 32 (1931) 65–94 [**2168**], by a studious descendant working from the printed and unprinted diplomatic correspondence of Otterbourg. Jordan and Pratt (no. 2092) reflects European opinion on the struggle between the Mexican expedition and Lincoln's emancipation policy for the favor of Frenchmen and Spaniards. F. E. Lalley, *French opposition to the Mexican policy of the second empire* (Baltimore, 1931) [**2169**], after study of the debates in the Chamber, and other French sources, the thesis rejects Duniway's (no. 2155) explanation of opposition in France as one of the principal reasons for withdrawal of French troops from Mexico. Owsley (no. 2117), ch. 17: " The Mexican pawn, 1862–65." Rippy, *U.S. and Mexico* (no. 3548) has chapters on " Mexican projects of the Confederates " and " Seward and French intervention." McPherson, *Colony in north Mexico* (no. 1865) shows relation between the projects of Sen. W. M. Gwin, Confederate sympathizer, and Napoleon III's Mexican policy. Perkins, *Monroe Doctrine, 1826–1867* (no. 1211), latest scholarly review, based on multi-archival research. Stolberg-Wernigerode, *Deutschland und Vereinigten Staaten* (no. 4314). Bertita Harding (Señora B. Leonarz de Harding), *Phantom crown; the story of Maximilian & Carlota of Mexico* (Indianapolis and N. Y., 1934) [**2169a**], an emotional biography of the "new" popular type of no scholarly value, of which the material is taken from the works of scholars like Corti.

Printed Sources

For general collections, see Sec. 1, above. See also Sec. 4, above, and Sec. 5, for printed diplomatic correspondence and other documents of the Confederate States.

U.S. OFFICIAL DOCUMENTS: For a " List of United States documents on the relations of the United States and France during the French occupation of Mexico, 1861–1867 ", see Griffin, *Internat. arbitration* (no. 4188), 106–113 [**2170**]. Some of the more important documents are listed in Perkins (no. 1211).

FRENCH OFFICIAL DOCUMENTS: *Documents diplomatiques,* 1861, 1862, 1863, 1866 (Paris, 1862, 1863, and 1866, 4 v.), and *Documents diplomatiques, 1866. Etats-Unis. Suite de la correspondance relative aux affaires du Mexique, no. VII* (Paris, 1866) [**2171**], all published by the " Ministère des Affaires Etrangères."

BRITISH PARLIAMENTARY (HOUSE OF COMMONS SESSIONAL) PAPERS: *Correspondence respecting British claims on Mexico* (1861, LXV) [**2172**]. *Convention between Her Majesty the Queen of Spain and the Emperor of the French, relative to combined operations against Mexico, signed at London, Oct. 31, 1861* (1862, LXIV) [**2173**]. *Correspondence respecting the affairs of Mexico* (1862, LXIV, 3 pts.) [**2174**]. *Despatches relating to British claims on Mexico* (1862, LXIV) [**2175**]. *Convention between Her Majesty and the Emperor of Mexico, for the investigation and settlement of British claims by a mixed commission, signed at Mexico, June 26, 1866* (1867, LXXIV) [**2176**].

MEXICAN OFFICIAL DOCUMENTS: *Correspondencia entre la legación de la República Mexicana en Washington, el Departamento de Estado de los Estados-Unidos de América y el Gobierno de México, con relación á la exportación de armas y municiones de guerra de los Estados-Unidos para puertos de naciones beligerantes,* 2d ed. (Mexico, 1867) [**2177**]. *Responsabilidades contraídas por el gobierno nacional de México con los Estados-Unidos, en virtud de los contratos celebrados por sus agentes, 1864–1867* (Mexico, 1867) [**2178**], includes extracts from the *Diario Oficial* and papers of M. Romero, Mexican minister to the United States. *Correspondencia de la legación mexicana en Washington con el Ministerio de Relaci-*

ones Exteriores de la República y el Departamento de Estado de los Estados Unidos, sobre la captura, juicio y ejecución de Don Fernando Maximiliano de Hapsburgo (Mexico, 1868, 2 v.) **[2179]**. *Circulares y otras publicaciones hechas por la legación mexicana en Washington, durante la guerra de intervención, 1862–1867* (Mexico, 1868, 2 v. in 1) **[2180]**. *Correspondencia de la legación mexicana en los Estados Unidos de América, sobre los contratos celebrados por Don Juan Bustamente, 1862–1863* (Mexico, 1869) **[2181]**. *Correspondencia oficial de la legación mexicana en Washington con el Ministerio de Relaciones Exteriores de la República y el Departamento de Estado de Washington, sobre la conducta de D. Jesús G. Ortega, 1865–1866* (Mexico, 1869) **[2182]**. *Correspondencia de la legación mexicana en Washington durante la intervención extranjera, 1860–1868* (Mexico, 1870–92, 10 v.) **[2183]**, of the greatest significance.[7] Four volumes, by Matías Romero, Mexican chargé d'affaires and minister to the United States, 1860–1868, published officially, are: *Responsabilidades contraídas* (no. 2178). *Apuntes para formar un bosquejo histórico del regreso a la República por los Estados Unidos de algunos de los prisioneros mexicanos deportados a Francia; accompañados de documentos oficiales para rectificar los Apuntes del sr. d. Epitacio Huerto* (Mexico, 1868) **[2183a]**. *Contratos hechos en los Estados-Unidos por los comisionados del gobierno de México durante los años de 1865 y 1866* (Mexico, 1868) **[2184]**. *Historia de las intrigas europeas que ocasionaron la intervención francesa en México; nota del Sr. Romero á Mr. Seward, el 2 de octobre de 1862* (Mexico, 1868) **[2185]**.

SPANISH OFFICIAL DOCUMENTS (dealing with the Santo Domingo affair): [*Documentos relativos á la cuestión de Santo Domingo, remitidos al Congreso de los Diputados*] *por el Ministerio de Estado* (Madrid, 1865) **[2186]**,[8] consisting of documents of the years 1843 to 1861. *Documentos relativos á la cuestión de Santo Domingo, remitidos al Congreso de los Diputados por el Ministerio de la Guerra* (Madrid, 1865) **[2187]**, consisting of documents of 1864.[9]

Two works by Michel Chevalier, *L'expédition du Mexique* (Paris, 1862) **[2188]**; and *La France, le Mexique, et les Etats-Confédérés*

---

[7] These documents (nos. 2177–2183) are published at Mexico: Imprenta de Gobierno; catalogued at Library of Congress under "Mexico. Legación. United States."

[8] Copy in the Harvard College Library.

[9] Copy in the Harvard College Library.

(Paris, 1863), published anonymously; also English edition, *France, Mexico, and the Confederate States*, by M. M. Chevalier, tr. by W. H. Hurlbut (N.Y., 1863) [2189], a plea for recognition of the Confederacy as an aid to France's Mexican policy. J. M. Gutiérrez de Estrada, *México y el Archiduque Fernando Maximiliano de Austria* (Paris, 1862; Mexico, 1863), also published in French, in more extended form (Paris, 1862) [2190] reflects public opinion in Spain. John Jay (the grandson), *Mr. Jay's letter on the recent relinquishment of the Monroe Doctrine* (N.Y., 1863) [2191], a warning against relinquishment. V. W. Kingsley, *French intervention in America; or, A review of La France, le Mexique, et les Etats-Confédérés* (N.Y., 1863) [2192], a replique. Joshua Leavitt, *The Monroe Doctrine* (N.Y., 1863) [2193], a plea for the support of the Monroe Doctrine as a bulwark against Popery and Absolutism. H. Mercier de la Combe, *Le Mexique et les Etats-Unis*, 2d ed., rev. and enl. (Paris, 1863), 1st edition issued under title, *Le Mexique, l'Amérique du Nord et l'Europe* (Paris, 1862) [2194], attack upon the Mexican policy of the Emperor. Manuel Bermúdez de Castro [and others], *La question du Mexique devant les Cortes d'Espagne; discours prononcés au Sénat et au Congrés par Mm. Bermúdez de Castro, Concha, Mon, et Ríos y Rosas* (Paris, 1863) [2195]. The following sources come from the pen of the able Mexican *chargé* (1860–63) and minister (1863–66) in the United States, Matías Romero: *The situation of Mexico;* speech delivered by Señor Romero . . . at a dinner in the city of New York, on the 16th of December, 1863 (N.Y., 1863) [2196]; and *Comisionados de la República Mexicana en los Estados Unidos, dos notas del Señor Romero á Mr. Seward* (Baltimore, 1867) [2197], an unofficial edition of his despatches. See also nos. 2181–2185 for his official correspondence and publications. Henry Moreau, *La politique française en Amérique—1861–1864* (Paris, 1864) [2198], an argument for getting out of Mexico. Montgomery Blair, *The Monroe Doctrine* (n.p., n.d.) [2199], " speech at Hagerstown, 12 July, 1865, exposing the alliance of the American secretary of state with Louis Napoleon to overthrow the Monroe Doctrine and establish a despotism on this continent." *Mexico and the Monroe Doctrine* (N.Y., 1865) [2200], an anonymous pamphlet arguing that Maximilian was the free choice of the Mexican people. F. J. Parker, *The Mexican Empire and the American union* (Boston, 1865)

[**2201**], argument for recognition by the United States of Maximilian lest he look too much to Europe for support. Napoleon III, *Letter to Gen. Forey. The cardinal idea of intervention in Mexico. What French nonintervention means. Comments of the London Times, June 20, 1863* (n.p., 1866?) [**2202**], a broadside [10] printing a letter of Napoleon III to Gen. Forey, July 3, 1862, taken from the *Moniteur* of Jan. 16, 1863; followed by the comments of the London *Times*. Léonce Détroyat, *L'intervention française au Mexique, accompagnée de documents inédits et d'un long mémoire adressé par l'empereur Maximilian à l'empéreur Napoléon et remis à Paris par l'impératrice Charlotte* (Paris, 1868) [**2203**], review by a French critic who ascribes the Mexican fiasco to personal government, which, unchecked by parliamentary responsibility, strayed from the true policy of protectorate over a Latin-American republic, to setting up a monarchy. Emmanuel Domenech, *Histoire du Mexique. Juárez et Maximilien; correspondance inédite des presidents, ministres et généraux Almonte, Santa Anna, Gutiérrez, Miramón, Márquez, Mejía, Woll, etc., de Juárez, de l'empéreur Maximilien et de l'impératrice Charlotte*, 3d ed. (Brussels, 1868, 3 v.) [**2204**]. Eugène Lefèvre, *Documentos oficiales recogidos en la secretaria privada de Maximiliano; historia de la intervención francesa en Méjico* (Brussels and London, 1869, 2 v.) [**2205**], published by authorization of President Juárez, who allowed the author to examine papers left by Maximilian in Mexico. It is also published in French, *Documents officiels . . .* (Paris, 1870, 2 v.). R. M. Walsh, "My mission to San Domingo", *Lippincott's magazine*, VII (1871) 293–307 [**2206**]. Louis Thouvenel, ed., *Le secret de l'empéreur; correspondance confidentielle et inédite échangée entre M. [Edouard] Thouvenel, le duc de Gramont et le général comte de Flahault, 1860–1863*, with notes and biographical index (Paris, 1889, 2 v.) [**2207**], record only in part of the views of the French foreign minister. J. L. Blasio, *Maximiliano íntimo, el emperador Maximiliano y su corte; memorias de un secretario particular* (Paris, 1905), recently issued in translation, *Maximilian, emperor of Mexico; memoirs of his private secretary, Jose Luis Blasio*, tr. and ed. by R. H. Murray (New Haven, 1934) [**2207a**]. Also Louis Thouvenel, *Pages de l'histoire du second empire, d'après les papiers de M. [Edouard] Thouvenel, ancien ministre des affaires*

---

[10] Copy in the Harvard College Library.

étrangères (*1854–1866*) (Paris, 1903) [2208]. Genaro García, ed., *Correspondencia secreta de los principales intervencionistas mexicanos, 1860–1862* (Mexico, 1905–07, 3 v.) (Documentos Inéditos . . . pub. por Genaro García y Carlos Pereyra, t. I, IV, XIII) [2209]. Charles Blanchot, *Mémoires; l'intervention française au Mexique* (Paris, 1911, 3 v.) [2210], as a young officer the author participated in the military intervention in Mexico, and wrote in his old age this undocumented narrative, apparently based in part on his diary. Henry Salomon, "Le prince Richard de Metternich et sa correspondance pendant son ambassade à Paris (1859–1871)" *Rev. Paris*, XXXI ann. (1924) 507–541, 762–804 [2211]. Comtesse Reinach-Foussemagne, "L'impératrice Charlotte et l'aventure mexicaine; lettres inédites", *Rev. deux mondes*, 7e pér., XXV (Feb. 15, 1925) 749–784 [2212], letters written by the Empress of Mexico, to various persons.   Cowley, *Paris embassy* (no. 1987). *Don Juan Prim y su labor diplomática en México* (Mexico, 1928) (Archivo Histórico Diplomático Mexicano, XXV) [2213], documents from the Mexican archives, preceded by an historical introduction.   Antonio de la Peña y Reyes, *Comentarios de Francisco Zarco sobre la intervención francesa* (*1861–1863*) (Mexico, 1929) (Archivo Histórico Diplomático Mexicano, XXX) [2214] does not deal directly with the United States.

The following special collections of printed sources deal with the Monroe Doctrine and Santo Domingo, 1861–65: Mariano Torrente, *Política ultramarina* (no. 1796), by a Spanish agent who went to Santo Domingo in 1852, and here argues for the protectorate. Felix de Bona, *Cuba, Santo Domingo, y Puerto Rico* (Madrid, 1861) [2215], another Spanish view. José Ferrer de Couto, *Reincorporación de Santo Domingo á España; breves consideraciónes sobre este acontecimiento* (Madrid, 1861) [2216], another Spanish view. Cayetano Martín y Oñate, *España y Santo Domingo* (Toledo, 1864) [2217].   J. F. Campuzano, *Remedio radical para su situación, la de Cuba y Puerto Rico* (Madrid, 1865) [2218].   *De la cuestión de Santo Domingo; nueve interesantes artículos que publicó el independiente*, anonymous (Madrid, 1865) [2219].   J. López de la Vega, *La cuestión de Santo Domingo* (Madrid, 1865) [2220].   Gaspar Núñez de Arce, *Santo Domingo* (Madrid, 1865) [2221] contains numerous comments from Spanish newspapers. *Documentos remitidos al Congreso de Diputados* (no. 2186). "Expediente instruído a consecuencia de una comunicación del consul de Hayti sobre la compra de la isla de Sn Thomas por los Estados Unidos ", *Bol. archivo nacional* (Havana), XIX (1920) 52–63 [**2221a**], despatches from the Spanish consul in Haiti, and other documents, 1854–55.

For the printed writings of Presidents Lincoln and Johnson, Secretary of State Seward, and diplomatists abroad (for names and tenure, see the latest *Register* of the Dept. of State (no. 5122)), see our list on p. 756. See also the printed writings of Confederate statesmen as given in Sec. 5, above.

MSS.: Suggestions

See Sections 1, 2, 4, and 5, for guides and indexes to the official archives of the United States and the various European countries. Any definitive history of the diplomacy of the Maximilian affair must search its ramifications among the archives of all these countries. For guides and indexes to Mexican archives, and photostats therefrom, see p. 910, below. The papers of Maximilian himself, very voluminous, are now in the *Haus-, Hof- und Staatsarchiv*, at Vienna. The Library of Congress has photostats of the great body of these pertaining to the diplomacy of the Maximilian affair, and of the diplomatic correspondence of the Austrian government with Maximilian's Mexican government. The custodian of the *Maximilian-archiv* had transcripts made of documents in the *Preussische Geheimes Staatsarchiv*, now at Berlin-Dahlem, relating to the Maximilian affair, and these transcripts have in turn been photostated by the Library of Congress.

See our list on p. 868 for the papers of Thomas Corwin (minister to Mexico, 1861–64), and J. L. Motley (minister to Austria, 1861–67).

The Bancroft Library at the University of California has a MS. dictated by Senator W. M. Gwin, of California, of "Memoirs on the history of the United States, Mexico, and California."

CHAPTER XIV

EXPANSIONIST EFFORTS AFTER THE CIVIL WAR
1865-1898

1. In General.
2. Alaska Purchase.
3. Danish West Indies.

4. Santo Domingo.
5. Hawaii.
6. Samoa.

1. In General

Bibliographical Aids

For general aids, see Sabin (no. 4655); Larned (no. 4657); Griffin (no. 4658); *Writings* (no. 4661); C. H. and T. (no. 4662); *Guide hist. lit.* (no. 4634); and bibliographies in *Am. secs. state* (no. 4796). Myers (no. 5399), for collections of treaties. Miller, *Treaties* (no. 5371), v. I, 39-54, for "Bibliography of United States treaty collections." See also the national historical bibliographies of the various European countries concerned (nos. 4726-4765).

For indexes to periodical literature, see nos. 4995-5003.

For lists of and indexes to newspapers, see nos. 5004-5047.

General Works

Of general histories of the United States, see Rhodes (no. 4783); Oberholtzer (no. 4785), an encyclopedic general work, after the style of McMaster, by an apparent disciple, but written before the appearance of some of the later monographic studies given below. See also *Am. secs. state* (no. 4796), v. XII-IX; and Wriston (no. 4799), for special agents.

Blaine, *Twenty years* (no. 5192). Henderson, *Am. dipl. questions* (no. 2821). T. C. Smith, "Expansion after the civil war, 1865-1871", *Pol. sci. quar.*, XVI (1901) 412-463 [**2222**], a scholarly and informative article, based on printed sources and secondary works. Rhodes, *McKinley and Roosevelt* (no. 2462), a sequel to his great history (no. 4783). Alice F. Tyler, *The foreign policy of James G. Blaine* (Minneapolis, 1927) [**2223**], an unusually thorough analysis of Blaine's foreign policy as revealed in the archives of the Dept.

of State, supplements the sketch by Lockey in *Am. secs. state* (no. 4796), v. VIII. A. L. P. Dennis, *Adventures in American diplomacy, 1896–1906* (N.Y., 1928) [**2224**], a perspicacious account by an acute student who used the State Department archives, and the personal papers of Theodore Roosevelt and John Hay. F. R. Dulles, *America in the Pacific; a century of expansion* (Boston and N.Y., 1932) [**2225**], a spirited and intelligent, but not definitive, outline of Anglo-American penetration into the Pacific area. Holt, *Defeated treaties* (no. 4837). Smith, *Republican expansionists* (no. 1918a).

For biographies of American presidents, secretaries of state, and diplomatists abroad (for names and tenure, see latest *Register* of the Dept. of State (no. 5122)), and for Charles Sumner, see the relevant articles and bibliographical data in the *D.A.B.* See also Allan Nevins' *Grover Cleveland* (no. 2467), for Cleveland's foreign policy; G. F. Howe, *Chester A. Arthur; a quarter century of machine politics* (N.Y., 1934) [**2226**]; C. E. Russell, *Blaine of Maine; his life and times* (N.Y., 1931) [**2226a**], and D. S. Muzzey, *James G. Blaine, a political idol of other days* (N.Y., 1934) [**2226b**].[1]

Printed Sources

For American official documents and general source collections, see *Jour. exec. proc. Sen.* (no. 5387); *Cong. Globe* (no. 5384); *Cong. Record* (no. 5385); *For. relations* (no. 5345); Wharton, *Digest* (no. 5366); Richardson (no. 5335); Moore's *Arbitrations* (no. 5364); *Repts. Sen. com. for. rel.* (no. 5388); Moore's *Digest* (no. 5365).

Myers (no. 5399), for collections of treaties. For texts of treaties, see Malloy (no. 5368); and Miller, *Treaties* (no. 5371). See also p. 822, below, for guide to treaties.

For guides to foreign official documents, see below, p. 836.

For contemporary periodical material, consult *Poole's index* (no. 4995).

For lists of and indexes to newspapers, see nos. 5004–5047.

For an analysis of the principal American newspapers and periodicals, 1848 to 1871, expressive of American opinion, see Gazley (no. 1424).

For printed writings of American presidents, secretaries of state, and diplomatists abroad (for names and tenure, see latest *Register* of the Dept. of State (no. 5122)), see our list on p. 756. See also

---

[1] Three biographies published after the appropriate volumes of the *D.A.B.*

the *Reminiscences* of F. W. Seward (no. 5291); and the *Works* and *Letters* of Charles Sumner, chairman of the Senate committee on foreign relations, 1861–71 (no. 5297).

MSS.: Suggestions

See below for official archives of the Department of State (p. 857), for the personal papers of Presidents (p. 862); secretaries of state (p. 865); and American diplomatists (p. 868) (for names and tenure, see latest edition of the *Register* of the Dept. of State (no. 5122)). The papers of Justin S. Morrill, senator from Vermont, 1866–98, anti-imperialist, who actively opposed the annexation of San Domingo in 1870, the acquisition of Cuba, and the annexation of Hawaii, are in the Library of Congress.

More particular suggestions are given in following sections of this chapter.

2. Alaska Purchase

Bibliographical Aids

For general aids, see Sec. 1, above.

Judson, *Pacific Northwest* (no. 1707). Cowan, *Pacific West* (no. 1570). James Wickersham, *A bibliography of Alaskan literature, 1724–1924* (Cordova, Alaska, 1927) [**2227**], a very comprehensive bibliography. Kerner, *Russian expansion to America* (no. 1710).

Special Works

P. Tikhmenev, *Istoricheskoe obozrienie obrazovaniia Rossiisko Amerikanskoi Kompanii i Dieistvii eia do nastoiashchago Vremeni* (St. Petersburg, 1861–63, 2 v.) [**2228**], historical review of the founding of the Russian American company and its history. For a translation into English, of a section of volume II, see *The Rezanov voyage to Nueva California in 1806; the report of Count Nikolai Petrovich Rezanov of his voyage to that provincia of Nueva España from New Archangel*, an English translation, rev. and cor., with notes, etc., by T. C. Russell (San Francisco, 1926) [**2228a**]. H. H. Bancroft, *History of Alaska, 1730–1885* (San Francisco, 1886) (*His* Works, v. XXXIII) [**2229**], a work said to be of composite authorship, written largely by Bancroft's paid writer, Ivan Petroff, whose reliability is alleged to have been questioned; generally superficial but valuable in places. Frederic Bancroft, "Seward's ideas of territorial expansion ", *No. Am. rev.*, CLXVII (1898) 79-89 [**2230**], an enlightening essay by Seward's principal biographer. J. M. Callahan, *The Alaska purchase and Americo-Canadian relations* (Morgantown, W.Va., 1908) [**2231**]. W. A. Dunning, " Paying for Alaska, some unfamiliar incidents in the process ", *Pol. sci. quar.*, XXVII (1912) 385-398 [**2232**], an exposure article based on an alleged Andrew Johnson MS. found by a student. Three studies by F. A. Golder: " The attitude of the Russian government toward Alaska ", in *The Pacific Ocean in history*, ed. by H. M. Stephens and H. E. Bolton (N.Y., 1917), 269-275 [**2233**], because Alaska was a colonial white elephant, Russia wished to cultivate good relations with the United States by a sale; " The purchase of Alaska ", *Am. hist. rev.*, XXV (1920) 411-425 [**2234**], most important monograph which has yet appeared on the purchase; extends backward of the negotiations to 1854; noticeably lacking in the use of American sources, but contains excerpts and extracts from Russian documents in translation and in French. It has had great influence in stimulating research in the purchase. See also his *Russ. Am. relations during Crimean war* (no. 1426). Four studies by V. J. Farrar: "Joseph Lane McDonald and the purchase of Alaska ", *Wash. hist. quar.*, XII (1921) 83-90 [**2235**], the career of a pioneer Pacific Coast fisherman who sought cod fishery privileges in Alaska in 1859 or 1860, and in 1866, and whose endeavors came to the attention of Senator Gwin and Secretary Seward; " The background of the purchase of Alaska ", *ibid.*, XIII (1922) 93-104 [**2236**], and " Senator Cole and the purchase of Alaska ", *ibid.*, XIV (1923) 243-247 [**2237**], Senator Cole, of California, represented Louis Goldstone (of the California Fur Company, later Alaska Commercial Company, in an endeavor to secure a fur-trading franchise in Alaska under the Russians; has to do with the Seward-Stoeckl negotiations; and *The purchase of Alaska* (Wash., privately printed, 1934) [**2238**], a short and convenient analysis of the Seward-Stoeckl negotiations and of the origin of the idea of buying Alaska. Hill, *Treaties* (no. 4794), ch. 12: " The Alaska purchase, 1867 ", the best summary account. Thomas, *Russo-Am. relations* (no. 1438), the writer has made use of most of the studies of others concerning the Alaska purchase. H. W. Clark, *History of Alaska* (N.Y., 1930) [**2239**] is a compendium of the valuable research of such scholars as Golder,

Stefansson, Farrar, and others. Douglas, *Boundaries* (no. 211).
Dulles, *America in the Pacific* (no. 2225), ch. 6: " Seward's folly."
Jordan, *Robert J. Walker* (no. 1535), Walker acted as " counsel "
for the Russian minister and Secretary Seward in putting the Alaska
purchase bill through Congress in 1868. T. A. Bailey, "Why the
United States purchased Alaska ", *Pacific hist. rev.*, III (1934) 39–49
[**2240**], analysis of 21 representative American daily newspapers and
debates in Congress to show that the American people bought
Alaska because they thought it a bargain. Hallie M. McPherson,
" The interest of William McKendree Gwin in the purchase of
Alaska ", *ibid.*, 28–38 [**2241**], from the Gwin papers in the Bancroft
Library of the University of California, traces the activities of the
" advance agent " for the purchase of Alaska, " if not the first of
the early negotiators."

For biographies of President Johnson, Secretary of State Seward,
C. M. Clay, minister to Russia, and other American statesmen and
individuals connected with the purchase (F. W. Seward, assistant
secretary of state, Charles Sumner, chairman Senate committee on
foreign relations, Senators Cornelius Cole and W. M. Gwin of California, etc.), see the relevant entries and bibliographical data in the
D.A.B. Note also, W. E. Dodd, *Robert J. Walker, imperialist* (Chicago, 1914) [**2242**].

Printed Sources

For general collections, see Sec. 1, above.

For index to the history of Alaska as found in United States
government documents, congressional series, and in other documents, see Judson (no. 1707). See also Wickersham (no. 2227),
for public documents printed in English, Russian, German, French,
Spanish, etc., relating to Alaska, 1724 to 1924. United States public
documents of particular note are: *Russian-America . . . Correspondence in relation to Russian America* (40th Cong., 2d sess.,
1867. House. Ex. doc. 177. Ser. no. 1339) [**2243**], complete correspondence on the purchase, contains also Sumner's speech, text of
treaty, opinion of E. Pershine Smith, of the Attorney General's
office, on the legal status of Alaska, and many historical items, newspaper comment, etc. It is the principal source for the study of
the purchase. *Alaska investigation. February 27, 1869 . . . Report [of the Committee on public expenditures]* (40th Cong., 3d

sess., 1869. House. Rept. 35. Ser. no. 1388) [**2244**], paying for Alaska; report on the charge of misuse of funds appropriated for the purchase of Alaska.

RUSSIAN GOVERNMENT DOCUMENTS: Few documents from the ministry of foreign affairs relating to the purchase or transfer have yet (apparently) appeared in print. Extracts from several of these documents are printed as translations—extracts in French in Dr. Golder's articles, especially in his *Purchase of Alaska* (no. 2234). A few copies of documents were obtained by the Library of Congress from Dr. Golder, and are inventoried according to the classification or file number system used by him in his *Guide* (no. 5779). These are Washington series, 1854, no. 652; I-9, nos. 4, 77, 165, 166, 208, 209, 210, 2901; I-13, no. 12. The above are either photostats or transcripts. Hallie M. McPherson, ed., " The projected purchase of Alaska, 1859-60 ", *Pacific hist. rev.*, III (1934) 80-87 [**2245**] prints a letter from Baron Stoeckl, Russian minister in Washington, to Prince Gorchakov, Russian foreign secretary, " 23 décembre 1859 (4 janvier 1860)." This is the first publication of the original or its translation (photostat in the Library of Congress); it reveals the preliminary steps to the purchase.

For text of the treaty, see the official *Correspondence* (no. 2243). For the printed writings of Secretary of State Seward, see no. 5292; and of C. M. Clay, minister to Russia, see no. 5204. Memoirs, etc., of other personalities connected with the purchase are: *Diary of O. H. Browning* (no. 1887), Browning was Secretary of the Interior; entries for March 15 and 19, 1867, extremely valuable for the treaty before the cabinet and fixing of the purchase price. *Memoirs of Cornelius Cole, ex-senator of the United States from California* (N.Y., 1908) [**2246**], Senator Cole represented Goldstone and others (the California Fur Company, later the Alaska Commercial Company) in his efforts to secure a lease hold for fur trading in Alaska, a participant in the Seward-Stoeckl negotiations. This forty-year-after account should be checked with inspired article in San Francisco *Daily Evening Bulletin*, June 5, 1867. E. L. Pierce, *Letters of Sumner* (no. 5297) contains Sumner's famous Alaska speech and estimate of his services. This speech is also printed in the official *Correspondence* (no. 2243). F. W. Seward. *Reminiscences* (no. 5291), by the assistant-secretary of state, and son of the Secretary; his account of the Alaska purchase is dramatic, but disappointing, coming from one who was in a position to know.

Cases under the Treaty of Cession: Callsen *v.* Hope, 75 Fed. Rep. 758. Kinkead *v.* U.S., 150 U.S.Rep. 483. Rassmussen *v.* U.S., 197 U.S.Rep. 516. U.S. *v.* Williams, Circuit Court, D. Oregon, Feb. 5, 1880, 2 Fed. 61.

MSS.: Suggestions

See Sec. 1, above. Note remarks on Russian archives, p. 933, paragraph on " Russian Government Documents ", above, and Kerner (no. 1710) for suggestions on the background of Alaska. The Library of Congress (see its *Handbook* (no. 5520), 456–458) has a collection of photocopies made by the late Professor Golder, of Russian documents relating to the earlier history of Alaska, then (1914) in the Imperial archives at Petrograd.

There are a few letters in the Library of Congress of Cassius M. Clay (U.S. minister to Russia, 1861–69). The Sumner papers are in the Harvard College Library. The papers of N. P. Banks (member of Congress, 1865–72, and chairman of the committee on foreign affairs of the House), an advocate of the purchase of Alaska, are in the Essex Institute, Salem, Mass. The Bancroft Library at Berkeley, California, has a MS. written in 1878 by Sen. W. M. Gwin of California, entitled, *Memoirs on the history of the United States, Mexico, and California, by Ex-Senator William M. Gwin, dictated by himself for the Bancroft Library.*

Maps: Suggestions

For maps relating to Alaska, see those published at the time of the Alaska boundary arbitration (no. 2627), below. See also, for maps in the Library of Congress, Phillips, *Alaska . . . maps in the Library of Congress* (no. 5133) ; and Paullin's *Atlas* (no. 213).

3. The Danish West Indies

Bibliographical Aids

For general aids, see Sec. 1, above. See also the Danish historical bibliographies (nos. 4730–4731).

A. P. C. Griffin, *A list of books (with references to periodicals) on the Danish West Indies* (Wash., 1901) (Library of Congress) [**2247**]. New York Public Library, *List relating to West Indies* (no. 4720), 212–214. *A bibliography of the Virgin Islands of the United States* (St. Thomas: Govt. Print. Off., 1922) [**2248**].

Special Works

[Sidney Andrews], *The St. Thomas treaty. A series of letters to the Boston Daily Advertiser* [Signed: Dixon, *pseud.* for Sidney Andrews] (N.Y., 1869) [**2249**] reports the proceedings in Washington while the treaty was pending, and includes the text of the treaty.   Olive R. Seward, "A diplomatic episode ", *Scribner's*, II (1887) 585–602 [**2250**], this article by an adopted daughter of Secretary Seward is an acrid attack on Senator Sumner for his opposition to the treaty of Oct. 24, 1867.   E. L. Pierce, *A diplomatic fiasco. The rejected treaty for St. Thomas* (Boston, 1889) [**2251**] is a refutation of the article by Olive R. Seward (no. 2250).   Bancroft, *Seward and territorial expansion* (no. 2230).   T. C. Smith, *Expansion after civil war* (no. 2222).   A. M. Stickles, " The Danish West Indies and American ownership ", *Jour. Am. hist.*, VII (1913) 849–874 [**2252**], a tolerable article based on obvious printed material.   W. F. Johnson, " The story of the Danish Islands ", *No. Am. rev.*, CCIV (1916) 381–390 [**2253**], nothing new; of limited value.   Fogdall, *Dan.-Am. dipl.* (no. 195), limited to obvious printed materials, for this period. C. C. Tansill, *The purchase of the Danish West Indies* (Baltimore, 1932) [**2254**], the standard account of Danish-American relations concerning the islands, based on study of documents from the archives of the United States, Germany, Great Britain, and Denmark.

For biographies of President Johnson, Secretary of State Seward, and American diplomatists abroad (for names and tenure, see latest *Register* of the Dept. of State (no. 5122), see the relevant entries and bibliographical data in the *D.A.B.*   See also biography of Sen. W. R. Doolittle, special commissioner to Denmark, 1867, negotiator of the treaty of that year, in the *D.A.B.*

Printed Sources

For general collections, see Sec. 1, above.

UNITED STATES OFFICIAL DOCUMENTS: *Report of Select committee to investigate facts connected with the purchase of the Danish West India Islands* (57th Cong., 1st sess. House Rept. no. 2749) [**2255**] contains all the hearings and the correspondence with reference to the activities of Captain Christmas during the years 1899–1900, and alleged corruption.   *Compilation of reports of the Committee on Foreign Relations, United States Senate, 1789–1901*, v. VIII (Wash.,

1901) (56th Cong., 2d sess. Sen. Doc. 231, pt. 8) [2256] contains a considerable amount of the diplomatic correspondence concerning the Danish-American treaty of Oct. 24, 1867, not in *Foreign relations* (no. 5345).

DANISH OFFICIAL PUBLICATION: (Denmark, Rigsdagen, Dansk Vestindiske Kommission), *Betænkning afgiven af den i henhold til lov nr. 294 af 30. september 1916 nedsatte Rigsdagskommission angaaende de Dansk vestindiske øer* (Copenhagen, 1916) [2257], p. 4–12 for "Konvention mellem Hans Majestæt kongen af Danmark og de amerikanske Forenede Stater angaaende overdragelsen af øerne St. Thomas, St. Jan og St. Croix i Vestindien" (Danish and English in parallel columns). For a list of references to material in the Danish *Rigsdagstidende*, 1867–1870, relative to negotiations for sale of the Danish West Indies, see Griffin (no. 2247), 17–18.

James Parton, *The Danish Islands: are we bound in honor to pay for them?* (Boston, 1869) [2258], Parton had access to the Seward-Raasloff correspondence but was paid by the latter, the Danish minister, to write this pamphlet.   Duane Mowry, " Government purchase of the Danish West Indies ", *Mag. of hist.*, XXI (1915) 178–181 [2259], correspondence from the papers of Sen. Doolittle of Wisconsin, 1866–67, regarding the proposed purchase.   Sarah Wambaugh, *A monograph on plebiscites; with a collection of official documents* (N.Y., 1920) [2260] includes extracts from the correspondence concerning the proposed cession of the islands of St. Thomas and St. John by Denmark to the United States, 1866–1867 (p. 945–976), from the *Compilation of reports of Senate committee on foreign relations* (no. 5388).

For the printed writings of Secretary of State Seward, and American diplomatists abroad (for names and tenure, see latest *Register* of the Dept. of State (no. 5122)), see our list on p. 756. M. F. Egan, *Ten years* (no. 5219), reminiscences of the American minister at Copenhagen contains an account of the difficulties that were encountered during the preliminaries to the purchase of the Danish West Indies.   See also the printed writings of Senator Sumner (no. 5297). Some of the correspondence from the papers of Sen. J. R. Doolittle of Wisconsin, relative to the purchase of the Danish West Indies by the United States, 1866–67, is printed in the *Magazine of history*, XXI (1915) 178–181 [2261].

MSS.: Suggestions

See Section 1, above.

For European archival collections, see below (Denmark, p. 932); (Germany, p. 924); (Great Britain, p. 890).

For the papers of Charles Sumner, and Nathaniel P. Banks, see Sec. 4, below. The Library of Congress has a portfolio of the papers of Senator J. R. Doolittle, who assisted in the negotiation of the unratified treaty of 1869. There is also a collection of pamphlets, clippings, several hundred letters, MS. speeches, etc., of Senator Doolittle, in the State Historical Society of Wisconsin, at Madison.

4. Santo Domingo

Bibliographical Aids

For general aids, see Sec. 1, above. See also New York Public Library, *List relating to West Indies* (no. 4720).

Special Works

J. D. Cox, " How Judge Hoar ceased to be attorney general ", *Atlantic*, LXXVI (1895) 162–173 [**2262**], Grant's secretary of the interior gives an " inside story " of the domestic politics of the annexation treaty, including the dismissal of Attorney General E. R. Hoar. St. Mérant, *Samana* (no. 2151). C. F. Adams, *Treaty of Washington* (no. 2518), important survey of Grant's annexation treaty based on study of Secretary Fish's personal papers. Treudley (no. 2161a) goes to 1866 only. Knight, *Americans in Santo Domingo* (no. 3912), a very general cynical and unscholarly account relying largely on secondary material. Welles, *Naboth's Vineyard* (no. 2167). Wriston (no. 4799) has important data on special missions to Santo Domingo (J. B. Hogan, David D. Porter, B. E. Green, R. M. Walsh, W. L. Cazneau, G. B. McClellan, Jonathan Elliott), 1845–60; Frederick Seward and Vice Admiral David D. Porter, 1867; and Brigadier General Orville E. Babcock, in 1869–70.

For biographies of presidents, secretaries of state, and diplomatists abroad (for names and tenure, see latest *Register* of the Dept. of State (no. 5122), see the relevant entries and bibliographical data in the *D.A.B.* Consult the *D.A.B.* also for biographies of the special agents mentioned above; and of B. F. Wade, A. D. White, and S. G. Howe, commissioners to Santo Domingo in 1871.

Printed Sources

For general collections, see Sec. 1, above.

The following U.S. official documents contain sources for the annexationist movement: *List of privileges—San Domingo treaty . . . April 6, 1870* (41st Cong., 2d sess. House. Ex. doc., No. 237) [**2263**], a statement by the Secretary of State, in response to a resolution of the House, that it would not be compatible with the public interest to transmit a list of privileges held by persons interested in Santo Domingo. *Information relative to the proposed annexation of the Dominican portion of the Island of San Domingo.* January 16, 1871 (41st Cong., 3d sess. Sen. Ex. doc., No. 17) [**2264**], report by the Secretary of State in response to Senate resolution, on previous (to 1870) negotiations and inquiries of the United States government in regard to Santo Domingo, and relevant documents. *Copies of correspondence with and orders issued to the commander of our naval squadron in the waters of the island of San Domingo since the commencement of the late negotiations.* February 7, 1871 (41st Cong., 3d sess. Sen. Ex. doc., No. 34) [**2265**]. *Dominican Republic. . . . Report of the Secretary of State relative to the Dominican Republic.* January 9, 1871 (41st Cong., 3d sess. House. Ex. doc. No. 42) [**2266**] contains the reports and relevant documents of J. B. Hogan, sent to Santo Domingo by President Polk; and Capt. G. B. McClellan, sent there by President Pierce. *Dominican Republic. . . . Report of Captain George B. McClellan upon the Dominican Republic, in the year 1854.* January 11, 1871 (41st Cong., 3d sess. House. Ex. doc., No. 43) [**2267**] contains report on possible naval bases. *Report of the Commission of inquiry to the Island of Santo Domingo.* April 5, 1871 (42d Cong., 1st sess. Sen. Ex. doc., no. 91) [**2268**] includes the introductory message of the President, special reports made to the commission, state papers furnished by the Dominican government, and the statements of witnesses; has also a map of the Island of Santo Domingo.

Contemporary periodical articles arguing for and against annexation: H. Hargrave, "The Dominican Republic and annexation", *Lippincott's*, VI (1870) 200–210 [**2269**]. A. G. Sedgwick, "The St. Domingo bargain", *Nation*, X (1870) 68 [**2270**]. "The annexation of St. Domingo", by Americus, *Galaxy*, XI (1871) 410–421 [**2271**]. G. A. Kroeger, "What will the San Domingo commission do?"

Nation, XII (1871) 68–69 [**2272**]. E. L. Godkin, " The new San Domingo scheme ", *ibid.*, XVI (1873) 52–53 [**2273**]. E. L. Pierce, "A senator's fidelity vindicated ", *No. Am. rev.*, CXXVII (1878) 61–80 [**2274**].

Annexation of San Domingo (N.Y., 1870) [**2275**] includes text of the annexation treaties and articles from the New York city newspapers. [W. L. Cazneau], *To the American press; the Dominican negotiacions:* [1] *I. Samana as a naval station. II. Samana as a free port. III. Samana and annexation* (Santo Domingo, 1870) [**2276**], Cazneau had been a special investigator of the Department of State to Santo Domingo in 1853–54, and later in 1859–60, and was an outstanding supporter of Grant's annexationist proposal. *The St. Domingo question. An American policy* (n.p., 1870?) [**2277**], anonymous undated argument for ratification of the treaty of annexation then pending before the Senate. *Breve refutación del informe de los comisionados de Santo Domingo, dedicada al pueblo de los Estados Unidos* (Curaçao, 1871) [**2278**], an antiannexation tract by " various Dominicans "; accuses the commissioners of subordination to the interested motives of Baez. S. G. Howe, *Letters on the proposed annexation of Santo Domingo, in answer to certain charges in the newspapers* (Boston, 1871) [**2279**], by one of Grant's committee of investigation, who says "I *know* that the investigation was made honestly, earnestly, and thoroughly." See also the *Letters and journals of Samuel Gridley Howe*, ed. by his daughter, Laura E. Richards (Boston, 1906–09, 2 v.) [**2280–1**]. Admiral Porter, *Missions to San Domingo* (no. 2146) contains important data relative to the secret missions of Porter to the Dominican Republic in 1846 and 1867. F. W. Seward, *Seward at Washington*, v. III of his *Autobiography* (no. 5292) is valuable for the account of F. W. Seward's mission to the Dominican Republic in 1867 for the purpose of leasing Samana Bay. " Partes sobre la salida de la fragata americana 'Albany' ", *Boletín del archivo nacional* (Havana), XXIX, nos. 1–6 (1930) 99–101 [**2282**] reprints reports of the Governor General of Cuba (from the *Ministerio de Ultramar*), 1870, concerning the sailing of the U.S. frigate "Albany " carrying a commission from the United States to the Dominican Republic for the purpose of negotiating for the use of Samana Bay.

---

[1] Spelled *Negotiacions* on title-page.

For the printed writings of Carl Schurz (who supported Senator Sumner in opposition to the treaty), the autobiography of Andrew D. White (one of Grant's commissioners to Santo Domingo and defender of his policy), and the works of Senator Sumner, see our list on p. 756.

MSS.: Suggestions

See Section 1, above. We know of no index to the archives of Santo Domingo.

In addition to the papers of Seward, Grant, and Fish, mentioned in Section 1, we have collections of various individuals who participated one way or another in the annexationist attempt: See our list on p. 868, for the papers of Andrew D. White and Carl Schurz; Charles Sumner papers largely printed (no. 5297) in the Harvard College Library. The papers of Nathaniel P. Banks (member of Congress, 1865-72, and chairman of the committee on foreign affairs of the House of Representatives) are in the Essex Institute, in Salem. Mass. There are a few letters of Samuel Gridley Howe in the Library of Congress.

5. Hawaii

Bibliographical Aids

For general aids, see Sec. 1, above.

Hawaiian Club, Boston, *Hawaiian club papers*, ed. by a committee of the Club (Boston, 1868) [2283] includes a " Catalogue of works published at, or relating to, the Hawaiian Islands " (p. 63-115). J. F. Hunnewell, *Bibliography of the Hawaiian Islands* (Boston, 1869) [2284], of little value for diplomatic history. *Catalogue of the bound books in the library of the Hawaiian Historical Society*, published by the Society (Honolulu, 1897) [2285]. A. P. C. Griffin, *List of books relating to Hawaii (including references to collected works and periodicals)* (Wash., 1898) (Library of Congress) [2286]. G. R. Carter, *Preliminary catalogue of Hawaiiana in the library of George R. Carter . . . collected largely by Professor H. M. Ballou* (Boston, 1915) [2287]. Vaughan MacCaughney, *The one hundred most important books and files relating to the Hawaiian Islands* (Boston, 1918) [2288], reprinted from the *Bulletin of Bibliography*, 1918.

Special Works

Three works by W. D. Alexander: *A brief history of the Hawaiian people* (N.Y., 1891) [**2289**], useful for a " list of all the cabinet ministers who have held office in the Hawaiian Islands, 1842–1897 " (p. 340–345) ; *History of later years of the Hawaiian monarchy and the revolution of 1893* (Honolulu, 1896) [**2290**]; *The uncompleted treaty of annexation of 1854* (Honolulu, 1897) (Hawaiian Historical Society Papers, IX) [**2291**], appendix contains a few relevant documents. E. J. Carpenter, *America in Hawaii; a history of United States influence in the Hawaiian Islands* (Boston, 1899) [**2292**], undocumented popular account. W. F. Blackman, *The making of Hawaii* (N.Y., 1899) [**2293**], a study of the social, political, and moral development of the Hawaiians. Callahan, *Pacific and Far East* (no. 3086) covers the pre-annexation period; based on United States official printed and unprinted documents. Foster, *Am. diplomacy in the Orient* (no. 3087), ch. 4: " Independent Hawaii." Walter Escott, "At the court of the Kamehamehas; an American diplomat in Hawaii during the civil war ", *Overland*, LX (1912), 419–426 [**2294**], picturesque account of the embassy of Dr. James McBride, first U.S. minister to Hawaii, 1863–67; apparently based on diary or other notes, with interesting early photographs. Paullin (no. 151), for early diplomatic negotiations of American naval officers. W. R. Castle, Jr., *Hawaii, past and present*, rev. and enl. (N.Y., 1917; 1st ed., 1913) [**2295**], colorful outline by a distinguished son of Hawaii. Scholefield, *The Pacific* (no. 2350). Three works by R. S. Kuykendall, *A history of Hawaii;* prepared under the direction of the Historical Commission of the Territory of Hawaii (N.Y., 1926) [**2296**], unusually good text of local island history; and "American interests and American influence in Hawaii in 1842 ", *Hawaiian hist. soc. ann. rep.*, for 1930, XXXIX (1931) 48–67 [**2297**], it was in 1842 that the United States recognized the independence of the Hawaiian Islands; and " Early Hawaiian commercial development ", *Pacific hist. rev.*, III (1934) 365–385 [**2297a**], valuable contribution particularly for the background of earliest American contacts. Dennis, *Adventures* (no. 2224), ch. 4: " Hawaii and Samoa." Wriston (no. 4799) has important data on special missions to Hawaii (of Capt. Thomas Ap Catesby Jones, 1825; Z. S.

Spalding, 1867; G. H. Bates, 1883; J. H. Blount, 1893). A. P. Taylor and R. S. Kuykendall, eds., *The Hawaiian Islands* (Honolulu: Archives of the Hawaii Commission, 1930) [2298] includes three valuable papers on the early diplomatic history of Hawaii which were read at the Captain Cook sesquicentennial celebration at Honolulu, August 17, 1928: F. W. Howay, "Early relations between the Hawaiian Islands and the northwest coast", based on early ship logs, 1786–1805; F. A. Golder, "Proposals for Russian occupation of the Hawaiian Islands", as revealed by the archives of the Russian ministry of foreign affairs; and G. V. Blue, "The policy of France toward the Hawaiian Islands from the earliest times to the treaty of 1846", based on archives of the French foreign office. T. A. Bailey, "The United States and Hawaii during the Spanish-American war", *Am. hist. rev.*, XXXVI (1931) 552–560 [2299] analyses the Hawaiian attitude of active assistance to the United States on the eve of the Spanish-American war, following McKinley's unratified treaty of annexation of 1897; uses all available sources, including State Department MSS. See also his *Japan's protest against the annexation of Hawaii* (no. 3279). Two studies by H. W. Bradley: "The American frontier in Hawaii", *Pacific Coast branch of Am. hist. assoc. proc.*, 1930 (1931) 135–150 [2300] sees Texas as the model; and "Thomas Ap Catesby Jones and the Hawaiian Islands, 1826–1827", *Hawaiian hist. soc. ann. rep., for 1930*, XXXIX (1931) 17–30 [2301] shows the commander of the *Peacock* important explanation of replacement of British prestige by American dominance. J. W. Pratt, "The Hawaiian revolution; a re-interpretation", *Pacific hist. rev.*, I (1932) 273–294 [2302] concludes that the revolution of 1893 was fundamentally the result of a desire for "stable government", and that its deliberate purpose was annexation, and the substance of the plan was known in Washington. Donald Rowland, "The United States and the contract labor question in Hawaii, 1862–1900", *ibid.*, II (1933) 249–269 [2303], based on correspondence in the Dept. of State, *For. relations* (no. 5345), and other printed sources. R. W. Van Alstyne, "Great Britain, the United States, and Hawaiian independence, 1850–1855", *Pacific hist. rev.*, IV (1935) 15–24 [2303a], Pierce's efforts to annex Hawaii in 1853, thwarted by British diplomacy.

For biographies of American presidents, secretaries of state, and commissioners and ministers to Hawaii, 1843–1897 (for names and tenure, see latest *Register* of the Dept. of State (no. 5122)), see the relevant entries and bibliographical data in the *D. A. B.*

Printed Sources

For general collections, see Sec. 1, above.

For United States official documents relating to Hawaii, 1828 to 1898, see Hasse's *Index* (no. 5344), to 1861; *Tables and index* (no. 5357) to 1893, and subsequent volumes of the *Document catalogue* (no. 5358); also, for the documents themselves, *Foreign relations* (no. 5345). *Foreign relations, 1894. Affairs in Hawaii* (Wash., 1895) (53d Cong., 3d sess. House. Ex. doc. No. 1, pt. 1, app. 2) [**2304**] consists of the report by Andrew H. Allen, Feb. 9, 1893 (" Report upon the official relations of the United States with the Hawaiian Islands from the first appointment of a consular officer there by this government ") and much correspondence. Noteworthy collections relating to annexation are: *Papers relating to the annexation of the Hawaiian Islands to the United States* (52d Cong., 2d sess. Sen. Ex. doc., Nos. 76–77) [**2305**]. *Correspondence with diplomatic and naval officers concerning the relations of the United States to the Hawaiian Islands, including a reprint of Senate executive documents nos. 76 and 77, fifty-second Congress, second session* (Wash., 1893) [**2306**], supporting the treaty of annexation of 1893; a compendium of principal official documents. [*Report from the committee on foreign relations, United States Senate, on Hawaiian Islands*], 1894 (53d Cong., 2d sess. Sen. Rept., No. 227) [**2307**], with accompanying testimony, and executive documents transmitted to Congress, from January 1, 1893, to March 10, 1894; a mine of information of all kinds. *President's message relating to the Hawaiian Islands, December 18, 1893* (53d Cong., 2d sess. House. Ex. doc. No. 47) [**2308**], the adverse report of Cleveland's special commissioner of investigation (J. H. Blount). *Hawaiian correspondence . . . A report of the Secretary of State, with copies of the instructions given to Mr. Albert S. Willis, the representative of the United States now in the Hawaiian Islands, and also the correspondence since March 4, 1889* (53d Cong., 2d sess. House. Ex. doc. No. 48) [**2309**]. *Annexation of Hawaii . . . Report* (55th Cong., 2d Sess. Sen. Rept. 681) ([**2310**]. . . . . *Report of the Hawaiian commission, appointed in pursuance of the " Joint resolution to provide for annexing the Hawaiian Islands to the United States ", approved July 7, 1898* (55th Cong., 3d sess. Sen., Doc. 16) [**2311**].

HAWAIIAN OFFICIAL DOCUMENTS:[2] *Report of the minister of foreign affairs,* 1843–1900 (Honolulu, 1845–1900, 21 v.) [**2313**]. *Correspondence between H.H.M. secretary of state and the United States commissioner, in the case of John Wiley, an American citizen,* 1844 (Honolulu, 1844) [**2314**]. *Correspondence between H.M.'s minister of foreign relations and the U.S. commissioner, on the case of John Wiley, an American citizen imprisoned at the instance of Viscount William de la Perrotière, M.D., a French subject,* 1845 (Honolulu, 1845) [**2315**]. *Official correspondence between Anthony Ten Eyck, esquire, commissioner of the United States, and Robert Crichton Wyllie, esquire, His Hawaiian Majesty's minister of foreign relations, upon the subject of alleged abuses in the registration of Hawaiian vessels* (Honolulu, 1848) [**2316**]. *Official correspondence between Anthony Ten Eyck, esquire, commissioner of the United States, and Robert Crichton Wyllie, His Hawaiian Majesty's minister of foreign relations, upon the subject of the mission to the governor of California of Theodore Shillaber, esquire* (Honolulu, 1848) [**2317**]. *Official correspondence between Anthony Ten Eyck, esquire, and Robert Crichton Wyllie, esquire, His Hawaiian Majesty's minister of foreign relations, showing the causes of cessation of official intercourse with Anthony Ten Eyck, esquire, as U.S. commissioner* (Honolulu, 1848) [**2318**]. *Official correspondence with Le Chevalier Dillon, consul of France, relating to charges brought by him against William Paty, esq., collector general of customs, and also relating to demands made, officially, by the consul of France, for the repeal of two laws of the Hawaiian Kingdom* (Honolulu, 1849) [**2319**]. *Report of the committee on foreign relations,* of the Legislature of the Hawaiian Islands (Honolulu, 1890) [**2320**], in regard to the matter of negotiations for renewal of the treaty with the United States, including charges against J. Austin, minister of foreign affairs. *Reply of Minister Austin to the majority report of committee on foreign relations in the Legislative Assembly, June 13th, 1890* (Honolulu, 1890) [**2321**], a reply to the report above (no. 2320).

For a selected list of articles in periodicals relating to Hawaii, 1839–1898, see Griffin (no. 2286), 22–26.

---

[2] Cf. J. T. Phillips, *A preliminary check list of the printed reports and correspondence of the minister of foreign relations of the government of the Hawaiian Islands, 1845 to 1862, inclusive* (Honolulu: Hawaiian Historical Society, 1928) [**2312**].

Treaties and conventions concluded between the Hawaiian Kingdom and other powers since 1825 (Honolulu, 1875) [**2322**] includes the texts of the convention with the United States, 1826, and the Postal convention, 1870. See also, for texts of treaties, Miller, *Treaties* (no. 5371), and remarks concerning treaty collections, p. 822, below.

Hawaiian almanac and annual, for 1875, 1876, 1883, 1888, 1897, compiled by T. G. Thrum (Honolulu, 1875–1897, 6 v.) [**2323**], handbooks of information on matters relating to the Hawaiian Islands, original and selected, of value to merchants, planters, tourists, and others. W. R. Castle [Sr.], *Brief digest and index of the various annexations of foreign territory made by the United States of America,* prepared by W. R. Castle, while Hawaiian minister in Washington in the year 1895. Published by the Annexation Club of Honolulu. (Wash., 1897) [**2324**]. J. A. Gillis, *The Hawaiian incident; an examination of Mr. Cleveland's attitude toward the revolution of 1893* (Boston, 1897) [**2325**], written to justify Cleveland's refusal to accept a treaty of annexation due to the connivance and assistance of the American minister aided by the presence in Honolulu of U.S. troops from the U.S.S. *Boston;* documents and testimony. *The Hawaiian crisis; correspondence between President Dole and U.S. minister Willis, December 1893* (Honolulu, 1893) [**2326**]. Abraham Hoffnung, *The recent revolution in Ḥawaii* (Woking, Eng., 1893?), reprinted from the *Imperial and Asiatic quarterly review,* April, 1893 [**2327**], by the Hawaiian *chargé* in London, who explains the revolution by expectations of Hawaiian sugar planters to find a panacea for their predicament. A. T. Mahan, "Hawaii and our future sea power", *Forum,* XV (1893) 1–11, also published in his *The interest of America in sea power* (Boston, 1897) 31–55 [**2328**], a highly important article presenting arguments from point of view of the military control of the Pacific, and especially the northern Pacific; Mahan was one of those who developed the policy of annexation in the United States. J. A. Palmer, Jr., *Memories of Hawaii and Hawaiian correspondence* (Boston, 1894) [**2329**], republication of reports from Hawaii in 1893 by a special correspondent of the Boston *Transcript,* writing from the dictates of independent judgment. W. R. Castle [Sr.] [*Letter concerning the annexation of Hawaii, dated March 1897*] [**2330**] is a letter written by the

" late Hawaiian minister in Washington " urging annexation. J. W.
Foster, *The annexation of Hawaii,* an address delivered before the
National Geographic Society at Washington, D.C., March 26, 1897
(Wash., 1897) [**2331**]. International Bureau of American Repub-
lics, *Hawaii* (Wash., 1897) [**2332**], factual information and a map.
L. A. Thurston, *A handbook on the annexation of Hawaii.* (St.
Joseph, Mich., 1897) [**2333**], by the leader in the islands of the
annexationists. J. D. Caton, *Argument favoring the annexation of
Hawaii* (Wash., 1898) (55th Cong., 2d sess. Sen. Doc. 214) [**2334**],
by a former justice of the Supreme Court of the United States.
H. E. von Holst, *The annexation of Hawaii* (Chicago, 1898) [**2335**],
plea of the eminent German-American historian against annexation.
G. S. Boutwell, *Hawaiian annexation* (Boston, 1898) [**2336**], an
example of numerous anti-annexation pamphlets. M. H. Krout,
Hawaii and a revolution (N.Y., 1898) [**2337**], the personal experiences of a correspondent in the Sandwich Islands during the crisis
of 1893 and subsequently; journalistic. Liliuokalani, *Hawaii's story
by Hawaii's queen* (Boston, 1898) [**2338**], the queen's defense against
the annexationist plot, apparently a narrative prepared with some
sort of literary assistance. Lucien Young, *The real Hawaii; its
history and present condition. (A revised and enlarged ed. of " The
Boston at Hawaii ")* (N.Y., 1899) [**2339**], written by an American
naval officer in 1893 to defend the navy against commissioner Blount's
charges of political interference, but suppressed till 1898; significantly dedicated to J. L. Stevens and G. C. Wiltse (Harrison's commissioners to Hawaii). F. R. Stoddard, "Annexation scheme of 1854
that failed ", *Hawaiian hist. soc. pap.,* XVII (1930) 39–52 [**2340–1**]
deals with Admiral Bailey's connection with the annexation movement of 1854, largely made up of letters, official and private, from
Admiral Bailey when in Hawaiian waters, 1854–55.

For the printed writings of American presidents, secretaries of
state (beginning about 1842 in the early period of American effort
to maintain the sovereignty of Hawaii against the encroachments of
France and Great Britain: particularly Webster, Clayton, Marcy,
Seward and Fish), and commissioners and ministers to Hawaii (for
names and tenure, see latest *Register* of the Dept. of State (no.
5122)), see our list on p. 756.

MSS.: Suggestions

See Sec. 1, above.

The Hawaiian Territorial Government has indexed the archives of the Department of State at Washington for material relating to Hawaii since 1820, when the first American agent was stationed there: R. S. Kuykendall, *Hawaiian diplomatic correspondence in the Bureau of Indexes and Archives of the Department of State, Washington, D.C.* (Honolulu, 1926) [**2342**]. There is a note on the archives of Hawaii by R. C. Lydecker, " The archives of Hawaii ", *Hawaiian hist. soc. pap.*, XIII (1906) 5–23 [**2343**] indicating that they were intact and safely housed, though not indexed. Since then the Hawaiian archives have been indexed by the local archivists, but no indexes are yet published. They contain: Foreign office files to 1885, and 1893–1900; private papers of Queen Liliuokalani, Sanford B. Dole, and others; and much other official and unofficial material relating to the islands. A set of photostats of correspondence that passed between the ministers of the Hawaiian kingdom and the secretary for foreign affairs at Honolulu, from January, 1889, through February, 1893, has been obtained by the University of Michigan.

The archives of foreign countries, described below (particularly France, p. 915; Great Britain, p. 890; Russia, p. 933; and Japan, p. 940) are certain to yield important data when examined; and such an examination would include naval ministries as well as foreign offices.

The only descriptions of the archives of the Department of the Navy of the United States, are those indicated in Van Tyne and Leland's *Guide* (no. 5495).

Note the papers of presidents and secretaries of state, referred to in Section 1.

The Library of Congress has a typewritten statement of facts relative to Hawaiian politics during Kalapaua's reign, 1874–1887, by D. W. Alexander, given in 1904 by Sen. H. C. Lodge.

6. Samoa

Bibliographical Aids

For general aids, see Sec. 1, above. See also German historical bibliographies (nos. 4740–4743).

A. P. C. Griffin, *A list of books (with references to periodicals) on Samoa and Guam* (Wash., 1901) (Library of Congress) [**2344**], most complete list. *Handbook of Western Samoa* (Wellington, N.Z., 1925) [**2345**], "Bibliography" (p. 140–174). Ryden (no. 2355), 582–592.

Special Works

Freeman Snow, *Treaties and topics* (no. 4786a). Paul Lefébure, "Le partage des Samoa et la politique dans le Pacifique Sud", *Annales des sciences politiques*, XV (1900) 116–129 [**2346**], a rather cynical summary. Callahan, *Pacific and Far East* (no. 3086). Henderson, *Am. dipl. questions* (no. 2821) gives extensive space to Samoa. J. W. Foster, *Am. diplomacy in Orient* (no. 3087). H. M. Herrick, *William Walter Phelps, his life and public services* (N.Y., 1904) [**2347**], a valuable study of the Samoan question in 1889. W. S. Penfield, *The settlement of the Samoan cases* (N.Y., 1913) [**2348**], reprinted from the *Am. jour. internat. law*, VII, 1913; a note summarizing the disposal of claims of American citizens for losses sustained in the bombardment of Apia, 1899. Zimmermann, *Kolonialpolitik* (no. 4303). Reventlow, *Deutsch. auswärtiges Politik* (no. 4304), this well-known presentation of German foreign policy to the world of 1913 has a meager mention of the Samoan settlement. R. M. Watson, *History of Samoa* (Wellington, 1918) [**2349**], a useful summary sketch with no pretenses to definitiveness. Keim, *Ger.-Am. relations* (no. 4305). G. H. Scholefield, *The Pacific, its past and future; and The policy of the great powers from the eighteenth century* (London, 1919) [**2350**], a scholarly short history of British foreign policy in the Pacific. Mary E. Townsend, *Origins of modern German colonization, 1871–1885* (N.Y., 1921) [**2351**], a study of the development of policy, rather than of consequent diplomatic activities; and by the same writer, *The rise and fall of Germany's colonial empire* (N.Y., 1930) [**2352**]. Valentin, *Deutsch. Aussenpolitik* (no. 4409). Felix Rachfahl, *Deutschland und die Weltpolitik, 1871–1914. I. Die Bismarck'sche Ära* (Stuttgart, 1923) [**2353**], one of the best treatments of German foreign policy from 1870 to 1890. Brandenburg, *Bismarck to world war* (no. 4310). Tyler, *For. pol. Blaine* (no. 2223), ch. 9: "The Samoan conference, 1889." T. T. Craven, "A naval episode of 1899", *U.S.N.inst.proc.*, LIV (1928) 185–200 [**2354**], by a junior officer of the expedition of the U.S.S. *Philadelphia* to Samoa in 1899 to guard American interests during the political disturbance there. Dennis, *Adventures* (no. 2224), ch.

4: "Hawaii and Samoa." Wriston (no. 4799) has much important material on special missions to Samoa (R. W. Meade, 1872; A. B. Steinberger, 1873; Gustavus Goward, 1878; G. H. Bates, 1886; Bartlett Tripp, 1899). Dulles, *America in Pacific* (no. 2225). G. H. Ryden, *The foreign policy of the United States in relation to Samoa* (New Haven, 1933) [2355], this comprehensive monograph will serve as the standard account for American policy, but must be supplemented with Stolberg and Masterman for the complete picture. Stolberg-Wernigerode, *Deutschland und Vereinigten Staaten* (no. 4314). Sylvia Masterman, *The origins of international rivalry in Samoa, 1845-1884* (London, 1934) [2355a] stresses British humanitarian and missionary interests. The author's use of British foreign office and colonial office archives makes this thesis a helpful supplement to Stolberg (no. 4314) who used German and American archives, and Ryden (no. 2355) who used only United States archives; but both Ryden and Stolberg seem unknown to Miss Masterman.

For biographies of presidents, secretaries of state, 1872-1899 (for names and tenure, see latest *Register* of the Dept. of State (no. 5122), and for commissioners to Samoa (noted above, under Wriston), also J. A. Kasson and W. W. Phelps, delegates to the Berlin Samoan conference, 1889, and H. C. Ide, chief justice of Samoa, see the relevant entries and bibliographical data in the *D.A.B. See also* Muzzey, *Blaine* (no. 2226).

Printed Sources

For general sources, see Sec. 1, above; note particularly Moore's *Digest* (no. 5365).

For United States official documents regarding Samoa (Congressional documents beginning with the 35th Cong. (1859) to the 56th Cong. (1899), and other relevant documentary material, including articles in U.S. consular reports, 1881-1901), see Griffin (no. 2344), 21-28, 42-44. The Library of Congress has a convenient [*Collection of congressional documents regarding Samoan affairs*] (Wash., 1874-95, 17 v. in 2) [2356], consisting of documents cited in the list above.

British Parliamentary papers dealing with Samoa, 1854-1899, are listed in Griffin (no. 2344), 10-12; as are also documents relating to Samoan affairs found in *Brit. and for. state pap.* (no. 5416), vols.

33 (1844–45), 70–86 (1878–1894). See also *Brit. docs. on origins of war, 1898–1914* (no. 5475), v. I, ch. 3: " Great Britain, Germany, and Samoa."

German documents on the Samoan affair were published as *Weissbücher*, in 1879, 1889, 1890, and 1893 (for description, see Sass, *Deutschen Weissbücher* (no. 5432). See also *Grosse Politik* (no. 5476), v. IV and VIII, containing a few documents throwing light on German policy in Samoa: IV. Bd., ch. 23: " Deutsch-Englische Beziehungen, 1885–1888 "; ch. 29: " Bismarcks Allianz-angebot an England. Verhandlungen über Helgoland." VIII Bd., ch. 44: " Die Bedeutung der Kolonialfragen für die Gruppierung der Mächte—b. England und Deutschland: Samoa-Kongo."

For a selected list of periodical articles on Samoa, 1840–1901, see Griffin (no. 2344), 30–41.

G. H. Bates, " Some aspects of the Samoan question ", *Century*, n.s. XV (1889) 945–949; XVI (1889) 25–33 [**2357**], Bates was special commissioner sent to Samoa in 1886. *Bismarck; the man and the statesman*, tr. by A. J. Butler (N.Y. and London, 1899) [**2358**]. *Die politischen Reden des fürsten Bismarck; historisch-kritische Gesammtausg.*, ed. by Horst Kohl (Stuttgart, 1892–1905, 14 v.) [**2359**]. R. L. Stevenson, *A footnote to history; eight years of trouble in Samoa* (N.Y., 1892) [**2360**], a narrative of international and native complications in Samoa; primarily a work of literary genius, but equally a contribution to history. Stevenson ran across these historical scenes while seeking health and recreation in Samoa. H. C. Ide, " Our interests in Samoa ", *No. Am. rev.*, CLXV (1897) 155–173 [**2361**], Ide was chief justice of the Supreme Court of Samoa, 1893–97. *Gedanken und Erinnerungen von Otto fürst von Bismarck,* ed. by Horst Kohl (Stuttgart, 1898–1921, 3 v.) [**2362**]. Albert Kautz, *Report of affairs in Samoa, by Rear Admiral Albert Kautz, U.S. Navy, to the Secretary of the Navy. March 6th to April 1st, 1899* (U.S.S. Philadelphia, Flagship Print, 1899) [**2363**]. Bartlett Tripp, *My trip to Samoa* (Cedar Rapids, Ia., 1911) [**2364**], Tripp was American commissioner to Samoa in 1899. Baron von Eckardstein, *Lebenserinnerungen und politische Denkwürdigkeiten* (Leipzig, 1919–21, 3 v.), also English translation, *Ten years at the court of St. James, 1895–1905*, tr. and ed. by George Young (London, 1921) [**2365**] discusses briefly the Samoan crisis of 1900. Cecil, *Marquis of Salisbury* (no. 2488), v. IV, contains brief allusions to the Samoan affair and prints a letter from Salisbury to Sir Edward Malet, April 24, 1889, in regard to Samoa. Von Bülow, *Memoirs* (no. 4328).

For the printed writings of American presidents and secretaries of state, 1872–1899 (for names and tenure, see latest *Register* of the Dept. of State (no. 5122)), and of American delegates to the Berlin conference on Samoa, 1889 (Geo. H. Bates, J. A. Kasson, and W. W. Phelps), see our list on p. 756.

MSS.: Suggestions

See Section 1, above.

The archives of Great Britain and Germany (below: Great Britain, p. 890; Germany, p. 924) are essential for a complete study of the diplomacy of Samoa which lies in a recent period for which official archives are not yet fully available to students. The archives of the Navy Department of the United States (in addition to those of the Department of State) are indispensable. The only indications are those in Van Tyne and Leland's *Guide* (no. 5495).

Maps: Suggestions

Several maps designating land owned by Americans, English, French, Germans, and Samoans, are published in 50th Cong., 1st sess. House. Exec. doc., no. 238 (*American rights in Samoa,* 1888) [2366].

CHAPTER XV

MISCELLANEOUS INTERNATIONAL CONFERENCES [1] AND MULTILATERAL TREATIES 1864–1914

Bibliographical Aids

For general aids, see Larned (no. 4657); Griffin (no. 4658); *Writings* (no. 4661); C. H. and T. (no. 4662); *Guide hist. lit.* (no. 4634); and bibliographies in *Am. secs. state* (no. 4796). Myers (no. 5399), for collections of treaties; also " Bibliography of United States treaty collections ", in Miller, *Treaties* (no. 5371), v. I, 39–54. See also the national historical bibliographies of the various foreign countries (nos. 4726–4765).

S. E. Baldwin, " List of memorable international conferences, congresses or associations of official representatives of governments, exclusive of those mainly concerned in dealing with the results of a particular war ", 1826–1907, *Am. jour. internat. law*, I (1907) 808–817 [**2367**], and " List of the more important international congresses, conferences, or associations of the past century, composed of private individuals ", *ibid.*, 817–829 [**2368**]. For a list of " International conventions and acts to which the United States is a party ", to 1923, see Malloy, *Treaties* (no. 5368), v. II, 1903–2420, and v. III, 2877–3140, 3699–3738 [**2369**], texts of 58 multilateral treaties, conventions, etc., arranged chronologically. H. H. B. Meyer and W. A. Slade, *Select list of references on the monetary question* (Wash., 1913) (Library of Congress) [**2370**]. *Serials of an international character;* tentative list prepared in the Columbia University Law Library (N.Y., 1921) (Institute of International Education. Bulletin, 2d ser., no. 3) [**2371**] contains a list of " Proceedings and

---

[1] For Central American Peace Conference, 1907, see Ch. XIX, sec. 4; for treaties and conventions dealing with Chinese affairs (Open Door, Boxer indemnity, loans, railways), see Ch. XVII; for Fur Seals convention of 1911 (Great Britain, Japan, Russia, and the United States), see Ch. XVI, sec. 7; for Hague Conferences and London Naval Conference of 1908–09, see Ch. XX; for Pan-American Conferences, see Ch. XIX.

reports of congresses and conferences " (p. 19–60), a most useful enumeration (alphabetically) of the really prodigious series of international conferences on all subjects and their published proceedings. This list is not limited to official congresses, in fact the majority are unofficial. Includes also a list of special periodicals of international character. Robert Doré, *Essai d'une bibliographie des congrès internationaux* (Paris, 1923) [**2372**], reprinted from the *Revue des bibliothèques*, XXXII° ann. (1922) 389–444; relates only to conferences of which at least one session has been held in a French-speaking country, concerns nonpolitical (social, industrial, economic) subjects, and is not limited to official conferences. Wriston (no. 4799), ch. 9: "Agents to international conferences " (p. 572–618) contains valuable data (giving personnel and relevant U.S. public documents), particularly of those conferences to which the delegate was chosen by the executive, rather than by nomination to the Senate. Miller, *Treaties* (no. 5371), v. I (short print) contains in its list of treaties, the multilateral treaties and conventions to which the United States has been a party; the first was the Geneva convention of 1864. *Treaties not gone into force* (no. 5367a) includes many multilateral treaties.

General Works

S. E. Baldwin, " The international congresses and conferences of the last century as forces working toward the solidarity of the world ", *Am. jour. internat. law*, I (1907) 565–578 [**2373**], a painstaking and valuable survey. Sir Ernest Satow, *International congresses* (London, 1920) [**2374**], a handbook of useful information prepared by a distinguished authority on diplomatic practice for the enlightenment of the British delegation to the Versailles peace conference in 1919. *Am. secs. state* (no. 4796). P. B. Potter, *An introduction to the study of international organization*, 3d edition, completely revised and enlarged (N.Y., 1928) [**2375**], ch. 12: " International conferences." A manual. N. L. Hill, *The public international conference; its function, organization, and procedure* (Stanford University, Calif., 1929) [**2376**], a scholarly summary of the history, organization, procedure, etc., of international conferences in general. C. E. Persinger, " Internationalism in the 60's ", *Hist. outlook*, XX (1929) 324–327 [**2377**] describes three movements: (1) a proposal by France and England for cooperation with the United States in the adoption of an international code of merchant-marine signals; (2) the invitation of the United States to participate in the preparation and adoption of a sanitary or Red Cross treaty providing for the improvement of the sanitary service of armies in the field; (3) the attempt to standardize the system of weights, measurements, and coinage of Europe and the Americas. Wriston (no. 4799), ch. 9: "Agents to international conferences", gives a comprehensive summary of American official participation in international conferences, particularly those to which the delegate was appointed by the President, rather than by nomination to the Senate, from the earliest time to and including the world war and post-war conferences.

Special Works

INTERNATIONAL POSTAL CONFERENCE (PARIS), 1863: J. E. Briggs, "Kasson and the first international postal conference", *Ia. jour. hist.*, XIX (1921) 366–388 [**2378**], John A. Kasson was United States representative at the International Postal Conference held at Paris in May 1863; this article is based on the printed official reports of the conference, the reports of the Postmaster-General, 1862–69, and *For. relations* (no. 5345), 1864.

INTERNATIONAL CONFERENCES FOR THE RELIEF OF THE SICK AND WOUNDED IN WAR (GENEVA) (RED CROSS), 1864 AND 1868: Gustave Moynier, *Étude sur la convention de Genève pour l'amélioration du sort des militaires blessés dans les armées, en campagne (1864 et 1868)* (Paris, 1870) [**2379**], historical introduction, and commentary on the convention by one of the Swiss delegates to the Geneva conferences of 1864 and 1868. Carl Lueder, *La convention de Genève au point de vue historique, critique, et dogmatique* (Erlangen, 1876) [**2380**], this work, by a German jurist and professor, received a prize offered in 1873 by the Empress of Germany for a work of the sort, and was translated into French under the auspices of the international Red Cross committee. J. S. Poland, *The conventions of Geneva and the St. Petersburg military commission for the amelioration of the condition of the wounded in armies in the field. Also convention between the United States and Mexico, 1882–83, for the reciprocal crossing of the international boundary line and other official information* (Fort Leavenworth, Kans., 1886) [**2381**], texts and proclamations only. Clara Barton, *The Red Cross; a* *history of this remarkable international movement in the interest of humanity* (Wash., 1898) [**2382**] refers more to the accomplishment of relief work than the diplomacy of the convention creating the Red Cross.   J. A. A. H. de Beaufort, *De herziening der Conventie van Genève* (Amersfoort, 1903) [**2383**], an Utrecht thesis analyzing the convention historically and legally.   G. W. Davis, *The Sanitary Commission—the Red Cross* (N.Y., 1910?), reprinted from the *Am. jour. internat. law,* and *supplement,* July 1910, and from v. I and II of the *supplement* for 1907 and 1908 [**2384**] traces the source of the later Red Cross in the Sanitary Commission of the American civil war.   M. T. Boardman, *Under the Red Cross flag at home and abroad* (Phila. and London, 1915) [**2385**], a general account of the history and activities of the Red Cross, particularly of women's part in it; it has interesting comments on the negotiation of the Geneva convention of 1864.

INTERNATIONAL MONETARY CONFERENCES, 1878, 1881: Henri Cernuschi, *Monetary diplomacy in 1878* (London, 1878) [**2386**], a polemical account of the International Monetary Conference at Paris, 1878, by an advocate of international "bimetallism."   J. L. Laughlin, *The history of bimetallism in the United States* (N.Y., 1892; 1st ed., 1885) [**2387**], a classic treatise; it touches international aspects of silver coinage.   E. B. Andrews, *An honest dollar* (Hartford, 1894) [**2388**], an international-bimetallist's essay on the monetary conference of 1892 at Brussels.   H. B. Russell, *International monetary conferences; their purposes, character, and results* (N.Y. and London, 1898) [**2389**] treats briefly the conferences of 1878, 1881, 1892, and the Wolcott commission of 1897.   Jeannette P. Nichols, "Silver diplomacy", *Pol. sci. quar.,* XLVIII (1933) 565–589 [**2390**], the only essay dealing with this subject, it discusses, from a wealth of material in the Department of State, the relation of domestic politics in the United States to attempts for international bimetallism.   This is a chapter from a larger work (in preparation) on the international aspects of bimetallism.

INTERNATIONAL COPYRIGHT CONFERENCES (1st, Berne, 1885): R. R. Bowker, *Copyright, its history and its law* (Boston, 1912) [**2391**], for brief discussion of copyright diplomatic agreements.

INTERNATIONAL CONFERENCE FOR THE PROTECTION OF INDUSTRIAL PROPERTY [Patent Laws], 1883 and 1911: Antoine Pillet, *Le régime international de la propriété industrielle; droit français et conventions internationales* (Grenoble, 1911) [**2392**], a thorough-going treatise on international aspects of patent law and other phases of industrial property that headed up in the Paris convention of 1911. Albert Osterrieth, *Die Washington Konferenz zur Revision der Pariser Nebereinkunft für gewerblichen Rechtsschutz* (Berlin, 1912) [**2393**], a systematic summary of the proceedings and agreement of the conference. S. P. Ladas, *The international protection of industrial property* (Cambridge, 1930) [**2394**], only work to date in English; a legal study which has much to do with the conference of 1883 for the protection of industrial property.

INTERNATIONAL CONFERENCE FOR THE PROTECTION OF SUBMARINE CABLES (Paris), 1884: Victor Perdrix, *Les cables sous-marins et leur protection international. Convention internationale du 14 mars 1884* (Paris, 1903) [**2395**], a doctoral thesis of the University of Paris. G. A. Schreiner, *Cables and wireless and their rôle in the foreign relations of the United States* (Boston, 1924) [**2396**].

BERLIN (CONGO) CONFERENCE, 1884–1885: J. S. Reeves, *The international beginnings of the Congo Free State* (Baltimore, 1894) (Johns Hopkins University Studies, 12th ser., XI–XII) [**2396a**], excellent pioneer diplomatic study. Riccardo Pierantoni, *Le traité de Berlin de 1885 et l'état indépendant du Congo* (Paris, 1901) [**2397**], French translation from the Italian treatise on the history, geography, and political disposition and status of the Congo Free State. A. B. Keith, *The Belgian Congo and the Berlin act* (Oxford, 1919) [**2398**], a study based on secondary works and British parliamentary publications designed to point out the defects of the Berlin act and to suggest amendments of a humanitarian nature; ignores Pierantoni (no. 2397). Stolberg-Wernigerode, *Deutschland und Vereinigten Staaten* (no. 4314) has much important material from the archives of Germany and the United States on this conference. R. S. Thomson, *Foundation de l'état indépendant du Congo; un chapître de l'histoire du partage de l'Afrique* (Brussels, 1933) [**2399**], admirable, well documented study; ends with the year 1885.

INTERNATIONAL CONFERENCE FOR THE SUPPRESSION OF THE AFRICAN SLAVE TRADE (Brussels), 1890: Henry Queneuil, *De la traite des noirs et de l'esclavage. La conférence de Bruxelles et ses résultats* (Paris,

1907)² [**2400**], a doctoral thesis of the University of Paris which gives the historical background for suppression of the slave trade and a judicial study of the conference at Brussels in 1890.

Algeciras Conference, 1906:³

André Tardieu, *La conférence d'Algésiras; histoire diplomatique de la crise marocaine (15 janvier–7 avril 1906)*, 3d ed., rev. and enl. (Paris, 1909) [**2402**], though now superseded by many later works, this study by a prominent French political personality retains value for its incisive tone and lucid arrangement. Hashagen, *Am.-deutsch. Beziehungen* (no. 4308). Dennis, *Adventures* (no. 2224), ch. 19: " The Algeciras conference." Adolf Hasenclever, " Theodore Roosevelt und die Marokkrisis von 1904–1906; ein Beitrag zur Geschichte der deutsch-amerikanischen Beziehungen vor der Weltkriege ", *Arch. Politik*, X (1928) 184–245 [**2403**], a very detailed study resting on papers and published documents of the German foreign office, including *Die Grossepolitik*, and printed American material; concludes that Roosevelt overreached the soft German government by not really responding to transparent flattery. E. N. Anderson, *The first Moroccan crisis, 1904–1906* (Chicago, 1930) [**2404**], excellent summary of an immense mass of printed material, official and unofficial; useful for the student who wants the most recent scholarly account as a basis for the special further study of American participation. Rouard de Card, *Etats-Unis et protectorat France au Maroc* (no. 4375). H. E. Brenning, *Die grossen Mächte und Marokko in den Jahren vor dem Marokko-Abkommen vom 8. April 1904 (1898–1904)* (Berlin, 1934) [**2405**].³ª

For the biographies of President Roosevelt, Secretary of State John Hay, and the American representatives at the Conference (Henry White and S. R. Gummeré), see the relevant entries and bibliographical data in the *D.A.B.* Note also Nevins, *Henry White* (no. 2468), and Dennett's *John Hay* (no. 2472).

---

² See also, for material on the abolition of the slave trade of an earlier period, Ch. XII, sec. 3, above.

³ We are omitting the material relating to the Algeciras conference which does not deal specifically with the participation of the United States in the conference. We are not listing works on African colonization in general; for this see: N. D. Harris, *Europe and Africa; being a revised edition of Intervention and colonization in Africa* (Boston, N.Y. [etc.], 1927) [**2401**]. See also the works on the origin of the world war (Ch. XXII, below) for discussion of the Algeciras conference.

³ª We have not been able to examine a copy of this book.

CONFERENCE ON WIRELESS TELEGRAPH (BERLIN), 1906: Alfred Landsberg, *Die drahtlose Telegraphie im deutschen und internationalen Verkehrsrecht mit besonderer Berücksichtigung des internationalen Vertrags vom 3. november 1906* (Leipzig, 1909) [2406], "inaugural dissertation" at Marburg.

INTERNATIONAL OPIUM COMMISSIONS AND CONFERENCES (1st Shanghai, 1909): W. W. Willoughby, *Opium as an international problem; the Geneva conferences* (Baltimore, 1925) [2407] includes a brief account of the Shanghai opium commission of 1909, and of the Hague opium conferences of 1911–12, 1913, and 1914.

Printed Sources

For American official documents and general source collections, see *Jour. exec. proc. Sen.* (no. 5387); *Cong. Globe* (no. 5384); *Cong. Record* (no. 5385); *For. relations* (no. 5345); Wharton, *Digest* (no. 5366); Richardson (no. 5335); Moore, *Digest* (no. 5363).

For text of treaties, see Malloy (no. 5368); and Miller, *Treaties* (no. 5371). For bibliographical guide to collections of treaties, see Myers (no. 5399).

For guides to foreign official publications, see below, p. 836.

For contemporary periodical material regarding international conferences, consult the periodical indexes (nos. 4995–5003).

For lists and indexes of newspapers, see nos. 5004–5047; particularly Library of Congress checklists (nos. 5030, 5032).

We know of no printed list of the delegates of the United States to the various international conferences. Membership must be ascertained by consultation of Wriston, *Executive agents* (no. 4799), and search through the published official documents regarding the specific conferences. In recent years the Department of State has printed in its annual *Register* (no. 5122) a list of the personnel of "American delegations to international conferences, congresses, etc.", held during the previous year. A list of the negotiators (or signers) of the various multilateral treaties may be ascertained by consultation of Malloy (no. 5368).

We have not attempted to extract from the document catalogues all the public documents dealing with the *many* international conferences and multilateral treaties participated in by the United States. For specific documentation, the investigator should consult the *Checklist* (no. 5361); *Tables and index* (no. 5357); *Document catalogue* (no. 5358).

For lists of international conferences, see above under "Bibliographical Aids"; particularly Baldwin (nos. 2367, 2368), and Wriston (no. 4799), the latter specifies the relevant U.S. public documents by serial number. For lists of multilateral treaties, see Malloy (no. 2369), and Miller, *Treaties* (no. 5371), v. I (short print), 39–54.

We note below certain special publications of documents dealing with some of these conferences: For the International Postal Conference of 1863, *For. relations* (no. 5345), 1864; and for J. A. Kasson's activities as special commissioner on behalf of the U.S. Post Office Dept. to negotiate new postal conventions with European governments, see the *Report* of the Postmaster General, 1862 (37th Cong., 3d sess. House. Exec. doc. v. IV, no. 1) ; 1863 (38th Cong., 1st sess. House. Exec. doc., v. V, no. 1) ; 1866 (39th Cong., 2d sess. House. Exec. doc., v. IV, no. 2) ; 1867 (40th Cong., 2d sess. House. Exec. doc., v. IV, no. 1) ; 1868 (40th Cong., 3d sess. House. Exec. doc., v. IV, no. 1) ; and 1869 (41st Cong., 2d sess. House. Exec. doc., v. I, no. 1) [**2408**].

GENEVA CONFERENCES FOR THE RELIEF OF WOUNDED SOLDIERS : *Report of Charles S. P. Bowles, foreign agent of the United States Sanitary Commission, upon the International Congress of Geneva, for the amelioration of the condition of the sick and wounded soldiers of armies in the field, convened at Geneva, 8th August, 1864* (London, 1864?) [**2409**]; . . . *Report of the Secretary of State with accompanying papers touching the Geneva convention for the relief of the wounded in war*, Dec. 12, 1881 (47th Cong., 1st sess. Sen. Exec. doc. no. 6) [**2410**]; . . . *Accession of the United States to the convention concluded at Geneva on the 22d August, 1864, between various powers and for the amelioration of the wounded armies in the field, and to the additional articles thereto signed at Geneva on the 20th October, 1868*, 1882 (47th Cong., 1st sess. Sen. Exec. doc. no. 177) [**2411**]; " Convention for the amelioration of the condition of the wounded in armies in the field, Geneva, 1906 ", in *International law topics and discussions*, published by the U.S. Naval War College (Wash., 1906), 125–140 [**2412**], a detailed analysis of the history and legal implications of problems within the purview of the convention.

INTERNATIONAL METRIC COMMISSION, 1875: *International Metric Commission at Paris. Papers relating to the meeting and proceedings of the diplomatic conference at Paris, for making provision, by means of a convention, for effecting the objects of the International Metric Commission,* published by Great Britain, Standards Department (London, 1875) (Gt. Brit. Parliament. Papers by command. C. 1331) [**2413**]; and Paris, Conférence Diplomatique du Mètre, *Documents diplomatiques de la Conférence du Mètre* (Paris, 1875) [**2414**], published by the " Ministère des Affaires Étrangères."

INTERNATIONAL MONETARY CONFERENCES: . . . *Report from the Secretary of State concerning the International Monetary Conference held at Paris in June 1867,* December 19, 1867 (40th Cong., 2d sess., Sen. Exec. doc. no. 14) [**2415–6**], Samuel B. Ruggles, delegate. *International monetary conference held, in compliance with the invitation extended to certain governments of Europe by the government of the United States, . . . in Paris, in August, 1878, under the auspices of the Ministry of Foreign Affairs of the republic of France* (Wash., 1879) (45th Cong., 3d sess., Sen. Exec. doc. no. 58) [**2417**] contains " Proceedings and exhibits, followed by the report of the American commission and an appendix containing correspondence submitted to the Department of State by Mr. [Reuben E.] Fenton, and historical material for the study of monetary policy contributed by Mr. [S. Dana] Horton." Also the *Procès-verbaux* (Paris, 1878) [**2418**], published by the " Ministère des Affaires Étrangères " of France. *Proceedings of the International Monetary Conference, held in compliance with the invitation extended to European governments by the governments of France and of the United States, in Paris, in May, June, and July, 1881, under the auspices of the Ministry of Foreign Affairs of the French republic,* printed by order of the Secretary of State (Cincinnati, 1881) [**2419**], a translation of the official French record of the proceedings of the conference. Same, with new table of contents and different index (Wash., 1887) (49th Cong., 1st sess. House. Misc. doc. 396, pt. 3; in Serial 2429). Conférence Monétaire Internationale, 1881, *Procès-verbaux* (Paris, 1881, 2 v.) [**2420**], published by the " Ministère des Affaires Étrangères ", of France. S. D. Horton, *Conférence Monétaire Internationale de 1881; discours prononcés et documents présentés par M. Dana Horton, délégué des Etats-Unis (extrait des v. I et II des Procès-verbaux)* (Paris, 1881) [**2421**]. Conférence Monétaire Internationale, 1892, *Procès-verbaux* (Brussels, 1892) [**2422**]. *Report of commissioners on behalf of the United States, and journal of the sessions of Novem-*

ber 22, 1892, to December 17, 1892 (Wash., 1893) (52d Cong., 2d sess. Sen. Exec. doc. no. 52) **[2423]** includes the report of the commissioners of the United States, signed: W. B. Allison, Jno. P. Jones, James B. McCreary, Henry W. Cannon, E. Benj. Andrews. E. B. Andrews, " The monetary conference of 1892 ", in his *An honest dollar* (Hartford, 1894), 127–156 **[2424]**, by a member of the American delegation to the conference. *Correspondence respecting the proposals on currency made by the special envoys from the United States* (Gt. Brit. Parliament. House of Commons. Sess. Pap., 1898, CV, 601) **[2425]**, for the Wolcott commission of 1897 in advance of an international bimetallic conference (members of the commission were E. O. Wolcott, C. J. Paine, and A. E. Stevenson).

CONFÉRENCE INTERNATIONALE POUR LES ÉCHANGES DES DOCUMENTS OFFICIELS. *Procès-verbaux* (Brussels, 1883) **[2426]**. J. B. Childs, *International exchange of government publications* (Wash., 1927) **[2427]** prints an English translation of the French originals of the " Convention for international exchange of official documents, scientific and literary publications, concluded at Brussels, March 15, 1886 ", and of the " Convention for the immediate exchange of official journals, parliamentary annals, and documents, concluded at Brussels, March 15, 1886."

BERLIN CONFERENCE, 1884–1885: *Acte générale de la Conférence de Berlin* (Berlin, 1885) **[2428]**. *Protocoles et acte générale de la Conférence de Berlin, 1884–1885* (n.p., 1885?) **[2429]**. France, Ministère des Affaires Étrangères, *Documents diplomatiques. Affaire du Congo et de l'Afrique occidentale* (Paris, 1885) **[2430]**. U.S., Dept. of State, *Congo conference. . . . Communication from the Secretary of State in relation to the Congo conference* (Wash., 1885) (48th Cong., 2d sess. House. Ex. doc. 247) **[2431]**; and . . . *Report of the Secretary of State relative to affairs of the Independent State of the Congo* (Wash., 1886) (49th Cong., 1st sess. Sen. Ex. doc. 196) **[2432]**, correspondence concerning the Berlin Congo conference, together with protocols and general act, and miscellaneous correspondence concerning the Independent State of the Congo; see also *Report by the Secretary of State, with accompanying correspondence, touching the condition of affairs in the Congo* (Wash., 1909) (61st Cong., 1st sess. Sen. doc. no. 147) **[2433]**, this deals with later alleged atrocious exploitation of natives in the Belgian

Congo. J. A. Kasson, " The Congo conference and the President's message ", *No. Am. rev.*, CXLII (1886) 119–133 [**2434**], the writer was American delegate to the Berlin Congo conference, 1884–85.

CONFERENCE FOR SUPPRESSION OF THE SLAVE TRADE, BRUSSELS, 1889–1890: Conférence Internationale et Commission de Bruxelles, 1890–1891, *Actes de la Conférence de Bruxelles (1889–1890)* (Brussels, 1890) [**2435**]. Same, *Correspondance diplomatique* (Paris, 1891) [**2436**], published by the French "Ministère des Affaires Étrangères." Same, *Documents diplomatiques, juillet-décembre 1891* (Paris, 1891) [**2437**], published by the French "Ministère des Affaires Étrangères." Same, *Protocoles et acte final* (Paris, 1891) [**2438**]. *Documents relatifs à la répression de la traite des esclaves, publiés en exécution des articles LXXXI et suivante de l'Acte général de Bruxelles, 1893–1913* (Brussels, 1893–1914, 23 v. in 16) [**2439**].

INTERNATIONAL CONFERENCE FOR THE SUPPRESSION OF THE WHITE SLAVE TRAFFIC: *Repression of the trade in white women. ... Projects of a convention and an additional arrangement adopted on July 25, 1902, by the delegates of the various powers* (Wash., 1902) (57th Cong., 2d sess. Sen. Exec. H. Confidential) [**2440**]. *Documents diplomatiques, Conférence Internationale pour le Répression de la Traite des Blanches* (Paris, 1902) [**2441**], published by the "Ministère des Affaires Étrangères." Also by the same, *Documents diplomatiques. Deuxième Conférence Internationale pour la Répression de la Traite des Blanches (18 avril-4 mai 1910)* (Paris, 1910) [**2442**]. Great Britain, Home Dept., *Correspondence respecting the international conferences on obscene publications and the " white slave traffic " held in Paris, April and May 1910)* (London, 1912) (Gt. Brit. Parliament. Papers by command. Cd. 6547) [**2443**].

INTERNATIONAL SANITARY CONFERENCES: Conférence Internationale Sanitaire, Paris, 1903, *Procès-verbaux* (Paris, 1904) [**2444**], published by the " Ministère des Affaires Étrangères " of France. Same, 1911–12, *Procès-verbaux* (Paris, 1912) [**2445**], published by the "Ministère des Affaires Étrangères."

INTERNATIONAL CONFERENCE CONCERNING HOSPITAL SHIPS: *Conférence Internationale concernant les Bâtiments Hospitaliers (La Haye, 13–21 décembre 1904)* (The Hague, 1904) [**2446**] consists of proceedings and texts. *Convention signed Dec. 20, 1904, by the*

United States and certain other countries . . . Feb. 2, 1905 (58th Cong., 3d sess. Senate. Exec. T. Confidential) **[2447]** includes reports of American delegates, but not proceedings.

ALGECIRAS CONFERENCE, 1906: France, Ministère des Affaires Etrangères, *Documents diplomatiques* . . . *Affaires du Maroc* (Paris 1905–12, 6 v.) **[2448]**. Algeciras, International Conference on Moroccan Affairs, 1906, *Conférence international d'Algeciras* (Madrid, 1906?) **[2449]** contains a list of the governments represented, the " procès-verbaux ", " comptes rendus ", and " acte générale et protocole additionnel." Great Britain, Foreign Office, *Despatches from the British delegate at the international conference at Algeciras forwarding the general act of the conference signed April 7, 1906, and other documents relating to the affairs of Morocco* (House of Commons. Sess. paper, 1906, CXXXVI, 331 (Cd. 3087)) **[2450]**. *Brit. docs. on origins of war* (no. 5475), v. III. *Grosse Politik* (no. 5476), XXI Bd.

CONFERENCE ON WIRELESS TELEGRAPH, BERLIN, 1906: Berlin, Conference on Wireless Telegraph, 1906, *Documents de la Conférence Radiotélégraphique Internationale de Berlin, 1906*, published by the " Département des Postes de l'Empire d'Allemagne " (Berlin, 1906) **[2451]**. U. S. Congress, Senate, Committee on Foreign Relations, *International wireless telegraphy. Hearing before the Committee on Foreign Relations, United States Senate* . . . *February 21, 1912* (Wash.: Govt. Print. Off., 1912) **[2452]**.

INTERNATIONAL OPIUM COMMISSION AND CONFERENCES: *Report of the International Opium Commission, Shanghai, China, February 1 to February 26, 1909* (Shanghai, 1909, 2 v.) **[2453]**. *Opium problem.* . . . *Report on the International Opium Commission and on the opium problem as seen within the United States, prepared by Mr. Hamilton Wright on behalf of the American delegates to the said commission, held at Shanghai in February, 1909* (Wash., 1910) (61st Cong., 2d Sess. Sen. Doc. 377) **[2454]**. . . . . *Communication of the Secretary of State covering the report of the American delegation to the International Opium Conference, held at The Hague, from December 1, 1911, to January 23, 1912* (62d Cong., 2d sess. Sen. Doc. no. 733, in v. 39) **[2455]**. *Communication from the Secretary of State, accompanied by a report prepared by Mr. Hamilton Wright on behalf of the American delegates to the second In-*

ternational Opium Conference, which met at The Hague on 1st day of July 1913, and adjourned on 9th day of same month, Aug. 9, 1913 (63d Cong., 1st sess. Sen. Doc. 157, in v. 21) **[2456]**. Great Britain, Foreign Office, *Instructions to the British delegates to the International Opium Conference held at The Hague, December 1911–January 1912* (London, 1913) (Parliament. Papers by command. Cd. 6605) **[2457]** includes letter of Mr. Carter to Sir Edward Grey, and " Circular instructions issued by the United States Department of State respecting international opium commission."

CONFERENCE FOR PROTECTION OF INDUSTRIAL PROPERTY: Great Britain, Foreign Office, *Industrial property and merchandise marks. Papers and correspondence relative to the recent conference at Washington, for the revision of the international convention for the protection of industrial property* (London, 1912) (Parliament. Papers by command. Cd. 5842) **[2458]**.

INTERNATIONAL CONFERENCES ON MARITIME LAW: *International convention for unification of certain rules of law with respect to assistance and salvage at sea, concluded at Brussels, Sept. 23, 1910, signed by the delegates of the United States to the 3d International Conference on Maritime Law* (62d Cong., 1st sess. Sen. Exec. K. Confidential) (not in Congressional set) **[2459]** includes the report of the American delegation. *Report of delegates of United States to International Conference on Maritime Law, 5th session, Brussels, Belgium, Oct. 17–26, 1922* (Wash., 1923) (Dept. of State) **[2460]**.

MSS.: Suggestions

Aside from the analysis of official archives to be found below, Pt. II, Ch. 3, we are at loss for any suggestions for further MS. sources.

The records of such conferences are often published. For the diplomatic discussions out of which the formal records spring one must go to the archives of the various countries (not usually open, at the present epoch, beyond 1888), and the extant personal papers (not yet listed) of the numerous negotiators.

The MS. correspondence of John A. Kasson, delegate to the International Postal Conference at Paris, in 1863, and to the Congo Conference at Berlin, 1884–85, are in the Historical Department of Iowa, at Des Moines.

The papers of Manton Marble, diplomatic agent on a special mission in 1885 to Great Britain, France, and Germany, with reference to bimetallism, are in the Library of Congress.

CHAPTER XVI

ANGLO-AMERICAN RELATIONS, 1867–1914[1]

1. In General

Bibliographical Aids

For general aids, see Larned (no. 4657); Griffin (no. 4658); *Writings* (no. 4661); C. H. and T. (no. 4662); *Guide hist. lit.* (no. 4634); and bibliographies in *Am. secs. state* (no. 4796). Myers (no. 5399) for collections of treaties. Miller, *Treaties* (no. 5371), v. I, 39–54, for "Bibliography of United States treaty collections." See also British and Canadian historical bibliographies (nos. 4744–4746) and (nos. 4671–4677), respectively.

For indexes to periodical literature, see nos. 4995–5003.

For lists and indexes of newspapers, see nos. 5004–5047; particularly Library of Congress check lists (nos. 5030, 5032).

Special Works

Of general histories of the United States, see Rhodes (no. 4783); and Oberholtzer (no. 4785), v. II, the chapter on the Alabama claims has an excellent recapitulation of Anglo-American relations. See also *Am. secs. state* (no. 4796), v. V–X; and Wriston, *Exec. agents* (no. 4799).

Foster, *Am. diplomacy* (no. 4788). Smith, *England and America* (no. 340). Henderson, *Am. dipl. questions* (no. 2821). Walpole, *Twenty-five years* (no. 1975). Low and Sanders, *History of England* (no. 1876). Kraus, *Monroe-Doktrin* (no. 1159). *Canada and*

---

[1] For the Samoan Affair, see Ch. XIV, sec. 6. For the Algeciras Conference, see Ch. XV.

its provinces; a history of the Canadian people and their institutions,
by one hundred associates. Adam Shortt, A. G. Doughty, general
editors (Toronto, 1914–17, 23 v.) **[2460a]**, a general undocumented
history. Dunning, *Brit. Emp. and U.S.* (no. 1335). C. R. Fish,
*The path of empire; a chronicle of the United States as a world
power* (N.Y., 1919) **[2461]**. Hart, *Monroe doctrine* (no. 1164).
Camb. hist. Brit. for. pol. (no. 209), v. III. Latané, *U.S. and
Lat. America* (no. 963), for the two Venezuelan episodes. Hyde,
Internat. law (no. 4810). J. F. Rhodes, *The McKinley and Roosevelt
administrations, 1897–1909* (N.Y., 1922) **[2462]**, a sequel to his great
history (no. 4783), it is not equal to it; but partakes of the nature
of recollections of a historian about his own times. There are
nevertheless excellent summaries of foreign affairs and a particularly
good note on the rise of the new navy. Sir Robert Falconer, *The
United States as a neighbour, from a Canadian point of view* (Cambridge, 1925) **[2463]**, Sir George Watson lectures for 1925 ; a sympathetic general analysis of the various problems (boundaries, fisheries,
nationalism, trade) of Canadian-American relations. Mowat, *Gt.
Brit. and U.S.* (no. 347a). Coolidge, *U.S. as world power* (no. 3345).
Tyler, *For. pol. Blaine* (no. 2223). Dennis, *Adventures* (no. 2224).
Rippy, *Lat. Am. in world politics* (no. 1076), ch. 7 : " Toward Anglo-
Saxon cordiality (1857–1927)." A. G. Dewey, *The Dominions and
diplomacy; the Canadian contribution*, v. I (N.Y., 1929, 2 v.)
[2464], a constitutional study of the relationship of Canadian
nationalism to imperial diplomacy. Keenleyside, *Canada and U.S.*
(no. 896). Douglas, *Boundaries* (no. 211). H. G. Hodges, *Diplomatic relations between the United States and Great Britain* (Boston, 1930) **[2465]**, incomplete and unreliable. Payne, *Eng. treatment of Am.* (no. 351). Brainerd Dyer, *The public career of
William M. Evarts* [2] (Berkeley, Calif., 1933) **[2466]**, a solid,
thoroughly documented monograph dealing primarily with Evarts'
political career, with the least valuable portion dealing with his
services in the Geneva arbitration. Beard, *National interest* (no.
4823).

For biographies of American presidents, secretaries of state, diplomatists abroad (for names and tenure, see latest *Register* of the Dept.
of State (no. 5122), and Charles Sumner, chairman of the Senate

---

[2] Published after the entry in the *D.A.B.*

Committee on Foreign Relations, see the relevant entries and bibliographical data in the *D.A.B.* Note also: Willson, *Ambassadors to England* (no. 348); Howe, *Chester A. Arthur* (no. 2226); two important biographies by Allan Nevins, *Grover Cleveland; a study in courage* (N.Y., 1933) [2467],[3] based on the Cleveland papers in the Library of Congress; and *Henry White; thirty years of American diplomacy* (N.Y. and London, 1930) [2468],[4] based on hitherto unpublished letters, which throw new light upon the two Venezuelan affairs, Anglo-American rapprochement at the time of the Spanish-American war, the Hay-Pauncefote treaty, and upon the insistence of the United States upon gaining all its objectives in the arbitration of the Alaska boundary. W. R. Thayer, *Theodore Roosevelt, an intimate biography* (Boston and N.Y., 1919) [2469]. J. B. Bishop, *Theodore Roosevelt and his time shown in his own letters* (N.Y., 1920, 2 v.) [2470]. H. W. Pringle, *Theodore Roosevelt; a biography* (N.Y., 1931) [2471] contains critical narrative of Roosevelt's diplomacy.[5] Two biographies of J. G. Blaine, by C. E. Russell (no. 2226a), and by D. S. Muzzey (no. 2226b). Tyler Dennett, *John Hay*[6] (N.Y., 1933) [2472], very important; a judicious and competent review by an authority on American diplomacy of this period who had access to Hay's papers, printed and unprinted, public and private, and unlimited use of the relevant files of the Department of State.

For biographies of British prime ministers, foreign secretaries, and diplomatists to the United States (for names and tenure of the foreign secretaries and diplomatists, see latest *Foreign office list* (no. 5125)), see relevant entries and bibliographical data in the *D.N.B.* See also Clive Bigham, *Prime ministers* (no. 242); and Algernon Cecil, *Foreign secretaries* (no. 821), for Granville, Salisbury, and Rosebery. More recent pertinent biographies are: J. A. Spender and Cyril Asquith, *Life of Herbert Henry Asquith, Lord Oxford and Asquith* (London, 1932, 2 v.) [2474]. Bernard Alderson,

---

[3] Published after the Cleveland entry in the *D.A.B.*

[4] Published in advance of the White entry in the *D.A.B.*

[5] We mention these Roosevelt entries in advance of fuller material expected in the *D.A.B.*

[6] Published after the Hay entry in the *D.A.B.* J. B. Moore, "John Hay: an estimate", *Saturday rev. lit.,* X (Nov. 11, 1923) [2473], an analysis of Hay embodied in a review of Dennett's *Hay,* in which the author gives certain autobiographical revelations of his own days in the "old Department."

Arthur James Balfour, the man and his work (London, 1903)
[**2475**]. *Retrospect; an unfinished autobiography, 1848–1886*, by
Arthur James, first Earl of Balfour (Boston and N.Y., 1930) [**2476**],
English edition has title, *Chapters of autobiography* (London, 1930).
H. A. L. Fisher, *James Bryce (Viscount Bryce of Dechmont, O.M.)*
(London, 1927, 2 v.) [**2477**]. J. L. Garvin, *The life of Joseph Cham-
berlain*, v. I–III (N.Y., 1932–34 [**2478**] touches upon his American
negotiations of 1887 on the fishery question, and efforts towards
Anglo-American understanding (Venezuela imbroglio). S. L. Gwynn
and Gertrude Tuckwell, *Life of the Right Honourable Sir Charles
Dilke, bart., M.P.* (London, 1917, 2 v.) [**2479**], Dilke was a brilliant
and well-informed under-secretary in the British foreign office when
Blaine was in office. Sir Percy Sykes, *The Right Honourable Sir
Mortimer Durand, P.C., G.C.M.G., K.C.S.I., K.C.I.E., a biography*
(London, 1926) [**2480**], ambassador to the United States, 1903–
1905. John Morley, *The life of William Ewart Gladstone* (N.Y.
and London, 1903, 3 v.) [**2481**]. Viscount Gladstone, *After
thirty years* (London, 1928) [**2482**], biography of W. E. Gladstone.
A. W. Gardiner, *The life of Sir William Harcourt* (London, 1923,
2 v.) [**2483**], Harcourt was member of Parliament; there is a chapter
dealing with the Alabama claims arbitration. Lord Newton, *Lord
Lansdowne; a biography* (London, 1929) [**2484**], notable biography;
the author had access to the 5th Marquis of Lansdowne's personal
correspondence (now preserved at Bowood, England). R. B. Mowat,
The life of Lord Pauncefote, first ambassador to the United States
(London, 1929) [**2485**], for the Bering Sea arbitration, Venezuelan
boundary affair, and the Hay-Pauncefote treaty. Lucien Wolf, *Life
of the first Marquess of Ripon* (London, 1921, 2 v.) [**2486**] contains
a narrative of the inception of the Alabama negotiations " based on
confidential documents which are now used for the first time." Marquess of Crewe, *Lord Rosebery* (N.Y. and London, 1931) [**2487**].
Tilby, *Russell* (no. 1927). Lady Gwendolen Cecil, *Life of Robert,
Marquis of Salisbury*, by his daughter (London, 1921–32, 4 v.) [**2488**].

See also Lytton Strachey, *Queen Victoria* (no. 1924); and Sir Sidney Lee, *King Edward VII; a biography* (N.Y., 1925–27, 2 v.)
[**2489**], with a few brief American references.

BIOGRAPHIES OF CANADIAN STATESMEN: Alexander Mackenzie, *The
life and speeches of Hon. George Brown* (Toronto, 1882) [**2490**],
George Brown was founder of the Toronto *Globe*, in 1874 he was

appointed co-plenipotentiary with Sir Edward Thornton, in an effort to secure a renewal of the reciprocity treaty of 1854; he was an ardent advocate of Confederation as an answer to annexation talk; and John Lewis, *George Brown* (Toronto, 1906) **[2491]**. Skelton, *Sir A. T. Galt* (no. 1928). J. S. Willison, *Sir Wilfrid Laurier and the liberal party; a political history* (Toronto, 1903, 2 v.) **[2492]**, Laurier was prime minister of Canada, 1896-1911, covering the period of the negotiations regarding the Alaska boundary, reciprocity, etc.; and O. D. Skelton, *The life and letters of Sir Wilfrid Laurier* (N.Y., 1922, 2 v.) **[2493]**. Sir Joseph Pope, *Memoirs of the Right Honourable Sir John Alexander Macdonald, G.C.B., first prime minister of the Dominion of Canada* (London, 1894, 2 v.) **[2494]**, Macdonald was prime minister of the Dominion of Canada, 1867-1873, and 1878-1891, and a member of the Joint High Commission at Washington in 1871; G. R. Parkin, *Sir John A. Macdonald* (London and Toronto, 1908) **[2495]**; and W. S. Wallace, *Sir John Macdonald* (Toronto, 1924) **[2496]**. C. R. W. Biggar, *Sir Oliver Mowat, . . . a biographical sketch* (Toronto, 1905, 2 v.) **[2497]**, Mowat was premier of Ontario, 1872-1896; there are several letters giving his views in regard to reciprocity, as an Imperialist he was opposed to commercial union with the United States considering it but the precursor of political union. J. W. Dafoe, *Clifton Sifton in relation to his times* (Toronto, 1931) **[2498]**, Sifton was attorney general of Canada, British agent at the Alaska boundary arbitration, and an active opponent of the reciprocity treaty of 1911. J. C. Hopkins, *Life and works of Sir John Thompson, prime minister of Canada* (Brantford, Can., 1895) **[2499]**, Thompson was a member of the Joint High Commission on the fisheries question in 1887, and arbitrator for Great Britain at the fur seal arbitration. J. W. Longley, *Sir Charles Tupper* (Toronto, 1916) **[2500]**, Tupper was a member of the Joint High Commission on the fisheries question in 1887.

Printed Sources

For American official documents and general source collections, see p. 810; particularly *Jour. exec. proc. Sen.* (no. 5387); *Cong. Globe* (no. 5384); *Cong. Record* (no. 5385); *For. relations* (no. 5345); Wharton's *Digest* (no. 5366); Richardson (no. 5335); Moore's *Arbitrations* (no. 5364), and *Digest* (no. 5365).

For guide to British official documents (Parliamentary debates, sessional papers, etc.), see p. 838.

For guide to Canadian official documents (legislative proceedings, etc.), see p. 840, n.

Particular documents are cited in separate sections of this chapter.

For contemporary periodical material, consult the indexes to periodicals (nos. 4995–5003).

For lists and indexes of newspapers, see nos. 5004–5047; particularly Library of Congress check lists (nos. 5030, 5032); and for English newspapers, *Tercentenary handlist* (no. 5013), and Library of Congress (no. 5032).

For printed writings of American presidents, secretaries of state, and diplomatists abroad (for names and tenure, see latest *Register* of the Dept. of State (no. 5122)), see our list on p. 756. Note also the writings of Sumner, in the same list. The political letters and diaries of John Hay are soon to be published, Tyler Dennett, editor.

G. W. Smalley, *Anglo-American memories* (N.Y. and London, 1911–12, 2 v.) [2501] consists of memories of personalities in Anglo-American public life, mostly written for the New York Tribune; they include sketches of Chamberlain, Balfour, Rosebery, Goldwin Smith, Sir Edward Grey, Haldane, Pauncefote, Whitelaw Reid, Carnegie, etc.).

MEMOIRS, LETTERS, ETC., OF BRITISH STATESMEN: Viscount Alverstone, *Recollections of bar and bench* (London, 1914) [2502], Lord Alverstone appeared for Great Britain in the Bering Sea arbitration in 1893, was a leading counsel in the Venezuelan arbitration in 1899, and arbitrator on the Alaska boundary question in 1903. Edith J. Archibald. *Letters of Sir E. M. Archibald* (no. 1984), as British consul general at New York, 1857–1883, he acted as treasurer of the award in receiving and paying over the Alabama claims accounts. Earl of Oxford and Asquith, *Memories and reflections* (Boston, 1928, 2 v.) [2503–4]. Viscount Grey, *Twenty-five years* (no. 4435). Andrew Lang, *Life, letters, and diaries of Sir Stafford Northcote, first Earl of Iddesleigh* (Edinburgh, 1890, 2 v.) [2505], one of the British commissioners who drew up the treaty of Washington. Roundell Palmer, *Memorials* (no. 1972), Pt. 2: " Personal and political, 1865–1895 "; the writer was counsel for Great Britain at the Geneva arbitration. *The letters and friendships of Sir Cecil Spring Rice; a record,* ed. by Stephen Gwynn (Boston and N.Y., 1929; London, 1929) [**2506**], valuable source for Anglo-American relations in the whole period after 1887. Lord John Russell, *Recollections* (no. 1966), has a chapter on the treaty of Washington. *Letters of Queen Victoria* (no. 1985).

MEMOIRS, LETTERS, ETC., OF CANADIAN STATESMEN: Mackenzie, *Speeches of George Brown* (no. 2490), for the reciprocity negotiations at Washington in 1874, conducted by Sir Edward Thornton and Mr. Brown as joint plenipotentiaries. *Speeches and public letters of Joseph Howe,* ed. by J. A. Chisholm (Halifax, 1909, 2 v.) [**2507**]. Skelton, *Letters of Laurier* (no. 2493), Laurier was prime minister of Canada, 1896–1911; there are occasional letters on United States affairs. J. P. Macpherson, *Life of the Right Hon. Sir John A. Macdonald* (St. John, N.B., 1891, 2 v.) [**2508**], Macdonald was prime minister of Canada, 1866–1891 (except for the years 1873–1878); this *Life* includes his speech in the Canadian Parliament on the Washington treaty, and others on United States affairs. Pope, *Memoirs Sir John Alexander Macdonald* (no. 2494) contains his correspondence in regard to the Washington treaty and other Canadian-American relations. *Correspondence of Sir John Macdonald; selections from the correspondence of the Right Honourable Sir John Alexander Macdonald, G.C.B., first prime minister of the Dominion of Canada* (Toronto, 1921) [**2509**]. Hopkins, *Life and works of Sir John Thompson* (no. 2499), while minister of justice of Canada he went to Washington as legal adviser to Sir Charles Tupper to arrange a fisheries treaty, 1887–88. Sir Charles Tupper, *Recollections of sixty years* (London, 1914) [**2510**], Tupper was Canadian minister of finance and one of the British plenipotentiaries at the Washington fisheries conference, in 1887. *The life and letters of the Rt. Hon. Sir Charles Tupper,* ed. by E. M. Saunders (London, 1916, 2 v.) [**2511**]; and *Supplement to The life and letters of Sir Charles Tupper,* ed. by Sir Charles H. Tupper (Toronto, 1926) [**2512**].

MSS.: Suggestions

For official archives of the United States, of Great Britain, and of Canada, see below, pp. 857, 890, and 896, respectively.

For papers of American presidents (Johnson, Grant, Hayes, Garfield, Arthur, Cleveland, Harrison, McKinley, Roosevelt, Taft,

Wilson), and secretaries of state (Seward, Washburne, Fish, Evarts, Blaine, Frelinghuysen, Bayard, Gresham, Olney, Sherman, Day, Hay, Root, Bacon, Knox, Bryan), see our lists on p. 862, and 865, respectively. For the private papers of American ministers and ambassadors to Great Britain, 1867 to 1914 (for names and tenure, see latest *Register* of the Dept. of State (no. 5122)), see our list on p. 868.

The papers of Queen Victoria are preserved, as royal archives, in the Round Tower of Windsor Castle (partly reprinted in *Letters of Queen Victoria* (no. 1985)). The papers of King Edward VII are also preserved in the same place. Among the private papers preserved of British prime ministers, foreign secretaries, and diplomatic representatives to the United States are: Gladstone (prime minister, 1868–74, 1880–85, 1892–94), at Hawarden Castle, Hawarden, Flintshire; Benjamin Disraeli (prime minister, 1868, 1874–80), the great mass of papers bequeathed by Lord Beaconsfield to the late Lord Rowton are now in the keeping of the trustees of the Beaconsfield estate; Lord Clarendon (foreign secretary, 1868–70) private papers for those years are in the Public Record Office; as are also the private collection of Lord Granville (secretary for foreign affairs, 1870–74, 1880–85); private papers of Lord Lansdowne (foreign secretary, 1900–05), are preserved at Bowood, Calne, Wiltshire. Lord Iddesleigh (Northcote) (foreign secretary, 1886, and one of the negotiators of the treaty of Washington), in the possession of the present Lord Iddesleigh. Letters and diaries of James Bryce, ambassador to the United States, 1907–1913, are in the possession of Lady Bryce and daughter.

In the Dominion Archives of Canada are 2 volumes of papers connected with the negotiations for the settlement of the boundary in Passamaquoddy Bay, arising out of the arbitration treaty of 1908; also portfolio of papers relating to Canada's claim to sovereignty in Arctic waters. Note the following collections of personal papers of Canadian statesmen: Sir James Douglas, governor of British Columbia (San Juan boundary controversy), in the archives of British Columbia, at Victoria, B.C.; Sir Alexander T. Galt (member of the Halifax fisheries commission), in the possession of his son, Sir Elliott T. Galt, Montreal. The Public Archives of Canada, at Ottawa, contains the papers of the following: Sir Wilfrid Laurier, whose papers (except for a few boxes burned with the Parliament buildings) were used by his biographer, O. D. Skelton (see no.

2493); Sir John A. Macdonald (prime minister of Canada, 1867-73, 1878-91); The Hon. Alexander MacKenzie, prime minister, 1873-78; Sir Richard W. Scott, secretary of state (Canada) from 1874 to 1878, and from 1896 to 1908, which contain material connected with the protest of the United States against the Ontario Provincial act of 1897 requiring that timber cut on crown lands should be manufactured in Canada, he was connected with the International Commission of 1899. In the same archives are some of the papers of Sir J. S. D. Thompson, minister of justice of Canada, 1885-94, prime minister, 1892-94, which include documents regarding international relations on the fisheries, pelagic sealing, and some connected with the Washington conference of 1887-88. The important collection of Baring papers (see no. 1331a) is now in the Public Archives of Canada.

The Library of Congress has the revealing diary, already noted (no. 1980) of Benjamin Moran, of the American legation at London, 1851-74.

2. Treaty of Washington; Geneva Arbitration [7]

Bibliographical Aids

For general aids, see Sec. 1, above. Hackett, *Alabama claims* (no. 2571), xiii-xvi. Reale, *Conflit de l'Alabama* (no. 2521), 139-141.

Special Works

Caleb Cushing, *The treaty of Washington; its negotiation, execution, and the discussions relating thereto* (N.Y., 1873) [**2513**], by the senior counsel of the United States at the Geneva arbitration. Arthur Mills, " Canada and the treaty of Washington ", *Contemp. rev.*, XXI (1873) 597-615 [**2514**], the principal issues and articles of the treaty settlement, reviewed by one who sees in this arrangement a strengthening of Canadian ties to the Empire. F. W. Hackett, *The Geneva award acts; with notes, and references to decisions of the court of commissioners of Alabama claims* (Boston, 1882) [**2515**], review of the legislation of Congress known as the " Geneva award acts ", June 23, 1874, and June 5, 1882; the author of this article was secretary to Caleb Cushing, senior American counsel at Geneva. J. C. Bancroft Davis, *Mr. Fish and the Ala-*

---

[7] See also Ch. XIII, secs. 2 and 3 (" Anglo-American Relations " and " Neutral Rights and Maritime Law ") during the Civil War.

bama claims (N.Y., 1893) [**2516**], the writer was assistant secretary of state at the time and had access to much first-hand material. T. W. Balch, *The Alabama arbitration* (Phila., 1900) [**2517**], " an attempt to tell the story of the *Alabama* arbitration, as far as possible, in the words of the participants in that drama ", author's preface. C. F. Adams, Jr., *Before and after the treaty of Washington* (N.Y., 1902), also published in his *Lee at Appomattox, and other papers* (N.Y., 1902) [**2518**], a careful study of American diplomacy in Grant's administration; the author had access to the papers of Secretary Hamilton Fish. This is the most penetrating analysis, to date, of the diplomacy preceding the treaty of Washington. D. H. Chamberlain, *Charles Sumner and the treaty of Washington* (Cambridge, Mass., 1902) [**2519**], examines the views of C. F. Adams, Jr., as presented in his study (no. 2518, above) of Senator Sumner's relations to the treaty of Washington, especially the matter of his removal from the chairmanship of the Senate committee on foreign relations in March, 1871, which the author believes " unwarrantable, grossly unjust, and inexcusable." Walpole, *Twenty-five years* (no. 1975), a history primarily of parliamentary legislation and administrative reforms, it contains a summary chapter on the treaty of Washington and the Geneva award. W. C. Church, " The arbitration of the 'Alabama claims'; with a series of cartoons from London ' Punch ' ", *Century*, LXXXV (1913) 703–720 [**2520**], interesting for the illustrations. Bigelow, *Breaches* (no. 1236). Hill, *Treaties* (no. 4794), ch. 13, one of the best summaries of the treaty of Washington. Egidio Reale, *Le règlement judiciaire du conflit de l'Alabama* (Geneva, 1929) [**2521**], a critical study of the judicial qualities of the dispute and arbitration, which does not neglect the political features: direct vs. indirect claims, and effect on England of the spectacle of the Franco-Prussian war. M. H. Long, " Sir John Rose and the informal beginnings of the Canadian high commissionership ", *Canad. hist. rev.*, XII (1931) 23–43 [**2522**], valuable narration of Rose's preliminary diplomacy in Washington, in preparation for the formal negotiation of the treaty of Washington, based on MS. material in the Canadian archives. Dyer, *Evarts* (no. 2466). Rising Lake Morrow, " The negotiation of the Anglo-American treaty of 1870 ", *Am. hist. rev.*, XXXIX (1934) 663–681 [**2522a**], a succinct monograph based more on British than on American archives, it shows how Seward endeavored to exploit the Fenian movement to secure British acquiescence to the American doctrine of the right of expatriation, which was finally written into this treaty.

For biographies of President Grant, American negotiators of the treaty of Washington (Hamilton Fish, R. C. Schenck, Samuel Nelson, E. R. Hoar, and G. H. Williams), Charles Sumner, chairman of the Senate Committee on Foreign Relations, and personalities connected with the Alabama arbitration (C. F. Adams, Jr., Caleb Cushing, J. C. Bancroft Davis, William Evarts, and M. R. Waite), see the relevant entries and bibliographical data in the *D.A.B.*

For biographies of British negotiators of the treaty of Washington (De Grey and Ripon, S. H. Northcote, Edward Thornton, Mountague Bernard) and personalities connected with the Alabama arbitration (Sir Alexander Cockburn, Sir Roundell Palmer, Lord Tenterden), see the relevant entries and bibliographical data in the *D.N.B.* Note also: Morley, *Gladstone* (no. 2481); Gardiner, *Harcourt* (no. 2483); Wolf, *Marquess of Ripon* (no. 2486); and Tilby, *Russell* (no. 1927).

For biographies of the Canadian signer of the treaty of Washington (Sir John A. Macdonald), see nos. 2494-2496.

Printed Sources

For general collections, see Sec. 1, above: particularly Moore's *Arbitrations* (no. 5364).

For text of the treaty of Washington, see Malloy (no. 5368); and analysis of treaty collections, p. 822, below.

UNITED STATES OFFICIAL DOCUMENTS: Three collections published by the Dept. of State: *Correspondence concerning claims against Great Britain, transmitted to the Senate of the United States in answer to the resolutions of December 4 and 10, 1867, and of May 27, 1868* (Wash., 1869-71, 7 v.) [2523], v. I-V published also as Senate Exec. Doc. no. 11, 41st Cong., 1st sess.); *Correspondence respecting the Geneva arbitration* (Wash., 1872) [2524]; and *Papers relating to the treaty of Washington* (Wash., 1872-74, 6 v.) [[2525], v. I-IV: Geneva arbitration; v. V: Berlin arbitration; v. VI: Washington arbitration and general appendix containing the report of Robert S. Hale (for detailed summary of contents of these volumes, see *Checklist* (no. 5361), 913-916). See also *Alphabetical list of the documents and correspondence submitted with the cases and counter cases of the United States and of Great Britain to the tribunal of arbitration at Geneva* (Geneva? 1872) [**2526**], a key to the evidence before the tribunal of arbitration, prepared by direction of the agent of the United States. Of the records of the Washington arbitration (American-British mixed claims commission), the Library of the Dept. of State, according to the *Checklist* (no. 5361), 916, contains 1 volume of *Memorials* and 1 volume of *Testimony* concerning claims of subjects of Great Britain vs. the United States, and 34 volumes of *Memorials* and 38 volumes of *Testimony* concerning claims of citizens of the United States against Great Britain. This last set (i.e. *Memorials* and *Testimony* concerning claims of citizens of the United States vs. Great Britain) is also in the Library of Congress. For a summary list of Records of the Court of Commissioners of Alabama Claims, 1st and 2nd, 1874-76, and 1882-85 (*Records* of cases, 151 v.; and general publications), see the *Checklist* (no. 5361), 1508-1511.

BRITISH PARLIAMENTARY (HOUSE OF COMMONS SESSIONAL) PAPERS: (Treaty of Washington)—*Correspondence, Despatch,* and *Instructions* for the Joint High Commission of 1871 (1871, LXX, 1, 9, and 25, respectively) [**2527**]; *Additional article to the treaty . . . 18th January 1873,* and *Protocol of conference . . . 7th June, 1873* (1873, LXXIV, 1 and 5) [**2528**]; and *Correspondence with the United States government respecting communication to other governments of rules of the treaty of Washington* (1874, LXXV, 1) [**2529**]. (Alabama Claims)—*Correspondence respecting the "Alabama"* (1863), LXII, 85 and 637; 1864, LXII, 1 and 109; 1865, LVII, 125; 1868-69, LXIII, 735; 1870, LXIX, 439 [**2530**]. Documents of the Geneva Tribunal (*Case* of Great Britain, and Appendix (7 v.), *Case* of the United States, *Correspondence, Counter-case* of Great Britain, *Counter-case* of the United States, *Correspondence respecting claims for indirect losses, Argument* of Great Britain, and *Argument* of the United States) (1872, LXIX, various nos.) [**2531**]. *Estimate of sum required in 1873-74 for payment . . . of "Alabama" claims* (1873, XXXIX, 101) [**2532**]. *Correspondence between the Board of Customs and Treasury . . . on the case of the "Alabama"* (1873, LIV, 223) [**2533**]. *Papers relating to the proceedings of the tribunal of arbitration at Geneva* (" Protocols, correspondence, &c.", and "Award of tribunal, and the reasons of Sir Alexander Cockburn for dissenting from the award "), and *Corre-*

spondence on the "Lafayette", captured and destroyed by the "Alabama" (1873, LXXIV, 9, 419, and 933, respectively) [**2534**]. *Report of . . . proceedings and award of Mixed [Claims] Commission . . .,* and *Papers respecting the proceedings of the Mixed Claims Commission* (1874, LXXV, 25 and 797, respectively) [**2535**].

CANADIAN OFFICIAL DOCUMENTS: Canada, Parliament, House of Commons, *The Washington treaty debate, in the House of Commons, at Ottawa, May 1872;* reports of speeches delivered on the occasion by Sir J. A. Macdonald, Sir Francis Hincks [etc.] (Toronto, 1872) [**2536**]. *Message, despatches, and minutes of the Privy Council, relating to the treaty of Washington* (Ottawa, 1872) (Sessional Papers, 1872, no. 18) [**2537**]. *Correspondence between the Government of the Dominion and the Government of the United States respecting the alleged violation of the treaty of Washington* (Sessional Papers, 1877, no. 14) [**2538**].

George Bemis, *Mr. Reverdy Johnson: the Alabama negotiations, and their joint repudiation by the Senate of the United States* (N.Y. 1869) [**2539**], defense of the Senate's rejection of the Clarendon-Johnson treaty. F. M. Edge, *Great Britain and the United States; a letter to the Right Honourable William Ewart Gladstone, M.P.* (London, 1869) [**2540**], an English defense of Sumner's leadership to defeat in the Senate the Johnson-Clarendon arbitration convention. [John Jay], *Remarks on the Clarendon-Johnson treaty, for adjusting the Alabama claims* (N.Y., 1869) [**2541**], an attack on the proposed treaty. Mountague Bernard, *Neutrality of Gt. Brit.* (no. 1895). J. W. Dwinelle, *American opinions on the "Alabama", and other political questions* (London, 1870) [**2542**], defenses of American attitude, by an American lawyer, prepared for English consumption. Great Western Insurance Company, *Correspondence relating to Alabama claims* (N.Y.? 1870?) [**2543**], 2 letters from J. A. Parker, president of the company, 1 from Reverdy Johnson to Parker, and 1 from George T. Curtis to Parker. Augusto Pierantoni, *La questione anglo-americana dell' Alabama; studio di diritto internazionale publico e marittimo* (Florence, 1870) [**2544**], a juridical analysis; the author's thesis is that there is an option for a power to recognize, or not, belligerency. (A marked copy of this pamphlet was presented to the Harvard College Library by Charles Sumner, on April 28, 1874). And by the same writer, *Gli arbitrati internazionale e il trattato di Washington* (Naples, 1872) [**2545**], an argument against any limitation by the treaty of Washington of the purview of the arbitrators. C. C. Beaman, Jr., *The national and private "Alabama claims" and their "final and amicable settlement"* (Wash., 1871) [2546], rather hastily prepared collection of notes on the origin of the Alabama claims and the treaty for their arbitration, with notes and opinions of others all tending to substantiate the American claims; also lists of vessels destroyed, and table of war premiums paid by Willet and Co., of New York. J. C. Bluntschli, *An impartial opinion on the Alabama question and the manner of settling it* (Wash., 1871) [2547], celebrated continental jurist concludes that the United States has a case against Great Britain on account of the "Alabama", but not for having recognized the belligerency of the Confederacy. B. F. Butler, *The treaty of Washington; an analysis of its provisions; our losses, England's gains* (Boston, 1871) [2548], an address at Music Hall, Philadelphia, Oct. 16, 1871; and by the same writer, *The treaty of Washington; an examination of its provisions, showing the advantages thereby gained to England over America* (Lowell, 1871) [2549], a letter to the Hon. A. Ames, U.S. senator. *The convention of Washington contrived for the destruction, not the reconciliation of Great Britain and the United States* (London, 1871) [2550], address to the Queen signed " by order and on behalf of the Foreign Affairs Committees of Cheshire and Lancashire, assembled in conference at Manchester, June 4, 1871 [etc.]." Reverdy Johnson, *A reply to a recent speech of Sir Roundell Palmer on the Washington treaty, and the Alabama claims* (Baltimore, 1871) [2551]; and by the same writer, *A letter from Hon. Reverdy Johnson to Hon. John A. Peters on the subject of the Washington treaty, and its construction in relation to the claim of the United States for consequential damages* (Baltimore, 1872) [2552]. Auguste Laugel, " Le traité de Washington du 8 mai 1871; règlement de la question de l'Alabama ", *Rev. deux mondes*, 2e pér., XCIV (1871) 795-810 [2553], a French publicist analyzes the diplomatic implications of the newly signed treaty. W. B. Lawrence, *The treaty of Washington* (Providence, 1871) [2554], ex-parte analysis by a British jurist. Also by the same, *The indirect claims of the United States under the treaty of Washington, of May 8, 1871, as submitted to the tribunal of arbitration at Geneva* (Providence, 1872) [2555]; and *Belligerent and sovereign rights as regards neutrals during the war of secession*, argument before the Mixed Commission on British and American Claims (Boston, 1873)

[2556], this argument is preceded by an introduction recording the history of the "non-Alabama" claims. *The Alabama case; list of articles and letters relating to the same which have appeared in the London newspapers* (n.p., 1872?) [2557], a scrapbook (10 bound volumes) in the Library of Congress. *The American commissioners and the statement of Sir Stafford Northcote at Exeter, in relation to an alleged promise of exclusion of the indirect claims of the United States* (Wash.: Govt. Print. Off., 1872) [2558]. *Consequential damages; three letters on the American doctrine*, by Saxe Brit. [*pseud.*] (London, 1872) [2559], supercilious and robust English repudiation of the idea of indirect claims. *The indirect claims; a chapter in the argument for the United States submitted to the tribunal of arbitration at Geneva, June 15th, 1872*, reprinted with a note (Paris, 1872) [2560], "Note: Opinions of statesmen, magazines, and journals of Great Britain and the continent on the construction of the treaty of Washington." Paul Pradier-Foderé, *La question de l'Alabama et le droit des gens* (Paris, 1872) [2561] points out the juridical impossibility of the American indirect claims. R. W. Russell, *Neutral relations and the treaty of Washington* (Wash., 1872) [2562] marshals historical facts to show that proposed legislation entrenching on neutral rights is inconsistent with the "Alabama" claims of the United States against Great Britain; arguments insisting on the rules of "due diligence." Conte Federigo Sclopis de Salerano, *Opinions sur les accusations, portées contre les navires nommés Florida, Alabama, & Shenandoah* (n.p., 1872) [2563]; and *Opinions sur les trois questions de droit sur lesquelles le tribunal d'arbitrage, dans sa séance du 25 juillet 1872, a demandé des éclaircissements aux conseils des hautes parties présentes à la barre* (n.p., 1872) [2564]. Three pamphlets by Jakob Staempfli, one of the arbitrators at the Geneva tribunal: *Exposé de M. Staempfli l' "Alabama"* (n.p., 1872) [2565]; *Exposé de M. Staempfli le "Florida"* (n.p., 1872) [2566]; and *Exposé de M. Staempfli relativement aux croiseurs le "Sumter", le "Retribution" et le "Shenandoah"* (n.p., 1872) [2567]. Viscount Bury (7th Earl of Albemarle), *Balance sheet of the Washington treaty of 1872 [i.e. 1871] in account with the people of Great Britain and her colonies*, by the Right Hon. Viscount Bury (London, 1873) [2568]. J. C. Bancroft Davis, *Mr. Sumner, the Alabama claims, and their settlement;* a letter to the New York Herald (N.Y., 1878) [2569], the author who was assistant secretary of state, con-

tends that Grant's removal of Motley and Sumner was not the
result of any political intrigue about Santo Domingo, but wise and
necessary political measures to secure the success of the treaty of
Washington. Also by the same writer, *Mr. Fish and the Alabama
claims* (Boston, 1893) [2569a]. J. F. Manning, *Epitome of the
Geneva award contest in the Congress of the United States* (N.Y.,
1882) [2570], arguments before the judiciary committee of the
House of Representatives for claimants to share in the award by reason of losses for so-called " outside cruisers " and " war premiums "
cases. F. W. Hackett, *Reminiscences of the Geneva tribunal of arbitration, 1872. The Alabama claims* (Boston and N.Y., 1911) [2571],
written forty years after by the secretary to Caleb Cushing, senior
American counsel. *Diary of Orville Hickman Browning* (no. 1887).

For printed writings of American statesmen and diplomatists (for
names, see p. 407), see our list on p. 756.

MEMOIRS, LETTERS, ETC., OF BRITISH STATESMEN: *Letters of Archibald* (no. 1984). T. W. Reid, *Life of the Right Honourable William
Edward Forster* (London, 1888, 2 v.) [2572], member of Parliament,
who took great interest in the Geneva arbitration; extracts from his
diary and correspondence are given. Lord Edmond Fitzmaurice,
The life of Granville George Leveson Gower, second Earl Granville,
2nd ed. (London, 1905, 2 v.) [2573] includes letters to and from
Granville, and a chapter on the Geneva arbitration. *Letters of
Northcote* (no. 2505). Roundell Palmer, *Memorials* (no. 1972).
Wolf, *Marquess of Ripon* (no. 2486). Lord John Russell, *Recollections* (no. 1966); Walpole, *Russell* (no. 1967); *Corres. Russell* (no.
1968).

See also, for the writings of Sir John A. Macdonald, Prime Minis-
ter of Canada and signer of the treaty of Washington: Macpherson,
Macdonald (no. 2508); Pope, *Macdonald* (no. 2494); and *Corres.
Macdonald* (no. 2509).

MSS.: Suggestions

See Sec. 1, above.

The archives of the Geneva Tribunal were deposited with the
Council of State at Geneva.

Of personal papers of American diplomatists connected with the
making and negotiation of the treaty of Washington and the Geneva
Arbitration, there are extant the following (for location, see our lists

on pp. 862 and 868) : C. F. Adams, Jr. (arbitrator at Geneva) ; Caleb Cushing (counselor at Geneva) ; J. C. Bancroft Davis[8] (agent at Geneva) ; W. M. Evarts (counselor at Geneva). The voluminous papers of Charles Sumner (chairman of the Senate Committee on Foreign Relations) are in the Harvard College Library; and those of N. P. Banks (chairman of the House Committee of Foreign Affairs) are in the Essex Institute, Salem, Massachusetts.

3. Boundary Disputes

A. San Juan Boundary

Bibliographical Aids

For general aids, see Sec. 1, above. Judson, *Pacific Northwest* (no. 1707). Smith, *Pacific Northwest Americana* (no. 1708). Turner and Merk, *References on West* (no. 307). Reid, *Brit. Columbia* (no. 1709).

Special Works

Viscount Milton (Wm. Fitzwilliam), *A history of the San Juan water-boundary question* (London and N.Y., 1869) [**2574**], by the leading advocate of the claim for Great Britain. E. C. Mason, " How we won the San Juan archipelago ", *Minn. hist. soc. coll.*, IX (1901) 35–54 [**2575**], the author was inspector general of the military department of the Columbia, and uses records of the War Department and memories of conversations concerning incidents of friction on the San Juan Islands in 1859 " not generally known to the public." Schafer, *Pacific N.W.* (no. 1718). Scholefield and Howay, *Brit. Columbia* (no. 1718a), v. II (by F. W. Howay) contains a chapter on " The San Juan difficulty." Andrew Fish, " The last phase of the Oregon boundary question; the struggle for San Juan Island ", *Oreg. hist. soc. quar.*, XXII (1921) 161–224 [**2576**]. W. N. Sage, *Sir James Douglas and British Columbia* (Toronto, 1930) [**2577**] sets forth Gov. Douglas' actions in the San Juan controversy, 1858–59. Alfred Tunem, " The dispute over the San Juan Island water boundary ", *Wash. hist. quar.*, XXIII (1932) 38–46, 133–137, 196–204, 286–300 [**2578**], based on printed documents. Fuller, *Pacific N.W.* (no. 1722).

---

[8] Extracts are printed in J. B. Moore's *Arbitrations* (no. 5364) of Davis's *Journal*, then in the Department of State, now in the Library of Congress.

Printed Sources

For general collections, see Sec. 1, above; particularly Moore's *Arbitrations* (no. 5364) ; and *Brit. and for. state pap.* (no. 5416), XV, 1211-1288 [**2579**], for " Correspondence between the British and United States commissioners [J. C. Prevost and Archibald Campbell] relative to the line of water boundary between the United States and British possessions on the northwest coast of America (Island of San Juan)."

UNITED STATES OFFICIAL DOCUMENTS: Dept. of State, *The northwest boundary. Discussion of the water-boundary question: geographical memoir of the islands in dispute, and history of the military occupation of San Juan Island* (Wash., 1868) [**2580**] includes diplomatic correspondence. *Papers relating to the treaty of Washington* (no. 2525), v. V: " Berlin arbitration " [**2581**].

BRITISH PARLIAMENTARY (HOUSE OF COMMONS SESSIONAL) PAPERS: *Correspondence respecting . . . San Juan water boundary* (1868-69, XIII, 735) [**2582**]. *Despatch from Lord John Russell to Lord Lyons, November 22nd, 1860* (1868-69, LXIII, 797) [**2583**]. The *Case* of Great Britain, *Memorial* of the United States, *Reply* of the United States, *Correspondence*, and *Maps* for the San Juan arbitration by the Emperor of Germany (1873, LXXIV, 681, 727, 765, 821, 869, 881, 911, and 927) [**2584**]. *Correspondence respecting determination of the northwestern boundary* (1875, LXXII, 51; 1876, LXXXII, 357) [**2585**].

" The beginning of the San Juan dispute ", *Wash. hist. quar.*, II (1908) 352-356 [**2586**], letter from Sir James Douglas, governor of British Columbia and Vancouver Island, to Gov. Stevens of Washington, Apr. 26, 1855, with reply from Gov. Stevens. " Captain William Hale Fauntleroy, a neglected character in northwestern history ", *ibid.*, XVIII (1927) 289-300 [**2587**], several documents regarding Captain Fauntleroy who commanded the U.S. ship *Massachussetts* during the San Juan Island negotiations of 1859.

MSS.: Suggestions

See Sec. 1, above.

There are some reports to the Prussian Government on the San Juan question, 1872, from the *Preussisches Geheimes Staatsarchiv* at Berlin, in the Library of Congress.

The MS. papers of George Bancroft relating to the arbitration by the German Emperor, including transcripts of documents and maps in Spanish archives and a journal of the meetings of the commission, are in the New York Public Library.

The papers of Sir James Douglas, governor of British Columbia and Vancouver Island, are in the provincial archives at Victoria.

Maps: Suggestions

Phillips (no. 5135), for a list of maps of the northwest part of North America in the Library of Congress. *The northwest boundary* (no. 2580) has a " geographical memoir of the islands in dispute " and 2 maps. " Karte des San Juan- od. Haro-Archipels mit den neuen Grenze nach der schiedsrichterlichen Entscheidung des Deutschen Kaisers am 21. Okt. 1872 ", in A. Petermann, *Mittheilungen*, XIX (Gotha, 1873), plate 4 [**2588**]. House of Commons, *Sessional papers*, 1873, LXXIV, 869 and 881 (no. 2584), for maps annexed to the *Case* of Great Britain, and to the *Memorial* of the United States Government, for the arbitration by the Emperor of Germany. Marcus Baker, *Survey of the northwestern boundary of the United States, 1857–1861* (Wash., 1900) (U.S. Geological Survey Bulletin, no. 174) [**2589**], " Maps " (p. 19–26) describes the original MS. maps, now in the Department of State, and British maps. Paullin's *Atlas* (no. 213), p. 71–72, and plate 96c.

B. Alaska Boundary

Bibliographical Aids

For general aids, see Sec. 1, above. Smith, *N.W. Americana* (no. 1708). Judson, *Pacific N.W.* (no. 1707). Wickersham, *Bibliog. Alaska* (no. 2227). Kerner, *Russian expansion* (no. 1710).

Special Works

Bancroft, *Alaska* (no. 2229). Marcus Baker, *The Alaskan boundary* (N.Y., 1896) [**2590**], reprinted from the *Bulletin* of the American Geographical Society, v. XXVIII, 1896; a statement of the conflicting claims, and their historical and geographical background on the eve of the agreement to arbitrate. David Glass, " The Alaskan boundary line ", *Anglo-Am. mag.*, II (1899) 315–325, 464–472, 548–563 [**2591**], from the Canadian point of view. J. B. Moore, " The Alaskan boundary ", *No. Am. rev.*, CLXIX (1899) 501–515 [**2592**].

J. W. Foster, "The Alaskan boundary", *Nation. geog. mag.*, X
(1900) 425–456 [**2593**]; and by the same writer, *The Alaskan boundary tribunal* (Wash., 1903), also pub. in the *Nation. geog. mag.*, XV,
1904 [**2594**], accompanied by a good map; a course lecture interesting because its author had been Secretary of State, and was one
of the members of the Joint High Commission appointed in 1898 to
consider Canadian-American questions. T. W. Balch, *The Alasko-
Canadian frontier* (Phila., 1902) [**2595**], reprinted from the *Journal*
of the Franklin Institute, CLIII (Phila., 1902), a valuable review
of the relation of the Russian-American negotiations of 1825 .to
the later Alaskan boundary controversy with reproductions of historic maps; this paper together with another, "La frontière alasko-
canadienne", which was printed in the *Rev. droit internat.*, 2ᵉ sér.,
IV (Brussels, 1902) are in part incorporated in the same writer's
The Alaska frontier (Phila., 1903) [**2596**]. Thomas Hodgins, *The
Alaska-Canada boundary dispute, under the Anglo-Russian treaty
of 1825; the Russian-American Alaska treaty of 1867; and the
Anglo-American conventions of 1892, 1894, and 1897; a historical
and legal review* (Toronto, 1902; 2d ed., 1903) [**2597**], Canadian plea
for arbitration. George Davidson, *The Alaska boundary* (San
Francisco, 1903) [**2598**], the author was engaged by the Alaska
Packers Association of San Francisco to write this treatise which is
a historical brief for the American claim. C. C. Hyde, "Concerning the Alaskan boundary", *Harv. law rev.*, XVI (1903) 418–435
[**2599**] analyzes solely the problem put before the tribunal in the
"fifth question": the intent of the convention of 1825 with reference to the boundary from the point on the 56th degree north latitude to the intersection of the 141st degree west longitude. Richard
Jebb, "The Alaska boundary", *Empire rev.*, V (1903) 185–193, also
published in his *Studies in colonial nationalism* (London, 1905) 40–
60 [**2600**], a contemporary account valuable for its example of one-
sided Canadian prejudice. Willison, *Laurier and liberal party* (no.
2492). *Canada's Alaskan dismemberment; an analytical examination of the fallacies underlying the tribunal award* (Niagara-on-the-
Lake, 1904) [**2601**], anonymous criticism of the award, reflecting indignant Canadian attitude. F. C. Wade, "Some comment on the
Alaskan award", *Canad. mag.*, XXII (1904) 336–342 [**2602**], severe
criticism of the award by one of the British counsel. D. A. Mac-
Arthur, "The Alaska boundary award", *Univ. mag.*, VI (1907) 412–

426 [**2603**], impartial review and conclusions by a Canadian historian who concludes: "Nothing has been taken from Canada to which she could establish a clear and positive right. Justice has been done." J. S. Ewart, "The Alaska boundary", in his *The kingdom of Canada* (Toronto, 1908) 299–347 [**2604**], exposition of the Canadian view. James White, "Alaska boundary", in *Canada and its provinces* (no. 2460a), v. VIII, 749–958 [**2605**], the author is a Canadian boundary specialist, who despite his conviction of the justice of the Canadian case, manages to give an objective summary of the principal facts in the arbitration. C. G. Washburn, "Memoir of Henry Cabot Lodge", *Mass. hist. soc. proc.*, LVIII (1925) 324–376 [**2606**] contains a revealing statement dictated by Lodge concerning Roosevelt's confidential preliminary draft of a convention for settlement of the Alaskan boundary. It is criticized by James White, a Canadian boundary specialist, in "Henry Cabot Lodge and the Alaska boundary award", *Canad. hist. rev.*, VI (1925) 332–347 [**2607**]. Dennis, *Adventures* (no. 2224), for new material. Keenleyside, *Canada and U.S.* (no. 896). Dafoe, *Clifton Sifton* (no. 2498), ch. 8, for an account of the Alaskan boundary dispute; Sifton was a member of the Laurier government and leader of the Liberal party in western Canada. Dennett, *Hay* (no. 2472).

For biographies of American statesmen and diplomatists connected with the dispute (for names of members of the Joint High Commission, 1898–99, and of the Alaska Tribunal, see the contemporary *Registers* of the Dept. of State), see the relevant entries and the bibliographical data in the *D.A.B.*

Printed Sources

For general collections, see Sec. 1 above.

U.S. OFFICIAL DOCUMENTS: *Report on the boundary line between Alaska and British Columbia* (Wash., 1889) (50th Cong., 2d sess. Sen. Ex. doc. no. 146) [**2608**], by T. F. Bayard, secretary of state, March 2, 1889, with documents and maps. Alaskan-Canadian Boundary Commission, *Joint report of United States and British Commissioners on Alaskan-Canadian boundary, Dec. 31, 1895* (Wash.: Govt. Print. Off., 1898) [**2609**]. *Proceedings of the Alaskan boundary tribunal, convened at London, under the treaty between the United States of America and Great Britain, concluded at Washington, January 24, 1903, for the settlement of questions . . .*

with respect to the boundary line between the Territory of Alaska and the British possessions in North America (Wash., 1904, 7 v.) **[2610]** includes the case, counter case, and argument of the United States, with the report of the agent of the United States, and the case, counter case, and argument of Great Britain, etc.

BRITISH OFFICIAL DOCUMENTS: (House of Commons Sessional Papers) *Exchange of notes between the United Kingdom and the United States of America, providing for the establishment of a provisional boundary between the Dominion of Canada and the Territory of Alaska, in the region about the head of Lynn Canal, October 20, 1899* (1900, CV, 879) **[2611]**. *Correspondence respecting the Alaska boundary* (London, 1904) (1904, CXI, 5) **[2612]**. The Foreign Office has published the British *Case, Counter Case, Argument, and Protocols, oral arguments,* [etc.] (London, 1903) **[2613]**, in several volumes.

CANADIAN SESSIONAL PAPERS: *Correspondence between the Dominion Government and the Government of the United States regarding the settlement of the boundary line between Alaska and British Columbia* (1876, no. 110) **[2614]**. *Extract from a report of the committee of the honourable the privy council, approved by His Excellency on the 23rd January 1897, referring to the delimitation of the Alaskan boundary* (1897, no. 51) **[2615]**. *Report of Major General Cameron on the proposed convention in reference to a portion of the Alaskan boundary, and memorandum thereon* (1897, no. 77) **[2616]**. *Protocol no. lxiii of the Joint High Commission, Washington, respecting the boundary between Alaska and Canada* (1899, no. 99) **[2617]**. *Correspondence and papers in relation to the Alaska boundary question* (1903, no. 149) **[2618]**. *The award of the Alaska boundary tribunal* (1904, no. 46) **[2619]**. *Correspondence respecting the Alaska boundary, together with the award of the Alaska boundary tribunal* (1904, no. 46a) **[2620]**.

David Mills, *The Canadian view of the Alaskan boundary dispute as stated by Hon. David Mills*, in an interview with the correspondent of the Chicago *Tribune* on the 14th August, 1899 (Ottawa: Govt. Print. Bureau, 1899) **[2621]**, by the Canadian Minister of Justice. E. S. Balch, ed., *Letters and papers relating to the Alaska frontier* (Phila., 1904) **[2622]**. G. W. Smalley, "Sir Wilfrid Laurier and the Alaska boundary", in his *Anglo-Am. memories* (no. 2501), 1st series, 260–276 **[2623]**. James White, "Treaty of 1825—correspondence respecting the boundary between Russian America (Alaska) and British North America ", *Royal soc. Canad. proc.*, 3d ser., IX, sec. 2 (1915) 65–77 [**2624**], hitherto unpublished correspondence (1823–1824) from the Bagot papers in the Canadian archives; written during the period when Bagot was trying to reach an understanding with Nesselrode respecting the conflicting claims of Great Britain and Russia on the Northwest coast, " they show the secret opposition of the United States and demonstrate the insincerity of Middleton, the American minister." F. W. Seward, *Reminiscences* (no. 5291).

For printed writings of American statesmen and diplomatists connected with the boundary question (for names of members of the Joint High Commission, 1898–99, and of the Alaska Tribunal, see the contemporary *Register* of the Dept. of State (no. 5122)), see our list on p. 756.

For printed writings of British and Canadian statesmen and diplomatists, see Sec. 1, above.

MSS.: Suggestions

See Sec. 1, above (particularly papers of presidents and secretaries of state; Elihu Root, member of the Alaska Boundary Tribunal).

The Alaska boundary issue is so recent in history that the personal papers of participants, some of whom are still living, are not much listed in bibliographies and catalogues. These persons or their families must be consulted.

See our list of papers of American diplomatists for Joseph Choate (U.S. ambassador to Great Britain, 1899–1905, and member of the Joint High Commission, 1898–99), John A. Kasson (member of the Joint High Commission, 1898–99), Henry White (U.S. ambassador to France, 1906–09, and member of the Joint High Commission, 1898–99), and Senator Lodge (member of the Alaska Boundary Tribunal).

Maps: Suggestions

W. H. Dall and Marcus Baker, " Partial list of charts, maps, and publications relative to Alaska and the adjacent region ", in U.S. Coast and Geodetic Survey, *Pacific Coast Pilot. Coasts and islands of Alaska*, 2d series (Wash., 1879) 163–223 [**2625**]. Phillips (no. 5135), for maps of Alaska in the Library of Congress. George

Davidson, "Available maps or charts of the northwest coast of America . . . at the first negotiations between Russia and the United States and Russia and Great Britain in 1822–1825", and "The American charts, 1867–1901", in his *The Alaska boundary* (no. 2598), 49–62, and 172–181 [**2626**]. "The evidence of the maps" (p. 84–86) and "Geographical and topographical information relative to southeastern Alaska", in the *Case of the United States* in the Alaska Boundary Tribunal *Proceedings* (no. 2610), 511–538 [**2627**]. The *Proceedings of the Alaskan boundary tribunal* (no. 2610) also includes the "United States atlas, maps, and charts accompanying the Case of the United States", "British atlas, maps, and charts accompanying the Case of Great Britain", and "Atlas of award, 25 sectional maps, and index map showing line fixed", and the *Appendix* to the *Argument* of the United States, has a list of maps and charts existing prior to the treaty of 1825. The British documents respecting the Boundary Tribunal (no. 2613) also contain many maps and summary accounts of maps. See also *Map to accompany correspondence respecting the Alaska boundary* (Gt. Brit. Parliament. House of Commons. Sess. Pap., 1904, CXI, 99) [**2628**]. Lawrence Martin, "Glaciers and international boundaries; how one nation gained hundreds of square miles of territory", *Sci. American*, supplement, LXXVI (1913) 129, 136–138 (summary in *Lit. digest*, XLVII (1913) 571–572, 871) [**2629**] shows how the movement of certain Alaska glaciers changed the Alaska-Canadian boundary line as settled in 1903, whereby Canada gained an unexpected harbor—but later the reversal of action of the glacier restored it to the United States. Paullin's *Atlas* (no. 213), p. 69–71, and plate 96A.

C. Other Boundary Matters

Lake of the Woods Boundary

H. L. Keenleyside, "The Lake of the Woods boundary (1871–1876)", in his *Canada and the U.S.* (no. 896), 238–242, for a brief account of the final demarcation of this boundary.

Northern Boundary Commission, *Reports upon the survey of the boundary between the territory of the United States and the possessions of Great Britain from the Lake of the Woods to the summit of the Rocky Mountains, authorized by an act of Congress approved March 19, 1872* (Wash., 1878) (44th Cong. 2d sess. Sen. Ex. doc.

no. 41) [2630], the immediate cause of the determination of the boundary line was a dispute between Great Britain and the United States regarding a certain portion (near Pembina) which left the Hudson Bay Company fort at Pembina within the territory of the United States. British Parliamentary (House of Commons sessional) papers: *Correspondence respecting the determination of the boundary between Canada and the United States* (1875, LXXXII, 51) [2631]; and *Further correspondence respecting the determination of the boundary* . . . (1876, LXXXII, 357) [2632] with inclosure of a set of 24 maps; these maps are in the Foreign Office Library.

International Joint Commission (U.S. and Canada)

L. J. Burpee, *The International Joint Commission* (Montreal? 1915?), reprinted from the *University magazine*, XIV (1915) 362–375 [2633]; and by the same writer (secretary of the Canadian section of the Commission), *A successful experiment in international relations* (Ottawa: King's printer, 1919) [2634], an account of the above-mentioned commission, which was established " speaking generally, to inaugurate an ordered régime for the use, obstruction, or diversion of the international waters of the long chain of rivers and lakes through which the common boundary passes." R. A. MacKay, " The International Joint Commission between the United States and Canada ", *Am. jour. internat. law*, XXII (1928) 292–318 [2635], a professional analysis and exposition of its functions and powers. *Papers relating to the work of the International Joint Commission* (Ottawa, 1929) [2636]. C. J. Chacko, *The International Joint Commission between the United States of America and the Dominion of Canada* (N.Y., 1932) [2637], the creation, powers, and accomplishments of that organization; a Columbia Ph.D. thesis based on printed sources and secondary works. A methodical study of this organization for the settlement of routine disputes along the undefended frontier, particularly power development and navigable waterways.

The International Joint Commission; organization, jurisdiction, and operation under the treaty of January 11, 1909, between United States and Great Britain (Wash.: Govt. Print. Off., 1924) [2638], an official analysis of the text of the treaty. *Report on the treaty with the United States relating to boundary waters and questions*

*arising along the boundary between Canada and the United States,
signed at Washington, January 11, 1909* (Ottawa, 1910) (Canada.
Parl. Sess. Pap., no. 19e) [2639]. *Orders or minutes of Council
. . . ; together with a copy of all despatches, letters, and telegrams
between the governor general, or the Government of Canada . . .
and the British ambassador at Washington, or the British Government . . . upon that subject* [*i.e.* treaty with the United States relating to boundary waters] (Canada. Parl. Sess. Pap., 1912, no. 119)
[2640].

International Boundary Commission

U.S. Dept. of State, *Canadian questions. Northern boundary of
the United States. The demarcation of the boundary between the
United States and Canada, from the Atlantic to the Pacific, with
particular reference to the portions thereof which require more complete definition and marking.* Report prepared for the Department
of State by Chandler P. Anderson, 1906 (Wash., 1906) [2641], an
objective historical account of the Canadian boundary questions between the United States and Great Britain, made in connection with
the treaty of 1908 for marking the boundary from the Atlantic to
the Pacific. Four reports by the International Boundary Commission (U.S. and Canada): *Joint report upon the survey and demarcation of the international boundary between the United States and
Canada along the 141st meridian from the Arctic Ocean to Mount
St. Elias,* in accordance with the provisions of article IV of the
convention signed at Washington, April 21, 1906 (Wash., 1918?)
[2642]. *Joint report upon the survey and demarcation of the boundary between the United States and Canada from the western terminus
of the land boundary along the forty-ninth parallel,* in accordance
with the provisions of article III of the treaty signed at Washington, April 11, 1908 (Wash., 1921) [2643]. *Joint report upon the
survey and demarcation of the boundary between the United States
and Canada from the source of the St. Croix River to the St. Lawrence River,* in accordance with the provisions of article III of the
treaty signed at Washington, April 11, 1908 (Wash., 1925) [2644].
*Joint report upon the survey and demarcation of the boundary be-
tween the United States and Canada from the northwesternmost
point of Lake of the Woods to Lake Superior,* in accordance with
the provisions of article V of the treaty signed at Washington, April

11, 1908, and article I of the treaty signed at Washington, February 24, 1925 (Wash., 1931) [**2645**].

Maps: Suggestions

The American section of the International Joint Commission transferred to the Library of Congress a considerable number of maps of the Lake of the Woods in the state of Minnesota and the Provinces of Ontario and Manitoba.

4. Isthmian Question[9]

Bibliographical Aids

For general aids, see Sec. 1, above.

Morrison, *Interoceanic canal* (no. 1212). Phillips, *Central America* (no. 4703). Frank, *Interoceanic canals* (no. 1213). Williams, *Isthmian diplomacy* (no. 1235), 331-345. Panama Canal, Washington Office, *Congressional history of the Panama Canal* (Wash., 1917?) [**2646-7**], index to references to the Panama Canal in the *Congressional record*, Dec. 2, 1901, to Mar. 4, 1917 (inclusive), 57th to 64th Congress. Meyer, *Panama Canal and Panama Canal Zone* (no. 1214).

Special Works

For material on the Clayton-Bulwer treaty, see Ch. VIII, sec. 3; particularly Keasbey, *Nicaragua canal* (no. 1226); and Travis, *Clayton-Bulwer treaty* (no. 1229).

J. B. Moore, *The interoceanic canal and the Hay-Pauncefote treaty* (Wash., 1900) [**2648**], reprinted from the New York *Times* of March 4, 1900; a defense of the policy of the first (unratified) Hay-Pauncefote treaty, which is significant because of the prestige of the writer. Samuel Pasco, " The Isthmian canal question as affected by treaties and concessions ", *Am. acad. pol. and soc. sci. ann.*, XIX (1902) 24-45 [**2649**], undocumented summary by a member (or attaché) of the U.S. Isthmian Canal Commission. J. H. Latané, " The neutralization features of the Hay-Pauncefote treaty ", *Am. hist. assoc. rep.*, for 1902, v. I (1903) 289-303 [**2650**], the writer believes that the terms of the Hay-Pauncefote treaty are so ambiguous that the United States will have pretty much her own way in regard to the Panama Canal. Achille Viallate, " Les Etats-

---

[9] For the Colombian negotiations, see Ch. XIX, sec. 3, below.

Unis et le canal interocéanique; un chapitre d'histoire diplomatique américaine ", *Rev. gén. droit internat. public*, X (1903) 5–65 [**2651**], an objective summary of the obvious facts, expanded in the author's own *Essai d'histoire diplomatique américaine* (Paris, 1905), 57–206 [**2652**], the book reviews in dramatic style American Isthmian diplomacy, stressing the change from a demand for neutralization to one for control. C. H. Huberich, *Le canal transisthmique; étude d'histoire diplomatique américaine* (Paris, 1903), reprinted from the *Revue du droit publique et de la science politique en France et à l'étranger*, XXIX (1903) 193–213; also in English, *The trans-Isthmian canal; a study in American diplomatic history (1825–1904)* (Austin, Tex., 1904) [**2653**], a short summary based on Travis (no. 1229), Moore's *Digest* (no. 5365), and obvious U.S. printed documents. Tavernier, *Canal interocéanique* (no. 3079). P. C. Hains, " Neutralization of the Panama Canal ", *Am. jour. internat. law*, III (1909) 354–394 [**2654**] doubts not that the Hay-Pauncefote treaty was made with the purpose of neutralizing the canal, " and if it fails to accomplish that purpose there is still time to correct its defects." Paul Müller-Heymer, *Der Panamakanal in der Politik der Vereinigten Staaten; eine völkerrechtspolitische Studie* (Berlin, 1909) [**2655**], a summary of the revision of the Clayton-Bulwer treaty by the Hay-Pauncefote treaty; and of the treaty relations between the United States and Panama, based on insufficient review of the printed literature. Two articles by H. S. Knapp, U.S.N., " The real status of the Panama Canal as regards neutralization ", *U.S.N. inst. proc.*, XXXVI (1910) 61–102 (reprinted in *Am. jour. internat. law*, IV (1910) 314–358) [**2656**]; and " The Panama Canal in international law ", *U.S.N. inst. proc.*, XXXIX (1913) 95–126 [**2657**], concludes that the canal is not neutralized in time of war as far as enemies of the United States are concerned. Arias, *Panama Canal* (no. 3681).   U.S. Dept. of State, *History of amendments proposed to the Clayton-Bulwer treaty* (Wash., 1911) [**2658**], amendments resulting in the treaty submitted Dec. 14, 1901, the history was prepared in the Department of State and sent by Secretary Hay to the Senate Committee on Foreign Relations. Eugene Wambaugh, " The right to fortify the Panama canal ", *Am. jour. internat. law*, V (1911) 615–619 [**2658a**], one of the most pointed analyses, which shows that the right to fortify the Panama Canal rests on the treaty of 1846 with New Granada unless estopped by later treaties, and

that it was not so estopped after the ratification of the 2d Hay-
Pauncefote treaty. Wilhelm Kaufmann, "La loi américaine du
24 août 1912 sur le canal de Panama et le droit international",
Rev. droit internat., 2d ser., XIV (1912) 581–613 [**2659**], professor of the University of Berlin discusses the treaties regarding
the canal in relation to the act of Aug. 24, 1912, fixing regulations for the use of the canal; and "Das Panama-kanalgesetz
der Vereinigten Staaten vom 24 August 1912 und das Völkerrecht",
Zeits. f. Völkerrecht, VI (1912) 407–435 [**2660**] shows how the
tolls statute violates the international obligations of the United
States. C. H. Stockton, Admiral, U.S.N., "Panama Canal tolls",
U.S.N. inst. proc., XXXVIII (1912) 493–499 [**2661**] argues
against discrimination against any country or citizen or subject
thereof. C. P. Anderson, *Panama Canal tolls; an address on the
issues between the United States and Great Britain in regard to
Panama Canal tolls, as raised in the recent diplomatic correspondence*
(Wash., 1913) (63d Cong., 1st Sess., Sen. Doc. 32) [**2662**], reprinted
from the *Proceedings* of the American Society of International Law,
VII (1913) 69–81; a *précis* by a former counselor for the Department of State. G. W. W. Gram, "The international interest in the
settlement of the Panama Canal toll question", *Am. soc. internat. law
proc.*, VII (1913) 41–52 [**2663**]. Two studies by Crammond Kennedy: "Comparison of the relative interests of the United States and
Great Britain in the western hemisphere at the different stages of
negotiations [Panama Canal]", *ibid.*, 6–69 [**2664**], the Clayton-Bulwer treaty and its supersedure by the Hay-Pauncefote treaty; and
"Neutralization and equal terms", *ibid.*, 27–50 [**2665**] advocates re-
affirmation and reconsecration of principles of neutralization to the
second Hay-Pauncefote treaty. Richard Lehmann, "Der Panamakanal; seine Geschichte, die Befestigungs- und die Gebührenfrage",
Zeits. internat. Recht, XXIII (1913) 46–102 [**2666**], a German review, advocating arbitration of the tolls controversy; an excellent
historical, strategical, and juridical analysis by a realist who writes
unusually well. Lewis Nixon, "Does the expression 'all nations'
in article 3 of the Hay-Pauncefote treaty include the United States?"
Am. soc. internat. law proc., VII (1913) 101–126 [**2667**], he argues it
does not; also by the same writer, *The canal tolls and American
shipping* (N.Y., 1914) [**2668**], a former associate of shipping interests examines the question of Panama tolls to show that the United

States had a right to levy tolls as it pleased; pertinent documents and diplomatic documents in appendix. L[assa] Oppenheim, *The Panama Canal conflict between Great Britain and the United States of America* (Cambridge, Eng., 1913) [2669], eminent British international lawyer points out the incompatibility of the tolls act with treaty obligations of the United States and favors arbitration. S. L. Parrish, *The Hay-Pauncefote treaty and the Panama Canal* (N.Y.? 1913) [2670]. Charlemagne Tower, " The treaty obligations of the United States relating to the Panama Canal ", *Am. phil. soc. proc.*, LII (1913) 234–242 [2671]. H. G. Miller, *The Panama Canal tolls controversy; or, A statement of the reasons for the adoption and maintenance of the traditional American policy in the management of the Panama Canal* (Boston, 1914) [2672], a book written to establish by an array of documents and arguments the correctness of President Wilson's Panama Canal tolls policy; and by the same writer, *The Isthmian highway; a review of the problems of the Caribbean* (N.Y., 1929) [2673], a statement of the history of the Panama Canal Zone, and a discussion of the international problems rising out of the operation of the canal and of the application of the Monroe Doctrine to these problems. G. A. Talley, *The Panama Canal; an elucidation of its governmental features as prescribed by treaties; a discussion of toll exemption and the repeal bill of 1914*, rev. ed. (Wilmington, Del., 1916) [2674], diffuse. Williams, *Isthmian question* (no. 1235), the standard authority. Hill, *Treaties* (no. 4794), ch. 15. Dennis, *Adventures* (no. 2224), ch. 7. Nevins, *Henry White* (no. 2468).

For further contemporary discussion of the Panama Canal tolls controversy, see Meyer (no. 1214), and *Readers' guide* (no. 4996).

For biographies of President Wilson, Secretary of State John Hay, see the relevant entries and bibliographical data in the *D.A.B.* See also Dennett's *John Hay* (no. 2472); and Mowat, *Pauncefote*, (no. 2485).

Printed Sources

See Sec. 1, above, for general collections; particularly *For. rel.* (no. 5345).

U.S. OFFICIAL DOCUMENTS: *Correspondence in relation to an interoceanic canal between the Atlantic and Pacific Oceans, the Clayton-Bulwer treaty and the Monroe doctrine, and the treaty between the United States and New Granada of December 12, 1846*

(Wash., 1900) (56th Cong., 1st Sess. Sen. Doc. no. 237) **[2675]** contains reprints of all important documents on the canal question as well as correspondence not theretofore communicated to Congress. *Canal treaties. Executive documents presented to the United States Senate, together with proceedings by the Senate thereon relative to the Panama Canal* (Wash., 1914) (63d Cong., 2d Sess. Sen. Doc. no. 456) **[2676]**. *Diplomatic history of the Panama Canal. Correspondence relating to the negotiation and application of certain treaties on the subject of the construction of an interoceanic canal, with accompanying papers* (Wash., 1914) (63d Cong., 2d Sess. Sen. Doc. no. 474) **[2677]**. See also [*Panama canal tolls. Debates in the 62d Cong., 2d sess., 1912; and 62d Cong., 3d sess., 1912–13*) (Wash., 1912–13, 2 v.) **[2678]**, extracts from the *Congressional record* of Jan. 4, 1912, to March 4, 1913; bound together for convenience, in the Library of Congress.

BRITISH PARLIAMENTARY (HOUSE OF COMMONS SESSIONAL) PAPERS: *Correspondence respecting projected Panama Canal* (1882, LXXX, 59 (c. 3110); and 1884, LXXXVII, 21 (c. 3446) **[2679]**. *Correspondence respecting the convention signed at Washington, February 5th, 1900, relative to the establishment of a communication by ship canal between the Atlantic and Pacific Oceans* (1901, XCI, 1045 (cd. 438)) **[2680]**. *Correspondence respecting the convention signed at Washington, November 18, 1901, relative to the establishment of a communication by ship canal between the Atlantic and Pacific Oceans* (1902, CXXX, 633 (cd. 905)) **[2681]**. *Despatch to His Majesty's ambassador at Washington respecting the Panama Canal act (1912), with a copy of the act and of President Taft's memorandum thereon* (1912–13, CXXII, 645 (cd. 6451)) **[2682]**. *Despatch from the Secretary of State at Washington to the United States chargé d'affaires, respecting the Panama Canal act, communicated to His Majesty's secretary of state for foreign affairs, January 20th, 1913* (1912–13, CXXII, 663 (cd. 6585)) **[2683]**. *Note addressed by His Majesty's ambassador at Washington to the United States secretary of state, February 28, 1913, on the subject of the Panama Canal act* (1912–13, CXXII, 671 (cd. 6645)) **[2684]**.

The following reflect contemporary opinion of notable British and American authorities on the tolls question: Wallace Nesbitt, *The Panama Canal and its treaty obligations* (Toronto, 1912?) **[2685]**, speech delivered by a Canadian lawyer at Montreal, Dec. 12, 1912, against the tolls act. American Society of International Law, *Proceedings*, at its seventh annual meeting, 1913 (Wash., 1913) [2686] is devoted to papers dealing with the Panama Canal tolls question, historical and juridical; appendix contains conventions, correspondence, memoranda, etc., between Great Britain and the United States. J. F. Dulles, *The Panama Canal controversy between Great Britain and the United States* (N.Y.? 1913) [2687] argues that the tolls act is justified by treaty and thinks it would be a nice question to arbitrate. D. O. Dykes, " The Panama Canal and treaty rights ", *Juridical rev.*, XXIV (1913) 261–273 [2688], a statement of the British case against alleged discrimination. J. R. Knowland, comp., *Panama Canal tolls; symposium of views protesting against a surrender of American rights and upholding the side of the United States in the toll-controversy* (Wash., 1913) [2689], extracts from the *Congressional record* and public documents. J. H. Latané, " The Panama Canal act and the British protest ", *Am. jour. internat. law*, VII (1913) 17–26 [2690], plea to repeal or modify the tolls act. Richard Olney, *Panama Canal tolls and the Hay-Pauncefote treaty* (Wash., 1913) (63d Cong., 1st sess. Senate. Doc. no. 33) [2691], an address before the American Society of International Law, Washington, D.C., April 25, 1913, and published in its *Proceedings*, 1913 (Wash., 1913) 81–93, a plea for arbitration of the tolls controversy. Edith M. Phelps, comp., *Selected articles on Panama Canal tolls* (Minneapolis, 1913) [2692] reprints selected articles and opinions as a handbook for debaters. Sir H. E. Richards, *The Panama Canal controversy;* a lecture delivered before the University of Oxford on October 25, 1913 (Oxford and London, 1913) [2693], British legal authority arraigns the tolls act. W. H. Taft, " *The time to test our faith in arbitration* ", and " *Should the Panama Canal tolls controversy be arbitrated?* " by A. S. Hershey (N.Y., 1913) (International Conciliation, no. 63) [2694], arguments for arbitrating the case. Root, *Addresses* (no. 5287), for his notable addresses in the Senate advocating repeal of the tolls act or submission to arbitration.

For printed writings of President Wilson and Secretary of State Hay, see our list on p. 756.

MSS.: Suggestions

See Sec. 1, above.

5. Great Britain and the Monroe Doctrine (Venezuela Boundary Controversy; Venezuela Debts Dispute)

A. Venezuela Boundary Controversy

Bibliographical Aids

See Sec. 1, above, for general aids. Meyer, *Monroe Doctrine* (no. 1140), see index for references to the Venezuela boundary case.

Special Works

G. S. Boutwell, *The Venezuelan question and the Monroe Doctrine* (Wash., 1896) [**2695**], the writer was secretary of the treasury in Grant's administration, international lawyer, and, from 1899–1900, president of the Anti-Imperialist League. C. P. Daly, *Is the Monroe Doctrine involved in the controversy between Venezuela and Great Britain?* (N.Y.? 1896), reprinted from the New York *Herald* of Jan. 19, 1896 [**2696**], seems to believe it is. Rowland Rugg, *Anglo-American boundary question as stated by Great Britain, Venezuela, and the United States, in their official despatches* (London, 1896) [**2697**], by the "geographical specialist to the late geographer to the Queen." Clinio Silvestri, *La questione anglo-venezuelana per la delimitazione dei confini territoriali della Guayana della Republica di Venezuela e breve confutazione delle asserzioni del geografo Prof. G. Cora della R. Univ. di Torino* (Rome, 1896) [**2698**], this is headed "Consolato generale degli Stati Uniti di Venezuela in Italia", and is apparently written to influence Italian opinion favorably. Three studies by Marcus Baker, one of the technical assistants to the Commission appointed by President Cleveland to examine into the Venezuela boundary: "The Venezuelan boundary commission and its work", *Nation. geog. mag.*, VIII (1897) 193–201 [**2699**]; "The Anglo-Venezuelan boundary dispute", *ibid.*, XI (1900) 129–144 [**2700**], a convenient summary of the geographical history of the dispute and its settlement; and *Geographical results of the Venezuela-British Guiana dispute* (Berlin, 1900) [**2701**], reprinted from the *Verhandlungen des VII. Internationalen Geographen-Kongresses in Berlin, 1899*. Georges Pariset, *Historique sommaire du conflit anglo-vénézuélien en Guyane; des origines au traité d'arbitrage, 1493–1897* (Paris, 1898) [**2702**], a concise summary, with an interesting conclusion that the papal award of 1493 may be too old a fundamental law for Venezuela to appeal to, and the Monroe Doctrine too new. G. L. Burr, "The search for the Venezuela-Guiana boundary", *Am. hist. rev.*, IV (1899) 470–477 [2703], excellent statement of the historical work of President Cleveland's boundary commission by a learned historical expert attached thereto. Grover Cleveland, *Venezuelan boundary dispute* (N.Y., 1901), also published in the *Century*, LXII (1901) 283–297, 405–419; and in his *Presidential problems* (N.Y., 1904; and Princeton, 1913) [2704], from the pen of the man who precipitated and followed triumphantly through with the issue, this has special value, and might also be included as a source. M. W. Hazeltine, "The United States and the late Lord Salisbury", *No. Am. rev.*, CLXXVII (1903) 720–724 [2705] attributes Salisbury's change of attitude in the Venezuela crisis to a desire to avoid a quarrel with her principal food-purveyor. I. Breukelman, "Lord Salisbury en Engelands buitenlandsche Staatkunde", *Tijdschrift v. geschiedenis*, XXI (1906) 241–261[2706] discusses the Monroe Doctrine and Venezuela, and analyzes Salisbury's concessions to the United States in the controversy in relation to other British problems, notably China and South Africa. Hart, *Monroe Doctrine* (no. 1164). C. R. Miller, "The Monroe Doctrine in the Venezuela dispute; how that controversy paved the way for the Panama Canal", *Century*, LXXXVI (1913) 750–764 [2707], an appreciation by the editor of the New York *Times*. Henry James, *Richard Olney and his public service* (Boston and N.Y., 1923) [2708]. J. F. Rippy, "Some contemporary Mexican reactions to Cleveland's Venezuelan message", *Pol. sci. quar.*, XXXIX (1924) 280–292 [2709], a study of one phase of the "attitude of the Hispanic Americans which might for the sake of convenience be termed the American policy of the United States." P. R. Fossum, "The Anglo-Venezuelan boundary controversy", *Hisp. Am. hist. rev.*, VIII (1928) 299–329 [2710], apparently an academic exercise, it is concerned mainly with the dispute from 1876 to 1896, when Venezuela was urging the United States either to use its good offices as an arbitrator or to make use of force to bring about a settlement; based on printed material. T. D. Jervey, "William Lindsay Scruggs, a forgotten diplomat", *So. Atlan. quar.*, XXVII (1928) 292–309 [2711], biographical notes on the American minister to Venezuela, 1889–1893, and his diplomacy; in 1894 he was made by

Venezuela its legal adviser and special agent charged with the work of bringing to friendly arbitration the conflicting claims of Great Britain and Venezuela in the British Guiana boundary dispute. A. R. F. Webber, *Centenary history and handbook of British Guiana* (Georgetown, 1931) [**2712**].

For biographies of American presidents, secretaries of state, diplomatists to Great Britain and Venezuela (for names and tenure, see the latest *Register* of the Dept. of State (no. 5122)), and for members of the Venezuela Boundary Commission (R. H. Alvey, A. D. White, F. R. Coudert, D. C. Gilman), see the relevant entries and bibliographical data in the *D.A.B.* Note particularly: Nevins, *Cleveland* (no. 2467), and his *Henry White* (no. 2468), White was semiofficial agent in England to handle the Venezuelan boundary question.

For biographies of British statesmen, and diplomatists to the United States (for names and tenure, see latest *Foreign office list* (no. 5125)), see the *D.N.B.* Note particularly: Gardiner, *Sir William Harcourt* (no. 2483), leader of the Opposition in Parliament at the time of the Venezuela boundary controversy. Mowat, *Lord Pauncefote* (no. 2485). Marquess of Crewe, *Lord Rosebery* (no. 2487). Cecil, *Salisbury* (no. 2488).

Printed Sources

For general collections, see Sec. 1, above; particularly Moore's *Digest* (no. 5365), v. VI.

UNITED STATES OFFICIAL DOCUMENTS: U.S. Dept. of State, *Correspondence in relation to the boundary controversy between Great Britain and Venezuela* (Wash.: Govt. Print. Off., 1896) [**2713**], reprint of Senate Executive Document no. 226, 50th Cong., 1st sess., and Senate Document no. 31, 54th Cong., 1st sess., contains correspondence sent to Congress in 1888, and in 1895. U.S. Commission to Investigate and Report upon the True Divisional Line between Venezuela and British Guiana, *Report and accompanying papers of the Commission appointed by the President of the United States " to investigate and report upon the true divisional line between the republic of Venezuela and British Guiana "* (Wash., 1896–97, 9 v.) [**2714**], the report of President Cleveland's commission of investigation (Justice D. J. Brewer, Judge R. H. Alvey, A. D. White, F. R. Coudert, and D. C. Gilman) appointed under act of Congress of Dec. 21, 1895. For description of contents of this report, which contains historical notes by Professor G. L. Burr, Professor J. Franklin Jameson, Dr. Justin Winsor, and Marcus Baker, see Baker's *Venezuelan boundary commission* (no. 2699).

BRITISH OFFICIAL DOCUMENTS: *Documents and correspondence relating to the question of boundary between British Guiana and Venezuela* (London, 1896) (Parliament. House of Commons. Sess. Pap., 1896, XCVII, 453, 473, 479, 841, 855, and 911) [**2715**], these British Blue Books are also printed in the United States official *Report* (no. 2714), v. V–VI. *British Guiana boundary. Arbitration with the United States of Venezuela. The argument on behalf of the government of Her Britannic Majesty* (London, 1898) ; . . . *The case [and Appendix] on behalf of the government of Her Britannic Majesty* (London, 1898, 8 v., and Atlas) and *The counter-case on behalf of the government of Her Britannic Majesty* [and Appendix] (London, 1898, 2 v.) [**2716**]; all three collections indexed in *British Guiana boundary. Arbitration with the United States of Venezuela. Index to cases, counter-cases, and printed arguments of the governments of Great Britain and Venezuela* (London, 1899) [**2717**].

VENEZUELAN OFFICIAL DOCUMENTS: Venezuela, Ministerio de Relaciones Exteriores, *Correspondence between the Venezuelan Government and H.B.M.'s Government about the question of the frontier* (Caracas, 1887) [**2718**]; *Latest correspondence on the question of limits of Guiana* (Caracas, 1887) [**2719**]; and *Memorandum del Ministerio de Relaciones Exteriores acerca de la nota de Lord Salisbury al Señor Olney, fechada a 26 de noviembre de 1895, y relativa á la cuestión de los límites de Venezuela con la Guyana Británica* (Caracas, 1896) [**2720**], this last memorandum is also published in the United States official *Report* (no. 2714). Venezuela, Ministerio de Relaciones Interiores, *Venezuela y la Gran Bretaña; cuestión límites de Guayana; estado en que la halló el gobierno inaugurado el 19 de marzo y su situación actual* (Caracas? Imprenta Nacional, 1890) [**2721**]. *Acuerdo del Congreso de los Estados Unidos de Venezuela, dictado el 9 de marzo de 1896 como expresión de reconocimiento á los altos poderes de los Estados Unidos de América, por su benéfica interposición en el asunto de los límites de Guayana*

(Edición del Ministerio de Relaciones Exteriores) (Caracas, 1896) [2722], expression of Venezuela's official gratitude to Cleveland. Venezuelan documents, and Venezuelan briefs comprise vols. VIII and IX of the U.S. official *Report* (no. 2714).
James Bryce, " British feeling on the Venezuelan question ", *No. Am. rev.*, CLXII (1896) 145-153 [2723], an eminent diplomatist and student of American affairs, after the shock of Cleveland's policy, concludes that British public opinion will not support any " weak " case for British Guiana.   Andrew Carnegie, " The Venezuelan question", *ibid.*, 129-144 [2724], a famous lover of peace analyzes the controversy to find that " no government can live in Britain which dares to persist in rejecting arbitration in a boundary dispute upon the American Continent.   There is too much religion, too much conscience, too much sincere desire for peace and good will, . . ."   H. C. Lodge, " England, Venezuela, and the Monroe Doctrine", *No. Am. rev.*, CLX (1895) 651-658 [2725], a new imperialist's lusty plea for Cleveland's interpretation, with " immediate action ", of the Monroe Doctrine.   [N. D. Davis], *Venezuelan international law* (Georgetown? Brit. Guiana, 1896) [2726], a sarcastic commentary on the Venezuelan blue book, published 1888 and (in translation) under the title *Venezuelan international law: British boundaries of Guayana*, by R. F. Seijas, Venezuelan jurist and diplomat, tr. from the Spanish (Paris, 1888).   Also by Rafael (R. F.) Seijas, *To the "London Times"* (Atlanta, Ga., 1896) [2727], translation of an article in the *Diario* of Caracas, Nov. 25, 1895, dealing with the Anglo-Venezuelan boundary dispute, with a foreword by W. L. Scruggs vouching for its fairness and dispassion. John Morley, "Arbitration with America ", *Nineteenth century*, XL (1896) 320-337 [2728], weighty comments by a distinguished Englishman on the published British correspondence relating to the Venezuela dispute and the scheme of general Anglo-American arbitration.   W. M. Salter, *The Venezuelan question* (Phila., 1896) [2729], a lecture before the Society for Ethical Culture of Philadelphia, January 26, 1896, by a speaker who was not of those who say " my country, right or wrong."   The following defensive articles and book were written by W. L. Scruggs (see no. 2711), who served as American minister to Venezuela, 1889-1893, and who was legal adviser of the Venezuelan Government and special coun-

sel before the Boundary Commission: *The Venezuelan question: British aggressions in Venezuela, or, The Monroe Doctrine on trial; Lord Salisbury's mistakes; Fallacies of the British " blue book " on the disputed boundary* (Atlanta, Ga., 1896) [**2730**] comprises three papers, each of which was previously published separately: *The Guayana boundary dispute. Important testimony by an English geographer. The Essequibo River recognized by England as the frontier line between Venezuela and British Guiana as late as 1822* (Wash., 1896) [**2731**]; and *The Colombian and Venezuelan republics* (Boston, 1900) [**2732**], with two chapters devoted to the Venezuelan boundary dispute. *Venezuelan and British Guiana boundary arbitration. Synopsis of the principal events in Guiana* [1498–1897], *arranged in chronological order, with special reference to the documents printed in the appendices of the British and Venezuelan governments* (n.p., 1897?) [**2733**], compiled chiefly by E. F. Im Thurn. Theodore Marburg, *Political Papers. I. The war with Spain. II. The Venezuelan dispute* (Baltimore, 1898) [**2734**], reprinted from the Baltimore *American* of Dec. 22, 1895; an American plea for peace: " If we are far-seeing we will not block the extension of English colonization in America." *Venezuela-British Guiana boundary arbitration. Digest of evidence arranged according to localities*, prepared for private use of Venezuelan counsel [by Marcus Baker] (N.Y., 1899) [**2735**].

For other contemporary expressions of opinion by American and British personalities, consult *Poole's index* (no. 4995), and *Readers' Guide* (no. 4996).

For printed writings of American presidents, secretaries of state, and diplomatists abroad (for names and tenure, see latest *Register* of the Dept. of State (no. 5122)), see our list on p. 756.

For printed writings of British statesmen and diplomatists, see Sec. 1, above. See also Gardiner, *Sir William Harcourt* (no. 2483), with several letters by the leader of the opposition in the Venezuela boundary controversy in the House of Commons. Wemyss Reid, *Memoirs and correspondence of Lyon Playfair* (N.Y. and London, 1899) [**2736**], member of Parliament who played an active part at the time of Anglo-American antagonism over the Venezuelan affair. Smalley, *Anglo-Am. memories* (no. 2501).

MSS.: Suggestions

See Sec. 1, above (notably papers of presidents and secretaries of state). The Library of Congress has a particular small collection of 16 letters written, 1896-1897, by ex-President Harrison to Mr. Severo Mallet-Prevost, secretary to the Venezuela-Guiana Boundary Commission, relating to the settlement by arbitration of the dispute. For the papers of Andrew D. White (member of Cleveland's Venezuela-Guiana Commission) see our list of papers of American diplomatists, p. 868. Note also, in the same list, the papers of Henry White, who was sent by Secretary Olney to England as semi-official agent to handle the Venezuelan boundary question in 1896.

The papers of Sir William Harcourt, leader of the Opposition in the House of Commons at this time (1896-1898), are supposedly in the possession of Mr. Lewis Harcourt, 2d Viscount Harcourt, Baron Nuneham, Nuneham Park, Oxford, England.

Maps: Suggestions [10]

Phillips (no. 5135), for maps in the Library of Congress. American Geographical Society, *Catalogue of maps of Hispanic-America* (no. 5153), v. III. O. A. Harris, *Sketch map of the territory in dispute between Venezuela and British Guiana* (London, 1888) [2737]. Daly, *Monroe Doctrine* (no. 2696) gives a review of the maps in the collection of the American Geographical Society of New York to show the essential uncertainty of the boundary. C. R. Markham, " Boundaries of British Guiana—evidence of maps ", *Geog. jour.*, VII (1896) 277-280 [2738] analyzes the maps in the collection of the Royal Geographical Society to show that Venezuela could have inherited no claim from Spain to the disputed region. Baker, *Venezuelan boundary commission* (no. 2699) gives an analysis of the maps relating thereto. U.S. Commission, *Report* (no. 2714), v. III: " Geographical "; v. IV: " Atlas "; v. V-VI: " British Blue Book " contains several maps. P. L. Phillips, " The value of maps in boundary disputes, especially in connection with Venezuela and

---

[10] Edward Nield, an English book-dealer of Bristol, published in his *Catalogue*, no. 21 (undated), " Guiana and Venezuela; a valuable and interesting collection of rare maps and books, relating to the disputed district." A copy of the catalogue is in the Harvard College Library.

British Guiana ", *Am. hist. assoc. ann. rep.*, for 1896, v. I (1897) 457–462 [**2739**]; and " Guiana and Venezuela cartography ", *ibid.*, for 1897 (1898) 681–776 [**2740**]. *Atlas to accompany the case presented on the part of Her Britannic Majesty to arbitral tribunal between Great Britain and the United States of Venezuela* (London, 1898) [**2741**].

B. Venezuelan Debts Dispute

Bibliographical Aids

See Sec. 1, above, for general aids. Griffin, *Internat. arbitration* (no. 4188), 114–131: " List of writings on the Venezuela case." Meyer, *Monroe Doctrine* (no. 1140).

Special Works

George Bohler, " La question du Vénézuéla ", *Quest. dipl. et col.*, XV (1903) 226–239 [**2742**] explains Germany's decision to arbitrate as due to her diplomatic isolation from Great Britain in any crisis with the United States. A. S. Hershey, " The Venezuelan affair in the light of international law. 1. Claims of the allies against Venezuela. 2. The conduct of the allies ", *Am. law reg.*, LI (1903) 249–267 [**2743**]; and " Calvo and Drago doctrines ", *Am. jour. internat. law*, I (1907) 26–45 [**2744**], a juridical analysis. T. E. Holland, " War sub modo ", *Law quar. rev.*, XIX (1903) 133–135 [**2745**], a British legal commentator stresses undesirability of obliterating the dividing line between peace and war. Rudolf Dillon, " The Venezuela arbitration once more: facts and law ", *Am. law rev.*, XXXVIII (1904) 648–661 [**2746**], justification of preference to the claims of the blockading powers as against the nonblockading creditors. Auguste Gaché, *Le conflit vénézuélien et l'arbitrage de La Haye* (Paris, 1905) [**2747**], a doctoral thesis of the University of Paris, based on printed state papers, journals, and newspapers. E. L. Bidau, *Las doctrinas de Monroe y Drago* (Buenos Aires, 1906) [**2748**] stresses the Drago Doctrine as a support to the objects of the Monroe Doctrine. H. W. Bowen, " Monroe, Calvo, and Drago doctrines ", *Indep.*, LXII (1907) 902–904 [**2749**], as presented to the American public by the ex-minister of the United States to Venezuela, who represented Venezuela in the Hague arbitration. L. M. Drago, *Cobro coercitivo de deudas públicas* (Buenos Aires, 1906) [**2750**]; and " State loans in their relation to international law ", *Am. jour. internat. law*, I (1907) 692–

726 [**2751**], an exposition by the distinguished author of the Drago doctrine. E. F. Baldwin, " Three South Americans and their doctrines ", *Outlook*, LXXXVII (1907) 118–123 [**2752**], Triana, Barbosa, Drago; by the staff correspondent of the *Outlook* at The Hague. Crammond Kennedy, " Forcible collection of contract debts ", *Am. soc. internat. law proc.*, I, 1907 (1908) 100–122 [**2753**], and a supplementary paper, " The Drago doctrine ", *No. Am. rev.*, CLXXV (1907) 614–622, argues that Mr. Drago misconceived the character and purpose of the tripartite intervention, which was really to obtain redress for outrages inflicted on the persons and property of subjects of the blockading powers. A. N. Vivot, *La doctrina Drago* (Buenos Aires, 1911) [**2754**], a juridical analysis of the history and fate of the doctrine since its utterance in 1902, pointing out that the reservations to the Hague Convention of 1907 make the doctrine far from completely accepted, and that Drago proposed it as a policy rather than a principle of international law. Latané, *U.S. and Latin America* (no. 963). *Camb. hist. Brit. for. pol.* (no. 209), v. III. Lauzanne, *Great men* (no. 4499) incidentally gives another version of Theodore Roosevelt's " ultimatum " to the German Kaiser in the Venezuelan crisis of 1902. Hill, *Roosevelt and the Caribbean* (no. 3864), one of the best accounts, is inclined to discount Roosevelt's pressure on Germany as revealed by his Thayer letter of Aug. 21, 1916 (printed). Victoriano Jiménez y Núñez, *La doctrina Drago y la política internacional* (Madrid, 1927) [**2755**], the Ibero-American peoples should follow the doctrine as a protector of weak nations. Dennis, *Adventures* (no. 2224) presents evidence to suggest that Roosevelt's account in his Thayer letter of Aug. 21, 1916, of pressure on Germany to arbitrate, was substantially correct. Rippy, *Latin America* (no. 1076).

For biographies of President Roosevelt, Secretary of State Hay, American diplomatists abroad (for names and tenure, see latest *Register* of the Dept. of State (no. 5122), W. L. Penfield and Wayne MacVeagh, agent and counsel respectively for the United States at the Hague Arbitration, and H. W. Bowen, American minister to Venezuela and agent for Venezuela at The Hague, see the relevant entries and bibliographical data in the *D.A.B.* Note in particular: Thayer, *Roosevelt* (no. 2469); Bishop, *Roosevelt* (no. 2470); Pringle, *Roosevelt* (no. 2471), containing a critical description of Roosevelt's diplomacy, including the Venezuela affair. Dennett, *Hay* (no. 2472), the most recent and authoritative account of Hay's diplomacy, including Venezuela. Nevins, *White* (no. 2468), a participant in the controversy as *chargé-d'affaires* at London in the absence of the ambassador (Choate) when the crisis came in 1902.

Printed Sources

For general collections, see Sec. 1, above, particularly Moore's *Digest* (no. 5365), v. VI.

UNITED STATES OFFICIAL DOCUMENTS: *Venezuela arbitrations of 1903, including protocols, personnel and rules of commissions, opinions, and summary of awards, with appendix containing Venezuelan yellow book of 1903, Bowen pamphlet entitled "Venezuelan protocols", and "preferential questions," Hague decision, with history of recent Venezuelan revolutions,* prepared by Jackson H. Ralston, assisted by W. T. Sherman Doyle (Wash., 1904) (58th Cong., 2d Sess., Senate. Doc. no. 316 (serial 4620)) [2756], prepared by the late umpire of the Italian Venezuelan Mixed Commission and the late assistant agent of the United States, etc. Hague, Permanent Court of Arbitration, *The Venezuelan arbitration before the Hague tribunal, 1903. Proceedings of the tribunal under the protocols between Venezuela and Great Britain, Germany, Italy, United States, Belgium, France, Mexico, The Netherlands, Spain, Sweden, and Norway, signed at Washington, May 7, 1903* (Wash., 1905) (58th Cong., 3d sess. Senate. Doc. no. 119 (serial 4769)) [2757] includes the "Final report of Hon. W. L. Penfield, agent of the United States", "Case of the United States", and "Oral argument on behalf of the United States", by Wayne MacVeagh, and complete proceedings of the arbitration.

BRITISH OFFICIAL DOCUMENTS: *Brit. and for. state pap.* (no. 5416), v. XCV-XCVI. *Correspondence respecting the affairs of Venezuela, 1902-1903* (Parliament. House of Commons. Sess. Pap., 1902, CXIII, 681 (cd. 1372); 1903, LXXXVII, 701 (cd. 1399)) [2758]. *Award of the tribunal of arbitration constituted in virtue of the protocols signed at Washington, May 7, 1903, between Germany, Great Britain, and Italy, on the one hand, and Venezuela on the other hand* (Parliament. House of Commons. Sess. Pap., 1904, CXI, 115 (cd. 1949)) [2759]. *Brit. docs. on origins of war* (no. 5475), v. II.

FRENCH OFFICIAL DOCUMENTS: *Archives diplomatiques* (no. 5430), 3. sér., LXXXVIII-LXXXIX.

GERMAN OFFICIAL DOCUMENTS: "Abkommen über die schiedsrichterliche Entschiedung gewisser Fragen wegen Bezahlung der deutschen Reklamationen. Speck von Sternberg. Herbert W. Bowen ", *Staatsarchiv* (no. 5434), v. LXIX (1904) 257-259 [**2760**]. *Grosse Politik* (no. 5476), v. XVII, 239-292.

VENEZUELAN OFFICIAL DOCUMENTS: Venezuela, Ministerio de Relaciones Exteriores, *Asuntos internacionales. Correspondencia del Ministerio de Relaciones Exteriores de los Estados Unidos de Venezuela con algunas de las legaciones acreditadas en la república, 1900-1903* (Caracas, 1905) [**2761**].

There is a vast amount of contemporary periodical literature relating to the Venezuelan debts controversy, see Griffin, *Internat. arbitration* (no. 4188); Meyer, *Monroe Doctrine* (no. 1140); Hill, *Roosevelt and Caribbean* (no. 3864); and consult also the *Readers' guide to period. lit.* (no. 4996).

Argentine Republic, Ministerio de Relaciones Exteriores, *La doctrine de Monroe; note diplomatique du Gouvernement Argentin à son réprésentant à Washington, en date du 29 décembre 1902. Lettre-circulaire de M. Carlos Calvo à quelques-uns de ses collègues de l'Institut de France et de l'Institut de Droit International* (Paris, 1903) [**2762**], " Note diplomatique " (signed: Luis M. Drago) embodies the principle known as the Drago doctrine. L. M. Drago, "La doctrine de Monroë—une note diplomatique du Gouvernement Argentin—consultations et axis ", *Rev. droit internat.*, XXXV (1903) 597-623 [**2763**], documents relating to the origin of the Drago doctrine; and *La república Argentina y el caso de Venezuela; documentos, juicios, y comentarios relacionados con la nota pasada al ministro argentino en Washington* (Buenos Aires, 1903) [**2764**], views of the distinguished author of the Drago doctrine. W. L. Penfield, " The Hague tribunal ", *Indep.*, LV (1903) 3001-3003 [**2765**]; and " The Venezuelan case at The Hague ", *ibid.*, 2560-2562 [**2766**], by the agent of the United States at the Hague Tribunal. Wayne MacVeagh, " The value of the Venezuelan arbitration ", *No. Am. rev.*, CLXXVII (1903) 801-811 [**2767**], by the American counsel at the debt question arbitration. Ramón Tello Mendoza, *Venezuela ante el conflicto con las potencias aliadas, Alemania, Inglaterra é Italia en 1902 y 1903* (Caracas, 1905, 2 v.) [**2768**], treaties, official documents, and editorials from the native and foreign press. Three articles by H. W. Bowen, American minister to Venezuela, 1901-

1905, and agent for Venezuela at The Hague: "Venezuela and The Hague", *Indep.*, LXI (1906) 1472–1475 [**2769**]; *Queer diplomacy with Castro* (no. 4013); and *Roosevelt's report on Venezuela* (no. 4014). G. W. Scott, "International law and the Drago doctrine", *No. Am. rev.*, CLXXXIII (1906) 602–610 [**2770–2**] advocates incorporation of the Drago doctrine into international law at the next Hague conference (which was done in a modified form). H. A. Moulin, *La doctrine de Drago* (Paris, 1908) [**2773**], a collection of articles and documents relating to the doctrine. Santiago Pérez Triana, *La doctrina Drago; colección de documentos* (London, 1908) [**2774**] contains documents (mostly state papers) on the antecedents of the Drago ´doctrine (1902–06), the relevant discussions at the Hague Conference in 1907, and selected press opinion.

For the printed writings of President Roosevelt, Secretary of State Hay, American diplomatists abroad (for names and tenure, see latest *Register* of the Dept. of State (no. 5122)), W. L. Penfield, and Wayne MacVeagh, agent and counsel respectively for the United States at the Hague Arbitration, and H. W. Bowen, American minister to Venezuela, 1901–05, and agent for Venezuela at the Hague Arbitration, see our list on p. 756. Bishop, *Roosevelt* (no. 2470) reproduces many documents from Roosevelt's own papers.

MSS.: Suggestions

See Sec. 1, above.

For the personal papers of President Roosevelt, Secretary of State Hay, and of Henry White (who was a participant in the negotiations in his capacity of *chargé d'affaires* at London in the absence of the ambassador (Choate) when the crisis came in 1902), see our lists on pp. 862–883.

6. Spanish-American War; Boer War

A. Spanish-American War [11]

Bibliographical Aids

For general aids, see Sec. 1, above. Reuter, *Anglo-Am. rel.* (no. 2775), 191–204.

---

[11] See also Ch. XVIII ("Cuba and Spain, 1861–1898").

Special Works

See Sec. 1, above. Benton, *Dipl. Sp.-Am. war* (no. 3443). Bertha A. Reuter, *Anglo-American relations during the Spanish-American war* (N.Y., 1924) [**2775**], this is a path-breaking study, unfortunately completed before the publication of the German (no. 5476) and English (no. 5475) documents on the origins of the world war; now in part superseded by Shippee (no. 3450). Latané, *Am. as world power* (no. 3344). Coolidge, *U.S. as world power* (no. 3345). Rippy, *Europe and Sp.-Am. war* (no. 3453). Zims, *Span.-Am. Krieg* (no. 3454). Guerra y Sánchez, *Camino de la independencia* (no. 3366). Nevins, *Henry White* (no. 2468). Dennett, *John Hay* (no. 2472).

Printed Sources

For general collections, see Sec. 1, above. *Brit. docs. origin of the war* (no. 5475), v. I, 105–121: "The Manila incident." *Grosse Politik* (no. 5476), v. XV, 31–105: "Die Philippen- und die Karolienfrage. Die Englisch-Amerikanische Annäherung 1898–1899."
A. T. Mahan, "Possibilities of Anglo-American reunion", *No. Am. rev.*, CLIX (1894) 551–573 [**2776**], a great historian and apologist for British naval policy believes that the ground is not yet prepared in the hearts of the American citizens and British subjects for a naval alliance. D. A. Wells, "Great Britain and the United States: their true relations", *ibid.*, CLXII (1896) 385–405 [**2777**], distinguished American economist deplores twisting the lion's tail. M. W. Hazeltine, "The United States and Great Britain: a reply to Mr. David A. Wells", *ibid.*, 594–606 [**2778**] asserts Wells' pacific views held by only a very small minority of his fellow citizens. Lyman Abbott, "The basis of an Anglo-American understanding", *No. Am. rev.*, CLXVI (1898) 513–521 [**2779**], writer believes an alliance would be of commercial and political advantage. Brooks Adams, "The Spanish war and the equilibrium of the world", *Forum*, XXV (1898) 641–651 [**2780**], "friends and enemies now agree that an Anglo-Saxon alliance, directed to attain common ends, might substantially make its own terms; but how it would stand, if opposed by a power capable of massing troops at pleasure in the heart of China, is less clear." James Bryce, "The essential

unity of Great Britain and America ", *Atlantic*, LXXXII (1898) 22–29 [**2781**], whether or not the two nations have a formal alliance they now have a league of the heart. Andrew Carnegie, " Distant possessions—the parting of the ways", *No. Am. rev.*, CLXVII (1898) 239–248 [**2781a**], this article provoked a number of contemporary writings on Anglo-American relations. Joseph Chamberlain, " Recent developments of a policy in the United States and their relation to an Anglo-American alliance ", *Scribner's*, XXIV (1898) 674–682 [**2782**] emphasizes community of aims of the new American imperialism with British policy; the author as Colonial Secretary had publicly hinted at an Anglo-American alliance. Also by Chamberlain, " Speech delivered at Birmingham, May 13, 1898 ", in the *London Times*, May 14, 1898 [**2783**], which declared in favor of an alliance with the United States. Sir G. S. Clarke, " England and America ", *Nineteenth century*, XLIV (1898) 186–195 [**2784**], writer thinks united action and permanent *rapprochement* may be possible without formal alliance. Walter Copeland, "An Anglo-American alliance ", *Westminster rev.*, CL (1898) 168–170 [**2785**], the writer wants to promote agitation for one. A. V. Dicey, " England and America ", *Atlantic*, LXXXII (1898) 441–445 [**2786**], alliance only a dream and hope of the distant future. Charles Dilke, "An Anglo-American alliance ", *Pall Mall mag.*, XVI (1898) 37–38 [**2787**], distinguished British authority believes alliance not probable; also by the same writer, " The future relations of Great Britain and the United States ", *Forum*, XXVI (1898) 521–528 [**2788**], says closer ties are up to the United States. H. N. Fisher, " The development of our foreign policy ", *Atlantic*, LXII (1898) 552–559 [**2789**], on the theme that the Anglo-Saxon is fitted to be trustee and guardian of inferior races. B. O. Flower, " The proposed federation of the Anglo-Saxon nations ", *Arena*, XX (1898) 223–239 [**2790**], thinks an alliance desirable to further common ideals of popular sovereignty. C. A. Gardiner, *The proposed Anglo-American alliance* (N.Y., 1898) [**2791**] does not say who proposes it, but advocates some sort of unwritten alliance. Washington Gladden, *England and America* (Columbus, O., 1898) [**2792**], pro-American addresses delivered in England during the summer of 1898 by a distinguished American Protestant clergyman. " Is there an Anglo-American understanding ", *Fortnightly rev.*, LXX (1898)

163–174 [2793], argues maybe there is. W. E. H. Lecky, " The relation between the United States and other powers ", *Indep.*, L (1898) 15–17 [2794], an eminent English historian's view that there will be growing mutual sympathy rather than a specific alliance. Sidney Low, " The change in English sentiment toward the United States ", *Forum*, XXVI (1898) 364–373 [2795], another discussion of incipient alliance. George McDermot, " The Anglo-American alliance and the Irish-Americans ", *Cath. world*, LXVIII (1898) 75–88 [2796], anti-British. Richard Olney, " International isolation of the United States ", *Atlantic*, LXXXI (1895) 577–588 [2796a], significant and far-reaching. Carl Schurz, " The Anglo-American friendship ", *Atlantic*, LXXXII (1898) 433–440 [2797], the most famous American statesman of German origin hesitates before an actual British alliance; also by the same writer, " Thoughts on American imperialism ", *Century*, LVI (1898) 781–788 [2798] warns against imperialism and its catchwords. Richard Temple, "Anglo-American versus European combination ", *No. Am. rev.*, CLXVII (1898) 306–317 [2799], an English publicist believes in superiority, physically and morally, of such a combination. Charles Waldstein, " The English-speaking brotherhood ", *No. Am. rev.*, CLXVII (1898) 223–238 [2800] stresses community of culture and ideals. *An American response to expressions of English sympathy*, printed for the Anglo-American Committee (N.Y., 1899) [2801]. Julian Ralph, "Anglo-Saxon affinities ", *Harper's*, XCVIII (1899) 385–391 [2802] thinks a " good understanding " more practical than an alliance. A. W. Tourgé, " The twentieth century peacemakers ", *Contemp. rev.*, LXXV (1899) 886–908 [2803], for an Anglo-Saxon peace of the world through alliance. A. M. Low, "An unwritten chapter in American diplomacy", *McClure's*, XV (1900) 255–261 [2804], by the distinguished American correspondent of the *London Chronicle;* a glowing discussion of Anglo-American diplomatic sympathies, 1896–1900. E. A. Ross, " England as an ally ", *Arena*, XXIII (1900) 583–592 [2805], the writer thinks Great Britain too vulnerable to be a good ally. J. R. Dos Passos, *The Anglo-Saxon century and the unification of the English-speaking people* (N.Y., 1902) [2806] advocates the union of all English-speaking peoples. Dewey, *Autobiography* (no. 3480), for the Manila Bay affair. See also Diederich's account (no. 3474).

MSS.: Suggestions

See Sec. 1, above.

B. Boer War

Bibliographical Aids

For general aids, see Sec. 1, above. A. P. C. Griffin, "List of books in the Library of Congress on the Boer war", in U.S. General Staff, 2d Division, *Selected translations pertaining to the Boer war* (Wash.: Govt. Print. Off., 1905) 207–231 [**2807**]. H. E. Haferkorn, *The South African war, 1899–1902; a bibliography* (Fort Humphreys, Va., 1924) [**2808**] emphasises military history.

Special Works

R. G. Campbell, *Neutral rights and obligations in the Anglo-Boer war* (Baltimore, 1908) [**2809**], analysis of the position of neutral powers, including the United States, as revealed by printed documents.[11a]

Printed Sources

Moore's *Digest* (no. 5365), v. I, 212–214, and v. VII, 19–21, for the South African Republics delegation to the United States, and the question of mediation. R. B. Roosevelt, *New York committee to aid the United Republics of South Africa, . . . to express American sympathy with the United Republics of South Africa fighting for independence and self-government* (N.Y., 1899) [**2810**]. H. H. Bowen, "American public opinion of the war", *Ninteenth century*, XLVII (1900) 744–752 [**2811**] analyzes opinion expressed by "broad minded and thinking classes" and editorial comment of newspapers. A pro-British analysis. E. J. Hodgson, "An American view of the Boer war", *Nineteenth century*, XLVIII (1900) 272–284 [**2812**] bespeaks sympathy of the American people for Great Britain's cause, remembering England's benevolent attitude during the Spanish American war. H. T. Peck, "American opinion on the South African war", *Bookman*, X (1900) 527–532 [**2813**], able journalist analyzes what seems an uncertain and nebulous state of American opinion. Mahan's *Asia* (no. 3714a), ch. 5.

[11a] There is soon to be published by the University of Pennsylvania a doctoral thesis, by John H. Ferguson, on *American diplomacy and the Boer war* [2813a]. This will be the first study of the subject. It is based on official sources, printed and unprinted.

MSS.: Suggestions

See Sec. 1, above.

7. Fisheries; Fur Seals

A. Fisheries [12]

Bibliographical Aids

For general aids, see Sec. 1, above. Elliott, *Northeast fisheries* (no. 2815), 135–144. McFarland, *New Eng. fisheries* (no. 2830) 338–363.

Special Works

H. Y. Hind, *The effect of the fishery clauses of the treaty of Washington on the fisheries and fishermen of British North America* (Halifax, N.S., 1877, 2 v.) [2814], a technical study of the operation of the fisheries, the habits of the fish, and the effect of the admission of American fishermen to the British North American coastal waters. Schuyler, *Diplomacy and commerce* (no. 2786). C. B. Elliott, *The United States and the northeastern fisheries; a history of the question* (Minneapolis, 1887) [2815], with Isham (no. 2817) one of the first methodical, scholarly studies: a Ph.D. thesis of the University of Minnesota, restricted to printed sources, mostly American. J. H. De Ricci, *The fisheries dispute, and annexation of Canada* (London, 1888) [2816], a perfervid polemic by a British writer, with an appendix of documents selected by himself to form the "United States' case", and the "Canadian case." Charles Isham, *The fishery question; its origin, history, and present situation* (N.Y. and London, 1887) [2817], an early Harvard thesis, like Elliott (no. 2815) restricted to printed sources; has a good map. J. I. Doran, *Our fishery rights in the north Atlantic* (Phila., 1888) [2818], a critical examination of the provisions and implications of the rejected Chamberlain-Bayard treaty; vindicates its rejection by the Senate. Heinrich Geffcken, "Question des pêcheries de Terre-Neuve et sur les côtes des Etats-Unis d'Amérique et du Canada", *Rev. droit internat. et legis. comp.*, XXII (1890) 217–233 [2819], short analysis by a famous jurist. Lewis Appleton, *The foreign policy of Europe* (London, 1891) [2820] contains (p. 172–228) an extended summary of the fisheries controversy between Great Britain and France, with copious

---

[12] See also Ch. II ("Peace Negotiations of 1782-1783 ").

extracts from documents unauthenticated by citations of sources. Snow, *Treaties and topics* (no. 4786a) gives one of the best treatises up to that date.   J. B. Henderson, Jr., *American diplomatic questions* (N.Y., 1901) [2821], an older general account, undocumented, of five specific questions (fur seals, Isthmian canal, Monroe Doctrine, Samoa, fisheries). Léon Guichard, *La question de Terre Neuve* (Paris, 1902) [2821a], a thin doctoral dissertation on the Anglo-French question of the fisheries. Willison, *Laurier* (no. 2492). Moore's *Digest* (no. 5365), v. I, 767–874, for a valuable treatise on the fisheries question.   Charles Godefroy, " Etats-Unis d'Amérique et Grande Bretagne; difficultés à propos des pêcheries sur les côtes de Terre Neuve ", *Rev. gén. droit internat. pub.*, XIV (1907) 287–302 [2822], a detailed analysis and discussion of the *modus vivendi* of October 8, 1906.   T. W. Balch, "The American-British Atlantic fisheries question ", *Am. phil. soc. proc.*, XLVII (1909) 319–353 [2823], a useful and scholarly summary based on the printed documents available at the time of the submission of the case to arbitration; and by the same writer, " La décision de la Cour Permanente d'Arbitrage au sujet des pêcheries de l'Atlantique dans le differend entre les Etats-Unis et l'Empire britannique ", *Rev. droit internat.*, 2d ser., XIII (1911) 5–23 [2824], comments by a distinguished and scholarly American lawyer.   E. M. Borchard, *North Atlantic coast fisheries arbitration. Coastal waters; English translations of extracts from the works of French, German, Austrian, Argentinian, Spanish, Swiss, Russian, Italian, and Belgian publicists* (Wash.: Govt. Print. Off., 1910) [2825], on all questions concerning coastal waters; comp. for the use of the Permanent Court of Arbitration at The Hague.   Also his " The North Atlantic coast fisheries arbitration ", *Columbia law rev.*, XI (1911) 1–23 [2826], analysis of the decision by a professor of international law, who believes that both countries will find the award acceptable.   L. M. Drago, *El arbitraje de las pesquerías del Atlántico norte entre la Gran Bretaña y los Estados Unidos de América* (Buenos Aires, 1911) [2827], summary of the juridical principles and their application by the eminent Argentine jurist and statesman.   Robert Lansing, " The North Atlantic coast fisheries arbitration ", *Am. jour. internat. law*, V (1911) 1–31 [2828], summary of the arbitration by a participant in preparation of the American case, later secretary of state.   J. de Louter, " L'arbitrage dans le conflit anglo-américain concernant la pêcheries de l'Atlantique ", *Rev. droit internat.*, 2d ser., XIII (1911) 131-157 [2829], another juridical analysis, by a Dutch professor of international law.   Raymond McFarland, *A history of the New England fisheries* (Phila., 1911) [2830], a valuable history of the fisheries of New England to the time of publication, with description of ways and practice, political and economic factors, and a résumé of international questions involved.   Jules Basdevant, *L'affaire des pêcheries des côtes septentrionales de l'Atlantique entre les Etats-Unis d'Amérique et la Grande-Bretagne devant la cour de la Haye* (Paris, 1912), reprinted from the *Révue générale de droit international public*, XIX (1912) 421-582 [2831], summary, by a French professor of international law, from the voluminous official proceedings. J. B. Scott, ed., *Argument of Elihu Root* (no. 2888), " Introduction " (p. ix-cli) gives a comprehensive survey of the question.   N. B. Wormwith, " The fisheries arbitrations ", in *Canada and its provinces* (no. 2460a), v. VIII, 681-748 [2832], summary account.   Johnson, *Dom. and for. comm.* (no. 227), ch. 36.   A. P. Daggett, " Fishery rights in territorial waters secured by international agreements ", in Harvard University, *Summaries of theses . . . 1931* (Cambridge, 1932) 120-123 [2833].

For biographies of American diplomatists and statesmen (H. E. Kellogg, commissioner, and Dwight Foster, agent, for the Halifax Commission, 1877-78; T. F. Bayard, W. L. Putnam, and J. B. Angell, members of the Joint High Commission, 1887-88, and negotiators of the convention of 1888; J. G. Blaine, convention of 1890; John Hay,[13] convention of 1902; and participants at The Hague Arbitration (Judge George Gray, member of the Tribunal; C. P. Anderson, agent; and S. J. Elder, Robert Lansing, Elihu Root, J. B. Scott, George Turner, and C. B. Warren, counsel)), see the relevant entries and bibliographical data in the *D.A.B.*

Printed Sources

For general collections, see Sec. 1, above.   Particularly Moore's *Arbitrations* (no. 5364), v. I, ch. 16, for the Halifax Commission. *Comp. repts. Sen. com. for. rel.* (no. 5388), v. V.

For a list of United States public documents dealing with the fisheries question, 1781-1887, see Elliott, *Northeast. fisheries* (no. 2815), 138-144.   Particular collections are: Dept. of State, *Memo-*

---

[13] Note also Dennett, *John Hay* (no. 2472), published since the Hay entry in the *D.A.B.*

randum respecting the North American fisheries, prepared for the information of the American commissioners who negotiated the treaty of May 8, 1871 (Wash.: Govt. Print. Off., 1871?) [2834]. Halifax Commission, *Award of the fishery commission. Documents and proceedings of the Halifax Commission, 1877, under the treaty of Washington of May 8, 1871* (Wash., 1878, 3 v.) (45th Cong., 2d Sess. House. Ex. Doc. 89) [2835]. *Relations with Canada. Testimony taken by the select committee on relations with Canada, United States Senate . . . 1890* (Wash., 1890) (51st Cong., 1st Sess. Senate. Rept. 1530) [2836] deals comprehensively with the fisheries question, fur seals, annexation, reciprocity, etc. *North Atlantic coast fisheries. Proceedings in the North Atlantic coast fisheries arbitration before the Permanent Court of Arbitration at the Hague. Under the provisions of the general treaty of arbitration of April 4, 1908, and the special agreement of January 27, 1909, between the United States of America and Great Britain* (Wash., 1912–13, 12 v.)   (61st Cong., 3d sess.   Senate.   Doc. 870) [2837].[14]   U.S. Congress, House, Committee on Foreign Affairs, *United States-Canada fisheries. Hearings . . . 1914* (Wash., 1914) [2839], hearings on a bill to give effect to the provisions of a treaty between the United States and Great Britain concerning fisheries in waters contiguous to the United States and Canada, signed at Washington, Apr. 1, 1908, ratified by the Senate, Apr. 13, 1908.

BRITISH PARLIAMENTARY (HOUSE OF COMMONS SESSIONAL) PAPERS: *Correspondence respecting the termination of fishery articles of the treaty of Washington of 8th May, 1871* (1884, LXXXVII, 15) [2840]. *Correspondence relative to North American fisheries, 1884–86* (1887, XCI, 637, 829; 1888, CIX, 583) [2841]. *Correspondence relating to proposed convention to regulate questions of commerce and fishery with Newfoundland* (1890–91, XCVI, 21, 73) [2842]. *Correspondence respecting the Newfoundland fisheries* (1906, CXXXVII, 389) [2843]. *Notes exchanged with the American ambassador on the subject of the Newfoundland fisheries, 1907* (1908, CXXV, 939, 943) [2844]. *Despatch from the British agent enclosing copy of the protocol containing the award of the Permanent Court*

---

[14] Text of the Hague award is printed in this official collection of *Proceedings,* also in *Am. jour. internat. law,* IV (1910) 948–1000 [2838] ; and in G. G. Wilson, *Hague arbitration cases* (no. 4018), containing documents relating to the submission of the controversy to arbitration and the award of the Tribunal.

of *International Arbitration at The Hague in the North Atlantic coast fisheries arbitration* (1910, LXXIV, 385) [2845]. North Atlantic Coast Fisheries Arbitration at The Hague, *Oral argument before the tribunal* . . . (London, 1910, 2 v.) [2846], arguments of British and American delegates; also *Counter-case presented on the part of the Government of His Britannic Majesty* . . . (London: Foreign Office, 1910, 2 v.) [2847].

CANADIAN OFFICIAL DOCUMENTS: Canada, Parliament, Legislative Assembly, *Return to an address from the Legislative Assembly for copies of reports or correspondence of Pierre Fortin, esquire, commanding the forces charged with the protection of the fisheries in the Gulf of St. Lawrence during the season of 1856* (Toronto, 1857) [2848], the annual report of the magistrate commanding the expedition for the protection of the fisheries in the Gulf of St. Lawrence, reports finding 8 United States fishing boats engaged in the cod fishery. Canada, Parliament, Legislative Assembly, Select Committee . . . , *Report of the Select committee on the working of the fishery act* (Quebec, 1864) [2849]. Two documents of the Dept. of the Secretary of State: *Return and supplementary return to an address of the Honorable the Legislative Assembly, dated 4th July, 1866; " for copies of papers having reference to the sea fisheries of the river and 'Gulf of St. Lawrence' "* (Ottawa, 1866) [2850]; and *Return of all licenses granted to American fishermen, to fish in the waters of the Dominion* . . . *for the years 1867 and 1868* (Ottawa, 1869) [2851]. Canadian Parliamentary (Sessional Papers): *Correspondence between the Government of the Dominion and the Imperial Government, on the subject of the fisheries, with other documents relating to the same* (1871, no. 12) [2852]. *Despatches and minutes of the Privy Council, having reference to the treaty of Washington,* also *Certain despatches and correspondence between the Governments of Nova Scotia, Newfoundland, and Prince Edward Island and the Imperial Government, in reference to the fishery clauses of the treaty of Washington* (1872, no. 18) [2853]. *Copies of all correspondence, etc., having reference to the notice given to the United States Government terminating the fisheries clauses of the Washington treaty, or relating to any steps taken by the Government, on the subject of the use by American fishermen of the sea fisheries of the Dominion in view of the approaching termination of the fishery clauses* (1884, no. 67a) **[2854]**. *Copies of despatches, correspondence, and papers having reference to the negotiations at Washington with respect to the termination of the fishery clauses of the treaty of Washington during the year 1884 and to the present date in 1885* (1885, no. 101) **[2855]**. *Copies of all minutes of Council, reports to Council, and of correspondence between the Canadian Government and the British Government, or any of its officers or members, not already laid before Parliament, relating to the so-called fishery question, from the 1st of July, 1867, up to the time of the signing of the Washington treaty* (1885, no. 101a) **[2856]**. *Correspondence relative to the fisheries question, 1885–87* (1887, no. 16b) **[2857]**. *Copy of the statement presented by the British plenipotentiaries to the fishery commission at Washington, in relation to reciprocal trade relations between Canada and the United States, and the answer of the American plenipotentiaries thereto* (1888, no. 36a) **[2858]**. *Two communications in relation to the fisheries question— one, written " personally and unofficially ", by the Hon. T. F. Bayard, secretary of state, Washington, United States, and dated the 31st May, 1887, and addressed to Sir Charles Tupper; and the other, the reply of Sir Charles Tupper to Mr. Bayard, also marked " personal and unofficial ", and dated the 6th June, 1887* (1888, no. 26b) **[2859]**. *Despatches and documents having reference to the fisheries question* (1888, no. 36c) **[2860]**. *Copies of papers relating to the mutual recognition by Canada and Newfoundland of licenses issued to United States fishing vessels, under the modus vivendi* (1892, no. 23c) **[2861]**. *Further papers respecting the fisheries on the Atlantic coast, including the separate arrangement proposed to be entered into by Newfoundland with the United States* (1892, no. 23e) **[2862]**. *Papers in regard to differences between Canada and the United States referred to the Hague tribunal* (1911, no. 97a) **[2863]**.

There is a considerable amount of contemporary periodical literature by competent observers and students, and even participants, in such publications as the *American law review, Atlantic monthly, Contemporary review, Empire review, Fortnightly review, North American review*, etc. See *Poole's index* (no. 4995), and *Readers' guide* (no. 4996).

G. R. Young, *Letters to the Right Hon. E. G. S. Stanley, M.P., upon the existing treaties with France and America, as regards their " rights of fishery " upon the coasts of Nova Scotia, Labrador, and*

Newfoundland (London, 1834) **[2864]**. *Corres. Castlereagh* (no. 864), v. XI (1815–1818), for letters of Sir Charles Bagot to Castlereagh on the fisheries. E. H. Derby, *Letter to the Hon. William H. Seward, secretary of state, in answer to one from him on the resolution of the Senate as to the relations of the United States with the British provinces, and the actual condition of the question of the fisheries* (Wash.: Govt. Print. Off., 1867) **[2865]**, by a special agent of the United States Treasury Department. W. H. Kerr, *The fishery question; or, American rights in Canadian waters* (Montreal, 1868) **[2866]**. *Review of President Grant's recent message to the United States' Congress, relative to the Canadian fisheries and the navigation of the St. Lawrence river* (Ottawa, 1870) **[2867]**, anonymous Canadian interpretation of the treaty of 1818; selected state papers in the appendix. Anglo-American Association, *Report on the questions between Great Britain and the United States with respect to the North American fisheries* (London and Cambridge, 1871) **[2868]**. *The fishery question—letters from the N.Y. Herald's special commissioners* (N.Y., 1871) **[2869]**, commissioners to Ottawa, Canada, and Gloucester, Mass. Royal Colonial Institute, *Report of the council of the Colonial Institute on the Newfoundland fishery question, November, 1875* (London, 1875) **[2870]**. H. Y. Hind, *Fraudulent official records of Government; correspondence with the late Lord Frederick Cavendish, M.P., published with the consent of the Right Hon. the Marquis of Hartington* (n.p., 1884) **[2871]** contends that the Halifax award of $5,500,000, gained by Great Britain was won disgracefully by the use of secretly concerted forged Canadian and forged United States statistics of trade between the two countries. *Memorial of the American fishery union* (n.p., 1885) **[2872]**, addressed to President Cleveland, and dated at Gloucester, May 12, 1885; on the controversy with Great Britain over fishery rights. *In the Vice-Admiralty court of Nova Scotia; Her Majesty the Queen, plaintiff, against the ship or vessel " David J. Adams ", and her cargo. Action for forfeiture of said vessel and cargo* (Wash.? 1887?) **[2873]** includes also papers in the case of the ship or vessel " Ella M. Doughty "; see also for record of the case of the " David J. Adams " in the Vice-Admiralty court of Nova Scotia, *American and British claims arbitration. The David J. Adams. Memorial of the United States in support of the claim* (n.p., 1913?) **[2874]**, Robert Lansing, agent of the United States. And for a similar case (in

1896) : *American and British claims arbitration. The Frederick Gerring, Jr. Memorial of the United States in support of the claim* (n.p., 1914?) [**2875**]. U.S. Dept. of State, [*Selected cases of maltreatment of American fishing vessels*] (Wash., 1887) [**2876**], relating to the " Ella M. Doughty " and the " David J. Adams." Canada, Dept. of Marine and Fisheries, *Reply to statement of selected cases of maltreatment of American fishing vessels* (Wash., 1887?) [**2877**], relating to the above-mentioned two ships. John Jay, *The fisheries dispute; a suggestion for its adjustment by abrogating the convention of 1818, and resting on the rights and liberties defined in the treaty of 1783* (N.Y., 1887) [**2878-9**], a letter to the Honourable William M. Evarts, of the United States Senate, by John Jay, late minister to Vienna, and grandson of the John Jay who signed the treaty of 1783 with the first fisheries clause. C. S. Davison, *Letters on the " proposed " fisheries treaty of 1888* (N.Y., 1888) [**2880**]. G. M. Oxley, " The Canadian view of the fisheries question ", *Our day*, I (1888) 132-136 [**2881**]. W. H. Trescot, *Letters reviewing the Bayard Chamberlain fishery treaty* (Wash., 1888) [**2882**]. *Speeches of the Rt. Hon. Sir Robert Bond, P.C., K.C.M.G., on the foreign fishing vessels bill, delivered on . . . April 7 and 12, 1905* (St. Johns? Newfoundland, 1905?) [**2883**], argument made in the House of Assembly of the colony of Newfoundland; also *Speech of the Rt. Hon. Sir Robert Bond . . . in relation to the modus vivendi between the United States and Great Britain respecting Newfoundland fisheries* (St. Johns? Newfoundland, 1907) [**2884**], delivered before the House of Assembly, Feb. 12, 1907. R. H. Dana, Jr., " Argument before the Halifax fishery commission ", in his *Speeches in stirring times and letters to a son*, ed. by R. H. Dana (3d) (Boston and N.Y., 1910) 345-426 [**2885**], also printed in the official proceedings of the commission (no. 2835). Gloucester, Mass., Board of Trade, *Canadian reciprocity; brief in opposition to the proposed tariff arrangement with Canada filed on behalf of the New England fisheries, filed by Gloucester Board of Trade and Master Mariners' Association, Gloucester, Mass.* (Boston, 1911) [**2886-7**], submitted to the Committee on Ways and Means, House of Representatives. *Letters of James Lloyd, 1815-1824* (no. 1698), some deal with the fisheries. Elihu Root, *Argument of the Honorable Elihu Root on behalf of the United States, before the North Atlantic coast fisheries arbitration tribunal at The Hague, 1910*, ed. with introduction and appendix, by J. B. Scott (Boston:

World Peace Foundation, 1912) [**2888**], appendix of documents (treaties, correspondence, statutes, circulars); and *North Atlantic coast fisheries arbitration at The Hague; argument on behalf of the United States*, by Elihu Root, ed. by Robert Bacon and J. B. Scott (Cambridge, Mass., 1917) [**2889**], a classic argument; also printed in the official proceedings (no. 2837). Sir Willoughby Maycock, *With Mr. Chamberlain in the United States and Canada, 1887–88* (London, 1914) [**2890**].

For printed writings of American diplomatists (for names, see p. 447), see our list on p. 756.

For printed writings of British diplomatists and statesmen, see Sec. 1, above.

For printed writings of Canadian diplomatists and statesmen, see Sec. 1, above: *Memoirs* and *Corres.* of Sir John A. Macdonald (nos. 2494 and 2509); *Works of Sir John Thompson* (no. 2499); *Letters of Sir Charles Tupper* (no. 2511).

MSS.: Suggestions

See Sec. 1, above.

The Dominion Archives, Ottawa (see *Report*, for 1908 (1909), 5) contain several thousands of folios of transcripts concerning the Newfoundland and Labrador fisheries taken from the colonial correspondence and Oswald, Shelburne, and Lansdowne collections for the years 1712–1715, 1772, 1783, 1819–1832, 1841–1850, described as most valuable for preparation of cases for arbitration.

Maps: Suggestions

Phillips (no. 5135), for list of maps in the Library of Congress. *Comp. repts. Sen. com. for. rel.* (no. 5388), v. VIII, for 4 maps from U.S. Coast and Geodetic Survey and British Admiralty, prior to 1888. The official *Proceedings* of the North Atlantic Coast Fisheries Arbitration (no. 2837), v. I, for two maps prepared at the office of the U.S. Coast and Geodetic Survey from British and Canadian maps, August 1909; these two maps are also printed in the *Argument on behalf of the United States by Elihu Root* (no. 2888).

B. Fur Seals

Bibliographical Aids

For general aids, see Sec. 1, above. Smith, *Pacific N.W. Americana* (no. 1708). Judson, *Pacific N.W.* (no. 1707). Wickersham, *Bibliog. Alaska* (no. 2227). Kerner, *Russian expansion* (no. 1710).

Special Works

Bancroft, *Alaska* (no. 2229). Russell Duane, *The case of the "Sayward"* (Phila., 1891) [**2891**], review of the case of the British sealer "Sayward" which precipitated the controversy concerning the right of the United States to protect seals in Bering Sea. F. H. H. Guillemard, "The seal-fisheries question; prospective and retrospective", *Blackwood's mag.*, CL (1891) 603–612 [**2892**] takes stock of the leading features of the controversy. S. B. Stanton, *The Behring Sea controversy* (N.Y., 1892) [**2893**], based on his pamphlet, *The Behring Sea in dispute* (privately printed), 1890, and brought down to Feb. 11, 1892; sheds the clear, cold light of international law upon the claims of the United States. [Henri de Blowitz], *The Behring Sea arbitration*, letters to *The Times* by its special correspondent (London, 1893) [**2894**], a sort of hand-book summary. Marcel Paisant, "La question de Behring", *Rev. hist. dipl.*, VII (1893) 375–413 [**2895**] analyzes the history of the controversy; concludes that if the United States is going to assume protection of the fisheries, the Canadians are entitled to some indemnity for seizures made and also for dislocation of capital caused. Joseph Stanley-Brown, "The Bering Sea controversy from an economic standpoint", *Yale rev.*, II (1893) 194–210 [**2896**], the secretary and son-in-law of President Garfield emphasizes the possibility of a continuous seal industry. Also by the same writer, "Fur seals and the Bering Sea arbitration", *Am. geog. soc. jour.*, XXVI (1894) 326–372 [**2897**]. J. C. Welling, *The Bering Sea arbitration; or "Pelagic sealing" juridically considered according to a particular analogy of municipal law* (Wash., 1893) [**2898**]. Andrew Wishart, *The Behring Sea question* (Edinburgh, 1893) [**2899**]. Henderson, *Dipl. questions* (no. 2821), "The fur seals and the Bering Sea award", (p. 3–62). Moore's *Digest* (no. 5365), v. I, 890–929. Howay, *Brit. Columbia* (no. 1718a), v. II, ch. 27: "The sealing industry and the fur seal arbitration." N. B. Wormwith, "The Bering Sea fur-seal disputes", in *Canada and its provinces* (no. 2460a), v. VIII, 723–748 [**2900**]. Johnson, *Dom. and for. com.* (no. 227), ch. 36. T. A. Bailey, "The North Pacific sealing convention of 1911", *Pacific hist. rev.*, IV (1935) 1–14 [**2900a**], useful description of the final settlement and regulation.

For biographies of members of the Bering Sea Arbitration Tribunal at Paris (Justice J. M. Harlan, Sen. J. T. Morgan, members; and F. C. Carter, F. R. Coudert, and E. J. Phelps, counsel), see such relevant entries and bibliographical data as may exist in the *D.A.B.*

Printed Sources

For general collections, see Sec. 1, above; particularly Moore's *Digest* (no. 5365), v. I; and *Arbitrations* (no. 5364), v. I, ch. 17.

U. S. OFFICIAL DOCUMENTS: *Report upon the seal fisheries in Bering Sea*, Feb. 12, 1889 (50th Cong., 2d sess. Sen. Ex. doc., no. 106) **[2901]**. *Relations with Canada*, 1890 (no. 2836). *Official correspondence . . . touching the seal fisheries of the Behring Sea since the nineteenth of July last* [1890] (Wash., 1890) (51st Cong., 2d sess. House. Ex. doc., no. 144) **[2902]**. *Papers touching the subjects of dispute between the Government of the United States and the Government of Great Britain in the Behring Sea, including all communications since March 4, 1889* (51st Cong., 1st sess. House. Ex. doc., no. 450) **[2903]**. *Recent correspondence upon the subject with the British Government* (Wash., 1892) (52d Cong., 1st sess. Senate. Ex. doc., no. 55) **[2904]**. Bering Sea Tribunal of Arbitration, *Fur seal arbitration. Proceedings of the Tribunal of Arbitration . . .* (Wash., 1895, 16 v.) (53d Cong., 2d sess. Senate. Ex. doc., no. 177) **[2905]**, the first volume contains a brief history of the tribunal's proceedings in the form of a final report of the United States agent (J. W. Foster), the protocols, etc.; the succeeding volumes contain the cases and countercases of both governments; the last volume is comprised of facsimiles of Russian documents in the Alaska archives. U. S. Revenue-Cutter Service, *Fur-seal, sea-otter, and salmon fisheries. Acts of Congress, President's proclamations, regulations governing U.S. vessels, acts of Parliament, orders in council, pertaining to the fur-seal fisheries in Bering Sea* (Wash., 1896) (Treasury Dept. Doc. no. 1850. Office of Division of Revenue Cutter Service) **[2906]**. *Fur-seal arbitration. In the matter of the claims of Great Britain against the United States of America before the Bering Sea claims commission. Argument for the United States in reply* (Wash., 1897) **[2907]**, counsel for the United States: D. M. Dickinson, Robert Lansing, C. B. Warren. Bering Sea Claims Commission, *Award of commissioners appointed pursuant to convention of Feb. 8, 1896, between the United States and*

Great Britain, for settlement of claims in virtue of convention of Feb. 29, 1892, Jan. 14, 1898 (55th Cong., 2d sess. Senate. Doc. no. 59) **[2908]**. *Work of commission appointed pursuant to convention of Feb. 8, 1896, between the United States and Great Britain, for settlement of claims presented by virtue of convention of Feb. 29, 1892,* Feb. 28, 1898 (55th Cong., 2d sess. Senate. Doc. no. 164) **[2909]**.

BRITISH PARLIAMENTARY (HOUSE OF COMMONS SESSIONAL) PAPERS: *Correspondence respecting the Behring Sea seal fisheries,* 1886–1897 (1890, LXXXII, c. 6131. 1890–91, XCVII, c. 6253 and c. 6368. 1892, XCVI, c. 6633, 6634, 6635. 1898, CV, c. 8662) **[2910]**. *Behring Sea arbitration. Case presented on the part of the Government of Her Britannic Majesty* (London, 1893, 1 v. and Appendix, 4 v.) (1893–94, CX, c. 6918) **[2911]**; and *Report of the Behring Sea commission, and report of British commissioners of June 21, 1892* (London, 1893) (1893–94, CX, c. 6919) **[2912]**; and *Countercase presented on the part of the Government of Her Britannic Majesty* (London, 1893) (1893–94, CX, c. 6920) **[2913]**; and *Argument of Her Britannic Majesty's Government* (London, 1893) (1893–94, CX, c. 6921) **[2914]**; *Case of the United States* (1893–94, CXI, c. 6949) **[2915]**; *Countercase of the United States* (1893–94, CXI, c. 6950) **[2916]**; *Argument of the United States* (1893–94, CXI, c. 6951) **[2917]**; *Award of the tribunal of arbitration* (1893–94, CXI, c. 7107) **[2918]**; *Papers relating to the proceedings of the tribunal of arbitration* (1893–94, CXI, c. 7161) **[2919]**. *Joint statement of conclusions signed by the British, Canadian, and United States delegates respecting the fur-seal herd frequenting the Pribyloff Islands in the Behring Sea* (1898, CV, c. 8703) **[2920]**.

CANADIAN PARLIAMENTARY (SESSIONAL) PAPERS: *Correspondence relative to the seizure of British American vessels in Behrings Sea by the United States authorities in 1886* (1887, nos. 48, 48a) **[2921]**. *Correspondence relative to the seizure of British American vessels in Behrings Sea by the United States authorities in 1886–87* (1888, nos. 65a, 65b, 65c) **[2922]**. *Correspondence relative to the seizure of British vessels in Behring Sea by United States authorities in 1886–91* (1891, no. 8b) **[2923]**. *Correspondence between Sir Wilfrid Laurier and Mr. Foster, of the United States of America, following the meeting of experts on the Behring Sea seal question* (1898, no. 39) **[2924]**.

There is a considerable amount of contemporary periodical literature in such publications as the *American law review, Atlantic monthly, Century, Forum, Harper's, Law quarterly review, Nineteenth century,* and *Scribner's.* See *Poole's index to period. lit.* (no. 4995).

A. B. Hart, ed., *Extracts from official papers relating to the Bering Sea controversy, 1790–1892* (N. Y., 1892) **[2925]** prints selected despatches, ukases, treaties, and conventions.

For the printed writings of American statesmen and diplomatists (Bering Sea Tribunal of Arbitration: Justice J. M. Harlan, Sen. J. T. Morgan, members; J. W. Foster, agent; F. C. Carter, F. R. Coudert, and E. J. Phelps, counsel), see the relevant entries and bibliographical data in the *D.A.B.*

For the printed writings of British statesmen, see Sec. 1, above. Note in particular Viscount Alverstone's *Recollections* (no. 2502).

Maps: Suggestions

"List of maps, with designation of waters, now known as the Behring Sea, with date and place of publication", *For. rel.,* 1890 (no. 5345), 504–507. Phillips (no. 5135), for maps of Alaska in the Library of Congress. *Corres. rel. seizure Brit. Am. vessels in Behrings Sea* (no. 2921) includes a map. *Fur-seal fisheries of Alaska* (Wash., 1889) (50th Cong., 2d sess. House. Rept. no. 3883) **[2926]** includes maps. House of Commons, *Sessional papers,* 1890–91, XCVII, c. 6368 (no. 2910). *Case presented on the part of the Govt. of Her Brit. Majesty* (no. 2911), Appendix, v. IV, consists of 2 maps: "Map of the northwest coasts of America, and the Aleutian and Kurile Islands, published in the Quartermaster-General's office, St. Petersburgh, 1802"; and "Map of the northern portion of the North Pacific Ocean." *Rept. of the Behring Sea commission* (no. 2912), 5 maps. *Fur seal arbitration; proceedings* (no. 2905), maps in v. III, V, VI, and VII. *Information relative to the enforcement of the regulations respecting fur seals, adopted by the Governments of the United States and Great Britain* (Wash., 1895) (53d Cong., 3d sess. Senate. Ex. doc. no. 67) **[2927]**, 3 maps. H. W. Elliott, . . . *Report of Henry W. Elliott on the condition of the fur-seal fisheries of Alaska* (Wash., 1896) (54th Cong., 1st sess. House. Doc. no. 175) **[2928]**, 14 maps. *Report by Mr. G. E. H. Barrett-Hamilton on his mission to the Russian seal islands* *in 1897* (London, 1898) [**2929**], maps of the Rookery, Bering Island, by Leonard Stejneger. *Seal and salmon fisheries and general resources of Alaska* (Wash., 1898) (55th Cong., 1st sess. House. Doc. no. 92) [**2930**], several maps. " Report of the fur-seal investigation, 1896–1897. Charts of the islands and fur-seal rookeries of St. Paul and St. George, Pribilof group, Alaska ", pub. with U.S. Treasury Dept., Commission on Fur-Seal Investigations, *The fur seals and fur-seal islands of the North Pacific Ocean* (Wash.: Govt. Print. Off. 1898–99, 4 v.) [**2931**].

MSS.: Suggestions

See Sec. 1, above.

The correspondence of Senator J. T. Morgan (member of the Bering Sea Tribunal, 1893), 1860–1907, is in the Library of Congress (26 portfolios).

8. Other Canadian Questions; Miscellaneous

A. Annexation

Bibliographical Aids

For general aids, see Sec. 1, above.

Special Works

De Ricci, *Annexation* (no. 2816). Goldwin Smith, *Canadian question* (no. 2942), argument in favor of commercial union with the United States by a famous British subject who favored annexation. Callahan, *Alaska purchase* (no. 2231) considers the acquisition of Alaska as a counter-movement against the future extension of the Canadian confederation westward; this study, somewhat rewritten, appears under the curious title *Americo-Canadian relations concerning annexation, 1846–1871* (see no. 1643). Bishop, *Canada rejected reciprocity* (no. 2947). Two works by T. C. Blegen: " James Wickes Taylor ", *Minn. hist. bul.*, I (1915) 153–219 [**2932**], special agent of the Department of State, 1869–70, to report upon conditions in the Canadian Northwest, and U. S. consul at Winnipeg, 1870–93; and "A plan for the union of British North America and the United States, 1866 ", *Miss. Valley hist. rev.*, IV (1918) 470–483 [**2932a**], a plan presented to the House of Representatives in 1866, by Gen. N. P. Banks, chairman of the committee on foreign affairs, but not supported by Grant's administration. Two works by R. G. Trotter:

Canadian federation; its origins and achievement (London, 1924), [**2933**] reviews in a scholarly fashion the influence of various factors in the United States (economic, including the ending of the reciprocity treaty; and political, including annexationist sentiment) on Confederation; and " Some American influences upon the Canadian federation movement ", *Canad. hist. rev.*, V (1924) 213–227 [**2933a**] shows how the Canadian Confederation was achieved " with one eye on the United States ", *i.e.* on annexationist sentiment. W. N. Sage, " The annexationist movement in British Columbia ", *Royal soc. Canad. proc.*, 3d ser., XXI, sec. 2 (1927) 97–110 [**2934**], the short-lived annexation movement, 1866–1871, growing out of the influx of American citizens during the gold rush to the Fraser River in 1858; the author has used the British Columbia archives and local prints. And by the same writer, " The critical period of British Columbia history, 1866–1871 ", *Pacific hist. rev.*, I (1932) 424–443 [**2935**], discussion of the annexation proposal as one of three courses open to British Columbia during the critical years, 1866–1871. H. L. Keenleyside, " British Columbia—annexation or confederation? " *Canad. hist. assoc. rep.* (1928) 34–40 [**2936**] shows how " manifest destiny " was " cheated of its prey " by Confederation. A. C. MacRae, " When annexation was in flower ", *Dalhousie rev.*, IX (1929) 282–286 [**2937**], the movement for annexation of Canada to the United States in 1866, when a bill was introduced into the House of Representatives at Washington for the admission of Canada into the Union. J. P. Pritchett, " The origin of the so-called ' Fenian raid on Manitoba in 1871 ' ", *Canad. hist. rev.*, X (1929) 23–42 [**2938**], a recently discovered letter from W. B. O'Donoghue to Jay Cooke, March 29, 1871, anent the O'Donoghue scheme for the annexation of Rupert's Land (no. 2940), corroborates the thesis that the raid was a private filibustering project. Ruth E. Sandborn, " The United States and the British northwest, 1865–1870 ", *No. Dak. hist. quar.*, VI (1932) 5–41 [**2939**] describes annexationist sentiment from United States documents, Canadian sessional papers, printed monographs, and archives of the Department of State (consular despatches from Winnipeg). Smith, *Republican expansionists* (no.1918a) is important. W. M. Whitelaw, *The Maritimes and Canada before Confederation* (Toronto, 1934) [**2939a**], carefully documented study, indispensable background for United

States relations with the Maritime Provinces, though not primarily concerned with diplomatic relations.

Printed Sources

For general collections, see Sec. 1, above. *Relations with Canada* (no. 2836). J. P. Pritchett, ed., " Letter from W. B. O'Donoghue to Jay Cooke, March 29, 1871, anent the O'Donoghue scheme for the annexation of Rupert's Land ", *No. Dak. hist. quar.*, V (1930) 49–53 [**2940**] concerns the origin of the Fenian raid into Manitoba in 1871, and shows the effort of O'Donoghue to enlist the aid of financial and political interests in the United States in his movement for the acquisition of the Canadian northwest.

MSS.: Suggestions [15]

See Sec. 1, above. The papers of James Wickes Taylor, special agent, 1869–70, to report upon conditions in the Canadian Northwest, and U. S. consul at Winnipeg, 1870–93, are in the Minnesota Historical Society.

B. Reciprocity [16]

Bibliographical Aids

For general aids, see Sec. 1, above. Griffin and Meyer, *Reciprocity* (no. 1333) ; H. H. B. Meyer, *Additional references relating to reprocity with Canada* (Wash., 1911) (Library of Congress) [**2941**], books and articles in periodicals relating to the proposed treaty of 1911. United States Tariff Commission, *The tariff; a bibliography* (Wash.: Govt. Print. Off., 1934) [**2941a**], a select list of references containing 6453 entries on all phases of the tariff.

Special Works

Goldwin Smith, " Reciprocity ", in his *Canada and the Canadian question* (London and N.Y., 1891) 281–301 [**2942**], argument in favor of commercial union with the United States by a famous British subject who favored annexation. Willison, *Laurier and the liberal party* (no. 2492). Edward Porritt, *Sixty years of protection in Canada, 1846–1907; where industry leans on the politician* (London, 1908) [**2943**], a free-trade polemic by an American writer, con-

---

[15] This applies to the various subdivisions in this section no. 8, *viz:* A, B, C, D.

[16] For the Reciprocity Treaty of 1854, see Ch. IX, sec. 2. For the abrogation in 1866 of the same treaty, see Ch. XIII, sec. 2, nos. 1943–1947, 1955–1958.

tains some interesting comments on the movement for reciprocity. O. D. Skelton, " Canada's rejection of reciprocity ", *Jour. pol. econ.*, XIX (1911) 726–731 [**2944**], with reciprocity given its quietus, discussion of the tariff may go on without flag-waving and brass-band distractions; and " Reciprocity, the Canadian attitude ", *ibid.*, 77–97 [**2945**], explaining the drift away from reciprocity in Canada. F. W. Taussig, " Reciprocity with Canada ", *ibid.*, 542–549 [**2946**], a defense of the proposal by arrangement by a distinguished authority on the tariff. [A. L. Bishop], " Why Canada rejected reciprocity "; by a Canadian, *Yale rev.*, n.s. I (1912) 173–187 [**2947**], because an eventual commercial union, if no more, with the United States was feared. A. H. Walker, " *Reciprocity* " *of William H. Taft* (N.Y., 1912) [**2948**], sharp attack. Edward Stanwood, " Trade reciprocity with Canada ", *Mass. hist. soc. proc.*, XLVII (1914) 141–178 [**2949**], a cogent historical review of the rise and fall of the idea of reciprocity. Trotter, *Canad. federation* (no. 2933). F. H. Soward, "American economic penetration of Canada ", *Canad. hist. rev.*, VIII (1927) 31–40 [**2950**], a useful study in connection with the subject of reciprocity. Keenleyside, *Canada and U.S.* (no. 896). W. G. Swartz, " The proposed Canadian-American reciprocity agreement of 1911 ", *Jour. econ. and business hist.*, III (1930) 118–147 [**2951**], a useful analysis, particularly of the domestic political issues involved, both in the United States and Canada.

See Sec. 1, for biographies of Canadian statesmen.

Printed Sources

For general collections, see Sec. 1, above. Griffin and Meyer, *Reciprocity* (nos. 1333 and 2941), for lists of United States, British, and Canadian official documents dealing with reciprocity with Canada, including speeches in Congress.

We note here collections dealing with the diplomatic phase of the subject in particular, and a few published since the above-mentioned lists.—*Message from the President . . . relative to negotiations for reciprocal trade with Canada*, 1892 (52d Cong., 1st sess. Senate Ex. doc., no. 114, pts. 1, 2) [**2952**]. Confidential memorandum for the use of the commissioners on the part of the United States in the American-British Joint High Commission, Washington, 1871 ", *For. rel.* (no. 5345), 1873, v. III, 292–305 [**2953**] deals with reciprocal trade between Canada and the United States. *Com-*

mercial reciprocity between the United States and the British North American provinces; memorandum of the British plenipotentiaries (Wash., 1875?) [2954]. *Relations with Canada*, 1890 (no. 2836). U.S. Congress, Senate, Committee on Finance, *Reciprocity with Canada; compilation of documents relating to the proposed agreement of 1911, and to the treaty of 1854* (Wash., 1911) [2955]. *Canadian reciprocity. Special message of the President . . . 1911. Correspondence embodying an agreement between the Dept. of State and the Canadian Government in regard to reciprocal tariff legislation* (Wash., 1911) (61st Cong., 3d sess. Senate. Doc. 787) [2956].

BRITISH PARLIAMENTARY (HOUSE OF COMMONS SESSIONAL) PAPERS: *Correspondence relating to the negotiations for a reciprocity treaty between Canada and the United States* (1874, LXXV, C. 1060) [2957]. *Papers relating to a proposed commercial arrangement between Canada and the United States of America* (1911, LIII, 17; Cd. 5512) [2958]. *Reports from His Majesty's ambassador at Washington respecting a reciprocal tariff arrangement between Canada and the United States* (1911, LIII, 35; Cd. 5523) [2959]. *Proposed customs tariff reciprocity arrangement between the Dominion of Canada and the United States of America* (1911, LIII, 53; Cd. 5537) [2960].

CANADIAN PARLIAMENTARY (SESSIONAL) PAPERS: *Correspondence which has passed since the 1st of May last between the Imperial Government, the Cabinet at Washington, and the Government of the Dominion of Canada on the subject of the renewal of the reciprocity treaty with the United States, and of all negotiations entered upon in consequence of the abrogation of the treaty* (1869, no. 47) [2961]. *Correspondence between the Government of the Dominion and the Government of the United States, on the subject of reciprocal trade* (1873, no. 40) [2962]. *Papers in connection with the negotiations with the Government of the United States for a treaty of commercial reciprocity* (1875, no. 51) [2963]. *Correspondence between the governments of Canada and the United States . . . upon the question of reciprocal trade relations between the two countries* (1883, no. 55) [2964]. *Copies of all memorials or papers relating to reciprocal trade between the United States and Canada, and of all correspondence . . . upon the subject of reciprocal trade relations* (1886, no. 65) [2965]. *Copy of the statement presented by the British plenipotentiaries to the Fisheries Commis-*

sion at Washington, in relation to reciprocal trade relations (1888, no. 36a) **[2966]**. *Documents relating to the negotiations at the conference recently held at Washington between the delegates from the Canadian government and the Secretary of State of the United States respecting the extension and development of trade between the United States and the Dominion of Canada* (1892, no. 37) **[2967]**. *Special report on the trade between Canada and the United States, for the use of the International Commission, Quebec, August 1898* (1899, no. 5a) **[2968]**. *Tariff relations between the United States and the Dominion of Canada; correspondence and statements* (1911, 109b) **[2969]**. *Papers relating to the conference held at Washington in February, 1892* (1893, no. 52) **[2970]**, question of a new treaty of reciprocity was discussed. *Correspondence between British ambassador at Washington and the government of Canada in connection with negotiations for a reciprocity treaty between Canada and the United States* (1912, no. 82a) **[2971]**.

There is a considerable amount of contemporary periodical literature by competent observers and students; this is listed comprehensively in Griffin and Meyer, *References on reciprocity* (nos. 1333 and 2941). See also *Poole's index* (no. 4995), and *Readers' guide* (no. 4996).

J. N. Larned, *Report on the state of trade between the United States and the British possessions in North America* (Wash., 1871) (41st Cong., 3d sess. House. Exec. doc., no. 94) **[2972]**, by a special agent of the Treasury Department. H. C. Carey, *The British treaties of 1871 and 1874; letters to the President of the United States* (Phila., 1874) **[2973]**, opposed to reciprocity. W. D. Kelley, *The proposed reciprocity treaty*, an address delivered by request of representatives of the leading manufacturing industries of the United States, at the Academy of Music, Phila., Oct. 28, 1874 (Phila., 1874) **[2974]**. Thomas Shaw, *Plain talks on commercial union between Canada and the United States* (Hamilton, Ont., 1887) **[2975]**. Sir E. W. Watkin, *Canada and the States; recollections, 1851 to 1886* (London and N.Y., 1887) **[2976]** has a discussion of the reciprocity treaty with the United States; by a British imperialist who regards Canadian confederation as a breakwater against the fell waves of annexation. G. M. Adam, ed., *Handbook of commercial union: a collection of papers read before the commercial Union Club, Toronto; with speeches, letters and other docu-*

ments in favour of unrestricted reciprocity with the United States
(Toronto, 1888) [2977]. J. N. Blake, *The true commercial policy
for Greater Britain;* an address delivered before the Commercial
Union Club, Toronto, April 5th, 1888 (Toronto, 1888) [2978], a
plea for renewal of reciprocity. A. H. U. Colquhoun, " Reciprocity
trips to Washington; a page from political history ", *Canad. mag.*,
VIII (1897) 423–429 [2979], visits of Canadian officials to Washington to obtain reciprocity treaties at different times. Albert
Clarke, *Reciprocity with Canada; status of negotiations and trade
relations* (Boston, 1902) [2980], speech before the Massachusetts
State Board of Trade, Jan. 21, 1902, to show that reciprocity was
more important to Canada than to the United States. E. G. Hay,
Reciprocity with Canada: report . . . to the advisory board of the
Minnesota branch of the National Reciprocity League (Minneapolis,
1903) [2981], the chief object of the National Reciprocity League
was to secure a reciprocity treaty with Canada. H. C. Lodge, " Reciprocity with Canada ", in *Speeches before the Home Market Club*
(Boston, 1903) 14–28 [2982], none too sanguine expectations from
reciprocity. Henri Bourassa, *The reciprocity agreement and its
consequences as viewed from the nationalist standpoint* (Montreal,
1911) [2983], by the chief editor of " Le Devoir." Canadian National League, Toronto, *Reciprocity with the United States; Canadian nationality, British connection and fiscal independence. How
the policy which has been pursued in Canada for more than thirty
years is reversed by the reciprocity agreement with the United
States, and how commercial and political union with the United
States would follow* (Toronto, 1911) [2984]. G. E. Foster, " The
reciprocity agreement, from a Canadian standpoint ", *No. Am. rev.*,
CXCIII (1911) 663–671 [2985], by a member of the Canadian Parliament. P. C. Knox, *Reciprocity with Canada* (Wash., 1911) (61st
Cong., 3d sess. House. Doc. 1418) [2986], an address before the
Chicago Association of Commerce, Feb. 15, 1911. H. L. Stimson,
Address [*on the proposed reciprocity agreement with Canada*], be-
fore the Intercolonial Club at Boston, May 24, 1911 (Boston? 1911?)
[2987]. W. H. Taft, " Reciprocity with Canada ", *Jour. pol. econ.*,
XIX (1911) 513–526; also pub. in Western Economic Society (no.
2992), and as Sen. Doc. 43, 62d Cong., 1st Sess. [2988], an address
delivered by the President of the United States before the Western
Economic Society, June 3, 1911. Also by President Taft, *Reci-*

procity, address . . . at the banquet of the Marion Club, Indianapolis, Ind., July 4, 1911, on Republican reciprocity (Wash., 1911)
(62d Cong., 1st Sess. Senate. Doc. 63) [**2989**]. Tariff Commission,
London, *The proposed reciprocal trade arrangement between Canada
and the United States of America* (London, 1911) [**2990**]; also by
the same commission, *Reciprocity with Canada. Most-favored-nation agreements in relation to the proposed reciprocal trade agreement between Canada and the United States of America* (London,
1911), also pub. (Wash., 1911) (62d Cong., 1st Sess. Sen. Doc. 66)
[**2991**]. Western Economic Society, *Reciprocity with Canada;* the
topic of the first meeting of the Society held in Chicago, June 3,
1911 (Chicago, 1911) [**2992**], a symposium by various authorities.
Clifford Sifton, " Reciprocity ", *Ann. Am. acad. pol. and soc. sci.*,
XLV (1913) 20–28 [**2993**], views of a Canadian statesman on the
reciprocity treaty of 1911. U.S. Tariff Commission, *Reciprocity
with Canada; a study of the arrangement of 1911* (Wash., 1920)
[**2994**], a brief but authoritative discussion of the Canadian reciprocity arrangement. A. H. U. Colquhoun, " The reciprocity negotiation with the United States in 1869 ", *Canad. hist. rev.*, VIII
(1927) 233–242 [**2995**], letter of Edward Thornton, British minister
at Washington, to the Earl of Clarendon, July 12, 1869, with enclosures, including " memorandum of conference held with Mr. Fish
on the question of reciprocity between Canada and the United
States, July 8, 1869 ".

For printed writings of American statesmen and diplomatists,
see Sec. 1, above. Also for British and Canadian statesmen.

C. Fenian Raids

Bibliographical Aids

For general aids, see Sec. 1, above.

Special Works

Gilbert McMicken, *The abortive Fenian raid on Manitoba* (Winnipeg, 1888) [**2996**], by the chief of the Canadian intelligence service.
J. A. MacDonald, *Troublous times in Canada, a history of the Fenian
raids of 1866* (Toronto, 1910) [**2997**]. Curtis, *Hostile military
expeditions* (no. 1797). Trotter, *Canad. federation* (no. 2933).
Pritchett, *So-called Fenian raid* (no. 2938). Pieper, *Fenian movement* (no. 1916).

Printed Sources

BRITISH PARLIAMENTARY (HOUSE OF COMMONS SESSIONAL) PAPERS: *Correspondence respecting the recent Fenian aggression upon Canada* (1867, XLVIII, 539) [2998]. *Despatch from Earl Granville to Governor General Sir John Young respecting the recent Fenian raid into Canada* (1870, XLIX, 331) [2999]. *Correspondence respecting publication in the United States of incitements to outrages in England* (1882, LXXX, 53) [3000].

Official report of Gen. John O'Neill, president of the Fenian brotherhood, on the attempt to invade Canada, May 25th, 1870 (N.Y., 1870) [3001]. O'Donoghue, *Letter* (no. 2940).

D. Miscellaneous

Special Works

" The Anglo-American joint high commission ", by a Canadian liberal, *No. Am. rev.*, CLXVII (1898) 165–175 [3002], extolling its importance for peaceful Canadian-American relations. Callahan, *Neutrality of American lakes* (no. 1642), ch. 7, details the adjustment of irritating questions of Anglo-American relations, 1861–1896, and the continuation of the agreement of 1817. Edward Farrer, " The Anglo-American commission ", *Forum*, XXV (1898) 652–663 [3003]. H. S. Boutell, " Is the Rush-Bagot convention immortal?" *No. Am. rev.*, CLXXIII (1901) 331–348 [3004] suggests that the agreement is of more value to Great Britain than the United States, and should be superseded by a more modern treaty. Two studies by P. T. McGrath: "A new Anglo-American dispute. Is the Hudson Bay a closed sea?" *No. Am. rev.*, CLXXVII (1903) 883–896 [3005], significance to Canadian-American relations of Canada's proposal to reaffirm exclusive sovereignty over Hudson's Bay and expel American whalers; and " The Hudson Bay dispute ", *Fortn. rev.*, LXXXIX (1908) 125–136 [3006], in which the author betrays anxiety lest Canada attempt to exercise some act of exclusive sovereignty over Hudson's Bay, giving ground to the United States for arbitration which might contest that sovereignty. A. S. Hershey, " The relations of the United States and England as affected by the Far Eastern question ", *Am. pol. sci. assoc. proc.*, II (1906) 59–72 [3007], writer believes our sympathies and interests are clearly enlisted on the side of the Anglo-Japanese alliance. T. W. Balch, " La baie d'Hudson, est-elle une mer libre ou une mer fermée?" *Rev. droit internat.*, 2d ser., XIII (1911) 539–586 [**3008**], an American lawyer, specialist in Anglo-American litigations and issues, supports the thesis that it is an open sea. Trotter, *Canad. federation* (no. 2933). H. L. Keenleyside, "American economic penetration of Canada", *Canad. hist. rev.*, VIII (1927) 30–40 [**3009**], an analysis of preponderating American capital ($3,000,000,000 by 1904) in Canada and its significance. H. A. Innis, "Interrelations between the fur trade of Canada and the United States", *Miss. Valley hist. rev.*, XX (1933) 321–332 [**3010**], general reflections and suggestions by an authority on this subject. Smith, *Republican expansionists* (no. 1918a) is important.

Printed Sources

BRITISH PARLIAMENTARY (HOUSE OF COMMONS SESSIONAL) PAPERS: *Correspondence respecting . . . naturalization* (1868–69, LXIII, 735) [**3011**]. *Correspondence between the Board of Trade and Mr. Burns, respecting a convention with the United States for putting British shipping in American waters on same footing as foreign ships in British waters, so far as regards liability* (1871, LXI, 35) [**3012**]. *Correspondence respecting the navigation of the United States canals by Canadian vessels* (1876, LXXXII, 323) [**3013**]. *Correspondence respecting the demand of the United States government for the recall of Lord Sackville from Washington* (1888, CIX, 601 and 609; LXXXVII, 661) [**3014**]. *Correspondence respecting a proposal made by the Government of the United States for the settlement of international disputes by arbitration* (1893–94, CXI, 1081 and 1101) [**3015**]. *Despatch from H.M.'s ambassador at Washington, forwarding treaty of general arbitration, Washington, 11th January 1897* (1897, CII, 429) [**3016**]. *Correspondence respecting the proposals on currency made by the special envoys from the United States* (1898, CV, 601) [**3017**], in advance of an international bimetallic conference.

BRITISH PARLIAMENTARY (HOUSE OF COMMONS SESSIONAL) PAPERS IN REGARD TO EXTRADITION: *Correspondence respecting extradition* (1876, LXXXII, 1, and 125; 1877, LXXXVIII, 1) [**3018**]. *Return of cases of extradition of prisoners under treaty between Great Britain and the United States* (1876, LXXXII, 199, 207) [**3019**]. *Des-*

patch from the Earl of Rosebery to Her Majesty's minister at Washington, enclosing a copy of a convention between Great Britain and the United States for the extradition of criminals, 1886 (1888, CIX, 597) [3020].

Correspondence or papers with the Colonial Office, or with the Government of the United States, in regard to the action of that Government in denying the free navigation of the United States canals, in accordance with the Washington treaty (Canada. Parliament. Sess. Pap., 1876, no. 111) [3021].

CHAPTER XVII

THE FAR EAST TO 1922

1. In General

Bibliographical Aids

For general aids, see Sabin (no. 4655); Larned (no. 4657); Griffin (no. 4658); *Writings* (no. 4661); C. H. and T. (no. 4662); bibliogs. in *Am. secs. state* (no. 4796); *Guide hist. lit.* (no. 4634). Myers (no. 5399), for collections of treaties. Miller, *Treaties* (no. 5371), v. I, 39-54, for " Bibliography of United States treaty collections."

For indexes to periodical literature, see nos. 4995-5003.

For lists and indexes of newspapers, see nos. 5004-5047.

For Chinese, Japanese, and Korean historical bibliographies, see nos. 4766-4777.

A. P. C. Griffin, *List of books (with references to periodicals) relating to the theory of colonization, government of dependencies, protectorates, and related topics*, 2nd ed., with additions (Wash., 1900) (Library of Congress) [**3022**]; his *Select list of books (with references to periodicals) relating to the Far East* (Wash., 1904) (Library of Congress) [**3023**], most useful; and his *Select list of references on Chinese immigration* (Wash., 1904) (Library of Congress) [**3024**]. R. E. Cowan and Dunlap Boutwell, *Bibliography of the Chinese question in the United States* (San Francisco, 1909) [**3025**], for references on Chinese immigration. K. S. Latourette, *Chinese hist. stud.* (no. 4770); and *Japan; suggested outlines for a discus-*

sion of Japan, her history, culture, problems, and relations with the United States (N.Y., 1921) **[3026]**, " Selected bibliography of books on Japan " (p. 37–39). Anderson and Hershey, *Handbook* (no. 4282). Boston Public Library, *The United States and Japan; selected references to books and periodicals in the Public Library of the City of Boston* (Boston, 1921) (Brief Reading Lists, no. 22) **[3027]**. Swingle, *Chinese hist. sources* (no. 4771). Dorothy P. Miller, *Japanese-American relations; a list of works in the New York Public Library* (N.Y., 1921) **[3028]**, reprinted from the *Bulletin*, v. XXV, 1921; is particularly useful. W. A. Slade, *Bibliography of China, Japan, and the Philippine Islands* (Concord, N.H., 1925) **[3029]**, also published in the *Annals of the American Academy of Political and Social Science*, Nov. 1925. J. M. Buell, " Problems of the Pacific; a bibliography ", in his *The Institute of Pacific Relations* (Worcester, 1926) (World Peace Foundation Pamphlets, no. 218) 29–53 **[3030]**. Louise M. Taylor, *Catalog of books on China in the Essex Institute* (Salem, Mass., 1926) **[3031]**. Hummel, *Chinese historians* (no. 4772). *A short list of books and pamphlets relating to the European intercourse with Japan (private collection of Professor Shigetomo Koda)*, exhibited at the Mitsukoshi, Eastern Room, from November 7th to 11th, 1930, under the auspices of the Tokyo Hibiya Library (Tokyo, 1930) **[3032]**. Hermann Hülle, *Neuerwerbungen chinesischer und manjurischer Bücher in den Jahren 1921–1930* (Leipzig, 1931) **[3033]**, books on politics and history, published in the Chinese language during those years. Kerner, *Russian expansion* (no. 1710). Morse and McNair, *Far East. internat. rel.* (no. 3045), 783–809. H. S. Quigley, *An introductory syllabus on Far Eastern diplomacy* (Chicago: Pub. for the American Council, Institute of Pacific Relations, 1931) **[3034]**. J. A. Robertson, *The Far East, with special reference to China; its culture, civilization, and history; an outline for individual and group study* (Chapel Hill, N.C., 1931) **[3035]**. C. S. Gardner, *A union list of selected western books on China in American libraries* (Wash.: American Council of Learned Societies, 1932) **[3036]**. Institute of Pacific Relations, *Publications on Pacific problems* (no. 5173). Langer and Armstrong, *Foreign affairs bibliog.* (no. 4399), 460–492.

General and Special Works [1]

Of general histories of the United States, see McMaster (no. 4781) to 1861; Rhodes (no. 4783) to 1909; Channing (no. 4784) to 1865; Oberholtzer (no. 4785) to 1888. See also *Am. secs. state* (no. 4796); and Wriston, *Executive agents* (no. 4799).

For contemporary periodical material consult the indexes to periodicals (nos. 4995-5003).

P. S. Reinsch, *World politics at the end of the nineteenth century as influenced by the Oriental situation* (N.Y., 1900) [**3037**], a suggestive examination of the international position by a professor at the University of Wisconsin who later became U.S. minister to China. Henri Cordier, *Histoire des relations de la Chine avec les puissances occidentales, 1860-1902* (Paris, 1901-02, 3 v.) [**3038**], comprehensive and accurate survey by one of the greatest authorities on Chinese history; and by the same writer, *Histoire générale de la Chine et de ses relations avec les pays étrangers depuis les temps les plus anciens* (Paris, 1920, 4 v.) [**3039**]. Bunyie Baba, *Japan, 1853-1864, or Genji Yume Monogatari*, translated by Sir Ernest Mason Satow (Tokyo, 1905) [**3040**]. F. E. Hinckley, *American consular jurisdiction in the Orient* (Wash., 1906) [**3041**], a thorough treatise on the subject as developed by United States treaties and practice with the Barbary States, Egypt, Turkey, the smaller Oriental States, China, and Japan. Ken Yamaguchi, *Kinse Shiriaku. A history of Japan, from the first visit of Commodore Perry in 1853 to the capture of Hakodate in 1869*, translated by Sir Ernest M. Satow, rev. ed., with supplementary notes, by Shuziro Watanabe (Tokyo, 1906) [**3042**]. H. B. Morse, *The trade and administration of the Chinese empire* (London and N.Y., 1908; 3d rev. ed., 1921) [**3043**], a more specialized work by the scholarly and authoritative

---

[1] The principal periodicals specializing on Far Eastern international relations are: *Asia;* the Journal of the American Asiatic Association (N.Y., 1898-). *The Asiatic review* (London, 1868-). Asiatic Society of Japan, *Transactions* (Tokyo, 1872-). *China weekly review;* devoted to the economic, political, and social development of China and intercourse with other nations (Shanghai, 1917-); title varies, formerly *Millard's review of the Far East*, etc. *Chinese social and political science review* (Peking, 1916-). *Far Eastern review;* engineering, commerce, finance (Shanghai, 1904-). *Far Eastern political science review* (Canton, 1919-). *New China review* (Shanghai, 1919-). *Revue du Pacifique* (Paris, 1922-). Royal Asiatic Society of Great Britain and Ireland, North China Branch, *Journal* (Shanghai, 1858-). *T'oung pao; archives pour servir à l'étude de l'histoire, des langues, de la géographie et de l'ethnographie de l'Asie orientale* (Leyden, 1890-). *The Trans-Pacific;* a financial and economic magazine of international service (Tokyo, 1919-).

author of no. 3045; and *International relations of the Chinese empire* (London and N.Y., 1910–18, 3 v.) [3044], one of the most important works, dispassionate and impartial survey supported " by the solid tramp of platoons of statistics ", it looks to the future redemption of China from foreign servitudes. Uses new material from European (notably British) archives, but is weaker on American sources. H. B. Morse and H. F. MacNair, *Far Eastern international relations* (Boston and N.Y., 1931) [3045], an excellent abridgment, the earlier parts relying on Morse's more comprehensive work, the later portion giving MacNair's perspicacious analysis of twentieth-century international affairs; uncompromising but dispassionate; voluminous bibliography. Frank Brinkley and Baron Dairoku Kikuchi, *A history of the Japanese people from the earliest times to the end of the Meiji era* (N.Y., 1915) [3046], reputed to be the most complete single-volume history, albeit tinctured with an exaggerated nationalistic viewpoint. Scholefield, *Pacific* (no. 2350), " the best general historical survey, covering the policy of the Powers from the 18th century to the present " (Langer (no. 4399), 492). Katsuro Hara, *An introduction to the history of Japan* (N.Y., 1920) [3047], one of the best cultural histories. Liu Yen, *Chung-kuo chin-shih wai-chiao shih* (History of Chinese foreign relations) (Shanghai, 1921, rev. ed.; 1st ed., *circa* 1905) [3048], first of its kind in Chinese. Rhodes, *McKinley and Roosevelt* (no. 2462). B. H. Williams, *The protection of American citizens in China* (N.Y., 1923) [3049], reprinted from the *Am. jour. internat. law*, XVI–XVII, 1922–1923. Otto Franke, *Die Grossmächte in Ostasien von 1894 bis 1914* (Brunswick and Hamburg, 1923) [3050], a solid work on an important period, written largely from printed state papers of the several powers. Sir R. K. Douglas, *Europe and the Far East, 1506–1912*, revised and corrected, with an additional chapter, 1904–1912, by J. H. Langford (N.Y., 1924; 1st ed., 1904) [3051], one of the best summaries; it is scanty on American affairs in eastern Asia. Two books by E. T. Williams: *China yesterday and today* (N.Y., 1923; 4th rev. ed., 1929) [3052], a general survey by a former professor of Oriental languages at the University of California and one-time chief of the division of Far Eastern affairs of the Department of State; and *A short history of China* (N.Y. and London, 1928) [3053], general treatment. Ch'ên Kung-fu, *Chung-kuo tsui-chin san-shih nien shih* (Chinese history of the last thirty years) (Shanghai, 1928) [**3054**]. *Ch'ing shih kao* (Draft history of the Ch'ing dynasty), published by the Chinese Historiographical Board (Pekin, 1928) [**3055**], 131 volumes in 536 sections, and including many biographies, which have been brought together in a separate work of 80 volumes (*Ch'ing-shih lieh-chüan*).[2] Dennis, *Adventures* (no. 2224) presents fresh material on the origin of the Open Door policy and on the United States and the Boxer rebellion. G. W. Keeton, *The development of extraterritoriality in China* (London and N.Y., 1928, 2 v.)[**3056**], a legal evaluation of historical facts with less regard for their political implications. The second volume consists entirely of documents. P. J. Treat, *The Far East; a political and diplomatic history* (N.Y., 1928) [**3057**], one of the best short reviews, believed by some to be apologetic for Japanese policy. K. S. Latourette, *A history of Christian missions in China* (N.Y., 1929) [**3058**], "the most complete and authoritative account" (Langer (no. 4399), 465). Dulles, *America in the Pacific* (no. 2225). Dennett, *John Hay* (no. 2472), and Moore, *John Hay; an estimate* (no. 2473). Dyer, *William M. Evarts* (no. 2466). Beard, *National interest* (no. 4823).

A Japanese publication of which we have been unable to find the date is: Nagao Ariga, *Kinji gaiko-shi* (Modern diplomatic history) (Tokyo) [**3059**]. See also Ariga's short but comprehensive chapter in Alfred Stead's *Japan by the Japanese* (London, 1904) [**3060**], probably the first scholarly survey by a Japanese who used (but did not cite) official Japanese sources.

Printed Sources

For American official publications and general source collections, see *Jour. exec. proc. Sen.* (no. 5387); *Cong. Globe* (no. 5384); *Cong. Record* (no. 5385); *For. relations* (no. 5345); Wharton, *Digest* (no. 5366); *Richardson* (no. 5335); Moore's *Arbitrations* (no. 5364); and his *Digest* (no. 5365); Hasse's *Guide* (no. 5344).

For texts of treaties, see Miller, *Treaties* (no. 5371), and Myers (no. 5399) for collections of treaties.

For guides to newspapers, see nos. 5004–5047. An analysis of the principal American newspapers and periodicals, 1848 to 1871, is given in Gazley (no. 1424). "Foreign language papers in Japan", in Treat (no. 3113), 568.

---

[2] For description of this work, see Latourette (no. 4770) and Peake (no. 5449a).

For United States government documents relating to the Far East, 1828 to 1861, see Hasse's *Index* (no. 5344). For selected material after 1861, to 1918, see *Foreign relations* (no. 5345), the volume for 1899 has an index for previous volumes. For thorough reconnaissance of all United States government documents since Hasse (1861), see the *Checklist* (no. 5361) and the serial indexes and catalogues (nos. 5358–5360).

For convenient lists of published United States official documents regarding the Far East, see (for 1894–1918), Henry Chung (no. 3265); (for Japan), D. P. Miller (no. 3028); and Treat (no. 3113); (for China), Latourette (no. 3097). For indexes and guides to foreign government documents, see p. 836. British parliamentary papers dealing with Japan are listed in Treat (no. 3113).

For Chinese official documents, see nos. 5442–5450. For Japanese official documents, see nos. 5451–5462.

Trescot, *Foreign policy of U.S.* (no. 1821), "the first to advocate an Anglo-American partnership in Far Eastern diplomacy." W. W. Rockhill, ed., *Treaties and conventions with or concerning China and Korea, 1894–1904, together with various state papers and documents affecting foreign interests* (Wash.: Govt. Print. Off., 1904) **[3061]**; and by the same editor, *Treaties, conventions, agreements, ordinances, etc., relating to China and Korea (October 1904–January 1908)* (Wash.: Govt. Print. Off., 1908) **[3062]**, both published by the Department of State. Huntington Wilson, *Government and foreign investment* (no. 3503a). Anderson and Hershey, *Handbook dipl. hist. Asia* (no. 4282). J. V. A. MacMurray, ed., *Treaties and agreements with and concerning China 1894–1919; a collection of state papers, private agreements, and other documents* . . . (N.Y., 1921, 2 v.) **[3063]**, published by the Carnegie Endowment for International Peace. It covers the same field as Rockhill (nos. 3061 and 3062) for a number of years, but more fully and completely, in that additional documents are included which were not available to Mr. Rockhill (has useful maps). H. F. MacNair, ed., *Modern Chinese history, selected readings; a collection of extracts from various sources chosen to illustrate some of the chief phases of China's international relations during the past hundred years* (Shanghai, 1923; 2d ed., 1927) **[3064]** does well for China's international relations what Robinson's well remembered *Readings* once did for European medieval and modern history.

MSS.: Suggestions

For official archives of the United States and the various European countries and of China and Japan, see below, Pt. II, ch. 3.

The archives of the Tokugawa family are said to be in the process of indexing. The location, preservation, indexing, calendaring, and publication of private archives in Japan for historical use has not developed to the degree of European practice.

In subsequent sections of this chapter are a few further suggestions for MSS., particularly private collections.

2. The 19th Century, to 1898

Bibliographical Aids

See Sec. 1, above.

Margaret Windeyer, " China and the Far East, 1889–99; contribution toward a bibliography ", *N.Y. state lib. bul.*, LIX (1901) (Bibliography 25) 563–679 [**3065**]. Griffin, *Chinese immigration* (no. 3024). Tien-lu Li, *Chinese immigration* (no. 3096), 126–132. Latourette (no. 3097), 145–200. Dennett (no. 3098), 695–703.

Special Works

Robert Tomes, " Perry's expedition to Japan ", *Harper's mag.*, XII (1856) 441–466, 733–756 [**3066**], " drawn from the most authentic sources ", evidently based on the official narrative of Perry's expedition (no. 3127). E. E. Hale, " Perry's expedition to Japan ", *No. Am. rev.*, LXXXIII (1860) 233–260 [**3067–8**], a review of the official narrative mentioned above. S. W. Williams, *Our relations with the Chinese empire* (San Francisco, 1877) [**3069**], Williams, originally a missionary, was successively secretary of the commission to China, to 1838, interpreter for Perry's expedition to Japan, 1853–54, secretary to the Legation of the United States in Japan, and seven times *chargé d'affaires.* J. M. Morrison, *Comprehensive statement of the circumstances surrounding the exaction of the Japanese indemnity* (Wash., 1880) [**3070**], favoring the return to Japan of the remainder of the Shimonoseki indemnity fund of 1864. G. F. Seward, *Chinese immigration in its social and economic aspects* (N.Y., 1881) [**3071**], by a former United States minister to Japan; one of the earliest temperate discussions, it is a plea for Chinese immigration, with exclusion (by cooperation with the Chinese

government) of contract labor and other undesirable elements.
J. B. Angell, "The diplomatic relations between the United States
and China", *Jour. soc. sci.*, XVII (1883) 24–36 [**3072**]. J. B. Angell
was one of three commissioners to negotiate the treaty of 1882; in
this work he emphasizes annoyance to the Chinese government of
features of inequality, summarized; a plea for moderate restriction
of Chinese immigration according to treaty provisions. J. K. Newton, *Obligations of the United States to initiate a revision of treaties
between the western powers and Japan* (Oberlin, O., 1887) [**3073**],
reprinted from *Bibliotheca sacra*, v. XLIV, Jan. 1887; it is an early
plea for revision on basis of modernization of Japan. G. H. Scid-
more, *Outline lectures on the history, organization, jurisdiction, and
practice of the ministerial and consular courts of the United States
of America in Japan* (Tokyo, 1887) [**3073a**], unique analysis of
the structure of American extraterritorial justice. Saburo Shimada,
Kaikoku shimatsu (Account of the opening of the ports) (Tokyo,
1888) [**3074**], a careful study from contemporary Japanese documents, principally from the family archives of Naosuke Ii; reproduces 8 letters of Naosuke Ii, official spokesman for the Shogunate
government, who is said to have been assassinated for having
urged the treaties. By the same author, *Life of Ii Naosuke* (Tokyo,
1888) [**3075**], see also nos. 3080 and 3093, for later biographies of
Ii. Three works by one of the foremost interpreters of Japanese-American historical contacts, who studied at Johns Hopkins,
1884–1887, in Herbert Baxter Adams' glorious seminar, now a professor in the University of Tokyo, a distinguished and well-balanced
Japanese authority on Japanese-American relations: Inazo Nitobé,
*The intercourse between the United States and Japan; a historical
sketch* (Baltimore, 1891) [**3076**], Hopkins Ph.D. thesis; though
founded largely on secondary accounts, it also makes use of letters
from individual Japanese and Americans who took part in these
earlier transactions of Japanese-American affairs. It is now superseded by Treat (nos. 3057 and 3113). See also, by Nitobé, *The Japanese nation; its land, its people, and its life; with special consideration to its relations with the United States* (N.Y. and London, 1912)
[**3077**] a fair-minded and distinguished Japanese historian's summary history of his country, with special reference to the influence of
American relations; a sobering background for present-day hot-
heads; and "American-Japanese intercourse prior to the advent of

Perry ", *Am. hist. assoc. ann. rep.*, for 1911, v. I (1913) 129–140
[**3078**]. Awa Katsu, *Kaikoku kigen* (Opening of the ports) (Tokyo,
1893, 3 v.) [**3078a**], diplomatic relations of the last period of
the Tokugawa era, 1830–68, based primarily on the Shogunate documents, and on memoirs of leading officials. Vi Kyuin Wellington
Koo, *The status of aliens in China* (N.Y., 1912) [**3079**], the doctoral
dissertation of a student later a leader in Chinese diplomacy. Henry
Satoh, *Agitated Japan. The life of Baron Ii Kamon-no-Kami
Naosuke*, based on the *Kaikoku shimatsu* of Shimada Saburo (Tokyo,
1896) [**3080**]. Kikutaro Kan, *Nichi-O kotsu kigen shi* (History
of the early intercourse between Japanese and Europeans) (Tokyo,
1897) [**3081**], based on documentary sources in the Imperial
Library of Tokyo, following official records of the Tokugawa, and
records of private families, supplemented by researches in American
and European archives. Little on American relations except early
expeditions of Nantucket whalers to Lew Chew waters. W. W.
Rockhill, "Diplomatic missions to the court of China; the Kotow
question ", *Am. hist. rev.*, II (1897) 427–442, 627–643 [**3082**], by an
eminent American diplomatist in the Far East, drawn from secondary accounts. *Kobe kaiko sanju-nen shi* (The thirty years since the
opening of Kobe harbor), ed. by the Committee for the Celebration
of the thirtieth anniversary of the opening of the harbor (Kobe,
1898, 2 v.) [**3083**], the first volume is concerned with the diplomatic
history of Japan, and emphasizes the importance of the American
expedition of 1853–54; it is based mainly on records of the Con-
troller of the Ports, and miscellaneous diaries. Charles Beresford,
The breakup of China (N.Y. and London, 1899) [**3084**], Beresford
contributed much to the ideology of the Open Door and the Anglo-
Japanese alliance. R. B. Hubbard, *The United States in the Far
East; or, Modern Japan and the Orient* (Richmond, 1899) [**3085**],
by the United States minister to Japan, 1885–1889; records negotiations of the Japanese-American treaty with bilateral immigration
clause, which President Harrison refused to send to the Senate.
J. M. Callahan, *American relations in the Pacific and Far East,
1784–1900* (Baltimore, 1901) [**3086**], based on printed American correspondence and well known secondary accounts; a pioneer monograph, now superseded by Dennett's more comprehensive work
(no. 3098). J. W. Foster, *American diplomacy in the Orient* (Boston and N.Y., 1903) [**3087**], for twenty years a standard, semi-

popular work by an eminent American diplomatist; it is now superseded by Dennett (no. 3098). W. E. Griffis, "Millard Fillmore and
his part in the opening of Japan ", *Buffalo hist. soc. pub.*, IX (1906)
53–79 [**3088**], an undocumented study, apparently based on such few
surviving Fillmore papers as remain in the Buffalo Historical Society. Kinnosuke Adachi, "The birth of the new Nippon",
Forum, XXXVIII (1906) 255–276 [**3089**], a stimulating and robust
review by a Japanese scholar of the significance to Japanese history
of the Perry (Shimoda) and Harris treaties. Yamaguchi Ken,
*Kinse Shiriaku. A history of Japan, from the visit of Commodore
Perry in 1853 to the capture of Hakodate by the Mikado's forces in
1869*, tr. from the Japanese by E. M. Satow; rev. ed., with supplementary notes by Shuziro Watanabe (Tokyo, 1906) [**3090**], a compact summary of the significant transformation of Japanese life from
1853, following the arrival of Perry's fleet, to 1869, by an official of
the Japanese foreign office under the administration of the Shoguns.
Henry Satoh, *Lord Hotta, the pioneer diplomat of Japan*, 2d ed.
(Tokyo, 1908) [**3091**], Hotta was the Shogun's minister who secured
the Mikado's consent to the Harris treaty, and who advocated diplomatic relations with foreign powers as the first step in eventual
Japanese hegemony over all nations. Mary R. Coolidge, *Chinese
immigration* (N.Y., 1909) [**3092**], the historical portion ends with
the fire in San Francisco in 1906. Shunkichi Akimoto, *Lord Ii
Naosuke and New Japan* (Translated and adapted by Shunkichi
Akimoto from the *Ii Tairo to kaiko* by Katsumaro Nakamura)
(Tokyo, 1909) [**3093**], Ii was spokesman for the Shogunate at the
time of the Perry mission. (See also nos. 3075 and 3080 for earlier
biographies of Ii Naosuke.) DuBois Patterson, "The great Japanese embassy of 1860, a forgotton chapter in the history of international amity and commerce and of the development of the Far East ",
Am. phil. soc. proc., XLIX (1910) 243–266 [**3094**], an undocumented
appraisal by an apparently informed person on the significance to
Japan of the information brought back from this epoch-making
embassy, which included American surgery, dentistry, and bank-
ing and postal systems. Paullin (no. 151) has important chapters on
early American relations with China, Japan, and Korea, based
largely on archives of the Navy Department. F. W. Williams,
Anson Burlingame and the first Chinese mission to foreign powers
(N.Y., 1912) [**3095**], careful study of a unique mission, based on

printed material, notably British and American diplomatic correspondence. Tien-lu Li, *Congressional policy of Chinese immigration; or, Legislation relating to Chinese immigration to the United
States* (Nashville, Tenn., 1916) [**3096**], history of Chinese immigration from about 1847, and giving particular consideration to treaties
and acts relating to Chinese immigration. K. S. Latourette, *The
history of early relations between the United States and China, 1784–
1844* (New Haven, 1917) [**3097**], "analytical, critical, and thoroughly documented account of trade and other relations ",[3] it utilized
the printed and unprinted American official sources, missionary records, trading ships' logs, but not Chinese sources. Morison, *Maritime history* (no. 1720). Tyler Dennett, *Americans in eastern
Asia; a critical study of the policy of the United States with
reference to China, Japan, and Korea in the 19th century* (N.Y.,
1922) [**3098**], a standard work, the best account of the subject,
based on the MS. archives of the Department of State and available printed sources. Some supplementary light is thrown by
Morse and MacNair (no. 3045), but on the other hand, Dennett
illumines Morse. Parts of the book have been presented in effect in
various scholarly reviews, 1921–1923. Among these is his " Seward's
Far Eastern policy ", *Am. hist. rev.*, XXVIII (1922) 45–62 [**3099**],
which stresses American " cooperation " with European powers in
the Far East as beginning with Seward. Hill, *Treaties* (no. 4794),
for the Perry and Harris treaties with Japan, 1854 and 1858. H. H.
Gowen, " The first Japanese mission to America ", *Wash. hist. quar.*,
XVI (1925) 8–16 [**3100**], mission in 1860 to exchange ratification of
the commercial treaty of 1858, as drawn from a Japanese work, entitled (in translation) *An illustrated account of the first Japanese
embassy to the United States, sent out in the year of Manen (1860).*
Takeshi Osatake, *Kokusaiho yori mitaru bakumatsu gaiko monogatari* (Diplomacy of the last years of the Tokugawa era from the
viewpoint of international law) (Tokyo, 1926) [**3100a**]. Sakuzo
Yoshino, ed., *Meiji bunka zenshu* (Cyclopedia of the Meiji civilization) (Tokyo, 1928–30, 24 v.) [**3101**], vol. VI deals with diplomatic
relations and foreign affairs, and includes an extended bibliography
of diplomatic sources, a chronology, diplomatic documents such as
speoial reports of the early missions sent to America, and prob-

---

[3] *Guide hist. lit.* (no. 4634), U, 2505b.

lems of mixed residence in the interior of Japan. A. E. Cook and J. J. Hagerty, *Immigration laws of the United States* (Chicago, 1929) [**3102**], a standard treatise which has a section on Chinese immigration laws. Jintaro Fujii, *Meiji ishin-shi kowa* (Lectures on the restoration of the Meiji era) (Tokyo, 1929, 5th ed.) [**3103**] contains sections dealing with foreign relations, with special emphasis on the social and economic background which led to the opening of the ports in Japan. Two studies by H. J. Noble: " The Korean mission to the United States in 1883 ", *Transactions of the Korea branch of the Royal Asiatic Society*, XVIII (1929) 1–27 [**3104**], as revealed in printed sources in the United States; and " The United States and Sino-Korean relations, 1885–1887 ", *Pacific hist. rev.*, II (1933) 292–304 [**3105**], a printed digest of the author's MS. thesis in the University of California; uses U.S. legation archives at Seoul. Rudolph Said-Ruete, " Relations of Said Bin Sultan with the United States of America ", *Essex inst. hist. coll.*, LXV (1929) 363–368 [**3106**], the official mission to Muscat, in 1833, of the American agent, Edmund Roberts, for the negotiation of a treaty of amity and commerce. F. C. Jones, *Extraterritoriality in Japan, and the diplomatic relations resulting in its abolition, 1853–1899* (New Haven, 1931) [**3106a**], a useful résumé which by no means exhausts the possibilities of the subject. T. F. Tsiang, " The extension of equal commercial privileges to other nations than the British after the treaty of Nanking ", *Chinese soc. and pol. sci. rev.*, XV (1931) 422–444 [**3107**] contains references and documents regarding Sino-American relations, based on the Chinese archival collection, the Palace Museum documents, *The beginning and end of the management of barbarian affairs* (no. 5446). Three studies by P. H. Clyde: " The China policy of J. Ross Browne, American minister at Peking, 1868–1869 ", *Pacific hist. rev.*, I, no. 3 (1932) 312–323 [**3108**], a new appraisal of the positive " cooperative " policy advocated by Burlingame's successor at Peking, based on State Department archives and published sources; and by the same writer, " Frederick F. Low and the Tientsin massacre ", *ibid.*, II, no. 1 (1933) 100–108 [**3109**], a sequel to the above; and " Attitudes and policies of George F. Seward, American minister at Peking, 1876–1880; some papers of the cooperative policy ", *ibid.*, II (1933) 387–404 [**3110**], the career in China of a minor American diplomatic personality, most carefully worked out from State Department records. Thomas

Kearny, " Commodore Lawrence Kearny and the open door and most favored nation policy in China in 1842 to 1843 ", *N. J. hist. soc. proc.*, n.s., L (1932) 162–190 **[3111]**, based on newly discovered Chinese documents, from which numerous quotations are made; and by the same author, " The Tsiang documents; Elipoo, Ke-ying, Pottinger, and Kearny and the most favored nation and open door policy in China in 1842–1844; an American viewpoint ", *Chinese soc. and pol. sci. rev.*, XVI (1932) 75–104 **[3112]**. P. J. Treat, *Diplomatic relations between the United States and Japan, 1853–1895* (Stanford University, Calif., 1932, 2 v.) **[3113]**, a reprint of the author's earlier study, *The early diplomatic relations between the United States and Japan, 1853–1865* (Baltimore, 1917), and an elaboration of his *Japan and the United States, 1853–1921, revised and continued to 1928* (Stanford University, Calif., 1928), a treatise on the same subject. It rests on an intensive study of the printed British and American state papers and the MS. archives of the Department of State; the private correspondence of R. H. Pruyn (minister of the United States to Japan, 1862–65) and of E. T. Sheppard (legal adviser to the Japanese ministry of foreign affairs, 1877–80), and a MS. doctoral thesis by H. J. Noble, *Korea and her relations with the United States before 1895*, submitted at Stanford University, 1931. Apparently the Japanese foreign archives, the necessary complement to those of the Department of State, have not been accessible to this, nor to any other historian of Japanese-American relations. For a translation of the volume on *Japan and the United States, 1853–1921* (Boston, 1921), by a professor of Western history in the Imperial University of Tokyo, see Kengo Murakawa, *Nichi-bei gaikoshi, 1853–1921* (Tokyo 1922) **[3114]**. Another study by Professor Treat is " The good offices of the United States during the Sino-Japanese war ", *Pol. sci. quar.*, XLVII (1932) 547–575 **[3115–6]**, based upon unpublished despatches from the United States minister at Tokyo (Edwin Dun), 1894. Ping-chia Kuo, " Caleb Cushing and the treaty of Wanghia, 1844 ", *Jour. mod. hist.*, V (1933) 34–54 **[3117]** has utilized the Chinese source *Ch'-ou pan yi-wu shih-mo* (The beginning and end of the management of barbarian affairs) (no. 5446), together with other printed sources, and Dennett (no. 3098). Reynoso, *Reminiscences* (no. 3479), for note regarding Japan and the Philippines in 1898. Stolberg-Wernigerode, *Deutschland u. Vereinigten Staaten* (no.

4314). E. H. Pritchard, "The struggle for control of the China trade during the eighteenth century", *Pacific hist. rev.*, III (1934) 280–296 [**3118**], the author studiously presents illuminating comparative statistics of the volume of trade of various nations, including the United States, to Canton. F. E. Ross, "The American naval attack on Shimonoseki in 1863", *Chinese soc. and pol. sci. rev.*, XVIII (1934) 146–155 [**3118a**] is based on United States official documents.

The following is a Japanese work of which we have been unable to find the place and date of publication: Count Shigenobu Okuma, *Kaikoku taise-shi* (Events leading up to the opening of Japan to foreign intercourse) [**3119**], a narrative of diplomatic history, based on source material; special emphasis on relations with the United States.

For biographies of American presidents, secretaries of state, and diplomatists to the Far East (for names and tenure, see latest Register of the Dept. of State (no. 5122)), see the relevant entries and bibliographical data in the *D.A.B.* There is a "Table of presidents, secretaries of state, and of diplomatic representatives in China, Japan, and Korea, 1842–1900", in Dennett (no. 3098), 705–707.

For biographical notes regarding Japanese members of the Iwakura embassy to the United States in 1871, see *Meiji restoration* (no. 3159), 351–388.

The biographies of individual Chinese and Japanese statesmen who had to do with relations with the United States have been cited above, as far as have been found. See also *A Chinese biographical dictionary*, by Herbert A. Giles (London and Shanghai, 1898) [**3120**] for an account of Sun Chia-ku (also called Chin Shih), co-envoy with Burlingame on a friendly mission to foreign countries in 1869. The Division of Orientalia of the Library of Congress has undertaken, for a limited period, the compilation of selected biographies of eminent Chinese of the past three centuries. This is to be in English, for Western use, primarily. For biographies of Chinese statesmen, in Chinese, see the biographical section of the "Draft history of the Ch'ing dynasty" (Ch'ing-shih lieh-chüan (no. 4981)).

Printed sources

For general collections, see Sec. 1, above. Note particularly Hasse (no. 5344) for index to United States public documents, to 1861. Dennett (no. 3098) lists United States government publications (congressional documents, etc.) and British parliamentary papers, dealing with the Far East in the 19th century. There is a complete list of printed U. S. public documents and British Parliamentary papers dealing with Japanese affairs in Treat (no. 3113). For comprehensive list of reports of debates in the *Congressional Record*, 1875–1902, and the Congressional documents, 1870–1902, dealing with Chinese immigration, see Griffin (no. 3024); for briefer list (continuing to 1911, see Tien-lu Li (no. 3096). Later documents are: *Compilation from the records of the Bureau of Immigration of facts concerning the enforcement of the Chinese exclusion laws* (Wash., 1906) [**3121**]; *Laws, treaty, and regulations relating to the exclusion of the Chinese* (Wash., 1909) [**3122**]; and *Treaty laws, and rules governing the admission of Chinese* (Wash., 1917) [**3123**], all three documents published by the Bureau of Immigration of the Department of Labor.

Edmund Roberts, *Embassy to the eastern courts of Cochin-China, Siam, and Muscat; in the sloop of war Peacock, . . . 1832–3–4* (N.Y., 1837) [**3124**]. *The journals of Major Samuel Shaw, the first American consul at Canton* (Boston, 1847) [**3125**]. *Imprisoned American seamen. Letter from the Secretary of the Navy, transmitting correspondence relative to the visit of the " Preble " to the port of Nagasacki, for the purpose of demanding imprisoned American seamen, Aug. 28, 1850* (Wash., 1850) (51st Cong., 1st Sess. House. Ex. Doc. 84) [**3126**], published by the Navy Department. *Narrative of the expedition of a squadron to the China seas and Japan, performed in the years 1852, 1853, and 1854, under the command of Commodore M. C. Perry, United States Navy, by order of the Government of the United States*, comp. from the original notes and journals of Commodore Perry and his officers, at his request, and under his supervision, by F. L. Hawks (Wash., 1856) [**3127**], published by the Navy Department. *Memorial of Townsend Harris, praying compensation for diplomatic services in negotiating a treaty with the Kingdom of Siam, while consul general at Japan, Feb. 27, 1857* (Wash.: Govt. Print. Off., 1857) [**3128**] gives details concerning his appointment as consul general to Japan, and of his arrival there. Also by Townsend Harris, " Consul Harris in Japan ", *Littell's Living age*, 3d ser., IV (v. LX of whole series) (1859) 567–574 [**3129**], letters of July 3 and 6, 1858, which were written to an unnamed friend, and " were not intended for the public eye."

See also Harris' *Journal* (no. 3156). A. H. Palmer, *Documents and facts illustrating the origin of the mission to Japan, authorized by the Government of the United States, May 10th, 1851; and which finally resulted in the treaty concluded by Commodore M. C. Perry, . . . 1854* (Wash., 1857) [**3130**], to which is appended a "list of the memoirs, &c., prepared and submitted to the Hon. John P. Kennedy, late secretary of the navy, by his order ". A. H. Foote, " Visit to Simoda and Hakodadi in Japan ", *Journal of the North China branch of the Royal Asiatic Society,* I (1858) 129–137 [**3131**], extract from a letter from Capt. A. H. Foote, U.S. ship Portsmouth, Sept. 15, 1857. Three journals by S. W. Williams: " Narrative of the American embassy to Peking ", *ibid.*, I, no. 3 (1859) 315–349 [**3132**], Williams, originally a missionary, was one of the secretaries to the famous embassy of 1844, and later served as interpreter for Commodore Perry. Also "A journal of the Perry expedition to Japan (1853–1854)", ed. by his son, F. W. Williams, *Transactions of the Asiatic Society of Japan,* XXXVII, pt. 2 (1910) 1–259 [**3133**]; and " The journal of S. Wells Williams, LL.D., secretary and interpreter of the American embassy to China during the expedition to Tientsin and Peking in the years 1858 and 1859 ", ed. by his son, Frederick Wells Williams, *Journal of the North China branch of the Royal Asiatic Society,* XLII (1911) 3–232 [**3134**]. J. D. Johnston, *China and Japan; being a narrative of the cruise of the U.S. steam-frigate Powhatan, in the years 1857, '58, and '60. Including an account of the Japanese embassy to the United States* (Phila. and Baltimore, 1860) [**3135**]. G. A. Matil, "ĪAaponskoe posol'sto v Soedinennykh Shtatakh v 1860 godu " (The Japanese mission in the United States in 1860), *Russkiĭ Vĭestnik* (Russian messenger), XXIX (1860) 3–25 [**3136**], a letter from New York, Aug. 24, 1860. G. F. Seward, *The United States consulates in China; a letter with enclosures of the consul-general in China to the Secretary of State* (Wash., Printed for private circulation, 1867) [**3137**], a letter of G. F. Seward to W. H. Seward, Secretary of State, July 31, 1867, with 33 enclosures, 1844–67, dealing with affairs of United States consulates in China. R. J. Hinton, "A talk with Mr. Burlingame about China ", *Galaxy,* VI (1868) 613–623 [**3138**], an expanded interview during his celebrated mission to America. *Addresses presented by the American and British communities of Shanghai to the Hon. J. Ross Browne, United States minister at Peking, and His Excellency's reply*

(Shanghai, 1869) [**3139**]. *Memorials on the revision of the treaty of Tientsin, forwarded to the governments of Great Britain and the United States by private residents in China*, reprinted from the *Supreme Court and Consular Gazette* (Shanghai, 1869) [**3140**]. Sir Rutherford Alcock, " Chinese statesmen, and state papers ", *Fraser's mag.*, LXXXIII (n.s., III) (1871) 328–342, 503–514, 613–628 [**3141**] gives a survey of the foreign office and conduct of foreign affairs, and data as to the prevailing opinions of the chief officers as they appear in a succession of state papers not originally meant to be seen by foreigners. The *Annual report of the Secretary of the Navy . . . for the year 1871* (Wash., 1871) [**3141a**] prints (p. 275–313) the report of Rear-Admiral John Rodgers on the expedition of F. F. Low, American minister to China, to secure a treaty with Korea which resulted in naval operations in May 1871. Thomas Walsh, *A letter addressed to the President of the United States on the existing diplomatic relations with Japan* (N.Y., 1871) [**3142**], a plea for more effective diplomatic representation in Japan lest rival commercial nations get the better of the United States. Johannes von Gumpach, *The Burlingame mission; a political disclosure, supported by official documents, mostly unpublished* (Shanghai, 1872; also London and N.Y.) [**3143**], to prove the mission a plot in support of the pretentions of the Emperor of China, a barbarous country not to be treated with on terms of equality, against the sovereign dignity and rights of the states of the western world. *Reports and official letters to the Kaitakushi by Horace Capron, commissioner and adviser, and his foreign assistants* (Tokyo, 1875) [**3144**]. Kunitake Kume, *Tokumei zenken-taishi Bei-o kwairan jikki* (Tokyo, 1878) [**3145**], account of the trip to the United States and Europe of the Iwakura mission. "Account of the first attempt of the United States to open communication with Japan ", *Mass. hist. soc. proc.*, 2d ser., II (1886) 258–261 [**3146**], anonymous letter, written by the purser of the U.S. steamer "Susquehanna ", Japan, July 14, 1853. W. Wyke and H. Keuchenis, *State papers of the Kingdom of Siam, 1664–1886*, comp. by the Siamese legation in Paris, by order of H. H. Prince Presdang (London, 1886) [**3147**]. Prince Hirobumi Ito, *A maker of new Japan; Marquis Ito's experience* (Nagasaki, 1904) [**3148**], career of a Japanese statesman who had much to do with the shaping of foreign policy. Taichi Tanabe, *Bakumatsu*

gaiko dan (Diplomacy of the Restoration period) (Tokyo? 1898)
[**3148a**], review of Japan's diplomatic relations during the last
years of the Tokugawa period, written by one who had personal
experience in international affairs as a high official of the Shogunate. *Dai-Nihon shiseki kyokai sosho* (Collected works, edited
by the Historical Association of Japan) (Tokyo, 1915, 143 v.)
[**3149**], one section, *Bakumatsu*, consists mainly of the private
papers of public men and others of eminence during the Restoration period, roughly 1840–1870, which have been kept in private archives. They include sources for the diplomatic history
of Japan, including its opening to foreign intercourse. Masanori
Muragaki, ed., *Manen gannen daiichi ken Bei shisetsu nikki* (Tokyo,
1918) [**3150**], diary of the Japanese mission to the United States
in 1860. America-Japan Society, *The first Japanese embassy to
the United States of America, sent to Washington in 1860 as the
first of the series of embassies sent abroad by the Tokugawa Shogunate* (Tokyo, 1920) [**3151**], compiled by C. Shibama; it includes
the diary of the first Japanese embassy to the United States written
by Murugaki Awajino-Kami, vice-ambassador, tr. by Shigehiko
Miyoshi, "The Japanese embassy as seen by Lieut. J. Johnston,
U.S.N.", and news items from American newspapers issued 60 years
ago. Tyler Dennett, ed., "American choices in the Far East in
1882 ", *Am. hist. rev.*, XXX (1924) 84–108 [**3152**] prints a despatch
of Oct. 2, 1882, from John Russell Young, American minister at
Peking (with enclosures) which proposes to induce the Japanese
to revise their treaty of 1876 with Korea conformably to the treaty
of 1882 with Korea, just signed by the United States. *Chung-hsi
chiao-t'ung shih-liao* (no. 5443). Munemitsu Mutsu, *Kenken roku*
(Memoirs) (Tokyo, 1929) [**3153**], important for the study of Japanese diplomatic relations between 1890 and 1910. T. F. Tsiang, ed.,
" China after the victory of Taku, June 25, 1859 ", *Am. hist. rev.*,
XXXV (1929) 79–84 [**3154**], 3 documents from a collection belonging to Mr. Wang Hsi-yun of Peking; they throw light on China's
attitude to J. E. Ward, American minister to China, and to America's participation in the fight at Taku. *Gaiko hen* [Diplomatic
matters] (Tokyo, 1930) (*Meiji bunka zens-hu* [Cyclopaedia of the
Meiji civilization] VI) [**3155**], documents dealing with Japanese
diplomatic relations, 1872–1893; contains a short bibliography (p.

563–572) on Japanese foreign relations. Townsend Harris, *The complete journal of Townsend Harris, first American consul general and minister to Japan*, introduction and notes by M. E. Cosenza (N.Y., 1930) **[3156]**, the earlier portion of the *Journal*, which includes his mission to Siam, is here published for the first time; the text of the Japanese portion is now for the first time given to the public in its full and complete form. W. F. Sands, *Undiplomatic memories* (N.Y., 1930) **[3157]**, the author, a member of the American diplomatic service, was personal adviser to the Emperor of Korea, 1896–1904. Osuke Hibata, *Beikoku shisetsu Perry teitoku raicho zui* (Tokyo, 1931) **[3158]**, a picture scroll of Commodore Perry's arrival in Yokohama in 1854, published by the artist's grandson. *Leaders of the Meiji restoration in America* (Tokyo, 1931) **[3159]**, an annotated translation, by Y. Okamura, of a volume published in Japanese in 1872, of which Charles Lanman, then American secretary of the Japanese legation in Washington was editor. It was published to give an account of the Iwakura embassy of 1871, to print a collection of essays written by the Japanese students then residing in the United States, and to publish a brief work on America compiled by Arinori Mori, then Japanese *chargé-d'affaires* at Washington.

The following are Japanese works of which we have been unable to find the place and date of publication: *Iwakura ko ikko ho-Bei shimatsu sho* [Report of the American visit of the Iwakura mission in 1871] **[3160]**. Takayoshi Kido, *Nikki* [Diary] (Tokyo, date?) **[3161]**, a diary of his visit to America and Europe in 1871.

For the printed writings of American presidents, secretaries of state, and diplomatists to the Far East (for names and tenure, see latest *Register* of the Dept. of State (no. 5122)), see our list on p. 756.

MSS.: Suggestions

See Section 1, above, for official archives.

C. O. Paullin (no. 151) has indicated valuable MS. collections (Shufeldt papers regarding Korea, and Hull-Biddle papers) in the archives of the Navy Department, which has also the original of Perry's official narrative (printed, no. 3127). The Library of Congress has photocopies from the *Rijksarchief* at The Hague of the reports of the Dutch factors in Japan concerning Perry's mission.

For the private collections of American presidents, secretaries of state, and diplomatists (Edmund Roberts, envoy to Zanzibar, Siam, Muscat; Caleb Cushing, minister to China, 1843–45; A. H. Everett, commissioner to China, 1845–47; T. A. R. Nelson, commissioner to China, 1851–52; W. B. Reed, minister to China, 1857–59; B. P. Avery, minister to China, 1874–76; John Russell Young, minister to China, 1882–84; and Townsend Harris, minister to Japan, 1859–61), see our lists on pp. 862–883.

Concerning the Perry expedition, the Library of Congress has the journals of J. G. Sproston and E. Y. McCauley, who were with Perry; and a volume of copy in Japanese character, made in 1885, from the original in the Japanese foreign office; also letters of S. W. Williams (see next paragraph).

Other collections: Papers, 1872–79, of E. T. Sheppard (special agent, 1868, of the Treasury Department in China, and legal adviser to the Japanese Government, 1877–80) in the Library of Congress, including a number of letters from S. Wells Williams (originally a missionary, successively secretary of the commission to China, to 1838, interpreter for Perry's expedition, 1853–54, secretary of the legation of the United States in Japan, and seven times *chargé d'affaires*. The papers of G. C. Foulk, naval attaché at the United States legation in Korea, in 1884, and of H. N. Allen, United States minister to Korea, 1897–1901, are in the New York Public Library. The papers of C. W. LeGendre, American consul at Amoy, China, 1866–72, from 1872 to 1875, foreign adviser to the Japanese Government, and from 1890 to 1899, vice-president of the Korean Home Office and adviser to the household department of the King of Korea, are in the Library of Congress. The papers of Rounseville Wildman, U. S. consul at Hong Kong, 1898–1900, are in the same library. The papers of Frederick Tudor, the " Ice King ", in the library of the Harvard School of Business Administration are mainly of economic interest, reflecting the advent of the Yankee ice trade to the Far East in the early and middle 19th century. The papers and memorials of Gen. F. T. Ward, a Salem, Mass., merchant in China, 1860–62, who took an active part in affairs of that country (particularly the Taiping rebellion) and at the time of the " Trent " affair laid plans to seize British ships in Chinese waters, are in the Essex Institute at Salem, Mass. This same Institute contains also papers of other Salem merchants trading in China in the 19th century, which should yield sidelights on international affairs.

Persistent inquiries directed to descendants and family relations of American agents to China, whose papers are not yet recorded, ought to turn up much more material. Latourette (no. 3097) lists MS. logs, ship accounts, bills of lading, and kindred documents of early American ships and trade to China.

3. The Open Door and Boxer Rebellion

Bibliographical Aids

For general aids, see Sec. 1, above. Note also the bibliographies in Clements (no. 3162), En-tsung Yen (no. 3208), and Steiger (no. 3164).

Special Works

Beresford, *Breakup* (no. 3084). P. H. Clements, *Boxer rebellion; a political and diplomatic review* (N.Y., 1915) [**3162**], a useful work (Columbia Ph.D. thesis) based on printed British and American state papers, with less attention to significant secondary accounts. Bau, *Open Door* (no. 3207). En-tsung Yen, *Open Door* (no. 3208). Hsia Chin-lin, *Studies in Chinese diplomatic history* (Shanghai, 1925) [**3163**], a doctoral thesis (University of Edinburgh), presenting the Chinese view of salient factors in the relations of China with the foreign powers since 1895, with special relation to questions submitted by China to the Paris Peace Conference. Blakeslee, *For. policy* (no. 4122) has a section on " Cooperation in the Far East: the Open Door and the Washington conference." Morey, *Dipl. episodes* (no. 552a), ch. 4: " The diplomacy of European Powers in the Far East: the threatened partition of China." G. M. Steiger, *China and the Orient; the origin and development of the Boxer movement* (New Haven, 1927) [**3164**], a careful description of an epochal event in Far Eastern history, the Boxer revolt, with emphasis rather on the humiliating consequences for China than any new contributions to the history of diplomacy. Dennis, *Adventures* (no. 2224). R. S. McCordock, *British Far Eastern policy, 1894–1900* (N.Y., 1931) [**3165**], a Columbia University doctoral thesis which stresses the interrelationship of British, American, and Asiatic affairs, particularly in the enunciation of the Open Door policy; but is inadequate if only because it does not go back of printed material.

For biographies of American presidents, secretaries of state, and diplomatists abroad (for names and tenure, see latest *Register* of the Dept. of State (no. 5122)), see the relevant entries and bibliographical data in the *D.A.B.* Note also Tyler Dennett's *John Hay* (no. 2472).

Note also the biographies of Li Hung Chang:[4] Mrs. Archibald Little (Alicia B.), *Li Hung Chang; his life and times* (London, 1903) [3167]; and J. O. P. Bland, *Li Hung-Chang* (N.Y., 1917) [3168].

Printed Sources

For general collections, see Sec. 1, above. See also Sec. 2, above.

Clements (no. 3162) prints a list of official publications of China, France, Great Britain, and the United States. Note particularly, *Affairs in China. Report of William W. Rockhill, late commissioner to China, with accompanying documents* (Wash., 1902) (57th Cong., 1st sess. House. Doc. no. 1) [3169], also published in *Foreign relations* (no. 5345) for 1901.

The British Parliamentary Papers (" Blue Books "), 18 in number, dealing with the Boxer affair are listed in Clements (no. 3162). The *British documents on the origins of the war* (no. 5475), v. II (1927) contains only a brief note (p. 58–59) in regard to the Boxer movement.

The French *Documents diplomatiques*, published by the " Ministère des Affaires Étrangères ", are: *Chine* (Paris, 1900), journal of the siege of Pekin; *Chine, 1898–1899* (Paris, 1900); *Chine, 1900–1901*, and *Chine, juin-octobre 1901* (Paris, 1901); *Évacuation de Shanghai, 1900–1903* (Paris, 1903); and *Affaires de Chine; négociations de Pékin, 1900–1902*, issued by the Pekin foreign representatives [3170]. See also *Documents diplomatiques français* (no. 5474), 2e sér., t. II (Paris, 1931), for Far Eastern affairs, 1900–1901, including some discussion of American policy and sentiment.

German Foreign Office documents for the Boxer period, beginning in May 1900 and continuing down to the evacuation of Shanghai in 1902, are found in the *Grosse Politik* (no. 5476), XVI. Bd.: *Die Chinawirren und die Mächte, 1900–2* (1924) [3171].

" Documents relating to the integrity of China and the " Open Door ", *Am. jour. internat. law*, suppl., v. I (1907) 378–398 [3172]

---

[4] Beware the *Memoirs of Li Hung Chang;* ed. by W. F. Mannix (Boston and N.Y., 1913) [3166], considered by specialists to be a literary forgery.

consist of six key documents, 1895–1907. *Indiscreet letters from Peking; being the notes of an eyewitness, which set forth in some detail, from day to day, the real story of the siege and sack of a distressed capital in 1900*, ed. by B. L. Putnam-Weale [*pseud.* for B. L. Simpson] (N.Y., 1907) **[3173]**. Eckardstein, *Lebenserinnerungen* (no. 2365) for international rivalries in China during the Boxer affair. Count von Waldersee's *Denkwürdigkeiten* (Stuttgart, 1923) **[3174]**, the reminiscenses of the commander in chief of the international forces in China; also published in English translation, *A field marshal's memoirs; from the diary, correspondence, and reminiscences of Alfred, Count von Waldersee, . . . commander in chief of the allied forces in China, 1900–1901*, tr. by Frederic Whyte (London, 1924). Nevins, *Henry White* (no. 2468). A. T. Mahan, *The problem of Asia* (Boston, 1900) **[3174a]** presents orthodox American expansionist views grown shaky with time.

For the printed writings of American presidents, secretaries of state, and diplomatists abroad (for names and tenure, see the latest *Register* of the Dept. of State (no. 5122)), see our list on p. 756.

MSS.: Suggestions

See Sec. 1, above, for official archives, and our lists (pages 862, 865, and 868) for papers of presidents (McKinley, Roosevelt), secretaries of state (Sherman, Day, Hay), also of Henry White. MSS. of official and unofficial participants in the Boxer troubles have not yet gotten into historical registry; and still must be ferreted out by the investigator. The archives of the American Board of Commissioners for Foreign Missions, at Boston, and other missionary groups, should be worth examination.

4. The Anglo-Japanese Alliance and Russo-Japanese War

Bibliographical Aids

See Sec. 1, above.

Special Works

Four books by B. L. Putnam-Weale (*pseud.*), the author, Bertram Lenox Simpson, has been a journalist and public servant for the Chinese government for many years. His books have the value of acute knowledge and intimacy with Far Eastern questions, concerning which he feels it his duty to warn the world against Japan:

Manchu and Muscovite; being letters from Manchuria written during the autumn of 1903 (London and N.Y., 1904) [3175]; *The reshaping of the Far East* (N.Y., 1905, 2 v.) [3176]; *The truce in the East and its aftermath; being the sequel to " The re-shaping of the Far East "* (N.Y. and London, 1907) [3177]; and *The coming struggle in eastern Asia* (London, 1908) [3178]. A. S. Hershey, *The international law and diplomacy of the Russo-Japanese war* (N.Y. 1906) [3179] has a chapter on " The relations of England and the United States as affected by the Far Eastern question and the war." He believes Anglo-American relations bettered by common problems in the Far East, even by the Anglo-Japanese alliance. E. J. Dillon, *The eclipse of Russia* (London, 1918) [3180], a vivid account of Czardom by a remarkable English journalist who was an intimate friend to Count Witte and had access to his papers. Dillon played a large part in the activities of the Russian delegation at Portsmouth. George Kennan, *E. H. Harriman; a biography* (Boston and N.Y., 1922, 2 v.) [3181], a defense of Harriman's career and his railway projects in Manchuria. A. L. P. Dennis, *The Anglo-Japanese alliance* (Berkeley, Calif., 1923) [3182], a careful analysis, especially of the American implications; also his *Adventures* (no. 2224). Tyler Dennett, *Roosevelt and the Russo-Japanese war; a critical study of American policy in Eastern Asia in 1902–5, based primarily upon the private papers of Theodore Roosevelt* (Garden City, N.Y., 1925) [3183], a very important work which had the advantage of use of the Roosevelt papers and MS. archives of the Department of State. It published the confidential Taft-Katsura " agreed memorandum " from the Roosevelt papers. Lord Newton, *Lord Lansdowne* (no. 2484). *Deutschland und die Mächte vor dem Krieg in amtlichen Schriften des Fürsten Bernhard von Bülow ohne seine Mitwirkung herausgegeben von einem Ungenannten* (Dresden, 1929, 2 v.) [3184] reveals important contacts of German embassy with Roosevelt, emphasizing his predisposition to see Japan control Korea and his anti-Russian attitude. Chung-fu Chang, *The Anglo-Japanese alliance* (Baltimore, 1931) [3185], professing to supplement Dennis' work (no. 3182) with subsequently available information, studies the alliance as a groundwork for Japan's aggressive ambitions in Asia.

There is a list of contemporary magazine and periodical articles in the bibliography in Dennett (no. 3183).

Printed Sources

For treaties, state papers, and published diplomatic correspondence of the several governments (United States, Great Britain, China, and Japan), see Sec. 1, above, and the notes in Dennett (no. 3183). The texts of the Anglo-Japanese alliances and relevant documents are reprinted by Dennis (no. 3182) from MacMurray's fundamental collection. There is a valuable note describing the published documents and sources covering nearly all phases of the discussions and issues of the Portsmouth Peace Conference in Dennett (no. 3183), 243-244; the same work also prints " all the important documents relative to Roosevelt's intervention ", p. 265-277.

For British documentary material, see *Brit. docs. on origins of the war* (no. 5475), v. II: *The Anglo-Japanese alliance and the Franco-British entente*, and v. IV: *The Anglo-Russian rapprochement. 1903-7* (Ch. 23 describes the British contribution to the mediation of President Roosevelt).

For German documentary material, see the *Grosse Politik* (no. 5476), XIX: *Der russisch-japanisch Krieg*, ch. 130: " Die Lokalisierung des Krieges—A. Deutschland-America und die Lokalisierung in Fernen Osten "; and ch. 139: " Deutschlands und Amerikas zusammengehen während des Krieges. Der Friedensschluss." These are reprinted in the English edition, ed. by E. T. S. Dugdale (no. 5477), v. III.

Useful Russian collections of state papers are: Russia, Mīnīsterstvo inostrannykh dîel (Russia, Ministry of Foreign Affairs), *Sbornīk dogovorov ī dīplomatīcheskīkh dokumentov po dîelam Dal'nîago Vostoka, 1895-1905* [Collection of treaties and diplomatic documents concerning the Far East] (St. Petersburg, 1906) **[3186]** includes not only Russian documents, but those of France, Germany, Great Britain, and the United States as well, printed in Russian and in the language of the particular country concerned; and E. D. Grimm, ed., *Sbornīk dogovorov ī drugīkh dokumentov po īstorīī mezhdunarodnykh otnoshenīī na Dal'nem Vostokîe* [Collection of treaties and other documents concerning the history of international relations in the Far East] (Moscow, 1927) **[3186a]** covering the period 1842 to 1925. It is a publication of the Institute for the Study of the Far East, created and controlled by the Soviet Government.

The secret memoirs of Count Tadasu Hayashi, ed. by A. M. Pooley (N.Y. and London, 1915) **[3187]**, a translation of such material as this Japanese diplomatist thought desirable to leave for publication. Has illuminating passages on the real purpose, for Japan, of the Anglo-Japanese alliance. J. J. Korostovetz (Ivan I. Korostovetz), *Pre-war diplomacy, the Russo-Japanese problem, treaty signed at Portsmouth, U.S.A., 1905; diary of J. J. Korostovetz* (London, 1920) [3188], the diarist was secretary and interpreter to Count Witte. M. E. Stone, *Fifty years a journalist* (Garden City, N.Y., 1921) [3189], p. 284-296: "The Portsmouth conference". Count Witte, *The memoirs of Count Witte;* translated from the original Russian manuscript and edited by Abraham Yarmolinsky (Garden City, N.Y., 1921) [3190], memoirs of the Russian plenipotentiary at the Russo-Japanese peace conference. Baron Rosen, *Diplomacy* (no. 4363), reminiscences of the Russian ambassador to the United States, 1905-1911; describe the Portsmouth conference. "Kaneko in America", *Living age*, 8th ser., XXXIV (1924) 179-185 [3191], summary of a confidential report of Viscount Kaneko's mission to America during the Russo-Japanese war, slightly revised from an English translation in the *Japan weekly chronicle*, May 1 and 8, 1924. *Letters of Sir Cecil Spring Rice* (no. 4439) include a number of letters regarding President Roosevelt's intervention in the Russo-Japanese war. Atsushi Hiratsuka, *Ito Hirobumi hiroku* (Tokyo, 1931) [3192] publishes the confidential papers of Prince Ito, throwing important light upon Japan's diplomacy and foreign policy from the beginning of the new regime to 1910. Described in detail in K. K. Kawakami's review in *Foreign affairs*, XI (1933) 490-500.

MSS.: Suggestions

See Section 1, above, for official archives; but we are now beyond the date after which governments (except the United States) allow their archives to be consulted.

For papers of President Roosevelt, and Secretaries of State Hay and Root, see our lists: presidents, p. 862; secretaries of state, p. 865.

5. China and The Powers, 1901-1914

Bibliographical Aids

See Sec. 1, above.

Carnegie Endowment for International Peace, Library, *Exterritoriality, with special reference to China* (Wash., 1927) (*Its* Reading List no. 9) [3193], M. Alice Matthews, librarian.

Special Works

Hershey, *U.S. and Eng., and Far East* (no. 3007). Three works by T. F. Millard, who dwelt long in the Far East and has an anti-Japanese tendency that used to be considered unduly alarming: *The new Far East; an examination into the new position of Japan, and her influence upon the solution of the Far Eastern question, with special reference to the interests of America and the future of the Chinese empire* (N.Y., 1906) [**3194**]; *America and the Far Eastern question; an examination of modern phases of the Far Eastern question, including the new activities and policy of Japan, the situation of China, and the relation of the United States of America to the problems involved* (N.Y., 1909) [**3195**]; *Our Eastern question; America's contact with the Orient and the trend of relations with China and Japan* (N.Y., 1916) [**3196**]. G. H. Blakeslee, ed., *China and the Far East* (N.Y., 1910) [**3197**], a symposium of papers by "experts", delivered at a conference at Clark University, touching leading political subjects of Far Eastern affairs at that time. S. K. Hornbeck, *Contemporary politics in the Far East* (N.Y., 1916) [**3198**], an unusually realistic and critical analysis by an American teacher who had much experience in China and who has since become chief of the division of Far Eastern Affairs in the Department of State. Ching Wen-sze, "The treaty relations between China and the United States relating to commerce", *Chinese soc. and pol. sci. rev.*, II (1917) 38–57 [**3199**], an interpretative but summary analysis. B. L. Putnam Weale, *The fight for the republic in China* (N.Y., 1917) [**3200**], and *The truth about China and Japan* (N.Y., 1919) [**3201**], for comment see no. 3175. T. W. Overlach, *Foreign financial control in China* (N. Y., 1919) [**3202**] contrasts disinterestedness of the United States with other powers in China. Chong-su See, *The foreign trade of China* (N.Y., 1919) [**3203**], " the author reviews the entire history of China's trade relations in what is a really valuable contribution " (Langer and Armstrong (no. 4399), 473). W. W. Willoughby, *Foreign rights and interests in China* (Baltimore, 1920; rev. ed., 1927) [**3204**], a careful analysis by a leading American political scientist who served as legal adviser to the Chinese Republic. There are notable chapters on Shantung, and the Lansing-Ishii agreement. G. A. Finch, "American diplomacy and the financing of China ", *Am. jour. internat. law*, XVI (1922) 25–42 [**3205**], informative summary based on printed sources. Two works by Ming-chien Joshua Bau (Pao Ming-ch'ien) : *The foreign relations of China; a history and a survey*, rev. and enl. ed (N.Y., 1922) [3206], a time-saving digest useful as introduction to the study of MacMurray's *Treaties* (no. 3063), but lacking in historical sense and insight; and *The Open Door doctrine in relation to China* (N.Y., 1923) [3207], a none too critical study of the origin, development, and implications of the doctrine as entrenched in the Washington treaties of 1922; but contains also a valuable interpretative introduction by Tyler Dennett. En-tsung Yen, *The Open Door policy* (Boston, 1923) [3208], more critical than Bau (no. 3207), he thinks that it is China herself who must hold the door open. Herbert Croly, *Willard Straight* (N.Y., 1924) [3209], the colorful biography of a young American diplomatist, who resigned from the service in the Far East to become the influential advance agent of American capital in China, based largely on his intimate and reflective diary. Pao-chao Hsieh, *The government of China (1644–1911)* (Baltimore, 1925) [3210] has a chapter on the foreign office. Shu-hsi Hsü, *China and her political entity* (N.Y., 1926) [3211] is said to be a reliable book on the background of diplomacy in regard to Manchuria by a historian who used Chinese sources. C. B. Malone, " The first remission of the Boxer indemnity ", *Am. hist. rev.*, XXXII (1926) 64–68 [3212], a brief note. Two works by C. F. Remer: *The foreign trade of China* (N.Y., 1926) [3213], a scholarly survey of the growth and distribution of Chinese trade, based largely on Chinese maritime customs reports and secondary works; and *Foreign investments in China* (N.Y., 1933) [3214], a work which assimilates and digests coöperative research, inspired by the Institute of Pacific Relations, and assisted by the Social Science Research Council. Sir Frederick Whyte, *China and foreign powers; an historical review of their relations*, published under the auspices of the Royal Institute of International Affairs, 1927 (London, 1927) [3215], a background of history, followed by a discussion of British policy, by a British Member of Parliament, who was political adviser to the National Government of China, 1929–32. Wu Yu-kan, *Chung-kuo kuochi mao-i shih* (Shanghai, 1928) [3216–7] is a history of the foreign trade of China. Luella J. Hall, *Abortive Ger.-Am. Chin. entente* (no. 4312). Shao-hua T'an, " The diplomacy of American investments in China ", in University of Chicago, *Abstracts of theses, Humanistic series*, VI (Chicago, 1929) 165–171 [**3218**], the abstract states that the study has used, in addition to the conventional sources of state papers, records supplied by the American Chamber of Commerce, and J. P. Morgan and Co. Concludes that there has been no application of equal opportunity to investments. A. G. Coons, *The foreign public debt of China* (Phila., 1930) [**3219**], a detailed study, from the standpoint of Chinese debts and credits, of official loans negotiated between China and foreign powers from 1865 to the present day. It deals, among others, with loans of American capital. P. H. Clyde, " Railway politics and the Open Door in China, 1916–1917 ", *Am. jour. internat. law*, XXV (1931) 642–657 [**3220**], based almost exclusively on the State Department's documentary publication *Foreign relations*. F. V. Field, *American participation in the China consortiums* (Chicago, 1931) [**3221**], a working summary prepared for the enlightenment of the Hangchow Conference of the Institute of Pacific Relations. Meribeth E. Cameron, "American recognition policy toward the republic of China, 1912–1913 ", *Pacific hist. rev.*, II (1933) 214–230 [**3222**], brings out two contrary tendencies: the one toward coöperative action with other powers, the other toward the pursuit of a purely individualistic course; it rests on the printed sources. Tyler Dennett, " The Open Door policy as intervention ", *Am. acad. pol. and soc. sci. ann.*, CLXVIII (1933) 78–83 [**3223**].

For biographies of American presidents, secretaries of state, and diplomatists abroad (for names and tenure, see the latest *Register* of the Dept. of State (no. 5122)), see the relevant entries and bibliographical data in the *D.A.B.* Note also Tyler Dennett's *John Hay* (no. 2472).

Printed Sources

See Sec. 1, above for general collections. Note particularly Mac-Murray (no. 3063).

For British official documents, see *Brit. docs. on origins of the war* (no. 5475), v. II, IV, and VIII. For British parliamentary papers, consult the indexes, noted below (p. 838). The Harvard College Library has a conveniently assembled collection of these documents relating to Chinese affairs, 1838 to 1921 (15 volumes).

For French official documents, see *Docs. dipl. franç.* (no. 5474), 2° sér., t. I and II.

For German official documents, see the *Grosse Politik* (no. 5476), v. XVI.

MSS.: Suggestions

See Section 1, above, for official archives, not open (except the United States to 1906) at this date.   Except for the papers of American presidents (Roosevelt, Taft, Wilson), and secretaries of state (Hay, Root, Bacon, Knox, Bryan), and of W. W. Rockhill, commissioner, 1900, and minister to China, 1905–09 (see our lists on pages 862, 865, and 868, respectively), we have no records in this late period of the private collections which undoubtedly exist, many of them in the hands of persons now living.

6. World War and Versailles Peace Conference

Bibliographical Aids

See Sec. 1, above; also bibliographical aids dealing with the world war (Ch. XXII).

Special Works

Four works by T. F. Millard (see no. 3194 for comment): *The great war in the Far East, with special consideration of the rights and interests of China and the United States of America* (Shanghai, 1915) [3224]; *Our Eastern question* (no. 3196); *Democracy and the Eastern question; the problem of the Far East as demonstrated by the great war, and its relation to the United States* (N.Y., 1919) [3225]; and *Shantung case at the conference* (Shanghai, 1921) [3226] concludes that the cumulative effect of the Peace Conference upon the psychology of the Orient is important and ominous.   M. T. Z. Tyau, " Diplomatic relations between China and the Powers since, and concerning the European war ", *Chinese soc. and pol. sci. rev.*, II (1917) 6–67 [3227], topical summary, undocumented.   P. J. Treat, " Japan, America, and the great war ", *League of Nations* (World Peace Foundation), I (1918) 417–442 [3228], sympathetic explanation of Japan's entry into the war as due to " a fine sense of honor."   W. R. Wheeler, *China and the world war* (N.Y., 1918) [3229], fair and clear contemporary account, by an American teacher in a Chinese college.   K. S. Latourette, " China, the United States, and the war ", *League of Nations* (World Peace Foundation), II (1919) 168–191 [3230], summary which stresses the

" almost quixotic " friendliness of the United States for China in its efforts to preserve her independence and integrity. B. L. Putnam-Weale, *The truth about China and Japan* (N.Y., 1919) [**3231**], see no. 3175 for comment. Willoughby (no. 3204) has notable chapters on Shantung and the Lansing-Ishii agreement. W. L. Godshall, *The international aspect of the Shantung problem* (Phila., 1923) [**3232**], " an American dissertation giving a thoroughly documented historical and analytical account of the problem." (Langer and Armstrong (no. 4399), 479.) R. T. Pollard, *China's foreign relations, 1917–1931* (N.Y., 1933) [**3233**], the latest survey, it gives the impression of scholarship and comprehensiveness.

Printed Sources

See also Sec. 7 (" Japanese-American Relations, 1898–1919 ").
U.S. OFFICIAL DOCUMENTS: *Occupation of Korea; in response to resolution, report submitting certain correspondence had between official representatives of United States and representatives of Korea relative to occupation of Korea, Feb. 23, 1916* (64th Cong., 1st sess. Sen. doc. 342) [**3234**]. *Agreement effected by exchange of notes between United States and Japan, mutual interest relating to the Republic of China; signed Nov. 2, 1917* (Wash., 1917) (Dept. of State. Treaty Series 630) [**3235**]. *Papers concerning German peace treaty, in response to resolution, information concerning purported German-Japanese treaty, adjustment in reference to Shantung, and intimidation of Chinese delegates by Japan, Aug. 11, 1919* (Wash., 1919) (66th Cong., 1st sess. Sen. doc. 72) [**3236**].
The principal documents regarding Japan, America, and the great war are given in *League of Nations* (World Peace Foundation), I (1918) 443–462 [**3237**]. Wheeler (no. 3229), 185–251, prints key documents regarding China and the world war. See also Latourette (no. 3230) for principal documents dealing with China and the world war. *Shantung: treaties and agreements* (Wash., 1921) [**3238**], published by the Carnegie Endowment for International Peace, Division of International Law (*Pamphlet series*, no. 42). Viscount Ishii, *Gaiko Yoroku* (no. 3295). *V. K. Wellington Koo's policy; some selected documents*, comp. by Wunsz King (Shanghai, 1931) [**3239**], mostly in regard to China's claims at Versailles, 1919; one on tariff autonomy, at the Washington conference of 1921–1922.

MSS.: Suggestions

See Section 5, above.

The papers of Secretary Lansing, partly in the Department of State and partly in the Library of Congress, contain vital material on the Lansing-Ishii conversations and agreement of 1917, which at present cannot be released for publication. Viscount Ishii's own papers seem to have been preserved by him, as portions are published in his *Gaiko Yoroku* (no. 3295).

MS. material for these recent episodes, still of an explosive nature politically, is under cover.

7. Japanese-American Relations, 1898–1919 [5]

Bibliographical Aids

See Sec. 1, above. Note particularly Miller (no. 3028); and Japanese historical bibliographies (nos. 4774–4777). Ina T. Firkins, "Japanese in the United States", *Bul. of Bibliog.*, VIII (1914) 94–98 [**3240**], a bibliography, including periodical literature, 1905–1913. Izura Shinmura, "Nichi-Ei kankei tosho tenkan-shi", *Geibun*, XIII (1922) no. 6, 57–72, no. 7, 53–70 [**3241**], notes on books relating to English-Japanese relations, primarily, but includes also many books that have to do with American-Japanese relations.

Special Works

Elihu Root, "The real questions under the Japanese treaty and the San Francisco school board resolution", *Am. jour. internat. law*, I (1907) 273–286 [**3242**], Root was Secretary of State at the time. Louis Aubert, *Américains et Japonais; l'émigration japonaise aux Hawaii, en Californie, au Canada et dans l'Amérique du Sud* (Paris 1908) [**3243**], the author thought that only in case of a paralysis of China could Japan expect to defend her rights and interests on the " white " shores of the Pacific. Comte de Blois (Louis), *En face du soleil levant. Les idées de Jean-Jacques Rousseau en Chine; le conflit américain-japonais et l'opinion publique américaine* (Paris, 1909) [**3244**]. G. H. Blakeslee, ed., *Japan and Japanese-American relations* (N.Y., 1912) [**3245**], a Clark University conference of " experts ", includes 22 separate articles by different writers on as many phases of contemporary Japanese affairs and Japanese-American

---

[5] See also Sec. 4 ("Anglo-Japanese Alliance and Russo-Japanese War ").

relations. The following books by K. K. Kawakami all have the same tendency: to put the defense of Japanese policy on all subjects in the most palatable and persuasive form for American public opinion, with the milieu of which the author is thoroughly familiar: *American-Japanese relations; an inside view of Japan's policies and purposes* (N.Y., 1912) [**3246**]; *Asia at the door; a study of the Japanese question in continental United States, Hawaii, and Canada* (N.Y., 1914) [**3247**]; *The Japanese question, a symposium*, ed. by K. K. Kawakami (San Francisco, 1915?) [**3248**]; *Japan in world politics* (N. Y., 1917) [**3249**]; *Japan and world peace* (N.Y., 1919) [**3250**]; *The real Japanese question* (N.Y., 1921) [**3251**]; *What Japan thinks*, ed. by K. K. Kawakami (N.Y., 1921) [**3252**]; and *Japan speaks on the Sino-Japanese crisis* (N.Y., 1932) [**3253–4**]. Dobson, *Edge of the pit* (no. 3526), a discussion of the foreign relations of the United States relating especially to Japan and Mexico. R. Tatsumi, *Kiokuto kinji gaiko shi*, 2nd ed. (Tokyo, 1914) [**3255**], a history of recent Far Eastern diplomacy. J. F. Abbott, *Japanese expansion and American policies* (N.Y., 1916) [**3256**] deprecates any chance of Japan successfully taking the northern Chinese provinces (since done); a sympathetic essay on Japanese-American relations, impressionistic. T. E. Green, *War with Japan?* (Wash.: The American Peace Society, 1916) [**3257**], a lively peace tract by an international lecturer. Toyokichi Iyenaga, ed., *Japan's real attitude toward America; a reply to Mr. George Bronson Rea's " Japan's place in the sun—the menace to America "* (N.Y. and London, 1916) [**3258**], a reply to the recently published pamphlet by the editor of the *Far Eastern review* (George Bronson Rea), to show that Japan is innocent of secretly arming for a war with the United States. J. A. B. Scherer, *The Japanese crisis* (N.Y., 1916) [**3259**], a " better understanding " discussion of the Japanese question in America; contains the text of the California land law and the American-Japanese treaty of 1911. Two works by S. L. Gulick, *Anti-Japanese war-scare stories* (N.Y., 1917) [**3260**]; and *American-Japanese relations, 1916–1920*, quadrennial report, Commission on Relations with the Orient of the Federal Council of Churches of Christ in America (N.Y.? 1921?) [**3261**] proposes plan to admit immigrants on basis of capacity for assimilation. Frederick McCormick, *The menace of Japan* (Boston, 1917) [**3262**], an experienced journalist's review, riding the theme " it will be finally determined by war." A. T. Mahan, *The interest of America in international conditions* (Boston, 1918) [**3263**], first published in 1910. Its thesis is that the rising naval power of Germany has fastened the British navy to European waters; this is followed by an argument for the transfer of the American fleet to the Pacific Ocean. J. T. Sunderland, *Rising Japan; is she a menace or a comrade to be welcomed in the fraternity of nations?* (N.Y. and London, 1918) [**3264**], dissuasions for Americans suspicious of a Japanese menace to them. Henry Chung, *The oriental policy of the United States* (N.Y., 1919) [**3265**], in the nature of a warning to the United States against letting Japan go ahead in China; particular attention to the Lansing-Ishii agreement; by a Korean. V. S. McClatchy, *The Germany of Asia; Japan's policy in the Far East, her " peaceful penetration " of the United States, how American commercial and national interests are affected* (Sacramento, 1919) [**3266**], by one of the organizers of Japanese exclusion. A. M. Pooley, *Japan's foreign policies* (London, 1920) [**3267**], a British writer's analysis of the interplay of Japanese, British, and American relations from the Anglo-Japanese alliances to the 21 Demands. Toyokichi Iyenaga and Kenoske Sato, *Japan and the California problem* (N.Y. and London, 1921) [**3268**], this is now superseded by Ichihashi (no. 3315). W. B. Pitkin, *Must we fight Japan?* (N.Y., 1921) [**3269**], journalistic lucubrations. Iichiro Tokutomi, *Japanese-American relations* (N.Y., 1922) [**3270**], translated from the Japanese; mainly a presentation, *suaviter in modo, fortiter in re,* of the Japanese case against American exclusion laws. R. L. Buell, " The development of the anti-Japanese agitation in the United States ", *Pol. sci. quar.,* XXXVII (1922) 605–638 [**3271**] discusses immigration in the 19th century (the first cause of friction), the San Francisco school incident, and the California land laws; also by the same writer, *Japanese immigration* (Boston, 1924) (World Peace Foundation Pamphlets, VII, nos. 5–6) [**3272**], a succinct summary, with appendix of relevant diplomatic notes, laws, court decisions, of the question to 1924. Prew Savoy, *La question japonaise aux Etats-Unis* (Paris, 1924) [**3273**], Ph.D. thesis by an American student at the University of Paris, based on judicial decisions and secondary material, but useful as an antidote to M. Yoshitomi's immoderate thesis (no. 3275). Blakeslee, *For. policy* (no. 4122) has a section on " Japanese immigration: statutory exclusion and American policy."

Conference on American Relations with China, *American relations with China*, report of a conference held at Johns Hopkins University, September 17–20, 1925 (Baltimore, 1925) **[3274]**, in a preliminary agenda the various aspects of Chinese-American affairs were set forth in detail, and these were then discussed by " experts " (mostly university professors) invited to the conference. Macaomi Yoshitomi, *Les conflits nippo-américains et le problème du Pacifique* (Paris, 1926) **[3275]**, a bitter denunciation of Yankee expansion and discriminatory legislation, addressed to French sympathies. It is not carefully documented, and not too accurate; for example it asserts that a law of California in 1921 drove the Japanese out of the State's public schools! Closes by a suggestion that the anti-Japanese policies of the United States will lead to war. J. Shinobu, *Taisho gaiko jugonen shi* (Tokyo, 1927) **[3276]**, a diplomatic history of the fifteen years of Taisho, 1912–1926. Rippy, *Latin America in world politics* (no. 1076) discusses the attitude of the United States toward the growing influence of Japan in Hispanic America. Teijun Wada, *American foreign policy towards Japan during the nineteenth century* (Tokyo, 1928) **[3277]**, the English is obviously acquired, style diffuse but earnest, content resting largely on printed American state papers and public documents, but also some publications of the Japanese foreign office. Yoshino, *Meiji bunka zenshu* (no. 3101). J. W. Pratt, *Lansing* (in no. 4796), unusually valuable chapter on the Lansing-Ishii agreement. P. H. Clyde, " Episode in American-Japanese relations; Manchurian freight rate controversy, 1914–1916 ", *Far East rev.*, XXVI (1930) 410–412 **[3278]**, summary of a little-known, but highly interesting episode, based on *Foreign relations*. Four studies by T. A. Bailey: " Japan's protest against annexation of Hawaii ", *Jour. mod. hist.*, III (1931) 46–61 **[3279]** uses the archives of Hawaii and the United States Department of State to suggest that the Japanese protest was due principally to internal politics; " California, Japan, and the alien land legislation of 1913 ", *Pacific hist. rev.*, I (1932) 36–59 **[3280]** considers the diplomatic phase of the question, involving the division of powers between the federal and state authority in the United States as affecting national foreign relations; " The world cruise of the American battleship fleet, 1907–1909 ", *ibid.*, 389–424 **[3281]** describes the cruise and explains it as principally caused by the Roosevelt administration's desire to exhibit a policy of greater firmness in dealing with Japan; and *Theodore Roosevelt and the Japanese-American crises; an account of the international complications arising from the race problem on the Pacific Coast* (Stanford University, 1934) [3281a], detailed study of Japanese-American relations, 1905–1909, based on files in the Department of State, Roosevelt papers, and other unpublished sources altogether in the United States. Most detailed account available of the negotiation of the gentlemen's agreement, but does not give the still unrevealed text. See also the same writer's *Sealing convention, 1911* (no. 2900a). Yamato Ichihashi, *Japanese in the United States* (Stanford University, Calif., 1932) [3282], a careful, detailed, and dispassionate analysis of numbers, character, employment, and economic, social, political, diplomatic, and psychological problems involved. See also Murakawa (no. 3116).

Printed Sources

For general collections, see Sec. 1, above. See Sec. 4, above, for United States' mediation in the Russo-Japanese war and the Portsmouth peace conference.

The policy of the United States and Japan in the Far East; text of notes exchanged on November 30, 1908 (N.Y., 1908) (International Conciliation, no. 12) [3282a], text of the Root-Takahira note. R. D. Evans, *An admiral's log; being continued recollections of naval life* (N.Y. and London, 1910) [3283], Admiral Evans was in command of the Pacific fleet when it sailed around the world in 1908. *American-Japanese discussions relating to land tenure law of California* (Wash., 1914) [3284], published by the Department of State (confidential). Naoichi Masaoka, ed., *Japan to America; a symposium of papers by political leaders and representative citizens of Japan on conditions in Japan and on the relations between Japan and the United States*, issued under the auspices of the Japan Society of America (N.Y. and London, 1914; published Tokyo, 1914, under title *Japan's message to America* [3285], a " good will " book. Lindsay Russell, ed., *America to Japan; a symposium of papers by representative citizens of the United States on the relations between Japan and America and on the common interests of the two countries* (N.Y., 1915) [3286], a " good will " complement to *Japan to America* (no. 3285). *Memoirs of Count Hayashi* (no. 3187). *The Imperial Japanese Government's special finance and economic commission to the United States, headed by Baron Tanetaro Megata (September 1917–*

April 1918) (Tokyo, 1918?) [3287], published by the Special Commission [etc.], consists of speeches, receptions, resolutions, etc. *The Imperial Japanese mission, 1917; a record of the reception throughout the United States of the special mission headed by Viscount Ishii; together with the exchange of notes embodying the Root-Takahira understanding of 1908 and the Lansing-Ishii agreement of 1917* (Wash., 1918) [3288], published by the Carnegie Endowment for International Peace, Division of Intercourse and Education. *The United States and Japan* (N.Y., 1918) (International Conciliation, no. 124) [3289] prints the texts of the Root-Takahira understanding and of the Lansing-Ishii agreement, and several addresses. Emile Laloy, *Les documents secrets des archives du ministère des affaires étrangères de Russie, publiés par les Bolcheviks* (Paris, 1919) [3290], no. 53: " Le traité entre le Japon et l'Amérique ", is an abstract of an article on this subject citing a large number of Russian secret despatches, published in the *Pravda* of Dec. 16/29, 1917. These despatches were published in the *Recueil de documents secrets*, published in Russia by the Bolcheviks, 1917–1918. *The verdict of public opinion on the Japanese-American question; a symposium instituted by Cornelius Vanderbilt, Jr., and founded on Peter B. Kyne's novel " The pride of Palomar "* (N.Y., 1921) [3291], " these comments from men of national prominence were gathered to help reflect public opinion on . . . Japanese-American relations." *The Lansing-Ishii agreement. Message from the President of the United States, transmitting in response to a Senate resolution of February 23 . . . 1922, information as to the present status and binding effect of the so-called Lansing-Ishii agreement, signed November 2, 1917* (Wash., 1922) (67th Cong., 2d sess. Sen. Doc. 150) [3292]. *Exchange of notes between the United States and Japan, canceling the Lansing-Ishii agreement of November 2, 1917. Signed April 14, 1923* (Wash., 1923) (Dept. of State. Treaty Series, no. 667) [3293]. *Diplomatic relations between the United States and Japan, 1908–1924* (Worcester, Mass., and N.Y., 1925) (International Conciliation, no. 211) [3294] consists of the texts of a number of official agreements, etc. Mutsu, *Kenken roku* (no. 3153). Viscount Kikujiro Ishii, *Gaiko yoroku* [6] (Tokyo, 1930)

---

[6] See R. S. Morris, " The memoirs of Viscount Ishii," *Foreign affairs,* X (1932) 677–687 [3296].

[3295], the memoirs of Viscount Ishii, containing such matter as he chose to publish concerning the Lansing-Ishii conversations and agreement. It is understood that an English translation is in progress. Hiratsuka, *Ito Hirobumi hiroku* (no. 3192) publishes the confidential papers of Prince Ito.

For the printed writings of American presidents, secretaries of state, and diplomatists abroad (for names and tenure, see latest *Register* of the Dept. of State (no. 5122)), see our list on p. 756.

8. The Washington Conference

Bibliographical Aids [7]

Ichihashi, *Washington conference* (no. 3315) has an extensive bibliography, including official publications of the various governments.

Special Works

A. O. Tuaner, " La maitrise du Pacifique et la diplomatie Yankee au dix-neuvième siècle ", *Rev. hist. dipl.*, XXX (1916) 268–301 [3297] builds the expansion of the United States from 1803 up to a climax of opposition to Japanese interests in the 20th century. S. F. Bemis, " Yap Island controversy ", *Pacific rev.*, II (1921) 308–328 [3298], brief summary based on printed United States government documents. H. C. Bywater, *Sea-power in the Pacific; a study of the American-Japanese naval problem* (Boston and N.Y., 1921) [3299], a very pertinent and perspicuous analysis of impending Japanese-American conflict in the Pacific on the eve of the Washington conference, it did much to awaken public opinion to the necessity of a peaceful adjustment. Kojiro Sato, *If Japan and America fight* (Tokyo, 1921) [3300], a translation by Jihei Hashiguchi. Three works by G. Zay Wood: *The Twenty-one demands; Japan versus China* (N.Y., 1921) [3301] prints the key documents; *China, the United States, and the Anglo-Japanese alliance* (N.Y., 1921) [3302], undocumented; written on the eve of the Washington conference by a Chinese publicist later attached to the publicity branch of the Chinese delegation, who imputes something unexpressed and sinister to the Anglo-Japanese alliance as renewed in 1911; and *Shantung question; a study in diplomacy and world politics* (N.Y., 1922) [3303], much of the material incorporated in the volume was prepared originally by

---

[7] The Carnegie Endowment for International Peace has unusually good card indexes on these contemporary subjects, which list many of the periodical articles.

the press department of the Chinese delegation to the Washington conference and used for publicity purposes. R. L. Buell, *The Washington conference* (N.Y., 1922) [3304] sees the conference as an unsuccessful effort to stay Japan's aggression in Asia; hastily done, but perhaps the best review yet available. S. Ito, *Kafu kaigi to sonogo* (Tokyo, 1922) [3305], the Washington conference and after. K. K. Kawakami, *Japan's Pacific policy* (N.Y., 1922) [3306], see no. 3246 for comment. B. L. Putnam-Weale, *An indiscreet chronicle from the Pacific* (N.Y., 1922) [3307], " a British adviser of the Chinese foreign office discusses the background of the Washington conference and the steps taken to bring about the abrogation of the Anglo-Japanese alliance ", (Langer and Armstrong (no. 4399), 475); see also no. 3175, for Putnam-Weale's books. Also by Putnam-Weale, *The vanished empire* (N.Y., 1926) [3308], a sequel to no. 3307. Mark Sullivan, *The great adventure at Washington* (N.Y., 1922) [3309], good copy by a sharp-eyed journalist on personalities and atmosphere. Iichiro Tokutomi, *Japanese-American relations*. Tr. by Sukeshige Yanagiwara (N.Y., 1922) [3310], extracts from Japanese publications by an influential publicist with candid observations on the precariousness of Japanese-American relations. W. W. Willoughby, *China at the conference* (Baltimore, 1922) [3311], of particular importance for China's problems at the Washington conference, by a legal adviser to the Chinese government. Godshall, *Shantung* (no. 3232). Camilo Barcía Trelles, *La política exterior norteamericana de la postguerra (hasta los acuerdos de Washington de 1922)* (Valladolid, 1924) [3312], author considers relations between the United States and Japan from point of view of Hispanic American states; regrets they were excluded from the Washington conference, but believes any war between the United States and Japan which would arise over Far Eastern questions of no vital interest to Hispanic America. T. F. Millard, *Conflict of policies in Asia* (N.Y., 1924) [3313], a study of the conflict of international policies in the Far East (see nos. 3194–3196). P. H. Clyde, *International rivalries in Manchuria, 1689–1922* (Columbus, 1926) [3314] now superseded by C. W. Young (nos. 3317–3320), but has a richer historical background. Shinobu (no. 3276). Yamato Ichihashi, *The Washington conference and after* (Stanford University, 1928) [3315], the author is professor of Japanese history at Leland Stanford, a scholar thoroughly immersed in the American *milieu* and *en rapport* with the Japanese government.

He was secretary to Admiral Kato at the conference. L. B. Tribolet, *The international aspects of electrical communication in the Pacific* (Baltimore, 1929) [3316] is concerned with the rivalry between the cable and radio companies of the various Powers for rights, privileges, and concessions in the Pacific world, especially in China. C. W. Young, *The international relations of Manchuria* (Chicago, 1929) [3317], a digest and analysis of treaties, agreements, and negotiations concerning the three eastern provinces of China, prepared for the 1929 conference of the Institute of Pacific Relations; followed by the author's more detailed three volumes of 1931, published after much further travel and study: *Japan's special position in Manchuria; its assertion, legal interpretation and present meaning* (Baltimore, 1931) [3318]; *The international legal status of the Kwantung leased territory* (Baltimore, 1931) [3319]; and *Japanese jurisdiction in the South Manchuria railway areas* (Baltimore, 1931) [3320], which form v. I–III of his *Japan's jurisdiction and international legal position in Manchuria.* These three volumes furnish a critical and objective analysis; the first has some particularly valuable analyses of the interpretation of the Lansing-Ishii agreement. Pollard, *China's foreign relations* (no. 3233) deals largely with the conference and its aftermath. H. W. Taft, *Japan and America; a journey and a political survey* (N.Y., 1932) [3320a], an intelligent American business man (brother of the late President Taft) comments on the Washington conference, and later Japanese-American relations. J. B. Brebner, " Canada, the Anglo-Japanese alliance and the Washington conference ", *Pol. sci. quar.*, L (1935) 45–58 [3320b], the efforts of the Canadian Prime Minister, Arthur Meighen, in 1921 to prevent the renewal of the alliance because it endangered good Anglo-American and Canadian-American relations.

Printed Sources [8]

U.S. OFFICIAL DOCUMENTS: *Conference on limitation of armament, Washington, Nov. 12, 1921–Feb. 6, 1922* (Wash., 1922) [3321], published by the Dept. of State (in English and French), consists of the official proceedings; also *Conference on limitation of armament. Subcommittees* (Wash., 1922) [3322], comprising the official proceedings of the subcommittees. *Conference on limitation of armament; address of President of United States submitting treaties*

---

[8] For detailed information regarding all editions of the Proceedings, etc., of the Conference, to date (1934), see the *Document catalogue* (no. 5358), v. XVI.

and resolutions approved and adopted by Conference . . . (Wash.,
1922) (67th Cong., 2d sess. Sen. Doc. 125) [**3323**], not included
in the Proceedings (no. 3321). *Nine powers treaty on China, treaty
submitted by President of United States, between United States,
Belgium, British Empire, China, France, Italy, Japan, Netherlands,
and Portugal, relating to principles and policies to be followed in
matters concerning China* [signed Feb. 6, 1922] (Wash., 1922) (67th
Cong., 2d sess. Sen. exec. P) [**3324**]. *Report of American delegation of proceedings of Conference on Limitation of Armament,
submitted to the President, Feb. 9, 1922* (Wash., 1922) [**3325**], not
included in the Proceedings (no. 3321). *Conversations between
Chinese and Japanese representatives in regard to Shantung question, Treaty for settlement of outstanding questions relative to Shantung,* [and] *Agreed terms of understanding recorded in minutes of
Japanese and Chinese delegations concerning conclusion of treaty
for settlement of outstanding questions relative to Shantung;* prepared by Japanese delegation (Wash., 1922) [**3326**], and Same, prepared by Chinese delegation (Wash., 1923) [**3327**], both published
by the Dept. of State.

The various official publications of the governments of Canada,
China, France, Germany, Great Britain, Japan, and the United
States, are listed in Ichihashi, *Washington conference* (no. 3315),
402–406. See also *Conferenza di Washington* (no. 4335), published
by the Italian foreign office.

For treaties, agreements, and resolutions, see MacMurray (no.
3063).

The Washington conference on limitation of armaments (N.Y.,
1921–22) (International Conciliation, nos. 169 and 172) [**3328**] prints
key documents. The Boston *Transcript* published some special reprints of its reports of the conference by J. T. Williams, Jr., which
are stimulating commentary.

MSS.: Suggestions

See Secs. 5 and 6.

The Hoover War Library at Stanford University has documents
and records, printed and unprinted, of the following delegations to
the Washington Conference: United States, Armenian, Belgian,
British, Canadian, Chinese, Far Eastern Republic, Egyptian,
Galician, Indian, Japanese, Korean, Latvian, Lithuanian, and Pri-
Amur Provisional Government, South China.

CHAPTER XVIII

CUBA AND SPAIN, 1861–1898

1. In General.
2. Cuban Question and the Outbreak of the War with Spain, 1860-1898.

3. Diplomacy of the War with Spain and the Peace of Paris, 1898.

1. In General

Bibliographical Aids

For general aids, see Larned (no. 4657); Griffin (no. 4658); *Writings* (no. 4661); C. H. and T. (no. 4662); *Guide hist. lit.* (no. 4634); and bibliographies in *Am. secs. state* (no. 4796). Myers (no. 5399) for collections of treaties.

Five bibliographies by A. P. C. Griffin: *Cuba* (no. 4722); *Colonization, dependencies, protectorates* (no. 3022), p. 13–22: " Expansion of the United States, 1898–1900; history, discussion of principles, etc." [3329]; *Porto Rico* (no. 4725); *A list of books (with references to periodicals) on the Philippines in the Library of Congress, . . . with chronological list of maps in the Library of Congress*, by P. Lee Phillips (Wash., 1903) (Library of Congress) [3330]; and *List of works relating to the American occupation of the Philippine Islands, 1898–1903* (Wash., 1905) (Library of Congress) [3331], which includes United States government documents. " Works relating to the Philippine Islands in the New York Public Library," *N.Y. pub. lib. bul.*, IV (1900) 19–29 [3332]. Four bibliographies by C. M. Trelles [y Govín]: *Bibliografía de la segunda guerra de independencia cubana y de la hispano-yankee* (Havana, 1902) [3333]; *Bibliog. cubana*, and *Biblioteca hist. cubana* (no. 4723); and *Bibliog. cubana doctrina Monroe* (no. 1141). J. A. Robertson, *Bibliography of the Philippine Islands* (Cleveland, 1908) [3333a]. *[Bibliography of] annexation of Cuba and independence of the Philippines* (Madison, Wis., 1912) (Univ. of Wisconsin Bulletin, 1911) [3334]. New York Public Library, *West*

Indies (no. 4720). G. H. Stuart, *Cuba and its international relations* (N.Y., 1923) (Institute of International Education. International Relations Clubs, syllabus no. XIV) [**3335**], with bibliographies. Reuter, *Sp.-Am. war* (no. 2775), 191–204, for Anglo-American relations. Slade, *Philippine Islands* (no. 3029). Sánchez Alonso, *Bibliog. de España* (no. 4759), v. II, 224–242, 246–252. Pedreira, *Bibliog. puertorriqueña* (no. 4725a).

For indexes to periodical literature, see nos. 4995–5003.

For lists and indexes of newspapers, see nos. 5004–5047; particularly Library of Congress check lists (nos. 5030 and 5032).

Special Works

Of general histories of the United States, see Rhodes (no. 4783). See also *Am. secs. state* (no. 4796), v. VII–IX; and Wriston, *Exec. agents* (no. 4799).

Of general histories of Cuba, see Jacobo de la Pezuela, *Historia de la isla de Cuba* (Madrid and N.Y., 1868–78, 4 v.) [**3336**]. Johnson, *Cuba* (no. 1798). C. E. Chapman, *A history of the Cuban republic; a study in Hispanic American politics* (N.Y., 1927) [**3337**], a realistic and objective analysis of political conditions in contemporary Cuba, preceded by a reliable survey of the Cuban question to 1898.

The following informing general histories of the Philippines deal with the acquisition of the islands, but not definitively from diplomatic records: J. A. Le Roy, *The Americans in the Philippines; a history of the conquest and first years of occupation, with an introductory account of the Spanish rule* (Boston and N.Y., 1914, 2 v.) [**3338**]. D. C. Worcester, *The Philippines, past and present* (N.Y., 1914, 2 v.; new ed., in one volume, with biographical sketch and four additional chapters by Ralston Hayden, N.Y., 1930) [**3339**]. C. B. Elliott, *The Philippines to the end of the military regime* (Indianapolis, 1917) [**3340**], "the background of history against which the American treatment of the Philippines must be projected, . . . to show the place which our Philippine policy holds in the history of colonization." Moorfield Storey and Marcial P. Lichauco, *The conquest of the Philippines by the United States, 1898–1925* (N.Y. and London, 1926) [**3341**], powerful and simply written indictment of American policy in the Philippines in 1898 and later. W. Cameron Forbes, *The Philippine Islands* (Boston and N.Y., 1928, 2 v.) [**3342**], the governor-general of the Philippines, 1909–13, gives an excellent summary of governmental and political activities and economic conditions during the American occupation, in which he has drawn largely upon his journal during tenure of office.

Callahan, *Am. relations in Pacific* (no. 3086). Harry Thurston Peck, *Twenty years of the republic, 1885–1905* (N.Y., 1906) [3343], brilliant journalist's review of American politics. J. H. Latané, *America as a world power, 1897–1907* (N.Y. and London, 1907) (The American Nation . . . XXV) [3344], a convenient if not penetrating summary of the principal diplomatic happenings. A. C. Coolidge, *The United States as a world power* (N.Y., 1908, later reprints) [3345] explains problems and international relations of the United States as developed in the decade following the Spanish war; the author was one of the most penetrating American observers of his time. Chadwick, *U.S. and Spain* (no. 108). Fish, *Path of Empire* (no. 2461). Hill, *Treaties* (no. 4794), 314–346: " The treaty of Paris." Rhodes, *McKinley and Roosevelt* (no. 2462). Bécker, *Relaciones exteriores España* (no. 723). Emile Bourgeois, *Manuel historique de politique étrangère. IV. La politique mondiale (1878–1919)* (Paris, 1926) [3346], probably the best general survey of diplomatic history, but one must discount the French point of view. Dennis, *Adventures* (no. 2224) introduces new material from the Department of State. Dulles, *Pacific* (no. 2225). H. F. Guggenheim, *The United States and Cuba* (N.Y., 1934) [3347], review of treaty relations between the United States and Cuba by a recent ambassador to Cuba who advocates the substitution of the intervention articles of the Platt amendment with a guarantee of independence similar to that of Panama. Savage, *U.S. maritime policy* (no. 22).

For biographies of American presidents, secretaries of state, and diplomatists abroad (for names and tenure, see latest *Register* of the Dept. of State (no. 5122)), see the relevant entries and bibliographical data in the *D.A.B.*

The best dictionary of Cuban biography is Calcagno, *Diccionario biog. cubana* (no. 4948).

Printed Sources

For American official documents and general source collections, see p. 810; particularly *Jour. exec. proc. Sen.* (no. 5387); *Cong. Globe* (no. 5384); *Cong. Record* (no. 5385); *For. relations* (no.

5345) ; Wharton's *Digest* (no. 5366) ; Richardson (no. 5335) ; Moore's *Arbitrations* (no. 5364), v. II, 1019–1053, for Spanish claims commission agreement of Feb. 12, 1871; and Moore's *Digest* (no. 5365). For contemporary periodical material, consult the indexes to periodicals (nos. 4995–5003).

For lists and indexes of newspapers, see nos. 5004–5047; particularly Library of Congress check lists (nos. 5030 and 5032).

For the printed writings of American presidents, secretaries of state, and diplomatists abroad (for names and tenure, see latest *Register* of the Dept. of State (no. 5122)), see our list on p. 756.

Particular documents are cited in separate sections of this chapter.

2. Cuban Question and the Outbreak of the War with Spain, 1860–1898

Bibliographical Aids

See Sec. 1, above.

Special Works

See Sec. 1, above.

Marqués de Olivart, *Del reconocimiento de beligerancia y sus efectos immediatos* (*escrito por encargo del Excmo. Sr. Ministro de Estado*) (Madrid, 1895) [**3348**], a careful study by an eminent Spanish international lawyer of the attitude of the United States toward Cuban belligerancy; and by the same writer, " Le différend entre l'Espagne et les Etats-Unis au sujet de la question cubaine ", *Rev. gén. droit internat. public*, IV (1897) 577–620; V (1898) 358–422, 499–555; VII (1900) 541–629; IX (1902) 161–202 [**3349**]. Olivart was a distinguished and temperate authority on international law, and his works may be considered dispassionate and valuable Spanish expositions of the Cuban issue with the United States. Two works by J. B. Moore: " The question of Cuban belligerency ", *Forum*, XXI (1896) 288–300 [**3350**] points out that to recognize the belligerency of Cuba would do the Cubans no good and would give Spain the right to visit and search neutral American ships; and " Maritime law in the war with Spain ", *Pol. sci. quar.*, XV (1900) 399–425 [**3351**], questions of blockade, contraband, etc., by a commentator who has since become the greatest authority in the United States.   J. H. Latané, " The diplomacy of the United States in regard to Cuba ", *Am. hist. assoc. ann. rep.*, for 1897 (1898) 217–278 [**3352**], a timely survey on the eve of the Spanish-American war, based on printed American state papers, but on no MS. material and no study of foreign works. This study is incorporated in his *U.S. and Latin America* (no. 963). Antonio Miró Quesada, *La intervención americana en Cuba* (Lima, Peru, 1898) [3353] is a doctoral thesis of the University of Lima. Callahan, *Cuba and internat. rel.* (no. 1805). A. Maurice Low, " Unwritten chapter in American diplomacy; war with Spain ", *Contemp. rev.*, LXXVIII (1900) 83–93 [3354] deals with John Hay's " unofficial warnings " to London that McKinley's prospective administration would not be so reasonable to deal with as Cleveland's! (cf. Dennett's *Hay*, no. 2472). Sidney Webster, " Revelations of a Senate document ", *No. Am. rev.*, CLXXII (1901) 867–881 [3355] comments on the political and international significance of withholding from publication the correspondence of the peace commission until after the ratification of the treaty [and after the election of 1900]. H. P. Willis, " Reciprocity with Cuba ", *Am. acad. pol. and soc. sci. ann.*, XXII (1903) 129–147 [3356] covers, in the first section, the period immediately after 1880 when it was sought to avoid tariff revision in this country by the introduction of a reciprocity policy, and traces the development of reciprocity relations from that time to 1903; ends with a deprecation of the value of reciprocity. H. E. Flack, *Spanish-American diplomatic relations preceding the war of 1898* (Baltimore, 1906) [3357], a very objective work demonstrating that American intervention was not justified on the ground of humanity, self-defense, loss of or danger to American life or property, or all of these together. Rudolph de Cordova, " The ' Virginius ' incident and Cuba ", *Nineteenth century*, LX (1906) 976–985 [3358], a narrative by the son of Altamont de Cordova, the consignee of the " Virginius ", whose efforts stayed some of the executions. Enrique Piñeyro, " José Morales Lemus, primer ministro de Cuba en los Estados Unidos ", in his *Biografías americanas* (Paris, 1906) 77–195 [3359], a sketch of the envoy of the Revolutionary government of Cuba in the United States, 1868–69. Manuel Márquez Sterling, *La diplomacia en nuestra historia* (Havana, 1909) [3360], a survey of the beginnings of Cuban diplomacy, 1868–98. L. A. Harding, *The preliminary diplomacy of the Spanish-American war* (Indianapolis, 1912) [3361], a short review of well-known facts, ending with a lame endeavor to justify American intervention in 1898. Martin, *Policy as regards intervention* (no. 4808). J. B. Soto,

Causas y consecuencias; antecedentes diplomáticos y efectos de la guerra hispano-americana (San Juan de Puerto Rico, 1922) [**3362**]. W. C. Deming, *How a letter of a country lawyer became international law* (Cheyenne, 1923?) [**3362a**], letter written by Frank E. Hutchins, of Warren, Ohio, Feb. 13, 1898, to Associate Justice W. R. Day, then acting secretary of state, stating the grounds upon which intervention in Cuba would be justifiable, which was embodied in the message of President McKinley, April 11, 1898, on the Cuban question. Salvador Salazar y Roig, *Discursos leídos en la recepción pública del doctor Salvador Salazar y Roig, la noche del 27 de septiembre de 1923* (Havana, 1923) [**3363**] has the half-title, *La gestión diplomática de Morales Lemus;* it is an essay on the Cuban revolution of 1868–78, and the question of recognition of belligerency by the United States, using some hitherto unpublished documents, by a professor in the University of Havana. Alberto Maury y Nodarse, "Relaciones políticas entre Cuba y los Estados Unidos", *Cuba contemporánea*, XXXV (1924) 101–128, 189–208 [**3364**], cursory summary, from the beginning of the 19th century to 1902. Morey, *Dipl. episodes* (no. 552a), ch. 3: "American policy as to the law of recognition; apropos of the Cuban revolt", deals with the controversy with Spain in regard to Cuba, 1868 to 1878, and in the later period, 1895–98. Jenks, *Our Cuban colony* (no. 3877), a review of the relations of the United States with independent Cuba, emphasizing the economic results of the Platt amendment, has a summary of Cuban affairs before 1898. J. K. Winkler, *W. R. Hearst, an American phenomenon* (N.Y., 1928) [**3365**] shows how Hearst worked through his press for a war. Ramiro Guerra y Sánchez, *En el camino de la independencia; estudio histórico sobre la rivalidad de los Estados Unidos y la Gran Bretaña en sus relaciones con la independencia de Cuba, con un apéndice titulado de Monroe a Platt* (Havana, 1930) [**3366**], a thoughtful review by a professor in the University of Havana, of the Cuban policy of the United States, based on an adequate study of the best secondary works, pointed to the Torriente thesis that the Platt amendment is incompatible with the joint resolution of Congress of April 20, 1898. L. M. Hacker, "The holy war of 1898", *Am. mercury*, XXI (1930) 316–326 [**3367**] explains the war as a Republican party maneuver contrived by party hacks, a trick to which McKinley gave his approval when he was convinced the nation was eager for blood. Walter Millis, *The martial spirit* (Boston and N.Y., 1931) [**3368**], most valuable for an analysis of the adolescent psychology of American nationalist sentiment that spurred on the war against Spain, drawn largely from newspaper sources; the author pays too little attention to some of the more important scholarly monographs. Sam Acheson, " Joseph W. Bailey and the Spanish war ", *Southw. rev.*, XVII (1932) 142–160 [**3369**], a study of one Congressman's (later Senator) emotional appeal for war. J. W. Pratt, " The ' large policy ' of 1898 ", *Miss. Valley hist. rev.*, XIX (1932) 219–242 [**3370**], an article of prime importance tracing the development of imperialistic policy and designs of Theodore Roosevelt, Henry Cabot Lodge, and A. T. Mahan; and "American business and the Spanish-American war ", *Hisp. Am. hist. rev.*, XIV (1934) 163–201 [**3370a**], based on the *Wall Street journal, Journal of commerce and commercial bulletin*, and other financial reviews and newspapers, it concludes that in the winter of 1897–98 American business generally preferred peace. H. S. Rubens, *Liberty; the story of Cuba* (N.Y., 1932) [**3371**], the author was general counsel to the Cuban Junta during the war of 1895–98, and thence familiar with the intricate episodes of gun running and problems of belligerency; the work carries on to the present time. It contains a spurious memorandum from the War Department to Gen. Miles on policy for conquest of Cuba (see article by R. M. Spaulding, " Propaganda or legend ", in *Am. hist. rev.*, XXXIX (1934) 485–488 [**3372**], which shows the spurious nature of this document) ; and also gives " inside " information on the theft of the De Lome letter and origin of the Teller amendment. M. M. Wilkerson, *Public opinion and the Spanish-American war; a study in war propaganda* (Baton Rouge, 1932) [**3373**], a useful but mechanical compilation of newspaper quotations, arranged under the implication of the title as an indictment of the war-mongering press. Dyer, *William L. Evarts* (no. 2466). J. E. Wisan, *The Cuban crisis as reflected in the New York press (1895–1898)* (N.Y., 1934) [**3373a**], a sort of " Literary Digest " analysis of the anti-Spanish hysteria of the New York press.

For biographies of American presidents, secretaries of state, and diplomatists abroad (for names and tenure, see latest *Register* of the Dept. of State (no. 5122)), see the relevant entries and bibliographical data in the *D.A.B.* Note in particular, Nevins, *Cleveland* (no. 2467), and *White* (no. 2468) ; and Dennett's *Hay* (no. 2472).

Printed Sources

For general collections, see Sec. 1, above.

For a list of " United States and British government documents (exclusive of resolutions, bills, and speeches), 1822–1896 ", see A. P. C. Griffin (no. 4722), 33–38.

For contemporary periodical material, not cited below, dealing with Cuba, 1825–1898, see A. P. C. Griffin (no. 4722), 23–32; and, for material dealing with the " Expansion of the United States, 1898–1900 ", *ibid.*, 17–22. For lists and indexes of newspapers, see nos. 5004–5047.

Special collections of United States official documents are: *Correspondence relative to the struggle for freedom in the Island of Cuba*, Feb. 22, 1870 (41st Cong., 2d sess. House. Ex. doc. no. 160) [**3374**]. *Information and . . . certain recommendations in relation to the existing insurrection in Cuba*, June 13, 1870 (41st Cong., 2d sess. Senate. Ex. doc., no. 99) [**3375**]. *Information in relation to the emancipation of slaves in Cuba*, July 14, 1870 (41st Cong., 2d sess. Sen. Ex. doc., no. 113) [**3376**]. *Information in relation to the seizure of American vessels, and injuries to American citizens, during the hostilities in Cuba*, July 9, 1870 (41st Cong., 2d sess. Sen. Ex. doc., no. 108) [**3377**]. *Correspondence between the United States government and Spain in relation to the Island of Cuba*, Jan. 21, 1876 (44th Cong., 1st sess. House. Ex. doc., no. 90) [**3378**], the Secretary of State (Fish) transmitted to Congress the note to Spain of Nov. 5, 1875, " together with a few carefully chosen extracts from the correspondence between himself and Mr. Cushing, but nothing was given that might indicate that the United States had appealed to the powers of Europe to countenance intervention " (Latané (no. 1803), 276). *Correspondence with European governments in regard to Cuba*, Jan. 25, 1876 (44th Cong., 1st sess. House. Ex. doc., no. 100) [**3379**], the House called the next day for whatever correspondence had taken place with foreign powers in regard to Cuba. Mr. Fish replied that . . . the note of November 5 had been orally communicated to several European governments ", but no correspondence had taken place; the correspondence was suppressed but finally after 20 years sent to Congress (54th Cong., 1st sess. Sen. Ex. doc., no. 213) (no. 3383 below) (cf. Latané no. 1803), 276. *The terms and conditions under which the surrender of the Cuban insurgents has been made, and in relation to*

the future policy of Spain in the government of the Island of Cuba,
1878 (45th Cong., 2d sess. Sen. Ex. doc., no. 79) **[3380]**. *Recogni-*
tion of Cuban independence, December 21, 1896 (54th Cong., 2d sess.
Senate. Rept. no. 1160) **[3381]**, report of the Committee on Foreign
Relations of the Senate. *Report from the Secretary of State, with*
accompanying correspondence, with regard to the claim of in-
demnity from Spain, for the execution at Santiago de Cuba of
persons who were on board the Virginius, 1875 (54th Cong., 1st
sess. Sen. Doc. no. 165) **[3382]**. *Correspondence of the Depart-*
ment of State between November 5, 1875, and the date of the pacifica-
tion of Cuba in 1878, relating to the subject of mediation or interven-
tion by the United States in the affairs of Cuba, Apr. 15, 1896 (54th
Cong., 1st sess. Sen. Ex. Doc. no. 213) **[3383]**. *Relations of the*
United States and Spain by reason of warfare in the Island of Cuba,
1898 (55th Cong., 2d sess. House. Doc. no. 405) **[3384]**. *Consular*
correspondence respecting the condition of the reconcentrados in
Cuba, the state of war in that island, and the projected autonomy
(55th Cong., 2d sess. House. Doc. 406) **[3385]**. *Report of the*
Committee on Foreign Relations, United States Senate, relative to af-
fairs in Cuba, Apr. 13, 1898 (55th Cong., 2d sess. Sen. Rept. no.
885) **[3386]**. *Report of the naval court of inquiry upon the destruc-*
tion of the United States battleship Maine in Havana Harbor, Febru-
ary 15, 1898, together with the testimony taken before the court, 1898
(55th Cong., 2d sess. Senate. Doc. no. 207) **[3387]**. Also a later
report on the " Maine ", *Final report on removing wreck of battle-*
ship " Maine " from harbor of Habana, Cuba, transmitted by the
Secretary of War, December 13, 1913 (Wash., 1914) (63d Cong.,
2d sess. House. Doc. no. 480) **[3388]** gives the engineer's description of the wreck without verdict of causes. *Filibustering expedi-*
tions; letter of Secretary of Treasury, concerning filibustering expeditions [to Cuba], Nov. 30, 1897 (Wash., 1897) (Treasury Dept.
Doc. 1989) **[3389]**, also in 55th Cong., 2d sess. House. Doc. 326.
Spanish diplomatic correspondence and documents, 1896–1900,
presented to the Cortes by the minister of state (Wash.: Govt. Print.
Off., 1905) **[3390]**, translation of Spanish documents (for Spanish
official publication of these documents, see no. 3397), includes the
general negotiations with the United States from Apr. 10, 1896,
until the declaration of war, the diplomatic negotiations from the
beginning of the war until the signing of the protocol at Wash-

ington, the conference at Paris and the treaty of peace of December 10, 1898, and negotiation for a treaty of cession to the United States of the islands of Sibutú and Cagayan de Joló, and includes some material not previously published. Spanish Treaty Claims Commission, *Final report* . . . , May 2, 1910 (Wash., 1910) [**3391**], the report alone, without the schedule of cases is also issued as Senate doc. 550, 61st Cong., 2d sess.

CUBAN OFFICIAL DOCUMENTS. "Noticia de los agentes secretos del gobierno español en los Estados Unidos de Norte América [1871] ", *Boletín del Archivo Nacional* (Havana), XVIII (1919) 426–433 [**3392**], documents from the *Archivo Nacional*, consisting of reports on Cuban revolutionary juntas in the United States. "Expediente relativo á la salida de New York de los hermanos Sanguilí, para Nueva Orleans y Cayo-Hueso, y de los actos ejecutados por estos y otros insurrectos para organizar expediciones filibusteras [1877] ", *ibid.*, XX (1921) 117–138 [**3393**], from the Consulate General of Spain in New York. "Expediente promovido por nuestro cónsul en Nueva Orleans acerca de la barca americana 'Venus'", *ibid.*, XX (1921) 139–155 [**3394**], despatches from the Spanish consul at New Orleans, 1877–78.

SPANISH OFFICIAL DOCUMENTS: Spain, Ministerio de Estado, *Documentos parlamentarios preparados para ser presentados a las Cortes en la legislatura de 1886; negociaciones con los Estados Unidos de América sobre la interpretación del convenio comercial del 13 de febrero de 1884* (Madrid, 1886) [**3395**]. Two collections of *Documentos presentados á las Cortes en la legislatura de 1898*, by the "Ministro de Estado"—[1] *Disposiciones de España y los Estados Unidos referentes á la guerra y declaraciones de neutralidad* (Madrid, 1898) [**3396**], declarations of neutrality by European governments; and [2] *Negociaciones diplomáticas desde el principio de la guerra con los Estados Unidos hasta la firma del protocolo de Washington y gestiones practicadas para su complimiento* (Madrid, 1898) [**3397**].

The Cuban question (N.Y., 1869) [**3398**], an attack upon Senator Sumner's hesitancy to favor recognition of Cuban belligerency. *The Cuban question and American policy, in the light of common sense* (N.Y., 1869) [**3399**], Cuban propaganda sent to President Grant and calculated to influence him to recognize Cuban belligerency. [Waldo Jiménez de la Romera], *Cuba no se vende* (Madrid,

1870) [**3400**], indignant Spanish statement that Cuba is not for sale.
[V. W. Kingsley], *Spain, Cuba, and the United States; recognition
and the Monroe Doctrine*, by Americus [*pseud.*] (N.Y., 1870) [**3401**],
a plea against recognition of belligerency, particularly now that
Spain had been " regenerated " by a liberal government; adds that
the Monroe Doctrine does not allow intervention within existing
colonies of European states in America. *The Cuban question in
England; extracts from opinions of the press* (London, 1871) [**3402**].
[José de Armas y Céspedes], *Position of the United States on the
Cuban question* (N.Y., 1872) [**3403**], Cuban propaganda for American recognition of belligerency.   Justo Zaragoza, *Las insurrecciones
de Cuba* (Madrid, 1872–73, 2 v.) [**3404**], for the Spanish point of
view.   G. T. Curtis, *The case of the Virginius, considered with reference to the law of self-defense* (N.Y., 1874) [**3405**] deems the seizure of the vessel entirely justifiable, but not the execution of some of
the persons found on board.   [Plutarco González y Torres], *The
"Virginius" case, as reviewed in England and regarded by the
New York Herald* (N.Y., 1874) [**3406**], letter from the owner of
the " Virginius " [J. F. Patterson], to the Secretary of State, Dec.
26, 1873.   José Ruiz de León, *Los filibusteros en Madrid y el apresa-
mento del "Virginius"* (Madrid, 1874) [**3407**], Spanish criticism
of the government for giving up the *Virginius*.   Cuban League of
the United States, *The present condition of affairs in Cuba;* a report
of a special committee of the Cuban League of the United States
(N.Y., 1877) [**3408**], propaganda of Cuban revolutionists.   *La
anexión de Cuba y los Estados Unidos, polémica entre . . .
Juan Bellido de Luna y Enrique Trujillo* (N.Y., 1892) [**3409**],
Bellido de Luna was director of the Cuban paper, *La Independencia*, published in New York in the 1870's.   Trujillo was a
Cuban writer resident in New York. *The Cuban question in its true
light . . .* , by an American (N.Y., 1895) [**3410**], a pro-Spanish
argument against recognition of Cuban belligerency.   Jerónimo
Bécker, *De los derechos de las naciones y del principio de intervención.   La neutralidad y la beligerancia.   España y los Estados
Unidos* (Madrid, 1895) [**3411**], against the right of the United
States to recognize the belligerency of Cuba; the author was later
archivist of the Spanish foreign office.   Segismundo Moret y Prendergast, " La insurrección de Cuba ante los Estados Unidos ", *España
moderna*, año VII, núm. 78 (1895) 46–72; núm. 79 (1895) 42–61

[3412], taking comfort from the appearance in Spain of a correspondent (Aubrey Stanhope) of the conservative New York *Herald*, the author proceeds to analyze the vagueness and lack of character of the Cuban revolutionary program. Calderon Carlisle, *Reports to E. Dupuy de Lome, Spanish minister* [*The law of neutrality of the United States, with reference to the Cuban insurrection*], Calderon Carlisle, legal adviser of the Spanish legation (Wash., 1896–97, 2 v.) [3413]. Cuban Society of Judicial and Economic Studies, *Cuban opinion on the President's message*, manifesto addressed by " The Cuban Society of Judicial and Economic Studies " to the American people (N.Y., 1896) [3414]. H. C. Lodge, " Our duty to Cuba ", *Forum*, XXI (1896) 278–287 [3415], apparently the author thought our duty was to take it, on grounds of humanity, from Spain because of its usefulness to the United States. Rafael Serra y Montalvo, *Ensayos políticos* (N.Y., 1896) [3416], Serra, with José Martí, was one of the Cuban revolutionary junta in New York; this contains some correspondence between the two. R. M. de Labra y Cadrana, *La cuestión de Cuba en 1897* (Madrid, 1897) [3417]; and *Aspecto internacional de la cuestión de Cuba* (Madrid, 1900) [3417a], political essays, rather than juridical studies, by a member of the Spanish opposition, attacking the government's diplomacy, and condemning also the policy and acts of the United States. J. T. Morgan, *Belligerent rights in Cuba;* speeches in the Senate of the United States, Jan. 29, 1896–May 4, 1897 (Wash., 1897) [3418]. Antonio Pérez Rioja, *Los Yankees en Cuba* (Havana, 1897) [3419], intemperate recital by a Spaniard, of " Yankee " politics in Cuba from the time of Jefferson. Charles Benoist, *L'Espagne, Cuba, et les Etats-Unis* (Paris, 1898) [3420], impressions of a French journalist among Spanish liberals. C. H. Butler, *The voice of the nation; the President is right;* a series of papers on our past and present relations with Spain (N.Y., 1898) (Cuba Must be Free Series, no. 1) [3421]. J. V. Findlay, *Some of the international aspects of the Cuban question* (Baltimore? 1898) [3422], a temperate argument to justify American intervention in Cuba. Theodore Marburg, *Political papers* (no. 2734), I. *The war with Spain* [3423] reprints a plea for war, printed in the Baltimore *American*, May 1, 2, 8, 1898, which may be taken as an example of an American intellectual's justification; " the loss of the island [Cuba] to Spain is but a just retribution for inhuman acts; its ultimate acquisition by the United States may

be an act of high state policy." Ricardo Monner Sans, *España y
Norteamérica; la guerra actual, antecedentes y consideraciones*
(Buenos Aires, 1898) [3424], a war-time plea for Spain against
unjust attack of the United States. Alberto Ruz, *La question cubaine* (Paris, 1898) [3425], a Cuban's complaint against the anti-
Cuban and anti-American tone of the French Press. Arthur de
Ganniers, "Les négociations secrètes relatives à Cuba, de 1822 à
1898 (d'après des documents inédits)", *Nouv. revue*, CXVI (1899)
48–65, 232–252 [3426], the documents are mostly from the State
Department, and have been published before or since. J. I. Rodríguez, *Estudio histórico sobre el origen, desenvolvimiento y mani-
festaciones prácticas de la idea de la anexión de la isla de Cuba á los
Estados Unidos de América* (Havana, 1900) [3427], reprint of
documents illustrating American policy toward Cuba, 1776–1898.
Juan Valera y Alcalá Galiano, *Estudios críticos sobre historia y
política (1892–1898)* (Madrid, 1914) [3428] contains a chapter,
"Los Estados Unidos contra España", an emotional "anti-Yankee"
war blast in 1896. Baron von Hengelmüller, "Die diplomatische
Vorgeschichte des Krieges der Vereinigten Staaten gegen Spanien",
Deutsche Rev., XLI (1916) 93–107, 164–179 [3429], written in 1902,
a perspicacious summary by the Austrian ambassador in the United
States at the time of the Spanish-American war. John D. Long,
America of yesterday, as reflected in the journal of John D. Long,
ed. by L. S. Mayo (Boston, 1923) [3430], the journal of the secre-
tary of the navy during the Spanish-American war. *Grosse Politik*
(no. 5476), XV Bd., 1–30: "Der Amerikanish-Spanische Krieg.
Schiedsspruch- und Interventionsfrage 1898." E. B. Underwood,
"An international incident", *U.S.N. inst. proc.*, LI (1925) 83–90
[3431], the *Virginius* affair, by an American naval officer, describes
filthy condition in which the *Virginius* was turned over to the
United States, and the loss of the vessel when being towed to New
York in a storm. E. F. Atkins, *Sixty years in Cuba; reminiscences*
(Cambridge, 1926) [3432], an American sugar planter in Cuba
who became a sort of informal spokesman of anti-interventionist
business element in Cuba to the McKinley Administration. J. A.
Saco, *Contra la anexión* (no. 1832). *Letters of General Tasker
Howard Bliss* (no. 4609b) are important for diplomacy preceding
the Spanish-American war, when Bliss was a peace-loving military
attaché at the Madrid legation.

For a numerous list of other contemporary (mainly Spanish, but including Hispanic American writers) discussion of the Cuban question and the Spanish-American war, see Sánchez Alonso (no. 4759), v. II, 224–252.

MSS.: Suggestions

For official archives of the United States, Great Britain, Spain, Cuba, and other countries, see below: United States, p. 857; Great Britain, p. 890; Spain, p. 898; Cuba, p. 912. The archives of the United States Department of State are now open to 1906; but at this writing (December, 1934), those of Spain and France are closed for such a late period as the Spanish-American war. The date line for investigators in the British archives is 1888. Paz, *Catálogo* (no. 5656) for MSS. relating to America in the Biblioteca Nacional, Madrid.

For papers of the American presidents and secretaries of state for this period, see our lists on pages 862 and 865, respectively (of the secretaries of state, Foster had been minister to Spain, 1883–85, 1891–92). For the papers of American diplomatists in Spain (J. P. Hale, 1865–69; D. E. Sickles, 1869–74; Caleb Cushing, 1874–77; Lucius Fairchild, 1880–81; J. W. Foster, 1883–85, 1891–92; J. L. M. Curry, 1885–88; T. W. Palmer, 1889–90; S. L. Woodford, 1897–98), see our list on p. 868.

Theodore Roosevelt's papers are in the Library of Congress. Senator H. C. Lodge's papers are in the Massachusetts Historical Society.

An interesting collection of papers of the Cuban revolutionary societies in New York are described by Joaquín Llaverías, *Inventario general del archivo de la delegación del partido revolucionario cubano en Nueva York (1892–1898)* (Havana, 1921) [**3433**], also published in the *Boletín del archivo nacional* (Havana), XVI–XXIX (1917–1930) *passim*.

See also " MSS. : Suggestions " in Sec. 3, below.

3. Diplomacy of the War with Spain and the Peace of Paris, 1898
Bibliographical Aids

See Sec. 1 above.

Special Works

Two volumes by A. T. Mahan: *The interest of America in sea power* (Boston, 1897) [**3434**], a group of essays published in magazines during the 1890's by the leading advocate of colonial and naval expansion; and *Lessons of the war with Spain* (Boston, 1899) **[3435]** a series of essays on significant questions of naval power and strategy raised by the war. Arthur Desjardins, " La guerre hispano-américaine et le droit des gens ", *Rev. deux mondes*, 4 pér., CXLVII (1898) 518–549 **[3436]** emphasizes the fact that the United States began the war without a declaration of war, and touches questions of neutrality, blockade, and bombardment. Louis Le Fur, *Etude sur la guerre hispano-américaine de 1898, envisagée au point de vue du droit international public* (Paris, 1899) **[3437]**, " of the secondary authorities . . . by far the most complete and satisfactory, though this book was written before the *Foreign Relations* of the United States for that period was published and is thus incomplete " (Flach). Ernesto Amador y Carrandi, *La guerra hispano-americana ante el derecho internacional* (Madrid, 1900) **[3438]**, bitter and polemic rather than an objective and calmly judicial analysis of legal cases. J. M. Gonzáles Benard, *Proceso histórico del tratado de Paris de 10 diciembre de 1898, con algunas ideas de derecho internacional público* (Valencia, 1903) **[3439]**, a stimulating study by a Spanish lawyer who, not prepared to accept any justification of the American intervention in Cuba, nevertheless views it in the light of race and geography, even as Spanish intervention in Morocco. Achille Viallate, " Les préliminaires de la guerre hispano-américaine et l'annexion des Philippines ", *Rev. hist.*, LXXXII (1903) 242–291, included later in his *Essais d'histoire diplomatique américaine* (Paris, 1905), 207–280 **[3440]**, factual summary from the documents published in *Foreign Relations* (no. 5345) for 1898, the Spanish red books (nos. 3462 and 3463), and the French *Négociations* (no. 3464) ; an unreliable alarmist discourse, rather than a scholarly treatise. Élie Lebraud, *La guerre hispano-américaine et le droit des gens* (Paris, 1904) **[3441]**, University of Paris thesis, characteristically thin in documentation but forcible in conclusion: " Really the conflict of 1898, long premeditated, was a brutal aggression against Spain, to be justified neither in war nor equity." Eugenio Montero Ríos, *El tratado de Paris* (Madrid, 1904) **[3442]**, the author was head of the Spanish peace delegation at Paris in 1898. E. J. Benton, *International law and the diplomacy of the Spanish-American war* (Baltimore, 1908) **[3443]**, among the most complete and impartial studies of the subject. S. B. Crandall, " Principles of international law applied by the Spanish treaty claims commission ", *Am. jour. internat. law*, IV (1910) 806-822 **[3444]**, the United States commission set up to adjudicate claims relinquished in the treaty as against Spain. F. E. Chadwick, *The relations of the United States and Spain; the Spanish-American war* (N.Y., 1911, 2 v.) **[3445]**, the last two chapters contain a narrative of the peace negotiations of 1898 drawn from American printed sources; this is a sequel to the author's work on Spanish-American diplomacy (no. 108). J. B. Moore, *McKinley as a diplomatist*, speech before the Ohio Society of Washington, D.C., on McKinley's birthday, Jan. 29, 1914 (Wash.? 1914) **[3446]**, valuable because of the author's great distinction as a jurist and his intimacy with the Department of State in McKinley's time. Charles Olcott, *The life of William McKinley* (Boston and N.Y., 1916, 2 v.) **[3447]** relates (v. II, 109-111) the incident of how the President was inspired by God to the decision to keep the Philippines, as told in a well-authenticated interview at the White House, Nov. 21, 1899, with a committee representing the General Missionary Committee of the Methodist Episcopal Church. Félix Iznaga, " Ecos del tratado de Paris; la deuda colonial ", *Cuba contemporánea*, XIII (1917) 214-280 **[3448]**, a Cuban writer shows how the United States delegates at Paris resisted any responsibility for the so-called colonial debt of Spain and kept it out of the treaty; this means Spain cannot collect it from *Cuba libre*, as there was in 1909 and 1910 some talk of doing, at least in Spanish newspapers. Keim, *German-Am. relations* (no. 4305). Tyler Dennett, *Americans in Asia* (no. 3098) explains reasons for insisting on the Philippines; see also his *John Hay* (no. 2472). H. H. Kohlsaat, *From McKinley to Harding; personal recollections of our presidents* (N.Y., 1923) **[3449]** reveals (p. 68) McKinley's astonishing geographical ignorance about the Philippines in May, 1898. Reuter, *Anglo-Am. relations* (no. 2775), this is a path-breaking study, unfortunately completed before the publication of the German (no. 5476) and English (no. 5475) documents on the origins of the world war; now in part superseded by L. B. Shippee, " Germany and the Spanish-American war ", *Am. hist. rev.*, XXX (1925) 754-777 **[3450]** reveals German policy in the Spanish-American war from documents in the *Grosse Politik* (no. 5476) showing Germany's disappointment at American acquisition of the Philippines and her frustrated appetite for them. Hashagen,

Am.-deutsch. Beziehungen (no. 4308). M. M. Kalaw, *The development of Philippine politics (1872–1920), an account of the part played by Filipino leaders and parties in the development of the Philippines* (Manila, 1927) [3451]. L. M. Sears, " French opinion of the Spanish American war ", *Hisp. Am. hist. rev.*, VII (1927) 25–44 [3452], as revealed by the *Journal des débats* and French periodical and pamphlet literature. J. F. Rippy, " The European powers and the Spanish-American war ", *James Sprunt hist. stud.*, XIX, no. 2 (1927) 22–52 [3453], included also in the author's *Latin America in world politics* (no. 1076). Bernhard Zims, *Die Grossmächte und der Spanisch-Amerikansche Krieg* (Quakenbrück, 1929) [3454], inaugural dissertation, Westfälische Wilhelms-Universitat in Münster; apparently unaware of Rippy's work (no. 3453) on the same subject, the author develops the matter as revealed by post-war archival publications of European powers. Mary E. Townsend, *Germany's colonial empire* (no. 2352) discusses Philippine affairs during the Spanish-American war. C. G. Bowers, *Beveridge and the Progressive era* (Boston, 1932) [3455], Senator Beveridge was an imperialist, wanted the United States to take its place in world politics, asserted " there was no such thing as isolation in the world today." Orestes Ferrara, *Tentativas de intervención Europea en América, 1896–1898* (Havana, 1933) [3456], based on material in French, Spanish, and Italian archives. Stolberg-Wernigerode, *Deutschland und Vereinigten Staaten* (no. 4314). Beard, *National interest* (no. 4823) has some stimulating philosophic chapters on the causes and results of this war.

For biographies of President McKinley, and secretaries of state (John Sherman, W. R. Day, and John Hay), and the American delegates to the Peace Conference at Paris (W. R. Day, Whitelaw Reid, Judge George Gray, Cushman K. Davis, W. P. Frye), see the relevant entries and bibliographical data in the *D.A.B.* Note also Dennett's *John Hay* (no. 2472); and F. H. Gillett, *George Frisbie Hoar* (Boston and N.Y., 1934) [3456a].[1]

Printed Sources

For general collections, see Sec. 1, above.

See also Sec. 2, above. For text of the Treaty of Paris, see Malloy (no. 5368); and guide to treaty collections, p. 822.

---

[1] Published too late for entry in the *D.A.B.*

UNITED STATES OFFICIAL DOCUMENTS (see also Sec. 2, above) : *A treaty of peace between the United States and Spain, signed at the city of Paris, on December 10, 1898*, 1898 (55th Cong., 3d sess., Senate. Doc. no. 62, pts. 1–3) [**3457**], treaty with Spain, text and map, and actual records of the conferences between the American and Spanish commissioners at Paris. U.S. Dept. of State, *Proclamations and decrees during the war with Spain* (Wash., 1899) [**3458**], proclamations and decrees of neutrality by foreign countries, etc. U.S. War Dept., *Report on legal status of islands acquired during the war with Spain* (Wash., 1900) [**3459**]. U.S. Dept. of State, *Papers relating to the treaty with Spain* (Wash., 1901) (56th Cong., 2d sess. Senate. Doc. no. 148) [**3460**]. U.S. War Dept., *Cuban pacification;* report of Secretary of War and Assistant Secretary of State, Dec. 11, 1906 (Wash., 1907) [**3460a**]; also by the War Dept., *Acts of Congress and treaties pertaining to the Philippine Islands in force and effect July 1, 1919* (Wash., 1920) [**3461**].

SPANISH OFFICIAL DOCUMENTS: *Conferencia de Paris y tratado de paz de 10 de diciembre de 1898* (Madrid, 1899) (Documentos presentados á las Cortes en la Legislatura de 1898, por el Ministro de Estado) [**3462**]. *Negociaciones de un tratado de cesión á los Estados Unidos de las islas de Sibitú y Cagayán de Jolo* (Madrid, 1900) (Documentos presentados á las Cortes en la Legislatura de 1900 por el Ministro de Estado) [**3463**].

Brit. docs. on origins of war (no. 5475), v. I, 105–107 : " The Manila incident (Germany and the United States)," prints a letter from the commanding officer of H.M. ship " Immortalité ", dated the 14th of July, together with enclosures reporting friction between the admirals of the United States' squadron and the German squadron at Manila, July 14, 1898.

France, Ministère des Affaires Étrangères, *Documents diplomatiques. Négociations pour la paix entre l'Espagne et les Etats-Unis, 1898* (Paris, 1898) [**3464**].

Grosse Politik (no. 5476), XV Bd., 31–105 : " Die Philippinen- und die Karolinienfrage. Die Englisch-Amerikanische Annäherung, 1898–1899 ", prints most of the German documents regarding the Manila affair.

The Harvard College Library has an extensive collection of anti-imperialist pamphlets. The Library of Congress also has, in its

Carnegie collection of MSS., a number of anti-imperialist pamphlets, 1899–1900, including a series of " Liberty Tracts " published by the American Anti-imperialist League.

Ricardo Becerra, *Cuestión palpitante; un poco de historia á propósito de la independencia de Cuba y Puerto Rico, y la doctrina Monroe y la intervención norte-americana en Cuba* (Caracas, 1898) [**3465**], a South American opinion. *Le traité de paix entre l'Espagne et les États-Unis* (n.p., 1898?) [**3466**], discussion from the Spanish point of view, of the questions of recognition and payment of Cuban debts, and of the occupation of the Philippines. Edmund Kelly, "An American in Madrid ", *Century*, LVII (1899) 450–457 [**3467**], enlightening in showing the courteous and even considerate treatment experienced in an enemy country. Rafael M. de Labra, *El tratado de Paris de 1898* (Madrid, 1899) [**3468**], the author was a member of the Spanish opposition in 1898. Whitelaw Reid, *Some consequences of the last treaty of Paris, advances in international law and changes in national policy* (London and N.Y., 1899) [**3469**], the author was one of the American peace delegation; also by the same writer, *The Treaty of Paris; some speeches on its policy and scope* (N.Y., 1899) [**3470**]. Carl Schurz, *American imperialism* (Chicago? 1899) [**3471**], address given at the 27th convocation of the University of Chicago, by an anti-imperialist; also by Schurz, *The policy of imperialism* (Chicago, 1899) [**3472**], address at the Anti-imperialist Conference in Chicago, October 17, 1899. G. S. Boutwell, *The president's policy; war and conquest abroad* (Chicago, 1900) [**3473**], published by the American Anti-Imperialist League, of which the writer was president. "A statement of events in Manila, May–October, 1898 ", by Admiral von Diederichs, translated, by permission, from the *Marine Rundschau*, is printed in the *Royal unit. ser. inst. jour.*, LIX (1914) 421–446 [**3474**], Diederichs' " statement " was intended as an answer to Dewey's *Autobiography* (no. 3480). Diederichs' cautious account must now be corrected by documents in the *Grosse Politik* (no. 5476), cf. Shippee (no. 3450). " The diplomatic correspondence (1898–1899) of Hon. Felipe Agoncillo ", *Philippine soc. sci. rev.*, II (1930) 140–150 [**3475**], some of the documents have never been published before; others have been published in the *Congressional Record* and in Taylor's *Philippine Insurgent*

Records.[2] " With the exception of a few . . . these documents constitute a complete record of Mr. Agoncillo's activities as foreign agent of the revolutionary government charged with the most difficult and delicate task of working for its recognition by the powers."
Souvenirs de Charles Benoist (Paris, 1932–33, 2 v.) [3478] has observations on Spain and the war written while the author was correspondent in Spain of the *Temps* and the *Revue des deux mondes*.
Francisco de Reynoso, *Reminiscences of a Spanish diplomat* (London, 1933) [3479], Reynoso was one of the Spanish commission which negotiated the peace of 1898. These memoirs say nothing about the negotiations, but contain the incidental interesting statement: " It would have been better for Spain to have accepted the offer of Marshall Yamagata, the Japanese victor of the Chinese war, made tentatively in Moscow during the coronation of Czar Nicholas II in 1894, to sell the Philippines to Japan for forty million pounds."

For printed writings of President McKinley, secretaries of state (John Sherman, W. R. Day, and John Hay), and the American delegates to the Peace Conference at Paris (W. R. Day, Whitelaw Reid, Judge George Gray, Cushman K. Davis, W. P. Frye), Theodore Roosevelt, and Sen. H. C. Lodge, see our list on p. 756.

Note also, *Autobiography of George Dewey, admiral of the Navy* (N.Y., 1913) [3480], for an account of the situation at Manila in 1898. George F. Hoar, *Autobiography of seventy years* (N.Y., 1903, 2 v.) [3481], Hoar was a Republican anti-imperialist, senator from Massachusetts. *Autobiography of Andrew Dickson White* (N.Y., 1905, 2 v.) [3482], ambassador to Germany, 1897–1902, gives notes of "America, Germany, and the Spanish-American war."

MSS.: Suggestions

See Sec. 2, above.

For papers of President McKinley and Theodore Roosevelt, see our list on p. 862; our list, p. 867, for papers of John Hay (ambassador to Great Britain, 1897–98, and secretary of state, 1898–

---

[2] Two publications prepared by J. R. M. Taylor, and issued by the War Department, Bureau of Insular Affairs: *Report on the organization for the administration of the government instituted by Emilio Aguinaldo and his followers in the Philippine Archipelago* (Wash., 1903) [3476], " the information utilized in preparing this report is a mass of records captured from the Philippine insurgents during the period of hostilities "; and *Compilation of Philippine insurgent records. I. Telegraphic correspondence of Emilio Aguinaldo, July 15, 1898, to February 28, 1899* (Wash., 1903) [3477].

1905); and our list on p. 883, for papers of Henry White (secretary of the American embassy in London, 1897–98), and Andrew White, ambassador to Germany, 1897–1902. For the American peace commissioners of 1898 (W. R. Day, Whitelaw Reid, Judge George Gray, W. P. Frye) inquiries might be made to their descendants. The Reid papers in the Yale Library are for the years 1872–73; but Royal Cortissoz's biography (v. I, ix) notes that he had " unrestricted access " to Reid's correspondence.

The papers of Senator J. T. Morgan, of Alabama, an active imperialist, are in the Library of Congress (restricted). The papers of Senator H. C. Lodge, leading imperialist with Roosevelt, are in the Massachusetts Historical Society. For anti-imperialist MSS.: Papers of Senator George F. Hoar, of Massachusetts, in the possession of his daughter-in-law, Mrs. Christine Rice Hoar Gillett, 34 Oak Ave., Worcester, Mass.; W. J. Bryan, see our list, p. 867; Carl Schurz, see our list, p. 881; Moorfield Storey, said to be in the possession of his son, Charles M. Storey, of Boston; and the William A. Croffut collection of papers of the Washington branch of the Anti-Imperialist League, recently (1933) acquired by the Library of Congress. The papers of Rounsevelle Wildman, U. S. consul at Hong Kong, 1898–1900, in the Library of Congress show relationships between the U. S. Government and the Filipino insurrectionists on the eve of the war.

Maps: Suggestions

P. L. Phillips, " Maps of Cuba, Porto Rico, and the West Indies in the Library of Congress ", in Griffin, *List relating to Cuba* (no. 4722), 41–57 [3482a]; " Maps relating to Cuba ", in Quesada, *Cuba* (no. 3483), 447–512 [3483]; and " Chronological list of maps [of the Philippines] in the Library of Congress ", in *Bibliog. Philippine Islands* (no. 3329), 269–378. *A treaty of peace with Spain* (55th Cong., 3d sess. Senate Doc. no. 62) (no. 3457), text and map.

CHAPTER XIX

HISPANIC AMERICA AND THE CARIBBEAN, 1861–1921

1. In General.
2. Mexico, 1867–1921.
3. Colombia and Panama.
4. Central America.
5. The Caribbean.

6. South America.
7. The Pan American Movement.
8. The Monroe Doctrine in the 20th century.

1. In General

Bibliographical Aids

For general aids, see Larned (no. 4657) ; Griffin (no. 4658) ; *Writings* (no. 4661) ; C. H. and T. (no. 4662) ; *Guide hist. lit.* (no. 4634) ; and bibliographies in *Am. secs. state* (no. 4796). Myers (no. 5399) for collections of treaties. See also the Hispanic American national historical bibliographies (nos. 4678–4725a) ; and Spanish historical bibliographies (nos. 4758–4760) ; particularly Sánchez Alonso (no. 4759), v. II, 253–263, for references to works on Pan Americanism, later phases of the Monroe Doctrine, United States expansion in the Caribbean, intervention, etc., but not so complete for Hispanic American history (especially contributions thereto in the United States) as for Spanish.

For indexes to periodical literature, see nos. 4995–5003; particularly *Poole's index* (no. 4995), *Readers' guide* (no. 4996), and *Internat. index* (no. 4997).

For lists and indexes of newspapers, see nos. 5004–5047; particularly Library of Congress check lists (nos. 5030, 5032).

A. P. C. Griffin, *Recognition in internat. law* (no. 4801). Griffin and Meyer, *References on reciprocity* (no. 1333), 93–100, for material relating to negotiations with the Spanish American states under the McKinley act, 1890–94. Boston Public Library, *A selected list of books on the commercial relations of South America, principally with the United States* (Boston, 1918) (Brief Reading List, no. 4)

[3484]. Robertson, *Hisp.-Am. and U.S.* (no. 1206), 431–455, for a comprehensive bibliographical list. Beman, *Intervention* (no. 3507) has a good bibliography, including a useful list of contemporary periodical articles on the subject. Two lists (mimeographed) issued by the Pan American Union, Columbus Memorial Library (C. E. Babcock, librarian): *Selected list of books and magazine articles on inter-American relations* (Wash., 1932; 2d ed., 1934) [3485] which is "limited to works in English and to books and magazine articles that should be readily available in large libraries"; and *Theses on Pan American topics prepared by candidates for degrees in universities and colleges in the United States* (Wash., 1933) [3486]. For bibliographical remarks upon the progress of Hispanic American studies in the United States, see Ch. 1 of Wilgus, *Modern Hisp. America* (no. 3502.)

For more special bibliographies on particular phases of Hispanic-American relations with the United States, see the following sections of this chapter.

General Works

Of general histories of the United States, see Rhodes (no. 4783), to 1909. Oberholtzer (no. 4785), to 1888.

For general histories of Hispanic America, see Ch. VIII, sec. 1. Latané, *America as world power* (no. 3344). F. A. Ogg, *National progress, 1907–1917* (N.Y. and London, 1918) (American Nation . . . XXVII) [3487]. Francisco García Calderón, *Latin America, its rise and progress* (N.Y., 1913) [3488], brilliant cultural interpretation, by a Peruvian diplomat and scholar. Fish, *U.S. as world power* (no. 2461). W. R. Shepherd, *The Hispanic nations of the new world* (New Haven, 1919) [3489]. Rhodes, *McKinley and Roosevelt* (no. 2462). Coolidge, *U.S. as world power* (no. 3345).

Special Works

B. G. Lewis, "Our trade relations with Latin America", *Jour. pol. econ.*, XIV (1906) 602–613 [3490] reviews rapidly growing trade in manufactures with South America in relation to political policy. Critchfield, *Am. supremacy* (no. 1205). G. H. Blakeslee, ed., *Latin America* (N.Y., 1914) (Clark University Addresses, November 1913) [3491], papers by specialists (mostly United States), read at the first of university conferences on Latin American affairs ever held in the United States. César Gondra, *Los Estados Unidos y las naciones americanas* [1] (Buenos Aires, 1918) [3492]. Latané, *U.S. and Lat. Am.* (no. 963). Raúl de Cárdenas y Echarte, *La política de los Estados Unidos en el continente americano* (Havana, 1921) [3493], one of the most dispassionate reviews of American imperialism, by a Hispanic American author, who sees the policy of the United States controlled by strategic rather than by economic motives. The author's views are also embodied in a shorter article, " La preponderencia de los Estados Unidos en el mar Caribe ", *Cuba contemporánea*, XXV (1921) 221-237 (English translation, " The preponderance of the United States on the Caribbean Sea ", *Inter-America*, IV (1921) 275-284 [3494]. J. F. Rippy, " Literary Yankeephobia in Hispanic America ", *Jour. internat. relations*, XII (1922) 350-371, 524-538 [3495], an instructive survey of selected contemporary South American writers (Rubén Darío, J. E. Rodó, F. García Calderón, R. Blanco-Fombona, Manuel Ugarte, Carlos Pereyra, S. R. Merlos, J. M. Vargas Vila). Robertson, *Hisp.-Am. and U.S.* (no. 1206). S. G. Inman, *Ventures in inter-American friendship* (N.Y., 1925) [3495a], after describing cultural development, the author expresses the fear of Hispanic Americans at the domination of South America politically by the influx of loans [mostly since defaulted without the United States lifting an eyebrow] from the United States. Scott Nearing and Joseph Freeman, *Dollar diplomacy; a study in American imperialism* (N.Y., 1925) [3496], this is the most representative of attacks by American citizens on the foreign policy of their country in Central America, the Carribbean, South America, the Far East, and elsewhere. P. A. Martin, *Latin America and the war* (Baltimore, 1925) (Albert Shaw Lectures on Diplomatic History, 1921) [3497], a detailed analysis of the diplomatic relations of the Hispanic American republics as affected by the world war, including of course their attitude toward the Wilsonian program. Manuel Ugarte, *The destiny of a continent*, ed., with an introduction and bibliography, by J. F. Rippey [*sic.*], tr. from the Spanish by Catherine A. Phillips (N.Y., 1925; Sp. ed., Madrid, 1923) [3498], a powerful book by one of the most brilliant thinkers and writers of Latin America, an Argentine, who became convinced that Latin America was in danger of being absorbed by

---

[1] We have not been able to see a copy.

the United States; probably the most influential utterance of this
kind. The English edition is preceded by an illuminating preface
by the noted North American Hispanic scholar, J. F. Rippy. Tyler,
For. policy Blaine (no. 2223). Cole, *Recognition policy* (no. 4815)
has section of value on President Wilson's policy of recognition.
C. H. Haring, *South America looks at the United States* (N.Y.,
1928) [3499], the most perspicuous of contemporary appraisals of
South American opinion of the United States; but Venezuela, Colombia, and Ecuador are largely neglected. We may hope the
author will give us another appraisal of the decade since. His
South American progress (Cambridge, Mass., 1934) [3499a] is a
popular survey of contemporary political, social, and economic development of the South American republics, with one chapter
appraising present-day South American relations of the United
States. Rippy, *Lat. Am. in world politics* (no. 1076), incorporating
results of earlier studies, this book extends to a luminous discussion
of the present problems of Latin America in relation to world politics. Also by the same author, *Hist. evolution Hisp. Am.* (no. 1204).
J. W. Stinson, " Our treaties with Latin America and its modern
constitutions ", *Am. law rev.*, LXII (1928) 834–847 [3500], a useful
and rare historical review of treaties of the United States with
those nations. Ernesto Quesada, *Die wirtschaftsbeziehungen zwischen Latein-Amerika und der Vereinigten Staaten* (Leipzig, 1931)
[3500a], accepting the different conditions of British and of Spanish settlements in North and in South America, the author stresses
the place of the Latin American nations in the 19th century as ex-
porters of raw materials. Distrustful of Pan Americanism, he
pleads for the removal of tariff barriers, particularly those of the
United States. Stuart, *Lat. Am. and U.S.* (no. 965) deals in a general way with contemporary problems. Dyer, *Evarts* (no. 2466)
deals with the public career of W. M. Evarts, secretary of state,
1877–81. J. L. McMahon, *Recent changes in the recognition policy
of the United States* (Wash., 1933) [3501] analyses Wilson's departure from the established principle of recognizing *de facto* governments, and Harding's reversion to the old practice; with particular relation to Central America and Mexico. A. C. Wilgus, ed.,
Modern Hispanic America (Wash., 1933) [3502], George Washington University conference by various specialists on contemporary Hispanic American affairs. Contains articles by J. F. Rippy,

" The British bondholder and the Roosevelt corollary of the Monroe Doctrine " (also printed in *Pol. sci. quar.*, XLIX (1934) 195–207), from reports of the council of British bondholders interested particularly in the San Domingo Improvement Co. the author concludes that they probably exerted some influence with Roosevelt's intervention in Santo Domingo and the development of this policy in the Caribbean, but were not wholly satisfied with it later because of scaling down of Dominican obligations; W. R. Manning, " The attitude of the United States toward the insurgent Spanish colonies "; C. C. Tansill, " The European background of the Monroe Doctrine "; R. F. Nichols, " Latin American guano diplomacy "; J. A. Robertson, " Intellectual cooperation between the Americas." Beard, *National interest* (no. 4823).

For biographies of American presidents, secretaries of state, and diplomatists to Hispanic American nations (for names and tenure, see latest *Register* of the Dept. of State (no. 5122)), see the relevant entries and bibliographical data in the *D.A.B.* Note also Muzzey, *Blaine* (no. 2226). Dennett, *John Hay* (no. 2472);[2] and Thayer, *Roosevelt* (no. 2469); Bishop, *Roosevelt* (no. 2470); and Pringle, *Roosevelt* (no. 2471)[3]

For biographies of Hispanic American diplomatists to the United States (for names and tenure, to 1874, see the *Register* of the Dept. of State, 1874) consult the Hispanic American biographical dictionaries (nos. 4932–4958).

Printed Sources

For American official documents and general source collections, see p. 810; particularly *Jour. exec. proc. Sen.* (no. 5387); *Cong. Globe* (no. 5384); *Cong. Record* (no. 5385); *For. relations* (no. 5345); Richardson (no. 5335); Moore's *Arbitrations* (no. 5364), and *Digest* (no. 5365).

For guide to Hispanic American official documents,[4] see p. 841.

For treaty texts, see Malloy (no. 5368); for collections of treaties, Myers (no. 5399) and analysis of treaty collections in Pt. II, ch. 2 (p. 822).

---

[2] Published after the Hay entry in the *D.A.B.*

[3] We mention these Roosevelt entries in advance of fuller material expected in the *D.A.B.*

[4] Manning's documentary series (no. 5342) is planned only to 1860. One would fain hope for its ultimate continuance! And for an Hispanic American counterpart to Manning.

For contemporary periodical material, consult the indexes to periodicals (nos. 4995–5003).

For lists and indexes of newspapers, see nos. 5004–5047; particularly Library of Congress check lists (nos. 5030, 5032) ; and, for list of Hispanic American newspapers, Pan American Union *Catalogue* (no. 5037).

For printed sources for particular countries and regions, see separate sections following in this chapter.

Woodrow Wilson, *United States and Latin America* (Wash., 1913) [3503], the famous Mobile national self-denial speech; it can be found also in the writings of Wilson (no. 5315). Huntington Wilson, " The relation of government to foreign investment ", *Am. acad. pol. and soc. sci. ann.*, LXVIII (1916) 298–311 [3503a] is a quasi-official exposition of dollar diplomacy in principle, by a former assistant secretary of state in the Taft administration. Elihu Root, *Latin America and the United States* (Cambridge, Mass., 1917) [3504] gives addresses which the Secretary of State made in various countries on his visit to Hispanic America in 1906–07; and other addresses on Hispanic American affairs. Isidro Fabela, *Los Estados Unidos contra la libertad; estudios de historia diplomática americana (Cuba, Filipinas, Panamá, Nicaragua, República Dominicana)* (Barcelona, 1921) [3505], a bitter and polemical indictment of American imperialistic policy towards Hispanic America and the Philippines and our intervention in these countries, by a Mexican diplomatist. W. R. Manning, ed., *Arbitration treaties among the American nations to the close of the year 1910* (N.Y., 1924) [3506]. L. T. Beman, comp., *Selected articles on intervention in Latin America* (N.Y., 1928) [3507], excerpts from selected articles, *pro* and *con*, for debates, with a bibliography. " Recent aspects of our relations with Latin America ", *Am. acad. pol. and soc. sci. ann.*, CXXXVIII (1928) 54–81 [3508], a symposium of views by public men, professors, and diplomatists. Louis Guilaine, *L'Amérique Latine et l'impérialisme américain* (Paris, 1928) [3509], another plea against North American " financial imperialism ", couched in the form of an (undocumented) historical essay. C. E. Hughes, *Our relations to the nations of the western hemisphere* (Princeton, 1928) [3510], here the former secretary of state develops his conceptions of foreign policy on the Monroe Doctrine, Latin America, intervention, recognition, Central America, arbitration, and international organization. W. R. Sutherland,

A debate handbook on the United States and the protection of capital invested in Central and Latin America; a collection of essays and addresses concerning our economic, political, and military developments under the Monroe Doctrine and our Caribbean policy (Lexington, 1928) [3511]. Max Winkler, *Investments of United States capital in Latin America* (Boston, 1928) (World Peace Foundation Pamphlets, XI, no. 6) [3512], a most useful book of statistics; shows among other things, that the United States has intervened most where it had least capital at stake. Horacio Blanco-Fombona, *Crímenes del imperialismo norteamericano* (Mexico, 1929) [3513], Mexican indictment of "Yankee imperialism." Léon Rollin, *El imperio de una sombra (Monroe y la América latina)*, tr. from the French by Javier Bueno (Madrid, 1930) [3514], the title tells the thesis; more fear of Hispanic America at the imperialistic shadow of the United States. Baker's *Life and letters of Wilson* (no. 5315), v. IV, 1913-1914, has discussion of Wilson's policy regarding Mexico, the Panama Canal tolls, Caribbean problems, the Colombian treaty, Nicaragua, the Dominican Republic, and Haiti.

For the printed writings of American presidents, secretaries of state, and diplomatists to Hispanic American nations (for names and tenure, see latest *Register* of the Dept. of State(no. 5122)), see our list on p. 756.

Printed writings of Hispanic American diplomatists to the United States so far as they have appeared, are entered in appropriate sections below.

MSS.: Suggestions

As so little listing of MS. material has been done outside of the United States, we are grouping suggestions for further research in MSS. here, instead of the individual sections of this chapter below. The greater part of the listed MSS. are to be found in the United States. Further cultivation of the Hispanic American field may locate a host of private MSS. of diplomatists, etc.

For official archives of the United States, and of the Hispanic American countries, see below, p. 857, and 909, respectively.

For papers of American presidents and secretaries of state, see below, pp. 862-867.

The papers of the following American diplomatists to Hispanic American countries can be indicated (see our list on p. 868): W. T.

Coggeshall (minister to Ecuador, 1866–67) ; J. W. Foster (minister to Mexico, 1873–80) ; T. H. Nelson (minister to Chile, 1861–65, and to Mexico, 1869–73) ; E. L. Plumb (secretary of legation in Mexico, 1866, and before and after that a consul at Havana).

The papers of Francis Lieber, who, in 1870, was chosen as umpire by the commission for settling claims between Mexico and the United States are in the Huntington Library, at San Marino, California.

The voluminous papers of General Leonard Wood, highly important for early relations with Cuba, are in the Library of Congress.

Senator Lodge's papers are listed below.

The personal papers of Mr. Philippe Bunau-Varilla, of Paris, would throw a flood of light on the origin of the Republic of Panama and on canal diplomacy.

Maps: Suggestions

The various maps relating to Hispanic America are pretty completely covered in the American Geographical Society, *Catalogue of maps of Hispanic America* (no. 5153). Wilgus, *Maps rel. to Latin America* (no. 5154).

2. Mexico, 1867–1921

Bibliographical Aids

For general aids, see Sec. 1, above. See also Mexican historical bibliographies: U.S. War Dept., *Index* (no. 4712) ; and New York Public Library, *List rel. to Mexico* (no. 4713).

Two bibliographies by Ignacio B. del Castillo: *Bibliografía de la imprenta de la Cámara de Diputados para servir a los historiadores de la época de Madero, Huerta y la convención, 1912–1915* (Mexico, 1918) [3515]; and *Bibliografía de la revolución mexicana de 1910–1916; historia, legislación, literatura, cuestiones sociales, políticas y económicas documentos, etc., marzo de 1908 a junio de 1916* (Mexico, 1918) [3516]. C. K. Jones, "Bibliography of the Mexican revolution", *Hisp. Am. hist. rev.*, II (1919) 311–314 [3517]. Pan American Union, Columbus Memorial Library, *Bibliography; books and magazine articles in the library of the Pan American Union on relations between the United States and Mexico* (Wash., 1924 [3518], mimeographed. Relyea, *U.S. and Mexico* (no. 3542), 90–91. Library of Congress, Division of Bibliography, *United States relations with Mexico and Central America, with special reference to intervention*, W. A. Slade, chief bibliographer (Wash., 1928) [**3519**], a mimeographed list. Römer, *Mexiko, 1910–1914* (no. 3550), 140–149, for a useful bibliography, particularly of periodical material, 1909–14. *Bibliografía mexicana* (Mexico, 1930–) [**3520**], a monthly publication listing recent works dealing with Mexico, and articles in periodicals treating of Mexican history and present affairs. Roberto Ramos, *Bibliografía de la revolución mexicana (hasta mayo de 1931)* (Mexico, 1931) [**3521**].

Special Works

For general histories of the United States, see Sec. 1, above. For general histories of Mexico, see Ch. X, above.

[J. T. Doyle], " History of the ' Pious Fund ' of California ", *Cal. hist. soc. pap.*, I, pt. 1 (1887) 41–60 [**3522**], an undocumented summary written long before the Hague arbitration of the question. Albéric Rolin, "L'affaire Cutting; conflit entre les Etats-Unis de l'Amérique du Nord et le Mexique en 1886 ", *Rev. droit internat.*, XX (1888) 559–577 [**3523**], Cutting was an American citizen arrested in Mexico for an alleged libel published in the United States against a citizen of Mexico. [Fernando Solís Cámara], *Biographical sketch of Señor Lic. Joaquín D. Casasús, ambassador of Mexico to the United States* (N.Y., 1905) [**3524**], later special ambassador, 1911. " The Chamizal arbitration between the United States and Mexico ", *Am. jour. internat. law*, V (1911) 782–833 [**3525**], summary of the question and arbitration; the Chamizal tract was disputed territory because of the shifting Rio Grande River. Miles Dobson, *At the edge of the pit* (Pasadena, Calif., 1914) [**3526**], a discussion of the foreign relations of the United States, especially with Japan and Mexico, and of the question of the Panama Canal tolls; lists atrocities and outrages on European and American citizens during the revolution following the fall of Díaz. E. E. Schulz, *El porvenir de México y sus relaciones con los Estados Unidos* (Mexico, 1914) [**3527**], by a Mexican professor writing under the slogan " Por la patria y por la raza." J. Singer, *Die mexicanischen Finanzen und Wilsons panamerikanische Politik* (Berlin, 1914) [**3528**], German study unsympathetic to the United States. Frederick Starr, *Mexico and the United States; a story of revolution, intervention, and war* (Chicago, 1914) [**3529**], an American who has lived long in Mexico writes a book, but not a history, to explain why the Mexican revolutions occurred after 1910, and warns of the folly of intervention. Ramón Guzmán, *El intervencionismo de Mr. Wilson en México* (New Orleans, La., 1915) [3530], by the director of the *Pan American review;* the author, not a Mexican, sees a great contrast between the words and deeds of President Wilson. Francisco Bulnes, *The whole truth about Mexico; President Wilson's responsibility*, authorized translation by Dora Scott (N.Y., 1916) [3531], the author was a Mexican publicist of the Díaz regime. A. M. Carreño, *Notas para una biografía del licenciado Joaquín D. Casasús* (Mexico, 1916) [3532], special ambassador of Mexico in 1911. W. R. Lewis, " The Hayes administration and Mexico ", *Southw. hist. nuar.*, XXIV (1920) 140–153 [3533], useful academic exercise, diligently constructed from United States printed documents. Professor H. I. Priestley, the leading American historian of Mexico (see no. 1462) has written two contemporary articles: " The relations of the United States and Mexico since 1910 ", *Univ. of Calif. chronicle*, XXII (1920) 47–60 [3534], and " The Carranza débâcle, *ibid.*, 138–252 [3535]. [F. H. Severance], " The Peace conference at Niagara Falls in 1914 ", *Buffalo hist. soc. pub.*, XVIII (1914) 1–75 [3536] contains a review of the A B C conference at Niagara Falls in 1914. R. E. L. Saner, " When President Díaz sought recognition; similarity of conditions imperiling Mexican-American relations in Hayes administration and international difficulties preceding Obregon's election ", *Am. bar assoc. jour.*, VI (1920) 195–197 [3537]. C. L. Jones, *Mexico and its reconstruction* (N.Y. and London, 1921) [3538], a reliable account of the recent history of Mexico, with considerable attention to its relations with the United States. Based on printed sources. F. W. Powell, *The railroads of Mexico* (Boston, 1921) [3539] contains much valuable material concerning concessions, construction, financing, with valuable bibliography in appendix. Carreño, *México y los Estados Unidos* (no. 1461). Two works by C. W. Hackett, *The recognition of the Díaz government by the United States* (Austin, Tex., 1924) [3540], reprinted from the *Southwestern historical quarterly*, v. XXVIII, 34–55; a careful study by a competent scholar, based almost exclusively on United States printed documents; and *The Mexican revolution and the United States, 1910-1926* (Boston, 1926) (World Peace Foundation. Pamphlets, IX, no. 5) [3541], a careful and understandable summary and analysis of a complicated problem, drawn from contemporary official printed documents. Pauline S. Relyea, *Diplomatic relations between the United States and Mexico under Porfirio Diaz, 1876–1910* (Northampton, Mass., 1924) (Smith College Studies in History, X, no. 1) [3542], an academic exercise based on diligent reading of printed United States documents. Launa M. Smith, *American relations with Mexico* (Oklahoma City, 1924) [3543], reviewing conditions since 1910 as revealed in the *Congressional record* principally— " If the two nations do ever go to war, American capital will cause it." George Creel, *The people next door; an interpretive history of Mexico and the Mexicans* (N.Y., 1926) [3544], loose journalitic history. Toribio Esquivel Obregón, *México y los Estados Unidos ante el derecho internacional* (Mexico, 1926) [3545] gathers momentum from a review of American expansion to indict the United States for damages to Mexico which " all the gold in the United States could not pay for ", but has less discussion of damages by Mexico to American citizens and property. Ernest Gruening, *Mexico and its heritage* (N.Y. and London, 1928) [3546], principally a history of Mexico's revolutions, church issues, and the general condition of the country at the time of writing, rather than foreign relations. J. F. Rippy, José Vasconcelos, and Guy Stevens, *Mexico* (Chicago, 1928) (Chicago Council on Foreign Relations) [3547], a symposium of three papers dealing with the relations between Mexico and the United States since the downfall of the Díaz régime, 1910–27. Also by J. F. Rippy, *The United States and Mexico*, rev. ed. (N.Y., 1931) [3548], the best general review, much original contribution except for the periods prior to 1848 and subsequent to 1910. Alfred Vagts, *Mexico, Europa, und Amerika unter besonderer Berücksichtigung der Petroleumpolitik; eine wirtschafts-diplomatische Untersuchung* (Berlin-Grunewald, 1928) [3549], an excellent and careful account, stressing America's international aspects, particularly the oil question, based on printed Mexican and American material and investigations by the author in Mexico and the United States. H. G. Römer, *Amerikanische Interessen- und Prinzipienpolitik in Mexiko, 1910–1914; ein Beitrag zur Kritik des Wilsonismus* (Hamburg, 1929) [3550] sees Wilson's Mexican policy as a piece of his world policy, and notes how Wilson got English approval for his Mexican policy by his solution of the Panama tolls question; based on the available printed Mexican and American documentary material. Frank Tannenbaum, *The Mexican agrarian revolution* (N.Y., 1929) [**3551**], investigation conducted under the auspices of the Brookings Institution, Institute of Economics, into the land institutions of Mexico as a basis for a proper understanding of the revolution; attempts to answer the question of the actual holding of land by foreigners, including citizens of the United States. Edgar Turlington, *Mexico and her foreign creditors* (N.Y., 1930) [**3552**], a convenient survey of the foreign loans of Mexico from the beginning of independence to July 1930. The writer used the archives of the Department of State, but not other archives. Howland, *Survey of American foreign relations*, 1931 (no. 3553), 1–315: "Mexico and the United States", instructive summary (exceptionally good account) of relations between the United States and Mexico, stressing the problems of the Mexican revolution, oil controversy, agrarian reform, church and state, and loans [**3553**]. Callahan, *Mexican relations* (no. 1465). Dunn, *Dipl. protection Americans in Mexico* (no. 1466), an iconoclastic juridical approach to a subject much investigated—the author still finds fresh material in the archives of the Department of State. A. S. MacCorkle, *American policy of recognition towards Mexico* (Baltimore, 1933) [**3554**], neither complete nor very thoughtful. W. E. McDonald, "The pious fund of the Californias", *Cath. hist. rev.*, XIX (1934) 427–436 [**3555**], short summary.

For biographies of American presidents, secretaries of state, and diplomatists to Mexico (for names and tenure, see latest *Register* of the Dept. of State (no. 5122)), see the relevant entries and bibliographical data in the *D.A.B.*

Printed Sources

For general collections, see Sec. 1, above; particularly *For. relations* (no. 5345), Moore's *Arbitrations* (no. 5364) for arbitrations with Mexico (v. II, 1287–2359, for "United States and Mexican claims commission: convention of July 4, 1868"), and his *Digest* (no. 5365).

UNITED STATES OFFICIAL DOCUMENTS: *Texas frontier troubles*, Feb. 29, 1876 (44th Cong., 1st sess. House Rept. no. 343) [**3556**]. *Claims on the part of citizens of the United States and Mexico under the convention of July 4, 1868, between the United States and Mexico* (Wash., 1877) (44th Cong., 2d sess. Sen. Exec. doc. no. 31) [**3557**]. *Reports from the secretaries of state and war in reference to Mexican border troubles*, November 13, 1877 (45th Cong., 1st sess.

House Exec. doc. no. 13) **[3558]**. *Report and accompanying documents of the Committee on Foreign Affairs on the relation of the United States with Mexico,* Apr. 25, 1878 (Wash., 1878) (45th Cong., 2d sess. House Rept. 701) **[3559]** is concerned with Mexican border difficulties, and contains voluminous appendixes with numerous documents. *Report of the boundary commission upon the survey and remarking of the boundary between the United States and Mexico . . . west of the Rio Grande, 1891 to 1896* (55th Cong., 2d sess. Senate Ex. doc. no. 247) **[3560]**. *Affairs in Mexico. Brief in support of Senate resolution of April 20, 1911, relative to [i.e. against] intervention in affairs in Mexico* (Wash., 1911) (62d Cong., 1st sess. Sen. Doc. 25) **[3561]**. *Mexican affairs. Address of the President of the United States, delivered at a joint session of the two houses of Congress, August 27, 1913* (Wash., 1913) (63d Cong., 1st sess. House. Doc. 205) **[3562]** includes also " Reply of Señor Gamboa to proposals of the American government through Hon. John Lind." *Address of the President of the United States delivered at a joint session of the two houses of Congress, April 20, 1914* (Wash., 1914) **[3563]**, on the arrest of United States sailors at Tampico, Mexico, on April 9, 1914. *Claims of American citizens against Mexico . . .* May 20, 1919 (66th Cong., 1st sess. Sen. Doc. no. 1) **[3564]**. *Claims against Mexico for the destruction of life and property of American citizens in that country,* August 1, 1919 (66th Cong., 1st sess. Sen. Doc. no. 67) **[3565]**. *Investigation of Mexican affairs. Preliminary report and hearings of the Committee on Foreign Relations, United States Senate, pursuant to S. Res. 106, directing the Committee on Foreign Relations to investigate the matter of outrages on citizens of the United States in Mexico* (Wash., 1920, 2 v.) (66th Cong., 2d sess. Sen. Doc. no. 285) **[3566]**, Fall committee report; 3,381 pages of source material of all kinds on American relations with Mexico to 1920.

The following are documents of the United States and Mexican Claims Commission, 1869–1876: *Dictamen del comisionado mexicano, y otros documentos, relativo a la cuestión sobre reclamaciones contra el gobierno de los Estados Unidos de América, por depredaciones de Indios barbaros* (Wash., 1872) **[3567]** includes correspondence between Gen. León Guzmán, Mexican commissioner, and W. H. Wadsworth, United States commissioner. *Reclamaciones de indemnización por depredaciones de los Indios; dictamen del Sr. D. Francisco*

Gómez Palacio (Mexico, 1872) [3568], by the Mexican member of the commission. J. I. Rodríguez, *La comisión mixta de reclamaciones mexicanas y americanas establecida conforme al tratado de 4 julio de 1868 entre México y los Estados Unidos. Historia de sus trabajos y procedimientos y exposición metódica de los principios establecidos en sus decisiones* (Mexico, 1873) [3569]. *Opiniones del comisionado de México en noventa y dos casos de la espedición Zerman y algunas constancias documentales relativas a los casos,* signed: M. de Zamacona (Wash., 1875) [3570]. *Opinión del comisionado Manuel M. de Zamacona en el caso de la Compañía Minera de la "Abra", contra México.* No. 489. (Wash., 1875) [3571]. *Opinión del comisionado Manuel M. de Zamacona en el caso de Thadeus Amat, obispo de Monterey y Joseph S. Alemany, arzobispo de San Francisco, contra México.* No. 493. (Wash., 1875) [3572], also published by the Mexican government printing office, *Tadeus Amat, obispo de Monterey, y Joseph S. Alemany, arzobispo de San Francisco, contra México. Reclamación núm. 493* (Mexico, 1876) [3573], papers laid before the commission relating to the claim against the Mexican government for payment of interest on the so-called " pious fund of the Californias." *Sinopsis histórica de la Comisión Mixta de Reclamaciones entre México y los Estados Unidos* (Mexico, 1876) [3574]. *Benjamin Weil contra México. Número 447. Petición de revisión* (Mexico, 1877) [3575]. *Claim of Benjamin Weil no. 447 vs. Mexico; award by the umpire of the United States and Mexican Claims Commission,* tr. by J. Carlos Méxia (Mexico, 1877) [3576]. *Claim of " La Abra Mining Co." vs. Mexico, no 489; award by the United States and Mexican Claims Commission and motion for rehearing,* tr. by J. Carlos Méxia (Mexico, 1877) [3577]. *Documento núm. 7; anexo a la memoria del secretario de estado y del despacho de relaciones exteriores, fechada el 10 de diciembre de 1877* (Mexico, 1877?) [3578]. *Case of Mexico upon the newly discovered evidence of fraud and perjury in the claims of Benjamin Weil and La Abra Silver Mining Company* (Wash., 1878) [3579].

INTERNATIONAL BOUNDARY COMMISSION, UNITED STATES AND MEXICO, 1882–1896: *Report of the Boundary Commission upon the survey and re-marking of the boundary between the United States and Mexico west of the Rio Grande, 1891 to 1896* (Wash., 1898) [3580], published also as Senate doc. 247 (v. XXIII) U.S. 55th Cong., 2d sess.

Note also *Memoria de la sección mexicana de la Comisión Internacional de Límites entre México y los Estados Unidos que restableció los monumentos de El Paso al Pacífico* (N.Y., 1901) [**3581**], not a U.S. official publication.

INTERNATIONAL BOUNDARY COMMISSION (UNITED STATES AND MEXICO) 1893—: *Proceedings of the International (Water) Boundary Commission, United States and Mexico, treaties of 1884 and 1889. Equitable distribution of the waters of the Rio Grande* (Wash., 1903, 2 v.) [**3582**]. *Proceedings of the International Boundary Commission, United States and Mexico. American section. Elimination of bancos, treaty of 1905* [First and second series, no. 1–89] (Wash., 1910–12, 2 v.) [**3583**]. *Chamizal arbitration. Argument of the United States of America* . . . (Wash., 1911) [**3584**]. *Chamizal arbitration. The case of the United States of America* . . . (Wash., 1911) [**3585**]; also *Appendix* (Wash., 1911, 2 v.) [**3586**] which includes diplomatic correspondence, miscellaneous correspondence, documents, etc. *Chamizal arbitration. The countercase of the United States* . . . (Wash., 1911) [**3587**]. *Chamizal arbitration. Minutes of the meetings of the International Boundary Commission June 10 and 15, 1911, containing the award in the Chamizal case* (Wash., 1911) [**3588**]. See also for the Chamizal case, Dept. of State, *Correspondence relating to the inspection of documents printed or relied on in the Mexican case and countercases* (Wash., 1911) [**3589**], correspondence between the two agents in the Chamizal case, W. C. Dennis and Señor Pereyra, and Mexican official publications below (nos. 3610–3613).

UNITED STATES OFFICIAL DOCUMENTS (Pious Fund of the Californias) : *Diplomatic correspondence between the United States and Mexico relative to the Pious Fund of the Californias, prepared for use of the Permanent Court of Arbitration in case of United States vs. Mexico* (Wash., 1902) [**3590**], in this print the correspondence is chronologically arranged; the same correspondence, differently arranged, appears as the 2nd part of the *Proceedings. Transcript of record of proceedings before Mexican and American Mixed Claims Commission [1869–76] with relation to the Pious Fund of the Californias, being claim 493, American docket, and entitled Thaddeus Amat, bishop of Monterey, Joseph S. Alemany, archbishop of San Francisco, vs. Mexico* (Wash., 1902) [**3591**]. *Report of Jackson H.*

*Ralston, agent of United States and counsel, in matter of Pious Fund
. . . with pleadings, appendix exhibits, briefs, and record of proceedings* (Wash., 1902) [**3592**], appeared also as Appendix 2 of *Foreign relations* (no. 5345), 1902. See also publication of the United States and Mexican Claims Commission, 1869–1876, *Opinión del comisionado Manuel M. de Zamacona* (no. 3572). *The case of the Pious Fund of the Californias. Replication of the United States of America, with exhibits* (The Hague, 1902) [**3593**]. *Recueil des actes et protocoles concernant le litige du " fonds pieux des Californies ", soumis au tribunal d'arbitrage constitué en vertu du traité conclu à Washington le 22 mai 1902 entre les Etats-Unis d'Amerique et les Etats-Unis mexicains* (The Hague, 1902) [**3594**]. *Reclamación Estados Unidos contra México resp. fondo piadoso* (no. 3605).

See also Moore's *Arbitrations* (no. 5364), v. II, 1348–1352, for the Pious Fund arbitration.

MEXICAN OFFICIAL DOCUMENTS: Mexico, Ministerio de Relaciones Exteriores, *Memorial*[*s*] (Mexico, 1823–(in progress)) [**3595**]. *Reclamaciones de indemnización por depredaciones de los Indios; dictamen del Sr. D. Francisco Gómez Palacio* (Mexico, 1872) [**3596**], the writer was Mexican member of the joint commission on United States and Mexican claims of 1869 to 1876. *Comisión Mixta de Reclamaciones* (no. 3574). *Benjamin Weil contra México. Número 447. Petición de revisión* (Mexico, 1877) [**3597**], arguments of the Mexican agent for a revision of the award by the United States and Mexican Claims Commission. *Memoranda y notas relativas cambiadas entre el Ministerio de Relaciones Exteriores y el ministro plenipotenciario de los Estados-Unidos* (Mexico, 1877) [**3598**]. *Correspondencia diplomática relativa a las invasiones del territorio Mexicano, por fuerzas de los Estados-Unidos de 1873 a 1877* (Mexico, 1878) [**3599**]. *Cuestión americana. Negocios diplomáticos con los Estados Unidos; notas y documentos relativos* (Guadalajara, 1878) [**3600**], composed chiefly of correspondence between the Mexican secretary of foreign relations, and the Mexican minister to the United States. *Exposición de la secretaría de hacienda de los Estados-Unidos Mexicanos de 15 de enero de 1879 sobre la condición actual de México, y el aumento del comercio con los Estados Unidos* (Mexico, 1879) [**3601**]. *Correspondencia diplomática cambiada entre el gobierno de los Estados Unidos Mexicanos y los de varias potencias extranjeras* (Mexico, 1882–92, 6 v.) [**3602**], from 1878 to

1892. *Correspondance diplomatique sur le cas du citoyen des Etats-Unis d'Amérique A. K. Cutting.* Traduction (Mexico, 1886) [**3603**]. *Caya Arenas y otras islas guaneras en los mares de Campeche y Yucatán. Correspondencia entre los gobiernos de México y los Estados Unidos de América acerca del dominio sobre dichas islas* (Mexico, 1895) [**3604**]. *Reclamación del gobierno de los Estados Unidos de América contra México respecto del fondo piadoso de las Californias. Documentos principales relativos* (Mexico, 1903) [**3605**]. *Entrevista Díaz-Taft. Documentación oficial. 16 de octubre de 1909.* (Mexico, 1909) [**3606**]. *Nota enviada por el gobierno constitucionalista, al de la Casa Blanca, con motivo de las incursiones de tropas americanas en territorio mexicano* (Mexico, 1916) [**3607**]. *Labor internacional de la revolución constitucionalista de México* (Mexico, 1918) [**3608**] contains correspondence with the United States government, 1913–17, and other documents. *Las memorias diplomáticas de Mr. Foster sobre México,* ed. by Genaro Estrada (Mexico, 1929) (Archivo Histórico Diplomático Mexicano, núm. 29) [**3609**], translation of the chapters relating to his Mexican mission given in v. I of the *Diplomatic memoirs* of J. W. Foster (no. 5223).

MEXICAN OFFICIAL DOCUMENTS (Chamizal Case) : *Argument submitted by the government of the United Mexican States to the honorable Arbitral Tribunal and to the agent of the government of the United States of America* . . . (Mexico, 1911) [**3610**]. *Brief presented by the government of the United Mexican States* . . . (Mexico, 1911) [**3611**]. *Reply which the government of the United Mexican States submits* . . . (Mexico, 1911) [**3612**]. *Memoria documentada del juicio de arbitraje del Chamizal celebrado en virtud de la convención de junio 24 de 1910* (Mexico, 1911, 3 v.) [**3613**].

Matías Romero was Mexico's diplomatic representative in Washington during the period of the American civil war and the Maximilian affair, and later during the greater part of the Díaz regime, 1882–1898, a man of solid merit and unassuming character who became of great influence in the peaceful diplomatic and commercial relations between the two countries. He was constantly presenting his country in lectures and publications. These appeared separately, as listed here (nos. 3614–3627), and were brought together in the voluminous volume *Mexico and U.S.* (no. 3627). His essays were intended to explain to the people of the United States that their southern neighbors were able to take care of themselves. *Tabla sinóptica de los tratados y convenciones que han negociado los Estados Unidos Mexicanos con las naciones extrangeras* . . . (Tabasco, 1859) [**3614**]. *Dinner to Señor Matías Romero, envoy extraordinary and minister plenipotentiary from Mexico, on the 29th of March, 1864* (N.Y., 1866) [**3615**]. *Refutación de las inculpaciones hechas al C. Matías Romero por el gobierno de Guatemala* (Mexico, 1876) [**3616**]. *Bosquejo histórico de la agregación a México de Chiapas y Soconusco y de las negociaciones sobre límites entabladas por México con Centro-América y Guatemala. Colección de documentos oficiales que sirve de respuesta al opusculo de D. Andrés Dardón, intitulado " La cuestión de límites entre México y Guatemala."* Tomo I. 1821–1831 (Mexico, 1877) [**3617**]. *Exposición de la comercio con los Estados Unidos* (nu. 3601). *Informe de Matías Romero al gobernador del estado de Oaxaca respecto de la compañía que organizó para construir el ferrocaril de Oaxaca, y del traspaso que le hizo de la concesión de 25 de agosto de 1880* (Mexico, 1881) [**3618**]. *Railways in Mexico; an article by Señor Don Matías Romero, Mexican minister to Washington, in answer to an article by the Hon. John Bigelow entitled, " The railway invasion of Mexico ", pub. in Harper's new monthly magazine for October 1882* (Wash., 1882) [**3619**]. *Reciprocidad comercial entre México y los Estados Unidos* (Mexico, 1890) [**3620**]. *Minutes of the International American Monetary Commission. Actas de la Comisión Monetaria Internacional Americana* (Wash., 1891) [**3621**], Matías Romero, president. *Artículos sobre México, publicadas en los Estados Unidos de América por Matías Romero en 1891–1892* (Mexico, 1892) [**3622**]. *El ferrocaril de Tehuantepec* (Mexico, 1894) [**3623**]. *The Tehuantepec Isthmus railway* (Wash., 1894) [**3624**]. " Mr. Blaine and the boundary question between Mexico and Guatemala ", *Am. geog. soc. jour.*, XXIX (1897) 281–330 [**3625**], concerned with the action of Secretary Blaine in the dispute. " Settlement of the Mexico-Guatemala boundary question, 1882 ", *ibid.*, 123–159 [**3626**]. *Mexico and the United States* (N.Y., 1898) [**3627**], " a study of subjects affecting their political, commercial, and social relations, made with a view to their promotion." W. S. Rosecrans, *El general W. S. Rosecrans, la " Doctrina Monroe ", el " destino manifesto ", y el ferrocaril de Tuxpán al Pacífico* (Mexico, 1870) [**3628**], plea for prompt ratification of Rosecrans' project; also English edition, " *Manifest destiny* ", " *The Monroe Doctrine* ", *and our relations with Mexico. A letter from Gen. Rosecrans to the people of the United States* (n.p., 1870). [Drake De Kay], *In relation to occurrences at Magdalena Bay, Lower California, Mexico* (San Francisco, 1871?) [**3629**], correspondence, protests, and documents, transmitted to the secretary of state by Drake De Kay, U.S. consul at Magdalena; relates to an attack made on the consul and other American citizens by Mexican revolutionists. Texas, Governor, *Mexican relations, letter of Gov. R. B. Hubbard, of Texas, to President Hayes.* (Austin? 1878) [**3630**], in regard to the extradition treaty. *Public opinion in the United States on the annexation of Mexico* (Wash.? 1892) [**3631**], " extracts from the public journals . . . on a proposition recently made in the Senate [and reported adversely] to change the boundaries so as to include large portions of . . . Mexico " (p. 3); significantly revealing widespread opposition to any annexation. *Les fondations californiennes et la question de la chose jugée en droit international. Etats-Unis contre le Mexique,* plaidoirie de M. le chevalier Descamps, conseil des Etats-Unis d'Amérique . . . (Brussels, 1902) [**3632**], plea of M. le chevalier Descamps, counsel of the United States at the Hague Pious Fund arbitration. Vicente Morales, *El Señor Root en México; crónica de la vista hecha en octubre de 1907 al pueblo y al gobierno de la República Mexicana* (Mexico, 1908) [**3633**]. J. P. Didapp, *Los Estados Unidos y nuestros conflictos internos* (Mexico, 1913) [**3634**], the author was agent in the United States of radical anti-Madero factions. Mexico (City), Committee of the American Colony, *Facts submitted by the Committee of the American Colony to President Wilson and Secretary of State Bryan relative to the Mexican situation and the record of the Hon. Henry Lane Wilson therewith* (n.p., 1913) [**3635**], requesting H. L. Wilson's continuance in his diplomatic office. Adolfo Ballivián, *Los designios de Bolívar, la doctrina Monroe y la mediación sudamericana en el Niagara* (N.Y., 1914) [**3636**] sees in the Niagara conference a resurrection of Bolívar's ideals of inter-American peace. Roberto Domenich, *Méjico y el imperialismo norte americano* (Buenos Aires, 1914) [**3637**], Argentine anti-American pamphlet written at the time of the Tampico incident. *International relations of the United States* (Phila., 1914) (Annals of the American Academy of Political and Social Science, LIV) [**3638**], a symposium of specialists analyzing various angles and problems. [Francisco Mallén], *Los Estados Unidos de Norte América y las repúblicas del Sur, reflexiones sugeridas por la insinceridad de los directors políticos del gran pueblo del Norte, con motivo del llamado incidente de Tampico* (Panama, 1914) [**3639**], Spanish English, and French; a protest to the United States government against treatment accorded the author when acting as Mexican consul in El Paso, Texas, in 1907, and comparing the case with the "Tampico incident." Rafael de Zayas Enríquez, *El caso México y la política del presidente Wilson* (Mexico, 1914), also English edition, *The case of Mexico and the policy of President Wilson*, tr. from the Spanish by André Tridon (N.Y., 1914) [**3640**], pro-Huerta and anti-Wilson pamphlet. William Lemke, *Crimes against Mexico* (Minneapolis, 1915) [**3641**], attack on the "dishonorable and cowardly" policy of President Wilson in dealing with the Mexican problem following the collapse of the "builder of Mexico", Porfirio Díaz. [Rafael Alducín], *La revolución constitucionalista, los Estados Unidos y el "A.B.C." Recopilación de documentos y artículos notables referentes a la intromisión de elementos extranjeros en los asuntos interiores de México y la patriótica actitud asumida por el C. primer jefe Venustiano Carranza* (Mexico, 1916) [**3642**]. Manuel Calero, *The Mexican policy of President Woodrow Wilson as it appears to a Mexican* (N.Y., 1916) [**3643**], the Mexican minister to the United States sees deep discouragement and humiliation. Ecuador, Ministerio de Relaciones Exteriores, *La mediación latino-americana en el conflicto entre los Estados Unidos y México.—La iniciativa del Ecuador* (Quito, 1916) [**3644**], diplomatic correspondence. W. R. Hearst, *Intervene in Mexico, not to make war but to end war, urges Mr. Hearst; letter of Mr. Hearst on the Mexican situation* (Brooklyn? 1916) [**3645**], reprinted from the *Brooklyn Eagle*, of June 6, 1916. F. K. Lane, *The President's Mexican policy*, presented in an authorized interview by Secretary of the Interior Franklin K. Lane (N.Y., 1916) [**3646**], reprinted from the Sunday *World*, July 16, 1916. Robert Lansing, *Remarks of Robert Lansing, secretary of state of the United States, at a luncheon to the American-Mexican joint commission at the Hotel Biltmore, New York City, September 4, 1916* (Wash., 1916) [**3647**], ceremonial. Mexican-American Peace Committee, *The Mexican-American league* (N.Y., 1916) [**3648**], signed: Crystal Eastman, secretary; report of the Joint Mexican-American Peace Conference, July 6-8, 1916, organized permanently as the Mexican-American Peace Committee. Henry Morris, *Our Mexican muddle* (Chicago, 1916) [3649], violent and vivid plea for intervention. Edith O'Shaughnessy (Mrs. Nelson O'Shaughnessy), *A diplomat's wife in Mexico; letters from the American embassy at Mexico City, covering the dramatic period between October 8th, 1913, and the breaking off of diplomatic relations on April 23rd, 1914, together with an account of the occupation of Vera Cruz* (N.Y. and London, 1916) [3650], by the wife of the secretary of the American Embassy at Mexico City at the time. The Mexican publicist and historian, Carlos Pereyra, who served as *chargé d'affaires* in the United States in 1911, has written hateful pamphlets against American policy: *Las dos supercherías diplomáticas norte-americanas* (Madrid, 1916) [3651]; and *El crimen de Woodrow Wilson. Su contubernio con Villa. Sus atentados en Santo Domingo. Su régimen corruptor en Nicaragua. Los dos polos de la diplomacia yanquí: la hipocresía y el miedo* (Madrid, 1917) [3652]. Caspar Whitney, *What's the matter with Mexico?* (N.Y., 1916) [3653], answered: she needs a strong-handed control. Woodrow Wilson, *The Mexican question* (Wash.: Govt. Print. Off., 1916) [3654], the article by President Wilson reprinted here, appeared in the issue of the *Ladies Home Journal* for October 1916, and dwells on the importance of the agrarian issue as key to the revolution's problems. José Gaxiola, *La frontera de la raza; Hispano-América, los Estados Unidos, la diplomacia de Venustiano Carranza, la Sociedad Internacional Americana* (Madrid, 1917) [3655], denunciation of imperialism of the United States under the guise of protection. Miguel Rebolledo, *México y Estados Unidos* (Paris and Mexico, 1917) [3656], a patriotic Mexican polemic against the role of the United States vis-a-vis Mexico and sister republics. L. J. De Bekker, *The plot against Mexico* (N.Y., 1919) [3657], " This is a fighting book. Its purpose is to expose and defeat the effort of a handful of pluto-cratic Americans to involve the United States in war with Mexico under pretext of intervention . . . " (Preface), principally republica-tion of a series of articles previously appearing in the *Nation*. S. G. Inman, *Intervention in Mexico* (N.Y., 1919) [3658] presents the Mexican rather than the American point of view; the author is one of the most voluminous American anti-imperialists, very sanguine as to the future of Mexican culture and political life. G. H. Blakeslee, ed., *Mexico and the Caribbean* (N.Y., 1920) (Clark University Ad-

dresses) [3659], Prof. Blakeslee was the first to get in motion, at
Clark University, the conference idea; and this book is a reprint of
varied papers by specialists on Mexico and the Caribbean. It may be
regarded as a source for authoritative opinion on contemporary problems of Mexico and the Caribbean. J. K. Turner, *Hands off Mexico*
(N.Y., Rand School of Social Science, 1920) [3660], title and contents characteristic of a large volume of American public opinion at
the time. I. J. Williams, *The menace of Mexico;* remarks before
the League of Free Nations Association, December 20, 1919, New
York City (N.Y.? 1920) [3661], intervention plea. Genaro Fer-
nández-MacGregor, *Artículos publicados en la Revista Mexicana de
Derecho Internacional, referentes a la investigación hecha por el sub-
comité senatorial de los Estados-Unidos acerca de los daños y per-
juicios sufridos por ciudadanos norteamericanos durante la revolución mexicana, y conclusiones de dicha investigación* (Mexico, 1921)
[3662], published to make the Mexican people aware of the ominous
significance of the hearings of the Fall committee (no. 3566). Fernando Iglesias Calderón, *La concesión Leese* (Mexico, 1924) (Archivo Histórico Diplomático Mexicano, XII) [3663], collection of
documents taken from the well-known *Correspondencia de la legación
Mexicana en Washington durante la intervención extranjera* (no.
2183) with analysis of the grant. Fernando González Roa, *El Dr.
Vicente G. Quesada y sus trabajos diplomáticos sobre México*
(Mexico, 1925) (Archivo Histórico Diplomático Mexicano, XIV)
[3664], only a small portion of the work relates to this Argentine
diplomatist's arbitration of the claims of two citizens of the United
States against Mexico (Oberlander and Messenger claims). *The
Rosalie Evans letters from Mexico*, arranged with comment by
Daisy Caden Pettus (Indianapolis, 1926) [3665], letters of a plucky
American woman defender of the rights of foreigners in Mexico,
depicting outrages on foreigners (she was herself killed). Moises
Sáenz and H. I. Priestley, *Some Mexican problems* (Chicago, 1926)
[3666], a Mexican educator and an American specialist on Mexican
history set forth essays on Mexican problems (including foreign in-
vestments, agrarianism, social rehabilitation, and relations with the
United States. It is an intelligent résumé of sober thought of each
country about the other. L. M. Rojas, *La culpa de Henry Lane
Wilson en el gran desastre de México* (Mexico, 1928) [3667], a

voluminous and diffuse defense of the Mexican revolution against "dollar diplomacy" and Henry Lane Wilson's support of Huerta (frustrated by Woodrow Wilson), accompanied by copious documents and narratives of adventures and perils of the author.

For the printed writings of American presidents, secretaries of state, and diplomatists to Mexico (for names and tenure, see latest *Register* of the Dept. of State (no. 5122)), see our list on p. 756. Note also the *Letters* of Francis Lieber (no. 5258), who in 1870 was chosen as umpire by the commission for settling claims between Mexico and the United States.

MSS.: Suggestions

See Sec. 1, above. The Garcia collection in the University of Texas Library has some material ("Papeles varios sobre la revolución, 1910–1915") containing manuscript documents showing what some prominent Mexicans thought of American activities in Mexico and the attitude of the American government at the time.

Maps: Suggestions

Boundary between the United States and Mexico, as surveyed and marked by the International Boundary Commission, under the convention of July 29th, 1882 (Wash., 1899) [**3668**] is an atlas (26 maps) published to accompany the *Report* of the commission (no. 3560). [*Planos de la*] *línea divisoria entre México y los Estados Unidos al oeste del Río Grande levantada y marcada . . . por la Comisión Internacional de Límites creada por la convención de julio 29, 1882* (N.Y.? 1901?) [**3669**], published with the *Memoria de la sección mexicana* (no. 3581). International (Water) Boundary Commission (no. 3582). International Boundary Commission, *Elimination of bancos* (no. 3583). For the Chamizal arbitration, see the *Case* and *Countercase* of the United States (nos. 3585–3587), with portfolios of maps; *Memoria documentada* (no. 3613); and Paullin's *Atlas* (no. 213), plate 95c and page 69. International Boundary Commission, 1893–, *Proceedings . . . American section. Joint report of consulting engineers on field operations of 1910–1911* (Wash.? 1913) [**3670**], with maps. American Geographical Society, *Catalogue* (no. 5153). Wilgus, *Maps* (no. 5154).

3. Colombia and Panama

Bibliographical Aids

For general aids, see Sec. 1, above. See also Colombian historical bibliographies (nos. 4707–4709). Morrison, *Interoceanic canal* (no. 1212). Griffin, *Recognition* (no. 4801), for material on recognition of Panama in 1903. Meyer, *Panama Canal* (no. 1214). Frank, *Interoceanic canals* (no. 1213). U.S. Superintendent of Documents, *Panama Canal, Canal Zone, Republic of Panama, Colombia treaty, Nicaragua;* publications relating to the above subjects for sale by the Superintendent of Documents (Wash., 1921) [3671]. Pan American Union, Columbus Memorial Library, *Bibliography; books and magazine articles in the library of the Pan American Union on relations between the United States and Colombia* (Wash., 1924) [3672], mainly of the 20th century. American Foreign Law Association, *Bibliographies of foreign law series.* No. 1. *Colombia* (N.Y., 1926) [3673].

Special Works

For general histories of Colombia, see nos. 1259–1260. .

Auguste Lucas, *Précis historique de l'affaire du Panama* (Paris, 1893) [3674], a history of the famous bankruptcy and political scandal of the French Panama Company. Diego Mendoza, " El canal interoceánico y los tratados ", *Anales de jurisprudencia* (Sociedad Colombiana de Jurisprudencia), 5th ser., V (1901) 1–281 [3675], review of the treaty background of Panama by a Colombian writer, who sees the possibility of the United States succeeding the French Canal Company, and desires in any treaty arrangements to provide for a complete neutralization of the canal. Pasco, *Isthmian canal* (no. 2649). Keasbey, *National canal policy* (no. 1227) advocates a Nicaraguan canal because Central America is bound to come within a United States sphere of influence. J. H. Latané, " The treaty relations of the United States and Colombia ", *Am. acad. pol. and soc. sci. ann.*, XXII (1903) 113–126 [3676], summary drawn from U.S. printed documents, but not from Colombian material. M. Sauvé, " La separation de Panama ", *Quest. dipl. et col.*, XVI (1903) 780–787 [3677], the writer feels that the French public ought not to be influenced by support which certain " interested " newspapers have given to the separation of Panama and Philippe Bunau-

Varilla. W. C. Dennis, "The Panama situation in the light of international law", *Am. law reg.*, LII (1904) 265–306 [**3678**]. Johnson, *Panama Canal* (no. 1222). Edouard Tavernier, *Étude du canal interocéanique de l'Amérique centrale, au point de vue diplomatique, juridique, et économique* (Paris, 1906) [**3679**], a doctoral thesis of the University of Paris, a review of well-known facts rather than a contribution, but interprets those facts to justify, realistically and without sentiment, the aggressive policy of the United States toward Colombia. Müller-Heymer, *Panamakanal* (no. 2655). Alfredo Vásquez Cobo, *Pro-patria; cuestiones internacionales* (Paris, 1910)[5] [**3680**], Ch. 5: "Negociaciones con los Estados Unidos y con Panamá." Harmodio Arias, *The Panama Canal, a study in international law and diplomacy* (London, 1911) [**3681**], a study of the legal status of the canal then nearing completion, with a summary of its diplomatic background, by a Panamanian, since become President. Carrera y Jústiz, *Cuba y Panamá* (no. 3873). Lehmann, *Panamakanal* (no. 2666). Tower, *Treaty obligations rel. to Panama Canal* (no. 2671). Norman Thomson, *Colombia and the United States. A juridical study of another "scrap of paper" and its supersession by the Colombian indemnity treaty for the settlement of the Panama question* (London, 1914?) [**3682**]. Lincoln Hutchinson, *The Panama Canal and international trade competition* (N.Y., 1915) [**3683**], economic implications good for an understanding of political movements in the diplomacy of the canal. J. C. Freehoff, *America and the canal title; or, An examination, sifting and interpretation of the data bearing on the wresting of the province of Panama from the republic of Colombia by the Roosevelt administration in 1903 in order to secure title to the Canal Zone* (N.Y., 1916) [**3684**], an indictment of Theodore Roosevelt's taking of Panama, to induce national repentance and unstinted compensation to Colombia. Belisario Porras and Francisco Filos, *Estudio sobre el tratado del canal* (Panama, 1920) [**3685**], assuming that the United States does not possess in the Canal Zone a *dominio directo* but rather a *dominio útil*. Two studies by I. J. Cox: "The Colombian treaty—retrospect and prospect", *Jour. internat. relations*, XI (1921) 549–570 [**3686**], informative essay on the justice of the indemnity treaty; and "'Yankee imperialism' and Spanish American solidarity; a Colombian in-

---

[5] Also published at Panama, 1910.

terpretation ", *Hisp. Am. hist. rev.*, IV (1921) 256–265 [**3687**], resentment felt in Colombia towards the United States on account of the occupation of Santo Domingo as seen in a resolution passed by the Congress of Colombia, Aug. 16, 1920. Martin, *Intervention policy* (no. 4808), ch. 4: " Intervention in the revolution of Panama, 1903." A. J. Uribe, *Las modificaciones al tratado entre Colombia y los EE. Unidos* (Bogota, 1921) [**3688**], important Colombian analysis of the modification of the original indemnity apology treaty of 1914 in the (finally negotiated) and ratified treaty of 1921. Also by the same author, *Colombia y los Estados Unidos de América. El canal interoceánico. La separación de Panamá. Política internacional económica. La cooperación* (Bogota, 1931) [**3689**], the author is one of the most eminent Colombian authorities and jurists, and onetime minister of foreign affairs. He presents a short review of the whole Panama question between the United States and Colombia, accompanied by voluminous reprints of his former articles, speeches, and other relevant documents. Hill, *Treaties* (no. 4794), ch. 15: " The Panama Canal treaties." Pierson, *Interoceanic canal* (no. 1237). W. W. Sullivan, *A study of the relations between Colombia and the United States, 1900–1924* (Urbana, 1926) [**3690**] stresses the canal question; the bibliography shows the thesis to be based solely on printed state papers of the United States and Colombia. Dennis, *Adventures* (no. 2224). Hill, *Roosevelt and Caribbean* (no. 3684). Hector Medina Planas, " Independencia de Panamá ", *Rev. de Arch. y Biblioteca Nacional de Honduras*, VII (1928) 180–189 [**3691**], Panama sooner or later would have become an independent country with or without the aid of the United States. L. E. Nieto Caballero, *La separación de Panamá. Conferencia* (Bogota, 1928) [**3692**].[6] Alvaro Bonilla Lara, *Los Estados Unidos y los canales interoceánicos de América* (Santiago de Chile, 1929) [**3693**], a balanced summary in an acceptable exercise by a Chilean student for academic requirements at the University of Chile; nothing new. J. Heinrich, *Kolumbien und der nordamerikanische Imperialismus* (Munich, 1929) [**3694**].[7] Alvaro Rebolledo, *Reseña histórico-política de la comunicación interoceánica, con especial referencia a la*

---

[6] This book is not listed in the Union Catalogue in the Library of Congress. We have not been able to see it.

[7] *Idem.*

separación de Panamá y a los arreglos entre los Estados Unidos y Colombia (San Francisco, 1930) [**3695**], a review of the international history of the Isthmian canal, designed to rectify previous works and to emphasize the importance of Colombia in that history. The writer sees the shadow of the colossus of the North fading as naval strategy of the canal gives way to aerial strategy. J. F. Rippy, *The capitalists and Colombia* (N.Y., 1931) (Studies in American Imperialism) [**3696**], American capital in Colombia and its significance; frank summary of the taking of Panama. Ernesto J. Castillero R., " La causa inmediata de la emancipación de Panamá; historia de los orígenes, la formación y el rechazo por el senado colombiano del tratado Herrán-Hay ", *Acad. Panameña hist. bol.*, I (1933) 255-427 [**3697**], this is a monograph on the abortive Hay-Herrán treaty, based on published diplomatic papers of the United States and Colombia, rather than of the Panamanian revolution which followed. G. J. B. Fisher, " Bunau-Varilla, protagonist of Panama ", *U.S.N. inst. proc.*, LIX (1933) 1313-1322 [**3698**], a dramatic sketch of the " single Frenchman " whose " invincible will " made possible the Panama Canal. Harold Tascher, *American foreign policy relative to the selection of the trans-isthmian canal route* (Urbana, Ill., 1933) [**3699**], abstract of thesis (doctor of philosophy in political science).

For biographies of American presidents, secretaries of state, and diplomatists to Colombia and Panama (for names and tenure, see the latest *Register* of the Dept. of State (no. 5122)), see the relevant entries and bibliographical data in the *D.A.B.* Dennett's *John Hay* (no. 2472) treats the Panama affair briefly.

Printed Sources

For general collections, see Sec. 1, above; particularly *For. relations* (no. 5345).

UNITED STATES OFFICIAL DOCUMENTS: U.S. Navy Dept., *Correspondence relating to the military occupation of bays of Panama and Colon, etc. . . . copies of all reports and of all correspondence in the Navy Department with naval or other officers of the United States on duty in the bays of Panama and Colon since April 1902, which relate to the military occupation of said bays and the region between them, and the cities of Colon and Panama, etc.* (Wash., 1903) (58th Cong., special sess., 1903. Sen. Doc. 10), also issued in 1904, with title, *Use*

*by the United States of a military force in the internal affairs of
Colombia* (58th Cong., 2d sess. Sen. Doc. 143) [**3700**]. *Relations of
the United States with Colombia and the Republic of Panama* (Wash.,
1904) (58th Cong., 2d sess. Sen. Doc. no. 95) [**3701**]. *Correspondence in regard to the relations of the United States with Colombia and
Panama* (Wash., 1908) (60th Cong., 2d sess. Sen. Doc. 542) [**3702**],
correspondence growing out of the secession of Panama. *Relations
between United States and the Republic of Colombia* (Wash., 1913)
(62d Cong., 3d sess. House Doc. 1444) [**3703**]. *The story of
Panama. Hearings on the Rainey resolution before the Committee
on Foreign Affairs of the House of Representatives* (Wash., 1913)
[**3704**], this is a capital and most extraordinary source for the inside
history of the Panama affair of 1903. *Diplomatic history of the
Panama Canal. Correspondence relating to the negotiation and
application of certain treaties on the subject of the construction of
an inter-oceanic canal, and accompanying papers* (Wash., 1914) (63d
Cong., 2d sess. Sen. Doc. 474) [**3705**], correspondence of 1901–13.
*The Panama Canal and our relations with Colombia. Papers relat-
ing to the acquisition of the Canal Zone* . . . (Wash., 1914) (63d
Cong., 2d sess. Sen. Doc. 471) [**3706**] includes an extract from the
message of President Roosevelt, Dec. 7, 1903, and the message
relating to the Isthmian canal, Jan. 4, 1904, an address by Elihu
Root before the Union League Club, on the " Ethics of the Panama
question ", an editorial from the *Outlook* of Oct. 7, 1911, on " How
the United States acquired the right to dig the Panama Canal ", the
letter of Secretary of State John Hay to Gen. Rafael Reyes, dated
Jan. 5, 1904, and an extract from the autobiography of Mr. Roosevelt. *Canal treaties. Executive documents presented to the United
States Senate, together with proceedings by the Senate thereon
relative to the Panama Canal* (Wash., 1914) (63d Cong., 2d sess.
Sen. Doc. 456) [**3707**]. *Settlement of differences with Colombia.
Diplomatic correspondence and documents submitted to the Committee on Foreign Relations, United States Senate, 63d Cong., 3d
session* (Wash., 1921) (65th Cong., special sess. Sen. Doc. 1)
[**3708**], March 16, 1917—Ordered printed in confidence for the use
of the Senate. *Diplomatic correspondence with Colombia in connection with the treaty of 1914, and certain oil concessions* . . . , Mar.
14, 1924 (68th Cong., 1st sess. Sen. Doc. 64) [**3709**].

COLOMBIAN OFFICIAL DOCUMENTS: *Documentos relativos al canal interoceánico* (Bogotá, 1870) [**3710**]. Colombia, Ministerio de Relaciones Exteriores, *Anales diplomáticas y consulares de Colombia*, edited by Antonio José Uribe (Bogotá, 1900–20, 6 v.) [**3711**], documents of contemporary years of publication. *Canal de Panamá. Documentos relacionados con este asunto, publicados por el senado de Colombia* (Bogotá, 1903) [**3712**]. *Canal de Panamá. Informes de las comisiones parlamentarias de Colombia* (Bogotá, 1903) [**3713**]. Colombia, Ministerio de Relaciones Exteriores, *Documentos diplomáticos sobre el canal y la rebelión del Istmo de Panamá* (Bogotá, 1904) [**3714**]. Colombia, Ministerio de Relaciones Exteriores, *Protest of Colombia against the treaty between Panama and the United States* (London, 1904) [**3715**], not an official edition. *La honra nacional y el ex-ministro Mendoza Pérez* (Bogotá, 1906) [**3716**], collection of selected documents reflecting on Mendoza's negotiations in Washington. Colombia, Ministerio de Relaciones Exteriores, *Exposición que presenta el ministro de relaciones exteriores á la honorable Asamblea Nacional Constituyente y Legislativa sobre los tratados celebrados por la República de Colombia con la repúblicas de los Estados Unidos y Panamá* (Bogotá, 1909) [**3717**], signed: Francisco José Urrutia. Colombia, Congreso, Senado, Comisión de Relaciones Exteriores, *Informe de la Comisión de Relaciones Exteriores del Senado, sobre el proyecto de ley "que aprueba las modificaciones introducidas por el Senado norteamericano al tratado de 6 de abril de 1914", entre Colombia y los Estados Unidos de América* (Bogotá, 1921) [**3718**], signed: Antonio José Uribe [and others]. Colombia, Congreso, Senado, Comisión de Relaciones Exteriores, *Las modificaciones al tratado entre Colombia y los EE. Unidos*, artículos y discursos por el doctor Antonio José Uribe (Bogotá, 1921) [**3719**].

PANAMA OFFICIAL DOCUMENTS: Panama (City) Instituto Nacional, *Documentos históricos sobre la independencia del Istmo de Panamá* (Panama, 1930) ("Publicaciones del Instituto Nacional de Panamá") [**3720**], preface signed: Ernesto J. Castillero R., "secretario del Instituto Nacional de Panamá"; contains not only copies of official documents (covering the period, 1821–1926), but historical treatises, including "La independencia del Istmo de Panamá, sus antecedentes, sus causas y su justificación", by Ramón M. Valdés, and "La secesión de Panamá y sus causes", by Pablo Arosemena.

Eustorjio Salgar, *El ministro colombiano en Washington i la adquisición del vapor "Rayo"* (Bogotá, 1867) [3721], papers relating to the steamer "Rayo", formerly the "R.R. Cuyler", bought by the Colombian government in New York and detained by the United States government. Three works by L. N. B. Wyse: *Le canal de Panama* (Paris, 1886) [3722], this is a history by a French engineer on the basis of whose concessions from Colombia the French canal was begun. It has a lengthy chapter summarizing public and private negotiations for canal rights. The author thinks the work of the Panama Company will forestall growing interest in the United States for an American canal on American soil; and *Canal interocéanique de Panama; mission de 1890–91 en Colombie* (Paris, 1891) [3723], Wyse was sent by the receiver of the French Panama Company to make a technical report and to secure an extension of time for completion of the canal. Carlos Martín, *Canal interoceánico; informe para segundo debate del tratado celebrado en 1870* (Bogota, 1870) [3724], the author was Colombian minister to the United States, 1872–76, favorable to alliance with the United States. R. W. Thompson, *The interoceanic canal at Panama. Its political aspects. The "Monroe Doctrine." Argument before the Committee of Foreign Affairs, House of Representatives* (Wash., 1881) [3725], an *ex parte* statement that the Monroe Doctrine *protects* the rights of the Panama Canal Company in Colombia. [Ramón Santodomingo Vila], *Para la historia de 1881 á 1902* (Panama, 1902) [3726], this is a memorandum written by the former Colombian plenipotentiary in Washington, at Bogotá, concerning his discussions with W. H. Trescot, of the U.S. Dept. of State about the Wyse concession in 1881. See also L. N. B. Wyse, *Canal de Panama* (no. 3722). Ricardo Arias and Pablo Arosemena, *La opinión sensata de Panamá tocante al tratado Herrán-Hay* (Panama, 1903) [3727]. Also by Pablo Arosemena, *La secesión de Panamá y sus causas* (Panama, 1903) [3728], and his *Escritos* (Panama, 1930, 2 v.) [3729], Arosemena (1836–1920) was a leading Panamanian political figure and diplomat, both under the Colombian regime and during and after the secession; his works are full of source material (for cautious handling) of the Panama revolution and of its background and of canal diplomacy afterward. *La question du Panama* (Paris, 1903) [3730], "Les Colombiens résidant en Europe, et au nom desquels nous agissons, ont, avec le désir de ies présenter à l'attention de ceux qui s'intéressent au triomphe de la justice, recueilli quelques-uns des nombreux articles que la presse française a consacrés à la cause de la Colombie, en cette crise du droit public dont elle apparaît la victime."—*Avant-propos*, signed Carlos Calderón, R. Samper, Marceliano Vargas. R. M. Valdés, *The independence of the Isthmus of Panama; its antecedents, causes and justification* (Panama, 1903) **[3731]**, a Panamanian self-vindication, the writer was minister to the United States from Panama, 1912–13. *The Panama canal question, a plea for Colombia* (N.Y., 1904) **[3732]**, much of the material in this collection corresponds to Abelardo Aldana's pamphlet: *The Panama canal question. A plea for Colombia*, 2d ed. (enl.) (Cardiff, 1903) **[3733]**, Abelardo Aldana was consul of Colombia at Cardiff. Rafael Reyes (Colombian minister to the United States, 1903–04), *Misión diplomática y militar, 1903–1904* (Bogota, 1904?) **[3734]**, official account of his special diplomatic mission to Washington, 1903–04, after the Panama revolution, with diplomatic documents; and *The two Americas*, . . . tr. from the Spanish, with added notes by Leopold Grahame (N.Y., 1914) **[3735]**; also his *Escritos varios* (Bogotá, 1920) **[3736]**, his travels, explorations, speeches, and other activities, including much material about Panama. Philippe Bunau-Varilla, the aggressive agent of the French Panama Canal Company vitally assisted the Panama revolution in order to salvage $40,000,000 for his principals out of the old fiasco by selling their rights to the United States. He became Panama's first representative to the United States and negotiated the treaty of 1904. His books are valuable *ex parte* sources to be used with great critical caution: "La question de Panama", *Nouv. rev.*, CXLVI (n.s., v. XXVII) (1904) 433–458 **[3737]**; *Le détroit de Panama. Documents relatifs à la solution parfaite du problème de Panama (détroit libre, large et profond). Ces documents renferment des détails sur la solution trés imparfaite adoptée par les Etats-Unis (canal à écluses) et sur les mauvais résultats des trois premières années de travaux du gouvernement américain* (Paris, 1907) **[3738]**; *Panama; the creation, destruction, and resurrection* (London, 1913; N.Y., 1914) **[3739]**, a colorful *ex parte* statement of the author's part in the intrigue for the revolution of Panama and the treaty with the United States (see also " Refutación al libro de Bunau-Varilla, *Panamá; la creación, la* *destruction, la resurreción*", por el Dr. Jorge E. Boyd, in *Documentos históricos sobre Panamá* (no. 3720), 313–351; and *Dr. Jorge E. Boyd's open letter to President Porras refuting Bunau-Varilla's book with regards to the independence of Panama. Reply of the president of the Republic of Panama to Dr. Jorge E. Boyd* (Panama, 1913?) [**3740**]. Also by Bunau-Varilla, *The great adventure of Panama; wherein are exposed its relation to the great war and also the luminous traces of the German conspiracies against France and the United States* (Garden City, N.Y., 1920) [**3741**], the purpose of this war-time book is to exhibit France's creative genius in relation to the Panama Canal as comfort to Frenchmen and friends of Frenchmen in their life and death struggle with Germany, a power of less creative value. *Docs. and corres. rel. transisthmian canal* (no. 1255). Scruggs, *Colombian republic* (no. 2732), ch. 26: "More about Panama Canal projects." Enrique Cortes, *Los tratados de Colombia con los Estados Unidos y Panamá* (London, 1909) [**3742**], an argument for the acceptance of the tripartite treaties (United States, Colombia, Panama) of 1909, in answer to the adverse committee report of Dr. P. Mateus to the Colombian national assembly. Theodore Roosevelt, "Charter day address", *Univ. of Calif. chron.*, XIII (1911) 131–145 [**3743**], the famous "I took the Isthmus" statement; "How the United States acquired the right to dig the Panama Canal", *Outlook*, XCIX (1911) 314–318 [**3744**]; "*I took the Isthmus.*" *Ex-president Roosevelt's confession, Colombia's protest, and editorial comment by American newspapers on "How the United States acquired the right to build the Panama Canal*", comp. by Francisco Escobar, consul general of Colombia (N.Y., 1911) [**3745**]; "The Panama blackmail treaty", *Metropolitan*, XLI (1915) 8–10, 69–72 [**3746**]; and "The Panama Canal", in *The Pacific Ocean in history; . . .* ed. by H. M. Stephens and H. E. Bolton (N.Y., 1917), 137–150 [**3747**], a narrative of the course of action by which the writer, as president of the United States, secured the right to build the canal under purely American control. See also the following replies to Roosevelt's *Panama blackmail treaty* (above): *Separation from Panama; reply to an article entitled "The Panama blackmail treaty", published in the February number of "The Metropolitan", 1915*, anonymous (Wash., 1916) [**3747**]; and by J. M. González Valencia, former Colombian minister of foreign affairs, *Separation* *of Panama from Colombia; refutation of the misstatements and erroneous conceptions of Mr. Roosevelt in his article entitled "The Panama blackmail treaty"* (Wash., 1916) [**3748**]. J. T. Du Bois, *Ex-U.S. minister to Colombia, James T. Du Bois, on Colombia's claims and rights* (Hallstead? Pa., 1914) [**3749**], relative to the pending treaty signed at Bogotá, April 6, 1914; a Republican who opposes Theodore Roosevelt's Panama diplomacy pleads for the Bryan treaty "of chivalrous regret" with Colombia. Earl Harding, "In justice to the United States—a settlement with Colombia", *Jour. race develop.*, IV (1914) 427–442 [**3750**] attacks the "blackmail thesis." J. Hampton Moore, *Panama's independence of Colombia.* Extension of remarks of Hon. J. Hampton Moore, of Pennsylvania, in the House of Representatives, including a historical review based on official records, by Wilfred H. Schoff . . ., July 13, 1914 (Wash., 1914) [**3751**], against reparation. Marco Fidel Suárez, *Tratado entre Colombia y los Estados Unidos* (Bogota? 1914) [**3752**], a badly printed Colombian analysis of the proposed indemnification treaty of 1914 as one of necessarily imperfect reparation. *El tratado de 6 de abril ante al Senado y pueblo de los Estados Unidos. 1914* (Bogota? 1914) [**3753**], articles by J. T. Du Bois, and Hannis Taylor, address of W. J. Bryan, etc. J. M. González Valencia, *Separation of Panama from Colombia* (Wash., 1916) [**3754**], extracts of letters addressed by J. M. González Valencia, former minister of foreign affairs of Colombia, to a friend of Colombia in the United States, as a reply to the assertions made by Mr. Wilfred H. Schoff in his pamphlet entitled: "Extension of remarks of Hon. J. Hampton Moore, of Pennsylvania, in the House of Representatives, including a historical review based on official records." Diego Martínez C., *On the treaty between United States and Colombia* (Wash., 1916) [**3755**], the author was sent by the Chamber of Commerce of Cartagena, Colombia, on a goodwill mission, and speaks here for the proposed Bryan reparation treaty with Colombia of 1914. Elihu Root, "The obligations of the United States as to Panama Canal tolls", January 21, 1913, in his *Addresses on international subjects* (Cambridge, 1916) [**3756**], a famous and eloquent speech advocating withdrawal of the tolls act or submission to arbitration. *Separation of Panama from Colombia. Reply to certain statements contained in the work entitled "History of the Panama Canal", by I. E. Bennet* [sic.] *Wash.*,

D.C., *1915* (Wash., 1916) [**3757**], " from official Colombian documents." H. C. Lodge, *Panama* (Wash., 1921) (67th Cong., 1st sess. Sen. Doc. 37) [**3758**], speech of Hon. Henry Cabot Lodge, of Massachusetts, in the United States Senate, January 5, 1904. Two works by Diego Mendoza (Colombian minister to the United States, 1905–06) : " Colombia y los Estados Unidos. Historia diplomática del Canal de Panamá. El avance de los Estados Unidos en el Caribe. La conquista de los trópicos ", *Boletín de historia y antigüedades* (Academia de Historia, Bogotá), XV (1921) 513 ff. [**3759**], Colombian appreciation of the menace of the advance of the United States southward; and *El canal interoceánico* (Bogotá, 1930) [**3760**], caption title: " El canal interoceánico y los tratados." L. E. Nieto Caballero, *El dolor de Colombia* (Bogotá, 1922) [**3761**], a collection of opinions and newspaper excerpts on the indemnity treaty. A copy in the Library of Congress has inscription (in handwriting) by the author: " To the noble man and noble President that did justice to my country. To Mr. Warren G. Harding." The memorandum of " J. B. M." [John Bassett Moore, assistant secretary of state] advocating intervention in Panama, in case Colombia should reject the Hay-Herrán treaty is printed in *International servitudes in law and practice*, by Helen D. Reid (Chicago, 1932), 241–246 [**3762**].

For the printed writings of American presidents, secretaries of state, and diplomatists to Colombia and Panama (for names and tenure, see latest *Register* of the Dept. of State (no. 5122)), see our list on p. 756.

4. Central America [8]

Bibliographical Aids

For general aids, see Sec. 1, above.

Nicaragua, Biblioteca Nacional, *Catálogo general* (no. 4714). San Salvador, Biblioteca Nacional, *Catálogo* (no. 4718). Morrison, *Interoceanic canal and railway routes* (no. 1212). Phillips, *Central America* (no. 4703). Honduras, Biblioteca Nacional, *Catálogo* (no. 4711). Frank, *Interoceanic canals* (no. 1213). Supt. Documents, *Panama Canal . . . Nicaragua*, price list (no. 5376). Two lists compiled by the Library of Congress, Division of Bibliography (W. A. Slade, chief bibliographer): *Recent references on Nicaragua* (*with*

---

[8] See also Sec. 3, above (" Colombia and Panama ").

special reference to her relations with the United States) (Wash., 1927) [**3763**], a mimeographed list; and *United States relations with Mexico and Central America, with special reference to intervention* (Wash., 1928) [**3764**], also mimeographed. Denny, *Dollars for bullets* (no. 3785), 397-402. Bradley, *Monroe Doctrine* (no. 1143), 23-29: "The United States and Nicaragua." Van Lieu Minor, "A brief classified bibliography relating to the United States intervention in Nicaragua", *Hisp. Am. hist. rev.*, XI (1931) 261-277 [**3765**]. For the Central American peace conference of 1907, see Library of Congress *List . . . on Internat. Am. conferences* (no. 4032), nos. 191-209.

Special Works

W. H. Webb, *Monroe Doctrine and control of the Isthmian canal, Nicaragua* (N.Y., 1881) [**3766**].⁹ Keasbey (nos. 1226-1227). J. G. Whiteley, *Dipl. U.S. re Central Am. canal* (no. 1231), substantially a plea for our adherence to the Clayton-Bulwer treaty. Pasco, *Isthmian canal question* (no. 2649). Huberich, *Canal transisthmique* (no. 2653). Viallate, *Canal interocéanique* (no. 2651). Luis Anderson, "Peace conference of Central America", *Am. jour. internat. law*, II (1908) 144-151 [**3767**], editorial summary by a leading American international lawyer. Angel Marvaud, "La paix dans le Centre-Amérique", *Quest. dipl. et col.*, XXV (1908) 691-712 [**3768**], another sympathetic French review, with map and essential documents. J. B. Scott, "The Central American peace conference of 1907", *Am. jour. internat. law*, II (1908) 121-143 [**3769**], the historical parts in this review are furnished by Mr. Francisco J. Yánes, secretary of the International Bureau of the American Republics, and the account of the proceedings and results of the conference of 1907 is based on the *Monthly bulletin* of the International Bureau of American Republics, XXV (1907) 1334-1373. Francis Rey, *La Unión Centro-Americana. Estudio relativo á las instituciones creadas en Washington por la Conferencia de Paz Centro-Americana de 1907* (Guatemala, 1911) [**3770**], translation of an article published in the *Revue générale de droit international public*, XVIII (1911) 69-89; an essay which approves in principle the plan for Central American union, except for any union of legislation of the different states.

---

⁹ We have not examined this book.

P. M. Brown, "American intervention in Central America ", *Jour. race develop.*, IV (1914) 409–426 [**3771**], the author had been United States minister to Honduras, and in this article stresses good motives of American policy in stimulating union of the Central American states. Also by the same author, "American diplomacy in Central America ", *Am. pol. sci. rev.*, VI, suppl. (1912) 152–163 (*Proceedings . . . at its eighth annual meeting*) [**3772**]. Otto Schoenrich, " The Nicaraguan mixed claims commission ", *Am. jour. internat. law*, IX (1915) 858–869 [**3773**], summary of the work of the commission by one of the American members. Williams, *Isthmian diplomacy* (no. 1235). W. H. Koebel, *Central America; Guatemala, Costa Rica, Honduras, Panama, and Salvador* (London, 1917) [**3774**], a very general account with much local color in "travelog" style, of little direct use for diplomatic history. D. G. Munro, *The five republics of Central America; their political and economic development and their relation with the United States*, by Dana G. Munro, ed. by David Kinley (N.Y., 1918) (Carnegie Endowment for International Peace. Division of Economics and History) [**3775**], standard work, furnishing historical background of the American intervention, and the history of the Washington conference of 1907 and sequents of diplomatic events to date; carried forward by his 1934 publication (no. 3869). K. E. Imberg, *Der Nikaraguakanal; eine historisch-diplomatische Studie* (Berlin, 1920) [**3776**], this short account is drawn off mostly from ill-selected American secondary accounts. Edward Perry, "Central American union", *Hisp. Am. hist. rev.*, V (1922) 30–51 [**3777**], a very summary analysis of the background and accomplishment of the conference of 1922. J. P. Young, *Central American currency and finance* (Princeton, 1925) [**3778**], summary by a competent scholar, but for Nicaragua, see R. R. Hill's more recent and detailed analysis (no. 3792). I. J. Cox, *Nicaragua and the United States, 1909–1927* (Boston, 1927) (World Peace Foundation Pamphlets, X, no. 7) [**3779**], a convenient summary by a conscientious scholar; the appendix includes a number of relevant official documents, 1909–1927. Tyler, *For. pol. Blaine* (no. 2223), for Central America and the Caribbean in 1881, and 1889–1892. *United States policy in Nicaragua; a review of American policy since 1909* (N.Y.: Foreign Policy Association, 1927) (*Its* Information Service, II, no. 24) [**3780**], convenient factual summary for college classes in current events. Laudelino Moreno, *Historia de las relaciones* *inter-estatuales de Centro-América* (Madrid, 1928?) [3781], a careful factual history (free from polemics) of the movement for a Central American union to the present time, including relations to it of the United States; best work in Spanish. C. Quijano, *Nicaragua; ensayo sobre el imperialismo de los Estados Unidos* (Paris, 1928) [3782], a very biased and inaccurate narrative. Anna A. Powell, "Relations between the United States and Nicaragua 1898-1916", *Hisp. Am. hist. rev.*, VIII (1928) [3783], apparently an academic exercise based on the available printed documents; see rather Cox (no. 3779) and Munro (no. 3775). Floyd Cramer, *Our neighbor Nicaragua* (N.Y., 1929) [3784], a realistic and benevolent journalistic appreciation of American imperialism in troubled Nicaragua. H. N. Denny, *Dollars for bullets, the story of American rule in Nicaragua* (N.Y., 1929) [3785], a journalist's vivid and chronological account of the American intervention in Nicaragua, supplemented by a modicum of historical research; sympathetic to intervention and says leading Nicaraguans are so. R. L. Morrow, "A conflict between the commercial interests of the United States and its foreign policy", *Hisp. Am. hist. rev.*, X (1930) 2-13 [3786] describes an incident involving the earlier relations of the United States with Nicaragua and the attitude of the United States toward the Monroe Doctrine in the last decade of the 19th century. *Unsettled boundary disputes in Latin America* (N.Y.: Foreign Policy Association, 1930) (*Its Information Service*, V, no. 26) [3787] gives summary to 1930 of the Guatemala-Honduras and Honduras-Nicaragua boundary disputes arbitrated by the United States. C. P. Anderson, "Our policy of non-recognition in Central America", *Am. jour. internat. law*, XXV (1931) 298-301 [3788], editorial opinion by a distinguished American international lawyer. R. L. Buell, *The United States and Central American stability* (N.Y.: Foreign Policy Association, 1931) (Foreign Policy Reports, VII, July 8 and 22) [3789], a convenient and well documented summary. M. O. Hudson, " The Central American court of justice ", *Am. jour. internat. law*, XXVI (1932) 759-786 [3790], the best summary of its history and achievements, including the famous cases involving the canal rights and other rights of Costa Rica, and of El Salvador vs. Nicaragua. F. C. Fisher, "The arbitration of the Guatemalan-Honduran boundary dispute", *Am. jour. internat. law*, XXVII (1933) 403-427 [3791], scholarly and useful summary with maps. R. R. Hill, *Fiscal intervention in Nicaragua*

(N.Y., 1933) [3792] deals with the desperate fiscal situation which the Dept. of State in 1911 endeavored to correct through provisions of the Knox-Castrillo treaty; the author was a member of the Nicaraguan High [Financial] Commission, and this may be considered an authoritative history.

For biographies of American presidents, secretaries of state, and diplomatists to Central American countries (for names and tenure, see latest *Register* of the Dept. of State (no. 5122)), see the relevant entries and bibliographical data in the *D.A.B.*

Printed Sources

For general collections, see Sec. 1, above.

For a comprehensive list of United States official documents, 1827–1900, see the " Bibliography of the United State public documents relating to interoceanic communication across Nicaragua, Isthmus of Panama, Isthmus of Tehuantepec, etc.", prepared in the office of the Superintendent of Documents, and reprinted in Morrison (no. 1212). Particular issues of U.S. official documents are: *The Clayton-Bulwer treaty and the Monroe Doctrine. A letter from the secretary of state to the minister of the United States at London, dated May 8, 1882, with sundry papers and documents explanatory of the same, selected from the archives of the Department of State* (Wash., 1882) (47th Cong., 1st sess. Sen. Ex. doc., no. 194) [3793]. *Correspondence touching the construction of a ship-canal through Nicaragua* (Wash., 1887) (49th Cong., 2d sess. Sen. Ex. doc. 50) [3794]. *Correspondence and other papers relating to the proposed ship canal*, being a reprint of an executive document of the special session of March 4, 1857, and of document no. 194 of the 47th Congress, 1st session, 1900 (56th Cong., 1st sess. Sen. Doc. 161) [3795]. For the United States vs. Salvador arbitration, 1902 (claims against Salvador of the Salvador Commercial Company), see *Report in the case of Salvador Commercial Company vs. Salvador* (Wash., 1901) [3796]; and *Argument. United States vs. Salvador* (Wash., 1902) [3797], consisting of the oral argument of William L. Penfield for the United States. U.S. Isthmian Canal Commission, *Report of the Isthmian Canal Commission, 1899–1901*, Rear Admiral John G. Walker, United States Navy, president (Wash., 1904) (58th Cong., 2d sess. Sen. Doc. 222); an incomplete edition of this report was published (in 2 pts.), 1901–02, as Senate doc. 54, 57th Cong., 1st sess.

[3798], this is the voluminous report which favored the Nicaragua route; see also *Supplementary report of the Isthmian Canal Commission* (57th Cong., 1st sess. Sen. Doc. no. 123) [3799], upon the proposition of the New Panama Canal Company to sell and dispose of all its rights, property, and unfinished work to the United States. *Nicaraguan affairs.* Hearing before a subcommittee of the Committee on Foreign Relations, United States Senate, sixty-second Congress, second session, . . . to investigate as to the alleged invasion of Nicaragua by armed sailors and marines of the United States [El Paso, Tex., Oct. 8, 1912] (Wash., 1913) [3800]. Conference on Central American Affairs, 1922–1923, *Conferencia sobre asuntos centro-americanos. Manuel especial para el uso de los delegados. Conference on Central American Affairs. Special handbook for the use of the delegates* (Wash., 1922) [3801] includes the Spanish and English texts of all the treaties and conventions of the Central American peace conference held at Washington, D. C., in 1907, as well as the invitation extended by the government of the United States to the governments of the Central American republics to attend the conference. U.S. Senate, Committee on Foreign Relations, *Foreign loans, hearings before subcommittee, 69th Congress, 2d session, pursuant to S.Con.Res. 15, relative to engaging responsibility of the Government in financial arrangements between its citizens and sovereign foreign governments* (Wash., 1927) [3802], hearings on the financial situation in Nicaragua, 1909 and after. U.S. Dept. of State, *The United States and Nicaragua; a survey of the relations from 1909 to 1932* (Wash., 1932) [3803], a complete and carefully prepared official history.

COSTA RICAN OFFICIAL DOCUMENTS: *Fallo arbitral del chief justice de los Estados Unidos de América en la controversia de límites de las repúblicas de Costa Rica y Panamá* (San José, 1914) [3804], this document was also printed in the *Memoria de la Secretaría de Relaciones Exteriores* (San José, 1915), 10–27 [3805]. *Demanda de la república de Costa Rica contra la de Nicaragua, ante la Corte de Justicia Centroamericana, con motivo de una convención firmada por la segunda con la república de los Estados Unidos de América, par la venta del río San Juan, y otros objetos* (San José, 1916) [3806], English translation (Wash., 1916). Costa Rica, Congreso Constitucional, *Documentos relativos al proyecto de contrato petrolero Pinto-Greulich* (San José, 1920) [3807].

NICARAGUAN OFFICIAL DOCUMENTS: *Documents and correspondence between the republic of Nicaragua and the representatives of the German Empire, the United States and England, in regard to the Eisenstuck affair, during the years 1876, '77, and '78* (N.Y., 1878) [3808]. Nicaragua, Presidente, *An important document; message of Adolfo Díaz, president of Nicaragua, Central America, to the national assembly at Managua concerning conventions with the United States of America* (Managua, 1911) [3809], English translation, with biographical notice of Díaz, by J. M. Moncada. Nicaragua, Ministerio de Relaciones Exteriores, *Memoria presentada al Congreso Nacional por el señor ministro del ramo, don Diego M. Chamorro, 1916* (Managua, 1917, 2 v.) [3810] includes the case of Nicaragua as opposed to El Salvador and Costa Rica before the Corte de Justicia Centro-Americana in connection with the controversy over the Bryan-Chamorro treaty; also *Memoria presentada al Congreso Nacional por el subsecretario encargardo del despacho, don Humberto Pasos D., 1920* (Managua, 1921, 3 v.) [3811], " Mediación amistosa del honorable secretario de estado de los Estados Unidos de América en el asunto de límites entre Nicaragua y Honduras ". v. II, 157-687; v. III, 1-133; and the *Memoria de relaciones exteriores presentada al Congreso Nacional por el señor ministro ingeniero don José Andrés Urtecho, 1923* (Managua, 1924) [3812], " Conferencia sobre asuntos centroamericanos reunida en Wáshington el 4 de diciembre de 1922 ": p. 173-294. *Compilación de contratos celebrados con los banqueros de New York, con el Ethelburga syndicate de Londres y con el Banco Nacional de Nicaragua Inc.— Leyes relativos á los mismos contratos* (Managua, 1928-29) [3813].

SALVADOR OFFICIAL DOCUMENTS: *Demanda del gobierno de El Salvador contra el gobierno de Nicaragua ante la Corte de Justicia Centro-Americana, 1916* (San Salvador, 1916) [3814], a demand occasioned by the convention between the United States and Nicaragua relative to an interoceanic canal and naval station in the Gulf of Fonseca. This document was also published in English translation (Wash., 1917). *Voto del magistrado por Nicaragua, Dr. Daniel Gutiérrez Navas. El Salvador versus Nicaragua . . . marzo de 1917* (San José, 1917) [3815], opinion in the case of Salvador against Nicaragua relating, among other matters, to the leasing by the United States of a naval base in the Gulf of Fonseca, and to the Nicaraguan canal. Salvador, Presidente, *Cartas políticas cruzadas entre los presidentes de El Salvador y de los Estados Unidos* (San Salvador, 1918) **[3816]**.

Central American Peace Conference, Washington, 1907, *Actas y documentos* (Wash.: Govt. Print. Off., 1907) **[3817]**, Spanish and English in parallel columns. *Conferencia de paz centroamericana, 20 de diciembre de 1907* (San José, Costa Rica, 1907) **[3818]**. *Documentos relativos á la conferencia de paz centroamericana. Tratados y convenciones concluídos por los delegados de las cinco repúblicas de Centro América* (San Salvador, 1908) **[3819]**. U.S. Delegate to Central American Peace Conference, 1907, *The Central American peace conference, held at Washington, D.C., 1907;* report of Mr. William I. Buchanan (Wash., 1908) **[3820]**, published by the Dept. of State.

Two publications of the Corte de Justicia Centro-americana: *Decision and opinion of the court on the complaint of the republic of Costa Rica against the republic of Nicaragua, growing out of a convention entered into by the republic of Nicaragua with the United States of America for the sale of the San Juan River and other matters (September 30, 1916)*, translation pub. by the Costa Rican legation (Wash., 1916) **[3821]**. *The republic of El Salvador against the republic of Nicaragua. Opinion and decision of the court.* Translation (Wash., 1917) **[3822]**, decision in the case of Salvador against Nicaragua, arising out of the treaty between Nicaragua and the United States, known as the Bryan-Chamorro treaty which relates, among other matters, to the leasing of a naval base in the Gulf of Fonseca.

Emilio Benard, *Nicaragua and the interoceanic canal* (Wash., 1874) **[3823]**, by the minister of Nicaragua to the United States; an argument for preference of Nicaragua as canal site. Alfred Williams, *The interoceanic canal and the Monroe Doctrine* (N.Y., 1880) **[3824]**, an undocumented historical essay pointed to the principle that the United States should own and operate the Isthmian canal. T. B. Atkins, *The interoceanic canal across Nicaragua and the attitude toward it of the government of the United States*, presented by the Nicaraguan Canal Company . . . 44 Wall Street, New York (N.Y., 1890) **[3825]**, Atkins was secretary of the Maritime Canal Company of Nicaragua, and wrote this book to further the idea of an American canal on American soil for the American people. Patrick Cudmore, *Buchanan's conspiracy; the Nicaragua* *canal and reciprocity* (N.Y., 1892) [**3826**], anti-British tone; a hodge-podge of information, documents, and statistics to support Blaine's reciprocity policy. *Homenaje a la memoria del general Don Luis Molina en el LXXIII aniversario de su nacimiento* (Guatemala, 1909) [**3827**], Honduran minister to the United States, 1860-67. Rafael Montúfar, *The Nicaragua treaty*. Reply by Rafael Montúfar . . . *to the memorandum submitted, on behalf of Nicaragua, to the Committee on Foreign Relations of the Senate of the United States* (n. p., 191-?) [**3828**], reply to a memorandum urging the ratification of the treaty negotiated by Secretary Bryan with the government of Nicaragua relative to an interoceanic canal and a naval station in the Gulf of Fonseca. J. S. Zelaya, *La revolución de Nicaragua y los Estados Unidos* (Madrid, 1910) [**3829**], relation by the exiled dictator of Nicaragua. R. Arévalo González, " Desvaneciendo objeciones ", *Atenas* (Caracas, Apr. 15, 1912) 831 ff. [**3830**], long article on Secretary Knox's visit to Central America and the influence of the Monroe Doctrine (for other sources re Knox's trip to South America, see *Am. secs. state* (no. 4796), v. IX, 404-410). Jacinto López, *The conquest of Nicaragua by the United States; letter to President Tyler* (N.Y., 1913) [**3831**]. Ramón Rojas Corrales, *El tratado Chamorro-Weitzel ante Centro-América y ante el derecho internacional* (San José, Costa Rica, 1914) [**3832**], the author here makes a formidable brief for the rights of Costa Rica and El Salvador in face of the canal treaty between the United States and Nicaragua (the Bryan-Chamorro treaty). Pío Bolaños, *The economical situation of Nicaragua. Intervention of North America and its results, the procedures of the government of Adolfo Díaz,* tr. by Amelia Babin (New Orleans, 1916) [**3833**], published by instruction of the " Delegación del Partido Liberal Nacionalista de Nicaragua en los Estados Unidos." Three works by Salvador Rodríguez G[onzález] : " The neutrality of Honduras and the question of the Gulf of Fonseca ", *Am. jour. internat. law,* X (1916) 509-542 [**3834**], tr. by Pedro Capó-Rodríguez; Honduran writer attacks the proposed Bryan-Chamorro treaty as violating Honduran sovereignty; *El Golfo de Fonseca en el derecho público centroamericano. La doctrina Meléndez* (San Salvador, 1917) [**3835**]; and *El Golfo de Fonseca y el tratado Bryan-Chamorro celebrado entre los Estados Unidos de Norte América y Nicaragua; doctrina Meléndez* (San Salvador, 1917) [**3836**], a collection of documents relating to the canal issue chosen and edited by the Honduran advocate, Rodríguez González. Several discussions by G. T. Weitzel, American minister to Nicaragua, 1912–13: *American policy in Nicaragua. Memorandum on the convention between the United States and Nicaragua relative to an interoceanic canal and naval station in the Gulf of Fonseca, signed at Managua, Nicaragua, on February 8, 1913* (Wash., 1916) (64th Cong., 1st sess. Sen. Doc. 334); also issued in Spanish (Granada, 1916) [**3837**]; "The United States and Central America; policy of Clay and Knox", *Am. acad. pol. and soc. sci. ann.*, CXXXII (1927) 115–126 [**3838**]; and *Nicaragua and the Bryan-Chamorro canal treaty* (Wash., 1927) [**3839**]. Two works by Alfredo González Flores:*Manifiesto a mis compatriotas, noviembre de 1919* (San José, Costa Rica, 1919) [**3840**], the returned President of Costa Rica tells his constituents about his interviews with Woodrow Wilson who refused to recognize the revolutionary government of 1917; and *El petróleo y la política en Costa Rica* (San José, 1920) [**3841**], a defense by President González, of his administration in 1917, and an account of the coup-d'état of I. Tinoco, whose usurpation, unrecognized by President Wilson, he attributes to New York petroleum interests maneuvered by one Washington Valentine. L. G. Valentine, *The case of Costa Rica* (N.Y., 1919) [**3842**], the author prints an assortment of documents designed to show that President Wilson's Mobile pronouncement of 1913 had resulted in Latin American concessions being deflected to European rather than American capital. *Proceso de la restauración; o, La intervención americana en Costa Rica* (San José, 1922) [**3843**], preface signed: Octavio Quesada Vargas; articles by various authors, chiefly reprints from newspapers and periodicals, and correspondence, proclamations, laws, etc. The "intervention" was President Wilson's diplomatic attitude. Enrique Gay Calbó, "Centroamérica intervenida", *Cuba contemporánea*, XXXII (1923) 126–137 [**3844**], typical anti-Yankee essay. Gustavo Alemán Bolaños, *El país de los irredentos, diciembre de 1927* (Guatemala, 1927) [**3845**], a Guatemalan takes nasty cracks at the Yankees in Nicaragua. Cox, *Nicaragua* (no. 3779), the appendix includes a number of relevant official documents, 1909–1927. H. L. Stimson, *American policy in Nicaragua* (N.Y., 1927) [**3846**], special agent sent by President Coolidge to investigate conditions and arrange elections in 1927, but the book has a review of earlier relations between the United States and Central America. R. Nogales, *The looting of Nicaragua* (N.Y., 1928) [3847], a bitter attack on American intervention, but its lack of system, hodge-podge character, and incoherence, make it ineffective propaganda. Rodolfo Huete Abella, *Los banqueros y la intervención en Nicaragua* (Managua, 1931) [3848], hostile examination of relationship of American bankers and Nicaragua. *The conference on Central American affairs, held in Washington, D.C., from December 4, 1922, to February 7, 1923.* Texts of treaties, conventions, and protocols adopted, with an introduction by Dr. Leo S. Rowe (N.Y., 1923) (International Conciliation, no. 189) [3849]. "Central American conference, inaugural session, December, 1922 ", *Pan Am. union bul.*, LVI (1923) 1–12 [3850]; and " Closing session ", *ibid.*, 217–229 [3851].

For the printed writings of American presidents, secretaries of state, and diplomatists to Central American countries (for names and tenure, see latest *Register* of the Dept. of State (no. 5122)), see our list on p. 756.

5. The Caribbean [10]

a. In General

Bibliographical Aids

For general aids, see Sec. 1, above. See also Secs. 3 and 4 of this chapter.

L. M. Pérez, *Guide to the materials for American history in Cuban archives* (Wash.: Carnegie Institution, 1907) [3852], p. 35–75: " Documents on the relations between Cuba and the United States." A. P. C. Griffin, " List of writings relating to the Santo Domingo question, 1904–1905 ", in his *International arbitration* (no. 4188), 132–137 [3853], listing government publications, and books and articles in periodicals; also Griffin and Meyer, *List on reciprocity* (no. 1333), p. 101–110: " Reciprocity with Cuba ", which includes United States documents, 1901–1909, and books and articles in periodicals. N.Y. Public Library, *West Indies* (no. 4720). Jones, *Caribbean interests* (no. 3860), 353–368, for a " selected list of recent discussions relating to the Caribbean." Trelles, *Bibl. Cubana* (no. 4723). Two

---

[10] See also Ch. XVIII (" Cuba and Spain, 1861–1898 ") ; and Sec. 3 (" Colombia and Panama ") and Sec. 4 (" Central America ") of this chapter. For the negotiations culminating in the purchase of the Virgin Islands from Denmark, see Ch. XXI, sec. 4, below.

lists by the Pan American Union, Columbus Memorial Library (C. E. Babcock, librarian): *Bibliography; books and magazine articles in the library of the Pan American Union on relations between the United States and Dominican Republic* (Wash., 1924) [**3854**]; and *Bibliography; books and magazine articles in the library of the Pan American Union on relations between the United States and Haiti* (Wash., 1924) [**3855**]. Hill, *Roosevelt and Caribbean* (no. 3864), 214–224. Three bibliographies published by the American Foreign Law Association (compiled by G. H. Lippitt): *Bibliographies of foreign law series. No. 5. Porto Rico.* (N.Y., 1928) [**3856**]; No. 7. *Dominican Republic* (N.Y., 1933) [**3856a**]; and No. 8. *Haiti* (N.Y., 1933) [**3857**].

Special Works

A. T. Mahan, "The Isthmus and sea power", *Atlantic*, LXII (1893) 459–473, reprinted in his *The interest of America in sea power* (Boston, 1897) [**3858**], perspicuous analysis of the interests of the United States in a future canal by the greatest authority on the history of sea power. Also by the same writer, "The Panama Canal and sea power in the Pacific", in his *Armaments and arbitration* (no. 4253) 155–180, and in the *Century*, LXXXII (1911) 240–248 [**3858a**], a very notable article by a very notable thinker, on the strategic significance of the canal in the foreign policy of the United States. Marquis [H. D.] de Barral-Montferrat, *De Monroë à Roosevelt, 1823–1905* (Paris, 1905) [**3859**], after reviewing Theodore Roosevelt's diplomacy, this French author suspects he is as much of a menace to the peace of the world as Wilhelm II of Germany. Evelio Rodríguez Lendián, *Los Estados Unidos, Cuba y el canal de Panamá* (Havana, 1909) [**3859a**], the Panama Canal as a formidable threat to Cuban sovereignty and independence. C. L. Jones, *Caribbean interests of the United States* (N.Y., 1916) [**3860**], a brief popular outline of the more important political and economic developments. When published this represented the best general account. W. R. Shepherd, *The attitude of the United States toward the retention by European nations of colonies in and around the Caribbean* (N.Y., 1917) [**3861**], wartime reflections with valuable generalities of the importance to the United States of the Caribbean islands. Wahrhold Drascher, *Das Vordringen der Vereinigten Staaten im westindischen Mittlemeergebiet; eine Studie über die Entwicklung* *und die Methoden des amerikanischen Imperialismus* (Hamburg, 1918) [3862] traces the growth of American influence (imperialism) in the Caribbean. Blakeslee, *Mexico and Caribbean* (no. 3659). Latané, *U.S. and Lat. Am.* (no. 963). Jacques Crokaert, *La Mediterranée américaine; l'expansion des Etats-Unis dans la Mer des Antilles* (Paris, 1927) [3863], a Belgian diplomatist sees romantic islands beckoning to Uncle Sam who will take them for new stars in his flag. H. C. Hill, *Roosevelt and the Caribbean* (Chicago, 1927) [3864], a scholarly analysis of Roosevelt's Caribbean policy, based on his own papers, the archives of the Dept. of State, and the *Grosse Politik* (no. 5476). Tyler, *For. pol. Blaine* (no. 2223). Dennis, *Adventures* (no. 2224). C. P. Howland, ed., *American relations in the Caribbean;* a preliminary issue of section I of the annual *Survey of American foreign relations*, 1929 (no. 5170) (New Haven, 1929) [3865], chapters on each of the three island republics and on the six republics in Central America; it is the best summary, to date of publication. C. L. Jones, H. K. Norton, and P. T. Moon, *The United States and the Caribbean* (Chicago, 1929) (Chicago Council on Foreign Relations) [3866], a symposium of views on imperialism of the United States in the Caribbean. Miller, *Isthmian highway* (no. 2673), this is very one-sided from the historian's point of view, but impressive in its emphasis of the fact that the control of the Panama Canal stands or falls with the Monroe Doctrine. T. M. Cestero, *Estados Unidos y las Antillas* (Madrid, 1931) [3867] concerns mainly the relations of the United States with Cuba, the Dominican Republic, and Haiti, anti-interventionist essays written in 1913, 1917, and 1918, and reprinted without change in 1931. Bailey, *World cruise Am. fleet* (no. 3281). R. F. Nichols, " Navassa; a forgotten acquisition ", *Am. hist. rev.*, XXXVIII (1933) 505–510 [3868], a bit of guano diplomacy. D. G. Munro, *The United States and the Caribbean area* (Boston, 1934) (World Peace Foundation) [3869], this is a satisfactory general account, based on published United States documents, and selected Hispanic American documents, and secondary accounts; it continues the author's *Five republics of Central America* (no. 3775) and sundry special articles. Its value is enhanced by the author's long diplomatic experience in this region before becoming a professor of Latin American history at Princeton.

b. Cuba [11]

Special Works [12]

Willis, *Reciprocity with Cuba* (no. 3356), a review of the history of the question ending with a depreciation of the value of reciprocity. A. G. Robinson, *Cuba and the intervention* (N. Y., 1905) [3870–1], a journalist's intimate description of the work of the United States during the period of intervention. A. Whitcomb, *La situation internationale de Cuba* (Paris, 1905) [3872], a careful study of the administration of Cuba during the American occupation, 1899–1902, with considerable tribute to General Wood; considers Cuba as a quasi-sovereign country. Rodríguez Lendián, *Los Estados Unidos, Cuba* (no. 3860). F. Carrera y Jústiz, *Orientaciones necesarias; Cuba y Panamá* (Havana, 1911) [3873], pro-United States; looks on the Panama Canal as a great and expensive work of civilization of immense value to Cuba. Rafael Martínez Ortiz, *Cuba; los primeros años de independencia* (Havana, 1911–12, 2 v.; 3d ed., Paris, 1929, 2 v.) [3874] is esteemed by Cubans to be a circumstantial chronicle not devoid of objective judgments and appreciation of political events. Raúl de Cárdenas, *Cuba no puede invocarse en testimonio del imperialismo norteamericano* (Havana, 1917) [3875], and *Política Estados Unidos* (no. 3494), author believes it is strategic necessity rather than imperialism which has dictated American policy in the Caribbean; he affirms that after having seen the independence of the Spanish colonies the United States became defenders of the new nations. Martin, *U.S. and intervention* (no. 4808), ch. 3: "Intervention in Cuba." J. B. Scott, "The Isle of Pines", *Am. jour. internat. law*, XVII (1923) 100–104 [3875a], a good summary. C. E. Chapman, *A history of the Cuban republic* (N.Y., 1927) [3876], a careful, objective and realistic study that reflects in a way uncomfortable to Cubans the ineptitudes of Cuban self-government and independence. Hill, *Roosevelt and the Caribbean* (no. 3864). L. H. Jenks, *Our Cuban colony; a study in sugar* (N. Y., 1928) [3877], a review of the relations of the United States with Cuba, emphasizing the economic results of the Platt amendment; sharply critical of the United States. L. J. Meyer, "The United States and the Cuban revolution of 1917", *Hisp. Am. hist. rev.*, X (1930) 138–166 [3878],

---

[11] For Cuba, to 1898, see Ch. XVIII ("Cuba and Spain, 1865–1898").

[12] Many books which reflect opinion have been classed as sources in this division rather than as special works, *q.v.* It is difficult to classify them in one or the other category.

drawn principally from such material as is published in *Foreign relations* (no. 5345) for 1917. Janet D. Frost, "Cuban-American relations concerning the Isle of Pines", *Hisp. Am. hist. rev.*, XI (1931) 336–350 [3879], academic exercise summarizing the controversy from the obvious American printed papers. P. G. Wright, *The Cuban situation and our treaty relations* (Wash., 1931) (Publications of the Brookings Institution, XLII) [3880], short, keen, excellent study of the Platt amendment and the reciprocity treaty, less attention to political considerations which have affected the economic situation. Carleton Beales, *The crime of Cuba* (Phila. and London, 1933) [3881], an undocumented polemic against alleged looting of Cuba by American capitalists in implied collusion with the Department of State. It is pointed up particularly to the gruesome Machado regime, but the first third of the book reviews emotionally and picturesquely the preceding relations of the United States with Cuba. Guggenheim, *U.S. and Cuba* (no. 3347), a recent ambassador of the United States reviews his own negotiations, but has also a review of preceding relations, and argues for a modification of the Platt amendment.

Printed Sources

Cuba, Convención Constituyente, *Opinión sobre las relaciones entre Cuba y los Estados Unidos* (Havana, 1901) [3882]. T. B. Mederos, *La enmienda Platt; como la consideramos para el presente y porvenir de Cuba* (Havana, 1901) [3883], argument in favor of it by a Cuban *nacionalista.* U. S. War Dept., *Acts of Congress, treaties, proclamations . . . relating to non-contiguous territory, Cuba and Santo Domingo* (Wash., 1907; later editions, 1909, 1912, and 1914) [3884]. Aurelio Hevia, comp., *Colección de artículos y documentos referentes á la condición actual de Cuba* (Havana, 1908) [3885], articles on the Platt amendment and the American protectorate, with an appendix of documents, mostly dealing with the year 1902. J. C. Gandarilla, *Contra el yanquí; obra de protesta contra la enmienda Platt y contra la absorción y el maquiavelismo norteamericanos* (Havana, 1913) [3886]. J. B. Scott, ed., *The recommendations of Habana concerning international organization, adopted by the American Institute of International Law at Habana, January 23, 1917* (N. Y., 1917) (Carnegie Endowment for International Peace, Division of International Law) [3887] includes an account of the "origin of

the [Platt] amendment which states and defines the relations between Cuba and the United States and which is capable of . . . a
larger application"; also by the same writer, *Cuba, la América
latina, los Estados Unidos* (Havana, 1926) [**3887a**], collected papers
and addresses, translated into Spanish, on inter-American relations
(Platt amendment, Isle of Pines, Pan Americanism, etc.), by an eminent American authority on international law; the essay on the Platt
amendment looks on that tie as an alliance rather than a protectorate.
Ramón Zaydín and Manuel Márquez Sterling, *La soberanía de Cuba
ante las conferencias de la paz* (Havana, 1919?) [**3888**], denunciation of the Platt amendment as not voluntarily accepted; by the
present (Feb. 1934) ambassador of Cuba to the United States. A. V.
López Hidalgo, *Cuba y la enmienda Platt* (Havana, 1921) [**3889**],
a Cuban objection to the "imposed" Platt amendment. Luis
Machado y Ortega, *La enmienda Platt* (Havana, 1922) [**3890**], one
of the sharpest Cuban examinations of the Platt amendment, with
statement of objections thereto; attempts to interpret the Platt
amendment as not permitting intervention by the United States
(unless asked by Cuba or an international tribunal) except to ward
off danger to Cuban independence. Emilio Roig de Leuchsenring,
*Análisis y consecuencias de la intervención norteamericana en los
asuntos interiores de Cuba* (Havana, 1923) [**3891**], bitter attack
on United States policy toward Cuba. Three studies by Cosme de la
Torriente [y Peraza]: "Las relaciones de la república de Cuba y los
Estados Unidos de América conforme al tratado permanente", *Rev.
derecho hist. y letras* (Havana), LXXV (1923) 321–350 [**3892**];
Cuba y los Estados Unidos (Havana, 1929) [**3893**], a series of speeches
on Cuba's foreign relations, particularly with the United States, by a
distinguished and heroic Cuban patriot, jurist, and diplomatist, in
1923 ambassador to the United States; and *La enmienda Platt y el
tratado permanente* (Havana, 1930) [**3894**], one of the most notable
of Cuban pleas agains the full terms of the Platt amendment, ampli-
fied from the author's article ("The Platt amendment") in *Foreign
affairs*, VIII (1930) 364–378. D. W. Knox, "An adventure in diplomacy", *U.S.N. inst. proc.*, LII (1926) 273–287 [**3895**], narrative of
the part played by an American naval officer at Guantanamo Bay,
Cuba, during the rebellion of 1917. U. S. Tariff Commission, *The
effects of the Cuban reciprocity treaty of 1902* (Wash., 1929) [**3896**]

" Documents and notes relating to the history of the reciprocity movement " (p. 421–436).

For the Isle of Pines Controversy: *Adjustment of the title to Isle of Pines*, 1906 (59th Cong., 1st sess. Sen. Doc. no. 205) [3897], containing the majority and minority reports from the Committee on Foreign Relations, with numerous documents. M. E. Clapp, " Have we mislaid a valuable possession ", *No. Am. rev.*, CXC (1909) 330–337 [3898], Isle of Pines controversy between Cuba and the United States, settled by treaty in 1925; written by a United States senator. Two works by Gonzalo de Quesada, a former Cuban minister at Washington: *Los derechos de Cuba á la Isla de Pinos* (Havana, 1909), published in English, " Cuba's claims to the Isle of Pines ", *No. Am. rev.*, XC (1909) 594–604 [3899]; and *The title of the Republic of Cuba to the Isle of Pines* (Wash., 1924) [3900] containing material on the geography, history, etc., of the Isle of Pines, and an article by Señor Gonzalo de Quesada, late Cuban minister to the United States (no. 3899 above), and the decision of the United States Supreme Court, case of Pearcy vs. Stranahan (1907) which declared that " the Isle of Pines was an integral part of the territory of Cuba." Evelio Rodríguez Lendián, *La Isla de Pinos, según el tratado de París* (Havana, 1913) [3901]. *In re treaty of Isle of Pines, an appeal to the United States Senate, by American citizens* (n.p., 1923?) [3902] in behalf of 10,000 American citizens . . . we earnestly protest against ratification of the pending treaty which transfers the ownership of the island to the republic of Cuba . . ." signed: Edward Yanish, Asa G. Briggs, T. J. Keenan . . . [and others], committee. *Isles of Pines; papers relating to the adjustment of titles to the ownership of the Isle of Pines* (Wash., 1924) (64th Cong., 2d sess. Sen. Doc. 166) [3903] contains a reprint of doc. no. 205, and a few other documents, previously published by the Senate, together with the report of Senator Lodge, Dec. 11, 1922, and Feb. 15, 1924, in favor of ratification of the treaty. Cosme de la Torriente, " Examination of the facts and questions. Isle of Pines treaty between the United States and Cuba ", *Rev. droit internat. sci. dipl.* (Geneva), III (1925) 201–218 [3904], the author was ambassador of Cuba to the United States and helped on the treaty arrangement. Sociedad Cubana de Derecho Internacional, *Statements and documents relative to the Isle of*

Pines treaty between the United States and Cuba, published by the Cuban Society of International Law (affiliated with the American Institute of International Law, Havana, Cuba) (Wash., 1925) [3905].

c. Virgin Islands

For the purchase of the Virgin Islands from Denmark, see Ch. XXI, sec. 4.

d. Dominican Republic [13]

For bibliographical aids, see Sec. 1, above. See also N.Y. Public Library, *List relating to West Indies* (no. 4720).

Special Works

J. H. Hollander, " The convention of 1907 between the United States and the Dominican Republic ", *Am. jour. internat. law*, I (1907) 287-297 [3906], Professor Hollander was an expert sent down by the Department of State to adjust the Dominican finances after the intervention of 1905. Antonio de la Rosa, " Les finances de Saint-Domingue et le contrôle américain ", *Rev. gén. droit internat.*, XVIII (1911) 401-448, 499-583, XIX (1912) 73-120, XXI (1914) 425-468 [3907], a well-documented and objective summary to 1911. Otto Schoenrich, *Santo Domingo; a country with a future* (N.Y., 1918) [3908], a fair-minded, conscientious, glorified guidebook rather than a serious historical or political study. Max Henríquez Ureña, *Los Estados Unidos y la República Dominicana; la verdad de los hechos comprobada por datos y documentos oficiales* (Havana, 1919) [3909], the author opposes President Wilson's intervention, and says it will destroy the Pan American movement (useful to the United States) by creating distrust of American motives. This volume comprises the first part of his later work, *Los yanquís en Santo Domingo; la verdad de los hechos comprobada por datos y documentos oficiales* (Madrid, 1929). Cox, ' *Yankee imperialism* ' (no. 3687) discusses the resentment felt in Colombia toward the United States on account of the American occupation of Santo Domingo. Carl Kelsey, *The American intervention in Haiti and the Dominican Republic* (Phila., 1922) (Annals of the American Academy of Political and Social Science, no. 189) [3910], this was written by an American professor (University of Pennsylvania) who made an investigation for the American Academy of Political and Social Science; one of the

---

[13] See also Ch. XIV, sec. 4.

best objective summaries. Tulio Franco-Franco, *La situation internationale de la République Dominicaine à partir du 8 février, 1907* (Paris, 1923) [**3911**], " a well-informed doctoral dissertation examining the legal justification for American intervention, and reviewing American and Spanish public opinion on the subject " (Langer (no. 4399), 202). M. M. Knight, *The Americans in Santo Domingo* (N.Y., 1928) [**3912**], this is one of the most censorious of the attacks by American writers on this country's policy in Santo Domingo; these polemics should be balanced by more objective studies like Kelsey (no. 3910), Howland (no. 3865), and Munro (no. 3869). Welles, *Naboth's Vineyard* (no. 2167). Rippy, *Roosevelt corollary* (no. 3502).

Printed Sources

War Dept., *Acts Cong. Santo Domingo* (no. 3884). Academia Colombiana, *Memorial de protesta contra la arbitraria ocupación militar de la República Dominicana por tropas de los Estados Unidos de Norte America*, 1916 (Santo Domingo, 1916) [**3913**], addressed to the ambassadors of Argentina, Brazil, and Chile, at Washington. J. D. Phelan, *Santo Domingo investigation;* copy of the report, findings, and opinion of James D. Phelan, commissioner named by the Secretary of State, with the approval of the President, to investigate charges against United States minister to the Dominican Republic. Charles H. Strong, counsel (Wash., 1916) [**3914**]. Emilio Roig de Leuchsenring, *La ocupación de la República Dominicana por los Estados Unidos y el derecho de las pequeñas nacionalidades de América* (Havana, 1919), also published in *Rev. mex. derecho internac.*, II (1920) 249-296 [**3915**], a defense of Dominican sovereignty against the American occupation of 1916. U.S. Congress, Senate, Select Committee on Haiti and Santo Domingo, *Inquiry into occupation and administration of Haiti and Santo Domingo. Hearings* . . . (Wash.: Govt. Print. Off., 1921-22, 7 pts.) [**3916**], this committee was authorized by the Senate to inquire into the occupation and administration of the territories of the Republic of Haiti and the Dominican Republic; the report contains a mass of information and testimony. E. H. Gruening, " Conquest of Haiti and Santo Domingo ", *Current hist.*, XV (1922) 885-896 [**3917**], indictment of American intervention in Haiti and Santo Domingo by the managing editor of the (socialist) *Nation*. La Información,

Santiago de los Caballeros, Santo Domingo, *La Información frente a la ocupación de la República Dominicana por las fuerzas armadas de los Estados Unidos de Norte América* (Santiago, Rep. Dom., 1922) **[3918]**, campaign of a (finally suppressed) anti-interventionist newspaper. Félix E. Mejía, *Al rededor y en contra del plan Hughes-Peynado* (Santo Domingo, 1922) **[3919]**, a Dominican protest.

e. Haiti

For general aids, see Sec. 1, above. See also N.Y. Pub. Lib., *List relating to West Indies* (no. 4720).

Special Works

Frederick Douglass, "Haiti and the United States; inside history of the negotiations for the Môle St. Nicholas", *No. Am. rev.*, CLIII (1891) 337–345, 450–459 **[3920]**, negotiations directed by Blaine to obtain a harbor lease in Haiti; account based on knowledge of the source material, Douglass, the eminent Negro and former slave, was U.S. minister to Haiti at the time. Joseph Justin, *Les réformes nécessaires. Questions haitiennes d'actualité* (Port-au-Prince, 1915) **[3921]** contains a section on "Haiti et les Etats-Unis." Kelsey, *Intervention* (no. 3910). C. E. Chapman, "The development of the intervention in Haiti", *Hisp. Am. hist. rev.*, VII (1927) 299–319 **[3922]**, based on the professor-author's study of the records and of conditions in the island; he doubts if Haiti, left alone, will live up to international obligations. P. H. Douglas, "American occupation of Haiti", *Pol. sci. quar.*, XLII (1927) 228–241, 368–396 **[3923]**, a narrative of the steps by which American control was secured and established. H. P. Davis, *Black democracy; the story of Haiti*, 2d ed., rev. (N. Y., 1929) **[3924]**, like most "stories" it is journalistic. It gives from Senate hearings, the "story" of American intervention, and an eulogistic account of what has been done and what should be done by the American occupation. Vilfort Beauvoir, *Le contrôle financier du gouvernement des Etats-Unis d'Amérique sur la république d'Haiti* (Paris, 1930) **[3925]**, the most critical and scholarly Haitian account (based, however, on insufficient knowledge of United States sources), by a Haitian diplomatist, for a doctoral thesis at the University of Bordeaux; it is not unsympathetic to the American intervention. A. C. Millspaugh, *Haiti under American control* (Boston: World Peace Foundation, 1931)

[3926] supersedes Howland (no. 3865); the author, a former professor of political science, was financial adviser-general under the American intervention, and this is an authoritative factual study, the best account of events and American policy in Haiti since the intervention. M. E. Malval, *La politique financière extérieure de la république d'Haïti depuis 1910*. *La Banque Nationale de la république d'Haïti ou nos emprunts extérieurs* (Paris, 1932) [3926a], a University of Paris thesis; study of the role of finance in foreign affairs of the republic, including the loan of 1910, and the convention between the United States and Haiti of 1915. Munro, *Carribbean* (no. 3869), important and latest.

Printed Sources

For general collections, see p. 535.

Haiti, Ministère des Relations Extérieures, *Documents diplomatiques. Réclamations Pelletier et Lazare. Rapport du sécrétaire d'état des Etats-Unis, et annexes* (Port-au-Prince, 1887) [3927]. Moore's *Arbitrations* (no. 5364), v. II, for claims of Pelletier and Lazare, 1884, and the case of Charles Adrian van Bokkelen, 1888. Anténor Firmin, *M. Roosevelt, président des Etats-Unis et la République d'Haïti* (N.Y. and Paris, 1905) [3928], miscellaneous essays by a former minister of state of Haiti who does not think Theodore Roosevelt a big bad wolf, and thinks Haiti has got to solve her own problems herself if to be worthy of independence. W. A. MacCorkle, *The Monroe Doctrine in its relation to the republic of Haiti* (N.Y., 1915) [3929], by a former governor of West Virginia who sees in the Monroe Doctrine a justification for regenerative interventionism in Haiti. Haiti, *Exposé général de la situation de la république d'Haiti* (Port-au-Prince, 1917) [3930], a government document; concerned especially with the intervention of the United States. Haiti, Ministère des Relations Extérieures, *Documents diplomatiques. Affaires diverses* (Port-au-Prince, 1921) [3931], ten "dossiers", 1918–20, including some dealing with relations with the United States. *Inquiry into occupation of Santo Domingo* (no. 3916) contains a mass of information and testimony. See pp. 194 and 264, for statement explaining the origin of the constitution prepared for Haiti during the American intervention, based on a report of a speech of August 18, 1920, printed in the N.Y. *Herald*, Oct. 18,

1920, p. 2). Foreign Policy Association, *The seizure of Haiti by the United States. A report on the military occupation of the republic of Haiti and the history of the treaty forced upon her* (N.Y., 1922) [**3932**], " report " by a self-constituted committee of private citizens deprecating American intervention and urging immediate abrogation of the treaty of 1915. Gruening, *Conquest* (no. 3917). For indictment of American intervention, by a Haitian diplomat, Dantès Bellegarde: *Haïti et les Etats-Unis devant la justice internationale* (Paris, 1924) [**3933**] ; " Le calvaire d'un gouvernement ", in his *Pour une Haïti heureuse.* II (Port-au-Prince, 1929) 76–172 [**3934**] ; and *L'occupation américaine d'Haïti; ses conséquences morales et économiques* (Port-au-Prince, 1929) [**3935**]. Two reports by the House Committee of Foreign Affairs: *Policies of United States in Haiti* (Wash., 1929) (71st Cong., 2d sess. House. Rept. 39) [**3936**], and *idem* (71st Cong., 2d sess. House. Rept. 52) [**3937**].

6. South America

a. Argentine Republic [14]

Bibliographical Aids

For general aids, see Sec. 1, above. See also Argentine historical bibliographies (nos. 4693–4695).

Special Works

For general histories of Argentine, see Ch. VIII, sec. 7.

L. M. Moreno Quintana, *La diplomacia de Yrigoyen; relación técnica, objetiva y documentada de la política internacional argentina durante el período de gobierno 1916–1922* (La Plata, 1928) [**3938**] has a chapter on Yrigoyen's Pan American policy and Argentine's neutrality, 1914–19. Higino Arbro, " El cincuentenario del fallo arbitral del presidente Hayes ", *Rev. derecho internacional*, XV (1929) 5–27 [**3938a**], arbitral decision of President Hayes, 1878, concerning boundaries in Argentina. Alberto Palcos, *Sarmiento, la vida, la obra, las ideas, el genio* (Buenos Aires, 1929) [**3939**], Sarmiento was minister of the Argentine in Washington, 1865–67; the biography is concerned mostly with his literary genius. Paul De Witt, " The commercial relations between the United States and Argentine ", *Southw. pol. and soc. sci. quar.*, XI (1930) 156–172

---

[14] For Drago Doctrine, see Ch. XVI, sec. 5, b.

[3940], historical review based on official publications of both countries. P. D. Dickens, "Argentine arbitrations and mediations with reference to United States participation therein ", *Hisp. Am. hist. rev.*, XI (1931) 464–484 [3941] notes the following: Argentina and Paraguay: the Middle Chaco arbitration (1867); Argentina and Chile: the Andean boundary (1899); Argentina and Brazil: the Misiones arbitration (1892–95); The United States and Mexico: the A.B.C. mediation (1914–15). H. F. Peterson, " Efforts of the United States to mediate in the Paraguayan war ", *ibid.*, XII (1932) 2–17 [3942], a convenient summary of the proffered but rejected mediation of the United States, based on the printed diplomatic correspondence of the United States and of the several countries concerned.

Printed Sources

For general collections, see Sec. 1, above. *Information concerning recent transactions in the La Plata, affecting the political relations of the United States with Paraguay, the Argentine Republic, Uruguay, and Brazil* (Wash., 1869) (40th Cong., 3d sess. Sen. Ex. doc. no. 5) [3943]. *Further information concerning transactions in the region of La Plata affecting the political relations [etc.]* (Wash., 1869) (40th Cong., 3d sess. Sen. Ex. doc. no. 5, pt. 2) [3944]. D. F. Sarmiento (Argentine minister to the United States), *Obras* (Paris, 1889–1909, 53 v.) [3945], v. XXXIV: " Cuestiones americanas " contains a short chapter on his mission to the United States; and various data relating thereto are scattered throughout the other volumes of the *Obras*. Also, *Cartas confidenciales de Sarmiento a M. R. García (1866–1872)* (Buenos Aires, 1917) [3946] contains several letters written from the United States during his diplomatic mission there. Argentine Republic, Ministerio de Relaciones Exteriores, *Reciprocidad comercial: negociaciones entre Estados Unidos y la República Argentina* (Buenos Aires, 1892) [3947], correspondence between the two governments. The following by E. S. Zeballos (Argentine minister to the United States, 1893–5): *International law of Spanish America; arbitration on Misiones; statement made by the late minister of foreign affairs of the Argentine Republic . . . to refute mistakes of Brazilian origin and to enlighten public opinion in South and North America* (Buenos Aires, 1893) [3948]; *Argument for the Argentine Republic upon the question with Brazil in regard to the territory of Misiones, submitted to the arbitration of the President of the United States, in accordance with the treaty of September 7, 1889* (Wash., 1894) **[3949]**, also issued in Spanish; and " Theodore Roosevelt y la política internacional americana ", *Rev. archivos, historia y letras,* XLVI (1913) 545–604 **[3950]**, speeches by Dr. E. S. Zeballos and Theodore Roosevelt at the University of Buenos Aires, Nov. 10, 1913. V. G. Quesada, *Los Estados Unidos y la América del Sur,* by Domingo de Pantoja [pseud.] (Buenos Aires, 1893) **[3951]** sets forth " the Yankees depicted by themselves " as a people frankly disdaining South America, and saying under a pseudonym what he did not venture to say in his *Recuerdos de mi vida diplomática; misión en Estados Unidos (1885–1892)* (Buenos Aires, 1904) **[9351a]** which devotes some pages to an account of the " Lexington " case arising out of the attack of that sloop of war on an armed vessel flying the flag of Argentina in 1831. C. A. Aldao, *La cuestión de Misiones ante el presidente de los Estados Unidos de América* (N.Y., 1894) **[3952]**, Argentine brief. Martín García Mérou, *Estudios americanos* (Buenos Aires, 1900) **[3953]**, reflections of an Argentine minister in the United States (1890–99, 1901–04) on the country, its people, its politics, its diplomacy; also *Apuntes económicos e industriales sobre los Estados Unidos* (Buenos Aires, 1905) **[3954]**. Gregorio Benites, *Anales diplomática y mílitar de la guerra del Paraguay* (Asunción, 1902, 2 v.) **[3955]**, memoirs of the author, an ex-Paraguayan diplomat, about his missions to Europe and the United States anent the diplomacy of the Paraguayan war, and the proffered but rejected mediation of the United States. Stimson, *United States* (no. 5295), narrative of world war intrigue in Argentina, to which country the writer was our ambassador, 1914 to 1921.

For printed writings of American presidents, secretaries of state, diplomatists to Argentine Republic (for names and tenure, see latest *Register* of the Dept. of State (no. 5122)), see our list on p. 756.

b. Bolivia

Bibliographical Aids

For general aids, see Sec. 1, above. See also Bolivian historical bibliographies (nos. 4696–4697); and American Foreign Law Association, *Bibliographies of foreign law series. No. 3. Bolivia,* comp. by Edward Schuster (N.Y., 1926) **[3956]**.

Special Works

See Sec. 1, above.

Christian Grotewald, " Die Vorgeschichte des Konfliktes zwischen Bolivien und Paraguay ", *Europäische Gespräche*, VII (1929) 417–429 [**3957**], concerned principally in giving the background of the Chaco war, it notes the place of President Hayes' arbitral decision of 1878, in favor of Paraguay, reserving the rights of Bolivia. Dennis, *Tacna and Arica* (no. 3980).

Printed Sources

For general collections, see Sec. 1, above.

Bolivia, Ministerio de Relaciones Exteriores, *Mediación de Estados Unidos en la guerra del Pacífico* (La Paz, 1880) [**3958**]. Chile, Dept. Rel. Exter., *Mediación Estados Unidos* (no. 3988). U.S., Dept. of State, *Corres. with Trescot and Blaine* (no. 3986) ; and *War in So. America* (no. 3987), for U.S. official correspondence regarding the mediation in the war of the Pacific. Gómez Sánchez, *Estados Unidos en el Pacífico* (no. 3985). *Mediación de Estados Unidos* (no. 3988).

For the printed writings of American presidents, secretaries of state, and diplomatists to Bolivia (for names and tenure, see latest *Register* of the Dept. of State (no. 5122)), see our list on p. 756.

c. Brazil

Bibliographical Aids

For general aids, see Sec. 1, above. For Brazilian historical bibliographies and catalogues, see nos. 4698–4702.

Special Works

A. G. de Araujo Jorge, *Ensaios de historia diplomatica do Brazil no regimen republicano.* 1. serie. 1889–1902 (Rio de Janeiro, 1912) [**3959**], this is not a thoughtful historical study; it is rather mostly a catalogue of succeeding diplomatic representatives of Brazil to foreign nations, with dates of incumbency, and only most meager account of diplomatic questions. Henri Lorin, " La politique américaine du Brésil ", *Quest. dipl. et col.*, XXXIII (1912) 95–105 [**3960**], light undocumented essay, concerns mostly the early 20th century. D. de Abranches, *Brazil and the Monroe Doctrine* (Rio de Janeiro, 1915) [**3961**], a Brazilian political leader points out the good in the Monroe Doctrine and makes a plea not to enlist in the ranks of those who oppose the United States by every weapon at their command. An English edition was sent by the author to various individuals in the United States. Helio Lobo, *Cousas diplomaticas* (no. 1272); also *Cousas americanas e brasileiras* (Rio de Janeiro, 1923) [**3962**], this deals largely with economic relationships of all phases. J. F. Rippy, " The United States and the establishment of the republic of Brazil ", *Southw. pol. sci. quar.*, III (1922) 39–53 [**3963**], brief review, emphasizing opinion of the American press, 1870's to 1895. C. A. Timm, " The diplomatic relations between the United States and Brazil during the naval revolt of 1893 ", *ibid.*, V (1924) 119–137 [**3964**], adapted from a section of the author's thesis on the diplomatic relations between Brazil and the United States. This chapter rests almost exclusively on *For. relations.* N. A. N. Cleven, " James Watson Webb, United States minister to Brazil, 1861–1869 ", *Revista de Instituto Histórico e Geographico Brasileiro*, tomo especial. *Congresso Internacional de Historia da America* (1922), v. I (Rio de Janeiro, 1925) 295–394 [**3965**]; also by the same writer, " Some plans for colonizing liberated negro slaves in Hispanic America ", *Southw. pol. and soc. sci. quar.*, VI (1925) 151–166 [**3966**], a digest drawn off from printed diplomatic correspondence of the United States for 1862; it is superseded by Hill's book (no. 1277). Carolina Nabuco, *A vida de Joaquim Nabuco*, by his daughter (São Paulo, 1929) [**3967**], sketch of the minister to the United States, 1905–10. Hill, *U.S. and Brazil* (no. 1277, the best account. Peterson, *U.S. and Paraguayan war* (no. 3942).

For biographies of American presidents, secretaries of state, and diplomatists to Brazil (for names and tenure, see latest *Register* of the Dept. of State (no. 5122)), see the relevant entries and bibliographical data in the *D.A.B.*

Printed Sources

For general collections, see Sec. 1, above.

Transactions in La Plata (no. 3943). Eduardo Prado, *A illusão americana*, 2d ed. (Paris, 1895), the first edition was confiscated by order of the Brazilian government, later a Spanish translation was published, *La ilusión Yanqui*, tr., with introduction and notes by Carlos Pereyra (Madrid, 1918?) [**3968**], argument of a Brazilian

monarchist, at the time of the establishment of the republic, against
following any constitutional or other models of the United States
of America; and stressing that the imperialism of the United States
was far more dangerous to Brazil than the imperialism of European
countries. It had a considerable influence in Brazil at the time. *The
Acre territory; documents concerning the controversy between Brazil and Bolivia over a contract made with American citizens,* anonymous (n.p., 1902?) [**3969**]. Benites, *Anales dipl. guerra del Paraguay* (no. 3955). J. O. Kerbey, *An American consul in Amazonia*
(N.Y., 1911) [**3970**], writer's experiences as consul at Pará, Brazil,
1890–91; colorful and naïve, of no value for diplomatic relations.
Salvador de Mendonça, *A situação internacional do Brazil* (Rio de
Janeiro and Paris, 1913?) [**3971**], essays on Brazilian foreign policy
by a former Brazilian diplomatist who was minister to the United
States, 1891–98; there are several chapters relating to the United
States.

For the printed writings of American presidents, secretaries of
state, and diplomatists to Brazil (for names and tenure, see the latest
Register of the Dept. of State (no. 5122)), see our list on p. 756.

d. Chile

Bibliographical Aids

For general aids, see Sec. 1, above. See also Chilean historical
bibliographies and catalogues (nos. 4704–4706). Sherman (no. 1067),
219–224. Evans (no. 1069), 221–234.

Special Works

See Sec. 1, above. For general histories of Chile, see nos. 4704–
4706.

A. B. Hart, " The Chilean controversy ", in *Practical essays on
American government* (N.Y., 1893), 108–114 [**3972**], a thoughtful
contemporary essay by a teacher in Harvard University. J. B.
Moore, " The late Chilean controversy ", *Pol. sci. quar.,* VIII (1893)
467–494 [**3973**], a simple narration of the circumstances surrounding
the *Itata* affair, as they are disclosed in the official publications of the
United States, by the third assistant secretary of state. [J. A.
Gillis], *An examination of the Chilean incident,* by a member of the
bar (anon.) (Boston, 1896) [**3974**], a review of the evidence in the
case of the attack upon sailors of the U.S.S. *Baltimore,* while ashore

in Valparaiso in 1891. Pío Ballesteros, "Un conflicto yankee-chileno; la cuestión Allsop", *España mod.*, CCLVII (1910) 89–102 [**3975**], summary of the Alsop claim. Four studies by Osgood Hardy: "The Itata incident", *Hisp. Am. hist. rev.*, V (1922) 195–226 [**3976**], rather an introduction to a definitive history of this incident, it has brought together information from a large variety of printed documents and secondary accounts; "Was Patrick Egan a 'blundering minister?'" *ibid.*, VIII (1928) 65–81 [**3977**] discusses the rather unjustified tradition which has grown up to the effect that much of the trouble that arose between the United States and Chile in 1891 was due to the incapacity of the American minister at Santiago de Chile, Patrick Egan; "The United States and Chile; an account of the early relations between the two young republic". *Chile* (N.Y.) VII, no. 40 (1929) 60–64, 151–152 [**3978**], a scholarly little summary, drawn from the leading secondary accounts, appears in a propagandist publication; and "When the Monroe Doctrine was forgotten", *ibid.*, VIII (1930) 115–119, 143–145 [**3979**], the refusal of the United States to protect Chile during the war between Chile and Spain, 1865–66, was strongly resented by the Chileans as a failure of protection due under the Monroe Doctrine; discusses also the relations between the two countries during the war of the Pacific. Sherman, *U.S. and Chile* (no. 1067). Evans, *Chile and U.S.* (no. 1069). Tyler, *For. pol. Blaine* (no. 2223) has chapters on "The war between Chile and Peru, 1879–1883," and "The Chilean revolution in its relation to the United States." W. J. Dennis, *Tacna and Arica; an account of the Chile-Peru boundary dispute and of the arbitrations by the United States* (New Haven, Conn., 1931) [**3980**], about the last word in English on this subject; it surveys the historical background and interprets the attempted mediations of the United States. F. W. Fetter, "The Chilean debt payment of 1891", *Economic history* (Royal Economic Society suppl. to *Economic journal*), II, no. 8 (1933) 609–616 [**3981**].

For a convenient list of "U.S. ministers to Chile", 1823–1916, see Sherman (no. 1067), 215–216; and for "Chilean ministers to the U.S.", 1828–1911, see the same, 217–218.

For biographies of American presidents, secretaries of state, and diplomatists to Chile (for names and tenure, see latest *Register* of the Dept. of State (no. 5122)), see the relevant entries and bibliographical data in the *D.A.B.*

Printed Sources

For general collections, see Sec. 1, above.

Chile, Ministerio de Relaciones Exteriores, *Documentos relativos á la mediación de la Francia i la Gran-Bretaña i de los Estados-Unidos en la guerra entre las repúblicas aliadas del Pacífico i la España* (Santiago de Chile, 1867) [3982]. Benjamín Vicuña Mackenna, *Diez meses de misión a los Estados Unidos* (Santiago de Chile, 1867, 2 v.) [3983], this eminent Chilean publicist came to Washington on a mission of propaganda in 1865–66, anent the Chilean-Spanish war and the Monroe Doctrine; the work includes many documents. Bolivia, Min. Rel. Exter., *Mediación Estados Unidos* (no. 3958), war of the Pacific. Chile, Departamento de Relaciones Esteriores, *Las conferencias en Aríca; documentos relativos á la mediación ofrecida por el gobierno de los Estados Unidos de Norte América para poner fin a la guerra entre Chile, Perú i Bolivia* (Santiago, 1880) [3984]. E. Gómez Sánchez, *Memorandum sobre la actitud del gobierno de los Estados Unidos de Norte América en el Pacífico*, presentado a las cancillerías del Plata por la legación Peruana (Buenos Aires, 1882) [3985]. Two collections issued by the U.S. Dept. of State: *Correspondence between that Department [State] and the Hon. William Trescot, special envoy extraordinary to the republics of Peru, Chili, and Bolivia, and Walker Blaine, third assistant secretary of state* (Wash., 1882) (47th Cong., 1st sess., Sen. Ex. doc., no. 181) [3986]; and *Papers relating to the war in South America, and attempts to bring about a peace, submitted to the Senate, January 26 and 27, 1882, and to the House of Representatives, January 26 and February 17, 1882, in reply to resolutions of those bodies, calling for correspondence touching the efforts of this government to bring about peace between Chili and Peru and Bolivia, and touching claims against or contracts respecting either of the belligerent governments* (Wash., 1882) [3987]. *Mediación de los Estados Unidos de Norte América en la guerra del Pacífico. El señor doctor don Cornelio A. Logan y el D. Francisco García Calderón* (Buenos Aires, 1884) [3988]. Chile, Ministerio de Relaciones Exteriores, *Estados Unidos i Chile. Notas cambiadas entre la legación de Estados Unidos de Norte-América i el ministro de relaciones esteriores de Chile, a propósito de las cuestiones suscitadas entre ambos países* (Santiago de Chile, 1891) [3989], correspondence between M. A. Matta and Patrick Egan, regarding the " asylum " question and the *Baltimore* affair. M. A. Matta (Chilean minister of foreign affairs), *Cuestiones recientes con la legación i el gobierno de los Estados Unidos de Norte América* (Santiago de Chile, 1892) [**3990**], an important collection of Chilean documents. *Message of the President of the United States respecting the relations with Chile* (Wash., 1892) (52d Cong., 1st sess., House. Ex. doc. 91) [**3991**] contains also the diplomatic correspondence, the correspondence with naval officials, the inquiry into the attack on the seamen of the U.S.S. *Baltimore* in the streets of Valparaiso, and the evidence of the officers and crew of the steamer *Keweenaw* respecting the ill-treatment of Patrick Shields by the Chilean police. United States and Chilean Claims Commission, 1892–94, *Minutes of proceedings* (Wash., 1894) [**3992**]. Robley D. Evans, *A sailor's log; recollections of forty years of naval life* (N.Y., 1901) [**3993**], Evans was in command of the U.S. gunboat *Yorktown* at Valparaiso during the winter of 1891–92; his diary contains valuable information on the Chilean situation. United States and Chilean Claims Commission, 1900–01, *Minutes of commission* (Wash., 1901) [**3994**]; also *Report. Final report of John Hoyt Perry, agent and counsel for United States* (Wash., 1901) [**3995**]. United States, *The Alsop claim. The case of the United States of America for and in behalf of the original American claimants in this case, . . . versus the Republic of Chile before His Majesty George V* (Wash., 1910) [**3996**]; also "Award pronounced by His Majesty King George V as 'amiable compositeur' between the United States and the republic of Chile in the matter of the Alsop claim ", London, July 5, 1911, *Am. jour. internat. law*, V (1911) 1079–1107 [**3997**].

For the printed writings of American presidents, secretaries of state, and diplomatists to Chile (for names and tenure, see latest *Register* of the Dept. of State (no. 5122)), see our list on p. 756.

e. Paraguay

Bibliographical Aids

For general aids see Sec. 1, above. See also Decoud, *List relating to Paraguay* (no. 4715).

Special Works

See Sec. 1, above. For general history of Paraguayan diplomacy, Báez, *Hist. dipl. Paraguay* (no. 1310).

Peterson, *U.S. and Paraguayan war* (no. 3942). P. H. Box, *The origins of the Paraguayan war* (Urbana, 1929, 2 v.; also 1930, 1 v.) [3998], only analysis in English, but has little reference to the United States.

Printed Sources

For general collections, see Sec. 1, above.

Correspondencia entre el gobierno del Paraguay y la legación de los Estados Unidos de América y el cónsul de S. M. el Emperador de los Franceses, publicada en " el Seminario " de la Asunción (Buenos Aires, 1863) [3999]. *Correspondencias cambiadas entre el ministerio de relaciones exteriores de la república del Paraguay y el Señor Charles A. Washburn, ministro residente de los Estados Unidos de América, sobre la conspiración fraguada contra la patria, y el gobierno en combinación con el enemigo; y el atentado de asesinato á la persona del exmo. Señor mariscal López por nacionales y extranjeros* (Luque, 1868) [4000]. P. C. Bliss, *Historia secreta de la misión del ciudadano norteamericano Charles A. Washburn, cerca del gobierno de la república del Paraguay* (n.p., 1868) [4001], the writer, P. C. Bliss, was interpreter of the mission. *Une question du droit des gens. M. Washburn, ex-ministre des Etats-Unis à l'Assomption, et la conspiration paraguayenne* (Paris, 1868) [4002], written anonymously, professes to reveal intrigues of Washburn and Paraguayan revolutionists in wars of Brazilian aggression. C. A. Washburn, *History of Paraguay* (no. 5305), by the United States minister to Paraguay, 1861 to 1868; a valuable work, but written subject to the atmosphere caused by López's reign of terror, and written to a certain degree as defense against censure by a congressional inquiry into his alleged participation in a conspiracy against López. *Transactions in La Plata* (nos. 3943-3944). Benjamín Aceval, *Chaco paraguayo; memoria presentada al arbitro por Benjamín Aceval, e. e. y ministro plenipotenciario del Paraguay en Washington* (Asunción, 1896) [4003] includes documents and copy of the decision. Benites, *Anales dipl. guerra Paraguay* (no. 3955).

For the printed writings of American presidents, secretaries of state, and diplomatists to Paraguay (for names and tenure, see latest *Register* of the Dept. of State (no. 5122)), see our list on p. 756.

f. Peru

Bibliographical Aids

For general aids, see Sec. 1, above. See also nos. 4716–4717.

Special Works

See Sec. 1, above. For general histories of Peru, see nos. 1319a, 1320, 1321.

Two works by Arturo García Salazar: *Resumen hist. dipl. Perú* (no. 1322) containing a section on "Las mediaciones norteamericanas" in the war of the Pacific; and *Historia diplomática del Perú. v. I. Chile, 1884–1922* (Lima, 1930) [**4004**], the author is a well-known Peruvian diplomat and professor of diplomatic history at the University of San Marcos, and one of the best-informed men on that subject. The book is saturated with the Peruvian point of view. It contains material on the arbitration of the United States in the Tacna-Aríca dispute under Secretary Hughes. Dennis, *Tacna and Arica* (no. 3980). Nichols, *Guano diplomacy* (no. 3502).

For biographies of American presidents, secretaries of state, and diplomatists to Peru (for names and tenure, see latest *Register* of the Dept. of State (no. 5122)), see the relevant entries and bibliographical data in the *D.A.B.*

Printed Sources

For general collections, see Sec. 1, above.

José Antonio García y García, *Correspondencia diplomática entre el enviado estraordinario y ministro plenipotenciario del Perú en Washington y el secretario de estado de los Estados Unidos de América, sobre la cuestión de los monitores peruanos " Atahualpa " y " Manco-Capac ", anteriormente llamados " Catawba " y " Oniota "* (N.Y., 1868), also English edition, *Correspondence between Señor don José Antonio García y García, minister of Peru, and the Hon. William H. Seward, secretary of state of the United States* (N.Y., 1869) [**4005**]. Bolivia, *Mediación Estados Unidos guerra Pacífico* (no. 3958). Chile, *Conferencias en Aríca* (no. 3984). Gómez Sánchez, *Estados Unidos en el Pacífico* (no. 3985). Dept. of State, *Corres. with Trescot and Blaine* (no. 3986), and *War in South America* (no. 3987), for United States official correspondence regarding mediation in the war of the Pacific. *Mediación Estados Unidos* (no. 3988). Peru, Ministerio de Relaciones Exteriores,

Reclamación del ciudadano americano Victor H. MacCord; alegatos y documentos justificativos (Lima, 1899) [4006], MacCord, an American citizen, was imprisoned at Arequipa during a revolutionary movement in 1885. Alejandro Garland, *South American conflicts and the United States* (Lima, 1900) [4007], a Peruvian plea to United States opinion that the United States suppress Chilean aggression and contempt for Peruvian rights under the treaty of Ancon (1883), it reviews *ex parte* American diplomacy and the war of the Pacific. Also published in Spanish (Lima, 1900). Elihu Root, *Vísita al Peru del secretario de estado de los Estados Unidos Excmo. Sr. Elihu Root. Visit to Peru of the Hon. Elihu Root, secretary of state of the United States* (Lima, 1906) [4008], résumé of the acts and ceremonies with which Mr. Root was welcomed during his visit to Peru, and a collection of the speeches delivered, given in English and Spanish; see also *Latin America and the United States*, addresses by Elihu Root (no. 3504) which gives Mr. Root's addresses on his South American trip and translation into English of the addresses of welcome and congratulation.

For the printed writings of American presidents, secretaries of state, and diplomatists to Peru (for names and tenure, see latest *Register* of the Dept. of State (no. 5122)), see our list on p. 756.

g. Uruguay

Bibliographical Aids

For general aids, see Sec. 1, above.

American Foreign Law Association, *Bibliographical notes on the laws and legal literature of Uruguay*, comp. by F. B. Rives (N.Y., 1933) (*Its* Bibliographies of Foreign Law Series, no. 9) [4008a].

Special Works

For general history of Uruguay, see no. 1309.

Box, *Paraguayan war* (no. 3998). Peterson, *Mediation in Paraguayan war* (no. 3942). See also Federico Castellanos, *Luis Alberto de Herrera, monografía histórico-política* (Montevideo, 1922) [4009], political campaign biography; and César Pintos Diago, *Luis Alberto de Herrera, su vida—sus obras—sus ideas* (Montevideo, 1930) [4010], Herrera was *chargé-d'affaires* of Uruguay in Washington, 1902–03.

Printed Sources

For general collections, see Sec. 1, above. *Transactions in La Plata* (nos. 3943–3944). Luis Alberto de Herrera, *Desde Washington—correspondencias enviadas a "El Día"* (Montevideo, 1903) [**4011**]; and *Labor diplomática en Norte-América* (Montevideo, 1905) [**4012**], chiefly a collection of the principal official papers of the author during his residence in Washington as diplomatic representative of Uruguay, 1902–03.

h. Venezuela [15]

Bibliographical Aids

For general aids, see Sec. 1, above. See also Sánchez, *Bibl. venezolanista* (no. 4719).

Special Works

See Sec. 1 above. For general history of Venezuela, see Humbert (no. 1259).

Two articles by H. W. Bowen, "Queer diplomacy with Castro", *No. Am. rev.*, CLXXXIV (1907) 577–580 [**4013**], relations with Venezuela under Roosevelt in 1905, regarding the dispute over the rights of the American asphalt companies in Lake Trinidad; and "President Roosevelt's report to the Senate on Venezuela", *Indep.*, LXIV (1908) 911–913 [**4014**], comment by the former minister to Venezuela on the report to the Senate following demand for correspondence in Venezuelan claims cases (Orinoco corporation, etc.) 1905–08. R. C. Morris, "Our controversy with Venezuela", *Yale law jour.*, XVIII (1909) 243–251 [**4015**] discusses the background of the claim of the Orinoco corporation and the Critchfield claim. W. C. Dennis, "The Orinoco steamship case before the Hague tribunal", *Am. jour. internat. law*, V (1911) 35–64 [**4016**], a legal analysis of the arbitration. Georges Scelle, "L'affaire de la Orinoco Steamship Company", *Rev. gén. droit internat.*, XVIII (1911) 164–202 [**4017**], summary by an eminent French historian. G. G. Wilson, "United States and Venezuela; Orinoco Steamship Company", in *Hague arbitration cases* (no. 4018), 206–299 [**4018**] prints award of court only. P. F. Fenton, "Diplomatic relations of the United States and Venezuela, 1880–1915", *Hisp. Am. hist. rev.*, VIII (1928)

---

[15] See also Sec. 5 ("The Caribbean"). For the Venezuelan boundary controversy, see Ch. XVI, sec. 5 a. For the Venezuelan debt question of 1902–03, see Ch. XVI, sec. 5 b.

330–356 [4019], apparently an academic exercise based on obvious American printed material. Nichols, *Guano diplomacy* (no. 3502).

For biographies of American presidents, secretaries of state, and diplomatists to Venezuela (for names and tenure, see latest *Register* of the Dept. of State (no. 5122)), see the relevant entries and bibliographical data in the *D.A.B.*

Printed Sources

For general collections, see Sec. 1, above.

W. A. Pile, *A plea for justice. Venezuela's appeal to the United States for redress and fair play. The conspiracy to plunder Venezuela and certain American citizens. The powers of Congress to set aside, for cause, awards of international commissions* (Wash., 1878) [4020], argument before the Committee on Foreign Relations of the United States Senate, Jan. 29, 1878; reprints selected documents to show that the United States commissioner in the Mixed Claims Commission conspired with the United States minister to Caracas, and an attorney, in favor of certain claimants. U.S. Dept. of State, *In the matter of the claim of the Venezuela Steam Transportation Company against the government of Venezuela. Correspondence between the Department of State of the United States and counsel for the claimant, 1879–1884* (N.Y.? 1884?) [4021]. Venezuela, Ministerio de Relaciones Exteriores, *Documentos relativos á la reclamación intentada por la legación de los Estados Unidos de América en Caracas, á favor del cuidadano norte-americano Hancox, ó de la Compañía de Trasporte por Vapor de Venezuela* (Caracas, 1890) [4022]. Commission to arbitrate claims of Venezuela, Steam Transportation Company of New York against Venezuela, *Report. Final report of Alexander Porter Morse, agent of the United States* (Wash., 1895) [4023]. [O. E. Thurber], *The Venezuelan question; Castro and the asphalt trust from official records* (N.Y., 1907) [4024], contains a reprint of official and semiofficial documents and other matter pertinent to the case of the New York and Bermudez Company. U.S. Dept. of State, *Correspondence relating to wrongs done to American citizens by the government of Venezuela* (Wash., 1908) (60th Cong., 1st sess. Sen. Doc. 413) [4025], concerning claims of A. F. Jaurett, Orinoco Corporation, Orinoco Steamship Company, United States and Venezuela Company, New York and Bermudez Company; also *Orinoco Steamship Company . . . papers . . . show-*

ing the settlement of the controversies which existed with the government of Venezuela with respect to the claims of the Orinoco Steamship Company, etc., against that government (Wash., 1909) (61st Cong., 1st sess. Sen. Doc. 13) [4026]. United States, *The case of the United States of America on behalf of the Orinoco Steamship Company against the United States of Venezuela* (Wash., 1910); *Appendix to the case of the United States of America . . .* (Wash., 1910, 2 v.) [4027], v. II contains diplomatic and other correspondence; *The counter case of the United States . . .* (Wash., 1910) [4028], the appendix contains diplomatic and other correspondence prior to the meeting of the mixed commission of 1903. *Protocoles des séances de tribunal d'arbitrage constitué en exécution du compromis signé entre les Etats-Unis d'Amérique et les Etats-Unis de Vénézuela le 13 fevrier 1909. Différend au sujet d'une réclamation de la Compagnie des Bateaux à Vapeur " Orinoco "* (The Hague, 1910) [4029]. C. F. Grisanti (Venezuelan agent at the Hague Orinoco Steamship Arbitration) and much later (1926–30), Venezuelan minister to the United States), *Los Estados Unidos de Venezuela y los Estados Unidos de América ante el tribunal de la Corte Permanente de Arbitraje de la Haya . . . Alegatos* (Caracas, 1909) [4030]; and *Affaire de The Orinoco Steamship Company limited* (Paris, 1910) [4031], the *contre-exposé* of the Venezuelan agent.

For the printed writings of American presidents, secretaries of state, and diplomatists to Venezuela (for names and tenure, see latest *Register* of the Dept. of State (no. 5122)), see our list on p. 756.

7. The Pan American Movement [16]

Bibliographical Aids

For general aids, see Sec. 1, above. See also Sec. 8 ("Monroe Doctrine") for important bibliographical aids for this subject.

Büchi (no. 4044), ix–xii. Library of Congress, Division of Bibliography, *List of references on international American conferences, 1826–1914* (Wash., 1917) [4032], a typewritten list. Scott, *Internat. conferences* (no. 4108), xli–xliv, for a bibliography of reports and proceedings of the international conferences of American states, 1889–1928. *Books recommended for reading, study, and reference*

---

[16] See also Sec. 8 ("Monroe Doctrine"), and Ch. XX ("International Arbitration and the Peace Movement").

in the new Pan Americanism (Boston, 1916) (World Peace Foundation. Pamphlets series, v. VI, no. 2) [**4033**]. For works on Pan Americanism and the Monroe Doctrine in its application to present day conditions (particularly those written by Spanish Americans), see Sánchez Alonso (no. 4759), v. II, 253–263.

Special Works

J. V. Noel, *History of the second Pan American congress* (Baltimore, 1902) [**4034**], a United States journalist's impressions. Martín García Mérou, "Diplomacia del Panamericanismo", in his *Diplomacia americana* (no. 4790), 151–231 [**4035**] has value in describing the Pan American movement as seen by an Argentine diplomatist-historian of the diplomacy of the United States. American Academy of Political and Social Science, *The Pan-American conferences and their significance* (Phila., 1906) (Supplement to the *Annals* . . . May 1906) [**4036**], proceedings of a special session in honor of the Mexican ambassador to the United States, Señor Don Joaquín D. Casasús, Feb. 24, 1906. Manoel de Oliveira Lima, *Pan-Americanismo* (*Monroe-Bolívar-Roosevelt*) (Rio de Janeiro and Paris, 1907) [**4037**], disparate articles here reprinted, with philosophical discussion of the implications of the Monroe Doctrine for the Pan American movement. The author, not unmindful of the historic significance of the Monroe Doctrine for Hispanic American independence, resists any tendency for the Pan American movement to follow the political tutelage of the United States. Achille Viallate, "Les Etats-Unis et le pan-américanisme", *Rev. deux mondes*, 5e pér., LI (1909) 419–445 [**4038**] sees Pan Americanism as a successful policy of the United States of moral and political tutelage in the new world. Two studies by Alejandro Álvarez: *Le droit international américain* (Paris, 1910) [**4039**], the author, a Chilean jurist, is one of that school which believes that the diplomatic history of the new world gives the background for the foundation of a distinctly American international law and stresses the part which the inter-American conferences have played therein; and "La doctrina de Monroe y la América latina", *Revista argentina de ciencias políticas* (Buenos Aires), I (1911) 613–624 [**4040**] develops distinctions and confusions between the Monroe Doctrine *per se* and the hegemony of the United States in certain areas, after the manner of his broader study, *Le droit international américain*. A. H. Fried, *Pan-Amerika;*

Entwicklung, Umfang und Bedeutung der pan-amerikanischen Bewegung (1810-1910) (Berlin, 1910; 2d ed., enl., Zurich, 1918) [**4041**], a standard general account, weak on Spanish sources; invokes the interesting figure: the relation of Europe to the American states may be compared to that of the British Empire to the Balkan States. The second edition carries the study down to the year 1916. John Barrett, *The Pan American Union* (Baltimore, 1911) [**4042**], a popular description by its first director-general. Edouard Gérardin, "La question de l'arbitrage aux conférences panaméricaines ", *Rev. sci. pol.*, XXX (1913) 241-260 [**4043**], as seen by this French writer in the first four conferences. He thinks America is no less exempt than the old world from difficulties inherent in the organization of peace. Robert Büchi, *Die Geschichte der panamerikanische Bewegung* (Breslau, 1914) [**4044**], apparently a doctoral thesis; a methodical exposition drawn mostly from secondary sources. Its bibliography is astonishing because it does not contain a Spanish title. R. G. Usher, *Pan-Americanism; a forecast of the inevitable clash between the United States and Europe's victor* (N.Y., 1915) [**4045**], this is a general and perspicuous essay on the insignificance of the Pan American movement as a constructive movement; but it looked forward to a serious rivalry between the United States and Europe for economic domination of South America. Francisco García Calderón, " El Panamericanismo; su pasado y su porvenir ", *Rev. hispanique*, XXXVII (1916) 1-60 [**4046**], brief review of the relations between Spanish America and the United States. *Proceedings of the second Pan American Scientific Congress, Washington, U.S.A., Monday, December 27, 1915, to Saturday, January 8, 1916. Section VI. International law, public law, and jurisprudence.* v. VII (Wash., 1917) [**4047**] contains an article by E. P. Wheeler on " The Pan American conferences " (p. 851-859). D. P. Myers, *The new Pan Americanism.* Part III. *Central American league of nations* (Boston, 1917) (World Peace Foundation Pamphlets, VII, no. 1) [**4048**], an exposition of President Wilson's Pan American concepts. Three works by F. J. Urrutia: *Un comentario a la declaración de los derechos de las naciones decha por el Instituto del Derecho Internacional Americano*, edición oficial (Bogota, 1917) [**4049**], " El texto inglés de este trabajo se publicó en Washington, y circuló en los Estados Unidos de América en mayo de 1916, después de que la Comisión de Relaciones Exteriores del Senado norteamericano presentá su informe sobre el tratado entre Colombia y los Estados Unidos de América, celebrado en Bogotá el 6 de abril de 1914 " (p. 3) ; *La evolución del principio de arbitraje en América* (Madrid, 1920) [4050], this is an historical treatise by an eminent Colombian publicist who develops the American arbitration movement in relation to the background of the Pan American conferences; and *Le continent américain et le droit international* (Paris, 1928) [4051], discusses the origins of the revolutions in both Americas, the development of international principles during the early period after independence, the 6 Pan American conferences, 1889–1928, from the point of view of a believer in a distinct American system of international law. The gist of several earlier articles by the author appears here. Fernando Berenguer, *El hispano-americanismo estudiado desde el punto de vista del derecho internacional y el problema territorial de América* (Havana, 1918) [4052], examination into the opposing forces of the " artful " policy of the United States to control Hispanic America under formula of Pan Americanism and " spontaneous, natural, and irresistible tendency " of those nations to form their own union of policy. Latané, *U.S. and Latin Am.* (no. 963), ch. 8: " Pan Americanism." Lockey, *Pan-Americanism* (no. 964). Edward Perry, "Anti-American propaganda in Hispanic America ", *Hisp. Am. hist. rev.*, III (1920) 17–40 [4053–4], at least worth reading. Cox, *Yankee imperialism* (no. 3687) calls attention to mischievous significance of anti-United States propaganda in Colombia. S. G. Inman, *Problems in Pan Americanism* (N.Y., 1921; new ed., with additional material, 1925) [4055], the author, a representative of American religious and missionary efforts in South America, has long been one of the most fluent critics of the policy and attitude of his country, the United States. Also by the same writer, " Pan American conferences and their results ", *Southw. pol. sci. quar.*, IV (Dec. 1923) 238–266, (Mar. 1924) 341–368 [4056], a summary of the movement, with a hopeful attitude, on the eve of the fifth (Santiago) conference. Three studies by A. C. Wilgus: " James G. Blaine and the Pan American movement ", *Hisp. Am. hist. rev.*, V (1922) 662–708 [4057], based on U.S. official printed documents, and newspapers; and similar, " The second international American conference at Mexico City ", *ibid.*, XI (1931) 27–68 [4058]; and " The third international American conference at Rio de Janeiro, 1906 ", *ibid.*, XII (1932) 420–456

[4059]. Manuel Márquez Sterling, *El Panamericanismo; acuerdos y orientaciones de la quinta conferencia internacional americana*, *reunida en Santiago de Chile* (Havana, 1923) **[4060]**, objective summary of the proceedings by a Cuban diplomatist. Robertson, *Hisp. Am. rel.* (no. 1206), ch. 10: "Pan Americanism." Blakeslee, *Recent for. pol.* (no. 4122) has a reflective summary of the significance of Pan Americanism on United States policy. L. M. Moreno Quintana, "Pan Americanism and the Pan American conferences", *Inter-America*, VIII (1925) 429–444 **[4061]**, translation of "La comunidad internacional americana" in *Revista ciencias económicas* (Buenos Aires); an essay on the general development of the movement, to 1923, from a lofty international liberalism to a basis of the economic aggrandisement of the United States even at the cost of the other American republics. Pablo García de la Parra, *Colombia en las conferencias panamericanas* (Bogotá, 1926) **[4062]**, a factual summary by the Secretary of the Colombian delegation to the 6th Pan American Sanitary Conference. Santiago Magariño, *Panhispanismo, su transcendia histórica, política y social* (Barcelona, 1926) **[4063]**, Pan Americanism and Pan Hispanism both aim at peace; but Pan Americanism aspires to increase economic ties between Hispanic American nations, and between them and the United States, while Pan Hispanism would increase them with the old mother-country. Miguel Cruchaga [Tocornal], "Les conférences panaméricaines, de 1889 à 1928; le bilan des faits et résultats", *Rev. gén. droit internat. public*, 3d ser., III (1929) 88–107 **[4064]**; and "Las conferencias pan-americanas", *Rev. chilena*, XI (June 1927) 7–26 **[4065]**, as their history appears to a Chilean publicist. J. F. Godoy, *Las conferencias panamericanas; breve reseña de los trabajos y resultados de la primera, segunda, tercera, cuarta, y quinta conferencias panamericanas y preparativos para la sexta* (Mexico, 1927) **[4066]**, popular summary by a Mexican diplomatist. Tyler, *For. pol. Blaine* (no. 2223), ch. 7: "The international American conference [Wash., 1889–90]." Néstor Carbonell, *Las conferencias internacionales americanas* (Havana, 1928) **[4067]**, a voluminous factual description of the work of the 1st to 5th, inclusive, Pan American conferences, based on agenda and proceedings, by a Cuban delegate to the 6th conference and director of the Pan American office of Cuba. Fens Fessen, "Die ökonomische Grundlage der panamerikanischen-Idee", *Schmollers Jahrb.*, LII Jahrg., no. 5 (1928) 79–112 **[4068]** would explain the motive of Pan Americanism in the expanding need of the United States for markets for manufactures. For. Pol. Assoc., *Arbitration on Am. continent* (no. 4222). Wriston (no. 4799), 601–603, for executive agents to Pan American conferences (including medical, financial, etc.). Ferrera, *Panamericanismo* (no. 4105). J. F. Rippy, " The significance of the Pan-American movement ", *So. Atlan. quar.*, XXX (1931) 280–289 [4069], convenient and reflective summary; shows achievements not impressive in total of ratified conventions and treaties, but not lacking altogether in a considerable measure of harmony and cooperation in America. See also same author's *Latin America in world politics* (no. 1076). Cory, *Compulsory arbitration* (no. 4233). Enrique Gil, *Evolución del Panamericanismo; el credo de Wilson y el Panamericanismo* (Buenos Aires, 1933) [4070], a new survey of inter-American relations with special attention to Pan Americanism, the Monroe Doctrine, and Wilson's " creed."

Printed Sources

For general collections, see Sec. 1 above, particularly Moore's *Digest* (no. 5365), v. VI, 599–604 and v. VII, 70–73.

For official publications (proceedings, reports, etc.) of international congresses, conferences, and commissions (except such as are appointed to settle international disputes) to 1909, see the *Checklist* (no. 5361), 944–949. For list of printed reports and proceedings of the international conferences of American states, 1889–1928, see Scott (no. 4108), xli–xliv. Lists of American delegations to international conferences, congresses, and expositions, and American representation on international institutions and commissions, with relevant data, are given in the contemporary volumes of the *Register* of the Dept. of State (no. 5122). For a list of delegates of all countries to the international conferences of American states, 1889–1928, see Scott (no. 4108), 511–520. See also the Department of State list of *Inter-American conferences, 1826–1933. Chronological and classified list*, prepared by Warren Kelchner (Wash., 1933) (Dept. of State. Conference series no. 16) [4071], most useful, enumerates dates, places, and subjects of the several inter-American international conferences and the various ancillary congresses; bankers, journalists, good roads, scientists, sanitation, etc.

For running comment and description of the several conferences, and the ancillary congresses, see the appropriate juridical journals:

American journal of international law; Revista de derecho, historia, y letras; Revue de droit international (Geneva); *Revue de droit international et de législation comparée; Revue générale de droit international public; Ibero-amerikanisches Archiv, Zeitschrift für Völkerrecht;* and the *American political science review, Annals of the American Academy of Political and Social Science, Hispanic American historical review, Pan-American magazine* (very popular), and the *Pan American Union bulletin.*

J. G. Blaine, *Foreign policy of the Garfield administration; peace congress of the two Americas* (Chicago, 1882) [**4072**], Blaine's apologia (from the *Chicago weekly magazine,* Sept. 16, 1882). C. A. O'Rourke, *Congreso internacional americano* (N.Y., 1890) [**4073**], mostly a description of the " grand excursion " which the delegates took about the industrial United States. C. de Varigny," J. G. Blaine et le Congrès des 3 Amériques ", *Rev. deux mondes,* 3e pér., XCVII (1890) 433–462 [**4074**] sees the Pan American conference as a stroke of Blaine, the "American Bismarck ", to cultivate new markets for American industries. International Bureau of the American Republics, *Hand book of the American republics* (Wash., 1891) [**4075**]. Amédée Prince, *Le congrès des trois Amériques, 1889–1890* (Paris, 1891) [**4076**], European and American press reports, and official documents; with a narration of the " grand excursion " about industrial United States. Romero, *Mexico and the United States* (no. 3627), for account of the Pan American conference at Mexico City, by the Mexican delegate to the conference. International American Conference (2d), *Algunos datos sobre tratados de arbitraje y buenos oficios celebrados por las naciones de América* (Mexico, 1901) [**4077**]; *Crónica social, 1901* (Mexico, 1902?) [**4077a**]; and *La adhesión de la segunda Conferencia Internacional Americana a las convenciones de La Haya* (Mexico, 1902) [**4078**], an explanatory statement from Señor J. D. Casasús, secretary general of the conference, with accompanying documents. Aníbal Maúrtua, *La idea pan-americana y la cuestión del arbitraje; estudio histórico á propósito del Congreso de México* (Lima, 1901) [**4079**], a sympathetic review of the Pan American movement during the 19th century, ending with a plea for a Pan American international arbitration treaty as a gauge against possible aggression by an overwhelmingly powerful United States of the future. Darby, *International tribunals* (no. 4250). Pan American Sanitary Conference (1st), *Transactions of the first general*

International Sanitary Convention of the American republics, . . . Washington, D.C., Dec. 2, 3, and 4, 1902 (Wash., 1903) (57th Cong., 2d. sess. Sen. Doc. 169) [4080]; and also *Transactions of the second International Sanitary Convention of the American republics . . . Washington, D.C., October 9, 10, 12, 13, and 14, 1905* (Wash., 1906). *Speeches incident to the visit of Senator Root to South America, July 4, to September 30, 1906* (Wash., 1906) [4081]. "What the Latin American republics think of the Pan-American conferences", *Nation. geog. mag.*, XVII (1906) 474–479 [4082], summaries of statements made by diplomatic representatives of Mexico, Brazil, Costa Rica, and Bolivia in conferences of the American Academy of Political and Social Science. Perú, Ministerio de Relaciones Exteriores, *Congresos y conferencias internacionales en que ha tomado parte el Perú; coleccionados sus trabajos*, by Ricardo Aranda (Lima, 1909–13, 4 v.) [4083]. Benjamín Vicuña Subercaseaux, *Los congresos pan-americanos* (Santiago de Chile, 1906; 2d ed., 1910) [4084], the author was Chilean delegate to the 3d (Rio de Janeiro) Pan American conference, which he describes. Henry White, "The fourth International Conference of American States", *Am. acad. pol. and soc. sci. ann.*, XXXVII (1911) 585–593 [4085], the author was chairman of the United States delegation to the conference. John Bigelow, *American policy. The western hemisphere in its relations to the eastern* (N.Y., 1914) [4086], an essay seeking to distinguish between the "expansion" of the Monroe Doctrine and the "perversion" of it, and to expound the doctrine of Pan Americanism, which the author believes to mean independence of the European concert. Policarpe Bonilla, *Wilson doctrine. How the speech of President Wilson at Mobile, Ala., has been interpreted by Latin American countries* (N.Y., 1914) [4087]. C. A. Becu, *El "A.B.C." y su concepto político y jurídico* (Buenos Aires, 1915) [4088], essays by an Argentine evoked by the A B C mediation in Mexico; it conceives such a phenomenon as presaging a salutary American "concert" for peace, analagous to the European concert, but thinks Uruguay should be included. Francisco García Calderón, "El panamericanismo; su pasado y su porvenir", *Cuba contemp.*, XII (1916) 126–178, also in *Rev. hispanique*, XXXVII (1916) 1–60 [4089], passionate rhetorical review of American expansion to show how Pan Americanism is a screen for imperialism of the United States. Jacinto López, "Monroísmo y panamericanismo", *Cuba contemp.*, X (1916) 329–343

[**4090**] asks why it should be necessary to go to Washington to seek solutions for Hispanic American problems. The following by Ernesto Quesada (eminent Argentine historian and professor ιt the University of Buenos Aires) : " El nuevo panamericanismo y el congreso científico de Washington ", *Univ. Buenos Aires rev.*, XXXII (1916) 257-274 [**4091**], by the president of the Argentine delegation, who sees quite a lot of good in United States scientific and university life anyway; he sums up the results of the conference for his government; " El punta de vista norteamericano en la doctrina del panamericanismo ", *Anales de la Facultad de Derecho* (Univ. of Buenos Aires), 3d ser., I (1916) 85-184 [**4092**], as gathered by this Argentine historian, from American newspapers and personalities, during his attendance upon the 2nd Pan American Scientific Congress; thinks Wilson's ideas of co-fraternity represent a new Pan Americanism, but they cannot go far beyond the vital interests of the United States; " La evolución del panamericanismo ", *Univ. Buenos Aires rev.*, XLI (1919) 289-358 [**4093**] points out the domination by the United States of the Pan American Union, which would control any serious issue which went outside of the conventional harmless and pious pathways of Pan Americanism as it is. *The new Pan Americanism* (Boston, 1916-17, 3 nos.) (World Peace Foundation. Pamphlet series, VI, nos. 1, 2; VII, no. 1) [**4094**], the object of this publication is to bring together the essential utterances and facts that contribute to a clearer definition of a Pan American league of peace, from Root to Wilson. Pedro Capó Rodríguez, " Porto Rico y el panamericanismo ", *Cuba contemp.*, XIII (1917) 155-162 [**4095**], a prominent Porto Rican, a lawyer in the United States, thinks Porto Rico would be equally happy, either as a state in the United States, or as independent, but that its present status is incompatible with the spirit of Pan Americanism. F. A. Pezet, *Pan-American cooperation in Pan-American affairs* (Baltimore, 1917) [**4096**], reprinted from the *American political science review*, v. XI, no. 2; defines Pan American cooperation as directed toward international American solidarity based on international conciliation and arbitration. J. F. V. Silva, *Reparto de América Española y Pan-Hispanismo* (Madrid, 1918) [**4097**], voluminous hispanophil thesis by an Argentine, against the *hispanophobia* and *yankización* of Hispanic America. S. G. Inman, " Imperialistic America ", *Atlantic monthly*, CXXXIV (1924) 107-116 [**4098-9**], the author is a champion of the South American objections to wicked imperialism of the United States. Manning, *Arbitration treaties* (no. 3506). Alberto Guani, *La solidarité internationale dans l'Amérique latine* (Paris, 1926) [**4100**], an enlightened international solidarity is a fact, he says, in Latin America, and thinks participation by the United States is inspired by highest concepts of moral and intellectual solidarity. Sumner Welles, " Is America imperialistic ? " *Atlantic*, CXXXIV (1924) 412–423 [**4101**], reply to Inman's *Imperialistic America* (no. 4098). Benjamín Fernández y Medina, *La política internacional en América (pasado—presente—futuro)* (Valladolid ? 1928) [**4102**], author was Uruguayan ministei in Spain; looks upon the Pan American movement as a fiction which ought not to maintain itself. C. E. Hughes, *Pan American peace plans* (New Haven, 1929) [**4103**], this was published after the author's service as chairman of the delegation of the United States to the Pan American conference, 1928; it is an exposition of the background of the arbitration policy of the United States and of the network of inter-American arbitration and conciliation treaties, and of the discussions of such at Havana in 1928. Walter Schück, "Wurzel und Gegenwartsgestalt des Pan-Iberoamerikanismus ", *Zeits. Politik*, XIX, no. 5 (1929) 316–329 [**4104**] stresses Pan-Iberoamericanism as an antidote to the ominous imperialistic tendencies of Pan Americanism.[17] Orestes Ferrara, *El panamericanismo y la opinión europea* (Paris, 1930) [**4105**], the author, who has served as Cuban ambassador to the United States and secretary of state in Cuba (Machado regime), reviews the Pan American movement sympathetically to the United States. He thinks the sinister pictures which have been set up of the policy of the United States should be replaced by the real picture of an international policy based on justice and reciprocal respect. J. M. Yepes, *El panamericanismo y el derecho internacional* (Bogota, 1930) [**4106**], review of one phase of the history of Pan Americanism. Ingeborg Richarz-Simons, " Chronik der interamerikanischen Rechtsbeziehungen ", *Ibero-am. Archiv*, IV (1931) 544–557 [**4107**], a most valuable outline of the various Pan American congresses and conferences, 1826–1928, with a synopsis of events and accomplishments, treaties, conventions, ratifications, and texts thereof. J. B. Scott, ed., *The Interna-*

---

[17] For the German historical organ of the Pan-Iberoamerican movement, see *Ibero-Amerikanisches Archiv*, ed. by Prof. Otto Quelle of the University of Bonn (Berlin and Bonn, 1924–).

tional conferences of American states, 1889–1928; a collection of the conventions, recommendations, resolutions, reports, and motions adopted by the first six international conferences of the American states, and documents relating to the organization of the conferences (N. Y., 1931) [**4108**]. H. L. Stimson, *The United States and the other American republics; a discussion of recent events* (Wash., 1931) (Publications of the Dept. of State. Latin American series, no. 4) [**4109**], address of the secretary of state before the Council on Foreign Relations, New York, Feb. 6, 1931; for a clear statement of American policy in regard to Hispanic America.

MSS.: Suggestions

The original MS. minutes of the proceedings of the 1st, 2nd, and 5th conferences are in the Pan American Union.

8. The Monroe Doctrine in the 20th Century

Bibliographical Aids

The thousands of books, articles, and other data on the Monroe Doctrine have been made the subject of more bibliographical study than any other phase of American diplomacy. We can present only a selected list of titles, referring the reader to the following bibliographical aids: *Writings on American history* (no. 4661) which has a special section on this subject. Kraus (no. 1159), 19–36. Hart (no. 1164), 405–421, for a " Bibliography of the Monroe Doctrine and its collateral doctrines ", to 1916. Edith M. Phelps, *Selected articles on the Monroe Doctrine*, 2d and enl. edition (White Plains, N.Y., and New York City, 1916) (Debaters' Handbook Series) [**4110**], "Bibliography " (p. xvii-xxxiii) includes also material on Pan Americanism; this handbook is a useful reprint of various significant articles for and against the Monroe Doctrine as a continuing policy, together with a brief of arguments which does some thinking for debaters. Meyer, *Monroe Doctrine* (no. 1140). Trelles y Govín, *Doctrina de Monroe* (no. 1141). Pan Am. Union, *Monroe Doctrine* (no. 1142). Sánchez Alonso (no. 4759), v. II, 253–263. Phillips Bradley, *Monroe Doctrine* (no. 1143).

Special Works

Reddaway (no. 1146). Hector Pétin, *Les Etats-Unis et la doctrine de Monroë* (Paris, 1900) [**4111**], a review of American foreign relations by a Frenchman become nervous about American imperialism in Theodore Roosevelt's time. Marquis de Barral-Montferrat, "La doctrine de Monroë et les évolutions successives de la politique étrangère des Etats-Unis (1823–1903)", *Rev. hist. dipl.*, XVII (1903) 594–619, XVIII (1904) 21–52, 379–405 [**4112**]. Edgington (no. 1149). Harrison, *Deutschtum and Monroe Doctrine* (no. 4296). Rio Branca, *Monroe Doctrine* (no. 1155). J. C. Dunning, *Die neuesten Anwendungen der Monroedoktrin* (Borna-Leipzig, 1908) [**4113**], inaugural dissertation, University of Heidelberg; the theory of the Monroe Doctrine remains the same as it was originally, but new circumstances and conditions require a different sort of application. Carlos Pereyra, *La doctrina de Monroe; el destino manifiesto y el imperialismo* (Mexico, 1908) [**4114**]; and *El mito de Monroe* (Madrid, 1914) [**4115**], Mexican author asserts the Monroe Doctrine has never protected any American people; considers it a model of impertinence and stupidity, and that the policy of the United States would have been the same without the Monroe Doctrine. Chadwick, *U.S. and Spain* (no. 108). J. Laferrière, "La résolution Lodge et la doctrine Monroe", *Rev. gén. droit internat. public*, XX (1913) 549–574 [**4116**], a lengthy analysis of the implications of the Lodge resolution; it applies the Monroe Doctrine to private operations not susceptible to control when the doctrine looked only at states. Hart, *Monroe Doctrine* (no. 1164). A. B. Hall, *The Monroe Doctrine and the great war* (Chicago, 1920) [**4117**], no historical contribution, contains a resumé of arguments for joining the League of Nations. Latané, *U.S. and Latin America* (no. 963). W. S. Robertson, "Hispanic American appreciations of the Monroe Doctrine", *Hisp. Am. hist. rev.*, III (1920) 1–16 [**4118**], a valuable analysis; also by the same writer, *Hisp. Am. and U.S.* (no. 1206). Julius Klein, "The Monroe Doctrine as a regional understanding", *Pan Am. union bul.*, LII (1921) 139–144 [**4119**], examination of economic developments between the United States and Latin America, 1914–18, which bear on political relationships (expansion of trade and loans) which should promote the idea of the Monroe Doctrine as a regional understanding. T. H. Mahoney, *The Monroe Doctrine; the vital necessity of its continued mainte-nance*, pub. by the Knights of Columbus Historical Commission (Boston?, 1921) [**4120**], historical exposition to prove it a vital neces-

sity. D. Y. Thomas, *One hundred years of the Monroe Doctrine,
1823–1923* (N.Y., 1923) [4121], the first half of this work is now
superseded by Perkins' more detailed studies (nos. 1172 and 1211),
and the last half deals mostly with the 20th century, in which much
American policy is viewed with disapproval, and the question is
asked why the Monroe Doctrine should be maintained today unless
extended to all the world. The study is limited principally to
printed American sources. G. H. Blakeslee, *The recent foreign
policy of the United States; problems in American co-operation with
other powers* (N.Y., 1925) [4122], this is a perspicuous analysis of
recent trends of American foreign policy (1) in relation to the
American continents, (2) the Far East, and (3) Europe, in each of
which three fields the author distinguishes a distinct policy of the
United States. J. B. Whitton, "L'isolement des Etats-Unis;
principe caduc de la doctrine de Monroe", *Rev. gén. droit internat.*,
3d ser., I (1927) 45–57 [4123] stresses consistency of the non-
entanglement principle, 1823–1923. W. A. Bewes, "The Monroe
Doctrine and entangling alliances", *Grotius soc. trans.*, XIII (1928)
1–29 [4124], a temperate English analysis of contemporary definitions and implications of the Monroe Doctrine, particularly hostility
to it in Hispanic America. Garner, *Am. foreign policies* (no. 4817), an
American professor leans over backward trying to be fair-minded
to foreign countries about various criticized phases of the foreign
policy of the United States, including the Monroe Doctrine. Otto
von Gottberg, *Die Entwicklung eines amerikanischen Völkerrechts
(Beiträge zur Geschichte der panamerikanischen Bewegung)*
(Königsberg, 1928) [4125] surveys the Pan American movement
and tendency for a distinct American law and the Monroe Doctrine;
lays great stress on the fact that that doctrine has become international law in the covenant of the League of Nations. Welles,
Naboth's Vineyard (no. 2167), for the Roosevelt corollary (p. 601–
639). Miller, *Isthmian highway* (no. 2673) for application of the
Monroe Doctrine to these problems. A. T. Wilson, "The Monroe
Doctrine and Latin-American states", *Edinburgh rev.*, CCXLIX
(1929) 247–259 [4126] develops protests of South American
political writers against the Monroe Doctrine article (XXI) of the
League of Nations; and of its implications for the United States.
Hans Römer, "Das Clarksche Memorandum über die **Monroe-Dok-**

trin; Sinn und Auswirkung ", *Zeits. Politik*, XX (1930) 590–606 [**4127**], an analysis of the significance of this quasi-official exegesis; the author does not fail to see the apparent purpose of the Clark memorandum: to slough off the "Roosevelt corollary." Barcía Trelles, *Doctrina de Monroe* (no. 1174). C. E. Chapman, "New corollaries of the Monroe Doctrine, with especial reference to the relations of the United States with Cuba ", *Univ. of Calif. chron.*, XXXIII (1931) 161–189 [**4128**], the "Roosevelt corollary " (of vicarious responsibility) and the "Wilson corollary " (of discouraging revolutions). Alfonso García González, *La doctrina Monroe y el pacto de la Sociedad de las Naciones* (Mexico, 1931) [**4129**], thesis, Universidad Nacional Autonomía, of Mexico. L. N. Summers, "La clause Calvo ", *Rev. droit international* (Paris), Vᵉ ann., t. VII (1931) 567–581; VIIᵉ ann., t. XII (1933) 229–233; and a revised and translated reprint in the *Va. law rev.*, XIX (1933) 459–484 [**4129a**], the Calvo clause is a clause inserted in a contract-concession between a Latin American government and an alien individual or corporation, by which the alien renounces diplomatic protection. Fleming, *U.S. and League of Nations* (no. 4545), highly valuable for the relation of the Monroe Doctrine to the famous controversy. T. A. Bailey, "The Lodge corollary to the Monroe Doctrine ", *Pol. sci. quar.*, XLVIII (1933) 220–239 [**4130**], careful analysis of the Lodge resolution and of the domestic and foreign reaction to it. Gaston Nerval [*pseud.* for Raúl Díez de Medina], *Autopsy of the Monroe Doctrine; the strange story of inter-American relations* (N.Y., 1934) [**4130a**] the son of a former Bolivian minister to the United States presents an "indictment written in the wavering period of American power."

Printed Sources

For general collections, see Sec. 1, above; particularly Moore's *Digest* (no. 5365), v. VI, 369–599, for a documentary history of official expressions of opinion and invocations of the Monroe Doctrine, 1823–1906; the most valuable single source for the history of the doctrine.

Hart and Channing, *Official declarations* (no. 1190). J. M. Céspedes, *La doctrina de Monroe* (Havana, 1893) [**4131**], undocumented treatise by a Cuban disillusioned of early admiration of the United States and of the early professions of the Monroe Doctrine contrasted with dawning imperialistic tendencies; written to dissuade Cubans from any annexation to the United States. The following by J. B. Moore: *The Monroe Doctrine; its origin and meaning* (N.Y., 1895) [**4132**]; "The Monroe Doctrine", *Pol. sci. quar.*, XI (1896) [**4133**], interesting as giving the opinion of this publicist in his earlier years at the time of the Venezuela boundary crisis; *Principles* (no. 4793); and "The Monroe Doctrine", *Am. acad. pol. and soc. sci. ann.*, XCVI (1921) 31–33 [**4134**], one article of a symposium of views by J. B. Moore, H. W. Taft, and Prof. W. E. Lingelbach. Compare with Mr. Justice Moore's ideas in 1895–1896 (nos. 4132–4133). [Henry Dustin], *The Monroe Doctrine up to date, with a life of President Monroe, from the press of the Illustrated American* (N.Y., 1896) [**4135**], eulogium for popular consumption in Venezuela crisis; cover illustration gives a blue-coat with fixed bayonet. Maurice D. de Beaumarchais, *La doctrine de Monroë; l'évolution de la politique des États-Unis au xixe siècle* (Paris, 1898) [**4136**], written during the Spanish-American war; sees in the Monroe Doctrine a supple juridical formula for the purpose of giving a legal attribute to a national policy; and the once *defensive* Monroe Doctrine now *offensive.* John Chetwood, *Manila, or Monroe Doctrine?* (N.Y., 1898) [**4137**], anti-imperialist statement against acquisition of the Philippines. Alberto del Solar, *La doctrina de Monroe y la América Latina* (Buenos Aires, 1898) [**4138**], an early Argentine diatribe against the egoism, rapacity, and gaucherie of the United States and its people, at least so conceived by this writer. F. B. Loomis, *The position of the United States on the American continent—some phases of the Monroe Doctrine* (Phila., 1903) [**4139**], reprinted from the *Annals* of the American Academy of Political and Social Science, v. XX, July 1903; written by the 1st assistant secretary of state. [Austin Harrison], *Deutschtum and Monroe Doctrine* (no. 4296). Daniel Antokoletz, *La doctrine de Monroë et l'Amérique latine* (Paris, 1905) [**4140–1**], a doctoral thesis, University of Paris; concludes danger from the United States is greater than any European intervention; and should be defended against by a resolute federated alliance of the South American republics. Bidau, *Doctrinas Monroe y Drago* (no. 2748), comments by an Argentine professor on the two supplementary doctrines; he is not hostile to Theodore Roosevelt's Dominican policy. E. C. Fiallos, *La doctrina de Monroe juzgada por un centro americano* (Tegucigalpa, 1907) [**4142**]. André Tardieu, "La doctrine de Monroe et le panaméricanisme ", in Paris, Ecole Libre des Sciences Politiques, Société des Anciens Élèves, *Les questions actuelles de politique étrangère dans l'Amérique du Nord* (Paris, 1911), 186–227 [4143], by a young French publicist who later became a national political figure; thinks Latin American future will be in more danger from the United States than from Europe and that it can no longer keep the United States in abstention from European affairs. P. C. Knox, *The Monroe Doctrine and some incidental obligations in the zone of the Caribbean* (N.Y., 1912) [4144], reprinted from the *Proceedings* of the New York State Bar Association, v. XXXV, 294–320, the Secretary of State argues for the extension of the Roosevelt " corollary " from Santo Domingo to Honduras and Nicaragua in the shape of the treaties of 1911 (subsequently rejected by the Senate). M. A. de S. Sá Vianna, *De la non-existence d'un droit international américain* (Rio de Janeiro, 1912) [4145], reply to a thesis by Dr. Álvarez in which the writer combats the idea advanced by Álvarez that there is an American international policy in which all the states of America are in accord. Two works by Hiram Bingham: *The Monroe Doctrine; an obsolete shibboleth* (New Haven, 1913) [4146]; and " The future of the Monroe Doctrine ", *Jour. internat. rel.*, X (1920) 392–403 [4147], as a Yale University professor of archaeology, the author thought it an obsolete shibboleth; but as U.S. senator he completely changed his mind (in this article). See also Rafael Uribe Uribe, *The Monroe Doctrine an obsolet* [sic.] *shibboleth by Hiram Bingham* (Bogota, 1914) [4148]. F. Capella y Pons, *Monroïsme? Notes-études sur la politique continentale américaine, à l'égard de l'Europe* (Paris, 1913) [4149], Uruguayan diplomat who thinks the once salutary Monroe Doctrine is no longer necessary; but a solidarity of the two Americas is. Kraus, *Monroe-Doktrin* (no. 1159). W. H. Taft, " The Monroe Doctrine ", *Indep.*, LXXVI (1913), 530, 540 [4150], and " The Monroe Doctrine; its limitations and implications ", in his *The United States and peace* (N.Y., 1914), 1–39 [4151], an ex-president defends the vitality and necessity of the Monroe Doctrine. " The present status of the Monroe Doctrine ", *Am. acad. pol. and soc. sci. ann.*, LIV (1914) 1–333 [4152], an important symposium of papers by academic men, publicists, naval and diplomatic authorities. American Society of International Law, " Monroe Doctrine ", in the *Proceedings . . . at its*

eighth annual meeting, . . . April 22-25, 1914 (Wash., 1914)
[**4153**], symposium of addresses by numerous international lawyers
and public men on various phases of the Monroe Doctrine (Elihu
Root, C. F. Adams, W. R. Manning, J. M. Callahan, J. H. Latané,
Eugene Wambaugh, W. I. Hull, Joseph Wheless, and Hiram Bingham). Blakeslee, *Latin America* (no. 3491) contains several papers
by specialists on the Monroe Doctrine reflecting contemporary judgments. Francisco Caraballo Sotolongo, *El imperialismo norteamericano* (Havana, 1914) [**4154**], does not think imperialism will en-
throne itself in the United States where opinion does not support it;
and believes the Monroe Doctrine a beneficent thing for Spanish
America and for Cuba especially. Carlos M. de Peña, "La doctrina americanista de Monroe; opiniones de distinguidos esta-
distas sobre su justicia y significación" *Boletín del Ministerio
de Relaciones Exteriores* (Montevideo), II (1914) 1038-1077
[**4155**]. Francisco García Calderón, "La doctrina Monroe y
la América latina", *Cuba contemp.*, VI (1914) 151-169, English
translation in *Atlantic*, CXIII (1914) 305-315 [**4156**], avers
that Latin Americans do not universally condemn the insistent
pressure of the North, the civilizing mission which does so much
toward maintaining internal peace; does not agree with Hiram
Bingham that the Monroe Doctrine is a formula the significance
of which has been allowed to lapse. Roque Sáenz Peña (one-time
president of the Argentine Republic), "Los Estados Unidos en
Sud-América; la doctrina de Monroe y su evolución", in his *Escritos y discursos* (Buenos Aires, 1914-15, 2 v.), v. I, 377-425 [**4157**],
very very anti-Monroe. Abranches, *Monroe Doctrine* (no. 3961), a
Brazilian plea against hasty enlistment in anti-Yankee ranks. M.
J. Bonn, "Germany and the Monroe Doctrine", *New Republic*,
VII (1916) 141-143, and *Am. acad. pol. and soc. sci. ann.*, LXVI
(1916) 102-105 [**4158**], very ambiguous and not reassuring war-time
statement by a professor at the University of Munich. C. H. Sher-
rill, *Modernizing the Monroe Doctrine* (Boston and N.Y., 1916)
[**4159**], late United States minister to Argentina, thinks that it is
the psychological time to chain the three republican Americas together by evoking a system of mediatory cooperation such as was
suggested by the A B C mediation in Mexico, in short: Pan Amer-
icanizing the Monroe Doctrine. G. G. Wilson, *The Monroe Doctrine*

and the program of the League to Enforce Peace (Boston, 1916) (World Peace Foundation Pamphlets, VI, no. 4) [**4160**], suggests that the United States ought to be willing to submit issues involving the Monroe Doctrine to the League of Nations; and by the same writer, " The Monroe Doctrine after the war ", *League of Nations* (World Peace Foundation), I (1918) 253–305 [**4161**], the Monroe Doctrine if it is to survive must rest on the broader support which its fundamental character merits, through a concert of nations. Carlos Castro Ruiz, " Monroe Doctrine and the government of Chile ", *Am. pol. sci. rev.*, XI (1917) 231–238 [**4162**], thinks concepts exaggerated which have (1) explained the preservation of the independence of the American states by the Monroe Doctrine, and (2) deny it any real influence in that direction. Stresses close harmony of Chilean and United States policy in maintaining naval supremacy on the west coast of the Pacific as a solemn confirmation of Chile's purpose to continue to maintain the principles of the " great doctrine." Octavio N. Brito, *O Monroismo e a sua nova phase* (Rio de Janeiro, 1918) [**4163**], Brazilian interpretation of the Wilsonian phase of Monroeism. Adolf Hasenclever, *Die Bedeutung der Monroedoktrin für die amerikanische Politik der Gegenwart* (Halle, Germany, 1918) [**4164**], a German war-time attack on Wilsonian policy. Edward Perry, " Central America and the Monroe Doctrine ", *Hisp. Am. hist. rev.*, III (1920) 407–408 [**4165**] prints a statement submitted by Dr. Policarpo Bonilla of Honduras to the World Peace Conference at Paris, Apr. 22, 1919, with comment. For text of the note of El Salvador to the United States requesting a definition of the Monroe Doctrine, Dec. 14, 1919, see the *Boletín del Ministerio de Relaciones Exteriores*, año XI, núm. 10, 11, and 12 (1919) 66–68 [**4166**], a French translation of the reply by the acting secretary of state of the United States (F. L. Polk) to the note, dated Feb. 26, 1920, is printed in *L'Europe nouvelle*, XI (July 7, 1928) 1296; the correspondence was not published by the United States government. See also the *Diario Oficial* (San Salvador) (Mar. 5, 1920) 361, and (Apr. 7, 1920) 577, for the same exchange of notes; the official definition of the United States on the Monroe Doctrine was cited by the United States in President Wilson's address to the 2d Pan American Scientific Congress. Ernesto Quesada, *La doctrina Monroe; su evolución histórica* (Buenos Aires, 1920) [**4167**], denies any juridical or legal quality in the Monroe

Doctrine but sees it as a purely political and elastic policy of the United States, primarily for advancement of interests of the United States and sometimes of incidental value to Hispanic American nations. This study was reprinted from the *Anales de la Universidad Nacional* (Buenos Aires) (Facultad de Derecho y Ciencias Sociales), XX (1919) 65–177. Alfonso Solorzano, *A propósito de la interpretación del gobierno de El Salvador al de los Estados Unidos sobre la doctrina de Monroe* (Managua, 1920) [**4168**], a Nicaraguan comes to the defense of the Monroe Doctrine, his remarks being called forth by the celebrated exchange of notes between El Salvador and the United States (no. 4166 above). E. S. Zeballos, "La diplomatie des Etats-Unis dans l'Amérique du Sud", *Rev. pol. et parl.*, CIV (1920) 328–346 [**4169**], temperate thoughts by a former minister of foreign affairs of the Argentine Republic who thinks the Monroe Doctrine has passed from a phase of political protection to economic protection. Cárdenas, *Política EE. UU.* (no. 3494), 89–186. Stuart, *Lat. Am. and U.S.* (no. 965). Carrie Chapman Catt, *The Monroe Doctrine and our Latin-American relations*, discussed by Mrs. Carrie Chapman Catt and Judge Otto Schoenrich; excerpts from stenographic report of a luncheon meeting at the Hotel Astor, New York, Dec. 15, 1923 (N. Y.: Foreign Policy Association, 1923) [**4170**], woman suffragist opinion. C. E. Hughes, *The centenary of the Monroe Doctrine* (Wash., 1923) [**4171**], Mr. Hughes was secretary of state at the time; also his *Observations on the Monroe Doctrine* (Wash., 1923), also printed in the *Am. jour. internat. law*, XVII (1923) 611–628 [**4172**] is of unusual significance as an exegesis; it explains away the Roosevelt corollary. H. C. Lodge, *One hundred years of the Monroe Doctrine* (Wash., 1923) (68th Cong., 1st sess. Sen. Doc. no. 8) [**4173**], a leading American imperialist asserts: (1) the Monroe Doctrine is vital as ever; (2) its sole interpretation rests with the United States. Alberto Ulloa Sotomayor, "La doctrina de Monroe", *Rev. universitaria* (Lima), XVII (1923) 8–28 [**4174**], a lecturer at the Peruvian University of San Marcos dissects the Monroe Doctrine to find it today a doctrine of self-preservation for the United States, closely associated with the Panama Canal, and not compatible with the idea of a "regional understanding." *Promulgation of the Monroe Doctrine.* Proceedings of the international centennial celebration of the promulgation of the Monroe Doctrine held at Richmond, Va., Dec. 2–4, 1923 (Wash., 1924) (69th Cong., 1st sess. Sen. Doc. no. 125) [4175], oratory by Congressmen and other, academic, dignitaries. Alejandro Alvarez, *The Monroe Doctrine; its importance in the international life of the states of the new world* (N.Y., 1924) [4176], selections made by a distinguished Chilean publicist, of expressions of opinion in Hispanic America, and in North America, showing how that doctrine has appealed to publicists and statesmen of the new world (1) Latin America: R. J. Alfaro (Panama), Alejandro Alvarez (Chile), Luis Anderson (Costa Rica), Clovis Bevilaqua (Brazil), Policarpo Bonilla (Honduras), L. M. Drago (Argentine Republic), F. García Calderón (Peru), J. V. Lastarria (Chile), Manoel de Oliveira Lima (Brazil), A. de Manos-Albas, Marcial Martínez (Chile), Emilio Mitre (Argentine Republic), M. B. Otero (Uruguay), Carlos Pereyra (Mexico), Santiago Pérez Triana (Colombia), Simón Planas Suárez (Venezuela), Victorino de la Plaza (Argentine Republic), Rafael Reyes (Colombia), Roque Sáenz Peña (Argentine Republic), Eduardo Suárez Mujica (Chile), Alberto Torres (Brazil), Alberto Ulloa (Peru), Raymundo Wilmart (Argentine Republic), and Estanislao S. Zeballos (Argentine Republic). (2) U.S.A.: John Barrett, G. H. Blakeslee, C. N. Chester, Geo. B. Davis, J. W. Foster, Charles Cheney Hyde, P. C. Knox, Robert Lansing, A. J. Montague, J. B. Moore, Richard Olney, Theodore Roosevelt, Elihu Root, L. S. Rowe, A. H. Snow, W. H. Taft, Charlemagne Tower, and Woodrow Wilson. *The centenary of the Monroe Doctrine*, addresses delivered at the sessions commemorative of the centenary of the Monroe Doctrine, Philadelphia, Pa., Nov. 30th and Dec. 1st, 1923 (Supplement to the Annals of the American Academy of Political and Social Science (Phila.), January 1924) [4177], ceremonial addresses by United States secretary of state, and ministers of Panama, Honduras, Uruguay; and Professors P. M. Brown and H. T. Collings. Sociedade Brasileira de Direito Internacional, *The Monroe Doctrine centenary;* addresses delivered at the Brazilian Society of International Law's solemn session, on December 2, 1923, in commemoration of the first centenary of President James Monroe's declaration of principles (Rio de Janeiro, 1924) [4178] exhibits temperate Brazilian opinion. S. G. Inman, " The Monroe Doctrine as an obsolete principle ", *Current hist.*, XXVI (1927) 875–881 [4179], characteristic of the author's distrust of the foreign policy of the United States. Jean Teyssaire, " La doctrine de Monroë et le pan-américanisme ", *Rev. pol. et parl.*, CXXXVII (1928) 87–100 **[4180]**, French lawyer sees the Monroe Doctrine leading to Pan Americanism and serving the cause of peace. Luis Izaga, *La doctrina de Monroe; su origen y principales faces de su evolución* (Madrid, 1929) **[4181]**, " a general brief account of the origin and chief phases in the evolution of the doctrine, interesting for the viewpoint disclosed rather than for any contribution of fact " (Langer (no. 4399), 183). J. R. Clark, *Memorandum on the Monroe Doctrine*, prepared by J. Reuben Clark, undersecretary of state, December 17, 1928 (Wash., 1930) (Dept. of State) **[4182]**, this is a collection of documents, edited by an undersecretary of state, calculated to show the development of official interpretation of the United States regarding the Monroe Doctrine. The historical work is hasty and loose; but the memorandum is important as a quasi-official expression; and apparently is put together to cast aside the so-called Roosevelt corollary. A. L. Delle Piane, *Doctrina de Monroe* (Montevideo, 1930) (" Publicaciones de jurisprudencia Uruguaya ") **[4183]**, an Uruguayan jurist investigates the origin and development of the Monroe Doctrine to 1921; examines putative excrescences, and suggests a proper interpretation of the doctrine: every attack or menace to the independence of an American state, whether from Europe, *or America*, is a violation of the Monroe Doctrine. J. W. Garner, " The recrudescence of the Monroe Doctrine ", *Pol. sci. quar.*, XLV (1930) 231–258 **[4184]**, discusses 20th century expositions, particularly in reference to the League of Nations and arbitration treaties. Thinks what once was a sound and defensible policy is being " overworked " and becoming a " national obsession." W. R. Castle, "Aspects of the Monroe Doctrine ", address of the Acting Secretary of State, University of Virginia, July 4, 1931, published in the *Press release*, no. 92, of the Dept. of State (*Its* Publication 206), p. 23–32 **[4185]**. Rippy, *Roosevelt corollary* (no. 3502).

CHAPTER XX

INTERNATIONAL ARBITRATION[1] AND THE PEACE MOVEMENT[2]

Bibliographical Aids

For general aids, see Larned (no. 4657); Griffin (no. 4658); *Writings* (no. 4661); C. H. and T. (no. 4662); *Guide hist. lit.* (no. 4634); and bibliogs. in *Am. secs. state* (no. 4796). Myers (no. 5399) for collections of treaties.

For indexes to periodical literature, see nos. 4995–5003; particularly *Poole's index* (no. 4995), *Readers' guide* (no. 4996), and *Internat. index* (no. 4997).

For lists and indexes of newspapers, see nos. 5004–5047; particularly Library of Congress check lists (nos. 5030 and 5032).

Brooklyn Public Library, *International peace; a list of books, with references to periodicals, in the Brooklyn Public Library* (Brooklyn, 1908) [4186]. A. H. Fried, *Verzeichnis von 1000 Zeitungsartikeln Alfred H. Fried's zur Friedensbewegung (bis März 1908). Nach Materien geordnet, mit bibliographischen Nachweisen und zum Teil mit kurzen Inhaltsandeutungen versehen . . .* (Berlin, 1908) [4187]. A. P. C. Griffin, *List of references on international arbitration* (Wash., 1908) (Library of Congress) [4188], with particular reference to the Hague conferences. M. H. Huntsman, *Peace bibliography* (London, 1910) [4189], reprinted from the *Peace year book*, 1910. E. D. Mead, *The literature of the peace movement* (Boston: International School of Peace, 1910) [4190]. F. C. Hicks, *Internationalism; a selected list of books, pamphlets, and periodicals* (N.Y., 1913) (International Conciliation . . . no 64)

---

[1] For the Geneva arbitration, see Ch. XVI, sec. 2. For the Alaska boundary arbitration, Ch. XVI, sec. 3B. For the Venezuelan arbitration of 1903, see Ch. XVI, sec. 5. For the Fisheries and Fur Seals arbitrations, see Ch. XVI, sec. 7. For the Pious Fund of the Californias arbitration, see Ch. XIX, sec. 2. For the Misiones Boundary arbitration, see Ch. XIX, sec. 6A. For the Orinoco Steamship Company arbitration, see Ch. XIX, sec. 6H.

[2] See also Ch. XIX, sec. 7 (" Pan American Movement ") ; and Ch. XXII, sec. 3 (" The Peace Settlement of 1919–1921 ").

[**4191**].   C. H. Livermore, *Suggestions for the study of international relations* (Boston, 1913) (World Peace Foundation. Pamphlet Series, v. III, no. 11, pt. 2) [**4192**]. R. C. Root, *Bibliographies on international peace topics* (n.p., 1914) [**4193**]. Hague, Palace of Peace, Library, *Catalogue*, by P. C. Molhuysen and E. R. Oppenheim (Leyden, 1916), *Premier supplément du Catalogue (1916)*, by P. C. Molhuysen and D. Albers (Leyden, 1922), and *Index alphabétique du Catalogue (1916) et du Supplément (1922)* (Leyden, 1922) [**4194**]. J. R. Metz, *Peace literature of the war, material for the study of international polity* (N.Y., 1916) (International Conciliation, Special bulletin, Jan. 1916) [**4195**]. Two lists of the Boston Public Library: *Problems of peace; racial and territorial, selected references to recent books and magazines* (Boston, 1919) (*Its* Brief Reading List, no. 8) [**4196**]; and *Disarmament and substitutes for war; selected references to books and periodicals in the Public Library of the City of Boston* (Boston, 1921) [**4197**]. Hague, Permanent Court of International Justice, *Bibliographical list of official and unofficial publications concerning the Permanent Court of International Justice*, prepared by J. Douma (The Hague, 1926) and *Supplement*, 1927– [**4198**]. D. S. Jordan, *For international peace; list of books, reviews, and other articles in the interest of peace, friendship, and understanding between nations, . . . 1898 to 1927* (Stanford University, Calif., 1927) [**4199**]. World Peace Foundation, *International relations publications available from a group of American organizations* (Boston, 1927) [**4200**]. Five lists issued by the Carnegie Foundation for International Peace (compiled by M. Alice Matthews, librarian): *Peace forces of today* (Wash., 1930) (Reading list no. 27) [**4201**]; *The Permanent Court of International Justice and the relation of the United States to the court* (Wash., 1930) (Reading list no. 28) [**4202**]; *The Permanent Court of Arbitration; select list of references on arbitrations before the Hague tribunals and the international commissions of inquiry, 1902–1908* (Wash., 1931) (Reading list no. 30) [**4203**]; *Disarmament and security* (Wash., 1931) (Reading list no. 32) [**4204**]; and *Education for world peace; the study and teaching of international relations and international law* (Wash., 1932) (Reading list no. 33) [**4205**]. League of Nations, Library, *Annotated bibliography on disarmament and military questions* (Geneva, 1931) [**4206**]. Library of Congress, Division of Bibliography, *Permanent*

Court of International Justice; references supplementing previous lists, compiled by Florence S. Hellman (1933) [**4207**], a mimeographed list; previous lists were issued in 1923, 1926, 1929, 1930, 1931, and 1932.

See also Ch. XXIII, sec. 13, for serial publications of " Present-day agencies for the dissemination of information on international affairs ", such as the Carnegie Endowment for International Peace, the World Peace Foundation, etc.

Special Works [8]

The material on the Hague conferences is so vast we must depend upon published bibliographies (see above, particularly Griffin (no. 4188)); and we are omitting here all but a few titles of the voluminous literature on the subject when it does not relate specifically to the United States.

For running comment and description of the several peace congresses and conferences, and the development of the peace movement, see the appropriate juridical journals: *American journal of international law, Revista de derecho, historia, y letras, Zeitschrift für Völkerrecht, Revue de droit international, Revue des sciences politiques*, and the *American political science review*. The first and still the most important treatise on the United States and international arbitration, to 1896, is J. B. Moore's *Arbitrations* (no. 5364), for special comment see this chapter, "Printed Sources", below, p. 626; but the narrative into which are inserted the documents make this also the most important history of international arbitrations of the United States, as well as digest of sources. F. W. Holls, *The peace conference at The Hague* (N.Y., 1900; 2d ed., 1914) [**4208**], written primarily for American and English readers; the author, secretary of the American delegation at this first Hague conference, had complete access to the files of the Dept. of State and all relevant documents, but observes a disappointing silence on important phases of his narrative, and is generally too indiscriminately eulogistic. J. W. Foster, *What the United States has done for international arbitration* (Albany? 1904) [**4209**], by a former secretary of state and lawyer active in arbitration. Crichfield, *Am.*

---

[8] The literature on the Court of International Justice (World Court) falls outside of the purview (to 1921) of this volume.

For a general list of treaties of arbitration, conciliation, etc., now in force, see the *Dictionnaire diplomatique* (no. 5057a) supplement, xxxv-xci.

supremacy (no. 1205), pt. V: "Arbitrations with Latin American countries." The following by **J. B.** Scott: *The Hague peace conferences of 1899 and 1907*, a series of lectures delivered before the Johns Hopkins University in the year 1908 (Baltimore, 1909, 2 v.), also issued in French, *Les conférences de la paix de La Haye de 1899 et 1907*, tr. by A. de Lapradelle (Paris, 1927, 3 v.) [**4210**], a lengthy survey, analysis, and commentary, by a recognized American authority on international law who served as a technical delegate to the 2d Hague conference (v. II of the English edition, and v. II and III, of the French edition consist of documents); *Peace through justice; three papers on international justice and the means of attaining it* (N.Y., 1917) [**4211**], three articles, here published in book form, relating to the aims and work of the American Peace Society; *The United States of America; a study in international organization* (N.Y., 1920) [**4212**], this study sees in the union of the United States an historical and practical example for international union; and " The third Pan-American conference and the second Hague conference: arbitration treaties ", in the *Am. secs. state* (no. 4796), v. IX, 216–226. Alexandre André, " Le traité anglo-américain d'arbitrage de 1897 ", *Rev. gén. droit internat.*, XVIII (1911) 654–666 [**4213**], analysis of the significance of the power of ratification of treaties possessed by the American Senate, as illustrated by the failure of the Anglo-American arbitration treaty of 1896. Norman Angell, *The great illusion; a study of the relation of military power in nations to their economic and social advantage*, 3d rev. and enl. ed. (N.Y. and London, 1911) [**4214**], this work, written by an English pacifist to prove war a great illusion, had a powerful influence on American public opinion. C. C. Hyde, " General arbitration treaties ", *No. Am. rev.*, CXCV (1912) 1–14 [**4215**], juridical analysis by an eminent American international lawyer. D. P. Myers, " The commission of inquiry: the Wilson-Bryan peace plan; its origin and development ", *World peace foundation pamphlet*, v. III, no. 11, pt. 1 (1913) 16–26 [**4216**]. K. E. Imberg, *Die Stellung der Vereinigten Staaten von Nordamerika zur internationalen Schiedsgerichtsfrage* (Berlin, 1914) [**4217**], an historical account of the place of the United States in international arbitration, 1794–1914, concluding that the United States has done more than any other nation to further it. Does not think the wars of 1812–14, 1846–48, and 1898 belie this; believes the union itself a powerful example. Jacob ter

Meulen, *Der Gedanke der internationalen Organisation in seiner Entwicklung* (The Hague, 1917–29, 2 v.) [4218], this monumental work has as its motto: " *Mais patience! Laisser passer quelques siècles: l'Utopie aura pris corps dans la société.*" It contains (v. II, 268–308), a chapter on English and American pacifists. Anderson and Hershey, *Handbook* (no. 4282) has sections on the two Hague conferences. Walther Schücking, *The international union of the Hague conferences*, tr. from the German by C. G. Fenwick (London and N.Y., 1918) (Carnegie Endowment for International Peace. Division of International Law) [4219], the author is one of the leading jurists and peace advocates of Germany and seeks in this volume to give a clear idea of the direction which the Hague conferences and conventions have given as a whole to the development of international law, particularly toward a world federation. Little specifically about the United States. J. B. Moore, *International law and some current illusions, and other essays* (N.Y., 1924) [4220], ch. 3 carries the author's discriminating essay ahead from ch. 8 of his *Principles* (no. 4793). Lawrence Egbert, *Les États-Unis et la Cour Permanente de Justice Internationale* (Paris, 1926) [4221], doctoral thesis, University of Paris; summarizes American participation in international arbitration from the point of view of those who would see it developing into support of a court of international justice. *Arbitration on the American continent* (N.Y., 1928) (Foreign Policy Association Information Service, IV, no. 17) [4222], convenient summary prepared on the eve of the sixth (Havana, 1928) Pan American conference. Arthur Bullard, *American diplomacy in the modern world* (Phila., 1928) [4223], an idealistic social worker envisages a " new diplomacy " centered on organization of peace movement. Dennis, *Adventures* (no. 2224) has a chapter on "Arbitration and the Hague conferences." Edith Dobie, "Attitude of the United States upon general arbitration treaties", *Southw. pol. and soc. sci. quar.*, VIII (1928) 413–424 [4224], the author feels that a general distrust of other nations, particularly England, rather than an examination of the merits of each treaty has impelled the Senate in its hostility to certain arbitration treaties (cf. the more complete studies of Dangerfield, *Defense of the Senate* (no. 4836), and Holt, *Defeated treaties* (no. 4837)). P. C. Jessup, *The United States and treaties for the avoidance of war* (Worcester, Mass., and N.Y., 1928) (International Conciliation, no. 239) [4225] contains a valuable "chart of United States treaty obligations for the pacific settlement of international disputes" (p. 213–243). E. L. Whitney, *The American Peace Society* (Wash., 1928) [**4226**], an account, based on the records of the society, of the first century of its existence, describing its organization, aims, methods, and progress. Hughes, *Am. peace plans* (no. 4103). J. H. Ralston, *International arbitrations from Athens to Locarno* (Stanford University, Calif., 1929) [**4227**], a pretentious general work by a retired American diplomatist; it gives a substantial portion of its contents to a review of the United States' participation in arbitration, this part being mostly a digest of Moore's *International arbitrations* (no. 5364). Fleming, *Treaty veto* (no. 4834). Christina Phelps, *The Anglo-American peace movement in the mid-nineteenth century* (N.Y., 1930) [**4228**], the author, covering the period 1815–1915, sees in this a period of incubation for some of the phases of present-day peace organization. Based on printed material. M. E. Curti, *The American peace crusade* (Durham, N.C., 1929) [**4229**] covers the organized movement for peace in the United States from 1815 to 1860, with some correlation to the same movement in Europe, particularly France and England. Also by the same writer, *Bryan and world peace* (Northampton, Mass., 1931) (Smith College Studies in History, XVI, no. 3–4) [**4230**], a study of the history of Bryan's thirty conciliation treaties by an advocate of peace who has a sympathetic approach to Bryan's latent pacifism. A. C. F. Beales, *The history of peace; a short account of the organized movements for international peace* (N.Y., 1931) [**4231**], a careful and scholarly summary of the peace movement in the last half of the 19th century, its breakdown in 1914, and an epilogue on the League of Nations. B. H. Williams, *The United States and disarmament* (N.Y., 1931) [**4232**] treats of the sea power theory of history, American naval wars, the naval conferences, cooperation with the League of Nations; and combats Mahan's doctrines. Helen M. Cory, *Compulsory arbitration of international disputes* (N.Y., 1932) [**4233**], a thoughtful, well-written and useful contribution to the scientific literature of international "compulsory arbitration." D. P. Myers, *World disarmament, its problems and prospects* (Boston, 1932) (World Peace Foundation) [**4234**], a general summary and handbook. W. F. Galpin, *Pioneering for peace; a study of American peace efforts to 1848* (Syracuse,

1933) [**4235**], analysis of the genesis and growth of peace efforts in the United States down to the outbreak of the Mexican war, based on archives of peace societies. Holt, *Defeated treaties* (no. 4837). M. O. Hudson, " The Permanent Court of Arbitration ", *Am. jour. internat. law*, XXVII (1933) 440–460 [**4235a**] reviews very briefly cases before the tribunals of the Permanent Court of Arbitration.

For biographies of American presidents, secretaries of state, and delegates to the Hague conferences (1st: A. D. White, Seth Low, Stanford Newel, A. T. Mahan, William Crozier, and F. W. Holls, secretary; 2nd: J. H. Choate, Horace Porter, U. M. Rose, D. J. Hill, G. B. Davis, C. S. Sperry, and W. I. Buchanan), see the relevant entries and bibliographical data in the *D.A.B.* See also B. J. Hendrick, *The life of Andrew Carnegie* (N.Y., 1932, 2 v.) [**4236**], an intimate biography, from the subject's voluminous papers, of the great philanthropist and advocate of peace.

Printed Sources

For American official documents and general source collections, see p. 810; particularly *Jour. exec. proc. Sen.* (no. 5387); *Cong. Record* (no. 5385); *For. relations* (no. 5345); Richardson (no. 5335); Moore's *Arbitrations* (no. 5364), this is the most exhaustive and authoritative publication on the United States and international arbitration to date of publication, monumental and erudite. Its voluminous excerpts of official papers are also a mine of source material. Despite its massive character, it is being supplemented by additional material in the author's *International adjudications* (no. 5367).

For texts of treaties, see Malloy (no. 5368), and Moore's *Arbitrations* (no. 5364), v. V, 4687–4820, for texts of " Treaties relating to arbitrations to which the United States has been a party " (to 1898). See also analysis of treaty collections, p. 822. *List of arbitration treaties and conventions submitted to and acted upon by the United States Senate* (Wash., 1912) (62d Cong., 2d sess. Sen. Doc. no. 373) [**4237**] lists 74 treaties or conventions.

The *Advocate of peace*, pub. by the American Peace Society (Boston, 1837–1910; Wash., D.C., 1911–31), continued as *World affairs*, v. I– (Wash., 1932–); the various publications of the Carnegie Endowment for International Peace, in several series (for list see latest *Yearbook* of the Endowment); *International conciliation*, pub. by the American Association for International Conciliation, no. 1 (Apr. 1907) to no. 199 (June 1924) (N.Y., 1907–24) and nos. 200– (in progress), pub. by the Carnegie Endowment for International Peace (for list of publications, nos. 1–265, see *International conciliation. List of documents, April 1907–December 1930*) (Worcester, Mass., 1931) and for later numbers, the latest *Yearbook* of the Carnegie Endowment); and the World Peace Foundation, *Pamphlet series* (Boston, 1910–17, 7 v.), superseded by *A League of nations* (Boston, 1917–23), continued as *World peace foundation* (Boston, 1923–) are organs of American organized efforts for international peace.

OFFICIAL DOCUMENTS RELATING TO THE HAGUE CONFERENCES (1899, 1907): *Conférence internationale de la paix. La Haye 18 mai-29 juillet 1899* (The Hague, 1899, 4 pts. in 1 v.) [**4238**] contains the " procès verbaux " of the sessions of the conference (with annexes) and of the *commission plénière*, its three subcommissions, and the *comité d'examen*. *Deuxième conférence internationale de la paix. La Haye, 15 juin-18 octobre 1907. Actes et documents* (The Hague, 1907, 3 v.) [**4239**]. *The second international peace conference held at The Hague from June 15 to Oct. 18, 1907. Instructions to and report from the delegates of the United States, conventions and declarations, final act* (Wash., 1908) (60th Cong., 1st sess. Sen. Doc. no. 444) [**4240**]. The Carnegie Endowment for International Peace has published the following collections of official documents under the editorship of J. B. Scott: *Texts of the peace conferences at The Hague, 1899 and 1907,* with appendix of related documents (Boston and London, 1908) [**4241**]. *The Hague conventions and declarations of 1899 and 1907, accompanied by tables of signatures, ratifications, and adhesions of the various powers and texts of reservations* (N.Y., 1915) [**4242**], also issued in French and Spanish editions; it reprints much of the documentary material in the same editor's broader publication (no. 4210). *Instructions to the American delegates to the Hague peace conferences and their official reports* (N.Y., 1916) [**4242a**], also issued in French. *The reports to the Hague conferences of 1899 and 1907; being the official explanatory and interpretative commentary accompanying the draft conventions and declarations submitted to the conferences by the several commissions charged with preparing them, together with the texts of the final acts, conventions, and declarations as signed, . . . as well as other documents laid* *before the commissions* (Oxford, 1916) [**4243**]. *The proceedings of the Hague peace conferences; translations of the official texts* (N.Y., 1920–21, 5 v.) [**4244**].

The World Peace Foundation also has published the *Instructions to the American delegates to the Hague conferences, 1899 and 1907*, by John Hay and Elihu Root, secretaries of state (Boston, 1913) (*Its* Pamphlets series, v. III, no. 4) [**4245**].

The several great national collections of diplomatic correspondence preceding the outbreak of the world war contain material relating to the Hague convention and other efforts for organization of international peace: *Brit. docs. on origin of war* (no. 5475), v. VIII, ch. 70; " The negotiation of a general arbitration treaty in 1911 between Great Britain and the United States which came to an end in the following year is the main theme "; the second part describes the negotiation of the so-called Bryan treaties. *Documents dipl. franç.* (no. 5474). *Grosse Politik* (no. 5476), XV Bd., ch. 100: "Die erste Haager Friedenskonferenz " (p. 137–364), and XXIII Bd., ch. 165–169: " Die Friedenskonferenz " of 1907.

American Conference on International Arbitration (1st), *The American Conference on International Arbitration held in Washington, D.C., April 22 and 23, 1896* (N.Y., 1896) [**4246**], this conference of eminent friends of arbitration was one of the factors which produced the abortive Olney-Pauncefote arbitration treaty of 1897. *The second American Conference on International Arbitration held in Washington, D.C., January 12, 1904* (Wash., 1904) [**4247**], the second conference of " friends of arbitration "; it was followed by the abortive Root arbitration treaties of 1904. J. B. Moore, *The United States and international arbitration* (Boston: American Peace Society, 1896) [**4248**], reprinted from the *Annual report* of the American Historical Association for 1891 (1892) 65–85, with additions; a sensible espousal of the arbitration movement written in his younger days by the great American authority on international arbitration. Two works by W. E. Darby: *The peace conference at The Hague; its history, work, and results* (London, 1899?) [**4249**], documents relating to the summoning of the conference of 1899, British arbitration proposals, and text of the convention for pacific settlement; and *International tribunals. A collection of various schemes which have been propounded; and of instances in the 19th century*, 4th ed., considerably enlarged (London, 1904) [**4250**], a reprint chronologically arranged, of various historical schemes and treaties, for the organization of international arbitration and peace. Seth Low, " The international conference of peace ", *No. Am. rev.*, CLXIX (1899) 625–639 [4251], the writer, a member of the United States delegation to the 1st Hague conference, endeavored to state accurately the attitude of the American delegation. A. T. Mahan, " The peace conference and the moral aspect of war ", in his *Lessons of the war with Spain, and other articles* (Boston, 1899), 207–238 [4252], believes it is premature to assume that nations will not resort to high-handed acts of aggression, and that oppressive war is better than acquiescence in recognized wrong. Also by the same writer, *Armaments and arbitration; or, The place of force in the international relations of states* (N.Y. and London, 1912) [4253], realistic and very pertinent and penetrating observations of a great naval historian on implications of treaties for arbitration, and the general peace movement. A. G. de Lapradelle, ed., *Recueil des arbitrages internationaux* (Paris, 1905–23, 2 v.) [4254], a digest by French jurists; history and commentary on all international arbitrations during the period from 1798–1872. Pearce Higgins, *The Hague peace conferences and other international conferences concerning the laws and usages of war* (Cambridge, Eng., 1909) [4255], texts of conventions with commentaries, includes the Declaration of London of 1909 as well as the Hague conventions of 1899 and 1907. Scott, *Hague conferences* (no. 4210), v. II of the English edition and v. II and III of the French edition consist of documents. Also *American addresses at the second Hague peace conference*, delivered by Joseph H. Choate, General Horace Porter, James Brown Scott, ed. by J. B. Scott (Boston and London, 1910) [4256]; and J. B. Scott, *An international court of justice* (N.Y., 1916) [4257], documents exhibiting the author's participation in proposals for a court of arbitral justice. Four publications by D. P. Myers: *Why the arbitration treaties should stand; the objections of the majority of the Senate committee on foreign relations answered point by point* (Boston, 1911) (World Peace Foundation. Pamphlet series, no. 3, pt. 1) [4258]; *Revised list of arbitration treaties; pacts to which pairs of nations are parties, with statistics and notes* (Boston, 1912) (World Peace Foundation. Pamphlet series, no. 6, pt. 5) [4259]; *The record of the Hague; results of the conferences, and tables showing the cases decided and the ratification of conventions* (Boston, 1914) (World Peace Foundation) [4260], to come more up to date see the Department of State's *Treaties in force, 1932* (no. 5367); and *Arbitration engagements now existing in treaties, treaty provisions and national constitutions* (Boston, 1915) (World Peace Foundation. Pamphlet series, v. V, no. 5, pt. 3) [4261], a list designed to show to what extent the pacific method of settling disputes has become institutional. U.S. Senate, Committee on Foreign Relations, *Report, with views of minority, upon general arbitration treaties with Great Britain and France, signed* [*Washington*], *Aug. 3, 1911*, . . . reprinted with additional matter Aug. 21, 1911 (Wash., 1911) (62d Cong., 1st sess. Sen. Doc. 98) [4262]. N. M. Butler, *The international mind; an argument for the judicial settlement of international disputes* (N.Y., 1912) [4263]. Ernest Lémonon, *La seconde conférence de la paix, La Haye* (*juin-octobre 1907*), 2 éd., rev., et précédée d'une introduction sur la première conférence de la paix (1899) et suivie d'un appendice sur l'arbitrage de 1907 à 1912, et la conférence navale de Londres (Paris, 1912) [4264]. W. H. Taft, *The proposed arbitration treaties with Great Britain and France* (Baltimore? 1911) [4265], address delivered by President Taft before the American Society for the Judicial Settlement of International Disputes, Cincinnati, Nov. 7, 1911, and reprinted from the *Proceedings* of the society. Also by ex-President Taft, *The United States and peace* (N.Y., 1914) [4266]. J. H. Choate, *The two Hague conferences* (Princeton, 1913) [4267], academic lecture by the chairman of the United States delegation to the 2d Hague conference. A. E. Pillsbury, *The arbitration treaties; an examination of the majority report of the Senate committee on foreign relations* (Boston, 1914) (World Peace Foundation. Pamphlet series) [4268]. G. G. Wilson, *The Hague arbitration cases* (Boston and London, 1915) [4269], compromise and awards, with maps, in cases decided under the provisions of the Hague conventions of 1899 and 1907, and texts of the conventions. G. W. Wickersham, *Our compulsory arbitration treaties should be abandoned* (Phila., 1917) [4270-1], reprinted from the *Annals* of the American Academy of Political and Social Science, LXXII (July 1917) 200-207; an argument against the advisability of the Bryan conciliation treaties. Dillon, *Eclipse of Russia* (no. 3180), this remarkable description of the Russian revolution by an English journalist relates the extraordinary circumstances which impelled the Czar to issue the call for the Hague peace conference of 1899 as a diplomatic coup in the race for armaments. Carnegie Endowment for International Peace, Division of International Law, *Treaties for the advancement of peace between the United States and other powers, negotiated by the Honorable William J. Bryan, secretary of state of the United States* (N.Y., 1920) **[4272]**. Manning, *Arbitration treaties among American nations* (no. 3506), 383–393. C. E. Hughes, *Pathway of peace* (no. 5241). Florence B. Boeckel, *The effort of the United States to bring about world peace*, pub. by the National Council for the Prevention of War (Wash., 1927) **[4273]**, popular sketch for peace propaganda. B. F. Trueblood, *The development of the peace idea, and other essays*, collected and newly issued (Boston, 1932) **[4274]**. F. C. De Wolf, *General synopsis of treaties of arbitration, conciliation, judicial settlement, security and disarmament actually in force between countries invited to the disarmament conference* (Wash.: Carnegie Endowment for International Peace, 1933) **[4275]**. J. W. Burgess, *Reminiscences of an American scholar* (N.Y., 1934) **[4276]**, the vivid autobiography of an eminent American scholar and advocate of peace who saw his life work ruined by the world crash of 1914.

For the printed writings of American presidents, secretaries of state, and delegates to the Hague conferences (for names, see above, p. 626), see our list on p. 756. See also the *Autobiography of Andrew Carnegie* (Boston and N.Y., 1920) **[4277]**, a retrospect, full of charm and personal touches, of a life magnificently devoted to humanitarian ideals and particularly to international peace, for which he was the leading American protagonist of his age. Also *Miscellaneous writings of Andrew Carnegie*, ed. by B. J. Hendrick (N.Y., 1933, 2 v.) **[4278]**, which contains among others, his noteworthy addresses of Oct. 17, 1905, on "A league of peace", and "'Honor' and international arbitration " of 1910, the Guildhall address which preceded his gift of $10,000,000 for the Carnegie Endowment for International Peace.

INTERNATIONAL NAVAL CONFERENCE LONDON, 1908–09: *Proceedings of the International Naval Conference, held in London, December 1908–February 1909* (London, 1909) (British Blue Book (Miscellaneous. No. 5, 1909)) **[4279]**. *Declaration of International Naval Conference, signed by the delegates of the United States to the International Naval Conference, held at London, England, from December 4, 1908, to February 26, 1909* (Wash., 1914) (63d Cong., 2d sess. Sen.

Doc. 563) [4280].   J. B. Scott, ed., *The Declaration of London, February 26, 1909;* a collection of official papers and documents relating to the International Naval Conference held in London, December 1908–February 1909 (N.Y., 1919) (Carnegie Endowment for International Peace. Division of International Law) [4281], "Bibliography" (p. 259–268).

MSS.: Suggestions

For official archives of the government of the United States and other governments, see Pt. II, ch. 3.

For personal papers of American presidents and secretaries of state, see our lists on pp. 862 and 865, respectively; and for those of Andrew D. White, president of the American delegation to the 1st Hague conference, and of J. H. Choate, chairman of the delegation to the second conference, see our lists of manuscripts of diplomatists (p. 868). The papers F. W. Holls, secretary of the American delegation to the 1st Hague conference, are in the custody of the librarian of Columbia University.

The voluminous papers of Andrew Carnegie are in the Library of Congress.

The correspondence of Rear Admiral C. S. Sperry, much of which is on the second Hague conference, is in the Library of Congress.

The library of the American Peace Society, Washington D.C., contains biographical MSS. relating to the early workers in behalf of arbitration and the peace movement; also printed material not to be found elsewhere.

The activities of the Carnegie Endowment for International Peace represent a distinct feature of the Peace movement; for information in regard to the records of the Endowment, application should be made to the Secretary, Mr. James Brown Scott, 700 Jackson Place, Washington, D.C.

The files of the World Peace Foundation, at 40 Mount Vernon St., Boston, with a special collection at Tufts College, Medford, Mass., are available to investigators under special arrangements.

CHAPTER XXI

THE UNITED STATES, EUROPE, AND AFRICA, 1865–1914[1]

1. In General

Bibliographical Aids

For general aids, see Larned (no. 4657); Griffin (no. 4658); *Writings* (no. 4661); C. H. and T. (no. 4662); *Guide hist. lit.* (no. 4634); and bibliographies in *Am. secs. state* (no. 4796). Myers (no. 5399) for collections of treaties.

See also the national historical bibliographies of the various countries (Ch. XXIII, sec. 1).

For indexes to periodical literature, see nos. 4995–5003.

For lists and indexes of newspapers, see nos. 5004–5047; particularly Library of Congress check lists (nos. 5030 and 5032).

Special Works

Of general histories of the United States, see Rhodes (no. 4783); Oberholtzer (no. 4785). See also *Am. secs. state* (no. 4796), v. V-X; and Wriston, *Exec. agents* (no. 4799).

For general histories of European countries, consult the *Guide hist. lit.* (no. 4634).

F. M. Anderson and A. S. Hershey, *Handbook for the diplomatic history of Europe, Asia, and Africa, 1870–1914,* prepared for the

---

[1] For the United States and Great Britain, see Ch. XVI ("Anglo-American Relations, 1867–1914"). For the United States and Spain, see Ch. XVIII ("Cuba and Spain, 1861–1898").

National Board for Historical Service (Wash., 1918) [4282], most helpful; contains handy and reliable digests of the principal diplomatic questions with references to pertinent documents and monographs. Rhodes, *McKinley and Roosevelt* (no. 2462). Coolidge, *World power* (no. 3345). Henri Hauser, ed., *Histoire diplomatique de l'Europe (1871-1914)* (Paris, 1929, 2 v.) [4283], a cooperative work of French scholars lacking the unity of the earlier studies of Fay, Gooch, Brandenburg, Bourgeois, and Pagès; little on commercial and industrial rivalry. Beard, *National interest* (no. 4823).

For biographies of American presidents, secretaries of state, and diplomatists to European countries (for names and tenure, see latest *Register* of the Dept. of State (no. 5122)), see the relevant entries and bibliographical data in the *D.A.B.* See also Dyer, *Wm. M. Evarts* (no. 2466), secretary of state, 1877–81; and two biographies of J. G. Blaine, by C. E. Russell (no. 2226a), and D. S. Muzzey (no. 2226b). For biographies of Roosevelt, see nos. 2469–2471. Dennett's *Hay* (no. 2472).

Printed Sources

For American official documents and general source collections, see p. 810; particularly *Jour. exec. proc. Sen.* (no. 5387), through 1901; *Cong. globe* (no. 5384); *Cong. record* (no. 5385); *For. relations* (no. 5345); Wharton's *Digest* (no. 5366); Richardson (no. 5335); Moore's *Arbitrations* (no. 5364), and *Digest* (no. 5365).

For guide to official documents of foreign governments, see p. 836.

Particular documents are cited in separate sections of this chapter.

For contemporary periodical material, consult the indexes to periodicals (nos. 4995–5003).

For lists and indexes of newspapers, see nos. 5004–5047; particularly Library of Congress check lists (nos. 5030 and 5032).

For printed writings of American presidents, secretaries of state, and diplomatists abroad (for names and tenure, see latest *Register* of the Dept. of State (no. 5122)), see our list on p. 756.

The printed writings of foreign statesmen which deal with diplomatic relations with the United States are entered in appropriate sections below.

MSS.: Suggestions

For guides, catalogues, and indexes of official archives of the United States, and of foreign governments, see below, Pt. II, Ch. 3.

For papers of American presidents and secretaries of state, see our lists on pp. 862–867.

For papers of the following American diplomatists,[2] see our list (p. 868): J. A. Kasson (minister to Austria-Hungary, 1877–81; to Germany, 1884–85); H. S. Sanford (minister to Belgium, 1861–70); J. A. Dix (minister to France, 1866–69); Elihu Washburne (minister to France, 1869–77); Henry White (ambassador to Italy, 1905–06; to France, 1906–09); George Bancroft (minister to Germany, 1871–74); J. C. Bancroft-Davis (minister to Germany, 1874–78); D. J. Hill (ambassador to Germany, 1908–11; minister to Switzerland, 1903–05; to The Netherlands, 1905–08); J. S. Pike (minister to The Netherlands, 1861–65); Benjamin Moran (minister to Portugal, 1874–82); J. W. Foster (minister to Russia, 1880–82 (see list of MSS. of secretaries of state)); C. C. Andrews (minister to Sweden and Norway, 1869–77); John Seys (minister resident and consul general in Liberia, 1866–70); G. H. Boker (minister to Turkey, 1871–75; to Russia, 1875–77).

In the Library of Congress are the papers of C. M. Dickinson, in 1897 appointed consul general in Turkey, and in 1901 also agent of the United States in Bulgaria, where, among other services, his most famous achievement was the rescue from brigands of Miss Ellen M. Stone, missionary.

The nearer we approach our own times, the fewer are the collections of private papers listed, but the greater the likelihood of their being extant and the easier to trace descendants likely to know of the whereabouts of such documents.

2. Austria-Hungary

Bibliographical Aids

For general collections, see Sec. 1, above.

For Austrian material, see Charmatz, *Literatur öesterreich. Geschichte* (no. 4726).

Special Works

We know of no special monograph on relations between Austria-Hungary and the United States during this period. For a general study of Austro-Hungarian diplomatic history, see Jean Larmeroux,

---

[2] For note regarding papers of American diplomatists to Spain of this period, see Ch. XVIII ("Cuba and Spain").

La politique extérieure de l'Autriche-Hongrie, 1875–1914, 2d ed. (Paris, 1918, 2 v.) [4284], which, however, contains nothing regarding the United States.

Printed Sources

For general collections, see Sec. 1, above.

3. Belgium

Bibliographical Aids

For general aids, see Sec. 1, above.

See also Pirenne, *Bibliog. hist. Belgique* (no. 4728).

Special Works

We know of no special monograph on Belgian-American diplomatic relations. For the Berlin (Congo) conference, 1884–1885, and the Brussels conference of 1890 for the suppression of the African slave trade, see Ch. XV ("Miscellaneous International Conferences").

Printed Sources

For general collections, see Sec. 1, above.

For guide to Belgian official documents, see below, p. 836, and no. 5431.

MSS.: Suggestions

See Sec. 1, above.

4. Denmark [3]

Bibliographical Aids

See Ch. XIV, sec. 3.

Special Works

The only monograph covering Danish-American relations as a whole is Fogdall, *Dan.-Am. dipl.* (no. 195). For the purchase of the Danish West Indies by the United States, see Ch. XIV, sec. 3.

Fogdall (no. 195) has a useful list of "United States representatives at Copenhagen [1810–1921]" (p. 157), and list of "Danish representatives at Washington [1800–1913]" (p. 157–158).

For biographies of American diplomatists to Denmark see the relevant entries and bibliographical data in the *D.A.B.*

---

[3] See Ch. XIV, sec. 3 ("Expansionist Efforts after the Civil War—The Danish West Indies").

Printed Sources

For American official documents and general source collections, see Sec. 1, above.

For guide to Danish official documents, see pp. 836 and 844.

L. de Hegermann-Lindencrone, *The sunny side of diplomatic life, 1875–1912* (N.Y. and. London, 1915) [4285] is a chatty account written by Madame de Hegermann-Lindencrone (Lillie Greenough), wife of the Danish minister to the United States, 1875–1880. M. F. Egan, *Ten years* (no. 5219), written by the American minister at Copenhagen who conducted the negotiations leading to the treaty of August 4, 1916, contains a first-hand account of the many difficulties that were encountered during the negotiations. See also his *Recollections* (no. 5219) for an account of his diplomatic experiences.

For the printed writings of American diplomatists to Denmark (for names and tenure, see the latest *Register* of the Dept. of State. (no. 5122)), see our list on p. 756.

MSS.: Suggestions

See Ch. XIV, sec. 3; and Sec. 1, this chapter.

5. France [4]

Bibliographical Aids

For general aids, see Sec. 1, above. See also French historical bibliographies (nos. 4732–4739).

American Foreign Law Association, *Bibliographies of foreign law series.* No. 4. *France* (N.Y., 1927) [4286].

Special Works

Paul Leroy-Beaulieu, " Les traités de commerce de l'Europe centrale, les conventions commerciales entre les états d'Amérique et le régime douanier de la France ", *Rev. deux mondes*, 3d ser., CIX (1892) 564–593 [4287], reflections on the implications of a tendency for commercial alliances (as illustrated in the Pan American conference, and central European developments) for France's policy of commercial isolation; thinks they will bring France back to a policy of real commercial treaties of fixed tariffs for fixed periods. Coolidge, *World power* (no. 3345). Curtis, *Am. opinion Fr. 19th cent. revols.* (no. 1416) analyzes public sentiment in the United States in

---

[4] For the " Venezuela Debts Dispute ", see Ch. XVI, sec. 5. For the " Spanish-American War ", see Ch. XVI, sec. 6. For the Algeciras Conference, see Ch. XV (" Miscellaneous International Conferences ").

regard to the French revolution of 1870. Sears, *Fr. opinion Sp. Am. war* (no. 3452). Rippy, *Lat. Am. in world pol.* (no. 1076), ch. 8: "France aggressive and critical (1857-1927)" deals with the attitude of France toward the expanding influence of the United States in the western hemisphere.

For the biographies of American diplomatists to France (for names and tenure, see latest *Register* of the Dept. of State (no. 5122)), see the relevant entries and bibliographical data in the *D.A.B.* See also Beckles Willson, *Am. ambassadors to France* (no. 68); and Robert McElroy, *Levi Parsons Morton, banker, diplomat, and statesman* (N.Y., 1930) [4288], a biography of the minister to France, 1881-85; and Nevins, *White* (no. 2468), biography of Henry White, ambassador to France, 1906-09.

Printed Sources

For general collections, see Sec. 1, above.

For guide to French official documents, see pp. 836 and 842.

U.S. OFFICIAL DOCUMENTS: "Correspondence between the Department of State and embassy of France, at Washington, as representing interests of Spain", Jan. 13, 1899, in *Treaty of peace between the U.S. and Spain* (no. 3457), 285-318. U.S. Senate, Committee on Foreign Relations, *Documents relating to reciprocity convention with France*, Mar. 16, 1900 (56th Cong., 1st sess. Sen. doc. 225; in v. XVI) [4289]. Idem, *Report . . . upon general arbitration treaties* (no. 4262).

For printed writings of American diplomatists to France (for names and tenure, see the latest *Register* of the Dept. of State (no. 5122)), see our list on p. 756. See also Hoffman (no. 5238), for reminiscences of Wickham Hoffman, secretary of legation at Paris, 1869-1871.

Jules Jusserand, *What me befell; reminiscences of J. J. Jusserand* (Boston and N.Y., 1933) [4290], reminiscences of an active life in diplomacy which brought him in contact with the America of Theodore Roosevelt's administration and later, by the French ambassador to the United States, 1903-25; goes only through the administration of Theodore Roosevelt, M. Jusserand having died before he brought his narrative beyond that point.

MSS.: Suggestions

See Sec. 1, above.

6. Germany [5]

Bibliographical Aids

For general aids, see Sec. 1, above. See also German historical bibliographies (nos. 4740-4743), particularly Dahlmann-Waitz (no. 4741). Keim, *Ger.-Am. pol. rel.* (no. 4305), 305-318. Stolberg-Wernigerode, *Deutschland u. Verein.-Staaten* (no. 4314).

Special Works

Friedrich Kapp, " Der deutsch-amerikanische Vertrag vom 22. Februar 1868 ", *Preuss. Jahrb.*, XXXVI (1875) 509-534, 660-683 [4291], this treaty adjusted the German claims to military service of returning naturalized Americans (see also Stolberg-Wernigerode (no. 4314)). Ernst Baasch, *Handelsbeziehungen Hamburg u. Amerika* (no. 1386). Two works by G. M. Fisk: *Die handelspolitischen und sonstigen völkerrechtlichen Beziehungen zwischen Deutschland und den Vereinigten Staaten von Amerika* (Stuttgart, 1897) [4292], the author was secretary of the American embassy at Berlin and had access to its archives, but not to those of the German government; and " German-American ' most favored nation ' relations ", *Jour. pol. econ.*, XI (1903) 220-236 [4293]. A. Sartorius Freiherr von Waltershausen, *Deutschland und die Handelspolitik der Vereinigten Staaten von Amerika* (Berlin, 1898) [4294], the author, after a study of German-American trade relations, makes a plea for a treaty fixing tariff rates for 10 years, and abolition of most-favored-nation privileges. Richard Calwer, *Die Meistbegünstigung der Vereinigten Staaten von Nordamerika* (Berlin, 1902) [4295], a liberal exposition of the commercial relations between Germany and the United States and plea for concerted middle-European tariff reprisals to force a modification of the Dingley tariff, by a socialist-democratic member of the German Reichstag; the author argues that the United States and Germany were without commercial treaty agreements, 1894-1900, after lapse of the Saratoga arrangements. [Austin Harrison], " Deutschtum in the United States of America—the Monroe Doctrine ", in his *The pan-Germanic doctrine* (London and N.Y., 1904), 316-348 [4296], the author has studied pan-Germanic litera-

---

[5] For the Samoan question, see Ch. XIV, sec. 6. For the Algeciras Conference, see Ch. XV. For the Venezuela debts dispute, see Ch. XVI, sec. 5. For the relations between Germany and the United States during the Spanish-American war, see Ch. XVIII.

ture, and discerns an ambition to use German-Americans to break down the Monroe Doctrine and leave Germany a freer hand in Hispanic America. Ludwig Bendix, *Fahnenflucht und Verletzung der Wehrpflicht durch Auswanderung; eine rechtswissenschaftliche und politische Studie zu den deutsch-amerikanischen Bancroftverträgen* (Leipzig, 1906) [4297], an important study based on printed state papers of Germany and of the United States and the commentaries of jurists and publicists, the relevant documentary sources being brought together in a voluminous appendix. N. L. Stone, " The most-favored-nation relations between Germany and the United States ", *No. Am. rev.*, CLXXXII (1906) 433–445 [4298], the author was a tariff expert in the U.S. Bureau of Statistics. For two special treatises on the history of naturalization legislation see F. G. Franklin, *The legislative history of naturalization* (Chicago, 1906) [4299], and J. S. Wise, *A treatise on American citizenship* (Northport, N.Y., 1906) [4300]. Heinrich Charles, *The commercial relations between Germany and the United States* (N.Y., 1907) [4301], the author professes to have been a mediator whose efforts produced the trade agreement of 1907. Coolidge, *World power* (no. 3345). Paul Curtius, *Kurd von Schloezer; ein Lebensbild* (Berlin, 1912) [4302], a biography of the German minister to the United States, 1871–78. Alfred Zimmermann, *Geschichte der deutschen Kolonialpolitik* (Berlin, 1914) [4303], a standard work, emphasizing the external history of the German colonies, by a prominent official of the old regime; has a section on " Samoa " (p. 288–302). Count Reventlow, *Deutschlands auswärtiges Politik 1888–1914*, 3d ed. (Berlin, 1916) [4304], superseded by Brandenburg (no. 4310). Reeves, *Pruss.-Am. treaties* (no. 287). Jeannette Keim, *Forty years of German-American political relations* (Phila., 1919) [4305], this was the first publication on the subject, based on such printed material as was available in 1919, stronger therefore for earlier episodes (like Samoa) than for more recent events like Manila Bay. Rudolf Walter, *Deutschland und die Vereinigten Staaten in ihrem gegenseitigen Warenverkehr seit der Wende dieses Jahrhunderts* (Greifswald, 1921)[6] [4306]. Clara E. Schieber, *The transformation of American sentiment toward Germany, 1870–1914* (Boston and N.Y., 1923) [4307], composed chiefly of excerpts and citations from

---

[6] We have not been able to get a copy of this work for examination.

American periodicals. Shippee, *Germany and Sp. Am. war*
(no. 3450), a highly valuable article revealing, from the recently
published *Grosse Politik*, the real attitude of Germany who hoped to
keep coveted Spanish islands from conquest by another power. Gazley, *Am. opinion Ger. unification* (no. 1424). Justus Hashagen,
"Zur Geschichte der amerikanisch-deutschen Beziehungen, 1897–
1907 ", *Zeits. Politik*, XVI, no. 2 (1926) 122–129 [**4308**], short monograph stimulated by the *Grosse Politik;* Samoa, Spanish-American
war, and Algeciras are discussed. Ludwig Prager, *Die Handelsbeziehungen des Deutschen Reiches mit den Vereinigten Staaten von
Amerika bis zum Ausbruch des Weltkrieges im Jahre 1914 (dazu
einen Nachtrag über die Entwicklung der Verhältnisse in der Nachkriegszeit bis 1924); eine kritisch-historische Wirtschaftsstudie*
(Weimar, 1926) [**4309**].[7]   Erich Brandenburg, *From Bismarck to
the world war; a history of German foreign policy, 1870–1914*, tr. by
Annie E. Adams (London, 1927) [**4310**], a masterly exposition and
criticism; the first history of the post-Bismarckian period to be written with a full acquaintance with all the documents in the German
foreign office (but not other foreign offices). It is concerned little
with German-American relations but there are short and revealing
passages on Samoa, Manila Bay, and Algeciras. Hermann Leusser,
Ein Jahrzehnt deutsch-amerikanischer Politik (1897–1906) (Munich
and Berlin, 1928) [**4311**], German dissertation based on the *Grosse
Politik* and American printed sources and secondary monographs; it
carries on the theme of German-American relations (Samoa, Spanish-American war, Hispanic America, Algeciras) from where Stolberg-Wernigerode's later book (no. 4314) stops. Rippy, *Lat. Am.
in world politics* (no. 1076), " German interests and activities (1870–
1927)" (p. 142–155) discusses briefly German policy as influenced
by the Monroe Doctrine. Germany's attitude during the Spanish-
American war has been reserved for subsequent treatment. Luella J.
Hall, " The abortive German-American-Chinese entente of 1907–08 ",
Jour. mod. hist., I (1929) 219–235 [**4312**], anent the Kaiser's
fiasco, revealed in *Die Grosse Politik*, for a German-American-
Chinese entente, supported by Russia, to counteract the Anglo-

---

[7] We have not been able to get a copy of this for examination; but there is one in
the New York Public Library (not subject to interlibrary loan).

French-Japanese agreements of 1904–06. Otto Graf zu Stolberg-Wernigerode, "Bismarck and his American friends", *Va. quar. rev.*, V (1929) 397–410 [**4313**], a by-product of his larger scholarly study (no. 4314), it reveals a pleasant relation of Bismarck with Motley, Bancroft, Bayard Taylor, Andrew White, and Carl Schurz. Also by the same writer, *Deutschland und die Vereinigten Staaten von Amerika im Zeitalter Bismarcks* (Berlin and Leipzig, 1933) [**4314**], a history of German-American relations in the nineteenth century. A work of major importance, resting on long and painstaking multiarchival research in the United States and Europe, together with digesting a prodigious body of secondary material and printed documents. Nevins, *Henry White* (no. 2468) throws new light upon Theodore Roosevelt's vigorous attitude toward Germany in the Venezuela imbroglio of 1902–03. Friedrich von Trotha, *Fritz von Holstein als Mensch und Politiker* (Berlin, 1931) [**4315**], biography of one of the most influential formulators of German foreign policy—from his papers. E. M. Borchard, "The effect of war on the treaty of 1828 with Prussia", *Am. jour. internat. law*, XXVI (1932) 582–586 [**4316**] comments on the Flensburger case 52 Sup. Ct. 645 (Feb. 8, 1932) which affirmed the continuing validity of the treaty. Joachim von Kürenberg, *Die Graue Eminenz; der Lebensroman des Geheimrats Fritz v. Holstein* (Berlin, 1932) [**4317**], the personal life of the Père Joseph of German diplomacy. L. L. Snyder, *Die persönlichen und politischen Beziehungen Bismarcks zu Amerikanern* (Darmstadt, 1932) [**4318**], points out how Bismarck's personal friendship for Motley influenced the chancellor's attitude toward the United States during the Franco-Prussian war. Alfred Vagts, *Deutschland und die Vereinigten Staaten in der Weltpolitik, 1890–1906* (N.Y., 1935) [**4318a**], based on extensive multiarchival scholarship, serves as a sequel to Stolberg (no. 4314).

For biographies of American diplomatists to Germany (for names and tenure, see latest *Register* of the Dept. of State (no. 5122)), see the relevant entries and bibliographical data in the *D.A.B.*

Printed Sources

For general collections, see Sec. 1, above.

For guide to German official documents, see pp. 836 and 843; particularly *Grosse Politik* (no. 5476).

Charles Munde, *The Bancroft naturalization treaties with the German states; the United States' constitution and the rights and privileges of citizens of foreign birth . . . An appeal* (Würzburg, 1868) [**4319**], a collection of documents and opinions relating to the subject; the compiler believes the naturalized citizens of German birth insufficiently protected by the Bancroft treaty. R. Schleiden, *Reise-Erinnerungen aus den Vereinigten Staaten von Amerika* (N.Y., 1873) [**4320**], the writer was formerly minister resident of the Hanseatic League in the United States. *Correspondence of E. B. Washburne* (Wash., 1878) (45th Cong., 2d sess. Sen. exec. doc., no. 24) [**4321**] relates to the custody of the German embassy in Paris during the war of 1870-71, by the United States legation. This official collection is to be supplemented by Adolf Hepner, *America's aid to Germany in 1870-71;* an abstract from the official correspondence of E. B. Washburne (St. Louis, 1905) [**4322**], the English text, with a German translation, and prefaced by Adolf Hepner. Emil Witte, *Revelations of a German attaché; ten years of German American diplomacy*, tr. from the German (N.Y., 1916) [**4323**], Witte was councillor of legation at Washington, 1898 to 1906. Kurd von Schlözer, *Amerikanische Briefe* (Stuttgart, 1927) [**4324**] includes letters from Washington, 1871-81, the writer was minister of the North German Confederation in the United States. The memoirs of successive German chancellors have been published: Otto, Fürst von Bismarck, *Gedanken und Erinnerungen*, ed. by Horst Kohl (Stuttgart, 1898, 2 v.; v. III, 1919), English translation, *Bismarck the man and the statesman; being the reflections and reminiscences of Otto, prince von Bismarck, written and dictated by himself after his retirement from office*, tr. by A. J. Butler (N.Y. and London, 1898, 2 v.), and the third volume issued in 2 editions, *The Kaiser vs. Bismarck; suppressed letters by the Kaiser and new chapters from the autobiography of the Iron Chancellor*, with a historical introduction by C. D. Hazen (N.Y., 1920), and *New chapters of Bismarck's autobiography*, tr. by Bernard Miall (London, 1921) [**4325**]. *Denkwürdigkeiten des Fürsten Chlodwig zu Hohenlohe-Schillingsfürst;* authorized by Prince Alexander zu Hohenlohe-Schillingsfürst, ed. by Friedrich Curtius (Stuttgart and Leipzig, 1906, 2 v.), English translation, *Memoirs of Prince Chlodwig of Hohenlohe-Schillingsfuerst*, authorized by Prince Alexander of

Hohenlohe-Schillingsfuerst and ed. by Friedrich Curtius; English ed. supervised by G. W. Chrystal (N.Y., 1906, 2 v.) ; also *Denkwürdigkeiten der Reichskanzlerzeit*, ed. by Karl Alexander von Müller (Stuttgart and Berlin, 1931), including documents covering the period from October 1894 to May 1901 [4326]. Wilhelm II (German Emperor), *The Kaiser's memoirs, 1888-1918* (N.Y., 1922) [4327]. Prince von Bülow, *Denkwürdigkeiten*, ed. by Franz von Stockhammern (Berlin, 1930-31, 4 v.) English translation, *Memoirs of Prince von Bülow*, tr. from the German by F. A. Voigt and Geoffrey Dunlop (Boston: Little, Brown and co., 1931-32, 2 v.; London and N.Y.: Putnam, 1931-32, 3 v.) [4328], brief reference to German jubilation over definite acquisition in 1899 of a share of the Samoan islands. *Friedrich von Holstein Lebensbekenntnis im Briefen an eine Frau*, ed. by Helmuth Rogge (Berlin, 1932) [4329], consists of letters from Holstein to his wife on all subjects (some from Washington during his service there, 1865-67, as attaché to the Prussian legation), from his youth to 1909.

For the printed writings of American diplomatists to Germany (for names and tenure, see latest *Register* of the Dept. of State. (no. 5122)), see our list on p. 756. See also the *Correspondence* of Carl Schurz (no. 5289).

7. Italy [8]

Bibliographical Aids

For general aids, see Sec. 1, above. See also Italian historical bibliographies (nos. 4748-4749).

Special Works

Gay, *Italia e gli Stati Uniti* (no. 1409), the author, an American, long resident in Italy (where he built up a notable collection on the *risorgimento*, now at the Harvard College Library) was the principal authority on recent Italo-American relations.

Printed Sources

For general collections, see Sec. 1, above.

For guide to Italian official documents, see pp. 836 and 845.

The most conspicuous subject of diplomatic negotiation between Italy and the United States (except for the Venezuela debts dispute, noted above) was the New Orleans affair of 1891. The " Corre-

[8] For the " Venezuela Debts Dispute ", see Ch. XVI, sec. 5.

spondence as to the killing of Italian prisoners at New Orleans, La., 1891 ", is printed in *For. relations* (no. 5345), 1891, p. 658–728. The Italian Ministry of Foreign Affairs ("Ministero degli Affari Esteri ") has published state papers regarding the affair as follows: *Incidente di Nuova Orléans, 30 aprile 1891* [date of presentation to the parliament] (Rome, 1891) ("Documenti Diplomatici " no. 73) [**4330**] and *Incidente di Nuova Orléans*, 4 maggio 1892 [date of presentation to the parliament] (Rome, 1892) ("Documenti Diplomatici " no. 75) [**4331**]. Unofficial contemporary discussion of the affair is found in G. T. Curtis, "The law and the lynchers ", *No. Am. rev.*, CLII (1891) 691–695 [**4332**], approving Sec. Blaine's attitude for federal reparation; and R. H. Marr, "The New Orleans Mafia case ", *Am. law rev.*, XXV (1891) 414–431 [**4333**], a New Orleans lawyer describes the lynching as a "movement conceived by gentlemen and carried out by gentlemen." Other publications of the Italian Foreign Office are: *Emigrazione e colonie. Raccolta dei RR. agenti diplomatici e consolari* (Rome, 1903–09, 3 v.) [**4334**], of which v. III (1909) contains a report on "Gli Stati Uniti d'America e l'immigrazione italiana "; and *Conferenza di Washington (1921–1922)* (Rome, 1922) ("Documenti Diplomatici " no. 135) [**4335**].

MSS.: Suggestions

See Sec. 1, above.

8. The Netherlands

Bibliographical Aids

For general aids, see Sec. 1, above. See also Dutch historical bibliographies (nos. 4750–4751).

Special Works

We know of no special monograph dealing with relations between The Netherlands and the United States during this period.

For biographies of American diplomatists to The Netherlands (for names and tenure, see latest *Register* of the Dept. of State (no. 5122)), see the relevant entries and bibliographical data in the *D.A.B.*

Printed Sources

For general collections, see Sec. 1, above.

For guide to official documents of The Netherlands, see below, pp. 836 and 843.

MSS.: Suggestions

See Sec. 1, above.

9. Norway

Bibliographical Aids

For general aids, see Sec. 1, above. See also Munthe, *Bibliog. Norges historie* (no. 4752). American Foreign Law Association, *Bibliographies of foreign law series.* No. 2. *Scandinavia* (N.Y., 1926) [**4336**], compiled by Axel Teisen.

Special Works

H. F. Swansen, " The attitude of the United States toward Norway in the crisis of 1905 ", in Norwegian-American Historical Association, *Studies and records*, IV (1929) 43–53 [**4337**], a few facts that relate to the attitude of the United States toward Norway in the crisis with Sweden during the summer of 1905, based on unpublished records in the Dept. of State.

For biographies of American diplomatists to Norway (for names and tenure, see the latest *Register* of the Dept. of State (no. 5122)), see the relevant entries and bibliographical data in the *D.A.B.*

Printed Sources

For general collections, see Sec. 1, above.

For guide to Norwegian official documents, see below, p. 836.

For the printed writings of American diplomatists to Norway (for names and tenure, see the latest *Register* of the Dept. of State (no. 5122)), see our list on p. 756.

MSS.: Suggestions

See Sec. 1, above.

10. Portugal

Bibliographical Aids

For general aids, see Sec. 1, above.

Special Works

There is no special monographic literature known to us on the relations between Portugal and the United States during this period.

Printed Sources

For general collections, see Sec. 1, above.

MSS.: Suggestions

See Sec. 1, above.

11. Russia [9] and the Balkans [10]

Bibliographical Aids

For general aids, see Sec. 1, above. See also Kerner, *Slavic Europe; bibliog.* (no. 4755); and Kornilov (no. 4757).

Library of Congress, Division of Bibliography (W. A. Slade, chief bibliographer), *List of references on the Russian policy of the United States* (Wash., 1922) [**4338**], a mimeographed list, issued March 14, 1922, and a supplementary list issued the same year.

Special Works

Ĭ. Butkovskiĭ, " Taĭnstvennaĭa ėkspedĭtsiĭa (kapĭtana Semechkĭna) v Amerĭku v 1878 godu." [The mysterious expedition (of Captain Semechkin) to America in 1878], *Istorĭcheskĭĭ Vĭestnĭk* [The Historical Messenger], XI (1883) 601–618 [**4339**], concerning the purchase and equipping of four cruisers in the United States by the Russian government in preparation for war against England; especially interesting because of the benevolent attitude of the United States government. R. Ĭ. Sementkovskiĭ, " Vooruzhennyĭ mir ĭ torgovye dogovory ", [The armed peace and trade agreements], *Istorĭcheskĭĭ Vĭestnĭk.* [The Historical Messenger], XLVII (1892) 766–798 [**4340**], a study of the political and economic sides of contemporary Franco-Russian relations, with special emphasis on the importance of American-Russian and American-French relations. Two works by O. S. Straus: *The United States and Russia; their historical relations* (N.Y.? 1905) [**4341**], reprinted from the *North American review*, August 1905; a short, popular summary by an American diplomat; and " Humanitarian diplomacy of the United States ", *Am. soc. internat. law proc.*, VI (1912) 45–54, also published in his

---

[9] For the "Alaska Purchase ", see Ch. XIV, sec. 2. For the Portsmouth Peace Conference, see Ch. XVII, sec. 4.

[10] Aside from occasional minor periodical articles (consult the guides to periodicals, nos. 4995–5003) we know of no special works on the relations between the Balkan States and the United States. Occasional U.S. printed documents may be found listed in the *Document catalogue* (no. 5358), annually. See also *For. relations* (no. 5345) annually.

The American spirit (N.Y., 1913), 19–38 [4342], collates and analyzes a number of notable instances of intermediation by the United States government in behalf of non-American religious and political victims of persecution, particularly Jews in Russia and the Balkans. Coolidge, *World power* (no. 3345) has a chapter on " The United States and Russia." J. V. Hogan, " Russian-American commercial relations ", *Pol. sci. quar.*, XXVII (1912) 631–647 [4343], an analysis of economic relationships. J. D. Whelpley, " What about Russia ", *Century*, LXXXVII (1914) 731–734 [4344], an unfriendly estimate of American policy in regard to negotiations with Russia regarding the Jewish passport question. Johnson, *Dom. and for. comm.* (no. 286) for the agreement of the United States, Great Britain, and Japan in regard to fur seal fisheries, 1911. M. Pavlovĭch (M. L. Weltman), *Sovetskaĭa Rossiĭa i kapitalĭsticheskaĭa Amerĭka* [Soviet Russia and capitalistic America] (Moscow, 1922) [4345], a general review of the relations between the two countries from 1780 to the Washington conference, interesting particularly for the later period. Jerome Davis, " One hundred and fifty years of American-Russian relations, 1777–1927 ", *Am. acad. pol. and soc. sci. ann.*, CXXXII (1927) 18–31 [4346], short popular summary pointed toward recognition of the Soviet Republic. B. J. Hovde, " Russo-American relations, 1917–1927 ", *Current hist.*, XXVII (1927) 233–237 [4347], is another short, popular summary by the author of (no. 4365). Dennis, *Adventures* (no. 2224) has a chapter on American diplomatic relations in regard to Jews in Rumania and Russia. L. I. Strakhovsky, " Russia's privateering projects of 1878 ", *Jour. mod. hist.*, VII (1935) 22–40 [4348], concerned with the building of cruisers in Philadelphia by Russia for use against England in case of war, after the Russian-Turkish war, based on archives of the United States Department of State and the British Foreign Office and private papers of Wharton Barker, Philadelphia banker, in the Library of Congress. Bailey, *Sealing convention, 1911* (no. 2900a).

For biographies of American diplomatists to Russia (for names and tenure, see latest *Register* of the Dept. of State (no. 5122)), see the relevant entries and bibliographical data in the *D.A.B.*

Printed Sources

For general collections, see Sec. 1, above.

For guide to Russian official documents, see below. p. 844.

U.S. OFFICIAL DOCUMENTS: U.S. Dept. of State, *Translation of the memorandum of the party claimant to the Honorable arbitrator, Mr. T. M. C. Asser, counselor to the ministry of foreign affairs of the Kingdom of the Netherlands, etc. . . . to adjust the differences be tween the government of the United States of America, party claimant, and the imperial government of Russia, party defendant, relative to the arrest and seizure of the American vessels* " *Cape Horn Pigeon* ", "*James Hamilton Lewis* ", " *C. H. White* ", *and* " *Kate and Anna* " (Wash., 1902) (57th Cong., 1st sess. Sen. Doc. no. 62) **[4349]**, whaling and sealing claims against Russia; published also, with additional documents in *For. relations*, 1902, app. 1 (1903). U.S. Congress, House, Committee on Foreign Affairs, *Termination of the treaty of 1832 between the United States and Russia. Hearing before the Committee . . ., Monday, December 11, 1911* (Rev. ed.) (Wash., 1911) **[4350]**. U.S. Congress, Senate, Committee on Foreign Relations, *Treaty of 1832 with Russia. Hearing before the Committee . . . December 13, 1911* (Wash., 1911) **[4351]**. J. F. Loubat, *Narrative of the mission to Russia, in 1866, of the Hon. Gustava Vasa Fox, assistant secretary of the navy; from the journal and notes of J. F. Loubat*, ed. by J. D. Champlin, jr. (N.Y., 1873) **[4352]**. T. M. C. Asser, "Arbitrage international entre les Etats-Unis d'Amérique et la Russie relatif aux navires *Cape Horn Pigeon, James Hamilton Lewis, C. H. White*, et *Kate and Anna* ", *Rev. droit internat.*, 2d ser., V (Brussels, 1903) 75–95 **[4353]**, statement of cases and awards. " Etats-Unis d'Amérique du Nord et Russie. Sentences arbitrales des 19 octobre 1901 et 29 novembre 1902, rendues par M. T.–M.–C. Asser relativement aux navires *Cape Horn Pigeon, James Hamilton Lewis, C. H. White*, et *Kate and Anna* ", *Rev. gén. droit internat.*, X (1903) docs. **[4354]**, the Hague arbitration award. Cyrus Adler, *Jews in the diplomatic correspondence of the United States* (Baltimore, 1906) (American Jewish Historical Society, Publications, v. XV) **[4355]**, Turkey, Switzerland, Morocco, Roumania, Russia, Persia. *The American Jewish yearbook, September 23, 1911, to September 11, 1912* (Phila., 1911) **[4356]**, " The passport question " (p. 19–128). A. K. Kuhn, *International law and the discriminations practiced by Russia under the treaty of 1832* (Wash., 1911) **[4357]**, " prepared by request for the board of delegates on civil rights of the Union of American Hebrew Congregations and the Independent Order of B'nai B'rith." Louis Marshall, *Russia and the American passport*, address to the delegates at the 22d Council Union of American Hebrew Congregations, Jan. 19, 1911 (N.Y., 1911) [**4358**]. B. P. Egbert, *The conflict between the United States and Russia* (St. Petersburg, 1912) [**4359**], a censorious account, condemning American abrogation. *Obshchee sobranie v S.-Peterburgîê 9 Fevralîâ 1912 goda po dîêlu ob otmîênîê S. Sh. A. dogovora 1832 goda s Rossieĭ.* [The general meeting held in St. Petersburg on February 9, 1912, in connection with the abrogation by the United States of the treaty of 1832 with Russia] (St. Petersburg, 1912) [**4360**], a publication of the Council of the All-Russian National Union. *Otmîêna Soedīnennymī Shtatamī Amerikī dogovora 1832 goda s Rossieĭ.* [The abrogation by the United States of the treaty of 1832 with Russia] (St. Petersburg, 1912) [**4361**], a popular publication by the Council of the All-Russian National Union. A. D. White, *The question between the United States and Russia* (Ithaca, N.Y., 1912) [**4362**], reprinted from *The Cornell era*, v. XLIV, 1912; address of a former minister of the United States to Russia (1892–94) condemning Russian discrimination against United States naturalized Jews, before a protest meeting at Carnegie Hall, N.Y. City, Dec. 6, 1911. Baron Rosen, *Forty years of diplomacy* (London and N.Y., 1922), 2 v. [**4363**], Russian consul-general at New York, 1884–86, *chargé-d'affaires* at Washington at intervals, 1886–90, and ambassador to the United States, 1905 to 1911. M. J. Kohler, *The United States and German Jewish persecutions—precedents for popular and governmental action*, 5th ed. (Cincinnati, 1934) [**4364**], current (1933) persecution of German Jews in Germany, this recapitulates the interest and diplomatic steps of the United States in preventing persecution of Jews in Russia and elsewhere in times past.

For the printed writings of American diplomatists to Russia (for names and tenure, see latest *Register* of the Dept. of State (no. 5122)), see our list on p. 756.

12. Sweden

Bibliographical Aids

For general aids, see Sec. 1, above. See also Setterwall, *Svenska hist. bibliog.* (no. 4761). *Bibliog. law ser., Scandinavia* (no. 4336).

Special Works

B. J. Hovde, *Diplomatic relations of the United States with Sweden and Norway, 1814–1905* (Iowa City, Ia., 1920) [**4365**], based on American printed sources. Frederick Tilberg, *The Development of commerce between the United States and Sweden, 1870–1925* (Moline, Ill., 1930) [**4366**], a trade study from American and Swedish printed consular reports, devotes some pages to the "Diplomacy of Swedish-American commerce, 1783–1925." Luthin, *St. Bartholomew* (no. 1390b) describes Swedish negotiations in the 1870's with the United States for the transfer of the island to this country.

For biographies of American diplomatists to Sweden, see the relevant entries and bibliographical data in the *D.A.B.*

Printed Sources

For general collections, see Sec. 1, above.

For guide to Swedish official documents, see below, p. 836.

For the printed writings of American diplomatists to Sweden (for names and tenure, see latest *Register* of the Dept. of State (no. 5122)), see our list on p. 756.

13. Turkey, the Near East, and Africa [11]

Bibliographical Aids

For general aids, see Sec. 1, above.

See also Voyslav M. Yovanovitch, *An English bibliography on the Near Eastern question, 1481–1906* (Belgrade, 1909) (Servian Royal Academy. Second series of Monuments, pt. XLVIII) [**4367**]. W. W. Rockwell, *Armenia; a list of books and articles* (N.Y., 1916) [**4368**].

Special Works

J. B. Angell, "The Turkish capitulations", *Am. hist. assoc. ann. rep.*, for 1900, v. I (1901) 511–519 [**4369**], short historical sketch of the background of the capitulations, and advocacy of their continuance so far as the United States is concerned; the author was minister to Turkey, 1897–98. Adler, *Jews in dipl. corres. U.S.* (no. 4355). Hinckley, *Am. consular jurisdiction* (no. 3041), a thoroughgoing treatise on the subject as developed by U.S. treaties and practice with the Barbary States, Egypt, Turkey, the smaller Oriental States,

---

[11] For the Berlin (Congo) Conference, 1884–85, the Conference for the Suppression of the African Slave Trade (Brussels), 1890–91, and the Algeciras Conference, see Ch. XV.

China, and Japan. Sir Harry Johnston, *Liberia* (London, 1906, 2 v.) [**4370**], this is a general history but has sketchy mention of the relations of the United States to the founding and welfare of Liberia. R. P. Falkner, " United States and Liberia ", *Am. jour. internat. law,* IV (1910) 529–545 [**4371**], the only special account, based largely on United States published documents; the writer was chairman of the American commission to Liberia in 1909. See also documents relating to Liberia (no. 4383). Philip Brown, " Turkey and the United States ", *Jour. race develop.,* I (1911) 447–459 [**4372**], general observations and historical reflections by a former secretary of embassy at Constantinople. G. W. Ellis, " Dynamic factors in the Liberian situation ", *Jour. race develop.,* I (1911) 255–276 [**4373**], the writer was for eight years secretary of the American legation in Monrovia. The article deals principally with boundary disputes between Liberia and France, and Great Britain, and the British loans of 1871 and 1906 and the tripartite agreement of 1908. Also by the same writer, " Political importance of the international loan in Liberia ", *ibid.,* III (1912) 109–116 [**4374**]. G. B. Ravndal, *The origin of the capitulations and of the consular institution* (Wash., 1921) (67th Cong., 1st sess. Sen. Doc. 34) [**4374a**], the writer was then American consul general at Constantinople. Dennis, *Adventures* (no. 2224) has chapters on the " Jews in Rumania and Russia ", "African questions " (Liberian question, commercial treaty with Abyssinia, 1903, and Morocco (Predicaris case)), and "Americans in Turkey ". Edgard Rouard de Card, *Les Etats-Unis d'Amérique et le protectorat de la France au Maroc* (Paris, 1930) [**4375**], an instructive examination into the uncertain relationship of the United States to the French protectorate in Morocco, from the point of view of old American treaties and France's new relationships. R. L. Jones, "American opposition to slavery in Africa ", *Jour. negro hist.,* XVI (1931) 266–286 [**4376**], American participation in international efforts to extirpate slavery in Africa, 1876–1931. L. J. Gordon, *American relations with Turkey, 1830–1930; an economic interpretation* (Phila., 1932) [**4377**], though the author had access to the archives of the U.S. legation at Constantinople the book, which stresses recent economic relations cannot be regarded as a definitive study of Turkish-American relations. F. J. Manheim, " The United States and Ethiopia; a study in American imperialism ", *Jour. negro hist.,* XVII (1932) 141–155 [**4378**], based on consular letters in the Department

of State; mainly the mission of Robert P. Skinner as consul to
Abyssinia in 1900 to negotiate a treaty of amity, reciprocal estab-
lishments, and commerce. Sousa, *Capitulatory régime* (no. 1443a).
For biographies of American diplomatists to Turkey, the Near
East, and Africa (for names and tenure, see latest *Register* of the
Dept. of State (no. 5122)), see the relevant entries and bibliographi-
cal data in the *D.A.B.*

Printed Sources

For general collections, see Sec. 1, above.

UNITED STATES OFFICIAL DOCUMENTS: U.S. Dept. of State, *Treaty
of commerce between the United States and Ethiopia, signed* [*Addis
Abeba*], *Dec. 27, 1903;* [and with *Our mission to Abyssinia, report
by R. P. Skinner*] Mar. 2, 1904 (58th Cong., 2d sess. [Senate] Confidential. Executive I) [**4379**], not in the Congressional set. Commission to Investigate Interests of the United States in Liberia,
*Report of commission which visited Liberia in pursuance of provi-
sions of act of Mar. 4, 1909, to investigate interests of United States
and its citizens in the Republic of Liberia, with consent of authorities of said republic*, Mar. 25, 1910 (61st Cong., 2d sess. Sen. Doc.
457) [**4380**].

F. D. Greene, *The American crisis in Turkey; the massacre of
1894, its antecedents and significance;* with a consideration of some
of the factors which enter into the solution of this phase of the
Eastern question (N.Y. and London, 1895) [**4381**]. R. P. Skinner,
*Abyssinia of today; an account of the first mission sent by the
American government to the court of the King of Kings (1903–1904)*
(London and N.Y., 1906) [**4382**], the writer was commissioner to
Abyssinia, 1903–04, to negotiate a commercial treaty with the Emperor Menelik's government; prints text of the treaty. "Documents
relating to Liberia", *Am. jour. internat. law supplement*, IV (1910)
188–229 [**4383**]. E. J. Scott, "Is Liberia worth saving? " *Jour.
race develop.*, I (1911) 277–301 [**4384**], the writer had recently been
commissioner of the United States to the Republic of Liberia; after
some review and analysis of current difficulties he opines the sovereignty of Liberia is worth saving by United States help against
European encroachments. M. J. Kohler and Simon Wolf, *Jewish
disabilities in the Balkan States; America's contributions toward
their removal, with particular reference to the Congress of Berlin*

(Baltimore, 1916) (Publications of the American Jewish Historical Society, no. XXIV) [4385], documents from Jewish source.

For the printed writings of American diplomatists to these countries (for names and tenure, see the latest *Register* of the Dept. of State (no. 5122)), see our list on p. 756.

MSS.: Suggestions

See Sec. 1, above.

CHAPTER XXII

THE WORLD WAR, AND PEACE SETTLEMENT, 1914-1921[1]

Bibliographical Aids

For general aids, see *Writings* (no. 4661); *Guide hist. lit.* (no. 4634), which presents critical choices of most important works on the causes of the war, and the peace settlement; and bibliogs. in *Am. secs. state* (no. 4796), v. IX–X.

H. H. B. Meyer, *List of references on Europe and international politics in relation to the present issues* (Wash., 1914) (Library of Congress) [**4386**]; also his *A check list of the literature and other material in the Library of Congress on the European war* (Wash., 1918) (Library of Congress) [**4387**], this is, as the title indicates, a check list, not a classified bibliography. It contains books and pamphlets, list of war periodicals including those general periodicals which have devoted a large space to war matters. Mez, *Peace literature* (no. 4195). G. H. Blakeslee, ed., "A selected list of books on the present war", *Jour. race develop.*, VIII (1917) 44–78 [**4388**] reveals what the academic world in the United States was reading then. R. A. Sawyer, Jr., *Diplomatic history of the European war; a list of references in the New York Public Library* (N.Y., 1917) [**4389**], reprinted from the *Bulletin*, v. XXI, 1917; it is particularly valuable for its listing of relevant United States and foreign official documents. G. M. Dutcher, *A selected critical bibliography of publications in English relating to the world war* (Phila., 1918) [**4390**], reprinted from A. E. McKinley, *Collected materials for the study*

---

[1] In the entries in this chapter the effort has been to list material which concerns the United States, but a few selected works of the diplomatic background of the World War are included. The bibliographical aids will supplement these latter titles, and take the reader as far as he cares to go.

of the war (Phila., 1918) [**4391**], which was much consulted by schoolmen and pupils. Boston Public Library, *Freedom, of the seas; selected references to recent books and magazines* (Boston, 1919) [**4392**]. National Board for Historical Service, *Peace and reconstruction: preliminary bibliography* (Boston, 1919) (League of Nations, v. II, special number) [**4392a**]. British Museum, Dept. of Printed Books, *Subject index of the books relating to the European war, 1914–1918, acquired by the British Museum, 1914–1920* (London, 1922) [**4393**]. Graham, *Neutral rights* (no. 4449), "Bibliography" (p. 183–187) lists source material found in *British and foreign state papers* and parliamentary papers. Sir G. W. Prothero, *A select analytical list of books concerning the great war* (London, 1923) [**4394**]. W. G. Leland and N. D. Mereness, *Introduction to the American official sources for the economic and social history of the world war* (New Haven, 1926) [**4395**], a valuable account of official activities. Carnegie Endowment for International Peace, Library, *League of Nations covenant* (Wash., 1928) (*Its* Reading list, no. 1a) [**4396**]. C. B. Falls, *War books, a critical guide* (London, 1930) [**4397**], principally military works and books of reminiscence. G. P. Gooch, *Recent revelations of European diplomacy* (London and N.Y., 1930) [**4398**], a most valuable discussion of the historical value of then recent publications on the origins of the war; it contains a chapter on the United States and the causes for its entrance, as revealed in recent literature on the subject. W. L. Langer and H. F. Armstrong, *Foreign affairs bibliography; a selected and annotated list of books on international relations, 1919–1932* (N.Y., 1933) [**4399**], a most valuable work, of great importance for this phase of American history, and (with Binkley) used liberally in estimating the items in this chapter. Library of Congress, Division of Bibliography, *The League of Nations; a selected list of recent references*, comp. by Ellen F. Chamberlin, under the direction of Florence S. Hellman (Wash., 1933) [**4400**]; also *Selected list of recent writings on internationalism*, comp. by Anne L. Baden (Wash., 1933) [**4401**]. R. H. Lutz, "Studies in world war propaganda", *Jour. mod. hist.*, V (1933) 490–517 [**4402**]. Seymour, *Am. diplomacy in world war* (no. 4460), 401–408, for latest and best selected bibliography of "absolutely indispensable" printed material (official documents, letters, diaries, memoirs, histories, special studies, and articles).

Alfred von Wegerer, *Bibliographie zur Vorgeschichte des Welt-krieges* (Berlin, 1934) [**4402a**], this bibliography contains more than 1200 titles. *The world war; a list of the most important books published before 1934* [**4402b**] is a mimeographed compilation recently (1934) issued by the Division of Bibliography of the Library of Congress.

The *Kriegsschuldfrage* (title varies) (Berlin, 1923–) [**4403**], and the *Revue d'histoire de la guerre mondiale* (Paris, 1923–) [**4404**] contain useful current bibliographical information and criticism.

Special Works

J. B. McMaster, *United States in the world war* (N.Y. and London, 1918–20, 2 v.) [**4405–6**], "among the best of the contemporary accounts of the part played by the United States in the world war, and in the making of the peace treaty" (*Guide hist. lit.*). Ogg, *Nation. progress, 1907–1917* (no. 3487). J. W. Garner, *International law and the world war* (London and N.Y., 1920, 2 v.) [**4407**], for legal aspects of the problems of neutrality. H. H. Powers, *America among the nations* (N.Y., 1921) [**4408**], a journalistic analysis of rather ephemeral value. Veit Valentin, *Deutschlands Aussenpolitik von Bismarcks Abgang bis zum Ende des Weltkrieges* (Berlin, 1921) [**4409**], a capable review of German foreign policy from Bismarck's fall to 1918. It has brief summaries of German-American relations, notably 1914–18: and blames the military for assuming control of foreign policy. Salvador Diego Fernández, "La misión del Conde Bernstorff en Washington", *Rev. mex. derecho internac.*, II (1920) 534–542, III (1921) 206–221, 543–553, IV (1922) 104–113, 249–259 [**4410**], merely a digest of the contents of Bernstorff's *Three years* (no. 4431). Hyde, *Internat. law* (no. 4810). Charles Seymour, *Woodrow Wilson and the world war* (New Haven, 1922) [**4411**], important popular account by accomplished authority, but now to be read in the light of much material since published, particularly the author's own work (no. 4460). In addition to Professor Seymour's edition of Colonel House's *Intimate papers* (no. 5239) and his *World war* (no. 4460), are his appreciations of House's influence on Wilson's foreign policy: "Wilson et House", *Le Flambeau* (Brussels), VIIe ann.

(1924) 392–410 [**4412**]; and "Oberst House; ein Kapitel amerikanischer Europapolitik", *Neue Rundschau*, XLIV (1933) 757–769
[**4413**]. *Camb. hist. Br. for. pol.* (no. 209). A. F. Pribram, *Austrian foreign policy, 1908–18* (London, 1923) [**4414**], a manual by
a scholarly and dispassionate authority, of use for summary of
Austrian diplomacy during the years of American intervention.
Charles Appuhn, "L'ambassade de Bernstorff à Washington", *Rev.
hist. guerre mondiale*, III (1925) 297–329 [**4415**], criticism of
Bernstorff's book (no. 4431) by a Frenchman who was remarkably well informed. Blakeslee, *Foreign policy* (no. 4122).
Maximilian Graf von Montgelas, *The case for the Central Powers,
an impeachment of the Versailles verdict* (N.Y., 1925) [**4416**],
an expert analysis of the diplomatic background of the war by
one of the most temperate German scholars. Bourgeois and
Pagès, *Politique étrangère* (no. 3346). Baker, *Woodrow Wilson*
(no. 5315), this is the standard biography of Wilson by his
designated biographer, writing intimately from the war President's
voluminous personal papers. The last-published volume advances
only to the year 1914. Brandenburg, *Bismarck to world war* (no.
4310). Latané, *For. policy* (no. 4797). S. B. Fay, *The origins of the
world war* (N.Y., 1928, 2 v.) [**4417**], a standard work, and one of
the first impartial and scholarly analyses. It integrates several notable articles which had previously appeared in the *American historical review*. It acquits Germany of deliberately and studiously
launching the war, but concludes there were serious German "blun-
ders." Pierre Renouvin, *The immediate origins of the war (28th
June–4th August, 1914)*, tr. by T. C. Hume (New Haven, Conn.,
1928) [**4418**], esteemed to be the most objective and scholarly of
French treatments. *Am. secs. state* (no. 4796), v. IX–X. Tien-kai
Lincoln Tan, "The foreign policy of Woodrow Wilson concerning
the world war, 1914–1917", in Stanford University, Leland Stanford Junior University, *Abstracts of dissertations, 1928–29*, v. IV
(Stanford University, Calif., 1929) 121–122 [**4419**], merely an outline of the plan and scope of the dissertation. Alfred Vagts,
"Colonel House", *Europäische Gesprache*, VII (1929) 430–442
[**4420**] describes Colonel House's diplomacy in Europe and explains
the break between Wilson and House by the willingness of House
to surrender principle. Wriston, *Exec. agents* (no. 4799), for ac-

count of agents to countries with which the United States has broken off relations (Germany and Turkey). B. E. Schmitt, *The coming of the war: 1914* (N.Y., 1930, 2 v.) [4421], scholarly, standard, exhaustive, judicious, though bitterly criticized by ardent revisionists.[2] P. W. Slosson, *The great crusade and after, 1914–1928* (N.Y., 1930) [4422], social aspects of the war and diplomacy. A. F. Pribram, *England and the international policy of the European great powers, 1871–1914* (Oxford, Eng., 1931) [4423], the primary concern of the author, who is a professor of history at the University of Vienna, has been with Anglo-German relations. An eminent authority on " the other side " writes in favor of the policy of one of the principal Allies. Carlo Marchiori, *Gli Stati Uniti dall' isolamento all' intervento nella guerra mondiale* (Pavia, 1932) [4424], the first half of the book is a none too critical summary of facts, 1776–1914, tending to show the breakdown gradually to isolation, concluding with the thesis of Vitetti (no. 621) ; the second half concerns Anglo-American relations after 1914, German-American relations, American mediation, etc., the author believing American entrance into the world war due to materialistic factors tinctured with idealism. H. G. Moulton and Leo Pasvolsky, *War debts and world prosperity* (Wash., 1932) (Brookings Institution. Institute of Economics. Publication no. 46) [4425], a careful investigation of the world war debts, interallied and reparations, their origin and their interrelation, with factors of domestic and world economy; many carefully prepared diagrams and tabulations. The best work on the subject. G. S. Viereck, *The strangest friendship in history, Woodrow Wilson and Colonel House* (N.Y., 1932) [4426], an unusual analysis of the personal relations of President Wilson and Colonel House which had a potent effect on American diplomacy. R. J. Sontag, *European diplomatic history, 1871–1932* (N.Y., 1932) [4427], a highly useful textbook which makes available the results of recent investigators. Ebba Dahlin, *French and German public opinion on declared war aims, 1914–1918* (Stanford University, Calif., 1933) [4428], an examination into the attitudes of the French and German people toward the war aims expressed by the groups controlling national war policy. Pierre Renouvin, *La crise europé-*

---

[2] M. H. Cochran, *Germany not guilty* (Boston, 1931) [4421a].

ene et la grande guerre (*1904–1918*) (Paris, 1934) [**4428a**], the most comprehensive treatment to date, judicious, fair.

For biographies of President Wilson, secretaries of state (W. J. Bryan, Robert Lansing, and Bainbridge Colby), and diplomatists abroad (for names and tenure, see latest *Register* of the Dept. of State (no. 5122)), and other statesmen of the period (for example, Senator Lodge), see the relevant entries and bibliographical data in the *D.A.B.*

Printed Sources

For American official documents and general source collections, see p. 810; particularly *Cong. record* (no. 5385); *For. relations* (no. 5345). This regular series of the official publications of the Department of State is now (1934) published through the year 1918. The documents are edited according to acceptable canons, and we feel that the material in them is inclusive rather than exclusive. Special supplements for the years 1914, 1915, 1916, and 1917, present the correspondence and other documents dealing with the question of neutral rights and duties [3] preceding the entrance of the United States into the war. Supplements for 1918 deal with a multitude of diplomatic questions of the United States during the war. There are three volumes for 1918 which deal with Russia. The American sources for the diplomatic history of the Peace Conference of 1919 [4] have not been published. Nor have those for any other Government, for that matter; nor any full official proceedings. "Statutes of the United States relating to the state of war, April 6, 1917, to May 20, 1918", and "Executive proclamations and orders, April 6, 1917, to April 10, 1918", are listed in McKinley (no. 4391).

For guides to official documents of foreign governments, see p. 836. For the several general series of official publications by various European governments of diplomatic documents relating

---

[3] These supplementary volumes reprint with extended addenda special publications on particular phases of neutral rights which appeared from time to time from the Department of State during the world war, and which are not listed in this *Guide*. They represent the editorial supervision and active scholarship of the late Dr. Joseph V. Fuller, who was also responsible for the three volumes on Russia for the year 1918. The greater part of these earlier publications of the Department of State was reprinted in supplements to the *American journal of international law* and in separate publications by the American Society for International Law.

[4] The American Historical Association has repeatedly petitioned the Secretary of State for the publication of the material dealing with the Peace Conference.

to the origins of the world war (France, *Docs. diplomatiques;* Germany, *Grosse Politik;* Great Britain, *Brit. docs. on origins of war,* etc.), see nos. 5474–5476, and Langer (no. 4399), 87–90 For British parliamentary papers dealing with this period, consult the *General alphabetical index . . . 1910–1919* (no. 5406). These papers, to 1917, are conveniently listed in the N.Y. Pub. Lib. list (no. 4389), and in Graham (no. 4449), 184–186.

Particular documents are cited in separate sections of this chapter. For contemporary periodical literature, consult the indexes to periodicals (nos. 4995–5003). For a list of war periodicals, including those general periodicals which have devoted a large space to war matters, see Meyer (no. 4387).

For lists and indexes of newspapers, see nos. 5004–5047; particularly Library of Congress check lists (nos. 5030, 5032). A list of foreign newspapers of the war period is given in Meyer (no. 4387).

E. E. Robinson and V. J. West, *The foreign policy of Woodrow Wilson, 1913–1917* (N.Y., 1917) [**4429**] publishes the most important utterances of President Wilson regarding foreign policy, and gives chronological tables of the leading events in American foreign relations for the period. J. B. Scott, ed., *President Wilson's foreign policy; messages, addresses, papers* (N.Y., 1918) (Carnegie Endowment for International Peace) [**4429a**]. Alexander Prince zu Hohenlohe-Schillingsfürst, *Vergebliche Warnungen* (Munich, 1919) [**4430**]. J. H. Graf von Bernstorff, *My three years in America* (N.Y., 1920) [**4431**], memoirs of Count Bernstorff, German ambassador to the United States, 1913–17. Theobald von Bethmann-Holweg, *Reflections on the world war,* tr. by George Young (London, 1920, 1 v.) [**4432**]. Hendrick, *Walter H. Page* (no. 5276), the first two volumes relate chiefly to the five years of his ambassadorship to Great Britain, including the period of the world war; the third volume contains the letters to Woodrow Wilson. V. E. Orlando, *I discorsi per la guerra e per la pace* (Foligno, 1924) [**4433**], speeches of former premier of Italy, made during and after the war. William C. Redfield, *With Congress and Cabinet* (Garden City, N.Y., 1924) [**4434**], memoirs of Wilson's secretary of commerce, throwing some light on discussions within the Cabinet. Viscount Grey, *Twenty-five years* (N.Y., 1925, 2 v.) [**4435**], account of his policy, by the former British foreign minister, reflects frankly the significance attached by

British policy in preventing any embargo by the United States that would shut off the export of the indispensable munitions (note also: Lutz, *Lord Grey and the world war*, and Montgelas, *British foreign policy under Sir Edward Grey*). Houston, *Eight years* (no. 5240), one of President Wilson's cabinet occasionally discusses Secretary Lansing's work as secretary of state, and other matters of policy. Raymond Poincaré, *Au service de la France* (Paris, 1926–33, 10 v.) [**4436**], detailed memoirs of one of the two greatest French statesmen of the period. Seymour, *Intimate papers of Colonel House* (no. 5239), the most important source yet published on the foreign policy of Woodrow Wilson. Herbert Henry Asquith, Earl of Oxford and Asquith, *Memories and reflections, 1852–1927* (Boston, 1928, 2 v.) [**4437**], British prime minister, 1914–16. Maximilian Prince of Baden, *Memoirs* (N.Y., 1928, 2 v.) [**4438**], German chancellor, 1917, before the armistice negotiations. *The letters and friendships of Sir Cecil Spring-Rice*, ed. by Stephen Gwynn (Boston, 1929, 2 v.) [**4439**], the author of these letters was British ambassador to the United States, to 1917, and friend of many American political personalities; the letters deal intimately with problems of Anglo-American relations, including neutrality. J. J. Jusserand, *Le sentiment américain pendant la guerre* (Paris, 1931) [**4440**], as analyzed by the brilliant mind of the French ambassador to the United States during the war. Constantin Dumba, *Memoirs of a diplomat*, tr. from the German by I. F. D. Morrow (Boston, 1932) [**4441**], reminiscences of ambassador from Austria-Hungary to the United States, 1913–15; whose mission was abruptly ended by the U.S. State Dept. on account of his undiplomatic action in trying to dissuade Austrian and Hungarian workmen from serving in American war industries. *War memoirs of David Lloyd George* (Boston, 1934, 4 v.) [**4442**] contains, among many valuable passages, most interesting interpretation of President Wilson's position, much more intelligent than that of most European contemporaries. Mark Sullivan, *Our times*, v. V, *Over here, 1914–1918* (N.Y., 1933) [**4443**], perspicacious journalist mirrors war-time feeling and action at home.

For the printed writings of President Wilson, secretaries of state (Bryan, Lansing), and of diplomatists abroad (for names and tenure, see latest *Register* of the Dept. of State (no. 5122)), see our list on p. 756. See also Lodge, *War addresses* (no. 5259.).

MSS.: Suggestions

Because of the live contemporary significance of their contents, government archives are not open, nor publicly catalogued. For the period before the outbreak of the war, and for certain countries (Russia) for the period of the war (the secret treaties, etc.) very extensive publications of archival material have been printed for various political motives. See below, p. 850 and Langer (no. 4399), 87–90.

For the very voluminous papers of Woodrow Wilson, see our list (p. 864). For papers of secretaries of state (Bryan, Lansing, Hughes) see our list (p. 867). The papers of Col. E. M. House are now in the Yale University Library (for description by Andrews Wanning, see *Yale university library gazette*, VII, no. 1 (1932) 4–9 [4444].

In addition to the voluminous and intimate *Diary* of Colonel House, much of which has not been printed, and which is not available to students until 1940, the collection of House papers at Yale contains: letters from members of the Cabinet, American diplomatists, and army and navy officials, and a host of private citizens who knew how to win the war; letters from foreign diplomatists and statesmen (Grey, Balfour, Plunkett, Bernstorff, etc.); minutes of conversations held in London and in Paris between the American War Mission and the Allies, particularly in connection with the Interallied Conference of November, 1917, with minutes of the second session of the Supreme War Council of Nov. 29, 30, Dec. 1, 1917; full notes of the conversations, respecting the armistice, of Lloyd George, Orlando, and House, and their conference with the Allied military, naval, and diplomatic leaders, which conversations were really more important than the minutes of the Supreme War Council, which merely rubber-stamped the decisions taken in these conversations; extensive minutes of the Council of Ten, the Council of Five, and Council of Four, in the Peace Conference, and the reports of the territorial commissions, and the very important minutes that were printed for the governments.

In the Library of Congress are the papers of Henry White (member of the American delegation to the Peace Conference), and of Breckinridge Long (3d assistant secretary of state in the Wilson administration), and certain photostats of the papers of Walter H. Page (ambassador to Great Britain, 1913–18).

The original MS. of the published Miller diary (no. 4600) and other peace conference papers of Dr. Miller are at the Council on Foreign Relations, New York (not available, however).

The Hoover War Library at Stanford University, California, has the papers of the Belgian Relief Commission (correspondence with governments), of the Inquiry (commission of experts under Col. House to prepare for peace negotiations); reports from the United States consulate at Petrograd, March–June 1914; from the U.S. military attaché to Italy, Oct.–Dec. 1918; U.S. Shipping Board agreements with Norwegian shipping commissioners, Apr. 20, and May 25, 1918; George D. Herron papers; minutes of various inter-allied and associated bodies (Finance Committee, Blockade Committee, Maritime Transport Council, Aviation Commission, Commission for Chemical Warfare Supplies, Food Council, Munitions Council, Rhineland Commission, Economic Council, Supply and Relief Council, Reparations Commission). In the voluminous collection of the papers of Col. House in the Yale University Library (not yet entirely catalogued) are important reports to him from the Inquiry and the MSS. of many technical reports by specialists in the Inquiry, also the important " Red Book " and " Black Book " with their information of historical and geographical character.

Such papers emanating from the Inquiry as are not to be found at the Hoover Library or the Yale University Library are presumably in the Department of State.

There is a valuable collection of mimeographed material (and many printed pamphlets) in the *Musée de la Guerre* at Vincennes, France, with an excellent unprinted catalogue, which is particularly important to the student of American diplomacy for three reasons: (1) for a study of French opinion regarding American policy during the period of neutrality; (2) for cooperation of the French with the British in maintaining the blockade of Germany and the problems arising between the British and the French and the United States; (3) for interallied co-ordination after the United States entered the war.

In the New York Public Library are photostatic minutes of commissions on territorial claims of the peace conference, for Jugo-Slavia and Rumania.

The late Professor Fred Morrow Fling, of the University of Nebraska, who was chief of the section on diplomatic history of the historical branch of the General Staff, U.S.A., in Paris during the peace conference, had an unique collection of material on the building, Place de la Concorde, which was used as an office by the American peace delegation, with blueprints and photographs, and biographies of the members of the groups which occupied each room; also a collection of contemporary *communiqués*, mimeographed memoranda prepared by R. S. Baker for the press; propaganda literature; newspaper clippings; as well as a large collection of newspapers and books relating to the peace.

Floods of ink were spent at Paris by delegates, attachés, experts, advisers, and hangers-on, all conscious of the historical importance of the occasion. It is too recent for these to have been indicated in the conventional apparatus of historical scholarship. They may be expected to come to light gradually all over the world during the remainder of the century.

2. American Neutrality and the World War, 1914–1918

Bibliographical Aids
See Sec. 1, above.

Special Works
See Sec. 1, above.

F. W. Wile, *The German-American plot, the record of a great failure, the campaign to capture the sympathy and support of the United States* (London, 1915) [**4445**], loose, war-time journalism. Treat, *Japan and great war* (no. 3228). Latourette, *China and the war* (no. 3230). Georges Lechartier, *Intrigues et diplomaties à Washington (1914–1917)* (Paris, 1919) [**4446**], vigorous French indictment of German activity in the United States. Pratt, *Brit. blockade* (no. 2002). M. E. Sprott, *A survey of British wartime propaganda in American issues* (Palo Alto, Calif., 1921) [**4447**], for the significance of Lord Northcliffe's propaganda and public opinion in the United States. Diego Fernández, *Misión Bernstorff* (no. 4410). Amy A. Bernardy and Vittorio Falorsi, *La questione adriatica vista d'oltre Atlantico (1917–1919); ricordi e documenti* (Bologna, 1923) [**4448**]. Montagu Consett, *The triumph of unarmed forces (1914–1918)* (London, 1923) [**4448a**] shows how the British foreign office and ministry of blockade allowed British goods to get into Germany via Scandinavia. M. W. Graham, Jr., *The contro-*

versy between the United States and the allied governments respecting neutral rights and commerce during the period of American neutrality, 1914–1917 (Austin, Tex., 1923) [**4449**], one of the earliest analyses of the controversy, based on printed documents then available, with a minimum of political interpretation; useful. M. F. Parmelee, *Blockade and sea power; the blockade, 1914–1919* (N.Y., 1924) [**4450**], a survey of the problems of sea power, blockade, etc., during the world war, and reflections of the author on possibilities of a world state. C. J. Colombos, *A treatise on the law of prize* (London, 1926) [**4450a**], best treatment for the world war period. L. H. Woolsey, " The personal diplomacy of Colonel House ", *Am. jour. internat. law*, XXI (1927) 706–715 [**4451**], mostly an informative review of Col. House's *Intimate papers* (no. 5239). J. M. Kenworthy and George Young, *Freedom of the seas* (N.Y., 1928) [**4451a**], a valuable discussion of the relation of international law to the realities of the war and neutral and belligerent interests. Johannes Kühn, " Die Friedensvermittlung des Präsidenten Wilson im Weltkrieg ", *Zeits. Politik*, XVIII (1928) 209–230 [**4452**], German analysis of the evangelical character of Wilson's peace offers. C. J. C. Street, *Lord Reading* (London, 1928) [**4453**], president of the Anglo-French loan mission to the United States, 1915; special envoy, 1917; and High Commissioner and special ambassador, 1918. C. H. Grattan, *Why we fought* (N.Y., 1929) [**4454**], a review of propaganda of the Entente Allies, and of the economic issues which are believed by the author to have made it expedient for the United States to go into the war once an emotional excuse was provided. C. T. Dix, " Colonel House abroad ", in Clark University, *Thesis abstracts, 1929* (Worcester, Mass., 1930), 111–114 [**4455**], the influence of House upon the formation of Wilson's foreign policy, based on House's *Intimate papers* and Hunter Miller's *Diary*. Hamilton Fyfe, *Northcliffe; an intimate biography* (N.Y., 1930) [**4456**] includes account of his mission to the United States in 1917, to create and direct an agency for the buying of supplies needed for England. Louis Guichard, *The naval blockade, 1914–1918*, tr. and ed. by C. R. Turner (London, 1930) [**4457**]. E. G. Trimble, " Violations of maritime law by the Allied Powers during the world war ", *Am. jour. internat. law*, XXIV (1930) 79–99 [**4457a**] stresses circuitous presumptions used by the British to condemn American cargoes en route to Swedish and Dutch ports.

Curti, *Bryan and world peace* (no. 4230). Frederick Palmer, *Newton D. Baker; America at war* (N.Y., 1931, 2 v.) [**4458**], this is an important contribution to the inner political and diplomatic history of the participation of the United States in the world war, based on Baker's personal papers, and official papers of great volume.   Two works by Charles Seymour: " Diplomatic background of America's entry into the war ", *Current hist.*, XXXIII (1931) 540–544 [**4459**], brief review based on documents published by the Dept. of State in *Foreign relations*, for 1916 (*The world war*); and *American diplomacy during the world war* (Baltimore, 1934) [**4460**], the best study of the development of American policy as related to the European belligerents, through the vexing problems of neutrality to intervention in the war and the drafting of the armistice, at which point the work stops.   Based on the printed sources and monographs, with footnotes containing statements by participants who reviewed Prof. Seymour's manuscript.   Esther C. Brunauer, " The peace proposals of December 1916–January 1917 ", *Jour. mod. hist.*, IV (1932) 544–571 [**4461**], based largely on the testimony to the German *Untersuchungsausschusses* (no. 4475).   M. P. Briggs, *George P. Herron and the European settlement* (Stanford University, Calif., 1932) [**4462**], Herron was an old academic friend of President Wilson who received permission to make secret peace approaches to Austria, here revealed in documents hitherto unused.   Two studies by T. A. Bailey, " World war analogues of the *Trent* affair ", *Am. hist. rev.*, XXXVIII (1933) 286–290 [**4463**], based on *Foreign relations*, 1915, 1916, and supplements; and " The United States and the blacklist during the great war ", *Jour. mod. hist.*, VI (1934) 14–36 [**4464**], sees in the blacklist an accepted instrument of warfare, objected to by the United States in neutrality, but adopted in wartime.   Ethel C. Phillips, "American participation in belligerent commercial controls, 1914–1917 ", *Am. jour. internat. law*, XXVII (1933) 675–693 [**4465**], worked out from U.S. official publication, *Foreign relations* and the files of the Textile Alliance.   R. W. Van Alstyne, " Private American loans to the Allies, 1914–1916 ", *Pacific hist. rev.*, II (1933) 180–193 [**4466**], $2,300,000,000 to the allies: $27,000,000 to Germany; implications of this, based largely on review of the press.   Charles Warren, " Troubles of a neutral ", *Foreign affairs*, XII (1934) 377–395 [**4467**], highly instructive article by eminent constitutional historian and lawyer, who as assistant attorney-general, 1914–17, had charge of enforcing legislation dealing with neutrality. He stresses the continuing uncertainty of neutral " rights ", the violation of which forced the United States into the world war, and offers a program to cope with problems in case of another war. Walter Millis, *The road to war: America, 1914–1917* (Boston, 1935) [**4467a**], journalistic recital of a bewildered nation blundering in.

Printed Sources

For general collections, see Sec. 1, above; particularly *Foreign relations* (no. 5345). For German sabotage in the United States during the period of neutrality and war, see C. R. Allison, ed., *Alien enemies and property rights under the trading with enemy act* (N.Y., 1921) [**4468**], composed largely of extracts from Congressional hearings and debates, committee reports, and other official documents; and reports of the Mixed Claims Commission (United States and Germany) as follows: *First and second reports of Robert C. Morris, agent of the United States before the . . .* (Wash., 1923) [**4469**], and *First report of Robert W. Bonynge, agent* (Wash., 1925) [**4470**].

For the sequestration of enemy property during the war, see the annual reports of the Alien Property Custodian and the *Report of the Alien Property Custodian* (Wash., 1922) (67th Cong., 2d sess. Senate. Doc. no. 181) [**4471**]. See also *Claims convention with Great Britain and France . . . Report regarding the negotiation of claims conventions with Great Britain and France for the arbitration and settlement of claims of American citizens between August 1, 1914, and April 6, 1917* (Wash., 1926) (69th Cong., 1st sess. Sen. Doc. 155) [**4472**].

For guide to foreign official publications, see Sec. 1, above. Note also the British *Manual of emergency legislation, comprising all the acts of Parliament, proclamations, orders, &c., passed and made in consequence of the war to September 30th, 1914*, ed. by Alexander Pulling (London: H. M. Stationery Off., 1914, and *supplements*) [**4473**] which contains British orders in council and other regulations dealing with neutral rights. Gt. Brit., Committee on Alleged German Outrages, *Report of the Committee on Alleged German Outrages* (London, 1915, 2 v. in 1) ([Papers by command] Cd. 7894–7895) [**4474**], a statement substantiated with photographs and affidavits, which, despite widespread skepticism of atrocities propaganda, has never been overthrown. It did much to create public indignation in the United States. The German official publication (Germany, Nationalversammlung, 1919/20), *Stenographische Berichte über die öffentlichen Verhandlungen des 15. Untersuchungsausschusses der verfassunggebenden Nationalversammlung* (Berlin, 1920, 2 v.) [**4475**], Nr. 2–4: "Aktenstücke zur Friedensaktions Wilsons 1916/17 "; and v. II, 702–703, for despatches of the German ambassador in the United States (von Bernstorff) and testimony of Generals Hindenburg and Ludendorff in regard to German diplomatic decisions on the peace offer of the United States, etc. For English translation, see the publication of the Carnegie Endowment for International Peace, Division of International Law, *Official German documents relating to the world war;* reports of the first and second subcommittees of the committee appointed by the National Constituent Assembly to inquire into the responsibility for the war (N.Y., 1923, 2 v.) [**4476**]. *Die Ursachen des Deutschen Zusammenbruchs im Jahre 1918,* ed. by Albrecht Philipp (Berlin, 1925) (" Das Werk des Untersuchungsausschusses der Deutschen Verfassunggebenden Nationalversammlung und das Deutschen Reichstages 1919– 1926 ", 4. Reihe. 3. Bd.) [**4477**].

Gabriel Alphaud, *L'action allemande aux Etats-Unis, de la mission Dernburg à l'incident Dumba (2 août, 1914–25 septembre, 1915)* (Paris, 1915) [**4478**], and by the same author, *Les Etats-Unis contre l'Allemagne, du rappel de Dumba à la déclaration de guerre (25 septembre 1915–4 avril, 1917)* (Paris, 1917) [**4479**], a French journalist, correspondent of the *Matin* in the United States, covers the field of German intrigue, with documents, in war-time publications. W. H. Skaggs, *The German conspiracies in America, from an American point of view, by an American* (London, 1915) [**4480**], violent denunciation of conspiracies for which there was unfortunately too much of a basis of real truth. G. H. Blakeslee, ed., *The problems and lessons of the war*; Clark University addresses, December 16, 17, and 18, 1915 (N.Y., 1916) [**4481**], useful source for academic state of mind. S. D. Fess, *The problems of neutrality when the world is at war. A history of our relations with Germany and Great Britain as detailed in the documents that passed between the United States and the two great belligerent powers* (Wash., 1917) (64th Cong., 2d sess. House. Doc. no. 2111) [**4482**], important documents topically and analytically arranged, ventilating the issues (submarine controversy and restraints of trade).   E. S. Martin, *The diary of a nation; the war and how we got into it* (Garden City, N.Y., 1917) [4483], a journalist's vivid diary.   Two works compiled under the editorship of J. B. Scott: *A survey of international relations between the United States and Germany, August 1, 1914–April 6, 1917*, based on official documents (N.Y., 1917) [4484], and *Diplomatic correspondence between the United States and Germany, August 1, 1914–April 6, 1917* (N.Y., 1918) [4485].   Sir Thomas Barclay, *Le président Wilson et l'évolution de la politique étrangère des Etats-Unis* (Paris, 1918) [4486], a war book, impressionistic in content, prepared to meet an urgent demand.   Three war-time journalistic revelations of German secret service and sabotage in the United States, 1914–17, of which the most valuable is Jones and Hollister: J. P. Jones and P. M. Hollister, *The German secret service in America, 1914–1918* (Boston, 1918) [4487]; French Strother, *Fighting Germany's spies* (N.Y., 1918) [4488]; Thomas Tunney and P. M. Hollister, *Throttled! The detection of the German and anarchist bomb plotters* (N.Y., 1919) [4489].   Stephen Osuský, " The secret peace negotiations between Vienna and Washington [1918] ", *Slavonic rev.*, IV (1926) 657–668 [4490], new light upon the attempt to detach Austria-Hungary from the Central Powers, the negotiations conducted by Prof. G. D. Herron during the war.   The author, a Slovak-American immigrant, was intelligence officer of the Czechoslovak national council; this article consists of translations of extracts from his pamphlet, *George D. Herron: Jeho práca v Našej Zahraničnaj Revolúcii*, published in Slovak (Brno, 1925).   Emile Hovelaque, *Les Etats-Unis et la guerre; de la neutralité à la croisade* (Paris, 1919) [4491], a series of essays written at various times during the war for the *Revue des deux mondes* on the development of American public opinion and idealism.   W. B. Stevens, " David R. Francis, ambassador and plenipotentiary to Russia ", *Mo. hist. rev.*, XIII (1919) 195–225 [4492], some information about Francis, mostly by his secretary (see also Francis, *Russia* (no. 5224)).   Grand-Admiral Alfred von Tirpitz, *My memoirs* (London and N.Y., 1919, 2 v.) [4493].   Achille Viallate, *Les Etats-Unis et le conflit européen, 4 août–6 avril 1917* (Paris, 1919) [4494] describes effect of the war on American trade and finance, with a review of

American colonial expansion. Rear-Admiral Sir Douglas Brown-rigg, *Indiscretions of the naval censor* (N.Y., 1920) [**4495**], recollections of service as chief censor at the Admiralty during the war; shows the all-pervasive cleverness of the British naval intelligence service. George Creel, *The war, the world, and Wilson* (N.Y., 1920) [**4496**], Creel was Director of Public Information, and close to Woodrow Wilson's propaganda. *V. Macchi di Cellere all' ambasciata di Washington, memorie e testimonianze*, by " Justus " [*pseud.*] (Florence, 1920) [**4497**], a defense of Count Vincenzo Macchi di Cellere, Italian ambassador at Washington during the war and the period of the peace conference; contains part of his diary. Campbell Stuart, *Secrets of Crewe House; the story of a famous campaign* (London, 1920) [**4498**], on Northcliffe's propagandist activity, particularly in undermining enemy morale; but is significant for its silence as to activity in the United States. Stephane Lauzanne, *Great men and great days* (N.Y., 1921) [**4499**], the editor of Paris *Matin* gives journalist's vivid and emotional impressions of leading American personalities of the period of the world war (Woodrow Wilson, Theodore Roosevelt, Col. House, and other, British and French, leaders). Romée de Villeneuve-Trans, *A l'ambassade de Washington, octobre, 1917-avril, 1919; les heures décisives de l'intervention américaine; les Etats-Unis et le traité de paix* (Paris, 1921) [**4500**]. Tasker H. Bliss, " The armistices ", *Am. jour. internat. law*, XVI (1922) 509-522 [**4501**], Gen. Bliss was member of the American war mission to Europe, 1917, military adviser to the Supreme War Council, and participant at the armistice conferences. *The Kaiser's memoirs* (no. 4327). " *Le journal de Lee Meriwether; attaché spécial de l'ambassade américaine à Paris, 1916, 1917, 1918* (Paris, 1922) [**4502**], author was inspector of German prisoners in France in 1917; later traveled in Spain and Italy, and France again in 1918. Bernardy and Falorsi, *Questione adriatica* (no. 4448). T. G. Masaryk, *The making of a state, memories and observations, 1914-1918.* An English version, by H. W. Steed (London, 1927) [**4503**], the reminiscences of the first president of the Czechoslovak Republic, who spent the period from Apr. 29 to Nov. 20, 1918, in the United States. H. P. Falcke, *Vor dem Eintritt Amerikas in den Weltkrieg; deutsche Propaganda in den Vereinig-*

ten Staaten von Amerika, 1914–1915 (Dresden, 1928) [**4504**], unrestrained revelations of German propaganda in the United States by a former German consul in New York. B. E. Schatzky, "La révolution russe de février 1917 et les Etats-Unis d'Amérique", *Monde slave*, V (1928) 353–376 [**4505**], the writer was sent to the United States in 1916 on a special mission in the interest of Russian-American accord. T. B. Mott, *Myron T. Herrick* (N.Y., 1929) [**4506**], a member of the ambassador's diplomatic staff pictures the man and his activities through his letters and papers, but does not present a critical biography. T. S. Gaffney, *Breaking the silence; England, Ireland, Wilson and the war* (N.Y., 1930) [**4507**], relation by a disappointed former American consul at Munich of his difficulties with the Department of State and recall after interference by the British government (apparently because of his Irish nationalist loyalties), with revelations about British propaganda service in the United States. *The memoirs of Marshal Foch*, tr. by T. Bentley Mott (Garden City, N.Y., 1931) [**4508**]. *Crowded years; the reminiscences of William G. McAdoo* (Boston, 1931) [**4509**], memoirs of the Secretary of the Treasury under Wilson. H. O. Yardley, *The American black chamber* (Indianapolis, 1931) [**4510**], how Major Yardley deciphered the secret state messages of foreign powers during the world war. H. J. Coolidge and R. H. Lord, *Archibald Cary Coolidge, life and letters* (Boston and N.Y., 1932) [**4511–2**], Professor Coolidge was one of the technical advisers to the American delegation to the peace conference. R. H. Lutz, ed., *Causes of the German collapse in 1918* (Stanford University, Calif., 1934) (Hoover War Library Publications, no. 4) [**4513**], translation of the documents of the fourth subcommittee of investigation of the German National Assembly and Reichstag, to determine the cause of the German collapse. J. V. Fuller, "The genesis of the munitions traffic", *Jour. mod. hist.*, VI (1934) 280–293 [**4513a**], important.

For printed writings of American statesmen and diplomatists, see Sec. 1, above. Note also J. J. Pershing, *My experiences in the world war* (N.Y., 1931, 2 v.) [**4514**], autobiography of the commander of the American expeditionary forces has much of political significance as well as military.

MSS.: Suggestions

See Sec. 1, above.

3. The Peace Settlement of 1918–1921

Bibliographical Aids

See Sec. 1, above.

Emily G. Balch, *Approaches* (no. 4518) prints selected peace program and has useful contemporary bibliography. Hoover War Library (of Leland Stanford Junior University), *A catalogue of Paris peace conference delegation propaganda in the Hoover War Library* (Stanford University, Calif., 1926) (Bibliographical Series, I) [4515], the most comprehensive list of propaganda materials actually used in Paris in support of various national claims. R. C. Binkley, " Ten years of peace conference history ", *Jour. mod. hist.*, I (1929) 607–629 [4516], this scholarly analysis of the peace conference must be read by every student of that chapter of American diplomacy. We have drawn on it directly for the major part of our appreciations of the significance of the following items. With it should be read the same author's " New light on the Paris peace conference ", *Pol. sci. quar.*, XLVI (1931) 335–361, 509–547 [4517], a brilliant summary in which he brings to date the new light thrown by later publications. Löffler, *Versailler Vertrag* (no. 4544), xii–xvi.

Special Works

See Sec. 1, above.

J. H. Latané, " The Monroe Doctrine and the American policy of isolation in relation to a just and durable peace ", *Am. acad. pol. and soc. sci. ann.*, LXXII (1917) 100–109 [4517a], argument for substituting the League of Nations for the Monroe Doctrine. Emily G. Balch, *Approaches to the great settlement*, published for the American Union against Militarism (N.Y., 1918) [4518]. R. S. Baker, *What Wilson did at Paris* (N.Y., 1919) [4519], by Woodrow Wilson's own biographical spokesman; now superseded by his *Woodrow Wilson and the world settlement* (N.Y., 1922, 3 v.) [4520] which uses Wilson's private papers; and until the appearance of the anticipated relevant volumes of the author's monumental biography of Wilson (no. 5315), is the most complete account of the President's participation in the peace negotiations. Walter Lippmann, *The political scene; an essay on the victory of 1918* (N.Y., 1919) [4521], a plea for a cooperative peace by one of the ablest American commentators.

Th. Čapek, *The Čechs (Bohemians) in America* (N.Y., 1920) [4522] has one short chapter on reverberations in the United States of the movement for Czech independence during the world war. G. A. Finch, *The treaty of peace with Germany in the United States Senate* (N.Y., 1920) (International Conciliation, no. 153) [4523], also published in the *Am. jour. internat. law*, XIV (1920) 155–206; an exposition and a review, rather than an interpretation. C. H. Haskins and R. H. Lord, *Some problems of the peace conference* (Cambridge, Mass., 1920) [4524], informing, scholarly, important. The authors, professors at Harvard University, and eminent authorities on European history, were advisers to the United States peace delegation. The problems: tasks and methods, Belgium and Denmark, Alsace-Lorraine, Rhine and Saar, Poland, Austria, Hungary, and the Adriatic, Balkans. Good maps. Marion I. Newbigin, *Aftermath; a geographical study of the peace terms* (Edinburgh and London, 1920) [4525]. A. P. Scott, *Introduction to the peace treaties* (Chicago, 1920) [4526], useful guide for review of negotiations and analysis of terms. H. W. V. Temperley, ed., *A history of the peace conference at Paris* (London, 1920–24, 6 v.) [4527] comes close to being an official British history of the peace conference, the editors had access pretty unrestricted to British archives. A contribution by the American historian, H. B. Learned, on " The attitude of the United States Senate towards the Versailles treaty, 1918–20 ", published therein (v. VI, 391–425) [4528] was until Fleming (no. 4545) the most useful summary and is more objective than Fleming. Also a chapter on " The Wilsonian principles and the negotiations leading to peace " (v. VI, 539–543). E. M. House and Charles Seymour, eds., *What really happened at Paris* (N.Y., 1921) [4529], Professor Seymour was one of the historical advisers to the peace delegation. A collection of articles by specialists attached to the American delegation; semi-official in tone. Also by Professor Seymour, " La politique de Wilson et le Sénat ", *Revue de l'Institut de Sociologie* (Brussels), II (1925) 1–19 [4530], a lucid explanation, for the benefit of European readers, of the political involutions of President and Senate during their conflict in 1918–19. Beer, *African questions* (no. 4593). Bernardy and Falorsi, *Questione adriatica* (no. 4448). T. H. Dickinson, *The United States and the League* (N.Y., 1923) [4531] analyzes the debate over the League in the United States as a phase of a struggle between the legislative and executive branches of the government for control over foreign affairs; and advocates United States entry. Believes proposal for ratification of the Court of International Justice a step in that direction. A. L. P. Dennis, *The foreign policies of Soviet Russia* (N.Y., 1924) [4532], a scholarly pioneer study of the years 1917–1923. Blakeslee, *Recent foreign policy* (no. 4122). Charles Pergler, *America in the struggle for Czechoslovak independence* (Phila., 1926) [4533], the author was secretary to President Masaryk during the latter's proselyting activities for Czechoslovak independence in the United States. F. H. Simonds, *How Europe made peace without America* (Garden City, N.Y., 1927) [4533a], clear and provocative review of rôles played by different allies in the peace and since the peace. Sidney Brooks, *America and Germany, 1918–1925*, 2d ed., rev. (N.Y., 1927) [4534], an able journalist's summary of peace negotiations and early post-war relationships between the United States and Germany. H. H. Fisher and Sidney Brooks, *America and the new Poland* (N.Y., 1928) [4535], thorough treatment of relation of the United States to the resurrection of the Polish nation. Hunter Miller, *The drafting of the Covenant* (London, 1928, 2 v.) [4536], the eminent author was a participant and adviser upon whom Wilson leaned heavily in the drafting of the Covenant; very authoritative and scholarly. F. L. Schuman, *American policy toward Russia since 1917; a study of diplomatic history, international law and public opinion* (N.Y., 1928) [4537], scholarly and well-documented analysis of Russian-American relations. H. M. Darling, "Who kept the United States out of the League of Nations?" *Canad. hist. rev.*, X (1929) 196–211 [4538], Lodge did, concludes the author. Mary R. Frear, "Did President Wilson contradict himself on the secret treaties?" *Current hist.*, XXX (1929) 435–443 [4539], it is not improbable, the author thinks, that they slipped his fatigued mind. J. J. H. Mordacq, *La verité sur l'armistice* (Paris, 1929) [4540], a defence of the armistice, as assurance of victory and of no need to fight on to Berlin. K. F. Nowak, *Versailles*, tr. by Norman Thomas and E. W. Dickes (London, 1928; N.Y., 1929) [4541] takes us behind the scenes with the German negotiators, using Schiff (no. 4603) as his source, and breaks lances with Wilsonian writers. Louis Fischer, *The Soviets in world affairs; a history of relations between the Soviet Union and the rest of the world* (N.Y., 1930) [4542], not definitive, but an important contribution in journalistic style, sympathetic to Russia. The author had advantage of intimate relations with Bolshevik and German statesmen, and to public and private papers. Fleming, *Treaty veto* (no. 4834). Nevins, *Henry White* (no. 2468) has material on the peace, especially on the liaison between the American delegation and the Republicans (Lodge, in particular), and the struggle in the Senate over the treaty of Versailles, based on White's correspondence. Williams, *U.S. and disarmament* (no. 4232). C. A. Berdahl, *The policy of the United States with respect to the League of Nations* (Geneva, 1932) [4543], lectures before the Graduate Institute of International Studies, at Geneva, which trace the history of the League idea in the United States together with its diplomatic and political vicissitudes, and supposedly gradual approach of the United States to entry, from a study of the printed secondary material and sources which does not include Fleming's important study (no. 4545). Martin Löffler, *Vereinigten Staaten von Amerika, Versailler Vertrag und Völkerbund; ein Beitrag zur Europa-politik der U.S.A.* (Berlin-Grunewald, 1932) [4544], a dissertation attempting a preliminary study of the subject objectively in its historical, legal, economic and political aspects. D. F. Fleming, *The United States and the League of Nations, 1918–1920* (N.Y. and London, 1932) [4545], though less objective than Learned (no. 4528), and avowedly sympathetic to the League, this is the most informing and important historical work that has yet appeared on the subject. Felix Morley, *The Society of Nations, its organization and constitutional development* (Wash., D.C.: Brookings Institution, 1932) [4546], a constitutional study. J. W. Swain, " Woodrow Wilson's fight for peace ", *Current hist.*, XXXV (1932) 805–812 [4547], Wilson's last stand for a negotiated peace. Viereck, *Wilson and House* (no. 4426). Holt, *Defeated treaties* (no. 4837) contains a careful and cogent analysis of political defeat in the treaty of Versailles in the U.S. Senate. Discusses in particular the motives of Senator H. C. Lodge. McMahon, *Recognition policy* (no. 3501) has several chapters on Russian recognition. Wilhelm Ziegler, *Versailles; die Geschichte eines mussglücken Frieden* (Hamburg, 1933) [4548], the most recent work on the conference as a whole. M. W. Graham, " Russian-American relations, 1917–1933; an interpretation ", *Am. pol. sci. rev.*, XXVIII (1934) 387–409

[4548a], a most helpful review. J. T. Shotwell, ed., *The origins of the International Labor Organization* (N. Y., 1934, 2 v.) (The Carnegie Endowment for International Peace. . . . The Paris peace conference, history and documents) [4549]. G. B. Noble, *Policies and opinions at Paris, 1919; Wilsonian diplomacy, the Versailles peace, and French public opinion* (N.Y., 1935) [4549a], a study of the effect on his diplomatic program of Wilson's anomalous political position at Paris.[5]

For biographies of President Wilson and deceased members of the American delegation to the peace conference (Lansing, Henry White), see bibliographical data in the *D.A.B.* Bowers, *Beveridge* (no. 3455) for League of Nations controversy.

Printed Sources

See Sec. 1, above.

Texts of treaties:[6] The treaty of peace of the Allied Nations with Germany is printed in the congressional series as follows: (66th Cong., 1st sess. Sen. Doc. 49); (66th Cong., 1st sess. Sen. Doc. 51); *Treaty of peace with Germany showing amendments reported by the committee on foreign relations* (66th Cong., 1st sess. Sen. Doc. 51) [4550]. Treaties of the United States with Austria, signed Aug. 24, 1921, and with Germany, Aug. 25, 1921, are published in the Dept. of State, *Treaty series*, as follows: *Germany and Austria; treaties of peace between the United States and Germany and Austria,* 1921 (Wash., 1921) (Treaty Series 658 and 659) [4551], combined issue; also issued separately. The treaty with Austria is also published in the congressional series (67th Cong., 2d sess. Sen. Doc. 98). The treaty with Germany in the same series (67th Cong., 1st sess. Sen. Doc. 70). See also the *Agreement between the United States and Germany for a mixed commission to determine the amount to be paid by Germany in satisfaction of Germany's financial obligations under the treaty concluded between the two governments on August 25, 1921, signed August 10, 1922* (Wash., 1922) (Treaty Series 665) [4552]. For " Treaties due to the negotiations of the Paris peace conference, signed by representatives of the United States, on which

---

[5] Professor L. I. Strakhovsky has ready for publication a study on *The origins of the American intervention in north Russia, 1918* [4549a].

[6] The entire series of treaties is available in the British *Parliamentary papers* [Foreign Office] *Treaty series,* 1919 and 1920).

no further action has been taken ", see Malloy, *Treaties* (no. 5368), v. III, 3699–3730.

UNITED STATES OFFICIAL DOCUMENTS: For the armistice negotiations, see *For. relations* (no. 5345), for 1918. *Assistance to France in the event of unprovoked aggression by Germany* . . . ; *agreement between the United States and France, which was signed at Versailles, June 28, 1919, to secure the Republic of France the immediate aid of the United States in case of unprovoked movement of aggression against her on the part of Germany* (Wash., 1919) (66th Cong., 1st sess. Sen. Doc. 63) [**4553**]. *Conditions of peace with Austria. Treaty of peace between Allied and Associated Powers and Austria* (Wash., 1919) (66th Cong., 1st sess. Sen. Doc. 92) [**4554**]. *Conditions of peace with Germany. Exchange of notes between the German peace delegation and the Allied and Associated Powers respecting the conditions of peace presented to Germany on May 7, 1919* (Wash., 1919) (66th Cong., 1st sess. Sen. Doc. no. 149) [**4555**]. U.S. Cong., Senate, Committee on Foreign Relations, *Maintenance of peace in Armenia;* hearings before subcommittee on S.J.R. 106 (Wash., 1919) [**4556**]. *Military occupation of the Rhine. Agreement between the United States, Belgium, British Empire, and France and Germany with regard to military occupation of territories of the Rhine signed at Versailles on June 28, 1919* (66th Cong., 1st sess. Sen. Doc. 75) [**4557**]. *Republic of Armenia. A memorandum on the recognition of the government of the Republic of Armenia, submitted by special mission of Republic of Armenia to United States* (Wash., 1919) (66th Cong., 1st sess. Sen. Doc. no. 151) [**4558**]. *Mandatory for Armenia; report* [and minority views] *to accompany S. Con. Res. 27 declining to grant to the Executive power to accept mandate over Armenia* (66th Cong., 2d sess. House. Rept. 1101. 2 pts.) [**4559**]. *Proposed reservations to the treaty of peace with Germany,* November 6, 1919 (Wash., 1919) (66th Cong., 1st sess. Sen. Doc. no. 150) [**4560**]. *Treaty of peace with Germany. Hearings before the committee on foreign relations, United States Senate, sixty-sixth Congress, first session, on the treaty of peace with Germany,* . . . *1919* (Wash., 1919) (66th Cong., 1st sess. Sen. Doc. no. 106) [**4561**], testimony before the Senate committee on foreign relations of President Wilson, Sec. Lansing, and others. *Treaty of peace with Austria. Letter of Allied and Associated Powers transmitting to the Austrian delegation the treaty of peace* *with Austria, together with the reply of the Allied and Associated Powers to the Austrian note of July 20, 1919, requesting certain modifications of the terms* (Wash., 1919) (66th Cong., 1st sess. Sen. Doc. no. 121) [**4562**]. *Treaty of peace with Germany. Report of the conference between members of the Senate committee on foreign relations and the president of the United States at the White House, Tuesday, August 19, 1919* (Wash., 1919) (66th Cong., 1st sess. Sen. Doc. no. 76) [**4563**]. *League of Nations* (Wash., 1921) (66th Cong., 1st sess. Sen. Doc. no. 7) [**4564**]. For status and disposal of alien property during the war and peace settlement, see the *Report of the Alien Property Custodian, 1917-* (Wash., 1918-) [**4565**], and *Report of the Alien Property Custodian. Letter . . . and a statement of property seized or demanded since the passage of the resolution declaring a state of peace to exist with Germany* (Wash., 1922) (67th Cong., 2d sess. Sen. Doc. no. 181) [**4566**].

For general series of official documents of foreign governments dealing with the world war and peace of Versailles, see p. 850. Note also: British parliamentary papers regarding the German peace offer, as follows: *Reply of the Allied Governments to the note communicated by the United States ambassador on 20th December 1916* (1917-18, XXXVIII (Cd. 8468)) [**4567**]; *Reply to the German peace note communicated by the French Government on behalf of the Allied Powers to the United States ambassador in Paris, 30th December 1916* (1917-18, XXXVIII (Cd. 8467)) [**4568**]; *Despatch to His Majesty's ambassador at Washington respecting the Allied note of 10th January 1917* (1917-18, XXXVIII (Cd. 8439)) [**4569**]. France, Ministère des Affaires Etrangères, *Documents diplomatiques. Documents relatifs aux négociations concernant les garanties de sécurité contre une agression de l'Allemagne (10 janvier 1919-7 décembre 1923)* (Paris, 1924) [**4570**]. *History of events immediately preceding the armistice. Official documents issued by the Office of the German chancellor by order of the federal government* (London, 1920) [**4571**], which is a translation of the German official publication, *Vorgeschichte des Waffenstillstande* (no. 5478).

For convenient reprints of official documents and expressions of opinion on American foreign policy, particularly projects and possibilities of peace and a league of nations, consult the publications of the American Association for International Conciliation (no. 5167); *American journal of international law;* the publications of the Car-

negie Endowment for International Peace (nos. 5165-5167); and of
the World Peace Foundation (no. 5168). *The treaties of peace, 1919-
1923* (N.Y.: Carnegie Endowment for International Peace, 1924, 2
v.) [4572], v. I. Containing the treaty of Versailles, the treaty of St.
Germain-en-Laye, and the treaty of Trianon. Maps compiled especially for this edition, and a summary of the legal basis of the new
documents, by Lt.-Col. Lawrence Martin. v. II. Containing the
treaties of Neuilly and Sèvres, the treaties between the United States
and Germany, Austria and Hungary respectively, and the treaty of
Lausanne, the convention respecting the regime of the Straits and
other instruments signed at Lausanne. Maps compiled . . . by
Lawrence Martin.

Handbook of the European war, ed. by S. S. Sheip (White
Plains, N.Y., 1914-16, 2v.) [4573], a debaters' handbook uncon-
sciously revealing source of a certain type of American public
opinion: the weigh-all-sides-impartially type of mind, but unwit-
tingly weighing material studiously published and furnished by
belligerent governments. *America's relation to the world conflict
and to the coming peace* (Phila., 1917) (Annals of the American
Academy of Political and Social Science, v. LXXII) [4574], a
symposium of academic views. Austria, Peace Conference Delegation, *Bericht über die Tätigkeit der deutsch-österreichischen Fried-
ensdelegation in St. Germain-en-Laye* (Vienna, 1919, 2 v.) [4575].
Bulgarskata delegatsiia za mira; dokumenti po dogovora v Neuilly
(Sofia, 1919) [4576]. Two journalist's accounts: Harry Hansen,
The adventures of the fourteen points (N. Y., 1919) [4477], and
Sisley Huddleston, *Peace-making at Paris* (London, 1919) [4578].
J. M. Keynes, *The economic consequences of the peace* (London,
1919) [4579], a world shaking indictment of the economic clauses
of the treaty and criticism of Wilson as a bamboozled old Presbyter-
ian; also by the same writer, *A revision of the treaty* (N.Y., 1922)
[4580], carrying into definite suggestions the criticisms of the
author's famous earlier tract. " Letter of Honorable Elihu Root
to Honorable Will H. Hays regarding the covenant of the League of
Nations ", *Am. jour. internat. law*, XIII (1919) 580-594 [4581],
six suggested reservations. B. M. Baruch, *The making of the reparation and economic sections of the treaty* (N.Y., 1920) [4582], author was principal economic adviser to the United States delegation; quasi-official in tone. Caroline K. Cumming and W. W. Pettit,

eds., *Russian-American relations, March 1917–March 1920*, documents and papers (N.Y., 1920) (League of Free Nations Association) [**4583**]. E. J. Dillon, *The inside story of the peace conference* (N.Y. and London, 1920) [**4584**], the author was one of the most accomplished journalists of his time, and a penetrating observer of international politics. He was present at the conference. This is an excoriation of the selfish motives and compromises of the diplomats, which events since then have justified. *Handbooks prepared under the direction of the Historical Section of the Foreign Office*, nos. 1–42 (London, 1920) [**4585**], prepared for the use of the British delegates to the peace conference. Herbert Kraus and Gustav Roediger, eds., *Urkunden zum Friedensvertrage vom Versailles vom 28 juni 1919* (Berlin, 1920–21, 2 v.) (Kommentar zum Friedensvertrage, ed. by Prof. Dr. Walther Schüking) [**4585a**], a convenient edition of documents. *Macchi di Cellere* (no. 4497), a defense of the Italian ambassador; includes part of his diary. C. T. Thompson, *The peace conference day by day; a presidential pilgrimage leading to the discovery of Europe* (N.Y., 1920) [**4586**], journalist's account. *The United States Senate and the treaty* (Boston, 1920) (League of Nations, v. III, no. 4) [**4587**], a record of all votes is indicated. *The Hungarian peace negotiations; an account of the work of the Hungarian peace delegation at Neuilly s./Seine from January to March 1920* (Budapest, 1921, 3 v.) [**4588**]. Lansing, *The big four* (no. 5253), the leading personalities, by the American secretary of state who met them; and *Peace negotiations* (no. 5253), giving his personal account, with searching illustrations on Wilson's program and policy. *Official statements of war aims and peace proposals, December 1916, to November 1918* (Wash., 1921) (Carnegie Endowment for International Peace) [**4589**]. André Tardieu, *The truth about the treaty* (Indianapolis, 1921) [**4590**], translated from *La Paix* (Paris, 1921) ; very important historical document because of the influence of this French participant, who was Clemenceau's right-hand man, and also an historian of international repute. It is a defense of the treaty, designed for French critics. Gabriel Terrail [Mermeux, pseud.], *Les negociations secrètes et les quatre armistices* (Paris, 1921) [**4591**], the only text available of Supreme War Council minutes at the time of the armistice; and by the same writer, *Le combat des trois; notes et documents sur la conférence de la paix* (Paris, 1922) [**4592**], material gathered to defend Clemenceau, includes some minutes of the Council of Four. G. L. Beer, *African questions at the Paris peace conference* (N.Y., 1923) [**4593**] publishes the material prepared on this question by Professor Beer for the Inquiry and used at the peace conference. Bernardy and Falorsi, *Questione adriatica* (no. 4448), for Italian efforts to influence American opinion favorably to Italian claims. Hamilton Foley, comp., *Woodrow Wilson's case for the League of Nations*, compiled with his approval (Princeton, 1923) [**4594**]. Wickham Steed, *Through thirty years, 1892–1922* (Garden City, N.Y., 1924, 2 v.) [**4595**]. H. C. Lodge, *The Senate and the League of Nations* (N.Y., 1925) [**4596**], for the view of the opposition, by its leader in the Senate, chairman of the committee on foreign relations. " Rapport présenté par la commission d'enquête américaine au Président Wilson, relativement aux buts de guerre et conditions de paix ' ", *Rev. hist. guerre mondiale*, IV (1926) 327–345 [**4597**], documents published in Ray Stannard Baker's *Wilson and world settlement* (no. 5315), v. III, 23–41. C. E. Callwell, *Field-Marshal Sir Henry Wilson, . . . his life and diaries* (N.Y., 1927, 2 v.) [**4598**]. Maximilian, Prince of Baden, *Memoirs*, tr. by W. M. Calder and C. W. H. Sutton (N.Y., 1928, 2 v.) [**4599**]. Hunter Miller, *My diary at the conference of Paris* (Priv. print., 1928, 21 v.; v. XXI consists of index and maps) [**4600**], the author was a special legal adviser to the United States delegation, and preserved with his day-to-day diary voluminous documentary records of negotiations, so that this is—with House's *Intimate papers*—the most valuable printed source for the participation by the United States. Unfortunately only 40 sets were printed. These were distributed in selected libraries throughout the United States and other countries (for list of these libraries, see the *Annual report* for 1929, of the Carnegie Endowment for International Peace). N. D. Houghton, *Policy of the United States and other nations with respect to the recognition of the Russian Soviet government, 1917–1929* (Worcester, Mass., and N.Y. City, 1929) (International Conciliation, no. 247) [**4601**], a most useful summary based on contemporary printed material. A. G. de Lapradelle, ed., *La documentation internationale. La paix de Versailles* (Paris, 1929– (in progress)) [**4602**], an important collection of minutes of peace conference commissions; each volume devoted to one particular phase of the peace negotiations. To date (1934) v. I–VI, IX, and XII have appeared. Victor Schiff, *The Germans at Versailles, 1919*, tr. by Geoffrey Dunlop (London, 1930) [**4603**], an insider's account by an expert in the German delegation. Coolidge and Lord, *Archibald Cary Coolidge* (no. 4511). W. S. Graves, *America's Siberian adventure, 1918-1920* (N.Y., 1931) [**4603a**], memoirs of the commanding officer of the American expedition to Siberia. R. H. Lutz, ed., *Fall of the German Empire, 1914-1918*, translations by D. G. Rempel and Gertrude Rendtorff (Standford University, Calif., 1932, 2 v.) (Hoover War Library Publications, nos. 1-2) [**4604**], a source book, mostly German documents, of the history of Germany from the onset of the world war to the collapse of the Hohenzollern rule in November 1918. No commentary on the documents which are carefully and comprehensively selected. Pershing, *Experiences* (no. 4514). *Development of the League of Nations idea; documents and correspondence of Theodore Marburg*, ed. by J. H. Latané (N.Y., 1932, 2 v.) [**4605**], a voluminous documentary history of one side of the development of the idea of the League of Nations down to the Covenant of 1919; does not supplant Miller. Luigi Aldrovandi, "La settimana di passione adriatica a Parigi, 17-27 aprile, 1919 ", *Nuova antologia*, anno LXVIII (1933) 161-186, 354-382 [**4606**], verbatim reports of conversations between Wilson, Lloyd George, Clemenceau, Orlando, Sonnino. H. H. Bandholtz, *An undiplomatic diary, by the American member of the Inter-Allied Military Mission to Hungary, 1919-1920, Maj. Gen. Harry Hill Bandholtz, U.S.A.*, edited with introduction and notes by Fritz-Konrad Krüger (N.Y., 1933) [**4606a**]. C. F. Brand, " The reaction of British labor to the policies of President Wilson during the world war ", *Am. hist. rev.*, XXXVIII (1933) 263-285 [**4607**], the materials used in the preparation of this article are in the Hoover War Library at Stanford University, California. Harold Nicolson, *Peace making, 1919* (London, 1933; N.Y. and Boston, 1933) [**4608**] supplants Keynes as the best inside story from a British delegate's point of view; it is a brilliant, important, and honest analysis of the labors of the conference. One part is an historical survey of the organization, methods, and problems of the conference presented in a topical manner; and the remainder is concerned with disputes, quarrels, and mistakes. *Lord Riddell's intimate diary of the peace conference and after, 1918-1923* (London, 1933) [**4609**], Riddell was a close friend of Lloyd George, and representative of the

Press at the peace conference. *Forty-two years in the White House,* by Irwin Hood (Ike) Hoover, chief usher (Boston and N.Y., 1934) [**4609a**], indiscreet close-ups of White House family life, it throws interesting light on the intimacy of Colonel House and Woodrow Wilson. Frederick Palmer, *Bliss, peacemaker; the life and letters of General Tasker Howard Bliss* (N.Y., 1934) [**4609b**], a famous war correspondent who had access to General Bliss's voluminous papers, sets forth the most significant, linked together with a biographical narrative. It is important for the negotiations at Paris in 1919, when Bliss was a member of the American peace commission. Nina Almond and R. H. Lutz, *The treaty of St. Germain; a documentary history of its territorial and political clauses* (Stanford University, Calif., 1935) (Hoover War Library Publications. No. 5) [**4609c**] prints documents ancillary to the peace settlement of Central Europe.

MSS.: Suggestions

See Section 1, above.

Maps: Suggestions

P. L. Phillips, *A list of atlases and maps applicable to the world war* (Wash., 1918) (Library of Congress) [**4610**]. Lawrence Martin, "Maps" in *Treaties of peace* (no. 4572). Isaiah Bowman, *The new world; problems in political geography,* 4th ed., with 257 maps (Yonkers-on-Hudson, N.Y., 1928) [**4611**]. Paullin, *Atlas* (no. 213). The valuable and numerous maps prepared by the Inquiry and used by the American delegation at the Peace Conference are now in the archives of the Department of State, but many are reproduced in Hunter Miller's *Diary* (no. 4600).

CHAPTER XXIII

GENERAL WORKS, HISTORICAL PUBLICATIONS AND AIDS

In the preceding bibliographical chapters of this guide we have attempted to classify appropriately the general works, monographs, (biographies through cross reference to the *D.A.B.*), and sources, printed and manuscript. But there is a class of general manuals, bibliographical aids, and categories of historical publications which we cannot so treat. Both general student and special investigator will desire to use them. In this chapter, we list this material. In consulting it the reader is reminded that there is a fuller treatment of sources in Part II.

1. General Bibliographical Aids

The practice of bibliography is to descend from the general to the particular. First we have bibliographies of general bibliography; then bibliographies of historical bibliography; then bibliographies of particular fields of history. The guidebook in the reader's hands professes to contain a bibliography of a special field: the diplomatic history of the United States.

The rapid growth of bibliographical publications makes it unnecessary for us to make here any extended remarks on general bibliography.[1]   We content ourselves with references to some of the recent manuals on bibliography, particularly historical bibliography, and with indicating specifically those bibliographical aids which are particularly useful for the diplomatic history of the United States.[2]

A. Historical Bibliographies in General

The principal manuals on historical bibliography are:

Langlois, C. V., *Manuel de bibliographie historique* (Paris, 1901–04, 2 v.), pt. 1: *Instruments bibliographiques;* pt. 2: *Histoire et organisation des études historiques.*   [4625

---

[1] For manuals on bibliography in general, see Henry Stein, *Manuel de bibliographie générale* (Paris, 1897) [4612]; Georg Schneider, *Handbuch der Bibliographie,* 4th, rev. ed. (Leipzig, 1930) [4613]; *Internationale Bibliographie des Buch- und Bibliothekswesens, mit besonderer Berücksichtigung der Bibliographie,* 1926– (Leipzig, 1928–) [4614], which supersedes the *Bibliographie des Bibliotheks- und Buchswesens,* 1904–25 (Leipzig, 1905–27); and H. B. Van Hoesen and F. K. Walter, *Bibliography; practical, enumerative, historical* (N.Y., 1928) [4615].

For manuals on reference books in general, see John Minto, *Reference books; a classified and annotated guide to the principal works of reference* (London, 1929) [4616]; Isadore G. Mudge, *Guide to reference books,* 5th ed. (Chicago, 1929) [4617]; and Isadore G. Mudge, Doris M. Reed, and Constance M. Winchell, *Reference books of 1929* [–1933], *an informal supplement to Guide to reference books, fifth edition* (Chicago, 1930–34, 3v.) (in progress) [4618].

For bibliographies of periodicals, see Van Hoesen and Walter, *Bibliography* (no. 4615), 194–197; and nos. 4982–5003 of this bibliography, below.

[2] Mention should also be made of the printed catalogues of the foremost libraries of the world, such as: British Museum, *Catalogue of printed books in the library of the British Museum* (London, 1881–1900, 393 pts. in 95 v.), and *Supplement* (1900–05); a new edition now appearing (1931–), which is an alphabetical list according to authors, but also containing subject entries [4619]; and idem, *Subject index of the modern works added to the library of the British Museum in the years 1880–1900* (London, 1902–03, 3v.); *idem* for 1901–05 (1906); 1906–10 (1911); 1911–15 (1918); 1916–20 (1922); 1921–25 (1927); 1926–30 (1933) [4620]. Preussische Staatsbibliothek, *Berliner Titeldrucke; Verzeichnis der von der Preussischen Staatsbibliothek und den Preussischen Universitätsbibliotheken erworbenen neueren Druckschriften* (Berlin, 1892–) [4621]. Bibliothèque Nationale, *Catalogue général des livres imprimés de la Bibliothèque Nationale; Auteurs* (Paris, 1897–) [4622]. *Catalogue of printed books in the library of the Foreign Office* [of Great Britain] (London: H. M. Stationery Off., 1926) [4623]. For others, see Van Hoesen, *Bibliography* (no. 4615), 244–245.

The Library of Congress catalogue, though not printed, is nevertheless available through its duplicate sets of cards (author entries) in more than fifty depository libraries throughout the United States and abroad. It forms one of the most important bibliographical aids. A list of the depository libraries will be found in the annual *Report of the Librarian of Congress,* 1932 (Wash., 1932), 251–253.

The Union Catalogue at the Library of Congress, containing titles received from all the large libraries of the United States and many of the smaller libraries, is useful in locating rare and unusual books, as well as the more obvious ones. At present it is only an author catalogue.

A recent development of the " union catalogue " is that of the Prussian State Library: *Gesamtkatalog der Preussischen Bibliotheken mit Nachweis des identischen Besitzes der Bayerischen Staatsbibliothek in München und der Nationalbibliothek in Wien,* ed. by the " Preussische Staatsbibliothek " (Berlin, 1931–) [4624].

Coulter, Edith M., *Guide to historical bibliographies; a critical and systematic bibliography for advanced students* (Berkeley, Calif., 1927).[2a]　　　　　　　　　　　　　　　　　　　　　　[4626

Histoire et historiens depuis cinquante ans (Paris, 1927, 2 v.), a survey of the methods, organization, and progress of historical work from 1876 to 1926, with bibliographical summaries of the historical publications of the leading countries of the world; it was prepared under the auspices of the *Revue historique*.　[4627

For lists of current bibliographies (including of course historical bibliographies), see American Council of Learned Societies, *Catalogue of current bibliographies in the humanistic sciences* (Wash., 1931) [4628], classified and annotated, and list by countries; "History": p. 36–50. *Index bibliographicus; international catalogue of sources of current bibliographical information (periodicals and institutions)*, 2nd edition, brought down to date and enlarged, ed. by Marcel Godet and Joris Vorstius (Berlin and Leipzig, 1931) [4629], issued under the auspices of the League of Nations International Institute of Intellectual Cooperation.

B. International Historical Bibliographies

The principal universal, or international, historical bibliographies are:

Jahresberichte der Geschichtswissenschaft, 1878–1913 (Berlin, 1880–1916, 36 v.), compiled under the auspices of the "Historische Gesellschaft zu Berlin."　　　　　　　　　　　　　　　　[4630

Annual bulletin of historical literature, 1911– (London, 1912–), published by the Historical Association, London; has a *General index*, 1911–22.　　　　　　　　　　　　　　　　　　　　　　　[4631

Social science abstracts; a comprehensive abstracting and indexing journal of the world's periodical literature in the social sciences, 1929–1932 (Menasha, Wis., 1929–32 (suspended publication with the Dec. 1932 number)), published under the auspices of the Social Science Research Council; presents from January 1, 1929, a monthly abstract of all periodical articles in 35 languages (not including Oriental) on the various fields of social sciences, including history, the various fields of which are divided into sections. Regrettably it does not cite books.　　　　　　　　　[4632

[2a] Professor Edith M. Coulter and Dr. Melanie Gerstenfeld are at work on a revision of this guide. The scope of the work is to be greatly enlarged.

International bibliography of historical sciences, 1926– (Paris, 1930–), edited by the International Committee of Historical Sciences, is a list of selected publications for each year in all fields of history, the only general international guide to current historical literature; a continuation on an international plan of the *Jahresberichte* (no. 4630). [4633

A guide to historical literature, ed. by G. M. Dutcher, H. R. Shipman, S. B. Fay, A. H. Shearer, W. H. Allison (N.Y., 1931), prepared by the Committee on Bibliography of the American Historical Association in co-operation with the American Library Association. This *Guide* is a monument to co-operative American scholarship which is bound to commend the respect of the historical world. It opens to the discriminating student the entire domain of history and historiography. [4634

A London bibliography of the social sciences (London, 1931–32, 4 v.), comp. under the direction of B. M. Headicar and C. Fuller; the subject catalogue of the British Library of Political and Economic Sciences at the London School of Economics and Political Science, and several other libraries. (To be followed by annual volumes, the first *Supplement* was published in 1934). [4635

The student will find that these several works cover the general field of historical bibliography.

For the most recent books one must watch publishers' lists and advertisements, and the review columns of current newspapers and periodicals.[3] The most responsible and authoritative reviews may be expected to appear in the professional historical reviews. We have noted these below, p. 716.

C. National Historical Bibliographies

Each principal occidental country, and China and Japan, has its group of national historical bibliographies, and of professional historical reviews or journals, which must be consulted by an investigator who desires to complete his own bibliography on a subject of

---

[3] In addition to the historical periodicals noted below, nos. 4838–4913, which currently list recent historical publications, one may consult the bibliographical review *Polybiblion; revue bibliographique universelle* (Paris, 1868 to date) [4636], issued in 2 sections: *Partie littéraire*, containing book reviews, and the *Partie technique*, giving a classified bibliography of recent books (mostly foreign), and a list of the contents of recent periodical publications, both parts devoting large sections to historical material.

American diplomatic history.[4] We must consult these bibliographies for accumulations of older works. We must watch the historical journals for the more recently published books not included in the bibliographies which so rapidly become out of date. Below are listed the principal national *historical* bibliographies and historical periodicals by countries. The reader is referred to the above mentioned manuals for further elaborations; also, particularly for historical

[4] In addition to the national historical bibliographies many countries have national or trade bibliographies consisting of general and comprehensive catalogues of books (on all subjects) printed and published in that country. For bibliographies of these catalogues, see W. P. Courtenay, *A register of national bibliography, with a selection of the chief bibliographical books and articles printed in other countries* (London, 1905–12, 3 v.) [4637], originally intended to be confined to English bibliographies, afterward expanded to include a selection from the literature of other countries. R. A. Peddie, *National bibliographies; a descriptive catalogue of the works which register the books published in each country* (London, 1912) [4638], a comprehensive list of the national bibliographies of 49 countries. Van Hoesen, *Bibliography* (no. 4615), 209–238. Mudge, *Guide* (no. 4617), 286–309. *Guide hist. lit.* (no. 4634), listed under separate countries. We list below the principal national bibliographies of a general character:

For the United States: Charles Evans, *American bibliography* (Chicago, 1903–34, 12 v.) (in progress) [4639], a chronological dictionary of all books, pamphlets, and periodical publications printed in the United States of America from the genesis of printing in 1639 down to and including the year 1820; with a classified subject index in each volume which brings together the historical items, of particular use to the historical student. Volume XII carries through the year 1799. W. O. Waters, *American imprints, 1648–1797, in the Huntington Library, supplementing Evans' American bibliography* (Cambridge, Mass., 1933) [4639a], is reprinted from the *Huntington Library bulletin*, no. 3, 1933. O. A. Roorbach, *Bibliotheca americana; catalogue of American publications, 1820–1861* (N.Y., 1849–61, 4 v.) [4640]. James Kelly, *The American catalogue of books . . . published in the United States, 1861–1871* (N.Y., 1866–71, 2 v.) [4641], continuation of Roorbach (above). For the period between Kelly (no. 4641) and *American catalogue* (no. 4643), *i.e.* 1872–1876, consult the *Publishers' weekly*, 1872– (N.Y., 1872–) (in progress) [4642]. *The American catalogue*, 1876– (N.Y., 1880–1911) [4643], supplemented currently by the *Publishers' weekly* (no. 4642 above). *The Cumulative book index (United States catalog supplement)* (Minneapolis, and N.Y., 1898–) [4644], cumulated annually (to date). *The United States catalog; books in print*, 1902, 1912, with supplements to 1924 (Minneapolis, 1903, 1912, 1924), and *The United States catalog; books in print January 1, 1928* (N.Y., 1928) [4645], kept up to date by the *Cumulative book index.*

For Great Britain: *English catalogue of books, 1801–* (London, 1864–) [4646], supplemented by the annual *English catalogue*, and currently by the Publishers' circular *and booksellers' record. Whitaker's cumulative book list*, 1924– (London, 1924–) [4647], a classified list of publications.

For France: O. H. Lorenz, *Catalogue général de la librairie française*, 1840– (Paris, 1867–) [4648] ; and the *Bibliographie de la France*, 1811– (Paris, 1811–) [4649].

For Germany: The Hinrichs publications: (1) *Wöchentliches Verzeichnis*, 1893– (Leipzig, 1893–; issued under title, *Allgemeine Bibliographie für Deutschland*, 1842–1892) ; (2) *Vierteljahrs-Katalog*, 1846– (Leipzig, 1853–) ; (3) *Halbjahrs-Katalog*, 1798– (Leipzig, 1798–) ; and (4) the *Fünfjahrs-Katalog*, 1851– (Leipzig, 1857–) [4650]. Nos. 1, 3, and 4 are continued (1916–) by the Börsenverein der deutsche Büchhandler, the five yearly catalogue under title: *Deutsches Bücherverzeichnis.* C. G. Kaiser's *Halbjahrsverzeichnis der im deutschen Buchhandel erschienen Bücher, Zeitschriften und Landkarten.* (Leipzig, 1798–) [4651], all of which are continued by the *Deutsches Bücherverzeichnis* (Leipzig, 1916–) [4652].

periodicals and serial publications of learned societies, to the " Enquête pour l'orientation des recherches dans la bibliographie historique des differents pays ", published in the *Bulletin of the International Committee of Historical Sciences*, I (1929) 217–249, 457–461,
II (1930) 763–803 [4653]. Because our subject concerns primarily
the diplomatic history of the United States, we presume to present
our own country first, next alphabetically the others mentioned.

America in General

Winsor, Justin, *Narrative and critical history of America* (Boston
and N.Y., 1884–89, 8 v.), each chapter followed by a valuable bibliographical and critical essay on sources and authorities.   [4654

Sabin, Joseph, *A dictionary of books relating to America, from its
discovery to the present time*, begun by Joseph Sabin, continued
by Wilberforce Eames, and completed by R. W. G. Vail, for the
Bibliographical Society of America (N.Y., 1868–1934, 24 v. (in
progress)), an author catalogue of books, pamphlets, and periodicals printed in America, and of works about America printed
elsewhere; has no subject index.   [4655

Oficina Panamericana de la República de Cuba. *Catálogo de obras
de derecho internacional e historia de América que el gobierno
cubano pone a disposición, para su consulta, de los señores delegados
a la sexta Conferencia Internacional Americana* (Havana, 1928), a
general collection of works on international law and the history
and diplomacy of the Americas, gathered together for the use
of members of the conference at Havana, in 1928.   [4656

United States

Larned, Josephus, *Literature of American history; a bibliographical
guide in which the scope, character, and comparative worth of
books in selected lists is set forth in brief notes by critics of authority* (Boston, 1902) and *Supplement for 1900 and 1901*, ed. by
P. P. Wells (Boston, 1902) consists of a compilation of the principal titles before 1901, with critical comment on the contents.
    [4657

Griffin, A. P. C., *Bibliography of American historical societies, the
United States and the Dominion of Canada*, rev. ed. (Wash.: Govt.
Print. Off., 1907) (Am. Hist. Assoc. Ann. Rep., for 1905, v. II).
    [4658

Richardson, E. C., and A. E. Morse, *Writings on American history, 1902* (Princeton, N.J., 1904). [4659

McLaughlin, A. C., W. A. Slade, and E. D. Lewis, *Writings on American history, 1903. A bibliography of books and articles on United States history published during the year 1903, with some memoranda on other portions of America* (Wash.: Carnegie Institution, 1905). [4660

Griffin, Grace Gardner, *Writings on American history, 1906–*(N.Y., New Haven, and Wash. (imprint varies), 1908–); now published as v. II of *Annual report* of the American Historical Association. This is a continuation of nos. 4659 and 4660. It aims to list all books and periodical articles on the history of the United States and British North America, with some memoranda on other portions of America (that is the material on Spanish America published in the United States and Europe). The titles are classified by subjects, and there is a comprehensive index. There are sections on the various chronological " periods " of United States history, on diplomatic history, and on the Monroe Doctrine. [4661

Channing, Edward, A. B. Hart, and F. J. Turner, *Guide to the study and reading of American history*, rev. ed. (Boston and London, 1912). [4662]. Professor Hart has also contributed some bibliographical guidance in his: (1) *Handbook of the history, diplomacy and government of the United States* (Cambridge, Mass., 1901) [4663], and (2) *Manual of American history, diplomacy and government for class use* (Cambridge, 1915). [4664

Greene, E. B., and R. B. Morris, *Guide to the sources for early American history (1600–1800) in the city of New York* (N.Y., 1929), in 2 parts: (1) Printed sources; (2) Manuscript collections. [4665

The general indexes to the various historical periodicals constitute useful bibliographical aids, particularly for our purpose the following:

American historical review, General index to volumes I–XXX, 1895–1925 (N.Y., 1906, 1916, 1926, 3 v.), prepared by D. M. Matteson. [4666

General index to Papers and Annual reports of the American Historical Association, 1884–1914, comp. by D. M. Matteson (Wash., 1918). [4667

An analytical index to the American journal of international law, and supplements, volumes 1 to 14 (1907–1920) and the Proceedings of the American Society of International Law, 1907–1920, prepared by G. A. Finch (Wash., 1921).   [4668

General index to the American political science review, volumes I–XX, and to the Proceedings of the American Political Science Association, 1904–1914 (Menasha, Wis., 1927).   [4669

There are a few bibliographical aids to the diplomatic history of the United States, of a comprehensive nature, such as the Carnegie Institution guides to material relating to American history in foreign archives, which are entered in the textual part of this *Guide* (Pt. II, Ch. 3: *Archives*), under the countries to which they relate. We refer the investigator to nos. 5764 (Austria), 5704 (France), 5746 (Germany), 5576, 5577, 5590 (Great Britain), 5791 (Italy), 5635, 5650, 5660 (Spain), and 5764 (Switzerland). Similarly, indexes and lists of printed diplomatic correspondence and state papers have been entered in their appropriate places in Part II, Ch. 2: *Printed State Papers.*

See also the *General index to the published volumes of the diplomatic correspondence and foreign relations of the United States, 1861–99* (no. 5345); Adelaide R. Hasse's *Index to United States documents relating to foreign affairs* (no. 5344); the price list of publications relating to foreign relations, issued by the Superintendent of Documents (no. 5376); *Trial bibliography of American diplomacy,* by A. B. Hart (no. 4788); and the bibliographies in Fish, *American diplomacy* (no. 4791); *Am. secs. state* (no. 4796); and Sears, *Hist. Am. for. relations* (no. 4798).

The Library of Congress Division of Bibliography has prepared a number of typewritten lists relating to foreign relations which, together with its mimeographed lists (entered above in relevant sections) are sent, from time to time, to the Public Affairs Information Service, New York City, where they are listed in its *Bulletin,* with the statement that the mimeographed lists may be obtained on request to the Division of Bibliography, Library of Congress, while the typewritten lists are obtainable of the Public Affairs Information Service for the cost of copying.

One of the principal purposes of this volume is to provide a detailed bibliography of the diplomatic history of the United States, topically and chronologically arranged, in the chapters which precede.

Canada [5]

Gagnon, Philéas, *Essai de bibliographie canadienne; inventaire d'une bibliothèque comprenant imprimés, manuscrits, estampes, etc., relatifs à l'histoire du Canada et des pays adjacents, avec des notes bibliographiques* (Quebec, 1895–1913, 2 v.), containing 5018 titles, alphabetically arranged by author, with no subject classification and no index. [4671

Review of historical publications relating to Canada, v. 1–22, 1896–1918 (Toronto, 1897–1919, 22 v.), a critical review of the historical publications of the given year; it is supplemented by the *Canadian historical review* (no. 4863) which includes in each number book reviews and a comprehensive bibliographical list of " Recent publications relating to Canada." [4672

Burpee, L. J., and A. G. Doughty, *Index and dictionary of Canadian history* (no. 5051) is useful as a bibliographical aid through its references to the principal printed material to be consulted for further information on each subject, its list of MS. sources in the Dominion archives, and partial list of scarce maps and plans relating to Canada.

Shortt, Adam, and A. G. Doughty, eds., *Canada and its provinces*, v. XXIII, *Index* (Toronto, 1917) contains convenient classified bibliographies, and itself constitutes a useful bibliographical aid. [4673

Trotter, R. G., *Canadian history; a syllabus and guide to reading* (N.Y., 1926; new and enl. ed., Toronto, 1934). [4673a

Catalogue of pamphlets in the Public Archives of Canada . . . with index, prepared by Magdalen Casey (Ottawa, 1931–2, 2 v.) supersedes the lists of pamphlets, journals, and reports, 1611–1867, issued in 1903 and 1916, and includes additional material published after 1867. These two recent volumes cover the years 1493–1931. [4674

Canadiana, 1698–1900, in the possession of the Douglas library, Queen's University, Kingston, Ont. (Kingston, 1932), list of books on all subjects published in Canada during the years specified. [4675

---

[5] See also *A bibliography of Canadian bibliographies,* compiled by the 1929 and 1930 classes in bibliography of the McGill University Library School (Montreal, 1930) [4670].

Lewin, Evans, *Subject catalogue of the library of the Royal Empire Society, formerly Royal Colonial Institute.* v. III. *The Dominion of Canada and its provinces, the Dominion of Newfoundland, the West Indies, and colonial America* (London: Published by the Royal Empire Society, 1932).   [4676

See also *The Cambridge history of the British Empire,* v. VI. *Canada and Newfoundland* (N.Y. and Cambridge, Eng., 1930) for a list of the "Manuscript sources of Canadian history", by A. G. Doughty, and a bibliography of printed works on the history of Canada and Newfoundland.   [4677

Hispanic America

BIBLIOGRAPHIES OF BIBLIOGRAPHIES

Jones, C. K., *Hispanic American bibliographies, including collective biographies, histories of literature and selected general works* (Baltimore, 1922), originally published in the *Hispanic American historical review,* v. III–IV, 1920–21; and 5 supplements published in *ibid.,* v. VI (1926), v. IX (1929), v. XI (1931), v. XIII (1933), and v. XIV (1934).   An outstanding piece of bibliographical research, of the greatest value to investigators.   [4678

Pan American Union, Columbus Memorial Library, *Bibliographies pertaining to Latin America in the Columbus Memorial Library of the Pan American Union,* comp. by C. E. Babcock (Wash., 1928), mimeographed.   [4679

Pan American Union, Columbus Memorial Library, *Sources of information for books on Latin America; magazines containing book reviews, library and book trade journals,* 2d ed., rev. (Wash., 1930); also *Fuentes de información sobre libros de la América latina* (Wash., 1933), mimeographed.   [4680

Wilgus, A. C., *The histories of Hispanic America* (no. 4688), "Selected list of bibliographical collections": p. 111–115.   [4681

GENERAL BIBLIOGRAPHIES

Pan American Union, Columbus Memorial Library, *List of Latin American history and description in the Columbus Memorial Library* (Wash., 1907), supplements pub. in 1909 and 1914.

     [4682

Keniston, Hayward, *List of works for the study of Hispanic-American history* (N.Y., 1920).   [4683

Hoskins, H. L., *Guide to Latin-American history* (Boston and N.Y., 1922), " Selected, classified bibliography of materials relating to Latin-American history ": p. 1–17. " Political and diplomatic history ": p. 10–12.   [4684

Sánchez Alonso, *Fuentes de la historia* (no. 4759) includes works dealing with Spanish American history to 1833.

University of California, *Spain and Spanish America in the libraries of the University of California, a catalogue of books* (Berkeley, Calif., 1928–30, 2 v.), the first volume is devoted to the general and departmental libraries, and the second volume is a catalogue of works dealing with Spain and Spanish America in the Bancroft Library.   While the catalogue itself is an alphabetical author or title list, the extensive subject index of 150 pages makes it easily adapted to use in historical research; a valuable contribution to the bibliography of Mexico and Central America.   [4685

Ibero-amerikanische Bibliographie, comp. by Hans Praesent (Berlin, 1930–(in progress)) (" Beiläge zu Ibero-amerikanisches Archiv "), a bibliographical review of recent works in German dealing with Hispanic America.   [4686

Williams, Mary W., *People and politics of Latin America* (Boston 1930) contains a list of the principal works dealing with the history of Latin America.   [4687

Wilgus, A. C., *A history of Hispanic America; a text book hand-book for college students* (Wash., 1931) contains bibliographical material; his *The histories of Hispanic America; a bibliographical essay* (Wash., 1932) (Pan American Union, Bibliographic series, no. 9) gives a list of the outstanding works dealing with Hispanic America history; and " List of articles relating to Hispanic America published in the periodicals of the American Geographical Society, 1852–1933 ", *Hisp. Am. hist. rev.*, XIV (1934) 114–130.   [4688

Bealer, L. W., " Some recent additions to the South American collections in the University of California libraries ", *Hisp. Am. hist. rev.*, XII (1932) 103–106, supplements *Spain and Spanish America in the University of California libraries* (no. 4685).   [4689

Robertson, J. A., " Recent accessions of German books in the Library of Congress referring to Hispanic America ", *Hisp. Am. hist. rev.*, XII (1932) 522-529, mainly books recently published.   [4690

Pan American Union, Columbus Memorial Library, *Selected list of recent books (in English) on Latin America* (Wash., 1933) (Bibliographical Series, no. 4 (3d ed., rev. and enl.)), C. E. Babcock, librarian.   [4691-2

Separate Countries

The contributions to the field of Hispanic American historical bibliography are slight, the outstanding exception being that of Cuba, with the comprehensive bibliographies of C. M. Trelles, noted below. In lieu of formal historical bibliographies for this region we note below, for certain countries, general bibliographies and catalogues of libraries, from which the investigator may derive partial bibliographical aid.

Argentine Republic

Argentine Republic, Biblioteca Nacional, *Catálogo metódico de la Biblioteca Nacional* (Buenos Aires, 1893-1925, 6 v.), v. II and VI devoted to history and geography, and containing sections on diplomacy, treaties, and archives.   [4693

Argentine Republic, Ministerio de Relaciones Exteriores y Culto, *Catálogo de la biblioteca, mapoteca y archivo del Ministerio de Relaciones Exteriores y Culto* (Buenos Aires, 1905), and *Apéndice: Servicios prestados en la carrera diplomática y administrativa, 1810-1910* (Buenos Aires, 1910).   [4694

Selva, Manuel, Fortunato Mendilaharzu, and L. J. Rosso, *Bibliografía general argentina; inventario analítico-crítico de todas las publicaciones argentinas desde el origen de la primera imprenta en el Río de la Plata, hasta el presente* (Buenos Aires, 1931-), to date (November, 1934), v. I (A-B) only has been published.   [4695

Bolivia

René-Moreno, Gabriel, *Biblioteca boliviano; catálogo de la sección de libros y folletos* (Santiago, 1879), with supplements pub. in 1900 and 1908, containing material from 1879-1899 and 1900-1908 respectively; arranged alphabetically, with author index only, not being classified it is difficult to use for our purpose.   [4696

Pan American Union, Columbus Memorial Library, *Catalogue of books, pamphlets, periodicals and maps relating to the republic of Bolivia in the Columbus Memorial Library* (Wash.: Govt. Print. Off., 1905). [4697

Brazil

Rio de Janeiro, Bibliotheca Municipal, *Catalogo da Bibliotheca Municipal* (*Publicação official*) (Rio de Janeiro, 1878), a classified list. [4698

Catalogo da exposição de historia do Brazil realizada pela Bibliotheca Nacional do Rio de Janeiro a 2 de Dezembro de 1881 (Rio de Janeiro, 1881, 2 v.; and suppl., 1883), comp. by B. F. Ramiz Galvão; includes sections, "Ministerio de extrangeiros", and "Historia diplomatica" (nos. 10201–10597). [4699

Brazil, Congresso, Senada. *Catalogo alphabetico, bibliotheca do Senado federal da Republica dos Estados Unidos do Brazil* (Rio de Janeiro, 1898). [4700

Garraux, A. L., *Bibliographie brésilienne; catalogue des ouvrages français et latins relatifs au Brésil* (*1500–1898*) (Paris, 1898). [4700a

Brazil. Archivo Publico Nacional. *Catalogo da bibliotheca do Archivo Publico Nacional* (Rio de Janeiro, 1901). [4701

Phillips, P. L., *A list of books, magazine articles and maps relating to Brazil, 1800–1900*, comp. for the International Bureau of American Republics (Wash., 1903). [4702

Manchester, A. K., "Descriptive bibliography of the Brazilian section of the Duke University Library", *Hisp. Am. hist. rev.*, XIII (1933) 238–266, 495–523; has 3 sections: "Bibliographical aids", "Contemporary accounts, 1500–1822", and "Works written since 1822." 4702a

Central America

Phillips, P. L., *A list of books, magazine articles, and maps relating to Central America, including the republics of Costa Rica, Guatemala, Honduras, Nicaragua, and Salvador, 1800–1900*, comp. for the International Bureau of the American Republics (Wash., 1902). [4703

Chile

Anrique Reyes, Nicolás, and L. Ignacio Silva A., *Ensayo de una bibliografía histórica i jeográfica de Chile* (Santiago de Chile, 1902), containing 2561 titles, classified. [4704

Phillips, P. L., *A list of books, magazine articles and maps relating to Chile*, comp. for the International Bureau of the American Republics (Wash., 1903).   [4705
Chile. Congreso. Biblioteca. *Catálogo de la Biblioteca del Congreso Nacional, 1921–2* (Santiago, 1922), arranged under subjects, with author index.   [4706

Colombia

Laverde Amaya, Isidro, *Bibliografía colombiana* (Bogotá, 1895), containing titles "Abadía Méndez-Ovalle"; only one volume published.   [4707
Bogotá. Biblioteca Nacional. *Catálogo de periódicos y libros de la Biblioteca Nacional de Bogotá* (Bogotá, 1914).   [4708
Posada, Eduardo, *Bibliografía bogotana* (Bogotá, 1917–25, 2 v.), arranged chronologically, 1738–1831, with author and subject indexes.   [4709

Ecuador

Rolando, C. A., *Catálogo de la bibliografía nacional del Dr. Carlos A. Rolando* (Guayaquil, 1913).   [4710

Honduras

Honduras. Biblioteca Nacional. *Catálogo metódico de la Biblioteca Nacional* (Tegucigalpa, 1915).   [4711

Mexico

U.S. War Department Library. *Index of publications, articles and maps relating to Mexico, in the War Department Library* (Wash., 1896) includes sections on general literature, interoceanic canals and railroads, Mexican war, 1846–48, Texan-Mexican war, and French intervention and Maximilian period.   [4712
List of works in the New York Public Library relating to Mexico (N.Y., 1909), reprinted from the *Bulletin*, v. XIII, 1909.   [4713

Nicaragua

Nicaragua. Biblioteca Nacional. *Catálogo general de los libros de que consta la Biblioteca Nacional de la República de Nicaragua* (Nicaragua, 1882).   [4714

Paraguay

Decoud, J. S., *A list of books, magazine articles, and maps relating to Paraguay* (Wash.: Govt. Print. Off., 1904).   [4715

Peru

René-Moreno, Gabriel, *Biblioteca peruana; apuntes para un catálogo de impresos* (Santiago de Chile, 1896, 2 v.), pub. by the Biblioteca del Instituto Nacional of Chile; contains list of Peruvian books and pamphlets in that library and in the Biblioteca Nacional of Chile, with bibliographical notes.   [4716

Peru. Congreso. Cámara de Senadores. *Catálogo de la biblioteca*, formado por el oficial primero, don Rafael Belaunde, 31 de julio de 1913 (Lima, 1913).   [4717

Salvador

San Salvador. Biblioteca Nacional. *Catálogo alfabético y por materias de todos los libros que contiene la Biblioteca Nacional de El Salvador*, formado por Rafael U. Palacios (San Salvador, 1887), and *Apéndice*, por E. M. López (San Salvador, 1890).   [4718

Venezuela

Sánchez, M. S., *Bibliografía venezolanista; contribución al conocimiento de los libros extranjeros relativos a Venezuela y sus grandes hombres* (Caracas, 1914), the Sánchez collection of books relating to Venezuela was purchased in 1913 for Harvard University Library, John Crerar Library, and Northwestern University Library, among which it was fairly equally divided. The present catalogue of books written by foreign authors on Venezuela represents about half the collection.   [4719

West Indies

GENERAL

List of works in the New York Public Library relating to the West Indies (N.Y., 1912), reprinted from its *Bulletin*, v. XVI, 1912.   [4720

British West Indies

Ragatz, L. J., *A guide for the study of British Caribbean history, 1763–1834, including the abolition and emancipation movements* (Wash., 1932) (Am. Hist. Assoc. ann. rep., for 1930, v. III), an invaluable bibliography, containing books, MSS., documents, and other items.   [4721

Cuba

Griffin, A. P. C., *List of books relating to Cuba (including references to collected works and periodicals)*, 2d ed. (Wash., 1898) (Library of Congress), including a bibliography of maps, by P. Lee Phillips; also a later list, with additions, published in *Cuba*, prepared by Señor Gonzalo de Quesada (Wash., 1905), these lists contain books, periodical articles, and government documents.   [4722

Trelles, C. M., *Bibliografía cubana del siglo XIX* (Matanzas, 1911–15, 8 v.); and *Bibliografía cubana del siglo XX (1900–1916)* (Matanzas, 1916–17, 2 v.); and *Biblioteca histórica cubana* (Matanzas, 1922–26, 3 v.).   [4723

Figaralo-Caneda, Domingo, " Bibliografía histórica cubana," *Anales de la Academia de la Historia de Cuba*, VIII (1926) 105–119.
                                                                    [4724

Porto Rico

Griffin, A. P. C., *A list of books (with references to periodicals) on Porto Rico* (Wash., 1901) (Library of Congress).   [4725

Pedreira, A. S., *Bibliografía puertorriqueña (1493–1930)* (Madrid, 1932), a classified list, with author and subject indexes.   [4725a

EUROPE

Austria

Charmatz, Richard, *Wegweiser durch die Literatur der österreichischen Geschichte* (Stuttgart and Berlin, 1912), a general bibliography of Austrian history.   [4726

Balkans

Savadjian, Léon, *Bibliographie balkanique 1920–1930* (Paris, 1931) " Biographies "; p. 235–253; supplemented by *Bibliographie balkanique, 1931–* (Paris, 1933–). It is divided as follows: Balkans, Albanie, Bulgarie, Grèce, Roumanie, Turquie, Yougoslavie, and Europe Centrale.   [4727

Belgium

Pirenne, Henri, *Bibliographie de l'histoire de Belgique méthodique et chronologique, des sources et des ouvrages principaux relatifs à l'histoire de tous les Pays-Bas jusqu' en 1598 et à l'histoire de Belgique jusqu' en 1914*, 3 éd. (Brussels, 1931), completely revised with the collaboration of Henry Nowé and Henry Obreen. [4728

Czechoslovakia

Český časopis historický (Czech historical magazine) (Prague, 1894–) publishes reviews of all important current works for Czech history and an annual bibliography of historical publications relating to Czechoslovakia (interrupted from 1916 to 1922, but the gap is covered by a summary in 1922).   [4729

Denmark

" Fortegnelse over historisk litteratur fra aret 1896 vecrorende Danmarks historie ", in *Historisk tidsskrift* (no. 4875), 1896 to date; an annual bibliography of the history of Denmark published in the periodical noted.   [4730

Erichsen, B., and Alfr. Krarup, *Dansk historisk bibliografi; systematisk fortegnelse over bidrag til Danmarks historie til udgangen af 1912* (Copenhagen, 1917–27, 3 v.), the third volume devoted to biography.   [4731

France

Monod, Gabriel, *Bibliographie de l'histoire de France; catalogue méthodique et chronologique des sources et des ouvrages relatifs à l'histoire de France depuis les origines jusqu'en 1789* (Paris, 1888), in 2 parts—(1) a subject arrangement; (2) a chronological arrangement in which the titles are listed under historical periods.   [4732

Bibliothèque Nationale, *Catalogue de l'histoire de France* (Paris, 1855–79, 11 v.; and supplements (1880, 1884, 1885, 1894, 1895)), minutely classified under 15 main and 904 subclasses. [4733

Lasteyrie, Robert de, *Bibliographie générale des travaux historiques et archéologiques publiés par les sociétés savantes de la France* (Paris, 1888–1913, 6 v.), published under the auspices of the Ministry of Public Instruction. The items are listed under the name of each society, and as there is no index it is difficult to use for our purpose. Covers the literature published to 1900; supplemented for material after 1900 by no. 4735.   [4734

Bibliographie annuelle des travaux historiques et archéologiques publiés par les sociétés savantes de la France, 1901/4–1909/10 (Paris, 1906–14, 3 v.).   [4735

Répertoire méthodique de l'histoire moderne et contemporaine de la France pour année 1898[-1913] (Paris, 1899–1933, 10 v.), comp. by Gaston Brière, Pierre Caron and others (the volume for 1907–1909 not published) ; an annual classified bibliography of French history, including books and articles in periodicals. Supplements Caron, *Bibliographie* (no. 4737).   [4736

Caron, Pierre, *Bibliographie des travaux publiés de 1866 à 1897 sur l'histoire de la France depuis 1789* (Paris, 1912), a classified bibliography, with an index to authors, persons, and places ; includes books, pamphlets, and articles in periodicals and society publications, and contains a section on diplomatic history. Supplemented for the material published after 1897 by no. 4736.   [4737

Répertoire bibliographique de l'histoire de France, 1920–1927, par Pierre Caron et Henri Stein (Paris, 1923–32, 4 v. (in progress)), a current bibliography covering the entire period of French history, and including biographies.   [4738

Peloux, Vicomte Charles du, *Répertoire général des ouvrages modernes relatifs au dix-huitième siècle français, 1715–1789* (Paris, 1926) and *supplément: Table méthodique* (Paris, 1927), the bibliography consisting of an alphabetical list by author's names, brief entries, no annotations ; includes an " Index des principaux personnages du XVIIIe siècle ayant fait l'objet d'études biographiques."   [4739

Germany

Bibliographie zur deutschen Geschichte, 1889– (Leipzig, 1889–1918; Dresden, 1920–), issued as a supplement to the *Historische Vierteljahrschrift* (no. 4890) ; a useful annual bibliography arranged by subjects, with author index; various compilers (the earlier numbers were compiled by Oscar Masslow).   [4740

Dahlmann, F. C. Dahlmann-Waitz. *Quellenkunde der deutschen Geschichte*, 9. Auflage, . . . hrsg. von Hermann Haering (Leipzig, 1931–32), a classified bibliography of German history, the standard work of its subject; lists practically all works of any importance on German history in the German language published prior to 1931; includes 16,337 titles, and is supplemented by an index (*Registerband*) issued separately (Leipzig, 1932). [**4741**

Jahresberichte der deutschen Geschichte, 1918–1924 (Breslau, 1920–26, 7 v.), comp. by Victor Loewe and others. [**4742**

Jahresberichte für deutsche Geschichte, 1925–, comp. by Albert Brachmann and Fritz Hartung (Leipzig, 1927–), supersedes no. 4742 above. [**4743**

Great Britain

Cambridge modern history (Cambridge, Eng., 1902–12, 13 v.) has useful bibliographies in each volume. [**4744**

Cannon, H. L., *Reading references for English history* (Boston, 1910), a selected list of references to English history, arranged chronologically; with author and subject index. [**4745**

Morgan, W. T., *Guide to the study of English history* (N.Y., 1926), a syllabus for college classes, with lists of readings at end of each chapter. [**4746**

Hungary [6]

Kont, Ignace, *Bibliographie française de la Hongrie, 1521–1910, avec un inventaire sommaire des documents manuscrits* (Paris, 1913), and *Supplément*, by A. Laval (Budapest, 1914). [**4747**

Italy

Annuario bibliografico della storia d'Italia, 1902– (Pisa and Pavia, 1903–), supplement to *Studi storici*, v. XI–XVIII. [**4748**

Calvi, Emilio, *Biblioteca di bibliografia storica italiana; catalogo tripartito delle bibliografia finora publicate sulla storia generale e particolare d'Italia* (Rome, 1903), and *Supplemento, 1903–1906* (Rome, 1907), reprinted from *Rivista delle biblioteche*, XVII (1906) 129–143; contains printed works, MSS. and documents, and statutes. [**4749**

The Netherlands

Fruin, Robert, and others, *Reportorium der verhandelingen en bijdragen, betreffende de geschiedenis des vaderlands, in mengelwerken en tijdschriften tot op 1860 verschenen* (Leyden, 1863; supplements, 1872, 1884, and 1893), a revised and enlarged edition

---

[6] See also under Austria, above.

incorporating all the material in the 1st edition and its 3 supplements, by L. D. Petit, was issued in 5 parts, 1905–07. Continued by supplementary volumes, under the editorship of H. J. A. Ruys (Leyden, 1913–33, 3 v.), covering the years 1901–1919. This is a useful index to the historical material appearing in periodicals.

[4750

Nijhoff, Martinus (Firm of), *Bibliotheca historiconeerlandica. Histoire des Pays-Bas; catalogue systematique de livres anciens et modernes en vente aux pris marqués chez Martinus Nijhoff* (The Hague, 1899), a trade bibliography which is of value as a historical bibliography.

[4751

Norway

Munthe, Wilhelm, and others, *Bibliografi til Norges historie*, 1916– (Oslo, 1917–), issued as supplements to the current numbers of the *Historisk tidsskrift* (no. 4902), of which separate numbers were compiled by Wilhelm Munthe, Leiv Amundsen, Jonas Hauer, and Reidar Omang.

[4752

Poland

Finkel, Ludwik, *Bibliografia historji polskiej* (Crakow, 1891–1914, 3 v. in 7 pts.), with supplements (1914–).

[4753

Portugal

Figanière, J. C. de, *Bibliographia historica portuguesa, ou Catalogo methodico dos auctores portuguezas, e de alguns estrangeiros domiciliarios em Portugal, que tractares da historie civil, politica e ecclesiastica d'estes reinos e seus dominios* (Lisbon, 1850).

[4754

Russia [7]

Kerner, R. J., *Slavic Europe; a selected bibliography in the western European languages comprising history, languages and literature* (Cambridge, Mass., 1918), a classified bibliography containing 4520 entries, and divided into 6 large parts: (1) Slavs (general); (2) The Russians; (3) The Poles; (4) The Slavs in Germany; (5) The Bohemians; (6) The southern Slavs (Serbs, Croats, and Slovenes) and other Balkan Slavs (Macedonians).

[4755

---

[7] For a helpful (brief) summary of Russian and other Slavic (Polish, Bohemian, Slovak, and southern Slav) historical bibliographies, see R. J. Kerner, "The foundations of Slavic bibliography", *Bibliog. soc. Am. pap.*, X. no. 1 (1916) 3–39 [4756].

Kornilov, Aleksander, *Modern Russian history* (N.Y., 1924) contains a " Bibliography ", by G. T. Robinson.   [4757

Spain

Ballester y Castell, Rafael, *Bibliografía de la historia de España; catálogo metódico y cronológico de las fuentes y obras principales relativos a la historia de España desde los orígines hasta nuestros días* (Gerona and Barcelona, 1921), a useful classified bibliography, but practically ends with the close of the 18th century.   [4758

Sánchez Alonso, Benito, *Fuentes de la historia española e hispanoamericana; ensayo de bibliografía sistemática de impresos y manuscritos que ilustran la historia política de España y sus antiquas provincias de ultramar*, 2d ed., rev. y ampliada (Madrid, 1927, 2 v. in 1), a catalogue of printed sources and monographs, classified by periods, also the principal manuscript sources; the most useful work for Spanish historical research. It is weak on publications in the United States. It may be supplemented by the current bibliographies in the *Revista de archivos* (no. 4904), and the *Revista de filología española* (no. 4760 below).   [4759

Revista de filología española (Madrid, 1914–) prints in each number a comprehensive bibliography of publications relating to Spanish and Spanish American literature, history, etc.   [4760

University of California. *Spain and Spanish America in the libraries of the University of California* (no. 4685).

Sweden

Setterwall, Kristian, *Svenska historisk bibliografi, 1875 [–1920]; systematisk förteckning öfver skrifter och uppsatser som röra Sveriges historia utkomna fran och med 1875 till och med 1920* (Stockholm, 1907; Uppsala, 1923, 2 v.), the best bibliography of recent literature on the history of Sweden; supplemented by annual lists in the *Svenska hist. tidskrift* (no. 4906).   [4761

Switzerland

Brandstetter, J. L., *Repertorium über die in Zeit und Sammelschriften der Jahre 1812–1890 enthaltenen Aufsätze und Mitteilungen schweizergeschichtlichen Inhaltes* (Basel, 1892), a closely classified list, with author index, and including a section on biography.   [4762

Barth, Hans, *Repertorium über die in Zeit- und Sammelschriften der Jahre 1891–1900 enthaltenen Aufsätze und Mitteilungen Schweizergeschichtlichen Inhaltes* (Basel, 1906), a continuation of Brandstetter's *Repertorium* (no. 4762).   [4763

Barth, Hans, *Bibliographie der Schweizer Geschichte enthaltend die selbständig erschienen Druckwerbe zur Geschichte der Schweiz bis Ende 1912 [–1913]* (Basel, 1914–15, 3 v.), comprehensive bibliography of Swiss history, comprising books only (for articles in periodicals, see *Repertorium* (nos. 4762–4763)).   [4764

Bibliographie der Schweizer-Geschichte, 1913–19, issued as a supplement to the *Anzeiger für schweizerische Geschichte* (Berne, 1914–20); since 1920 as a supplement to the *Zeitschrift für schweizerische Geschichte* (Zurich, 1921–).   [4765

Asia

GENERAL

Orientalische Bibliographie, 1–25 Bd., 1897–1911 (Berlin, 1887–1922, 25 v.), a comprehensive annual bibliography, each issue of which contains a section on the history of Asiatic countries; it is preceded by Zenker's *Bibliotheca orientalis*, 1846–61, *Wissenschaftlicher Jahresbericht über die morgenländischen Studien*, 1859–81, Friederici, *Bibliotheca orientalis*, 1876–83, and *Literaturblatt für orientalische Philologie*, 1883–86.   [4766

Robertson, J. A., *The Far East, with special reference to China, its culture, civilization and history* (Chapel Hill, N.C., 1931), an outline for individual and group study, with useful bibliographical surveys of publications now in print, in regard to China, Japan, Korea, and other regions of the Far East.   [4767

China

Maspero, Henri, " Chine et Asie centrale ", in *Histoire et historiens* (no. 4627), v. II, 517–559, gives a survey of the material produced in China and Central Asia during the past half century.   [4768

Cordier, Henri, *Bibliotheca sinica; dictionnaire bibliographique des ouvrages relatifs à l'Empire chinois*, 2d ed., rev. and enl. (Paris, 1904–08, 4 v.), a closely classified bibliography, containing a valuable section on historical works relating to China.   [4769

Latourette, K. S., " Chinese historical studies during the past seven years ", *Am. hist. rev.*, XXVI (1921) 705–716, is a survey of works relating to Chinese history during the seven years prior to 1901, forming a valuable aid to research in this field; and his " Chinese historical studies during the past nine years ", *ibid.*, XXXV (1930) 778–797, continues the survey, for the subsequent years.　　[4770

Swingle, W. T., " Chinese historical sources ", *Am. hist. rev.*, XXVI (1921) 717–723, is a useful summary of printed and unprinted records, including documents and collections of historical works.
　　[4771

Hummel, A. W., " What Chinese historians are doing in their own history ", *Am. hist. rev.*, XXXIV (1929) 715–724, a valuable account.　　[4772

North China Union Language School. *Books on China* (Peiping, China, 1931), a useful classified catalogue of western books on China (including exterritoriality, foreign relations and history) in the library of the North China Union Language School at Peiping.
　　[4773

National Library of Peiping, *Quarterly bulletin of Chinese bibliography* (Peiping, China, 1934–　), ed. by Dr. T. K. Koo, of the National Library of Peiping, in a Chinese, and English, and a " combined " edition.　　[4773a

Japan

Wenckstern, Friedrich von, *A bibliography of the Japanese Empire; being a classified list of all books, essays, and maps in European languages relating to Dai Nihon (Great Japan) published in Europe, America, and in the East*, from 1859 to 1906 (Leyden, 1895, and Tokyo, 1907, 2 v.), closely classified, with author and title index.　　[4774

Cordier, Henri, *Bibliotheca japonica; dictionnaire bibliographique des ouvrages relatifs à l'Empire japonais rangés par ordre chronologique jusqu'à 1870, suivi d'un appendice renfermant la liste alphabétique des principaux ouvrages parus de 1870 à 1912* (Paris, 1912).　　[4775

Elisseev, Serge, " Japon ", in *Histoire et historiens* (no. 4627), v. II, 560–579, gives a brief survey of the material produced in Japan during the past half century.　　[4776

Nachod, Oskar, *Bibliography of the Japanese Empire, 1906–1926; being a classified list of the literature issued in European languages since the publication of Fr. von Wenckstern's " Bibliography of the Japanese Empire ", up to the year 1926* (London and Leipzig, 1928, 2 v.), issued in German. It contains 9526 entries.   [4777

2. General Histories

A. General Histories of the United States

Bancroft, George, *A history of the United States from the discovery of the American continent* (Boston, 1834–75, 10 v.; varied imprints and numerous editions), foreign relations meagerly based on the author's extensive transcripts from European archives.
[4778

Hildreth, Richard, *The history of the United States of America* (N.Y., 1856–60, 6 v.), extends only to the end of the 16th Congress, 1821; a valuable factual narrative, undocumented.   [4779

Holst, Hermann von, *The constitutional and political history of the United States*, by H. von Holst, tr. from the German by J. J. Lalor (Chicago, 1881–92, 8 v.), a constitutional history woven about the slavery question.   [4780

McMaster, J. B., *History of the people of the United States from the revolution to the civil war* [8] (N.Y., 1883–1913, 8 v.), a voluminous work which is increasingly more scholarly in successive volumes, relying at first perhaps too heavily on newspaper sources. [4781

Winsor, Justin, *Narrative and critical history of America* (Boston and N.Y., 1884–89, 8 v.), v. VII: *The United States;* most of the articles are followed by a critical essay on the sources of information, and notes. This is a cooperative history under the editorship of Justin Winsor.   [4782

Rhodes, J. F., *History of the United States from the compromise of 1850* [9] (N.Y. and London, 1900–28, 9 v.; issued in several editions), really exclusively a careful narration of the rise of the slavery question, the civil war, and reconstruction after that conflict.

[4783

Channing, Edward, *A history of the United States* [10] (N.Y., 1905–25, 6 v.); supplementary volume: *General index*, comp. by Eva G.

---

[8] See W. T. Hutchinson, " John Bach McMaster, historian of the American people ", *Miss. Valley hist. rev.*, XVI (1929) 23–49.

[9] See L. B. Shippee, " Rhodes's History of the United States ", *Miss. Valley hist. rev.*, VIII (1921) 133–148; and W. W. Stephenson, " Mr. Rhodes as historian ", *Yale rev.*, n.s. X (1921) 860–865.

[10] See R. R. Fahrney, " Edward Channing ", *Miss. Valley hist. rev.*, XVIII (1931) 53–59.

Moore (N.Y., 1932), the only one man history from 1492, it is today
the most comprehensive and best; stops at 1865.   [4784
Oberholtzer, E. P., *A history of the United States since the civil
war* (N.Y., 1917-31, 4 v.) continues McMaster in style and character.   [4785

B. Manuals on the History of American Diplomacy

The general histories of the United States and other countries are
sufficiently indicated in the *Guide hist. lit.* (no. 4634). There is at
present no adequate comprehensive diplomatic history of the United
States.[11] There are a number of short surveys and textbooks, and
one general study in the form of a particular biographical series:
Schuyler, Eugene, *American diplomacy and the furtherance of commerce* (N.Y., 1886).   [4786
Snow, Freeman, *Treaties and topics in American diplomacy* (Boston,
1894) contains texts of important treaties with numerous quotations from well-known state papers.   [4787
Hart, A. B., *The foundations of American foreign policy; with a
working bibliography* (N.Y. and London, 1901), a textbook for
college use; now out of date. The bibliography was also published in the *Am. hist. rev.*, VI (1901) 848-866, as "A trial bibliography of American diplomacy."   [4788
Foster, J. W., *A century of American diplomacy; being a brief review of the foreign relations of the United States, 1776-1876*
(Boston and N.Y., 1900), superseded by later works.   [4789
García Merou, Martín, *Historia de la diplomacia americana; política
internacional de los Estados Unidos* (Buenos Aires, 1904, 2 v.),
the author was Argentine minister to the United States, 1896-99,
1901-04.   [4790
Fish, C. R., *American diplomacy* (N.Y., 1915; 5th ed., 1929), a textbook for college use; in this fifth edition the text has been revised,
particularly that following the world war, and the bibliographical
references extended to include material brought out since the 4th
edition in 1923. Gives a broad synthesis brilliantly written, but
it is meager in its account of American diplomacy since 1914.
          [4791

---

[11] For Mr. Justice J. B. Moore's monumental digests of *International law, International arbitrations, International adjudications,* which range in their special ways over
the whole field of American diplomacy, see nos. 5364, 5365, 5367.

Johnson, W. F., *America's foreign relations* (N.Y., 1916, 2 v.), a readable popular account, not altogether reliable as to some details.   [4792

Moore, J. B., *The principles of American diplomacy* (N.Y. and London, 1918) incorporates substantially the entire text, with few alterations or amendments, of the volume published by the author in 1905, under the title, *American diplomacy; its spirit and achievements*, and brings the history of that policy down to date. A study of general principles illustrated by particular topics.
                                                                    [4793

Hill, C. E., *Leading American treaties* (N.Y., 1922) gives the historical setting and chief provisions of fifteen of the leading American treaties from the treaties with France, 1778, to the Panama Canal treaties.   [4794

Adams, R. G., *A history of the foreign policy of the United States* (N.Y., 1924), too rapidly executed.   [4795

The American secretaries of state and their diplomacy, S. F. Bemis, editor; J. F. Jameson, H. B. Learned, J. B. Scott, advisory board (N.Y., 1927–29, 10 v.) consists of historical sketches by a number of writers of the different secretaries of state and analyses of their diplomacy, from R. R. Livingston, secretary for foreign affairs of the Continental Congress, 1781 to 1783, through the secretaryship of Charles Evans Hughes, 1921 to 1925.   Though this series ranges through the whole diplomatic history of the United States and contains important contributions on that subject, it is not designed as a synthetic comprehensive history.   The sketches are of uneven value.   We note below the contents.   [4796

Vol. I: J. B. Scott, *Historical introduction*.   M. L. Bonham, jr., *Robert R. Livingston, secretary for foreign affairs of the Continental Congress, 1781–1783*.   S. F. Bemis, *John Jay, secretary for foreign affairs of the Continental Congress, 1784–1790*.

Vol. II: S. F. Bemis, *Thomas Jefferson, 1790–1793*.   D. R. Anderson, *Edmund Randolph, 1794–1795*.   A. J. Montague, *John Marshall, 1800–1801*.

Vol. III: C. E. Hill, *James Madison, 1801–1809*.   C. C. Tansill, *Robert Smith, 1809–1811*.   J. W. Pratt, *James Monroe, 1811–1817*.

Vol. IV: Dexter Perkins, *John Quincy Adams, 1817–1825*. T. E. Burton, *Henry Clay, 1825–1829*.   J. S. Bassett, *Martin Van*

Buren, 1829–1831. Francis Rawle, *Edward Livingston, 1831–1833.* E. I. McCormac, *Louis McLane, 1833–1834;* and *John Forsyth, 1834–1837.*

Vol. V: C. A. Duniway, *Daniel Webster, 1841–1843.* R. G. Adams, *Abel Parker Upshur, 1843–1844.* St.G. L. Sioussat, *John Caldwell Calhoun, 1844–1845;* and *James Buchanan, 1845–1849.*

Vol. VI: Mary W. Williams, *John Middleton Clayton, 1849–1850.* C. A. Duniway, *Daniel Webster (second term) 1850–1852.* Foster Stearns, *Edward Everett, 1852–1853.* H. B. Learned, *William Learned Marcy, 1853–1857.* Lewis Einstein, *Lewis Cass, 1857–1860.* R. F. Nichols, *Jeremiah Sullivan Black, 1860–1861.*

Vol. VII: H. W. Temple, *William H. Seward, 1861–1869.* J. V. Fuller, *Elihu Benjamin Washburne, 1869;* and *Hamilton Fish, 1869–1877.* C. G. Bowers and Helen D. Reid, *William M. Evarts, 1877–1881.* J. B. Lockey, *James Gillespie Blaine, 1881 (first term).*

Vol. VIII: P. M. Brown, *Frederick Theodore Frelinghuysen, 1881–1885.* L. B. Shippee, *Thomas Francis Bayard, 1885–1889.* J. B. Lockey, *James Gillespie Blaine, 1889–1892 (second term).* W. R. Castle, Jr., *John Watson Foster, 1892–1893.* Montgomery Schuyler, *Richard Olney, 1895–1897.*

Vol. IX: L. M. Sears, *John Sherman, 1897–1898.* L. B. Shippee and Royal B. Way, *William Rufus Day, 1898.* A. L. P. Dennis, *John Hay, 1898–1905.* J. B. Scott, *Elihu Root, 1905–1909;* and *Robert Bacon, 1909.* H. F. Wright, *Philander Chase Knox, 1909–1913.*

Vol. X: *William Jennings Bryan, 1913–1915* (Anon.). J. W. Pratt, *Robert Lansing, 1915–1920.* John Spargo, *Bainbridge Colby, 1920–1921.* C. C. Hyde, *Charles Evans Hughes, 1921–1925.*

Latané, J. H., *A history of American foreign policy* (Garden City, N.Y., 1927), a most readable and rapid account but thin on some phases and weak where knowledge of foreign monographs and sources is demanded. Later edition, revised and enlarged by D. M. Wainhouse (Garden City, N.Y., 1934). [4797

Sears, L. M., *A history of American foreign relations* (N.Y., 1927), a well proportioned account, resting principally on American monographs. [4798

Wriston, H. M., *Executive agents in American foreign relations* (Baltimore and London, 1929), a valuable encyclopedic work covering from this point of view the whole diplomatic history of the United States. See also no. 5328a below. [4799

Jones, R. L., *History of the foreign policy of the United States* (N.Y. and London, 1933), really a text on the history of American diplomacy, has the advantage of devoting more space than former manuals to events since 1898. [4800

C. American Foreign Policy and Conduct of Foreign Relations [12]

Olney, Richard, " Growth of the foreign policy of the United States," *Atlantic,* LXXXV (1900) 289–301. [4801

Jones, C. L., *The consular service* [13] *of the United States, its history and activities* (Phila., 1906), a methodical historical and juridical analysis. [4802

Foster, J. W., *The practice of diplomacy; as illustrated in the foreign relations of the United States* (Boston and N.Y., 1906), intended " primarily to set forth the part taken by American diplomatists in the elevation and purification of diplomacy; and, secondarily, to give in popular form, . . . the rules and procedure of diplomatic intercourse." [4803

Bigelow, John, *American policy; the western hemisphere in its relation to the eastern* (N.Y., 1914) deals with American policies in their broader aspects, with political problems of the United States and of all America. [4804

Balch, T. W., " The United States and the expansion of the law between nations ", *Univ. of Penn. law rev.,* LXIV (1915) 113–140. [4805

Gibbons, H. A., " The evolution of the foreign policy of the United States since the Spanish American war ", *New world,* I (1919) 119–134. [4806

Carnegie Endowment for International Peace. Division of Intercourse and Education. *American foreign policy, based upon statements of presidents, secretaries of state of the United States, and of publicists of the American republics,* 2d ed. (Wash., 1920). [4807

---

[12] For a bibliography of a special phase of American foreign policy, see A. P. C. Griffin, *List of references on recognition in international law and practice* (Wash., 1904) (Library of Congress) [4800a].

[13] For bibliography, see A. P. C. Griffin, *List of references on the United States consular service* (Wash. 1905) (Library of Congress) [4802a].

Martin, C. E., *The policy of the United States as regards intervention* (N.Y., 1921) deals with the formation and development of the policy of nonintervention and departures from that policy.   [4808

Wright, Quincy, *The control of American foreign relations* (N.Y., 1922), based on the sources (court reports, acts of Congress, treaties, presidential messages, diplomatic correspondence, congressional debates, reports, and documents).   [4809

Hyde, C. C., *International law chiefly as interpreted and applied by the United States* (Boston, 1922, 2 v.).   [4810

Blakeslee, George H., *The recent foreign policy of the United States; problems in American cooperation with other powers* (N.Y., 1925), one of the best broad interpretations of our relations (1) with Europe, (2) with the Orient, and (3) with Hispanic America.   [4811

Culbertson, W. S., *International economic policies; a survey of the economics of diplomacy* (N.Y., 1925).   [4811a

Dealey, J. Q., *Foreign policies of the United States; their bases and development* (Boston and N.Y., 1926).   [4812

Kellogg, F. B., *Some foreign policies of the United States* (N.Y., 1926), an address delivered before the Council of Foreign Relations, at New York City, Dec. 14, 1925; also his *Some objectives of American foreign policy* (Wash., 1926), an address delivered before the Associated Press, April 20, 1926.   [4813

Carter, John, *Conquest; America's painless imperialism* (N.Y., 1928).   [4814

Cole, Taylor, *The recognition policy of the United States since 1901* (Baton Rouge, 1928), an academic exercise based on Moore's *Digest, For. relations*, etc.; has a section of value on President Wilson's policy of recognition.   [4815

Donaldson, John, *International economic relations* (N.Y., 1928).   [4816

Garner, J. W., *American foreign policies; an examination and evaluation of certain traditional and recent international policies of the United States* (N.Y., 1928), an American professor leans over backward trying to be fair-minded to foreign countries about various phases of the foreign policy of the United States, including the Monroe Doctrine.   [4817

Mathews, J. M., *American foreign relations, conduct, and policies* (N.Y. and London, 1928) incorporates (for the most part) his earlier book (1922) on the *Conduct of American foreign relations*, and adds a general survey of the formation and content of the principal American foreign policies that are of present importance.   [4818

Offutt, Milton, *The protection of citizens abroad by the armed forces of the United States* (Baltimore, 1928).   [4819

Williams, B. J., *Economic foreign policy of the United States* (N.Y., 1929), brief historical account and exposition of the diplomacy of investment and of commerce.   [4820

Wright, Quincy, ed., *Interpretations of American foreign policy* (Chicago, 1930) consists of 5 lectures on various phases of American foreign policy, including G. H. Blakeslee, " The foreign policy of the United States ", advancing the thesis that the fundamental policies are clear-cut and have been maintained, in the main, with exceptional consistency.   [4821

Morrow, R. L., " The early American attitude toward the doctrine of expatriation ", *Am. jour. internat. law*, XXVI (1932) 552–564.

[4822

Beard, C. A., *The idea of national interest; an analytical study of American foreign policy* (N.Y., 1934), a stimulating and provoking historical inquiry into the meaning of national interests of the United States, which the author shows to have been a fluctuating group of special private interests with little relationship to the common weal. He selects historical facts in an effort to prove that the Federalist-Whig-Republican political power has sought to advance special industrial interests, by thrusts from the homeland; and that the agrarian Democratic party power has more prudently resisted this. The latter thesis will not hold water for the period before the civil war, but the general argument of the book cannot be overlooked. *The open door at home* (N.Y., 1934), the author's maturely-formulated opinion as to a proper policy for foreign and domestic affairs, calculated to secure the defense of the continental homeland only, with foreign relations limited principally to an exchange of goods fitting into a planned economy.

[4823

Savelle, Max, " Colonial origins of American diplomatic principles ", *Pacific hist. rev.*, III (1934) 334–350, the author seeks to find in colonial expressions, and occasional official colonial action, prece-

dents for some of the later guiding principles of foreign policy
of the United States. [4824

D. Treaty-Making Power [14]

Butler, C. H., *The treaty making power of the United States* (N.Y.,
1902, 2 v.), a comprehensive exposition and analysis of every
phase, extensively documented; Pt. 2 (v. I, 110-318) : " Historical
review of the treaty-making power of the United States." [4825

Crandall, S. B., *Treaties; their making and enforcement* (N.Y., 1904;
2d ed., rev. and enl., 1916) deals with treaties of the United
States and of foreign countries; an historical treatment of the
subject, based on extensive research in both published and unpublished sources. [4826

Moore, J. B., " Treaties and executive agreements ", *Pol. sci. quar.*,
XX (1905) 385-420. [4827

Corwin, E. S., *National supremacy; treaty power vs. state power*
(N.Y., 1913) ; and *The President's control of foreign relations*
(Princeton, 1917). [4828

Tucker, H. S., *Limitations on the treaty-making power under the
Constitution of the United States* (Boston, 1915) seeks to eliminate
the prevalent error of the " unlimited " scope of this power.
[4829

Griffin, A. P. C., *Ratification of treaties; methods and procedure in
foreign countries relative to the ratification of treaties, also extracts from the executive journal of the Senate relative to proceedings in cases of treaties rejected by the Senate* (Wash., 1919)
(66th Cong., 1st sess. Senate Doc. 26). [4830

*Treaty reservations. A compilation of reservations made to treaties
and conventions by the Senate of the United States* (Wash., 1919)
(66th Cong. 1st sess. Sen. Doc. no. 148). [4831

Hayden, Ralston, *The Senate and treaties, 1789-1817* (N.Y., 1920)
treats of the development of the treaty-making functions of the
United States Senate during their formative period. [4832

Stone, I. M., " The House of Representatives and the treaty-making
power ", *Ky. law jour.*, XVII (1929) 216-257, certain general and
historical considerations. [4833

---

[14] For bibliography, see H. H. B. Meyer, *List of references on the treaty-making power*
(Wash., 1920) (Library of Congress) [4824a], dealing with the treaty-making power in
foreign states (particularly Great Britain), and in the United States.

Fleming, D. F., *The treaty veto of the American Senate* (N.Y. and London, 1930), the author, convinced that the unique Senate veto of the United States is unfortunate, particularly in the rejection of treaties for the organization of peace, makes this pioneer study into the historical background in order to establish his point. [4834

McClendon, R. E., " Origin of the two-thirds rule in Senate action upon treaties ", *Am. hist. rev.*, XXXVI (1931) 768–772; and " The two-thirds rule in Senate action upon treaties, 1789–1901 ", *Am. jour. internat. law*, XXVI (1932) 37–56, examines treaties which have been defeated by the $\frac{2}{3}$ requirement, and concludes (as does Dangerfield (no. 4836)) that it has played a minor part; but see Holt, *Treaties defeated* (no. 4837). [4835

Dangerfield, R. J., *In defense of the Senate; a study in treaty making* (Norman, Okla., 1933), a systematic analysis of the effect of the Senate's participation in the ratification of treaties, measuring quantitatively the effect of the Senate's action in dealing with treaties from 1778–1928. [4836

Holt, W. S., *Treaties defeated by the Senate; a struggle between the President and Senate over the conduct of foreign relations* (Baltimore, 1933), a careful and luminous historical analysis, based on documentary study, of the reasons for the defeat of those treaties which the Senate has rejected. [4837

3. Historical Journals and Publications of Learned Societies [15]

For bibliographical lists of historical periodicals see the following: [16]

Griffin, A. P. C., *Bibliography of American hist. societies* (no. 4658).

---

[15] For general periodicals, see p. 730, below. We include here periodicals dealing with international affairs, and a few devoted to political science, as well as the strictly historical journals.

[16] For guides to the historical material published by historical societies in the United States and abroad see: *Handbook of American historical societies,* prepared by the Committee on Handbook of the Conference of Historical Societies (Madison, 1926), giving brief data regarding the history, activities, and publications of the societies [4838]. " Guide to the historical publications of the societies of England and Wales; supplement[s] : 1929 [–1930] ", *Inst. hist. research bul.*, supplements nos. 1–2 (Nov. 1930 and 1931) 47, 45 p., which aims to include all publications in the English language issued by societies in England and Wales and bearing on the history and archeology of the English and Welch peoples (the supplements have been issued prior to the *Guide* itself) [4839]. " Canadian historical societies ", *Canad. hist. rev.*, XII (1931) 356–363, giving a list of Canadian historical societies, with short notes indicating the scope and nature of their activities [4840].

Stock, L. F., *List of American journals devoted to the humanistic and social sciences* (Wash., 1928), reprinted from the *Bulletin* of the American Council of Learned Societies, no. 8, October 1928; and *A list of American periodicals and serial publications in the humanities and social sciences* (Wash., 1934) (American Council of Learned Societies, Bulletin no. 21). [4841

Enquête pour l'orientation des recherches dans la bibliographie historique (no. 4653).

Ker, Annita M., *A survey of Mexican scientific periodicals* (Baltimore, 1931) includes a "Bibliography of Mexican periodicals" and a list of "Historical periodicals." [4842

Ulrich, Carolyn F., *Periodicals directory: a classified guide to a selected list of current periodicals, foreign and domestic* (N.Y., 1932–), for list of leading periodicals dealing with history, international relations, etc. [4843

We list below the most important for our subject (arranged by countries) and include the most significant (for our purpose) of those regional historical periodicals published in the United States which frequently contain material dealing with international relations (such, among others, as colonial border rivalries and boundary disputes of the national period).[17]

United States: General

Of the earlier periodicals the most valuable for its historical material is *Niles' weekly register* (title varies) (Baltimore, 1811–1849, 76 v.). [4844

American Historical Association, *Annual report*, 1885– (N.Y., 1885–89; Wash., 1890–). [4845

American historical review (N.Y., 1895–) prints in each number reviews of books on general, modern European, and American history, and notices of recent publications appearing in historical journals and publications of societies. [4846

American journal of international law, pub. for the American Society of International Law (N.Y., 1907–), and *Supplements* comprising official documents and contemporary diplomatic correspondence. [4847

---

[17] Do not overlook, when they exist, the cumulated indexes to these journals. They constitute useful bibliographical aids to the material for the particular subjects treated.

American political science review, 1906– (Baltimore, 1907–) publishes currently a list of documents of the United States and foreign countries recently issued.   [4848

Current history, pub. by the New York Times Company (N.Y., 1915–).   [4849

Foreign affairs; an American quarterly review (N.Y., 1922–), giving in each number useful bibliographical lists of recent books on international relations in English and foreign languages and lists of public documents officially printed, and other source material on the same subject.   [4850

Hispanic American historical review (Baltimore, 1918–22; Durham, N.C., 1926–).   [4851

Journal of economic and business history (Cambridge, Mass., 1928–1932).   [4851a

Journal of modern history, pub. by the University of Chicago (Chicago, 1929–).   [4852

Political science quarterly, a review devoted to the historical, statistical, and comparative study of politics, economics, and public law (Boston and N.Y., 1886–).   [4853

There are also in the United States numerous regional historical reviews, the contents of which are regularly listed in the *American historical review*. These frequently contain valuable articles on diplomatic history.[18] We list below those most pertinent to our subject.

United States: Regional

California Historical Society, Quarterly of the (San Francisco, 1922–).   [4854

Florida Historical Society quarterly (Jacksonville, 1917–),   [4855
Georgia historical quarterly (Savannah, 1917–).   [4855a

Massachusetts Historical Society, Proceedings of the, 1791– (Boston, 1859–).   [4856

Mississippi Valley historical review (Lincoln, Neb., pub. by Mississippi Valley Historical Association (Lincoln, Neb., 1914–).
                                                                  [4857

---

[18] For example: T. M. Marshall, "Diplomatic relations of Texas and the United States, 1839–1843", *Tex. hist. assoc. quar.*, XV (1912) 267–293; T. C. Elliott, "The surrender of Astoria", *Ore. hist. soc. quar.*, XIX (1918) 271–282; Annie Middleton, "Donelson's mission to Texas in behalf of annexation", *Southw. hist. quar.*, XXIV (1921) 247–291; Henry Commager, "England and the Oregon treaty, 1846", *Ore. hist. quar.*, XXVIII (1927) 18–38; and W. P. Cresson, "Francis Dana; an early envoy of trade", *New Eng. quar.*, III (1930) 717–735.

New England quarterly (Cambridge, Mass., 1928–).   [4858
North Carolina historical review (Raleigh, N.C., 1924–).   [4859
Oregon historical quarterly, pub. by the Oregon Historical Society (Eugene, Oreg., 1900–).   [4860
Pacific historical review, issued quarterly by the Pacific Coast Branch of the American Historical Association (Glendale, Calif., 1932–).   [4861
Southwestern historical quarterly (Austin, Tex., 1897–), formerly *Quarterly of the Texas State Historical Association*, still published by the same association.   [4862

Canada

Canadian historical review (Toronto, 1920–), continuing the *Review of historical publications relating to Canada*.   [4863

Hispanic America [19]

Argentine Republic

Boletín del Instituto de Investigaciones Históricas (Buenos Aires, 1922–).   [4864

Brazil

Revista do Instituto Historico e Geographico Brasileiro (Rio de Janeiro, 1839–).   [4865

Chile

Revista chilena de historia y geografía (Santiago de Chile, 1912–).   [4866

Colombia

Boletín de historia y antigüedades; organo de la Academia Colombiana de Historia (Bogotá, 1902–).   [4867

Cuba

Anales de la Academia de la Historia (Havana, 1919–), published annually.   [4868

Ecuador

Boletín de la Academia Nacional de Historia (Quito, Ecuador, 1920–), formerly the *Boletín de la Sociedad Ecuatorial de Estudios Históricos.* (1918–1920).   [4869

[19] For bibliographical list of Hispanic American periodicals, see *Catalogue of newspapers and magazines in the Columbus Memorial Library of the Pan American Union* (no. 5037).

Peru

Revista del archivo nacional del Perú (Lima, 1920–).   [4870

Porto Rico

Boletín histórico de Puerto Rico (San Juan, 1914–).   [4871

Uruguay

Revista del Instituto Histórico y Geográfico del Uruguay (Montevideo, 1920–).   [4872

Venezuela

Boletín de la Academia Nacional de la Historia (Caracas, 1912–).   [4873

Europe [20]

Belgium

Revue de droit international et de législation comparée (Brussels, 1869–1925).   [4874

Denmark

Historisk tidsskrift, udgivet af den Danske Historiske Forening (Copenhagen, 1840– (in progress)).   [4875

France

Académie Diplomatique Internationale, Séances et travaux (Paris, 1930–).   [4876
Affaires étrangères (Paris, 1931–).   [4877
Questions diplomatiques et coloniales (Paris, 1897–1914).   [4878
Revue d'histoire diplomatique, publiée par les soins de la Société d'Histoire Diplomatique (Paris, 1887– (in progress)), the sole journal exclusively devoted to diplomatic history.   [4879
Revue d'histoire moderne, publié par la Société d'Histoire Moderne (Paris, 1926–).   [4880
Revue de droit international, 1927– (Paris, 1927–).   [4881
Revue des études historiques, Société des Etudes Historiques (Paris, 1834– (in progress)).   [4882

---

[20] For further lists of European and Asiatic historical periodicals the reader is referred to the *Guide to historical literature* (no. 4634) under the separate countries. " Publicazioni periodiche italiane viventi che contengono notizie bibliografiche riguardanti la storia d'Italia ", International Committee of Historical Sciences, *Bulletin*, I, pt. 2 (1927) 238–246, lists Italian historical periodicals.

Revue des questions historiques (Paris, 1866– (in progress)).
[4883

Revue générale de droit international public (Paris, 1894– (in progress)).   [4884

Revue historique (Paris, 1876– (in progress)).   [4885

Revue politique internationale (Paris and Lausanne, 1914– (in progress)).   [4886

Germany

Archiv für Politik und Geschichte (Berlin, 1923–).   [4887

Europäische Gespräche; Monatshefte für auswärtige Politik (Hamburg, 1923–), publishes currently a list of publications on politics and international relations, particularly useful for its foreign titles.   [4888

Historisches Jahrbuch (Münster and Munich, 1880– (in progress)).
[4889

Historische Vierteljahrschrift (Leipzig, 1898–), a continuation of the *Deutsche Zeitschrift für Geschichtswissenschaft* (Freiburg, 1889–98).   [4890

Historische Zeitschrift (Munich, 1859– (in progress)).   [4891

Zeitschrift für Völkerrecht, 1906– (Breslau, 1907–).   [4892

Great Britain

Bulletin of the Institute of Historical Research, 1923– (London, 1925–).   [4893

Cambridge historical journal (Cambridge, Eng., 1923–).   [4894

English historical review (London, 1886– (in progress)).   [4895

International affairs, pub. by Royal Institute of International Affairs (London, 1931–), formerly *Journal of the Royal Institute of International Affairs* (1922–30).   [4896

Political quarterly, 1930– (London, 1930–).   [4897

Royal Historical Society, Transactions (London, 1872– (in progress)).   [4898

Italy

Archivio storico italiano (Florence, 1842– (in progress)).   [4899

Rivista storica italiana (Turin, 1884– (in progress)).   [4900

The Netherlands

Tijdschrift voor geschiedenis, land- en volkenkunde (Amsterdam and Groningen, 1886– (in progress)).   [4901

Norway

Historisk tidskrift, udgivet af den Norske Historiske Forening (Christiana (Oslo), 1871– (in progress)).   [4902

Roumania

Revue historique du Sud-Est européen (Bucharest, 1924–).   [4903

Spain

Revista de archivos, bibliotecas y museos (Madrid, 1871– (in progress)).   [4904

Real Academia de la Historia, Boletín (Madrid, 1877– (in progress)), now the *Boletín* of the "Academia de la Historia ", without the " Real."   [4905

Sweden

Historisk tidskrift, utgifven af Svenska Historiska Föreningen (Stockholm, 1881– (in progress)).   [4906

Switzerland

Revue de droit international de sciences diplomatiques et politiques, organe à l'International Law Association (Geneva, 1923–).   [4907

Zeitschrift für Schweizerische Geschichte, hrsg. von der Allgemeinen Geschichtsforschenden Gesellschaft der Schweiz (Zürich, 1921–), continues the *Anzeiger für Schweizerische Geschichte.*   [4908

Pacific Area

Pacific affairs, pub. monthly at Honolulu by the International Secretariat of the Institute of Pacific Relations, May 1928–.   [4909

China [21]

T'oung Pao, ou Archives concernant l'histoire, les langues, la géographie, l'éthnographie et les arts de l'Asie orientale, 1890– (Leyden, 1890–), contains current bibliographical summaries and reviews of new books.   [4910

Journal of the North China branch of the Royal Asiatic Society (Shanghai, 1858–) contains in addition to contributed articles, reviews of recent books on the Far East, particularly China.   [4911

---

[21] Periodicals in the Chinese language containing articles of importance for historical studies are noted in Latourette, *Chinese historical studies* (no. 4770), 705.

Japan

Contemporary Japan; a review of Japanese affairs, pub. by the Foreign Affairs Association of Japan (Tokyo, 1932–).   [4912

Gaiko Jiho (*Revue diplomatique*), published semimonthly (Tokyo, 1905–), entirely in Japanese except for the subtitle " Revue diplomatique."   [4913

4. Biographical Dictionaries [22]

For practically all of the larger countries and some others there are general biographical dictionaries or encyclopedias. The important *Dictionary of American biography* (no. 4927) (now 1934) through the name " Platner ", is the most valuable for American diplomacy.

We list below those of the principal countries with which American diplomatic relations have been most extensive (for others the investigator is referred to Mudge, *Guide* (no. 4617), 209–232, and the *Guide hist. lit.* (no. 4634), which lists such material in a separate section under each country). In presenting this list we give (1) Bibliographies and indexes of biographical material; (2) Universal biographical dictionaries; and (3) Biographical dictionaries limited to persons of a particular nationality, arranged alphabetically by countries.

Bibliographies and Indexes of Biographies

Oettinger, E. M., ed., *Bibliographie biographique; ou, Dictionnaire de 26,000 ouvrages, tant anciens que modernes relatifs à l'histoire de la vie publique et privée des hommes célèbres de tous les temps et de toutes les nations*, 2d ed. (Brussels, 1854, 2 v.), a useful list, giving references to published material regarding eminent persons.   [4914

Phillips, L. B., *Dictionary of biographical reference, . . . together with a classified index of the biographical literature of Europe and America*, new ed., rev., corr. and augm., with supplement to date by Frank Weitenkamp (London and Phila., 1889).   [4915

A conspectus of American biography, being an analytical summary of American history and biography . . . comp. by George Derby (N.Y., 1906) forms a useful dictionary of American biography.   [4916

---

[22] See also the national historical bibliographies (nos. 4654–4777) of the various countries, which invariably list biographical material.

Sears, Minnie E., *Standard catalog; Biography section*, 2d ed., rev. and enl. (N.Y., 1927) contains about 1,150 titles of the most representative biographies, based on the first edition (1,000 titles). [4917

Hefling, Helen, and Eva Richards, *Index to contemporary biography and criticism* (Boston, 1929), in which the compilers have as a rule " chosen books which contain biography and criticism of persons whose birth occurred around the year 1850 or later." [4918

Iguíniz, J. B., *Bibliografía biográfica mexicana*, t. I: *Repertorios biográficos* (Mexico, 1930), a biographical index to 703 selected works relating to Mexico in all fields of literature, including historical publications. [4919

Riches, Phyllis M., *An analytical bibliography of universal collected biography, comprising books published in the English tongue in Great Britain and Ireland, America and the British dominions* (London, 1934) is of value in the search for biographical particulars about various persons including those " of some importance in their own day and in their own special sphere, whose memory is lost in the mist of ages." [4919a

Biography: General

Biographie universelle (Michaud) ancienne et moderne, rev. ed. (Paris, 1854–65, 45 v.), 2nd, rev. and enl. ed. of the work begun by J. F. Michaud and L. G. Michaud and published 1811–62, in 85 v.; the foremost of the large dictionaries of universal biography. [4920

Nouvelle biographie générale . . ., publiée sous le direction de M. le Dr. Hoefer (Paris, 1853–66, 46 v.), which should be used to supplement the *Biographie universelle*. [4921

Vapereau, Gustave, *Dictionnaire universel des contemporains, contenants toutes les personnes notables de la France et des pays étrangers* (Paris, 1893). [4922

Garollo, Gottardo, *Dizionario biografico universale* (Milan, 1907, 2 v.), useful for Italian biographies in particular. [4923

Thomas, Joseph, ed., *[Lippincott's] Universal pronouncing dictionary of biography*, 5th ed. (Phila. and London, 1930). [4924

National Biographies

American

Appleton's cyclopedia of American biography, ed. by J. G. Wilson and John Fiske, rev. ed. (N.Y., 1900, 6 v.), and supplements, v. VII–IX (1900, 1918, 1922).   [**4925**

Biographical directory of the American Congress, 1774–1927 (Wash.: Govt. Print. Off., 1928) includes the Continental Congress, 1774–1788, and the Congress of the United States, 1789–1927.   [**4926**

Dictionary of American biography, ed. by Allen Johnson and Dumas Malone (N.Y., 1928–), produced under the auspices of the American Council of Learned Societies; modeled after the British *Dictionary of national biography*, but superior in scope and scholarship; (to date (1934) it has been carried through v. XIV, " Oglethorpe to Platner." For biographical references we have dovetailed this *Dictionary* by cross references into the bibliographical chapters of this *Guide*.   [**4927**

Canadian

Charlesworth, Hector, *A cyclopaedia of Canadian biography* (Toronto, 1919), containing brief biographies of persons distinguished in the professional, military and political life, and the commerce and industry of Canada in the twentieth century.   [**4928**

Wallace, W. S., *The dictionary of Canadian biography* (Toronto, 1926), the most useful general dictionary of Canadian biography.   [**4929**

Le Jeune, L. (Louis M.), *Dictionnaire général de biographie, histoire, littérature, . . . du Canada* (Ottawa, 1931, 2 v.).   [**4930**

Hispanic American [23]

Cortés, J. D., *Diccionario biográfico americano* (Paris, 1875), though including both Americas is largely devoted to Hispanic American biography.   [**4931**

Aspurúa, Ramón, *Biografías de hombres notables de Hispano-América* (Caracas, 1877, 4 v.).   [**4932–3**

---

[23] For bibliographies of Hispanic American biography, see Jones, *Hisp. Am. bibliographies* (no. 4678), which includes titles of collective biography and bio-bibliography.

Professor P. A. Martin is now getting ready for publication a *Who's who* of Hispanic America.

See also Mudge, *Guide* (no. 4617) for biographical dictionaries of individual Hispanic American nations.

Argentine Republic

Gutiérrez, J. M., *Apuntes biográficos de escritores, oradores y hombres de estado de la República Arjentina* (Buenos Aires, 1860).   [4934

República Argentina, *Album nacional. Galería de hombres públicos de actualidad. Comprendiendo: poder ejecutivo de la nación, parlamento, ejército y armada* (Buenos Aires, 1903).   [4935

Muzzio, J. A., *Diccionario histórico y biográfico de la República Argentina* (Buenos Aires, 1920? 2 v.).   [4936

Brazil

Sisson, S. A., *Galeria dos brasileiros illustres (os contemporaneos); retratos dos homens mais illustres do Brasil, na politica, sciencias e letras desde a guerra da independencia até os nossos dias* (Rio de Janeiro, 1861, 2 v.).   [4937

Dias da Silva, M. F., *Diccionario biographico de brasileiros celebres nas letras, artes, politica, philantropia, guerra, diplomatica . . .* (Rio de Janeiro, 1871).   [4938

Chile

Desmadryl, Narciso, *Galería nacional, o, Colección de biografías y retratos de hombres célebres de Chile* (Santiago de Chile, 1854-61, 2 v.).   [4939

Suárez, J. B., *Rasgos biográficos de hombres notables de Chile* (Santiago de Chile, 1863).   [4940

Amunátegui, M. L., *Ensayos biográficos* (Santiago de Chile, 1893-96, 4 v.).   [4941

Figueroa, P. P., *Diccionario biográfico de Chile*, 4th ed., enl. (Santiago de Chile, 1897-1902, 3 v.).   [4942

Fuenzalida, E. A., *Galería contemporánea de hombres notables de Chile (1850-1901).* Tomo 1. (Valparaiso, 1901), no more published.   [4943

Figueroa, Virgilio, *Diccionario histórico y biográfico de Chile* (Santiago de Chile, 1925- (issued in parts)).   [4944

Colombia

Arboleda, Gustavo, *Historia contemporánea de Colombia* (*desde la disolución de la antigua república de ese nombre hasta la época presente* (Bogotá, 1918) contains much biographical information. [4945

Libro azul de Colombia. Blue book of Colombia. Bosquejos biográficos de los personajes más eminentes (N.Y., 1918), Spanish and English. [4946

Samper, J. M., *Galería nacional de hombres ilustres ó notables; ó sea Colección de bocetos biográficos* (Bogotá, 1879). [4947

Cuba

Calcagno, Francisco, *Diccionario biográfico cubano* (N.Y., 1878), the library of the Sociedad Económica de Amigos del País, Havana, has a copy completed to 1905 by Vidal Morales, prepared for a new edition. [4948

Ecuador

Campos, Francisco, *Galería biográfica de hombres célebres ecuatorianos* (Guayaquil, 1885). [4949

Destruge, Camilo, *Album biográfico ecuatoriano* (Guayaquil, 1903–05, 5 v.). [4950

Arboleda R., Gustavo, *Diccionario biográfico de la República del Ecuador* (Quito, 1910). [4951

Ceballos, P. F., *Ecuatorianos ilustres* (Quito, 1912). [4952

Mexico

Arróniz, Marcos, *Manual de biografía mejicana, o, Galería de hombres célebres de Méjico* (Paris and N.Y., 1857). [4953

Sosa, Francisco, *Biografías de mexicanos distinguidos* (Mexico, 1884) ; and *Efemérides históricas y biográficas* (Mexico, 1883, 2 v.). [4954

Paz, Ireneo, *Los hombres prominentes de México* (Mexico, 1888). [4955

Leduc, Alberto, and L. Lara y Pardo, *Diccionario de geografía, historia y biografía mexicanas* (Mexico, 1910). [4956

Panama

Aguilera, Rodolfo, *Galería de hombres públicos del Istmo* (Panama, 1906). [4957

Peru

Diccionario biográfico del Perú, comp. and ed. by Manuel de Mendiburu; 2d ed., with additions and bibliographical notes by Evaristo San Cristóval (Lima, 1931–33, 6 v.). [4957a

Uruguay

De Marie, Isidro, *Rasgos biográficos de hombres notables de la república oriental del Uruguay* (Montevideo, 1879–80, 3 v.). [4958

Europe [24]

Wurzbach, Constantin von, *Biographisches Lexikon des Kaisertums Oesterreich* (Vienna, 1859–61, 60 v.), containing biographies of the period from 1750 to date of publication. [4959

Neue österreichische Biographie, 1815–19; begrundet von Anton Bettelheim [and others] (Vienna, 1923–31, 8 v.) includes a bibliography of Austrian biography. [4960

Biographie nationale, publiée par l'Académie Royale des Sciences, des Lettres et des Beaux-Arts de Belgique (Brussels, 1866–1932, 25 v. (in progress)). [4961

Dansk biografisk lexikon, tillige omfattende Norge for tidsrummet, 1537–1814 (Copenhagen, 1887–1905, 19 v.), ed. by C. F. Bricka and others; and *Dansk biografisk leksikon* (Copenhagen, 1933–), founded by C. F. Bricka, ed. by Povl Engelstoft, under the direction of Svend Dahl. [4962

Dansk biografisk haandleksikon (Copenhagen, 1920–26, 3 v.), ed. by Svend Dahl and P. Engelstoft. [4963

Finsk biografisk handbok (Helsingfors, 1903, 2 v.). [4964

Dictionnaire de biographie française, sous la direction de J. Balteau, M. Barroux et M. Prevost, avec le concours de nombreux collaborateurs (Paris, 1933–), now (1934) completed through "Amb"; modeled after the *D.N.B.*, contains bibliographical data. [4965

Allgemeine deutsche Biographie (Leipzig, 1875–1912, 56 v.), published under the auspices of the "Historische Commission, Akademie der Wissenschaften" of Munich; contains biographies of

---

[24] Arranged alphabetically by countries.

prominent Germans from the earliest period to the end of the
19th century. [4966
Biographisches Jahrbuch und deutscher Nekrolog, 1896-1913 (Berlin,
1897-1917, 18 v.), ed. by Anton Bettelheim. [4967
Deutsches biographisches Jahrbuch, hrsg. von Verbunde der Deutschen Akademien (Berlin and Leipzig, 1925-), supersedes the
Biographisches Jahrbuch, above. [4968
Dictionary of national biography, ed. by Leslie Stephen and Sidney
Lee [and others] (London, 1885-1901, 66 v.) and supplements
(1904, 1912, and 1927), and a reissue of the first 66 volumes (London, 1908-09, in 22 v.); the foremost reference book on British
biography, containing signed articles and valuable bibliographical
data. For systematic corrections, see files of no. 4893. [4969
Jásznigi, Alexander, and Imre Parlagi, *Das geistige Ungarn, bio-
graphisches Lexikon* (Vienna and Leipzig, 1918, 2 v.). [4970
Szinnyei, József, *Magyar irok* (Budapest, 1891-1914, 14 v.), continued by *Magyar électrajzi lexikon* (Budapest, 1925-). [4971
See also Wurzbach, *Biographisches Lexikon* (no. 4959) which in
cludes Hungarian biographies.
Nieuw Nederlandsch biografisch woordenboek, onder redactie van
P. C. Molhuysen en P. J. Blok (Leyden, 1911-33, 9 v.). [4972
Norsk biografisk leksikon (Christiana, 1921-), ed. by E. Bull, and
others; now (1934) completed through "Jensen" (6 v.). [4973
For Spanish biographical material one must depend mainly upon
the *Enciclopedia universal ilustrada europeo-americana* (Espasa-
Calpe) (Barcelona, 1907?-30, 70 v. in 72; and *Apendice*, 1930-33,
10 v.). [4974
Alemany y Bolufer, José, ed., *Diccionario enciclopédico ilustrado de
la lengua española* (Barcelona, 1919, rev. ed., 1928), very useful
for identifying Spanish statesmen. [4974a
Svenska biografiskt lexikon (Örebro and Stockholm, 1857-1907, 10
v.). [4975
Biografiskt lexikon öfver namnkunnige svenska män (Stockholm,
1874, 23 v.). [4976
Svenskt biografiskt lexikon (Stockholm, 1918-), now (1934) complete through "De La Gardie" (10 v.). [4977
Dictionnaire historique et biographique de la Suisse (Neuchâtel,
1921-33, 7 v.), issued in French and German editions. [4978

Asia

Giles, H. A., *A Chinese biographical dictionary* (London and Shanghai, 1898).   [4979

Mayers, W. F., *The Chinese reader's manual; a handbook of biographical, historical, mythological, and general literary reference* (Shanghai, 1924), reprinted from the original edition; includes brief biographical accounts of about 900 of the chief personages of China.   [4980

The biographical material from the *Ch'ing shih kao* [Draft history of the Ch'ing dynasty] (no. 3055) has been brought together in a separate work of 80 volumes and given the title *Ch'ing shih lieh chüan* (Shanghai, China: Chung Hwa Book Co.).   [4981

For an account of a recent project of compilation of a Chinese biographical dictionary, see p. 482.

5. Guides and Indexes to General Periodicals

General periodicals are an important element in research work, particularly in furnishing the latest information available in print, in giving older material which often does not get into book form, and as source material in showing contemporary opinion on a subject. As a guide to this material of a general nature (not limited to history), there are a number of periodical indexes (American, English, and European) of which we note below the leading ones, and for further references refer the reader to the *Periodicals directory; a classified guide to a selected list of current periodicals, foreign and domestic*, ed. by Carolyn F. Ulrich (N.Y., 1932–) [4982], which consists of (1) A classified list of periodicals with a key to subjects and title index, and (2) Bibliographies of periodical literature; lists, indices, and directories; to Mudge, *Guide* (no. 4617) 6–18; and to the *Guide hist. lit.* (no. 4634), 52–53.

For lists of American periodicals, consult Kenny's *American newspaper directory* (no. 5004a); *Ayer's American newspaper annual* (no. 5007); H. O. Severance, *A Guide to the current periodicals and serials of the United States and Canada*, 5th ed. (Ann Arbor, Mich., 1931) [4983]; Roorbach, *Bibliotheca Americana* (no. 4640) contains a "List of periodicals published in the United States", 1820–1852 (p. 644–652); Columbia University Law

Library, *Serials of an international character;* tentative list (N.Y., 1921) [4984]; and William Beer, *Checklist of American periodicals, 1741–1800* (Worcester, Mass., 1923) [4985], reprinted from the *Proceedings* of the American Antiquarian Society, n.s. XXXII, pt. 2, 1922; Tinker, *French periodicals of Louisiana* (no. 5020).

For Hispanic American periodicals: Buenos Aires, Bibliotheca Nacional, *Catálogo de las revistas y periódicos existentes en la Biblioteca Nacional* (Buenos Aires, 1904) [4986]; New York Public Library, *Latin-American periodicals current in the reference department* (N.Y., 1920) [4987]; *Catalogue of newspapers . . . Pan American Union* (no. 5037); *Guía periodística argentina y de las repúblicas latino-americanas,* 1928–, F. A. Le Rose, director-proprietario (Buenos Aires, 1928–) [4988]; Gabriel René-Moreno, *Ensayo de una bibliografía general de los periódicos de Bolivia, 1825–1905* (Santiago de Chile, 1905) [4989]; Manuel Odriozola, " Catálogo de los periódicos nacionales existentes en la Biblioteca Nacional ", *Boletín bibliográfico,* I (Lima, 1924) 170–179, 234–265 [4990]; and J. E. Machado, *Lista de algunos periódicos que vieron la luz en Caracas de 1808 a 1900* (Caracas, 1929) [4991] lists 128 periodicals, arranged chronologically.

For British: *Sell's world press* (no. 5008), which is a bibliography of English newspapers and periodicals; *Willing's press guide* (no. 5005); and the *Tercentenary handlist of English and Welsh newspapers, magazines, and reviews* (no. 5013). For Canadian: W. S. Wallace, "A checklist of Upper Canadian periodicals, 1793–1840 ", *Canad. hist. rev.,* XII (1931) 4–22 [4992].

For French: *Annuaire de la presse française* (no. 5006).

For German: *Sperlings Zeitschriften- und Zeitungs- Adressbuch; Handbuch der deutschen Presse . . .,* 57. Ausgabe, 1931 (Leipzig, 1931) [4992a]; and for others, see Mudge, *Guide,* (no. 4617), 21–22.

For a guide in identifying and locating periodicals in all subjects and in all languages, see the *Union list of serials in libraries of the United States and Canada,* ed. by Winifred Gregory (N.Y., 1927), and *Supplement, January 1925 [–Dec. 1932],* ed. by Gabrielle E. Malikoff (N.Y., 1931–32, 2 v.) [4993], a comprehensive list of serial publications and guide to their location in many libraries; and Edith M. Phelps and Eleanor E. Ball, *Periodicals of international importance; a selection of 600 useful in libraries everywhere* (N.Y., 1926) [4994]

Indexes to Periodicals

An Index to legal periodical literature (Boston, 1888–1924; Indianapolis, 1933–), to date (1934) five volumes have been issued, containing material prior to 1887 through 1932.   [4994a
Poole's index to periodical literature, rev. ed. v..I, 1802–1881 (Boston, 1893, 1 v. in 2), and 5 *Supplements*, 1882–1907 (Boston and N.Y., 1893–1908, 5 v.), an extensive subject index to American and English periodicals.   [4995
Readers' guide to periodical literature (cumulated), 1900– (N.Y., 1905–).   [4996
International index to periodicals, devoted chiefly to the humanities and science, 1907– (N.Y., 1907–), which covers the more scholarly journals; later volumes include many foreign references.   [4997
The Magazine subject-index; a subject index to seventy-nine American and English periodicals, 1907– (Boston, 1908–), which specializes in history; continued by the *Annual magazine subject-index* (Boston, 1909–), ed. by F. W. Faxon.   [4998
Index to legal periodicals (Chicago, 1908–13; N.Y., 1914–), official organ of the American Association of Law Libraries.   [4999
Subject index to periodicals (*English and foreign*), 1915– (London, 1919–), published by the (British) Library Association; index to a large number of periodicals, chiefly British and American.   [5000
Social science abstracts (no. 4632).
Essay and general literature index, ed. by Minnie E. Sears and Marian Shaw, 1931– (N.Y., 1931–), an index to 6350 essays and articles in 284 volumes of collections of essays and miscellaneous works.   [5001

Foreign Periodical Indexes

Bibliographie der deutschen Zeitschriftenliteratur, 1897– (Leipzig, 1897–).   [5002
Bibliographie der fremdsprachigen Zeitschriftenliteratur, 1911– (Leipzig, 1911–), a subject list only; indexes periodicals in the non-German languages only; is valuable to the student for the large amount of French and Italian material.   [5003
For Belgian, Dutch, French, Italian, Norwegian, and Russian periodical indexes, see Mudge, *Guide* (no. 4617), 9–12.

6. Guides and Indexes to Newspapers

For newspapers, which, when properly used, form a valuable medium for historical work,[25] we offer the following guides, giving first the principal catalogues and directories of newspapers. For some of the larger collections of newspapers (notably those of the Library of Congress), and many of the smaller and regional collections, there are published lists; these we enumerate second; and third, memoranda regarding the foremost newspaper indexes, which are of great value in locating material in the current press. The political affiliations and tendencies of newspapers are indicated in *Ayer's newspaper annual* (no. 5007) and in the *Political handbook of the world* (no. 5082).

Catalogues and Directories of Newspapers

The newspaper press directory (Mitchell's) (London, 1847– (in progress)) contains the " latest information about newspapers published in the British Isles, in the Dominions overseas, and in foreign countries."   [5004

Kenny, D. J., *The American newspaper directory and record of the press. Containing an accurate list of all the newspapers, magazines, reviews, periodicals, etc. in the United States and British provinces of North America* (N.Y., 1861).   [5004a

Willing's press guide . . . , 1874– (London, 1874– (in progress)), a concise and comprehensive index to the press of the United Kingdom.   [5005

Annuaire de la presse française et étrangère et du monde politique, 1880– (Paris, 1880– (in progress)).   [5006

Ayer and sons' American newspaper annual and directory; a catalogue of American newspapers (Phila., 1880– (in progress)), a list of all newspapers and periodicals published in the United States, territories, and Dominion of Canada, Cuba and the West Indian Islands; giving detailed information about each, including its character or politics.   [5007

Sell's world press (London, 1884–1921), a bibliography of English newspapers and periodicals.   [5008

---

[25] For discussion of their value, see Lucy M. Salmon, *The newspaper and the historian* (N.Y., 1923).

Nelson, William, *Some account of American newspapers, particularly of the eighteenth century, and libraries in which they may be found* (Paterson, N.J., 1894, 1895, 1897, 3 v.), now superseded by Brigham (no. 5012).   [5009

The Canadian newspaper directory (Montreal, 1899–), a complete list of the newspapers and periodicals published in the Dominion of Canada and Newfoundland.   [5010

Ayer, Mary F., *Checklist of Boston newspapers, 1704–1780, with bibliographical notes by Albert Matthews* (Boston, 1907) (Collections of the Colonial Society of Massachusetts, v. IX) lists the Boston newspapers found in 14 libraries of the United States.
                                              [5011

Brigham, C. S., "Bibliography of American newspapers, 1690–1820", *Am. antiq. soc. proc.*, n.s. XXIII–XXVII (1913–1927), various paging.   [5012

Tercentenary handlist of English and Welsh newspapers, magazines and reviews (London, 1920), published by The Times; a chronological bibliography of English periodicals and newspapers, 1620–1919.   [5013

Adressbuch der fremdsprachigen Zeitschriften und Zeitungen; die wichtigsten Zeitschriften und politischen Zeitungen des Auslandes und Deutschlands in fremden Sprachen (Leipzig, 1927).   [5014

Crane, R. S., and F. B. Kaye, *A census of British newspapers and periodicals, 1620–1800* (Chapel Hill, N. C., and London, 1927) lists those accessible in American libraries separately.   [5015

Fox, Louis H., "New York city newspapers, 1820–1850; a bibliography", *Bibliog. Soc. Am. pap.*, XXI, pts. 1 and 2 (1927) 1–131.
                                              [5016

A political handbook of the world; parliaments, parties and press, 1927– (N.Y., 1927–), published by the Council on Foreign Relations.   [5017

L'Argus de la presse; nomenclature des journaux et revues en langue française paraissant dans le monde entier (Paris, 1930–31, 6th edition).   [5018

Handbuch der Weltpress; eine Darstellung des Zeitungswesens aller Länder, herausgegeben von Deutschen Institut für Zeitungskunde [of the Universität, Berlin] (Berlin, 1931), compiled by Karl Bömer.   [5019

Tinker, E. L., *Bibliography of the French newspapers and periodicals of Louisiana* (Worcester, Mass.: American Antiquarian Society, 1933), reprinted from its *Proceedings*, n. s., v. XLIII. [5020

Berlin, Deutsches Institut für Zeitungskunde, *Standortskatalog wichtiger Zeitungsbestände in deutschen Bibliotheken* (Leipzig, 1933), catalogue of German and foreign newspapers, giving the location of important sets of newspapers in German libraries and archives of publishing houses. [5021

Collections in Libraries [26]

Check list of newspaper and periodical files in the Department of Archives and History of the state of Alabama (Montgomery, 1904). [5022

Newspapers in libraries of metropolitan Chicago; a union list prepared by the University of Chicago libraries, . . . 1931 (Chicago, 1931), mimeographed list. [5023

Chicago, University of, *The Durrett collection now in the library of the University of Chicago*, by E. A. Henry (Chicago, 1914). [5024

District of Columbia, "A list of newspapers published in the District of Columbia, 1820–1850", *Bibliog. soc. Am. pap.*, XIX, pt. 1–2 (1927) 43–65. [5025

Duke University. *A check list of United States newspapers (and weeklies to 1900) in the general library*, comp. by Mary Wescott and Allene Ramage (Durham, N.C., 1932–). [5026

Gabler, A. J., "Check list of English newspapers and periodicals before 1801 in the Huntington Library", *Huntington lib. bul.*, no. 2 (1931) 1–66. [5027

Illinois. *A list of newspapers and periodicals in Illinois libraries . . .*, by F. W. Scott (Springfield, Ill., 1910), published by the Illinois State Library. [5028

Indiana. *A list of Indiana newspapers available in the Indiana State Library, the Indianapolis Public Library, the library of Indiana University, and the Library of Congress* (Indianapolis, 1916). [5029

---

[26] Arranged alphabetically by library or region.

Compilation has recently been started of a *Union list of newspapers in the libraries of the United States and Canada,* Winifred Gregory, editor, under the auspices of the Bibliographical Society of America. It is expected that the work will be ready for publication in 1937.

Library of Congress. *A check list of American newspapers in the Library of Congress*, comp. under the direction of A. G. Slauson (Wash., 1901). New edition is in preparation, under the direction of H. S. Parsons, chief, Division of Periodicals.   [5030

——— *A check list of American eighteenth century newspapers in the Library of Congress*, comp. by J. Van Ness Ingram (Wash., 1912). New edition is completed; ready for printing (1935).   [5031

——— *A check list of foreign newspapers in the Library of Congress*, newly compiled under the direction of H. S. Parsons (Wash., 1929).   [5032

Missouri, State Historical Society of. *List of old newspapers in the library of the State Historical Society of Missouri* (Columbia, Mo., 1910).   [5033

New York Public Library. *Checklist of newspapers and official gazettes in the New York Public Library*, comp. by D. C. Haskell (N.Y., 1915), reprinted from the *Bulletin*, July–Dec. 1914, and July 1915.   [5034

North Carolina State Library. *A bibliography of bound newspapers in the North Carolina State Library* (Raleigh, N.C., 1926).   [5035

Ohio State Library. *Newspapers and periodicals in the Ohio State Library, other libraries of the state, and lists of Ohio newspapers in the Library of Congress and the Historical Society of Wisconsin*, comp. by C. B. Galbreath (Columbus, 1902).   [5036

Pan American Union. *Catalogue of newspapers and magazines in the Columbus Memorial Library of the Pan American Union* (Wash., 1931), mimeographed.   [5037

Historical Society of Western Pennsylvania, *Inventory of files of American newspapers in Pittsburgh and Allegheny county, Pennsylvania* (Pittsburgh, 1933), mimeographed.   [5307a

Pennsylvania State Library. "Annotated catalogue of newspaper files in the Pennsylvania State Library", by Nathan E. Hause, in *Report of the State librarian of Pennsylvania, 1900* (Harrisburg, 1901), 185–308.   [5038

Philadelphia. *List of serials in the principal libraries of Philadelphia and its vicinity*, by J. P. Lamberton (Phila., 1908), and supplement (1910), includes newspapers.   [5039

Virginia. "A list of Virginia newspapers in the library of the Virginia Historical Society and the Virginia State Library ", *Va. mag. hist. and biog.*, IX–X (1901–03), passim. [5040

—— *A list of newspapers in the Virginia State Library, Confederate Museum and Valentine Museum* (Richmond, Va., 1912).

[5041

Washington (State). *Union list of periodicals currently received by the Library of the University of Washington and by the Seattle Public Library during the year 1909; also a list of newspapers in the Seattle Public Library* (Seattle, Wash., 1909). [5042

Wisconsin, State Historical Society of. *Annotated catalogue of newspaper files in the Library of the State Historical Society of Wisconsin*, 2nd ed., comp. by Ada T. Griswold (Madison, 1911), and supplementary catalogue, 1911–1917, pub. in 1918. [5043

Yale University. *A list of newspapers in the Yale University Library* (New Haven, 1916) includes a large number of South American newspapers. [5044

Newspaper Indexes

New York Daily Tribune index, 1875–1906 (N.Y., 1876–1907, 31 v.), discontinued. [5045

The Times (London), *Official index to the Times*, Jan. 1914– (London, 1914–), absorbed the *Annual index to the Times*, 1906–13 (1907–14) 8 v.) and the *Monthly index to the Times*, Jan. 1906– June 1914 (1906–14, 22 v.). [5046

New York Times index; a master-key to all newspapers, 1913– (N.Y., 1913–). [5047

7. Encyclopedias

Aside from the general encyclopedias the following special ones are particularly valuable for the purpose of this *Guide*. The investigator will find the principal encyclopedias of a general character listed and described in Mudge, *Guide* (no. 4617), 37–46, and in the *Guide hist. lit.* (no. 4634), in the latter are listed under each country, those which are the product of that particular country and especially likely to contain material dealing specifically with affairs of that country. We attempt here to enumerate only those which deal with subjects contributory to a study of foreign relations.

Appleton's annual cyclopaedia and register of important events,
1861–1902 (N.Y., 1862–1903, 42 v.) ; each volume devoted to events
of the given year.   [5048

Lalor, J. J., ed., *Cyclopaedia of political science, political economy,
and of the political history of the United States* (Chicago, 1881–84,
3 v.).   [5049

*Harper's encyclopaedia of United States history from 458 A.D. to
1902* (N.Y., 1902, 10 v.).   [5050

Burpee, L. J., and A. G. Doughty, eds., *Index and dictionary of
Canadian history* (Toronto, 1911), consisting of an analytical index to the entire series of 20 volumes of the *Makers of Canada,*
with additional information, and including a list of MS. sources
in the Dominion archives, and a partial list of scarce maps and
plans relating to Canada.   [5051

McLaughlin, A. C., and A. B. Hart, eds., *Cyclopedia of American
government* (N.Y. and London, 1914, 3 v.), containing a detailed
index; there are discussions of the principles of international law
which are supported by numerous articles on the history of
American international relations.   [5052

Larned, J. N., *New Larned history for ready reference, reading, and
research* . . . the work of J. N. Larned, completely revised, enlarged and brought up to date under the supervision of the publishers, by Donald E. Smith, editor-in-chief, . . . (Springfield,
Mass., 1922–24, 12 v.).   [5053

Americana annual, an encyclopedia of current events, 1923–1927
(N.Y., 1923–27, 5 v.), which serves as a supplement to the *Encyclopedia Americana,* and includes many biographies.   [5054

Low, Sidney J. M., and Frederick S. Pulling, *Dictionary of English
history,* revised edition, enlarged (London and N.Y., 1928).

                                                                     [5055

Encyclopaedia of the social sciences, editor-in-chief, E. R. A. Selig-
man, associate editor, Alvin Johnson (N.Y., 1930– (in progress)) ;
the endeavor has been to include all of the important topics in
politics, economics, law, anthropology, sociology, penology and
social work, and history is represented only to the extent that historical episodes or methods are of especial importance to the student of society.   [5056

Jameson, J. F., *Dictionary of United States history, alphabetical,
chronological, statistical, from the earliest explorations to the*

present time, based upon the original work prepared in 1893, by
J. F. Jameson. Rev. edition, edited under the supervision of Albert E. McKinley (Phila., 1931). [5057

Académie Diplomatique Internationale, *Dictionnaire diplomatique*,
publié sous la direction de M. A.-F. Frangulis . . . (Paris, 1933,
2 v.), cooperative work; includes bibliographies. [5057a

Keller, Helen Rex, *The dictionary of dates* (N.Y., 1935, 2 v.), v. I:
" The old world "; v. II: " The new world ". [5057b

8. Year Books

Annual register; a review of public events at home and abroad,
1758– (London, 1761– (in progress)), this general year book is
an important repository for contemporary British state papers
(and occasionally others), and for annual summaries of international events. [5058

Europaischer Geschichtskalendar, 1861– (Munich, 1861–), now called
Schulthess' Europaischer Geschichtskalendar. [5059

World almanac and encyclopedia (N.Y., 1861?– (in progress)), contains statistics of industry, politics, governments, finance, etc.;
most comprehensive of American almanacs. [5060

[*Whitaker's almanack*] *An almanack for the year* . . ., by Joseph
Whitaker (London, 1869– (in progress)) statistical information
relating to Great Britain particularly. [5061

*Statesman's year-book; statistical and historical annual of the states
of the world, 1864–* (London, 1864– (in progress)), a mirror of
the political and economic conditions of the countries of the world. [5062

*Year book of the scientific and learned societies of Great Britain
and Ireland*, 1884– (London, 1884– (in progress)) includes lists
of papers read, and publications of each society. [5063

Minerva; Jahrbuch der gelehrten Welt, 1891/92– (Strassburg, 1891–
1914; Berlin and Leipzig, 1920–), a year book of universities,
colleges, and learned institutions of the world. [5064

International year book; a compendium of the world's progress,
1898–1902 (N.Y., 1899–1903, 5 v.), planned as a supplement to this
is the *New international year book*, 1907– (N.Y., 1908–), and
together these year books are used as a supplement to the *New
international encyclopaedia*, and are especially useful for biography. [5065

Canadian annual review of public affairs, 1901–, ed. by J. C. Hopkins (Toronto, 1902–), an exhaustive annual digest of the current history of Canada.   [5066

International peace year book (title varies), 1910–18; 1921– (London, 1910–).   [5067

American year-book; a record of events and progress, 1910– (N.Y., and London, 1911–20, 1926–), ed. by S. N. D. North and E. G. Wickware, 1910–19; by A. B. Hart (and W. M. Schuyler), 1925–; contains a section on " international situations affecting the United States."   [5068

American statesman's yearbook, from official reports of the United States government, state reports, consular advices, and foreign documents (N.Y., 1912–), a statistical yearbook.   [5069

Carnegie Endowment for International Peace, *Year book* (Wash., 1912–) includes a list of its publications.   [5070

Official digest of the world, 1912– (N.Y., 1912–).   [5071

Britannica year-book, 1913–; a survey of the world's progress since the completion in 1910 of the *Encyclopaedia Britannica*, 11th ed. (London, 1913–).   [5072

Grotius, annuaire international, 1913– (The Hague, 1913–), including a section: " Bibliographie des publications parus aux Pays-Bas sur le droit international et les matières connexes."   [5073

Jahrbuch des Völkerrechts (Munich and Leipzig, 1913–).   [5074

Index generalis; annuaire général des universités, grandes écoles, académies, archives, bibliothèques, instituts scientifiques, jardins botaniques et zoologiques, sociétés savantes, 1919– (Paris, 1919–).   [5075

British year book of international law, 1920/21– (London, 1920–), containing an annual bibliography of books dealing with international law, and a diary of international events of the preceding year.   [5076

The armaments year-book; general and statistical information, 1924–, pub. by the League of Nations (Geneva, 1924–) contains detailed articles on armaments.   [5077

Survey of international affairs, 1920/23–, by A. J. Toynbee (London, 1925–), pub. under the auspices of the Royal Institute of International Affairs.   [5078

The Europa year-book; an annual survey of economic and social conditions, a directory of the League of Nations and of interna-

tional societies, a European who's who in politics, trade, science, art and literature (subtitle varies slightly), 1926–29 (London, 1926–29) includes sections on "European bibliography", and lists of international associations; it is merged into *Europa; with which is incorporated the Europa year book* (London, 1930–).
[5079

Annuaire de la Société des Nations, 1920/27– (Lausanne and Geneva, 1927–). [5080

Annuaire de la vie internationale; politique-économique-juridique, 1927– (Paris, 1928–) includes a chronology of events of international interest, lists of treaties, decisions of tribunals, international conferences, publications on international law, public documents, and current bibliographical summary of articles in reviews and periodicals of all nations dealing with political and economic affairs. [5081

Political handbook of the world; parliaments, parties, and press, published by the Council on Foreign Relations (Cambridge, Mass., 1928–) gives information on the composition of governments of the world, the character and aims of political parties, and the affiliation and tendencies of leading newspapers. [5082

Annual digest of public international law cases; being a selection from the decisions of international and national courts and tribunals given during the years 1925/1926– (London and N.Y., 1929–), ed. by A. D. MacNair and H. Lauterpacht, and pub. under the direction of the Dept. of International Studies of the London School of Economics and Political Science (Univ. of London).
[5083

Jahrbuch für auswärtige Politik; internationale Wirtschaft und Kultur, Weltverkehr und Völkerrecht, 1929– (Berlin, 1929–).
[5084

Minerva-Handbücher, ergänzungen zu "Minerva", Jahrbuch der gelehrten Welt, 1929– (Berlin and Leipzig, 1929–), 1. Abt.: *Die Bibliotheken* (Bd. 1: *Deutsches Reich*. Bd. 2: *Oesterreich*). 2. Abt.: *Die Archive* (1932–). [5085

Annuaire interparlementaire, publié sous le patronage de l'Union Interparlementaire, par Léopold Boissier, and B. Mirkine-Guetzévitch, avec la collaboration de J. Laferrière, 1931– (Paris, 1931–) contains information regarding political organizations, statistics, etc., of all countries. [5086

National Council for the Social Studies, *Yearbook*, 1931– (Phila., 1931–), including bibliographies.   [5087

The League year-book, 1932– (N.Y., 1932–), edited by Judith Jackson and Stephen King-Hall; the first volume (1932) comprises a fully documented reference book on the organization and working of the League of Nations, the second volume (1933) contains a complete survey of the proceedings of the League, 1932–33.   [5088

9. Doctoral Dissertations

Considerable material of more or less value, treating of special subjects accumulates in the form of theses for degrees at the various universities. There are several national lists of dissertations submitted at all universities in a given country, references to which are given below. Furthermore many of the universities in this country have issued lists of theses submitted at those institutions. Both types of lists are useful in rendering available to scholars much unpublished original work, found in university libraries only, and reveal what subjects have already been written on. We note below (first) national lists—American, English, French, and German (others to be found in Mudge, *Guide* (no. 4617), 30–32; and (second) lists issued by a number of American universities and colleges.

American

" List of doctoral dissertations in political science ", *Am. pol. sci. rev.*, IV (1910–), listing those in preparation at American universities.   [5089

Jameson, J. F., " List of doctoral dissertations in history now in progress at the chief American universities ", 1902–; the list for 1912, pub. in *Hist. teach. mag.*, IV (1913) 8–15; from 1913– (Wash., 1913–), issued by the Department (now Division) of Historical Research of the Carnegie Institution, reprinted from the *American historical review*, 1914–.   [5090

Library of Congress, *A list of American doctoral dissertations printed in 1912 [–1933]* (Wash., 1913–35 (in progress)), recent numbers prepared by Mary W. MacNair; not limited to history, but with a classified list and subject index by which the historical items may be easily identified.   [5091

Association of Research Libraries, *Doctoral dissertations accepted by American universities, 1933–1934*, ed. by D. B. Gilchrist (N.Y., 1934) is the first of a series which is intended to be annual.

[5091a

American Universities [27]

California, University of, *Record of theses submitted in partial fulfillment of the requirements for the degree of doctor of philosophy at the University of California, 1885–1926* (Berkeley, 1926), a mimeographed list. [5092

Catholic University of America, *Doctoral dissertations published by the students of the Catholic University of America, 1897–1928* (Wash., 1928). [5093

Chicago, University of, *Register of doctors of philosophy of the University of Chicago, June 1893–June 1927* (Chicago, 1927). [5094

Chicago, University of, *Abstracts of theses, humanistic series*, 1922– (Chicago, 1925–). [5095

China Institute in America, *Theses and dissertations by Chinese students in America* (N.Y., 1927), and supplementary list (1928). [5096

Clark University, *List of degrees granted at Clark University and Clark College, 1889–1920* (Worcester, Mass., 1920); and *Thesis abstracts*, 1929– (Worcester, Mass., 1930–). [5097

Columbia University, *A bibliography of the faculty of political science of Columbia University, 1880–1930* (N.Y., 1931), listing the doctoral dissertations written under the Faculty of Political Science. [5098

Harvard University, *Doctors of philosophy and doctors of science who have received their degree in course from Harvard University, 1873–1926, with the titles of their theses* (Cambridge, 1926). [5099

Harvard University, Graduate School of Arts and Sciences, *Summaries of theses accepted in partial fulfilment of the requirements for the degree of doctor of philosophy*, 1925– (Cambridge, 1928–). [5100

Iowa, State University of, *Graduate theses, including schedule of dissertations of approved candidates for advanced degrees with major and minor subjects* (Iowa City, 1924–). [5101

---

[27] Arranged alphabetically by universities.

Iowa, State University of, *Abstracts in history from dissertations for the degree of doctor of philosophy as accepted by the Graduate College of the State University of Iowa, 1922–1930* (Iowa City, 1932), ed. by Louis Pelzer. [5102

Johns Hopkins University, *List of dissertations submitted in conformity with the requirements for the degrees of doctor of philosophy . . . 1876–1926* (Baltimore, 1926). [5103

Kansas, University of, *Titles to theses presented in partial fulfillment of the requirements for advanced degrees in the Graduate School* (Lawrence, 1920). [5104

Minnesota, University of, *A register of the Ph. D. degrees conferred by the University of Minnesota, 1888–1932* (Minneapolis, 1932). [5104a

Northwestern University, Evanston, Ill., Graduate School, *Summaries of Ph. D. dissertations . . .* v. I– (Chicago and Evanston, 1933–). [5104b

Ohio State University, *Abstracts of doctors' dissertations* (Columbus, 1929–). [5105

Pan American Union, Columbus Memorial Library, *Theses on Pan-American topics prepared by candidates for degrees in colleges and universities in the United States* (Wash., 1931; 2d ed., rev. and enl., 1933), mimeographed list. [5106

Stanford University, *Abstracts of dissertations for the degree of doctor of philosophy*, 1924– (Stanford University, Cal., 1927–). [5107

Washington, University of, *Digests of theses, 1914–1931* (Seattle, Wash., 1931). [5108

Yale University, *Doctors of philosophy of Yale University, with the titles of their dissertations, 1861–1915* (New Haven, 1916). [5109

British

" Titles of theses accepted for the degree of doctor ", in the *Yearbook of the universities of the empire*, 1914– (London, 1914–). [5110

" Summaries of theses [in history] ", published in various numbers of the *Bulletin* of the Institute of Historical Research [of the University of London], v. I– (London, 1923–). [5111

Brown, G. W., and Alison Ewart, " Graduate theses in Canadian history and economics ", *Canad. hist. rev.*, VIII– (1927–), an annual list of theses in one number of the *Review* for each year. [5112

Cambridge University, "List of subjects of theses by Cambridge University students working for the PH.D. or M.LITT. degrees in history ", *Cambridge hist. jour.*, III– (1929–).   [**5113**

French

France, Ministère de l'Instruction Publique et de Beaux-Arts, Direction de l'Enseignement Supérieur, *Catalogue des thèses et écrits académiques*, 1884/89– (Paris, 1885–), the official French list.
[**5114**

Paris, Bibliothèque Nationale, *Catalogue des dissertations et écrits académiques provenant des échanges avec les universités étrangères et reçus par la Bibliothèque Nationale*, 1882– (Paris, 1884–), a general list, not limited to French theses, and useful particularly for countries for which there is no national list.   [**5115**

Maire, Albert, *Répertoire alphabetique des thèses de doctorat des lettres des universités françaises, 1810–1900* (Paris, 1903), which partially supplies the lack of an official list before 1884.   [**5116**

German

Jahresverzeichnis der an den deutschen Universitäten und Hochschulen erschienenen Schriften, 1885– (Berlin, 1887–), the standard official German list, including the theses of all German universities.   [**5117**

Monatsbericht über neu erschienene schul- und universitätsschriften, 1889/90– (Leipzig, 1890–).   [**5118**

10. Diplomatic Lists, Registers, Etc.

The principal countries of the world publish more or less regularly diplomatic year books or registers, which contain lists of diplomatic officials. These may be located in Myers, *Manual* (no. 5399), American Library in Paris (no. 5399a), and Gregory (no. 5400), and *A provisional list of printed lists of ambassadors and other diplomatic representatives*, ed. by J. F. Jameson (Paris, 1928) [**5119**], an extract from the *Bulletin* of the International Committee of Historical Sciences, no. 4, Mar. 1928, for enumeration of printed lists, in general and by particular countries. We give below memoranda regarding the American, British, French, and German manuals, and refer the student for further references to the above-named bibliographical aids.

The International Committee of Historical Sciences is now preparing an international compilation of historical lists of diplomatic representatives (with full names, titles, and exact dates of incumbency and sojourn) at the several courts and capitals of the world.[28]

General

Almanach de Gotha, annuaire généalogique, diplomatique et statistique (Gotha, 1764– (in progress)), issued simultaneously in French and German, and containing in each issue a section "Annuaire diplomatique et statistique", giving statistical and descriptive information about the various countries of the world, and lists of the principal executive, legislative, and diplomatic officials of each. From 1926 the *Gothäisches Jahrbuch für Diplomatie, Verwaltung und Wirtschaft* continues the lists of officials which formed part 2 of the *Almanach de Gotha*. [5120

Annuaire du corps diplomatique et consulaire, 1931– (Geneva, 1931–), consists of (1) lists of diplomatists and members of consular service of all nations, and (2) biographical notices of the same. [5121

United States

U.S. Dept. of State, *Register of the Department of State* (Wash., 1869– (in progress)); 1882–1904 volumes contain lists of papers concerning foreign relations. Particularly to be noted is the *Register . . . corrected to March 1, 1874,* of which Pt. II is a *Historical register,* containing a "List of diplomatic agents of the United States prior to the adoption of the Constitution", "List of diplomatic agents of the United States since March 4, 1789", a list of "Heads of foreign missions and diplomatic agents in the United States" to 1874, and a list of members of "International arbitrations and claims commissions", 1796 to 1871. The list of diplomatic agents of the United States since 1874 is brought up to date in the latest *Register* of the Department of State. See also page 825, section V ("Diplomatic Registers and Lists") for a more comprehensive account of such lists published by the Department of State. The lists of foreign diplomatic agents in the United States since 1874 may be expected in the projected international compilation above mentioned. [5122

[28] *Bulletin* of the International Committee of Historical Sciences, no. 8 (v. II, pt. 3) (1930), 417–420.

France

Annuaire diplomatique et consulaire de la République Française,
1860– (Paris, 1860– (in progress)).   **[5123**

Germany

Deutsche Gesandschaften, Konsulate und Pastellen, herausgegeben
vom Auswärtigen Amt (Berlin, 1923–) beginning with the 1929
volume title changed to *Verzeichnis der deutschen diplomatischen·
und konsularischen Vertretungen im Ausland.*   **[5124**

Great Britain

Foreign Office list and diplomatic and consular year book, 1859–
(London, 1859– (in progress)), ed. for Godfrey E. P. Hertslet
by members of the Staff of the Foreign Office, contains in each
number a chronological list of secretaries of state for foreign
affairs, 1782 to date, of ambassadors, envoys, ministers, etc., accredited to foreign states, 1851 to date, and of " Papers relating
to foreign affairs laid before Parliament " in the given year.
      [5125

See also *British diplomatic representatives, 1689–1789,* ed. for the
Royal Historical Society by D. B. Horn (London, 1932) (Camden
third series, v. XLVI), containing lists of British diplomatic agents
to various countries, giving dates of credentials and instructions and
indications of where amongst the Record Office papers these documents are to be found.   **[5126**

Mexico

*Personas que han tenido a su cargo la secretaría de relaciones ex-
teriores desde 1821 hasta 1924* (Mexico, 1924), pub. by the Ministry of Foreign Relations ("Ministerio de Relaciones Exteriores"), gives a list, with dates, of the secretaries of the foreign
office of Mexico from the beginning.   **[5127**

Peru

García Salazar, Arturo, *Guía práctica para los diplomáticos y cónsules peruanos* (Lima, 1918, 2 v.) contains chronological lists of the
presidents, ministers of foreign affairs, and diplomatic representatives, to 1917.   **[5127a**

11. Official Gazettes

Most countries have official journals, or gazettes, like the British *London gazette*, 1665– (in progress) [5127b]; the French *Journal officiel* (varying title), 1789– (in progress) [5127c] which includes, in addition to records of legislative debates, texts of laws and decrees, and occasional bills or reports upon bills, and administrative documents; and the Spanish *Gaceta de Madrid*, 1700– (in progress) [5127c] which publishes the most important decrees, orders, legislation, etc., regarding foreign affairs. They are the media for the publication of current items regarding public matters. They may be located by consulting Myers, *Manual* (no. 5399), for material in 1922, and further identified for later dates in the American Library in Paris, *Official publications* (no. 5399a), and Winifred Gregory, *Serial publications of foreign governments* (no. 5400). For the official gazettes of the Spanish American countries, see (in addition to the Gregory List (no. 5400)), Childs, "*Hisp. Am. govt. documents in Libr. of Cong.* (no. 5425), which includes a checklist of official gazettes and legislative proceedings of Hispanic American countries in the Library of Congress.

12. Bibliographies of Maps

Harvard University. Library. *A catalogue of the maps and charts in the library of Harvard University* (Cambridge, 1831) (Catalogue of the Library of Harvard University, v. III, pt. 2). [5128

British Museum. *Catalogue of the manuscript maps, charts, and plans . . . in the British Museum* (London, 1844–61, 3 v.), v. III includes maps of America. [5129

Royal Geographical Society. Library. Map Room. *Catalogue of map room of the Royal Geographical Society* (London, 1882). [5130

British Museum. *Catalogue of the printed maps, plans, and charts in the British Museum* (London, 1885, 2 v.). [5131

Winsor (no. 4782), v. VII: *The United States*, contains many maps and bibliographical data regarding maps. [5132

Phillips, P. L. *Alaska and the northwest part of North America, 1588–1898; maps in the Library of Congress* (Wash., 1898) (Library of Congress). [5133

——— "Maps of Cuba, Porto Rico, and the West Indies, in the Library of Congress", in Griffin (no. 4722), 41–57. [5134

Phillips, P. L. *A list of maps in the Library of Congress* (Wash., 1901) (Library of Congress).   [5135

—— *Checklist of large scale maps published by foreign governments (Great Britain excepted) in the Library of Congress* (Wash., 1904) (Library of Congress).   [5136

—— *A list of geographical atlases in the Library of Congress, with bibliographical notes* (Wash., 1909–20, 4 v.) (Library of Congress).   [5137

California. State Library. *List of printed maps contained in the map department* (Sacramento, 1899).   [5138

Spain. Depósito de la Guerra. *Catálogo general del archivo de mapas, planos y memorias del Depósito de la Guerra* (Madrid, 1900, 2 v.)   [5139

Torres Lanzas, Pedro, *Relación descriptiva de los mapas, planos, &c., de México y Florida existentes en el Archivo General de Indias* (Seville, 1900, 2 v.).   [5140

Hulbert, A. B., *The Crown collection of photographs of American maps* (Cleveland, O., 1904–08, 5 v.), maps of American rivers, forts, and other military and regional maps in the Crown collection of MSS. in the British Museum.   [5141

Winsor, Justin, *The Kohl collection (now in the Library of Congress) of maps relating to America* (Wash., 1904) (Library of Congress), a reprint of *Bibliographical contribution* number 19 of the Library of Harvard University.   [5142

Great Britain. Colonial Office. *Catalogue of maps, plans, and charts in the library of the Colonial Office* (1910), a bound list of 3 excerpts from printed lists, separately paged, of maps of (1) "America (North and South)"; (2) " Canada "; (3) " North American colonies (afterwards United States of America)"; a copy of which is in the Division of Maps in the Library of Congress (source not identified).   [5143

Holmden, H. R., *Catalogue of maps, plans, and charts in the map room of the Dominion Archives*, pub. under the direction of the archivist (Ottawa, 1912) (Publications of the Canadian Archives, no. 8).   [5144

Lowery, Woodbury, *The Lowery collection; a descriptive list of maps of the Spanish possessions within the present limits of the United States, 1502–1820*, ed. by P. L. Phillips (Wash., 1912) (Library of Congress).   [5145

Canada. Geographic Board. *Catalogue of maps in the collection of the Geographic Board* (Ottawa, 1918).   [5146

Toronto. Public Reference Library, *Map collection of the Public Reference Library of the city of Toronto* (Toronto, 1923).
          [5147

Library of Congress. Division of Maps. *Noteworthy maps . . . accessions*, 1925/26–, comp. by Lawrence Martin and Clara Egli (Wash., 1927–), a continuation of the lists included in the annual reports of the Librarian of Congress for the years 1899–1925.
          [5148

Karpinski, L. C., "Manuscript maps relating to American history in French, Spanish, and Portuguese archives", *Am. hist. rev.*, XXXIII (1928) 328–330; the many maps mentioned in a general way in this article, and photographed for five American libraries (Library of Congress, N.Y. Public Library, Huntington Library, Newberry Library, and W. L. Clements Library) are listed in MS. catalogues in those libraries. Sets, or partial sets, are available also in several other libraries, listed in the article mentioned above. They contain many items on Louisiana and Florida and form a highly valuable source.   [5149

—— *Bibliography of the printed maps of Michigan, 1804–1880, with a series of over one hundred reproductions of maps constituting an historical atlas of the Great Lakes and Michigan* (Lansing, Mich., 1931).   [5150

St. Louis. Public Library. *Maps in the St. Louis Public Library*, by Mildred Boatman (St. Louis, 1931).   [5151

Leland, W. G., *Guide* (no. 5704), 221–237, for a classified list of MS. maps relating to North America and the West Indies in the Bibliothèque Nationale.   [5152

American Geographical Society, *A catalogue of maps of Hispanic America, including maps in scientific periodicals and books and sheet and atlas maps, with articles on the cartography of the several countries and maps showing the extent and character of existing surveys* (N.Y. [1933], 4 v.).   [5153

Wilgus, A. C., *Maps relating to Latin America in books and periodicals* (Wash., 1933) (Pan American Union. Bibliographical Series, no. 10), this is an index to page numbers of books and periodicals, the indicated maps being classified under appropriate geographical, historical, political, and other headings.   [5154

13. Present-day Agencies for the Dissemination of Information on International Affairs

The second decade of the twentieth century witnessed the beginning of numerous agencies for the dissemination of information on current international affairs, and the stimulation of study. The conviction that, unrestricted, war, under present-day dynamics, will destroy contemporary civilization is responsible for the foundation and endowment of the majority of these agencies, which generally pursue the persuasion that educational endeavor and achievement in that field presents the best if not indeed the only hope. The objective historian should be on his guard against the general and laudable *tendenz* of these organizations toward the promotion of international peace.[29]

Many of them have organs of publication and print, or sponsor studies in international relations. Many of them broadcast reprints of state papers [30] which are sources for diplomatic history, which as a consequence become cheaply and easily obtainable. Frequently these publications furnish the most convenient and effective means of keeping close up to date on day-to-day developments in our own times. Recently there have appeared five manuals which list such agencies and their publications:

League of Nations, *Handbook of international organisations (associations, bureaux, committees, etc.)* (Geneva, 1929; earlier editions, 1921, 1923, 1925) and *Supplement . . .* (Geneva, 1931), the chief purpose of which is to give most recent information on international organizations the world over, but enterprises " whose activity is international but whose organisation is built on a national basis are . . . omitted." [31]   [5155

Harley, J. E., *International understanding; agencies educating for a new world* (Stanford University, Cal., 1931).   [5156

---

[29] Incidentally, for example, one is likely to meet in such publications assertions that the United States has no foreign policy. As a matter of fact, few nations have had a more definite set of principles of foreign policy than the United States. Persons disagreeing with American foreign policy persuade themselves that the nation has none.

[30] See also Chapter II of Part II of this *Guide* for further information on printed state papers, particularly the League of Nations publications.

[31] See also S. A. Heald, *A directory of societies and organizations in Great Britain concerned with the study of international affairs* (London, 1929) [5157], published under the joint auspices of the Royal Institute of International Affairs and the Information Service on International Affairs.

International Institute of Intellectual Co-operation. *Handbook of reference centres for international affairs*, compiled by the International Institute of Intellectual Co-operation (League of Nations) (Paris, 1931).   [5158

Peace year book, 1931 (London, 1931), published by the National Peace Council.   [5159

Savord, Ruth, *Directory of American agencies concerned with the study of international affairs* (N.Y., 1931), published by the Council on Foreign Relations.   [5160

Among the many agencies listed in such manuals one may call attention to (1) Official international organizations; [32] and (2) the following in the United States:

Pan American Union [33] (estab. 1890) (Washington, D.C.), as the Commercial Bureau of the American Republics, later the International Bureau of American Republics, and in 1910 changed to the present title. It publishes a *Monthly bulletin*, 1893– [5164], in English, Portuguese and Spanish, which is the official organ of the Union, and constitutes a record of actual conditions and trends in each of the countries which are members of the Union; and other series of pamphlets and reports which, however, are concerned rather with commercial and economic conditions, etc., than with diplomatic relations.

Carnegie Endowment for International Peace (estab. 1910) (Washington, D.C.), the purpose of which as described in Mr. Carnegie's bequest of $10,000,000, is " to hasten the abolition of war, the foulest blot upon our civilization." It is organized into a number of divisions for particular purposes, among which one finds the following series of publications: [34] (1) *Classics in international law*, 1917–, the editing of which is directed by Dr. J. B. Scott, published by the Division of International Law, which also publishes a miscellaneous *Pamphlet series* [5165], dealing with international af-

---

[32] Official international organizations are: Pan American Union (see no. 5164, below); League of Nations (see its list of *Publications* (no. 5470a); and the Permanent Court of International Justice, at The Hague.

[33] See W. H. Kelchner, *The founding and development of the Pan American Union* (Wash., 1930) [5161]; L. S. Rowe, *The Pan American Union in Pan American affairs* (Wash., 1931) [5162]; and C. B. Casey, "The creation and development of the Pan American Union", *Hisp. Am. hist. rev.*, XIII (1933) 437–456 [5163].

[34] For a complete list of the publications of the Endowment see its *Yearbook* (no. 5070).

fairs. (2) *Economic and social history of the world war* [**5166**], a voluminous series, from different nations, edited by Professor J. T. Shotwell, and published by the Division of Economics and History; not directly connected with political history. (3) *International conciliation*, 1907– [**5167**], published in pamphlet form, about ten numbers per annum, each number devoted to some special contemporary problem; many of the numbers are devoted to documents and state papers. Distributed to subscribers at a nominal price, these pamphlets, in the hands of discriminating students, are of great value.[35]

World Peace Foundation (estab. 1910) (Boston), its purposes are similar to the Carnegie Endowment for International Peace, but its resources are much more limited. Its publications include books and a *Pamphlet series*, 1910–17, 7 v.; 1917–30, 20 v. [**5168**], consisting of short monographs on timely topics of international interest, similar in content to *International conciliation* (no. 5167).[36] This series (issued at irregular intervals at first) was published in 1917–1923 under the title *League of Nations*. Since the completion of v. XII, the term *Pamphlet* has not been used. The Foundation also issues: *International book news* [**5169**], a bibliographical periodical, each number being devoted to the publications in a selected field of international relations and cooperation.

The Foundation also serves as a general distributing agent for documents issued by other agencies, both in America and Europe, including the League of Nations,[37] the Permanent Court of International Justice, and other official and semiofficial international cooperative bodies.

Council on Foreign Relations (estab. during the world war) (New York) is an organization similar to the Foreign Policy Association, seemingly of a more sober and discriminating cast. Besides

---

[35] During 1907–1909 issued by the American Association for International Conciliation. In 1910 the Association went under the control of the Division of Intercourse and Education of the Carnegie Endowment for International Peace, but continued to issue this publication under its own name until July 1924, after which *International conciliation* bears in the imprint the above division of the Carnegie Endowment in place of the original association.

[36] For list of pamphlets, etc., see Harley, *International understanding* (no. 5156), 385–388.

[37] See below, p. 849.

sponsoring the excellent quarterly, *Foreign affairs* (no. 4850), it maintains the following publications: (1) *Survey of American foreign relations*, 1928– (New Haven, 1928–) [5170], published annually, edited by C. P. Howland, and printed by the Yale University Press. It selects, in each number, specific subjects for treatment, with careful sketches of the historical background. Highly objective, it is indispensable for the student of contemporary American diplomacy. It is not, however, a complete account of American foreign relations for the given year. Beginning with the 1931 volume (published in 1932), its annual publication has been edited by Walter Lippmann and W. O. Scroggs, and its scope altered to present an annual survey of American foreign relations of the previous year as recorded and interpreted in newspapers, official documents, and other immediately available accounts, as follows: *The United States in world affairs; an account of American foreign relations*, 1931– (N.Y. and London, 1932–) [5171]. It contains a " Selected bibliography " (compiled in 1931 by Ruth Savord), listing printed works, source material dealing with recent events, and list of " periodicals and regularly published official and unofficial reports and bulletins which should prove especially useful to students of current history or international relations ", and a " Chronology of events affecting American foreign relations " of the specific year.

The Foreign Policy Association (estab. 1918) (New York) issues the following publications: [38] (1) *Information service*, 1925–, containing monthly articles, frequently generously documented, on current international problems. Beginning with the issue for March 18, 1931 (v. VII, no. 1) this publication appears under the name *Foreign policy reports*. (2) *Pamphlet series*, 1922–, containing separate short monographs on subjects of current international interest. (3) *Foreign policy bulletin* (formerly the *News bulletin*) 1923–, issued weekly, and containing brief comment on important international events. (4) *Study outlines*, with selected bibliographies.

So far as American foreign policy is concerned the attitude of the Foreign Policy Association appears to have been generally one of adverse criticism and attack.

---

[38] They are listed, to 1929, in Harley, *International understanding* (no. 5156), 258–263.

Chicago Council on Foreign Relations (organized 1922, incorporated 1923) publishes a series of small books on *American policies abroad*, 1928– [5172], the first volume related to Mexico, the second to the Caribbean, and the third to the *United States and Great Britain*, by C. R. Fish, Sir Norman Angell and C. L. Hussey [5172a]. It also publishes occasional (separate) volumes on special subjects.

Institute of Economics (estab. 1922) [39] (Washington, D.C.) publishes a series of *Investigations in international commercial policies* and *Investigations in international economic reconstruction* [5173], consisting of monographs on special subjects.

Institute of Pacific Relations (estab. 1925) [40] (headquarters, Honolulu, Hawaii) is concerned with promoting the best relations between the Pacific peoples; its main efforts devoted to collecting and elucidating the facts of international significance which may assist constructively the development of the countries concerned. Publishes *Problems of the Pacific* (Chicago, 1925–) giving the proceedings of the biennial conferences of the Institute. For list, see *Some publications on Pacific problems;* a list of papers and books published by or in cooperation with the Institute of Pacific Relations (Honolulu, Hawaii, 1932) [5175].

There are a number of university institutes of international relations, listed in Savord, *Directory* (no. 5160), which from time to time publish material on international problems of the day, like the Institute of Politics, founded at Williamstown, Massachusetts, in 1921; and the Institute of International Relations, which is a project of the Los Angeles University of International Relations, and publishes annual *Proceedings*, 1927–.

The foreign agencies will be found listed in the above-mentioned manuals, but we note here in particular one not included there:

American Library in Paris, Reference Service on International Affairs, which includes among its series of publications a *Bulletin*, 1924– [5176], issued several times a year, each number being devoted to a specific subject of international affairs; no. 3 (1924) consisting of a *Summary of source material* dealing with the character, scope, and method of securing the principal and most acces-

---

[39] Since December 1927, united with the Brookings Institution.
[40] J. M. Davis, *The Institute of Pacific Relations* (Worcester, Mass.) (International Conciliation, no. 218) [5174].

sible publications on international affairs of the principal international organizations, and of the governments of the United
States, Great Britain, and France. See also its *Official publications of European governments* (no. 5399a). From 1925 to 1929
(4 v.) it published fortnightly a *European economic and political
survey* [5177].

Biographies of American Statesmen and Diplomatists

The original intention of the compilers of this *Guide* was to present a list of selected biographies of American statesmen and diplomatists who had to do with the foreign relations of the United
States. On more mature consideration such a list has appeared to
us a work of supererogation in view of the careful and compendious
labor of scholars presented in the *Dictionary of American Biography*. We refer the reader particularly to the bibliographical summaries appended to the pertinent entries in the *D.A.B.* (no. 4927).
We anticipate that by the time this *Guide* is in the reader's hand
the publication of the *D.A.B.* will have advanced well into the last
letters of the alphabet; and we understand it is scheduled for completion in 1936. In the bibliographical chapters of our volume we
are giving citations of biographies which have been printed since the
entry in the D.A.B.

The reader is reminded that particular studies of the diplomacy
of each secretary of state are to be found in the series *The American
secretaries of state and their diplomacy* (no. 4796). Each one of the
biographical sketches in this series contains a bibliographical
appendix.

Brief accounts of American diplomatists to England and France
are found in Beckles Willson, *America's ambassadors to England
(1785–1928)* (London, 1928; N.Y., 1929) and his *America's ambassadors to France (1777–1927)* (N.Y. and London, 1928).

Writings of American Statesmen and Diplomatists

In this section are listed the writings (including mainly collected
works, correspondence, and autobiographical reminiscences) of
American diplomatists and of those statesmen who are particularly
identified with American diplomatic history, or whose writings contain comment of value on foreign affairs of their period. As a rule
speeches made in Congress or anywhere else where a regular record

has been kept (such as international commissions, the Hague Conventions, etc.) have been excluded. Nor have isolated speeches, letters, etc., unless of extraordinary value been entered here, and in any case only those which are not included in collected works or correspondence. Writings of diplomatists or statesmen dealing with a specific subject have been entered in the appropriate section of the *Bibliography* rather than in this general list.

See also the bibliographical notes appended to relevant articles in the *D.A.B.* for detailed information regarding the writings (MS. and printed) of the persons discussed.

A

Adams, Charles Francis, *A cycle of Adams letters, 1861–1865*, ed. by W. C. Ford (Boston and N.Y., 1920, 2 v.), a collection of family letters forming a valuable contribution to the social, military, and diplomatic history of the period; they were written during the period of his mission to Great Britain.   [5178

Adams, John, *The works of John Adams, second president of the United States: with a life of the author, notes and illustrations*, by his grandson, Charles Francis Adams (Boston, 1850–56, 10 v.); and *Statesman and friend; correspondence of John Adams with Benjamin Waterhouse, 1784–1822*, ed. by W. C. Ford (Boston, 1927).   [5179

Adams, John Quincy, *Memoirs of John Quincy Adams, comprising portions of his diary from 1795 to 1848*, ed. by C. F. Adams (Phila., 1874–77, 12 v.). "Letters of John Quincy Adams to Alexander Hill Everett, 1811–1837", *Am. hist. rev.*, XI (1905–06) 88–116, 332–354, the greater number of which are not included in the *Writings. Correspondence of John Quincy Adams, 1811–1814* (Worcester, Mass., 1913), reprinted from the *Proceedings* of the American Antiquarian Society, for April 1913, includes a few letters, written from Russia, not included in the *Writings. Writings of John Quincy Adams*, ed. by W. C. Ford (N.Y., 1913–17, 7 v.), covering the years 1779 to 1823. *The diary of John Quincy Adams, 1794–1845; American political, social, and intellectual life from Washington to Polk*, ed. by Allan Nevins (N.Y. and London, 1928), being a selection from his *Memoirs* giving emphasis on the more dramatic political and diplomatic events of the time.   [5180

Adams, Samuel, *The writings of Samuel Adams*, ed. by H. A. Cushing (N.Y., 1904–08, 4 v.).   [5181

Adams, T. B., *Berlin and the Prussian court in 1798; journal of Thomas Boylston Adams, secretary to the United States legation at Berlin*, ed. by V. H. Paltsits (N.Y., 1916), reprinted from the *Bulletin* of the New York Public Library, for November 1915. *Letters of Thomas Boylston Adams* (Cincinnati, 1917), consisting of letters written by Adams to Joseph Pitcairn, from The Hague and Berlin, 1795–98, while he was acting as secretary to his brother, J. Q. Adams.   [5182

Allen, Horace N., *Things Korean; a collection of sketches and anecdotes, missionary and diplomatic* (N.Y. and Chicago, 1908), the writer was minister to Korea, 1897–1905.   [5183

Ames, Fisher, *Works of Fisher Ames, with a selection from his speeches and correspondence*, ed. by his son, Seth Ames (Boston, 1854, 2 v.), v. I: *Letters, 1789–1807*, some of which throw light on our relations with France and Great Britain, from the Federalist anti-French viewpoint.   [5184

Andrews, C. C., *Christopher C. Andrews, . . . diplomat, general in the civil war; recollections, 1829–1922*, ed. by his daughter, Alice E. Andrews (Cleveland, O., 1928), minister to Sweden and Norway, 1869–77; there is a chapter of pleasant recollections of his service there, with diary entries.   [5185

Angell, James B., *The reminiscences of James Burrill Angell* (N.Y. and London, 1912), minister to China and member of commission to negotiate a new immigration treaty with that empire, 1880–81, member of the Canadian Fisheries Commission and the Canadian-American Deep Waterways Commission, 1887–89, and minister to Turkey, 1897–98.   [5185a]

B

Bacon, Robert, *Robert Bacon, life and letters*, by J. B. Scott (Garden City, N.Y., 1923), ambassador to France, 1909–12.   [5186

Barlow, Joel, *Life and letters of Joel Barlow, LL.D., poet, statesman, philosopher, with extracts from his works and hitherto unpublished poems*, by C. B. Todd (N.Y. and London, 1886), consul to Algiers, 1796–97, and negotiator of treaties with Tunis, Algiers, and Tripoli; while minister to France, 1811–12, he endeavored to intercede with Napoleon for a more generous treatment of American commerce.   [5187

Bayard, J. A., *Letters of James Asheton Bayard, 1802–1814* (Wilmington, Del., 1901), previously published in the *Bulletin* of the New York Public Library, IV (1900) 228–248; consists of letters to Caesar A. Rodney. *Papers of James A. Bayard, 1796–1815*, ed. by Elizabeth Donnan (Wash., 1915) (American Historical Association, Annual Report, 1913, v. II), Bayard was a member of the mediation commission to Russia, 1813, and of the peace commission at Ghent, in 1814. [5188

Belmont, Perry, *Public record of Perry Belmont, a member of the House of Representatives* . . . (Albany, 1898–1902, 6 v. in 4) includes some material dealing with his mission as minister to Spain, 1888–89. [5189

Benton, Thomas Hart, *Thirty years' view; or, A history of the working of the American government for thirty years, from 1820 to 1850; chiefly taken from the Congress debates, . . . and the speeches of ex-Senator Benton* (N.Y., 1854–56, 2 v.). [5190

Bigelow, John, *Retrospections of an active life* (N.Y., 1909–13, 5 v.), containing many letters; the writer was minister to France, 1865–66. [5191

Blaine, James G. (secretary of state, 1881, and 1889–1892), *Twenty years of Congress: from Lincoln to Garfield* (Norwich, Conn., 1884–86, 2 v.). *Political discussions; legislative, diplomatic, and popular, 1856–1886* (Norwich, Conn., 1887). [5192

Boudinot, Elias, *The life, public services, addresses, and letters of Elias Boudinot, LL.D., president of the Continental Congress*, ed. by J. J. Boudinot (Boston and N.Y., 1896, 2 v.). [5193

Bowen, Herbert W., *Recollections, diplomatic and undiplomatic* (N.Y., 1926), minister to Venezuela, 1901–05, and counsel for Venezuela at the Venezuela arbitration before the Hague tribunal in 1903. [5194

Bryan, W. J., *The memoirs of William Jennings Bryan, by himself and his wife* (Phila. and Chicago, 1925) discusses briefly his activities as secretary of state, 1913–15, and the peace treaties which he sponsored. [5195

Buchanan, James. *The works of James Buchanan, comprising his speeches, state papers, and private correspondence*, ed. by J. B. Moore (Phila. and London, 1908–11, 12 v.) contains a biographical sketch, by J. B. Henry, and an autobiographical sketch, 1791–

1828, and includes all the more important instructions of Buchanan and a few of the especially important despatches.   [5196

Burr, Aaron. *Memoirs of Aaron Burr with miscellaneous selections from his correspondence*, by Matthew L. Davis (N.Y., 1836–37, 2 v.), Davis was intimately acquainted with Burr; his editing of the correspondence is unreliable and untrustworthy. *The private journal of Aaron Burr*, reprinted in full from the original manuscript in the library of Mr. William K. Bixby of St. Louis (Rochester, N.Y., 1903, 2 v.), comp. and ed. by W. H. Samson; corrects errors made by Davis (above), gives the material " as nearly as possible as Burr wrote it."   [5197

C

Cabot, George, *Life and letters of George Cabot*, by Henry Cabot Lodge (Boston, 1877), the letters of the 1790's and early 1800's reflect the views of the more moderate type of Federalist leader of this period in regard to French affairs, relations with Great Britain, the embargo, neutral rights, etc.   [5198

Calhoun, J. C. *The works of John C. Calhoun*, ed. by R. C. Crallé (N.Y., 1851–56, 6 v.) includes the most important of his instructions as secretary of state, 1844–45. *Correspondence of John C. Calhoun*, ed. by J. F. Jameson (Wash., 1900) (American Historical Association, Annual Report, 1899, v. II) contains a few instructions not given in his *Works*. " Correspondence addressed to John C. Calhoun, 1837–1849," ed. by C. S. Boucher and R. P. Brooks, *Am. hist. assoc. ann. rep.*, for 1929 (1930) 125–533, 551–570, throws new and additional light upon the Oregon question.   [5199

Cathcart, J. L., *Tripoli . . . Letter book by James Leander Cathcart, first consul to Tripoli, and last letters from Tunis*, comp. by his daughter, J. B. Cathcart Newkirk (La Porte, Ind., 1901), the journal of his negotiations with the regency of Tripoli, 1799 and years following, containing letters from Tripoli and Tunis, 1799–1802.   [5200

Child, Richard Washburn, *A diplomat looks at Europe* (N.Y., 1925), by the ambassador to Italy, 1921–24, containing reminiscences of the conference at Genoa, 1922, and his diary at the Lausanne conference, in 1923.   [5201

Choate, J. H., *American addresses at the second Hague peace conference, delivered by Joseph H. Choate* [and others], ed. by J. B. Scott (Boston and London, 1910). *The two Hague conferences* (Princeton, 1913). "Mr. Choate in England; extracts from his letters showing his activities while ambassador", *Scribner's*, LXVIII (1920) 403–417. *Arguments and addresses of Joseph H. Choate*, ed. by F. C. Hicks (St. Paul, 1926).   [5202

Choate, Rufus, *The works of Rufus Choate, with a memoir of his life*, by S. G. Brown (Boston, 1862, 2 v.) contains a speech in the Senate, June 11, 1841, in defense of Webster's conduct in the McLeod case.   [5203

Clay, C. M., *The writings of Cassius Marcellus Clay: including speeches and addresses*, ed. with preface and memoir, by Horace Greeley (N.Y., 1848) does not, however, extend to the period of his mission to Russia, 1861–62.   [5204

Clay, Henry, *Works of Henry Clay, comprising his life, correspondence, and speeches*, ed. by Calvin Colton (N.Y., 1863, 6 v.; 1897, 7 v.), secretary of state, 1825–29.   [5205

Cleveland, Grover, *Addresses, state papers and letters*, ed. by A. E. Bergh (N.Y., 1909) includes his lectures on the Venezuela boundary dispute given at Princeton University, 1901. *Letters of Grover Cleveland, 1850–1908*, selected and edited by Allan Nevins (Boston, 1933), that part of the material used by the editor in writing his *Life of Grover Cleveland*.   [5206

Collier, William M., *At the court of His Catholic Majesty* (Chicago, 1912), the writer's reminiscences as minister to Spain, 1905–09.
     [5207

Coolidge, T. J., *The autobiography of T. Jefferson Coolidge, 1831–1920* (Boston and N.Y., 1923), minister to France, 1892–93, and in 1898, member of the Joint High Commission of Great Britain and the United States, to examine the questions of the Alaskan boundary, fisheries, destruction of fur seals, etc.   [5208

Crawford, W. H., *The journal of William H. Crawford*, ed. by D. C. Knowlton (Northampton, Mass., 1925) (Smith Coll. Stud. in Hist., v. XI, no. 1) covers the period of his diplomatic mission to France (1813–15) from the time of his departure on June 4, 1813, to his interview with Napoleon on Nov. 14 of the same year.   [5209

Cullom, S. M., *Fifty years of public service; personal recollections of Shelby M. Cullom, senior senator from Illinois* (Chicago, 1911), chairman of the Senate committee on foreign relations, 1901 to 1913.   [5210

D

Dallas, A. J., *Life and writings of Alexander James Dallas*, by his son G. M. Dallas (Phila., 1871), his writings as secretary of the treasury, 1814–15, throw light on Jay's treaty, the foreign relations of the war period and the question of neutral rights.
        [5211

Dallas, G. M., *A series of letters from London written during the years 1856, '57, '58, '59, and '60*, ed. by his daughter Julia (Phila., 1869), of which many are addressed to Secretaries Marcy and Cass, and, though touching on matters behind the screen of diplomacy, are nevertheless wholly apart from his official correspondence. *Diary of George Mifflin Dallas, while United States minister to Russia, 1837 to 1839, and to England, 1856 to 1861*, ed. by Susan Dallas (Phila., 1892).   [5212

Dana, Francis. *Francis Dana, a Puritan diplomat at the court of Catherine the Great*, by W. P. Cresson (N.Y. and Toronto, 1930) contains letters now for the first time printed, taken from his letter books or the originals preserved in the Adams family archives.   [5213

Davis, Jefferson, *Jefferson Davis, constitutionalist, his letters, papers, and speeches*, ed. by Dunbar Rowland (Jackson, Miss., 1923, 10 v.).
        [5214

Deane, Silas, *The Deane papers*, ed. by Charles Isham (N.Y., 1887–90, 5 v.) (N.Y. Hist. Soc. Coll., v. XIX–XXIII) cover the period from 1774 to 1790, and include a biographical sketch by the editor. *The Deane papers; correspondence between Silas Deane, his brothers and their business and political associates, 1771–1795* (Hartford, 1930) (Conn. Hist. Soc. Coll., v. XXIII).
        [5215

Denby, Charles, *China and her people; being the observations, reminiscences, and conclusions of an American diplomat* (Boston, 1906, 2 v.), by the minister to China, 1885–97.   [5216

Draper, William F., *Recollections of a varied career* (Boston, 1908), the writer was minister to Italy, 1897–1900.   [5217

E

Eaton, William, *The Hull-Eaton correspondence during the expedition against Tripoli, 1804–1805*, ed. from a letter book in the library of the society, by C. H. Lincoln (Worcester, Mass., 1911), reprinted from the *Proceedings* of the American Antiquarian Society, n.s., v. XXI, pt. 1.   [5218

Egan, Maurice Francis, *Ten years near the German frontier* (N.Y., 1919), the writers's experiences as minister to Denmark, 1907–15, revealing glimpses of German-American relations at the outbreak of the war, as well as negotiations leading up to the purchase of the Danish West Indies, in 1916; and his *Recollections of a happy life* (N.Y., 1924).   [5219

Evarts, W. M., *Arguments and speeches of William Maxwell Evarts*, ed. by his son, Sherman Evarts (N.Y., 1919, 3 v.), his legal rather than diplomatic, writings and speeches; includes his argument before the international tribunal at Geneva, on behalf of the United States, under the treaty of Washington (Alabama claims), 1871, and argument before the mixed commission on British and American claims under the treaty of Washington, 1873.   [5220

Everett, Edward, *Orations and speeches on various occasions* (Boston, 1850–68, 4 v.), these do not however reflect his brief diplomatic career of 4 months as secretary of state, 1852–53. *Cuba; the Everett letters on Cuba* (Boston, 1897), including his letter to the French minister, the Comte de Sartiges, Dec. 1, 1852, on the project of a convention between France, Great Britain, and the United States to guarantee Cuba to Spain.   [5221

F

Fillmore, Millard. *Millard Fillmore papers*, ed. by F. H. Severance (Buffalo, N.Y., 1907, 2 v.) (Buffalo Hist. Soc. Pub., v. X–XI), containing a bibliography of publications of Fillmore or relating to his career and services.   [5222

Foster, John W., *Diplomatic memoirs* (Boston and N.Y., 1909, 2 v.), being his reminiscences as minister to Mexico, 1873–80, and secretary of state, 1892–93. The more significant of his publications on American diplomacy are enumerated in *The American secretaries of state* (no. 4796), v. VIII, 342–344.   [5223

Francis, David R., *Russia from the American embassy, April 1916–November 1918* (N.Y., 1921), consisting of his recollections and letters while minister to Russia, 1916–18. [5224

Franklin, Benjamin, *The works of Benjamin Franklin, . . . with notes and a life of the author*, ed. by Jared Sparks (Boston, 1836–40, 10 v.). *Benjamin Franklin's life and writings; a bibliographical essay on the Stevens' collection of books and manuscripts relating to Doctor Franklin*, by Henry Stevens (London, 1881), the collection is now in the Library of Congress. *The complete works of Benjamin Franklin*, comp. and ed. by John Bigelow (N.Y. and London, 1887–88, 10 v.). *List of the Benjamin Franklin papers in the Library of Congress*, ed. by W. C. Ford (Wash., 1905) (Library of Congress). *The writings of Benjamin Franklin*, ed., with a life and introduction, by A. H. Smyth (N.Y. and London, 1905–07, 10 v.). *Calendar of the papers of Benjamin Franklin in the library of the American Philosophical Society*, ed. by I. M. Hays (Phila., 1908, 5 v.). William L. Clements Library of American History, *An exhibition of books and papers relating to Dr. Benjamin Franklin from the collections in this library and the library of William Mason Smith* (Ann Arbor, Mich., 1926), the Clements Library has " several original letters exchanged between Franklin and Oswald, as well as all the original correspondence between Oswald and the British prime minister Shelburne to whom Oswald gave lengthy and detailed reports of his negotiations with the Doctor." *Benjamin Franklin, bibliographie et étude sur les sources historiques relatives à sa vie* [by] Bernard Faÿ (Paris, 1931). [5225

G

Gallatin, Albert, *The writings of Albert Gallatin*, ed. by Henry Adams (Phila., 1879, 3 v.), member of the commission sent to Russia in response to the offer of mediation in the war with Great Britain, in 1813, member of the peace mission at Ghent, 1814, minister to France, 1816–23, and to Great Britain, 1826–27. [5226

Gallatin, James, *A great peacemaker; the diary of James Gallatin, secretary to Albert Gallatin, 1813–1827*, ed. by Count Gallatin (N.Y., 1914; new ed., 1916), containing his journal of the peace negotiations at Ghent. [5227

Garfield, J. A. *The works of James Abram Garfield*, ed. by B. A. Hinsdale (Boston, 1882–83, 2 v.), dealing with national affairs rather than international relations.   [5228

Gerard, James W., *My four years in Germany* (London and N.Y., 1917), and *Face to face with Kaiserism* (N.Y., 1918), consisting of his experiences and observations while ambassador to the German empire, during the first years of the world war, 1913–17.   [5229

Gibson, Hugh, *A journal from our legation in Belgium* (N.Y., 1917), the "private journal jotted down hastily from day to day", of the secretary of legation at Brussels during the year 1914.   [5230

H

Hamilton, Alexander, *The works of Alexander Hamilton; containing his correspondence and his political and official writings, exclusive of the Federalist, civil, and military*, ed. by J. C. Hamilton (N.Y., 1850–51, 7 v.). *The works of Alexander Hamilton*, ed. by H. C. Lodge (N.Y., 1885–86, 9 v.). The arrangement of the earlier edition is more convenient.   [5231

Harris, Townsend, *The complete journal of Townsend Harris, first American consul general and minister to Japan*, ed. by Mario Emilio Cosenza (Garden City, N.Y., 1930), covering the years, 1855–58.   [5232

Harrison, Benjamin, *Public papers and addresses of Benjamin Harrison, twenty-third president of the United States, March 4, 1889, to March 4, 1893* (Wash., 1893).   [5233

Hay, John, *Letters of John Hay and extracts from diary* (Wash., 1908, printed but not published, 3 v.); *The life and letters of John Hay*, by W. R. Thayer (Boston and N.Y., 1915, 2 v.), ambassador to Great Britain, 1897–98, and secretary of state, 1898–1905.   [5234

Hayes, R. B., *Diary and letters of Rutherford Birchard Hayes, nineteenth president of the United States*, ed. by C. R. Williams (Columbus, O., 1922–26, 5 v.). See also the *Index and list of letters and papers of Rutherford Birchard Hayes* (no. 5513).   [5235

Hillard, H. W., *Politics and pen pictures at home and abroad* (N.Y., 1892) gives an account of his mission to Belgium, 1842–44, and to Brazil, 1877–81.   [5236

Hoar, George F., *Autobiography of seventy years* (N.Y., 1903, 2 v.), a valuable political autobiography, by a leading anti-imperialist senator (from Massachusetts) of the late 19th century.   [5237

Hoffman, Wickham, *Camp, court and siege; a narrative of personal adventure and observation during two wars: 1861-1865, 1870-1871* (N.Y., 1877), the writer was secretary of the legation at Paris, 1869-1871, and here relates his experiences during the Franco-Prussian war.   [5238

House, Edward M., *The intimate papers of Colonel House arranged as a narrative* by Charles Seymour (Boston and N.Y., 1926-28, 4 v.), extending over the period from 1912 to 1919, a most valuable printed source of " inside " details of United States foreign policy during a critical period.   [5239

Houston, David F., *Eight years with Wilson's cabinet, 1913 to 1920* (Garden City, N.Y., 1926, 2 v.), the reminiscences of the secretary of agriculture; throws some light upon foreign relations.   [5240

Hughes, Charles Evans, *The pathway of peace; representative addresses delivered during his term as secretary of state (1921-1925)* (N.Y. and London, 1925) contains addresses by the former secretary of state on various phases of his foreign policy (limitation of armaments, Russia, Latin America, Monroe Doctrine, World Court, etc.). *Our relations to the nations of the western hemisphere* (Princeton, 1928).   [5241

Humphreys, David, *Life and times of David Humphreys*, by F. L. Humphreys (N.Y. and London, 1917, 2 v.) prints his letters and despatches covering his diplomatic career as secretary to the commission for negotiating treaties with foreign powers, in France and England, 1784-86, as minister to Portugal, 1791-97, and to Spain, 1797-1801.   [5241a

I

Izard, Ralph, *Correspondence of Mr. Ralph Izard, of South Carolina, from the year 1774 to 1804; with a short memoir* (N.Y.,1844) includes his correspondence during his residence in Europe as commissioner to the court of Tuscany during the American revolution. *Some letters of Ralph Izard to Thomas Jefferson*, contributed by W. C. Ford (Charleston, 1901), reprinted from the *South Carolina historical and genealogical magazine* for July 1901; among them are several of 1785-1789 discussing our relations with France, Great Britain, and the Barbary States.   [5242

J

Jackson, Andrew, *The statesmanship of Andrew Jackson as told in his writings and speeches*, ed. by F. N. Thorpe (N.Y., 1909). *Correspondence of Andrew Jackson*, ed. by J. S. Bassett (Wash.: Carnegie Institution, 1926–33, 6 v.), the sixth volume contains the most important letters by Jackson in a valuable acquisition of Jackson MSS. recently acquired by the Library of Congress, the " cream " of the Jackson papers which had been taken out by the general for an intended biography by Eaton.   [5243

Jay, John, *The life of John Jay; with selections from his correspondence*, by his son, William Jay (N.Y., 1833, 2 v.). *The correspondence and public papers of John Jay*, ed. by H. P. Johnston (N.Y., 1890–93, 4 v.). *The diary of John Jay during the peace negotiations of 1782; being a complete and faithful rendering of the original manuscript, now published for the first time*, ed. by Frank Monaghan (New Haven, 1934).   [5244

Jefferson, Thomas, *The writings of Thomas Jefferson*, ed. by H. A. Washington (Wash., 1853–54, 9 v.). *The writings of Thomas Jefferson*, ed. by P. L. Ford (N.Y., 1892–99, 10 v.).[41] *Calendar of the correspondence of Thomas Jefferson* (Wash.: Dept. of State, 1894–1903, 3 v.). *The Jeffersonian cyclopedia; a comprehensive collection of the views of Thomas Jefferson classified and arranged in alphabetical order* . . . ed. by J. P. Foley (N.Y. and London, 1900). *The Jefferson papers* (Boston, 1900) (Mass. Hist. Soc. Coll. 7th ser., v. I), a selection from the private papers of Thomas Jefferson in the Massachusetts Historical Society. *The writings of Thomas Jefferson*, memorial edition, ed. by A. A. Lipscomb and A. E. Bergh (Wash., 1903–04, 20 v.). *The letters of Lafayette and Jefferson*, ed. by Gilbert Chinard (Baltimore, Md., and Paris, 1929), " most of the letters and documents printed in this volume have never been published before and were copied from the originals in the Library of Congress." *Correspondence between Thomas Jefferson and Pierre Samuel du Pont de Nemours, 1798–1817*, ed. by Dumas Malone (Boston and N.Y., 1930), " except for

---

[41] C. M. Thomas, " Date inaccuracies in Thomas Jefferson's Writings ", *Miss. Valley hist. rev.*, XIX (1932) 87–90 [5245], notes two instances where incorrect dates of cabinet meetings in 1793 lead to erroneous conclusions, as given in Ford's edition of the *Writings*.

one letter . . . all have been taken from the Jefferson papers in the Library of Congress "; ch. 4: " The Louisiana purchase, 1802–1803 " (p. 46–79). *The correspondence of Jefferson and Du Pont de Nemours, with an introduction on Jefferson and the physiocrats,* by Gilbert Chinard (Baltimore, Paris, and London, 1931), covering the period 1781–1826; contains documents in the original French, not in Malone's edition. " Letters of Thomas Jefferson to William Short ", *Wm. and Mary coll. quar. mag.,* 2d ser., XI (1931) 242–250, 336–342; XII (1932) 145–156, a collection of hitherto unprinted letters, in the library of the College of William and Mary, from Jefferson to Short, when Jefferson was minister to France, letters of 1785 to 1789. For critical summary of the various editions of the Writings of Jefferson, see Channing, *History of the United States,* v. IV, 272–273.   [5246

K

Kasson, J. A., " John A. Kasson; an autobiography ", *Annals of Iowa,* 3d ser., XII (1920) 346–358; Kasson's wide range of diplomatic service included: commissioner for making of postal conventions, 1867; minister to Austria-Hungary during the Congress of Berlin of 1878; to Germany during the Congo conference of 1884 at Berlin; head of the American delegation to the Berlin conference of 1889 in regard to Samoa; special commissioner, 1899, for the negotiation of commercial treaties; member of the British-American High Commission for the settlement of disputes with Canada.   [5247

King, Rufus, *The life and correspondence of Rufus King; comprising his letters, private and official, his public documents, and his speeches,* ed. by his grandson Charles R. King (N.Y., 1894–1900, 6 v.) includes his despatches while minister to Great Britain, 1796–1803.   [5248

Koerner, Gustave, *Memoirs of Gustave Koerner, 1809–1896, life-sketches written at the suggestion of his children,* ed. by T. J. McCormack (Cedar Rapids, Ia., 1909, 2 v.), minister to Spain, 1862–65.   [5249

L

Lafayette, Marquis de, *Mémoirs, correspondance et manuscrits du général Lafayette,* pub. par sa famille (Brussels, 1837–39, 12 v.), of which the first three volumes deal with the American revolution; is also issued in later French editions, and in 2 English editions (London, 1837, 3 v.; N.Y., 1837, 1 v.). *Correspondance inédite de La Fayette 1793–1801; lettres de prison—lettres d'exil*, précedée d'une étude psychologique par Jules Thomas (Paris, 1903). "Letters from the Marquis de Lafayette to Hon. Henry Laurens, 1777–1780", *S. C. hist. mag.*, VIII–IX (1907–1908), passim. "Letters from Lafayette to Luzerne, 1780–1782", ed. by W. G. Leland and E. C. Burnett, *Am. hist. rev.*, XX (1915) 341–376, 577–612. *The letters of Lafayette and Jefferson*, with an introduction and notes by Gilbert Chinard (Baltimore and Paris, 1929) comprises letters of 1781 to 1826, published here for the first time, and covering the most eventful period in Franco-American relations. [5250

Lamar, M. B., *Calendar of the papers of Mirabeau Buonaparte Lamar*, prepared from the original papers in the Texas State Library by Elizabeth H. West (Austin, Tex., 1914). *The papers of Mirabeau Buonaparte Lamar*, ed. from the original papers in the Texas State Library, by C. A. Gulick, jr., with the assistance of Katherine Elliott (Austin, Tex., 1921–27, 6 v.), consisting of the state papers and correspondence of the president of the Republic of Texas. [5251

Lane, F. K., *The letters of Franklin K. Lane* (Boston and N.Y., 1922), personal and semiofficial letters of the secretary of the interior, 1913–15, which throw light upon world war events and relations. [5252

Lansing, Robert, *The big four and others of the peace conference* (Boston, 1921), description of the leading personalities by the American secretary of state who met them; and *The peace negotiations, a personal narrative* (Boston, 1921), with searching illustrations on Wilson's program and policy. [5253

Lee, Arthur, *Life of Arthur Lee, LL.B., joint commissioner of the United States to the courts of Spain and Prussia, during the revolutionary war*, by Richard Henry Lee (Boston, 1829, 2 v.) includes his political and literary correspondence and his papers on diplomatic and political subjects and the affairs of the United States during the same period. *Calendar of the Arthur Lee manu-*

scripts in the library of Harvard University (Cambridge, Mass., 1882). *Calendar of the correspondence relating to the American revolution of . . . Hon. Arthur Lee, . . . in the library of the American Philosophical Society* (Phila., 1900), also published in its *Proceedings*, v. XXXVIII, 1899. *Catalogue of the manuscripts in the collection of the Virginia Historical Society* (Richmond, 1901) includes a catalogue of the letters of Arthur Lee, Richard Henry Lee, and William Lee, during the period from 1766 to 1789.   [5254

Lee, Richard Henry, " Selections and excerpts from the Lee papers ", *Southern literary messenger*, XXVII-XXIX (1858-1860) passim, consists of selections from the papers of Richard Henry Lee, including letters to Arthur Lee, from the collection in the University of Virginia. *Calendar of the correspondence relating to the American revolution of . . . Hon. Richard Henry Lee, Hon. Arthur Lee, . . . in the library of the American Philosophical Society* (Phila., 1900), also published in its *Proceedings*, v. XXXVIII, 1899. *The letters of Richard Henry Lee*, ed. by J. C. Ballagh (N.Y., 1911-14, 2 v.), written during the years 1762-1794. (See v. I, p. viii-x, for an account of collections of the Lee papers and previous publication of the same).   [5255

Lee, William, *Letters of William Lee, sheriff and alderman of London; commercial agent of the Continental Congress in France; and minister to the courts of Vienna and Berlin, 1766-1783*, ed. by W. C. Ford (Brooklyn, N.Y., 1891, 3 v.). His letters from Paris, London, and Brussels, etc., are calendared in the *Catalogue of manuscripts in the Virginia Historical Society* (Richmond, 1901).   [5256

Legaré, H. S., *Writings of Hugh Swinton Legaré . . . consisting of a diary of Brussels, and . . . extracts from his private and diplomatic correspondence; orations and speeches* (Charleston, S.C., and N.Y., 1845-46, 2 v.), reminiscences of the chargé d'affaires at Brussels, 1832-37.   [5257

Lieber, Francis, *The life and letters of Francis Lieber*, ed. by T. S. Perry (Boston, 1882) contains extracts from his diary; in 1870 he was chosen as umpire by the commission for settling claims between Mexico and the United States.   [5258

Lodge, H. C., *War addresses, 1915–1917* (Boston, 1917); *Selections from the correspondence of Theodore Roosevelt and Henry Cabot Lodge, 1884–1918* (N.Y., 1925, 2 v.); and *The Senate and the League of Nations* (N.Y., 1925).   [5259

M

McKinley, William, *Speeches and addresses of William McKinley, from March 1, 1897, to May 30, 1900* (N.Y., 1900).   [5260

McLane, Robert M., *Reminiscences, 1827–1897* (n. p., 1903), commissioner to China, 1853–55, and minister to Mexico, 1859–60.
                                                                    [5261

Madison, James, *The writings of James Madison, comprising his public papers and his private correspondence, including numerous letters and documents now for the first time printed,* ed. by Gaillard Hunt (N.Y., 1900–10, 9 v.) supersedes the earlier Gilpin edition. *Calendar of the correspondence of James Madison* (Wash.: Dept. of State, 1894–95; reprinted, 1902).   [5262

Marsh, G. P., *Life and letters of George Perkins Marsh,* comp. by Caroline C. Marsh (N.Y., 1888, 2 v.), minister to Turkey, 1849–53, and to Italy, 1861–82, but the volume ends with the appointment to Italy, in 1861.   [5263

Marshall, John. *The political and economic doctrines of John Marshall . . . also his letters, speeches, and hitherto unpublished and uncollected writings,* by J. E. Oster (N.Y., 1914) contains most of his published letters.   [5264

Mason, J. M., *The public life and diplomatic correspondence of James M. Mason, with some personal history,* by his daughter (Virginia Mason) (Roanoke, Va., 1903) includes his correspondence while agent of the Confederate States to Great Britain.
                                                                    [5265

Monroe, James, *Calendar of the correspondence of James Monroe,* new ed., with corrections and additions (Wash.: Dept. of State, 1893; reprinted 1902), covering the years 1783–1831. *The writings of James Monroe, including a collection of his public and private papers and correspondence now for the first time printed,* ed. by S. M. Hamilton (N.Y., 1898–1903, 7 v.). *Papers of James Monroe, listed in chronological order from the original manu-*

scripts in the Library of Congress, ed. by W. C. Ford (Wash., 1904) (Library of Congress), intended to complement the alphabetical *Calendar* . . . issued by the Dept. of State.   [5266

Morgenthau, Henry, *All in a lifetime* (Garden City, N.Y., 1922), being the reminiscences of the ambassador to Turkey, 1913–16; includes a report on the mission to Poland to investigate Jewish matters, in 1919. *Ambassador Morgenthau's story* (Garden City, N.Y., 1918) contains his reminiscences at Constantinople.

[5267

Morris, Gouverneur, *The life of Gouverneur Morris, with selections from his correspondence and miscellaneous papers*, by Jared Sparks (Boston, 1832, 3 v.). *The diary and letters of Gouverneur Morris, minister of the United States to France*, ed. by Anne C. Morris (N.Y., 1888, 2 v.), covering the years 1776–1816.   [5268

Morris, I. N., *From an American legation* (N.Y., 1923), containing the reminiscences of the American minister to Sweden during the world war.   [5269

Morris, Robert, *Description and analysis of the remarkable collection of unpublished manuscripts of Robert Morris, the first financial minister of the United States from 1781 to 1784, including his official and private diary and correspondence* . . . by H. A. Homes (Albany, 1876).   [5270

Motley, J. L., *The correspondence of John Lothrop Motley*, ed. by G. W. Curtis (N.Y., 1889, 2 v.), consisting mainly of private correspondence, and omitting that dealing with his resignation of the mission to Austria, and of his retirement from the English mission, which, according to the Preface of the *Correspondence*, are " told accurately and adequately in Dr. Holmes's *Memoir*." " John Lothrop Motley ", in *Ralph Waldo Emerson and John Lothrop Motley*, two memoirs by Oliver Wendell Holmes (Cambridge, Mass., 1892) (Holmes's *Writings*, v. XIV), p. 326–526.

[5271

Murray, William Vans, " Letters of William Vans Murray to John Quincy Adams, 1797–1803 ", ed. by W. C. Ford, *Am. hist. assoc. ann. rep.*, for 1912 (1914) 343–715, consists of his correspondence while minister to France.   [5272

N

Newlands, F. G., *The public papers of Francis G. Newlands*, edited and placed in historical setting by A. B. Darling (Boston and

N.Y., 1932, 2 v.), consisting mainly of his speeches in Congress
as member of the House of Representatives, 1893–1903, and of
the Senate, 1903–1917; in the former he served on the committee
on foreign affairs, and in the latter on the committee on foreign
relations.   [5273

O

Richard Olney and his public service, by Henry James; with documents including unpublished diplomatic correspondence (Boston
and N.Y., 1923).   [5274–5

P

Page, W. H., *The life and letters of Walter H. Page*, by B. J. Hendrick (Garden City, N.Y., 1922–25, 3 v.), containing material concerning his work as ambassador to Great Britain during the world
war (1913–18), and including his letters to Woodrow Wilson.
                                                                [5276

Paine, Thomas, *The writings of Thomas Paine*, ed. by M. D. Conway
N.Y., 1884–96, 4 v.). Later editions: Independence edition (N.Y.,
1908, 10 v.), ed. by D. E. Wheeler; and Patriots' edition (New
Rochelle, N.Y., 1925, 10 v.), ed. by W. M. Van der Weyde, seems to
contain no new material. The Conway edition contains only part
of the Paine correspondence in regard to the Deane affair, while he
was secretary to the committee on foreign affairs of the Continental Congress, 1777–1779. For this correspondence the investigator should consult the *Papers of the Continental Congress* in
the Library of Congress, no. 55, folios 1–69, and 75–101, these last
folios dealing with his negotiations with Congress in 1783, and
later, to obtain reimbursement for his expenses.   [5277

Parker, Peter, *The life, letters, and journals of the Rev. and Hon.
Peter Parker*, by the Rev. George B. Stevens (Boston and Chicago,
1896), containing material on his activities as secretary of legation and United States commissioner to China in the 1840's.
                                                                [5278

Perry, Matthew C., *Narrative of the expedition of an American
squadron to the China seas and Japan, performed in the years
1852, 1853, and 1854, under the command of Commodore M. C.
Perry, U.S. navy* (Wash., 1856, 3 v.), describing the negotiation
of the treaty with Japan in 1852.   [5279

Pierce, Franklin, *Calendar of the papers of Franklin Pierce, prepared from the original manuscripts in the Library of Congress* by W. R. Leech (Wash., 1917) (Library of Congress).   [5280

Pinkney, William, *Some account of the life, writings, and speeches of William Pinkney*, by Henry Wheaton (N.Y., 1826), commissioner of the United States under Jay's treaty to determine claims of American merchants to compensation for losses and damages by the British, 1796–1804, commissioner (with James Monroe) to treat with the British government respecting violation of rights of neutrals in 1806, minister to Great Britain, 1807–11, and minister to Russia and special envoy to Naples, 1815–18.   [5281

Polk, J. K., *The diary of James K. Polk during his presidency, 1845 to 1849, now first printed from the original manuscript in the collections of the Chicago Historical Society*, ed. by M. M. Quaife (Chicago, 1910, 4 v.). *Polk, the diary of a president, 1845–1849; covering the Mexican war, the acquisition of Oregon, and the conquest of California and the Southwest*, ed. by Allan Nevins (London and N.Y., 1929), containing selections only from the *Diary* (noted above).   [5282

R

Reinsch, P. S., *An American diplomat in China* (Garden City, N.Y., 1922), comprising reminiscences of his mission to China, 1913–20.   [5283

Roberts, Edmund, *Embassy to the eastern courts of Cochin-China, Siam, and Muscat . . . 1832–3–4* (N.Y., 1837), the writer was special agent to these countries to negotiate a treaty of amity and commerce.   [5284

Rockhill, W. W., *Diplomatic audiences at the court of China* (London, 1905), the writer was commissioner to China in 1900, and minister from 1905 to 1909.   [5285

Roosevelt, Theodore, *The works of Theodore Roosevelt*, memorial ed. (N.Y., 1923–26, 24 v.), prepared under the auspices of the Roosevelt Memorial Association, and ed. by Hermann Hagedorn. *Selections from the correspondence of Theodore Roosevelt and Henry Cabot Lodge, 1884–1918* (N.Y., 1925, 2 v.), the correspondence as a whole is general in character, but much of it reflects political affairs. "An exhaustive bibliography of Roosevelt's writings has been completed and will be published, it is expected, eventually, and a cyclopedia of Roosevelt's sayings is in preparation, with publication definitely in view ", by the Roosevelt Memorial Association, cf. F. F. Holbrook, *Survey* (no. 5569).

[5286

Root, Elihu, *Addresses on international subjects*, collected and edited by Robert Bacon and James Brown Scott (Cambridge, Mass., 1916) includes addresses on " The real Monroe Doctrine ", " The Hague peace conferences ", " Foreign affairs, 1913–1916 ", and three on the Panama Canal tolls question. *The United States and the war; the mission to Russia* (Cambridge, 1918). The writings and speeches of Secretary Root are extensive and are to be found in many periodicals as well as in separate publications. A considerable number are listed in *The American secretaries of state* (no. 4796), v. IX, 383–384.

[5287

Rush, Richard, *Memoranda of a residence at the court of London* (Phila., 1833; issued in several editions, 3d ed., 1872. London editions read *Narrative of a residence at the court of London*), this first series comprises events from 1817 to Jan. 1819; is followed by second series as follows: *Memoranda of a residence at the court of London, comprising incidents official and personal from 1819 to 1825, including negotiations on the Oregon question, and other unsettled questions between the United States and Great Britain* (Phila., 1845; another ed., London, 1845), written by the minister to Great Britain at that time.

[5288

S

Schurz, Carl, *The reminiscences of Carl Schurz* (N.Y., 1907–08, 3 v.) describes his mission to Spain in 1861. *Speeches, correspondence and political papers of Carl Schurz*, ed. by Frederic Bancroft (N.Y. and London, 1913, 6 v.).

[5289–90

Seward, F. W., *Reminiscences of a war-time statesmen and diplomat, 1830–1915* (N.Y., 1916), written by an assistant secretary of state during the administrations of Lincoln, Johnson, and Hayes.

[5291

Seward, W. H., *The works of William H. Seward*, ed. by G. E. Baker, new ed. (Boston, 1884, 5 v.). *William H. Seward, an autobiography, with a memoir of his life and selections from his letters*, by his son, Frederick W. Seward (N.Y., 1891, 3 v.).

[5292

Sharp, W. G., *The war memoirs of William Graves Sharp, American ambassador to France, 1914-1919*, ed. with a biographical introduction and notes by Warrington Dawson (London, 1931).
[5293

Sherman, John, *John Sherman's recollections of forty years in the House, Senate, and Cabinet; an autobiography* (Chicago and N.Y., 1895, 2 v.), written prior to his secretaryship of state, 1897-98.
[5294

Stimson, Frederic J., *My United States* (N.Y., 1931) is an autobiography, dealing especially with the author's diplomatic experiences in Argentina during the world war.   [5295

Straus, O. S., *Under four administrations, from Cleveland to Taft* (Boston and N.Y., 1922) comprises the recollections of Oscar S. Straus, who was minister to Turkey, 1887-88, 1898-1900, and 1909-10.   [5296

Sumner, Charles, *Memoir and letters of Charles Sumner*, by E. L. Pierce (Boston, 1877-93, 4 v.) contains valuable material on the Alabama claims and the Dominican question. *Charles Sumner, his complete works*, statesman ed. (Boston, 1900, 20 v.) contain numerous speeches on foreign relations made during his chairmanship of the committee on foreign relations of the United States Senate, 1861-1871.   [5297

T

Taylor, Bayard. *Life and letters of Bayard Taylor*, ed. by Marie Hansen-Taylor and Horace E. Scudder (Boston, 1884, 2 v.) contains material on his Russian mission, 1862-63, when he was secretary of legation at St. Petersburg.   [5298

Thompson, Waddy, *Recollections of Mexico* (N.Y., and London, 1846) gives his reminiscences of Mexico while minister to that country, 1842-44, and includes some diplomatic correspondence.
[5299

Thomson, Charles, *The papers of Charles Thomson, secretary of the Continental Congress* (N.Y., 1879) (N.Y. Hist. Soc. Coll., v. XI) consists of the correspondence between Thomson and Franklin, Jay, R. R. Livingston, and others, 1765-1816, and the debates in the Congress of the Confederation, July 22 to September 20, 1782.
[5300

Trumbull, John, *Autobiography, reminiscences and letters of John Trumbull from 1756 to 1841* (N.Y. and London, 1841), Jay's secretary in 1794 and member of the commission under article VII of Jay's treaty which sat at London, 1797–1804.   [5301

Tyler, John. *The letters and times of the Tylers*, by Lyon G. Tyler (Richmond, Va., 1884–85, 2 v.) includes many letters of President Tyler.   [5302

V

Van Buren, Martin, *Calendar of the papers of Martin Van Buren*, from the original manuscripts in the Library of Congress, by Elizabeth Howard West (Wash., 1910) (Library of Congress). *Autobiography of Martin Van Buren*, ed. by J. C. Fitzpatrick (Wash., 1920) (Am. Hist. Assoc. Ann. Rep., for 1918, v. II).   [5303

Vopicka, C. J., *Secrets of the Balkans; seven years of a diplomatist's life in the storm centre of Europe* (Chicago, 1921), the reminiscences of the minister to Rumania, 1913–1920.   [5304

W

Washburn, C. A., *The history of Paraguay, with notes of personal observations, and reminiscences of diplomacy under difficulties* (Boston, 1871) describes his diplomatic experiences as minister to Paraguay from 1861 to 1868.   [5305

Washburne, E. B., *Recollections of a minister to France, 1869–1877* (N.Y., 1877, 2 v.).   [5306

Washington, George, *A calendar of Washington manuscripts in the Library of Congress*, comp. under the direction of Herbert Friedenwald (Wash., 1901) (Library of Congress). *Calendar of the correspondence of George Washington, commander in chief of the Continental army with the Continental Congress*, prepared from the original manuscripts in the Library of Congress by J. C. Fitzpatrick (Wash., 1906) (Library of Congress). *Calendar of the correspondence of George Washington, commander in chief of the Continental army with the officers*, prepared from the original manuscripts in the Library of Congress by J. C. Fitzpatrick (Wash., 1915, 4 v.) (Library of Congress). *The writings of George Washington from the original manuscript sources, 1745–1799*, ed. by J. C. Fitzpatrick (Wash., 1931–), prepared under the direction of the United States George Washington Bicentennial Commission, to date (1934) 11 volumes, 1745– May 31, 1778, have appeared. This edition supersedes both the Sparks and the Ford editions.   [5307

Webster, Daniel, *Diplomatic and official papers of Daniel Webster, while secretary of state* (N.Y., 1848). *The works of Daniel Webster* (Boston, 1851, 6 v.). *The letters of Daniel Webster, from documents owned principally by the New Hampshire Historical Society*, ed. by C. H. Van Tyne (N.Y., 1902) presents new material especially rich in details of his work in connection with the " Caroline " and " McLeod " cases, the northeastern boundary dispute, and the impressment question. *The writings and speeches of Daniel Webster*, national ed. (Boston, 1903, 18 v.), ed. by J. W. McIntire, is a substantially complete edition of his writings, and thus supersedes earlier publications.   [5308

Weed, Thurlow, *Life of Thurlow Weed, including his autobiography and a memoir* (Boston and N.Y., 1883–84, 2 v.) reflects the political events of the time, and in both autobiography and memoir gives accounts of his semi-official mission in 1861–62, with Archbishop Hughes and Bishop McIlvane, to prevent the intervention of foreign governments, especially England and France, in behalf of the Confederacy.   [5309

Welles, Gideon, *Diary of Gideon Welles, secretary of the navy under Lincoln and Johnson*, with an introduction by J. T. Morse, jr. (Boston and N.Y., 1911, 3 v.).   [5310

White, A. D., *Autobiography of Andrew Dickson White* (N.Y., 1905, 2 v.) describes his diplomatic experiences in various positions, as commissioner to Santo Domingo in 1871, minister to Germany, 1879–1881, and ambassador to that country, 1897–1903, minister to Russia, 1892–94, and as president of the American delegation at the peace conference at The Hague, 1899.   [5311

Whitlock, Brand, *Belgium; a personal narrative* (N.Y., 1919, 2 v.) comprises his reminiscences while minister, and later ambassador, to Belgium, during the world war, 1913–22.   [5312

Williams, S. W., *The life and letters of Samuel Wells Williams, LL.D., missionary, diplomatist, sinologue*, by his son F. W. Williams (N.Y. and London, 1889), Williams, originally a missionary, was successively secretary of the commission to China, to

1838, interpreter for Perry's expedition to Japan, 1853–54, secretary to the legation of the United States in Japan, and seven times *chargé-d'affaires.*   [5313

Wilson, Henry Lane, *Diplomatic episodes in Mexico, Belgium, and Chile* (Garden City, N.Y., 1927) describes his experiences in Chile, 1897–1902, Belgium, 1905–09, and Mexico, 1909–13.   The memoirs of this American diplomatist, who differed from President Wilson on the non-recognition of Huerta in Mexico in 1913, are of value principally for Mexican-American relations.   [5314

Wilson, Woodrow, *Addresses delivered by President Wilson on his western tour, September 4 to September 25, 1919, on the League of Nations, etc.* (Wash.: Govt. Print. Off.). *Woodrow Wilson and world settlement, written from his unpublished and personal material,* by Ray Stanard Baker (Garden City, N.Y., 1922, 3 v.), the third volume of which is devoted wholly to the texts of letters, memoranda, minutes, and other crucial documents referred to or quoted from in the narrative. *The public papers of Woodrow Wilson,* authorized ed., by R. S. Baker and W. E. Dodd (N.Y. and London, 1925–27, 6 v.), v. III–VI, consisting of presidential messages, addresses, and public papers, 1913–1924. *Woodrow Wilson; life and letters* (Garden City, N.Y., 1927–31, 4 v.), this is the standard biography of Wilson by his designated biographer, Ray Stannard Baker, writing intimately from the war President's voluminous personal papers. The last volume advances only to the year 1914. Sequent volumes may be looked forward to as vitally important for the period of the world war.
      [5315

Winthrop, R. C., *Addresses and speeches on various occasions* (Boston, 1852–86, 4 v.).   [5316

Wolcott, Oliver, *Memoirs of the administrations of Washington and John Adams* (N.Y., 1846, 2 v.) gives voluminous selections from the papers of Oliver Wolcott, second secretary of the treasury.   [5317

Y

Young, John Russell, *Men and memories; personal reminiscences* (N.Y., 1901) is the work of a former minister to China, 1882–85.
      [5318

PART II

REMARKS ON THE SOURCES

INTRODUCTION TO PART II

"Diplomatic history" is a phrase in recent years commonly used to indicate the history of diplomacy. We at once distinguish it from the more recondite subject of "diplomatics", which is the study of ancient documents, their deciphering and interpretation. To be sure, "diplomatics" must occasionally be part of the equipment of the investigator into diplomatic history, though usually the study of this subject does not involve questions of establishing the authenticity of obscure texts and discovering their meaning.

The principal function of this second part of our manual is to guide the investigator in the sources for the diplomatic history of the United States. Here we wish to say something about the nature of the sources; to present a general analysis of the printed sources; finally to give some general guidance through the realm of MS. material, suggesting here and there bypaths which may be explored from the main highways. We intend that the reader in using these chapters shall refer back to the first part of the book, where more specific bibliographic data have been assembled topically and chronologically.

783

CHAPTER I

NATURE OF THE SOURCES FOR THE DIPLOMATIC HISTORY OF THE UNITED STATES

The sources for the diplomatic history of the United States are relatively modern. That history began in 1775, although America as a factor in European diplomacy dates back to the beginning of modern history, which commenced with the discovery of the New World. Provided one is familiar with the languages in which they are written and has fairly good eyesight, there is usually little difficulty in reading these sources, except in those cases where for safety against interception a despatch may have been put into secret cipher.[1]

---

[1] Most ciphers can be broken down with skill and patience by experts; but for the most part translations are preserved in archives, for the simple reason that untranslated despatches were of no use to the persons for whom they were intended.

The reader is presumed to be aware that historical sources are the traces, generally written or printed, of happenings left by those who participated in or witnessed them, or, lacking such participants and witnesses, by those who were nearest to them. For diplomatic history, at least, this definition suffices. Our body of knowledge for the history of the conduct of diplomacy rests on documentary records. This does not mean that portions, sometimes essential portions, of what actually happened have been always recorded, or if recorded were not later lost or destroyed, by accident or purposely. Diplomacy is a business where things can be done and have been done orally or even by gestures, traces of which speedily evaporate. In the name of diplomacy, too, things have been done—let us use the perfect—of which, without documents, only the angels in heaven are witnesses. But when all is said and done, only the remaining record of what was said or done, or its obvious results, is available for the historian.

The record itself is not meager. Practical reasons impel governments to preserve detailed records, and it is usual to find not only despatches minutely relating diplomatic affairs, but minutes of oral conversations, sometimes on most trivial matters. Even the reports of secret service agents—than which nothing is more likely to shrink from the light of public knowledge—are occasionally preserved, much to the enlightenment of historians. With the mass of public and private documents it is possible to state that for diplomatic history the sources are fairly complete, if all are not immediately available. Indeed, with the increasing volume of international intercourse with foreign nations in which a great power like the United States is engaged, the historian is embarrassed not by a paucity but by a plethora of sources. So voluminous has become the record that it is doubtful whether any one historian can write from the sources the full history of American diplomacy in recent times. The diplomatic history of the United States during the twentieth century, during any appreciable period of our own times must rest on a foundation of monographs, themselves based on a first-hand working of the sources. Diplomatic history thus becomes like other forms of social study a matter of organized effort. A less exalted part of that division of labor is the preparation of such a guide as this.

As we indicate the variety of principal sources, official and unofficial, printed and manuscript, for the diplomatic history of the

United States, we must insist that the investigator of necessity has a familiarity with the methods of historical research and the elements of historical criticism;[2] with the terms and definitions, the principles and practices, the offices and customs on which rests the practice of diplomacy;[3] and with the principles of international law.[4] The historian of diplomacy cannot ignore these essentials of the diplomatists' profession.

A primary distinction in describing the sources is between official and private records: that is, between the records kept by governments in their state archives, and the private papers of official personages or even of private individuals. The latter category of documents is often more revealing than the official documents written over the signature of the writer in his official capacity. The fact that the original draft of the Ostend Manifesto is in the handwriting of James Buchanan,[5] found among his personal papers, has a significance beyond that flowing from the official copy duly signed by Soulé, Mason, and Buchanan. The private letter of Señor Dupuy de Lome to a friend in Cuba, intercepted and published by the press in 1898, is a far more revealing description of what that diplomatist really thought of President McKinley than we might expect to find in his official despatches. The private letters of Colonel E. M. House to President Wilson give the inside history of American diplomacy during the World War more vividly and more valuably than the official despatches in the Department of State.

The private papers of diplomatists are sometimes quasi-public in their nature and it is often difficult, at least for historical pur-

---

[2] There is a constantly expanding list of manuals on historical method and criticism. Like the elements of strategy, the elements of criticism are everlasting, and old manuals are not necessarily obsolete. Two well-known standbys are: Ernst Bernheim, *Lehrbuch der historischen Methode und der Geschichtsphilosophie* (Leipzig, 1889; 6th ed., 1908) [5319–21] and Ch. V. Langlois and Ch. Seignobos, *Introduction to the study of history* (London and N.Y., 1898), translated from the French, *Introduction aux études historiques* (Paris, 1897) [5322]. Two more recent manuals, somewhat simplified by American professors, are: J. M. Vincent, *Historical research; an outline of theory and practice* (N.Y., 1911) [5323], and Allen Johnson, *The historian and historical evidence* (N.Y., 1926) [5324]. For the mechanics of research (note taking, etc.) see H. C. Hockett, *Introduction to research in American history* (N.Y., 1931) [5325]. For others, see *Guide to historical literature* (no. 4634), 25–30.

[3] For diplomatic practice the standard treatise is Sir Ernest Satow, *Guide to diplomatic practice*, 2d and rev. ed. (London, 1922, 2 v.) [5326].

[4] A standard treatise, particularly for the historical aspects of international law, is John Westlake, *International law* (Cambridge, Eng., 1904–1907, 2 v.; 2d ed., 1910–1913, 2 v.) [5327].

[5] In facsimile in the Appendix to Nichols, *Franklin Pierce* (no. 1792).

poses, to tell where the official tinge comes in or fades out. Indeed the question of what portion of a diplomatist's personal files should be turned over to the state has been a perplexing problem for the archivists of foreign offices. Not to mention retaining their private letters to diplomatic officers, some foreign ministers have taken away with them official correspondence to keep as their personal property.[6]

Aware of the difficulty of always distinguishing between official and private sources, we shall say something of both classes, classifying them by the three great branches of modern governments: executive, legislative, and judicial.

Official Sources

I. Sources of the Executive Branch

A. The Foreign Office, or Department of State

1. Diplomatic Correspondence

The basic source for our interest is the great body of diplomatic correspondence that exists in the archives of the United States Department of State, of the several foreign offices, and in the diplomatic posts abroad. This consists of:

a. **Communications, with enclosures,** from the minister of foreign affairs—in the United States of course he is called the Secretary of State—or from an official under his responsible direction [7] to the diplomatic agents abroad; these outgoing letters are commonly called Instructions.

---

[6] The editors of *British documents on the origins of the war, 1898–1914* (no. 5475) state in their introduction to volume I that Lord Salisbury carried away to his own house the greater part of his official correspondence when he quit official life (in 1902).

[7] During the first few years of our national history the Secretary of State personally wrote or dictated practically every instruction of the least significance. For nearly a century he signed everything that went out. Now he does not even sign most of them. Only instructions of primary importance today can be read, or even signed, personally by the Secretary. An elaborate organization of labor and responsibility has grown up leading up to the Secretary, and involving (in 1934), in addition to the foreign service abroad, approximately 700 employees. It requires an under secretary, four assistant secretaries, and twenty or more heads of divisions. There is an Office of the Historical Adviser which has custody of the archives of the Department and a Division of Research and Publication which is charged with the editing and compilation of the diplomatic correspondence of the United States. The same is generally true of the foreign offices of other governments. For the history of the Department of State, see Gaillard Hunt (no. 205).

b. Communications, with enclosures, from diplomatic representatives abroad to the minister of foreign affairs; these incoming letters are commonly called Despatches. It is customary to number instructions and despatches serially, and of course to keep duplicates for office files. The serial numbers have obvious advantages to prevent confusion, only one of which is to distinguish between different despatches bearing the same date. In the former days of uncertain communication it was usual to send despatches in duplicates and triplicates to ensure delivery as soon as possible of at least one copy. In times of war resort 'was made to quadruplicates and even quintuplicates. One can imagine the scraping quills of foreign office clerks, some of whom were young apprentices in diplomacy. It is customary to endorse the date of receipt of all incoming communications, both at the foreign office at home and at diplomatic stations abroad. The date of reception of a document is often of supreme importance for the historian, enabling him to place the exact time of and explain the reason for important crystallizations of policy.[8]

So there accumulate at the foreign office of a particular government: (a) drafts or copies [9] of instructions to diplomatic representatives abroad, (b) signed despatches, in duplicate, perhaps in multiple signed copies, from diplomatic agents abroad. On the other hand, there accumulate at the embassies and legations [10] abroad: (a) signed instructions from the foreign office at home, with possible multiple signed copies, (b) office copies (or drafts) of despatches sent to the foreign office at home. Thus at both sides of the ocean or of the frontier, there is a complete set of the correspondence with that legation. It is obvious that the historian prefers to read the signed instructions and despatches, rather than the drafts or unsigned copies, because the signed documents are more authentic and moreover they frequently vary in small details, sometimes important, from the

---

[8] For example, see the controversy between A. P. Whitaker and S. F. Bemis as to whether the Spanish minister, Godoy, certainly knew of the text of Jay's treaty between the United States and Great Britain when he signed Pinckney's treaty between the United States and Spain: Bemis (no. 506); Whitaker (nos. 503–504).

The same sort of data is important in determining whether or not there was collusion between France and Spain in closing the navigation of the Mississippi in 1802. See Lyon (no. 708) and Whitaker (no. 505). The hour, and even minute, of receipt of diplomatic despatches is of great importance to the historian of the diplomacy preceding the outbreak of the World War of 1914–1918.

[9] A draft may be very rough notes, considerably reshaped in the actual instruction.

[10] For convenience we shall use hereafter the term *legation* as a general description for a diplomatic post abroad.

drafts. Furthermore, it is only with the originals that enclosures
are found, lists only of these important documents are filed with
drafts. After the passage of time dead correspondence in legation
archives is usually sent home for preservation. The practice of the
United States in this matter has not been fixed, and the archives of
most legations have never been thus transferred.[11] In some cases
the normal chapter of accidents and carelessness has sadly depleted
their contents.[12] With the new National Archives Building of the
United States and the recently created organization, we hope that
the practice of periodic transfer of old files of legations abroad will
be systematically pursued, as is the case with well-organized national
archives in other countries. Needless to say, this has convenience for
the historian in assembling at the same spot the legation files (for
authentic signed instructions) and the foreign office archives (for
authentic signed despatches). It has also the advantage of greater
safety [13] through scientific custody.

c. Notes. These are the communications passed between the minister
for foreign affairs and the resident diplomatic representatives of
other powers. They may be distinguished as follows: (1) Notes from
the foreign office to the foreign diplomatic resident at the capital.
Office copies of these are kept for files. The originals are usually
retained in the files of the foreign legation, from which copies (generally with translations) are in turn sent to the legation's foreign
office at home, although the signed original may be sent home and a
legation copy preserved. Thus there are three sets of these notes.[14]
(2) Notes from the foreign diplomatic residents to the minister of
foreign affairs of the government to which they are accredited.

---

[11] See *Archives of government offices outside of the city of Washington* (Wash., 1913)
(62d Cong., 3d sess. House. Doc. 1443) [5328] for a statement of archives of United
States legations and consulates abroad. See also Hunter Miller, *Transfer to Department
of State of the older archives of certain embassies, legations, and consulates* (no. 5497).

[12] This is the case, for example, in the records of early American legations in the
Italian states.

[13] A national archives should of course be of fireproof and earthquakeproof construction.
It should also be located reasonably free from danger of floods or bombardment, where
the air is clean and not abnormally damp, and where there is room for expansion.
When beginning a new archives building, as in the United States, choice was free for
these advantages. The location of the new national archives building in the "quad-
rangle" at Pennsylvania, Constitution Avenues, 7th and 9th Sts., Washington, departs
somewhat from proper caution in these respects in favor of the general architectural
symmetry of the government building program.

[14] That is: (a) copies, or drafts, of notes going out from the foreign office of Power A;
(b) signed originals, or copies thereof, delivered to the legation of Power B; (c) incoming
copies, or signed originals (as the case may be) in the foreign office of Power B.

These notes may have been prepared either by the diplomatic envoy himself, or by his superior at home. If prepared and signed by himself he keeps an office copy in the legation files, and sends another copy home; if prepared by his minister at home, an office copy remains in the foreign office there, and an office copy is taken for the legation files before the original is delivered. Thus there are likely to be three separate copies of these notes.[15] The historian of course prefers the authentic signed note, when available.

2. Memoranda of Conversations

Most foreign offices have files of memoranda of diplomatic conversations. It has been customary to include these in files along with the diplomatic correspondence, although practice cannot be said to be uniform on this detail. These memoranda are recorded by foreign ministers or their clerks after diplomatic interviews. Their departmental value is obviously for future reference and for the information of successors following a change of ministers. There are of course instances where records of conversations have been carefully avoided, if only to conceal them from successors of different political allegiance; and sometimes diplomatists feel that they can have franker discussions with each other if they know that no minutes are to be kept. When an exchange of views is desired in formal record by one or both parties it is customary for the participants to initial agreed minutes thereof.[16] When it embodies an agreement or particular statement of policy it is the practice to put an agreed version into an exchange of diplomatic notes, like " the agreed memorandum " between Secretary of War Taft (acting as the personal representative of President Roosevelt) and Count Katsura, in 1905; or, to take other more formal instances from Japanese-American diplomacy, the Root-Takahira agreement of 1908, and the Lansing-Ishii agreement of 1917. Such exchanges

---

[15] Present day practice frequently instructs the envoy to read to the foreign minister of the government to which he is accredited the note in question, and " to leave with him a copy if he desires to have one ". The practice of transmitting notes by telegraph removes much of the distinction between *signed* originals and office copies; the delivered copy may be presumed to be the authentic note.

[16] For example, the Count de Vergennes, in discussing peace overtures with an agent of the expiring North Government of Great Britain, in 1782, insisted (as a record to show his allies) that the agent initial as authentic Vergennes' summary of the conversation. See Doniol (no. 40), v. V, 40.

of course may enter into the category of international agreements
with more or less treaty force, according to the constitutional forms
of the exchanging parties.

Where there is no agreed minute there is no agreed version of the
interview, and the historian must decide critically, from the evidence,
what was said. A record of the same interview may usually be
found in the despatches of the diplomatist to his home government,
and in memoranda kept by the minister with whom he has been
conversing. These accounts naturally vary in emphasis, phraseology,
and sometimes in content. There are many familiar examples where,
if space permitted, it would be interesting to put the two accounts
in parallel columns: the conversations between Benjamin Franklin
and Richard Oswald in the preliminary peace negotiations at Paris
in 1782; Thomas Jefferson's and George Hammond's accounts, respectively, of their conversation in 1792 concerning the northwest
boundary gap; the separate version of Stratford Canning, and of
John Quincy Adams, in 1821, in regard to the possession of the
mouth of the Columbia River. One does not always find two accounts; then the historian must critically interpret the one-sided
report. The writer does not remember having seen any account by
a diplomatist of an interview in which that diplomatist felt the
slightest confusion, was reduced to the least embarrassment by his
confabulator, or betrayed any vestige of awkwardness in handling
the business. For such manifestations one must always look in the
reports of the other participant. The voluminous diaries of John
Adams and his famous son John Quincy Adams, both of them distinguished American diplomatists, do not suggest that either was
ever set out of countenance in a diplomatic conversation therein recorded, nor do they evidence the slightest *gaucherie*, on their parts;
but they are full of instances in which they detected such indications
in the words or appearance of their interviewers. Indeed, if a diplomatist should admit in his writings any awkwardness or lack of
resourcefulness he would not be a diplomatist. From such sources,
to recapitulate what was said, or the nature of what was said, becomes then, a nice problem for the historian.

3. Memoranda of Policy

A group of official records not a part of the actual diplomatic
correspondence or conversations with a given country, but equally if

not more important than either for the historian, is memoranda on policy. Here in full confidential nakedness are set down the paragraphs which elucidate the particular chapters of diplomacy, and which reach back of all formal diplomatic correspondence. When the authorship of these can be established,[17] they are of supreme and certain value. The archives of the French foreign office are replete with such revealing memoranda, and Mr. Doniol (no. 40) published many of them for the period of the American Revolution, much to the enlightenment of historians, who without them would have gained from the diplomatic correspondence an insufficient understanding of French policy toward the United States. Then there is the celebrated memorandum of Sir Eyre Crowe on British relations with Germany, written in 1907, which is said to have had a great influence in determining the German policy of Sir Edward Grey, the British foreign minister, in the diplomatic crises preceding the outbreak of the World War of 1914–1919.

These memoranda of policy may be variously filed, according to the source from which they emanate. In the case of the French archives there is a particular file *Mémoires et Documents*, in which one looks for them. They are not so common or so neatly formulated, in the archives of other countries; and are more likely to be filed with despatches from legations.

4. Records of Secret Service or Intelligence Operatives

These may be found as enclosures to despatches, or, when submitted directly to the foreign minister, they may be found in separate files, generally classified under the name of the country to which they relate. For example, there is indicated in the index of foreign office papers in the British Public Record Office, under the general head of France, the volume " Notes and Intelligence, 1782 ", into which the student of the peace settlement of 1782 might well look. To cite some examples from episodes with which we are personally familiar, we find thus preserved in England and France the confidential reports of British intelligence operatives,

---

[17] The authorship is not always revealed, sometimes is purposely disguised. But there is at least one celebrated instance of attributing to a minister a spurious memorandum on policy, notably the alleged memoir of Vergennes on French policy in regard to Louisiana, which Professor P. C. Phillips (no. 44), 30–32, demonstrated to be factitious, written in 1802 after Vergennes' death to strengthen Napoleonic policy with the support of consistency with former French policy.

and of French trailers tracing them, concerning the movements of Benjamin Franklin and his colleagues at the Court of France in 1777–1778. The activity of these British secret agents, as observed by French informers, was actually what precipitated the French offer of an alliance to the United States. Again, British tapping of French diplomatic correspondence at Hamburg, en route from Copenhagen to Paris, was an important factor in the diplomacy of the epoch-making Jay's Treaty between the United States and Great Britain in 1794. The reports of a Spanish spy, who considered himself to be accounted in a way a British informer and who took expense money from both sides, reveal the real policy of Spain toward the American Revolution. Coming down to the twentieth century, the interception of the famous Zimmermann note from Germany to Mexico in January 1917, by the British secret service, was a dramatic and, in its consequences, an important episode in the diplo·*·atic history of our own times. When we can find such abundant and revealing records on file for matters of such a fine nature, we can be pretty confident that the less dramatic and colorful, the ordinary narrative of diplomacy is usually well preserved in the conventional type of records. A rather rare type of source which, occasionally encountered, yields rich results consists of the petitions to neglectful governments by spies or intelligence agents for rewards or pensions for past services rendered. In such petitions the individual recounts with considerable detail his services, not only conclusively revealing his real character to the historian, but narrating, and probably exaggerating for his own advantage, the significance of his accomplishments. By such a document was conclusively established the real identity and services of the famous British spy, Dr. Edward Bancroft, secretary to Silas Deane, and later to Franklin and the American commissioners in France during the American Revolution.[18]

5. Miscellaneous

In many foreign offices files exist for a series of miscellaneous correspondence, classified under the country to which it relates (sometimes indexed, sometimes not).[19] Such may contain documents writ-

---

[18] See *Am. hist. rev.*, XXIX (1924), 474–495 (no. 59).

[19] In the case of the French foreign office archives, these miscellanea are included in "*Mémoires et Documents*", classified by countries, and inventoried in a printed inven-

ten by almost anybody and relating to almost anything and among them the historian can often find enlightening pieces.

6. Correspondence with and of other States

Very frequently the diplomatic activities between two countries, A and B, are reflected not only in their own diplomatic correspondence and conversations and supplementary foreign office records, of the kind described above, but in the correspondence of A with C, and D; or of B with C and D, or X, or even of C and D with E, F, and X. Professor Dexter Perkins showed in his standard studies of the origin, and subsequent development of the Monroe Doctrine (nos. 1172 and 1211) that it was necessary to consult not only the diplomatic record of Great Britain and the United States, but of Great Britain and France, Russia and France, Prussia and France, etc., etc. The exposition of Anglo-American relations during the American Civil War required Professor E. D. Adams (no. 1909) and Professor F. L. Owsley (no. 2117) to consult, among other sources, the diplomatic exchanges between France and Great Britain. Professor Golder (no. 2086) threw light on Britain's attitude during that war by consultation of diplomatic correspondence in the Russian archives. The history of the Franco-American alliance of 1778 cannot be wholly understood from an investigation restricted to a study of the diplomatic correspondence, and closely related documents, exchanged between France and the United States; one must consult the correspondence of each of these governments with Spain, The Netherlands, and even Austria, Prussia, and Russia. The historian of the diplomatic relations between two countries should examine the diplomatic correspondence of each of these governments with such other countries as may be indicated by the nature of the research.

7. Legation Papers

By this we mean the matter not sent home immediately in the regular diplomatic despatches. Generally speaking such matter is relatively unimportant, because all important papers would have been enclosed in the regular despatches. But in days of poorer communi-

---

tory (see below, p. 916). In the case of the British Public Record Office, there is a miscellaneous series listed by countries in the *List of Foreign Office records to 1878* (no. 5578). The miscellaneous documents in the Department of State have a general manuscript index with subjects and names arranged alphabetically.

cation it was quite usual for diplomatic envoys of the same government, both residing at some distance from their own capital, to indulge in a good deal of cross correspondence of greater or less importance.[20] Legation files are not unlikely to contain letters of this nature; on the other hand they may have been abstracted into the personal files of the diplomatists. The legation files of those European powers who had colonial possessions in America contain a great quantity of correspondence between the legation at the capital of the United States and the colonial officials in America; the British legation was in constant correspondence with the Governor-General of Canada, and the Lieutenant-Governor of Upper Canada, and frequently with the West Indian officials; the French minister had a voluminous correspondence with the French colonial officials in the West Indies; and the Spanish envoys at Philadelphia and Washington constantly exchanged numerous letters and documents with the authorities commanding in Louisiana, Florida, Cuba, Mexico, etc. This correspondence has proven to be of great importance to the historian of American diplomacy. In those cases where the legation archives have been periodically sent home for deposit in the national archives, it is quite practical to consult them; but the archives of American legations abroad are still widely scattered.[21]

8. Consular Despatches and Instructions

These may be described (as to instructions and despatches) in practically the same way as the diplomatic correspondence. Often the appointment of consuls, or of agents for commerce and seamen, has preceded the opening of regular diplomatic intercourse, and the first relations between two countries may be followed in consular correspondence. Such was the case in the beginning of our diplomacy with some of the new republics of South America. After the establishment of regular diplomatic intercourse it is not ordinarily [22]

---

[20] Examples are the cross correspondence between William Short, commissioner to Spain in 1793 and 1794, and James Monroe, minister to France, which was revealed first from the private papers of those men ; Lord Malmesbury's printed despatches (no. 179) include cross correspondence of this kind. There was, for example, a considerable amount of cross corresponding between American ministers in London, Paris, and The Hague concerning the imprisonment of Lafayette in 1792–1797.

[21] For their content, see note 11, p. 790, above.

[22] Professor F. L. Owsley (no. 2117) has made good use of United States and foreign consular despatches in his study of the ineffectiveness of the federal blockade of the southern states during the American Civil War.

practicable for the investigator to concern himself with the multiplying mass of consular records.

9. International Congresses and Conferences, Mixed Commissions, and Arbitrations

Foreign offices preserve special files for this sort of material, which includes instructions and despatches, copies of proceedings, etc. In some instances papers relating to an international congress may be found in the despatches from a particular legation, when the incumbent acted also as a delegate to the congress.

10. Special Agents

Under this heading comes the record of special agents and missions assigned for purposes outside the function of regular diplomatic agents. In the archives of the Department of State there is a particular file for special agents, whose functions and diplomacy, and whose constitutional status in American diplomacy, is almost a discipline of study in itself.[23] Such agents have existed throughout the history of most countries, to a greater or less extent, from the *secret du roi* of Louis XV to the peregrinations of Colonel House, and with greater or less supervision by foreign offices.

The archivist of the Department of State, Mrs. Natalia Summers, has compiled a card catalogue of special agents of the United States, 1789 to 1906, with data on the objects of their missions and with citation of United States archival references [5328a]. It is arranged in two series: alphabetical and chronological. This valuable aid is available to investigators.

Where the mission is under the control of the foreign office, the records of such agencies appear as diplomatic correspondence, and frequently they are included in the regular series of diplomatic correspondence, classified by countries.

11. Treaties

These consist of the original texts, or authenticated copies, of all ratified treaties, which are kept in every foreign office. The authoritative text of a treaty is that which was ratified, usually found im-

---

[23] The work of special agents in American diplomacy has been made the subject of an elaborate and encyclopedic study by H. M. Wriston (no. 4799).

bedded in an instrument of ratification. These original archives are important to the historian, who may consult their contents instead of the generally published editions, (1) for the revelation of secret treaties, (2) verification of texts. In the United States there is now no such thing as a secret treaty, not only because of custom, but because the democratic control of foreign policy by the directly elected Senate makes secrecy impossible. The only examples of secret treaties or secret articles, all of which occurred in our early history, and did not actually remain secret, are: [24]

1778. Treaty of Alliance with France, which contained a secret article providing for the possible accession of Spain.

1782. Preliminary Articles of Peace with Great Britain, which contained a secret contingent article in regard to the southern boundary of the United States. It was not included in the final articles of the definitive peace.

1790. Treaty with the Creek Indians.

1830. Treaty with Turkey, contained a secret article envisaging the construction of ships, including warships, in the United States for Turkey. The Senate found this article inacceptable and excluded it from the ratified treaty.

1848. Treaty of Peace with Mexico had a secret article providing for extension under certain conditions of the time limit for exchange of ratifications.

12. Interdepartmental Communications

These are communications between the foreign office and the other official departments or ministries (war, navy, treasury, colonies, interior, etc.), and in the case of federal governments occasionally between the foreign office and state governments within the federation, subordinate to the federal government in matters of foreign affairs; or between imperial governments and their colonies, dominions, or self-governing commonwealths.[25]

---

[24] We are indebted to Dr. Hunter Miller, Historical Adviser to the Department of State, for these data on the treaties of 1830 and 1848, which he assembled during his erudite labors in preparing a scholarly edition of the texts of the treaties of the United States.

[25] We have already suggested above (p. 796) that the correspondence of the colonial offices of European powers with American colonies is a source for the diplomatic history of the United States. In Great Britain the correspondence between the imperial government and the self-governing commonwealths now centers in the Ministry of Dominions,

Similarly one might look into the correspondence of the Governor-General of the Philippines under American dominion, with the United States Secretary of War, and into interdepartmental communications between War and State for material relating to American diplomacy in the Far East in the twentieth century. The records of the ministries of war, navy, and treasury, and occasionally of other ministries and departments (as the subject of research may suggest), and their communications with the department for foreign affairs, can be of greatest importance. A good example in American history is the Panama episode of 1903, where the correspondence of the Navy Department with commanders of vessels operating near the Isthmus vividly illustrates the correspondence of the Department of State with the United States consul on the eve of the revolution.

One could not expect to get the complete history of the Washington Conference of 1921-1922 or the London Naval Conference of 1930, both for the purpose of limiting naval armaments, without consulting the interdepartmental communications of the participating countries.

B. Other Executive Departments

The last paragraph suggests that behind the interdepartmental communications the archives of those several departments themselves may occasionally contain material relating to foreign affairs. In American history naval officers have been frequently entrusted with diplomatic business. In addition to their reports directly to the Department of State there are files of their correspondence in the archives of the Navy Department.[26] One may safely assume

---

between which and the Foreign Office one would expect an interdepartmental correspondence touching foreign affairs at many points, particularly Anglo-American relations. Before the establishment of a Canadian legation in Washington in 1927, the correspondence of the British Colonial Office (predecessor of the Ministry of Dominions) was a prime source for Anglo-American relations. The correspondence of the Spanish Ministry for the Indies (the colonial office of Spain) with the Minister for Foreign Affairs is a voluminous and important source for American frontier history, much of it illustrating Spanish-American relations. The local reports of Spanish colonial officials on the continent of North America were delivered to the Governor-General of Cuba, who covered them in his despatches to the Minister for the Indies. Thus the colonial archives of Cuba, which were transferred to Spain during the period from June 25, 1888, to Oct. 28, 1889, are a mine of information for the student of American history. They have been described in detail in a very painstaking catalogue prepared for the Carnegie Institution of Washington by Dr. R. R. Hill (no. 5650).

[26] Paullin, *Dipl. negotiations Am. naval officers* (no. 151).

that the files of the Department of the Treasury are replete with records reflecting (among other subjects) our diplomatic relations with the debtor governments of Europe since 1919, as indeed they are with sources for our diplomacy with at least one of these governments when the tables were reversed, 1778–1795, and the United States was a debtor government. So also with the ministries or departments of finance of foreign governments. We must therefore bring these other departmental records within the purview of the historian of American diplomacy as important supplements to the archives of the department of foreign affairs.

C. Records of the Chief of State

The foreign office and the several other executive departments or ministries are of course only subordinate parts of the executive power. It is customary for diplomatists, at least of the higher grade, to have direct access when desired to the sovereign or chief of state. Such contacts however are by no means the most important producers of documents interesting to the readers of this guide; the correspondence of the chief of state with all sorts of persons, official and unofficial, is full of material relating to the formulation of foreign policy. This has been abundantly evident to the few scholars who have had access to Theodore Roosevelt's papers now in the custody of the Library of Congress. And of course there are the splendid examples of the papers of George Washington and of Woodrow Wilson. The correspondence of George III (no. 143), published in 1927–1929—unfortunately without enclosures to letters printed—is a mine of new information for the diplomatic history of the American Revolution. So are the letters of Queen Victoria (no. 1985) for Anglo-American relations during the Civil War. An even more formidable example of this kind is that colossal piece of editing of the correspondence of Frederick the Great (no. 201), who directed and commanded his diplomats as vigorously as he did his generals.

Insofar as they enter into the formal diplomatic record the papers of the chief of state are usually embodied in the archives of the foreign offices. The remainder, often the more important, rest with the personal papers of the chief of state and do not always reach state archives. In the United States the papers of nearly all of the presidents have been brought together, for historical purposes, in the Library of Congress,[27] which from this point of view—among others—we may consider as a national cultural library rather than a service library to the legislative branch of the government. Some of these papers of the presidents, like those of General Washington, have been purchased by the federal government from the heirs or subsequent owners and deposited in that library. A lofty public spirit has frequently ordered the bequest or gift of other such collections (for example, the Garfield, Harrison, Cleveland, Roosevelt, Taft, and Coolidge papers) to the nation for custody in the Library. In this way collections of priceless value have been donated to history. That so many presidents, and their heirs, often persons of moderate means, have taken this point of view, is a matter for national gratulation. The same sentiment applies to the papers of the secretaries of state,[28] and of other important public servants, which are being deposited in increasing volume at the Library of Congress.

Another class of documents emanating from the chief of state consists of executive decrees and ordinances. In the United States such documents, after being signed by the President, are issued through the Secretary of State. In some governments of an autocratic nature such decrees arise out of the sovereign's prerogative. In our times most of them are expressions of power delegated to the executive by the legislative authorities or by written constitutions, or tolerated by unwritten constitutions. Such decrees often relate to foreign affairs, for example: the Russian Czar's ukase of 1821 claiming sovereignty on the northwest coast of North America down to 51 degrees north latitude and 100 miles out to sea; the numerous British orders-in-council containing instructions to commanders of public and private ships of war, which affected the navigation of neutral vessels and were consequently the cause of much diplomatic controversy, particularly with the United States. Such proclamations are normally filed in the archives of the subordinate executive department to which they relate, and are usually though not always printed.

---

[27] See below, pp. 861–862.
[28] Idem.

II. Sources of the Legislative Branch

While the greater volume of the records of the history of diplomacy, particularly of the active phases of it, rests in executive files, as above outlined, we must not overlook the legislature. We refer not only to the legislative record, the debates of parliaments and of congresses, the books of statutes enacted, all of this usually available in the larger libraries, and (in the United States) to the Senate Executive Journals. There are also the confidential files of the Senate,[29] and the proceedings and reports of committees, and the testimony presented to such committees. There are regular committees which deal with foreign affairs, like the committee on foreign relations of the United States Senate, and the committee on foreign affairs of the House of Representatives. Committee records are full of material for diplomatic history, and it is often easily available because printed and widely distributed. A celebrated example in American history may be found in the hearings before the foreign relations committee of the Senate in 1919 on the Treaty of Versailles, and the hearings, before the foreign affairs committee of the House in 1912, on the Rainey resolution to arbitrate the grievance with Colombia arising out of intervention by the United States in the Isthmus of Panama. One must not rely on the completeness of printed committee reports. The committee files of the two houses of Congress, as well as of the two houses of Parliament, are full of unprinted matter, particularly for the earlier decades of American history. The national legislature is of course the recipient of masses of informative data, presented through committees, or by members, or by individuals, which relate to their deliberations on foreign affairs. The practice of having much of this printed is of great value to the historian. In both the United States and Great Britain the legislative branch has until recently been the principal authentic medium for the publication of public documents.[30]

III. Sources of the Judicial Branch

Finally, among official sources, we must note the records of the judiciary. Matters relating to foreign affairs become involved in domestic court procedure, and all kinds of claims arise out of treaties.

---

[29] Not known to be accessible, but in view of the relation of the U.S. Senate to foreign affairs they are most important.

[30] See below, Ch. II.

One of the most notable sources for the diplomatic controversy between Spain and the United States preceding the war of 1898 may be found in the proceedings of the United States Court of Claims which adjudicated the historic French spoliation, and the claims of American citizens against Spain which had been assumed by the United States in the treaties of 1800 with France, and 1898 with Spain. Again, the claims of British creditors presented to state courts, in pursuance of the treaty of peace of Versailles of 1783, reflect much light on a particular chapter of early American diplomacy. In addition to the records of the domestic courts there are the records of international arbitrations and mixed claims commissions, referred to above.[31]

IV. Non-Official Sources

Such is an outline of the main body of official records on which diplomatic history can be based. There is in addition a body of non-official sources which cannot be so concisely described. These consist of the private papers of participants in diplomacy, which frequently expand and enlighten the official record. One would not gather from the exchanges of notes between Secretary of State John Quincy Adams and Minister Luis de Onís, leading to the signature of the Florida treaty of 1819, the explanation of Adams' successful effort to get the boundary between the two nations delimited clear through to the Pacific Ocean, but this is set forth luminously in John Quincy Adams' notable *Diary*, which is strictly speaking a private document . The private letters of Henry White, an American career diplomatist of the twentieth century, enlighten the formal record of American diplomatic correspondence with the embassies in England and France in this period.[32] Then there are the records of interested, and of interesting bystanders, like Henry Adams' letters illustrative of Anglo-American affairs, or informed commentators like Gouverneur Morris. There are also the records of banks, corporations, and business firms—such as the papers of the financial house of Baring, now preserved in the Canada archives— and individuals, which touch foreign affairs, a type of source material till now generally neglected. Then comes the press, with all its

---

[31] P. 797.
[32] Nevins, *Henry White* (no. 2468).

varied character of information true and false about contemporary diplomacy and contemporary conditions, a source above all for the temper of public opinion. It is necessary to emphasize that the historian of diplomacy must use the press most warily, weighing the party allegiance, the relation of the press to the government, or to the opposition, or to various social movements.[33] One could scarcely get the same opinion of American affairs from the communist *Rote Fahne* of Berlin and the nationalist *Deutsches Tageblatt* or the democratic right-wing *Vossische Zeitung*.[34] The comments and information in the socialist weekly, *The Nation*, and the independent New York *Times* on American diplomacy, say in Nicaragua, would scarcely give the intelligent reader the same information and impression.

While discussing the nature of the sources of diplomatic history of the United States, we must stress the truth that scarcely any portion of the international relations of this country can be written adequately from one nation's sources. Although this dictum has been recognized quite generally, it has not been unreservedly practiced. There is an inveterate persistence on the part of investigators in the United States as well as abroad, who still insist on writing from one set of sources monographs which have to be rewritten as soon as other national archives are studied on the same subject. One cannot write, for example, a history of the diplomatic relations of the United States and Spain without consulting both Spanish and American sources, and indeed to a lesser extent those of several other countries, yet both Spanish and American historians have attempted to do so. Curiously enough, university teachers have been among the chief culprits in this respect. Perhaps because of the hitherto comparative inaccessibility of the archives of the foreign offices of governments abroad, they have continued to allow doctoral dissertations to be based on one set of national records. As this is written a doctoral dissertation appears from the press of a well-known university, on Russian-American relations, by a person who has not had access to the Russian sources,

---

[33] See Lucy M. Salmon, *The newspaper and authority* (N.Y., 1923) [5329], and *The newspaper and the historian* (N.Y., 1923) [5330]; and J. F. Scott, "The press and foreign policy", *Jour. mod. hist.*, III (1931) 627-638 [5331].

[34] This was written before the Nazi Revolution. A controlled press such as exists in 1934 in Russia, Germany, and Italy is always of value as an historical source because of its close expression of official opinion, or of official desire to mould public opinion.

and who apparently does not know the Russian language. To demonstrate the limitations of such investigations one may ask how the history of Anglo-German relations from 1904–1914 could be written by merely perusing the records of only the British foreign office. If a study is based on the records of only one party to the events recorded, let the title and preface and the conclusion clearly and candidly limit the scope of the investigation and acknowledge the incompleteness of the work. The study above signalized ought to have been entitled *American policy toward Russia as revealed by*, etc., etc. In other words, to know the whole history of the game the historian must seek to turn up the cards of all the players who sat at the table, not of one player alone.

In the following chapters we shall tell how the investigator can best get at the sources, printed and unprinted, the nature of which has been described above.

CHAPTER II

PRINTED STATE PAPERS

I. United States:
  A. Published Records of the Executive Branch:
    1. Papers of the Presidents.
    2. Department of State:
      i. Diplomatic Correspondence.
      ii. Treaties.
      iii. International Congresses, Conferences, Commissions, Expositions, Exhibitions, etc.
      iv. General and Occasional Publications.
      v. Diplomatic Registers and Lists.
      vi. Foreign Commerce, including Consular Reports.
      vii. The new State Department Series.
    3. Published Records of other Departments of the Executive Branch which may touch Foreign Affairs.
  B. Printed Records of the Legislative Branch:
    1. Laws.
    2. Treaties.
    3. Proceedings, Debates, etc.
    4. Senate Executive Documents.
    5. Committee Reports.
  C. Printed Records of the Judicial Branch:
    1. Reports of the Federal Courts.
    2. Reports of the State Courts.
    3. Prize Court Decisions.
    4. Opinions of the Attorney-General.
  D. Independent Commissions.
  E. Mixed Commissions and other Arbitral Tribunals.
  F. State Publications.
II. Printed State Papers of Foreign Governments:
    Bibliographical note
    Great Britain.
    Portugal.
    Hispanic America.
    France.
    The Netherlands.
    Germany.
    Denmark.
    Russia.
    Italy.
    Far East: China; Japan.
III. Published Records of International Organs, League of Nations, etc.
IV. Documentary Publications relating to the Diplomatic History of the Origins of the World War of 1914 to 1918, to the Armistice of 1918, and to the Peace Settlements concluding the War.

Any distinction between printed and unprinted sources is at best an artificial one. A document may be a source of the same value whether printed or unprinted, and it would be a curious species of erudition which would regard it as necessarily more valuable only because it has never been printed. The more valuable a source is the more quickly it tends, other things being equal, to become printed. Provided it is accurately printed, it is of course equally valuable in its published form—for practical reading purposes— and more valuable in the sense of being accessible, though one might always desire to fall back on the original MS. to make sure that no liberties had been taken with the text, or that no errors had been made, or to distinguish between original text and later emendations before printing.[1] Nevertheless extremely valuable sources for the diplomatic history of the United States remain unprinted, and there is a mass of documents simply too voluminous to print.

Of course the confidential nature of diplomatic documents and other source material often prohibits publication. We have said in the previous chapter that frequently political reasons prevent the printing of essential material. It is often impossible for governments to arrive at results except through the frank exchange of confidence, which if betrayed would have serious results for individuals and for peoples. There are therefore honorable agreements not to reveal such documents except by mutual consent. On other occasions a political régime withholds documents from publication because of fear of furnishing ammunition for the opposition. Sometimes a negotiator holds back from the papers turned over by him to the archives of his government some document or draft which he thinks it desirable not to have on record.[2] Sometimes, at least in the United States, the President withholds diplomatic papers called for by the Senate or House, because he thinks it incompatible with the public interest to reveal them. In the case of Great

[1] Example of such emendations making significant changes are the *Diary of Gideon Welles*, Secretary of the Navy under Abraham Lincoln—see H. K. Beale, " Is the printed diary of Gideon Welles reliable ? " in *Am. hist. rev.*, XXX (1925) 547–552 [5332] ; and *Mémoires, correspondance et manuscrits du général Lafayette, publiés par sa famille*— see *Corres. inédite de La Fayette par Jules Thomas* (no. 5250), and L. R. Gottschalk, " Lafayette ", *Jour. mod. hist.*, II (1930) 281–287 [5332a].

[2] A notable example is John Jay's draft of September 30, 1794, for a treaty with Great Britain. When compared with the actual treaty which Jay signed on Nov. 19, 1794, it shows that he made great concessions from his original demands. To have included that in his despatches would have been to demonstrate this to his government; and had it been submitted to the Senate along with the remainder of his papers relating to the treaty negotiations, it might have resulted in the defeat of the treaty. See no. 551, pp. 243, 286.

Britain, Sir Edward Grey withheld from the public until the last moment in 1914 the nature of the oral understandings which he had reached with France for common defense in case Germany should declare war on France. To have revealed these to Parliament before a crisis might have precipitated the emergency which he hoped to avoid.

Often public papers which have become subject to the control of private persons are withheld for personal or for capricious reasons. Even the remote descendants of a diplomat often refuse to allow to be printed, without censorship, all the political papers of their ancestor, for fear something may damage the reputation of the distinguished but distant progenitor. Then, too, governments in the past have frequently made secret agreements, understandings, and even treaties, the purpose of which might have been frustrated by publication.[3] Now, such confidential documents as these are of supreme importance to the historian and are far more enlightening than printed material. They are to be found finally only in the extant archival records of the governments concerned. But, we repeat, they tend to get printed quickly once they are discovered or released to the public. Sometimes they are not released until another age, when the public has completely forgotten what they refer to. Then they remain unprinted until the historian discovers their importance. So the historical investigator may make many discoveries among MS. collections, particularly in state archives. In the next chapter we shall indicate aids to exploitation of unprinted material. But first we are interested to know what has been printed and how to reach it. When the investigator has

---

[3] A notorious example of this is the agreement during the Russian counter-revolutionary movement in 1919 between France and the Wrangel *de facto* counter-revolutionary Russian government, by which France in return for military supplies and assistance is believed to have extracted an economic bondage of Russia should the Wrangel Government have succeeded. See L. I. Strakhovsky, " The Franco-British plot to dismember Russia ", *Current history*, XXXIII (1931) 839–842 [5333].

Other well-known examples are the secret treaties of the Entente Allies, made *after* the outbreak of the war of 1914, (1) compensating Italy and Rumania for entering the war; (2) marking out certain partitions of enemy territory in case of victory. Though these treaties did not cause the war, their texts if published would have had a damaging effect on the morale of those citizens who believed they were fighting to make the world safe for democracy and to secure the rights of small nations. The British tried to tell President Wilson about some of them after the United States entered the war, but he appears to have preferred to remain officially ignorant of them. The Bolsheviks were quick to publish them for political purposes, to discredit the old régime, after the November revolution of 1917 gave them possession of the official records.

found and digested the printed sources relating to his subject, he may turn to the more refined and exhausting searches for further MS. material, to which there is guidance in the last chapter of this volume.

In describing the printed sources for the diplomatic history of the United States, we shall give most emphasis to printed state papers, both American and foreign, supplementing these indications with remarks on privately printed sources. This is because most of the printed sources are official records, generally the product of public presses. In our analysis of these state papers, we shall devote the greatest space to American prints, because (1) despite the indispensability of foreign material, the American sources are the most voluminous for this particular subject; (2) because the American official records are on the whole more copiously printed, and certainly the best indexed; in fact the lack of indexes to printed public documents issued by many foreign governments makes it impracticable to attempt as much analysis of them.

I. United States

A. Published Records of the Executive Branch

1. Papers of the Presidents.—The published official papers of the President consist of annual and special messages; executive orders; inaugural addresses; proclamations; and general publications.[4] Any one of these may contain material dealing with foreign relations. The standard publication for presidential messages is J. D. Richardson's *A compilation of the messages and papers of the presidents, 1789–1897* (Wash.: Govt. Print. Off., 1896–99, 10 v.) (Congressional series, 3265) [**5335**] of which there is a later edition " with additions and encyclopedic index by private enterprise " (N.Y., 1917, 20 v.)[5] which contains the remainder of McKinley's papers and those of later presidents, including Coolidge. Almost any paper written by a president may have historical significance.

---

[4] All that had been officially printed to the end of 1909 are listed, according to these categories, in the *Checklist of United States public documents, 1789–1909,* compiled under direction of the Superintendent of Documents (Wash.: Govt. Print. Off., 1911), 874–891 [**5334**]. For the period since 1909 one must consult the *Document catalogue* (no. 5358).

[5] They may also be found, insofar as they are messages which deal with foreign relations, in the series *Foreign relations* (no. 5345), which is now (1934) published through 1918. For such presidential documents since 1918, see the *Document catalogue* (no. 5358).

For certain presidents who have assumed heroic proportions the Government in the past has subsidized the official publication of voluminous editions of selected papers; and on other occasions it has published calendars of the MS. collections of such papers possessed by the Government.[6] Private enterprise, increasingly organized under the leadership of learned societies, institutions, and foundations, has also been responsible for printing large parts of the papers of presidents.[7]

2. Department of State [8]

i. Diplomatic Correspondence

The printed correspondence of the United States is easy of access, but there is no means of telling what proportion of the total is printed. For 1774–1789, nearly all is printed. From 1789–1828, Professor McLaughlin's estimate of not more than one-fourth printed (and that omitting some of the most important matter)[9] is as good as any. We have no way of estimating how much of the total has been printed for the period since 1828. In 1930 there were some 1,242 cubic feet of diplomatic correspondence preserved in the archives of the Department of State for the period prior to 1907; that is the nearest estimate of its quantity! Although the experience of investigators who have made soundings here and there seems to

---

[6] Congress in 1850 subscribed for 1,000 copies, and later, 1857, for additional copies, of C. F. Adams' *Works of John Adams* (Boston, 1850–56, 10 v.), selected and edited by his grandson. The H. A. Washington edition of the *Writings of Thomas Jefferson* was published under authority of an act of Congress of 1848. At the present time as a feature of the 200th anniversary of the birth of George Washington, there is being edited by J. C. Fitzpatrick and published by the United States George Washington Bicentennial Commission, under act of Congress of December 2, 1924, a definitive edition of everything that Washington wrote (except for his *Diaries*, edited by J. C. Fitzpatrick and published for the Mount Vernon Ladies' Association in 1925) [5335a].

The Library of Congress has published calendars of large portions of the papers of Washington and Martin Van Buren, now in its possession. Previously the Bureau of Rolls and Indexes of the Department of State had published calendars of the Jefferson, Madison, and Monroe Papers, which went to the Library of Congress.

[7] For list of printed writings of presidents, see above, p. 756. For MS. papers of the presidents, see below, p. 862.

[8] Cyril Wynne, "Publications, available documents, and archives of the Department of State", in its *Press releases*, weekly issue no. 234, March 24, 1934 (*Its* Publication no. 571), 164–169; and a later comprehensive statement by Dr. Wynne, chief of the Division of Research and Publication of the Department of State: *Department of State publications,* issued by the Department of State (Wash., 1935) [5336].

[9] A. C. McLaughlin, *Diplomatic archives of the Dept. of State* (no. 5496), 4.

65215—35——53

confirm the impression that a pretty comprehensive representation of the diplomatic correspondence is in print, particularly since 1860, and while we can give reasonable assurances on that score for the diplomatic correspondence relating to the period of American neutrality and belligerency, 1914–1918, it is never safe for the investigator to assume that important material, even in quantity, does not lie behind the printed record. At the most, only a small part of the total is generally printed.

The student should be familiar with the standard sets of printed diplomatic correspondence of the United States. For the period of the American Revolution there are two well-known collections: Jared Sparks, *The diplomatic correspondence of the American revolution* (Boston and N.Y., 1829–30, 12 v.; new ed., Wash., 1857, 6 v.) [5337], was published under the direction of the President of the United States, conformably to a resolution of Congress of March 27, 1818. Sparks was not only careless but occasionally used his own judgment discreetly (as he thought) to edit some despatches, modifying and even omitting certain passages.[10] The result was that a new edition had to be published, which has completely superseded Sparks: Francis Wharton, *The revolutionary diplomatic correspondence of the United States* (Wash.: Govt. Print. Off., 1889, 6 v.) [5339]. Though Wharton missed a few diplomatic documents, it may be said that for all practical purposes his edition is complete. His helpful and good index is not infallible. Sparks and Wharton stop with the year 1783. The printed diplomatic correspondence is continued in *The diplomatic correspondence of the United States of America, from the signing of the definitive treaty of peace, 10th September, 1783, to the adoption of the Constitution, March 4, 1789* (Wash., 1833–34, 7 v.; 2d ed., 1837, 7 v.; 3d ed., 1855, 3 v.) [5340]. It was printed, under government contract, by F. P. Blair (1st edition), and Blair and Rives (2d and 3d editions), without any editing. For the period from 1789, the beginning of the federal government under the Constitution of 1787, we rely for printed diplomatic correspond-

---

[10] For Sparks as an editor see J. S. Bassett, *The middle group of American historians* (N.Y., 1917), 100–113. For parallel columns comparing passages from Sparks's edition with the original, see Wharton (no. 5339), v. I, iv–viii; and J. B. Moore, "The diplomatic correspondence of the American revolution", *Pol. sci. quar.*, VIII (1893), 33–47 [5338].

ence on *American state papers. Class I. Foreign relations* (Wash., 1832–1859, 6 v.) **[5341]**.[11] The diplomatic notes reprinted in *American state papers* were often originally printed at the time of delivery, either in the press or particular pamphlets, for the sake of influencing public opinion. Though these are significant because of their publication we make no attempt to mention them here. This series covers foreign affairs from 1789 to 1828. It was printed by the firm of Gales and Seaton, on contract with the Government, and edited by Walter Lowrie and Matthew St. Clair Clarke. It assembles all the previously printed diplomatic correspondence, together with presidential messages, reports of the secretary of state, and other relevant material. It thus supersedes the successive editions of *State papers* on foreign relations, 1789–1815, published by T. B. Wait in 1814–15 (1st edition).[12] In all these old prints of diplomatic correspondence, or indeed in dealing with any such American collections dated before the twentieth century, the investigator should be cautioned that the printing is likely to prove carelessly done.

For relations between the United States and Hispanic America a notable supplement to the *American state papers, Foreign relations,* is the collection published by the Carnegie Endowment for International Peace, and edited by W. R. Manning: *Diplomatic correspondence of the United States concerning the independence of the Latin-American nations* (N.Y., 1925, 3 v.) **[5342]**, containing documents of the years 1809 to 1830. As a sequel to this is the series (to contain ten or more volumes) of *Diplomatic correspondence of the United States; inter-American affairs, 1831–1860,* also selected and arranged by W. R. Manning (Wash.: Carnegie Endowment for International Peace, 1932–) **[5343]**, of which Volume I, *Argentina;* II, *Bolivia and Brazil;* III, *Central America, 1831–1850;* IV, *Central America, 1851–1860,* and V, *Chile and Colombia,* have already appeared.

---

[11] Other series of *American state papers* to be consulted for special subjects are Class IV. *Commerce and navigation,* 1789–1823 (Wash., 1832–34, 2 v.) **[5341a]**; Class VI. *Naval affairs,* 1794–1836 (Wash., 1834–61, 4 v.) **[5341b]**; Class IX. *Claims,* 1790–1823 (Wash., 1834) **[5341c]**.

[12] The several editions of Wait's *State papers* (as well as the standard editions of U.S. diplomatic correspondence) are listed in D. P. Myers' invaluable *Manual of collections of treaties* (no. 5399), 353–354, and also in the *Checklist* (no. 5361).

For the period 1828–1861, we have no general collection of the diplomatic correspondence of the United States, although a great deal of such matter was published in scattered public documents:[13] congressional and departmental publications. It would be impossible to locate these without great labor and consumption of time if fortunately we did not have a justly celebrated index compiled by Adelaide R. Hasse and published by the Carnegie Institution of Washington: *Index to United States documents relating to foreign affairs, 1828–1861* (Wash., 1914–21, 3 v.) [5344]. This monument of bibliographical labor and intelligent and lucid organization " affords reference to the entire published record of documents, papers, correspondence, and, to a considerable extent, legislation and decisions upon international or diplomatic questions. In addition to the reports of Congress, the following series of docu-

---

[13] For many of the individual years there are, however, published collections, of which the following list is taken from Hart's *Trial bibliography* (no. 4788):

1835 : *House doc., 24 Cong., 1 sess.,* v. I, no. 2.
1836 : *Sen. doc., 24 Cong., 2 sess.,* v. I, no. 1.
1837 : *Sen. doc., 25 Cong., 2 sess.,* v. I, no. 1 ; *House doc., 25 Cong., 2 sess.,* v. I, no. 3.
1838 : *Sen. doc., 25 Cong., 3 sess.,* v. I, no. 2 ; *House doc., 25 Cong., 3 sess.,* v. I, no. 2.
1839 : None.
1840 : None.
1841 : *Sen. doc., 27 Cong., 2 sess.,* v. I, no. 1 ; *House doc., 27 Cong., 2 sess.,* v. I, no. 2.
1842 : *Sen. doc., 27 Cong., 3 sess.,* v. I, no. 1 ; *House doc., 27 Cong., 3 sess.,* v. I, no. 2.
1843 : *Sen. doc., 28 Cong., 1 sess.,* v. I, no. 1 ; *House doc., 28 Cong., 1 sess.,* v. I, no. 1.
1844 : *Sen. doc., 28 Cong., 2 sess.,* v. I, no. 1 ; *House doc., 28 Cong., 2 sess.,* v. I, no. 2.
1845 : *Sen. doc., 29 Cong., 1 sess.,* v. I, no. 1 ; *House doc., 29 Cong., 1 sess.,* v. I, no. 2.
1846 : *Sen. doc., 29 Cong., 2 sess.,* v. I, no. 1 ; *House doc., 29 Cong., 2 sess.,* v. I, no. 4.
1847 : *Sen. doc., 30 Cong., 1 sess.,* v. I, no. 1.
1848 : *House exec. doc., 30 Cong., 2 sess.,* v. I, no. 1, pt. 1.
1849 : *House exec. doc., 31 Cong., 1 sess.,* v. III, pt. 1, No. 5, pt. 1.
1850 : None.
1851 : *Sen. exec. doc., 32 Cong., 1 sess.,* v. I, no. 1, pt. 1 ; *House exec. doc., 32 Cong., 1 sess.,* v. II. pt. 1, No. 2, pt. 1.
1852 : None.
1853 : *Sen. exec. doc., 33 Cong., 1 sess.,* v. I, no. 1, pt. 1 ; *House exec. doc., 33 Cong., 1 sess.,* v. I, pt. 1, No. 1, pt. 1.
1854 : *Sen. exec. doc., 33 Cong., 2 sess.,* v. I, no. 1, pt. 1 ; *House exec. doc., 33 Cong., 2 sess.,* v. I, No. 1, pt. 1.
1855 : *Sen. exec. doc., 34 Cong., 1 sess.,* v. 1, no. 1, pt. 1 ; *House exec. doc., 34 Cong., 1 sess.,* v. I, pt. 1, No. 1, pt. 1.
1856 : *Sen. exec. doc., 34 Cong., 3 sess.,* v. II, no. 5, pt. 1 ; *House exec. doc., 34 Cong., 3 sess.,* v. I, pt. 1, No. 1, pt. 1.
1857 : *Sen. exec. doc., 35 Cong., 1 sess.,* v. II, no. 2, pt. 1 ; *House exec. doc., 35 Cong., 1 sess.,* v. II, pt. 1, No. 2, pt. 1.
1858 : *Sen. exec. doc., 35 Cong., 2 sess.,* v. I, no. 1, pt. 2 ; *House exec. doc., 35 Cong., 2 sess.,* v. II, pt. 1, No. 2, pt. 1.
1859 : *Sen. exec. doc., 36 Cong., 1 sess.,* v. I, no. 2, pt. 1.
1860 : None.

ments have been indexed: *The Senate Executive Journal,* for diplomatic and consular appointments and treaty ratifications; the Opinions of the Attorneys General, for decisions on questions of international controversy; the *Statutes-at-Large,* for acts and resolutions relating to international affairs; and the *Congressional Globe* and its predecessors for speeches and correspondence." Though one sees by this description from the compiler's explanatory note that it goes farther afield than diplomatic correspondence in its indexing, it nevertheless lists all the diplomatic correspondence, which may quickly and easily be located. Of course it still remains a task for the librarian to assemble the numerous separate volumes in which the investigator, with the assistance of Miss Hasse's index, has located the desired publications. Such is the inconvenience of not having a regular series of published diplomatic correspondence for those years, 1828–1861.

Among the useful research aids compiled in the archives section, Office of Historical Adviser, of the Department of State, is a card catalogue of United States executive documents relating to foreign affairs, 1861–1881. It is arranged in the form of an index, with many cross references, by subjects and persons. This catalogue was prepared by Mrs. Natalia Summers, archivist.

The diplomatic correspondence of the United States during this period can now be supplemented by that of Texas, which has been printed in three volumes, by the American Historical Association in its *Annual reports* for 1907, and 1908, edited by Professor George P. Garrison (no. 1555).

Beginning 1861 we have the noteworthy series *Papers relating to the foreign relations of the United States, with the annual message of the President to Congress* (Wash.: Govt. Print. Off., 1862–1934) [5345] covering to date (1934) the years 1861–1918. This is more widely known by the shorter binder's-title *Diplomatic correspondence,* to 1868 (no volume was issued for 1869), and since then, *Foreign relations of the United States.* There is a *General index* to the volumes 1861–1899 (Wash., 1902), but none since. Individual volumes are indexed. The volumes include a collection of official papers relating to the foreign relations of the United States, with the annual message of the President to Congress. The diplomatic correspondence relating to the World War of 1914–1918 is published in this series in separate volumes (supplements) for the respective years.[14] Since 1916 there have been published additional volumes, containing the *Diplomatic correspondence with belligerent governments relating to neutral rights and commerce* [*or duties*] (Wash.: Govt. Print. Off., 1915–1918, 4 v.) [5347], also published as supplements to the *American journal of international law*, v. IX (July 1915); v. X (Oct. 1916); and v. XI (Oct. 1917), which had never been communicated to Congress. Other such supplementary volumes in the series are the *Papers relating to the foreign relations of the United States*, 1918, *Russia* (Wash., 1931–) [5348–9]. In this connection the Department of State has been pursuing a policy of historical publication, in the interests of education and historiography as much as of administration. The diplomatic correspondence of the United States, so far as this regular series is concerned, is now (1934) fifteen years in arrears, the last printed volume having appeared for the year 1919 (published 1934). The expanding volume of diplomatic correspondence, and the increasing number of subjects to which it refers, brought on by growing governmental activity everywhere in the world, has raised a serious problem of printing. Delay in publication is explained as due to the difficulty of securing release from other governments of promises made by the United States not to publish certain matter without mutual consent; this is particularly true for the matter relating to the peace negotiations of 1919, and the negotiations preceding the Washington Conference of 1921.[15]

This *Foreign relations of the United States* can be supplemented during the Civil War, with J. D. Richardson's *A compilation of the messages and papers of the Confederacy, including the diplomatic correspondence, 1861–1865* (Nashville, 1905, 2 v.)[16] [5350]; and *Official records of the Union and Confederate navies in the war of the rebellion* (no. 1883), *Series II, volume 3*, which contains the

---

[14] U.S. Dept. of State, *Papers relating to foreign relations of the United States. Supplement, World War*, 1914–1918 (Wash.: Govt. Print. Off., 1928–34, 9 v.) [5346].

[15] Historians sincerely hope that these bars will be let down soon. The American Historical Association has petitioned the Secretary of State repeatedly (in 1931 and in 1932) to publish the documents relating to the peace conference of 1919.

[16] For a " Bibliography of the official publications of the Confederate States of America ", see H. A. Morrison, in the *Proceedings and papers of the Bibliographical Society of America*, v. III, 1908 (N.Y., 1909) 92–132 [5351], and *A list of the official publications of the Confederate States government in the Virginia State Library and the Confederate Memorial Literary Society* (Richmond, Va., 1911) [5352], published as the *Bulletin of the Virginia State Library*, v. VI, no. 1.

diplomatic correspondence of the Confederate government with its agents abroad. For printed diplomatic correspondence since the latest volume of *Foreign relations* one must rely on the scattered publications that have appeared from time to time in congressional documents, or on " occasional publications " of the Department of State, which must be hunted down in the several catalogues to government documents. These form a unique series which requires a brief analysis.

After the publication of several indexes to congressional documents for particular periods, there appeared in 1885, *A descriptive catalogue of the government publications of the United States, September 5, 1774–March 4, 1881,* compiled by Benjamin Perley Poore (Wash.: Govt. Print. Off., 1885) (48th Cong., 2d sess. Senate. Misc. doc. 67) [5353]. This purported to present titles, with brief descriptive matter generally taken from the title-page, of all government publications, chronologically arranged. Being the only comprehensive work of its kind in existence, it was a great boon to reference workers, but it was seriously deficient in departmental publications, because Poore relied on the cooperation of departmental authorities for his lists. It has a useful alphabetical index without which the chronological lists would not be workable; but the limitations of this index for the student of diplomatic history are indicated by the entry; " Foreign relations (see under different countries, missions of the United States, and foreign missions in the United States)." Later specialists going over Poore's *Catalogue* have found lacunae.

Following a gap of eight years which intervened after the end of the period covered by Poore, there began a series of catalogues and indexes to government documents since 1881. The first of these was the work of J. G. Ames, *Comprehensive index of the publications of the United States government, 1889–93* (Wash.: Govt. Print. Off., 1894) [5354]. A second volume, published in 1905, *Comprehensive index . . . 1881–1893* (Wash.: Govt. Print. Off., 1905) [5355] went back and filled in the gap between Poore's catalogue and Ames's first index. It is by no means a " comprehensive index." It is really an alphabetical listing of the subject (but not of the precise title) of each public document, with the serial number and other enumeration of the congressional document in which it is found, with page references. In so listing, it utilizes a scheme, invented by Dr. Ames, for numbering serially the documents issued by Congress beginning with 1817 (the first year in which both houses of Congress began numbering their public documents according to sessions). Documents for years before 1817 had been reprinted in the collection *American state papers*, and are fully cited in A. W. Greely, *Public documents of the first fourteen congresses, 1789-1817* (Wash.: Govt. Print. Off., 1900) **[5356]**, and *Supplement* (1904). Ames's index also gives an indication of the author or person, or the department of the government, or both, from which the congressional document emanated.

In 1902 the Superintendent of Documents' Office published its *Tables of and annotated index to the congressional series of United States public documents* (Wash.: Govt. Print. Off., 1902) **[5357]**, commonly called "Tables and index." It contains (Part I) tables of documents arranged by serial numbers, 1817-1893 (15th to 52d Congress). These are classified by numbered congresses, only under the headings of Journals, Executive Documents, Miscellaneous Documents, Committee Reports, without any enumeration of the *titles* of separate documents; but there is in Part II a detailed alphabetical subject index to the documents listed in the tables.

Ames's remarkable work, and the "Tables and Index" were continued under provision of an act of Congress of January 12, 1895, in a series of volumes the first of which was entitled *Catalogue of the public documents of the fifty-third Congress and of all departments of the government of the United States for the period from March 4, 1893, to June 30, 1895* (Wash.: Govt. Print Off., 1896) **[5358]**. To date (1934) twenty sequent volumes proceed through the 71st Congress of 1929-1931. This publication known as the "Document Catalogue" is an alphabetical catalogue of all government documents by author and by detailed subject, with appropriate enumeration and description of the particular document. There is no separate classification for all documents relating to foreign relations; one must look under the names of the various countries, individuals, subjects, etc. We understand that valiant efforts are being made to bring the arrears of this catalogue reasonably close to the present date. The Superintendent of Documents' Office has published a *Consolidated Index*, called usually the "Document Index", for the congressional series of public documents, Dec. 2, 1895-Mar. 4, 1933. It is an alphabetical subject index, similar to the ordinary book index, valuable particularly for recent publications, and appears under the title: *Index to the reports and documents of the 54th Congress, 1st session to [the 72nd Congress, 2d session, Dec. 5, 1932–Mar. 4, 1933]* Wash.: Govt. Print. Off., 1897–1933, 43 v.) [5359]. The "Document Catalogue", when it appears supersedes this "Document Index." After 1933, pending appearance of these arrears of the *Document catalogue*, one may carry forward in the successive numbers of the *Monthly catalogue, United States public documents* [5360] (which began to appear in 1895) for which annual indexes are issued (see immediately above); and one may even advance right up to last Saturday in the *Weekly list of selected United States government publications*, published by the Superintendent of Documents, July 11, 1928, to date.

The most concise and valuable of all guides to public documents of the United States is the *Checklist of United States public documents, 1789–1909.* 3d ed., revised and enlarged. Vol. I. (Wash.: Govt. Print. Off., 1911) [5361] containing lists of congressional documents to the close of the sixtieth Congress (1908), and of departmental publications to the end of the year 1909. Congressional documents are listed chronologically by sessions, with serial number, sessional number. Departmental publications are listed by departments alphabetically, with subdivisions according to various departmental agencies (there is also a special classification number for each publication, devised to give it its proper place in the complete collection in the library of the Superintendent of Documents.

This checklist has the advantage of separating into one group the publications of the Department of State, of obvious convenience to us here. The various categories of titles grouped under the general heading of Department of State include: diplomatic correspondence published in the series *Foreign relations*; general publications (of a most voluminous and varied nature, alphabetically arranged); consular regulations; register of the Department of State; diplomatic and consular service (lists of officers); diplomatic lists (of foreign diplomatists in Washington); commercial regulations of foreign countries; instructions to diplomatic and consular officers (a few only); information regarding appointments and promotions; arbitrations and mixed commissions to settle international disputes; foreign commerce bureau; international congresses, conferences, and commissions; international exhibitions and expositions; laws of the

United States; Bureau of Rolls and Library (sponsoring many general publications of historical import); treaties; Puerto Rico (1900–1909); and trade relations bureau. They originally intended to bring out a second volume to the *Checklist*, which would contain an index. It has not appeared to date; and now the paramount need is rather for supplementary volumes to carry the *Checklist* after 1909. The checklist is invaluable for the student of diplomatic history as a key to congressional documents dated before 1909 and already described in the several document catalogues and indexes above mentioned. At first practically all public documents were printed as congressional documents; but gradually various departments began printing directly through the public printer, of course under appropriations voted by Congress. Some of these also appear as congressional documents. The Department of State began independent publications by series in 1929 (see below, p. 826).

We now have an excellent manual on the organization and use of United States government publications: Anne M. Boyd, *United States public documents as sources of information for libraries* (N.Y., 1931) [5362]. It is supplemented, for current material, by J. K. Wilcox, *United States reference publications; a guide to the current reference publications of the federal government* (Boston, 1931) [5363].

Before we leave the subject of printed diplomatic correspondence we must make especial notice of the three notable and erudite compilations of John Bassett Moore, which are of paramount importance for both the student and the investigator of American diplomacy. They deserve special mention and emphasis as the most important compilations in the history of American foreign relations. We refer to the two compendious and learned digests of Judge Moore: *History and digest of the international arbitrations to which the United States has been a party, together with appendices containing the treaties relating to such arbitrations, and historical and legal notes* (Wash.: Govt. Print. Off., 1898, 6 v.) [5364]; and *Digest of international law, as embodied in diplomatic discussions, treaties, and other international agreements, international awards, the decisions of municipal courts, and the writings of jurists, and especially in documents, published and unpublished, issued by presidents and secretaries of state of the United States, the opinions of attorneys-general, and the decisions of courts, federal and state*

(Wash.: Govt. Print. Off., 1906, 8 v.) **[5365]**.[17] Judge Moore is now occupied with a third great publication, a monumental edition of all international arbitrations: *International adjudications, ancient and modern; history and documents* (N.Y., 1929 to date (1934), 6 v.) **[5366]**. This contains additional information, with voluminous source material, including a fully documented report of all judicial decisions of international questions not recorded in the ordinary law reports. It is appearing as a publication of the Carnegie Endowment for International Peace.

There is no other extensive series of American diplomatic correspondence, printed either publicly or privately. Various small lots containing in part official documents of peculiar historical interest have come from non-official presses. They are appropriately mentioned in the bibliographical part of this volume.[18]

The various endowments and societies for the promotion of international peace *reprint* and thus make universally available much contemporary correspondence and other official documents relating to American diplomacy.[19] Such are the publications of the American Association for International Conciliation (now under the control of the Carnegie Endowment for International Peace), the Carnegie Endowment for International Peace, World Peace Foundation, Council on Foreign Relations, Foreign Policy Association. Of course a quantity of official diplomatic correspondence is printed (much of it reprinted) in the various " Writings " and " Works " of American statesmen and diplomatists,[20] or reproduced in part in their biographies.[21] For this sort of material the student must keep abreast of the various historical publications.[22]

---

[17] This supersedes an older three-volume digest by Francis Wharton, *A digest of the international law of the United States, taken from documents issued by presidents and secretaries of state, and from decisions of federal courts and opinions of attorneys-general*, 2d ed. (Wash.: Govt. Print. Off., 1887, 3 v.) **[5367]**.

[18] For example, *Letters relating to the negotiations at Ghent, 1812–1814* (no. 915); *The papers of James A. Bayard, 1796–1815* (no. 5188); *Letters of William Vans Murray* (no. 5272); *Despatches from the United States consulate in New Orleans, 1801–1803* (no. 706); and *The treaties of 1778, and allied documents* (no. 22a).

[19] These are surveyed in detail in League of Nations, *Handbook of international organizations* (no. 5155) and *Handbook of institutions for the scientific study of international relations*, compiled by the League of Nations' Institute of Intellectual Co-operation (Paris, 1929) **[5367a]**; Harley, *International understanding* (no. 5157); Heald, *Societies and organizations in Great Britain concerned with study of internat. affairs* (no. 5156); and Savord, *American agencies concerned with study of internat. affairs* (no. 5160).

[20] See list, p. 756 above.

[21] See bibliographical notes at end of short biographies in *Dictionary of American biography* for full information as to such biographical literature.

[22] See above, Part I.

ii. Treaties

All the ratified [23] treaties of the United States with foreign powers are printed. Because they are the law of the land, they appear in the various collections of statutes and laws.[24] They have also been reprinted in many collections of treaties of the United States, all of which may be found listed in Myers (no. 5399), 342–347. Until most recently the standard compilation has been William M. Malloy's edition of *Treaties, conventions, international acts, protocols, and agreements between the United States of America and other powers, 1776–1909* (Wash.: Govt. Print. Off., 1910, 2 v.) [5368] with a supplement 1910–1923 by Charles Garfield in 1923, in shape of a third volume.[25] Since Malloy, treaties may be found in the more recent editions [26] of United States Statutes at Large and, of course, in the Congressional Record. Since 1908 the Department of State has been publishing its "Treaty Series", numbered serially (beginning with no. 489, prints issued prior to no. 489 bore no numbers), including all treaties signed by the United States, which until 1929 included also executive agreements; since then the latter have appeared in a separate "Executive Agreement Series." See for description, the following: *Subject index of the treaty series and the executive agreement series, July 1, 1931* (Wash., 1932) [5370], published by the Department of State; it covers all the treaties of the United States which have at any time been in force, but does not cover all of the executive agreements. In 1929 the Department of State began, under the editorship of Mr. Hunter Miller, a definitive edition of *Treaties and other international acts of the United States of America* (Wash.: Govt. Print. Off., 1931–) [5371], of which to date (1935) four volumes have been published as follows: Vol. I (1931)[27]; Vol. II: 1776–1818 (1931); Vol. III: 1819–1835 (1933); and Vol. IV: 1835–1846 (1935). All previous treaty series have been imperfect reproductions, for the editors or printers often relied for printer's copy on previously printed texts.

---

[23] See the Department of State's *List of treaties and other international acts of the United States of America in force December 31, 1932* (Wash., 1933) [5367a]. For unratified treaties, see its *List of treaties submitted to the Senate, 1789–1931, which have not gone into force.* October 1, 1932 (Wash., 1932) [5367b].

[24] See below, p. 828.

[25] Congressional documents, vols. 5646–47, and 6350.

[26] For bibliography see Myers (no. 5399), and a "Bibliography of United States treaty collections", in Hunter Miller's *Treaties* (no. 5371), v. I, 39–54 [5369].

[27] A preliminary print of Vol. I contains lists and indexes, to be replaced later by a definitive Vol. I.

The result was the repetition or commission of an incredible number of small errors in typography, spelling, capitalization, and punctuation, and occasionally even more serious errors. Miller's official edition proceeds from original texts, or facsimiles thereof, with the most scrupulous collation, in the original language or languages of the authorized version of the treaties (accompanied by translation when the text is not English). The historical notes, of great value, become increasingly detailed with the progress of the volumes. It will supersede all previous compilations and is arranged so that it may carry ahead chronologically in future years as long as the treaty-making power shall last. There are also to be supplementary volumes of historical and judicial notes, and maps, on the individual treaties, the texts of which are printed in the several previous volumes of the publication.

Before American independence the treaties between European powers dealt frequently with the North American continent, including the region now within the limits of the United States and its dependencies. At first America was an incident to European international relations, but as the commercial importance of the New World became emphasized these regions became the object of European diplomacy, often the cause of European wars, and frequently the principal subject of European treaties. To search through the historical treaty collections [28] for treaties relating to the territory now within the United States is a tremendous task. The Carnegie Institution of Washington, Department of Historical Research, assisted by the erudition of the late Miss Frances Gardiner Davenport, began the preparation of a collection of *European treaties bearing on the history of the United States and its dependencies* (Wash.: Carnegie Institution of Washington, 1917–34, 3 v.) [5372]. Miss Davenport's lamented death in 1927 stopped the work at the year 1713. Volumes II and III were published posthumously.[29] Under Miss Davenport's editorship the publication was not limited to a scrupulous reproduction of the original texts of the relevant treaties. It included, in addition, copious bibliographical notes and historical introductions, both of the greatest value to the student of America

---

[28] For the classical collections see Myers (no. 5399), 16.

[29] Volume II, 1650–1697, was published in 1929. Volume III, 1698–1715, in 1934. A fourth volume is in preparation.

as a factor in European diplomacy, or of European diplomacy as a factor in American history.

iii. International Congresses, Conferences, Commissions, Expositions, Exhibitions, etc.

Beginning in 1863 the United States Government has published the proceedings of an increasingly large number of international congresses, conferences, commissions, expositions, exhibitions, etc., to which it has been a party. These include not only international congresses and conferences of a political nature, such as the Geneva Conferences, the Congress of Berlin, the Spanish-American Peace Commission, the Hague Conferences, the Inter-American (Pan-American) Conferences, but also a heterogeneous array of conclaves and parleys of all kinds, many of them of a scientific or literary nature, including the lengthy run of international exhibitions and expositions. In the *Checklist* (no. 5361, 944–953), the reports and other relevant printed documentary material thereto relating are catalogued chronologically. For the period 1909 to 1929 one must hunt through the *Document catalogue* (no. 5358); beginning 1929 see the cumulative quarterly lists of *Publications of the Department of State* (no. 5374). The Department of State publishes at the Government Printing Office such matter in its series of occasional publications (here so called to distinguish them from its serial publications) which are named in the cumulative quarterly lists of publications of the Department. There is in this material a vast amount of sources for the diplomatic history of the United States, which are not included in the published diplomatic correspondence, and which frequently are more important than diplomatic correspondence. There is no general index to it.[30]

iv. General and Occasional Publications

In the *Checklist* (no. 5361) are indicated alphabetically voluminous amounts of divers material dealing with diplomatic history.

---

[30] It is greatly to be desired that an index be prepared for the period since 1861 modeled on Miss Hasse's for 1828–1861, which would locate and list and index *all* printed government documents dealing with foreign relations. The expansion of diplomatic affairs since 1861 would make this enterprise so many times larger and more difficult than the Hasse *Index* that it would require the organization of a small staff of bibliographers, and some expense, but not so much as many of the rivers-and-harbors bills items, and the result in the long run possibly would be much more valuable. If the Department of State itself cannot be persuaded to undertake the project, some scientific endowment or learned society might well do so.

Such titles as the following suggest the variety and possibilities of this general and occasional type of publication: "Abyssinia: Our mission to Abyssinia, Robert P. Skinner's report, February 1, 1904 "; " Fox, Gustavus Vasa: Russian account of official mission of G. V. Fox, in 1866, translated by S. N. Buynitzky, 1867 "; " Portraits: Descriptive catalogue of collection of portraits in the Department of State, 1900." Similar items are grouped also under *Bureau of Rolls and Library* (a division of the State Department which has been obsolete since 1921). These are of great importance because they comprise the publications of strictly defined " historical " matter, like the *Documentary history of the Constitution* and the various calendars and indexes to the MS. collections such as the correspondence of the Virginia presidents. Among the occasional publications issued by the Department of State since the publication of the *Checklist* (no. 5361) are such very recent books and pamphlets as, for example: " Proceedings of the International Conference of American States on Conciliation and Arbitration "; " Report of the chairman, Commission of Inquiry and Conciliation, Bolivia and Paraguay "; " The American foreign service." [31]

v. Diplomatic Registers and Lists

Beginning in 1837, next in 1855, and thereafter annually have been printed *Lists of ministers, consuls, and other diplomatic and commercial agents of the United States in foreign countries* [5373]. This publication has been continuous under different titles and has been printed at varying intervals; it is now known as the *Foreign service list*, which is published quarterly. Since 1869, the annual *Register of the Department of State* (no. 5122) [32] has been issued; this publication contains lists of persons employed in the Department and in the Foreign Service, information regarding the latter being largely reprinted from the *Foreign service list*. Lists of diplomatic and consular representatives of foreign countries resident in the United States, formerly printed in the *Register*, now appear in the monthly *Diplomatic list* and the semiannual *Foreign consular offices in the United States*, respectively. Noteworthy here is the *Register* for the year 1874, now a rare publication, which contains

---

[31] *Foreign affairs,* VIII (1930) 303.
[32] For catalogue of various issues see *Checklist* (no. 5361), 904–907. For recent lists see the *Document catalogue* (no. 5358), and from 1933, the *Monthly catalogue* (no. 5360).

a historical register, giving " a succession of persons charged with
the care of foreign relations of the country and of diplomatic representatives or agents to or from the United States during the century ", 1774–1874. This is extremely useful to the student for
identifying diplomatic agents and their appointments,[33] but is not
impeccably accurate, and card catalogues of a more precise detail
are now kept in the archives of the Department of State.

vi. Foreign Commerce, including Consular Reports

This includes the voluminous series beginning 1856, of annual reports on commercial relations, consular reports, a few general publications on foreign commerce, exports declared for the United
States, reviews of the world's commerce, etc.[34]

vii. The New State Department Series (1929)

In 1929 the Department of State began a new departure in publications, by the institution of a number of separate series, which
bids fair in the future to multiply. They now include: *Press releases* (weekly printings of mimeographed releases of various information to the press); *Publications of the Department of State*
(quarterly list); *Treaty information*, a monthly bulletin giving detailed information concerning treaties to which the United States
is or may become, a party; *Arbitration series; Conference
series* (continuing in a more methodical form the publication of material relating to all sorts of international conferences: Nos. 1 and 2
of this series, for example, deal respectively with the London Conference of 1929 on safety of life at sea, and with the London Conference of 1930 for the limitation of naval armaments); *Executive
agreement series; Latin American series; Near Eastern series; West-*

---

[33] An international committee appointed by the International Committee of Historical
Sciences is preparing an international historical diplomatic register, for all countries.
The Department of State is compiling, in the case of the United States, the list of
diplomatic representatives sent to all countries. This catalogue, compiled by Miss
Alice M. Brown, is now on cards and available for use at that department (Archives
section) [5373a]. The list of diplomatic agents received, from all countries, has been
compiled by Mrs. Mary P. Ragatz, under the direction of Dr. J. Franklin Jameson, chairman of the international committee mentioned, and is to be printed ultimately by the
International Committee of Historical Sciences [5373b]. A list of " Principal diplomatic agents, March 4, 1789–" (American only) is published in each recent number of
the *Register* of the Department of State (no. 5122).

[34] Listed in the *Checklist* (no. 5361), 921–943. For this matter since 1909, see the
Document catalogue, Monthly catalogue, etc. (nos. 5358, 5360).

ern European series; and *Passport series.* This material[35] is of the highest value to the student of contemporary American diplomacy, but specialists have been importuning the Department to make some of the series more inclusive: for example, the proceedings of the Havana Inter-American Conference of 1928 have not yet (1934) been fully published by the United States Government. When not published by the United States, however, the proceedings of the various international conferences of the present time may be found in the League of Nations Publications,[36] and there is something forceful to be said against duplicating such matter in a publication by the Department of State. As above remarked the Treaty Series, which until 1929 published some executive agreements, dates back to 1908, prior to which date the treaties were published " occasionally ", that is not in a regular series.

As noted below the published laws of the United States issue from the Department of State after being signed by the President.

viii. Writings and Works of the Secretaries of State

The "writings" or " works " of some of the Secretaries have been privately published (in the case of Jefferson there is the official edition). Such editions frequently publish official documents, as well as the sometimes more interesting private correspondence. We refer the reader to the list of the Secretaries of State in an earlier part of this volume, and to our lists of writings and works of American statesmen, for this printed matter.[37]

3. Published Records of other Departments of the Executive Branch which may touch Foreign Affairs

Although there is no index since Miss Hasse's which covers the period 1828–1861, by which the reader can sift out of the vast amount of printed volumes of documents published by the executive departments other than the Department of State, one should not overlook a considerable quantity of printed material to be found in the War, Navy, Treasury, Interior, Commerce, Justice,[38] and Labor Depart-

---

[35] It is listed in *Publications of the Department of State; a list cumulative from October 1, 1929* (Wash., 1934) [5374]. Quarterly lists of such publications carry forward.
[36] See no. 5470a.
[37] For lists of MS. papers of the Secretaries of State, see p. 865.
[38] For opinions of attorneys-general, see below, p. 835.

ments.[40] We indicate in a footnote below a few of the more suggestive titles that appear in the catalogue of this departmental literature.[41] In searching for this matter one must use the *Checklist* and the several later indexes and catalogues of public documents.

Since 1915 the Superintendent of Documents has been printing periodically a price-list, *Foreign relations of the United States; list of publications . . . for sale by the Superintendent of Documents* [5376], which consists of a list of publications of government documents on that subject which are *in stock at the time of going to press* and for sale. This is of course incomplete. Many documents are no longer in stock,[42] and others dealing with foreign relations (for example, on occasions, the proceedings of mixed claims commissions) are not for sale. Others may be " printed but not published."

B. Printed Records of the Legislative Branch

1. Laws

The laws of the United States, and of the several states touch the subject of foreign affairs in multitudinous ways: one would need

---

[40] See the excellent analysis of departmental publications in Boyd (no. 5362), 91–260.

[41] The War Department provides few publications of use to the student of diplomatic history; some, however, put forth by the Bureau of Insular Affairs may prove valuable. Among them we mention the following : *Report on legal status of islands acquired during the war with Spain* (no. 3459) ; *Cuban pacification* (no. 3460) ; *Acts and treaties, etc., Cuba and Santo Domingo* (no. 3884) ; and *Philippines* (no. 3461). There are also reports on Dominican and Haitian customs receiverships, with summary of commerce, published in 1908 and 1918, respectively.

The Navy Department published Commodore M. C. Perry's *Journal* (no. 3127). Of special interest is the diplomatic correspondence of the Confederate government with its agents abroad, published in the concluding volume of the series of records of the navies in the civil war (no. 1883). The Naval War College (under the Navy Department) has published a series of volumes of *International law situations* (or *topics and discussions,* title varies) (Wash., 1901–1930) [5375] which has a *General index . . . vols. I to XXX,* 1901–1930 (Wash., 1933).

Among the publications of the Treasury Department we find a number dealing with foreign relations, including documents relating to trade with Canada (nos. 1349, 1958, 1959), *Filibustering expeditions to Cuba* (no. 3389), also reports of Pan-American financial conferences ; and of the Inter-American High commission, laws, decisions, and regulations relating to Chinese exclusion, published by the " Special Agents Division, 1896–1902 " (after 1902 similar publications were issued by the Immigration Bureau of the Department of Commerce).

The Department of Commerce, through its Bureau of Foreign and Domestic Commerce, issues two groups of publications, *Periodicals* and *Special bulletins.* See *Condensed list of publications issued by Bureau of Foreign and Domestic Commerce* (Wash. : Govt. Print. Off., 1932) [5375a].

[42] For a complete list beginning with 1915, all editions of the price list should be consulted. The Superintendent of Documents publishes and distributes free, the following similar price lists : *American history and biography* (first published, 1910, continued periodically to date), *Political science* (first published, 1911, and continued periodically to date).

only mention tariff, immigration, neutrality laws, prohibition, naturalization, alien land acts, etc. A convenient description of the publication of the Federal laws is given in the list of *Publications of the Department of State* (Wash., 1934), page 12, as follows: The following editions of Federal laws are published by the Department of State: *Slip Laws*. The first form in which the laws are printed for public distribution. *Session Laws*. At the close of each session of Congress the slip laws are collected, edited, and indexed, and, together with the concurrent resolutions, treaties and conventions, and Executive proclamations issued during the same session, are published in large pamphlets entitled "Statutes of the United States of America." They are generally known as "session laws." *Statutes at Large*.[43] At the close of each Congress the session laws are assembled, their indexes are consolidated, and they are then published under the title "Statutes at Large." These comprise the acts and joint resolutions, public and private, and concurrent resolutions, treaties, conventions, and Executive proclamations published during the 2-year term of each Congress. Beginning with the Seventy-second Congress, second session, the session laws and the Statutes at Large also include the Executive agreements.

2. Treaties (see above, p. 822).

3. Proceedings, Debates, etc.

The printed record of debates of the two houses of Congress begins in 1789 with the inauguration of the Government of the present Constitution. The Continental Congress kept only a journal of motions, bills, laws, committee appointments, committee reports (to a limited degree), in other words a journal of action taken, *but not* of discussion and debate. These journals were incompletely printed by a contract printer in two sets: the *Journals*, which ran to thirteen octavo volumes from September 5, 1774, to November 3, 1788 (second

---

⁴³ *The Statutes at large of the United States of America* (Boston, 1845–73; Wash.: Govt. Print. Off., 1875–1934, 48 v. (in progress)) [5377] from the organization of the government in 1789 to date, contain acts and resolutions relating to international affairs. There is an *Index analysis of the federal statutes (general and permanent law) 1789–1873, 1873–1907* (Wash.: Govt. Print. Off., 1911, 1908, 2 v.) (Library of Congress) [5378], by G. W. Scott, M. G. Beaman, and others, under the direction of the Librarian of Congress. *Index to the federal statutes, 1874–1931; general and permanent law contained in the Revised statutes of 1874 and volumes 18–46 of the Statutes at Large. Revision of the Scott and Beaman Index analysis of the federal statutes*, by W. H. McClenon and W. C. Gilbert (Wash.: Govt. Print. Off., 1933) (Library of Congress) [5378a].

ed., 4 v., 1924) ; and the *Secret journals*, 4 v., from September 5, 1774, to September 16, 1788. A modern edition of the whole journals, public and secret, printed from the original MSS. has recently been published by the Library of Congress, edited successively by W. C. Ford, Gaillard Hunt, J. C. Fitzpatrick, and R. R. Hill : *Journals of the Continental Congress, 1774–1789* (Wash. : Govt. Print. Off., 1904–34, 31 v.) [5379].[44] Not until the year 1785 was reached did the editors begin to avail themselves of the material to be found in despatch books, committee reports, and committee books, beginning 1779 (Papers of the Continental Congress, MSS., nos. 185–191), which are necessary for the complete tracing of committee work, much of which concerned foreign affairs. The intention announced, at the publication of the first volume, to print all the papers and documents of the Continental Congress was never carried out. The *Journals* are well indexed, and are indispensable to the historian of the diplomacy of the American Revolution. But they do not contain the debates and discussions, of which no record was kept. To supply this gap the Carnegie Institution of Washington, Department of Historical Research, began in 1921 the publication of the *Letters of members of the Continental Congress*, edited by E. C. Burnett (Wash., 1921–34, 7 v.) [5380]. Seven volumes, through the year 1784, have been printed, and the completion of the task is expected at a relatively early date. In lack of any preserved debates all that one can know about what was said in Congress is to be found in such accounts of them as are contained in these private letters of members who were present. The *Letters* supplement the *Journals* and like them are indispensable to the student of the beginnings of American diplomacy. The editing and indexing of this set is supreme in American historiography.

Similarly only a journal was kept of the proceedings of the Philadelphia Constitutional Convention of 1787; but some of the members, James Madison, in particular, and Robert Yates and James McHenry to a much lesser degree, kept personal notes in debates. Numerous editions of the proceedings, including Madison's *Journal* have been published,[45] but they are superseded by Max Farrand's

---

[44] Publication now extends through the year 1786, with subsequent volumes through 1788 in preparation.

[45] See *Checklist* (no. 5361), 1668–1670. Note also v. III of the *Documentary history of the United States of America, 1787–1870* (Wash. : Govt. Print. Off., 1894–1905, 5 v.) [5380a], published by the Department of State.

Records of the Federal Convention (New Haven, 1911, 3 v.) [5381], the purpose of which was to print every scrap of source material relating to that convention.[46] The Constitution itself, and the exegesis of it published by Alexander Hamilton, James Madison, and John Jay[47] in *The Federalist* in 1788, will ever be vital to the student of the constitutional origins of American foreign affairs.

With the beginning of the present national legislature in 1789, a printed record of the debates in both houses of Congress exists. "Though these records have been issued under various titles and auspices, they form a continuous and connected documentary chronicle, and the different series of which it is composed have had the sanction of Congress as official and have been distributed as government publications."[48] The series containing the proceedings are as follows: *Annals of Congress*, 1789–1824 (Wash., 1834–56, 42 v.) [5382] containing records of debates,[49] not taken verbatim, but prepared by the compilers from contemporary newspaper reports; *Register of debates in Congress, 1824–1837* (Wash., 1825–37, 14 v. in 29) [5383], debates not literally reported in all cases, but substantially reliable; *Congressional Globe*, 1833–1873 (Wash., 1834–73, 46 v. in 111) [5384], a full record but not verbatim; the *Congressional Record* (Wash.: Govt. Print. Off., 1874– (in progress) [5385], being a complete stenographic record, padded with "extensions of remarks" never uttered in Congress. Mention should also be made of T. H. Benton's *Abridgment of the debates of Congress from 1789 to 1856* (N.Y., 1857–1861, 16 v.) [5386] which is based on the *Annals* and the *Register of debates*. In the *Annals*, *Register*, and *Globe*, the indexes are printed in each volume; in the *Record*, except for one session, the index for each volume is printed separately from it. There is also the *Journal* of the House of Representatives, 1789– (N. Y. [1789–1790], Phila., 1791–1800; Wash., 1801–   ); and *Journal* of the Senate (N. Y. [1789–1790], Phila., 1791–1800; Wash.,

---

[46] A new scrap, in the shape of a hitherto unknown copy of a Madison manuscript relating to the Federal Convention, turned up in 1930. See C. R. Keller and G. W. Pierson in *Am. hist. rev.*, XXVI (1930) 17–30 [5381a]. The Library of Congress also acquired recently another little scrap, a part of a speech of Luther Martin.

[47] For references to the mooted authorship of certain numbers of the *Federalist*, see the article on the Federalist in the *Cyclopedia of American government* (N.Y., 1914).

[48] *Checklist* (no. 5361), 1463.

[49] The Senate proceedings are meagerly reported before 1794, because that body (with slight exception) sat behind closed doors till then.

1801–); and the *Journal of the executive proceedings of the Senate of the United States of America* (Wash., 1828–1909, 32 v. in 34) [5387] covering the period from the commencement of the first congress, 1789, to March 9, 1901. It is reported that further publication (to 1931) is contemplated. It is needless to remark that these proceedings, because of the special relation of the Senate to treaties, are of major importance to the student of foreign relations.[50]

The legislative proceedings of the Congress of the Confederacy are printed in the *Journal of the Congress of the Confederate States of America, 1861–1865* (Wash.: Govt. Print. Off., 1904–05, 7 v.) [5387a].

4. Senate Executive Documents

The Senate being an organic controlling body in the exercise of foreign policy, under the treaty-making power, there are a great many so-denominated executive documents, publications at first printed as confidential documents or reports, from which the injunction of secrecy has been subsequently removed.[51] Of most of these very numerous documents very few examples are extant; if available, they would be of real value and interest as some of them contain material not to be found in other sources.

5. Committee Reports

These are to be found in the miscellaneous unclassified publications of both House of Representatives and Senate, *i.e.*, the " Congressional Documents " which are not generally indexed and which must be worked, after 1861, for foreign affairs with the help of the various indexes and catalogues of government documents.[52] For the student of diplomatic history, however, one notable printed series stands out: *Compilation of reports of committee on foreign relations, United States senate, 1789–1901* (Wash.: Govt. Print. Off.,

---

[50] For description, and list of the Proceedings of Congress to 1909, see *Checklist* (no. 5361), 1463–1475; continued after 1909 in periodic publications by the Superintendent of Documents of a catalogue (price-list), *Proceedings of Congress*.

[51] Such confidential documents as are in the Public Documents Library are listed on pages 1476–91 of the *Checklist* (no. 5361), " but the library does not claim that its set is complete, only a few issues prior to the 55th Congress having been secured." For issues subsequent to 1909, when the *Checklist* was published, one must consult the several volumes of the *Document catalogue* (no. 5358), under " Senate: Confidential publications."

[52] See note on catalogues and indexes to United States public documents, above, p. 817.

1901, 8 v.) [**5388**]. "In making this compilation search was made through the original files of the Senate, the American State Papers on Foreign Relations, the Legislative and Executive Journals of the Senate, the Annals and Debates of Congress, the Congressional Globe and Record, and the bound volumes of Senate reports." So says the editor, Mr. Hawkins Taylor, who was clerk of the Committee on Foreign Relations.[53] There is no similar compilation of the reports of the Committee on Foreign Affairs of the House; for this one must rely upon McKee's compilation of reports, described below (this page), using the index volume for this particular committee as a key, and for later years the *Document index* (no. 5358) where they are listed under the committee. The hearings of the Senate Committee on Foreign Relations and the House Committee on Foreign Affairs have been frequently issued in separate pamphlets not included in the Congressional series. These will be found listed in: *Index of congressional committee hearings (not confidential in character) prior to March 4, 1929, in the United States Senate Library* (Wash.: Govt. Print. Off., 1929) [**5389**], by Edward C. Goodwin, librarian of the Senate; and a later edition, to March 4, 1933, by the present librarian of the Senate, James D. Preston.

C. Printed Records of the Judicial Branch

1. Reports of the Federal Courts

Since the foundation of the present federal union in 1787 a pretty complete report of cases tried in the federal courts has existed in several editions. Questions of international significance frequently get into the federal courts, either by original jurisdiction, or by appeal from state courts.

---

[53] By a law of 1886 the compilation of a series of the printed reports of the committees of each house of Congress, 1815–1887, was authorized, and the work was undertaken and completed in 1887 by Mr. Thomas Hudson McKee, clerk of the Document Room, United States Senate, in the shape of 512 volumes, not of reprints, but of reassembly of the various reports, already printed, of the respective committees, which had been taken out of other volumes of otherwise irrelevant matter and rebound in order. There are 58 volumes of indexes for the reports of the committees of the House and 36 for the reports of the committees of the Senate. The indexes are arranged under committees, with subjects alphabetically ordered, and reference to the sessional number of the document in which the subjects are to be found. These compilations were for the use of the several standing committees of the two houses of Congress, and are inaccessible outside of Washington. They are known as "McKee's Compilations."

For the Supreme Court a complete report exists, in eight successive editions of reporters.[54] The Library of Congress contains a complete file of the printed *briefs* and *records* in the cases before the United States Supreme Court, which should prove helpful in understanding the ramifications of the cases. The lower federal courts are well reported except for the earliest years.[55]

2. Reports of the State Courts

For the period 1776–1789 state reports are meager, but afterward fairly complete.[56] They may not always be overlooked by the student of international affairs; for example, the famous McLeod case in New York.

3. Prize Court Decisions

Prize cases are decided by the nearest federal district court to the port to which the prize is taken in, and they must be sought accordingly in the federal court reports.[57] In 1923 the Carnegie Endowment for International Peace published a compilation, made under the supervision of Dr. James Brown Scott, *Prize cases decided in the United States Supreme Court, 1789–1918* (Oxford, 1923, 3 v.) [**5393**].

---

[54] See the following table:

Consisting of—	Period covered	Volumes
Dallas (or 1–4 U.S.)	1790–1800	4
Cranch (or 5–13 U.S.)	1801–1815	9
Wheaton (or 14–25 U.S.)	1816–1827	12
Peters (or 26–41 U.S.)	1828–1842	16
Howard (or 42–65 U.S.)	1843–1860	24
Black (or 66–67 U.S.)	1861–1862	2
Wallace (or 68–90 U.S.)	1863–1874	23
United States (91 to date)	1875 to date	

See F. C. Hicks, *Material and methods of legal research* (Rochester, N.Y., 1923) 121 [**5390**].

[55] For lists of reports, see Hicks (no. 5390), 556–559. For recent material, see the abstracts of current " Judicial decisions involving questions of international law ", published in the *American journal of international law* (no. 4847), v. I (1907), to date.

[56] For complete description, see Hicks (no. 5390), 110–134, and C. C. Soule, *The lawyer's reference manual of law books and citations* (Boston, 1883) [**5391**], 1–64.

[57] *American maritime cases* (Baltimore, 1923–1931) [**5392**] is a periodical reporter begun in 1923, since when (to 1934) there have been no American prize cases.

4. Opinions of the Attorney General [58]

The Department of Justice publishes the *Official opinions of the Attorney General of the United States* (Wash.: Govt. Print. Off., 1852–1932, 36 v.) [5394] covering the years 1791–1932; and *Digest of the official opinions of the attorneys-general of the United States* (Wash.: Govt. Print. Off., 1885–1926, 3 v.) [5395] covering volumes 1 to 32, for the years 1789 to 1921, which contain decisions on questions of international controversy.

D. Independent Commissions

There are the various independent federal commissions which cannot be classed with either executive, legislative, or judiciary. The work of some of these, like the Tariff Commission, established 1917,[59] and the World War Foreign Debts Commission (1922–1927) touch foreign affairs. For each of these latter-named commissions there is a very considerable body of printed documents. These publications of these independent establishments are adequately analysed in Boyd's manual (no. 5362). Some notable examples are the official publications, 1925–1927, of the World War Foreign Debts Commission.

E. Mixed Commissions and other Arbitral Tribunals

Publications of the work of these bodies have often emanated from the Department of State as public documents;[60] but sometimes the documents pertaining to these commissions have come directly from the commissions or tribunals, and have been printed for them by the Government Printing Office, or in some instances by private printers. In such cases they have not been for sale as government documents, and their distribution has been limited.

F. State Publications

The official publications of the several states of the Union are catalogued in the following: R. R. Bowker, *State publications; a*

---

[58] These really emanate from the executive branch of the government, but are so clearly related to the judicial matter that we rather arbitrarily class them here.

[59] See *Publications of the Tariff Commission* (Wash., 1931) [5396], mimeographed edition.

[60] See above, p. 824.

*provisional list of the official publications of the several states of the
United States from their organization* (N. Y., 1908) [**5396a**]; and
the *Monthly list of state publications*, January 1910– (Wash.: Govt.
Print. Off., 1910– (in progress)), compiled by the Division of Documents of the Library of Congress and published by that Library
[**5396b**].

II. Printed State Papers of Foreign Governments

In listing these published sources we do not undertake any such
detailed analysis as above for American public documents. Such a
presentation would needs be preceded by some analysis of the political structure of the several foreign governments [61] and elaborate
researches in many countries. With a few exceptions, " no attempt
has been made by individual governments to list their respective
publications, and such official material as exists is scattered among
numerous libraries. Even in these, methodical research is extremely
difficult owing to the absence of catalogues or the imperfection of
such as do exist." The editors of the manual, noted below, of the
American Library in Paris, estimate that such a bibliography would
require a prolonged stay in every European capital and would
probably occupy ten or fifteen years and during that decade and
a half the unindexed and uncatalogued publications of these governments would multiply beyond the registry. According to his
needs the student must seek out in the official publications of other
governments the counterparts of the American sources, if so they be
published. From the relatively few available catalogues and indexes
we have already drawn off such material as specifically relates to
American diplomatic history, and dropped it into the appropriate
headings of the strictly bibliographical chapters in the first part of
this guide. The following general bibliographical aids will intro-
duce the investigator into these realms of foreign state papers:

J. B. Childs, *An account of government document bibliography
in the United States and elsewhere. Revised July 1930* [61a] (Wash.:

---

[61] For an analysis of the relation of various national legislatures to the conduct of
foreign relations, see D. P. Myers, " Legislatures and foreign relations ", *Am. pol. sci.
rev.*, XI (1917) 643–684 [**5397**], with a very useful chart.

[61a] See also his pamphlet on *Recent bibliography of foreign government publications*
(Wash., 1932) [**5397a**], which is reprinted from the *Proceedings* of the Fifth Conference
of Teachers of International Law and Related Subjects, Washington, D. C., April 26–27,
1933.

Govt. Print. Off., 1930) (Library of Congress) [5398]. This most valuable booklet lists the guides to published state papers for the various countries, insofar as such guides exist. With the aid of these individual guides (the more important of which we list hereafter) one can find one's way into the public documents of the several powers with which the United States has maintained diplomatic relations. D. P. Myers, *Manual of collections of treaties and of collections relating to treaties* (Cambridge, 1922) (Harvard Bibliographies, Library series, v. II) [5399] extends its scope much further than the title implies, and includes collections of diplomatic correspondence, judicial decisions, state papers, etc., for all countries up to 1919 (not therefore including the new " succession states " of Europe). The works are listed in sections on: (1) bibliographies; (2) general collections; (3) collections by states, in alphabetical order; (4) collections by subject matter; (5) international administrations. It is an indispensable bibliography for the student of international law and diplomacy.

The American Foreign Law Association (New York) has published a series of *Bibliographies of foreign law*, of which to date (1934), the following have appeared: (1) Colombia; (2) Scandinavia; (3) Bolivia; (4) France; (5) Porto Rico; (6) Soviet Law; (7) Dominican Republic; (8) Haiti; (9) Uruguay.

American Library in Paris, Reference Service on International Affairs,[61b] *Official publications of European governments*, pt. I, compiled by José Meyer (Paris, 1929) [62] [5399a] is an outline bibliography of serials and important monographs, including diplomatic documents, *farbenbücher* (" color books " of state papers which include particularly diplomatic correspondence), issued by European governments and ministries. It was compiled following a detailed questionnaire sent to the different ministers of the various governments, and other efforts, and is the most informative list to date. The work includes the succession states, but, as the title indicated, does not include non-European states. Only the first volume, comprising Albania, Austria, Belgium, Bulgaria, Czechoslovakia, Denmark, Esthonia, Finland, and France, is so far

---

[61b] Since disbanded.

[62] A mimeographed volume containing *all* European countries was issued in 1926. The printed list noted here is a revision and expansion of this preliminary list, but to date (1934) only this first part has been issued.

published. Information on published diplomatic correspondence is particularly full.[63]

Winifred Gregory, *List of the serial publications of foreign governments, 1815-1931* (N.Y., 1932) [5400]. This is a check list only, but very useful in identifying and locating copies of the collections of proceedings and debates of legislative bodies, as well as the serial publications (bulletins, reports) and, in Hispanic America, the *Memorias* of the ministries of foreign affairs. Under each country, *without classification*, it presents in alphabetical order the titles of official serial publications. It is consequently difficult to extract desired categories of titles.

Great Britain

H. B. Lees-Smith, *A guide to parliamentary and official papers* (London, 1924) [5401] lists very lucidly the various indexes for British public documents. This should be supplemented by the account of British " Government publications ", by Sidney Horrocks, in the *Library assoc. rec.*, n. s. VIII (London, 1930) 93-104 [5402] where more detailed information is given concerning the sessional papers, the command papers, and non-parliamentary papers. Margaret I. Adam, John Ewing, and James Munro, *Guide to the principal parliamentary papers relating to the dominions, 1812-1911* (Edinburgh and London, 1913) [5403] [64] covers the corresponding material for the dominions.

For printed British official papers since 1800 there are adequate catalogues and indexes, somewhat simpler than the corresponding American catalogues and indexes.[65] British sessional papers which

---

[63] A bibliography of *Farbenbücher* is now being compiled by Ludwig Bittner, of Vienna, secretary of the subcommittee on Diplomatic Lists, of the International Committee of Historical Sciences.

[64] More recent official publications of the dominions and colonies, since 1927, are listed in *Overseas official publications* (London: Royal Empire Society, 1927-1932, 5v.) [5404], " being a quarterly bulletin of official publications . . . issued in the overseas British Empire or relating thereto ", edited by the librarian of the Royal Empire Society, London; and *Bibliography of Canadian bibliographies* (no. 4670), giving a useful bibliographical list of Canadian documentary material on pages 16 to 19. See also Evans Lewin, *Dominion of Canada* (no. 4676), which features specially parliamentary and official publications of the overseas dominions.

[65] The printed British state papers consist of parliamentary papers and nonparliamentary or stationery-office (corresponding to the United States Superintendent of Documents office) papers.

Parliamentary papers are: (a) those documents put before either or both houses of Parliament at command of the King (i.e., of the actual government), and hence known as *Command papers;* and (b), papers summoned to either or both houses by parliamentary

deal with diplomatic relations between the United States and Great
Britain are entered in the appropriate sections in the *Bibliography*
given in Part I of this *Guide*. There is much material respecting

order, and known as House of Commons papers and House of Lords papers. Up to
1900 each house printed its own papers separately, frequently duplicating the other's.
Since 1900 the command papers have appeared only as *House of Commons papers*. Parliamentary papers, commonly called *sessional papers*, are divided into four categories:
public bills, reports of committees, reports of commissioners (royal commission and similar bodies), accounts and papers, which last cover the great bulk of papers each year
(including correspondence of the foreign office, and other ministries).

The nonparliamentary papers issue directly from the various ministries through the
Stationery Office without a particular parliamentary order. They are departmental,
administrative, technical, and historical. They include, among many things, publications
of the Admiralty, Public Record Office, Colonial Office, Foreign Office, etc. The investigator must consult these as well as parliamentary papers. For a brief, but helpful,
survey of the publications of the Stationery Office, see Angus Fletcher, " His Majesty's
Stationery Office ", *Library jour.*, LII (1927) 461–464 [5405].

The principal indexes for parliamentary papers and for nonparliamentary or Stationery
Office papers are as follows:

Parliamentary Papers: 1. House of Commons, *Catalogue of parliamentary reports and
a breviate of their contents;* . . . *1696–1834* (London, 1836) ; *Catalogue of papers printed
by order of the House of Commons from the year 1731 to 1800* (London, 1807) ; *General
index to the bills printed by order of the House of Commons, 1801–1852* (London, 1854) ;
General index to the reports of select committees, . . . *1801–1852* (London, 1854) ; *General
index to the accounts and papers,* . . . *1801–1852* (London, 1854) ; *General alphabetical
index to the bills, reports, estimates, accounts, and papers* . . . *1852–1899* (London, 1909) ;
General alphabetical index to the bills, reports, estimates, accounts and papers . . . *1900–09*
(London, 1912) ; *General alphabetical index to the bills, reports, estimates, accounts,
and papers* . . . *1910–1919* (London, 1927) ; *General alphabetical index to the bills, reports,
estimates, accounts, and papers* . . . *1920–1929* (London, 1931) [5406]. L. J. Ragatz, *A
checklist of House of Commons sessional papers relating to the British West Indies and
to the West Indian slave trade and slavery, 1763–1834* (London, 1923, reissued, 1928)
[5407].

2. House of Lords, *A general index to the sessional papers printed by order of the
House of Lords or presented by special command* (London, 1860–1890, 3 v.), covering the
period 1801–1885. *Tables of the papers ordered by the House of Lords and of the papers
presented by His Majesty's command* . . . *followed by an alphabetical index to the titles
of all the papers of the session* (London, 1886–1920, 35 v.) [5408].

L. J. Ragatz, *A checklist of House of Lords sessional papers relating to the British
West Indies and the West Indian slave trade, 1763–1834* (London, 1931) [5409].

Beginning with 1921, the *Sessional papers printed by order of the House of Lords* have
only a general table of contents in the first volume for each session.

The records of the House of Lords and House of Commons are issued in a continuous
series ever since the sixteenth century. The volumes up to 1803 are called *Parliamentary history* and are not an actual record of debates ; with 1803 begins the series *Parliamentary
debates,* 1803 to date (London, 1804 to date) [5410]. Since 1909 the debates of each
House have been issued in separate series.

Non-parliamentary or Stationery Office Papers : " Non-parliamentary papers are issued
under the authority of the various departments of administration and are classified under
the names of the departments responsible for their contents, in alphabetically numbered
Lists. Until 1920 they were comprised in a *Catalogue of works (other than parliamentary
papers and acts of Parliament) published by His Majesty's Stationery Office* [(London,
1921) [5411]]. In 1921 a *Quarterly list of official publications . . . issued by His
Majesty's Stationery Office* was published, that for the last quarter of the year being
cumulative for the year. In 1922 this *List* was combined with that of ' Parliamentary
papers ' . . . under the title *Consolidated list of parliamentary and Stationery Office pub-*

imports and exports, shipping, trade, etc., which we have not itemized, but which may be found by consulting the *General indexes* (nos. 5406, 5408). We specially mention, for printed diplomatic correspondence: (1) The parliamentary papers (sessional papers) *Accounts and Papers*,[66] which are abundantly indexed (see preceding footnote), and (2) The *British and foreign state papers* . . . , 1812–1929, v. 1–131 (London, 1841–1934 (in progress)) **[5416]**, published from vol. 1 to 78 by private publishers, and beginning with vol. 79 (*i.e.* beginning 1888) by H. M. Stationery Office, being a publication of the Foreign Office. This series is intended to comprise the principal documents which have been made public relating to the political and commercial affairs of nations (treaties, laws, etc.) not only of Great Britain, but with each other, since the end of the Napoleonic wars (1814). It totals to date (1934) 131 volumes. Also the series *Hertslet's commercial treaties* (London, 1827–1925, 31 v.) **[5417]**, which ceased as a separate publication of the Foreign Office with v. XXXI, being incorporated with the *British and foreign state papers* (no. 5416) beginning with v. CXVI of the latter series; it is described as a " collection of treaties and conventions, between Great Britain and foreign powers; and of the laws, decrees, orders in council, &c., concerning the same, so far as they relate to commerce and navigation, slavery, extradition, nationality, copyright, postal matters, &c."

The House of Lords *Journals*, 1509– date (London, 165 v. (in progress)), and House of Commons *Journals*, 1547– date (London, 1742–1933, 188 v. (in progress)) **[5418]** contain items dealing with American relations which may be located by consulting the *General indexes* to the *Journals*,[67] and Paullin and Paxson, *Guide* (no. 5577),

lications . . . which in the following year became simply the *Consolidated list of government publications issued by His Majesty's Stationery Office from, etc.* **[5412]**, the present form of the title." *cf.* Fletcher (no. 5405), 462.

P. S. King and Son, of London, published as a private venture some catalogues to parliamentary papers, viz: *Catalogue of parliamentary papers, 1801–1900, with a few of earlier date* (London [1904]) **[5413]**, compiled by Hilda Vernon Jones. *Catalogue of parliamentary papers, 1901–1910, being a supplement to Catalogue of parliamentary papers, 1801–1900* (London, 1912) **[5414]**, compiled by Hilda Vernon Jones; *Catalogue of parliamentary papers, 1911–1920* (London, 1922) **[5415]**.

[66] Of this series, the " Papers relating to foreign affairs laid before Parliament " are conveniently listed, for the given year, in each volume of *The Foreign Office list* (no. 5125).

[67] For similar material in the Canadian Legislative Assembly and House of Commons *Journals*, see the *General index* to the same (containing such items as reciprocity treaty, customs, fisheries, Indians and Indian lands, trade relations, treaty of Washington, Alaska boundary) : *General index to the Journals of the Legislative Assembly of Canada, 1841–1866* (Montreal, 1855–67, 2 v.) ; and *General index to the Journals of the House of Commons of the Dominion of Canada and of the sessional papers of Parliament, 1867–1930* (Ottawa, 1880–1932, 5 v.) **[5419]**.

328–360, containing a calendar of House of Lords papers (including printed documents) relating to America, 1783–1903, based upon the indexes of the *Journals*. All entries relating to colonial affairs for North America and the West Indies are superbly edited and printed in L. F. Stock, *Proceedings and debates of the British parliaments respecting North America* (Wash.: Carnegie Institution of Washington, 1924–30, 3 v.) [5420], covering in these 3 volumes the years 1542–1727 (to be continued in later volumes), and drawn for the most part (for the *Proceedings*) from the printed *Journals*, (for *Debates*) from many printed and unprinted sources. Relations with the British dominions are similarly noted in reports on proceedings (debates and acts) published in the *Journal of the parliaments of the Empire*, issued under the authority of the Empire Parliamentary Association (United Kingdom branch) v. I–, 1920– (London, 1920–) [5421].

The Royal Historical Society has published six volumes of *British diplomatic instructions, 1689–1789* (London, 1922–34) [5422], comprising instructions to British diplomatic envoys in three countries (Sweden, France, and Denmark), from 1689 to 1789. Two volumes of despatches from France, 1784–1790, also occur in this series.[68] The great historical *Calendars of state papers, foreign series* (London, 1861–), *Domestic series* (London, 1856–), *Colonial series, America and the West Indies*, 1574–1721 (London, 1860–1933, 27 v. (in progress)), *Acts of the Privy Council of England, colonial series* (London, 1908–12, 6 v.), and *Journal of the Commissioners for Trade and Plantations*, 1704– (London, 1920–) concern only colonial times.

Portugal

Catálogo de livros à venda em 1929 (Lisbon: Imprensa nacional, 1929) [5423], and other editions in 1924 and 1927, lists briefly Portuguese official documents, but only those on sale at the time.

Hispanic America

A valuable guide to a group of Hispanic American government publications useful for diplomatic history is: J. B. Childs, *The memorias of the Republics of Central America and of the Antilles* (Wash.: Govt. Print. Off., 1932) [5424], published by the Library

---

[68] *Despatches from Paris, 1784–1790,* selected and edited from the Foreign Office correspondence, by Oscar Browning (London, 1909–10, 2 v.) [5422a], published by the Royal Historical Society, in its *Camden third series,* v. XVI and XIX.

of Congress. It includes the many *memorias* (reports) of the foreign offices of the separate republics of this region. Note also his account of " Hispanic American government documents in the Library of Congress ", printed in the *Hisp. Am. hist. rev.*, VI (1926) 134–141 [5425] ; in this collection the files of official gazettes and legislative proceedings constitute the outstanding feature. See also Myers (no. 5399) in which special attention has been given to Latin American reports or *memorias* of the ministers of foreign relations, which, as they are not published in formal series, are easily lost to sight. The various official publications of the several Hispanic American governments, issued serially, are included in the Pan American Union *Catalogue of newspapers* (no. 5037), and in Gregory, *Serial publications of foreign governments* (no. 5400). For publications of the foreign offices of these countries (to 1919), see also Myers (no. 5399). For a convenient list of Mexican treaties now in force, see " Tratados y convenciones vigentes ", in the *Memoria de la secretaría de relaciones exteriores*, 1930–1931, t. I (Mexico, 1931) 11–56 [5426]. For analysis of the 32 volumes of documents on selected subjects of diplomatic relations of Mexico, the *Archivo histórico diplomático* (Mexico, D. F., 1923–1930) see J. F. Rippy, " The diplomatic monographs of the Mexican government ", in *Hisp. Am. hist. rev.*, X (1930) 247–254 [5427]. For further information one must rely on Gregory (no. 5400).

France

Reference to Myers (no. 5399), 156–158, will show a series of published French diplomatic correspondence since 1862, several volumes of which concern the United States.[69] Though it concerns American diplomacy very little because of the limitation of dates, and then only insofar as reflected in instructions to French diplomatists in other states, we should at least mention : *Recueil des instructions données aux ambassadeurs et ministres de France depuis les traités de Westphalie jusqu' à la révolution française*, publié sous les auspices de la Commission des Archives Diplomatiques au Ministère des Affaires Étrangères (Paris, 1884–1929, 25 v. in 26) [5429].

---

[69] See also R. Doré, *Bibliographie des " livres jaunes "* à *date du 1er janvier 1922* (Paris, 1922) [5428], which is reprinted from the *Revue des bibliothèques*, XXXII (1922), 109–136. This list is reprinted in the American Library in Paris list (no. 5399a), pt. 1, 211–244, with some additional titles.

The countries covered so far are Austria, Sweden, Portugal, Poland, Rome, Bavaria, Palatinate, Deux-Ponts, Naples and Parma, Russia, Spain, Denmark, Savoy-Sardinia and Mantua, Prussia, the German Diet, Florence, Modena and Geneva, Holland, and England. *Archives diplomatiques; recueil mensuel de diplomatie, d'histoire et de droit international* (Paris, 1861–1914, 193 v. in 112) [5430], a semiofficial publication which contains texts of treaties, conventions, and protocols of international conferences and congresses, diplomatic correspondence, despatches, and notes, laws, etc., and *chronique*.

The Netherlands

In 1930 the International Exchange Service of the Royal Library of the Netherlands issued the first annual list of Dutch official publications: *Nederlandsche overheidsuitgaven; lijst van officieele uitgaven verschenen in Nederland en Nederlandsch Oost- en West-Indië*, bewerkt door het Ruilbureau der Koninklijke Bibliotheek (The Hague: Algemeene landsdrukkerij, 1930) [5431].

Germany

For printed German state papers we have fewer guides. Johann Sass, *Die deutschen Weissbücher zur auswärtigen Politik, 1870–1914; Geschichte und Bibliographie* (Berlin and Leipzig, 1928) [5432] restricts itself to publications of German diplomatic correspondence since the foundation of the German Empire, with a historical sketch. There is a detailed inventory of each volume of published correspondence. The editor adds a list, compiled from Myers (no. 5399) and the American Library in Paris manual (no. 5399a), of the " color-books " (*Farbenbücher*), or official diplomatic correspondence, of Austria-Hungary, England, France, Italy, and Russia; and has a valuable section on *Farbenbücher* as historical sources.[70] The great German compilation of documents, including diplomatic correspondence, *Das Staatsarchiv; Sammlung der offiziellen Aktenstücke zur Geschichte der Gegenwart* [5434] (see Myers (no. 5399), 49), ran (86 volumes) from 1861–1919, and commenced a new series in 1928. More recent printed German items on foreign affairs may be consulted or traced, in the official *Reichsministerialblatt* and

---

[70] André Ganem, " La valeur historique des documents diplomatiques ", *Rev. hist. guerre mond.*, VII (1929) 1–9 [5433].

Reichsgesetzblatt, and the publications (*Drucksachen*) of the German Reichstag. For the German diplomatic collections dealing with the world war and peace settlement, see nos. 5475a–5479.

The *Monatliches Verzeichnis der reichsdeutschen amtlichen Druckschriften* (Berlin: Reichs- und Staatsverlag, 1928– (in progress)) [5435], which includes not only the official and semiofficial publications of the federal government but also those of the state governments, and of the larger municipalities, may be used as a continuation of Sass (no. 5432).

Denmark

K. A. Hansen, comp., *Oversigt over Beretninger, m. v udgivet ved statens foranstaltning i tiden 1848–1929* (Copenhagen, 1929) [5436] is a survey of the Danish state papers published by the government. Chapter III has items on the Danish West Indies, Ch. XIII on foreign relations.

Russia

There is no general bibliography of Russian government documents, but for a valuable list of serial publications of the Russian government under the Russian Empire, the Provisional Government, and the Union of Soviet Socialist Republics, compiled by Mr. Vladimir Gsovski and Mr. George Novossiltzeff, of the Library of Congress, see Gregory (no. 5400), 577–693. Particularly, for our purpose, *Krasnyĭ Archiv* [Red Archives], 1922– (Moscow, 1922– (in progress)) [5436a], published by the Russian Central Archives (" TSentral'nyĭ Arkhiv "); it contains considerable material on Russian pre-war diplomacy, though bearing the imprint of selection with a view to sensational discovery. Also *Mezhdunarodnaĭa politika noveĭshego vremeni v dogovorakh, notakh i deklaratsiĭakh* [Modern international policy presented in treaties, notes, and declarations], compiled by I. V. Klĭuchnikov (Moscow, 1925–, 3 pts.) [5437], from the French Revolution to the tenth anniversary of the October Revolution. There is a list of " Décrets et resolutions de la RSFSR depuis 1917[–1922]", in the *Bulletin de l'Institut Intermédiare International* " (The Hague), VIII (1923) 344–385; IX (1924) 173–201, 399–415; X (1925) 138–164, 352–365 [5438].

Italy

Pubblicazioni edite dallo stato o col suo concorso (1861–1923).
Catalogo generale (Rome: Libreria dello Stato, 1924) **[5439]** published by the " Provveditorato Generale dello Stato " is a very extensive catalogue of all Italian public documents, a model of its
kind which all other nations might well follow. In the 2nd group,
devoted to foreign affairs, are listed the 138 diplomatic documents or
green books, 1861–1923. It is supplemented by *Pubblicazioni edite
dallo stato o col suo concorso. Spoglio dei periodici e delle opere
collettive, 1901–1925* (Rome: Libreria dello Stato, 1926–31, 4 v.)
[5440]. These reveal few American items.

China

For Chinese official publications we have the following catalogue
published by the official Bureau of International Exchange, of the
"Academia Sinica " at Shanghai, for the Nationalist Government:
A list of Chinese government publications (Shanghai, 1930) **[5441]**,
with titles given in Chinese and English in double columns. See
also the valuable notes by Latourette (no. 4770), Swingle (no. 4771),
Hummel (no. 4772), A. K'aiming Ch'iu (no. 5448), and Peake (no.
5449a).

Special collections of Chinese official publications are: *Tung-hua
lu* (Official records of the Ch'ing dynasty) (Peking, 1887, 129 books)
[5442], covering the period 1820–1860. *Chung-hsi chiao-t'ung shih-
liao* (Sources for a history of Sino-foreign relations), by Chang
Hsing-lang (Peking, 1928, 6 v.) **[5443]**, the editor is head of the
Dept. of History, Catholic University, Peking. Two series of documents from official archives now being published by the Palace
Museum: (1) *Chang-ku ts'ung-pien* (Peking, 1928–), series publishing select documents from the archives of the Grand Council
of State; the first 10 volumes are entitled *Chang-ku ts'ung-pien*, the
later volumes, *Wên-hsien ts'ung-pien* (Peking, 1930–) **[5444]**; and
(2) *Shih-liao hsün-k'an* (Peking, 1930–) **[5445]**, documents from
the archives of the Grand Secretariat, dealing with foreign relations
prior to 1836. *Ch'ing-tai ch'ou-pan yi-wu shih-mo* (The beginning
and end of the management of barbarian affairs under the [Ch'ing]
dynasty) (Peking, 1930, 130 v.) **[5446]**, a compilation of official

documents relating to foreign affairs, 1836 to 1874.[71] *Ching-chi wai-chiao shih-liao* (Documents on the foreign relations of the last two reigns of the Ch'ing dynasty) (Peking, 1932, 120 v.) [5450], documents of the years 1875–1911.

Japan

Entries of printed government documents before 1926 are to be found in the catalogues of the Imperial Library of Tokyo and of the libraries of the imperial universities of Kyoto and Kyushu.[72] The first official catalogue of Japanese government documents begins in 1927: *Kancho kanko tosho mokuroku* [Catalogue of the official documents of Japan], published quarterly (beginning 1927) by the Naikaku Insatsu-kyoku [The Imperial Cabinet Printing Office] (Tokyo, 1927– (in progress)) [5455]. There are several collections of printed documents relating in part to foreign relations: *Tokugawa kinrei-ko* [Edicts of prohibitions under the Tokugawa régime, 1603–1867], first series in 6 volumes, edited by the Judiciary Department (Tokyo, 1894–95, 6 v.) [5456], this series was compiled between 1878 and 1883 from the documents in the archives of the Edo government, and each act of prohibition is preceded by a short description which includes date, author, relation to others if any, and other matters. *Tokugawa kinrei-ko koshu* [Edicts of prohibitions under the Tokugawa régime, 1603–1867], *second series* in 4 volumes, edited by the Judiciary Department (Tokyo, 1895, 4 v.) [5457], this series was compiled between 1883 and 1890, the main part consists of the *Kajo ruiten*, an encyclopedia of laws and ordinances of the Edo government from its beginning to the year 1742, with additional notes and corrections. The most notable for American relations concerns

---

[71] For description and analysis of this series, and the following series, see Ping Chia Kuo, in *Am. hist. rev.*, XXVI (1931) 870–875 [5447]; T. F. Tsiang. "New light on Chinese diplomacy, 1836–49", *Jour. mod. hist.*, III (1931) 578–591 [5448]; A. K'aiming Ch'iu, "Chinese historical documents of the Ch'ing dynasty, 1644–1911", *Pacific hist. rev.*, I (1932) 324–336 [5449]; and C. H. Peake, "Documents available for research on the modern history of China", *Am. hist. rev.*, XXXVIII (1932) 61–70 [5449a].

[72] *Teikoku toshokan wakan-sho kenmei mokuroku* [Classified catalogue of the Chinese and Japanese books in the Imperial Library] (Tokyo: Teikoku Toshokan, 1905) [5451]. *Monthly bulletin of books added to the Imperial Library of Japan*, 1905– (Tokyo: Imperial Library, 1905– (in progress)) [5452]. *Quarterly bulletin of books added to the Imperial University Library of Kyoto*, 1914– (Kyoto: Kyoto Imperial University Library, 1914– (in progress)) [5453]. *Kyushu teikoku daigaku tosho mokuroku* [Catalogue of the Kyushu Imperial University Library], v. 1– (Fukuoka: Kyushu Imperial University Library, 1932– (in progress)) [5454] is of more limited value.

the period of the opening of Japan to foreign intercourse: *Dai-nihon komonsho* [73] [Ancient documents of Japan], a collection consisting of many volumes, including a series: *Bakumatsu gaiko kankei bunsho* [Documents relating to the foreign relations of Japan during the restoration period] (Tokyo: Printed by the Imperial University, 1910–1933, 24 v. (in progress)) [**5459**]. This collection, says the preface, includes all the records known to exist for the foreign relations of the period, 1853–1867. These were the documents which were turned over by the Shogunate government to the newly-created foreign office in 1867. Most of them are dated after 1853. Earlier documents had been scattered through various departments of the government and unfortunately irreparably lost. Some others were destroyed when the Edo (Yedo) castle burned (in Tokyo) in 1859, including—it is presumed—the originals of documents from Perry and the Russian mission. This published series contains: (1) notes between the Japanese and foreign governments; (2) short-hand records of oral negotiations; (3) correspondence between the Imperial court and the Shogunate; (4) notices from the provincial governors and other officials; (5) petitions, grants, etc., concerning local governments; (6) memoranda of officials; (7) memoranda by private individuals. *Dai Nihon komon-sho. Bakumatsu gaikoku kankei bunsho* (Documents relating to foreign relations in the last years of the Tokugawa period) (Tokyo, 1910–) [**5459a**] is a collection of documents in process of publication, under the editorship of the Japanese historical manuscripts commission. They cover the period from 1853 to 1858.

Koji rui-en [Encyclopedia of antiquities], published by the Bureau of Shrines (Tokyo, 1897–1903, 53 v.) [**5460**], with copious transcriptions of ancient documents and a detailed index. One volume (unnumbered) *Gaiko-bu* [Section on foreign relations] contains selected documents concerning Japan's relations with Belgium, China, Denmark, France (including Anan), Germany, Great Britain, Italy, Korea, The Netherlands (including Java), Portugal, Siam, Spain, Switzerland, and the United States (including the Philippines). The section on the United States contains documents regarding: knowledge in Japan concerning the origin of the name

---

[73] *Dai-nihon shiryo* [Source material for Japanese history], printed by the Imperial University (Tokyo, 1902–1934, 132 v. (in progress)) [**5458**], at present extends to 1630, but will continue until the present time.

United States of America, commercial intercourse, diary of Miyaki-Toyo, the attending physician to the embassy to America, 1860; negotiations for the lease of land in Japan, treaties, legations, Shimonoseki affair, shipwrecked marines, etc. An official publication of the Japanese foreign office (but of which we are unable to find the date of publication) is *Gaiko-shiko* [Diplomatic source material] (Tokyo, 2 v.) [5461], a collection of official documents dealing with Japanese diplomatic history.

For Japanese treaty collections, see Myers (no. 5399). A series of collections of treaties, published by the Japanese foreign office is: *Joyaku iho* (Tokyo, 1858 to date) [5462].

To date (1935) we know of no other general guides to, or bibliographies of, public documents of other nations. Every nation has its compilation of laws, of judicial decisions, legislative proceedings, and of foreign office publications, including *farbenbücher*, i.e. color-books (white books, blue books, etc.). These have been listed in Myers (no. 5399), and it would be supererogatory for us to repeat his findings.[74]

In lack of guides to the printed state papers of other governments, we endeavored to include in the bibliography which forms the first part of our *Guide*, under the section headings " printed sources ", such foreign public documents as relate to diplomatic relations with the United States. This is usually in the form of published diplomatic correspondence. While we believe the bibliographical entries

---

[74] Treaty collections since Myers are listed in his current bibliography of " Source material—I. Public documents officially printed ", in current numbers of *Foreign affairs* (no. 4850, 1922 to date, and in *Documents on international affairs, 1928–*, ed. by J. W. Wheeler-Bennett (London, 1929–) [5463], to date (1934) 6 volumes have appeared. We note in particular the publication of the United States Tariff Commission: *Handbook of commercial treaties, digests of commercial treaties, conventions and other agreements of commercial interest between all nations* (Wash.: Govt. Print. Off., 1922) [5464]; the most recent Canadian edition of treaties, *Treaties and agreements affecting Canada in force between His Majesty and the United States of America with subsidiary documents, 1814–1925* (Ottawa, 1927) [5465], compiled in the Department of External Affairs of Canada; The British *Handbook of commercial treaties, etc., with foreign powers*, 4th ed. London: H. M. Stationery Off., 1931) [5466], published by the Foreign Office, which contains copies of the treaties; Max Habicht, *Post-war treaties for the pacific settlement of international disputes; a compilation and analysis of treaties of investigation, conciliation, arbitration, and compulsory adjudication, concluded during the first decade following the world war* (Cambridge, Mass., 1931) [5467]; and *Treaties and other international acts of the United States,* ed. by Hunter Miller (see no. 5371 for fuller account of this publication).

Convenient lists of treaties published by the British Foreign Office are: *Lists of treaties, &c., relating to commerce and navigation between Great Britain and foreign powers, January 1st, 1929* (London, 1929) [5468], and *List of commercial treaties, etc., with foreign powers, January 1, 1930* (London, 1930), continued in later editions [5469].

to be fairly comprehensive, we caution the investigator to consult Childs (no. 5398), Myers (no. 5399), the American Library in Paris (no. 5399a), Gregory (no. 5400), and such national guides as exist to public documents in order to go farther afield with the various categories of public documents for the respective states.

III. Published Records of International Organs, League of Nations, etc.

The advent of the twentieth century witnessed the first permanent international bodies which have archives and published records not under the control of any one state. Such are The Hague Permanent Court of Arbitration, the League of Nations, and its judicial organ, the Permanent Court of International Justice.[75] The Secretariat of the League has been efficiently organized, and its publications carefully catalogued; viz, The text of the Covenant, and amendments; the *Official journal*, beginning 1920 (well indexed), with special supplements; *Treaty series* (with several indexes); *Monthly summary of the League of Nations*, giving a survey of the League's work during the previous month; *Monthly bulletin of statistics; Monthly epidemiological report; Quarterly bulletin of information on the work of international organizations; Educational survey; Fortnightly list of selected articles; Monthly list of books catalogued in the library of the League of Nations; Bulletin of international university information office; Records of the assembly*, and *Minutes of the council; Reports of the various administrative commissions; Protection of minorities;* multifarious series of publications of the sections of Economics and Finance, Health, Social Questions; Law (including the Permanent Court of International Justice);[76] Mandates, Slavery, Politics, Communications and Transit, Disarmament, Financial administration of the League, Traffic in opium and other dangerous drugs; Intellectual cooperation, International bureaux, Refugees, etc.

The United States though not a member of the League, played a fundamental role in its creation, and has officially participated in many of its non-political activities. The already voluminous publications of the League are increasingly important for the diplomatic history of the United States. The published records of the

---

[75] The Pan-American Union publishes no such documents.
[76] Publications of the Court are separately listed in the *Sixth annual report of the Permanent Court of International Justice* (Leyden, 1930) [**5470**] p. 329-337.

League are completely listed in a catalogue of *Publications issued by the League of Nations*, issued by the Publications Department of the League of Nations (Geneva, Switzerland, 1929) [5470a], containing titles to the end of October 1929, which is kept up to date by means of supplements. See also Marie J. Carroll, *Key to League of Nations documents placed on public sale, 1920–1929* (Boston: World Peace Foundation, 1930) and *Supplement*, I–, 1930– (Boston, 1931–) [5471]; and a *Short bibliography of the publications of the League of Nations* (Geneva, 1931), which is a classified list, published by the Library of the League of Nations [5472].

IV. Documentary Publications relating to the Diplomatic History of the Origins of the World War of 1914 to 1918, to the Armistice of 1918, and to the Peace Settlements concluding the War

The Austrian, British, French, and German governments have issued voluminous collections of documents on the origins of the World War.[77] These collections have value of varying importance for the history of American diplomacy from 1870 to 1914.

Austria

Diplomatische Aktenstücke zur Vorgeschichte des Krieges 1914; Ergänzungen und Nachträge zum österreichisch-ungarischen Rotbuch (Vienna, 1919, 3 v.) [5473], published by the Austrian " Staatsamt für Ausseres." *Oesterreich-Ungarns. Aussenpolitik von der bosnischen Krise, 1908, bis zum Kriegsausbruch 1914; diplomatische Aktenstücke des Oesterreichisch-Ungarischen Ministeriums des Aussern*, ausgewählt von Ludwig Bittner, Alfred Francis Pribram, Heinrich Srbik, und Hans Uebersberger, bearbeitet von Ludwig Bittner und Hans Uebersberger (Vienna and Leipzig, 1930, 9 v.) [5473a].

France

Documents diplomatiques français (1871–1914) (Paris, 1929–33, 13 v. (in progress)) [5474], published by the French " Commission de Publication des Documents relatifs aux Origines de la Guerre de 1914."

---

[77] For a survey of the *unofficially printed* collections of diplomatic correspondence and documents on the origins of the world war, see *Guide hist. lit.* (no. 4634), 377–383.

Great Britain

British documents on the origins of the war, 1898–1914, ed. by G. P. Gooch and Harold Temperley (London: H. M. Stationery Office, 1926–33, 10 v. (in progress)) [**5475**].

Germany

Die deutschen Dokumente zum Kriegsausbruch; vollständige Sammlung der von Karl Kautsky zusammengestellten amtlichen Aktenstücke mit einigen Ergänzungen, im Auftrage des Auswärtigen Amtes nach gemeinsamer durchsicht mit Karl Kautsky, hrsg. von Graf Max Montgelas und Prof. Walter Schücking (Charlottenburg, 1919, 4 v.) [**5475a**], see also, for English translation of a selection of the documents, *Outbreak of the world war; German documents collected by Karl Kautsky,* ed. by Max Montgelas and Walter Schücking . . . tr. by the Carnegie Endowment for International Peace (N.Y., 1924, 1 v.); and a selection of some of the most important of the documents in the *Die deutschen Dokumente,* pub. by the American Association for International Conciliation, *German secret war documents, covering the period June 15 to August 5, 1914* (N.Y., 1920). *Die Grosse Politik der europäischen Kabinette, 1871–1914; Sammlung der diplomatischen Akten des Auswärtigen Amtes,* hrsg. von Johannes Lepsius, Albrecht Mendelssohn-Bartholdy, Friedrich Thimme (Berlin, 1922–27, 40 v. in 54) [**5476**], issued by the German "Auswärtiges Amt"; a publication of the secret and important papers from the archives of the Foreign Office. An abridgment (in English) of the *Grosse Politik* is: *German diplomatic documents, 1871–1914,* selected and translated by E. T. S. Dugdale (London, 1928–31, 4 v.) [**5477**], being a selection of those documents which specially concern Great Britain. Germany, Reichskanzlei, *Vorgeschichte des Waffenstillstande, 1918* (Berlin, 1919) and enlarged edition, *Amtliche Urkunden zur Vorgeschichte des Waffenstillstandes, 1918. Auf Grund der Akten der Reichskanzlei des Auswärtigen Amtes und des Reichsarchivs herausgegeben vom Auswärtigen Amt und vom Reichsministerium des Innern.* 2., um 41 neue Dokumente vermehrte Ausgabe (Berlin, 1924) [**5478**], published by the German "Auswärtiges Amt"; an English edition was published in London. Germany, Waffenstillstandkommission, 1918–1919, *Der Waffenstillstand, 1918–1919, das dokumenten Material,* Edmund Marhefka, ed. (Berlin, 1928, 3 v.) [**5479**].

Russia

A Russian "Orange Book", published at St. Petersburg in 1914 (in Russian, English, and French editions) is: Ministerstvo Inostrannykh Dîel [Ministry of Foreign Affairs], *Sbornik diplomaticheskikh dokumentov. Peregovory ot 10 do 24 Iûlîa predshestvovavshïe voînê* [Collection of diplomatic documents. Negotiations from 10 to 24 July, 1914, preceding the war] (St. Petersburg, 1914) [5480], English edition, *Documents respecting the negotiations preceding the war 10/23 July–24 July/6 August, 1914* (St. Petersburg? 1914?) A later, German edition of this "Orange Book" is: *Das russische Orangebuch von 1914; ergänzt durch die inzwischen bekanntgewordenen neuen Dokumente*, ed. by Alfred von Wegerer (Berlin, 1925) [5481], the Russian edition contains only 79 documents (telegrams), this German edition prints 218 documents and telegrams. Other publications of Russian official documents dealing with the world war are: *Materialy po istorii Franko-Russikh otnoshenii za 1910–1914* (Moscow, 1922) [5482], published by the "Narodnyï Komissariat po Inostrannym Delam"; materials for the history of Franco-Russian relations, 1910–1914, from the Russian archives, mainly in Russian, and consisting for the most part of the secret correspondence between the Russian minister of foreign affairs, Sazonov, and the Russian ambassadors in Paris and London, Izvolski and Benckendorff. *How the war began in 1914, being the diary of the Russian Foreign Office from the 3rd to the 20th (old style) of July, 1914, published by the "Red Archives" department of the Russian Soviet government in their "Historical journal", vol. IV, 1923*, translated from the original Russian by Major W. Cyprian Bridge (London, 1925) [5483], this is also published in German, *Der Beginn des Krieges, 1914. Tages-Aufzeichnungen des ehemaligen Russischen Aussenministeriums*, ed. by Alfred von Wegerer (Berlin, 1924). Russia (U.S.S.R.), Komissiîa po Izdaniîû Dokumentov Epokhi Imperialisma, *Die internationalen Beziehungen im Zeitalter des Imperialismus; Dokumente aus den Archiven der Zarischen und der Provisorischen Regierung*, herausgegeben von der Kommission beim Zentralexekutivkomitee der Sowjetregierung unter dem Vorsitz von M. N. Pokrowski, ed. by Otto

Hoetzsch (Berlin, 1931–) [5484],[78] the authorized German translation, issued by the "Deutsche Gesellschaft zum Studium Osteuropas". To date (1934) 5 volumes (Reihe I: *Das Jahr 1914 bis zum Kriegsausbruch*) have been issued. These 5 volumes cover the period from January 14 to August 4, 1914 and comprise the first 5 volumes of series III (1914–1917) of the great collection of Russian documents (1878–1917) now in course of publication by a commission appointed by the Central Executive Committee of the Soviet Government. They include many hitherto unpublished documents, some of which concern the United States.

United States

The diplomatic correspondence of the United States during the world war is published in the series of *Papers relating to the foreign relations of the United States* (no. 5346), as supplements, 1914 to 1918. The regular series of *Foreign relations* for 1919 (Wash., 1934) includes a few documents dealing with the representation of the United States in the Peace Conference and related international bodies.

Paris Peace Conference, 1919

An official edition of the proceedings of the Paris Peace Conference of 1919 is in process of publication by the French Government: *Conférence de la paix, 1919–1920; recueil des actes de la conférence* (Paris: Imprimerie Nationale, 1923–) [5485]. It is a strictly confidential publication (therefore not available for general use), and its distribution is confined to the governments which were represented on each commission.

---

[78] For a valuable analysis, see B. E. Schmitt, "Russia and the war", *Foreign affairs*, XIII (1934) 133–153 [5484a].

Reihe II. Bd. 6 (1 und 2 Halbbände), recently issued (Berlin, 1935) covers the period from August 5. 1914, to January 13, 1915.

CHAPTER III

MANUSCRIPT SOURCES: ARCHIVAL COLLECTIONS
IN THE UNITED STATES AND ABROAD

The body of prime sources which forms the originals of those printed records reviewed in the last chapter, and which extends in content to an unknown degree behind and beyond the fraction of records that are printed consists of collections of archival material:[1] state archives, institutional archives, and collections, and the archives of individuals, and scattered and isolated pieces and groups of MS. material, to be found in libraries, museums, and private ownership everywhere. It is impossible to round up all the extant MSS. which touch the diplomatic history of the United States, but we can say something about important state deposits and library collections

---

[1] For the history of archives, see Eugenio Casanova, *Archivistica* (Siena, 1928) [5486]. For archival structure and organization, see Franz von Löher, *Archivlehre* (Paderborn, 1890) [5487]; Georg Holtzinger, *Handbuch der Registratur- und Archivwissenschaft* (Leipzig, 1908) [5488]; Hilary Jenkinson, *A manual of archival administration including the problems of war archives and archive making* (Oxford, 1922) [5489]; Samuel Muller, J. A. Feith, and R. Fruin, *Handleiding voor het ordenen en beschrijven van archieven; ontworpen in opdracht van de Vereeniging van archivarissen in Nederland* (Groningen, 1905, 1st ed.; 1920, 2d ed.) [5490], translated into French as *Manuel pour le classement et la description des archives* (The Hague, 1910), also into German and Italian. For bibliographies on archival history and procedure: August Hettler, *Archivalische Bibliographie* (Halle, 1910) [5491]; and " Bibliography of the history of the public records ", in the *First report of the Royal Commission on Public Records* (London: H. M. Stationery Off., 1912), v. I, pt. 2, 164–168 [5492]. In the *Bulletin of the Institute of Historical Research*, v. II–VII (1924–1930) [5493] appear some very helpful data in shape of answers to a questionnaire sent out to archival authorities in various countries, on the accessibility of archives. For effect of conquests and annexation on archives, see Louis Jacob, *La clause de livraison des archives publiques dans les traités d'annexion* (Paris, 1915) [5494].

and indicate listed private collections. In so doing we rely on
the numerous printed guides, inventories, catalogues, indexes, and
calendars which make this material known to the scholar. We shall
classify the material according to countries, taking the United
States first because of its relative importance to our specialty.

At the outset it is well to note that although various guides, catalogues, and indexes, either printed or manuscript, have existed for
many archives, such apparatus was not designed to take care especially of the student of American diplomatic history, but was fash-
ioned, obviously, for the convenience of the local archivist and his
official responsibilities. To provide aids for stimulating research in
American history, one of the first and steadily one of the principal
activities of the Department of Historical Research of the Carnegie
Institution, was to prepare suitable guides to MS. material relating
to the history of the United States to be found in archives and
libraries at home and abroad. Under the direction of that sterling
teacher and mentor of historians, Dr. J. Franklin Jameson, a corps
of scholars prepared a shelf of volumes of guides to this archival
material. Taken with the local archival catalogues and indexes, they
describe the archives, locate the important material, and put the
investigator in touch with it in the quickest and most practical way.
The Carnegie Institution of Washington pursuing the plan mapped
out by Professor Jameson, provided for scholars a wealth of apparatus which has been the one greatest material factor in making
known the sources of the history of the United States, including its
foreign relations. With the assistance of these guides we can generally make our way directly to the sources concerned, avoiding false
leads. Unfortunately for present and future investigators in American history the program mapped out by Dr. Jameson suffered a decline after the retirement of that energetic and erudite scholar from
this particular post, though fortunately it deflected his still youth-
ful energies into other valuable channels of endeavor most useful
to the historical investigator. As a result guides for some of the
European countries that fall within the original plan [2] have not been
completed. In the pages which follow we shall have occasion fre-

---

[1] The guides completed before Dr. Jameson's retirement in 1927 were: Washington,
Great Britain, Spain, Italy, Switzerland, Austria, Germany, Russia, Cuba, and Mexico.
Work on the Scandinavian countries, the Netherlands, and France have been interrupted.
A volume on MSS. in Paris libraries (but not archives) has been published. Two other
volumes on French archives are still in preparation.

quently to mention such of these " Carnegie Institution Guides " as have been completed.

The United States

Until 1934 the United States had no national archival organization (though a national archives building is now nearing completion in Washington). The archival records of the federal government were scattered about the capital (and elsewhere). Those of the executive departments and the various independent offices overflowed, in many instances, from the buildings which housed them into a great variety of obscure and unsafe lofts, cellars, attics, commercial storehouses, etc., which had already subjected some of the records to the ravages of fire, mildew, and various accidents. The National Archives is being finished as this guide is published, and first steps are being taken to organize the Archives. It is expected that soon the transfer of the records (except for live files needed for current business) from the various present locations will commence and that a program of indexing and cataloguing of material will be put in motion. The first Archivist of the United States, Professor R. D. W. Connor, was appointed in October, 1934.

The MS. records of the legislative and judicial branches of the federal government are now housed in the Capitol building, in the office buildings of the House and Senate, respectively, and in the Library of Congress. One may assume that when the new Supreme Court building is completed all court records will be deposited there.

The lack of any national archival organization in the United States has prevented hitherto any uniformity of custody and arrangement of the priceless records of our government. Nor do we have the organized accumulation of archival reports, with their catalogues, calendars, lists, indexes, and documentary prints, such as are found in so many other countries. Again, there is lacking in North America any journal or printed organ of archivists [3] and archival practice such as are to be found in the principal European countries, journals which are media for the printing of such matter. As a result comparatively little is known in detail of the con-

[3] The American Historical Association established in 1899 a Public Archives Commission within its organization, the activities of which, reflected in its annual reports, may be traced in the *Annual reports* of the American Historical Association; but its work has been confined to state and local archives.

tents of large portions of the still disorganized archives of the
United States. However, one of the first tasks of the Department
of Historical Research of the Carnegie Institution of Washington
was to institute a survey of these records, which resulted in the publication of C. H. Van Tyne and W. G. Leland's *Guide to the archives
of the United States in Washington* (Wash.: Carnegie Institution,
1904; 2d ed., revised and enlarged, 1907) [5495]. This work presents a general " survey of all the branches, bureaus, and divisions
of the federal government in Washington." It included, in addition
to a description of their records, some analysis of the evolution of
the offices from which the records come (so necessary to a proper
understanding of the archives), and references to bibliography and
printed authorities. This is the only general description of our national archives in existence, and has serious limitations: (1) it is
already out of date for the many new functions of federal government that have developed since its publication, (2) the inadequacy
of existing archival organization, custody, and indexing made it
impossible for the authors to indicate anything in detail about many
important *fonds*,[4] and (3) many changes of place have occurred.
Nevertheless it will acquaint the investigator with at least the
existence of the various *fonds* to 1903, and to a degree, with the
general nature of their contents. The nature of the sources for
diplomatic history, as we have said, requires the investigator not
to overlook other archives than those of the department of foreign
affairs. In the case of the Department of State, the archives are
in good order and custody (though the building itself is not strictly
fireproof). We have already said something [5] about the nature of
these MSS., the larger (but not necessarily the most important) part
of which is still unprinted.[6] Up to 1906 despatches and instruc-

---

[4] A standard but untranslatable French word generally used to indicate a major
collection.

[5] Above, page 788.

[6] Professor A. C. McLaughlin made a *Report on the diplomatic archives of the
Department of State, 1789–1840* (Wash.: Carnegie Institution, 1903; rev. ed., 1906) [5496]
in which he reproduced some very important documents as samples of what had remained
unpublished. He estimates the published documents for the period 1789–1828 printed
in *American state papers, Foreign relations,* at not more than one-fourth the total mass.
For recent transfer of legation archives in foreign countries to the Department of State,
see H[unter] M[iller] "Transfer to the Department of State of the older archives of
certain American embassies, legations, and consulates ", *Am. hist. rev.,* XXXIX (1933)
184–185 [5497]. To date (December, 1934), the legation archives of Brazil, Ecuador,

tions were filed by countries, or by " special agents ", which makes it fairly simple, if laborious, for the student to follow the history of our relations with a given country. The multiplying diversity and details of the business of modern diplomacy, however, so increased the subject matter and the volume of this business, that it seemed expedient at that time to desert the traditional system of filing and to compromise with a new system of *dossiers* by subjects, for example: neutral rights (with various subdivisions: contraband, blockade, submarine warfare, etc.), international telegraphic communications, League of Nations, Pan America, etc. This classification simplifies certain types of historical research but runs counter to the sacred *principe de provenance*, hitherto inviolable by archivists; but the principle finds refuge in a card-index catalogue, under headings of countries, in which each document outgoing and incoming is listed, with a direct reference to the subject file in which it is to be found. For the historian, this card catalogue becomes very precious. If it were destroyed he would be almost hopelessly at loss to locate and disentangle from the actual files the documents relating to all affairs with any one country. The volume and diversification of material emphasizes the importance of an expanded program of publication in the Department; for without this, rendered by a corps of specialists, the future historian of our present-day diplomacy will not be unlikely to find himself well-nigh helpless.

We understand that the archives of the Department are at present open to perusal by qualified consultants for documents dated not later than August 14, 1906.

Such papers as belonged to the old government of the Confederation before 1789, *i.e.*, Papers of the Continental Congress, including diplomatic correspondence, 1774–1789; and the Washington, Madison, Jefferson, Hamilton, Monroe, and Franklin papers, were transferred (except for a few pieces), beginning 1903, to the Division of Manuscripts of the Library of Congress.[7] The only calendar pub-

---

Venezuela, the Republic of Texas, and of the Kingdom of Hawaii, have been brought back to the Department of State. A start has been made on the transfer of those of the Caribbean region and Central America.

[7] *Catalogue of the papers of the Continental Congress* (Wash.: Dept. of State, 1893) [5498]. Those acquired by the Library of Congress to 1918 are listed in the *Handbook* (no. 5520) ; later acquisitions are given in C. W. Garrison's *List of manuscript collections* (no. 5522), 143–145, which notes the volumes transferred to the Library of Congress in 1922, and a few coming from other sources. The Department of State still (1934) retains a few volumes, including certain records of the office of the Department of

lished of material now existing in the Department of State (aside from the calendars of "historical" collections, *i.e.*, papers of the Continental Congress, Washington, Jefferson, Hamilton, Franklin, Madison, and Monroe) is the *Calendar of miscellaneous letters received by the Department of State from the organization of the government to 1820* (Wash.: Govt. Print. Off., 1897) [5507]. Much diplomatic and consular material is in the earlier volumes of this series, as also in the companion series (not calendared) of *Domestic Letters*. Theoretically, both of these series consist of correspondence of the Secretary of State, not diplomatic or consular in character.[8]

The archives of the old monarchical regime of Hawaii have been preserved [9] and are described in *Report of the Board of Commissioners of Public Archives*, 1926–1928 (Honolulu, 1928) [5509]. This material now partially indexed by the librarian of the Board of Commissioners of Public Archives, Miss Maude Jones, is arranged chronologically under departments and is readily accessible. The foreign office files to 1885, also 1893–1900, have now (1934) been indexed; also the historical and miscellaneous files, and the private collections of Queen Liliuokalani, Sanford B. Dole, and Miers. The Historical Commission of the Territory of Hawaii has published a pamphlet catalogue by R. S. Kuykendall, *Hawaiian diplomatic correspondence in . . . the Department of State, Washington, D.C.*

Foreign Affairs. Of the collections of the papers of statesmen, all but the Hamilton papers have been calendared: *Calendar of the correspondence of George Washington, commander in chief of the Continental army, with the officers* (Wash.: Govt. Print. Off., 1915, 4 v.) [5499]; *Calendar of the correspondence of George Washington, commander in chief of the Continental army, with the Continental Congress* (Wash.: Govt. Print. Off., 1906) [5500]; *List of Washington manuscripts, from the year 1592 to 1775* (Wash.: Govt. Print. Off., 1919) [5501], these three calendars (published by the Library of Congress) were prepared from the original MSS. in that library by J. C. Fitzpatrick. *Calendar of the correspondence of James Monroe*, new edition, with corrections and additions (Wash.: Dept. of State, 1893) [5502] and *Papers of James Monroe, listed in chronological order from the original manuscripts in the Library of Congress*, comp. under the direction of W. C. Ford, chief, Division of Manuscripts (Wash.: Govt. Print. Off., 1904) (Library of Congress) [5503] which is intended to complement the alphabetical *Calendar* issued by the Department of State; *Calendar of the correspondence of Thomas Jefferson* (Wash.: Dept. of State, 1894, 1895, 1903) [5504], in three parts; *Calendar of the correspondence of James Madison* (Wash.: Dept. of State, 1894 [reprinted 1902]) [5505]; *List of the Benjamin Franklin papers in the Library of Congress*, comp. under the direction of W. C. Ford, chief, Division of Manuscripts (Wash.: Govt. Print. Off., 1905) (Library of Congress) [5506]. See also calendar of the main collection in the American Philosophical Society (no. 5225).

[8] Van Tyne and Leland (no. 5495), 20.

[9] R. C. Lydecker, "The archives of Hawaii", in *Hawaiian hist. soc. pap.*, no. 13 (1906) 5–23 [5508].

(Honolulu, 1926) [5510]. It is, more strictly described, a catalogue of correspondence of the United States, relative to the subject of Hawaii, which has some considerable footnote indication of those portions which are already printed.

One specific category of MSS. in federal archives that has been pretty well described in detail by a Carnegie Institution guide is: D. W. Parker, *Calendar of papers in Washington archives relating to the territories of the United States (to 1873)* (Wash.: Carnegie Institution, 1911) [5511]. This is a rounding-up and archival description and analysis of these papers in the Departments of State,[10] War, and the Interior, also the files of the House of Representatives, Senate, and the Library of Congress. " Documents bearing upon subjects of an international character have been listed when it was clearly apparent that the question directly affected a territory."

Publication of these papers has recently begun, under the editorship of Professor C. E. Carter: *Territorial papers of the United States* (Wash.: U. S. Govt. Print. Off., 1934–) [5511a], of which three volumes (Vol. I: *General*, preliminary printing; Vols. II–III: *The Territory Northwest of the River Ohio, 1787–1803*) were issued in 1934.

In view of the lack of catalogues and indexes for other archives of the federal government, one can only refer, except for the papers relating to the territories, to the general descriptions given by Van Tyne and Leland. Attention must be given to the great MS. collections, still mostly uncalendared, in the Library of Congress. Though originally this was only a reference library for the use of members of Congress, its expanding resources and the enterprise of its Librarian since 1899, Dr. Herbert Putnam, have magnified its significance into that of a real national library, incomparably the richest and most important in the world for the study of American history. Of the materials therein collected, the original MSS., and more recently, the facsimiles of original MSS. from other (principally foreign) libraries and archives, in the custody of the Division of Manuscripts are the most important. These include the greater part of the original papers of nearly all the

---

[10] For a " List of the territorial and state records deposited in the Bureau of Rolls and Library," of the Department of State, see its *Bulletin* no. 7, September 1894 (Wash., 1895), 5–8 [5511b].

successive Presidents of the United States,[11] and similarly of the secretaries of state, with many other supporting collections of papers, or of isolated MSS., from other individuals in many cases of American diplomatists. The following lists indicate the whereabouts of papers of presidents, secretaries of state, and American diplomatists, as known to us.

Papers of the Presidents

Washington, George: J. C. Fitzpatrick estimates that approximately 98 percent of the mass of extant personal papers of George Washington are in the great collection of the Library of Congress. (For calendars, see nos. 5499–5501.) The others are widely scattered, but have been brought together at that Library in facsimile for printing in the Bicentennial Edition (no. 5307). Washington's diaries and correspondence may be said now to have been completely printed (for editions, see nos. 5307 and 5335a).

Adams, John: The main collection of the personal papers of John Adams is in the papers of the Adams family, in the possession of that family, and closed to historical investigators.

Jefferson, Thomas: Official papers are in the Library of Congress, calendared (but not entirely) (see no. 5504); most of the private papers in the Massachusetts Historical Society, see no. 5246. See also for the papers of Jefferson, a brief analysis in Channing (no. 4784), v. IV, 272–274, reprinted in the *Am. secs. of state* (no. 4796), v. II, 288–290.

Madison, James: Papers in the Library of Congress; for calendar, see no. 5505, which calendars the portion formerly held in the Department of State, comprising about two-thirds of the whole collection.

Monroe, James: The main collection in the Library of Congress; for calendar, see no. 5502. The Library of Congress also has a MS. Calendar of the Gouverneur collection of Monroe papers now owned by Mr. L. G. Hoes of Washington, D.C. For the Monroe papers in the New York Public Library (about 1,200 items), see

---

[11] The papers of Presidents, now in the Library of Congress, are: Washington, Jefferson, Madison, Monroe, Jackson, Van Buren, W. H. Harrison, Tyler, Polk, Pierce, Lincoln, Johnson, Garfield, Arthur, Cleveland, Benjamin Harrison, Roosevelt, Taft, and Coolidge; and of Secretaries of State: Jefferson, Madison, Monroe, Robert Smith (in part) Clay, Van Buren, Webster, Clayton, Marcy, Black, Washburne, Olney, Sherman, Gresham, Root, Knox, Bryan, and Lansing.

Greene and Morris (no. 5531). Hitherto unpublished notes written by Monroe when he was ambassador to England to Count Vorontsoff, Russian ambassador at London, have recently (1935) been discovered in the Vorontsoff family library. They will be published by the Academy of Sciences of the U. S. S. R.

Adams, J. Q.: Papers of the Adams family are in the possession of the family and closed to historical investigators. Some letters from J. Q. Adams before and while he was secretary of state, relative to political and diplomatic affairs, to William Eustis, of Massachusetts, are in the Eustis papers in the Library of Congress.

Jackson, Andrew: The voluminous surviving papers are in the possession of the Library of Congress, including a very important supplementary collection (of Amos Kendall) acquired in 1932. The essential documents are printed (see no. 5243). For calendar of the Jackson-Lewis letters, 1806–1864, see *N.Y. pub. lib. bul.*, v. IV (1900) 292–320 [**5511a**], partially printed in *ibid.*, passim.

Van Buren, Martin: Papers in the Library of Congress; see *Calendar of the papers of Martin Van Buren*, prepared from the original manuscripts in the Library of Congress, by Elizabeth H. West (Wash., 1910) (Library of Congress) [**5512**].

Harrison, W. H.: No great collection; a few papers widely scattered. Of these the Library of Congress is believed to have the largest lot.

Polk, J. K.: The main collection of personal papers in the Library of Congress; MS. of *Diary* printed (see no. 5282).

Taylor, Zachary: Apparently no collection; a few letters and a short MS. autobiographical sketch in the Library of Congress.

Fillmore, Millard: Most of the papers of President Fillmore were burned by his son's executor in 1891, in accordance with a mandate in the son's will.[12]

Pierce, Franklin: Two collections—Library of Congress and New Hampshire Historical Society; and some in private hands.

Buchanan, James: Main collection in the Historical Society of Pennsylvania (most important printed in no. 5196); a small collection in the Library of Congress.

Tyler, John: The main collection (8 vols.) in the Library of Congress. All the papers, public and private, left to his widow's

---

[12] W. E. Griffis, "Millard Fillmore and his part in the opening of Japan", *Buffalo hist. soc. pub.*, IX (1906) 65.

care at his death were destroyed in the burning of Richmond in 1865.[13]

Lincoln, Abraham: In the Library of Congress (not accessible until 1947). There are two important smaller collections: the Herndon collection now in the possession of Mr. T. W. Weik of Greencastle, Indiana; and a collection belonging to Mrs. O. R. Barrett, of Chicago. Scattered individual pieces of Lincolniana are in the hands of many collectors. The papers used by Nicolay and Hay in preparing their life of Abraham Lincoln are in the Library of Congress, with restrictions ("not to be open to inspection until 21 years after his [R. T. Lincoln] death ").

Johnson, Andrew: In the Library of Congress.

Grant, U. S.: Still in the possession of various descendants.

Garfield, J. A.: In the Library of Congress.

Arthur, C. A.: Only known collection consists of the small group in the Library of Congress.

Hayes, R. B.: Main collection in the Hayes Memorial at Fremont, Ohio. For description, see *An index and list of the letters and papers of Rutherford Birchard Hayes, nineteenth president of the United States; with notes on other source material at the Hayes Memorial Library, Spiegel Grove State Park, Fremont, Ohio,* published by the Ohio State Archaeological and Historical Society (Columbus, O., 1933) [5513].

Cleveland, Grover: Papers of Cleveland dated subsequently to 1885 are in the Library of Congress. Earlier papers believed to be in private hands. The New York State Library has a sealed box of Grover Cleveland MSS. not to be consulted without the permission of the donor until 1939.

Harrison, Benjamin: In the Library of Congress.

McKinley, William: In the Library of Congress.

Roosevelt, Theodore: In the Library of Congress.

Taft, W. H.: In the Library of Congress.

Wilson, Woodrow:[14] At present (1934) his personal papers are in the custody of his biographer, Mr. Ray Stannard Baker, of Amherst, Mass.

---

[13] Letters from Mrs. Julia G. Tyler, in *Tyler's quar. mag.,* III (1921) 255–256.
[14] See R. S. Baker's *Life of Woodrow Wilson* (no. 5315), v. 1, for an analysis of Wilson's papers, very voluminous, total weight (including containers) five tons.

Harding, Warren: In the possession of the Harding Memorial Association, of Marion, Ohio.

Coolidge, Calvin: Papers relating to his presidency are in the Library of Congress.

Hoover, Herbert: In February, 1933, President Hoover's papers were shipped to his home in Palo Alto, California.

Papers of the Secretaries of State

Livingston, R. R.: In the library of the New York Historical Society; a few are in the New York State Library; and the Missouri Historical Society has recently (1925) acquired a number of Livingston letters.

Jay, John: Correspondence and public papers [15] are only partially printed; private papers are in the possession of a descendant, Mrs. Arthur Iselin (Eleanor Jay), of Katonah, N.Y. His diplomatic papers are among the Papers of the Continental Congress now in the Library of Congress. A letterbook of Jay's official correspondence from Spain and France (mostly printed in Wharton) from Dec. 14, 1779 to Nov. 17, 1782, is in the Huntington Library at San Marino, Calif.; the Library of Congress has photostats of these letters.

Jefferson, Thomas: See under "Papers of the Presidents", p. 862.

Randolph, Edmund: The last trace of the personal papers of Randolph is those printed in Moncure Conway's *Omitted chapters of history disclosed in the life and papers of Edmund Randolph* (N. Y., 1888). There are a few pieces in the Library of Congress, and in the Thomas Addis Emmet collection in the New York Public Library, and a small collection in the Virginia Historical Society, at Richmond (see list in *Catalogue of the manuscripts in the collection of the Virginia Historical Society* (Richmond, Va., 1901) 99–100) [5514].

Pickering, Timothy: In the Massachusetts Historical Society, for calendar, see *Historical index to the Pickering papers* (Boston, 1896) (Mass. Hist. Soc. Coll., 6th ser., v. VIII) [5515]; large excerpts from them are printed in C. W. Upham's *Life of Timothy Pickering* (Boston, 1867–73, 4 v.) [5516]. There is an account

---

[15] Mr. Frank Monaghan, of Yale University, is preparing a definitive edition of the writings of John Jay.

book of Pickering as secretary of state, 1796–1799, in the Library of Congress. For other Pickering items, see *MSS. in public and private collections* (no. 5530).

Marshall, John: There is no important major collection. The Library of Congress has photostats of letters, etc., brought together by the late Senator A. J. Beveridge from scattered sources in preparing his biography of Marshall. The journal of Marshall, in Paris, Sept. 27, 1797, to Apr. 11, 1798, is in the Massachusetts Historical Society; photostat copy in the Library of Congress.

Madison, James: See under "Papers of the Presidents", p. 862.

Smith, Robert: A small collection in the Library of Congress.

Monroe, James: See under "Papers of the Presidents", p. 862.

Adams, J. Q.: See under "Papers of the Presidents", p. 863.

Van Buren, Martin: See under "Papers of the Presidents", p. 863.

Clay, Henry: In the Library of Congress.

Van Buren, Martin: See under "Papers of the Presidents", p. 863.

Livingston, Edward: In the possession of Gen. John Ross Delafield, of New York.

McLane, Louis: All papers burned in the fire in Baltimore in 1904.

Forsyth, John: No collection known to exist.

Webster, Daniel: Largest collection of personal papers in the library of the New Hampshire Historical Society, at Concord; the Library of Congress has an important collection; some are in the American Antiquarian Society, Massachusetts Historical Society, Yale University Library, and in the possession of individuals; the Fillmore papers in the Buffalo Historical Society contain over 300 letters from Webster to Fillmore.

Upshur, A. P.: No collection known to exist.

Calhoun, J. C.: Private papers (mostly printed, see no. 5199) are in the library of Clemson College, Fort Hill, S.C.

Buchanan, James: See under "Papers of the Presidents", p. 863.

Clayton, J. M.: Collection in the Library of Congress, consisting mainly of letters to Clayton, a few by him.

Everett, Edward: The Everett papers and diary in the possession of the family have been deposited with the Massachusetts Historical Society, but are not available to historical investigators. The Fillmore papers in the Buffalo Historical Society contain a considerable number of letters from Everett.

Marcy, W. L.: In the Library of Congress.

Cass, Lewis: A small collection in the possession of a descendant is believed to have no material of importance as to foreign affairs.

Black, Jeremiah: In the Library of Congress; and a number of his letters are in the Buchanan MSS. in the Historical Society of Pennsylvania.

Seward, W. H.: In the possession of Wm. H. Seward, a grandson, in Auburn, N.Y.

Washburne, E. B.: In the Library of Congress.

Fish, Hamilton: Voluminous collection in the possession of Mr. Hamilton Fish, of Garrison, N.Y.

Evarts, W. M.: A small and unimportant collection believed to be in the possession of descendants.

Blaine, J. G.: In the Library of Congress.

Frelinghuysen, F. T.: In the possession of a descendant.

Bayard, T. F.: In the Library of Congress. Include, among others, such subjects as the Alaskan fisheries, Samoa, Hawaii, etc.

Foster, J. W.: In the Library of Congress (only a few), dealing in large part with the fur seals arbitration.

Gresham, W. Q.: In the Library of Congress.

Olney, R. F.: In the Library of Congress.

Sherman, John: Library of Congress has about 550 vols., but only a few pieces pertain to foreign relations.

Day, W. R.: In the possession of Judge Day's sons.

Hay, John: In the possession of his daughter, Mrs. J. W. Wadsworth, Jr.

Root, Elihu: In the Library of Congress.

Bacon, Robert: Believed to be in the possession of the family.

Knox, P. C.: In the Library of Congress.

Bryan, W. J.: In the Library of Congress.

Lansing, Robert: Public papers in his collection were deposited in the Department of State; the private papers in the Library of Congress (time restrictions on his diary to 1951).

Colby, Bainbridge: Still in Mr. Colby's possession.

Hughes, C. E.: In the Library of Congress (on deposit only).

Kellogg, F. B.: Mr. Justice Kellogg is understood to have left his business papers in the possession of his law firm, and to have turned over to the Department of State all papers relating to his public service.

Stimson, H. L.: Still in Mr. Stimson's possession.

Papers of American Statesmen and Diplomatists

A

Adams, J. Q.: See p. 863; a small lot of papers written while minister to the court of St. Petersburg, including accounts against the United States, in the Library of Congress.

Adams, John: See p. 862.

Adams, Samuel: Correspondence with Arthur Lee and others, in the New York Public Library (Bancroft Collection).

Allen, Horace N. (minister to Korea, 1897–1901): In the New York Public Library.

Andrews, C. C. (minister to Sweden and Norway, 1869–77): In the Minnesota Historical Society.

Armstrong, John (minister to France, 1804–1810): In the Library of Congress.

Avery, Benjamin P. (minister to China, 1874–76): MSS. regarding interviews with Li-Hung-Chang, 1874, in the Library of the University of California, Berkeley.

B

Bancroft, George (minister to Great Britain, 1846–49; to Prussia, 1867–71; to Germany, 1871–74): In the Massachusetts Historical Society. The Library of Congress has a collection of several hundred pieces (letters, newspaper clippings, etc.); and papers relating to the arbitration by the German Emperor of the northwestern boundary dispute, 1872, in the New York Public Library. The Massachusetts Historical Society has an extensive collection of the George Bancroft papers (for the period of his service in England, 15 vols.; for his years in Germany, 24 vols.). There are some family letters of George Bancroft, including those to Mrs. J. C. Bancroft Davis, his nephew's wife, and to his son-in-law John Davis, written while minister abroad, and containing political comments, in the collection of the American Antiquarian Society, at Worcester, Massachusetts. There are thirteen odd letters of George Bancroft, mostly academic in nature and of minor importance in the Yale University Library.

Banks, N. P. (Congressman from Massachusetts, 1853–57, 1865–73, 1875–79; advocated acquisition of Alaska and a bold policy in regard to Alabama claims) : Papers in the Essex Institute, Salem, Mass.

Barbour, James (minister to Great Britain, 1828–29) : In the New York Public Library, partly calendared in its *Bulletin*, VI (1906) 22–34.

Barlow, Joel (consul to Algiers, in 1795, effected treaties with Tunis, Algiers, Tripoli; minister to France, 1811–12) : In Harvard College Library.

Barnard, D. D. (minister to Prussia, 1850–53) : In the New York State Library, Albany; and letters to Webster in the Webster Collection in the Library of Congress.

Bayard, J. A. (commissioner at the Ghent peace negotiations) : Correspondence and diary (1813–1815) in the Library of Congress; some letters in the New York Public Library (about 30 letters, including some from Copenhagen, St. Petersburg, London, and Ghent, 1813–14, printed in its *Bulletin*, IV (1900) 228–248. See also no. 5188.

Bayard, R. H. (*chargé d'affaires* in Belgium, 1850–53) : In the Library of Congress.

Bayard, T. F. (minister to Great Britain, 1893–97) : See p. 867.

Bigelow, John (consul general at Paris, 1861–65; minister to France, 1865–66) : In the New York Public Library.

Bleecker, Harmanus (*chargé d'affaires*, The Netherlands, 1839–42) : Some letters in the Van Buren papers in the Library of Congress.

Boker, G. H. (minister to Turkey, 1871–75; Russia, 1875–77) : At Princeton University.

Butler, Anthony (*chargé d'affaires* in Mexico, 1829–36) : In the Texas State Library at Austin (regarding conditions in Mexico and the purchase of Texas) ; and some pieces in the Van Buren and Sumter collections in the Library of Congress.

C

Cameron, Simon (minister to Russia, 1862–63) : Some letters relating to his earlier years in the Coryell and Buchanan papers in the Pennsylvania Historical Society; others, written in later life, in the Library of Congress in the MS. collections of his political contemporaries.

Campbell, G. W. (member of Congress, 1803–09; senator, 1811–14, 1815–18; secretary of the treasury, 1814; minister to Russia, 1818–

20) : In the Library of Congress. Include a long report made to the Department of State while commissioner under the convention of 1831 with France.

Carmichael, William (assistant to Silas Deane, secret agent of Congress at Paris, 1776–77; mission to Berlin, 1776; secretary to John Jay, and *chargé d'affaires*, Madrid, 1779–94) : In some of his last letters written just before his death early in 1795 in Madrid, Carmichael mentions that he had sent a trunk of his own correspondence to Cadiz, whence he had expected to embark for the United States. We have no trace of the trunk or its contents since then. Papers presented to Congress with claims of his heirs are found in the *House miscellaneous papers* in the Library of Congress (see Tilton, *House misc. papers* (no. 5523). Some transcripts in the New York Public Library (Bancroft Collection).

Carr, D. S. (minister to Turkey, 1843–49) : In the Library of Congress (a few letters).

Cass, Lewis (minister to France, 1836–44) : See p. 867.

Cass, L. J., jr. (*chargé d'affaires* and minister to the Papal States, 1849–58) : A few letters in the Library of Congress.

Cathcart, J. L. (consul at Tripoli) : Correspondence (1785–1806) relating to negotiations between the United States and Tripoli, in the New York Public Library.

Chandler, W. P. (consul at Tunis, 1854–1856) : Letter book of correspondence with other consuls and a diary in 4 vols., both covering the above period, in the Library of Congress.

Choate, J. H. (ambassador to Great Britain, 1899–1905) : Papers on deposit in the Library of Congress.

Clay, C. M. (minister to Russia, 1861–62) : All papers prior to the Civil War were burned during that conflict; few papers in the Library of Congress.

Clay, Henry: See p. 866.

Clay, J. Randolph (*chargé d'affaires* in Russia, 1836–37) : Diary and letter book regarding this mission, in the Library of Congress.

Clayton, J. M.: See p. 866.

Clemson, T. G. (*chargé d'affaires* in Belgium, 1844–51) : Letters to Calhoun in Clemson Agricultural College, Fort Hill, South Carolina.

Clifford, Nathan (minister to Mexico, 1846–48): Papers in the Maine Historical Society, Portland; many of his letters printed in P. Q. Clifford, *Nathan Clifford* (N.Y., 1922) [**5516a**].

Coggeshall, W. T. (minister to Ecuador, 1866–67): Papers and diaries in the possession of his son-in-law, Mr. T. A. Bushey, of South Vienna, Ohio.

Conkling, Alfred (minister to Mexico, 1852–53): A few letters in the New York Historical Society.

Coxe, C. D. (consul to Tunis): Letter book, 1806–1809, in the Library of Congress.

Crawford, W. H. (minister to France, 1813–15): Letter book when he was minister to France, in the Library of Congress. It contains 81 communications to the French government, July 27, 1813–Mar. 14, 1815. (Indemnity for confiscation of American vessels by French cruisers, neutral rights, prizes and privateers, and the decree repealing the Berlin and Milan decrees, are the subjects of the notes). Also photostat copies of 33 letters received by Crawford while he was in Paris, from the American commissioners at Ghent.

Curry, J. L. M. (minister to Spain, 1885–88): Papers (correspondence, letter books, scrap books) in the Library of Congress.

Cushing, Caleb (commissioner to China to negotiate a commercial treaty in 1844; minister to Spain, 1874–77): Fuess's biography notes 40 large wooden boxes of papers which the heirs allowed him to use; some pieces in the Library of Congress.

D

Dana, Francis (alternate to John Adams in the negotiation of a loan in The Netherlands, 1780; minister to Russia, but never received at court, 1780–83): The Dana papers (mostly printed in published works of John Adams) are in the Massachusetts Historical Society, Boston.

Davie, W. R. (peace commissioner to France, 1799–1800): Papers in the possession of the University of North Carolina Library, at Chapel Hill.

Davis, J. C. Bancroft (*chargé d'affaires* in Great Britain, 1849–52; assistant secretary of state at different periods; agent for the

United States before the Geneva tribunal of arbitration (Alabama claims) ; minister to Germany, 1874–78) : In the Library of Congress (54 vols.). Include a dairy (1870–71) while he was assistant secretary of state; journal of the negotiations of the treaty of Washington, 1871; and much material on the Alabama claims. Extracts from his MS. journal are printed in the chapter on " The Geneva arbitration ", in v. I of Moore's *International arbitrations* (no. 5364).

Deane, Silas (secret agent in France, 1776; joint commissioner with Franklin and (later) Arthur Lee, 1776–77) : The Deane papers are in the collections of the Connecticut Historical Society, printed by the New York Historical Society and ed. by Isham, and by the Connecticut Historical Society (no. 5215), and a few transcripts are in the Library of Congress, see Garrison (no. 5522). There is a smaller collection of Deane papers in the Yale University Library (see C. M. Andrews, *Franklin-Deane mission* (no. 101). The Library of Congress has a fairly large collection (over 100 pieces) of original accounts and receipts relating to Deane's French mission.

Dix, J. A. (minister to France, 1866–69) : In the New York State Library, Albany.

Dodge, A. C. (minister to Spain, 1855–59) : In the State Historical Society of Iowa, Iowa City. See Louis Pelzer, " The diplomatic correspondence of Augustus Caesar Dodge ", *Miss. Valley hist. assoc. proc.*, I (1909) 111–120 [5517]. Some of the correspondence deals with negotiations regarding Cuba.

Donelson, A. J. (*chargé d'affaires* in Texas at the time of annexation (1844–45) ; minister to Prussia, (1846–49)) : In the Library of Congress.

Dudley, T. H. (consul at Liverpool) : Correspondence relating to blockade of southern ports, 1861–1865, in the Huntington Library, San Marino, California.

Dumas, C. W. F. (secretary to John Adams, minister to The Netherlands, 1781–82; *chargé d'affaires*, 1782) : Papers acquired from descendants by the *Rijksarchief* (for calendar, see no. 5731). The Library of Congress has photocopies of both the official Dutch diplomatic correspondence and the Dumas papers. There are a few original Dumas pieces (outside the Papers of the Continental Congress) in the Library of Congress.

E

Eaton, Gen. William (consul at Tunis) : Correspondence, 1801–08 (26 vols.) in the Library of Congress. (Barbary States).

Ellis, Powhatan (*chargé d'affaires* and minister to Mexico, 1836–42) : Some letters in the voluminous Ellis-Allan papers in the Library of Congress.

Ellsworth, H. W. (minister to Sweden and Norway, 1845–49) : A few letters to Thomas Ewing in the Ewing papers in the Library of Congress, 1849.

Erving, G. W. (minister to Spain, 1814–19) : Several letters in the Library of Congress. (For the Floridas, 1815–19).

Eustis, William (minister to The Netherlands, 1814–18) : Correspondence in the Library of Congress, includes his despatches to the secretary of state, and other diplomatic correspondence dealing with his mission.

Everett, A. H. (*chargé d'affaires* at The Hague, 1818–25; minister to Spain, 1825–29; commissioner to China, 1845–47) : Official and private correspondence in the Massachusetts Historical Society. The Library of Congress has a few letters to and from Everett in the Joseph Blunt papers (1817–1854).

Everett, Edward: See p. 866.

F

Fairchild, Lucius (minister to Spain, 1880–81) : Papers, letters, and voluminous scrapbooks are in the Museum of the State Historical Society of Wisconsin.

Faulkner, C. J. (minister to France, 1860–61) : A few letters and copies of speeches are in the possession of his son, C. J. Faulkner, at Martinsburg, W.Va.

Forbes, J. M. (consul in Copenhagen, 1817–18; *chargé d'affaires* in Argentina, 1825–32) : Papers in the Library of Congress, consist of letter book, 1817–18; and account book, 1825–30.

Forsyth, John (minister to Spain, 1819–23) : Account book of expenses while on his mission to Spain, in the Library of Congress.

Foster, J. W. (minister to Mexico, 1873–80; Russia, 1880–82) : See p. 867.

Franklin, Benjamin (commissioner and minister to France, 1776–85; for other missions, see latest *Register* of the Dept. of State) : For calendars of the Franklin MSS. in the Library of Congress, most of which are printed, see no. 5225. See also no. 5536, for calendar of the papers of Franklin in the Library of the American Philosophical Society, and no. 5559 for calendar of the papers of Franklin in the library of the University of Pennsylvania. There are some other valuable Franklin papers in the private library of Mr. W. S. Mason, of Evanston, Ill., which deal with foreign relations. A full account of the various collections in the Library of Congress, Department of State, American Philosophical Society, and the University of Pennsylvania, is given in Smyth's edition of the *Writings* (no. 5225). There is believed to be an important collection of Franklin papers in the possession of the Bache family in Philadelphia.

G

Gallatin, Albert (special envoy to Russia regarding mediation offer, 1813; member of Ghent peace commission, 1814; minister to France, 1815–23; to Great Britain, 1826–27): Papers in the New York Historical Society include material on the northwest boundary question, etc.

Gerry, Elbridge: The Library of Congress has one volume of letters and miscellaneous MSS. of Elbridge Gerry, 1797–1801, and memoranda of diplomatic negotiations made while on his special mission to France, and copies of his accounts against the United States for expenses of this mission, 1800. Others in private hands; there are important letters from Gerry to President Adams in the Adams papers (see p. 862); and some in the Pierpont Morgan Library, in New York City. The Huntington Library has a letter book (contemporary copies) of the " X.Y.Z." commissioners, 1797–98. There are some papers in the possession of Mrs. Townsend Phillips, 277 Park Avenue, New York City, who is understood to be engaged upon a life of Elbridge Gerry.

Green, Duff (unofficial representative in England and France in 1841; consul at Galveston, 1844, and emissary to Mexico in regard to the Texas matter, aided in molding public opinion in regard to Oregon boundary dispute): Collection of letters in the Library of Congress; larger one in private hands at Chapel Hill, North Carolina.

H

Hale, John P. (minister to Spain, 1865–69): Considerable collection of letters and miscellaneous MSS. relating to John P. Hale in the New Hampshire Historical Society, Concord.

Harris, Townsend (consul to Japan, 1857–59, minister, 1859–61): Papers in the College of the City of New York; a small collection of personal papers in the New York Public Library. For brief analysis of these papers, see his *Journal* (no. 5232), viii.

Hill, D. J. (minister to Switzerland, 1903–05; The Netherlands, 1905–08; ambassador to Germany, 1908–11): Personal papers are in the possession of his son, Walter L. Hill, Scranton, Pa.

Hilliard, H. W. (*chargé d'affaires* in Belgium, 1842–44): A few letters in the Library of Congress.

Houston, Sam (President of the Republic of Texas, 1836–38, 1841–44): Professor E. C. Barker has been engaged in compiling and editing the letters, papers, and speeches of Houston (cf. *Am. hist. rev.*, XXXVIII: 424). See also page 264.

Hughes, Christopher (minister to Sweden and Norway, 1818–26, 1830–42; The Netherlands, 1842–45): Occasional pieces in the Library of Congress.

Humphreys, David (minister to Portugal, 1791–95; Spain, 1795–1801): Uncollected letters in the New York Historical Society, Massachusetts Historical Society, and the Library of Congress.

Hunter, R. R. (consul at Cowes, Eng.): Letter book, 1822–1827, in the Library of Congress.

I

Irving, Washington (secretary of legation and *chargé d'affaires* at London, 1829–31; minister to Spain, 1842–46): In the New York Public Library, Harvard College Library, Pennsylvania Historical Society, Library of Congress (5 pieces), Peabody Institute in Baltimore, Huntington Library, and in the possession of Mr. Roderick Terry, of Newport, R.I.

Izard, Ralph (commissioner to the court of Tuscany, 1777–79): A collection in the Library of Congress.

J

Jay, John (minister to Spain, 1779–82; joint commissioner to negotiate peace with Great Britain, 1782–83; envoy extraordinary to

Great Britain, and negotiator of the treaty with that nation, 1794) : See p. 865.

Johnson, Reverdy (minister to Great Britain, 1868–69) : In the Library of Congress. " The major portion of them deal with the social side of Johnson's residence in England, while United States minister to that country, but scattered through these are diplomatic letters of more than ordinary interest. There are several letters of Gladstone, relative to the failure of Johnson's negotiations, and the subsequent treaty."

K

Kasson, J. A. (minister to Austria-Hungary, 1877–81; Germany, 1884–85; delegate to the International Postal Conferences at Paris, 1863) : Correspondence in the Historical Department, Des Moines, Iowa.

Kavanagh, Edward (minister to Portugal, 1835–41) : Some papers and scrap books are in the possession of Miss Blanche Bryant, of Damariscotta Mills, Maine. (See also *D.A.B.*)

King, Rufus (minister to Great Britain, 1796–1803, 1825–26) : Papers in the New York Historical Society; some letters to Oliver Wolcott in the Connecticut Historical Society; letters to N. Vansittart, British secretary to the treasury, 1802, 1803, 1806, respecting British duties on imports and exports, and other matters, in the British Museum (Add. MSS. 31229). The papers of Rufus King in the New York Historical Society are mostly printed in C. R. King's *King* (no. 5248). There is also a collection of letters to King (about 600 items) of which many have been printed, in the Huntington Library. They were written 1791 to 1805, when King was minister to England, and are mostly from American ministers to France, Holland, and Russia, in regard to American foreign policy.

King, W. R. (secretary of legation in Russia, 1816–18; minister to France, 1844–46) : A few of his letters are in the Buchanan MSS. in the Historical Society of Pennsylvania.

Kinney, W. B. (*chargé d'affaires* to Sardinia, 1850–53) : Diary in the possession of W. B. Kinney II, Newark, N.J.

L

Lamar, M. B. (president of the Republic of Texas, 1838–41; U.S. minister to Costa Rica and Nicaragua, 1858–59) : Papers in the Texas State Library (see the *Calendar of the papers of Mirabeau Buonaparte Lamar*, prepared . . . by Elizabeth Howard West (Austin, Tex., 1914) bound in the *Second biennial report* of the Texas Library and Historical Commission [**5518**]. This collection is particularly valuable for the Texas question.

Larkin, T. O. (consul at Monterey, Cal.) : Letters and papers, 1845–47, in the Bancroft Library, University of California.

Laurens, Henry (minister to The Netherlands to negotiate a treaty and loan, 1779–80; captured by the British, 1780–82; signed the preliminary articles of peace, 1782) : Papers in the South Carolina Historical Society, including the "Tower" narrative (printed in the *S.C. hist. soc. coll.*, I, 18–83) [**5519**].

Lawrence, Abbott (minister to Great Britain, 1849–52) : In the Library of Congress (Blunt Collection).

Lear, Tobias (commissioner to Tripoli, 1805) : Letters and documents, 1797–1813, in the Library of Congress.

Lee, Arthur (secret agent in London, 1775; commissioner to France, 1776–78; to Spain, 1776–77) : The Library of Congress has a private journal of Arthur Lee (Dec. 16, 1776–Sept. 5, 1777) covering in part the period of his mission to Spain. The New York Public Library has a journal or autobiography (in transcript) of Arthur Lee describing his diplomatic activities in 1777, interviews with foreign ministers, and his relations with Franklin and Deane. For calendars of Arthur Lee MSS., see no. 5254.

Lee, William (diplomatic agent in Europe, 1777–78) : Letters . . . calendared in the *Catalogue of the manuscripts in the collection of the Virginia Historical Society* (Richmond, 1901).

Legaré, H. S. (*chargé d'affaires* in Belgium, 1832–37) : Occasional letters in the Library of Congress.

Letcher, R. P. (minister to Mexico, 1849–52) : Some letters among the J. J. Crittenden papers in the Library of Congress.

Livingston, Edward (minister to France, 1833–35) : See p. 860.

Livingston, R. R. (minister to France, 1801–04) : See p. 865.

Lodge, H. C. (member and chairman of the Senate committee on foreign relations, including the period of the World War; member of Alaska boundary tribunal, 1903; U.S. representative at the Conference on the Limitation of Armament, 1921–22) : Papers in the Massachusetts Historical Society.

Long, Breckinridge (assistant secretary of state, 1917–20) : Correspondence and documents in the Library of Congress.

M

McLane, Louis (minister to Great Britain, 1829–31, 1845–46) : See p. 866.

Mann, A. D. (Confederate commissioner to Europe) : Some papers among the James M. Mason and Pickett papers in the Library of Congress.

Marsh, G. P. (minister to Turkey, 1849–53; Italy, 1861–82) : In Dartmouth College (small collection).

Marshall, John (mission to France, 1797–98) : Library of Congress has MS. journal. For other papers, see p. 866.

Mason, J. M. (Confederate diplomatic envoy to Great Britain) : Papers and despatches in the Library of Congress; include many letters of John Slidell, Confederate envoy at Paris, to Mason.

Maxcy, Virgil (*chargé d'affaires* in Belgium, 1837–42) : Correspondence in the Library of Congress.

Monroe, James (minister to France, 1794–96; Great Britain, 1803–06) : See p. 862.

Moran, Benjamin (secretary to Minister Buchanan in London and secretary of the American legation through the terms of G. M. Dallas, C. F. Adams, Reverdy Johnson, J. L. Motley, and R. C. Schenck, 1853–1870; minister to Portugal, 1874–82) : In the Library of Congress.

Morgan, J. T. (U. S. senator, 1876–1907, long a member of the committee on foreign relations and arbitrator on the Bering Sea fisheries dispute, 1892) : Papers (1860–1906) in the Library of Congress (restricted).

Morris, Gouverneur (special agent to Great Britain, 1789–91; minister to France, 1792–94) : Papers in the Library of Congress include the original MS. of the diary (the text printed by A. C. Morris having been, it is understood, expurgated by a pious widow).

Several letters (1790) to the Duke of Leeds in regard to British-American affairs, in the British Museum.

Morris, Robert (member of the Committee on Foreign Affairs of the Continental Congress): In the Pennsylvania Historical Society. The papers of Robert Morris in the Library of Congress include some of Beaumarchais' accounts during the Revolution. See also no. 612, above.

N

Nelson, Hugh (minister to Spain, 1823–25): Letters, 1808–33 (40 pieces) in the Library of Congress.

Nelson, T. A. R. (commissioner to China, 1851–52): Political papers, 1840–73, in the Lawson McGhee Library, Knoxville, Tenn. (Calvin Morgan McClung historical collection).

Nelson, T. H. (minister to Chile, 1861–65; Mexico, 1869–73): Official letter books, 1861–65 (2 vols.) in the Library of Congress; deal with affairs of other South American nations besides Chile.

Niles, Nathaniel (secretary of legation at Paris, 1832–33; special agent to Austria, 1837–38; *chargé d'affaires* at Sardinia, 1838–50): Letters to Niles, many from foreign cities, 1824–50, in the Library of Congress.

P

Page, W. H. (ambassador to Great Britain, 1913–18): Library of Congress has correspondence with President Wilson (photostats of letters from Page (62 letters) and originals of letters from Wilson (61 letters); restricted.

Palmer, T. W. (minister to Spain, 1889–90): Diaries, letter books, and files in the Detroit Public Library.

Perry, M. C.: The Library of Congress has treaty negotiations (1854) with the Japanese (1 vol.); copy in Japanese character, made in 1885, from the original in the Tokio foreign office (1 vol.); a journal of John G. Sproston, who was with the expedition (1854) (1 vol.).

Pickett, John (Confederate diplomatic agent in Mexico): Correspondence (8 vols.) in the Library of Congress.

Pierrepont, Edwards (minister to Great Britain, 1876–77): In Yale University.

Pike, J. S. (minister to The Netherlands, 1861–66): Letters, mainly to W. P. Fessenden, 1849–69, in the Library of Congress.

Pinckney, C. C. (minister to France, 1796–1801) : Papers in the South Carolina Historical Society, at Charleston.

Pinckney, Charles (minister to Spain, 1801–04) : Papers in the South Carolina Historical Society, at Charleston.

Pinckney, Thomas (minister to Great Britain, 1792–94; envoy extraordinary to Spain, 1794–96) : Letter books in the South Carolina Historical Society, at Charleston.

Pinkney, William (minister to Great Britain, 1806–11; the Two Sicilies, 1816; Russia, 1816–18) : Some papers at the Harvard College Library.

Plumb, E. L. (secretary of legation in Mexico, 1866–67, *chargé d'affaires*, 1867–68; consul-general at Havana subsequently) : Letters and papers in the Library of Congress; include some regarding the policy to be adopted by the United States toward Díaz and other insurrectionists.

Poinsett, J. R. (special mission to South America as observer, in 1809; minister to Mexico, 1825–29) : Papers in the Library of Congress and the Historical Society of Pennsylvania; the New York Public Library has letters to Poinsett, 1814–40, from Mexican and Chilean officials, mostly during his ministry to Mexico. Paper regarding the boundary commission (Mexico), 1825, is among the Mexican transcripts in the Library of Congress.

Pollock, Oliver (commercial agent of the United States at New Orleans during the Revolution) : Letters to, and his accounts, 1767–81, in the Library of Congress.

Pruyn, R. H. (minister to Japan, 1862–65) : Correspondence in the possession of Robert C. Pruyn, Albany, N.Y.

R

Randolph, John (minister to Russia, 1830–31) : Letters, 1807–34, and diary, 1818–19, in the Library of Congress; also letter book of the American legation in Russia, Sept.–Dec. 1830.

Reed, W. B. (minister to China, 1857–59) : Private diary of his mission, with MS. letters from British officials and others in the Orient inserted, in the Library of Congress.

Reid, Whitelaw (minister to France, 1889–92; ambassador to Great Britain, 1905–13) : Some papers in Yale University Library.

Roberts, Edmund (first American diplomatist in the Orient) : Letters, 1829–1836, in the Library of Congress. In 1832 was sent as special envoy to Siam and Muscat, with which powers he made treaties; was consul at Demarara in 1823, at Batavia in 1832.

Robinson, Jeremy (agent for commerce and seamen at Lima, Callao, and other places in South America, in 1817): Papers, including letters to J. Q. Adams, secretary of state, in the Library of Congress.

Rockhill, W. W. (commissioner to China, 1900; and minister, 1905–1909): Papers are understood to be in the possession of Mrs. W. W. Rockhill, Gramercy Park, N.Y.

Rush, Richard (minister to Great Britain, 1817–25; secretary of state (*ad interim*), 1817): In the New York Historical Society; few letters in the Library of Congress, which also has diary (London), 1821, and an autograph draft of his opinion on the proposed transfer, by Spain, of Cuba to Great Britain, 1823.

Russell, Jonathan (one of 5 commissioners who negotiated the treaty of Ghent, and minister to Sweden and Norway, 1814–18): Chief collection in the Brown University Library.

S

Sanford, H. S. (minister to Belgium, 1861–70): In the Connecticut Historical Society, Hartford.

Schenck, R. C. (minister to Great Britain, 1870–76): Few letters in the E. B. Washburne collection in the Library of Congress.

Schurz, Carl (minister to Spain, 1861–62): Papers (about 80 portfolios) in the Library of Congress; restricted.

Seys, John (minister resident and consul general in Liberia, 1866–70): Papers among the slave trade and African colonization papers in the Library of Congress.

Shaler, William (appointed agent for commerce and seamen at Havana and Vera Cruz in 1810, in Havana and on the Mexican border to 1813; attached to mission to negotiate peace with Great Britain, 1814; commissioner to and consul general at Algiers, 1815–29; consul at Havana, 1829–33): MSS. in the possession of Mrs. Willoughby Webb, Martha's Vineyard, Mass.

Short, William (*chargé d'affaires*, France, 1790–92; minister to the Batavian Republic (The Netherlands), 1792–94; minister to Spain, 1794): Correspondence (52 vols.) in the Library of Congress.

Sickles, D. E. (minister to Spain, 1869–74) : Drafts of reports to the secretary of state, also other letters and documents, in the Library of Congress.

Smith, Wm. L. (minister to Portugal, 1797–1806) : Papers, including discussion of Jay's treaty, in the Library of Congress.

Squier, E. G. (*chargé d'affaires* at Guatemala, 1849–53) : Papers in the Huntington Library, many letters and documents, 1852 to 1858, regarding the project known as the Honduras Interoceanic Railroad, and correspondence with Hispanic American diplomatists and others.

Stevenson, Andrew (minister to Great Britain, 1836–41) : In the Library of Congress.

T

Thompson, Waddy (minister to Mexico, 1842–44) : Papers in the library of the University of Texas, at Austin; a few, to Thompson, and from Thompson to Daniel Webster (Webster collection), in the Library of Congress.

Todd, C. S. (minister to Russia, 1841–46) : In the Historical and Philosophical Society of Ohio, at Cincinnati.

Trist, N. P. (special envoy to negotiate peace with Mexico, 1847–48) : Papers and letter books in the Library of Congress, record fully the diplomatic negotiations which terminated the Mexican war.

V

Vroom, P. D. (minister to Prussia, 1853–57) : Diaries, 1850–72, including mission at Berlin, in the Detroit Public Library (Burton Historical Collection).

W

Washburne, E. B. (minister to France, 1869–77) : Letters and papers (94 vols.) in the Library of Congress; and a letterpress copy book (54 vols.) in the Chicago Public Library.

Wheaton, Henry (*chargé d'affaires* in Denmark, 1827–35; *chargé d'affaires* and minister to Prussia, 1835–46; special agent to Hanover, 1837, and to Bavaria, Hesse Cassel, Saxony, and Württemburg, in 1843) : Papers for period 1835–46, in the Massachusetts Historical Society.

White, A. D. (minister to Russia, 1892–94; ambassador to Germany, 1897–1902; commissioner to Santo Domingo (Grant's administration)) : Papers in Cornell College Library.

White, Henry (ambassador to Italy, 1905–06; France, 1906–09; Versailles peace commission, 1919) : Papers in the Library of Congress (restricted). They throw light on the Venezuelan boundary dispute, upon Anglo-American *rapprochement* at the time of the Spanish-American war, the " open door " and Boxer rebellion in China, Hay-Pauncefote treaty, Theodore Roosevelt's handling of the Venezuela imbroglio, 1902–03, Alaska boundary arbitration, Algeciras conference, and the peace conference of 1919.

Woodford, S. L. (minister to Spain just before the war of 1898) : Few MSS. in the Library of Congress.

Y

Young, J. R. (minister to China, 1882–84) : Papers, 1858–98 (33 vols.) in the Library of Congress.

The great historical collections of the revolutionary period and of the Continental Congress, 1774–1789, above-mentioned as transferred from the Department of State are the basic sources for the early diplomatic history of the United States before the adoption of the present Constitution. The numerous other collections in the Library throw new light on our diplomatic history from many points and angles. They are enumerated in the *Handbook of manuscripts in the Library of Congress* (Wash.: Govt. Print. Off., 1918) [5520] which should be supplemented by the annual *Report[s] of the Librarian of Congress* (Wash.: Govt. Print. Off.) [5521] each of which from 1901 to date records the MS. accessions of the respective years; and *List of manuscript collections in the Library of Congress to July 1931*, by C. W. Garrison (Wash., 1932) [5522], reprinted from the *Annual report* of the American Historical Association for 1930. A special collection in the Library of Congress, is described by A. C. Tilton: *House miscellaneous papers in the Library of Congress* (Madison, 1913) [5523], reprinted from the *Proceedings* of the State Historical Society of Wisconsin, for 1912.

A more recent departure of the Library of Congress, of the greatest value to research into the diplomatic history of the United States consists of the acquisition of hundreds of thousands of copies of documents relating to American history, taken from European archives. In 1904 a modest though systematic program of continued acquisition of transcripts from British archives, to which were added in 1914, France, and Spain, and beginning in 1919, Mexico, was initiated. These transcripts commenced with the acquisition in 1906 of the B. F. Stevens collections relating to the diplomacy of the Revolution: 18 portfolios containing 10,928 pages of transcripts from the English and French archives (in all, about 1,100 documents) relating to the peace negotiations of 1783, between the United States and Great Britain, and dating from March 22, 1782, to May 25, 1784; and 19 portfolios containing transcripts of documents (about 820 documents and about 4,680 folios relating to the French alliance with the American colonies, which date from April 11, 1778, to May 17, 1784. The work was expanded in 1927 to far greater dimensions by a five-year project subsidized by Mr. John D. Rockefeller, Jr., for the acquisition of source materials on American history from foreign archives. From the beginning of that period the plan proceeded by photographic methods, reaping in a harvest of facsimiles carefully indexed (on cards at the Library) and inventoried. The first five years of this project yielded the enormous total of 1,750,000 pages of facsimiles.[16] In the main, these are facsimiles of the series of documents indicated in the several Carnegie Institution guides to MS. material in European archives relating to American history; but the facsimiles are not limited to that. They fall roughly, and allowing for many minor groups, into three great categories: (1) documents relating to the colonial regime of European powers in North America; (2) emigration to the United States; (3) the largest, diplomatic correspondence of various European foreign offices with their diplomatic representatives in the United States. The wide circulation of these guides in American

---

[16] A portion of these are still in the form of miniature impressions on a non-inflammable type of cinematographic films, from which enlarged prints are made at convenience. Investigators interested in particular documents would do well before visiting the Library to ascertain by correspondence whether prints have been made from the films. Though readable by projection, it is still impracticable to use these films in any great numbers without enlargements.

See the reports of the directors of the Library of Congress European mission for the acquisition of source material in foreign archives, 1927–1933 (S. F. Bemis, 1927–1929. W. C. Ford, 1929–1933), published in the annual *Report of the Librarian of Congress* (Wash.: Govt. Print. Off.) for those years; and separately (1928–29, 1929–30), with the report of the Division of Manuscripts, for those years. For additional acquisitions of facsimiles since then see successive annual reports of the Librarian of Congress.

libraries makes it possible for the investigator residing in almost any locality, even remote, to have knowledge of the existence of documents in various foreign archives pertinent to his interests. The useful system of interlibrary loans makes it possible for him to summon to a responsible library of his own locality a loan of designated facsimiles. Thus the investigator, say in Walla Walla, Washington, or Santa Fé, New Mexico, who for practical reasons cannot go to Washington, much less to Europe, can with little trouble or expense have available infallible copies of documents from European archives. The existence and ready accessibility of these facsimiles of non-American foreign office records will do much to promote multiple-archive research in the diplomatic history of the United States, which, as we have already remarked, is indispensable for its proper presentation. As we proceed to note MS. collections for our subject in foreign archives we shall refer to such portions as are thus available in transcript or in facsimile in the Library of Congress.

In addition to the official archives of the federal government, there are of course the archives of the several states, many of which are in better organization than those of the nation. We cannot say that material in them does not touch on foreign affairs, but we pass them by, as to any detailed description, because of their subordinate nature. Investigators having particular reason to consult them will find available a series of catalogues and indexes.[17] The greater wealth of American MS. material supplementary to the official archives lies in the collections of various public and private libraries, endowments, universities, institutions, and individuals.

---

[17] Adelaide R. Hasse, "Materials for a bibliography of the public archives of the thirteen original states, covering the colonial period and the state period to 1789", *Am. hist. assoc. ann. rep.*, 1906, v. II (1908) 239–572 [5524]. This is really a bibliographical list of *printed records* of colonial executive and legislative bodies. Most of them are not in the state archives at all, but in London. The American Historical Association in its *Annual reports* has printed reports on the public archives of thirty-seven of the states (omitting Arizona, Mississippi, Nevada, New Hampshire, North Dakota, Oklahoma, Oregon, South Carolina, South Dakota, Utah, and West Virginia), see *Annual reports* of the American Historical Association, from 1900 to 1917 [5525], most of the states are represented therein before 1914, in which year a comprehensive index to previous reports was published. Other States are noticed after the 1914 *Report* in later reports of the Association and in special publications and reports of state archival authorities. The most recent listing of guides, surveys, and reports for state archives is: A. R. Newsome, "Unprinted public archives of the post-colonial period; their availability", *Am. hist. rev.*, XXXIX (1934) 682–689 [5525a].

This is particularly true of the collections of private papers of individuals which have passed out of family custody. To undertake a statement of all such material which might in some way touch on the diplomatic history of the United States is at this time impractical if not impossible; but we can refer the reader to the following list of inventories of manuscripts in outstanding repositories (other than national) in the United States.

In the listing of these data the Historical Manuscripts Commission (established 1895) of the American Historical Association has played an active part, beginning with its first report of 1896.

"A list of printed guides to and descriptions of archives and other repositories of historical manuscripts ", first report of the Historical Manuscripts Commission, in *Am. hist. assoc. ann. rep.*, for 1896, v. I (1897) 481–512 [5526], compiled by E. C. Burnett. A. P. C. Griffin, *Bibliog. Am. hist. societies* (no. 4658), for lists of MSS. noted in reports and proceedings of various historical societies; [18] *Writings on American history* (no. 4661), sections on "Archives and manuscript collections "; general and comprehensive guides: American Historical Association, Historical Manuscripts Commission, " Items respecting historical manuscripts ", *Am. hist. assoc. ann. rep.*, 1898 (1899) 573–590, and Additional items . . .", *ibid.*, 1900, v. I (1901) 595–607 [5528]. *Checklist of collections of personal papers in historical societies, university and public libraries, and other learned institutions in the United States* (Wash.: Govt. Print. Off., 1918) [5529], compiled by J. C. Fitzpatrick and published by the Library of Congress; a sequel to the same (enlarged edition) in 1924, *Manuscripts in public and private collections in the United States* (Wash.: Govt. Print. Off., 1924) [5530], listing 131 collections. E. B. Greene and R. B. Morris, *A guide to the principal sources for early American history (1600–1800) in the city of New York* (N.Y., 1929) [5531]. J. A. Robertson, *List of documents in Spanish archives which have been printed or of which transcripts are in American libraries* (Wash.: Carnegie Institution, 1910) [5532].

---

[18] The data in this publication may be brought up to date, to a limited degree, by consulting the *Handbook of American historical societies*, prepared by the Committee on Handbook of the Conference of Historical Societies (Madison, Wis., 1926) [5527], this Conference is a *protégé* of the American Historical Association.

For proposed Social Science Research Council project for survey and cataloguing of all historical manuscripts in the United States and Canada, see no. 5569.

The work of the Conference of Historical Societies may be traced in the annual reports of its meetings (since 1905) in the *Annual reports* of the American Historical Association.

C. W. Smith, *Manuscripts in libraries of the Pacific Northwest* (Seattle, 1931) [5533]. W. S. Thomas, "American revolutionary diaries . . . and personal memoirs", *N. Y. hist. soc. bul.*, VI (1922) 32–35, 61–71, 101–107 [5534]. Justin Winsor, "The manuscript sources of the history of the United States of America, with particular reference to the American revolution", in his *Narrative and critical history of America*, v. VIII (Boston and N.Y., 1889), 413–468 [5535] includes the federal archives, state and personal archives, and foreign archives. Catalogues of special collections: Two calendars by the American Philosophical Society, *Calendar of the papers of Benjamin Franklin in the library* . . . ed. by I. M. Hays (Phila., 1908), 5 v.) [5536]; and "Calendar of the correspondence of Richard Henry Lee and Arthur Lee", *Am. phil. soc. proc.*, XXXVIII (1899) 114–131 [5537]. Buffalo Historical Society, *Rough list of manuscripts in the library of the Buffalo Historical Society* (Buffalo, 1910) [5538], reprinted from the *Publications*, v. XIV. Detroit Public Library, *The Burton historical collection of the Detroit Public Library* (Detroit, 1928?) [5539], this collection consisting of records, both printed and MS., dealing with the history of Detroit and the Old Northwest. J. A. Robertson, *The Spanish manuscripts of the Florida State Historical Society* (Worcester, Mass., 1929) [5540], reprinted from the *Proceedings of the American Antiquarian Society*, for April 1929 and describing MSS. of the period 1518–1819. J. A. Robertson, "The archival distribution of Florida manuscripts", *Fla. hist. soc. quar.*, X (1931) 35–50 [5541] describes the MSS. on Florida in archival institutions both within and without the United States. Harvard College Library, *Calendar of the Arthur Lee manuscripts in the library of Harvard University* (Cambridge, 1882) [5542]; and *Calendar of the Sparks manuscripts in Harvard College Library, with an appendix showing other manuscripts*, by Justin Winsor (Cambridge, 1889) [5543]. "Huntington Library collections", *Huntington Library bulletin*, no. 1 (May 1931) 33–106 [5544]. Illinois State Historical Library, *Alphabetic catalog of the books, manuscripts, maps* . . . *of the Illinois State Historical Library* (Springfield, Ill., 1900) [5545]. *Materials for historical research afforded by the University of Illinois*, published by the University of Illinois (Urbana, 1922) [5546] contains a list of the larger MS. collections in the Illinois Historical Survey which is a branch of the graduate school of the University of Illinois. "Alphabetical list of manuscript collection in the Historical, Memorial, and Art Department of Iowa, as of April 1, 1929 ", *Annals of Iowa*, 3d ser., XVI (1929) 610–621 [5547], this collection includes the public archives of Iowa. Library of Congress, *Handbook of manuscripts* (no. 5520), which should be supplemented by the *Annual reports* of the Librarian of Congress, each of which, since 1901, contains a description of the more important accessions of the year; and C. W. Garrison, *List of manuscript collections in the Library of Congress to July 1931* (no. 5522). Massachusetts Historical Society, *Historical index to the Pickering papers* (Boston, 1896) [5548], its *Collections*, 6th ser., v. VIII; and "List of the principal manuscripts belonging to the Society ", *Mass. hist. soc. proc.*, X (1869) 158–165 [5549]. "An account of manuscripts, papers, and documents in public repositories within the state of Mississippi ", *Miss. hist. soc. pub.*, V (1902) 119–227 [5550] compiled by F. L. Riley and J. M. White. "An account of manuscripts, papers, and documents pertaining to Mississippi in public repositories beyond the state ", *ibid.*, 49–117 [5551], including foreign archives (by P. J. Hamilton), federal archives (by T. M. Owen), state archives (by F. L. Riley), and libraries and societies (by J. M. White). "An account of manuscripts, papers, and documents in private hands ", *ibid.*, 229–293 [5552], by J. M. White and F. L. Riley. J. S. Kendall, " Historical collections in New Orleans ", *N.C. hist. rev.*, VII (1930) 463–476 [5553], giving a survey of the collections of source material (MSS., newspapers, etc.) for the history of Louisiana, found in libraries of New Orleans. New York Public Library, *Calendar of the Emmet collection of manuscripts, etc., relating to American history* (N.Y., 1900) [5554]; *Manuscript collections in the New York Public Library* (N.Y., 1901) [5555], appearing also in its *Bulletin*, v. V, 1901; V. H. Paltsits, *The Manuscript division in the New York Public Library* (N.Y., 1915) [5556], reprinted from the *Bulletin*, v. XIX, and containing a " Supplement to the list of ' Manuscript collections ' of 1901 noted above, embracing principal additions and accessions to the end of 1914 ", and " Historical texts that have been printed in the Bulletin for 1897–1914." New York State Library, *Annotated list of the principal manuscripts in the New York State Library* (Albany, 1899) [5557]. North Carolina

Historical Commission, *Calendars of manuscript collections*, v. I, prepared from the original MSS. in the collections of the North Carolina Historical Commission by D. L. Corbitt (Raleigh, 1926) [5558], see also its *Biennial reports* which list recent acquisitions. Historical Society of Western Pennsylvania, *Inventory of the manuscript and miscellaneous collections of the Historical Society of Western Pennsylvania* (Pittsburg, 1933) [5558a]; University of Pennsylvania, *Calendar of the papers of Benjamin Franklin in the library of the University of Pennsylvania* (Phila., 1908) [5559]. University of Texas, " The historical manuscript collections of the University of Texas ", by W. A. Whatley, *Texas hist. teach. bul.*, IX no. 1 (1920) 19–25 [5560]. Virginia Historical Society, *Catalogue of the manuscripts in the collection of the Virginia Historical Society* (Richmond, 1901) [5561]. Virginia State Library, *Calendar of transcripts, including the annual report of the Department of Archives and History* (Richmond, 1905) [5562], describing the archives and MSS. in the library. William L. Clements Library, *An exhibition of books and papers relating to Dr. Benjamin Franklin from the collections in this library and the library of William Mason Smith* (Ann Arbor, 1926) [5563], the *Bulletin* no. 12 of the William L. Clements Library. R. G. Adams, "A new library of American revolutionary records ", *Current history*, XXXIII (Nov. 1930) 234–238 [5564], a brief description of the MS. collections, including the Shelburne papers, recently acquired by the William L. Clements Library; see also the annual *Report[s] of the William L. Clements Library*, 1925– (Ann Arbor, 1926–) [5565] which describe acquisitions of MSS. of the given year, and its *Bulletins*, published from time to time, which include among other items summaries of special collections of MSS. in the library (see for example (no. 5596 below)). State Historical Society of Wisconsin, *Descriptive list of manuscript collections of the State Historical Society of Wisconsin, together with reports on other collections of manuscript material for American history in adjacent states*, ed. by Reuben Gold Thwaites (Madison, 1906) [5566]; this society has also published *The Preston and Virginia papers of the Draper collection of manuscripts* (Madison, 1915) [5566a]; *Calendar of the Kentucky papers of the Draper collection of manuscripts* (Madison, 1925) [5567]; and *Calendar of the Tennessee and King's Mountain papers of the Draper collection of manuscripts* (Madison, 1929) [5568].[19]

Great Britain

Of all public archives, those of Great Britain, in the Public Record Office, London, are most systematically and extensively indexed.[20] In this central archive now repose the great mass of British public records, particularly political (including of course departmental) records.[21]

The contents of the British Public Record Office are described in M. S. Giuseppi, *A guide to the manuscripts preserved in the British Record Office* (London: H. M. Stationery Off., 1923-24, 2 v.) [5575]. Material relating to American history in the Record Office is noted particularly in C. M. Andrews, *Guide to the materials for American history, to 1783, in the Public Record Office of Great Britain* (Wash.: Carnegie Institution, 1912-14, 2 v.) [5576]; and C. O. Paullin and F. L. Paxson, *Guide to the materials in London archives for the*

---

[19] A comprehensive survey and summary inventory and classification of all historical MS. material in the United States available to the public has been projected as a joint enterprise of the American Council of Learned Societies and the Social Science Research Council. They propose to incorporate the data on printed cards, and to set up card catalogues therefor in several libraries located in strategic places on the continent. These catalogues would incorporate the various inventories, indexes, and catalogues already in existence, such as those listed above. It is planned to distribute published summaries of the work from time to time. Meanwhile a preliminary survey of material available for research in the United States has been published in photolithographic reproduction by the American Council of Learned Societies: Franklin F. Holbrook, *Survey of activities of American agencies in relation to materials for research in the social sciences and the humanities* (Wash. and N.Y., 1932) [5569], compiled for the Joint Committee on Materials for Research of the American Council of Learned Societies and the Social Science Research Council.

[20] See *Lists and indexes* of papers in the Public Record Office (London: H. M. Stationery Off., 1892-1931, 53 v.) [5570].

[21] The English public records, central and local, are surveyed in Hubert Hall, *Repertory of British archives. Part I. England* (London, 1920) [5571], published by the Royal Historical Society. Anyone desiring comprehensive and detailed information as to the history and present status of the public records of Great Britain may turn to *Report[s] of the Royal Commission on Public Records . . .* (London: H. M. Stationery Off., 1912-19, 3 v.) [5572], 1st report, 1912 (reprinted 1914) with appendices, command papers 6361, 6395, 6396; 2d report, 1914, with appendices, command papers, nos. 7544, 7545, 7546; 3d report, 1916-19, with appendices, command papers, nos. 367, 368, 369, which contain conclusions as well as recommendations on almost every aspect of the subject. An orderly survey of English archival procedure is Walther Holtzmann and Alex Bein, "Das englische Archivwesen in Vergangenheit und Gegenwart", *Archiv. Zeitschrift*, 3d ser., VI (1930) 1-42 [5573]. C. K. Webster, "The study of British foreign policy (nineteenth century)", *Am. hist. rev.*, XXX (1925) 728-737 [5574] surveys and analyzes briefly the archival sources for British foreign policy.

history of the United States since 1783 (Wash.: Carnegie Institution, 1914) [5577]. Of this, much for the diplomatic history of the United States is contained in the records of the British Foreign Office, which are deposited in the Record Office. The archives of the Foreign Office are catalogued in *List of Foreign Office records to 1878 preserved in the Public Record Office* (London, 1929) (*Its* Lists and Indexes, LII) [5578].[22] The records are open to students who wish to consult documents not later in date than 1885. The material relating to the United States consists of the American correspondence in the following series: " General correspondence "—in Series F. O. 4 (1781–1792), and F. O. 5 (1793–1878) from which year the archives were closed to the public, at the time of the printing of the *List;* " Ratifications of treaties "—Series F. O. 94; " Miscellanea "—Series F. O. 95; " Embassy and consular archives "—Series F. O. 115, 116, 117, 281, 282, 283, 284, and 285; "Archives of commissions "[23]— Series F. O. 301, 302, 303, 304, and 305; " Slave trade "—Series F. O. 84; " Commissions "—Series F. O. 301, 302, 303; "American claims, 1794 "—Series F. O. 304, 305; " Private collections "—Series F. O. 362 (Granville), F. O. 353 (F. J. Jackson), F. O. 352 (Stratford Canning). The list [24] enables the student to identify immediately the archive number of the volume of papers he wishes to consult; and once the call is presented at the Record Office, the manuscripts can be on his desk in a few minutes.

A significant collection of peculiar documents in the British Museum helps to interpret certain files of diplomatic correspondence in the Foreign Office: " Deciphers of despatches passing between foreign governments and their ministers in England, with cipher-

---

[22] See also the Public Record Office *List of state papers, foreign* (London, 1904) (*Its* Lists and Indexes, XIX) [5579].

[23] These series contain British and American claims, and associated papers, accounts, journals, and printed papers, with names of claimants listed.

[24] One may note for special purposes, L. J. Ragatz, *A guide to the official correspondence of the governors of the British West India colonies with the secretary of state, 1763–1833* (London, 1923) [5580], which lists the correspondence from the several colonies to be found in the Public Record Office where the papers have been deposited ; Hubert Hall, *British archives and the sources for the history of the world war* (London and New Haven, 1925) [5581], a publication of the Carnegie Endowment for International Peace, Division of Economics and History ; and " Notes from the archives of Scotland concerning America ", by Dr. J. Franklin Jameson, in *Am. hist. assoc. ann. rep.*, for 1930, v. I (1931) 97–122 [5582]. The Irish archives perished in the Easter Rebellion of 1916. See Herbert Wood, " The public records of Ireland before and after 1922 ", *Royal hist. soc. trans.*, XIII (1930) 17–49 [5583].

keys ", Br. Museum, Additional MSS., " America ", 1780–1841, no. 32303.

The Library of Congress has in transcript or photostatic reproduction the following British Foreign Office material obtained at the Record Office: Transcripts of diplomatic correspondence relating to the Peace Negotiations at Paris, 1782–1783. These were formerly grouped in a separate collection known as the *B. F. Stevens transcripts relating to the peace negotiations of 1782–1783*, comprising selections from the diplomatic correspondence of France, Great Britain (including private papers of Lord Shelburne, the then prime minister), and The Netherlands; but the collection has now been split up into original archival provenance, and filed accordingly in the Library.

The Library of Congress has a facsimile and transcript collection of the British consular correspondence, 1783–1791 (F.O. Series 4, vols. 2–10) preceding the establishment of formal diplomatic relations in 1791, but has refrained from duplicating the matter covered in the Carnegie Institution transcripts of correspondence of British ministers in the United States, 1791–1806.[25] Beginning with the year 1806, the Library has secured a complete photostatic record of the main series of despatches from and instructions to the British legation in the United States to December 1870, taken from the papers of the Foreign Office now deposited in the Record Office,[26] (F.O. Series 5). The reproductions do not include printed material (which is editorially indicated) already available at the Library of Congress, nor do they include, with a few exceptions, other papers than strictly despatches and instructions with enclosures.[27] The photostats of instructions are of drafts, until 1835,

---

[25] The Carnegie Institution of Washington has recently (June, 1935) transferred these transcripts of the correspondence of the British ministers in the United States, 1791–1806 (F. O., Series 4 and 5), despatches and instructions, to the Library of Congress. The material is now being edited by Professor Bernard Mayo.

[26] The papers of the British legation are stored in Cambridge, England, but are under the control of the Record Office.

[27] Facsimiles of volumes listed in the series F.O. 5, containing other than diplomatic correspondence, will not (with a few exceptions) be found at the Library of Congress. The volumes of diplomatic correspondence reproduced in facsimile in the Library of Congress are as follows: F.O. Series 4, vols. 2–10, 12 (Paullin and Paxson, 13–15), and F.O. Series 5, vols. 1 and 4 (selections only from these volumes, *i.e.*, correspondence between Alexander Hamilton and George Hammond, 1792 and 1794) (Paullin and Paxson, 30–31) ; vols. 52, 54, 56–58, 62–64, 68–70, 74–77, 83–88, 100, 101, 102, 105–110, 112–115, 120–123, 129–133, 141–143, 148–150, 156–159, 165–169, 174–177, 184–186, 191, 192, 197–199, 209–213, 222–225, 235–238, 247–249, 258–260, 265, 266, 271–273, 280–283, 288–293, 299–301, 306, 307, 313, 314, 322, 323, 325 (selections), 332–334, 340 (selections),

after that date they are reproductions of the signed instructions in the series F.O. 115 of embassy and consular archives, which are stored outside of London.

As in the case of other countries, the investigator may need to consult the records of other departments, war, admiralty,[28] colonies (dominions), etc. These are indexed similarly to the Foreign Office material.[29] There is also an abundant amount of well indexed MS. material to be found in English libraries, and in private archives. The MSS. in the British Museum,[30] and other London libraries—as well as in the libraries of Oxford and Cambridge—have been indexed in C. M. Andrews and Frances G. Davenport, *Guide to the manu-*

---

347 (selections), 348, 349, 359, 360–364, 377–380, 391–393, 404–410, 424–430, 446–451, 464–467 (correspondence of Lieut. Col. Estcourt, British commissioner appointed to trace the northeast boundary, 1843–48), 469–472, 484–487, 498–501, 511–515, 527–531, 544–548, 563–567, 589 (Lord Elgin correspondence, 1854), 593–600, 619–624, 640–647, 670–675, 690–695, 711–716, 734–740, 759–777, 823–840, 874–900, 938–942 (selections), 943, 965, 1000–1003 and 1008 (correspondence regarding ironclad steamers built at Birkenhead, 1863–64), 1009–1012 (selections), 1013–1022, 1059–1061 (selections), 1062–1068, 1104–1109, 1128–1133. F.O. Series 7, vol. 148 (selections). F.O. Series 27, vols. 2, 3, 5–9, 151, 265, 285, 296, 297 (selections only from each), 2356. F.O. Series 35, vol. 58 (selections). F.O. Series 64, vol. 123 (selections). F.O. Series 72, vols. 1, 127, 128, 177, 184, 196, 222, 262 (selections only from each). F.O. Series 83, vols. 2204–2226 (reports of law officers, 1781–1876). F.O. Series 84, vols. 296, 332, 376, 423, 538, 596 (selections only from each). F.O. Series 92, vols. 35, 36, 41 (selections only from each). F.O. Series 95, vol. 512 (John Jay correspondence, 1794), 515 (treaty signed London, Dec. 31, 1806, and papers relating thereto). F.O. Series 97, vols. 1 (Citizen Genet correspondence, 1793), 17–18 (selections: Gov. of New Brunswick, etc., correspondence, 1837–43), 157 (correspondence with Oswald, 1782–83). F.O. Series 115, vols. 68, 70–75, 77–83, 85, 87–89, 91, 94–96, 98, 99, 102–104, 106–108, 113–115, 120, 121, 128–130, 136–142, 151–156, 163–166, 173–180, 188–192, 201–207, 220–225, 238–250, 251–259, 284–306, 341–357, 402–409, 432–438, 449–454, 462–466, 472–477. This series (F.O. 115) has not been copied in full, the material selected is supplementary to that from F.O. 5, and consists in the main of signed instructions, of which the drafts are in F.O. 5. F.O. Series 353, vol. 30 (F. J. Jackson's correspondence, 1809).

[28] For an excellent example of the use of British admiralty records in the diplomatic history of the United States, see James P. Baxter, 3d, "The British government and neutral rights, 1861–1865 ", *Am. hist. rev.*, XXXIV (1928), 9–29.

[29] *List of Admiralty records, preserved in the Public Record Office* (London, 1904) (Lists and Indexes, no. 18) [5584]. *List of War Office records, preserved in the Public Record Office* (London, 1908) (Lists and indexes, no 28) [5585]. *List of Colonial Office records, preserved in the Public Record Office* (London, 1911) (Lists and Indexes, no. 36) [5586]. *Lists of the records of the Treasury, . . . and the Board of Trade, to 1837, preserved in the Public Record Office* (London, 1921) (Lists and Indexes, no. 46) [5587]. *An alphabetical guide to certain War Office and other military records, preserved in the Public Record Office* (London, 1931) (Lists and Indexes, no. 53) [5588].

[30] One should not fail to consult the *Catalogue of additions to the manuscripts in the British Museum* (London, 1911–33, 3 v.) [5589] covering additions, 1906–1910, 1911–1915, and 1916–1920, for acquisitions since the publication of Andrews and Davenport's *Guide* (no. 5590) ; for example there have come in since that time the following papers: Official and private correspondence and papers of William Huskisson, 1782, 1790–1831 ; papers of the Earls of Liverpool (1st and 2d) ; of Sir Robert Peel, Home Secretary, 1822–1830, and Prime Minister, 1834–35, 1841–46; and of the Marquis of Wellesley, Secretary of State for Foreign Affairs, 1809–1812.

script materials for the history of the United States to 1783, in the British Museum, in minor London archives, and in the libraries of Oxford and Cambridge (Wash.: Carnegie Institution, 1908) [5590], which is continued, for documents after 1783, in Paullin and Paxson's *Guide* (no. 5577). For other libraries one should note D. M. Matteson, *List of manuscripts concerning American history preserved in European libraries and noted in their published catalogues and similar printed lists* (Wash.: Carnegie Institution, 1925) [5591]. The Library of Congress has transcripts or photostatic copies of most of the manuscripts relating to American history in these libraries as noted in these two guides including practically all of the American items in the British Museum.

The British Government has cooperated splendidly with British historical scholars in locating, indexing, calendaring, and even printing, collections of private papers. This has been done through the agency of the Historical Manuscripts Commission, appointed in 1869, which " for all practical purposes . . . may be regarded as a branch of the Record Office, an arrangement which, though somewhat anomalous, has worked well." [31]

The numerous and voluminous (some of the reports contain several volumes, *i.e.*, report and appendixes) printed *Reports* of the Commission contain the best indication of the nature and contents of many (but by no means all) collections now privately owned. The Reports [32] not only indicate the existence of important private records, survey and index them, but frequently calendar them, in calendars so extensive (as in the case of the Dropmore Papers) as to amount to a printing *in toto* of the important documents. [33] Among the papers thus indicated, which are useful to the history of American diplomacy are: " Manuscripts of Sir Henry Strachey ", in the 6th *Report*, appendix, p. 396-404 (London, 1877) [5595], concerning the war of independence and peace of 1782; " Stopford-

---

[31] *First report of the Royal Commission on Public Records* (London, 1912), 12. For lists of reports issued to 1931, see the pamphlet published by the Commission : *The Royal Commission on Historical Manuscripts* (Harrow, Eng., 1931) [5592].

[32] R. A. Roberts, *The reports of the Historical MSS. Commission* (London, 1920) [5593] gives a résumé of the contents of the reports to 1920.

[33] For shifting locations of sources, see " Migrations of historical manuscripts ", a feature of the *Bulletin of the Institute of Historical Research* (London), I-, 1923- [5594].

Sackville papers ",[34] 9th *Report*, appendix 3 (London, 1884), reissued as appendix to the 15th report (London, 1904–10, 2 v.) [5597], papers relating to the American war, 1775–1782; *Report on American manuscripts in the Royal Institution of Great Britain* (London, 1904–09, 4 v.), report on historical MSS., unnumbered series [5598], papers of Sir Guy Carleton, later Lord Dorchester, now in the possession of the Williamsburg Holding Corporation at Williamsburg, Va.; *Manuscripts of the Marquis of Lansdowne* [Lord Shelburne], published in the 3rd *Report*, appendix, p. 125–147, and the 5th *Report*, appendix, p. 215–260 (London, 1872 and 1876) [5599], which are very important for the Peace of 1782;[35] *Manuscripts of J. B. Fortescue, Esq., preserved at Dropmore* (London, 1892–1927, 10 v.) [5602] vol. 1: appendix to the 13th report, vol. 2: appendix to the 14th report, vols. 3–9: appendixes to the 15th report, vol. 10: independent volume (letters of Lord Grenville, 1791–1820—Grenville was Secretary of State for Foreign Affairs, 1791 to 1801—and his notable correspondents); *Report on the manuscripts of Earl Bathurst, preserved at Cirencester Park* (London, 1923) [5603]. The material covered by these reports has become so extensive that particular guides to it have been published: Frances G. Davenport, " Materials for English diplomatic history, 1509–1783, calendared in the reports of the Historical Manuscripts Commission, with references to similar materials in the British Museum ", in *Eighteenth report of the Royal Commission on Historical Manuscripts* (London, 1917), appendix II, 357–402 [5604]; and J. Franklin Jameson, " Guide to the items relating to American history in the reports of the English Historical Manuscripts Commission and their appendixes ", *Am. hist. assoc. ann. rep.*, for 1898 (1899) 611–708 [5605].

---

[34] The papers are now in the possession of the William L. Clements Library, at the University of Michigan. See R. G. Adams, *The papers of Lord George Germain; a brief description of the Stopford-Sackville papers now in the William L. Clements Library* (Ann Arbor, 1928), which is the *Bulletin* no. 18 of the same Library [5596].

[35] The papers of this collection relating to public affairs are now in the possession of the William L. Clements Library, at the University of Michigan, where they are known as the " Shelburne Papers." For note as to their contents: C. W. Alvord, " The Shelburne manuscripts in America ", *Inst. hist. research bul.*, I (1924) 77–80 [5600]; and " Calendar of Shelburne correspondence ", in *Report of the Public Archives [of Canada] for the year 1921* (Ottawa, 1922), 229–281 [5601].

For a guide to the historical publications of the societies of England and Wales, see no. 4839, above. For the British West Indies: H. C. Bell and D. W. Parker, *Guide to British West Indian archive materials, in London and in the islands, for the history of the United States* (Wash.: Carnegie Institution, 1926) [5606]; and Richard Pares, " Public records in British West India islands ", *Inst. hist. research bul.*, VII (Feb. 1930) 149–157 [5607]. See also *Archives of British Honduras*, ed., with historical note, by Sir John Alder Burdon (London, 1931– (in progress)) [5607a]. To date, volumes I and II have appeared, carrying the records from the earliest date through 1840.

Dominion of Canada [36]

The systematic organization of a federal collection of Canadian archives was begun in 1872.[37] There is a Carnegie Institution guide to material in these archives for United States history: D. W. Parker, *Guide to the materials for United States history in Canadian archives* (Wash.: Carnegie Institution, 1913) [5610]. Among the additions to the Dominion Archives since Parker's *Guide* are: transcripts from the *Ministère des Affaires Etrangères, Corres. pol.*, *Etats-Unis*, 1–25 (1776–83) and *Angleterre*, 537–542 (1782–83), which duplicates that in the Library of Congress; British *Foreign Office*, 5 (America) covering the years 1806 to 1837 (also in the Library of Congress); and a large further consignment of papers from the office of the governor-general (Series G), bringing the correspondence of the governors-general down to 1904. Beginning with the year 1872 the annual reports of the Dominion archivist constitute a mine of information as to the rapidly increasing acquisi-

---

[36] We make no attempt to analyze the archives of South Africa, New Zealand, or the Irish Free State. Direct diplomatic relations of the United States with South Africa and the Irish Free State are of such recent origin as not to give unlimited access to their archives for historical purposes for a long time to come. Historical and limitrophal factors, of course, put Canada on a different basis.

[37] For an account of the history of these archives the investigator is referred to the following publications : J. Edmond Roy, " Les archives du Canada à venir à 1872 ", *Royal soc. Canada proc.*, 3d ser., v. IV, sec. 1 (1911) 57–123 [5608]; D. A. McArthur, " The Dominion archives ", *Am. hist. assoc. ann. rep.*, for 1911, v. I (1913) 343–352 [5609]; and D. W. Parker's *Guide* (no. 5610), 1–9.

tions of the Canadian archives.[38] In addition to these reports the Dominion Archives issues a series of *Publications of the Public Archives
of Canada* (Ottawa, 1909–32, 14 v. (in progress)) [**5613**], also
printed in French, which consist of special reports, calendars of
particular collections, and printings of source material (journals,
etc.) from the collections in the Archives.

The material contained in the Public Archives is indicated briefly
in " Manuscript sources in the Dominion Archives ", in the *Index
and dictionary of Canadian history*, ed. by L. J. Burpee and A. G.
Doughty (Toronto, 1911), 419–433 [**5614**]; D. N. McArthur (no.
5609); A. G. Doughty, *The Canadian archives and its activities*
(Ottawa, 1924), 83–88 [**5615**]; and H. P. Biggar, " The Public
Archives at Ottawa ", *Inst. hist. research bul.*, II (Feb. 1925) 66–79,
and III (June 1925) 38–44 [**5616**], giving a brief résumé of the
various series of records preserved in the Public Archives at Ottawa.
For further details these should be supplemented by the various calendars and guides: *Inventory of the military documents in the
Canadian archives*, prepared by Lieut. Col. Cruikshank (Ottawa,
1910) [**5617**], although dealing in the main with military affairs
these papers will be found to contain much useful information in
regard to relations with the United States; *Catalogue of maps, plans
and charts in the Dominion Archives* (no. 5144); D. W. Parker, *A
guide to the documents in the manuscript room at the Public
Archives of Canada*, v. I (Ottawa: Govt. Print. Bureau, 1914)
[**5618**], most important of all; *Catalogue of pamphlets, journals
and reports in the Public Archives of Canada, 1611–1867, with index*,
second edition, prepared by Norman Fee (Ottawa: King's printer,
1916) [**5619**]; " Manuscript sources of the history of New France
and the French régime in the Public Archives, Ottawa ", in *Canada*

---

[38] The reports for 1872 to 1880, inclusive, were issued as supplements to the Reports
of the Minister of Agriculture; but in 1881 a separate series began: *Report of the Public
Archives [of Canada] for the year[s] 1881* (to date) (Ottawa, 1881–) [**5611**], which
include reports on MS. acquisitions during the given year and calendars of special collections (such as " Calendar of Shelburne correspondence ", published in the *Report* for the
year 1921 (Ottawa, 1922), 229–281) [**5611a**], issued as appendixes to the *Reports*.
For a detailed account of the contents of these reports, to 1908, see *Index to reports of
Canadian archives, from 1872 to 1908* (Ottawa, 1909) [**5612**] (Also issued in French)
which gives a bibliographical and analytical list, chronologically arranged, of the reports,
followed by an author and subject index of material contained therein.

and its provinces, v. XXIII (Toronto, 1917), 224–228; and " Manuscript sources of the history of Canada under British rule in the Public Archives, Ottawa ", *ibid.*, 229–230 [5620].

Three of the provinces of Canada have issued reports of their activities and publications of source material, the Province of Ontario being first in priority of publication.[39]

The Library of Congress contains reproductions (photofilm enlargements) from the Public Archives of Canada at Ottawa, of " Diplomatic and military correspondence relating to the war of 1812 ": Series C, vols. 676–688E (27 bound volumes in the Library of Congress), and all the correspondence between the British ministers in Philadelphia and Washington with the Canadian government and other officials, 1791–1875, including the Bagot papers, 1791–1843, 1816–1866.

Spain

The manuscript material in Spanish archives for American history is outranked only by the English in importance, and by no state archives in volume. For the history of American diplomacy it is extremely rich; one need only mention the American Revolution, Nootka Affair, Mississippi Question, Western Boundaries, Louisiana, Florida, Texas, South American Independence, Cuba, Santo Domingo, the Philippines, in order to suggest vistas of investigation

---

[39] The Bureau of Archives of the Province of Ontario was organized in 1903, and an account of its scope and its collections is given in: A. S. Fraser, " The Ontario archives ", *Am. hist. assoc. rep.*, for 1911, v. I (1913) 353–363 [5621], written by the provincial archivist. It has published reports on its collections as follows: *Report[s] of the Bureau of Archives of the Province of Ontario, 1903[–1933]* (Toronto, 1904–1934, 22 v.) [5622], which consist mainly of publication of source material on special subjects contained in the archives. Note particularly the *Second report . . .*, by Alexander Fraser, provincial archivist, 1904 (Toronto, 1905) [5623], containing the proceedings and evidence taken before the special commission sent to Canada by Great Britain, 1785–1789, in regard to claims of Canadian loyalists for losses and services during the American Revolution.

The Archives of the Province of Quebec has published seven volumes of reports, which are made up to a large extent of reprints of source material found in the archives. We refer to the *Rapport[s] de l'archiviste de la Province de Québec, 1920/21 [–1932/1933]* (Quebec, 1921–1933, 12 v.) [5624]. It has also published a *Collection de manuscrits contenant lettres, mémoires, et autres documents historiques relatifs à la Nouvelle-France, recueillis aux archives de la province de Québec, ou copiés à l'étranger* (Quebec, 1883–85, 4 v.) [5625], covering the period 1492–1789.

For the Province of British Columbia we note the *Report of the Provincial Archives Department of the Province of British Columbia for the year ended December 31st, 1913* (Victoria, B.C., 1914) [5626], with appendixes containing transcripts of original material in the archives. It has also published a series of *Memoirs* (8 volumes to date), which are monographs on special subjects based on MSS. in the archives.

that indispensably require the Spanish archives. The principal categories of material which bear on American diplomacy consist of: papers of the Spanish Department of State (and incidentally of the other ministries); and papers of the Spanish colonial authorities. From 1776 to 1823 the Spanish-American frontier was the main subject of diplomacy between the new republic and that monarchy. Although the decisive turns of this diplomacy are to be gauged as much by European situations (to be derived from European foreign office archives) as by frontier conditions, the advance of the American frontier-line was the paramount object of the United States, as its defense was the principal desire of Spain, in that half-century of relations between the two countries. Hence the reports of Spanish colonial officials in Louisiana, the Floridas, and Texas, to Spain, generally via Cuba, and the instructions to them, are full of revelations; this phase of the diplomatic history of the United States is now being rewritten from a perusal of these bountiful sources, which were not *fully* studied by early distinguished historians such as Henry Adams, who relied on selections from European foreign office records.

There are four principal archives in Spain: the Archives of Simancas (*Archivo General de Simancas*), at Simancas, near Valladolid; the Archives of the Indies (*Archivo General de Indias*), in Seville; the National Historical Archives (*Archivo Histórico Nacional*), in Madrid; and the Archives of Aragon (*Archivo General de la Corona de Aragón*), in Barcelona. The last named repository has little of anything to do with American diplomacy.

The Simancas archives,[40] established 1540, served for about 300 years as a storehouse of public documents overflowing from the administrative offices, and from other organs of the monarchy, including the Department of State with its diplomatic correspondence, both foreign office records and recalled legation archives. More recently this class of diplomatic correspondence has been deposited by the Department of State in the *Archivo Histórico Nacional* in Madrid. There is no distinct line of division, marking off records

---

[40] The comparative isolation of this archive and the impossible living conditions in its vicinity presented real hardships to early investigators, who developed an alarming mortality rate there. Motor transit makes it now possible to live comfortably in Valladolid while working in the archive at Simancas, seven miles away. Without desiring to be public admonishers in the manner of Baedeker, we earnestly advise people not to eat or drink in Simancas.

included in deposits at Simancas from those to be found in deposits at the *Archivo Histórico Nacional.* The investigator must ascertain that for himself. Generally speaking one may say that the diplomatic correspondence of Spain for the 18th century (which includes the American Revolution) and before, is at Simancas; but there are important exceptions to this: the papers of the Spanish legation at Paris (correspondence of Count de Aranda (drafts) and Floridablanca (originals)) are in the *Archivo Histórico Nacional,* as are also selected *dossiers* of the corresponding foreign office material for the same series.[41] It is desirable at this point to note that it has been the custom for secretaries to select out of a main file of diplomatic correspondence the documents relating to a specific subject—say the right of deposit for the Mississippi River—and to associate them, with other relevant documents, perhaps from other ministries, in a particular *dossier* (*expediente*) for the minister's perusal. These extracted pieces are not always restored to their original file, though slips are left to denote their withdrawal and archival whereabouts, but are kept in a special file. So in working the *Estado* papers of the *Archivo Histórico Nacional* one must constantly search for the documents which have been withdrawn (*documentos extraidos*) in another series; frequently these are the most important of the original unbroken series.[42] These breaks do not occur, of course, in the corresponding series of documents which have accumulated in the legation papers. The papers of the Spanish legation in the United States through 1910 have been transferred to Spain, and at present lie in unbroken series (original signed instructions and draft despatches) in the Spanish Department of State, in Madrid. The diplomatic correspondence of Spain with the United States is therefore all of it in Madrid—foreign office in

---

[41] Señor Gómez del Campillo, archivist of the *Archivo Histórico Nacional* has compiled a manuscript list: *Indice de la correspondencia entre el conde de Aranda, embajador en Paris* (*minutas*) *y los secretarios de estado* (*originales*), *1775–1786* [5627] (with *legajo* references) of all the despatches from and instructions to Aranda, Spanish Ambassador to France, including draft despatches and signed instructions, 1775 to 1786. There is a typescript copy of this in the Division of Manuscripts of the Library of Congress, with indications of what photocopies of the documents mentioned therein had been acquired to date.

[42] Miss Irene A. Wright had copied for the Library of Congress a MS. calendar of the United States file of the diplomatic correspondence of the Spanish Department of State now in the *Archivo Histórico Nacional, 1808–1823;* and a supplementary calendar of the documents which had been withdrawn from that series into other *expedientes.* There is a typescript copy of this calendar in the Division of Manuscripts of this library.

the *Archivo Histórico Nacional*, and legation archives in the *Ministerio de Estado*.[43] Most of the colonial sources, on the other hand, are in the Archives of the Indies, in Seville, as will presently be explained.

There is an excellent general guide to all Spanish archives, a cooperative work prepared under the direction of Francisco Rodríguez Marín: *Guía histórica y descriptiva de los archivos, bibliotecas y museos arqueológicos de España* (Madrid, 1916, 2 v.) [5628], of which volume I is *Sección de archivos; archivos históricos*. A later general notice, in the form of a brief tabular analysis of the principal *fonds* of the Spanish archives, such as might be drawn off from Rodríguez Marín, is the publication of the Argentine scholar, José Torre Revello, *Los archivos españoles* (Buenos Aires, 1927) (Universidad Nacional, Facultad de Filosofía y Letras, Publicaciones del Instituto de Investigaciones Históricas, núm. XXXVI) [5629].

There is a special guide for the archives of Simancas:[44] Francisco Díaz Sánchez, *Guía de la villa y archivo de Simancas* (Madrid, 1885 [5630]. The later one, Mariano Alcocer Martínez, *Guía del investigador* (Valladolid, 1923) [5634] is by no means as helpful as the Díaz Sánchez, which is more difficult of purchase. The material at Simancas (as well as in Madrid and Seville) relating to American history, so far as it could be summarily noted from the Díaz Sánchez and the local MS. indexes, is suggested in W. R. Shepherd, *Guide to the materials for the history of the United States in Spanish archives* (*Simancas, the Archivo Histórico Nacional, and Seville*) (Wash.: Carnegie Institution, 1907) [5635]. Unfortunately Shepherd's very general guide is lacking in one very important detail: it gives no reference to the indispensable *legajo* (bundle) numbers, by which documents are to be located in the archives.

For the Archives of the Indies at Seville, the great repository (established 1785) for Spanish colonial history there are now avail-

---

[43] The Library of Congress has typescript papers of the original instructions to Spanish diplomatists in the United States, 1796–1838, taken from these legation papers (vols. 203–242, 274). Also *legajo* 270 which contains drafts of legation despatches, 1835, and *legajo* 272 which contains correspondence with the Intendant at Havana, 1835.

[44] For a readable sketch (among others) of this archive, see: G. A. Bergenroth's introduction to Vol. I of *Calendar of letters, despatches, and state papers, relating to negotiations between England and Spain, preserved in the archives at Simancas and elsewhere* (London, 1862), i–xvi [5631]; also G. Constant, "Simancas", *Revue historique*, XCVI (1908) 50–68 [5632]; and Walter Heins, "Das spanische Generalarchiv in Simancas", *Archiv. Zeitschrift*, 3d ser., III (1926) 31–34 [5633], with complete bibliography thereon.

able a series of guides, indexes, and catalogues—in addition to the general descriptions in Rodríguez Marín, and in Shepherd. The veteran archivist, Pedro Torres Lanzas, prepared (anonymously) a useful description of the general contents of the archive in *El Archivo de Indias y la Sociedad de Publicaciones Históricas* (Madrid, 1912) [5636]; and the section on the Archives of the Indies, in the *Guía histórica* (no. 5628). One should also note: Pedro Torres Lanzas and Germán Latorre, *Catálogo; cuadro general de documentación* (Seville, 1918) [5637], of the *Archivo General de Indias*, which is a publication of the "Biblioteca Oficial de Estudios Americanistas de Sevilla", and also published in its *Boletín*, años III-V, 1915-1918. The most recent general survey, with valuable notes to other literature,[45] is José Torre Revello, *El Archivo General de Indias de Sevilla; historia y clasificación de sus fondos* (Buenos Aires, 1929)

---

[45] There are many special indexes, lists, and calendars to particular classes of documents in the Archives of the Indies, particularly those bearing on the colonial history of individual Hispanic-American republics, but also of European states. For lists of these see: José Torre Revello, *Inventario del Archivo General de Indias* (Buenos Aires, 1926) [5638], v. XXVIII of the *Publicaciones del Instituto de Investigaciones*, see below, (no. 5673). Examples are: Pedro Torres Lanzas, *Catálogo de legajos del Archivo General de Indias* (Seville, 1919- 21, 2 v.; 1921-22, 4 v.) [5639], the first two sections dealing with: *Patronato y contaduría general del Consejo de Indias* (Seville, 1919-21, 2 v.); the third: *Casa de la Contratación de Indias* (Seville, 1921-22, 4 v.); and by the same editor, *Independencia de América; fuentes para su estudio; catálogo de documentos conservados en el Archivo General de Indias de Sevilla* (Madrid, 1912, 6 v.; and 2d ser., Seville, 1924-25, 2 v.) [5640]; and (for Mexico) *Indice de documentos de Nueva España existentes en el Archivo de Indias de Sevilla* (Mexico: Imprenta de Secretaría de Relaciones Exteriores, 1928-31, 4 v.) [5641]; *Catálogo de los fondos cubanos del Archivo General de Indias*, tomo I, vol. 1 (Madrid, 1929) [5642], containing "consultos y decretos, 1664-1783"; Luis Rubio y Moreno, *Inventario general de registros cedularios del Archivo General de Indias de Sevilla* (Madrid, 1930) [5643]. Useful special notes are: Luis Rubio y Moreno, "Archivo General de Indias; movimiento de fondos, investigación y catalogación", *Centro estud. Americanistas Sevilla bol.*, año III (1915) 15-39 [5644]; C. E. Chapman, "A description of certain legajos in the Archivo General de Indias", *Hisp. Am. hist. rev.*, I (1918) 209-230, 352-371 [5645]; A. S. Aiton and J. L. Mecham, "The Archivo General de Indias", *Hisp. Am. hist. rev.*, IV (1921) 553-567 [5646]; J. T. Lanning, "A descriptive catalogue of some legajos on Georgia in the Spanish archives", *Ga. hist. quar.*, XIII (1929) 410-421 [5647]; and R. R. Hill, "Reforms in shelving and numbering in the Archivo General de Indias", *Hisp. Am. hist. rev.*, X (1930) 520-524 [5648]. The Library of Congress has transcripts of two MS. guides to special *fonds* in this archive: *Documentación de la Florida Occidental* (no. 5651); and *Corres. capitanes generales de Cuba* (no. 5652).

Many of the Hispanic American republics have archival societies and organs which pursue and publish researches indexing and cataloguing documents for the history of their respective countries, at Seville and elsewhere in Spain. Among others one should note in this respect the publications of the *Centro de Estudios Americanistas de Sevilla* and the *Instituto Histórico Hispano-Cubano*, the Spanish archival publication, *Revista de archivos, bibliotecas y museos*, and the publications of the *Instituto de Investigaciones Históricas*, of the *Facultad de¹ Filosofía y Letras, Universidad Nacional* (Buenos Aires).

[5649], vol. L of the *Publicaciones del Instituto de Investigaciones Históricas*, (see below, no. 5673).

In addition to the very general indications in the section for the Archives of the Indies in Shepherd's guide to American material in Spanish archives there are two particular guides to special categories of material relating to the history of the United States: Roscoe R. Hill, *Descriptive catalogue of the documents relating to the history of the United States in the Papeles Procedentes de Cuba deposited in the Archivo General de Indias at Seville* (Wash.: Carnegie Institution, 1916) [5650].　This is a thorough and painstaking catalogue, a model for this kind of work, of the most important *fonds* for the history of the United States at this archive.　It details, with *legajo* numbers, a mass of colonial papers dealing principally with Louisiana, Florida, and the Spanish-American frontier,[46] in the 18th and early 19th centuries, and has come to be indispensable to the investigator of those subjects.　The other special guide, not of a particular *fonds*, is C. E. Chapman, *Catalogue of the materials in the Archivo General de Indias for the history of the Pacific coast and the American southwest* (Berkeley, Calif., 1919) [5653].[47]

The *Archivo Histórico Nacional* at Madrid, the youngest of Spanish archives (founded 1850, but in activity really only since 1896) has not been so carefully cultivated by the guide-makers and cataloguers.　Aside from the general Spanish archival guide by Rodríguez Marín, with its section on the *Archivo Histórico Nacional*, and the very general suggestions of American material noted (without *legajo* numbers) in Shepherd, there are no printed catalogues or indexes for this important archive.[48]　The present archivist, Mr.

---

[46] When the *Papeles de Cuba* were shipped from Cuba to Spain lists were kept of the bundles and their titles.　Two such lists were copied in 1911 in Havana for the Carnegie Institution of Washington and are now in the Library of Congress: *Indice de la documentación de la Florida Occidental desde el año 1729 á 1823* [5651], with *legajo* numbers; and *Indice de la correspondencia de los capitanes generales de la Isla de Cuba, desde el año 1766 á 1823, Ramo de Guerra* [5652].　There is nothing in these not to be found in Hill's *Catalogue*.

[47] One should consult these catalogues to materials for the colonial history of Spain in North America in connection with H. E. Bolton's *Guide to materials for the history of the United States in the principal archives of Mexico* (no. 5674), for frequently the Mexican archives contain duplication of papers in the Spanish.

[48] A provisional catalogue, with some historical remarks, was printed in: G. Desdevises du Dézert, "Les archives historiques nationales de Madrid (historique et inventaire provisoire)", in *Bibliographie moderne*, V (1901) 19–46, 157–184 [5654].

Gómez del Campillo,[49] has prepared a typescript index to material for the history of the United States to 1800, a copy of which he generously furnished to the Library of Congress. This is the best thing of the kind, and is now being continued beyond the year 1800.[50] Julián Paz, *Catálogo de manuscritos de América existentes en la Biblioteca Nacional* (Madrid, 1933) [5656] contains a list of scattered MSS. relating to the United States, 1776–77, also to Cuba, and occasionally to relations with the United States regarding Cuba. These are in the Division of MSS. of the *Biblioteca Nacional* as distinct from the *Archivo Histórico Nacional* in the same building.

We know of no general attempt, similar to the English, Dutch, and French historical manuscripts commissions to survey, list, and index historical manuscripts in private hands in Spain.[51] The American items appearing in the few published catalogues of Spanish libraries are, of course, noted by Matteson (no. 5591); and there are some big collections of printed documents—*inédits*—for Spanish history; [52–53] but these deal little with our subject.

The Library of Congress has a collection of several hundred thousand pages of reproductions from Spanish archives of documents relating to the history of America.[54] A great deal of this concerns the history of Spanish colonization in territory now a part of the United States. Much of it concerns the early diplomatic relations of Spain and the United States. These reproductions consist of transcripts (both hand-written and typed), of photostats, and of photofilms in miniature on cinema film many of which have been enlarged

[49] Note also his "Chronological statement of papers and documents relative to Louisiana in the National historical archives of Madrid", *La. hist. soc. pub.*, IV (1908) 1124–1144 [5655].

[50] The *Archivo Histórico Nacional* has been enriched by the transfer of departmental records from a smaller state papers office, the *Archivo General Central de Alcalá de Henares*, which served as a depository after the *Archivo General de Simancas* had been filled up. José Torre Revello describes these deposits and transfers in *El Archivo General Central en Alcalá de Henares, reseña histórica y clasificación de sus fondos* (Buenos Aires, 1926) [5657].

[51] There are notes in Ulla Deibel's article "Literaturberichte, VII. Spanien und Portugal", in *Archiv. Zeitschrift*, 3d ser., V (1929) 218–248 [5658], which contains useful data on Spanish archives in general.

[52–53] For bibliography, see Sánchez Alonso (no. 4759), nos. 2893–2958.

[54] T. P. Martin, "Transcripts, facsimiles, and manuscripts in the Spanish language in the Library of Congress, 1929", *Hisp. Am. hist. rev.*, IX (1929) 243–246; and "Spanish archive materials and related materials in other national archives, copied for the Library of Congress, project "A" gift fund, 1927–1929", *ibid.*, X (1930) 95–98 [5659].

and printed.[55] The collection has been built up, at first in a fragmentary way, more recently according to a methodical plan. We need notice here only such reproductions as relate to the diplomatic history of the United States.

Archivo Histórico Nacional, Madrid

Photocopies of the diplomatic correspondence with Spanish diplomatic representatives in the United States, 1784–1861, together with other material relating to the United States and the American Colonies as far back as 1737. This material was photocopied following the indications in Mr. Gómez del Campillo's typescript guide, above mentioned [56] (no. 5655).

Archivo General de Indias, Seville

Photocopies of a great volume of the material from the *Papeles de Cuba* listed in Hill's *Catalogue* (no. 5650), namely the *legajos* listed in the footnote.[57] These comprise material from the archives of the offices of the governor of Louisiana, the commandant of Pensacola, and the captain general at Havana. They include documents dealing with the political, military, and economic affairs of the province;

[55] The library is proceeding with its program of enlarging and printing these films.

[56] Only those portions of this guide which extend to 1800 are in copy in the Library of Congress. Mr. Gómez del Campillo has expanded the guide beyond the year 1800. Its publication is greatly to be desired. The photocopies in the Library of Congress from the *Archivo Histórico Nacional*, Section *Estado*, are *legajos* nos.: 94, 105, 112, 114, 116, 118, 215, 745, 918–927, 2848, 2952, 3412, 3420, 3457, 3567, 3882–3902, 4062, 4068, 4072, 4079, 4101, 4116, 4119, 4143, 4164, 4168, 4199, 4200, 4202, 4203, 4206, 4210, 4211, 4215, 4220, 4224, 4232, 4233, 4246, 4250, 4255, 4256, 4268, 4280, 4281, 4284–4291, 4296, 5207–5210, 5537–5589 (5630–5632 in transcript only), 5633–5663, 6557, 6609, 6644, 6797. Of these *legajos*, numbers 4062–4246, 4268, 4280, 4281, 4284, and 6609 consist of correspondence (1773–1783) of the Spanish minister of state with the Spanish ambassador in Paris, and related documents dealing with the war between Spain and England. *Legajos* 5537–5589, 5630–5663 consist of the regular series of diplomatic correspondence with the Spanish diplomatic envoys in the United States, and related documents, 1797–1861. These photocopies now supplant certain transcripts made by Henry Adams from the diplomatic correspondence, 1800–1807, and other typescripts supplementary thereto, made later by one of the authors of the volume in the reader's hands, Mr. Bemis, both of which sets are in the Library of Congress. Exception should be made in reference to *legajos* 5630–5632 which are still in transcript only.

[57] *Legajos* from *Papeles de Cuba*, now in photocopies in the Library of Congress: 2, 21 (selection), 36–40, 102, 104, 149 B, 150–156, 158, 171, 203, 267, 569, 584, 593–595, 633, 638, 1319, 1335, 1336, 1377, 1387, 1394, 1395, 1409 (selections), 1425, 1432, 1436–1447, 1483, 1484, 1500–1502, 1550–1559, 1561–1575, 1708, 1737, 1750, 1789–1797, 1809, 1837, 1856, 1873–1877, 1898, 1900, 1931, 1944, 1945, 1950, 1958, 1963, 2343, 2351–2356, 2369–2375. There are also transcripts (selections) of *legajos* 11, 16, 17, 22, 70, 148, 149 A, 1354, 1355, 1368, 1375, 1376, 1393.

correspondence with the governors of Louisiana and the Floridas, with the diplomatic agents of Spain in the United States, and with the ministries in Spain, and others. They extend from about 1780 to 1820. There is also some correspondence of the consuls of Spain in France, Holland, and the United States, with the governors of Louisiana and the commandants of Pensacola, 1786 to 1816; and correspondence of Gen. Wilkinson with Spanish officials, and others, 1786–1809.

From this same archive, the Library also has photocopies from the *Audiencia de Santo Domingo*, of approximately the same period. The documents in this section of the archive are derived from the ministerial offices in Spain (especially Indies and the Treasury), and include among others, correspondence and documents regarding affairs in Louisiana and the Floridas. The Library also has extensive typescripts (Dunn transcripts) from various *audiencia* series at Seville (Guadalajara, Santo Domingo) and other transcripts which do not primarily relate to the diplomacy of the United States.

Another series of importance from this Archive is *Estado*, containing material concerning the large general relations of the United States to Spain and the Spanish in the New World during the period of the revolutions of the Spanish colonies in America (documents of about 1700 to 1836). The Library of Congress is including in its collections photostats of *legajos* 86–105 (formerly *América en General* nos. 1–20) from this series.

Archivo General de Simancas

Documents selected from the papers of the Spanish embassy at Paris, 1761–1783, relating to the War of American Independence and its antecedents.[58] Documents from the Foreign Office files [59]

---

[58] The Embassy papers (signed instructions and draft despatches) at Simancas, are duplicated by the Foreign Office files for the same business (signed despatches and draft instructions) now in the *Archivo Histórico Nacional* at Madrid. As noted above, Mr. Miguel Gómez del Campillo has compiled a typescript list of that portion of the Foreign Office deposit which includes the correspondence of Aranda, the Spanish ambassador at Paris, and Floridablanca, Spanish minister of foreign affairs, between 1775 and 1786 (no. 5655).

From Simancas then the Library of Congress has selections of the material relating to America from the following *legajos* of the diplomatic correspondence of the Spanish government with its Paris embassy, 1761–1783: Series *Estado, moderno* nos. 1715–1720, 1734, 1735–1740, 1742.

[59] Note that the *Francia* series at Simancas is Embassy papers (Foreign Office files are at the *Archivo Histórico Nacional*), but the *Inglaterra* series at Simancas is Foreign Office files.

deposited at Simancas, consisting of selections of American material, from the correspondence of Spain with its Embassy in England, 1761 to 1822, from the following *legajos*, series *Estado, moderno*, nos.: 2352, 2354–2357, 2360, 2361, 2363, 2364, 2676, 2677.

Similarly, material relating to America, selected from the diplomatic correspondence (Foreign Office files) of the Spanish government with its legation in Holland, 1776–1782, Series *Estado, moderno*, 2177–2180.

There is also some ancillary material [60] relating to Spanish colonial activities on the frontier of the United States, 1779–1804, viz: Series *Guerra, moderno, legajos* no. 6912–6917, 6921, 6922, 6928–6930, (all these are imperfect Cunningham transcripts) (see note 60); and films of 6913–6925, 6929, 6930, 7019–7026, 7029, 7030, 7041, 7042, 7044–7047, 7302, 7303.

Scattered through various American libraries are isolated originals, and series of transcripts, of a great deal of source material from Spanish archives. A chronological list of such pieces was compiled and published in 1910 by the Carnegie Institution of Washington: J. A. Robertson, *List of documents in Spanish archives relating to the history of the United States, which have been printed or of which transcripts are preserved in American libraries* (Wash., 1910) [5660]. Since then such collections have been built up apace. The Florida State Historical Society, for example, under the direction of the same diligent scholar, J. A. Robertson, has secured photocopies of practically all the MS. material in Spanish archives relating to the Floridas, to 1819.[61] The Newberry Library, at Chicago, has in the Ayer collection, probably three hundred thousand pages of transcripts from Spain, and documents from the Ramírez Library and elsewhere, for the history of California, Louisiana, and other Spanish parts of the United States.[62] The North Carolina Historical

---

[60] In addition to the Simancas photocopies above listed there is a series of films made of selected documents, relating to America, from the diplomatic correspondence of Spain, with its Embassy in England, 1480–1678, viz: *Estado, moderno, legajos* no. 303–306, 308–315, 984–987, 989–999, 1003, 1007–1012.

The above-mentioned photocopies from Simancas relating to the diplomacy of the American Revolution displace several thousands of unreliable typescripts, irresponsibly and inaccurately made, known as the "Cunningham transcripts."

[61] Robertson, *Spanish manuscripts of the Florida State Historical Society* (no. 5540).

[62] R. D. Hussey, "Manuscript Hispanic Americana in the Ayer collection of the Newberry Library, Chicago", *Hisp. Am. hist. rev.*, X (1930) 113–118 [5661].

Commission has a collection of transcripts and photostats from Spanish archives.[63]

Portugal

" The beginnings of the Portuguese royal archives are lost in the dusk of history." [64] The present national archives (*Archivo Nacional da Torre do Tombo*) is the counterpart, for that kingdom, of the English Record Office. The standard description of its organization and contents is Pedro A. de Azevedo and Antonio Baião, *O Archivo da Torre do Tombo, sua historia, corpos que o compõem e organisação* (Lisbon, 1905) [5664]. A less detailed but useful later guide is A. Mesquita de Figueiredo, *Arquivo nacional da Torre do Tombo* (Lisbon, 1912) [5665]. V. S. Robaina, "Archivos Portugueses ", *Revista histórica* (Montevideo) IX (1919) 629–638 [5666] gives a brief survey of the several archives of Portugal. There are no adequate catalogues, but there are a number of inventories and lists of special *fonds*, none of which is of use to the student of American diplomacy.[65] There is no guide to material for American history in the Portuguese archives.

The contents of the Portuguese archives for the student of diplomatic history are best described in Antonio Ferrão, *Da importancia dos documentos diplomáticos em história, estudo sucinto, de alguns arquivos diplomáticos estrangeiros e nacionais* (Coimbra, 1917) [5669], reprinted from the *Trabalhos da Academia de Sciencias de Portugal*, v. VI. In addition to its description of diplomatic material in Portuguese archives, this pamphlet is the only publication which we know of that attempts a general essay on the archival sources for diplomatic history in general.[66] The main body of diplo-

[63] See its *Eleventh biennial report*, 1924–1926 (Raleigh, 1927), p. 22; and *Twelfth biennial report*, 1926–1928 (Raleigh, 1928), p. 16 [5662], for descriptions of the Spanish material in the archives of the Commission.

[64] Carl Erdmann, " Vom Archivwesen Portugals ", *Archiv. Zeitschrift*, 3d ser., V (1929) 197–217 [5663], a highly useful summary of Portuguese archives and *Archivwesen*.

[65] See " Some Portuguese archives ", *Inst. hist. research bul.*, II (1924) 4–7 [5667], which lists them; and gives a few notes on other Portuguese archives. Antonio Ferrão, *Os arquivos e as bibliotecas em Portugal* (Coimbra, 1920) [5668], an official report on the Portuguese archives, contains a chapter on inventories and catalogues.

[66] It is a plea for a more general realization of the importance of diplomatic correspondence as historical sources, and for their extensive publication everywhere, with brief analyses of the organization of diplomatic archives in France, England, Italy, the Vatican, Belgium, The Netherlands, Germany, Austria-Hungary, and Spain. It pleads

matic correspondence of Portugal for the eighteenth and nineteenth centuries is in the archives of the Ministry of Foreign Affairs, in Lisbon, but it is not complete, thanks to the presumption of officials in carrying away official papers connected with their incumbency, and because of some removals to the *Archivo da Torre do Tombo*, in the same capital. Mr. Ferrão lists important MS. collections of various Portuguese ministers and diplomatists in the *Biblioteca Nacional de Lisboa*, and the *Biblioteca de Ajuda*. The generally serene character of a century and a half of Portuguese-American relations possibly explains the lack of any mention by Mr. Ferrão of material relating to American diplomacy. A few MSS. in Portuguese libraries relating to the United States are listed by Matteson (no. 5591).

Hispanic America

There is to date no general inventory of the content of Hispanic-American public archives.[67] Nor is there a general guide to MS. material in Hispanic American archives relating to the history of the United States, despite the crying need.[68] The development of the several South American archives has not been uniform. For several of the states of Hispanic America there are, to our knowledge, no guides to public archives. However, the rapidly awakening interest in archives, together with the well-known bibliographical propensities of Hispanic American scholars,[69] may at almost any time make the above remarks obsolete. We indicate such guides and catalogues as are available, making no mention of states for which we have observed no aids of this nature:

particularly for a more enlightened archival policy in Portugal, especially in the archives of the Foreign Office: opening the archives to historical research, up to the year 1858; preparation and publication of catalogues and indexes of all the Portuguese archives dealing with diplomatic history; publication of instructions and other diplomatic correspondence. The diplomatic archives of Portugal are open only to 1815, though subject to some conditions, series from 1815 to 1840 may be examined (see *Inst. hist. research bul.*, II, no. 4 (1924), 6).

[67] José Torre Revello made some interesting suggestions on supplying such, in *Los archivos de la República Argentina* (Seville, 1925) [5670], reprinted from the *Boletín del Centro de Estudios Americanistas de Sevilla*, año XII, nos. 94–96 (1925) 105–132. There are some brief but valuable notes by Ulla Deibel, "Die lateinamerikanischen Freistaaten", in *Archiv. Zeitschrift*, 3d ser., V (1929) 252–254 [5671].

[68] C. E. Chapman, "South America as a field for an historical survey", *Am. hist. assoc. ann. rep.*, for 1916, v. I (1919) 201–209 [5672].

[69] The remarkable work, and publications, of the Department of History of the University of Buenos Aires is described by J. A. Robertson, "The publications of the Instituto de Investigaciones Históricas de la Facultad de Filosofía y Letras", *Hisp. Am. hist. rev.*, X (1930) 101–113 [5673].

Mexico

The archives of the Foreign Office of Mexico, separately housed in that department, are not arranged in the conventional order of foreign office files, *i. e.*, diplomatic correspondence, instructions and despatches, classified by countries and proceeding chronologically. Instead, there was at first an attempt to classify diplomatic correspondence and foreign office papers by subdivisions of the Foreign Office, *i.e.*: *Political Department*, with geographical sections (North, Central, and South America), each section subdivided into divisions such as treaties, boundaries, uncivilized Indians, extradition, claims; reception, retirement, and correspondence with the diplomatic agents of countries named in each section; appointment of diplomatic, consular, and secret agents, and their correspondence. *Commercial Department. Chancellery.* Each section had a separate MS. index of its groups of papers, with separate indexes by names of foreign countries. Such was the general arrangement when Professor H. E. Bolton compiled, for the Carnegie Institution of Washington, a *Guide to materials for the history of the United States in the principal archives of Mexico* (Wash., 1913) [5674] (see p. 221–223).[70] But even then a plan of reclassification of the archives of the Foreign Office on a subject basis was in process.[71] A reclassification has now been carried through for the archives of the Foreign Office (*Relaciones Exteriores*) and Treasury (*Hacienda*), the subject division being recatalogued on a decimal system.[72] This means that the old

---

[70] For special subjects see: H. E. Bolton, "Material for southwestern history in the central archives of Mexico", *Am. hist. rev.*, XIII (1908) 510–527 [5675]; F. V. Scholes, "Manuscripts for the history of New Mexico in the National Library in Mexico City", *New Mex. hist. rev.*, III (1928) 301–323 [5676]. Everything listed in this last is now in the Library of Congress in photostat form.

[71] W. R. Manning, "The Mexican foreign office archives", *Pan American union bulletin*, XXXVII (1913) 657–661 [5677].

[72] *Cuadro de clasificación decimal e instrucciones para la tramitación y archivo de los documentos de la secretaría de relaciones exteriores*, published by the "Ministerio de Relaciones Exteriores" (Mexico, 1929) [5678]. For a description of the reform, see E. A. Chávez and others, *Manual de organización de archivos* (Mexico City: Departamento de Approvisionamientos Generales, 1920) [5679]. We understand, however, that only a small portion of the documents listed in the Bolton *Guide* for *Relaciones Exteriores* are at present available. All the material of the colonial period has been transferred to the *Archivo General de la Nación*, while much of the later material is not as yet listed under the new system of classification. There is, however, a copy of the Bolton *Guide* in the archive of *Relaciones Exteriores,* and investigators wishing to consult documents listed by Bolton have only to consult this archive copy to obtain the new classification number. The officials of the archive make a conscientious effort to annotate the *Guide* as the work of reclassification progresses. The materials now accessible have been entered in the specific categories in the bibliography given in part I of this *Guide*.

numbered series of diplomatic correspondence and cognate papers by which the historian is able carefully to trace a diplomatic relation in all its ramification, has been broken up, and reassigned into subject groups, violating the *principe de provenance*, so sacred to archivists. Archives are supposed to reflect the history of the organ of government from which their documents emanate.[73] This arbitrary rearrangement by the decimal system and subject index turns the archives into a museum. Unless some sort of key-index between the old classification by countries and the new system exists one cannot be sure that he has reassembled the original documents in the original provenance because one cannot imagine the various subjects into which it has been classified. It is like separating the pages of a book from their ordered sequence and then trying to put the book together again in alphabetical order of the index subjects.

The investigator must not overlook the important section War and Navy (*Guerra y Marina*) and other departments (*Gobernación*, *Hacienda*), the only printed index to which is Bolton's *Guide*.

The Library of Congress, subject to some supervision and consequent restriction from complete reproduction, and excluding some divisions (on which recataloguing was under way),[74] has photostated the archives of the Mexican Foreign Office insofar as they relate to the United States, 1821–1890, and insofar as the material can be located in the decimal reclassification. This includes the material listed in Bolton's *Guide* (no. 5674), 221–268, and a great deal not listed. The problem of relating the old archival indications to the new system is by no means easy. Little more can be said here than to refer the invesigator to the MS. inventories of the photostats in the Library of Congress, or to the MS. indexes of the Mexican archives themselves and to the card-catalogues now in process in the archives of the departments of foreign affairs and treasury, on the scheme of their reclassification.[75] This unique classification,

---

[73] " . . . No archivist, even in the cases where these documents have been taken over direct from the original owners and custody has consequently been preserved unbroken, could possibly allow full archive value to documents which have been violently torn from the connexion in which they were originally preserved, a connexion which in nine cases out of ten is important, if not vital, for the full understanding of their significance." cf. Hilary Jenkinson, *A manual of archive administration* (Oxford, 1922) [5680], 42.

[74] The Library of Congress has a list of the restricted material.

[75] The photostat collection in the Library of Congress of documents from the *Secretaría de Relaciones Exteriores* of Mexico is very voluminous. The peculiar nature of the archival numbering system employed by the Mexican Government makes it impracticable to indicate even in an abridged manner the precise identity of these photostats. They

while promising certain advantages as to subject indexing, places on the historian a handicap [76] in following the consecutive diplomatic history of Mexico with a particular country.

We know of no other printed analyses of Mexican archives, public or private. Such may be expected in the near future, in the newly established (1930) *Boletín del Archivo General de la Nación* (Mexico). Plans are said to be on foot for publication of calendars of materials in the Foreign Office according to the new decimal arrangement.

Cuba

The history of the Cuban archives, with lists of periodical deposits, is set forth in Joaquín Llaverías, *Historia de los archivos de Cuba* (Havana, 1912) [5681]. Previously there had appeared L. M. Pérez's *Guide to the materials for American history in Cuban archives* (Wash.: Carnegie Institution, 1907) [5682], which has little to do, of course, with the history of *Cuba Libre*.

The *Boletín del Archivo Nacional* (Havana, 1902–) contains inventories of various *fonds*, of which the following should be noted here: Joaquín Llaverías, " Inventario general del archivo de la delegación del partido revolucionario cubano en Neuva York (1892–1898 (no. 3433). The Cuban Academy of History has recently (July 3, 1930) received a valuable collection of historical documents from the private archives of the first president, Don Manuel de Céspedes y Céspedes.[77]

Argentine Republic

Some very summary indexes have been published for the archives of the Argentine Republic. The national archives of that nation are " the largest, most important and significant of South America." [78] *Los archivos de la República Argentina*, by José Torre

---

cover the years 1821–1890 and include almost all on the Texas question and Mexican war, filibustering, border difficulties, and numerous important treaty negotiations.

[76] The disadvantages of this to the investigator appear also when he wishes to relate Mexican diplomatic sources to the corresponding sources of another, conventionally classified, archive, say the United States, Great Britain, or France.

[77] *Pan American Union bul.*, LXIV (Sept. 1930), 967 [5683].

[78] Herbert Koch, " Das argentinische Hauptstaats Archiv in Buenos Aires ", *Minerva-Zeitschrift*, I (1925), 131–133 [5684]. There is a short but informative report on the national archives of the Argentine in J. J. Biedma, "Archivo General de la Nación", *Rev. derecho, hist. y letras*, LI (Buenos Aires, 1915), 237–253 [5685]. This archive has undertaken the publication of a series of source material, which is described by the same author, " Publicaciones del Archivo General de la Nación Argentina ", *ibid.*, III (1927) 39–41.

Revello (no. 5670) is a trial index which dismisses the archives of the nation in a summary of two pages. There is a five-page general inventory of the national archives, "Archivo General de la Nación, República Argentina, inventario de índices parciales", in the *Boletín del Instituto de Investigaciones Históricas* (published by the "Facultad de Filosofía y Letras" of the "Universidad de Buenos Aires"), II (1924) 364-369 [5686]. A much more detailed catalogue of the archives of the Argentine Foreign Office appears in that ministry's official publication *Catálogo de la biblioteca, mapoteca y archivo* (Buenos Aires, 1910, 3d edition) [5687]. It has big gaps. Material for relations with the United States is summarily indicated.

Since 1928 there have been appearing in the *Bol. Inst. Investigaciones Hist.* (no. 5686), some indexes of *fonds* in the Archivo General de la Nación, República Argentina, viz.: " Indices de gobierno, correspondiente á los años 1810-1812 ", in v. III-IV (1924-1925) *passim.* [5688] and " Indice de decretos, órdenes, reglamentos, 1813-1821 ", in v. VII- (1928-(in progress)) *passim.* [5689], from the *División Nacional, sección gobierno.*

This same Institute is publishing a series of inventories of the various provincial archives of the Argentine.[79]

Brazil

For Brazil there is a very general indication of the various *fonds* in the National Archives: " Catalogo dos livros da secção historica do Archivo Nacional precedido do respectivo plano ", in *Publicações do Archivo Nacional*, XIII (Rio de Janeiro, 1913) 5-124 [5691]. We have not been able to discover anything in the way of an index to those archives for the national period.[80]

For comments on earliest Brazilian diplomatic archives, see Mario de Vasconcellos (formerly Director of the Itamaraty Archives), *Motivo de historia diplomática do Brasil* (Rio de Janeiro, 1930) [5693],

---

[79] See also Herbert Koch, "Die argentinischen Provinzialarchive ", *Minerva-Zeitschrift,* III (1926), 119-125 [5690].

[80] There is a catalogue of royal letters, decrees, notices, etc., for the colonial period, 1662-1821, " Catalogo das cartas régias, provisões, alvarás, avisos, portarias, etc., de 1662 a 1821, existentes no Archivo Nacional ", in the first volume of *Publicações do Archivo Publico Nacional* (Rio de Janeiro, 1886; reprinted in 1922) ; and an "Indice da correspondencia da corte de Portugal com os vice-reis do Brasil no Rio de Janeiro de 1763 a 1807 ", in *ibid.,* III (1901) c, 204 p. [5692].

225–251: "Os archivos do Itamaraty." The Itamaraty Archives comprise the foreign office archives.

Chile

The Archivo Nacional of Chile was created out of the MSS. division of the National Library in 1925.[81] To date (1934) no catalogues, indexes, or inventories of *fonds* have been published.

Colombia

There is an index to the national archives of Colombia by F. J. Vergara y Velasco, *República de Colombia, Archivos Nacionales, índice analítico, metódico y descriptivo* (Bogotá: Imprenta nacional, 1913) [5697]. It covers only the colonial period, 1544–1819; but sequels were promised. Some indications of the diplomatic correspondence of Colombia in the first years, during the revolution and the period of the establishment of independence are given in the bibliographical appendix to Zubieta (no. 1057).

Paraguay

The "Instituto de Investigaciones Históricas" of the University of Buenos Aires (Universidad Nacional) has published a history and description: Juan F. Pérez, *Los Archivos de la Asunción del Paraguay* (Buenos Aires, 1923) [5698], which has short appraisals of the size of the various *fonds*, but no catalogue of contents.[82]

Peru

The "Indice del Archivo Nacional del Perú", which is appearing in instalments in the *Revista del Archivo Nacional del Perú*, v. II–, 1921– [5699] has so far concerned only the colonial period.

---

[81] A *Memoria preliminar* on plans for the archives was published by the Ministry of Public Instruction at Santiago de Chile, in 1926 (see also the *Boletín del Instituto de Investigaciones Históricas* (no. 5686), IV (1926) 570–581 [5694], which gives extracts from the *Memoria*). T. T. Ojeda describes the MSS. division (and its contents) of the National Library of Chile, in "La sección de manuscritos de la Biblioteca Nacional de Chile", *Hisp. Am. hist. rev.*, IV (Feb. 1921), 156–197 [5695], written in Spanish, and followed by an English translation. A brief account of the history and organization of the archives is given in "Archivo Histórico Nacional", *Revista chilena de historia y geografía*, LI, no. 55 (1926) 5–33 [5696]. Beginning with v. LIII, no. 57 (1927), this *Revista*, published by the Sociedad Chilena de Historia y Geografía (Santiago de Chile), became the organ of the *Archivo Histórico Nacional*, and is now issued jointly by the two organizations.

[82] The archival organ, *Archivo Nacional* (Asunción) is principally devoted to publication of documents.

Venezuela

The *Boletín del Archivo Nacional* (estab. 1923) (Caracas) contains archival indexes, devoted to the contents of the new national archives, inaugurated in 1911; but so far this has not touched the subject of foreign affairs. There is an *Indice del archivo del General Miranda* (Caracas, 1927) [5700], published by the "Ministerio de Instrucción Pública" of Venezuela. The MSS. themselves are now being published (no. 1126 above).

France

The public archives of France [83] are admirably organized and catalogued and, to a great extent, indexed [84] for everything but American history. The Department of Historical Research of the Carnegie Institution of Washington has been for some years engaged in the preparation of a guide to MS. materials relating to American history in the libraries and archives of Paris. One of the volumes dealing with the libraries of Paris has been published: W. G. Leland, *Guide to materials for American history in the libraries and archives of Paris.* v. I. *Libraries* (Wash., 1932) [5704]. The other volumes of this guide have not yet been completed.[85] Consequently investigators into American historical MSS. in France must use the various French catalogues, which naturally make no special classification of American material. For the student of the foreign relations of the United States the archives of the Ministry of Foreign Affairs (*Archives du Ministère des Affaires Étrangères*) at the *Quai d'Orsay* are of supreme importance. They

[83] For detailed description see C. V. Langlois and Henri Stein, *Les archives de l'histoire de France* (Paris, 1891) [5701].

[84] For statements of catalogues and indexes supplementing the lists in Langlois and Stein (no. 5701), see *État des inventaires des archives nationales au 1er janvier 1914* (Paris, 1914) [5702], published by the "Ministère de l'Instruction Publique et des Beaux Arts"; and Robert Doré, *État des inventaires et répertoires des archives nationales, départementales, communales et hospitalières de la France à la date du 1er décembre 1919* (Paris, 1921) [5703], which is reprinted from the *Revue des bibliothèques,* v. XXIX, 1919; also supplementary items 1919–1921, *ibid.,* XXXI (1921) 174–280; and the *Répertoire bibliographique de l'histoire de France,* 1923 (no. 4738), section on "Archives et bibliothèques."

[85] Subsequent volumes (probably three in number) are in preparation. They deal with the *Archives Nationales,* Ministries of War, Marine, and Colonies, and one volume will be devoted largely to the Ministry of Foreign Affairs alone. Much material on the United States is to be found indicated in J.-E. Roy, *Rapport sur les archives de France relatives à l'histoire du Canada (Ottawa, 1911)* [5704a], which is no. 6 of the *Publications des archives du Canada.*

are not wholly inventoried, and some of the parts not inventoried are those which touch diplomacy with the United States. The notable *Inventaire sommaire des archives du Département des Affaires Étrangères, Mémoires et documents* (Paris: Imprimerie Nationale, 1883–96, 3 v.) [5705], and *Correspondance politique* (Paris: Imprimerie Nationale, 1903–20, 3 v.) [5706], both published by the "Ministère des Affaires Étrangères", note contents of these two important *fonds* to the year 1830. The *Inventaire* of the series *Correspondance politique* takes up the various countries alphabetically, and in these 3 volumes (v. I and II, pts. 1 and 2) extends through "Espagne" only. The next volume, containing the inventory for the United States, is now in page proof, and covers the period, 1774–1830. In the archives of the French foreign office there are the following great *fonds* or major divisions of diplomatic documents:

1. **Mémoires et Documents,** which comprise papers of all kinds other than correspondence of strictly diplomatic officials. This is a most valuable repository, particularly because of the habit of Frenchmen, official and private, of writing *mémoires* and *rapports* on phases of foreign affairs. There are two prime series in this section which interest us:

a. **Mémoires et Documents, Amérique.** This consists of fifty volumes relating to the two Americas during the French régime and thereafter (1682–1830). They relate principally to the diplomacy of colonial rivalry from the 16th to the 19th centuries and to the independence and development of the Hispanic American republics, and are inventoried in the *Inventaire sommaire* (no. 5705), *Mémoires et Documents*, v. II, *Fonds divers*, 41–52; and v. III, *supplément*, 81–90.

b. **Mémoires et Documents, États-Unis.** Similarly are inventoried, *ibid.*, v. II, 219–223; v. III, 122–124, eighteen volumes of documents relating to the United States, 1766–1830; the catalogue also notes four volumes (v. 18–21) of documents dated after 1830, the nature of which is not indicated. The documents relate to: the diplomatic background of the American Revolution, French policy during the Revolution, the peace negotiations of 1782–3, commerce, international debts, Franco-American relations, 1795–1830, etc.

c. **Mémoires et Documents, France.** Similarly are inventoried, *ibid.*, v. I. This contains volumes of divers material much of which bears on the United States and is of prime importance.

In addition to these series, *Amérique*, *États-Unis*, and *France*, the investigator would do well to run his eye, for American material, over the series *Angleterre*, *Espagne*, *Hollande*, *Prusse*, etc., inventoried in the same volume.

2. Correspondance Politique, and Correspondance Politique Supplémentaire.

This contains the regular series of diplomatic correspondence, instructions, and despatches, between the French Foreign Office and its diplomatic representatives in the United States, and separately as a supplementary series, the ancillary correspondence of the Legation, often very important. The *Inventaire sommaire* (no. 5705) devotes three volumes to inventorying, in alphabetic order, these series: Allemagne, Angleterre, Argentine (République), Autriche, Bade, Bâle, Bavière, Brésil, Brunswick-Hanovre, Chili, Cologne, Colombie, Corse, Danemark, Dantzig, Espagne. We have noted that a volume for *États-Unis*, the publication of which American investigators eagerly await, is still in proof. These inventories extend to the year 1830. For the period after 1830 there is no guide nor catalogue. The investigator would, however, expect to go forward chronologically in the same *fonds* and series. The Texas series should be included here. The Library of Congress has for some years past been engaged in collecting transcripts and facsimiles of the *fonds*, *Mémoires et Documents*, series *Amérique*, and series *États-Unis;* and of the *fonds*, *Correspondance Politique*, series *États-Unis* and *États-Unis supplémentaire*. See section Ia, b, and c below.

In addition to the purely American series in the Foreign Office archives, one may have reason to consult the series of diplomatic correspondence (*Correspondance Politique*), and the *Mémoires et Documents*, for various other countries,[86] *Espagne*, *Prusse*, *Autriche*, *Danemark*, etc. Again, the archives of the other ministries, particularly of Marine [87] (which includes colonial affairs [88] to 1894), and

---

[86] See *Inventaire sommaire* (no. 5705). For printed Instructions for these countries, see *Recueil des instructions* (no. 5429). For list of the calendars of particular collections, see Doré (no. 5703), and Langlois and Stein (no. 5701), 47–50.

[87] See *Etat sommaire des Archives de la Marine antérieures à la révolution* (Paris, 1898) [5707], prepared by Didier Neuville; and *Inventaire des Archives de la Marine, service général* (Paris, 1885–1914, 7 v.) [5708], compiled by Didier Neuville (first 6 volumes) and G. Bourgin (1914 volume); and Charles Braibant, *L'état présent des archives et des bibliothèques de la Marine* (Besançon, 1921) [5709], which is reprinted from the periodical *Bibliographie moderne*, XX (1920–1921) 113–137. *Inventaire sommaire des archives historiques (archives anciennes)—correspondance* (Paris, 1898–1930,

War. These are remoyed from the respective ministries when considered as no longer of political importance and deposited in the National Archives, the ministries retaining control over them—as distinct from control by the National Archives where they lie—for documents dated after 1814. Investigators wishing to look into these *fonds* after that date must seek permission from the ministry which retains control. All documents released to the control of the National Archives are open to perusal.

The entire archives of the Foreign Office are kept in the separate custody of the Foreign Office, *Quai d'Orsay*, where they are understood to be open to the investigator to 1871.

The provincial, or departmental, archives, and the communal records of France are numerous and voluminous. A complete list of inventories, lists, catalogues, etc., to 1919, for these archives, appears in Langlois and Stein (no. 5701) to 1891 *ca.*, and Doré (no. 5703) (to 1919).

There is a monumental *Catalogue général des manuscrits des bibliothèques publiques des départements* (Paris, 1849–85, 7 v. of the 1st series; 1886–1923, 47 v. of the 2d series) [5716], published under the auspices of the " Ministère de l'Instruction Publique "; as are also the following: *Catalogue général des manuscrits des bibliothèques publiques de France: Université de Paris et universités des départements* (Paris, 1918) [5717]; *Catalogue général des manuscrits des bibliothèques publiques de France: Paris, Bibliothèque de l'Institut, ancien et nouveau fonds* (Paris, 1928) [5718], by M. Bouteron and J. Tremblot; and *Catalogue général des manuscrits des bibliothèques publiques de France: Sociétés savants*, t. I (Paris, 1931) [5719], containing Amiens, Poitiers, Evreux, Montpellier, Nancy,

---

7 v.) [5710] ; and *Inventaire sommaire des archives historiques (archives modernes)* (Paris, 1905) [5711], both published by the "Archives de la Guerre."

88 W. G. Leland, " Les sources de l'histoire américaine (période de la colonisation française) à Paris ", *Rev. hist. moderne,* III (1928), 297–299 [5712]. For history of archives in the French colonies, see Paul Roussier, " Le dépôt des papiers publics des colonies, *ibid.,* IV (1929), 241–262 [5713]. *Calendar of manuscripts in Paris archives and libraries relating to the history of the Mississippi Valley to 1803,* ed. by N. M. Miller Surrey (Mrs. F. M. Surrey) (Wash.: Carnegie Institution, 1926–28, 2 v.) [5714]. Mr. Wirth, formerly of the Ministry of the Colonies, made a MS. calendar: *Manuscrits de l'inventaire sommaire de la correspondance générale de la Louisiane* [5715] giving an inventory of *Correspondance générale* (C13 A), to 1758, transferred to the *Archives Nationales* some years ago. The Wirth calendar was not so transferred.

and Paris. The MS. material relating to the diplomatic history of
the United States in these archives and libraries is very small, and
may be picked out in Matteson's well-indexed *List of manuscripts
concerning American history in European libraries* (no. 5591). The
Paris libraries, notably the *Bibliothèque Nationale* and its rich MS.
deposits are not all included in the above-mentioned catalogues.
These are combed for American MS. material in Leland's *Guide* (no.
5704). See also Bibliothèque Nationale, *Catalogue général des manuscrits français. Table générale alphabétique des anciens et nouveaux
fonds* (*nos. 1–33264*) *et des nouvelles acquisitions* (*nos. 1–10000*), by
A. Vidier and P. Perrier (Paris, 1931–1933, 2 v. (in progress))
[5720], I: A–B; II: C–D.

An official commission, mostly of distinguished historical scholars,
established by the historian and statesman, Guizot, in 1834, and since
1881 known as the *Comité des Travaux Historiques et Scientifiques*,
under the *Ministère de l'Instruction Publique et des Beaux-Arts*, as-
sists the direction and superintendence of researches and publications of unprinted MSS. relating to the history of France. Its
publications [89] are the best guide to the private MS. collections in
France, but they reveal little which bears on the history of American
diplomacy.

I. Transcripts and Facsimiles in the Library of Congress

Special note should be made of extensive collections of transcripts
and facsimiles in the Library of Congress from French archives and
libraries. A great part of these relate to diplomatic history. The
collections began with the acquisition 1898–1906, of the B. F. Stevens
Indexes, Facsimiles, Transcripts relating to the French Alliance,
1778–1784, and Peace Transcripts, 1782–1784.[90] As noted above,
p. 884, these Stevens transcripts and facsimiles are reproductions of
documents selected from the archives by Mr. Stevens. The three
collections have now been broken up and filed according to their

---

[89] Ministère de l'Instruction Publique et des Beaux-Arts, Comité des Travaux Historiques et Scientifiques, *Collection des documents inédits sur l'histoire de France* (Paris,
1836–) [5721].

[90] *Catalogue index of manuscripts in the archives of England, France, Holland, and
Spain, relating to America, 1763 to 1783* [5722] ; *Facsimiles of manuscripts in European
archives relating to America, 1773–1783* [5723] ; *Transcripts relating to the peace negotiations of 1782–1783*, between the United States and Great Britain, and *Transcripts relating
to the French alliance, 1778–1784* [5724].

original archival designations and provenance. They thus have become the basis of an attempt, as resources permit, to complete transcripts of the entire volumes from which Stevens made selections. The Library now has the following reproductions:

a. From the Archives du Ministère des Affaires Étrangères:

Transcripts and facsimiles—France, *Affaires Étrangères: Correspondance Politique, Angleterre*, vols. 508–523 (1775–1777) (photofilms and enlargements), and 515–519, 521–526, 528–529, 536–545 (selections, from Stevens transcripts). *Correspondance Politique, Espagne*, vols. 583, 586–588, 606–609 (1777, 1782). *Correspondance Politique, Etats-Unis*,[91] vols. 1–79 (1774–1822); and *Correspondance Politique, Etats-Unis, supplémentaire* (1777–1814), 1–8, 10–33, 36–38 (films and prints). *Mémoires et Documents, Amérique*, vols. 1–18, 20–22, 24, 25, 33 (comprising documents anterior to 1814). *Mémoires et Documents, Etats-Unis*, vols. 1–10, 14, 15, 17, 18 (comprising documents anterior to 1814). *Mémoires et Documents, France*, vols. 140, 410, 446, 463, 518, 525, 530, 531, 535, 565, 566, 582, 584, 586, 587, 792, 1258, 1276, 1351, 1352, 1353, 1385, 1387, 1389, 1425, 1426, 1427, 1770, 1786, 1794, 1806, 1809, 1888, 1969, 1990–1992, 1994, 1996, 2005–2028, 2031, 2034–2036, 2100. (Selections of American material. Films and prints.) Main headings in this series, since 1776, are: Commerce, neutrality, prizes, etc.

b. From the Archives Nationales

A great amount of material relating to French colonies in America, which touches on international relations at many angles. The pieces already transcribed and in the possession of the Library of Congress are checked in Surrey (no. 5714). But one should note accessions since the date of publication of Surrey's *Guide*, 2 vols., 1926–1928.

A voluminous collection of facsimiles of records of French naval operations during the war of American independence. These are indexed on cards and inventory sheets in the Manuscript Division of the Library.

---

[91] Photocopying of this series (with *Mémoires et Documents*) is to extend through 1830. For printed extracts from this series, *Etats-Unis*, also *Espagne, Hollande*, etc.; and similarly from *Mémoires et Documents;* and from other French series, for the period 1775–1784, see Doniol (no. 40). The correspondence of the French Ministers to the United States, 1791 to 1797, is edited by Turner (no. 476).

c. From the Bibliothèque Nationale and other Paris libraries: Arsenal (Archives of the Bastille), Institut, Mazarine, Museum, and Sainte Geneviève.

All the original material touching the history of the United States and preceding English colonies. The content of this is indicated in Leland's *Guide* (no. 5704). There are also some scattered pieces (photostated) from libraries at Avignon, Carpentras, Lyons, Marseilles, Toulon, most of which are indicated in Matteson's *Guide* (no. 5591).

The Bancroft transcripts (in the New York Public Library) from the French and other foreign office archives, relate to the diplomacy of the American Revolution. See Greene and Morris (no. 5531). The Jared Sparks transcripts in Harvard College Library (no. 5543) touch the same sources.

The Netherlands

The public records of the Kingdom of The Netherlands are adequately stored and indexed in the model *Rijksarchief*, or national state archive, at The Hague.[92] The archives of the Foreign Office as well as of other political departments of the Confederation and later monarchy may be found there, where they are available without restriction to historical investigators, up to the date line of 1878. In the case of the records of the Confederation, the peculiar nature of the Dutch constitution of that time gave increased significance to provincial affairs in the history of Dutch diplomacy. The archives of the seven provinces are in each case well organized. Inventories, lists, indexes, and calendars of *fonds* (including acquisitions of private papers) in national, provincial, and other archives, are to be found in the annual reports published by the *Rijksarchief: (Verslagen omtrent's rijks oude archieven)*, 1878– (The Hague, 1879– (in progress)) [5728].[93] Volumes XLI, pt. 1 (1918) 291–469; XLIV, pt. 1, 1921 (1923) 111–240, and XLVI, pt. 1, 1923 (1924) 174–207, contain full inventories of the various series of records of the Foreign Office (*De archieven van het Departement van Buitenlandsche*

---

[92] For historical sketch see Th. Morren, " Het Rijksarchief te 's-Gravenhage ", *Nederl. Archievenblad*, XVI (1908), 28–44 [5725]. For description, with photographs and diagrams, see A. Loran, " Het Algemeen Rijksarchief te 's-Gravenhage ", *ibid.*, XXIII (1915), 36–44 [5726]. For the Republic, see T. H. F. van Riemsdijk, *De griffie van Hare Hoog Mogenden* (The Hague, 1885) [5727].

[93] See also *Inventarissen van Rijks- en andere archieven van rijkswege uitgegeven*, I, 1928– (The Hague, 1929 (to 1933, 4 v.)) [5729], formerly included in the *Verslagen* . . .

Zaken), and of the various Dutch legations. Beginning 1928 the archival inventories [94] are printed together each year in separate volumes *Inventarissen* (no. 5729). The Association of Dutch Archivists is planning a general guide to Dutch state archives.[95] A particular guide to the *Rijksarchief* is *The general state archives and their contents* (The Hague, 1932) [5730], a revised edition translated into English, of a survey of the contents of the general state archives which was published in the *Verslagen omtrent 's rijks oude archieven* (no. 5728), v. XLIX, no. 1, 1926 (The Hague, 1927), 87–160.

The reports also list the contents of new acquisitions which are being continually made, including private papers [96] that come in. Among these there is a collection of particular importance to early Dutch-American relations and to the history of American diplomacy: the papers of C. W. F. Dumas, the first agent of the United States in the Netherlands (see *Verslagen* (no. 5728), XLI, pt. 1 (1918) 481–503, for inventory ("Beschrijving eener verzameling stukken, afkomstig van C. W. F. Dumas")) [5731].

The Library of Congress has a complete record, on films (enlarged prints in some parts) of the diplomatic correspondence of The Netherlands in the United States, 1783–1879, including despatches (from Foreign Office papers) and instructions (from legation papers), and ancillary documents, together with miscellaneous material relating to Dutch policy and the American Revolution, 1777–1783, all photographed in the *Rijksarchief*. It also has facsimiles of the papers of C. W. F. Dumas,[97] insofar as they relate to the United States. These include his notable 1,000-page letterbook, kept by him during his experience as American agent.

D. M. Matteson (no. 5591) notes the American MS. pieces which are indicated in the published catalogues of the various Dutch libraries. For private collections in The Netherlands, one may consult the publications of the Advisory Committee for National Historical Publications (*Commissie van Advies voor 's Rijks Geschied-*

---

[94] The papers of the Dutch admiralty colleges in the *Rijksarchief* are inventoried in J. de Hulu, *De archieven der admiraliteitscolleges* (The Hague, 1924) [5729a].
[95] *Inst. hist. research bul.*, III (1926), 146.
[96] Private collections are not otherwise inventoried or indexed.
[97] On enlarged positive prints from the miniature films.

kundige Publicatiën), established in 1902, which undertook, after the manner of the British Historical Manuscripts Commission— adapted to Dutch requirements—to survey the materials available for the study of the various periods of Dutch history, then to outline and to execute plans for the analysis and publication of it:[98] and the excellent periodical organ of the well-organized Dutch professional archivists: *Nederlandsch archievenblad*, established at Groningen, 1892.

Belgium

The diplomatic relations of the United States and Belgium since the independence of that kingdom in 1831 still require to be investigated in archival sources. There is no guide to material for American history in Belgian archives. The Belgians, like the Dutch, have cultivated assiduously archival procedure and historical research.[99]

The Belgian archivists have analysed their archives in a comprehensive way. In 1902 began a notable series of inventories: *Inventaires des archives de la Belgique* in which the investigator can rapidly run his eye over the principal *fonds*.[1]

Belgium under the Hapsburgs, until overrun by the wars of the French Revolution and Napoleon, was an Atlantic outpost for the

---

[98] H. T. Colenbrander, " The work of Dutch historical societies ", *Am. hist. assoc. ann. rep.*, 1909 (1911) 243–256 **[5732]** ; and " The Commission of Advice for National Historical Publications ", *First report of the [British] Royal Commission of Public Records*, v. I, pt. 2 (London, 1912) **[5733]**, 162. The notable publications and projects of this active and learned commission may be found listed in the *Jaarverslag van de Commissie voor 's rijks geschiedkundige publicatien over 1929* (The Hague, 1930) **[5734]**.

The archives of the House of Orange have been pretty extensively printed, and for the period of 1779–1789 are valuable for American diplomacy (see no. 164).

[99] The Royal Historical Commission (*Commission Royale d'Histoire*, of the *Académie Royale des Sciences, des Lettres et des Beaux-Arts de Belgique*), founded in 1834, has produced: (a) a series of annual *Bulletins* (*Compte-rendu des séances* . . . Brussels, 1834–1902; *Bulletin*, 1903 to date) with accounts of proceedings, notices, documents, papers read, etc. **[5735]** ; (b) an impressive series of historical narratives and of documentary collections (*Collection de chroniques belgiques inédites*, 1836–) **[5736]**, totaling to date nearly 200 volumes. In 1898 the Commission began a general survey of all materials at home and abroad for the history of Belgium, and after some years of deliberation entered upon schematic publications. None of the work so far done by the Commission concerns the United States.

[1] In the first volume 1903 (p. 28–34) of the organ of the Belgian archivists, *Revue des bibliothèques et archives de Belgique*, is a " Tableau synoptique " of the Royal Archives at Brussels **[5737]**, with plans for inventorying, *i.e.* the beginning of the work since incorporated in this series.

Holy Roman Emperor and his ambitions for overseas activities.[2] One should therefore not overlook the relevant inventories of 18th century *fonds*, as well as 19th century material after 1831, published by the "Archives Générales du Royaume ": E. de Breyne, " Inventaire sommaire des archives de la chancellerie autrichienne du Pays-Bas, conservées à Bruxelles ", in the *Inventaire sommaire des archives des anciens gouvernements des Pays-Bas, conservées aux Archives Générales du Royaume à Bruxelles*, I (Brussels, 1906) [5738]; and in the same volume, " Inventaire des archives de la sécretairerie d'état allemande ", by A. Gaillard and E. de Breyne [5739]; and *Inventaire des archives de la sécretairerie d'état allemande*, by Edouard Laloire (Brussels, 1929) [5740].

Germany

The political division of Germany before the nineteenth century produced a multiplicity of state archives, large and small, the principal function of which was to preserve and support the legal titles, prerogatives, perquisites, and claims of those states and principalities. Most of these archives were regarded as secret and confidential, closed to historians, until the petty states themselves disappeared in the increasing unification of Germany. To this day the completely modern Prussian archives at Berlin-Dahlem are still called the Prussian Secret State Archives. In the nineteenth century accessibility to and scientific organization of the great archival resources of the German states lagged behind the brilliant achievements of the new German historiography. Since the completion of German unity there has been a rapid development of archival technique and of the professional solidarity of German archival officials.[3] The many state archives within the *Reich* are professionally

[2] See documents relating to "American commercial conditions, and Negotiations with Austria, 1783-1786 (no. 291), which include a number drawn from the relations of Baron de Beelen-Bertholff, Austrian diplomatist in the United States, found in the *Archives générales* in Brussels ; and the *Berichte des ersten Agenten oesterreichs in den Vereinigten Staaten von Amerika, Baron de Beelen-Bertholff* (no. 290).

[3] For a review of archival history and technique in Germany, with a sketch of the various state archives, see Victor Loewe, *Das deutsche Archivwesen; seine Geschichte und Organisation* (Breslau, 1921) [5741]. There is a note on the most recent developments in *Archiv. Zeitschrift*, 3d ser., VIII (1932) 304-307 [5742], and further information in the *Berichte über Archivwesen* which are a feature (since 1927) of the *Jahresberichten für deutsche Geschichte* (no. 4742). For special technical instruction to Prussian archival personnel, given in the *Institüt für Archivwissenschaft und geschichtswissenschaftliche Fortbildung*, see A. Brackmann, *Archiv. Zeitschrift*, 3d ser., VII (1930) [5743].

staffed and organized to a high degree. Their contents are highly accessible, though sometimes only through local MS. indexes. The organization of the German *archives* has developed two periodicals [4] of professional interest, which should be known to every investigator interested in German historical sources: the *Korrespondenzblatt des Gesamtvereins der deutschen Geschichts- und Altertumsvereine* and the *Archivalische Zeitschrift;* the former the organ of the associated German historical societies (*Gesamtverein der deutschen Geschichts- und Altertumsvereine*) with which the German-Austrian *Archivtage* meet annually: and the latter is a publication of the Bavarian State Archives at Munich. Of recent years the *Archivalische Zeitschrift* has extended its purview beyond the strictly German archival field, and today stands as the most comprehensive and informing journal on archival arts and sciences the world over.

This awakening of professional archival consciousness in Germany had as its field of endeavor until very recently the many state archives and their vast and invaluable contents. In the years since the world war the German states have built numerous [5] new archival edifices among the most up-to-date and best equipped and staffed in the world. One of these—the most notable and, in our opinion, one of the best planned archive buildings in the world—is the new Prussian Archives at Berlin-Dahlem (*Preussisches Geheimes Staats-archiv*).[6] But it was not until 1921 that the first German national archives, the *Reichsarchiv* was established in improvised quarters (the former military school and its barracks) at Potsdam for the custody of the records of the new German Empire, since 1871. This archive is intended to be not only a national record office, but a great archival museum for the history of the German people. It is acquiring private papers and nonofficial collections.[7] An Historical Com-

---

[4] There was also the now defunct *Mittheilungen der K. Preussischen Archivverwaltung* (Leipzig, 1900–1913) which contains a survey of the archives of Hannover, Schleswig (now Kiel), Koblenz, Düsseldorf, Danzig, the province of Posen, and of German city archives. Resumption of publication is intended.

[5] "Eine ganze Reihe", says Dr. Lothar Gross, in *Archiv. Zeitschrift*, 3d ser., III (1926) 237 [5743a].

[6] For description, photographs, and plans, see Ernst Posner, "Der Neubau des Geheimen Staatsarchivs in Berlin-Dahlem", *Archiv. Zeitschrift*, 3d ser., II (1925) 23–40 [5744]; see also the description, photographs, and plans of the new Saxon State Archives Building, by Woldemar Lippert, *ibid.*, 40–60; and of the new Königsberg State Archives, *ibid.*, VII, 25.

[7] For sketch of the history of the *Reichsarchiv*, a reference to the existing literature on it, and a brief analysis and tabulation of the principal *fonds* (including private

mission composed of eminent German historians and archivists has been attached to the Archives to direct publications.

Strangely enough, German professional industry, though prodigiously and minutely concerned in listing the contents of small state archives, has not yet emphasized the printing of inventories and indexes to the major *fonds* so admirably preserved in the larger state archives, although we may expect rapid progress in this direction.[8] It seems to be the German manner rather to write general descriptions of the history and contents of the archives. Consequently rapid initiation of a foreign, or even of a German investigator, into the precise content of an archive is sometimes more difficult than, for example, into the admirably catalogued, indexed, and inventoried English, Dutch, and French archives.

The Carnegie Institution of Washington has again eased the way of the American investigator by the publication of M. D. Learned's *Guide to the manuscript materials relating to American history in the German state archives* (Wash.: Carnegie Institution, 1912) **[5746]**. This has been supplemented voluminously by a more recent typescript report now in possession of the Library of Congress. Division of Manuscripts: *Supplements, corrections and new inventory-lists to be added to M. D. Learned's Guide to the manuscript materials relating to American history in the German state archives,* made by the German staff of the European Historical Mission of the Library of Congress, 1929–1932, 2 vols. **[5747]**. The United States maintained at various times regular diplomatic relations before 1871 with Prussia, the Hanse cities (Bremen, Lübeck, and Hamburg), Hannover, and Bavaria; and consistently with Prussia and the later German Empire; there were also special missions to Baden, Nassau, Oldenburg, Saxony, and Württemberg. Of these the Prussian Archive at Berlin-Dahlem is of the greatest importance.

The archives of these states, so far as the diplomatic history (and indeed other history) of the United States is concerned, are abundantly revealed up to 1848 in Learned's *Guide;* and copies of some of this material have been secured for the Library of Congress,

---

papers) see Helmuth Rogge, " Das Reichsarchiv ", *Archiv. Zeitschrift,* 3d ser., II (1925) 119–133 **[5745]**.

  [8] A series of inventories of state and city archives is now being prepared, *Korrespondenzblatt,* v. LXV (1927), 224. Printing of definitive inventories is said to be delayed by continuing deposits from official sources. From 1901–1910 appeared the *Inventare des Grossherzöglichen Badischen General-Landes Archivs,* in 4 vols.

which has been able to complete work in the Prussian series (with a few exceptions) to 1862, and the Hanse series (Bremen, Hamburg, and Lübeck) to 1868. There are also in the Library of Congress facsimiles from the Prussian archives of the documents relative to the United States, 1776–1817, preceding the establishment of a Prussian legation (see Learned (no. 5746), 18–39) including the despatches, to Frederick the Great, of Prussian ministers in Great Britain, France, and Holland (the latter not recorded in Learned), 1776–1784. There are also reproductions of various bundles (not recorded in Learned) dealing with Texas, 1844–45, Mexico, 1837–62, Panama, 1854–55, Central America, 1857, the West Indies, and Antwerp (Ostend Manifesto), 1854.

The student of American diplomacy for the period before the North German Confederation and the German Empire will find little else than above indicated in the way of official diplomatic MSS. Matteson's *Guide* (no. 5591) lists the MS. material in German libraries relating to American history. The private papers of various German diplomatists having to deal with the United States remain to be discovered and exploited. There is (so far as we know) no general catalogue of such; but there is a published list (*Korrespondenzblatt des Gesamtvereins der deutschen Geschichts- und Altertumsvereine*) (Berlin), v. LII (1924) 97–104 [5748] of 130 collections of private papers now in the Prussian State Archives. It includes the correspondence of Ludwig von Roenne, Prussian diplomatist in Washington, 1834 to 1845. The *Korrespondenzblatt* publishes from time to time lists of similar acquisitions of various German archives.[9] The student would do well to search through the various German bibliographical guides (see nos. 4740–4743) and archival organs, and the publications of the numerous learned societies,[10] and state historical commissions (for which there is no general guide), none of which has dealt with private MS. collections so systematically as the British Historical Manuscripts Commission.

There is on foot in Germany, however, an increasingly concerted movement, sponsored by German archival administrations, to have local and private papers of historical value deposited for proper

---

[9] See note 11, p. 928, below.
[10] The *Korrespondenzblatt* has a section devoted to a review of publications of numerous historical societies.

custody in state archives, if only temporarily for the purpose of being inventoried, in cases where deposits are impracticable or it is impossible to have the contents inventoried on the spot under the auspices of the pertinent one of the various numerous regional historical commissions.[11] We may hope this work will lead to an eventual inventorying of all the most important nonofficial German records, perhaps to a consolidated general inventory.

Though the new German *Reichsarchiv* allows general free access to documents not later than 1890,[12] as a matter of fact, the German Foreign Office has not yet deposited any of its records, including diplomatic correspondence, therein.[13] The *Reichsarchiv* is rapidly acquiring bequests of private papers, which should not be overlooked.[14]

Austria and Austria-Hungary

It is the archives of the former Empire, rather than the present succession states, which interest us in this treatise; the diplomatic relations of the United States with the new states are of too recent origin to be investigated by conventional archival research. The principal political records of Austria (archives founded in 1749) and of the dual empire are in Vienna,[15] notably in the relatively new building of the *Haus-, Hof- und Staatsarchiv*, constructed in 1899.

---

[11] See remarks of Archivar Dr. Hermann Grotefend, " Die Inventarisation der nichtstaatlichen Archives ", *Korrespondenzblatt des Gesamtvereins der deutschen Geschichts- und Altertumsvereine*, LXVIII (1920) 225-236 [5749], to the fourteenth German *Archivtag*, Weimar, September 27, 1920.

These historical commissions have had a valuable function in breathing new life into the more than 300 local German historical societies, and marshalling the resources of the latter for broader and more important work than the petty local antiquarianism into which they, like similar societies in other countries (notably France and the United States) were tending to sink. See H. E. Bourne, " What we can learn from the publishing activities of European societies ", *Am. hist. assoc. ann. rep.*, for 1909 (1911) 293-302 [5750]; Victor Loewe, " Die historischen Kommissionen Deutschlands ", *Korrespondenzblatt des Gesamtvereins der deutschen Geschichts- und Altertumsvereine*, LXXIII (1925) 45-52 [5751]. The activities of these numerous societies, of the historical commissions, and publication institutes are recorded succinctly year by year in the *Korrespondenzblatt*.

[12] R. P. Oszwald, " Das Deutsche Reichsarchiv ", *Nederlandsch Archievenblad*, XXXIII (1926) 26-37 [5752].

[13] Rogge (no. 5745), 122.

[14] For a list to 1927, see Helmuth Rogge, " Nachlässe und private Archive im Reichsarchiv ", *Korrespondenzblatt*, LXXV (1927) 53-61 [5753].

[15] For bibliography of the history of the Austrian archives, see Joseph Cuvelier, " Les archives autrichiennes ", *Rev. bibliothèques et archives de Belgique*, IV (1906) 178-200 [5754]; A. B. Faust (no. 5764), p. 186; Lothar Gross, " Das Wiener Haus-, Hof- und Staatsarchiv in Wien ", *Archiv. Zeitschrift*, 3d ser., II (1925) 134-140 [5755]; Ludwig Bittner, " Das Wiener Haus-, Hof- und Staatsarchiv in der Nachkriegszeit ", *ibid.*, 141-

It is here that the archives of the old foreign office have been deposited, and where they are open without restriction to historical investigators down to the year 1894.

No printed indexes exist for the contents of the state archives in Vienna, except the records of the Ministry of the Interior, and the Ministry of Finance, which appear in the abortive series, *Inventare Österreichischer Staatlicher Archive:* I, *Inventar des allgemeinen Archive des Ministeriums des Innern* (Vienna, 1909) [5762]; II, *Inventar des Archivs des k. k. Finanzministeriums* (Vienna, 1911) [5763].[16] The compilation and publication of a long-needed adequate inventory of the *Haus-, Hof- und Staatsarchiv*, is now expected within a reasonable time.[17] The provincial archives of the old empire are insignificant for the diplomatic history of the United States.

While awaiting the publication of comprehensive indexes to the various *fonds* of the *Haus-, Hof- und Staatsarchiv*, the student of the diplomatic history of the United States can profit by A. B. Faust's *Guide to the materials for American history in Swiss and Austrian archives* (Washington: Carnegie Institution, 1916) [5764], which lists the American items to be found from an examination of the various manuscript indexes to the *fonds* of that archives, and also to the records, housed in Vienna, of the several ministries

203 [5756]; and by the same author, "Die zwischenstaatlichen Verhandlungen über das Schicksal der Osterreichischen Archive nach dem Zusammenbruch Oesterreich-Ungarns", *Archiv. Politik u. Geschichte*, III (1925) 58–96 [5757]; and "Zu Neuorganisation der oesterreichischen Archivwesens", *Archivstudien, Festschrift für W. Dippert* (Dresden, 1931) 36–41 [5758]; O. Brunner. "Literatur zur Kenntnis der Wiener Haus-, Hof- und Staatsarchivs", *Oesterreich. Inst. Geschichtsforschung Mitteil.*, XLI (1926) 374–376 [5759]; Eduard Strassmayr, *Bibliographie zur oberösterreichischen Geschichte*, 1891–1926 (Linz, 1927–29, 4 pts.) [5760], section on "Archivkunde" (p. 26–29); and most important of all the first volume of the new official series, Lothar Gross, *Die Geschichte der Deutschen Reichshofkanzlei von 1559–1806* (Vienna, 1933) (*Inventare des Wiener Haus-Hof- und Staatsarchivs*, I) [5761].

16 The records of the *Finanzministerium* are still in its own custody. The former *Archiv des Ministeriums des Innern* is now organized independently under the name *Staatsarchiv des Innern und der Justiz*, which contains a *fonds* of some importance for diplomatic history, that of the *Polizeihofstelle*. This archive was badly damaged by the fire of 1927. The archives of the Ministry of War, *Kriegsarchiv*, contain papers of high political interest especially for the 19th century and the war of 1914–1918. (Anton Langer, *Das k. u. k. Kriegsarchiv von seiner Gründung bis zum Jahre 1900*, 2nd ed. (Vienna, 1900) [5763a]). *The Hofkammerarchiv* has scanty material on diplomatic history.

17 Lothar Gross (no. 5755), 134; Ludwig Bittner (no. 5756), 184–193; O. Brunner (no. 5759), 374–375. The first volume only of the new inventory series, which is a history of the archives, appeared in 1933 (no. 5761).

which have not yet been deposited in the *Haus-, Hof- und Staatsarchiv*. At the time Professor Faust prepared his *Guide*, the state archives at Vienna were open only to 1848 for historical investigation. Since the war the date has been extended to 1894. The *Guide* gives no indication of material later than 1848; but the investigator can assume that the several series analyzed by Faust to that date can naturally be followed for later years, though no index exists. Not noted in this *Guide* are the papers of the Archduke Maximilian, ephemeral sovereign of Mexico, which are in the Haus-, Hof- und Staatsarchiv. They are vastly rich in material relating to a significant phase of American diplomacy.

The Library of Congress has reproductions of practically all the unprinted diplomatic material listed in Faust's *Guide* (no. 5764), 185–216, which includes the diplomatic correspondence of the Chancellor with Austrian representatives in the United States, 1819–1894, despatches, instructions, and miscellaneous matter. It should be noted that the Library's photostatic collection of this material extends, beyond Faust's limit, through 1894. Faust's *Guide*, p. 217–237, lists certain documents mentioning the United States, and matters of American diplomacy, contained in the despatches, 1768–1821, of Austrian diplomatic representatives in Holland, Spain, England, France, and Portugal. The list of items was made by Dr. Hans Prankl, who, we have reason to believe, drew it off from heads of items appearing in an adequate MS. index in the Haus-, Hof- und Staatsarchiv.[18]

The Library of Congress also has photostatic copies of those voluminous portions of the *Maximilian Archiv*, above mentioned, which relate to the Mexican adventure. These photostats are supplemented by similar facsimiles of the relevant documents selected out of the diplomatic correspondence of the Austrian Foreign Office with its representatives in France and Mexico. Austrian archivists had caused to be made, as a supplement to the Austrian archives, transcripts of the documents in the Prussian archives relating to the Mexican imbroglio. The Library of Congress has photostated, from the originals in Prussia, the documents represented in these transcripts (*Preussen, Auswärtiges Amt, Centralbüro I. C. Amerika, Mexiko*). The Library of Congress has also documents concerning

---

[18] Only portions of this miscellaneous material are in photostatic form in the Library of Congress.

commercial relations with the United States, from the *Hofkammer Archiv*, in Vienna, to about 1830, from the *Archiv des Finanzministeriums*, to 1855, and from the *Staatsarchiv des Innern und der Justiz, Präsidialakten des Handelsministeriums*, 1850–1892.

For a list of deposits of political papers in official Austrian archives, see Fritz Reinöhl, " Politische Nachlässe des 19. Jahrhunderts in den staatlichen Archiven Oesterreichs ", *Korrespondenzblatt des Gesamtvereins der deutschen Geschichts- und Altertumsvereine*, LXIV (1926) 209–219 [5765].

For indications of private collections of MSS. in Austria-Hungary, see the inventories published by the " Kommission für neuere Geschichte Oesterreichs ", in *Archivalien zur neueren Geschichte Oesterreichs* (Vienna, 1913) [5766]. Matteson (no. 5591) lists the few American items which appeared in the catalogues of libraries.

Scandinavian Countries

The archives of the Scandinavian countries [19] are well organized and partially inventoried in published matter, but entries for the United States are very meager.

Sweden

The contents of the Swedish Royal Archives at Stockholm (which exercise an official supervision over the local archives) as well as of the local archives are inventoried, for various *fonds*, in the publication of the Swedish archives, *Meddelanden från Svenska Riksarkivet*, established in 1875 [5773]. They reveal only meager mention of material relating to American diplomacy.[20] A general card-catalogue

---

[19] See A. D. Jörgensen, *Udsigt over de danske rigsarkivers historie* (Copenhagen, 1884) [5767] ; V. A. Secher, " Das Archivwesen im skandinavischen Norden ", *Archiv. Zeitschrift*, IV (1879) 249–259, V (1880) 40–50, VI (1881) 77–106 ; Danish original is published in *Meddelelser fra det kongelige Gehejmearkiv*, 1901–05, p. 145–166, under the title " Om organisationen af Arkivvaêsent i Norden." [5768] ; Severin Bergh, " Notice sur les archives de Suède ", *Rev. internat. archives et musées*, I, 1895–1896 (1897) 148–153 [5769] and *Svenska Riksarkivet, 1618–1847* (Stockholm, 1916–27, 2 v.) [5770] gives the history of the Swedish archives, with respect to organization, arrangement, personnel, buildings, regulations, and acquisitions ; G. W. Kernkamp, " Over Zweedsche, Noorsche en Deensche Archieven ", *Nederl. Archievenblad*, IX (1901) 181–200 [5771]; Herman Brulin, " Das schwedische Archivwesen ", *Archiv. Zeitschrift*, 3d ser., V (1929) 151–177 [5772].

[20] " Förteckning öfver i Riksarkivet förvarade Ministerriella handlingar, XVI : Americana ", *Meddelanden Svens. Riksark.*, XXV (1901) (bound vol. V, 1901) 318 [5774], notes three volumes of despatches, etc., and treaty negotiations with the United States, 1783–1813. There is another brief mention of documents relating to the Swedish-American treaty of 1783 in *ibid.*, XIX (1895) (bound vol. IV, 1897) 333 [5775].

index, and a general printed guide to Swedish archives is now under preparation.[21] The Swedish archival authorities have made rich acquisitions of private papers. The series of diplomatic correspondence with the Swedish legation in the United States, despatches and instructions; and ancillary material relating to the United States, is preserved in the *Riksarkiv* from the beginning in 1783 to date. The Library of Congress has facsimiles of this series 1812–1878; also 1 roll of film (25 pages) dealing with negotiations between Sweden and the United States, 1783–1813; and despatches from Swedish consuls, 1784–1818.

Denmark

The only printed catalogue for the Danish archives is given in the *Meddelelser fra det Kongelige Gehejmearkiv*, 1883–1888 (Copenhagen, 1886–89, 2 v.) [5776]; this contains a very general index to the classification of the papers of the Danish Chancery (*Danske Kancelli*) and the German Chancery (*Tyske Kancelli*) to 1848, which departments successively—and sometimes concurrently—handled the foreign affairs of Denmark. We are aware of no published index [22] to the Danish Foreign Office records. Kristian Erslev, *Rigsarkivet og hjaelpemidlerne til dets benyttelse, en oversigt* (Copenhagen, 1923) [5777] is a description, by sections, of the contents of the royal Danish archives, from which it would appear that since 1848 the papers relating to foreign affairs have not been deposited in the archives, and that the papers for foreign affairs, 1771–1848, which are deposited there are not yet definitely organized. This publication lists the numerous private papers of political personalities that have been acquired by the archives. The important *Bernstorffske papirer* have been printed (no. 181). Among the political records of the Danish Government are upwards of 3000 volumes and bundles of MS. material of a local nature and significance relating to the Danish West Indies, transferred to Denmark in execution of the treaty of cession between the United States and

---

[21] Brulin (no. 5772), 159, 172.

[22] Langlois and Stein (no. 5701), p. 810, note that the Danish archivist, A. D. Jörgensen held forth prospects of a set of indexes on these and other papers. He died in 1897 without completing the task.

that kingdom, of 1917.[23] This supplements the bulk of the administrative documents relating to the islands, which has long since been
in the Rigsarkiv.[24]

Norway

Diplomatic relations with Norway as a separate kingdom began
so recently, in 1905, that its independent state archives can scarcely
be open for investigations of the historian of Norwegian-American
relations for any stretch of years. Until 1814 that country was
united with Denmark, and its diplomacy conducted from Copenhagen; after 1814, following the union with Sweden, the Foreign
Office at Stockholm managed the joint international concerns of
Sweden and Norway, until the separation in 1905.

Russia

The Russian archives, if taken too literally as indicating the
thousands of small collections of official documents of any kind,
might constitute the most voluminous of any in the world. But for
all practical purposes for this manual, we may limit our survey
to the principal national archives, which are now centralized in
Moscow under the administration of the Central Archives of the
Russian Socialist Federated Soviet Republic, which controls all
archival activities within the strictly Russian parts of the Republic
and renders advice to the remainder. Before the October revolution
of 1917 relatively little progress in modern archival arts and sciences
(*Archivwesen*) had developed in Russia. The Bolshevists, conscious
of the desirability of preserving the historical sources of their great
experiment, have established professional education on western
models for their archivists, inaugurated (1923) an archival journal,
Arkhivnoe delo, and have turned eagerly to the reform and reor-
ganization of their archives along (for records since 1917) conventional lines: custody, inventorying, cataloguing, calendaring, and
publication. The Russian archivists divide their records into two

---

[23] This mass of material is still relatively unorganized. In 1928 we observed one of
the archival staff at work on it; but we know of no printed catalogue.
[24] Waldemar Westgaard, *The Danish West Indies, under company rule (1671–1754)
with a supplementary chapter, 1755–1917* (N.Y., 1917) [5778].

clean-cut categories. The "historical," already considered as a closed book, consisting of everything before the year 1917. The "Archives of the October Revolution" comprise all records since the beginning of the year 1917; these comprise, strictly-speaking, an archival section, that is, the records turned over to archival custody, which extend generally up to within five years of the present; and the contemporary records—generally those of the last elapsed five years—still in the files of the government offices from which they emanate. It is with the Revolutionary Archives that the new school of Russian archivists is concerning itself pretty exclusively, for the purpose of strengthening political morale with what they deem a properly oriented historiography. They are compiling a card index of the various *fonds* of the Central Archive—better stated Central Archives, for they are brought together in separately located buildings—; and printed inventories may be expected to follow. Already 27 volumes of selections of diplomatic correspondence anteceding the world war have been published, in the *Krasny Archiv* (no. 5436) and plans are on foot to extend publication of this material back to the 1870's, paralleling the similar German series *Grosse Politik* (no. 5476) and other English, French, and Austrian series (see p. 850).

The late Professor F. A. Golder prepared in 1914 and 1915 for the Carnegie Institution of Washington a remarkable *Guide to materials for American history in Russian archives* (Wash., 1917) [5779], which describes rather minutely (frequently by individual documents) the material in the Russian Foreign Office before 1854 that deals with American affairs.[25] He indicated also the indexes and inventories, printed and unprinted, which existed before the Revolution. It is not to be presumed that the Soviet archivists have yet concerned themselves with any further indexing of the "historical" archives before 1917.

Supplementing the information in Golder's *Guide* the investigator should remark that the archives of the Czarist Foreign Office at St. Petersburg, which contained diplomatic correspondence from 1800

---

[25] The Carnegie Institution of Washington, Division of Historical Research, has a MS. supplement to 1867, which Prof. Golder was later allowed to make. (Information from Dr. J. F. Jameson.)

to 1917, are now in Moscow, intact, somewhat shuffled up by a confused and round-about transit during the revolution and civil war, but at last now united in one and the same archive with the records of Russian diplomacy before the nineteenth century when Moscow was the capital.[26]

The Library of Congress has transcripts and photostats of selected documents relating to Russian-American relations:

Documents on commercial relations in the northern Pacific, 1781–1783, 1785: Archive of the State, Petrograd, XIX, no. 360 (Golder, *Guide*, 14).

Memoir on the relations of the North American states with Russia in the time of Empress Catherine II, 1784 (a F. O. *précis* summarizing Dana's mission): Archive of the State (formerly) Petrograd, XV, no. 214.

Report of Committee appointed to study the interpretation of Article I of the Treaty of Ghent, Mar. 4, 1822: Ministry of Foreign Affairs, Petrograd, Doklad series, 1822, no. 5190 (Golder, *Guide*, 16).

Relations between Russia, Great Britain, and the United States, 1821–1826: *ibid.*, no. 1213 (Golder, *Guide*, 16).

Documents relating to the early history of Alaska—Activities of Shelikov, missionaries, and others: Ministry of Foreign Affairs, Petrograd, Asiatic Dept., 1783–1796, II–3, no. 1 (Golder, *Guide*, 111).

Documents relating to Baranov; the early history of Sitka, 1805–1808: *ibid.*, 1805–1808, I–13, no. 12 (Golder, *Guide*, 111).

Instructions to the diplomatic agent in Washington (Pahlen), Dec. 28, 1809: Ministry of Foreign Affairs, Petrograd, Wash. series, 1809–1811, carton I, 1809, no. 5.

Instructions to the diplomatic agent (appointee, never served) in Washington (Tuyll) June 7, 1817: *ibid.*, 1817, carton VII, no. 24 (Golder, *Guide*, 31).

---

[26] For the Russian archives since the October Revolution, see V. V. Adoratskij, "Das Archivwesen der Russischen Sozialistischen Föderativen Sovet-Republik", in Otto Hoetzsch, ed., *Aus der historischen Wissenschaft der Sovet-Union* (Berlin, 1929) 33–57 [5780]; H. O. Meisner, "Uber das Archivwesen der Russischen Sowjet-Republik", *Archiv. Zeitschrift*, 3d ser., V (1929) 178–196 [5781], and bibliography therein cited; and report on recent literature and developments by Fritz Epstein, *ibid.*, 3d ser., VI (1930) 282–308 [5782]. A list of the publications of the Central Archives is *Centrarchiv RSFSR, Katalog izdanij* (Moscow and Leningrad, 1928) [5783]. For centralization of archival *fonds*, 1918–1923, see E. Nersisjan, *Arkhivnoe delo*, V–VI (1926) 25–44 [5784].

Relations between Russia, Great Britain, and the United States, 1821–1826: Ministry of Foreign Affairs, Petrograd, Doklad series, 1826, no. 1213 (Golder, *Guide*, 16).

Correspondence relating to the transfer of Alaska, 1854–1868 (selected by F. A. Golder): Ministry of Foreign Affairs, Petrograd, Wash. series, 1854, no. 6652; *ibid.*, 1854–1868, v. I–9, nos. 77, 165, 166, 208, 209, 210, 290 (and documents relating to the transfer of Alaska, *ibid.*, 1857, I–9, no. 4); correspondence, Asiatic dept., 1857–1867, I–9, no. 4.

Letters from Stoeckl to Chancellor Gortchakoff regarding the civil war in the United States, Dec. 26, 1860–July 14, 1863, photostats (selected under the direction of Mr. V. Adoratsky) from the Central Archive, Moscow, Foreign Affairs, vol. 49.

The documents of the Russian American Company (approximately 1820–1857), in the Department of State, acquired from the Russian Government when Alaska was purchased, have recently been photofilmed for the Institute of Social Sciences of the University of California at Berkeley, under the direction of Professor R. J. Kerner. Copies will later be made available at the Library of Congress.

A collection of documents of the Russian American Company recently (1935) discovered among the private correspondence of the company's founders in Russia, will be published by the Academy of Sciences of the U. S. S. R.

Balkan States

There are no published catalogues for the archives of these countries.

Greece

In the case of Greece, it has been officially stated, no access is allowed to the archives of the Foreign Office, although Messrs. Édouard Driault and Michel Lhéritier made thorough use of them in their formidable *Histoire diplomatique de la Grèce*.[27] It would be difficult to conceive that such a fair-minded government as that of the Greek Republic would deny to responsible historians of one country what it has previously allowed to those of another. Its diplomatic archives are intact and well ordered. In Rumania only

---

[27] (Paris, 1925–26, 5 v.) from 1821 to 1923 [**5785**].

in particular cases are the archives open to investigators.[28] The Greek archives were established in 1915. Greece is of course the oldest of the present incarnation of Balkan States (excluding Turkey). The relatively recent establishment of these states, their turbulent history and frequent wars have delayed the organization of archives and the development of archival procedure. We can list no study of American diplomatic relations with them based on Balkan archives. This may be a rich field for investigation in the future.

Ottoman Empire

We know of no index or other guide to the Turkish archives aside from the thorough and rather prodigious analysis of the Turkish archives at Cairo: Jean F. Dény, *Sommaire des archives Turques du Caire* (Le Caire, 1930) [5786], the name " United States " does not appear in the index.

Succession States (Hungary, Jugoslavia (including Serbia and Montenegro), Czechoslovakia, Poland, Latvia, Esthonia, Finland)

The diplomatic history, not to mention the independence of these states, is too recent for archival investigations, although here will be a rich field for research, notably for relations of the United States with Czechoslovakia and Poland, as archives are organized and their contents made accessible to historical scholars.[29]

Italy and the Papal States

Italy is full of MSS. and archives of all times.[30] Those which concern the diplomatic history of the United States fall into these cate-

---

[28] We are dependent, for our information as to these two states, on the material printed, after responses to questionnaires, in the *Bulletin of the Institute of Historical Research,* IV, no. 10 (June 1926) and V, no. 15 (Feb. 1928).

[29] For some notes on archives in these States, see the answers sent in to the questionnaire composed by the Committee of Intellectual Co-operation of the League of Nations and published in the *Bulletin of the Institute of Historical Research,* III, 75 (Finland), 78–81 (Hungary), 139–140 (Esthonia) ; V, 160–162 (Poland) ; VII, 158–161 (Czechoslovakia) [5787] ; Ludwig Bittner (no. 5757) ; and Alexis Bachulski, " Polnische Staatsarchive ", *Archiv. Zeitschrift,* 3d ser., IV (1928) 241–261 [5788] ; *Bulletin of the International Committee of Historical Sciences,* no. 15, pp. 206–277 [5789].

[30] Eugenio Casanova, *Archivistica* (no. 5486). The authors of this guide wish to acknowledge the valuable assistance given them by Doctor Casanova in the preparation of material for these paragraphs on Italy. *Ad Alessandro Luzio, gli archivi di stato italiano: miscellanea di studi storici* (Florence, 1932? 2v.) [5790] deals especially with questions of the organization of archives ; useful information is given on those of Zara, Trente, Trieste, and Bolzano, as well as the better known collections of Naples, Florence, Venice, and Palermo.

gories: (1) The archives of the several Italian States, 1775–1866, from the beginning of the American Revolution until the establishment of the Kingdom of Italy. (2) The archives of the Kingdom of Italy. (3) Papal archives. (4) Collections of private papers which might touch American relations. The first and third of these categories are adequately inventoried, for American material, in the Carnegie Institution guide by C. R. Fish, *Guide to the materials for American history in Roman and other Italian archives* (Wash., 1911) [5791]; and it suffices to refer the student to this excellent work for sources in the relations of the United States with the Italian States,[31] and the Papal States.

The archives of the modern Kingdom of Italy are of such recent date as not to have been generally opened to historical investigation (though it is understood that they may be consulted for particular purposes under special conditions).[32]

The records since 1861 of the Ministries of Foreign Affairs, War, and Navy are kept in the archives of those respective offices: [33] in fact in the Foreign Office archives records, notably the "historical" series, go back of 1861. The records of the other ministries, after

---

[31] A handbook of contents (uncatalogued) of the principal state archives of Italy is *L'ordinamento delle carte degli archivi di stato italiani; manuale storico archivistico* (Rome, 1910), published by the "Direzione Generale dell' Amministrazione Civile", of the "Ministero dell' Interno", of Italy [5792]. See also Angelo Pesce, *Notizie sugli Archivi di Stato* (Rome, 1906) [5793]. The following printed inventories describe the contents of the archives of the several Italian states that were sovereign when American independence was achieved: Kingdom of Sardinia: Nicomede Bianchi, *Le materie politiche relative all' estero, degli archivi di stato piemontesi* (Bologna and Modena, 1876); and by the same editor, *Le carte degli archivi piemontesi politici, amministrativi, giudiziari* . . . (Turin, 1881) [5794]; Michele Giuseppe Canale, *Degli archivi di Venezia, Vienna, Firenze, Francia e Genova* (Florence, 1857) [5795]; Giuseppe Mazzatinti, *Archivi di Genova negli inventari dei nos, degli archivi d' Italia* (Forli, 1891) [5796], Venice: *L' archivio di stato in Venezia* (Venice, 1881) [5797]. Modena: Giovanni Ognibene, *Le relazioni della Casa d'Este coll' estero* (Modena, 1903) [5798]. Lucca: Salvatore Bongi, *Inventario del R. Archivio di Stato in Lucca* (Lucca, 1872–88, 4 v.) [5799]. Rome: Armando Lodolini, *Guida metodica e analitica dell' Archivio di Stato di Roma* (Rome 1932) [5800]. Naples and Sicily: Francesco Trinchera, *Degli archivii napoletani* (Naples, 1872) [5801]; *Inventario officiale del grande archivio di Sicilia* (Palermo, 1861) [5802]. The Royal Italian Historical Institute has commenced the publication of a *Storica e bibliografica degli archivi e delle biblioteche d'Italia* under the direction of Luigi Schiaparelli. The first volume (Rome, 1932) [5803], on "Provincia di Firenze" contains nothing on diplomatic documents.

[32] *Bulletin of the Institute of Historical Research,* V (1928) 160.

[33] It is understood that preparation is well advanced, under the direction of Senator. Salata Francesco, of a series of the diplomatic correspondence of the Kingdom of Italy from 1861 to 1915, the first four volumes of which are expected to appear within the year 1932. This series will contain documents bearing on Italo-American relations.

ten years, are deposited in the *Archivio del Regno* which is now united with the *Archivio di Stato di Roma.*

Italian law allows seizure for the state archives of official papers left in personal possession by deceased officials; these then are filed with the relevant archival series. There are no printed indexes to privately owned collections of diplomatic correspondence of former regimes; but there are voluminous printed collections of the works and writings of men like La Marmora, Cavour, Ricasoli, Pasolini, Minghetti, Crispi, Mazzini, Garibaldi, etc., for which see the Italian historical bibliographies (nos. 4748, 4749); and one may consult the files of the organ *Il Risorgimento italiano,* and *Rassegna storica del Risorgimento* (see also *Inventario della raccolta donata da Achille Bertarelli al comune di Milano* (Bergamo, 1925, 3 v.)) [5804].

Fish (no. 5791), and the handbooks above [34] noted, list the various collections of private libraries and private deposits in state archives. Matteson (no. 5591) gives MSS. listed in catalogues of libraries outside Rome and touching American history.

Switzerland

The Swiss, with their rich historical background, have been most active in organized publications [35] but have done less in the way of inventories.[36] A summary inventory, *Inventare Schweizerischer Archive* (Bern, 1895–99, 2 v. in 1) [5806], published under the auspices of the *Allgemeine geschichtsforschende Gesellschaft der Schweiz,* reveals no American material. The diplomatic correspondence is preserved in the federal archives at Bern. A. B. Faust's *A guide to the materials for American history in Swiss and Austrian archives* (no. 5764) mentions that material for our early (mostly consular) relations with Switzerland—an American minister was not appointed to Switzerland until 1853. We know of no inventory of private collections in Switzerland, Matteson (no.

---

[34] Note 31, p. 938.

[35] See for example the remarkable series *Quellen zur Schweizer Geschichte,* published at Basel in several series since 1877, by the Swiss Society for Historical Research (*Allgemeine geschichtsforschende Gesellschaft der Schweiz*) [5805].

[36] Langlois et Stein (no. 5701), 823. For a list of inventories to Swiss official archives, see *Bibliographie der Schweizer Geschichte* (no. 4764), II, 18–19; and *Bibliographie der Schweizergeschichte* (no. 4765), sections on archives.

5591) notes the items of American MSS. listed in Swiss library catalogues.

The Far East

China

Chinese archives, though voluminous in the extreme, are still unorganized. Sad losses have occurred because of war, accidents, and ignorance as to custody. Highly useful descriptions of them were recently published by C. H. Peake, " Documents available for research on the modern history of China ", *Am. hist. rev.*, XXXVIII (1932) 61–70 [5807], and A. K'aiming Ch'iu " Chinese historical documents of the Ch'ing Dynasty, 1644–1911 ", *Pacific hist. rev.*, I (1932) 324–336 [5808]. Any information we present is taken from these easily available articles to which the reader is referred for further details. The bulk of this valuable archival material is to be found in Peking: (1) in the Historical Museum (Palace Museum), (2) in the Sinological Research Institute of the Peking National University, (3) at a number of places in the Palace Museum, (4) at the Imperial Rain-Temple (*Ta Kao Tien*), which has the archives of the Grand Council of State, covering the period 1729–1911, and containing 184 volumes of documents relating to foreign affairs.[87] A general preliminary catalogue of these archives, prepared by Liu Ju-lin, the curator, appeared in the *Bulletin* of the Library Association of China, v. III (1928) 9–15, under the title of " Ch'ing Chün Chi Ch'u Tang An I Lan Piao " [5811]. " With this considerable collection of documents, both published and unpublished,[88] awaiting the scholar's careful reading, it is apparent that anything like a definitive history of the Ch'ing dynasty will not appear for decades." The forces of modernism must still be awaited to make accessible to the research worker the valuable material located in provincial repositories and innumerable private libraries.

Japan

The archives of the Japanese Foreign Office are not open to historical scholars, or anyone, without the special permission of that

---

[87] For historical summary of the organization of administration of foreign affairs in China : Yü-chüan Chang, " The organization of the Waichiaopu [foreign office] ", *Chinese soc. and pol. sci. rev.*, I, no. 1 (1916) 21–55 [5809] ; and same author's " The provincial organs for foreign affairs in China ", *ibid.*, I, no. 3 (1916) 47–70 [5810].

[88] For printed documentary series, see nos. 5442–5450.

office. We are informed that there are two main series of unpublished diplomatic correspondence in those archives: (1) *Tsushin Zenran* (Diplomatic correspondence, 1st Series), (2) *Zoku Tsushin Zenran* (Diplomatic correspondence, 2d Series). These documents are arranged chronologically, but are not otherwise classified, nor indexed. We know of no historical publication which has made use of this unpublished material.[89] But see *Bakumatsu Gaiko* (no. 5459).

Periodical Publications relating to Archives   [5812]

Anais das bibliotecas e arquivos de Portugal. Coimbra and Lisbon, 1915–.

Anais das bibliotecas, arquivo e museus municipais (Lisbon, 1931–), official publication of the " Inspecção das Bibliotecas, Arquivo e Museus Municipais."

Annuaire des bibliothèques et des archives. Paris, 1886–1903 (irregular, 1904–1927), 1927–.

Anuario del cuerpo facultativo de archiveros, etc. Madrid, 1881–1882, 2 v.

Archivalische Zeitschrift. Stuttgart, 1876–1880; Munich, 1881–1915, 1925–.

Archivalisches Centralblatt. Halle, 1903–.

Archivi italiani. Naples, 1914–1921.

Archivo nacional (Paraguay). Asunción del Paraguay, 1900–1902.

Arquivo historico português. Lisbon, 1903–.

Bibliographie moderne; courrier international des archives et des bibliothèques. Paris, 1897–.

Boletim das bibliothecas et archivos nacionaes. Coimbra, 1902–.

Boletim de bibliographia portugueza e revista dos archivos nacionaes. Coimbra, 1879–.

Boletín del Archivo Nacional [Cuba]. Havana, 1902–.

Boletín del Archivo General de la Nación [Mexico]. Mexico, 1930–.

Boletín del Archivo Nacional [Venezuela]. Caracas, 1923–.

Bulletin des bibliothèques et des archives. Paris, 1884–1889. Preceded by *Le Cabinet historique,* 1854–1883.

---

[89] Inquiries directed through the United States Department of State to the lesser independent nations of Asia elicited replies which indicate no published indexes to archives.

Meddelanden fran Svenska riksarchivet. Stockholm, 1877–.

Meddelelser fra det danske Rigsarkiv. Copenhagen, 1906–.

Mittheilungen der Königlich Preussischen Archivverwaltung. Leipzig, 1900–1901.

Mittheilungen der dritten (Archiv-) Section der k. k. Central-Commission zur Erforschung und Erhaltung der kunst- und historischen Denkmale. Vienna and Leipzig, 1888–.

Nederlandsch Archievenblad; orgaan van de Vreeniging van Archivarissen in Nederland. Groningen, 1893–.

Revista chilena de historia y geografía; organo de la Sociedad chilena de historia y geografía y del Archivo Histórico Nacional. Santiago de Chile, 1927–.

Revista de archivos, bibliotecas y museos. Madrid, 1871–.

Revista del Archivo y de la Biblioteca Nacional de Honduras. Tegucigalpa, 1904–.

Revista del Archivo Nacional del Perú. Lima, 1920–.

Revista histórica (published by the "Archivo y Museo Histórico Nacional," Uruguay). Montevideo, 1907–.

Revue des bibliothèques. Paris, 1891–.

Revue des bibliothèques et archives de Belgique. Brussels, 1903–.

Revue internationale des archives, des bibliothèques et des musées. Paris, 1895–1897. (Superseded by *Bibliographie moderne*).

Rivista delle biblioteche e degli archivi. Florence, 1888–.

INDEX OF COLLECTIONS OF PERSONAL PAPERS

[Numbers refer to pages, not to items]

Papers of the Presidents, Secretaries of State, and American diplomatists are given on pages 862–865, 865–867, 868–883, respectively. We give here references to papers of other American statesmen and personalities, and of foreign statesmen and diplomatists.

943

R

Roenne, Ludwig von, 927.
Rost, P. A., 349.
Russell, Earl (Lord John), 229.
——— Jonathan, 154.
Rutledge, John, 94.

S

Saunders, J. L., 271.
Scott, Sir R. W., 405.
Shelburne, Lord (2d Earl of Shelburne, 1st Marquis of Lansdowne), 43, 44.
Sheppard, E. T., 488.
Simcoe, J. G., 104.
Slidell, John, 348.
Smith, Albert, 287.
Sperry, C. S., 632.
Sproston, J. G., 488.
Stephens, A. H., 348.
Storey, Moorfield, 530.
Strachey, Sir Henry, 43, 44.
Stuart, Sir William, 331.
Sumner, Charles, 320.

T

Taylor, J. W., 460.
Thiers, Adolphe, 240.
Thompson, Sir J. S. D., 405.
Thornton, Edward, 104.

Tornel y Mendivil, J. M., 264.
Townshend, Thomas, 43, 44.
Trumbull, John, 103.
Tudor, Frederick, 488.

V

Vallejo, Gen. M. G., 271.
Vaughan, Sir Charles, 198.
Victoria, Queen, 331.

W

Ward, Gen. F. T., 488.
Warden, D. B., 147.
Wellesley, Marquis of, 146.
Whitefoord, Caleb, 44.
Wilding, Henry, 330.
Wildman, Rounseville, 488.
Wilkinson, James, 135.
Williams, S. W., 488.
Wilson, Sir R., 189.
Wolcott, Oliver, 70.
Wood, Gen. Leonard, 538.

Y

Yancey, W. L., 349.
Yorke, Philip. See Hardwicke.
Yrujo. See Irujo.

AUTHOR INDEX

[Numbers refer to items]

A

Abbey, K. T., 120, 121.
Abbott, J. F., 3256.
―――― Lyman, 2779.
―――― W. C., 208a.
Abel, Annie H., 1640, 1856.
Abella. *See* Huete Abella.
Aberdeen, Earl of, 1383, 1685, 1695, 1776.
Abernethy, T. P., 29.
Abranches, D. de, 3961.
Acal. *See* Puga y Acal.
Aceval, Benjamín, 4003.
Acevedo, Eduardo, 1309.
Acheson, Sam, 3369.
Acosta de Samper, Soledad, 1262.
Adachi, Kinnosuke, 3089.
Adam, G. M., 2977.
―――― M. I., 5403.
Adamov, E. A., 2091, 2104.
Adams, Brooks, 411, 1904, 2780.
―――― C. F., 2124, 5178–5180.
―――― C. F., *Jr.*, 1898–1900, 1996–1999, 2115, 2518, 4153.
―――― E. D., 537, 1516, 1519a, 1558, 1586, 1673, 1909.
―――― Henry, 634, 656, 696, 909, 1983, 5226.
―――― J. Q., 251, 886, 897, 903, 912, 915, 918, 986, 987, 1193, 1391, 5180.
―――― J. T., 1919.
―――― Jane E., 1275.
―――― John, 98, 370, 5179.
―――― R. G., 4795, 4796, 5564, 5596.
―――― Samuel, 98, 5181.
―――― T. B., 5182.
Adet, P. A., 460.
Adler, Cyrus, 4355.
Adoratskij, V. U., 5780.
Agan, Joseph, 1058, 1421.
Agoncillo, Felipe, 3475.
Agostini, Enrico de, 942.
Aguilar y López, Mariano, 1608.
Aguilera, Rodolfo, 4957.
Aiton, A. S., 685, 5646.
Akers, C. E., 1203.
Akimoto, Shunkichi, 3093.

946

Alamán, Lucas, 1486, 1491, 1498.
Alaux, Gustave d', 2136.
Albemarle, George Thomas, Earl of, 245.
―――― 7th Earl of (Viscount Bury), 2568.
Albers, D., 4194.
Albion, R. G., 861.
Albrecht, Emil, 173.
Alcalá Galiano. *See* Valera y Alcalá Galiano.
Alcázar Molina, C., 128.
Alcocer Martínez, Mariano, 5634.
Alcock, *Sir* Rutherford, 3141.
Aldana, Abelardo, 3733.
Aldao, C. A., 3952.
Alderson, Bernard, 2475.
Aldrovandi, Luigi, 4606.
Alducín, Rafael, 3642.
Alemán Bolaños, Gustavo, 3845.
Alemany y Bolufer, José, 4974a.
Alexander, W. D., 2289–2291.
Allen, A. H., 2304.
―――― G. W., 936.
―――― H. N., 5183.
Allin, C. D., 1340.
Allison, C. R., 4468.
―――― W. B., 2423.
―――― William, 4634.
Almond, Nina, 4609c.
Alphaud, Gabriel, 4478, 4479.
Álvarez, Alejandro, 1041, 4039, 4040, 4176.
Álvarez, V. Salado. *See* Salado y Álvarez.
Alverstone, Viscount, 2502.
Alvord, C. W., 228, 5600.
Amador y Carrandi, Ernesto, 3438.
Ambler, C. H., 2132.
Ames, Fisher, 5184.
―――― H. V., 477.
―――― J. G., 5354.
―――― Seth, 5184.
Ammidon, Otis, 920.
Amunátegui, M. L., 4941.
Amunátegui y Solar, Domingo, 1101, 1316a.

González y Torres, Plutarco, 3406.
Gooch, G. P., 209, 1968, 4398, 5475.
Goodwin, Cardinal, 678, 1601, 1616.
—— E. C., 5389.
Gordon, *Sir* Arthur (1st Baron Stanmore), 1252, 1503.
—— H. T., 1671a.
—— *Capt.* John, 1772.
—— L. J., 4377.
Gorostiza, M. E. de, 1542, 1543, 1547.
Gottberg, Otto von, 4125.
Gottschalk, L. R., 32, 298, 5332a.
Gowen, H. H., 3100.
Gower, G. G. L., 2d earl Granville. *See* Granville.
Grafton, A. H., third Duke of, 256.
Graham, G. S., 559.
—— John, 1099.
—— M. W., 4449, 4548a.
Gram, G. W. W., 2663.
Grandmaison. *See* Geoffroy de Grandmaison.
Grant, U. S., 878.
—— W. L., 224.
Granville, *Earl* (William Windham), 1982, 2573, 2999.
Grattan, C. H., 4454.
—— T. C., 1949.
Graves, W. S., 4603a.
Gray, Edward, 1675.
Greeley, Horace, 5204.
Greely, A. W., 363, 5356.
Green, Duff, 1854.
—— F. M., 2119.
—— T. E., 3257.
—— T. M., 493.
Greene, E. B., 4665, 5531.
—— F. D., 4381.
Greenhow, Robert, 932, 1712, 1713, 1781.
Greenlee, J. A., 1390a.
Gregory, Winifred, 4993, 5400.
Grenville, Lord, 577.
Greville, Charles, 1700.
Grey, Sir Edward, *Viscount*, 4435.
Griffin, A. P. C., 30, 1009, 1333, 2134, 2247, 2286, 2344, 2807, 3022–3024, 3330, 3331, 4188, 4658, 4722, 4725, 4802a, 4830.
—— G. G., 4661.
Griffis, W. E., 3088.
Grisanti, C. F., 4030, 4031.
Griswold, A. T., 5043.
Gronsky, P., 1755.
Gross, Lothar, 5743a, 5755, 5761.
Grotefend, Hermann, 5749.
Grotewald, Christian, 3957.
Gruening, Ernest, 3546, 3917.

Grund, F. J., 1820a.
—— J. P., 2102.
Gsovski, Vladimir, 5436.
Guani, Alberto, 4100.
Guedalla, Philip, 1926, 1986.
Guerra y Sánchez, Ramiro, 3366.
Guggenheim, H. F., 3347.
Guggenheimer, J. C., 280.
Guichard, Léon, 2821a.
—— Louis, 4457.
Guilaine, Louis, 3509.
Guillemaud, H. H., 2892.
Guillén, J. F., 1777.
Guiness, R. B., 688.
Guion, Capt. Isaac, 528.
Gulick, C. A., 5251.
—— S. L., 3260, 3261.
Gumpach, Johannes von, 3143.
Gurowski, Adam, 1888.
Gutiérrez, J. M., 4934.
Gutiérrez de Estrada, J. M., 2190.
Gutiérrez de Lara, José, 1125.
Gutiérrez Navas, Daniel, 3815.
Guttridge, G. H., 138.
Guyot, Raymond, 412, 440.
Guzmán, León, 3567.
—— Ramón, 3530.
Gwynn, S. L., 2479.
—— Stephen, 2506, 4439.

H

Habicht, Max, 5467.
Hacker, L. M., 895, 3367.
Hackett, C. W., 786, 1075, 3540, 3541.
—— F. W., 979, 2515, 2571.
Hadfield, Joseph, 362.
Haferkorn, H. E., 1571, 2808.
Hagedorn, Hermann, 5286.
Hagerty, J. J., 3102.
Hains, P. C., 2654.
Hale, E. E., 3067.
—— R. S., 2525.
Haliburton, R. G., 1664.
Hall, A. B., 4117.
—— F. R., 433.
—— Hubert, 535, 5571, 5581.
—— L. J., 4312.
Hallam, Oscar, 423.
Hamer, P. M., 586.
Hamilton, Alexander, 376a, 626, 5231.
—— J. C., 5231.
—— P. J., 5551.
—— S. M., 1191, 5266.
Hammond, O. G., 1673a.
Hanfstaengl, E. F. S., 198.
Hansen, Harry, 4577.
—— K. A., 5436.

Polovtsov, A. A., 1194.
Pons. *See* Capella y Pons.
Poole, R. L., 335.
Pooley, A. M., 3187, 3267.
Poore, B. P., 5353.
Pope, *Sir* Joseph, 2494.
Porras, Belisario, 3685.
Porras Barrenechea, Raúl, 1136.
Porritt, Edward, 2943.
Porros Troconis, Gabriel, 1052.
Portell Vilá, Herminio, 1810–1812.
Porter, D. D., 2146.
—— Horace, 4256.
—— K. W., 1758a.
Portiez, Louis, 465.
Posada, Eduardo, 1232, 1263, 4709.
Posey, W. B., 555.
Posner, Ernst, 5744.
Posthumus, N. W., 1392, 1393.
Potter, P. B., 2375.
Powell, A. A., 3783.
—— F. W., 3539.
Powers, H. H., 4408.
Pradier-Foderé, Paul, 2561.
Prado, Eduardo, 3968.
Pradt, Dominique de Fourt de, 1103, 1131.
Praesent, Hans, 4686.
Prager, Ludwig, 4309.
Pratt, E. J., 1084, 2092.
—— J. W., 725, 1538, 1752, 2002, 2302, 3370, 3370a, 4796.
Preble, *Commodore* Edward, 957, 958.
Prentiss, Charles, 950.
Preston, J. D., 5389.
Prevost, J. C., 2579.
Prévost, Michel, 4695.
Pribram, A. F., 4414, 4423, 5473a.
Priestley, H. I., 1462, 3534, 3535, 3666.
Prim, *Don* Juan, 2213.
Prime, R. E., 1411.
Prince, Amédée, 4076.
Pringle, H. W., 2471.
Pritchard, E. H., 3118.
Pritchett, J. P., 2938, 2940.
Prittwitz und Gaffron, F. W. von, 172.
Prothero, *Sir* G. W., 4394.
Puelles, J. M., 1557.
Puga y Acal, Manuel, 1073.
Pulling, Alexander, 4473.
—— F. S., 5055.
Putnam, G. H., 1903.
—— Herbert. *See* Librarian of Congress.
—— Rufus, 581.
Putnam-Weale, B. L., *See* Simpson, B. L.

Q

Quaife, M. M., 783, 5282.
Queen Victoria, 1985.
Queneuil, Henry, 2400.
Quesada, A. M., 3353.
—— Ernesto, 3500a, 4091, 4092, 4167.
—— Gonzalo de, 3899, 3900.
—— V. G., 1293, 3951.
Quesada Vargas, Octavio, 3843.
Quigley, H. S., 3034.
Quijano, C., 3782.
Quincy, Edmund, 816.
Quintana. *See* Morena Quintana.
Quisenberry, A. C., 1806.

R

Rachfahl, Felix, 2353.
Radaelli, S. A., 1299.
Rados, Constantin, 1165.
Ragatz, L. J., 1345, 4721, 5407, 5409, 5580.
—— Mary P., 5373b.
Raines, C. W., 748.
Ralph, Julian, 2802.
Ralston, J. H., 2756, 3592, 4227.
Ramage, Allene, 5026.
Ramírez, J. F., 1636.
Ramiz, Galvão, B. F., 4699.
Ramos, Roberto, 3521.
Randall, E. O., 667.
—— J. G., 623, 1887.
Randolph, Edmund, 456.
Rankin, R. R., 539.
Ratchford, B. U., 607a.
Rather, Ethel Z., 1517.
Rattenberry, J. F., 989.
Ratterman, Elleanore (Callaghan), 1868.
Ravignani, Emilio, 1120.
Ravndal, G. B., 4374a.
Rawle, Francis, 4796.
Ray, William, 949.
Rayneval. *See* Gérard de Rayneval.
Rea, G. B., 3258.
Reale, Egidio, 2521.
Rebello, Silvestre, 1123.
Rebolledo, Alvaro, 3695.
—— Miguel, 3656.
Reddaway, W. F., 1146.
Redfield, W. C., 4434.
Reed, D. M., 4618.
—— Joseph, 139.
Reeves, J. S., 287, 1024, 1459, 2396a.
Reid, H. D., 3762, 4796.
—— R. L., 1709.